# Twentieth-Century Literary Criticism

# Guide to Gale Literary Criticism Series

**When you need to review criticism of literary works, these are the Gale series to use:**

| **If the author's death date is:** | **You should turn to:** |
|---|---|

**After Dec. 31, 1959 (or author is still living)**

### CONTEMPORARY LITERARY CRITICISM

for example: Jorge Luis Borges, Anthony Burgess, William Faulkner, Mary Gordon, Ernest Hemingway, Iris Murdoch

**1900 through 1959**

### TWENTIETH-CENTURY LITERARY CRITICISM

for example: Willa Cather, F. Scott Fitzgerald, Henry James, Mark Twain, Virginia Woolf

**1800 through 1899**

### NINETEENTH-CENTURY LITERATURE CRITICISM

for example: Fyodor Dostoevsky, Nathaniel Hawthorne, George Sand, William Wordsworth

**1400 through 1799**

### LITERATURE CRITICISM FROM 1400 TO 1800 (excluding Shakespeare)

for example: Anne Bradstreet, Daniel Defoe, Alexander Pope, François Rabelais, Jonathan Swift, Phillis Wheatley

### SHAKESPEAREAN CRITICISM

Shakespeare's plays and poetry

**Antiquity through 1399**

### CLASSICAL AND MEDIEVAL LITERATURE CRITICISM

for example: Dante, Homer, Plato, Sophocles, Vergil, the Beowulf Poet

## Gale also publishes related criticism series:

### CHILDREN'S LITERATURE REVIEW

This series covers authors of all eras who have written for the preschool through high school audience.

### SHORT STORY CRITICISM

This series covers the major short fiction writers of all nationalities and periods of literary history.

### POETRY CRITICISM

This series covers poets of all nationalities and periods of literary history.

### DRAMA CRITICISM

This series covers dramatists of all nationalities and periods of literary history.

ISSN 0276-8178

*R*

Volume 41

# Twentieth-Century Literary Criticism

**Excerpts from Criticism of the
Works of Novelists, Poets, Playwrights,
Short Story Writers, and Other Creative Writers
Who Died between 1900 and 1960,
from the First Published Critical Appraisals
to Current Evaluations**

**Laurie DiMauro
Editor**

**David Kmenta
Marie Lazzari
Thomas Ligotti
Bridget Travers
Thomas Votteler
Associate Editors**

 *Gale Research Inc.* · DETROIT · LONDON

## STAFF

Laurie DiMauro, *Editor*

David Kmenta, Marie Lazzari, Thomas Ligotti, Bridget Travers, Thomas Votteler, *Associate Editors*

John P. Daniel, Rogene M. Fisher, Ian A. Goodhall, Elizabeth P. Henry, Andrew M. Kalasky, James Poniewozik, *Assistant Editors*

Jeanne A. Gough, *Permissions & Production Manager*

Linda M. Pugliese, *Production Supervisor*

Maureen Puhl, Jennifer VanSickle, *Editorial Associates*

Donna Craft, Paul Lewon, Lorna Mabunda, Camille Robinson, Sheila Walencewicz, *Editorial Assistants*

Maureen Richards, *Research Supervisor*

Paula Cutcher-Jackson, Judy L. Gale, Robin Lupa, Mary Beth McElmeel, *Editorial Associates*

Jennifer Brostrom, Amy Kaechele, Tamara C. Nott, *Editorial Assistants*

Sandra C. Davis, *Permissions Supervisor (Text)*

Maria L. Franklin, Josephine M. Keene, Denise M. Singleton, Kimberly F. Smilay, *Permissions Associates*

Rebecca A. Hartford, Michele Lonoconus, Shelly Rakoczy (co-op), Shalice Shah, Nancy K. Sheridan, *Permissions Assistants*

Patricia A. Seefelt, *Permissions Supervisor (Pictures)*

Margaret A. Chamberlain, Pamela A. Hayes, *Permissions Associates*

Keith Reed, *Permissions Assistant*

Mary Beth Trimper, *Production Manager*

Mary Winterhalter, *Production Assistant*

Arthur Chartow, *Art Director*

C. J. Jonik, *Keyliner*

# Contents

Preface   vii

Acknowledgments   xi

Alain (1868-1951) ..............................................................................................................1
   *French philosopher*

John Buchan (1875-1940)..................................................................................................32
   *Scottish novelist*

Robert W. Chambers (1865-1933) ....................................................................................86
   *American novelist*

Elizabeth (1866-1941) ......................................................................................................116
   *English novelist*

Paul Eluard (1895-1952)...................................................................................................141
   *French poet*

Marcus Garvey (1887-1940).............................................................................................170
   *Jamaican essayist*

Louise Imogen Guiney (1861-1920).................................................................................202
   *American poet*

William Dean Howells (1837-1920)..................................................................................231
   *American novelist; entry devoted to* The Rise of Silas Lapham

Johannes V. Jensen (1873-1950) .....................................................................................288
   *Danish novelist*

Claude McKay (1889-1948) .............................................................................................315
   *American poet*

Oscar Wilde (1854-1900).................................................................................................347
   *Irish novelist; entry devoted to* The Picture of Dorian Gray

Emile Zola (1840-1920) ..................................................................................................404
   *French novelist*

Literary Criticism Series Cumulative Author Index   459

Literary Criticism Series Cumulative Topic Index   511

*TCLC* Cumulative Nationality Index   515

Title Index to *TCLC*, Vol. 41   519

# Preface

Since its inception more than ten years ago, *Twentieth-Century Literary Criticism* has been purchased and used by nearly 10,000 school, public, and college or university libraries. *TCLC* has covered more than 500 authors, representing 58 nationalities, and over 25,000 titles. No other reference source has surveyed the critical response to twentieth-century authors and literature as thoroughly as *TCLC*. In the words of one reviewer, "there is nothing comparable available." *TCLC* "is a gold mine of information—dates, pseudonyms, biographical information, and criticism from books and periodicals—which many libraries would have difficulty assembling on their own."

## Scope of the Series

*TCLC* is designed to serve as an introduction to authors who died between 1900 and 1960 and to the most significant interpretations of these authors' works. The great poets, novelists, short story writers, playwrights, and philosophers of this period are frequently studied in high school and college literature courses. In organizing and excerpting the vast amount of critical material written on these authors, *TCLC* helps students develop valuable insight into literary history, promotes a better understanding of the texts, and sparks ideas for papers and assignments. Each entry in *TCLC* presents a comprehensive survey of an author's career or an individual work of literature and provides the user with a multiplicity of interpretations and assessments. Such variety allows students to pursue their own interests; furthermore, it fosters an awareness that literature is dynamic and responsive to many different opinions.

Every fourth volume of *TCLC* is devoted to literary topics that cannot be covered under the author approach used in the rest of the series. Such topics include literary movements, prominent themes in twentieth-century literature, literary reaction to political and historical events, significant eras in literary history, prominent literary anniversaries, and the literatures of cultures that are often overlooked by English-speaking readers.

*TCLC* is designed as a companion series to Gale's *Contemporary Literary Criticism,* which reprints commentary on authors now living or who have died since 1960. Because of the different periods under consideration, there is no duplication of material between *CLC* and *TCLC*. For additional information about *CLC* and Gale's other criticism titles, users should consult the Guide to Gale Literary Criticism Series preceding the title page in this volume.

## Coverage

Each volume of *TCLC* is carefully compiled to present:

- criticism of authors, or literary topics, representing a variety of genres and nationalities

- both major and lesser-known writers and literary works of the period

- 12-16 authors or 4-6 topics per volume

- individual entries that survey critical response to each author's work or each topic in literary history, including early criticism to reflect initial reactions; later criticism to represent any rise or decline in reputation; and current retrospective analyses.

## Organization of This Book

An author entry consists of the following elements: author heading, biographical and critical introduction, list of principal works, excerpts of criticism (each preceded by an annotation and followed by a bibliographic citation), and a bibliography of further reading.

- The **author heading** consists of the name under which the author most commonly wrote, followed by birth and death dates. If an author wrote consistently under a pseudonym, the pseudonym will be listed in the author heading and the real name given in parentheses on the first line of the biographical and critical introduction. Also located at the beginning of the introduction to the author entry are any name variations under which an author wrote, including transliterated forms for authors whose languages use nonroman alphabets.

- The **biographical and critical introduction** outlines the author's life and career, as well as the critical issues surrounding his or her work. References are provided to past volumes of *TCLC* and to other biographical and critical reference series published by Gale, including *Short Story Criticism, Children's Literature Review, Contemporary Authors, Dictionary of Literary Biography,* and *Something about the Author.*

- Most *TCLC* entries include **portraits** of the author. Many entries also contain reproductions of materials pertinent to an author's career, including manuscript pages, title pages, dust jackets, letters, and drawings, as well as photographs of important people, places, and events in an author's life.

- The **list of principal works** is chronological by date of first book publication and identifies the genre of each work. In the case of foreign authors with both foreign-language publications and English translations, the title and date of the first English-language edition are given in brackets. Unless otherwise indicated, dramas are dated by first performance, not first publication.

- **Criticism** is arranged chronologically in each author entry to provide a perspective on changes in critical evaluation over the years. All titles of works by the author featured in the entry are printed in boldface type to enable the user to easily locate discussion of particular works. Also for purposes of easier identification, the critic's name and the publication date of the essay are given at the beginning of each piece of criticism. Unsigned criticism is preceded by the title of the journal in which it appeared. Some of the excerpts in *TCLC* also contain translated material. Unless otherwise noted, translations in brackets are by the editors; translations in parentheses or continuous with the text are by the critic. Publication information (such as publisher names and book prices) and parenthetical numerical references (such as footnotes or page and line references to specific editions of works) have been deleted at the editors' discretion to provide smoother reading of the text.

- Critical excerpts are prefaced by **annotations** providing the reader with information about both the critic and the criticism that follows. Included are the critic's reputation, individual approach to literary criticism, and particular expertise in an author's works. Also noted are the relative importance of a work of criticism, the scope of the excerpt, and the growth of critical controversy or changes in critical trends regarding an author. In some cases, these annotations cross-reference excerpts by critics who discuss each other's commentary.

- A complete **bibliographic citation** designed to facilitate location of the original essay or book follows each piece of criticism.

- An annotated list of **further reading** appearing at the end of each author entry suggests secondary sources on the author. In some cases it includes essays for which the editors could not obtain reprint rights.

## Cumulative Indexes

- Each volume of *TCLC* contains a cumulative **author index** listing all authors who have appeared in Gale's Literary Criticism Series, along with cross-references to such biographical series as *Contemporary Authors* and *Dictionary of Literary Biography.* For readers' convenience, a complete list of Gale titles included appears on the first page of the author index. Useful for locating authors within the various series, this index is particularly valuable for those authors who are identified by a certain period but who, because of their death dates, are placed in another, or for those authors whose careers span two periods. For example, F. Scott Fitzgerald is found in *TCLC,* yet a writer often associated with him, Ernest Hemingway, is found in *CLC.*

- Each *TCLC* volume includes a cumulative **nationality index** which lists all authors who have appeared in *TCLC* volumes, arranged alphabetically under their respective nationalities, as well as Topics volume entries devoted to particular national literatures.

- Each new volume in Gale's Literary Criticism Series includes a cumulative **topic index,** which lists all literary topics treated in *NCLC, TCLC, LC 1400-1800,* and the *CLC* Yearbook.

- Each new volume of *TCLC,* with the exception of the Topics volumes, contains a **title index** listing the titles of all literary works discussed in the volume. The first volume of *TCLC* published each year contains an index listing all titles discussed in the series since its inception. Titles discussed in the Topics volume entries are not included in the *TCLC* cumulative index.

## A Note to the Reader

When writing papers, students who quote directly from any volume in Gale's Literary Criticism Series may use the following general forms to footnote reprinted criticism. The first example pertains to material drawn from periodicals, the second to material reprinted from books.

[1] T. S. Eliot, "John Donne," *The Nation and the Athenaeum,* 33 (9 June 1923), 321-32; excerpted and reprinted in *Literature Criticism from 1400 to 1800,* Vol. 10, ed. James E. Person, Jr. (Detroit: Gale Research, 1989), pp. 28-9.

[2] Clara G. Stillman, *Samuel Butler: A Mid-Victorian Modern* (Viking Press, 1932); excerpted and reprinted in *Twentieth-Century Literary Criticism,* Vol. 33, ed. Paula Kepos (Detroit: Gale Research, 1989), pp. 43-5.

## Suggestions Are Welcome

In response to suggestions, several features have been added to *TCLC* since the series began, including annotations to excerpted criticism, a cumulative index to authors in all Gale literary criticism series, entries devoted to criticism on a single work by a major author, more extensive illustrations, and a title index listing all literary works discussed in the series since its inception.

Readers who wish to suggest authors or topics to appear in future volumes, or who have other suggestions, are cordially invited to write the editors.

# Acknowledgments

The editors wish to thank the copyright holders of the excerpted criticism included in this volume, the permissions managers of many book and magazine publishing companies for assisting us in securing reprint rights, and Anthony Bogucki for assistance with copyright research. We are also grateful to the staffs of the Detroit Public Library, Wayne State University Purdy/Kresge Library Complex, and the University of Michigan Libraries for making their resources available to us. Following is a list of the copyright holders who have granted us permission to reprint material in this volume of *TCLC*. Every effort has been made to trace copyright, but if omissions have been made, please let us know.

## COPYRIGHTED EXCERPTS IN *TCLC*, VOLUME 41, WERE REPRINTED FROM THE FOLLOWING PERIODICALS:

*Afro-Americans in New York Life and History,* v. 10, July, 1986. © 1986 Afro-American History Association of Niagara Frontier, Inc. Reprinted by permission of the publisher.—*American Literary Realism 1870-1910,* v. 21, Winter, 1989. Copyright © 1989 by the Department of English, The University of Texas at Arlington. Reprinted by permission of the publisher.—*American Norvegica,* v. III, 1971. Reprinted by permission of the publisher.—*The American Scholar,* v. 51, Summer, 1982. Copyright © 1982 by the author. Reprinted by permission of the publishers.—*Biography,* v. 2, Fall, 1979. © 1979 by the Biographical Research Center. All rights reserved. Reprinted by permission of the publisher.—*Chicago Review,* v. II, Fall-Winter, 1948. Copyright 1948, renewed 1975 by *Chicago Review.* Reprinted by permission of the publisher.—*CLA Journal,* v. XVIII, December, 1974; v. XXIII, March, 1980; v. XXIV, March, 1981; v. XXXII, March, 1989. Copyright, 1974, 1980, 1981, 1989 by The College Language Association. All used by permission of The College Language Association.—*College English,* v. 26, February, 1965 for "Howells' Mansion and Thoreau's Cabin" by William Wasserstrom. Copyright © 1965 by the National Council of Teachers of English. Reprinted by permission of the publisher and the Literary Estate of the author.—*Crypt of Cthulhu,* v. 3, Roodmas, 1984 for "Robert W. Chambers" by S. T. Joshi. Copyright © 1984. Reprinted by permission of the author.—*English Literature in Transition: 1880-1920,* v. 24, 1981 for "The Villain in the Spy Novels of John Buchan" by Philip E. Ray; v. 29, 1986 for "John Buchan and the Path of the Keen" by Alistair McCleery. Copyright © 1981, 1986 *English Literature in Transition: 1880-1920.* Both reprinted by permission of the publisher and the respective authors.—*L'Esprit Créateur,* v. XXI, Fall, 1981. Copyright © 1981 by *L'Esprit Créateur.* Reprinted by permission of the publisher.—*The Listener,* v. LXXV, April 21, 1966 for "Emile Zola" by F. W. J. Hemmings. © British Broadcasting Corp. 1966. Reprinted by permission of the author.—*The Midwest Quarterly,* v. XXII, Spring, 1981; v. XXIV, Winter, 1983. Copyright, 1981, 1983, by *The Midwest Quarterly,* Pittsburg State University. Both reprinted by permission of the publisher.—*Modern Fiction Studies,* v. VIII, Winter, 1962-63. Copyright © 1963 by Purdue Research Foundation, West Lafayette, IN 47907. All rights reserved. Reprinted with permission.—*The New York Times Book Review,* February 25, 1923. Copyright 1923 by The New York Times Company. Reprinted by permission.—*The New Yorker,* v. XXI, April 28, 1945. Copyright 1945, renewed 1973 by The New Yorker Magazine, Inc. Reprinted by permission of the publisher.—*The Old Northwest,* v. 13, Winter, 1986. Copyright © Miami University 1986. Reprinted by permission of the publisher.—*Poetry,* v. LXXXIII, January, 1954 for "Claude McKay's Art" by M. B. Tolson. Copyright 1954, renewed 1982 by the Modern Poetry Association. Reprinted by permission of the Editor of *Poetry* and the Literary Estate of the author.—*The Romantist,* n. 3, 1979. Copyright © 1979 by The F. Marion Crawford Memorial Society. All rights reserved. Reprinted by permission of The F. Marion Crawford Memorial Society.—*The Round Table,* v. LXII, July, 1972 for "John Buchan's Thrillers: The Ideology of Character" by Patrick Cosgrave. Reprinted by permission of the author.—*Scandinavian Studies,* v. 61, Winter, 1989 for "The Absent Father and the Inauguration of Discourse in Johannes V. Jensen's 'Kongens Fald' " by Jorgen Steen Veisland. Reprinted by permission of the publisher and the author.—*Studies in the Literary Imagination,* v. XVI, Fall, 1983. Copyright 1983 Department of English, Georgia State University. Reprinted by permission of the publisher.—*The Times Literary Supplement,* n. 3526, September 25, 1969; n. 3734, September 28, 1973; n. 4453, August 5-11, 1988. © Times Supplements Limited 1969, 1973, 1988. All reproduced from *The Times Literary Supplement* by permission.—*The Victorian Newsletter,* n. 63, Spring, 1983, for "Parody and Homage: The Presence of Pater in 'Dorian Gray' " by Robert K. Martin. Reprinted by permission of *The Victorian Newsletter* and the author.—*Wagner Literary Magazine,* no. 3, 1962 for "Paul Eluard: Poet in the World of Painters" by Anne Fessenden. Copyright 1962 by *Wagner Literary Magazine.* Reprinted by permission of the author.—*The Western Political Quarterly,* v. XVIII, September, 1965 for "The Philosopher Alain and French Classical Radicalism" by Ronald F. Howell. Copyright © 1965, by the University of Utah. Reprinted by permission of the publisher.

# Alain

## 1868-1951

(Pseudonym of Emile-Auguste Chartier; also wrote under the pseudonym Criton) French philosopher, essayist, critic, and educator.

An influential philosopher and educator in France during the first half of the twentieth century, Alain is best known for his writings in a literary form that he termed the *propos,* a brief, informal essay commenting on a philosophical, cultural, or political subject. His major works, including *Mars ou la guerre jugée (Mars; or, The Truth about War),* a collection of *propos* condemning war, and *Les dieux (The Gods),* a book-length study of metaphysics, have been lauded for their witty and insightful observations on modern society, religion, and literature. Widely read during his lifetime, Alain's *propos* have earned him recognition as a notable figure in French philosophy.

Born in Mortagne in the Normandy region of France, Alain was the son of a veterinarian. He attended a Catholic elementary school in Mortagne and from 1886 to 1889 he studied at the Lycée Michelet in Vanves, where he developed a strong interest in philosophy. Alain spent the next three years studying philosophy and literature at the Ecole normale supérieure in Paris. After graduating in 1892 he taught philosophy at various lycées during the next four decades. In addition to teaching Alain wrote a weekly column for the newspaper, the *Dépêche de Rouen,* between 1903 and 1906. He subsequently conceived of the *propos* as a form requiring less effort to produce than a full-length column. Under the pseudonym Alain he published daily *propos* during the next eight years to much popular acclaim. At the beginning of World War I Alain volunteered to serve in a French artillery unit; although he was an ardent pacifist, he believed that one must experience war to pass judgment on it. Wounded in action, he returned in 1917 to teach philosophy at the Lycée Henri-Quatre in Paris, while writing numerous *propos* for national periodicals, and four years later *Mars; or, The Truth about War* was published. Throughout the 1920s and 1930s Alain produced several book-length works primarily on philosophical and literary subjects. He retired from teaching in 1933 and his autobiography, *Histoire de mes pensées,* appeared three years later. Alain was awarded the first Grand Prix national de littérature shortly before his death in 1951.

During his lifetime Alain wrote more than five thousand *propos,* many of which have been gathered in collections that focus on such recurring topics in his writing as war, religion, political authority, and literature. Working under the pressure of daily deadlines, Alain limited each *propos* to two handwritten pages, often containing fewer than a thousand words, and rarely revised his ideas after they had been initially transcribed. Alain's *propos* characteristically begin with a specific reference to a common experience or a well-known incident, such as the sinking of the *Titanic,*

and then develop a general observation or assertion. In discussions of his numerous volumes of *propos* Alain has been especially praised for his balanced commentary on the relationship between individual responsibility and governmental authority. Critics observe that *The Gods* and many of his book-length studies are arranged in short sections similar in scope to *propos,* and these works are commended for their philosophical insight and poetic prose style. While a few commentators criticize Alain for failing to offer a formally elaborated system of thought and find his writing style obscure, many note that Alain never claimed to offer a systematic philosophy and respond favorably to the intuitive quality of his writings. Both supporters and detractors of Alain attribute part of his critical reputation to the continuing adoration of his former students. While Alain's works have gained international recognition, critical discussion and translations of his writings have been relatively limited in English-speaking countries. In France, however, Alain is acknowledged as a significant teacher and writer of modern French philosophy, and his works are considered representative of French political thought during the interwar era.

## PRINCIPAL WORKS

*Les cent un propos d'Alain.*   5 vols.  (essays)  1908-28
*Quatre-vingt-un chapîtres sur l'esprit et les passions*  (essays)  1917
*Les propos d'Alain.*   2 vols.  (essays)  1920
*Système des beaux-arts*  (philosophy)  1920
*Mars ou la guerre jugée*  (essays)  1921;  also published as *Mars ou la guerre jugée* [enlarged edition], 1936
   [*Mars; or, The Truth about War,* 1930]
*Propos sur l'esthétique*  (essays)  1923
*Propos sur le christianisme*  (essays)  1924
*Eléments d'une doctrine radicale*  (essays)  1925
*Le citoyen contre les pouvoirs*  (essays)  1926
*Les idées et les âges.*  2 vols.  (philosophy)  1927
*Propos sur le bonheur*  (essays)  1928
   [*Alain on Happiness,* 1973]
*Entretiens au bord de la mer*  (philosophy)  1931
*Idées: Platon, Descartes, Hegel*  (philosophy)  1932; also published as *Idées: Introduction à la philosophie—Platon, Descartes, Hegel, Comte* [enlarged edition], 1939
*Propos sur l'éducation*  (essays)  1932
*Les dieux*  (philosophy)  1934
   [*The Gods,* 1974]
*Propos de littérature*  (essays)  1934
*Stendhal*  (criticism)  1935
*Histoire de mes pensées*  (autobiography)  1936
*Avec Balzac*  (criticism)  1937
*Propos sur la religion*  (essays)  1938
*Lettres à Sergio Solmi sur la philosophie de Kant*  (letters)  1946
*Cahiers de Lorient.*   2 vols.  (notebooks)  1963-64

---

### André Maurois   (essay date 1930)

[*A former student of Alain, Maurois was a French literary figure whose versatility is reflected in the broad scope of his work. However, it was as a biographer that he made his most significant contribution to literature. Following the tradition of Lytton Strachey's "New Biography," Maurois believed that a biography should delve into the psychological aspects of personality to reveal its subject's multiplicity, contradictions, and inner struggles, as well as serve as a personal expression of the biographer. In the following excerpt from his introduction to* Mars; or, The Truth about War, *Maurois surveys Alain's early career and describes his worldview.*]

I write to introduce to English readers a contemporary French thinker, who is not yet translated and not yet known outside his own country; a writer whose fame is likely to grow with time, and in whom I believe.

The contemporary influence of an author depends nearly as much upon his character as his work. Art is a means of escape from the slavery of actuality, and men are disappointed if a writer's life proves that he also was only a bondman, and if his recorded actions destroy the illusion

which his writings have created. Tolstoy was Tolstoy because he had written *War and Peace, Anna Karenina,* and *Ivan Ilyitch,* but he was also 'Tolstoy,' thanks to the legend of Yasnaya Polyana; Byron would never have fired the imagination of Europe if his readers had not divined him in *The Corsair, Childe Harold,* and *Lara;* and Proust, if he is the greatest French novelist of his time, is also the sick man in a cork-lined room, feverishly set upon the 'recapture of the past' before he dies.

In the case of philosophers and moralists, we expect the link between a man's life and his work to be even closer. It is hard to feel respect for one who, while writing a treatise on morality, is canvassing his election to an academy, and while he is scheming for his own ends, expounds those ends of which the whole Universe is in travail. 'The genuine Socrates is fearless and satisfied; one, who without wealth, influence, or worldly adroitness, lives contented. Doubt in itself is the sign of a strong soul, and indifference to possessions and opinions are proofs of a noble doctrine, independent of others.'

The growing prestige of the philosopher, who signs himself Alain, and whose real name is Chartier, is due, in part, to such ancillary causes. He is a professor in the Lycée Henri IV, and the feelings he inspires in his pupils are not unlike those which Socrates inspired in his followers. So many want to attend his lectures that no hall on the premises can hold them. Men who have long finished their academic careers seek in vain the privilege of becoming again his pupils, and many of these are writers. They look up to him as to a master, who not only once influenced them profoundly, but one whose praise and blame still far outweigh the blame and praise the world can give. Jean Prévost, who is such a writer, published in *La nouvelle revue française* the story of his eighteenth year. He describes Alain thus:

> We waited for him on the morning of his first lecture in a room which looks out on the Panthéon: we heard the sound of his footsteps and were silent; he entered limping a little from his wound. At first I only noticed his shoulders and his enormous hands. Then he took off a soft hat, the brim of which had seemed to reach down to a great fat nose, peering over a ragged moustache. Had he kept it on and his forehead hidden, I should have taken him for a heavy dragoon. I awaited his famous exposition, fortifying my heart like a Christian about to hear profane doctrines: I was astounded. What he was reading and translating and commenting upon was that Ode in Horace in which Teucer addresses his comrades, and I remember well his joyous gesture, expressive of the assent of the whole of his robust body, to the final verse: *Cras ingens iterabimus æquor.*

Let me mention a few actions characteristic of him: Alain, though a passionate pacifist, volunteered as a private soldier and served four years in the artillery. As soon as he was free he wrote a terrible book against soldiers, **Mars ou la guerre jugée** (in my opinion too severe, but salutary as a counterblast). Again, this professor, the most brilliant of his generation, could, by conciliating the authorities in some small degree, have secured any sort of promotion;

the Sorbonne, the Collège de France, the Institut were all within his reach. But he has deliberately turned aside from such prizes. He has kept his Lycée post to preserve his independence. (pp. 9-12)

[Alain also wrote many thousands of propos (some of which have been collected under such titles as *Propos d'Alain, Propos sur le bonheur, Propos sur le christianisme*) that were first published in a small provincial newspaper, the *Dépêche de Rouen*.]

Alain, who at that time was a master at the Lycée in Rouen, supplied this paper daily with such comments, fifty to sixty lines in length. They were upon anything and everything: poets, God, the seasons, Catholicism, myths, prostitutes, Stendhal, Beethoven, Goethe. They were certainly the most curious and remarkable kind of journalism written under the Third Republic. Providing these paragraphs has had a great influence on Alain himself, inculcating in him a habit of thinking in short chapters.

The first important work in which his doctrine found expression was called *Quatre-vingt-un chapitres sur l'esprit et les passions,* and many of the ideas contained in it have been developed since . . . *Les idées et les âges.*

During the war, in his artillery dug-out, he pondered the problems of æsthetics, and conceived there what is perhaps the best of all his books, his *Système des beaux-arts.* In that book he examines the principles underlying the different arts, and the proper part of each in the life of man. According to Alain the function of Art is to discipline the imagination and to rescue imagination from the disastrous madness of mere dreaming, by linking it on to realities—real forms, whether sculptured or created in literature. A list of the titles of the different parts into which [*Mars; or, The Truth about War*] is divided will give some notion of its contents: 'De l'imagination créatrice,' 'De la danse et de la parure,' 'De la poésie et de l'eloquence,' 'Du théâtre et de l'architecture,' 'De la peinture,' 'Du dessin,' 'De la prose.'

It will be seen that the book moves from the concrete art-forms to those which are most abstract. To Alain, the art of prose is at once the most difficult and the most beautiful of all; but he only rates thus highly prose which is simple and severe; for brilliant and many-faceted prose he shows much contempt. (pp. 14-16)

Alain himself is far from being a facile writer. He sacrifices nothing to appearances; he exacts much from his readers. You must, before you take him up, resolve to respect him, and continue to read him in spite of all forbidding initial difficulties. He presses so hard on his pen that it goes, so to speak, through the paper till it reaches thought itself; and such readers as persevere can make that thought their very own. The region of his mind is enclosed by a few large simple boundary lines. No writer cares less about being up to date, or in touch with new ideas or authors. He is a man of few books: Plato, Spinoza, Descartes, Kant, Hegel, Auguste Comte, are the springs which feed the river of his thought; there is also no doubt that he is the best reader that Stendhal and Balzac have ever found in France. With some hesitation he has recently adopted Proust, and more recently Paul Valéry. He is an admirer of Retz and Saint-Simon. Add to these Goethe, occasionally Shakespeare, a few of George Sand's novels—and he has all the reading he wants; for he knows how both to ignore and to select; precious gifts in this age, when intellects are a prey to miscellaneous curiosity.

It is, of course, impossible in an article to give an accurate account of Alain's extremely personal philosophy. Moreover, he has himself a horror of analysis, and he would think poorly of me if I attempted it. Interpreters are apt to be obscurer than their masters. If you wish to see how he himself re-creates the system of another thinker, read his little book on *Spinoza,* or his *Onze chapitres sur Platon.* He thinks *with* Plato, *with* Spinoza; stationing himself first at that point from which they saw the world, and then re-thinks as it were their thoughts as though they were his own. His own view is that this is the only reliable critical method. He has a deep disdain for dialectical discussion—even for 'proofs.' He holds that the methods of mathematics, so trustworthy in sciences dealing with definable elements, become absurd in the case of such complex entities as the soul, as feelings, as thoughts: 'Every proof is, as far as I am concerned, invalid.' For Alain, philosophy is more akin to Poetry than to Science.

Some time ago there was, at the Ecole normale, a professor, M. de la Coulonche, famous for reducing writers to descriptive formulas. He would say, for instance: 'Lucretius! He is the St. Paul of Epicureanism; a Schopenhauer in metre mitigated by Victor Hugo.' I fancy that if M. de la Coulonche were still alive he would be tempted to define Alain as 'a graver Chesterton, with an admixture of Ruskin; a Santayana of greater vitality, on whose countenance one occasionally catches the expression of Carlyle.' (pp. 16-18)

*André Maurois, in an introduction to* Mars; or, the Truth about War, *by Alain, translated by Doris Mudie and Elizabeth Hill, Jonathan Cape & Harrison Smith, 1930, pp. 9-18.*

**Felix Morrow   (essay date 1930)**

[*An American publisher and writer, Morrow is the author of several books on the civil war in Spain. In the following review of* Mars; or, The Truth about War, *Morrow criticizes Alain for neglecting a substantial body of scholarly works on the economic and social causes of war, as well as disparaging what he views as the obscure form and weakly interrelated content of Alain's* propos.]

There is a reading public, composed of literati, which knows almost nothing about philosophy and the social sciences, but which nevertheless feels an interest in philosophical and social ideas—an interest not entirely satisfied by reading the current reviews of important works. It is this public that has given importance to a kind of writing that is neither belles-lettres nor yet sustained thought: short, undocumented, "suggestive," unsystematic, and very literary books, usually collections of essays. Their typical writers are Paul Valéry, T. S. Eliot, and A. R. Orage. Alain, who has an enormous reputation in France and who is now for the first time translated into English [in *Mars; or, The Truth about War*], belongs to this class.

It is significant that all the writers mentioned have been interested first in aesthetic problems, for it is their writing in this field that has given them their model. Their over-concise, elliptical style, with its false air of precision (created by a parade of qualifying phrases) cloaking the essential absence of definition, their obscure and allusive manner are especially suitable to the field of aesthetics and literature, subjects whose principles remain vague, whose boundaries are unmapped, with which documentation can do little to induce intuitive agreement, and to which dialectic proof is inapplicable. Yet even in this field such an endeavor as I. A. Richards's (in his *Principles of Literary Criticism*) to write with some science and system makes the work of these others appear that of amateurs and dilettantes.

Certainly the attempts of these writers to deal with philosophical and social ideas, fields intensively, fruitfully, and systematically cultivated in well-established traditions, in the same fragmentary way that they deal with literature are not to be taken very seriously. One's judgment on this aspect of their work is made more harsh than necessary by the serious attention one sees lavished on it by men who should know better. It is not so much this kind of writing as the uninformed praise of it that should be condemned. There is a certain, though very subordinate, value in Valéry's ideas about the nature of thought, Eliot's ideas about politics, or Orage's psychological exercises. Such work is at least a kind of journalism of thought. But it is never more. And for this reason it is unfortunate that Alain should be introduced to the English public by these little essays on a subject which—unlike aesthetics and religion, on which he has written a number of books usually referred to by thinkers who praise him—is comparatively amenable to analysis. War is a phenomenon with economic and social causes, and there is already a considerable literature upon it in economics and social psychology; anyone who writes about war with any hope of saying something important must take this literature into consideration, and must certainly be prepared to elaborate fully his ideas. Besides Trotter's *Instinct of the Herd in War and Peace*—I compare it to a book which is also a psychological study, tentative and speculative—Alain's essays appear thin, pontifical in their brevity, and literary in the worst sense of that word.

Alain hates war, thinks it not inevitable, and considers its cure to be the reduction of the power of the state, which he considers at best a necessary evil. He considers the conflict of interests to be "only the occasion" for war, its cause is "the passions." The conflict of interests and the passions are talked of as if they were individual as well as social phenomena; which they are at any point is not quite clear; and their relation to the war-waging state is not developed. An individualistic psychology—Alain tells us that Descartes has said the last word on the passions—is scarcely the instrument with which to analyze a group phenomenon like war. Though the essays were written to stand together, there is no attempt to relate the various ideas to each other. The best bits in the book are discussions of the minutiae of war: the psychology of commanding officers, of civilians, of army doctors. This gives us a hint as to what is wrong with the book. Alain is, perhaps, attempting

nothing more than to tell us how he *feels* about war, but he has selected the form most unadapted to this. A narrative, interspersed with reflections, should have been its style, not this highly abstract and obscure prose. The result of this war between a narrational motive and an ideational form has been that neither emotion nor idea has come through. We shall have to read something of his much more successful in form and impressive in content before we can understand the awe and admiration with which André Maurois [see excerpt above] and Denis Saurat write the foreword and introduction.

*Felix Morrow, "Alain," in* The Nation, *New York, Vol. CXXXI, No. 3409, November 5, 1930, p. 500.*

### Albert Guérard   (essay date 1957)

[*A French-born American critic, historian, philologist, and educator, Guérard has written several studies of French history and of French and comparative literature. In the following excerpt, he praises Alain's literary artistry and the iconoclasm of his philosophical thought.*]

A book by Maurice Barrés has this appealing title: *Le mystère en pleine lumière,* "Mystery in Broad Daylight." It might well be applied to the enigma of Alain's widespread, prolonged, and yet esoteric fame. Everything is obvious about him, and everything is strange. A philosopher writing daily "columns" in a provincial newspaper, and by imperceptible steps establishing himself as a power in French thought and literature; a political theorist wearing without shame the outmoded and almost seamy garb of the small-town radical, and maintaining stubbornly his position against the mighty hosts of Maurrasian reaction on the right and Marxism on the left; a profoundly religious man, a catholic in the fullest sense, who also professed to be a free-thinker and a determined anticlerical—Alain is the most improbable of chimeras. Yet he did exist in the flesh, and labored in the spirit, for our education and our delight.

First of all, why *Alain?* The name, with a medieval flavor, and familiar in Brittany, is not frequent in modern France. Fifty years ago, Alain Fournier and Alain Gerbault were unknown. Seeking a clue in the past, the inquirers first came across the great and elusive Alanus de Insulis, or Alain of Lille, the *Doctor Universalis,* author of *De Planctu Naturae;* but it proved a false scent. The one obvious Alain in French annals was Alain Chartier, in the darkest days of the Hundred Years' War. Every schoolboy knows, as Macaulay loved to say, that he wrote the *Quadrilogue invectif*—a title so fascinating that I never went beyond it—and, four centuries before Keats, "La Belle Dame sans Merci." While he was asleep, a Princess bent over him and kissed his honeyed lips. This time, the guess was correct: the man who signed "Alain" was called Chartier (a name famous at the time for a chain of popular restaurants), and he was a teacher of philosophy. (pp. 171-72)

Alain was an unconventional, and withal an admirable, teacher. His courses, and even his individual lectures, never were formally organized. He read and commented on some great text—Plato and Spinoza were his favorites—and thought aloud. This great free-thinker did not encourage free discussion in the classroom. Not that he was a dogmatist: his teaching was truly Socratic, a liberation and a stimulant. But he was conscious that the Socratic game often is a waste of time; that, in serious thought, improvisation is mostly futile; that the objections raised by the best students were probably what the teacher was planning to say next; and above all, that the young men who had least to say were those most anxious to say it at great length. At any rate, the testimony of his former pupils, in the *Hommage à Alain* published by the *Nouvelle revue française,* is unanimous. Alain taught no system, encouraged no chatter; but he made young men think for themselves. So great was his influence in the classroom that it gave deeper significance to his writings: when the last of his actual disciples has died, it is possible that much of the halo will fade. I, who never met Alain, approve of his work, and relish it; but my appreciation is tepid, compared with the fervor of the initiates. There was, and there still is, a chapel with an altar to Saint Alanus, miracle worker. But the congregation is shrinking, and it may be doomed to disappear.

In this uneventful academic life, there were only two dramatic episodes, created by outward events: the Dreyfus Case and the First World War. Alain, a young teacher, threw himself ardently into the Dreyfus crisis. The famous "Affair" was not a mere technical miscarriage of justice: it involved a conflict of ideals. Alain served his cause by teaching at a "Popular University," a sort of voluntary adult education center, intended to initiate workingmen into careful methods of thought, and above all to foster the critical spirit. It was this agitation also that induced him to become a local journalist. All this, of course, without thought of self or fame.

The other episode was the Great War of 1914. When it broke out, Alain was beyond military age. He had never been a militarist, and his Dreyfusism had strengthened his bias. Yet he volunteered—out of pride, no doubt, but also out of conviction. France, in his eyes, was fighting not for life or happiness but for liberty. He enlisted as a private. Many safe and comfortable staff jobs were open to him: an office, not the trenches, was the normal place for a middle-aged professor. He insisted on going to the front. He got on very well with his comrades in the ranks; at times, an officer was found to recognize his moral greatness and address him as "Sir." An artillery observer on the front line, he rose to the high rank of technical sergeant. He was not embittered by the hard experience—at least not against men, not even against the enemy. But he brought back from the trenches a book, **Mars ou la guerre jugée,** which is a formidable indictment. There still are men who believe like Napoleon that "there is no substitute for victory," and that truth, justice, peace, and brotherhood can be attained if only you massacre a sufficient number of men. Against that poison, Alain provides a powerful antidote.

Beyond the classroom, Alain's activity was manifested chiefly through the daily press. He wrote several thousand miniature essays, each under a thousand words, which he called *propos.* The literal meaning is "chats," but with a

particular shade. There is no chitchat, no smalltalk in Alain. Each of his brief articles has a definite *purpose* and offers us a *proposition.* The brevity, the daily publication, the variety of subjects, the freedom from pedantry would make the *propos* similar to some of our columns; and I have read remarks by Will Rogers and Heywood Broun akin, in spirit and form, to Alain's *propos.* Oddly, a mightier name suggests itself to us—Emerson. Both Alain and Emerson were professional philosophers; but both wrote without pedantry, in an alert, lucid style, homely, somewhat jerky, full of unexpected sallies and paradoxes, all the shrewder, all the wiser, for a constant background of humor. No wisecracking: their chief purpose is not to make us laugh, or even smile, as did Mark Twain, Mr. Dooley, and Will Rogers. Irony is present but not obtrusive; and even more subdued is Irony's melancholy twin, Pity. There is a constant check on pretense and pretension. Both Emerson and Alain, with the limpidity of a mountain spring, are difficult to follow at times, because their thought refuses to be systematic, and because their expression is willfully elliptical. Emerson is the worse offender: it is easier to get lost and weary in a twenty-page Essay than in a two-page *propos.* Emerson, I firmly believe, deliberately indulged in lofty nonsense: his Yankee shrewdness could not quite shake off German transcendentalism. Alain managed to keep his paradoxes within reason.

In a collection, *Thinkers and Philosophers,* a volume, by Paul Foulquié, is devoted to Alain. Philosopher he certainly was, by training and calling; but he never wrote a treatise or elaborated a system. The word philosopher, however, has many meanings. To be a philosopher, first of all, is to adopt an attitude of haughty fortitude in the trials of life; to view contingencies—including death—from the heights of thought and character: this elevation, this stoicism, were present in Alain. But a philosopher need not be harsh in his personal pride, stiff in his moral certitude: he must know how to take our tribulations *philosophically,* i.e., with a smile and a shrug, and Maurois was not wrong in calling Alain our Montaigne. Finally a philosopher, or more precisely a *philosophe,* is one who reflects, but in the hope of guiding human progress: on the intellectual front, a servant of civilization. In this capacity, Alain was not untrue to the spirit of Voltaire, and some of his *propos* could take their place in the *Dictionnaire philosophique.*

But, philosopher or not, Alain undoubtedly qualifies as a thinker. First of all, he believes in the primacy of thought. Descartes was his guide, and for Alain also thought was the sole evidence of our existence. It is essential that we learn how to conduct our thought, yet the goal of thinking is not the elaboration of an infallible system: systems soon harden, and become impediments to free—i.e., fluid—thought. Our thought, while remaining free, must not be loose. It should be able to discern trends in the apparent chaos and to accept the discipline of laws, even if only as working hypotheses. A mind soberly reflecting on realities, in the hope of guiding action, is a *moralist* in the best sense of the term; and a long line of such moralists is a tradition of which France may well be proud. A moralist is not a mere satirist; not a rigid agent of the law, ever-anxious to reprove and rebuke; not a disenchanted old bachelor like Koheleth; but a shrewd and realistic adviser, in whom occasional gruffness is tempered by kindly humor.

If he had no system, Alain had ideas and opinions. Increasingly at the end of his career, he was interested in the fine arts, which include the finest of all, literature. (The title, **Système des beaux-arts** is a misnomer; but the book is a pregnant one.) In this domain, he was in close agreement with Paul Valéry, whom he had distrusted at first; and in our age of confusion, there was something reassuring, even ennobling, in the active sympathy between those two great minds. Alain professed to be an anticlerical, but only in the sense in which the very best Catholics would be anticlericals. The community should not be dictated to by any single group—business, labor, the military, the clergy. Religion is the center of Alain's philosophy; with Hegel, he holds that "to philosophize is to reflect upon religion." For the myths of the past, he has nothing but respect. He only complains that living myths, instinct with spiritual power, have been fossilized into dogmas, turned into pseudo-science, and thus bereft of their true significance and of their potency. Man must constantly create new myths to guide his constant quest.

In politics, he called himself a Radical of the Emile Combes persuasion. The basis of this "radicalism" is equality: never give official recognition to superiorities which cannot be tested at all times, and without fear. Accept no permanent master: every master is an enemy, as La Fontaine had said long before Blanqui. Alain's attitude is a curious compound of reluctant conformity—it is prudent and wise to obey—and indomitable inner resistance. Had he lived in this country, he would have rebelled against "hundred-per-centism, or else . . . "—the enforced "American way of life," because he would have considered it destructive of our fundamental Americanism, which is liberty. He is a law-abiding citizen, the reverse of a subversive, but with the soul of an anarchist: very much after the heart of Herbert Spencer and Herbert Hoover.

The average Frenchman (a myth, no doubt, but myths may throw a searching light upon reality) is an Alain. He obeys, but saves his self-respect by grumbling. He believes in checks and balances, which protect the individual, rather than in the sensational achievements of dictators, giant concerns, elaborate organizations—all *démesurés,* beyond the common measure. He shudders at the ruthless—and barely conscious—collectivism of American life: nationwide standardization, a day formally appointed to love and honor your mother. If one fourth of the French electorate vote the Communist ticket, it is because most of them are Alains who refuse to be coerced even into the right path, and who believe that it is healthy for a government to be faced with a genuine opposition. A country in which "the other side" has not a single representative in Congress seems to the French Alains to be in grave spiritual jeopardy.

I have read many of Alain's innumerable works over the last thirty years; I was glad to renew, extend, and organize my acquaintance by perusing his best books again, and the tributes of his friends. After this scrupulous inquiry, I find it hard to pass a general judgment upon him. I owe nothing to him: the first *book* of his I read, **Mars,** appeared in 1931, when my own thought was well formed. On most points I agree with him: both of us men of the people, both teachers by profession, both rebels against the same imperious masters, both deeply stirred by the Dreyfus Case, both religious free-thinkers. My verdict ought to be: "Marvelous! Just what I have said myself!" On the contrary, Alain's message is so familiar to me that it appears a trifle trite.

It is as a literary artist that Alain is to be judged. "Only well-written works will pass to posterity," said Buffon, who could redeem natural history from the blight of naturalness. There is no more "thought" of a startling nature in Montaigne and in Voltaire than in Alain. The problem is one of style, and style is personality. Alain's teaching manifestly had a style of its own: I am not so sure about the esthetic quality of his *propos.* He wrote too many; he wrote them too fast; he made it a principle never to correct himself. Compared with Montaigne, his picturesqueness is not sufficiently vivid, and his humor is tame. The chief difference is that Montaigne offers us "a man, not a book": Alain refuses to take us into his familiar confidence. A man of the people, and garrulous, he is actually more distant than Count Alfred de Vigny, the apostle of stoic silence. For those who have not known him in the flesh, Alain does not become a permanent friend, as Montaigne does.

André Maurois, who knew him well, and who distilled an admirable summary of his teaching, brings him the most glowing tribute of all.

> I prophesy that his work, within a hundred years, will be in the literary history of our days what Montaigne's was in his time. Among the writers of this century, which are destined to survive? In the case of most, I should not like to commit myself. But about this one, I have no hesitation; and the only glory I crave with our descendants is to have been the herald of his glory.

This was written in 1950, when Alain was still alive: I am glad that Maurois's wreath was not laid down on a tomb. Funeral orations should be antehumous. Now Alain is dead, and it is not inconceivable that he will stay dead. Time will tell? Time *may* tell: but will it tell the truth? Time has preserved mummies, and destroyed beauties which should have been imperishable. But to crave for the interminable afterglow of a text and of a name is vanity—a vanity that Alain himself would have scorned. He did good, and he had his fun doing it: what other reward is needed? (pp. 174-80)

*Albert Guérard, "The Enigma of Alain," in his* Fossils and Presences, *Stanford University Press, 1957, pp. 171-80.*

**John Hampton** (essay date 1961)

[*In the following essay, Hampton examines Alain's views on individualism, civilization, and religion.*]

It is strange that the voluminous writings of Alain—the pseudonym of Emile-Auguste Chartier, 1868-1951—should be so little known in this country, whereas in France his prestige was great enough, at his death, to warrant a special number of the *Revue de métaphysique et de morale* and the *Nouvelle revue française,* two national journals of very high standing. M. André Maurois has prophesied that Alain's name will rank alongside that of Montaigne when the final assessment has been made.

This comparison is indeed significant, for just as one naturally thinks of Alain as the philosophical counterpart of the *poet* Valéry, so one has no difficulty in placing him in the great French tradition of philosopher-*moralists* who have, like Jean-Paul Sartre and Gabriel Marcel today, always had one foot in philosophy and the other in literature. Such a marriage not only helps the writer to maintain contact with the "laity", but is also the best guarantee that he will not leave the sure path of experience. We assume too readily that experience is something given. This is true only in the grossest sense. Experience is rather a function of consciousness which develops with the cultivation of attention. And philosophy itself demands not only rigour, but also the *finesse* of perception which results from such pursuits as the practice of literature.

Alain's approach to his subject is interesting in itself. Nearly everything he wrote, including those books in which he treats a single overall theme, like religion or art, was presented in the form of short articles or *propos* of two, three or four pages. The habit of writing in this way was acquired at an early stage in his career, probably when he was a contributor to the *Dépêche de Rouen,* but it was not the product of chance. Alain's whole aim was to produce *ideas* which would help his readers to see reality more clearly. These ideas he compares to spectacles, and leaves it to the reader to judge for himself whether they give him clearer vision or not. But, he points out, if an idea does not give us a better grasp of things, no amount of argument will make us accept it as true.

On the other hand, ideas which illuminate the world for us can do without proof. "La preuve est la compagne de l'ignorance," he says in **Vigiles de l'esprit.** That is to say that one tries to prove only what cannot be immediately seen, or in other words, what one does not and cannot *know* in the most concrete sense of the word. The task of the philosophers, in the words of Alain, is to "reveal the world as it is and man as he is". If their teachings are rarely understood, that is because, in most men, vision is obscured by passion. Prior to all valid thought, therefore, there must be a moral preparation, a real purification, without which it is useless to go further. Argument, however clever, will merely be the slave of passion.

Each *propos* of Alain aims at pointing to one particular "view" of a given theme. This was usually expressed by Alain on the four sides of a sheet of folded writing-paper. If it could not be done in this way, it had better not be done at all. Indeed the author tells us that very often, especially in the early days before the First World War, it just didn't "come off". Nevertheless, whenever he wrote, Alain insisted on putting down on paper the genuine and authentic expression of his mind as it was at the moment of writing,

as it freely *perceived* and *judged* in face of the problem it had set itself. The mind must be faithful only to itself.

Alain hardly ever corrected what he had written, confident as he was that the naked expression of his living judgment was more likely to awaken the mind of his reader than a whole shopful of logical devices. Such an attitude affects his style considerably: it is, as it were, an anti-style, devoid of transitions, of rhythm, of any striving after effect, and the shock of such candour has a greater effect than anything the author could have invented. The result of this was to make Alain the centre of an enthusiastic band of disciples, but his success never led him to seek high office. He remained a schoolteacher all his life, refusing a post at the Sorbonne as he had, during the war, refused a commission, in order that he should not debase himself by rising. To his motto *rester peuple* he remained faithful to the end of his life.

One might well be tempted to see egoism in such a cross-grained individualist as Alain seems to be. But I am sure one would be quite wrong. To convince ourselves of this, we need only consider Alain's attitude towards his own life. He was quite unable to take any serious interest in himself, to such a degree that when pressed to write his autobiography, he confined his study entirely to the development of his impersonal ideas, refusing to relate these to external events or to those influences so beloved of the psycho-analysts.

> "I do not like confessions," he wrote in his ***Histoire de mes pensées,*** so much so that I have been unable even in the form of a novel, to write anything about my private life; it is perhaps because I do not like to think about it too much, or because I have found other consolations. *I have learnt how to forget and begin again;* and this practical method cannot be put into maxims, *since it breaks the sequence of the story.* Not to talk about oneself thus becomes a kind of rule, an almost merciless one, designed to lead to forgetting.

Of his childhood he tells us little, and what he does say is merely meant to stress the childishness of his childhood. "I wish to speak here," he continues, "of hours of complete sobriety, that is to say of that part of my existence for which I am joyfully responsible."

I mention this attitude of the author, first because it helps us to distinguish, using this example, between a legitimate individualism and an immature egoism, and secondly because it gives us already a glimpse of Alain's philosophy. For where there is a complete biographical explanation of a man's philosophy, to that extent it comes under suspicion as being *inauthentic,* that is, of having been inculcated by circumstances and institutions. And inauthentic it remains until such time as it is—if ever it is—confirmed in a moment of freedom and lucidity by the person involved, acting as a centre of responsibility. Alain would insist that such an act transcends the possibilities of the body, confined as it is to the causal flux of sensation and emotion. *L'esprit,* the mind or the spirit, is the only aspect of human nature characterized by *autonomy.* It is the only source of the human in man, and any civilization which does not recognize its supremacy is a mockery.

It is important to remember that for Alain the intellectual and spiritual life of man begins in society, rather than as a result of an individual contact with nature as such. The child has first to recognize the signs sent out from the people about him, for his survival depends upon this. The understanding of these signs consists at first in nothing else but the recognition that they *are* signs, and in the imitation of them. Eventually ideas are born within this system of communication, and these express at first only social relationships, being applied later on to nature itself. Art is essentially a system of signs, from which thought may arise, but in themselves the signs are more elemental than thought: *"Le beau nous somme de penser"*—beauty summons us to thought.

Ceremony plays a particularly important part in Alain's philosophy of art, and hence in his philosophy of man. The individual left to himself, the author points out, would be the victim of his own formless, chaotic, emotional outbursts. But by expressing these in an orderly and socially acceptable way, then, far from being repressed and tyrannized by convention, he is in fact *saved,* in a quasi-religious sense, from his own animality, and enabled to *create himself as man.* "Human passions," writes Alain, "do not rule over the arts, but on the contrary it is the arts which rule over man, showing him, through architectural laws, his own form more beautiful than himself and wiser than himself. That is why every true statue demands a prayer from us, and always obtains it." Human nature is not something covered up by a veneer of civilization, but *is* the veneer, and its value has nothing to do with its material bulk.

Art, then, is a form of language, but one which consists of action immediately understood and imitated. It is a sort of absolute language: "And this is what I understand," says Alain, "by absolute language. There is a part of language which has no other object than itself; there is a moment of language in which language occupies one's whole thought. To understand is merely to know that one is communicating; it is to imitate without looking any further." The meaning of a work of art is what one feels in its presence. It cannot mean anything but itself, and no commentary can ever exhaust its meaning. And this sign, which is a materialization of the human spirit, is for Alain a genuine form of salvation, and indeed a real solution to man's problem in the world. That is to say it is simply one aspect of the cult of man which can also express itself in the incarnation called religion.

Alain was one of the early thinkers of the twentieth century to realize the need for a new approach to what he terms the religious myth. It should not be regarded as a piece of wrong reasoning, nor as an ornament for expressing something which could be put more clearly in purely intellectual terms. It has a peculiar value, saying, as it does, something which cannot otherwise be said about the fundamental *structure* of man. And religion itself is not something external to man, handed down from on high, but is the very reflection of his existential situation, of his participation in the *being* of the world. Man first emerges into the realm of the human when he attains to an awareness of his own presence in the world, that is to say, when he realizes that he is, as consciousness, distinct from the objective world, and that he at the same time confronts it. This new awareness is not, of course, expressed in sophisticated philosophical language. It is grasped in the form of a haunting feeling of the presence of *something else.* This is in fact himself. It is as though man were behind himself all the time, felt to be mysteriously present and yet never appearing.

The feeling of being haunted is however relieved, according to Alain, when it is projected into the material world in the form of material objects—the signs referred to above—in which, in a very real sense, there now dwells the spirit of man. Yet this liberation is only a moment in a dialectical process. Mind, instead of confronting the world from an undefinable position, now confronts *man* from within the image, and demands an explanation of itself. This results in the creation of a myth, of a story woven round the image and felt darkly but intensely to be *right.* And it is right, not because something has been proved, but because something has been *recognized.* Such recognition of man by man is the real ground of religion and the source of its tenacity in the face of purely conceptual thought. "People like to think," writes Alain,

> that man made images because he was religious. This is the same as saying that he made tools because he was scientific; but on the contrary science is simply the observation of tools and of the work done by tools. In the same way I would prefer to say that the first act of contemplation had an idol as its object, and that man became religious because he made idols. The power of the sign had to be explained, and mythology was invented to explain beauty.

All this means, in fact, that for Alain the true essence of religion is to be found in the creative work of the latter, as distinct from its theological doctrines. To *explain* religion in terms of dogmas is like trying to translate poetry into plain prose. For religion is a *sign* of the presence of man: "There is something lifeless about all theology," writes Alain. So we see that for our author the images themselves are more alive and more significant because they are more human. This is what all theology forgets—that religion is for man, not for God, who, under whatever name he may go, has no need of it.

Alain, therefore, in spite of his extreme radicalism, regards the efforts of enlightened people to purge religion of its visible signs as misguided. "For," he writes in a passage referring to Auguste Comte, "according to his views, to which each day brings added support, the old fetishism is indeed the essential religion, whilst intellectualized and purified religion is only the negation of religion which, under the name of theology and metaphysics, extracts the god from the sign, and even from the temple, itself a sign, and casts us into the insubstantial infinite, from which we must forthwith return."

Alain often writes, quite deliberately, under the influence of one or more of the great philosophers of the past. He did not believe in the possibility of radical progress in philosophy—all the essential ideas of which the human mind is capable have already been put forward, and what really matters is that we should remain in constant *contact* with these, for they provide an inexhaustible field for study, reflection and spiritual enrichment. Culture is the *cult* of the *static* element in man, that is to say, of his permanent and essential structure. For man's structure explains his history, the static being the basis of the dynamic, and not *vice versa*. And we have seen that for Alain the structure of man is found in art, religion and philosophy, without which there is no humanity. If one can speak of progress, it is not of movement in a horizontal direction, as it were, towards any historic goal set in the future, but rather of the ever-present possibility of a vertical movement which consists simply of being fully human, here and now.

Man is at all times capable of living on a number of levels, of which the sub-human basis is always present, but of which the truly human levels can be made manifest only through the *will*. No system of education, no society can be foolproof against its own foolishness. We are always free to choose barbarism. It is for this reason that Alain prefers to speak of *les étages de l'homme,* the storeys or planes of man, rather than *les étapes de l'homme,* the stages through which man has passed. He even goes so far as to say, in his **Propos sur l'education,** that we are as intelligent as we decide to be, as we *will* to be. Thus the cultivation of the will is central to his philosophy of education, and takes him far away from the educational trends of our day, which he characterizes as "insane". The victory, of course, is never definitively won. Even for Alain each day represented, as he put it, *une bêtise à surmonter*—a stupid tendency to be overcome.

When he comes to a closer examination of religion, Alain again adds his commentary to what has been said by one of the great philosophers, this time Hegel. Just as Hegel had divided the history of religion into three stages, nature religion, aesthetic religion and spiritual religion, so Alain divides the house, as it were, of religion, into three storeys, each of which is always there, though not always lived in. The first one, Pan, as he calls it, represents the agrarian level of religion, and is the expression of man's natural reactions in the face of nature. His dominant emotion at this stage is fear, but religiously significant fear is fear of what is not there: "It is *nothingness* which frightens, and all fear is fear of fear, fear of oneself, fear of the gods."

The transformation of this kind of religion into the next kind—the one which Alain calls Jupiter—is a process which occurs in all civilized people. The first reaction of fear of the world gives way, eventually, to the religion of Caesar, of the physical power of man. It has its beauty, and it is a first manifestation of the spirit, in so far as this is bound up with the development of man's self-consciousness. But in the long run it is a failure, because the worship of material power finally drives the spirit in upon itself, so that now it comes to be revealed in its place of refuge, in the slave, not in the master.

And finally the true manifestation of the human spirit is seen in the *negation of power,* symbolized, for example, in such an image as that of the infant Jesus: "This being," says Alain, "who would perish without our care, is God." Now, the human spirit manifests itself in its purity, for

what it is, and *without any guarantee of success* in the world. Indeed, for Alain, whom, if we have any use for such words, we must call an agnostic, the figure of the crucified Jesus represents the permanent, vital and essential *powerlessness* of the human spirit in the face of material force. Its purpose, in manifesting itself, is not success or conquest, and whenever it is diverted towards these aims, it perishes. It shines simply because it is light, without any desire to get anywhere or have anything.

Alain closes his study of the gods with a tribute to those who devote their lives to the seemingly futile task of training subnormal children. "A friendly word, now," he writes,

> for those doctors who care for the retarded and who watch, like prophets, for the slightest gleam of understanding; they never tire, and they are right. There is therefore a truth which is the core of all truth, and which defies fate. And I could show, following Descartes, that there is no truth, even proved, even useful, which is not the child of truth unproved, of useless truth, of truth bereft of all power. But industrial truth is an ungrateful child, moreover punished a hundredfold by her rewards. Perhaps these ideas will be made known, and the spirit of man will know how to deprive itself of power, of every kind of power; such is the highest reign. And Calvary reveals this very thing in such an eloquent and moving way, that I will add no commentary.
>
> (pp. 92-7)

*John Hampton, "The Humanism of Alain," in* Contemporary Review, *Vol. 199, February, 1961, pp. 92-7.*

## Ronald F. Howell    (essay date 1965)

[*In the following excerpt, Howell discusses Alain's political thought within the context of his general philosophy, noting its relation to French radicalism during his lifetime.*]

The judgment that France today still suffers from the French Revolution and the wars of Napoleon I requires no other empirical confirmation than a casual examination of French political history since 1789 will afford. The life of any nation is sustained by its symbols; the French deprived themselves of theirs the moment they escorted King Louis XVI to the guillotine. As symbols of a national consensus, the *Marseillaise,* the tricolor, and Bastille Day have proved to be quite inadequate substitutes for the *fleur-de-lis* and the majesty and pageantry of a royal dynasty, themselves found wanting earlier. For in their political temperament the French have remained both monarchical *and* republican (radical), never being really certain which of these poses best depicts their true self. The malaise of that republic in the nineteenth and twentieth centuries is perhaps most accurately diagnosed in terms of the psychological effects of periodic oscillations between those two states of mind, with no viable synthesis or midpoint compromise ever attained. The French are reputedly the world's supreme individualists, who dislike the restraint of being governed much more decisively than they lack the knowledge of how to govern.

Astonishing it therefore is that nowhere in the English literature that concerns France is there available a full exposition of the political thought of the one man who since the eighteenth century has most vividly exhibited the French political spirit or, more specifically, the spirit of French classical radicalism during the Third Republic. That man is the philosopher Alain, pseudonym for Emile-Auguste Chartier, who lived from 1868 to 1951. Now, it is true that Alain is frequently cited and quoted in British and American books on political science, particularly those on comparative government. Usually, however, only his "radicalism" is mentioned, and the content of even that "radicalism" is not adequately or clearly disclosed. In Great Britain and the United States, Alain is simply *not known.* This neglect, if not countered, will continue to leave a hiatus in the knowledge of every Britisher and American who aspires to understand the French situation today. (pp. 594-95)

Embarrassing to admit, Alain has fared markedly better outside the English-speaking world. His works, encompassing nearly every sphere of human thought and activity, are contained in over sixty published volumes, many of which have been translated into German, Spanish, Italian, Turkish, and almost all into Japanese! Yet only one of these, *Mars ou la guerre jugée,* has found its way into English, in a translation that is extremely poor. On the other hand, Alain's importance in French letters and pedagogy was acknowledged in a leading (page one) article in the *Times Literary Supplement* as recently as August 1, 1958 [see Further Reading]. After recognizing that "Alain was, in the first place, a teacher—by far the most famous one in France between 1919 and 1933," the *Supplement* continued:

> It is no exaggeration to say that for the average literary minded young Frenchman of the 1930's there were five great contemporary authors: Proust, Gide, Valéry, Claudel, and Alain. Alain, as a matter of fact, helped to create this conviction not, of course, by placing himself on a level with the other four, but by praising Valéry, Claudel, and Proust in such a way as to imply that no other writers were worth bothering about. (For reasons which remain unexplained, he had no patience with Gide. . . . ) The Big Five are now all dead and each of the first four has, provisionally at least, been settled in a niche. Only Alain remains unplaced.

Even Alain's own countrymen have conceded the vexing difficulty of properly appraising and "placing" him within the French philosophic tradition. The fact that throughout his life he refused to categorize himself or to accept the categorization of others may in part explain why his works are of such perennial interest and value. Nominally a professor of philosophy, *un professeur de khâgne,* in several *lycées* and finally at the Lycée Henri-Quatre in Paris, Alain was always a great teacher. The subject-matter of his teaching did not really matter; he could discourse with equal agility and insight on philosophy or politics or literature or music or economics or religion or mathematics or

the physical sciences. He was truly a man of *virtù,* akin to the highly versatile and profoundly humanistic Renaissance man of parts. Life he would never compartmentalize; to do so was ultimately to destroy its meaning. In his words [from *Histoire de mes pensées*], "I am certain . . . that all truths would perish in a system of truths." Hence, any attempt (except for purely analytical purposes) to isolate and label his philosophic orientation or his literary criticism or (especially) his political thought would do major violence to his own stated intent. Alain can be wedged into no classifiable slot prearranged either by the conservation of tradition or the revolutionary nature of those passing intellectual fads to which others of his time succumbed. Perhaps it is enough to say that he was "a radical," a philosopher, and the Third Republic's "moralist of liberty."

It is thus more appropriate to speak of Alain's political thought than of his political theory. Theory implies unity and system; Alain's thought was not, and indeed he never meant it to be, unified and systematic. Although he was the author of many works employing a "standard" prose style, the principal genre through which he expressed his ideas in effect precludes the construction of theory *qua* unified, coherent system. That genre is the *propos,* a restricted prose form resembling a short newspaper feature article with editorial comment. More precisely, an Alain *propos* is a proposition for discourse, a brief thesis tersely conveyed, a scholarly chat, a sketch, an essay-vignette, a provocative commentary written on almost every conceivable topic. It recalls in its more elongated form a maxim of La Rochefoucauld and in its briefer compass an essay of Montaigne. It has been compared to the type of sonnet that proceeds from a reflection on particulars to the tentative statement of a universal [in Georges Pascal, *Pour connaître la pensée d'Alain* (1946)]. And because of its nontechnical language, its rich imagery, its familiar and often earthy examples, its classical allusions, and its polyphonic prose, it is analogous to unversed poetry generally.

Alain rigidly limited the length of a *propos,* which for many years he wrote daily for French provincial newspapers (more often than not against the "Parisian elite"), to two handwritten pages (about fifty lines). He made virtually no revisions of the first draft; rather than correct, he began anew. Because the *propos* is thus circumscribed, indicating a predilection for strict form in the rationalistic, neoclassic heritage of the Enlightenment, much is necessarily left unsaid, unexplained, unsystematic, paradoxical, elliptical, enigmatic, laconic, merely suggested, or implied. Accordingly, the ramifications of a discrete idea could not possibly be developed in any one *propos.* Observable, nevertheless, from the total corpus of his works, those sixty-odd volumes, is a consistent thread of interpretation of political and other matters. André Maurois, probably Alain's most celebrated student, has pointed out that while Alain was purposefully unsystematic, he did express with constancy, throughout his life, "certain preferences and dislikes." To be sure, there is considerable repetition in Alain's writing, and partly by design. He complained that though everything has been said, little has been heard, so everything must be said at least twenty times again. Such repetition ought not to be denigrated.

Its positive merit in underscoring an enduring commitment to certain fundamental ideas (constants, universals) surely outweighs the negative criticism that Alain belabors those ideas to the point of prolixity.

Further, Alain writes more in the style and spirit of the older French *politiques et moralistes,* the counterpart of moral philosophers in eighteenth-century England, than in that of contemporary political scientists. (He has been variously acclaimed as a twentieth-century Montaigne or Montesquieu or Voltaire.) His political terms are often nebulously defined, primarily because he had no interest in giving them specific substantive content. That he would have had an honest dislike for the recent "scientific" direction of a segment of American political scientists is attested by Jacques Brenner's statement that "Alain's distrust of 'proofs' was reinforced by political and economic [scholars] who pretended to reason with the rigor of mathematicians and physicists." His own political concepts are sometimes dogmatically advanced, but this is so because he was faithful to a pungent formula of his own personal political creed: one must make a choice among political value-alternatives early in life and then unswervingly hold fast to that choice. (That such a position augurs a rather static *Weltanschauung* cannot be lightly dismissed.) Alain, moreover, writes intuitively and from insight, and the signification of his thought reaches the reader by a sharpening and refining of the reader's acumen, which does in fact occur from a wide reading of the *propos* and from thoughtfully reflecting upon their maxims, parables, aphorisms, and epigrams. Alain also writes impressionistically; in any concise resume of his thought, the impressions have to be pinned down, arranged, and ordered (at least mentally) by the critic. A *propos,* though aesthetically well-contoured within its restricted limits, often leaves an idea open-ended and dangling. Fortunately, in copious later *propos,* Alain returns to the idea to dissect and embellish it further, though rarely definitively.

It is impossible to understand, analyze, synthesize, systematize, and then evaluate Alain's political thought except in collation with the totality of the *propos* that touch on his analysis of the political order. It is equally impossible to assess his political thought except within the perspective of the totality of his general philosophy. General philosophy, as Alain taught and wrote it, was sufficiently broad in compass to embrace every human endeavor. From that totality the generating *élan* of a metaphysical, epistemological, and ethical persuasion may be discerned, supplying the root premises from which his political thought implicitly develops.

According to Alain, any attempt to effectuate a separation, whether metaphysically or epistemologically, between *la pensée* (thought) and *l'action* (action) is neither viable, valid, nor realistic. Thought and action cannot be dichotomized. The problems engendered by purely abstract thoughts are simply those that admit of no solution, no passage to the active, actual world. Such a belief might eventuate in a "law" of causality according to which "every reasonable man recognizes necessity in things, on the theory that everything is connected to everything else, as the tides to the moon." Alain refused to concede the affinity of such a statement with the pantheistic determinism of Spinoza. For though confessedly skeptical and doubting—doubting what is certain being more crucial than doubting what is doubtful, he remained an optimistic apostle of freedom, if not freedom in the processes of nature, assuredly freedom in man's confrontation with those processes.

From his own highly esteemed professor, Jules Lagneau, at the Lycée Michelet at Vanves from 1886 to 1889 (the time of Boulangism), Alain had decided that the mind (spirit) orders concrete objects, but always in the immediate or potentially immediate presence of those concrete objects. This decision would appear to parallel a conclusion of the subjective idealism of Kant, whose philosophy Alain lavishly praised and even explicated in a short book, *Lettres à Sergio Solmi sur la philosophie de Kant.* In the revolutionary *Critique of Pure Reason,* Kant had pronounced *ex cathedra:* "In respect of time . . . no knowledge of ours is antecedent to experience, but begins with it. But, though all our knowledge begins with experience, it by no means follows that all arises out of experience." Note, however, the amendment proposed by Georges Pascal in his exposition of Alain's philosophy:

> Idealism is true if it means only that the world is at each instant a construction of the spirit, but it is unacceptable if it pretends to make the world a contingent matter whose very existence would depend on the spirit. Common sense rebels against such a fantastic doctrine that reduces existence to a human decree. Essence, not existence, is of the spirit. The world is nothing but an immense and indivisible existence that appears to the spirit as chaos which must be ordered.

Hence follows the standard that Alain appropriated from Lagneau: *"la pensée est la mesureuse."* Thought is the measuring instrument for ordering external existence, as Anaxagoras had argued in pre-Socratic times, and "the spirit is nothing more than an ensemble of *a priori* ideas." Ideas must relate to experience, however, and in a Kantian way. Lagneau had lectured that "there is no [purely] subjective knowledge." There are ideas because there are things for there to be ideas about. Ideas are "the pincers for seizing the objects of experience." It is only the modes of ordering, e.g., space and time, that are not contingent upon and not known by human experience. Otherwise, object and subject are necessarily related: *una eademque res.* As Alain explains, "we formulate ideas only in the actual perception of an object." Yet apart from the modes of ordering, may there be an idea with which an actual human perception has never been associated? The idea of God? Alain, intrepidly anticlerical and forsaking formal religion at the age of twelve, once confided: "I sometimes think that if I had never thought about God in some way, I would not have thought at all."

An appreciation of Alain's theological position, cryptically complex, is somewhat difficult to communicate intelligibly. In the first place, he would deny as fallacious the assumptions of an anthropomorphic deity and of personal immortality. Second, "God cannot be said to *exist.*" Now, this is not the same as saying there "is" no God. Existence is a purely human construct of all that is external to man in nature. If God "is" "anything," His properties cannot be described in finite human terms. If there "is" a God, then by apodictic definition He must be transhuman, transmundane, transspatial, transtemporal, transcausal, *trans* everything perceived as existence. "To prove the existence of God is to deny Him." (Alain, in fact, was highly skeptical of the possibility of *proving* anything.) God, therefore, is not existence; He is essence. "Existence is hypothesized by essence," and "eternity is the mirror of time."

Perceptible glimmerings of Alain's meaning now pierce the opacity of a paradoxical denial *and* affirmation of deity. Using his favorite pedagogical method, *clarum per obscurius* (clarify by obscuring), Alain (*pace* Plato) entices his reader to find his own way out of the cave. So, as Auguste Comte had demonstrated, polytheism precedes monotheism: "If I could think of all the gods as being in God and as God, all the gods would be true." External existence, unlike active, willing, judging essence (God, *esprit*) that abides in man, is nature. And "nature is inertia," known only as phenomena and only through the forms of thought *when* the forms of thought have coherently ordered it. Order is thus subsequent to chaos, the superior (*epistêmê*: knowledge) to the inferior (*doxa*: opinion), Christianity to paganism, philosophy to theology, the ellipsis (Kepler) to the circle (Copernicus), music to noise, adults to children, free men to slaves, the republic to the monarchy, Alain to Emile-Auguste Chartier.

The map to Alain's epistemology, inextricable from his metaphysics, is perhaps now more decipherable despite the subtle detours indicated. Basically, it is Cartesian: I think, therefore I am—*and I am free.* The will to think makes freedom determined. Man is free when he acts, and his actions are willed by *la pensée*. To think is to construct—that is, to act. Thinking is as much an "act" (action, activity) as the visible, concrete act in which thinking, prompting will into motion, may abide. The concrete, manifested, experiential, and observable act, though chronologically successor to thought, is finally an integral and inseparable aspect of thought, just as thought is an integral and inseparable aspect of the act. "The universe of things is also a fact of thought." *Ordo et connexio idearum* and *ordo et connexio rerum* are but facets of the same reality, as Spinoza had cogently reasoned. The Aristotelian metaphysical premise *universalia in re* Alain here reaffirms. Thought directing the will (*élan*) incites, advances, and enhances the act and serves as its terminal criterion. Alain's implication, however, is emphatically *not* that the philosopher is thereafter obliged to *arrange* thoughts, ideas, "truths" in a logical and hierarchical system, even if the system could then withstand empirical tests for validation. Far from it, he warns. Life cannot thus be bound. Curiously, Alain's own personal life was almost as narrowly regimented by methodical routine as was Kant's, and the *propos* is an aptly tangible examplar of his self-permission to roam at will philosophically, but only within self-prescribed cognitional limits and inflexible stylistic rules.

Beneath this most highly generalized perspective, from his own Mount Olympus, Alain subsumed his ideas on the more specific topics of politics, literature, economics, religion, music, painting, the physical sciences, and education. Always he credited Lagneau with having inculcated in him the desire to think, and to think freely. Probably, then, free judgment (*le jugement libre*), perception (*la perception*), and will (*la volonté*) constituted the matrices of Alain's philosophy, nascent but emerging during his tutelage under Lagneau. Even as a young man he had recognized that independence of judgment, perception, and will presupposes a lively acceptance of personal responsibility:

> To safeguard that power to think, not to submit it to anything, not to dishonor it by any kind of intoxication—is not that the true moral philosophy, my Master? . . . Perhaps he [Lagneau] might return to remind me that the true moral philosophy does not have as its primary objective the judgment of others, but rather the self-control of oneself.

From his metaphysical and epistemological "*doctrine de la volonté*" Alain derived his ethical and political thought, which, written with reference to activities of the will (made aware by perception and guided by judgment), is devoted primarily to a surgical dissecting of the component parts of his concepts of personal and political liberty. These are the concepts he emphasized in all of what are somewhat incorrectly designated as his ethical and political writings. Yet *political* liberty is ancillary to *personal* (moral) liberty. Indeed, political liberty can legitimately be attained only insofar as the exercise (by will) of personal liberty evokes reliable guidelines for judgment. For to Alain personal liberty does not mean freedom from external restraint so decidedly as it means obedience to the internal restraint and discipline that an individual freely imposes upon himself. That this view should seem essentially Rousseauistic (and certainly Kantian) is not surprising in view of the acknowledged debt that Alain professed he owed to "that French-speaking Swiss with the most German of hearts." "Rousseau," he admitted, "was always my master."

Alain's concept of personal liberty is grounded in the postulate that one should not submit to his own whimsical and capricious passions. Rather, he should recognize his duty to the internal order of his reason. One is truly and genuinely free only in the thought and the act of refusing to surrender as a slave to the domination of his partial and thus prejudicial self-interests. Political liberty is meaningless and valueless if it is not regarded as a prize less worthy to be won than personal liberty, or ethical victory over one's self. It is better to bow before a political tyrant than to acquiesce in capitulation to the larger tyranny of one's own personal, particularistic desires. Alain here concurs with Kant that the personally *free* individual must be the successfully self-legislating individual. Self-realization comes through self-limitation, and happiness is the byproduct of the fulfillment of duty. Hence: "Today, even more than in earlier times, I understand how the doctrine of Duty supports the doctrine of Liberty." The individual's dutiful confrontation with, and effective vitiation of, the willfulness of his intrinsic nature is therefore the focal point of reference and departure for understanding his relationship to those who are his governors in the impersonal state.

Alain's ethics exalted the "integrity" and the "decency" of individual freedom, coupled with mandatory, thought usually personally objectionable and disrespectful, social responsibility. His prescription? Criticize resolutely and energetically, yet obey unsullenly. Recognize that minimal social order demands limitations on overt political activity, but permit no restraint on freedom of thought and expression. The greater the freedom of thought and its expression, operative in something like John Stuart Mill's "market place of ideas," the greater the likelihood that the "best" people will rule in a democracy. The ideal politics is the politics of criticism and resistance and control. In one of the most typical and memorable passages of all his political *propos*, Alain trenchantly proclaims: "Resistance and obedience, those are the virtues of the citizen." Obedience insures order; resistance insures liberty. But order and liberty are not separable; they are correlatives rather than opposites. Liberty cannot exist without order, and order is worthless without liberty. "To obey while resisting, that is the whole secret. Whatever destroys obedience is anarchy; whatever destroys resistance is tyranny. . . . Obey physically, never spiritually." This is the incisive thematic advice of Alain's "radicalism."

In that radicalism, both the monarchical and republican sides of his political temperament merge, complement, and act as catalysts one for the other, with no violation of consistency. In a certain indirect sense Alain *was* a monarchist. He enjoyed recalling that voters in his native Perche voted "royalist," not because they favored the return of a king, but because their mere act of voting against "republicans in power" made them obstinate republicans. His own humble lifelong aspiration was: "*rester peuple*," "*rester simple soldat*," to live his life as a courageous pacifist, a relentless opponent of all forms of militarism and human oppression, close in memory to the rustic peasant soil of his Normandy birthplace, possessing "the Stoic serenity of an Epictetus," and displaying the quiet patience and the stern will of '*un boeuf laboreur*." Maurice Savin, one of Alain's best-known students, probes deeply [in "Discours sur Alain," *Alain (Emile Chartier) au Lycé d'Alençon, 1881-1886* (1958)]:

> There was something of the spirit of Monarchy in him, about which he was not ashamed. A Republican of the purest sort, yes, and even fiercely so. But Monarchy first of all, just as noise precedes music; and the Republic would be nothing without the Monarchy, which was a natural thought to him, just as it is natural to our country, which is a country of insurgent peasants. There was a peasant spirit in Alain, and he did not hide it: a rejection of all the nonsense in fashion, a native resistance, undiminishable, to everyone who promises the moon and all the pleasures of civilization without [first enduring] a peasant austerity.

Alain emerges as a radical republican. Never departing from the conviction so deeply imprinted on his thought from childhood that one must not be unctuous or sycophantic towards those in political authority, he "ridiculed the clever speech-makers and their platitudes, which so often went unquestioned." He had no wish "to deify society." Any "master" is an enemy; thought must therefore be kept free and flexible; a perfect society on earth is an extravagantly absurd chimera, the ideal of an infantile human mythology.

Alain was therefore certainly no revolutionary or fanatical anarchist. He had no desire to replace one political system with another, one set of rulers with another. A change in the form or functions or personnel of political institutions does not automatically improve the government; usually a change occasions not progress but retrogression. Even so, to criticize and censure government is an indisputable prerogative (*libre arbitre*) of the individual—to be exercised even during the very act of obeying. Alain insisted unexceptionally on the necessity of protecting the freedoms of judgment, perception, and will of the unfettered human spirit. The individual must exercise an unrestrained free will in evaluating political, social, religious, and economic ideas and institutions, even if the result be nonconformity, "the nonconformity that is itself the genius of the [French] race, the concern for the worth and the dignity of man, the informed awareness of the dangers of power and of the imperativeness of controlling it." Such intense, uncompromising individualism is the cornerstone of Alain's radicalism.

French classical radicalism, which received its intellectual cast and tone from Alain, was a philosophical movement long before its institutional espousal by that identifiable political party whose ranks included Combes, Clemenceau, Herriot, Daladier, and Mendés-France. (Alain considered Auguste Comte "the father of French radicalism.") The Radical party (and the Radical-Socialists), while the oldest of contemporary parties in France and the country's most important and most powerful left-wing group until 1936, was not founded until 1901. In considerable measure, the history of the Third Republic after the *Seize Mai* defeat of General MacMahon in 1877 was the history of radicalism, and the chief philosopher of radicalism was Alain. Whereas Alain, who eschewed doctrines himself, wrote in 1925 a kind of prolegomenon for radicalism entitled **Eléments d'une doctrine radicale**, the party itself was never committed to any doctrinaire set of political specifics. "Politically progressive but socially conservative," it saw as its task "to build" the Republic from the blueprint of the "immortal principles of 1789." Radicalism, then, was an *état d'esprit*, not a statement of a party program. This *état d'esprit* was nonetheless made visible in various particularized radical attitudes about France and its political culture. Implicit was the belief that political institutions must be rooted in small natural societies, such as the family, the village, the farm, and small individual businesses and professions. In its dedication to the protection of local interests, it stood intransigently against "the State" and the Paris political, cultural, and economic monopoly. At the same time, it stood defiantly against "the Church," and its intensive, embittered anticlericalism (for Father Combes the essential ingredient of radicalism), particularly after the Dreyfus Affair, led straightway to the passage of the Separation Act of 1905. Belated efforts of the Roman Catholic church hierarchy to make certain liberal amends were unavailing. Francis de Tarr has written of members of the Radical party [in *The French Radical Party* (1961)]:

> They have stressed their love of country and their respect for private property; they have defended Individualism, Democracy, and the Republic; they have rejected both Catholicism and Marxism which, they complain, place Church and State above the individual and demand conformity to a revealed body of doctrine; they have identified the Radical Party with the Republic and with France.

These "preferences and dislikes" were of course wholly consistent with Alain's own subjective principles, and his works became the vehicle for succinctly purveying radical ideas. As Jean Touchard has noted, "above all, Alain is *against*. Against the prince, against the chateaux, the academies, important personages, against the administration, against militarism and against war, against the Church, against political powers." An inveterate enemy of all sham and hypocrisy, of all pomp and circumstance, of all the "merchants of sunshine," Alain refused a chair of philosophy at the Sorbonne, refused membership in academic, literary, and political associations, refused every academic and literary honor proffered him except one to gratify his friends a few weeks before his death. He was the *citoyen contre les pouvoirs*, who envisaged the special mission of the Radical party to be the party of governmental opposition. Understandably, the Radical party claimed Alain as its own. Even today, "the halls of Radical congresses always include banners that quote some of his memorable slogans; to the *Comité exécutif* of the Radical Party, a party official [Antonin Douzet] described him, in 1949, as 'the greatest of modern philosophers.' " Elsewhere, Douzet recalled André Maurois's prediction that "in a hundred years people will speak of Alain as they spoke of Descartes a century after his death." Alain's impress on the political culture of France is kept indelible by the ubiquitous presence of new editions of his books at Radical party headquarters and by the activities and the publications of *L'association des amis d'Alain* at Le Vésinet, in suburban Paris.

Subsequent to the decisive surrender of MacMahon and other conservative forces on *Seize Mai*, the unsettling characteristics of the Third Republic began to become apparent. Pronounced governmental instability was the hallmark of French political life until the demise of the Third Republic in 1940. The antagonistic relationship of the legislature and the executive culminated in legislative supremacy in face of almost every important policy decision. And within the legislature, within the frenetic Chamber of Deputies and the dilatory Senate, large groups did not conceal the fact that they were unassuageable enemies of the Constitution, prepared to commit violent and irrational acts against the regime. The two traditions in French political culture remained unreconciled and, it seemed, irreconcilable. The Constitution of the Third Republic blatantly signified a truce, not a compromise between those two traditions. They were mythically couched in the metaphors of the Red and the Black, the Black representing the dark forces of monarchical, authoritarian, bureaucratic,

Bonapartist, and ecclesiastical reaction, the Red exalting the humane, republican, libertarian, egalitarian, and radical principles of 1789. Yet oddly, despite the divisive individualism of the French people, the two in varying degrees seem still at war in every Gallic soul, accounting perhaps for the ambivalent attitude of Frenchmen towards political authority. As Nicholas Wahl has lucidly argued [in "The French Political System," Samuel H. Beer and Adam B. Ulam (eds.), *Patterns of Government* (1962)], the Frenchman prefers

> to have decisions made centrally by some impersonal and presumably expert but distant authority. Thus one of the reasons advanced for the long maintenance of the centralized bureaucracy created by Napoleon is simply that Frenchmen approve of having many delicate political decisions made for them by experts in order to assure some sort of abstract justice. It explains, too, why there has never been more of a movement in favor of autonomous local government in France. On the other hand, Frenchmen are also very eager to protect their individual liberty of action, to prevent abuses of power by the centralized political authority, and to have a constant veto over its decisions.

Astutely aware of the prevalence of this ambivalent attitude, Alain characteristically admonished his countrymen to obey silently, but to reprove and resist audaciously. To reprove and resist and control is the function of *Le Contrôleur* (connoting more than the English word "controller"), which Alain finds to be French democracy's (or any democracy's) most impermeable shield for protecting liberty.

The concept of *Le Contrôleur*, which significantly reveals so much about Alain's political thought, is introduced by the rather obvious remark that democracy cannot exist "by itself" (any more than "can politics save itself")—that is, in its pure (classical) form. In every constitution, there are elements of monarchy, oligarchy, and democracy, held (ideally) in relative equilibrium. Unfortunately, true mixed government, boasting that relative equilibrium of the three forms, as in the United Kingdom, did not exist in the Third Republic of France. Indeed, Wahl has maintained: "Mixed government has *never* existed in France because the aristocratic principle of command and the democratic principle of consent, instead of becoming blended within each institution and thus assuring balance and cooperation among them, individually became *fully* embodied in *different* and ultimately antagonistic institutions."

Principally accepting a modified Polybian schema of mixed government or the mixed constitution, in which status and class orders in society parallel and are reflected in functional branches of government, Alain finds the monarchical element manifested in the executive branch and the oligarchic in the legislature. The democratic element, however, is not located in a specific branch of government, but rather in *Le Contrôleur*, "which Political Science has in no way defined." And what is *Le Contrôleur*? Alain's reply is that it is "nothing more than the continually effective power of deposing kings [ministers] and specialists [bureaucrats] at the very moment when they no longer manage affairs according to the interests of the greatest number. The power was long exercised in revolutions and barricades. Today, it is exercised by means of Interpellation . . . the endless effort of the governed to oppose the abuses of power." *Le Contrôleur* thus stands always suspiciously and skeptically on guard, and democracy becomes a system of diligent surveillance of the voters over the elected: of the people over the deputies ("controlled controllers"), of the deputies over the ministers.

Alain consistently exhibited a deep and enduring faith in democratic government, as he defined it. A vital element in his definition was a doctrine of equality, which served him well first in gauging and then in contesting the presumptuousness of all "*Les Importants*" of society. But a doctrine of equality of rights and responsibilities is by no means democracy's only essential. A monarchy or a tyranny can be democratic in this way, "with many obligations and few rights" shared equally. Offering an explanation reminiscent of that of Hobbes and Rousseau, Alain continues: "If liberty of thought existed for no one, that fact in itself would suggest a kind of equality." A "politics of nature" underlining the truism that every society must be governed is to be distinguished from a "politics of the spirit" demanding that freedom of personal judgment must be preserved. For democracy is inconceivable without laws, without government, and without limitation on the liberty of action of every citizen.

Another essential of democracy, for Alain and the Radical party, is universal (women included) and secret-ballot suffrage. Such an extensive private franchise maximizes the number of people who might vote against the "abuses of power." Universal suffrage will not, however, lead to anything new: "its role is rather to reaffirm vigorously those old truths that Power is naturally inclined to forget." As an electoral mechanism, even universal suffrage is not restricted to a democratic order. "The election of the Pope by universal suffrage did not make the Church democratic. . . . A tyrant can be elected by universal suffrage." In addition, "a law is never (if it is a true law) a servitude imposed by the greatest number of the smallest number, but a servitude imposed equally on all, so that it is impossible for a true law to be very far removed from the general will." To Alain, the crucial test for determining whether a particular regime is "democratic" is "not the origin of powers, but the continuous and effective control that the governed *then* exercise upon the governors." Again, *Le Contrôleur:* just as the Radical party considered that it was its function *par excellence* to be the party of governmental opposition, rarely the party in power. The party's intrinsic *ethos* dictated that it was more important to control power than to seize it.

The radical individual within the democratic order is the man who is unreservedly committed to *droit* (law, right) and equality. The disparate individual is therefore irrevocably linked in his relations and his activities to the social group, and, as the "politics of nature" decrees, his liberty is inconceivable outside social confines. Once more Alain refers to the Comtean social philosophy: even though the individual is the supreme political entity, he is and always

has been an inescapable fact of society. "Comte has propounded a momentous idea, the physics of our sentiments and our thoughts: namely, that man is man only because there is a society of men, which is as natural and inevitable as the solar system." The doctrinal fallacy, then, of some self-professed "individualists" is the assumption that freedom of belief and opinion also embodies a crass license to *disobey* political authority. Alain answers:

> I can testify that the contrary is true. As far as I can see, those who respect and approve [political authority] obey poorly. Why? Because they do not govern themselves—they are consequently very weak in opposing their own passions. For example, it is a commonplace that the soldier who accepts those in authority unquestioningly and as a matter of fact is also the one who most readily neglects small chores when the officer is away.

Though natural and inevitable, society—"always blind and always powerful," produces war, slavery, and superstition. It is of the very essence of society to encourage barbarism, while in the individual spirit "humanity finds itself again." Moral man and immoral society? And, for "society" read *state*? [The critic adds in a footnote that"Alain's distinction between *society* and *state* is rather unclear; wherever he seems to use the terms synonomously is parenthetically indicated."] Alain concludes that the most notable attribute of the democratic spirit is that it is antisocial (antistatist). To the true democrat, "society is a gross animal," a "Leviathan" of which individuals are but submissive units; it is uncivilized, an "infant," a "savage." Society, as he reifies it, cannot differentiate between right and force. It becomes readily entangled in war, which is "compatible with justice and humanity in *no* sense whatever." If on one decisive issue Alain is at all well known to the British and the Americans, that issue is his inordinate abhorrence of war.

It all started with the Dreyfus Affair at the close of the nineteenth century. Emile Chartier, teaching at the Lycée de Lorient at the time, was soon to adopt the pseudonym Alain in signing his first *propos* for the *Dépêche de Lorient.* He proclaimed himself a Dreyfusard, an unflinching opponent of all forms of war, militarism, and human oppression. It was obvious to Alain that Dreyfus was an innocent Jewish artillery officer who was being sacrificed in the dishonest name of "national security" to save the French Army from embarrassment and to bolster a reactionary elite that would use the Republic to achieve its own selfish designs. David Thomson, incorrectly it would seem, gives equal weight to both sides of the controversy:

> Some of the many issues involved in the Dreyfus affair were the issues between the claims of individualism and personal rights and the claims of authoritarianism and "national security." Largely as a result of the affair, Radicalism came to be stated in the extreme and anarchistic form of the philosophy of "Alain," whilst authoritarianism was stated in an equally extreme form: the traditionalist *étatisme* of the *Action française* and the postwar semi-Fascist movements.

In any event, Alain's decision to ally himself with the

"Dreyfusards" was immediate and final; he never altered his initial verdict in the matter. And from that bleak period on, the unfortunate Dreyfus was a constantly recurring theme in his political writings. The man and the event made bitterly clear all the reasons why the Army, the Church, and the State must be opposed—why war, the unavoidable objective of militarism, must be prevented by all peaceable means.

Alain's opposition to war, which "always" massacres the nation's best, was almost obsessively intractable. Nevertheless, he enlisted as a "simple soldier" in World War I, when there was no obligation whatever for him to do so; he was already forty-six years old. Yet he felt that he must personally endure the experience of war in order to earn the right to judge it. Throughout his life, his beliefs remained those of a fervently unshakable pacifist. War puts the Republic in danger of becoming tyrannical by abetting an expansion of executive and military power. "To believe in war aggravates the risk." And "every measure of force, even for preventing war, is a menace to peace." These judgments Alain continually reaffirmed, as when he shared with Langévin and Rivet the leadership of the Vigilance Committee of Anti-Fascist Intellectuals in 1934, supported Léon Blum's Popular Front in 1936, and unremittingly refused to participate in the "crusade" or "holy war" against Hitler. While never an active participant, he remained in spirit and in his writings an adherent of the Vigilance Committee long after the resignation, for reasons of expediency, of its Communist membership. (In fact, firmest resistance to both communism and fascism seemed to him to be concentrated in the poorer provinces towards which he was most favorably disposed.) Alain's conviction was not so much that war was to be dreaded more than fascism as it was that fascism, in both its German and Italian models, could be eventually defeated by delaying tactics and reasonable measures short of armed conflict. Alain's beliefs (personal reflections) concerning war are most poignantly, though not exclusively, revealed in **Mars ou la guerre jugée,** the only one of his works in an English translation. A fervid declaration of the rightness of non-violence, it is *sui generis* and deserves serious perusal even today.

Beginning with an analysis of patriotic sentiments in wartime, Alain finds that while love of one's own country is natural enough, such love alone is not sufficiently strong to support a massive war effort. Other factors must be present and propitious if war is to be portrayed as a tenable enterprise for its participants. For Alain deems it to be ironically true that citizens are more willing to give their lives for their country than to part with their money. Are wars then fought principally for economic gain? Though recognizing that some persons do indeed profit financially, he does not consider the economic motive primary. A spirit of individual courage and honor must somehow be engendered. Are hate and anger significant driving forces? Hate in war, which is collective hate, is somehow not only to be expected but is fully accepted by society. Human nature is so constructed that it endures a great misfortune like war more stoically than it endures a small one; for since war is waged and suffered collectively, the problem of individual responsibility either is minimized or does not arise at all. Observance of duty to one's country, in war duty to the military specifically, eliminates irresolution, to Alain (as to Descartes earlier) the "greatest of human evils." But the individual has not thereby obviated his personal irresoluteness; he is now merely acting in obedience to the fiat of the great Leviathan—society and the state. "If I obey voluntarily, I am no longer a slave." *Pacifists,* however, cannot obey *voluntarily* in war.

When a society (state) in the aftermath of war makes promises by negotiating treaties, it premises the terms of the agreements with the international law proviso, *rebus sic stantibus.* That is, it rarely assumes that it is ultimately bound by its word. If war is "politics exasperated," politics is but the continuation of war by nonbellicose means. "Statesmen" illumined by that impersonal (albeit personified) Leviathan irresistibly adopt, or adapt themselves to, its conscienceless maxims. Its immorality becomes their immorality. If "statesmen" are politically and otherwise successful, it is by the criterion of success alone that they are presumed to be nonaccountable for their behavior. Yet they must *not* be absolved of their guilt, Alain insists, even though society in its corporate capacity must be primarily blamed for the initial and greater malfeasance.

In his defense of democracy, conceived as the only effective weapon against society (state), Alain contends that "every democratic movement is directed against the reactionism of that great animal, and tends to balance the social organism by a kind of contract incorrectly called the social contract because it is, in reality, the *antisocial contract.*" Adumbrating a more generic definition of democracy or, to be more exact, stating what democracy generically is not, Alain says:

> Democracy is not the rule of numbers; it is the rule of law. It is advisable to reflect upon this formula at this moment in our history . . . because all the proportionalists seem to me to have an entirely different conception of the Republic. According to them, it is enough merely that power be given to the numerically strongest, [since] for them justice demands nothing more.

Decidedly different was Alain's conception of "the Republic." A democracy is not a legitimized tyranny of the majority, since "force of numbers can never create the barest foundation of right." The majority is not necessarily just in what it thinks and does. The numerically strongest party or coalition might convince itself that it has a right to be unjust, or that, because it *is* the numerically strongest party or coalition, its beliefs and actions are *ipso facto* just. Stressing the fact that right and majority will are not automatically conjoined, Alain first defines right (*droit*) as the equal access to *rights;* e.g., it would be an infringement of the right of a dozen religious dissenters in a state if the majority should attempt to impose its own religion upon them. The protection of the minority, even the minority of one dissenting individual, is thus indispensable to a truly just democratic order.

As a corollary of this conviction, Alain was convinced that he must favor the electoral system *scrutin uninominal d'arrondissement* over *scrutin de liste,* the latter advocated by the proportional representationists (or "proportional-

ed the law on workmen's compensation [*accidents du travail*]. But elsewhere, Alain makes complete freedom of criticism a condition for arriving at the unanimous decision of the community, which presumably determines whether or not the law on workmen's compensation will be adopted, and the suffrage—as opposed to absolute rule—is the symbol of this freedom.

The significance of Alain's neglect of the role of political leadership may be illustrated by comparing Alain's liberalism with the liberal doctrine which prevailed, at least until the nineteen thirties, in the United States. Both liberal doctrines contain an *a priori* suspicion of the exercise of political power which is absent, by way of contrast, from all the main currents of English political thought. Neither the framers of the American constitution nor Alain shared anything like the English utilitarians' reliance on state power to achieve desired social goals or the Burkean veneration of political institutions, provided they be old, which conduces much more to confidence in the beneficence of governmental decisions than to suspicion of them. The United States' system of divided power, expressed in federalism, the separation of powers, and bicameralism, has its doctrinal counterpart in Alain's rejection of numerical majority rule and his approval of close and continuing parliamentary control over the executive.

Yet there is an important difference between the implications of these two liberalisms, outwardly so similar, which springs from the different contexts in which they appeared. When American liberal theory was being made explicit at the time of the drafting of the constitution, Americans were in the process of changing their institutions from a situation in which they contained inadequate provisions for leadership to one in which this leadership could be supplied, and their concern with controlling the exercise of power by establishing numerous checks and balances was a logical corollary to their efforts to build an institutional structure through which governmental authority could be more firmly exercised than it had been before. Alain's doctrine was implicit in the activities of French Republican leaders and the French citizenry even before Alain reached adulthood. It was first expressed in the processes by which the Republican leaders sapped the powers of the Presidency and put all incumbent and prospective Prime Ministers in a position of permanent subordination to the elected deputies. This French development was precisely the opposite of what had occured in the United States a century earlier. While Americans had strengthened the provisions for political leadership, Frenchmen were weakening them. A liberal doctrine which casts suspicion on the exercise of political power is bound to have different consequences when it appears in a society where the suspect institutions are already weak than when it appears in a society where those institutions are strong. American liberalism operated against the abuse of power, but American institutions permitted power to be exercised; Alain's liberalism served to reinforce an existing institutional tendency towards governmental inaction.

The view that because governmental activity can be dangerous virtually no governmental activity should be undertaken can be acceptable only so long as society is free

of significant conflicts or as it can furnish nongovernmental institutions through which those conflicts which exist can be resolved. It may be said that until the First World War, France generally fulfilled those conditions. During the decade between 1919 and 1929 they were already breaking down, and by the nineteen thirties they no longer existed. A doctrine which urges governmental idleness until such time as social unanimity permits governmental activity to pass unnoticed, without prescribing the methods or sketching the institutions by which such unanimity can be brought about, is useless for a society where various social groups are competing for wealth, status, or power. It would be a serious mistake, however, to think that Alain's doctrine, or at least all the elements out of which it is constructed, have disappeared from French political thought. His student, Simone Weil, who was to surpass him in inventiveness and intellectual rigour, never fully escaped his pessimistic influence. Bertrand de Jouvenel has expressed in different form themes which resemble those of Alain. Raymond Aron criticizes the use which Alain made of the distinction between temporal and spiritual power, but he retains the importance of the distinction itself. At the same time, however, it may also be said that when, during the nineteen thirties and later, a reaction developed against the politics of the Third Republic, the efforts of political thinkers to produce a political theory appropriate to France's needs was in large part an effort to overcome the influence of Alain. (pp. 4-10)

> *Roy Pierce, "French Political Thought on the Eve of the Thirties," in his* Contemporary French Political Thought, *Oxford University Press, 1966, pp. 1-23.*

## Robert D. Cottrell    (essay date 1973)

[*Cottrell is an American educator and critic. In the following excerpt from his introduction to* Alain on Happiness, *he examines the structure and style of Alain's* propos *and focuses on his use of this form in the collection.*]

When he died in 1951 at the age of eighty-three, Emile Chartier, the brilliant philosophy professor who had published numerous books and thousands of articles under the pseudonym of Alain, had been loved and revered by several generations of Frenchmen. He had left an indelible mark on the minds and lives of not only his most gifted pupils, including André Maurois, Simone Weil, and Maurice Schumann, but on all who had had the good fortune to attend his classes. Like any great teacher, Chartier taught more than books. He instilled in his many pupils a love for truth, a sense of hope, and the firm conviction that they could fashion their own future. Robust, frank, and generous, he won the admiration and lasting devotion of his students who often called him, with eloquent simplicity, *L'Homme*—The Man.

For us of a different language and of a later generation it is not Chartier the teacher we know, but Alain the writer. Of course, the philosophy teacher and the writer were inseparable. Alain aimed, as he said, to change philosophy

ists"). Because no really significant political improvements in society are possible anyway, the vigilant democrat (radical) must attempt only to prevent government from getting worse. Alain's political skepticism is clearly evident in his statement: "Many people say that the important thing is to advance; I believe that the important thing is not to slide backwards." *Scrutin uninominal d'arrondissement* was simply a way to prevent government from "sliding backwards." By contrast, proportional representation in the Chamber of Deputies would make the general conduct of political affairs impossible *ab initio*. The inevitable multiplication of parties would favor certain leaders who, by an inexorable law of politics, would grasp for more and still more power. The control of the *arrondissement* voters over their deputy would consequently be reduced. Furthermore, the elected deputies would find it imperative to expend so much time and energy fighting among themselves that the general will or even its modest approximation could hardly be realized. And by the default of impotent ministers, the power of the administrative bureaucracy would rapidly increase. According to Alain, the central mistake of the proportionalists was the suspicious assumption that the deputy of the single-member district is concerned only with the purely local interests of the people who have voted for him. In reality, in order to act as their delegate to protect their interests, he must also act as a representative of the nation, constantly compromising and conciliating among other deputies similarly elected and thus similarly circumstanced. To the rationally persuasive argument of the proportionalists that proportional representation and *scrutin de liste* would more precisely mirror the variegated shades of the French political complexion than any alternative electoral system, Alain counters that the precision of the mandate given the deputy is much less essential to democracy than the immediate and continual contact of the deputies with the voters. Alain wanted to vote for a man, not for a party label.

Moreover, it is overly facile, he states, to believe that representatives in a democracy are selected uniquely through the operation of the suffrage, "the sovereign's brief moment." That "society with its representatives is as much a product of [human] nature as are plants and animals" must never be "forgotten." As Montesquieu had pointed out, the complex structure of society, the interaction of its needs, wants, passions, customs, history, geography, economic resources, climate, religion, language, and a plethora of other considerations, must be understood. The weight and the interplay of all these factors are reflected in public opinion, that synchronization of an aggregate of "opinions dependent upon opinions." Against unquestioning credulity, "man has invented the free circulation of opinions, which universal suffrage represents symbolically." But because an individual may be too strongly influenced by what he thinks is public opinion, "it is useful for every person to decide for himself privately what is his own opinion before learning that of his neighbor." Once more, the specter of Rousseau intrudes. Such insulated personal decision-making is manifestly impossible, however, and an *informed* public opinion as ordinarily understood is the only remedy for naïve public credulity. The

suffrage provides an outlet for the expression of that opinion "against the abuses of power."

Yet does the utilization of the suffrage confer power on "the people?" No. "To say that the people have power in a democratic regime is soft-thinking, [for] deception follows." Rather, the people exercise a control (ideally) over the pre-existing powers, over a long-prevailing governmental structure. The people can merely "modify a pre-existing order"; they cannot "create a new order." Historically, society has developed (without fundamentally changing) more by a gradual accretion of customs, mores, usages, sentiments, and attitudes than by abrupt, *ad hoc* formulations of rationalistic constitutions, codified laws, and mechanically contrived political systems. "Custom is stronger than law; moreover, a true law is always extracted from custom and necessity, almost by blind experience, as jurisprudence proves." Acknowledgment and application of this principle of social, political, and legal growth Alain finds to be one of the many commendable features of British constitutionalism.

In every age and in every country, each person ideally merits a share in governing to the extent of the contribution of his individual force. One may be Machiavelli's "lion" and thus stronger and more agile; another may be Machiavelli's "fox" and thus more guileful, cunning, and intelligent. Accordingly, Alain favors that the distribution of force be ascertained in terms of individual functional abilities. Some people are capable of conducting war, others of making policy, others of managing finances, others of judging and persuading, and still others of playing less auspicious and more menial community roles. Justice decrees that each must have his place, and order is the societal harmony that results from a proper division of labor.

In delineating that division of labor, Alain employs the terms *proletariat* and *bourgeoisie*. However, he disavows the Marxian classification according to ownership or non-ownership of capital and private property. The extent of an individual's property holdings and other financial resources is thus not necessarily correlated with his socioeconomic class. The true proletariat consists of those who *act* and *do*, primarily artisans, laborers who work with their hands and with simple machines and tools. They are basically irreligious. Into this category the peasant also falls, but the proletarian character of peasants is modified by the fact that many of them have remained superstitious and have retained an awesome feeling of dependence on the gods of sun and rain and earth. The bourgeoisie, by contrast, consists of those who *persuade;* and politicians, those never desisting persuaders, are always of the bourgeois class. Now, Alain admits that there is no such simplistically exact division in any society. Some people, for instance surgeons, who are both doers and persuaders, fit into both classes. In varying degrees, in fact, all people combine in their occupations proletarian and bourgeois elements. A person's *perception* of his social status, moreover, may be as much a determinant of his class as the nature of the community tasks he performs. Alain's refusal to accept Marx's definitions and his consequent formulation of his own classifications show clearly how he could consistently entertain a prejudice in favor of workers and peasants and still defend and exalt the ownership of private property.

Although a radical, Alain never accepted the tenets of socialism or communism, which he condemned as debasing to human freedom, dignity, and personality. He considered socialists without exception to be "stupid" and socialist ideas "a little too simple for my taste." Whereas Alain's radicalism posited only one justice, one humanity, one human nature whose politics "has not, and will only slightly change," socialists are fundamentally "historians," who see one society, one law, one machine, one justice inevitably replacing another. "All socialism kills the spirit with dogma."

When the Radical party joined the Socialists to form coalition governments, it did so only for the purpose of presenting a united front against the far Right, despised by Radicals and Socialists alike. The enemy of my enemy is my friend. The Radicals of Alain's persuasion, however, never concurred in socialist prescriptions for governmental control of the means of production, or for accelerated technological advance, or for a really equitable leveling of propertied interests. The socialist program would necessitate even more inhibiting governmental power exercised by an inflexibly centralized administration in Paris. Technological advance could only bring an increased need for scientific specialists in government and thus would further strengthen an already too powerful and officious bureaucracy. Rigid organization of doctrine and people was a socialist tactic that Alain could not approve. Besides, the long-range objective of socialism seemed impossible to achieve. Where the socialist experiment had been tried, the result was that society "was not governed according to the ideas of the workers, but according to the ideas of the administrators instead."

Alain's radicalism, and hence French radicalism generally during the Third Republic, was actually extreme liberalism in its political and religious connotations only. To an American the word *radical* may suggest social and economic, as well as political, extremes. To the French, not necessarily. Politically and religiously liberal, Alain's social and economic views must be adjudged uncompromisingly conservative—in the economic, individualistic, *laissez-faire* meaning of the term. He allied himself with *rentiers* and weaker peasants, with artisans and retail traders, with small shopkeepers and less successful professional men of the middle class; with all who were suspicious of big government, big church, big city, big industry, big finance, big men, big ideas. That he could foresee only the humanly deleterious possibilities of industrialization, urbanization, bureaucratic regimen, automation, technocracy, polemical advertising, destructive nuclear devices, and space-probing ventures (all non-radical) is obvious. In 1921 he claimed to be the only radical still alive—radical, that is, in the Combist, pre-Gaullist, negative sense of one who is anti-Church, anti-State, anti-Army, anti-Power, anti-Psychology, and anti-Relativity, but yet who had a positive love of right, equality, humanity, and justice as he understood those concepts.

In an incomparable Gallic *ambiance* at the Lycée Henri-Quatre in Paris and at his small cottage in Le Vésinet, Alain taught and wrote prodigiously to help educate two generations of Frenchmen and to provide an intelligible political ideology for the whole nation. Whether that ideology was truly constructive and liberating for the individual, or merely paralyzing and demoralizing for the government, depends in considerable measure on the political commitment and the reasoned judgment of the critic who evaluates it. What may be stated positively, however, is that more than anyone else in his lifetime, this unassuming philosopher impressed upon his countrymen the mood and spirit of French radicalism, which in many respects remains the mood and spirit of France today. André Maurois has concluded that Alain's "politics was modest, prudent, and invincibly resolute. . . . No adversary could hold fast before him, [a man] who wished for nothing. A simple soldier in the army of citizens." And perhaps it will be possible, some time, some place, to have efficient, workable government while "building each day," in the hallowed name of liberty, "a little barricade against the insensible Leviathan." (pp. 595-614)

*Ronald F. Howell, "The Philosopher Alain and French Classical Radicalism," in* The Western Political Quarterly, *Vol. XVIII, No. 3, September, 1965, pp. 594-614.*

## Roy Pierce (essay date 1966)

[*Pierce is an American professor of political science who has written studies of French politics. In the following excerpt from his* Contemporary French Political Thought, *he focuses on the liberalism of Alain's political theories and evaluates his influence on political thought in twentieth-century France.*]

Alain's liberalism, which came to be known as 'la doctrine radicale'—the description of and justification for the behavior of the Radical Socialists who played such a prominent role in the government of the French Third Republic—is not so much a systematic political theory as a series of reflections on the central theme of the corrupting influence of power. 'Power corrupts all those who exercise it', Alain wrote in 1910, and this remained the guiding principle of his thought throughout the entire decade between 1919 and 1929 as well. But while Alain was constantly concerned with the permanent threat to the liberty of the citizens presented by the exercise of political power, he was not an anarchist. Political organization is essential to the maintenance of order, and without order there can be no liberty. How to maintain both order and liberty, how to avoid the twin evils of tyranny and anarchy (which only leads, in turn, to tyranny), are the problems towards which Alain's thought was directed. The solutions which he proposed are of three kinds, although they are closely related. One is to limit sharply the functions of the state; a second is to exercise constant control over the people who exercise power; and the third is to combine one's obedience to the laws with an underlying attitude of resistance.

Alain's political theory is perhaps the most classic example of those liberal theories which take an essentially negative view of the role of the state. His conception of the proper function of the political system was literally exhausted in the statement that 'the role of the political authorities is to ensure the fulfilment of contracts, and not to dictate the contracts'. Alain was not only radically opposed to grand designs for pursuing social reform through political means, but he also was sceptical of the possibility of the government promoting any positive programme without doing more damage than there would be if the state remained inactive. 'Voter, do not ask for too much', he wrote in 1924. 'It may be that the State will be generous and beneficent in the future. In our time the State proves itself to be naturally injurious. . . . Let us not ask the State to enrich us; let us ask it first of all not to ruin us.' The state must be closely confined within the limits of an essentially minimal police function, because if it is permitted or encouraged to extend its activities, the natural inclination of the people who hold power will be to abuse it at the expense of the liberty of the citizens.

Limiting the role of the state and counteracting the corrupting influence of power requires constant vigilance on the part of the citizens. Democracy, for Alain, meant exclusively the control of political power. The role of the elected deputy is to check and limit the action of the executive and the bureaucracy; the role of the voter is to pick and choose among candidates who best fulfil this controlling function. The whole democratic political process was viewed by Alain as constituting negation. It hardly occurred to him that the initiative for positive action might spring from the electorate, so convinced was he that these initiatives would come from ambitious governors. It is true that his perspective on the democratic system allows for the acceptance of government activities of which the deputies and their voters approve, but 'the first article' of Alain's hypothetical 'Charter of the Governed' was that one must 'moderate this ambition that all governors have to settle [*régler*] everything by laws'.

The state's functions are narrowly circumscribed and the role of both the citizens and their elected representatives is essentially negative, but the state still does have a function and the citizens must be governed. Alain's method of reconciling these conditions was to urge that the citizens both obey and resist. 'Resistance and obedience, those are the two virtues of the citizen. By obedience he guarantees order; by resistance he guarantees liberty.' The distinction between obedience and resistance was based on the more fundamental distinction which Alain made between the temporal and the spiritual orders. The temporal order is the domain of force, action, and the body. The spiritual order is the domain of the mind and spirit. By obedience, Alain meant simply carrying out the orders of the legitimate authorities. It is the duty of the citizens to obey the laws. By resistance, he meant constant application of the critical function; the maintenance of a permanently sceptical attitude towards all authority; the refusal to commit one's mind as well as one's body to the duty of obedience.

This theory, or rather this body of political prescriptions, has been widely criticized for its negativeness. It has been called the doctrine of 'the disgruntled citizen', described as 'negative, desiccated, small-minded' and held partially responsible for the political and moral weakness of French democracy during the later years of the Third Republic. Some of these criticisms rest more solidly on the cynical tone of Alain's homilies than on the sceptical philosophy which underlies them. Moreover, it is impossible to determine the extent to which Alain's writings actually affected the attitudes of his fellow-citizens and the extent to which they simply rationalized existing behavioural patterns. One balance, however, the logic of these criticisms is sound. His doctrine has serious shortcomings and these were magnified in their effects by the particular context in which it was produced.

Alain's doctrine, like all liberal theories, makes a distinction between the state and society. The state's role must be confined, and social forces must be given free play within an atmosphere of critical liberty. It is this free play of social forces which actually determines what the laws will be and not the conscious decisions of the legislators. The state, in other words, is a reflection of society, in the sense that it ratifies the rules of conduct that have already been decided upon by the 'good sense' of the citizens acting with a critical spirit. ' . . . Reforms, social organization, new laws, all that is determined much more by circumstances and the conditions of labour than by the will of the voters.' Up to a point, this view is consistent with the theory of a much more positive liberal, Ernest Barker. Barker writes [in *Principles of Social and Political Theory* (1951)] that 'the action of the legislature is not creation, but declaration; and its essential function is to declare the implications of the idea and ideal of justice, or the right ordering of human relations in an organized society, and to declare them as they are generally felt by the members of that society and as they are expressed in the form of its common conviction'. This analysis is essentially the same as Alain's view that 'the laws are made by common agreement and without any partisan spirit'. 'In short,' he adds, 'in the legislative sphere I do not see that the majority makes its pressure felt; it is, rather, unanimity, which requires public debates, continuous and impartial work, and complete liberty for every opinion and for every criticism.' For Alain, as for Barker, the legislature simply expresses in law what has already been decided upon as proper by the whole community.

It is a weakness of this view, as expressed by both theo
rists, that the process by which the whole communit
makes its common will known to the legislature is not ad
quately explained. But Barker, who is by far the more ri
orous of the two thinkers, at least includes a theory of p
litical institutions within his overall framework. It is r
relevant to this argument to examine Barker's instituti
al theory; it is enough simply to point out that he has o
and that because he does, he necessarily establishes so
framework for the organization of community opir
and for the exercise of political leadership. Alain, how
er, pays almost no attention at all to institutions and
treatment of leadership—in so far as there is one—is v
in his familiar framework of suspicion and distrust r
than related to the problem of how social opinion bec
translated into legislative decisions. In fact, Alain is
different to institutions that he sees no difference
consequences for legislation of different forms of pc
system. 'An absolute king undoubtedly would have

ists"). Because no really significant political improvements in society are possible anyway, the vigilant democrat (radical) must attempt only to prevent government from getting worse. Alain's political skepticism is clearly evident in his statement: "Many people say that the important thing is to advance; I believe that the important thing is not to slide backwards." *Scrutin uninominal d'arrondissement* was simply a way to prevent government from "sliding backwards." By contrast, proportional representation in the Chamber of Deputies would make the general conduct of political affairs impossible *ab initio.* The inevitable multiplication of parties would favor certain leaders who, by an inexorable law of politics, would grasp for more and still more power. The control of the *arrondissement* voters over their deputy would consequently be reduced. Furthermore, the elected deputies would find it imperative to expend so much time and energy fighting among themselves that the general will or even its modest approximation could hardly be realized. And by the default of impotent ministers, the power of the administrative bureaucracy would rapidly increase. According to Alain, the central mistake of the proportionalists was the suspicious assumption that the deputy of the single-member district is concerned only with the purely local interests of the people who have voted for him. In reality, in order to act as their delegate to protect their interests, he must also act as a representative of the nation, constantly compromising and conciliating among other deputies similarly elected and thus similarly circumstanced. To the rationally persuasive argument of the proportionalists that proportional representation and *scrutin de liste* would more precisely mirror the variegated shades of the French political complexion than any alternative electoral system, Alain counters that the precision of the mandate given the deputy is much less essential to democracy than the immediate and continual contact of the deputies with the voters. Alain wanted to vote for a man, not for a party label.

Moreover, it is overly facile, he states, to believe that representatives in a democracy are selected uniquely through the operation of the suffrage, "the sovereign's brief moment." That "society with its representatives is as much a product of [human] nature as are plants and animals" must never be "forgotten." As Montesquieu had pointed out, the complex structure of society, the interaction of its needs, wants, passions, customs, history, geography, economic resources, climate, religion, language, and a plethora of other considerations, must be understood. The weight and the interplay of all these factors are reflected in public opinion, that synchronization of an aggregate of "opinions dependent upon opinions." Against unquestioning credulity, "man has invented the free circulation of opinions, which universal suffrage represents symbolically." But because an individual may be too strongly influenced by what he thinks is public opinion, "it is useful for every person to decide for himself privately what is his own opinion before learning that of his neighbor." Once more, the specter of Rousseau intrudes. Such insulated personal decision-making is manifestly impossible, however, and an *informed* public opinion as ordinarily understood is the only remedy for naïve public credulity. The

suffrage provides an outlet for the expression of that opinion "against the abuses of power."

Yet does the utilization of the suffrage confer power on "the people?" No. "To say that the people have power in a democratic regime is soft-thinking, [for] deception follows." Rather, the people exercise a control (ideally) over the pre-existing powers, over a long-prevailing governmental structure. The people can merely "modify a pre-existing order"; they cannot "create a new order." Historically, society has developed (without fundamentally changing) more by a gradual accretion of customs, mores, usages, sentiments, and attitudes than by abrupt, *ad hoc* formulations of rationalistic constitutions, codified laws, and mechanically contrived political systems. "Custom is stronger than law; moreover, a true law is always extracted from custom and necessity, almost by blind experience, as jurisprudence proves." Acknowledgment and application of this principle of social, political, and legal growth Alain finds to be one of the many commendable features of British constitutionalism.

In every age and in every country, each person ideally merits a share in governing to the extent of the contribution of his individual force. One may be Machiavelli's "lion" and thus stronger and more agile; another may be Machiavelli's "fox" and thus more guileful, cunning, and intelligent. Accordingly, Alain favors that the distribution of force be ascertained in terms of individual functional abilities. Some people are capable of conducting war, others of making policy, others of managing finances, others of judging and persuading, and still others of playing less auspicious and more menial community roles. Justice decrees that each must have his place, and order is the societal harmony that results from a proper division of labor.

In delineating that division of labor, Alain employs the terms *proletariat* and *bourgeoisie.* However, he disavows the Marxian classification according to ownership or non-ownership of capital and private property. The extent of an individual's property holdings and other financial resources is thus not necessarily correlated with his socioeconomic class. The true proletariat consists of those who *act* and *do,* primarily artisans, laborers who work with their hands and with simple machines and tools. They are basically irreligious. Into this category the peasant also falls, but the proletarian character of peasants is modified by the fact that many of them have remained superstitious and have retained an awesome feeling of dependence on the gods of sun and rain and earth. The bourgeoisie, by contrast, consists of those who *persuade;* and politicians, those never desisting persuaders, are always of the bourgeois class. Now, Alain admits that there is no such simplistically exact division in any society. Some people, for instance surgeons, who are both doers and persuaders, fit into both classes. In varying degrees, in fact, all people combine in their occupations proletarian and bourgeois elements. A person's *perception* of his social status, moreover, may be as much a determinant of his class as the nature of the community tasks he performs. Alain's refusal to accept Marx's definitions and his consequent formulation of his own classifications show clearly how he could consistently entertain a prejudice in favor of workers and peasants and still defend and exalt the ownership of private property.

Although a radical, Alain never accepted the tenets of socialism or communism, which he condemned as debasing to human freedom, dignity, and personality. He considered socialists without exception to be "stupid" and socialist ideas "a little too simple for my taste." Whereas Alain's radicalism posited only one justice, one humanity, one human nature whose politics "has not, and will only slightly change," socialists are fundamentally "historians," who see one society, one law, one machine, one justice inevitably replacing another. "All socialism kills the spirit with dogma."

When the Radical party joined the Socialists to form coalition governments, it did so only for the purpose of presenting a united front against the far Right, despised by Radicals and Socialists alike. The enemy of my enemy is my friend. The Radicals of Alain's persuasion, however, never concurred in socialist prescriptions for governmental control of the means of production, or for accelerated technological advance, or for a really equitable leveling of propertied interests. The socialist program would necessitate even more inhibiting governmental power exercised by an inflexibly centralized administration in Paris. Technological advance could only bring an increased need for scientific specialists in government and thus would further strengthen an already too powerful and officious bureaucracy. Rigid organization of doctrine and people was a socialist tactic that Alain could not approve. Besides, the long-range objective of socialism seemed impossible to achieve. Where the socialist experiment had been tried, the result was that society "was not governed according to the ideas of the workers, but according to the ideas of the administrators instead."

Alain's radicalism, and hence French radicalism generally during the Third Republic, was actually extreme liberalism in its political and religious connotations only. To an American the word *radical* may suggest social and economic, as well as political, extremes. To the French, not necessarily. Politically and religiously liberal, Alain's social and economic views must be adjudged uncompromisingly conservative—in the economic, individualistic, *laissez-faire* meaning of the term. He allied himself with *rentiers* and weaker peasants, with artisans and retail traders, with small shopkeepers and less successful professional men of the middle class; with all who were suspicious of big government, big church, big city, big industry, big finance, big men, big ideas. That he could foresee only the humanly deleterious possibilities of industrialization, urbanization, bureaucratic regimen, automation, technocracy, polemical advertising, destructive nuclear devices, and space-probing ventures (all non-radical) is obvious. In 1921 he claimed to be the only radical still alive—radical, that is, in the Combist, pre-Gaullist, negative sense of one who is anti-Church, anti-State, anti-Army, anti-Power, anti-Psychology, and anti-Relativity, but yet who had a positive love of right, equality, humanity, and justice as he understood those concepts.

In an incomparable Gallic *ambiance* at the Lycée Henri-Quatre in Paris and at his small cottage in Le Vésinet,

Alain taught and wrote prodigiously to help educate two generations of Frenchmen and to provide an intelligible political ideology for the whole nation. Whether that ideology was truly constructive and liberating for the individual, or merely paralyzing and demoralizing for the government, depends in considerable measure on the political commitment and the reasoned judgment of the critic who evaluates it. What may be stated positively, however, is that more than anyone else in his lifetime, this unassuming philosopher impressed upon his countrymen the mood and spirit of French radicalism, which in many respects remains the mood and spirit of France today. André Maurois has concluded that Alain's "politics was modest, prudent, and invincibly resolute. . . . No adversary could hold fast before him, [a man] who wished for nothing. A simple soldier in the army of citizens." And perhaps it will be possible, some time, some place, to have efficient, workable government while "building each day," in the hallowed name of liberty, "a little barricade against the insensible Leviathan." (pp. 595-614)

> *Ronald F. Howell, "The Philosopher Alain and French Classical Radicalism," in* The Western Political Quarterly, *Vol. XVIII, No. 3, September, 1965, pp. 594-614.*

## Roy Pierce (essay date 1966)

[*Pierce is an American professor of political science who has written studies of French politics. In the following excerpt from his* Contemporary French Political Thought, *he focuses on the liberalism of Alain's political theories and evaluates his influence on political thought in twentieth-century France.*]

Alain's liberalism, which came to be known as 'la doctrine radicale'—the description of and justification for the behavior of the Radical Socialists who played such a prominent role in the government of the French Third Republic—is not so much a systematic political theory as a series of reflections on the central theme of the corrupting influence of power. 'Power corrupts all those who exercise it', Alain wrote in 1910, and this remained the guiding principle of his thought throughout the entire decade between 1919 and 1929 as well. But while Alain was constantly concerned with the permanent threat to the liberty of the citizens presented by the exercise of political power, he was not an anarchist. Political organization is essential to the maintenance of order, and without order there can be no liberty. How to maintain both order and liberty, how to avoid the twin evils of tyranny and anarchy (which only leads, in turn, to tyranny), are the problems towards which Alain's thought was directed. The solutions which he proposed are of three kinds, although they are closely related. One is to limit sharply the functions of the state; a second is to exercise constant control over the people who exercise power; and the third is to combine one's obedience to the laws with an underlying attitude of resistance.

Alain's political theory is perhaps the most classic example of those liberal theories which take an essentially negative view of the role of the state. His conception of the proper function of the political system was literally exhausted in the statement that 'the role of the political authorities is to ensure the fulfilment of contracts, and not to dictate the contracts'. Alain was not only radically opposed to grand designs for pursuing social reform through political means, but he also was sceptical of the possibility of the government promoting any positive programme without doing more damage than there would be if the state remained inactive. 'Voter, do not ask for too much', he wrote in 1924. 'It may be that the State will be generous and beneficent in the future. In our time the State proves itself to be naturally injurious. . . . Let us not ask the State to enrich us; let us ask it first of all not to ruin us.' The state must be closely confined within the limits of an essentially minimal police function, because if it is permitted or encouraged to extend its activities, the natural inclination of the people who hold power will be to abuse it at the expense of the liberty of the citizens.

Limiting the role of the state and counteracting the corrupting influence of power requires constant vigilance on the part of the citizens. Democracy, for Alain, meant exclusively the control of political power. The role of the elected deputy is to check and limit the action of the executive and the bureaucracy; the role of the voter is to pick and choose among candidates who best fulfil this controlling function. The whole democratic political process was viewed by Alain as constituting negation. It hardly occurred to him that the initiative for positive action might spring from the electorate, so convinced was he that these initiatives would come from ambitious governors. It is true that his perspective on the democratic system allows for the acceptance of government activities of which the deputies and their voters approve, but 'the first article' of Alain's hypothetical 'Charter of the Governed' was that one must 'moderate this ambition that all governors have to settle [*régler*] everything by laws'.

The state's functions are narrowly circumscribed and the role of both the citizens and their elected representatives is essentially negative, but the state still does have a function and the citizens must be governed. Alain's method of reconciling these conditions was to urge that the citizens both obey and resist. 'Resistance and obedience, those are the two virtues of the citizen. By obedience he guarantees order; by resistance he guarantees liberty.' The distinction between obedience and resistance was based on the more fundamental distinction which Alain made between the temporal and the spiritual orders. The temporal order is the domain of force, action, and the body. The spiritual order is the domain of the mind and spirit. By obedience, Alain meant simply carrying out the orders of the legitimate authorities. It is the duty of the citizens to obey the laws. By resistance, he meant constant application of the critical function; the maintenance of a permanently sceptical attitude towards all authority; the refusal to commit one's mind as well as one's body to the duty of obedience.

This theory, or rather this body of political prescriptions, has been widely criticized for its negativeness. It has been called the doctrine of 'the disgruntled citizen', described as 'negative, desiccated, small-minded' and held partially responsible for the political and moral weakness of French democracy during the later years of the Third Republic. Some of these criticisms rest more solidly on the cynical tone of Alain's homilies than on the sceptical philosophy which underlies them. Moreover, it is impossible to determine the extent to which Alain's writings actually affected the attitudes of his fellow-citizens and the extent to which they simply rationalized existing behavioural patterns. One balance, however, the logic of these criticisms is sound. His doctrine has serious shortcomings and these were magnified in their effects by the particular context in which it was produced.

Alain's doctrine, like all liberal theories, makes a distinction between the state and society. The state's role must be confined, and social forces must be given free play within an atmosphere of critical liberty. It is this free play of social forces which actually determines what the laws will be and not the conscious decisions of the legislators. The state, in other words, is a reflection of society, in the sense that it ratifies the rules of conduct that have already been decided upon by the 'good sense' of the citizens acting with a critical spirit. ' . . . Reforms, social organization, new laws, all that is determined much more by circumstances and the conditions of labour than by the will of the voters.' Up to a point, this view is consistent with the theory of a much more positive liberal, Ernest Barker. Barker writes [in *Principles of Social and Political Theory* (1951)] that 'the action of the legislature is not creation, but declaration; and its essential function is to declare the implications of the idea and ideal of justice, or the right ordering of human relations in an organized society, and to declare them as they are generally felt by the members of that society and as they are expressed in the form of its common conviction'. This analysis is essentially the same as Alain's view that 'the laws are made by common agreement and without any partisan spirit'. 'In short,' he adds, 'in the legislative sphere I do not see that the majority makes its pressure felt; it is, rather, unanimity, which requires public debates, continuous and impartial work, and complete liberty for every opinion and for every criticism.' For Alain, as for Barker, the legislature simply expresses in law what has already been decided upon as proper by the whole community.

It is a weakness of this view, as expressed by both theorists, that the process by which the whole community makes its common will known to the legislature is not adequately explained. But Barker, who is by far the more rigorous of the two thinkers, at least includes a theory of political institutions within his overall framework. It is not relevant to this argument to examine Barker's institutional theory; it is enough simply to point out that he has one, and that because he does, he necessarily establishes some framework for the organization of community opinion and for the exercise of political leadership. Alain, however, pays almost no attention at all to institutions and his treatment of leadership—in so far as there is one—is within his familiar framework of suspicion and distrust rather than related to the problem of how social opinion becomes translated into legislative decisions. In fact, Alain is so indifferent to institutions that he sees no difference in the consequences for legislation of different forms of political system. 'An absolute king undoubtedly would have enacted the law on workmen's compensation [*accidents du travail*]. But elsewhere, Alain makes complete freedom of criticism a condition for arriving at the unanimous decision of the community, which presumably determines whether or not the law on workmen's compensation will be adopted, and the suffrage—as opposed to absolute rule—is the symbol of this freedom.

The significance of Alain's neglect of the role of political leadership may be illustrated by comparing Alain's liberalism with the liberal doctrine which prevailed, at least until the nineteen thirties, in the United States. Both liberal doctrines contain an *a priori* suspicion of the exercise of political power which is absent, by way of contrast, from all the main currents of English political thought. Neither the framers of the American constitution nor Alain shared anything like the English utilitarians' reliance on state power to achieve desired social goals or the Burkean veneration of political institutions, provided they be old, which conduces much more to confidence in the beneficence of governmental decisions than to suspicion of them. The United States' system of divided power, expressed in federalism, the separation of powers, and bicameralism, has its doctrinal counterpart in Alain's rejection of numerical majority rule and his approval of close and continuing parliamentary control over the executive.

Yet there is an important difference between the implications of these two liberalisms, outwardly so similar, which springs from the different contexts in which they appeared. When American liberal theory was being made explicit at the time of the drafting of the constitution, Americans were in the process of changing their institutions from a situation in which they contained inadequate provisions for leadership to one in which this leadership could be supplied, and their concern with controlling the exercise of power by establishing numerous checks and balances was a logical corollary to their efforts to build an institutional structure through which governmental authority could be more firmly exercised than it had been before. Alain's doctrine was implicit in the activities of French Republican leaders and the French citizenry even before Alain reached adulthood. It was first expressed in the processes by which the Republican leaders sapped the powers of the Presidency and put all incumbent and prospective Prime Ministers in a position of permanent subordination to the elected deputies. This French development was precisely the opposite of what had occured in the United States a century earlier. While Americans had strengthened the provisions for political leadership, Frenchmen were weakening them. A liberal doctrine which casts suspicion on the exercise of political power is bound to have different consequences when it appears in a society where the suspect institutions are already weak than when it appears in a society where those institutions are strong. American liberalism operated against the abuse of power, but American institutions permitted power to be exercised; Alain's liberalism served to reinforce an existing institutional tendency towards governmental inaction.

The view that because governmental activity can be dangerous virtually no governmental activity should be undertaken can be acceptable only so long as society is free

of significant conflicts or as it can furnish nongovernmental institutions through which those conflicts which exist can be resolved. It may be said that until the First World War, France generally fulfilled those conditions. During the decade between 1919 and 1929 they were already breaking down, and by the nineteen thirties they no longer existed. A doctrine which urges governmental idleness until such time as social unanimity permits governmental activity to pass unnoticed, without prescribing the methods or sketching the institutions by which such unanimity can be brought about, is useless for a society where various social groups are competing for wealth, status, or power. It would be a serious mistake, however, to think that Alain's doctrine, or at least all the elements out of which it is constructed, have disappeared from French political thought. His student, Simone Weil, who was to surpass him in inventiveness and intellectual rigour, never fully escaped his pessimistic influence. Bertrand de Jouvenel has expressed in different form themes which resemble those of Alain. Raymond Aron criticizes the use which Alain made of the distinction between temporal and spiritual power, but he retains the importance of the distinction itself. At the same time, however, it may also be said that when, during the nineteen thirties and later, a reaction developed against the politics of the Third Republic, the efforts of political thinkers to produce a political theory appropriate to France's needs was in large part an effort to overcome the influence of Alain. (pp. 4-10)

*Roy Pierce, "French Political Thought on the Eve of the Thirties," in his* Contemporary French Political Thought, *Oxford University Press, 1966, pp. 1-23.*

## Robert D. Cottrell    (essay date 1973)

[*Cottrell is an American educator and critic. In the following excerpt from his introduction to* Alain on Happiness, *he examines the structure and style of Alain's* propos *and focuses on his use of this form in the collection.*]

When he died in 1951 at the age of eighty-three, Emile Chartier, the brilliant philosophy professor who had published numerous books and thousands of articles under the pseudonym of Alain, had been loved and revered by several generations of Frenchmen. He had left an indelible mark on the minds and lives of not only his most gifted pupils, including André Maurois, Simone Weil, and Maurice Schumann, but on all who had had the good fortune to attend his classes. Like any great teacher, Chartier taught more than books. He instilled in his many pupils a love for truth, a sense of hope, and the firm conviction that they could fashion their own future. Robust, frank, and generous, he won the admiration and lasting devotion of his students who often called him, with eloquent simplicity, *L'Homme*—The Man.

For us of a different language and of a later generation it is not Chartier the teacher we know, but Alain the writer. Of course, the philosophy teacher and the writer were inseparable. Alain aimed, as he said, to change philosophy into literature and literature into philosophy. Like the sixteenth-century essayist Montaigne, who maintained that "there is nothing more joyful, more jovial, more light-hearted, and I might almost say more playful" than philosophy, Alain wished to free men from fear and "to cleanse this world of all the human vapors" that cloud our perceptions. Opposed to any form of dogmatism and to tyranny, whether of the body or the mind, he constantly displayed a strong streak of practicality and common sense typical of the Norman peasants who were his ancestors.

Born in 1868, Alain was the son of a successful veterinarian. A brilliantly gifted student, he could have elected a career in medicine, science, music, or any of a dozen other professions. He chose instead to study philosophy and literature at the *Ecole normale,* the most rigorous and glorious of French institutions of higher learning. After earning his degree in 1892, he began teaching, first at Pontivy and then at Lorient. In 1894 the Dreyfus Affair bitterly divided French public opinion. Alain, who was fervently interested in politics and incensed at the treatment accorded Dreyfus, wrote a series of articles for a radical newspaper, *La dépêche de Lorient,* defending Dreyfus and exposing the hypocrisies and duplicities of Dreyfus' accusers. During the next ten years he pursued his teaching career, engaged from time to time in political and journalistic activity, and published numerous articles on philosophical topics as well as a book-length study on Spinoza.

From 1900 to 1902 Alain taught at Rouen, and although he moved to Paris in 1903, his friends in Rouen convinced him to contribute articles to a local newspaper. Beginning in 1903 *La dépêche de Rouen* carried a rather long weekly article by Alain.

Every writer discovers by trial and error the rhythm and pace that suit him best. Alain, whose thought is incisive and tends to be aphoristic, felt ill-at-ease writing a column of considerable length. "Those articles poisoned my whole week," he later noted in his memoirs. For some three years, however, he doggedly continued to write his weekly column. Then, early in 1906 he decided to try writing a short article every day instead of a longer one each week; "that would permit me to make amends immediately for a botched article."

These shorter articles began appearing in the same newspaper, *La dépêche de Rouen,* on February 16, 1906, eleven days after the demise of the longer column. The title of the new daily column was "Propos d'un Normand"; it was signed simply "Alain," the pseudonym Emile Chartier had derived from the name of the fifteenth-century Norman poet, Alain Chartier. From 1906 until the outbreak of World War I, Alain continued to write a two-page article each evening, changing philosophy not only into literature, but into journalism as well. By 1914 he had published 3,078 such articles, which he called *propos* (remarks). After the war he wrote some 2,000 additional *propos* for various newspapers and magazines, but never again did he adhere to the schedule of one a day. However, he was by then writing books as well as *propos,* and for the next thirty years scarcely a year passed without the publication of one or more of Alain's remarkable books on philosophy,

politics, esthetics, or literature. His fame as a writer was soon firmly established.

From time to time some of the *propos* were rescued from that limbo to which most journalism is consigned, and were published in book form. Out of the mass of nearly 5,000 *propos,* editors chose to collect and publish in individual volumes those that dealt with one particular subject. Thus, in 1928 ninety-three *propos* dealing with the general theme of happiness were published under the title of *Propos sur le bonheur.*

The word *propos,* as Alain used it, is virtually untranslatable. Montaigne, to whom Alain has frequently been compared, had used a common noun, *essai,* or essay, meaning trial or test, to define what it was that he was writing, and the word soon came to denote a particular literary genre whose distinctive characteristics were those of an essay by Montaigne. Similarly, Alain used the common noun, *propos,* a word rich in meanings, to define his newspaper articles; in so doing he created a unique literary genre as distinctive as the essay Montaigne had created. Basically, the French word *propos* means spoken words, or words exchanged in the course of a conversation. It therefore suggests something relatively informal and social. Furthermore, it contains the notion of proposing; Alain's *propos* are propositions which the reader is invited, and indeed urged, to examine. The overlapping meanings of the word itself indicate in a general way the rhythm and tonality of Alain's *propos.* Short aphoristic pieces of fifty or sixty lines, they move along easily and wittily.

Alain made it a principle never to rewrite or modify what he had once written down. Years later he recalled how he wrote the *propos:* each evening he would sit down before two sheets of paper, knowing before he started that the last line would be written on the bottom of the second page, and that within the confines of those two pages he would write a piece which, if he succeeded, would have "movement, air, and elevation." He also knew that he would make no corrections, erasures, or changes; since the piece would be published the next day, he did not have time for the niceties of anguished composition. He saw the bottom of the second page approach, and ruthlessly suppressed every idea that was not germane to his theme. "The final barrier approached as other ideas began to appear; they were repressed; but, and I don't know how, they succeeded in filling out the principal idea. . . . The result was a kind of poetry and strength."

The urgent necessity of meeting a journalistic deadline taught Alain another lesson: he learned the importance of exercising the will. There is, he realized, only one way for a man to create anything, whether it be the writing of an article, the making of a chair, or the planting of a garden, and that is simply to do it. Here we approach the heart of Alain's message on happiness: there is no happiness except what a man creates for himself by exercising his will. "Certainly we do not become what we want to become," he wrote in an article entitled **"Comments on the Art of Knowing Others and Oneself"**; "but we do not become anything at all if first we do not exercise our will." And the ninetieth *propos* on happiness begins with the assertion: "We must will to be happy, and work at it." The very discipline required in the composition of the *propos* gave Alain an opportunity to exercise his will. A product of the will, the *propos* on happiness are a series of richly embroidered variations on the theme of judicious use of the will.

But in order to exercise one's will wisely and to procure the maximum happiness from life while suffering only the minimum amount of unhappiness, one must first perceive the causes of both happiness and unhappiness, of joy and sadness. In short, one must be able to perceive reality clearly. Indeed, Alain devoted the first three months of his famous philosophy courses to lectures on perception. A similar approach may be seen in the *propos*.

A *propos* by Alain nearly always begins with a reference to something precise and immediately recognizable. Sometimes it is an incident familiar to all his readers, such as the sinking of the *Titanic;* sometimes it is a personal anecdote; often it is a reference to those activities of the human body with which we are all familiar—sneezing, coughing, yawning, scratching, or swallowing.

The first *propos* in **Alain on Happiness** is not only typical of Alain's style but also contains the major themes that will be treated with considerable virtuosity throughout the entire book. It opens with the evocation of a crying baby; his nurse, trying to determine the cause of the infant's distress, imagines numerous fanciful causes to explain the very audible effect. Finally, she perceives the obvious, that a pin is the real cause of the trouble. Alain, not content with this homey anecdote illustrating the futility of abstract speculation when detached from the reality of the concrete world, then relates another story illustrating the same theme. This time, however, the story is remote in time and place, it is the legendary account of how young Alexander tamed the untameable horse, Bucephalus.

Although Alain's *propos* are firmly rooted in physical reality, they often bear, lightly and even gaily, a rich cargo of legend, myth, philosophy, and literature. Alexander, of course, perceived that Bucephalus was afraid of his own shadow, and, turning the horse's head toward the sun, managed to calm him and then to train him. "We have no power at all over our passions as long as we do not know their true causes," declares Alain, restating in slightly extended form the conclusion he had reached at the end of the first anecdote. The *propos* then moves from the specific to the general. The body of the article is devoted to a series of remarks and observations suggested to the author by the two stories he has just related. Like leitmotifs, the words crying, fear, and pin reappear in various guises. Comments and reflections which, in the work of another writer, might well serve as a springboard for speculation, are constantly checked and brought back to the real world by concrete examples that are artfully spaced throughtout the *propos*. Thus, in a brief sentence Alain rapidly relates a comic incident in the life of Marshal Masséna; in the following paragraph he refers to a remark of Talleyrand; several sentences later he evokes "the evils of 1914."

The central part, or development section, of a *propos* is not constructed like a philosophical demonstration, one idea leading logically and irrefutably to another. Instead, Alain's remarks circle around the single idea which was contained in the opening sentences. They spiral around the basic theme, illuminating it from unexpected angles. The tone is alert, relaxed, and friendly. The conclusion, which is usually a succinct final sentence, pointing, like a fable or a parable, to a practical lesson, often takes the reader by surprise. It is nearly always pungent. Generally, it returns the reader to the familiar world of common experience which had been evoked at the beginning of the *propos*. Often, as in the first *propos,* it brings him back abruptly to the initial incident. "Look for the pin," concludes [the first propos of **Alain on Happiness**], but now the word "pin" is laden with all the metaphorical meanings that have accrued to it throughout the course of the *propos*.

Agreeing with the Stoics, with Descartes, and with Spinoza, "that master of contentment," as he called him, Alain affirms that, except for real physical pain and the few genuine misfortunes that befall us only infrequently, our unhappiness is caused by our passions, which in turn are nurtured by our thoughts and imagination. Fear, despair, anger, irritation, in a word, all our passions alter the functioning of our body. The muscles become tense, the heart beats faster, and breathing becomes difficult. "Still, our passions can be managed," declares Alain. Not easily, however, and not without an understanding of the relationship between our thoughts and our body. We are not free to control our thoughts directly, nor are we able to rid ourselves of the passions that promote unhappiness by simply wanting to. We can, however, control our bodily movements. "Man's will has no control over his passions, but does have direct control over his movements." And direct control over our movements is precisely the means whereby we can indirectly control our passions. For, and this is the wise man's secret which was first demonstrated by Descartes, the passions are not autonomous; they are in fact dependent upon the movements of the body. "A man who is bored," writes Alain, "has a way of sitting down, of getting up, of speaking, which is calculated to promote boredom." Therefore the only way to counteract our passions is by governing the body; in short, by judicious action.

To illustrate his concept of action as an indirect control of the passions, Alain introduces the notion of gymnastics. "Once accustomed to doing certain things, once the muscles are trained and exercised by gymnastics, we can act as we wish." Thus, he points out the powerful effects that posture, ritual, politeness, and ceremonies can have in controlling passions and in creating happiness. For happiness must be created. Joy must be cultivated. In a world that is neither hostile nor friendly, there is nothing favorable to man except what he makes through his own efforts.

One of Alain's favorite myths, referred to twice in **Alain on Happiness,** is the myth of Er which Plato relates in the closing pages of *The Republic*. Er, who had been thought dead, descended to Hades, and when the error was discovered, returned to earth where he told his friends what he had seen down there. The souls, explained Er, were given the choice of a new destiny. Still remembering their past life, they chose according to their desires and regrets. Each soul then took his destiny, drank of the river of Forgetfulness, and returned to earth to live as he had chosen. Whether our destiny be happiness or unhappiness, Alain suggests, is largely a matter of our own choice. "We must stand firm," he once wrote, "between two kinds of madness: the belief that we can do anything; and the belief that we can do nothing." Alain's work is an act of faith in the human spirit. It dispels fear, and fosters hope. When old and severely crippled by arthritis, Alain looked back over his long life, his numerous works, and wrote with the serene confidence that characterized him: "There is a way of singing which shows that one is not afraid, and which reassures the world of men." (pp. xi-xix)

> *Robert D. Cottrell, in an introduction to* Alain on Happiness, *translated by Robert D. Cottrell and Jane E. Cottrell, Frederick Ungar Publishing Co., 1973, pp. xi-xix.*

## Richard Pevear  (essay date 1974)

[*In the following excerpt from his foreword to* The Gods, *Pevear places Alain's method of discourse within the tradition of the ancient Greek storyteller.*]

"Ulysses, wrapped up and sleeping under the leaves, like a shepherd's fire, is Ulysses none the less." This one sentence from *The Gods* is a paradigm of the constructive principles of Alain's thought and a model of his prose. The image of Ulysses, fire under leaves, the powerful nature of the man hidden behind a tattered appearance, is a condensed figuration of two widely separated moments in the *Odyssey.* But in context it is more than an allusion, it is a primary, active image. Alain is talking about the Homeric idea of gods wandering the world in human disguises, of which Ulysses, since he is not a god, is a metaphor: just as Ulysses is hidden under a beggar's rags, so it might be a god; the reserved fire of his nature is godlike, an image of the god-in-disguise. But the sentence contains something else, the mention of the shepherd's fire, which is the most memorable thing about it. The counterpart of that brief image, in Homer, is a long simile that describes the way a man who must spend the night in the open, not by a hearth, will conserve his fire for morning by burying a fresh stick in the embers. That is why Alain says, with such odd precision, a *shepherd's fire.* In neither case is the image merely a "vehicle." The construction of the Homeric simile is dialectical, it is more of a disruption than an illustration, it argues with the main line of the narrative and corrects or adjusts our view of it. The texture of the simile, the question of its structure, is the basic question of *The Gods.*

In his essay "The Storyteller," Walter Benjamin observed that "an orientation toward practical interests is characteristic of many born storytellers." *The Gods* is a book of images and image-readings. But for Alain the realm of images is wider than we would expect: the gesture of an old farmer resting during a walk over his fields, the shape of a loaf of bread, the layout of an iris garden, the cobwebs in stable windows, the angular intersections of city streets, the furrow drawn by a plow, the paths that cows make across a meadow, the balance, the yard-sentence from *The Gods* as a paradigm of the constructive stick, the coin are

all readable images. The figures of the gods are familiar to us, their world is the perpetual world of statues, pictures, myths. But the lore that Alain has gathered belongs to another perpetual world, one that has no "status" in the categories of thought or in the partial records of history, and which might be called the world of labor. The meeting, opposition, and interpenetration of these two worlds is the source of the old art of storytelling, and is therefore both the source and the subject of Alain's thinking in *The Gods.*

"Counsel woven into the fabric of real life is wisdom," says Benjamin, using an appropriate metaphor. The resident craftsman, the weaver, is one prototype of the storyteller. War stories are not invented at the front; storytelling naturally accompanies the peacetime arts. Stories are, besides, literally woven out of hundreds of intersections known as words. And the fabric of our existence is such that people who are constantly at war, whose peacetime life is also a kind of war, will lose the art of storytelling and will find themselves speaking a language of migratory ciphers. "The art of storytelling is reaching its end," Benjamin writes, "because the epic side of truth, wisdom, is dying out." And further, "The earliest symptom of a process whose end is the decline of storytelling is the rise of the novel at the beginning of modern times. . . . What differentiates the novel from all other forms of prose literature—the fairy tale, the legend, even the novella—is that it neither comes from oral tradition nor goes into it." It is a curious fact, in this connection, that Alain once thought of becoming a novelist. He did not follow that inclination, perhaps because he was already too much of a philosopher, that is, a lover of wisdom. What was natural to him was not the novelist's long form, the construction of a definitive "world," but the brief, provisional images of the storyteller, the opposing of the world of myths and the world of labor, the storyteller's freedom to bring diverse materials together, to create anachronisms. The novelist is an observer of life, but in the end his observations are wholly transformed into fiction and take on the consistency of fiction. His images are not constructed on the dialectical principle of the Homeric simile or the storyteller's story. Dreams, myths, and the history of historicism have the consistency of fiction, as does the reasoning of the systematic philosopher. But thought implies the interruption of reasoning. That is the function of Alain's method, and of his humor, which is a quality of the free spirit. The storyteller is an older figure than the novelist, and even older than the epic poet; yet the remarkable thing is not that he is older but that he persists alongside them, which means that he stands in a place that is not visible to history. From there he is able to interrupt and ask questions.

That, roughly speaking, has been the place of popular culture, by which I mean the inner life of working people and its poetic objects, in relation to the ruling powers of historical civilization. And that explains why certain political convictions are inseparable from Alain's study of religious images, why in one aspect *The Gods* is a critique of power and of political idolatry. It may also explain his rather humorous references to Marx. Alain's socialism was not based on the "laws" of history, it was, as he would have said, physiological. His dialectic is more pervasive and detailed than Marx's because it takes place in individuals, not only between classes, and because it is recurrent rather than successive. But Marx is furthest from Alain in his methods, which he adopted from historicism and systematic philosophy, and with which he fashioned an obligatory, inevitable truth, a truth based on the notion of power.

The attitude of the teller and of the listener to the story is in each case a free one. The teller does not disappear into the story and the listener is not absorbed by it; the one is always a man speaking, the other a man listening, and the story is something offered and considered between them. Its truth can only be tested experimentally. Thought offered and considered in the same way is counsel, the most humble face philosophy can show us, the most familiar, the most reminiscent. The naïveté of the story as an instrument of thought is its best recommendation. It is that kind of naïveté, I think that Bertolt Brecht had in mind when he said, "The naïve is an aesthetic category, the most concrete of all. . . . The opposite of a naïve approach is naturalism." Naturalism in the theater is like empiricism in philosophy; they are both born of a distrust of representations, and that distrust leads them to attempt an absolute representation, which is the highest degree of illusion. "Let them see that you are not conjuring, but working," Brecht advised his actors. The naïve method is the most concrete because it lets the teller be seen in the act of telling, the actor in the act of acting, the thinker in the act of thinking, and thus reaffirms the living world. Paradoxically, the naïve image in its provisional nature is a more complex form of utterance than the most difficult proposition. Its complexity is dramatic, not semantic. The script only comes to life when it is performed, and each time it is performed under new circumstances. There is no definitive performance of a play, no definitive telling of a story, no idea that puts an end to thought.

The material of **The Gods** comes from daily life and common tradition, but also from the works of philosophers, novelists, poets, physicists, historians. If Alain tells many stories, he also recounts many ideas. His discovery of the recountability of ideas marks the extent of his break with the philosophy of his own youth, what he always called "the philosophy of the schools," which was a mixture of mathematics, psychology, and historical criticism. It would be a great misunderstanding of **The Gods** to consider it a historical study of religion. It would also be a misunderstanding to consider **The Gods** an attempt to reconstitute past beliefs, a work of cultural anthropology, in the manner of Kerényi. Though Kerényi seems close to Alain when he writes, in *Prometheus,* "Our assumption that *human existence* was the chief determinant of these mythical figures . . . distinguishes our mode of observing and interpreting ancient mythology from all previous attempts characterized by astral or 'naturist' theories," he is still a scholar; his work is the careful excavation of a site that is no longer there. Whereas Alain says, "In some way I am reading two texts one on top of the other. . . . The past leads me back to the present, and always presupposes the present in my thought." The world that appears in Kerényi's words is "spiritually" reconstructed in the scholar's mind's eye. The world that appears in Alain's words is physically construed. The trees, flowers, birds, animals, seas, springs, winds and tides, sun and moon in

**The Gods** have their own natural being and presence; they must be sensed physically in order to be understood metaphorically as the substance of the gods. The provisional nature of images is answered by the continuity of the material world through time. That is the configuration of Alain's thought, the ground of storytelling and of the realism of poetry. He does not locate truth on one side or the other. Instead he takes us into the workshop, he demonstrates the cross-grained, intricate, dialectical process of image-making itself.

Alain's prose is extremely concise. That is the only difficult thing about it. He has a way of depicting and interpreting an image in the same breath, and his thought moves by quick associations that are not always marked in the writing. His style is abrupt, elliptical, and gnomic. (pp. 1-5)

Alain worked by improvisation. He once described his handwriting as a kind of carving: " . . . my pen is always trying to go through the paper . . . ; my writing is like wood sculpture, and I have to make shift with the cut of the chisel; how can I revise it?" (*propos* of 14 April 1923). He believed, as he says in the same place, that an artist "can only invent as he works and as he perceives what he is working on." But he also wrote, in the **Système des beaux-arts** (1917): "When a man gives himself up to inspiration, I mean to his own nature, I see nothing but the resistance of the material that could save him from hollow improvisation and the instability of the spirit." Alain's material sense was very strong. And, for example, the art of psychological shading was foreign to him. He was not a modeler. He dispensed with certain ramifications of sensibility as he dispensed with much of the rhetoric of French prose. Style, for him, was a question of heightening the resistance of language. And for the same reason he preferred to work within strict formal limits.

The basic model for all of Alain's writings was the brief essay he called the *propos.* The word means a conversation, a talk. . . . In a note written in 1908, he compared the *propos* to the *stretto* in a fugue, the abbreviated repetition of the subjects, which come together "as if they were passing through a ring. The material crowds in, and it has to line up, and pass through, and be quick. That is my acrobatic stunt, as well as I can describe it; I have succeeded perhaps one time in six, which is a lot. . . ." In the same note he says, "It is not the desire for fame that makes me write, but rather a lively political passion, which will not let me consider without horror the present state of letters, emptied of all richness and force. One would like to have talent and not sell it to the highest bidder. I am trying to find out what my talent is, and what sort of virtue I claim to have." Each of these statements is clear in itself, but they have to be taken together. Pure play (art plus acrobatics) is one term in Alain's writing; ethical conscience and a passionate involvement in the world are the other. There is no simple way to read him.

A number of Alain's later books are collections of *propos.* And the form turns up again in the short chapters of **The Gods.** The beautifully integrated structure of the book, which is at once temporal, hierarchical, and circular, does not preclude the fact that it was produced in a single, sustained act of improvisation. Alain first touched on the subject of *The Gods* in a note written in 1911: "If religion is only human, and if its form is man's form, it follows that everything in religion is true." Twenty-two years later the book was written out, in the month of September, while he was staying at the village of Le Pouldu on the coast of Brittany. (pp. 5-7)

> *Richard Pevear, in a foreword to* The Gods, *by Alain, translated by Richard Pevear, New Directions, 1974, pp. 1-7.*

## John Weightman    (essay date 1982)

[*Weightman is an English educator and translator. In the following excerpt, he discusses the importance of Alain's work as an educator in the development of his philosophy and reputation, and observes the limitations of his philosophical rhetoric and thought.*]

Émile-Auguste Chartier (1868-1951), the philosopher-essayist who wrote under the pen name Alain, is a unique case of a French intellectual figure celebrated in his own country but virtually unknown in the English-speaking world, even today, more than thirty years after his death. Yet he was one of the most prolific writers of his generation. He invented a particular genre, the short essay or *propos,* of which he produced some five thousand examples, in addition to turning out other more structured works. Since the 1950s, the Gallimard publishing house has reissued the bulk of his writings in the special Pléîade edition, and this is the recognized sign of admission to classic status. His name is familiar, of course, to English and American students of French culture who have lived in France, many of whom, like myself, were introduced to his works at an early stage; but no one, as far as I know, has produced an extended study of him in English. Nor does the British Museum Library catalogue record more than two attempts to present him in English translation: *Mars ou la guerre jugée,* a series of *propos* on the psychological attitudes behind war, was brought out in 1930 as *Mars; or, the Truth About War,* and the philosophico-anthropological study, *Les dieux,* appeared in 1974 as *The Gods*; but neither volume seems to have made much impact in England or America. If we believe that all great writers—especially prose writers, whose work can usually, to some extent, survive in translation—must sooner or later have a universal appeal, this raises a problem: was, or is, Alain's reputation within France a local cultural illusion that would repay analysis, or, on the contrary, was he a truly great man, whom the Anglo-American public has yet to discover?

There is one immediate circumstance that goes some way toward explaining the anomaly. Alain was not simply, or even primarily, a writer. He was a teacher, a *professeur de lycée,* and more particularly a *professeur de philosophie.* His fame depended in the first place on his prestige in the classroom, and his writings were in large measure an extension of his oral instruction. In France, under the system in force until the Second World War, teachers of philosophy were especially important, since it was they who introduced seventeen- or eighteen-year-olds to the major works of world philosophy and trained them in the general discussion of ideas and moral issues that has traditionally been such a notable feature of French life. Chartier's career, in outline, followed the usual pattern. He was a lower-middle-class boy, the son of a Normandy veterinary surgeon, and brought up in the country against a peasant background. His academic ability won him a place at the Ecole Normale Supérieure in Paris; he passed *l'agrégation,* the national competitive examination that gave access to posts in secondary education, and was appointed in the normal way to a succession of schools in the provinces. He must have made a name for himself quite early because, by the turn of the century, he had graduated to Paris, and in 1909 he was given the most coveted position in the system, that of *professeur de philosophie* at the Lycée Henri Quatre, the outstanding boys' school and the most famous of all forcing grounds for young intellectuals.

He stayed there—with a break for war service between 1914 and 1917—until his retirement in 1933. During the postwar years, he also taught certain classes at the best girls' schools. The intense centralization of French education meant that the great majority of academically gifted pupils passed through the Parisian *lycées* on their way to the *grandes écoles* and the university. Alain, being so strategically placed, came to exercise an enormous personal influence. His classes had such a reputation that they attracted outsiders, that is, members of the general public and pupils playing truant from other schools. So magnetic, indeed, was his personality that his prestige quite eclipsed that of most university professors, and it was generally agreed that there had been no comparable draw since the early years of the century when Henri Bergson lectured at the Collège de France. Eventually, there were few people of note in the intellectual world who had not been taught at some stage either by Alain himself or by one of his many fervent disciples. He loomed so large that his presence could even seem irksome to a few jealously independent spirits. Jean-Paul Sartre, for instance, explains that he deliberately avoided Alain's classes so as not to come under his sway, although one may suspect that the twin doctrines of absolute freedom and social commitment, later developed by Sartre, owe something, either directly or indirectly, to Alain. However, most people were glad to accept Alain's teaching and, with rare exceptions, responded to it positively. This being so, it was natural that they should approach his written works in a spirit of admiration and respect.

My own experience as a foreign student may have some relevance here. When I first went to France in 1935, I was taught by one of Alain's ex-pupils who so revered the master that he had given the name Alain to his eldest son. In England, I had encountered one or two good teachers, but this man's classes were a revelation to me. Whatever the subject under discussion, there was never a dull moment, and ideas poured forth in a constant, jovial stream. This made me wonder with awe what it must have been like to drink at the fountainhead, and I was immediately converted to a belief in Alain. But his writings, when I came to look at them, were something of a puzzle and a disappointment, and I remember the effort I had to make to bring myself even to hint at this. However, my mentor assured me that I should have faith. He, who had sat at Alain's feet, could vouch for the fact that the philosopher was a great man. If I persevered in my reading, the works would eventually fall into place as the compelling expression of a whole universe of thought. Things have not turned out quite like that, but because I continued to admire Alain through my admiration for his epigone, it took me years to see him in any sort of perspective, and even now I cannot be sure that I have got him properly into focus.

What Alain illustrates is the phenomenon of *le maître à penser,* which is perhaps more in evidence in France than elsewhere. In one sense, it is a peculiar virtue of the French that, because of their intense intellectual tradition and their feeling that they all descend ultimately from Descartes, they should have heroes of the mind as well as stars of the theater, the cinema, pop music, and sport. It is also understandable that young people especially should polarize their attention on charismatic figures in the intellectual field, since the star system, with its spontaneous partisanship, simplifies the welter of the given. But, in another sense, this means that the intellectual life itself tends to take on show-business characteristics. Alain became a star, in the first place, because of his great ability as a teacher of adolescents, as a *réveilleur d'esprits,* and this implies that he had certain features that appealed to young people as daring, exciting, and unorthodox. If I may anticipate a view I shall amplify later, I suspect that, through achieving this particular kind of stardom in early middle age, he was isolated from criticism by his peers and confirmed in some of his less satisfactory tendencies. His enormous prestige also inhibited impartial discussion of his role and his writings because his pupils were everywhere and, with one or two exceptions, never publicly questioned the fervent admiration of their youth or subjected his works to objective analysis, even though, in many cases, they might have gone on to do things of which Alain would certainly have disapproved. For example, André Maurois, a very early disciple and the author of the introduction to the first Pléîade volume, had become a member of the French Academy, in spite of Alain's ironical comments on all institutions of that kind. One may suppose that the memory Alain's pupils had of him was associated with the springtime of their careers and that they could not express the slightest reservation about him or his writings without seeming to deny the intellectual lyricism of adolescence. His ready admission to the Pléîade series may have been, in some measure, an act of piety that later generations will question.

By now, having lived through the reigns of several subsequent *maîtres à penser*—Jean-Paul Sartre, Albert Camus, Jacques Lacan, and Roland Barthes, all of whom taught at some point in their careers—and having observed the current luminary, Michel Foucault, I have developed a keen mistrust of the phenomenon, while recognizing that it may be unavoidable. The temptation to commit oneself to a guru, particularly in youth, is no doubt universal; it is a sort of intellectual equivalent of falling in love; but in the end, all fan clubs are breeding grounds for falsehood and have a bad effect on both the guru and his disciples. Of the five writers mentioned above, only one, Albert

Camus, was clearly and painfully aware of the danger of adulation, which produces subjective dogmatism. In fact, this is precisely the theme of his last completed work, *La chute.* If the other four writers are still difficult to evaluate, it is partly because of the haze of emotionalism that surrounded them as leaders of thought and that reacted only too obviously on their writing.

In Alain's case, there is a degree of paradox. He declares in his autobiography, ***Histoire de mes pensées,*** that he had no wish to recruit disciples and, in fact, never really enjoyed being a teacher. Besides, the center of his doctrine, all during his career, was the principle of individual liberty and responsibility, combined with truth to oneself. It can be argued that he remained at heart an anarchist, who discovered collective realities only by a process of ratiocination, and that his young audiences took to him instinctively because they sensed this unquenchable rebelliousness. However, he never appealed to his classes in a modern, comradely way, since he believed in keeping relations between teacher and pupils strictly formal and impersonal. In this respect, he may have modeled himself on a master by whom he had been enormously impressed in his own school days. This was Jules Lagneau, a philosopher who wrote very little and would by now no doubt have been quite forgotten had Alain not published a small volume, ***Souvenirs,*** celebrating him as an intellectual genius in exactly the same tone as Alain's pupils were later to celebrate him. But the crypto-anarchist was, in practice, authoritarian. From 1917 onward, he always spoke ex cathedral, did not allow discussion in his classes, and overawed his pupils with his dominant personality, even when he was preaching non-dominance.

A curious feature of Alain's spontaneous, or unconscious, dogmatism was his decision, which he explains at length, to treat any author commented on in class as being infallible, that is, wholly true in his own way and needing only elucidation. This corresponded to his oft-repeated dictum that "everything is true," by which he meant that even wrong perceptions may be right in their given context. An example he never tired of using was that of a stick that appears bent if partly immersed in water, even when it is known to be straight. The illusion is optically true, although factually wrong, and this illustrates the essential point that there is no such thing as a unitary grasp of the external world or of mental phenomena; the problem is how to establish a hierarchy of simultaneous "truths." This is a valuable pedagogic principle. It is undoubtedly better, in the first instance, to suppose that anything said by Plato, for example, is justifiable from his point of view and in his cultural situation. This is the willing suspension of disbelief necessary for any understanding and is much to be preferred to the itch to refute, which Alain, correctly or not, denounced as the besetting sin of most of his fellow teachers of philosophy. However, as he practiced it, the principle led to some questionable consequences.

In the first place, since he concentrated on the texts themselves, without being much interested in relating them to their cultural contexts (insofar as these can be reconstituted), he tended to reinterpret them according to his own lights, so that his enthusiastic, but never very particular, commentaries on Plato, Descartes, Kant, Hegel, Comte, et cetera, seem to run these very dissimilar thinkers into the same Alain-like blur, in spite of the contrary implications of another of his favorite dicta: "Differences are more instructive than resemblances." He was not historically minded. Here and there in the *propos,* he scores telling points against the "factual," pseudoscientific, overconfident school of historians that was strong in France in his day, but he appears not to see the absurdist point that, while history is inevitably approximate and always grossly simplified, it is absolutely indispensable. It is inseparable from thought itself, which is always groping to reconstitute the past. Since we live in time, what happened yesterday, or what I think about the book I read last week, is a historical problem. At the level of separate cultures, all thought, in the last resort, has to be history of thought. (The point is made with admirable clarity in the intellectual autobiography of the English philosopher-historian R. G. Collingwood.) But Alain was strangely indifferent to this intellectual dimension. He was a dogmatic humanist who constantly reasserted the fundamental immutability of human nature, in opposition to the believers in progress or decline, or in any form of significant evolution. Culture, he keeps saying, depends on man, and man does not change; he exercises his freedom within a permanent framework. In this respect Alain stands at the opposite pole from Sartre and existentialism; Sartre declares that man is free at any moment to fashion himself as he wills, that there is no such thing as a given human nature, and that the belief in human nature is no more than a reactionary illusion of "bourgeois humanism" as it has existed since the eighteenth century.

Both of these points of view appear to me to be too extreme in their opposite ways, and I would support the intermediate hypothesis put forward by Claude Lévi-Strauss. In the deepest sense, human nature is probably definable, but its possibilities are so multiform that no culture ever expresses, or has expressed, them fully. Each distinct culture represents a particular and limited crystallization of certain possibilities. The historical urge consists in trying to understand crystallizations other than that in which one happens to have grown up, in order to throw light on them all, including one's own. And, in this sense, the past of one's own country may be as exotic as any foreign territory. There is perpetual change, but no overriding logic of history, such as the Hegelian self-realization of the World Spirit, or inevitable progress in the Marxist sense, or even a clearly distinguishable sequence of ages, such as Comte postulated. But the perpetual change is significant and needs to be elucidated if we are going to understand anything at all. There remains, of course, the very difficult problem of historical relativity ("crystallization" is too static a metaphor); the historian himself is on a moving platform of time while he is trying to assess other movements—the shifting is trying to assess the shifting. Lévi-Strauss hints at this dilemma without suggesting a solution, and indeed there may be none. But I cannot help feeling it a limitation in Alain that he does not recognize these complexities. Also, while it is understandable that, with his static concept of human nature, he should admire Plato, it is less easy to see how he can praise essentially evolutionary or dialectical thinkers en bloc without dis-

torting them unconsciously to fit his own pattern; in fact, he admits at times that he is not worried by the possibility of reading his own ideas into his favorite authors. That pattern itself may be seen as a consequence of a certain cultural crystallization: the French post-Enlightenment tradition in which the constant nature of man tended to be assumed as a necessary condition for the elaboration of the moral law.

In the second place, Alain tends to set up a canon of consecrated writers—the philosophers already quoted together with such literary figures as Montaigne, Rousseau, Balzac, Stendhal, Dickens, and Valéry—who are the repositories of the permanent truth about human nature and against whom no criticism is to be leveled. His procedure is comparable to that of a recent English *maître à penser* Dr. F. R. Leavis, who established a list of writers to be admitted to the Great Tradition of the English novel. Here again, the effects are partly good. Alain's repetitious insistence enable him to make some interesting new points about these very well known authors. But he can also be willfully partisan. What he says, for instance, in **Propos de littérature** about Rousseau's novel *La nouvelle Héloïse* strikes me as being demonstrably wrong-headed, ignoring as it does the moral complexity of that rather monstrous and very eighteenth-century work. At the same time, he has a number of bêtes noires—Taine, Sainte-Beuve, Renan, Flaubert, et cetera—whom he frequently dismisses without discussion, as if they were self-evidently beyond the pale. In other words, instead of evaluating the details of the given work, he tends to take the author as the unit of excellence or execration, and this is a vicious critical principle. Since Rousseau wrote *La nouvelle Héloïse,* Alain decrees that it must be good and argues accordingly. (However, Judith Robinson, in her Sorbonne thesis, "Alain, lecteur de Balzac et de Stendhal," shows, mainly on the basis of oral evidence, that in the case of Stendhal, Alain disliked the *Journal* and confessional writings. The reader cannot guess this from his uniformly eulogistic approach. Alain chose to ignore Stendhal's self-analysis, although it may have had some relevance for the composition of the novels.)

Alain is also on record as saying of Simone Weil, one of his brilliant pupils, that she had only to put pen to paper to produce writing of genius, whereas it is clear, even to admirers of Simone Weil, that her genuine insight and pathological features need to be carefully disentangled before one can arrive at any valid critical judgment of her. Incidentally, Alain passed on his absolutist tendency to Simone Weil; she, in her turn, celebrates Rousseau as one of the very few "pure" spirits in French literature. Rousseau was undoubtedly a genius, but he is also remarkable for his fascinating impurities.

Alain may have developed these characteristics partly through the demagogic temptation to sharpen the distinction between the "good" and the "bad" when addressing young people. But other factors probably came into play as well. His temperament, he admits, was whimsical, impulsive, and impatient of the traditional academic approach. Also, at a relatively early age, he acquired a particular intellectual technique. Although he believed in the virtues of hard work, he was unable to undertake any sustained effort in composition at the beginning of his career because of attacks of extreme fatigue, which convinced him that he had not long to live. The disability later turned out to be due to ear trouble, but by then he had long become accustomed to the *propos* as his normal form of written expression. While still in the provinces, he took part in political and educational activities outside the *lycée,* at first through conviction, but also through the need to find relief from mental exhaustion. As part of this extracurricular amusement, he was invited to write newspaper articles, and he hit on the form of the *propos,* a short essay of about seven hundred fifty words on any subject under the sun, which he could compose in one sitting. These mini-articles were first published in *La dépêche de Rouen,* and they were naturally colored by his philosophical teaching. He himself claims, with a certain boastfulness that breaks out from time to time in **Histoire de mes pensées,** that he raised the newspaper article to the level of metaphysics. This is true enough, if we take metaphysics in the general sense of serious reflection about any aspect of life. But it leaves open the question of the value of the *propos* as an intellectual genre, especially in the light of the rules that Alain evolved for himself.

He made it a condition that each *propos* should be a complete improvisation with no crossings out or corrections. This was partly because he felt that the tension thus created gave his style a sort of lift, and partly, no doubt, because of his principle that "everything is true." If he could not go back on his initial sentence, even if he was not absolutely sure of it, he had to find a way of "saving" it, that is, of ingeniously molding the subsequent argument in order to give it, retrospectively, a justifiable meaning. Each *propos* is, then, a sort of gamble, and he admits that several, even of the published ones, did not come off, although he refrains from pointing out which. One could also say that, when they are successful, they often achieve their effect through a kind of sophistry that amuses and stimulates for a moment and then becomes less appealing when it is repeated in various forms and cannot be convincingly related to a wider pattern of thought. Some of the best of the early *propos* have the charm of perfectly expressed little moral fables. Many, belonging to all periods, offer short and dense sequences of statement of a high quality. Jules Romains, in his panoramic novel about French life in the first half of the century, *Les hommes de bonne volonté,* makes one of his heroes, a young *normalien,* refer very aptly to "sentences by Alain, stuck together like crystals." But, at their worst, the *propos* may be sententious, even hectoring, and are too often rounded off by vague or obscure generalizations forced on the author by the limitations of the allotted span of words. After reading any series grouped around a single theme—education, politics, literature, et cetera—one may be left with the feeling that Alain's thoughts on these subjects have remained tantalizingly incomplete, because arguments are developed in short spurts and then broken off.

Suggestiveness, rather than developed statement, may be excellent as an oral teaching technique, but it is not so satisfactory on the printed page. With Alain, impressionism and the constant shelving of unsolved difficulties becomes a mannerism; in his later writings, he is only too ready to be gnomic and to hint at meanings beyond the limits of normal expression. In **Histoire de mes pensées,** he elevates this practice to the level of a principle and argues that a sound and solid obscurity is often to be preferred to clarity. In this respect, he eventually came to appear as an opponent of *la clarté française,* in spite of the fact that he continued to champion Descartes, the original master of French philosophical clarity. At the same time, he put himself into the modernist, avant-garde literary camp, where hermeticism has been a dominant tendency since the days of Mallarmé. (This is why his contemporary, the out-and-out rationalist Julien Benda, launched a violent attack on him, with particular reference to the style of **Système des beaux-arts,** in *La France byzantine.*)

The cult of obscurity, which began in poetry as an understandable reaction against the rhetorical transparency of nineteenth-century Romantic verse, has long since spread to French analytical and expository prose, which, in the hands of some practitioners such as Jacques Lacan or Roland Barthes, may be as sibylline as the most abstruse poetic formulations. Alain was not as extreme as these two, and his liking for obscurity was rather more noticeable in middle life, when he took an interest in "difficult" poetry and became personally acquainted with Paul Valéry and other representatives of the literary avant-garde. Sometimes, when the opaque nature of his writing is related to a genuinely complex issue, one can feel that it is justified and that a certain limit of expression has been reached, as in good hermetic verse. But the danger of hermeticism as a method is that it can become a kind of facility; instead of striving for clarity and being genuinely defeated by the inherent difficulty of the subject, the writer may fall into the habit of depending on dubiety and mystery as a means of pseudopoetic effect, as a narcissistic indulgence in the abundant uncertainties of all language. Alain is less prone to this than Lacan or Barthes, but it is a feature of his prose and may help to explain the apparent lack of keenness to translate his works, since nothing is more difficult to render in another language than a margin of possibly gratuitous mystery. However, while Alain may be difficult to translate, Lacan and Barthes, who add punning to hermeticism, are, strictly speaking, untransposable into English, and the so-called translations of their most characteristic works bear only an approximate relationship to the originals.

Given the circumstances I have outlined, it was perhaps inevitable that Alain should have evolved the *propos* as his main form of written expression, or more accurately as his only form, since the books that purport to be structured, such as **Système des beaux-arts** or **Les idées et les âges,** are made up of short chapters only loosely articulated into larger units and open to the criticisms I have suggested. But one might hazard a deeper, more philosophical explanation for his choice of the genre. Although at first sight so far removed from existentialism, he not infrequently adopts an existentialist stance by emphasizing that all thought exists in time and therefore comes into being and perishes from moment to moment. All linguistic expression is a function of time. A written sentence only relives by becoming part of the existential temporal sequence of the reader, with all the possibilities of misunderstanding that this implies. An author, rereading his own work, is subject to the same existential uncertainties: how can the self of today be sure of understanding the self of yesterday? et cetera. This line of argument, if followed far enough, leads to the extreme absurdist conclusion that "truth" is what is valid for the instant and that consciousness is a series of discrete events. This process of atomization can appear, in the first instance, to annihilate systematic thought and to make a nonsense of morality, as existentialist literature has amply demonstrated. Alain never openly formulates the issue in this way, but he can often be felt moving in this direction, in spite of being dogmatically assertive and strongly moralistic in certain respects. It could be that the *propos,* a short essay pinpointing a moment of perception, was his instinctive reaction to the dilemma, a Heraclitus-like compromise on the part of an otherwise Platonic idealist.

He himself maintained that his philosophy could not be systematized, because it only existed "in action," and more especially in his oral teaching, not in the *propos.* But if the *propos* are metaphysical, as he also said, the reader cannot help looking for the outlines, at least, of a system. This is true even for the reader who is a convinced absurdist and who therefore accepts the principle of "not knowing" as the ultimate experience. Since that experience itself can only be formulated through language, absurdism, too, is a function of language; and language can therefore be used, with relative confidence, to make the widest possible synthesis. Instead of suggesting such a synthesis, Alain's thousands of *propos* are, in the last resort, like the beads of a broken necklace that one has to unscramble as best one can, with the unhappy feeling that a quantity of clouded glass may have got mixed up with the pearls.

The *professeur de philosophie* has, or had, a double function: to explain how things came to be as they are, since there must be a valid reason for everything that exists; and to teach morality, that is, the reasons for preferring some things to others. Although the doctrine that "everything is true" may seem to indicate that Alain stressed the first role rather than the second, the overall tone of his writing is strongly moralistic, too much so, perhaps, for readers unacquainted with, or unsympathetic to, the French tradition of republican virtue dating back to the Revolution, and beyond to Rousseau's seminal text, *Du contrat social.* Alain constantly emphasizes the tension between the individual, whose first duty is to be free and true to himself, and the necessary constraints of society. He does not say theatrically, like Sartre, that we are "condemned" to be free; he echoes Rousseau and Renouvier to the effect that individual freedom and the rejection of determinism is the only hypothesis compatible with our inherent consciousness of spiritual autonomy. While strongly anticlerical in his earlier phase, he was always a deist in the sense that God is the Universal Something, inside and outside himself, that the individual postulates when trying to think or feel most genuinely. At the same time, he was a Stoic, in that he preached serene acceptance of the play of natural forces, and even considered happiness as a sort of hygienic obligation. I remember once lending his *Propos sur le bonheur* to a distressed woman friend, who returned the vol-

ume half-read with the comment that it was *"primaire."* No doubt she would have said the same about Bertrand Russell's *The Conquest of Happiness.* Alain and Russell share what one might call a male-chauvinist determination not to be miserable and an insistence on distinguishing between the two forms of necessity: the absolute necessity of the workings of the universe, which we can only contemplate, and the relative necessity of human conventions, which the virtuous citizen agrees to obey provisionally while always retaining his right to call them into question.

Alain produces innumerable variations on this theme. For instance, he declares himself a radical, not a socialist, because he believed in a compromise between private property—being true to individual human nature—and civic morality—recognition of the citizen's proper subordination to the state. Instead of grumbling about paying taxes, he says, we should be delighted to live in a community where certain essential services are ensured collectively in return for a reasonable contribution. This is an echo of *Du contrat social,* where Rousseau makes the same point very forcefully by arguing that the individual who finds himself condemned to death for a murder that he has committed should go gratefully to his execution and congratulate himself on living in a society in which the rule of law prevails. Alain would no doubt add that the convicted murderer should not be in awe of the judge, the jury, or the executioner, since they are his equals, citizens like himself, who just happen to be administering the law—as a policeman directs the traffic. In ***Propos sur l'éducation*** he is cynically commonsensical about examinations, which he presents as conventional exercises that the candidate should understand as such and prepare for accordingly, provided he really wants the ends to which examinations lead, which may not be the best ends. In his attitude toward himself, he applied a sort of harsh wisdom. There is an admirable passage in an early letter to a friend where he says that it is unfitting for a teacher to try to "make a career" for himself; a teacher—that is, a *professeur de philosophie*—is someone who should be happy to accept a living wage in order to think on behalf of the community. This could be generalized as a motto for all academics. Although he believed in the family as the natural unit of society and enjoyed many relationships with women, he never had children and married only very late in life. It is clear from the posthumously published, early notebooks, ***Cahiers de Lorient,*** that commitment to a particular woman and to offspring would have been irksome for his willful temperament, but it would also have compromised his vocation as a lay monk of thought. Finally, the supreme proof of his civic virtue is that, while detesting war, he volunteered for active service in 1914 and served for three years as an ordinary soldier, first in the heavy artillery and then as a front-line telephonist.

All this is coherent enough, but as he grew older and more famous, he seems to have become less self-critical and to have undergone a slight "dissociation of sensibility" in the opposite directions of increased tetchiness and incipient sentimentality. He had always had a choleric nature, which tended to express itself in outbreaks of intolerance and irascibility—*des sautes d'humeur,* as he said. One of the rare ex-pupils of Alain who disliked him was a onetime colleague of mine, later a distinguished writer; he said he found Alain overbearing and could never forgive him for having one day dismissed Rimbaud, in front of a whole class, as a poet of no importance. Conversely, Alain's desire to understand and his confident idiosyncrasy caused him to lean over backward in the effort to be fair to the Fascists and the Nazis before the Second World War. It is true that, having lived through the First World War, he clung desperately to pacifism. Also, ever since the Dreyfus Affair, he had had a profound mistrust of the French military hierarchy and the governing elite. Perhaps, too, his claim to understand human nature made it impossible for him to apprehend the unprecedented extremes of evil to which the totalitarian nations were heading. Whatever the explanation, some of the *propos* he wrote during that period make rather embarrassing reading today, and it is a slight blot on his memory that he should have allowed one or two of his articles to appear in the phony, German-sponsored *Nouvelle revue française,* edited by the Fascist sympathizer, Drieu La Rochelle. (Raymond Aron, who had known Alain without being his pupil, criticized him fiercely in the French wartime periodical, *La France libre,* writing under the name of René Avord. After Alain's death, he wrote another critical, but more balanced, article in *Hommage à Alain.*) Alain even went back a little on his republican virtue and displayed a weakness for strong leaders; at least, that is how I interpret a curious passage in **Portraits de famille** where he says that he now believes the best government to be at once aristocratic and democratic, since it is controlled by the most able with the consent of the governed. He concludes: "In my view, the statesman who has best understood and practised this new democracy is Stalin, following on from Lenin." This unexpected shift from democracy to autocracy may not be new at all, but another echo from Rousseau. It will be remembered that, in the latter, and weaker, part of *Du contrat social,* the Legislator suddenly pops up like a deus ex machina to give form to the general will. Be that as it may, it is sad to have to number Alain among the people who were taken in by Stalin.

At the same time that Alain's political opinions become more disparate, the general quality of the *propos* seems to deteriorate. Familiar ideas tend to recur in much the same words, but with a greater reliance on enigmatic throwaway formulas. He expatiates again and again on art and natural phenomena in a vague and euphoric style that is neither properly analytical nor fully poetic in its own right. This tendency had already been present in **Système des beaux-arts** and **Les idées et les âges,** but it becomes much more pronounced in **Entretiens chez le sculpteur, Vingt leçons sur les beaux-arts, Entretiens au bord de la mer,** and **Les dieux,** which really belong to a hybrid genre of poeticized meditation, drawing on rather archaic, pastoral sensibilities. Not that pastoral sensibilities are necessarily to be criticized in themselves, but in Alain's case they represent something of a mystic retreat from his hard initial stoicism and veer toward a Rousseauistic acceptance of Nature, however indefinable that term may be, as being by definition good. Perhaps we can sum up the change by saying that the robust republican with a clear view of necessity had, to some extent, turned into an opin-

ionated rhetorician with an inclination to applaud the universe. **Les dieux,** which he wrote after his retirement and obviously thought of as a kind of masterpiece, is a disappointing illustration of all the weaknesses of the *propos* form.

Having formulated this judgement, I am surprised by its harshness and also by my temerity in criticizing a writer who was central to my own education, such as it was. But Alain taught freedom and honesty, and these two principles now oblige me to admit that he did not, as far as I can see, think his way through to a fully valid philosophy, or evolve an entirely satisfactory form of literature. I do not expect him eventually to be recognized as a great writer of international status. However, he certainly deserves to be better known in the English-speaking world than he is, and it is to be hoped that, sooner or later, some Anglo-American publisher will bring out a properly organized anthology of the best *propos,* together with a version of **Histoire des mes pensées,** a volume that is very worthy of a place in the international literature of intellectual autobiography. (pp. 381-89)

> John Weightman, "Alain: For and Against," in The American Scholar, *Vol. 51, No. 3, Summer, 1982, pp. 381-89.*

---

## FURTHER READING

Cruickshank, John. "The Emotional Response (I): Alain and Rational Pacifism." In his *Variations on Catastrophe: Some French Responses to the Great War,* pp. 138-54. Oxford: Clarendon Press, 1982.

Analyzes Alain's arguments against war in *Mars ou la guerre jugée.*

Howell, Ronald F. "Letters of a Wilful Sage." *The Times Literary Supplement,* No. 2,948 (29 August 1958): 483.

Letter responding to unfavorable commentary about Alain's philosophy. See Further Reading entry under the *Times Literary Supplement.*

———. "Emile Chartier Becomes Alain." *The Emory University Quarterly* 17, No. 1 (Spring 1961): 13-23.

Discusses Alain's life and the development of his philosophical thought.

Maurois, André. "Alain." In his *From Proust to Camus: Profiles of Modern French Writers,* pp. 96-121. Garden City, N.Y.: Doubleday & Co., 1966.

Provides biographical information, examines Alain's writings and political thought, and summarizes the content of *Système des beaux-arts* and *Les dieux.*

Robinson, Judith. "The Centenary of a Neglected French Thinker: Alain on the Subject of War." *Australian Journal of French Studies* 5, No. 3 (September-December 1968): 235-56.

Examines Alain's arguments against war, praising their relevance to contemporary world events.

Saurat, Denis. Foreword to *Mars; or, The Truth about War,* by Alain, translated by Doris Mudie and Elizabeth Hill, pp. 19-24. New York: Jonathan Cape & Harrison Smith, 1930.
>   Praises Alain's egalitarianism and belief in humanitarian values.

"Letters of a Wilful Sage." *The Times Literary Supplement,* No. 2,944 (1 August 1958): 429-30.
>   Reviews *Correspondance avec Elie et Florence Halévy,* a collection of Alain's letters, discussing Alain's life and analyzing the limitations of his philosophical thought.

Turnell, Martin. "Human Aspirations." *The Times Literary Supplement,* No. 3,834 (5 September 1975): 1004.
>   Reviews *The Gods,* praising Alain's approach to discussing religion and suggesting that current neglect of his works can be attributed to his paradoxical style of writing.

# John Buchan

## 1875-1940

(Also wrote under the pseudonyms Cadmus and H. de V.) Scottish novelist, biographer, historian, short story writer, essayist, poet, journalist, and editor.

For related criticism, see the entry on Detective Fiction in *TCLC,* Volume 38.

A prominent political figure and prolific author, Buchan is best known today for his espionage adventure novels that he called "shockers." His most popular work, *The Thirty-Nine Steps,* characterizes these novels, featuring an amateur sleuth who undergoes a series of narrow escapes and hurried journeys in his attempt to thwart an international terrorist conspiracy. In addition to espionage novels, Buchan wrote a number of highly regarded biographies and histories.

Born in Perth, Scotland, Buchan was the oldest of six children of a Calvinist minister in the Free Church of Scotland. In 1876 his family moved to Pathhead in Fife, and during his childhood there Buchan became acquainted with Scottish ballads, the Bible, and John Bunyan's allegory *The Pilgrim's Progress* (1678). He entered Hutcheson's Grammar School in Glasgow in 1888, where he studied English and classical Greek and Roman literature. In 1892 Buchan won a scholarship to Glasgow University and there he wrote essays that were published in *Macmillan's* and the *Gentleman's Magazine.* Having earned another scholarship, Buchan transferred to Brasenose College at Oxford in 1895, and during that year his first novel, *Sir Quixote of the Moors,* appeared. The success of Buchan's early novels and essays, combined with the income from his scholarship and his work as a publisher's reader and book reviewer, enabled him to become financially self-sufficient. Buchan graduated from Oxford with a humanities degree in 1899 and moved to London, where he worked as a journalist while studying to become a barrister. Soon after he passed the bar in 1901, Buchan accepted a position on the staff of the British high commissioner for South Africa in Johannesburg, and he later wrote *The African Colony,* a history of South Africa which included details of his two years of service there.

Returning to London in 1903, Buchan maintained several occupations during the following decade, working as a barrister, journalist, and as an adviser and book editor with Thomas Nelson, a major British publisher, while writing essays, fiction, and histories. At the beginning of World War I, Buchan was suffering from a duodenal ulcer that precluded him from military service, and during his convalescence he wrote the entirety of *The Thirty-Nine Steps* and began writing *Nelson's History of the War,* a study of the First World War that he completed in 1919. Buchan was partially recuperated by mid-1915, and he subsequently became a war correspondent, later serving as an intelligence officer and as Britain's director of information. After the war Buchan became the director and depu-

ty chairman of Reuters news agency and continued to write prolifically in a variety of genres. Throughout the late 1920s and 1930s he developed his career in public service: he was elected as a member of Parliament for the Scottish Universities in 1927; he was appointed high commissioner to the General Assembly of the Church of Scotland in 1933; and two years later Buchan was named governor-general of Canada and raised to the peerage as Baron Tweedsmuir of Elsfield. Buchan completed his memoirs in 1940, shortly before he died in Montreal.

Most critical attention has been focused on Buchan's novels, particularly his shockers. In the dedication of *The Thirty-Nine Steps,* Buchan defined the shocker as a "romance where the incidents defy the probabilities, and march just inside the borders of the possible." The protagonists of these works are frequently such amateur sleuths as the retired Glasgow grocer Dickson McCunn, the lawyer Sir Edward Leithen, and the mining engineer Richard Hannay, who sometimes get out of difficult situations through coincidence or luck. Throughout his espionage novels Buchan focuses on the theme of the vulnerability of civilization to the constant threat of international conspiracies. In *The Power-House,* for example, the villain

Andrew Lumley states: "You think that a wall as solid as the earth separates civilisation from barbarism. I tell you the division is a thread, a sheet of glass. A touch here, a push there, and you bring back the reign of Saturn." Critics often note the influence of Bunyan's *Pilgrim's Progress* on Buchan's novels, finding numerous allusions to the struggle between good and evil in Bunyan's Christian allegory. While some recent commentators assert that Buchan's portrayals of racial minorities are derogatory, others argue that his works have been misinterpreted and underrated. Buchan's historical romances, including *Sir Quixote of the Moors* and *Witch Wood,* have also been critically acclaimed and have been compared to the novels of Robert Louis Stevenson for their quickly paced plots and to those of Sir Walter Scott for their regional Scottish settings.

Buchan considered his scholarly writings, especially his four major biographies, *Montrose, Oliver Cromwell, Augustus,* and *Sir Walter Scott,* to be his most important works. His biography of Scott is particularly esteemed for its comprehensive treatment of the early nineteenth-century novelist's life and literary works. *Nelson's History of the War* has also been praised for presenting complicated incidents both accurately and concisely. While some commentators believe that Buchan glorified powerful and successful men, minimizing or neglecting negative aspects of the events and personalities he described, critics note his exhaustive research and commend his polished prose style. Once highly regarded, Buchan's biographies and historical studies receive little critical attention today. His shockers, however, continue to receive recognition as important works of English mystery and spy fiction. John G. Cawelti maintains: "Buchan was instrumental in giving both a model of form and an inner spirit to the story of espionage, giving it through his vision of the world a capacity to express in terms of contemporary international politics and intrigue the yearning for a lost world of fullness and heroism."

(See also *Contemporary Authors,* Vol. 108 and *Dictionary of Literary Biography,* Vols. 34 and 70.)

## PRINCIPAL WORKS

*Essays and Apothegms of Francis Lord Bacon* [editor] (essays and aphorisms)   1894
*Sir Quixote of the Moors*   (novel)   1895
*Scholar Gipsies*   (essays and short stories)   1896
*John Burnet of Barns*   (novel)   1898
*Grey Weather: Moorland Tales of My Own People*   (short stories and poetry)   1899
*A Lost Lady of Old Years*   (novel)   1899
*The Half-Hearted*   (novel)   1900
*The Watcher by the Threshold, and Other Tales*   (novella and short stories)   1902; also published as *The Watcher by the Threshold, and Other Tales* [enlarged edition], 1918
*The African Colony*   (history)   1903
*Some Eighteenth Century Byways, and Other Essays*   (essays)   1908
*Prester John*   (novel)   1910; also published as *The Great Diamond Pipe,* 1910

*The Moon Endureth*   (short stories and poetry)   1912
*Salute to Adventurers*   (novel)   1915
*The Thirty-Nine Steps*   (novel)   1915
*Nelson's History of the War.* 24 vols.   (history)   1915-19; also published as *A History of the Great War.* 4 vols. [revised edition], 1921-22
*Greenmantle*   (novel)   1916
*The Power-House*   (novel)   1916
*Poems, Scots and English*   (poetry)   1917; also published as *Poems, Scots and English* [revised and enlarged editon], 1936
*Mr. Standfast*   (novel)   1918
*The Path of the King*   (novel)   1921
*Huntingtower*   (novel)   1922
*Midwinter*   (novel)   1923
*The Three Hostages*   (novel)   1924
*John Macnab*   (novel)   1925
*The Dancing Floor*   (novel)   1926
*Witch Wood*   (novel)   1927
*Montrose*   (biography)   1928
*The Runagates Club*   (short stories)   1928
*The Courts of the Morning*   (novel)   1929
*Castle Gay*   (novel)   1930
*The Blanket of the Dark*   (novel)   1931
*The Gap in the Curtain*   (novel)   1932
*Sir Walter Scott*   (biography)   1932
*A Prince of the Captivity*   (novel)   1933
*The Free Fishers*   (novel)   1934
*Oliver Cromwell*   (biography)   1934
*The House of the Four Winds*   (novel)   1935
*The Island of Sheep*   (novel)   1936; also published as *The Man from the Norlands,* 1936
*Augustus*   (biography)   1937
*Memory Hold-the-Door*   (memoirs)   1940; also published as *Pilgrim's Way,* 1940
*Sick Heart River*   (novel)   1941; also published as *Mountain Meadow,* 1941

---

**The Bookman,** New York (essay date 1895)

[*In the following excerpt, the critic favorably reviews* Sir Quixote of the Moors.]

We understand that [*Sir Quixote of the Moors*] is the first piece of fiction by a new writer. If so, it is a decidedly promising bit of work, full of humour and vitality, and it deserves to be successful. . . . It is hard to say just what Mr. Buchan will yet do, but there are strong evidences of a master hand at work in this delicious little idyll. To be sure he will suffer by comparison with Stevenson and Crockett, and it may be fair to say that but for these writers the tale had never been written. But it is by no means an imitation. There are traces of their influence in his manner, and there are characteristic touches which remind us of Weyman as well as of the writers already mentioned; but there is an individual quality in his work and a certain bewitchment which belongs to the higher forms of imagination. Poor Sir Quixote is very human, and is next of kin to most of us; but we are particularly grateful for the heroine, who is so real as to enlist our sympathies from the first, and whose presence in the story becomes a living memory long after the book is closed. We could never have forgiven the Sieur de Rohaine had he deserted her in the end. The story is told with great delicacy and grace of diction, and pervading it is an air of gentle romance like the fragrant aroma of sweet lavender in an old garden. Whatever defects exist in the story arise from immaturity, but the power of reserve which is evident on every page makes us hope great things of the author. We shall certainly look with eagerness for his next book.

*A review of "Sir Quixote of the Moors," in* The Bookman, *New York, Vol. II, No. 4, December, 1895, p. 329.*

### The Bookman, London (essay date 1912)

[*In the following excerpt, the critic examines Buchan's early literary career.*]

Among those who have set the seal of their individuality on modern letters none stands out in a more distinctive light and deserves more honourable mention than Mr. John Buchan. He has breathed a new life into the moribund art of the novel; he has made the short story what a cameo might be when it is cut by the hand of a master, and he has even contrived to make the light essay and occasional article an entertaining and scholarly production. Mr. Buchan has "played the sedulous ape" to one great master with success—R. L. Stevenson—and with the brilliant exception of Sir A. T. Quiller-Couch he has inherited more of the Stevensonian spirit and tradition than any other modern writer, although with more classical restraint. Stevenson would not only have found in him a literary disciple; we feel sure that the spirit of the elder Scot would have responded gaily to the author of **Scholar Gipsies** and **Grey Weather** and found in him a boon companion; Borrow would have loved him; and we know that Mr. Hilaire Belloc who has roamed a continent throwing conventions to the wind in his mode of progression finds in him a congenial spirit on many a ramble among the Sussex Downs. For the author of **Scholar Gipsies** loves the sun and the wind; the purple moorland lying under grey skies attracts him as the Dartmoor landscape attracts Mr. Eden Phillpotts; his feet as a mountaineer are set in perilous places; the high hill has an irresistible charm for him; the silver stream winds its way through all his dreams as well as through the prose he writes; and we believe at odd moments when he is not brooding over some obscure point connected with the practical side of publishing his mind is off to the Spanish Main; he is back in the great sea fights of history with Raleigh and Drake and Morgan. It is this peculiar blend of what one might call the pastoral and the picaresque that one finds so attractive in the writings of Mr. Buchan. He may lay his scene in lowland Scotland when the sheep shearing is on the hills and nothing breaks the drowsy stillness of the summer afternoon but the sharp bark of the farmer's dog and the cries of huddled sheep, but it is ten to one that the vagrant spirit of the author will throw off the burden of the peaceful scene and plunge light-heartedly into his favourite atmosphere. At one mo-

ment he is playing on an oaten reed a caressing pastoral; the next he is wielding a cutlass. (pp. 140-41)

It is difficult, and always invidious, to define the exact place a contemporary man of letters holds in modern literature. In the case of Mr. John Buchan the difficulty becomes even more accentuated. The very scope and variety of his achievements perplex the critic. Besides novels and stories he has written on law, history, politics, metaphysics and sport. The probability that he will produce as much again before he has done coquetting with the "grisette of literature" as Mr. Barrie whimsically calls her, makes the duty of the critic both premature and supererogatory. We may, however, lightly sketch the character of the author, dwell on his style and methods and call attention here and there to a glowing phrase, a felicity of expression, perhaps even a conceit, but beyond that we dare not venture. Mr. Buchan is essentially Stevensonian both in the matter of literary style and in his outlook on life. He is the child of fancy. The world in which he moves has no attraction for him as an author except when he deals with a contemporary type that has no real place or business in the modern world; ordinary life has no meaning for him beyond the fact that it has got to be lived. We do not mean to say that he would go so far as to consider it a desecration of the printed page to introduce a vignette from real life; he has done so more than once; but he finds his inspiration in the romantic past and in the shadows of things that have become romantic. His great background is Jacobite Scotland, when he is not rapt in some peculiar myth or lost in the maze of some weird superstition. His earlier works, **Scholar Gipsies** and **Grey Weather** were in the true pastoral vein; his romances such as **John Burnet of Barns, A Lost Lady of Old Years,** and **Prester John** are all cast in the true Stevensonian mould. It is only in his . . . book **The Moon Endureth,** that he has broken away in some respects from the traditions of the Stevensonian manner. In this book he has probably found his true *métier* in the short story, which he has developed and brought to artistic perfection in such tales as **"The Grove of Ashtaroth"** and **"The Lemnian."** The Moon Endureth contains his best and most mature work, and in this perhaps more than in any other of his books he represents the classical-romantic school, with all its restraint and severity of style; its poise and balance; the coldness even of its romance; the clear-cut, concise phrase:

> The little more and how much it is,
> The little less and what worlds away!

In his own peculiar manner he is probably the best modern exponent of the short story. His stories are perfect cameos of expression, delicately cut and delicately rounded, that stand out clear and distinct from their background of romance. **"The Lemnian"** opens with an almost Homeric dignity and roll. It is a brilliant example of the cold classical restraint that distinguishes the author's best work:

> He pushed the matted locks from his brow as he peered into the mist. His hair was thick with salt, and his eyes smarted from the green-wood fire on the poop. The four slaves who crouched beside the thwarts—Carians with thin bird-like faces—were in a pitiable case, their hands blue with oar weals and the lash marks on their

shoulders beginning to gape from sun and sea. The Lemnian himself bore marks of ill usage. His cloak was still sopping, his eyes heavy with watching, and his lips black and cracked with thirst. Two days before the storm had caught him and swept his little craft into mid-Aegean. He was a sailor, come of sailor stock, and he had fought the gale manfully and well. . . .

And this beautiful vignette from the same source deserves quotation:

> Then, while the waves lapped on the white sand, Atta made a song. He was thinking of the homestead far up in the green downs looking over the snows of Samothrace. At this hour in the morning there would be a tinkle of sheep-bells as the flocks went down to the low pastures. Cool winds would be blowing and the noise of the surf below the cliffs would come faint to the ear. In the hall the maids would be spinning, while their dark-haired mistress would be casting swift glances to the doorway, lest it might be filled at any moment by the form of her returning lord. Outside in the chequered sunlight of the orchard the child would be playing with his nurse, crooning in childish syllables the chanty his father had taught him. And at the thought of his home a great passion welled up in Atta's breast. It was not regret but joy and pride and aching love. In his antique island creed the death he was waiting for was not other than a bridal. He was dying for the things he loved, and by his death they would be blessed eternally. He would not have long to wait before bright eyes came to greet him in the House of Shadows.

Mr. John Buchan has gone further than most men go in a life twice as long and he has achieved much in many rôles. He is an accomplished writer in a rare and difficult manner; he was written verse that will at least stand the test of contemporary poetry; he is the author of some half a dozen novels and he has visualised the African Colony for us in a vivid volume of travel. We feel that he will go further in the future, and it is of interest to note in view of the many-sided character of the man that he has of late devoted himself to politics and has been adopted as Unionist candidate for the counties of Peebles and Selkirk, with which he has been so long associated. As a writer he has to some extent freed himself from the shackles of tradition and he has proved himself a brilliant artist in the short story. If we may intrude a note of personal criticism we feel that he has but to weave some of the joy and laughter of his own sunny personality into his work to reach that wider public that demands that an author shall amuse as well as enthral. Let him launch out into a new atmosphere by giving real life a chance now and again; let him deal with things as he sees them; not the abnormal but the commonplace; not the supernatural, but the natural; the everyday things that lie about his feet; for a little real life is worth a great deal of tradition. Romance does not always lie buried in some half-forgotten legend. It is often the things that are commonplace to-day that are the legends of to-morrow. Mr. John Buchan has now attained his literary majority; we still wait for the great work; the more ambitious flight of his matured imagination. (p. 142)

"John Buchan," in The Bookman, *London,* Vol. 43, No. 255, December, 1912, pp. 140-42.

## The Spectator  (essay date 1915)

[*In the following excerpt, the critic favorably assesses* The Thirty-Nine Steps.]

The genesis of this spirited and ingenious story [**The Thirty-Nine Steps**] is told in a brief dedicatory epistle. Mr. Buchan confesses to having long shared with the soldier friend to whom he inscribes his book an affection for the American "dime novel" and the native "shocker"—"the romance where the incidents defy the probabilities, and march just inside the borders of the possible. During an illness last winter I exhausted my store of those aids to cheerfulness, and was driven to write one for myself." . . .

Readers of **Prester John, The Moon Endureth,** and **The Watcher by the Threshold** need not to be reminded that [Buchan] is a first-rate hand at spinning a yarn, and though he is working here on a somewhat lower plane and appealing to a wider audience, his literary craftsmanship remains as sound as ever. He cannot suppress his love of landscape, even in the midst of the most thrilling and sensational incidents. There are no purple patches, and the tender passion does not enter into the scheme at all: indeed, no single female character is directly concerned in the plot. But still the presentation has just that quality of literary amenity which the average "shocker" conspicuously lacks; it lifts the book out of the ruck without being so pronounced as to repel the unlettered reader. To a certain extent the story may be regarded as an essay in literary discipleship; Mr. Buchan has learnt something, as he implies in his dedication, from the study of the American "dime novel," but he is influenced much more by the methods of Stevenson—the Stevenson of *The New Arabian Nights, The Wrecker,* and *The Wrong Box.* Yet it would be unfair to press the parallel; the story is frankly eclectic, but not imitative, and so far as Stevenson is concerned, the resemblance is that of a family likeness, for, after all, Mr. Buchan is also a Scotsman, a romantic with a bent towards the fantastic, and a poet.

As for the plot, without revealing anything that might discount the joys of perusal, we may content ourselves with saying that it is an ingenious variation on the conditions that immediately preceded the outbreak of the war. The narrator-hero, who has just returned to England after many years of residence in South Africa, and finds himself unutterably bored by the futile feverishness of life at home, is suddenly confronted with a problem which exceeds his wildest dreams of adventure. In order to compass a patriotic end of vital importance, he incurs the suspicion of murder, and exposes himself to the double risk of capture by the police and assassination by the members of a powerful and relentless secret society. To carry out his plans he must disappear for a time. Hence the need of flight, and a constant change of disguises, accompanied by a policy of confiding—where advisable—in those who shelter him, and it is the alternation of the methods of elusion with those of audacity which lends the narrative much of its charm.

*A review of "The Thirty-Nine Steps," in* The Spectator, *Vol. 115, No. 4558, November 6, 1915, p. 630.*

## R. Brimley Johnson   (essay date 1922)

[*In the following essay, Johnson surveys Buchan's early fiction, especially praising the realistic portrayal of his protagonists.*]

Mr John Buchan I accept gratefully as a sign of the times, a sound type of competent efficiency. He has, of course, been many things besides a novelist, all of them with conspicuous, if not supreme, success. As a novelist, he is a master of his craft. The man who does what he undertakes well, in an interesting fashion, represents one, at least, of the conspicuous influences of our generation.

What one may call the material of his novels and short stories is not modern: their manner does not follow the road dear to his more strenuous contemporaries. They would annoy the "highbrow"; they do not satisfy those who yearn for a stricken soul, or love to plunge into the glamour and grime of sin. They are "plain tales" of romance and adventure, with only atmosphere and furniture up to date. And Mr Buchan admits, too, that fondness for crisp and knowing generalisations which youth always affects.

One may conveniently, and quite justly, illustrate his work in fiction by the consideration of three complete novels and two collections of short tales.

There is not, perhaps, much to say—with profit—about **Prester John** save that it is a quite admirable yarn, packed with murderous intrigue, hair-breadth escapes, deeds of reckless daring and the glamour of strange folk. Its canny hero adventures into the far corners of the earth, learns the secrets of many a coloured fanatic, helps to build the Empire, and triumphs over the tricks of his most deadly foes. The villainous, and yet inspired, Prester John himself long dreams, and indeed nearly achieves, a mystical Return of the Savage—to something approaching World-Power. A man born to kingship, holding himself an ally of God, this black-hearted pagan was a sincere enthusiast, believing in the divinity of his mission, feeling "behind him all the armies of heaven." His "blood-thirsty savage" followers were actually "consecrated to the meek service of Christ." His was the vision of a new

> Ethiopian Empire, so majestic that the white man everywhere would dread its name, so righteous that all men under it would live in ease and peace. . . . Ye, the old masters of the land, are now the servants of the oppressor. And yet the oppressors are few, and the fear of you is in their hearts. . . . What have ye gained from the alien?" save "a bastard civilisation which has sapped your manhood; a false religion which would rivet on you the chains of a slave.

All of which may not be very much like real life anywhere, yet is not altogether foreign to human nature: it serves to stir the imagination, to rest the mind. Besides which there is sound stuff in our good Mr David Crawfurd, who has wit enough to confound the mystic.

In **Greenmantle** Mr Buchan has chosen a different field of adventure, leading his hero a devil's dance over the by-ways of Armageddon. This is a spy story of the Great War, wherein a plain Englishman, carrying his life in his hands, strives to penetrate and circumvent one of those baffling intrigues of the wily Teuton, by which they were credited with having attached the fighters of Islam to their side: "some tremendous sacred sanction, some holy thing, some book or gospel or some new prophet from the desert, something which would cast over the whole ugly mechanism of German war the glamour of the old torrential raid which crumpled the Byzantine Empire and shook the walls of Vienna." Here is, indeed, another and a more venomous Holy War to be encountered, which would "let hell loose in those parts pretty soon."

This "forlorn hope," to the solution of which those in authority had practically no clue whatever, carries our Richard Hannay into strange places among wild men. It may not, perhaps, be said that he achieves any material success, but he does penetrate to the very heart of the great mystery; he does see, and learn, much of the lady Greenmantle, whose long-looked-for coming should summon the Eastern hordes and "madden the Moslem peasant with dreams of Paradise." He finds, indeed, but small reason to "quite believe in Islam becoming a back number."

Incidentally we learn from these absorbing pages to echo the judgment of Mr John S. Blenkiron—of the United States—that "you Britishers haven't any notion how wide awake your Intelligence Service is. I reckon it's easy the best of all the belligerents."

We shall not, probably, go far wrong if we accept, for all it attempts to reveal, the following account of the German mind:

> It is only boldness that can baffle them. They are a most diligent people. They will think of all likely difficulties, but not of all possible ones. They have not much imagination. They are like steam engines which must keep to prepared tracks. There they will hunt any man down, but let him trek for open country and they will be at a loss. Therefore boldness, my friend; for ever boldness. Remember as a nation they wear spectacles, which means that they are always peering.

**The Thirty-Nine Steps** is a war novel also. Here, however, the adventures occur mainly in Scotland; partly in London and Bradgate, Kent. We have here German agents, mingling in high politics, murdering a Greek Premier, stealing State secrets, and, in the process, disclosing a very considerable ingenuity, tireless energy, and reckless indifference to human life. There are chapters that recall *Kidnapped*— with a difference: for our hero is driven to exert all those fascinating devices of the trek-expert who yet, after all, owes so much to his genius for good luck. Mr Buchan, of course, is quite at home in the Highlands, and uses his knowledge with great effect. It is once more Richard Hannay who plays many new parts, a veritable master of make-up, true sportsman, and man of mettle. This is, as the author admits frankly, just a "dime novel" or "shocker," a "romance where the incidents defy the probabilities and march just inside the borders of the possible." Like Mr Buchan himself, however, "I have long cherished an affection for that elementary type of tale," which is truly an "aid to cheerfulness." The work is thoroughly well done; humorously varied, crowded with thrills and shocks, just sufficiently spiced with dramatic coincidences that please and startle, without strain or offence.

I am personally disposed to rate one quality in Mr Buchan's achievements rather exceptionally high. He resists, always and everywhere, the temptations towards perfectability. He does not plague us with the "complete" hero. His adventurers, inevitably, record many a hard-won triumph, and often score off their adversaries at the eleventh hour; but they are not invariably a success, not always cool and courageous, not masters of every weapon or of all men. They miss a chance, miscalculate and misjudge, do not perform miracles. Just because they are human; therefore our very good friends.

It is inevitable, perhaps, that we should ask how much these two novels have gained from that "inside" information about the war which their author was no doubt, in a most favourable position to acquire. They, probably, gain much: though I should presume that each actual framework, or plot, is quite imaginary. *Greenmantle,* in particular, reads more like a very ingenious hint—as it were—of what *might* have been happening behind the scenes, than like a dramatic adaptation of actual dangers afoot. Here, as in *The Thirty-Nine Steps,* it is most probable that Mr Buchan has only used his knowledge for the colouring of the atmosphere, to perfect the realism in detail, which is essential to modern romance.

Yet just because he was able to do this, and has done it, these tales remain (what many of their contemporaries have no pretence to be) a passably true picture, and most suggestive record, of certain phases in human experience, during a period when life was, in an ugly sense, romantic, and when many experiences we had long grown accustomed to call impossible, might actually come upon any of us at any moment.

It might be naturally supposed from the above analysis that Mr Buchan's Short Stories would follow the same lines in a more concentrated form. But they do, in fact, introduce a new element which, for want of a better word, we must call "supernatural." This is, indeed, characteristic of his generation. As we grow material, we become superstitious. The loosening of orthodoxy as a governing force in life has been always accompanied by keen interest, if not faith, in the older forms of religion; and, particularly since the war, average man has grown credulous. The historical investigation of Christianity, too, has induced many to find in all forms of belief some message from the one God, at least from the Spiritual Force behind creation generally so called.

Mr Buchan has skilfully used these tendencies, or forms of faith, for atmosphere, both in *The Moon Endureth* and in *The Watcher by the Threshold.* Each contains tales of men possessed by the devil, haunted by strange visions, in touch with mysteries behind the veil. He attempts, also, to analyse the mind of those scientists who go mad over

the fourth dimension, or perish in the pursuit of some almost miraculous discovery, carrying their great secret with them to the silent grave. He gives new life to many an old legend of the countryside, casting the weird, powerful influence of "place"—the local superstition—over the normal man. His wise men become as children, in their morbid seeking after the unknown truth, set in an old wives' tale. He introduces us, for example, in **"No-Man's-Land"**—a gruesome tragedy, to "the history of the craziest survival the world has ever seen . . . fragments of old religions, primeval names of god and goddess . . . the key to a hundred puzzles." His hero visits "the folk," hears and sees the "unmentionable deeds in darkness" of the half-animal Picts, lingering among the scarts of the Muncraw.

He writes of men, feeling the call of Wild Waters, stealing away to the woods that they may celebrate strange pagan rites, playing the hero in the old border raids, driven from fame and power at the bidding of a boy's dream.

The men and women of these "twice-told" tales are all on the verge of mania, super-normal, obsessed by the tyranny of One Idea, which must disturb the mind's balance, putting them "beyond the pale." It is attractive material for fiction, wisely handled in miniature, food for thought, not without service to the student of humanity who loves the "lands behind the mist."

For "the moon," said St Francis, "signified the dominion of all strange things in earth and air, such as were beyond the comprehension of man's reason or the authority of his temporal will." Also "the back-world of Scotland is a wise place to travel in for those who believe it is not bounded strictly by kirk and market-place, and who have an ear for old songs and lost romances."

Mr Buchan has given us, then, two versions of modernity, neither of them elsewhere so prominent among contemporary novelists, presented with equal skill: action and vision in the most extreme forms of which man is capable, the will to do and the will to dream. These are the two chief elemental forces in human nature, most contradictory, leading to thoughts ever opposed, yet for ever the very stuff and fibre of our nature. From life we shall always demand both; each provides first-class matter for the real drama of romance.

Though not formally a collection of short stories, his . . . novel, *The Path of the King,* is actually a series of episodes with a new hero, or heroine, to each. They are all, however, members of one family; descended, more or less directly, from one Viking ancestor; and, having royal blood in their veins, are destined one day to achieve kingship. Mr Buchan contends, and ingeniously illustrates his contention, that

> however heroism may lapse for more than a generation, it will emerge at the long last. It will not, most probably, appear in the direct line—among the first-born, from whom much comforting hath driven out the devil—but a younger son of younger sons will, in due course, rise from the gutter, and, by force of the character he has inherited from bygone centuries, become the man.

The theme affords ample opportunity for brisk drama and varied adventure. It carries us through many centuries into the far corners of the world. It provides costume and atmosphere, of many colours. Mr Buchan controls his motley crew with great craft and easy mastery. He recaptures the past, and gives us a well-drawn pocket History of the World.

It is all, as usual, very competent, very pleasing and sufficient unto itself. What he attempts, he achieves. (pp. 183-91)

> R. Brimley Johnson, "John Buchan," in his Some Contemporary Novelists (Men), *Leonard Parsons, 1922, pp. 183-92.*

## John Buchan   (essay date 1940)

[*In the following excerpt from his memoirs* Pilgrim's Way *(originally published as* Memory Hold-the-Door*), Buchan elaborates on his literary techniques and aesthetic objectives.*]

I suppose I was a natural story-teller, the kind of man who for the sake of his yarns would in prehistoric days have been given a seat by the fire and a special chunk of mammoth. I was always telling myself stories when I had nothing else to do—or rather, being told stories, for they seemed to work themselves out independently. I generally thought of a character or two, and then of a set of incidents, and the question was how my people would behave. They had the knack of just squeezing out of unpleasant places and of bringing their doings to a rousing climax.

I was especially fascinated by the notion of hurried journeys. In the great romances of literature they provide some of the chief dramatic moments, and since the theme is common to Homer and the penny reciter it must appeal to a very ancient instinct in human nature. We live our lives under the twin categories of time and space, and when the two come into conflict we get the great moment. Whether failure or success is the result, life is sharpened, intensified, idealised. A long journey, even with the most lofty purpose, may be a dull thing to read of if it is made at leisure; but a hundred yards may be a breathless business if only a few seconds are granted to complete it. For then it becomes a sporting event, a race; and the interest which makes millions read of the Derby is the same, in a grosser form, as when we follow an expedition straining to relieve a beleaguered fort, or a man fleeing to a sanctuary with the avenger behind him.

In my undergraduate days I had tried my hand at historical novels, and had then some ambition to write fiction in the grand manner, by interpreting and clarifying a large piece of life. This ambition waned, and apart from a few short stories I let fiction alone until 1910, when, being appalled as a publisher by the dulness of most boys' books, I thought I would attempt one of my own, based on my African experience. The result was **Prester John,** which has since become a school-reader in many languages. Early in 1914 I wrote **Salute to Adventurers,** the fruit of my enthusiasm for American history. In that book I described places in Virginia which I had never seen, and I

was amazed, when I visited them later, to find how accurate had been my guesses.

Then, while pinned to my bed during the first months of [World War I] and compelled to keep my mind off too tragic realities, I gave myself to stories of adventure. I invented a young South African called Richard Hannay, who had traits copied from many friends, and I amused myself with considering what he would do in various emergencies. In **The Thirty-Nine Steps** he was spy-hunting in Britain; in **Greenmantle** he was on a mission to the East; and in **Mr. Standfast,** published in 1919, he was busy in Scotland and France. The first had an immediate success, and, since that kind of thing seemed to amuse my friends in the trenches, I was encouraged to continue. I gave Hannay certain companions—Peter Pienaar, a Dutch hunter; Sandy Arbuthnot, who was reminiscent of Aubrey Herbert; and an American gentleman, Mr. John S. Blenkiron. Soon these people became so real to me that I had to keep a constant eye on their doings. They slowly aged in my hands, and the tale of their more recent deeds will be found in **The Three Hostages, The Courts of the Morning,** and **The Island of Sheep.**

I added others to my group of musketeers. There was Dickson McCunn, the retired grocer, and his ragamuffin boys from the Gorbals, whose saga is written in **Huntingtower, Castle Gay,** and **The House of the Four Winds.** There was Sir Edward Leithen, an eminent lawyer, who is protagonist or narrator in **The Power-House, John Macnab, The Dancing Floor,** and **The Gap in the Curtain;** and in his particular group were the politician, Lord Lamancha, and Sir Archibald Roylance, airman, ornithologist, and Scots laird. It was huge fun playing with my puppets, and to me they soon became very real flesh and blood. I never consciously invented with a pen in my hand; I waited until the story had told itself and then wrote it down, and, since it was already a finished thing, I wrote it fast. The books had a wide sale, both in English and in translations, and I always felt a little ashamed that profit should accrue from what had given me so much amusement. I had no purpose in such writing except to please myself, and even if my books had not found a single reader I should have felt amply repaid.

Besides these forthright tales of adventure I was busy with a very different kind of romance. The desire to recover the sense of continuity, which had brought me to Elsfield, prompted my first serious piece of fiction. It was called **The Path of the King,** and was based on the notion that no man knows his ancestry, and that kingly blood may lie dormant for centuries until the appointed time. The chapters began with a viking's son lost in a raid, and ended audaciously with Abraham Lincoln.

After that I varied my tales of adventure with this kind of romance, over which I took a great deal of pains, and which seems to me the most successful of my attempts at imaginative creation. Being equally sensitive to the spells of time and of space, to a tract of years and a tract of landscape, I tried to discover the historical moment which best interpreted the *ethos* of a particular countryside, and to devise the appropriate legend. Just as certain old houses, like the inns at Burford and Queensferry, cried out to Robert Louis Stevenson to tell their tales, so I felt the clamour of certain scenes for an interpreter.

The best, I think, is **Witch Wood,** in which I wrote of the Tweedside parish of my youth at the time when the old Wood of Caledon had not wholly disappeared, and when the rigours of the new Calvinism were contending with the ancient secret rites of Diana. I believe that my picture is historically true, and I could have documented almost every sentence from my researches on Montrose. In **The Free Fishers** I tried to catch the flavour of the windy shores of Fife at a time when smuggling and vagabondage were still rife. I had always felt keenly the romance of the Jacobite venture, but less in its familiar Scottish episodes than in the dreary ebb of the march to Derby, so I took that period for my attempt in *Midwinter* to catch the spell of the great midland forests and the Old England which lay everywhere just beyond the highroads and the plough- lands. Finally, in **The Blanket of the Dark** I chose the time when the monasteries fell and the enclosures began, and I brought all the valleys of Cotswold into the picture.

These were serious books, and they must have puzzled many of the readers who were eager to follow the doings of Richard Hannay or Dickson McCunn. That is the trou- ble with an author who only writes to please himself; his product is not standardised, and the purchaser is often dis- appointed. I once had a letter from an Eton boy who, hav- ing a taste for a bustling yarn, was indignant at anything of mine which did not conform to that pattern. He ear- nestly begged me to 'pull myself together.'

Though my hand is vile and scribing has always bored me, I found the writing of my romances almost a relaxation. Less so my excursions in biography. The subject of my first was Montrose. From my Oxford days I had been fas- cinated by his military genius and the sorrows of his life, and I gradually began to read myself into his period. I found that the Whig historians had dismissed him as at the best a bandit of genius, and had beatified the theocrats who opposed him. To this view I could not assent, and as my studies progressed I came to the conclusion that he was the most balanced and prescient mind in Scotland at the time, as well as the greatest of Scottish soldiers. Mate- rials for his life had been collected by Mark Napier with an enthusiasm which was not always critical, and I decid- ed to go over them again, and try to present an authentic picture of a very great man. In 1913 I published a short sketch, which presently went out of print, and after the War, when my military histories had been completed, I set myself to elaborate the portrait. The book was issued in 1928, and I am happy to think that my view of Montrose, foreshadowed by Carlyle and presented briefly in their his- tories by S. R. Gardiner and Andrew Lang, is now gener- ally accepted. I could ask for no greater honour than to help to restore to his country's pantheon the hero of my youth.

Cromwell was bound to follow. I had long shared Lord Rosebery's view of him as the greatest of Englishmen, and, when I began to study his campaigns, I felt that as a sol- dier he was very near the first rank. I had the supreme ad- vantage of having been brought up in a Calvinistic atmo- sphere, so I was able to write of his religious life with some

*Buchan in his library at Elsfield Manor.*

understanding. For several years I lived chiefly in the sev- enteenth century, reading acres of its divinity and many hundreds of its pamphlets. Cromwell with all his imper- fections seemed to me not only admirable but lovable, and I tried in my book to present the warm human side of him. I cannot claim that there was anything in my work which could not be found in Gardiner and Firth, but I think I elaborated certain neglected aspects, and I took special pains with the background.

When *Cromwell* was published in 1934 the subject had be- come acutely topical, for dictators were arising in Europe who claimed, without warrant, to follow in his steps. This made me return to what had been an undergraduate ambi- tion, a portrait of Augustus. I had already done a good deal of work on the subject, and my first two winters in Canada gave me leisure to re-read the Latin and Greek texts. I have rarely found more enjoyment in a task, for I was going over again carefully the ground which I had scampered across in my youth. Augustus seemed to me to embody all the virtues of a dictator, when a dictator was needed, and to have tried valiantly to provide against the perils. The book was kindly received by scholars in Brit- ain, America, and on the Continent, though my Italian friends jibbed at some of my political deductions.

In my book on Sir Walter Scott, published in the centenary year of his death, I tried not only to pay tribute to the best-loved of Borderers, but to repeat my literary *credo.* All these four books were, indeed, in a sense a confession of faith, for they enabled me to define my own creed on many matters of doctrine and practice, and thereby cleared my mind. They were a kind of diary, too, a chronicle of my successive interests and occupations. They were laborious affairs compared to my facile novels, but they were also a relaxation, for they gave me a background into which I could escape from contemporary futilities, a watch-tower from which I had a long prospect and could see modern problems in juster proportions. That is the supreme value of history. The study of it is the best guaranty against repeating it. (pp. 194-99)

> *John Buchan, in his* Pilgrim's Way: An Essay in Recollection, *Houghton Mifflin Company, 1940, 336 p.*

## Graham Greene    (essay date 1941)

[*Greene is considered one of the most important novelists in modern English literature. In his major works, he explores the problems of spiritually and socially alienated individuals living in corrupt and corrupting societies of the twentieth century. Greene is also esteemed as a film critic, biographer, and literary critic, and has written several notable spy novels. In the following review of* Sick Heart River, *Greene criticizes the importance of the success ethic in Buchan's works.*]

More than a quarter of a century has passed since Richard Hannay found the dead man in his flat and started that long flight and pursuit—across the Yorkshire and the Scottish moors, down Mayfair streets, along the passages of Government buildings, in and out of Cabinet rooms and country houses, towards the cold Essex jetty with the thirty-nine steps, that were to be a pattern for adventure-writers ever since. John Buchan was the first to realize the enormous dramatic value of adventure in familiar surroundings happening to unadventurous men, members of Parliament and members of the Athenaeum, lawyers and barristers, business men and minor peers: murder in 'the atmosphere of breeding and simplicity and stability'. Richard Hannay, Sir Edward Leithen, Mr Blenkiron, Archie Roylance, and Lord Lamancha; these were his adventurers, not Dr Nikola or the Master of Ballantrae, and who will forget the first thrill in 1916 as the hunted Leithen—the future Solicitor-General—ran 'like a thief in a London thoroughfare on a June afternoon'?

> Now I saw how thin is the protection of civilization. An accident and a bogus ambulance—a false charge and a bogus arrest—there were a dozen ways of spiriting one out of this gay and bustling world.

Now [in *Sick Heart River*] Leithen, who survived the perils of the Green Park and the mews near Belgrave Square, has died in what must seem to those who remember *The Power-House* a rather humdrum way, doing good to depressed and starving Indians in Northern Canada, anticipating by only a few months his creator's death.

What is remarkable about these adventure-stories is the completeness of the world they describe. The backgrounds to many of us may not be sympathetic, but they are elaborately worked in: each character carries round with him his school, his regiment, his religious beliefs, often touched with Calvinism: memories of grouse-shooting and deer-stalking, of sport at Eton, debates in the House. For men who live so dangerously they are oddly conventional—or perhaps, remembering men like Scott and Oates, we can regard that, too, as a realistic touch. They judge men by their war-record: even the priest in *Sick Heart River,* fighting in the desolate northern waste for the Indians' salvation, is accepted by Leithen because 'he had served in a French battalion which had been on the right of the Guards at Loos'. Toc H and the British Legion lurk in the background.

In the early books, fascinated by the new imaginative form, the hair-breadth escapes in a real world, participating whole-heartedly in the struggle between a member of the Athenaeum and the man who could hood his eyes like a hawk, we didn't notice the curious personal ideals, the vast importance Buchan attributed to success, the materialism . . . *Sick Heart River,* the last adventure of the dying Leithen seeking—at Blenkiron's request—the missing business man, Francis Galliard, who had left his wife and returned to his ancestral North, has all the old admirable dry ease of style—it is the intellectual content which repels us now, the Scotch admiration of success. 'Harold has a hard life. He's head of the Fremont Banking Corporation and a St Sebastian for everyone to shoot arrows at.' Even a nation is judged by the same standard: 'They ought to have made a rather bigger show in the world than they have.' Individuals are of enormous importance. Just as the sinister Mr Andrew Lumley in *The Power-House* was capable of crumbling the whole Western world into anarchy, so Francis Galliard—'one of Simon Ravelston's partners'—must be found for the sake of America. 'He's too valuable a man to lose, and in our present state of precarious balance we just can't afford it.'

But though *Sick Heart River* appears at the moment least favourable to these ideas (for it is not, after all, the great men—the bankers and the divisional commanders and the Ambassadors, who have been holding our world together this winter, and if we survive, it is by 'the wandering, wavering grace of humble men' in Bow and Coventry, Bristol and Birmingham), let us gratefully admit that, in one way at any rate, Buchan prepared us in his thrillers better than he knew for the death that may come to any of us, as it nearly came to Leithen, by the railings of the Park or the doorway of the mews. For certainly we can all see now 'how thin is the protection of civilization'. (pp. 223-25)

> *Graham Greene, "The Last Buchan," in his* Collected Essays, *The Bodley Head, 1969, pp. 223-25.*

## Richard Usborne    (essay date 1953)

[*An English critic, Usborne has written on and edited works by P. G. Wodehouse and is the author of* Clubland Heroes: A Nostalgic Study of Some Recurrent Characters in the Romantic Fiction of Dornford Yates, John

Buchan and Sapper. *In the following excerpt from that work, he discusses Buchan's characterizations of the major figures in his espionage fiction.*]

[In] the long interim of comparative pot-boilers between *Greenmantle* and *Sick Heart River,* Buchan's thrillers were [still] all 'rattling good yarns'. But, when I re-read them, I find that I have forgotten practically everything about them except that they are rattling good yarns. Why?

Buchan failed in character-drawing. His plots were exciting, but his people dull, heroes *and* villains. The heroes had no amiable weaknesses, the villains were never really juicy fiends. Hannay, Sandy Arbuthnot and the others were not quite prigs. But they had hardly any sense of humour. The good fellowship in which they moved was of the approved Cock House type. There is, throughout the Buchan canon, a slight but persistent propaganda for the decencies as preached by the enthusiastic housemaster—for cold baths, for hard work, for healthy exhaustion in the playing-field, for shaking hands with the beaten opponent, for the attainment of Success in after-life. As a schoolboy I used to read Buchan, and I admired his heroes. But Yates's Berry and Sapper's Bulldog Drummond—they were, for me, the heroes with real glamour. It was they who took me out of school, out of myself, into a world of laughter, lazy riches, topping girls, and villains that I could hiss with relish. I remembered Yates's and Sapper's books for the people in them rather than for their stories.

If, in my schooldays, not exactly the author set for homework, Buchan was certainly strongly recommended to the schoolboy by parent, uncle, guardian, pastor and master. Buchan backed up their directives and doctrines. Buchan wrote good English. Buchan taught you things. Buchan was good for you. Buchan himself, quite apart from authorship, was a man of success and, at the end, eminence beyond even his own fictional heroes. Had he persisted in the law for a career, he would possibly, like Leithen, have attained the Attorney Generalship. As it was, he died as Governor-General of Canada, a higher post than Leithen's, and one that would never have been offered to Hannay or Sandy Arbuthnot. No parent or schoolmaster could go wrong recommending to a boy the reading and study of John Buchan.

I have chosen to concern myself here with fewer than twenty of the fifty-seven books that Buchan wrote. They are the ones that Buchan called his 'shockers'. When today reviewers refer to a book as being 'in the Buchan manner', they mean the manner of the shockers. I am specifically studying the recurrent characters, Hannay, Leithen, Arbuthnot, Pienaar, Roylance and McCunn. The canon thus establishes itself as nineteen books: *The Half-Hearted, The Moon Endureth, Prester John, The Power-House, The Thirty-Nine Steps, Greenmantle, Mr Standfast, Huntingtower, The Three Hostages, John Macnab, The Dancing Floor, The Courts of the Morning, Castle Gay, The Gap in the Curtain, A Prince of the Captivity, The House of the Four Winds, The Island of Sheep, Sick Heart River* and *The Runagates Club.*

*The Half-Hearted, The Moon Endureth, Prester John* and *A Prince of the Captivity* only just squeak into my

category. The second and last bring Leithen in very briefly. *Prester John* brings in Arcoll, the policeman-intelligence officer in South Africa who had at one time employed Peter Pienaar. And *The Half-Hearted* (as you've probably forgotten) momentarily brings in Sandy Arbuthnot's mother and elder brother.

If you're a student of the Buchan mind behind the Buchan books, you certainly oughtn't to ignore *The Half-Hearted,* which Buchan published when he was twenty-five. There was a gap of more than a dozen years before Buchan tried the style again with *The Thirty-Nine Steps* and *Greenmantle.* Personally I put *The Half-Hearted* among the three most interesting of the nineteen. [The critic adds in a footnote that 'the other two are *Greenmantle* and *Sick Heart River.*'] It is in some ways more revealing of the Buchan 'decent-fellow' ethic than any other till the last, *Sick Heart River.* Buchan hadn't quite found his wavelength for the adventure story when he was twenty-five. (Youthfully, he gave *The Half-Hearted* an unhappy ending.) But he had found his main character. Lewis Haystoun of *The Half-Hearted* is a young Scottish laird, a fine scholar, good at games, keen on a cold plunge before breakfast, rich, an embryo politician, and a great traveller. He dies nobly in one of the far places of the world (the Northwest Frontier), saving British India from a Russian invasion.

There is much of Sandy Arbuthnot in Haystoun, and something of Hannay. The Scottish laird with a passion for lonely travel is Sandy of the later books. The courageous man afflicted with doubts about his own courage is Hannay. Haystoun's death is to some extent a foreshadowing of Leithen's in *Sick Heart River.* There is a villain, Marka, in *The Half-Hearted* who has much in him of the later, greater villain, Dominick Medina of *The Three Hostages.* There is a girl, Alice Wishart, in *The Half-Hearted* who, in her boyish grace and athletic, out-of-door predilections, is the forerunner of all Buchan's heroes' wives. In *The Half-Hearted* there are the first descriptions of swagger London clubs, the first suggestion that Lord This and Lord That of the Cabinet made their decisions on foreign policy over coffee at their club, bringing out a gazetteer in the library to assess just where the next foreign threat is coming. There is the first long journey taken by a worried man who doesn't know what he is going to find at the end. There is the first of those Kiplingesque paragraphs to evoke the smell of the distant places where fine deeds look finer still because a man is cut off from his own country, but facing a world of foreigners *for* his country.

> The place was the same as ever. The same medley of races perambulated the streets. Sheep-skinned Central Asians and Mongolians from Yarkand still displayed their wares and their cunning; Hunza tribesmen, half-clad Chitralis, wild-eyed savages from Yagistan mingled in the narrow streets with the civilised Persian and Turcoman from beyond the mountains. Kashmir Sepoys, an untidy race, still took their ease in the sun, and soldiers of South India from the Imperial Service troops showed their odd accoutrements and queer race mixtures. The place looked and smelled like a kind of home, and Lewis, with one eye on the gun-cases and one on

the great hills, forgot his heart-sickness and had leisure for the plain joys of expectation.

This type of man-of-the-world, know-it-all passage, clever trick-writing that is effective if infrequently offered, occurs several times in *Greenmantle* and once or twice in each of *Mr Standfast* and *The Three Hostages.* On second readings and second thoughts you will probably agree that this style of thing is Buchan pulling high-quality wool over his readers' eyes. Where he is uncertain of his ground, he goes out of his way to sound as though he knows it backwards. He does it very successfully, and, though the later books seem to have been written with an equanimity, and perhaps speed, that prevented him indulging in *trompe l'œil* writing, he really perfected the science into an art, and added it to his several others.

Buchan had an artistic ear for the suggestive music of names (real names), particularly of far-away people and places. South Africa, which he knew, gave him a name vocabulary and a knowing jargon which he knowingly used. Scotland and the Cotswolds, which he knew, were his favourite scenes for his stay-at-home books. The Swiss Alps, which he knew, and America and Canada, which he also knew, he could place on paper from memory. But he did not need memory to hold the door. He became just as adept, and almost more felicitous, in describing places he did not know. Sapper and Yates fairly obviously put their stories in countries and places where they themselves had been. Unhemmed by memory, Buchan could paint a memorable landscape, from an imagination electrified by a conversation with somebody else or, I suspect, from ten minutes reading in encyclopedia or gazetteer. He did not know the Northern Punjab, of which he wrote in *The Half-Hearted,* nor, then, the Germany, Danubian litoral or Turkey that he evoked in *Greenmantle.* He had not, we know, visited the distant places where Sandy Arbuthnot wandered. He did not know the Balkans that gave him Evallonia, the South America that gave him Olifa, or the Arctic of Adam Melfort's journey in *A Prince of the Captivity.*

He is as happy with houses as with country and scenery. Sandy's Border house, Laverlaw; Haystoun's house, Etterick; Hannay's own beloved Fosse; Sir Walter Bullivant's fishing cottage on the Kennet; Archie Roylance's Crask; even Haraldsen's place on the Island of Sheep, and Shelley Arabin's murky house on the Isle of Plakos. For some reason, Leithen's Cotswold house, Borrowby, and his Down Street flat, both described more than once, lack the usual magic.

Buchan's narrative style is of unassuming ease. Even when he stops the movement of his story to describe a numinous place or a successful man, he retains a quiet austerity. If, knowing Buchan's 'shockers', you read his book on Walter Scott, you will find it doubly interesting. It suggests a host of parallels, between Scott himself and some of Buchan's heroes, and between Scott and Buchan himself. Buchan says, of Scott's early training in the law: 'Its complexity and exactness formed a valuable corrective to a riotous imagination.' That could stand exactly for Buchan and his writing style. Buchan's tricks and repetitions are of thought rather than phrase or rhythm. He has certain

favourite words (totem, *rastaquouère,* breeding). But if you tried to parody Buchan in a paragraph, you'd go for the matter rather than the manner. The First in Greats mind and constant writing made him very smooth to read. When he stopped the running and the scrapping and the dialogue to explain obscure philosophies or parallels from history, he changed his gears without a sound. If you listen to the voice behind the written words, the voice seems to go on at the same speed, and it is only when the scrapping and movement start again in the story that you realise that you have just read, and absorbed, two or three pages of scholarship with most flattering ease. The Buchan 'shockers' may lack something in warmth, as, in my opinion, do the Buchan heroes. Perhaps the reason is the same in both cases; books and heroes lack obvious and endearing faults.

Buchan was less good at building the character of a man than evoking the character of a place. With the possible exception of Leithen at the end, none of the heroes is at any time three-dimensional. Buchan's stories came first. The stories kept the heroes constantly on the move. But the rolling stones gathered no atmospheric moss of character. Stevenson and Scott, two of Buchan's exemplars, had the art of giving character to men on the move. Buchan had not. He spent several books writing about Hannay, but he never made him more than a doer of deeds, hare or hound in excellent chases. You would recognise Hannay's Fosse if you saw it from the train. Would you recognise Hannay if he got into your carriage at Fosse station?

I had heard that the real-life source for Buchan's Hannay was supposed to be Lord Ironside. I wrote to Lord Ironside and asked him. With his permission, I quote from his reply.

> You ask me about my connection with [Buchan's] book character, Richard Hannay. The most direct evidence that I was [connected], is that his son, the present Lord Tweedsmuir, told me that his father had said so.
>
> I first met John Buchan in the South African War. He was what we young soldiers called one of Lord Milner's young men. He stayed on after the War for nearly a year, and it was then that I formed a friendship with him.
>
> He was some five years older than I was. A very highly educated product of Oxford. I was a Horse Artillery subaltern, who had been through the whole of the South African War. We were both Scotsmen . . .
>
> My education had been very different from that of the great scholar. I was a linguist, speaking French, German and Dutch with equal facility. After three years of war in South Africa, I spoke the Taal like any Boer.
>
> We had many talks together. I was interested in his power to observe things he saw. And in his power to put things on paper. His articles as an eye-witness were so good that I was most impressed. He was interested in my knowledge of the Boers, gained at first hand in the war. Naturally, he being the elder and the best educated, he drew me out. I told him that I intended to stay in South Africa, and I told him of how I

hoped to be able to do Intelligence work, if I could.

After the war, I served in the country for some ten years, and off and on we kept up our friendship. I worked for two years in the Intelligence, mostly in the remote corners of Cape Colony and German South West Africa. I do not think that any correspondence ever passed between us, but I used to see him and have a talk on all sorts of subjects, all through life until his death. I read his books with interest. He never once suggested to me that he had drawn me in one of these books, but undoubtedly he used what he had drawn out of me in our talks.

That is all I can tell you of the matter.

I asked Lord Tweedsmuir [Buchan's son John] if he could add to this. He replied:

Lord Ironside has expressed himself admirably as regards his connection with my father's 'Richard Hannay'. I have heard my father say specifically that Ironside was the main figure from which he drew his hero. When I say the main figure, I mean it advisedly. Most of my father's characters were two or three real people, put together to create one character of fiction, very often undergoing the adventures that happened to several other real life figures.

As regards Peter Pienaar, he was a real man, a friend of my father's in South Africa days. However, I have read no less than three obituary notices, at different times, of South African heroes each of whom was identified by their friends with Pienaar.

As to what extent Lawrence is Arbuthnot, I cannot say, but certainly Herbert forms the greater part of his inspiration.

There perhaps is the clue to Buchan's success as a storyteller, and his comparative failure as a delineator of character. He went for the achievements. His methods of placing a man in the reader's mind is to pile his achievements on top of one another.

And what achievements they were! Not only the mountain scaled, the citadel captured, the cipher cracked, the villain caught. Not only was each hero successful in what he undertook. He was a Success in Life. The books present a succession of successes, and the Buchan success ethic has to be examined. As a grown-up I have long found it unattractive. I think I was slightly suspicious of it when I was a boy.

Success in Buchan is competitive. It was not enough to have done a good job well. You had to have made a name for yourself by doing it better than anybody else. Heroes and villains, they almost all 'made big names for themselves'. Quiet achievement of a chosen object in life was not sufficient. You had to be known and talked about. You had to merit at least a column in *The Times* when you died.

The early pages of Buchan's last novel, **Sick Heart River,** bring in nearly a dozen men, most of them quite unimportant to the plot, most of them dropped after a quick men-

tion. Admittedly it was a picked party of Americans who were asked to meet Leithen when he went to New York. Blenkiron fixed the party. Blenkiron had persuaded Leithen to go and look for Galliard. Blenkiron's own brief irruption, in London, on the privacy of the great English lawyer whom he scarcely knew was fairly typical.

'They tell me that Sir Archibald Roylance is making quite a name for himself in your Parliament, and that Lord Clanroyden cuts a deal of ice with your Government . . .'

Then Blenkiron mentions Galliard:

'Francis Galliard, one of old Simon Ravelston's partners. Young Galliard's gotten a great name in the city of New York . . .'

Later, at the New York dinner-party, someone else adds to the Galliard dossier:

'Today he's forty-three, and there ar'n't five men in the United States whose repute stands higher. Not bad for a farm boy, I'll say . . .'

(Just as the villains [in Buchan] . . . , are the most dangerous, or the second most dangerous on earth at that moment, so the dinner-party connoisseur has a list in his mind of the first five men in order of repute in the United States. Villainy and success cannot be measured by yardsticks. The question is whether you are more villainous or more successful or more influential than other people. What is your place in the form?)

Here is a guest asked to dinner to meet Leithen:

On paper Bronson Jane was almost too good to be true. He had been a noted sportsman and was still a fine polo-player; his name was a household word in Europe for his work in international finance; he was the Admirable Crichton of his day and it was rumoured that in the same week he had been offered the Secretaryship of State, the Presidency of an ancient University, and the control of a great industrial corporation.

Here's another at the dinner:

He was president of one of the chief private banking houses in the world . . . No man ever saw him rattled or hustled, and this Olympian detachment gave him a prestige in two continents.

Another guest:

He's on the Johns Hopkins staff and is making a big name for himself in lung surgery.

And another:

He has flown and mushed and tramped over most of the Arctic, and there are heaps of mountains and wild beasts named after him.

It is a good list of guests. Leithen, far from home, at least starts his last adventure in surroundings which he, the most solidly successful of all the recurrent Buchan heroes, must feel he understands.

Think back among the smaller characters of the earlier books. Haystoun and Wratislaw of **The Half-Hearted,** the one a man born to weary success, the other a man who worked for a deserved name. Sir David Warcliff ('seriously spoken of for India') and Julius Victor (the richest man in the world) in *The Three Hostages.* Palliser Yeates (rugby international and wizard in foreign finance) in *John Macnab.* Lamancha, flitting royally through half a dozen books. Vernon Milburne of *The Dancing Floor,* and the Jew international financier, Theodore Ertzberger. Almost all the story-tellers in *The Runagates Club.* The house-party at Flambard in *The Gap in the Curtain.* Adam Melfort and the American millionaire he rescued in *A Prince of the Captivity.* Randal Glynde, gentleman scholar-gypsy who wore his Brigade tie, and rode an elephant, in the Balkans (*The House of the Four Winds*). And back again to Sandy Arbuthnot, Leithen, Hannay, Peter Pienaar. Even Dickson McCunn, the retired Glasgow grocer, had been a success; and his two young protégés, Jaikie and Dougal, are set fair for Buchan success when we last hear of them. The decent fellows in Buchan do all things well, and they do them better than other people. They are at or near the top of the form. They make good names for themselves, and are thus justified.

If success is the strophe, the antistrophe is honourable exhaustion. The main Buchan story moves fast, from the problem to the clue (generally in cipher), to the chase, to the loom of tragedy, due on a day ringed in black on the calendar, to tragedy averted in the nick of time, to the success of heroes, to the villains scolded, to the happy ending. But virtue triumphs only through ardours and endurances.

In Buchan exhaustion is an end in itself. It is not just the result of the endeavour necessary in any good tale of adventure. Odysseus was from time to time exhausted almost to the death. But exhaustion was not part of his character. Buchan's heroes are attracted to exhaustion as a drinker to the bottle, as Sherlock Holmes to cocaine. Hannay three or four times managed to resolve a crisis (when he was absolutely stumped for a flicker of light in the darkness of the problem) simply by being so exhausted, with malaria or hunger or the sheer distance he had had to run, that his brain cleared and he became simple. In his simplicity he saw the light, solved the cipher, spotted the clue.

In *The Gap in the Curtain,* Leithen, the narrator, tells of an experiment in Time organised by a brilliant Swedish professor with the help of a Whitsun house-party of eminent people at the Flambards' in the Cotswolds. Professor Moe's idea is to give, to each of six or seven chosen fellow guests, a momentary glimpse of a copy of *The Times* dated a year in the future. In preparation for this revelation, the Professor asks his guinea-pigs to go into a sort of reverse-Buchan training:

> Too much exercise was forbidden, for it was desirable that our health should be rather an absence of ailments than a positive, aggressive well-being. There were to be no cold baths . . .

> I went to bed feeling that I should probably get a liver attack from the lack of exercise.

In the world of Buchan's shockers, exercise and cold baths (or swims in icy tarns before breakfast) are necessary to the well-being, aggressive or otherwise, of all decent fellows. Without exercise a man becomes liverish. Without cold baths he becomes hot-eyed. It is the schoolboy formula of the Cock House. But exercise produces regenerative exhaustion. At Flambard that weekend most of the guests were honourably exhausted with over-work already. Leithen, now in Opposition, but recently Attorney-General, had come down a tired man. He had been over-working, in court, in chambers and in the House, and the world had begun to go grey at the edges. This was the honourable exhaustion of the spirit, curable only by honourable exhaustion, in the open air, of the body. The former was a tribute that Buchan's heroes paid to success. The latter was the only cure they knew. Leithen hoped that Flambard would give him day-long opportunity to avoid his fellow-mortal, to go fishing, and to enjoy extensive solitary downland rides on his host's horses. In that way he would try to reacquire some of the 'aggressive well-being' that he regarded, presumably, as his norm, however seldom he had time to engender it.

> As I took my place at the dinner table, I recognised that I was not the only tired mortal in Lady Flambard's Whitsuntide party. Mayot, who sat opposite me, had dark pouches under his eyes and the unwholesome high complexion which in a certain type of physique means that the arteries are working badly. I knew that he had been having a heavy time in the House of Commons over the Committee stage of his Factory Bill. Charles Ottery, who generally keeps himself fit with fives and tennis, and has still the figure of an athletic schoolboy, seemed nervous and out of sorts . . . Our hostess had her mid-season look—her blue eyes were drained of colour. But it was Arnold Tavanger farther down the table who held my attention. His heavy sagacious face was a dead mask of exhaustion. He looked done to the world and likely to fall asleep over his soup.

That's a wide-awake first paragraph for a book. It is the opening paragraph of *The Gap in the Curtain.*

Much ink had flowed from Buchan's romantic pen since, in *The Half-Hearted,* Lewis Haystoun had died, far from frowstily, on the North-West Frontier. David Crawford, in *Prester John,* was so painfully exhausted for so much of the time that he began to think that he was only safe from being a coward by *being* exhausted. Hannay was always at his healthiest when on the run. Peter Pienaar was hardly the indoor type. Sandy Arbuthnot was ready for a fifteen-mile walk any time at Laverlaw, and, given a broad enough field of operation, as in *The Courts of the Morning,* could tire himself to dropping point. In that book, when he conducted the war against Castor's people in the Gran Seco of Olifa, Sandy's favourite entrance to his own H.Q. was as one totally exhausted by deeds of derring-do over the last forty-eight hours, and now requiring a round-the-clock sleep before he even reported to his lieutenants.

Leithen had a history of exhaustion, since he won the Mile at Eton. He later spent his holidays rock-climbing in Chamonix, hunting with the Bicester or the Mivern, fishing in Norway, Canada or the Cotswolds, and stalking in Scotland. Hannay always got liverish in London, and his doctor could only advise squash (though Hannay chose rowing). Archie Roylance rode, steeplechased, played polo, flew aeroplanes and watched inaccessible birds even after acquiring a limp in the war. His bride, Janet, wouldn't let him go to Africa for their honeymoon, since he would certainly be wanting to go and shoot big game: which he mustn't with his bad leg. And, when Dr Christoph, in *The House of the Four Winds,* fixed Archie's leg up for him, his first thought was to go rock-climbing. He had heard such good accounts of it from Hannay.

Mr Craw, the self-made newspaper emperor in *Castle Gay,* kidnapped by mistake and left a captive with Mrs Macgregor, finds his health and outlook improving in the specific absence of hot baths. He is such a reformed character by the end of that book that he wins in marriage the outspoken old aristocrat, Aunt Harriet. This is the nearest that Buchan comes, though here it is only by implication, to condemning hot baths. Elsewhere, and in their proper contexts, he is prepared sometimes to speak highly of a hot bath, especially after an exhausting day on the hill. But, though a hot bath may be bad, a cold bath never is. Better go without your hot bath in the evening than your cold bath before breakfast. If you have both, you should, in between, for aggressive well-being, have walked about twenty miles, ridden thirty or bicycled forty. Jaikie Galt once proposed to circumnavigate England in a canoe.

Dickson McCunn put colour into his middle-aged cheeks and flattened his figure by marching for the wide-open spaces. An off-day for a good Buchan type was: a cold bath or plunge, a big breakfast, a quiet pipe, and then off to the hills in filthy tweeds. A lunch of sandwiches on the high tops, descent towards a distant, solitary lighted window, surprise of, and friendly treatment by, goodwife in the gloaming, a meal of branxsome ham and scones, and an exhausted sleep in a sweet-smelling hayloft.

*John Macnab* is a whole book devoted to the Highland defrowsting of three eminent but apparently restive Londoners. Leithen, Pallister Yeates and Lord Lamancha descend on Archie Roylance at Crask, and make far-ranging poachers of themselves in order to get the roses back into their cheeks. *The Dancing Floor* shows the forty-ish Leithen exhausted near to death in an Ægean island, trying to rescue a twenty-year-old girl whom he thinks he loves. Luckily he is prevented from making an ass of himself, and Koré Arabin becomes the bride of Vernon Milburne, also, in his earlier days, an Oxford Miler. Indeed, Koré only comes to Vernon's arms after he has saved her from an inflammable end by winning a long-distance race disguised as a Greek. The ardours and endurances of Adam Melfort in *A Prince of the Captivity* are the most exhausting of any book. Starting in the comparative quietude of prison (it's his nasty wife's fault that he's there), he emerges to long-distance runs and racing in the Fells, arduous war-work as a spy behind the German lines, an arduous trip across ice in the Arctic to rescue an American millionaire; and he ends up nobly dead on the *aiguilles* and *coulisses* of some arduous Alp in Italy. *A Prince of the Captivity* is, frankly, rather tiring to read. After a stiff course of Buchan, it is refreshing to go back to Sapper and

Yates, and notice that their heroes are all keen after-luncheon-nappers.

Exhaustion apart, the Buchan hero is a modest, polite, faithful-to-his-wife, sober doer of deeds. He is successful, liked by his friends, far too merciful (when he has beaten them) to his enemies. He can be of humble or noble birth, but he justifies his protagonism by action. If, as in the case of Lewis Haystoun, the silver spoon in his mouth dulls his taste for strife and striving, saps his eagerness to win political elections and makes him slow to dive into a dangerous pool to rescue a girl, he is given an opportunity to show the readers, and himself, that the easy life has not softened him irrevocably. Haystoun dies happily and nobly in his private Thermopylae. He is a sportsman.

> 'Then they're all alone at Nazri?'
>
> 'Except for the Khautmi men.'
>
> 'Will they try to hold it?'
>
> 'I should think so. They're all sportsmen. Gad, there won't be a soul left alive.'

As Haystoun awaits certain death, he reviews his past life, smoking his last pipe on earth, and relishing it 'as if the essence of all the pipes he had ever smoked was concentrated in this last one'. He remembers his friends, and the times when he was happy (compare Leithen at the end of *Sick Heart River*). He will meet death now, not only without fear, but with exhilaration.

> A broken neck in a hunting field, a slip on rocky mountains, a wounded animal at bay . . . such was the environment of death for which he had prayed. But this . . . this was beyond his dreams.

It was the death of a sportsman, in the line of duty for which he had volunteered.

Lewis Haystoun had gone out to India with a girl on his mind. Lewis died and Alice Wishart married a somewhat Second Eleven character at home. It was a pity about Alice. She was the first, and about the only faintly real, *jeune première* in the nineteen books. Buchan could write a perfectly good adventure story without girls. When he brought girls in, it was without emphasis. His girls don't retard the story; but the fact is that Buchan was really no good at women at all. Two more quotations from Buchan's *Life of Scott* are relevant here. Buchan's own comment on Scott's general treatment of women in his novels is: 'For women he had an old-fashioned reverence, and regarded them very much as a toast to be drunk after King and Constitution.' And Buchan quotes Bagehot on the same subject: 'The same blunt sagacity of imagination, which fitted him to excel in the rough description of obvious life, rather unfitted him for delineating the less substantial essence of the female character.'

In Buchan the girl the hero loves and marries is the same throughout the books. She may be Scots, English, American, Danish or Russian. But she is the open-air type always, clean-run, boyish and a sportsman. Alice went for long walks on the moors and fell into a tarn. Janet Raden, who married Archie, was a great walker and 'famous for her wind'. She also hunted. Mary Hannay was brave, and high up in the British Secret Service. Alison Westwater, when Jaikie first met her, was up a tree; the wind-blown type again. Sandy fell in love with Barbara Dasent when, in his Olifa campaign, he saw her handle a stampede of horses at his H.Q. Anna the Dane was a child of nature, barefoot queen of the Island of Sheep, and eager to go canoeing and hawking with Hannay's son, Peter John. Saskia the Russian (*Huntingtower*) ran so well across country, pursued by her beastly Bolshevik enemies, that Archie Roylance, watching, said in admiration, 'Gad! She's a miler!'

Half girl, half boy (is there a single Buchan heroine who is not at some time praised for her boyish looks, lines, stride, manner, health or hips?), the Buchan girl represents courage, fresh air and decency. She is not very interesting. And when she marries, she spends her time egging her husband on to be a success. [In a footnote, the critic observes, 'On the other hand, some of the heroes had feminine characteristics. Sandy Arbuthnot, for instance, had "a pair of brown eyes like a pretty girl's". Even old Peter Pienaar had "a face as gentle as a girl's". Hilda Von Einem in *Greenmantle* has the masculine attributes of command, decision, ruthlessness and riding breeches. So has Princess Araminta Troyos in *The House of the Four Winds.*']

But the heroines were only a small part of the heroes' lives. The men took to themselves wives only when they had won their position of worthiness by deeds. By and large it was always a man's world. A man was of your 'totem', or he was not. The men of the totem joined the same sort of clubs, didn't quarrel with each other's politics (they sat loose to politics and party anyway), talked the same language, travelled adventurously when young, always kept fit and tried to make something of their lives. They were slightly anti-Semitic, but no more so than was polite in any author in the pre-Hitler period. They had few dislikes, the men of the totem. Nationally, they were against the Irish and the Portuguese (often called Portugooses). Russia was behind some of the villainy in *The Half-Hearted, Huntingtower* and *The House of the Four Winds;* but it was the stateless Jewish element in Russia that was causing the trouble. Two or three Jews in Buchan's books were sympathetic characters, and Adela Victor, one of the three hostages, was married suitably in the end to a French nobleman, nicknamed Turpin, of the French Embassy in London. Turpin could have been of the totem. When, at one stage in *The Three Hostages,* he was captured and kept locked up in close confinement for several days, he kept himself fit by boxing.

The men of the totem were considerably disturbed by modern dancing and night-clubs. But not quite to the extent of condemning them. Men of the totem very rarely absolutely condemned anything. But Hannay was obviously made uncomfortable by the apparently joyless gyrations, in stuffy, frowsty rooms, of smooth young men with painted and revealingly-frocked young women. Archie Roylance was a keen student, though not specifically a performer, of the modern dance. But you get the feeling that he was the only one of the group of friends who could be allowed to dabble in anything so frowsty and frivolous.

There are several night-club scenes in *The Three Hostages,* all handled very gingerly.

Buchan was much happier when he had his characters in the open air, on the move, with someone after them. (pp. 81-99)

> Richard Usborne, "John Buchan," in his Clubland Heroes: A Nostalgic Study of Some Recurrent Characters in the Romantic Fiction of Dornford Yates, John Buchan, and Sapper, *revised edition, Barrie & Jenkins, London, 1974, pp. 81-99.*

## Gertrude Himmelfarb    (essay date 1968)

[*Himmelfarb is an American historian whose writings focus on English Victorian society and its philosophical background. In the following essay, an earlier version of which appeared in the journal* Encounter *in September 1960, she argues that Buchan's works express a conservative Victorian ethos.*]

John Buchan—novelist, biographer, historian, member of parliament, Governor-General of Canada, and, in his final years, Lord Tweedsmuir of Elsfield—died in 1940, one of the last articulate representatives of the old England. He is the paradigm (the parody, some would have it) of a species of English gentleman now very nearly extinct. The manners and morals celebrated in his books, the social prejudices unwittingly disclosed in them, and the attitudes and philosophy suggested by them have already acquired the faded tint of a period piece. Before they vanish altogether, it may be interesting to take pause, to inquire into an ethos that for some is an embarrassing memory, for others a remembrance of lost grandeur.

There is indeed matter for embarrassment in Buchan's novels. There is the clean, good life which comes with early rising, cold baths, and long immersion in fog and damp, in contrast to the red-eyed, liverish, sluggish, dissolute town dweller. There is the casual bravery, classically understated, of his heroes. ("There's nothing much wrong with me. . . . A shell dropped beside me and damaged my foot. They say they'll have to cut it off.") There is the blithe provincialism and amateurishness of his spy-adventurer who complains that the natives in a Kurdish bazaar do not understand any "civilised tongue," of his member of parliament who cannot pronounce "Boche" names and confuses Poincaré with Mussolini, of the cabinet minister who will not be bothered to read the newspapers while on vacation. There is the penchant for sports that requires every hero (and every respectable villain) to be a first-class shot, and looks upon politics, espionage, and war alike as an opportunity to practice good English sportsmanship. Richard Hannay, his principal hero, is much distressed at not "playing the game" when he abuses the hospitality of a particularly heinous villain; elsewhere he permits a German agent, plotting to spread anthrax germs through the British army, to escape rather than ignobly shoot him in the back; and another hero, Sandy Arbuthnot, during a tremendous cavalry attack involving Cossack, Turkish, German, and British troops, can be heard crying, "Oh, well done our side!"

*Buchan in South Africa.*

Even more reminiscent of the English public school boy is the curious blurring of sexual lines. All Buchan's heroes turn out to have "something girlish" about them. A husky mountain guide has hair "as flaxen as a girl's"; Peter Pienaar, the uncouth Boer adventurer, has a face "as gentle as a girl's," as does a general in the same novel; Sandy Arbuthnot has "a pair of brown eyes like a pretty girl's"; and a six and-a-half foot Negro chieftain has hands "more like a high-bred woman's than a man's." Even some of his historical heroes have the same ambiguous sexuality, Augustus, for example, having "features so delicately modelled as to be almost girlish." Conversely, his heroines have more than a little of the boy in them: boyish hips, boyish stride, wholesome boyish manners and interests. Even these reassuring qualities, however, cannot entirely allay the unease of the hero. When Hannay, then well in his forties, meets the bewitching Hilda von Einen, he is thrown into panic at the thought of sitting beside her: "I had never been in a motor-car with a lady before, I felt like a fish on a dry sandbank." His friend, Archie Roylance, had also been "as shy as a woodcock" of those "mysterious and unintelligible" creatures. "Fresh and unstaled by disillusion," he finally falls in love with Janet, but he succumbs, the author proudly reports, not to the vulgar charms of "swelling bosoms and pouting lips and soft curves and languishing eyes"; the fresh and unstaled phrases that come to his lips are "jolly," "clean-run," "a regular sportswoman," and, as an afterthought, "amazingly good-looking." Occasionally, Buchan might be found to poke fun at this priggishness. Of Walter Scott he once said: "For women he had an old-fashioned reverence, and . . . regarded them very much as a toast to be drunk after King and Constitution." Nevertheless, he respected Scott's diffi-

dence: "I do not suggest the severe doctrine that no man can write intimately of sex without forfeiting his title to gentility, but I do say that for Scott's type of gentleman to do so would have been impossible without a dereliction of standards."

So far the Buchan ethos amuses more than it offends. It becomes displeasing when private foibles begin to impinge upon public morality. The most serious item in Richard Usborne's indictment of Buchan (in *Clubland Heroes* [see excerpt dated 1953]) is Buchan's preoccupation with success, his top-of-the-form ethic. A dinner party in a Buchan novel assembles a typical assortment of guests: Bonson Jane "had been a noted sportsman and was still a fine polo player; his name was a household word in Europe for his work in international finance, . . . it was rumoured that in the same week he had been offered the Secretaryship of State, the Presidency of an ancient University, and the control of a great industrial corporation." Simon Ravelstone is president of "one of the chief banking houses in the world," his son is "making a big name for himself in lung surgery," and another guest is "about our foremost pundit, . . . there were few men alive who were his equals in classical scholarship." So closed is the universe inhabited by these Calvinist-minded characters that they can agree to the precise rank and order of their success. Thus Sandy Arbuthnot is "one of the two or three most intelligent people in the world," Julius Victor is the "richest man in the world," Medina is the "best shot in England after His Majesty," Castor is the "greatest agent-provocateur in history," and there is one of whom it is said, with a fine conjunction of precision and vagueness, that "there aren't five men in the United States whose repute stands higher."

Yet closer attention to the novels suggests that these marks of success are not the ends toward which his heroes—or villains—strive. They are the preconditions of their being heroes or villains at all, much as the characters in fairy tales are always the most beautiful, the most exalted, the most wicked of their kind. They are the starting points for romance, not the termination. Indeed the theme of the more interesting of the novels is the ennui, the *taedium vitae* afflicting precisely those who have attained the highest state—precisely because they have attained that state. In ***John Macnab,*** three of the most eminent men in England, dispirited by a surfeit of success, deliberately engage in an adventure in illegality in order to court exposure and disgrace. And in ***Mountain Meadow,*** a famous American financier and an equally famous English barrister leave their comfortable establishments to suffer pain and death in the far north. All Buchan's heroes are periodically beset by fatigue and lassitude, a "death-wish" that is overcome by divesting themselves of their urban identities—success being an urban condition—and donning the shabby, anonymous clothes of the countryman. Only when the perils of nature and of the chase have roughened up the smooth patina of success, leaving the body scarred and the mind tormented, can they resume their normal lives and identities.

If Buchan's heroes are not, in fact, obsessed by success in the vulgar sense, neither are they the mindless philistines that casual memory would have us think. It is true that Sandy, revisiting Oxford in 1938, complains that the youth have become "a bit too much introverted—isn't that the filthy word?" (Too *much* introverted: if Sandy is obliged to use the filthy word, he at least takes care to use the right syntax.) Yet Sandy himself is far from being an extrovert. He is given to spells of moodiness and despair, to a never-ending quest for an unattainable grail and a new identity (hence his predilection for exotic disguises).

Indeed, the introvert-intellectual is the hero of several of Buchan's works. One of these, Launcelot Wake in *Mr. Standfast,* is so far gone in introversion and intellectualism as to be a pacifist. He is represented in the opening of the book as the stock intellectual, sallow of complexion and red of eye, partial to modern poetry and modern art. Yet by the end of the book, as a result of one of those typical reversals of which Buchan, like other romancers, is fond (his critics seem not to realize that the ostensible truths of the prologue have turned into the half-truths of the epilogue), Wake has emerged as the hero. He has abandoned neither his intellectualism nor his pacifism and is still incapable of the easy sentiments of patriotism and duty:

> I see more than other people see, and I feel more. That's the curse on me. You're a happy man and you get things done, because you only see one side of a case, one thing at a time. How would you like it if a thousand strings were always tugging at you, if you saw that every course meant the sacrifice of lovely and desirable things, or even the shattering of what you know to be unreplaceable? . . . For me to fight would be worse than for another man to run away.

When he dies, after a gallant exploit, Hannay delivers his eulogy: "If the best were to be taken, he would be chosen first, for he was a big man, before whom I uncovered my head."

Buchan's portraits of Montrose and Cromwell are similarly tributes to the complicated man torn by conflicting ideas and emotions who barely manages to maintain a precarious balance: Montrose, starting as a Covenanter in rebellion against the king, and ending as the "noblest Cavalier" while still a Presbyterian; Cromwell, the "practical mystic," the revolutionist with a passion for law and order, the leader given to spells of withdrawal and self-doubt. In history as in fiction, his heroes are by no means the simple clean-cut men of action who shoulder their way to victory. They are sensitive souls, fated to noble failures and Pyrrhic victories.

There is no denying that Buchan is as remote as can be from the modern intellectual in his tastes and judgments. His description of the "advanced" community of Biggleswick in *Mr. Standfast* is as much a parody of such a community as it is of the writer capable of describing and judging it as he does: the pretentious, arty folk with their gimcrack houses and "demented modish" paintings, who were determined "never to admire anything that was obviously beautiful, like a sunset or a pretty woman, but to find surprising loveliness in things which I thought hideous." One does not know whether to be more dismayed

by this blithe confusion of the artsy-crafty with the avant-garde, or by the appalling clichés used to condemn both. One might even be tempted to assume that both the description and the judgment were intended as parodies, were it not that the judgment does essentially correspond to what Buchan himself has told us of his views. In his autobiography, he related his efforts to "get on terms with my contemporaries"—this in the 1920's—but he could only record a series of failures. Their verse (he was apparently referring to T. S. Eliot) seemed to him "unmelodious journalism, . . . a pastiche of Donne." He disliked the "hothouse world" of Proust although he granted his literary skills. He deplored the "tortuous arabesques" of the later Henry James. With the exception of *War and Peace* and a story or two by Turgenev, he found nothing of merit in the Russians and "resolved never to attempt them again." Some contemporaries, to be sure, pleased him: Sinclair Lewis and Booth Tarkington had the narrative gift of the good novelist, and some of H. G. Wells's novels "were destined to live as long as the English tradition endured." But for the rest—the "rebels and experimentalists"—he confessed a "radical defect of sympathy": "Their merits were beyond doubt, but their method and the whole world which they represented seemed to me ineffably dismal."

Yet, alien as he was from the typical literature of modernity, his mind had a range and seriousness that has to be respected. It was not only Scott, Tennyson, and Macaulay whom he (and the heartier characters in his novels) fondly quoted, but also such varied writers—to select only a few of those most often cited in his pages—as Shakespeare, Hakluyt, Thomas Browne, Bunyan, Hazlitt, Walton, Thoreau, Whitman, Johnson, Chateaubriand, Calvin, and Augustine. Impatient with experiments in the arts as in politics, fearful of attempts to probe the unconscious in novels as in life, he was obviously limited in his esthetic responses. Yet it can hardly be judged philistine to prefer Homer in the Greek to T. S. Eliot in English, "low brow" to admire Tolstoi more than Dostoevski, or "anti-intellectual" to write serious works of historical scholarship that are also refreshingly literate.

What is involved is a different cultural tradition emerging in a different set of intellectual and literary manners. The English intellectual of Buchan's generation was loath to parade his intelligence; his Double First at the university had to be acquired without visible swotting or cramming. (Buchan's characters never admitted to memorizing anything; they had "fly-paper memories" to which long passages of poetry or facts adhered effortlessly.) And his writing suggested not the anguish of creation but the casualness of civilized conversation. In this relaxed manner, Buchan was able to produce fifty-seven books in the interstices of his other more absorbing occupations—the law, interrupted by a short period of service with Milner in South Africa, then business, parliament, and finally the Governor-Generalship of Canada.

Such productivity could only be attained if one wrote not merely *as* one spoke, but also *what* one spoke. This is the real clue to Buchan's (as to the Victorians') prodigious output. There are many today who are as rich in intellectual resources; there are few who feel so free to draw upon their capital. Buchan had confidence not only in his knowledge, but also in his opinions, attitudes, intuitions, and prejudices. What he wrote for the public was what he felt in private; he did not labor for a subtlety or profundity that did not come spontaneously, or censor his spontaneous thoughts before committing them to paper. He had none of the scruples that are so inhibiting today. He was candid about race, nation, religion, and class, because it did not occur to him that anything he was capable of feeling or thinking could be reprehensible. His creative strength was the strength of character.

It is not only productivity but also authenticity that is enhanced by this assertion of personal authority. His familiarity with the Scottish countryside does more than provide the background of many of the stories. The hunting and fishing scenes in *John Macnab,* described in great and exciting detail, are not appendages to the plot; they *are* the plot. The homely details of the domestic life of a retired Glasgow merchant, interspersed with comments about Freudianism, communism, and international politics, lend verisimilitude to the fairy-tale character of the Russian princess and the wild improbabilities of plot of *Hunting-tower.* Verisimilitude, not verity—for his novels remain unashamed romances. It was his theory that fantasy and reality should be permitted to feed upon and nurture each other. This is why he did not trouble himself overmuch with plot, relying on coincidence, hunch, luck, the stock character and situation, to an extent that no popular writer today would dare to do. It is also why he did not trouble himself unduly with niceties of style, why he was unembarrassed by the cliché, the occasional longeur or discursive aside. The very laxity of plot and style served his purpose, not only to advance the tale with a minimum of effort, but also to provide the commonplace background against which the romantic adventure is best played out. In an essay on Scott, Buchan argued the case for a *punctum indifferens,* a calm center around which rages the storm of romance: "The kernel of romance is contrast, beauty and valour flowering in unlikely places, the heavenly rubbing shoulders with the earthly. The true romantic is not the Byronic hero; he is the British soldier whose idea of a *beau geste* is to dribble a football into the enemy's trenches."

The modern reader probably finds it less difficult to accept Buchan's style and mode of thought than the substance of his opinions. On the subject of race especially he appears as the English gentleman of a vintage now gone sour. At least one American publisher recently considered and then had to abandon the idea of reissuing one of his most successful novels, *Prester John,* because it might offend liberal sensibilities. First published in 1910, *Prester John* is the story of a native African uprising led by a Western-educated Negro who seeks to harness the primitive religion and nationalism of the savages to set himself up as the demi-god of a native republic. If this theme is calculated to outrage the liberal, Buchan's language (the hero, a white boy, speaks of the "niggers" with their "preposterous negro lineaments") does nothing to mitigate the offense. Yet while he dwells on racial differences and assumes natural racial inferiorities and superiorities, he does

so not to justify exploitation or inhumanity but rather to inculcate the duties of an enlightened humanitarianism. Laputa, the native leader, is represented as a noble figure and worthy antagonist. When he is defeated in honorable battle, the classical note of the White Man's Burden is sounded:

> I knew then the meaning of the white man's duty. He has to take all risks, recking nothing of his life or his fortunes and well content to find his reward in the fulfilment of his task. That is the difference between white and black, the gift of responsibility, the power of being in a little way a king; and so long as we know this and practice it, we will rule not in Africa alone but wherever there are dark men who live only for the day and for their own bellies. Moreover, the work made me pitiful and kindly. I learned much of the untold grievances of the natives and saw something of their strange, twisted reasoning.

*Prester John* was one of Buchan's earliest and least mature books, or possibly the fact that it was intended as a boy's book was responsible for the shrillness of its message. Elsewhere the racist overtones were more a matter of instinct and sentiment than of ideology or doctrine. Buchan was not conscious of race as a "problem" to which racism provided a solution; it was precisely because he was so unconscious of it that he could say: "A nigger band, looking like monkeys in uniform, pounded out some kind of barbarous jingle." And it is precisely because we today are so acutely, unhappily conscious of it that we find this language objectionable, whether in Buchan or in a writer of such distinction and delicacy as Conrad, who had no qualms about speaking of the "repulsive mask of a nigger's soul," the "black mist," the "subtle and dismal influence" emanating from him.

In spite of the usual protestations, to explain is, in large measure, to excuse. The familiar racist sentiments of Buchan, Kipling, even Conrad, were a reflection of a common attitude. They were descriptive not prescriptive; not an incitement to novel political action, but an attempt to express differences of culture and color in terms that had been unquestioned for generations. Today, when differences of race have attained the status of problems—and tragic problems—writers with the best of motives and finest of sensibilities must often take refuge in evasion and subterfuge. Neutral, scientific words replace the old charged ones, and then, because even the neutral ones— "Negro" in place of "nigger"—give offense, in testifying to differences that men of good will would prefer forgotten, disingenuous euphemisms are invented—"non-white" in place of "Negro." It is at this stage that one may find a virtue of sorts in Buchan: the virtue of candor, which has both an esthetic and an ethical appeal.

The same observations may be made of Buchan's alleged anti-Semitism. What some have condemned as insensitivity or condescension may also be taken as a forthright expression of opinion—or not so much opinion, because that is to dignify it as a conscious judgment, but rather impression or experience. One cannot reasonably object to references to Jewish rag dealers and pawnbrokers, Jewish

Communists and financiers, when these were in fact conspicuous both as individuals and as types in an otherwise ethnically homogeneous society—unless one is prepared to impose a decree of silence on the entire subject of Jews. Nor is it reasonable to take offense at the patently fairy-tale account of an international conspiracy devised by Jewish anarchists and Jewish financiers for different and ingenious reasons, and led by a "little white-faced Jew in a bath-chair with an eye like a rattlesnake" who is avenging himself for centuries of persecution. If Buchan's Jewish villains are to be kept account of, the ledger ought also to include the Jewish heroes: the "richest man in the world," who is an entirely honorable and sympathetic figure and who is made the victim of another conspiracy precisely because his mission was to secure peace in the world; or his beautiful daughter, the fiancée of the Marquis de la Tour du Pin, one of Hannay's oldest and noblest friends. And even the Jewish villain is not necessarily the nastiest of villains; in **Mr. Standfast** he is the most decent of the lot.

This is not to suggest that Buchan's novels can be acquitted of the charge of anti-Semitism. They were anti-Semitic in the same sense that they were anti-Negro. If the Jews, unlike the Negroes, were not in all ways inferior, they were most certainly different, and as one of Buchan's American heroes said of one of his Jewish heroes (vulgar Americans could be relied on to voice what polite Englishmen only thought), he simply "didn't like his race." But this kind of anti-Semitism, indulged in at that time and place, was both too common and too passive to be scandalous. Men were normally anti-Semitic, unless by some quirk of temperament or ideology they happened to be philo-Semitic. So long as the world itself was normal, this was of no great consequence. It was only later, when social impediments became fatal disabilities, when anti-Semitism ceased to be the prerogative of English gentlemen and became the business of politicians and demagogues, that sensitive men were shamed into silence. It was Hitler, attaching such abnormal significance to filiation and physiognomy, who put an end to the casual, innocent anti-Semitism of the clubman. When the conspiracies of the English adventure tale became the realities of German politics, Buchan and others had the grace to realize that what was permissible under civilized conditions was not permissible with civilization *in extremis.* **Mountain Meadow,** his last book, composed on the eve of World War II and in the shadow of his own death, was a tract exalting "brotherhood," as that term is understood in the now orthodox liberal lexicon. It is amusing to note that among the many financiers appearing in its pages, there is not a single Jew.

Nor was it only in his later novels that Buchan displayed an admirable sense of social responsibility. Early in 1934, long before most Englishmen had even discovered the fact, Buchan publicly denounced Hitler's anti-Semitism, and, like Milner before him, espoused the cause of Zionism. It is tempting to remark upon the irony of the fact that the fictional perpetrator of Jewish-capitalist-communist conspiracies should have had his name inscribed, in solemn ceremony, in the Golden Book of the Jewish National Fund. Buchan himself would have found nothing "ironic" about this. Fiction was fiction, reality re-

ality. Moreover his Zionism, like his fiction, was concerned not to obliterate differences but to respect them, not to deny, in more conventional liberal fashion, the Jewish identity, but to assert and promote it. His speech acknowledging the honor that had been paid him by the Jewish National Fund took as its theme the racial similarities of Scotsmen and Jews with particular reference to their high regard for learning. A participant in that ceremony, sharing the platform with Buchan, recalled his speech and also his behavior during the address following his, when Buchan leaned forward and watched, with unconcealed delight and fascination, the ample gestures and bodily movements of a Yiddish-speaking rabbi.

In the clubman syndrome, acute class consciousness was second only to race consciousness. It is sometimes suggested that for Buchan this class consciousness was both aggravated and made more reprehensible by its having been acquired rather than being indigenous. The son of a modest Presbyterian minister, attending village schools, a grammar school, and finally the university at Glasgow, he was far removed from the upper-class English characters he described so lovingly. He did not even like school games, and although he did enjoy country sports—hunting, fishing, naturalizing—it was without the ritual that the rich Englishman brought to them. Only when he entered Oxford at the age of nineteen did he get a glimpse of upper-class life. And for some time it was just a glimpse. Older than most freshmen, much poorer and more puritanical, he associated at first only with the other scholarship students. It was not until his third year, when prizes and literary work had made him relatively affluent, that his circle expanded to include rowing and rugby stars as well as poets, writers, and orators. His social initiation was completed in London where he read law and then in South Africa with Milner.

What redeems Buchan from the double charge of either not knowing the clubman society he purported to describe, or if he did know it, of having gained entrée into it only by such an effort as to suggest social-climbing and snobbery, is the fact of his Scottishness. For the Scot is neither an outsider nor an interloper in the sense in which a Cockney or suburbanite might be. Like the American, he is alien enough to be assimilated and mobile enough to expect to be assimilated. His culture is not a despised subculture, but a culture in its own right. His accent and schooling are a token of national peculiarity, not of class inferiority. This is not to say that there was no climbing involved. Men accustomed to social mobility are accustomed to climbing. But it is not the same demeaning process to the foreigner that it would be to the native, does not involve the same repudiation of his past or alienation from himself.

It was his Scottishness, too, that made Buchan a Tory with a difference. For the Scottish Tory was a special breed, as he himself recognized: "A youth in Scotland who called himself a Tory was almost certain to be thinking about politics, and not merely cherishing a family loyalty." He was a Tory by will and principle rather than personal or class interests. He thought the existing class structure was both inevitable and desirable. Like William Morris, he could say that he respected the working class too much to want to turn it into a middle class. And like Disraeli, he wanted to cultivate the alliance between aristocracy and working class. "Democracy and aristocracy," Buchan said, "can co-exist, for oligarchy is their common enemy." The word "oligarchy" was used advisedly, for what Buchan deplored was the tendency to make of class an exclusively economic category and to use social position as an economic instrument. He had no liking for the "genuine reactionaries" of his own party who "woke to life only in the budget season." Not committed to the principles of laissez-faire, he had no prejudice against socialist controls, public authorities, or welfare economics.

If class or social position was not identical with economics, neither was it fixed by birth, for history and character could alter what birth and money had established. It was the possibility, the actuality, of such alteration that attracted Buchan to the study of the English Civil War. And it was the nicety of his judgment that made him choose as his heroes Montrose rather than Charles, Cromwell rather than Lilburne: Montrose for recognizing that there were occasions when revolution was warranted, Cromwell for recognizing that there came a time in a revolution when authority had to be reasserted. Cromwell, he said, "was no Leveller or egalitarian, for the world could not do without its masters, but why reverence a brocaded puppet larded by a priest with oil, when there were men who needed no robes or sacring to make them kingly?" Authority remained, even as authorities were overthrown, and there were some more than others who were the natural repositories of authority: "It is a melancholy fact which exponents of democracy must face that, while all men may be on a level in the eyes of the State, they will continue in fact to be preposterously unequal."

This declaration of inequality might have appeared in Buchan's *Cromwell;* in fact it appeared in his novel *John Macnab.* The theme of this novel is not only the natural and rightful authority exercised by some men by virtue of their breeding, experience, and character, but also the natural and rightful impulse to rebel against that authority. John Macnab's gallant wager, to kill and remove against great odds a stag and salmon from his neighbor's property, is not the paean to adventure that it may seem on the surface—sheer, gratuitous, gentlemanly adventure, *le sport* at its most absurd. It is rather a parable about authority and property and the perpetual challenge to which they are both subject. The ancient families, cherishing the tokens of their glorious antiquity and trying to remain unsullied by modern enterprise, are doomed to extinction, and justly so. The heroine describes her sister: "She's a sentimentalist and she'll marry Junius and go to America, where everybody is sentimental, and be the sweetest thing in the Western hemisphere." The old Gaelic family motto, "Sons of Dogs, come and I will give you flesh," has given way to the genteel invention of the Herald's College, "Pro Deo et Rege," and the will to fight has succumbed to the wish to survive—as a result of which Lancashire cotton spinners are succeeding to the ancient houses and heirlooms. And the Lancashire manufacturers are advised to pay heed too, for the right of property "is no right at all." Neither property nor rank nor power has a right in perpetuity.

Everything is held under sufferance; every privilege must be defended and legitimized anew.

Misled by the romantic cast of Buchan's novels, critics have assumed that his Toryism was of the romantic variety that loves a lord, venerates the past, and despises the clerks and entrepreneurs of the middle class. In fact, his Toryism was radical rather than romantic, and he respected enterprise as he respected labor. While agreeing with Samuel Johnson that "life is barren enough surely with all her trappings; let us be therefore cautious of how we strip her," he had no fondness for trappings that interfered with the business of living, and no regrets for the regime that died in World War I: "The radicalism which is part of the Tory creed was coming uppermost, and I looked forward to a clearing out of much rubbish."

If Buchan's attitude to race and class is apt to cause dismay, his attitude to nation and empire may be even more distressing. "For King and Country," the homily of generations of housemasters, is taken to be the archaic and fatuous message of his work. He himself described, in retrospect, the imperial vision of his youth: "I dreamed of a world-wide brotherhood with the background of a common race and creed, consecrated to the service of peace; Britain enriching the rest out of her culture and traditions, and the spirit of the Dominions like a strong wind freshening the stuffiness of the old lands." This ideal is now commonly regarded as a utopian fantasy. But Buchan himself was no innocent, and when he confessed to his dream it was with the knowledge that his words had become irredeemable platitudes. "The 'white man's burden,' " he complained toward the end of his life, "is now an almost meaningless phrase; then it involved a new philosophy of politics, and an ethical standard, serious and surely not ignoble."

If there was rhetoric and fancy in the imperialist circles around Milner, there was also a truth and grandeur which today is too little appreciated. In his biography of Cromwell; Buchan quoted Captain John Smith: "The greatest honour that ever belonged to the greatest monarchs was the enlarging of their dominions and erecting Commonwealths"; and Harrington: "You canot plant an oak in a flower-pot; she must have earth for her roots, and heaven for her branches." This is not to say that the impulse behind the imperial enterprise is always honorable, or that its consequences, whatever the impulse, are always desirable. But to impugn the motives of all imperialists is surely to have a crabbed view of both the past and the present. A respect for the integrity and independence of others is admirable, but so is a respect and faith in oneself; and while the missionary or proselytizing temperament is to be suspected and feared, it is also, on occasion, to be esteemed. If self-serving motives are attributed to the imperialists, they can also be attributed to the "Little-Englanders." Prudence and aristocratic disdain were the not particularly lofty terms in which Raymond Asquith defended Little-Englandism to Buchan:

> The day of the clever cad is at hand. I always felt
> it would come to this if we once let ourselves in
> for an Empire. If only Englishmen had known
> their Aeschylus a little better they wouldn't have

bustled about the world appropriating things. A gentleman may make a large fortune, but only a cad can look after it. It would have been so much pleasanter to live in a small community who knew Greek and played games and washed themselves.

The dilemma of the imperial ideal was also the dilemma of the national ideal. Here too Buchan had a finer sensibility and at the same time a broader sympathy than he and his kind have generally been credited with. Thus he did not finally decide between the creeds of Cromwell and Montrose—Cromwell, as Buchan saw it, seeking to create a "spiritualized and dedicated" nation; Montrose satisfied with a homely, modest, judicious government of checks and balances. He saw the glory of the first, but he realized that men might become satiated with high communal, as with high spiritual, ideals, and might prefer to devote themselves to their private concerns. He did not pretend that the first path was without its dangers, or the second without its virtues.

There was certainly a romantic streak in Buchan that invaded his politics. It was not, however, the sentimental romanticism with which the conservative is often associated—a sentimental attachment to tradition, rank, and pomp. It was rather a Gothic, almost apocalyptic vision of the dark, destructive forces contained in human beings and society. His villains are permeated by this sense of the infernal. The typical Victorian or Edwardian villain was a bounder and cad, a seducer of shopgirls, extortionist of money, sometimes a trafficker in national secrets. The Buchan villain deals in a different order of villainy. He is not a fallen gentleman but a fallen man, the personification of evil. He dabbles in black magic rather than sex, seeks not money but power, and trafficks in the secrets of the soul as much as those of the nation. Compared with him, even the sadist of the contemporary thriller is frivolous, for instead of private sexual perversions, Buchan's villains are satisfied with nothing less than the subversion of society.

Long before the H-bomb, A-bomb, and even ordinary old-fashioned aerial bombing, before the threat of fascism and in the infancy of communism, Buchan felt what later events seemed to confirm—that "civilization anywhere is a very thin crust." The danger in revolution was not that it would overthrow any particular political or social institutions, but rather that it would undermine all government and society. Bolshevism itself was less menacing than the nihilism that it would release:

> A civilisation bemused by an opulent materialism has been met by a rude challenge. The free peoples have been challenged by the serfs. The gutters have exuded a poison which bids fair to infect the world. The beggar-on-horseback rides more roughshod over the helpless than the cavalier. A combination of multitudes who have lost their nerve and a junta of arrogant demagogues has shattered the comity of nations. The European tradition has been confronted with an Asiatic revolt, with its historic accompaniment of janissaries and assassins. There is in it all, too, an ugly pathological savour, as if a mature society

were being assailed by diseased and vicious children.

But the poison that was now infecting the world had always lain dormant in it; the diseased and vicious children are, after all, our own progeny. What terrifies Hannay in *The Three Hostages* is the fact that the villains are high in the Establishment, that they might be found next to one at a shoot in Suffolk or a dinner party in St. James'. Even when the villain in one of the spy stories was a German, Buchan took pains to absolve him from the lesser villainy of nationality (Buchan was neither a Germanophobe nor a Russophobe) and even of espionage, in order to convict him of the greater villainy of a moral depravity bordering on diabolism.

This is hardly the housemaster's credo of king and country. Again, what distinguished Buchan was his Scottishness, the Calvinist sense of the unquiet depths that lay beneath the human surface. He suspected that once the subconscious, lawless instincts of men were permitted to break through the barrier erected by civilization, "there will be a weakening of the power of reasoning, which after all is the thing that brings men nearest to the Almighty; and there will be a failure of nerve." It was thus not the reason of state, even of a hostile state, that alarmed him, but the force of unreason itself. Shortly after World War I he foresaw the development of a new kind of propaganda, compared with which the old-fashioned Prussian militarist variety was innocuous and innocent. As Sandy Arbuthnot reminds Hannay, the new threat came from the manipulator of minds: "We are only beginning to realize the strange crannies of the human soul. The real magician, if he turned up to-day, wouldn't bother about drugs and dopes. He would dabble in far more deadly methods, the compulsion of a fiery nature over the limp things that men call their minds." Buchan's villains do not simply bribe, blackmail, or torture their victims; they operate by means of hypnotism, hysteria, fanaticism, and a quasi-religious mysticism. Hannay, fortunately, is not susceptible to hypnotism, as he repeatedly comforts himself, but he is liable to his "one special funk," the mob. "I hated the thought of it—the mess, the blind struggle, the sense of unleashed passions different from those of any single blackguard. It was a dark world to me, and I don't like darkness."

Hannay may be an innocent, but his creator is not. When Buchan pits the "jolly party of clean, hard, decent fellows" against the "abominable hinterland of mystery and crime," he seems to be subscribing to the decent-fellow ethic that belongs to the caricature of the phlegmatic, obtuse Englishman. But in fact the ethic has acquired the urgency of a desperate counter-measure; it is inseparable from the evil that called it into being. As befits a good Calvinist, Buchan is hard, realistic, unsentimental, apprehensive: "It was a dogma of the elder liberalism that violence can never achieve anything, and that persecution, so far from killing a thing, must inevitably nourish it. For such optimism there is no warrant in history; time and again violence has wholly achieved its purpose, when it has been carried to its logical conclusion."

What makes Buchan, and the ethos with which he is identified, so unpalatable today is not one or another cause for distaste: the idea that the good life is a matter of cold baths, rousing games, and indifferent sex; the apparent philistinism that put a high premium on success and a low premium on intelligence; an unseemly preoccupation with race and class; and a still more unseemly glorification of nation and empire. It is each of these and more: the sense of a temperament and mentality that is inimical to the prevailing "liberal imagination." The liberal celebrates the likenesses of men rather than their differences; individuals rather than race, class, or nation; the benevolent and malleable character of men rather than their recalcitrance. He chooses to understand rather than judge, and he is discreet where understanding fails him. He is as much repelled by intuition and prejudice as by the usages and prescriptions of tradition. He regards violence, like evil, as a negative quality, a temporary aberration, unreal both in its impulse and in its effect.

Buchan—Calvinist in religion, Tory in politics, and romantic in sensibility—is obviously the antithesis of the liberal. It is no accident that he was addicted to a genre, the romantic tale of adventure, which is itself alien to the liberal temper. For what kind of romance would it be that feared to characterize or categorize, to indulge the sense of evil, violence, and apocalypse? It is no accident, either, that the predominance of liberal values has meant the degeneration of a literary form so congenial to the Tory imagination. (pp. 249-72)

> *Gertrude Himmelfarb, "John Buchan: The Last Victorian," in her* Victorian Minds, *Alfred A. Knopf, 1968, pp. 249-72.*

## Patrick Cosgrave   (essay date 1972)

[*Cosgrave is an Irish-born English essayist and biographer with a special interest in twentieth-century English political history. In the following excerpt, he favorably examines Buchan's plot and characterization techniques in his espionage novels.*]

Within a given *genre*—that of the adventure story—there is no doubt that John Buchan was supreme; as supreme in his field as Conan Doyle was with the detective story. Considered purely technically, one can say that everything Buchan started—the exotic environments (*Greenmantle*), the car chases (*The Island of Sheep*), the loneliness of the hero (*The Thirty-Nine Steps*)—is still going strong. But there is a useful distinction to be drawn between Buchan and Doyle. It is this: when we think of a Buchan story we think of the author; when we think of Doyle we think of Sherlock Holmes, of the character. This is partly because, on analysis, Holmes is engaging while Hannay—Buchan's main hero—is dull. He is designedly so, describing himself in *The Thirty-Nine Steps* merely as a man who "had got my pile—not one of the big ones, but good enough for me . . .".

The student of Buchan is thus thrown back on the man. Since John Buchan was a young Imperialist of the Milner school, a Tory M.P., a go-between linking Baldwin and Macdonald, and Governor-General of Canada, it is understandable that critics have seen the adventure stories as an offshoot of the author's public character. Thus the early

American chapters of *Sick Heart River* are a paean to capitalism; *The Courts of the Morning* is to be remembered for its supreme nostalgia—the statement that, in *modern* war, cavalry would continue to be of the utmost importance; and *Greenmantle* to be considered as a celebration of the Anglo-American alliance. And there is some truth in all of these propositions.

But there is another truth, albeit partial. In the chapter on the thrillers in her biography of Buchan [see Further Reading], Mrs. Janet Adam Smith quotes Lumley, the villain of Buchan's first tale of adventure, *The Power-House:* Lumley is explaining to the hero, Leithen, why he believes he can achieve his aim of destroying civilization.

> You think that a wall as solid as the earth separates civilisation from barbarism. I tell you the division is a thread, a sheet of glass. A touch here, a push there, and you bring back the reign of Saturn.

Later in this short and powerful story Leithen is walking in London, conscious of being surrounded and threatened by emissaries of his enemy and being unable to call on help:

> Now I saw how thin is the protection of civilisation. An accident and a bogus ambulance—a false charge and a bogus arrest—there were a dozen ways of spiriting me out of this gay, bustling world.

It is Mrs. Adam Smith's contention that this concept of the fragility of order is central to Buchan. Her argument cannot be questioned, but there is still a great deal more to be said on the subject. What has to be said enables us to separate an understanding of Buchan's thriller technique from an understanding of his ideas taken as a whole. It enables us, further, to appreciate the importance of his work as a representation of British cultural and political history at a particular historical moment: supreme though he is as a story-teller, he is not a novelist of great distinction—nor would he claim that he was—and so his usefulness to the historian of culture lies in what he said and stood for rather than in what, as an artist, he achieved. Then again, moving outwards into the work from its central preoccupation, we learn to understand the true place in Buchan's thinking of certain ideas and subjects which have assumed a disproportionate standing in the minds of several critics who have written about him—Imperialism, money and the self-made man, comradeship between heroes, and strongly expressed views on race, to name but a few. In my view, however, none of these things are as important in Buchan's work as his view of the function of character, defined not so much as individual character but as the essence of human nature, in relation to experience: Buchan was an existential writer, and the purpose of this essay is to show that.

It should be said, however, that not all of his large output of stories are of equal importance. The two main series— the Hannay books and the Leithen books—are the most important, since they represent the consummation of his art as a story-teller; and because both show the development of certain key themes over a long period of years. The Dickson McCunn books, which were Buchan's trib-

*Front cover of* Greenmantle.

ute to the Glasgow bourgeoisie and the Gorbals diehards, are not, in my view, of great importance, nor are the historical novels, save in so far as they show Buchan's interest in his native country and the fertility of his imagination. His numerous stories of the occult, the bizarre and the semi-supernatural are of greater moment, but they are not commonly distinguished in their execution, nor is the development of their main ideas more than superficial. There are, however, two novels—*The Courts of the Morning* and *A Prince of the Captivity*—which, though they are not among his best, and though they are overloaded with incident and excessive in length, are of significance. The first of these tells the story of a revolution in a South American republic, led by Sandy Clanroyden, Hannay's great friend and hero, who appears first in *Greenmantle,* the story immediately following *The Thirty-Nine Steps.* Hannay does not himself appear in this book, save to introduce it, but Clanroyden is helped by the American John S. Blenkiron, and several of the minor characters in the Hannay saga, notably Sir Archibald Roylance and Geordie Hamilton, the Scots Fusilier, who begins his fictional life as Hannay's batman and ends it as Clanroyden's major-domo on his Scottish estate. The second novel—*A Prince of the Captivity*—is outside both the main series. It tells the story of a talented young Army officer Adam Melfort who, in 1912, takes on himself the blame for forging a cheque, al-

though the crime was his wife's. He leaves his regiment and goes to prison. But, though his life as he has known it until then is destroyed, he re-emerges as an espionage hero in the First World War, and afterwards engages in a heroic struggle to save civilization from the threat of dissolution created by the events of the war and exploited by a shadowy conspiracy of villains in the mould of Lumley and the Black Stone—the villain of both *The Thirty-Nine Steps* and *Mr. Standfast. A Prince of the Captivity* is perhaps Buchan's most important *roman à thèse.*

There are three striking characteristics of Buchan's method as an adventure story-writer. The first is the pace and detail of his stories; the second is the way in which the theme of the fragility of order is used to heighten excitement, and the third is the inconsistency of both event and characterization. A good Buchan invariably moves at high speed—one of the weaknesses of *The Courts of the Morning* and *A Prince of the Captivity* is that they do not. Even when, as in the case of the last Hannay story, *The Island of Sheep,* there are long introductions to the main story these introductions themselves are full of variety and incident and, in the case of Hannay's account of how he became involved in the affairs of the Haraldsen family, thus contracting an obligation of honour to the persecuted victim of the villains in the main story, the introductory material constitutes a good short story in its own right. Indeed, there is a distinct fragmentation of the main structure of the story in most of the Buchan classics: *The Thirty-Nine Steps,* for example, consists of ten chapters several of which could quite easily be left out without detriment to the main development of the story. *Greenmantle* contains a lengthy prelude telling of the adventures of Hannay and his Boer companion Pieter Pienaar in Germany on their way to the Middle East where the main events of the tale take place. Though this prelude serves to introduce two of the main characters who appear again later in the story, and though it is extremely and claustrophobically exciting, it is not essential. And in what eventually becomes one of the best of the Leithen books, *The Dancing Floor,* there is an extremely long prefatory account of the strange dreams enjoyed by Vernon Milburne before he and Leithen turn up together on a Greek island to fight the forces of evil. Economy in pursuit of his main theme was not one of the characteristics of Buchan.

This, however, matters only to the purist. The fragmentation allows Buchan to pack incident and excitement into different sections of his books and enables him, further, to develop both different environments and the special gift he has for knowing and entrancing references to strange places and events and the past experiences of his characters: "I got the first hint" Scudder, the American who introduces Hannay to adventure in *The Thirty-Nine Steps,* says "in an inn on the Achensee in Tyrol. That set me inquiring, and I collected my other clues in a fur shop in the Galician quarter of Buda, in a Strangers' Club in Vienna and in a little bookshop off the Rackitzstrasse in Leipsic. I completed my evidence ten days ago in Paris . . .". If there is a general purpose to these references, apart from their introduction of variety and the excitement of strange places into the story, it is to develop the idea of the widespread nature of evil and the totality of the threat the villains in any given story pose to the world. It was also natural, of course, that, in a period when Englishmen thought unself-consciously in world-wide terms Buchan should write in this way, thus incidentally satisfying his own taste for the strange and the bizarre. But there was also a deliberate and technical reason for the variety.

As Dr. Greenslade explains in *The Three Hostages,* giving an account of Buchan's own story-telling method:

> I want to write a shocker, so I begin by fixing on one or two facts which have no sort of obvious connection . . . Let us take three things a long way apart . . . say, an old blind woman spinning in the Western Highlands, a barn in a Norwegian *saeter,* and a little curiosity shop in North London kept by a Jew with a dyed beard. Not much connection between the three? You invent a connection—simple enough if you have any imagination, and you weave all three into the yarn. The reader, who knows nothing about the three at the start, is puzzled and intrigued and, if the story is well arranged, finally satisfied. He is pleased with the ingenuity of the solution, for he doesn't realise that the author fixed upon the solution first, and then invented a problem to suit it.

The irony and the jest is that the three things mentioned by Greenslade become important clues in the story that follows.

Each fragmented facet of the main story also serves another purpose. It enables Buchan to split up his usually large cast of characters and give each of them a separate set of adventures before they all come together for the climax (although this does not apply to the Leithen books, which use a different technique—to which I will return). Each group is continually worrying about what has happened to the others and aware of the threat posed to whatever mission is in hand by the danger to themselves. Thus, in one of the best examples of this technique, in *The Island of Sheep* Lombard the banker, ill-equipped physically for adventure, is at one stage forced to drive furiously from the Home Counties to the fastness and safety of Clanroyden's estate in Scotland, chased by the villains and bringing with him the young daughter of the victim, Haraldsen, whom the villains wish to use as a hostage. Hannay knows of the threat to the girl, but must wait helplessly at Laverlaw while Lombard struggles alone with evil: Clanroyden, as is common with him, has disappeared into some by-way of the story. He, indeed, constantly worries his friends by mysterious disappearances, the purpose of which is not always very clear. Later in *The Island of Sheep* the main party of heroes is besieged on the island, anxiously awaiting the promised arrival of Clanroyden, whose absence seriously endangers them: he does not appear until the last moment, and then without assistance of any kind, the party being saved by luck and the intrepidity of two children. All this makes for intense excitement, but not for any very logical development of the overall story: nor does it enhance our respect for the intelligence of the heroes. Nonetheless, the excitement is sustained. This is partly because of the authenticity of detail in the incidents—the exact plotting of Lombard's route to the north, for example—and the economy of the writing. It is also because fragmentation of the story enables Buchan to draw out the contrast between the weakness of good and the all-knowing efficiency of evil: individual heroes are continually opposed to the mass, and the superior forces, of the enemy and the theme of loneliness and fragility thus developed and emphasized.

Nonetheless, this inconsistency of event and characterization are worthy of note. The principal oddity in the Hannay saga centres around the character and function of Clanroyden. He appears in all but two of the Hannay books and is treated throughout as a master-mind of good. In *Greenmantle* he is chosen by Hannay, who has only recently met him, as one of a desperate group of heroes to go on a highly dangerous mission to the Middle East, the purpose of which—it is 1916—is to subvert German attempts to start a Holy War. In *The Three Hostages* Clanroyden accidentally enters the story at a point when Hannay has unwillingly taken on the mission of tracking down three young people kidnapped by the villains as surety for their own safety. Hannay's investigations have led him to Dominick Medina, a brilliant rising politician of unexampled charm and courtesy. Clanroyden thinks Medina evil and has evidence to this effect culled from his own travels and investigations in far corners of the world. Eventually Hannay believes his old friend and together they unmask Medina as head of a virulently anti-British world-wide conspiracy. After this Clanroyden has an adventure of his own, in *The Courts of the Morning,* where he meets his wife Barbara, who is Blenkiron's niece. Finally, in *The Island of Sheep* Clanroyden comes to Hannay's aid when the latter is trying to save the son of an old friend from persecution by blackmailers: there is a particular logic to his intervention since the leader of the villains is a survivor from *The Courts of the Morning,* and Clanroyden does not regard his "Olifa job" as completed until this villain, D'Ingraville, is dead.

Clanroyden is Hannay's hero. He is invariably regarded as the fount of wisdom, courage, experience, intelligence and ability. Yet, save in the adventure in which Hannay does not appear, Sandy Clanroyden is almost the essence of incompetence, and temperamentally unstable to boot. In *Greenmantle* he is half hypnotized into evil by the German agent Hilda von Einem, who has fallen in love with him; and he does not recover his stability until he is rejoined by his friends and has their support in confronting her. A large part of *The Three Hostages* he spends off-stage, pursuing research into arcane magical practices at which Medina is adept, but to no eventual purpose. In *The Island of Sheep,* as I have already mentioned, he places his friends in serious danger. It is indeed—save in this last book—Hannay who invariably wins the victory for good, though he is in every way a duller, less experienced, less brilliant man than Clanroyden. Moreover, as Mrs. Adam Smith has acutely observed, Clanroyden is a different man in *The Courts of the Morning,* a fact partly to be explained by Buchan's decision to model him on Auberon Herbert in the other books, while he is a simulacrum of T. E. Lawrence in the South American adventure. *The Courts of the Morning* is in many respects a text-book illustration of Lawrence's theory of war and, as such, was appended to the bibliography of Sir Basil Liddel Hart's *The Future of Infantry*. The exclusively military preoccupation of this book meant that Buchan was less concerned with his more general, psychological themes of good and evil and this—together with its exceptional length—took much of the pace and excitement which was characteristic of him out of the story.

This indicates the sense in which *The Courts of the Morning* is an exception to the other books in which Clanroyden appears: it does not explain the anomaly of his and Hannay's respective roles in the stories where they appear together. It seems to me, however, that there is an explanation. Just as there is an enormous amount of background, often intensely and acutely rendered, in the Buchan books—the material on stalking in *The Three Hostages*, on bird life in *The Island of Sheep*, on, in fact, whatever happened to interest himself or his family at the time of writing—which floats above the central core of their argument, so I believe the character of Clanroyden testified to the lighter side of Buchan's nature and Hannay to the more serious. The ideal character for Buchan, the one who brings about the defeat of evil, has "a good commonplace intelligence," "a quite irrelevant gift of imagination" and is "a foursquare being bedded in the concrete of our civilization". This will do as a description of Hannay, but never as an analysis of Clanroyden, who is a fey and neurotic being. Likewise, for all that Hannay continues to tell us throughout *The Island of Sheep* about how much more able Clanroyden is than himself, and how much more likely to bring the villains to book; and although we are also told that the story is essentially about a settling of accounts between Clanroyden and D'Ingraville, nonetheless, at the outset of the book, when Hannay is consulting his old friend, the shrewd Scotland Yard detective Mac-Gillivray, he is told that none of the villains who have so far appeared are really dangerous: they would become so only if they acquired a leader, "a really desperate fellow—like yourself".

There is thus a series of contradictions in how Buchan sees the roles of the two friends, to whom all other friends and allies are ancillary. Yet, in my judgment, the writer's subterranean instinct which made the straightforward and uncomplicated Hannay the essential agent of good, while Clanroyden is a decoration on the surface of the action, was a true one. If complexity and conspiracy are the marks of villainy, and simplicity and vulnerability the marks of good, then Hannay is a far better hero for bringing out the essence of the conflict. For it is another essential part of the Buchan morality that the villain is in every technical respect the superior of the hero. Lumley is cleverer than Leithen; the Black Stone is immensely superior to Hannay as, even more so, is Medina. In *The Courts of the Morning* this principle is given an unusual twist when the villain, Castor, is kidnapped by Clanroyden and made first the theoretical and then the actual leader of the rebels, whose collective instinct for good reforms his character—though he dies at the end, to expiate his earlier sins. So vastly superior, indeed, are the villains that the triumph of good is incredibly difficult to bring about, and can be achieved only by the most stringent assertion of the simple verities and virtues, accompanied by the character-

istics conferred on the heroes by their possession of small and entertaining abilities, like Hannay's capacity for cracking codes and Pieter Pienaar's facilities for tracking and disguise.

If Hannay is the real hero and Clanroyden an appendage to him there is nonetheless something powerful and important in common between them. It is an anarchic contempt for the institutions and practices of the civilization they are defending. In *The Thirty-Nine Steps* Hannay gibes at Imperialism. When, in *The Island of Sheep*, he is an M.P., he is a singularly unconscientious one. Clanroyden is both bored by his inheritance of his title and rather borne down by the responsibilities attached to it. The Empire as such, and its institutions, are rarely if ever the subject of praise: patriotism comes out only when England herself is in peril or when what might be called the morality of the Secret Service comes into play. Clanroyden escapes from his estates for a dangerous jaunt in South America; he is singularly contemptuous of the House of Lords and, when sitting on a government commission in China, spends most of his time hunting in junk shops. The coherence and order which the heroes are defending is one established by their tastes, their willingness to make sacrifices to defend the basic stability of Western civilization which, it is clear, has little necessarily to do with the outward forms of that civilization, and their going into action principally at the behest of what might be called the conspirators of good—men like themselves, Sir Walter Bullivant and Blenkiron, who spend their lives defending things by stealth and in secret, against evil and desperate conspiracies. Of course it is easy to see what Buchan liked and, in his public life, valued: South Africa, the Anglo-American connection, his beloved Canada. But his vision of these things is not integrated into the struggle between good and evil which he describes, which is far more elemental and far more abstract. So much is this the case that, in the later books, Buchan moved the scene of conflict away from civilization altogether, and out into the wilds. In *The Island of Sheep*, when the heroes are eventually assembled in the safety of Laverlaw, with all their possessions about them, and in no danger from the villains, the remarkable decision is taken to move the scene of the conflict to a wild and lonely island in the Norlands. In part this is because Haraldsen, having spent years fleeing from his enemies, and conscious of the burden he has imposed on Hannay and Clanroyden, wants to find his soul by defying his enemies on his own ground. In part it is for an even more remarkable—and rather spurious—reason: that Clanroyden feels D'Ingraville, essentially an urban desperado, will be easier to deal with in a wild environment. (It is perhaps unnecessary to remark that the initial conflict with D'Ingraville, in South America, takes place in what Clanroyden considers to be an unfavourable situation for the villain and in which he nonetheless wreaks considerable damage).

These inconsistencies do not affect the excitement of the books, partly because they are devices to get everybody into the most desperate situation, one in which physical combat will become unavoidable; but largely because they encapsulate Buchan's determination to reduce the conflict between good and evil to its elements. That his use of the devices was not, however, wholly unconscious is shown by Hannay's thoughts on Clanroyden's decision to set out for the island of sheep: he reflects that, at the end of the previous adventure—*The Three Hostages*—when Medina was vanquished, but still alive, Clanroyden had sent him to a deer forest in Scotland to get away in isolation from the threat Medina posed to his life: the sequence of events ended with a grim battle between Hannay and Medina, in which the former was badly injured and the latter killed.

There is thus an awareness on the part of the author that he is contriving a situation in which his heroes are at a disadvantage. Not only do they regularly find themselves in this position, but they are also willing to put the values and the civilization they are supposed to be defending in danger as well. At the end of *The Three Hostages* when Medina, who has been engaged in a conspiracy to destroy civilization, is beaten, the heroes recall his political ambitions: they undertake to release him in return for the release of the final hostage, and to leave him free to pursue his political career unharmed and unhampered. It is only because Medina rejects this offer that he is finally destroyed.

The elemental theme is given a further twist in the Leithen books and it is, indeed, predominant in all the later works. The Leithen saga is less coherent and developed than that featuring the adventures of Hannay but, since Leithen is a figure rather based on Buchan himself there is an intimacy about his adventures. The first Leithen book features the conspiracy preoccupation at its most intense and abstract. The last to be completed—*Sick Heart River*—is concentrated on an individual finding his soul. Though the adventure—a trek in search of a lost man through the wilds of Canada—is exciting, there are no less than three separate characters who set out for the wilds to find themselves, and who abandon the comforts as well as the responsibilities of civilization. The first is Leithen, who is dying of a cancer; the second is a French-Canadian who has settled and made good in America but who suffers a nervous breakdown and must return to his roots; the third is a mad half-breed guide, searching for the Sick Heart River which is the source of happiness. One of the most interesting features of the book is the way in which Buchan dwells in the early stages—when Leithen is preparing to undertake the mission of searching for the missing man, with a growing awareness that he is doing the job to help himself rather than for any other reason—on the nature and lineaments of the American upper class society which he so admired and which he regarded as having made an indispensable contribution to the Anglo-American alliance. The valuation he places on this society is clear beyond dispute: but he nonetheless concludes that the troubled French-Canadian who has been injected into it was right to flee, and to find his own *raison d'être* away from it.

Great though the emphasis is in this novel on the existential, individual personality, however, and much though Buchan seems to opt for the individual over his duties to society, there is a definitive resolution at the end. Leithen catches up with the two men he is chasing and the discovery that the Sick Heart River is a deadland, a source of evil rather than joy, restores the two to sanity. Meanwhile,

through his exertions and the climate Leithen recovers from his disease, and has every prospect of a long life. Two events then occur. The Second World War breaks out, and attention is drawn to an Indian village whose inhabitants are dying of apathy and disease. Leithen immediately devotes his remaining strength to helping the Indians, sacrificing his life in so doing; the guides depart for the war; and the French-Canadian, restored in mental and spiritual health, returns to the United States. The thesis then is that a period of self-discovery, self-exploration and self-fulfilment, especially through toil and adventure, is necessary, but only as a prelude to undertaking duty. The self-discovery in *Sick Heart River* is, of course, the counterpart of the adventures in the Hannay books which, though they take place outside the comforting borders of established civilization, and concentrate essentially on the personalities and adventures of the heroes, are nonetheless about the defence of civilization's fragile order.

On the subject of duty and inclination Hannay's mind is divided. In *The Three Hostages* he is extremely reluctant to undertake the search for the kidnapped victims of Medina: he was good at that sort of thing, he explains, only during the war, when he was strung up to an exceptional pitch of endeavour. Now he has settled in his rut in the country and, though his conscience is troubled, he will have no part of future adventure. In *The Island of Sheep,* however, he is, though older again, hungry for adventure, and discontented with the pleasant lot he enjoys, though he feels it irresponsible in a man of his years to thirst for the excitements of youth. The dilemma in the latter book is resolved by his discovery that he has a long contracted family obligation to Haraldsen. In *The Three Hostages* he undertakes the task because his wife brings home to him the realization that the parents of the kidnapped victims are in the same position as the Hannays would be if their own child were subjected to a similar threat, and that it behoves Hannay, as a parent, to act in defence of other parents. The civilizational stability, then, which the Buchan heroes are defending is much less a matter of state and high politics, of Empire and national defence—though all these things come into it—than a matter of the common fabric of life and the dangers which threaten it.

If good, then, is elemental and flattens out the important characters—making Hannay less interesting than Clanroyden—evil is also elemental though, paradoxically, it enlivens the characters. All the Buchan villains have some element of grandeur about them. "Mad and bad she might be" he wrote of Hilda von Einem, "but she was also great". During one of his periods offstage in *The Island of Sheep* Sandy Clanroyden spends a weekend with D'Ingraville in the latter's chateau. When a horrified Hannay rebukes him for his folly Clanroyden explains that D'Ingraville, who was descended from a Crusader family fallen on evil days, would never harm a guest in his own home. There are, of course, other characters in the novels who are unsympathetic to the Buchan ethos of struggle and duty—notably Lancelot Wake, the courageous pacifist in *Mr. Standfast*—who are dealt with honourably and sympathetically, but they are not villains. The sympathy and respect his characters show for the villains—though these, as T. E. Lawrence wrote were "superhuman and grotesque"—revealed another aspect of his concern for the elemental. For no character in his books is wholly evil: he is merely driven along by the force of evil. There can thus exist, side by side in a single character, elements of good and elements of evil: it is when the evil predominates that danger, desperation and adventure arise. Thus the struggle of the stories is with Nature herself and, though this comes out most clearly in the outdoor scenes—the Alpine trekking of *Mr. Standfast* and the North Canadian journey of *Sick Heart River*—it is also clearly present in the more human struggles between heroes and villains. It is a curious fact, moreover, that these struggles, though they often end in physical combat, end in combats of different types. At the end of *The Three Hostages* there is the fight to the death between Hannay and Medina already mentioned. It is perhaps Buchan's most powerful piece of action writing, in which a combination of Hannay's skill—characteristically, he is at a disadvantage, having no ammunition for his gun—and luck serve to defeat the enemy. Victory and defeat in the battle are wholly logical, and quite justified in the telling. At the end of *The Island of Sheep,* however, not only does D'Ingraville mount a most incompetent siege of the house, but the heroes mount a singularly incompetent defence. Both Hannay and Clanroyden offer exceptionally tempting targets to the enemy, of which he does not avail; and they, likewise, deliberately forgo opportunities to gun him down. The situation is resolved only when Haraldsen, in an insane fit, rushes the whole body of the enemy, carries D'Ingraville off, and throws him into the sea. While the other villains are still dumb with shock reinforcements, discovered by the children, arrive and apprehend them.

This situation, which is complemented in less complete ways in many other Buchan stories, is something that makes him almost unique among the great thriller writers, whose heroes as well as whose villains are supermen or quasi-supermen. There is much accident and much self-denial in the Buchan stories. Hannay, for example, at the end of his struggle with Medina offers to help his enemy. The German count who is the villain of *Mr. Standfast* dies accidentally. The ingenuity, intelligence and skill of the heroes is best deployed in minor episodes rather than in the grand conclusions. Thus Lombard's escape to Scotland is, for ability and skill, greatly superior to the actions of Hannay and Clanroyden—supposedly the true men of action—at the climax of the book. In so skilful a writer this calls for some explanation. It seems that Buchan resisted bringing things to final and brutal conclusions through human agency: obscure and mysterious forces of fate had to take a hand. His interest in such forces comes out most clearly in the large number of his short stories dealing with the magical, the supernatural and the long buried myths of the ages. There can hardly be any doubt that, for all his own practicality of temperament, and in spite of the fact that he could discipline his imagination and bring it to order with great success, he was deeply moved by his inability to resolve his own view of human life and identity and by his inability to banish from his mind the concern with mystery and the movements of fate inherited with his Celtic temperament. He dramatized—some would say trivialized—these matters in order to find material for his thrillers, but they retained a powerful hold

over him, and the climaxes of his adventures are deeply influenced by a sense of outside intervention in the resolution. As therefore he was concerned with the existential elements of the human character, and with the most abstract conception of civilization and the forces threatening it, so he was equally but obscurely influenced by a sense of powers and forces beyond him, and beyond his heroes.

The Buchan stories offer a rich seam for endless speculation about his preoccupation, enthusiasms and ideas. Mrs. Adam Smith has shrewdly pointed out how current interests and hobbies enter in great detail into the sinew of the novels. But it is possible, by close study, to separate intermittent from continuing concerns. The things that have been most often associated with Buchan's novels by his critics—the ethic of success (Graham Greene), the snobbery (Gertrude Himmelfarb) [see excerpts dated 1941 and 1968], Eton (Janet Adam Smith), are in fact fairly superficial. When he tried, in *A Prince of the Captivity,* to treat of a great variety of political subjects which then preoccupied him, and to integrate them fully into his judgment of the struggle between good and evil in the book, he became wordy and ponderous. Yet the book itself reveals more than any other what fired his imagination. In it he tries to inject the elemental into everything—labour disputes, party politics, industrial relations, big business; and he tries to see each of these phenomena as, in their different ways, summarizing a basic, inescapable and simple conflict. It does not come off, not only because the subjects are intractable, but because his imagination did not grasp that they were inessential to—hostile to—his genius, which was for getting down to the basics of his story, and the basics of his characters, while giving the illusion that he and they had a very wide range of interests. These, in so far as they are complicated, though enjoyable, are as spurious as the multitude of geographical references designed to give excitement and substance to the off-stage lives of his characters.

It is his concern with the elemental and the existential that gives Buchan his core of fascination. While a novelist proper tries to deal with these themes through complexity and analysis, a story-teller tries to do so through clash, conflict and simplicity. There is something of the dramatist—in the simple sense of that word—about any thriller-writer worth his salt. He projects and throws up on a screen conflicts which are basically serious and complicated, and he resolves them simply and in favour of the good. It is not necessarily an intellectual process—and Buchan was scornful of people who took his "shockers" too seriously—but it is a process in which deep preoccupations make their appearance, even if unconsciously. Buchan was, after all, a serious man, who took his public duties with the utmost conscientiousness. He did not metamorphose his personality when he came to write adventure stories: he merely relaxed, and indulged some of the whims of his temperament and imagination. But the subjects and the problems that most motivated his professional and public life most exited him also, particularly when he wrote fiction. What is therefore particularly striking about his career is that a man so much in the thick of a complicated and arduous public life should have sat so lightly on the things that went to make up that life, and should have, so close to the surface of his mind, a concern with things very basic and even very primitive.

It is, of course, part of the delight of the adventure story that it should be serious without being ponderous: when the hero is in difficulties we care nothing about him if he is merely a frivolity; we care only if we have been persuaded that what he is doing is important, and that the struggle he is waging is consequential. Far from being light-hearted and escapist, the outstanding thriller is about very serious things indeed, but dealt with in a way and in a form which eliminates the complexities of both life and art. That is the fundamental source of its attraction and, in conveying that attraction with the aid of all the pyrotechnics of which he was master, Buchan established his supremacy in his field. (pp. 375-86)

*Patrick Cosgrave, "John Buchan's Thrillers: The Ideology of Character," in* The Round Table, *Vol. LXII, No. 247, July, 1972, pp. 375-86.*

## Barbara B. Brown   (essay date 1979)

[*In the following excerpt, Brown contrasts Buchan's major biographies with those characteristic of the "New Biography" movement of his time, praising Buchan's thorough scholarship, balanced judgment of his subjects, and accomplished prose style.*]

Biography, established by the works of Johnson and Boswell as a literary genre at the end of the eighteenth century, should have flourished under the stimulus of the Romantic revolution with its emphasis upon subjectivity and individuality. Yet despite the continuance of all forms of life-writing, particularly autobiography, in the early nineteenth century, and despite such biographies as Moore's *Byron,* Lockhart's elaborate *Life of Scott,* and the works of Froude, Gosse, and Carlyle, by the 1840's pseudo-biography, neo-hagiography, had stifled biography. Carlyle's often-quoted comment is descriptive: "How delicate, how decent, is English biography, bless its mealy mouth!" In the early twentieth century, biography as a literary art was revived by the movement labelled by Edward Hayes O'Neill as "The New Biography," dominated in England by the works of Lytton Strachey. With Boswell's *Johnson* acclaimed as a masterpiece and with Strachey's critical strictures and examples of biographical writing—*Eminent Victorians* (1918), *Queen Victoria* (1921), *Elizabeth and Essex* (1928)—stimulating discussions by Sir Harold Nicolson, Virginia Woolf, and others of the Bloomsbury Group, biography was recognized once more as a form of literary art.

The critical problem now was to examine, to describe, to define that form of art. Strachey's insistence upon the biographer's right to "maintain his own freedom of spirit" and to "lay bare the facts of the case as he understands them," his ironic detachment and tone, his artistic control of style, his dramatic touch were influential in establishing the form of "The New Biography" and also the awareness that biography, *sui generis,* is a work of art.

But the excesses of "The New Biography"—emphasis upon self-expression of the biographer, upon the extravagant and irresponsible use of literary devices such as irony and symbolism, and upon the free interpretation, even deliberate distortion of biographical facts—proved more harmful than beneficial to the definition as well as to the development of the new and increasingly popular art form. These very excesses, particularly as found in Strachey's many imitators in both England and America, revealed not only the potentialities but also the dangers of biographical writing. By 1939, for instance, Virginia Woolf, evaluating Strachey's experiments in biography, concluded that Strachey's works proved that the art of biography, not he, had failed. The movement that was "The New Biography" was ending, and after the Second World War its qualities were to become part of fictionalized biographies.

Yet contemporary with "The New Biography" but quite apart from the popular movement of Strachey and his imitators, writers like John Buchan were producing major biographies that attest to the continuing validity of the tradition established by Johnson and Boswell, a tradition centering around basic values of truth, historical accuracy, completeness, the worth of the individual, and a belief in the power of biographical writing to contribute to both knowledge and virtue. Buchan's four full-length biographies—**Montrose, Sir Walter Scott, Oliver Cromwell,** and **Augustus**—the **Scott** called by G. M. Trevelyan the "best one-volumed biography in the language," provide evidence that the main stream of English-American biography continues to be defined by the tradition of Johnson and Boswell.

The position of biographers like Buchan in the history of twentieth-century biography is only now becoming apparent; but it is their works, their artistic and scholarly principles, which provide a steady foundation for such solidly constructed contemporary biographies as Clifford's *Young Sam Johnson,* Lash's *Eleanor and Franklin,* Catherine Drinker Bowen's *The Lion and The Throne,* Fraser's *Cromwell,* Longford's *Wellington,* and the literary biographies of Walter Jackson Bate. Consequently a fresh examination of the biographical works of Buchan and of their critical reception in England and America not only provides a measure of belated justice to one of the principal biographers of the early twentieth century, but also helps to fill one evident gap in our understanding of the English-American biographical tradition.

Buchan's interest in biography spans his literary career, beginning with such essays as **Sir Walter Raleigh** (1897) and **"Nine Brasenose Worthies,"** one of whom is Walter Pater (1899), written while he was an undergraduate at Brasenose College, Oxford, through the four full-length works, shorter biographies, three memoirs, several collections of sketches, and the autobiographical **Memory Hold-the-Door,** sent to his publisher only two weeks before his death in 1940. In addition to his extensive contribution to biography, Buchan wrote thirty novels, seven books of short stories, sixty-six other books, twenty-six pamphlets and sixty-three contributions to other books, plus a great number of articles, many of them sketches reflecting his interest in biography. (pp. 328-30)

Many contemporaries knew John Buchan, or Lord Tweedsmuir, only as politician and statesman. Many readers knew Buchan only for his fiction, his series of exciting adventures of Richard Hannay and Edward Leithen, men of action, memorable for their courage and spirited intelligence and cool daring. But those readers who knew him as serious historian and as biographer, a group admittedly smaller in number, knew the works which Buchan himself believed to represent his most lasting contribution to literature. Popular and scholarly reviewers on both sides of the Atlantic poured lavish praise on Buchan as biographer, historian, and master stylist.

That so prolific and successful a writer as Buchan has not received more critical attention since his death in 1940 is difficult to understand. In the 1940's and '50's, while his popular fiction continued to be read all over the world, perhaps it and his reputation as Lord Tweedsmuir, statesman, overshadowed that of John Buchan, historian and biographer. But a more persuasive reason would seem to be that critical examination of biographical writing as literature continues to be tardy even in the twentieth century. Some assessment of his contributions as a writer was included in the memoir *John Buchan by His Wife and Friends* [see Susan Tweedsmuir entry in Further Reading], with statements, among others, by A. L. Rowse and G. M. Trevelyan. In 1949 a brief life of Buchan, no longer in print, *Mr. Buchan, Writer, Life of the First Lord Tweedsmuir* by Arthur C. Turner [see Further Reading] cited his *Montrose, Sir Walter Scott,* and *Augustus* as "standard works on their subjects, though enjoyed also by the general public." A fine biography in 1965 by Janet Adam Smith, *John Buchan* [see Further Reading], provides factual material concerning Buchan's life and career, but offers little critical assessment. Vivian Newport's American dissertation, "The Biographical Writing of John Buchan," and David Daniell's British publication, *The Interpreter's House* [see Further Reading], have given evidence of continuing scholarly interest. But, although the dissertation contains one chapter of analysis, the work is overburdened with summary, and there is little attempt to consider Buchan and the biographical tradition. Daniell's perceptive volume is devoted largely to Buchan's adventure stories, and allows only a few pages for an account of his biographies. Indeed, it is fair to say that there has been no extended critical discussion of Buchan's role in the development of twentieth-century biographical tradition.

The significance of Buchan's position in that tradition is founded largely upon his four full-length biographies and upon the principles of biographical art that emerge from them. The first, *Montrose* (1928), establishes Buchan's methods as a biographer.

From his Oxford days Buchan had been fascinated by the military genius and tragic end of the early seventeenth-century Scots leader James Graham, fifth Earl and first Marquis of Montrose. An early sketch, *The Marquis of Montrose,* was published in 1913. The book drew mixed reviews, perhaps a natural result of the controversial nature of Montrose, but also an indication of certain strengths and weaknesses of the biographer. One reviewer found the work "very readable" and declared that "best of all is the author's sense of proportion and perspective." Another spoke of Buchan's "vivid, incisive, and picturesque style." Still another, however, attacked the work for "elementary blunders, all of which told in favor of Montrose," and objected to the work as a "perfunctory performance, biased and inaccurate, unfair and untrustworthy," and urged Buchan to "eschew historical writing and devote himself to avowed fiction."

But the result of such strictures was to make Buchan all the more determined to prove himself a serious writer of history and biography. During the next fifteen years he devoted time (in the midst of a host of other activities) to a study of manuscript sources dealing with Montrose, supplemented by an exhaustive reading of the voluminous pamphlet literature of the period. As he states in the Preface to the 1928 *Montrose:*

> In September, 1913, I published a short sketch of Montrose which dealt chiefly with his campaigns. The book went out of print very soon, and it was not reissued because I cherished the hope of making it the basis of a larger work, in which the background of seventeenth-century politics and religion should be more fully portrayed. I also felt that many of the judgments in the sketch were exaggerated and hasty. During the last fifteen years I have been collecting material for the understanding of a career which must rank among the marvels of our history, and of a mind and character which seem to me in a high degree worthy of the attention of the modern reader.

In the same Preface, Buchan states his aim as a biographer is to "present a great figure in its appropriate setting." He acknowledges the controversial nature of Montrose's character and career, and the difficulties of unbiased interpretation: "In a domain where the dust of controversy has not yet been laid, I cannot hope to find for my views universal acceptance, but they have not been reached without an earnest attempt to discover the truth." He thus learns early the importance to the biographer of exhaustive research in primary materials, of the need for balanced, judicial assessment of both his subject and of those materials, and, above all, of a conscious devotion to truth as his first aim and final goal. In this 1928 version, Buchan, still fascinated by Montrose's romantic nature and career, is at last enabled to understand him as a man.

To write with appreciation of the life of Montrose was a task Buchan was uniquely prepared to perform by his devotion to the Scottish past, his Presbyterian heritage, his own nature. In Montrose, Buchan found the qualities that most appealed to his image of the ideal in man: physical courage and daring, the courage of intelligence, and a devout commitment to "pure duty and pure reason." The Marquis had that "single-hearted gift for deeds which usually belongs to the man whose vigour is not impaired by thought." Clearly Montrose, the "Presbyterian Cavalier," was for Buchan a symbol of the possible synthesis in man of thought and action: "armed and mailed Reason, Philosophy with its sword unsheathed." The Marquis comes to life because of Buchan's knowledge of the seventeenth-century manuscripts he had studied, his own walks on the Scottish hills, his knowledge of the art of war, and the attitudes and feelings he himself had for Scotland and the Kirk. "I am sending you my Montrose," he writes to his friend Stair Gillon, "because (1) it is a guide to the topography of nearly all Scotland and (2) it contains most of my philosophy of life."

In this first major biography Buchan illustrates that special relationship, particularly descriptive of much twentieth-century biography, in which an intimate bond develops between a subject long dead and his live biographer, called by Paul Murray Kendall "a simulated life-relationship" and by Mark Schorer a "symbiotic relationship." And this relationship, more and more evidenced in twentieth-century biography, has replaced the significant life-relationship of such great biographical works of the past as Boswell's *Life of Johnson,* Roper's *Life of Sir Thomas More,* or Tacitus' *Agricola.* Only from such a relationship can a biographer hope to bring his subject to life. It is significant that Buchan's view of Montrose, foreshadowed by Carlyle and presented briefly in the histories of S. R. Gardiner and Andrew Lang, is now generally accepted, and that his book has been recognized as the standard work on the subject, affecting the interpretations of all later writers.

For Buchan it was the book that established his reputation as serious historian and biographer. A. L. Rowse considered it Buchan's "chief contribution to historical research . . . it is written wholly from original sources and he had various additions and corrections of his own to offer in writing it. . . . It all goes to make a masterly historical biography." Or from Augustus Muir: "***Montrose*** put him in the front rank as delineator of character and it showed his grasp of the complex movements and fiery ideals of a period that had been dimmed by the dust of controversy . . . it was acclaimed as the definitive life of the Marquis of Montrose." ***Montrose*** is also a demonstration of Buchan's power as a literary artist. Reviews repeatedly cite his masterful prose style: the work is "narrated by Mr. Buchan in prose of a quality which few historians achieve," and—from *The Spectator*—"the great Marquis has found a great chronicler."

In 1932, the centenary of the death of Scott, Buchan published his second Scottish biography, ***Sir Walter Scott.*** There had been no new life of Scott since the seven volumes of Lockhart. The centenary, Buchan said, is "my excuse for the cutting of some of the lines of Lockhart's imperishable memorial, and for an attempt at a valuation of the man and his work after the lapse of a hundred years. It is a book I was bound one day to write, for I have had the fortune to be born and bred under the shadow of that great tradition." Again Buchan's subject had chosen him. Scott, in Buchan's words, was "the greatest, because the most representative of Scotsmen, since in his mind and character he sums up more fully than any other the idiomatic qualities of his countrymen and translates them into a universal tongue. . . . He is, with Burns, her [Scotland's] great liberator and reconciler."

Buchan's task as Scott biographer was for several reasons more difficult than it had been in writing the life of Mon-

*Buchan as a lieutenant colonel in 1916.*

trose. ***Sir Walter Scott,*** like the earlier book, is based on extensive research, the life fully documented, not only from Lockhart and other biographers of Scott such as R. P. Gillies, James Skein, and James Hogg, but also from Scott's *Private Letter-Books, Familiar Letters,* and the *Journal.* Buchan, however, is less free to make original use of his sources, here re-telling a life whose details and accomplishments are made familiar by one of the most complete of the lengthy Victorian biographies. The carefully detailed summary of Scott's life and career is arranged with stress on chronology and with an unswerving focus on the subject that was perhaps not possible in the treatment of Montrose. That Buchan was successful in his compression of the details of Scott's life is attested by Theodore Spencer's review in *The Atlantic:* "Comparison with Lockhart's great work only increases one's respect for the way in which Mr. Buchan has included, in so short a space, nearly everything that illuminates his subject."

And, as in the ***Montrose,*** Buchan is obliged to place his subject fully into context, describing Scottish Border society, Scott's financial disaster in terms of nineteenth-century credit and publishing practices, the tangled business arrangements with Ballantyne and Constable. The review in the *Times Literary Supplement* (3 March 1932) stated that Buchan "brings to his study just that trained historical imagination which by placing Scott accurately in his time and place shows us the real man in the comprehensiveness of his genius. . . ."

Further, and of great significance, Buchan is here writing not only a life but a literary or critical biography, containing a review and evaluation of most of the novels, citing their best passages, analyzing characters and themes, all without serious interruption to the narrative details of the life. Critics had tended to linger over Scott's personality at the expense of his books; Buchan's examination of Scott as writer was a needed corrective to this tendency and a stimulation for further critical discussion. In his words, "The wide popular acceptance as a classic has had a paralyzing effect on the critical study of Scott." In one of two summary chapters at the end of the book, "The Writer," Buchan gives an enthusiastic, possibly too enthusiastic, appraisal of Scott's achievements. Perhaps David Cecil's review in *The Spectator* (19 March 1932) best assesses Buchan's critical judgment:

> It is the conspicuous merit of Colonel Buchan's book that it does justice to Scott as writer. . . . Buchan is the first man to try to give a full and adequate estimate of Scott's work. He is perhaps a trifle over-reverent. No service is done to Scott's reputation by praising his constructive powers or defending the tepid nullity of so many of his heroes. Still, it is more important to praise rightly than to blame rightly; and Colonel Buchan praises superbly. He looks below the surface; he admires Scott for his intrinsic not for his superficial merits; he discerns and brilliantly analyzes his magnificent Shakespearean sympathy with human nature; and he has that wider culture which enables him to assess his merits by comparison with the great writers of other schools and other countries.

Or this from *The New Statesman and Nation:* "the criticism is perhaps the best that has been written on the subject. . . . Buchan understands what Scott attempted, and judges him in terms of it—a rare gift in critics of fiction. . . . The book leaves one richer in experience not only of Scott but of the craft of letters" (12 March 1932).

And finally, there is the difficulty of dealing with Scott's character, "the real man," both sympathetically and, at the same time, impartially. Buchan, despite the tendency toward hero-worship, sees Scott's faults: his opposition to Parliamentary Reform, his extravagance, his unkindness to Constable, his secrecy over money. In summing up Scott's character in a final chapter, "The Man," Buchan exhibits, as he himself said of another biographer: "the discriminating affection which enables him to read deep into the heart of the man." This "discriminating affection," illustrating again the stimulated life-relationship between live biographer and dead subject, is that affection which produces the sense in the biography of the reality of a life's being lived, of the re-creation of the personality and character of the living person. It is to this quality in Buchan's *Sir Walter Scott* that George M. Trevelyan most likely paid tribute in his memorable dictum: "It is

not only the best one-volumed book on Scott, but the best one-volumed biography in the language."

In the same month in which the *Scott* was published, March 1932, Buchan began specific work for his next biography, *Oliver Cromwell,* finished by January of 1934. The years of study for his *Montrose* had served to prepare Buchan for the writing of its natural collateral work. Again Buchan had selected as his subject one of the most controversial figures in English history; he correctly calls Cromwell "a mystery to his contemporaries and an enigma to his successors." It is significant that the life of Cromwell continues to be re-written and is, for the biographer, not so much a task of original research as of re-interpretation. In his Preface Buchan declares that his aim is two-fold: to produce a "companion piece" to his *Montrose* and to provide his own interpretations of the man he considers the "greatest figure" in England during the seventeenth century and the "greatest of English monarchs." Acknowledging that he disagrees with some earlier portrayals of Cromwell, Buchan sums up his purpose:

> My aim has been, in the words of Edmund Gosse, to give "a faithful portrait of a soul in its adventure through life." I hope I may claim at any rate I have not attempted to constrain a great man in a formula.

Buchan's portrayal of Cromwell is balanced, judicial. He does not deny, or hide, for example, atrocities committed by Cromwell's troops during the Civil War, but he describes Cromwell's attitudes in such phrases as "in war he had been notably merciful," "great mercy," and "wistful tenderness." Central to Buchan's interpretation is the inconsistency he sees between Cromwell's character and the actions he was forced to take:

> Paradox is the fiber of his character and career. . . . a devotee of the law, he was forced often to be lawless; a civilian to the core, he had to maintain himself by the sword; with a passion to construct, his task was chiefly to destroy; the most scrupulous of men, he had to ride roughshod over his own scruples and those of others; the tenderest, he had continually to harden his heart; the most English of our greater figures, he spent his life in opposition to the majority of Englishmen; a realist, he was condemned to build that which would not last.

Cromwell was, in Buchan's words, "in his good and ill, his frailty and strength, typical in almost every quality of his own English people, but with these qualities so magnified as to become epic and universal." Essentially sympathetic, then, Buchan attempts to explain but not to deny Cromwell's faults. And because Cromwell, for Buchan, was the "iron man of action whose consuming purpose was at all times the making of his soul," the biography examines the Protector's spiritual life in close detail; and it is with a summary of Cromwell's religious, not his political creed, that Buchan concludes his account. He was conscious of his own special knowledge of Cromwell's intellectual milieu, a knowledge which clearly produced again that "symbiotic relationship" between dead subject and live biographer stressed by Kendall and Schorer. In Buchan's words, "I had the supreme advantage of having been brought up in a Calvinistic atmosphere, so I was able to write of his religious life with some understanding. For several years I lived chiefly in the seventeenth century, reading acres of its divinity and many hundreds of its pamphlets. Cromwell with all his imperfections seemed to me not only admirable but lovable, and I tried in my book to present the warm human side of him."

For historical background Buchan uses primarily the works of S. R. Gardiner and Sir Charles Firth, but repeatedly reveals his intimacy with Cromwell's own letters and speeches, as well as with state papers and historical manuscripts. He gives "full reference for all Oliver's own written and spoken words." Structured on a firm historical basis, the biography gives evidence of considerable research and scholarship, setting Cromwell in the context of his period with complex details of strife in the halls of Parliament as well as on the field of battle. His first chapter, documenting the condition of England in the years before the Civil War, is a superb historical reconstruction of the milieu. And the scene in which Charles is sent to the scaffold is so dramatically striking and successful that it has been included by David Cecil in his *Anthology of Modern Biography*. A. L. Rowse also commends Buchan's portrait of seventeenth-century life:

> He read, conscientiously and critically, all the sources and authorities he visited, as an historian should, the places and studied the battlefields. He had a very good understanding of military history. . . . But he brought something more to his study of Cromwell—his own gifts of mind. . . . Here we see the breadth of his sympathies at their most advantageous, enabling him to thread his way with fairness and understanding through the maze of sects and sectaries. . . . There is an essential justice of mind—the proper attitude of the historian, though not all possess it—in his treatment of men on both sides, Cromwell and Charles, Laud and Strafford, Ireton and Vane. . . . With Cromwell himself . . . Buchan had an inner sympathy that makes him at last clear to one. I believe that his view of Cromwell—that character so open to controversy, the subject of so much debate—is essentially right.

The reception of *Cromwell* confirmed Buchan's reputation, established by his *Montrose* and *Scott.* For example, this from the English *Saturday Review:* "It is no exaggeration that this is probably the most convincing biography that has appeared of a great Englishman" (15 Sept. 1934). G. M. Trevelyan called the biography the "best book of all pictures of Cromwell as a man" and declared Buchan's "the best book on him that our generation is likely to produce." "Buchan," he added, "is one of the few really effective historical writers of our time" (*The Spectator,* 7 Sept. 1934).

At the time of the publication of *Cromwell* in 1934, the subject of dictators was becoming a pressing reality for many of the countries of Europe. Threats to established power, and perhaps his own position of high political rank, if not power, as Governor-General of Canada in 1935, moved Buchan to return to an ambition of his undergraduate days, a biography of Augustus, published in 1937. "I am conscious that my interpretation of Augustus is a personal thing," he writes in the Preface, "coloured insensibly by my own beliefs. But, since the historian is most at home in an age which resembles his own, I hope that the convulsions of our time give an insight into the problems of the early Roman empire which was perhaps unattainable by scholars who lived in earlier days" (*Augustus*). Buchan also points out the difficulty of finding reliable source materials for the life and times of Augustus: "Imperfect literary sources can be supplemented by important archeological and epigraphical matter"; but since other materials are scant, a principal guide must be tradition. In preparing to write the biography Buchan had spent many months rereading the Latin and Greek texts. What his careful scholarship produces is much more than a life of Augustus: it is a picture, a wide panorama, of Augustus and his times, of the whole life of the civilized world during his remarkable century. Buchan proposes no formula, no organic pattern of history; if he hints at a thesis, it is perhaps the examination of power politics.

Buchan gives to his portrait of Augustus the same intuitive sympathy he had for Cromwell. "The more I study him" he wrote to L. S. Amery, "the more I feel that he was probably the greatest practical genius in statesmanship the world has ever seen. He was the Scotsman *in excelsis,* not rich in ideas, but immensely good at giving practical effect to those of other men." Augustus was a great man, a man of genius, because he was a man of mind: "he gave the world a new and rational way of life." He had a great instinct for reality and was the "least romantic of great men." A builder, a creator of empire, with "that practical wisdom which is the proper attitude of a ruler," he developed a government at once "expert and professional." Buchan affirms his belief that "the Augustan constitution remains one of the major products of human intelligence" and that "The true achievement of Augustus is that he saved the world from disintegration."

In 1940 Buchan wrote in the autobiographical *Memory Hold-the-Door:* "Augustus seemed to me to embody all the virtues of a dictator, when a dictator was needed, and to have tried valiantly to provide against the perils. The book was kindly received by scholars in Britain and America. . . ." In his last statement Buchan was being characteristically modest. The reception of his *Augustus* was significant not only as evidence of Buchan's final achievement as biographer—his masterpiece, in the opinion of many reviewers—but as an indication that the influence of the stylistic characteristics of "The New Biography" was coming to an end. Critics accorded extravagant praise to *Augustus* as a work of biography:

> its wise, eloquent and sensitive pages everywhere bear traces of a scholar's scrupulous diligence . . . excels in characterization;

> the work of a real scholar and trained historian. . . . it is the work of a brilliant stylist . . . who does not . . . contribute thrills by means of brilliant but unconvincing hypotheses. . . . The economic and social life of the early Roman empire is brilliantly portrayed.

> steers with admirable success a middle course

between the uncritical hero-worship which denies the existence of the least defect and the unjust detraction which ascribes Augustus' successes to his coadjutors. . . .

it is nearly a perfect biography . . . it supersedes
all other English books now existing on its subject.

Such praise clearly demonstrates what Buchan had
achieved. His biographical writing exhibits brilliance of
style without literary extravagance of irony and symbolism, capturing the reader's interest with a sweep of narrative that is based upon historical truth and a scrutiny of
all available sources, not upon distortions of fact to fit
some pre-conceived interpretation. Here is well-balanced
estimate of character that does not put the subject of the
work on a pedestal nor debunk that subject to make the
work more sensational. In his full-length biographies
Buchan had exhibited mastery of three biographical
forms: historical biography, literary biography, and, in
**Augustus,** the life-and-times biography. In them all he had
demonstrated anew that a biographer's devotion to historical truth and to a sympathetic yet balanced presentation
of his subject can result in life-writing that is at once instructive and entertaining.

It seems evident that both the impact of "The New Biography" and Buchan's contribution to biography are bene-
fiting from a needed perspective. Early twentieth-century
biographers like Buchan, who continued to write outside
"The New Biography" movement, have been inadequately treated by literary historians and by critics of English-
American biography, critics whose attention has been
drawn to the movement in either excessive praise or condemnation.

Today a re-assessment of the post-World War I development of English-American biography is needed, taking
into greater account biographers like Buchan, who wrote
in what now may be considered the main stream of the
biographical tradition, reaching from Johnson and Boswell to the works of contemporary biographers. Johnson's
devotion to truth, his belief in the inherent didactic value
in the presentation of any life, his refusal to write panegyric, and his mastery of style were the guideposts that Boswell was to follow. Boswell's thoroughness, painstaking
accuracy, and original research, combined with brilliance
of style, demonstrated that a biography could become a
masterpiece of literature. Over a century later, Strachey,
disregarding Johnson's and Boswell's principles of biography, again proved that biographical writing could achieve
stylistic artistry. What Strachey lacked, however, was an
understanding of the fundamental integrity that had made
biography a unique literary genre.

But in the biographies of John Buchan and others writing
during this same period the traditional principles established by Johnson and Boswell were once more united
with masterful prose style. Moreover, Buchan, like Boswell, evidenced that passionate zest for life that inflames
the biographer's curiosity about the human life he proposes to investigate. Buchan further advanced the tradition by extending original research into diverse areas of
modern scholarship: psychology, politics, topography, re-

ligion, archeology, economics, military science—all in an
effort to set the life of his subject firmly in his milieu. Im-
mersing himself in all available source materials, Buchan
kindled that special bond, that "symbiotic relationship"
or "discriminating affection," once thought possible only
between live biographer and live subject. A study of Buchan as biographer affirms the continuity in the twentieth
century of the biographical tradition of Johnson and Boswell, a tradition to which John Buchan made a most significant contribution. (pp. 330-40)

> *Barbara B. Brown, "John Buchan and Twenti-
> eth-Century Biography," in* Biography, *Vol. 2,
> No. 4, Fall, 1979, pp. 328-41.*

## Jeanne F. Bedell    (essay date 1981)

[*In the following essay, Bedell examines parallels between Buchan's espionage fiction and John Bunyan's allegory* The Pilgrim's Progress *(1678).*]

My first acquaintance with John Buchan, an author "fascinated by hurried journeys" began ironically or, perhaps,
ideally, when I purchased a copy of **The Thirty-Nine Steps**
in San Francisco, America's most romantic city, and read
it during a return flight to Rolla, Missouri, bastion of middle-class protestant morality. The book was teasingly familiar, but the obvious parallels in other espionage novels
or in Scott and Stevenson, while assuredly present, did not
satisfy me. The familiarity was older, earlier, and, I suspected, not solely a question of literary ancestors or descendants. Halfway through **Greenmantle,** I found part of
my answer: after escaping from German intelligence agent
Colonel von Stumm, a man of gigantic physical stature
whose home is a "big black castle," Richard Hannay begins a mid-winter journey through a dense Bavarian forest; feverish and exhausted, he stumbles blindly through
falling snow and comes upon a "woodcutter's cottage"
where he finds shelter. The six and one-half foot tall von
Stumm, "hideous as a hippopotamus" and a perfect
mountain of a fellow," is surely an ogre, just as Hilda von
Einem, who makes Hannay feel like a "chattel" and as if
she were "trying to cast a spell over me," is a witch. The
implicit allusions become explicit when Hannay, in an Istanbul nightclub called the Garden-House of Suliman the
Red, watches a wild gypsy dance and feels that he is "looking at my first youth" and sees the dancers as "kindly wiz-
ards, who had brought me into fairyland." **Greenmantle**
recreates the Märchen-landscape of childhood: a brave
hero who possesses superior intelligence, skill, and physical endurance embarks on a dangerous journey to uncover
a great secret; deceitful and threatening enemies in a multiplicity of disguises attempt to imprison or kill him, but
in time of greatest need, help is always available. He survives to triumph over his adversaries, discover the secret,
and be rewarded with a great prize at the completion of
his journey.

The pattern was clear, yet somehow incomplete, and only
with the reading of **Mr. Standfast** did its full dimensions
emerge. Intentionally paralleling Hannay's journey with
that of Christian in John Bunyan's *The Pilgrim's Progress,*
Buchan presents the espionage agent as a "seeker after

truth" and fuses romance with protestant morality. Examining the espionage novels from this dual perspective, although it must be supplemented by consideration of his imperialist political stance, reveals that their overt form, that of "the romance where the incidents defy the probabilities and march just inside the borders of the possible," is linked structurally and linguistically with *The Pilgrim's Progress* and the Christian's journey towards salvation.

The roots of this crucial fusion lay in Buchan's childhood where, as the son of a minister in the John Knox Free Church, he grew up with two imaginative worlds: "We were," he says, "a noted household for fairy tales." The world of witches and warlocks was overshadowed by a sterner discipline, that of Calvinism, and by more serious reading matter, the Bible and *The Pilgrim's Progress*. The child who peopled the woods and hills of the Border Country with "stolen princesses and robber lords" and saw the imagery of the Psalms in "every sylvan corner" had *Pilgrim's Progress* as his "constant companion": "its spell was due largely to its plain narrative, its picture of life as a pilgrimage over hill and dale, where surprising adventures lurked by the wayside, a hard road with now and then long views to cheer the traveller and a great brightness at the end of it."

Buchan's love of both Bunyan and fairy tales is evident in an early novel, ***Prester John*** (1910). Opening in the Scottish countryside of his childhood, the novel relates the adventures of David Crawfurd who goes out to Blaauwildebeestefontein in the northern Transvaal to make his fortune. When he hears tales of illicit diamond smuggling and "weird natives" and learns that the area "gives the ordinary man the jumps," he vows that "I was going to a place with a secret and I meant to find it out." After a "weariful" journey, he reaches Blaauwildebeestefontein, "a haven of green," and is reminded of the moment when Christian and Hopeful reach the Delectable Mountains and see Canaan in the distance. Readers familiar with Bunyan will immediately note the irony in Crawfurd's response: before Christian is allowed to see the gates of the Celestial City, he must first look into hell.

While exploring the beautiful natural landscape that surrounds him, Crawfurd realizes that his movements are being watched. The natives disappear, the drums sound in the hills, and he is soon caught up in a native rebellion led by the Rev. John Laputa, whom he had first seen performing "strange magic" on a beach beside the Firth of Forth. Drawn into intelligence work by Captain James Arcoll, he sets out to discover the natives' plan of march. He meets Laputa again, feigns belief in the idea of Africa for the Africans, and overhears a conversation between Laputa and his lieutenant, a Portuguese named Henriques, from which he learns of the existence of a great treasure in a cave on the Rooirand. Confessing to himself his "lust" for the jewels and gold, Crawfurd gains entrance to the cave and witnesses the purification ceremony which precedes active rebellion: "It spoke of old kings and great battles, of splendid palaces and strong battlements, of queens white as ivory . . ." Like most of Buchan's villains, Laputa has a silver tongue, and for a moment Crawfurd finds his mind "mesmerized" by the sermon he hears. Laputa

prays to the Christian God, but he cannot long deceive the Scottish minister's son who recognizes his genius but knows that his heart is "black with all the crusts of paganism" and hears in his prayer "a tone of arrogant pride."

Discovered and captured, Crawfurd escapes with the great necklace of rubies known as Prester John's collar, only to be recaptured. Bargaining his life for the necklace, he evades Laputa and reaches Arcoll with information that enables him to crush the uprising. Eventually rewarded with a share of the treasure found in the cave, Crawfurd returns home with over a quarter million pounds.

But, as I have indicated, ***Prester John*** is not only a novel about a young man's successful search for a fortune. Laputa, who perverts Christianity for his own ends, dies nobly, his last words Antony's "Unarm, Eros. The long day's task is done," but there is no doubt that the river roaring beneath the Rooirand cave into which Laputa makes his suicide plunge is the entryway to hell, just as there is none that Crawfurd's journey is a moral as well as a material triumph. Relying on Providence to sustain him, he faces his own fear and passes through the hidden turnstile into the cave and towards his final confrontation with Laputa knowing that he "had quite forgotten the meaning of the fear of death." That is, he reaches the state of grace which Christian attains when he emerges from the Slough of Despond and passes through the Wicket Gate.

One can, with accuracy, call ***Prester John*** a Protestant fairy tale. But it is also a defense of British imperialism and embodies the "vision of what the Empire might be" that Buchan gained during his tenure as Private Secretary to Lord Milner, High Commissioner for South Africa (1901-1903). David Crawfurd, working, as Buchan did, with the resettlement of natives in the aftermath of war, comes to understand the "white man's duty": "He has to take all risks, recking nothing of his life or fortune, and well content to find his reward in the fulfillment of his task. That is the difference between white and black, the gift of responsibility . . . and so long as we know this and practise it, he will rule not in Africa alone but whenever there are dark men who live only for the day and their bellies." Not even Kipling put it more plainly. The last pages of the novel show Blaauwildebeestefontein transformed by a Scottish schoolmaster into a land of milk and money: instead of shabby mud huts, there are now a training college with technical workshops and experimental farms, libraries and playing fields, orchards and tobacco factories; the native chiefs are "members of our county council." The Delectable Mountains have, after all, provided a vision of paradise. But it is a white man's paradise, one which implicitly emphasizes the superiority of European civilization and leaves unanswered Laputa's question: "You call yourself a patriot? Will you not give me leave to be a patriot in turn?"

Although less overtly moral and imperialistic than many of Buchan's books, ***The Thirty-Nine Steps*** (1915) clearly implies that Providence favors England and links German spies with the devil. Richard Hannay, a South African mining engineer who has made his "pile" and returned to England, is at first disappointed because it is not the "Arabian nights" of his dreams. But once he decides to "play the game" in place of Franklin Scudder, an agent murdered in his apartment, Hannay embarks on a series of adventures compared, at various times, to "wild melodrama," "a penny novelette," and a "crazy game of hide-and-seek." Chased across Scotland by Germans who wish to silence him before he can reveal their plans to secure the mobilization disposition of the Home Fleet and by British police who think him a murderer, Hannay is "miraculously lucky" in eluding his pursuers until he takes temporary refuge in a moorland farmhouse with an elderly gentleman who on first glance resembles Mr. Pickwick. But Hannay, who had earlier told Sir Harry Bullivant of his plight because "I saw by this man's eyes that he was the kind you'd trust," notices the old man's eyelids and is immediately reminded of Scudder's statement that the man he feared most in the world could "hood his eyes like a hawk." Scudder's predatory image is reinforced and given a new dimension when Hannay says, "There was something weird and devilish in those eyes, cold, malignant, unearthly, and most hellishly clever. They fascinated me like the bright eyes of a snake." Later he specifically refers to the German as "that old devil with the eyelids." Of a second German agent, who will reappear as the arch-villain, "the most dangerous man in the world," in *Mr. Standfast,* Hannay says, "He hadn't a face, only a hundred masks that he could assume when he pleased."

In his autobiography, *Pilgrim's Way,* Buchan says that as a boy he could not take the Calvinist devil seriously and saw him as a figure of fun. Yet the novels tell a different story: his villains are men of exceptional ability who pervert their talents to destroy civilization and consider traditional morality a weakness. Buchan's description of one of them is precise: he has "A face like an angel—a fallen angel." Moxon Ivery is "puffed up with spiritual pride"; when Colonel von Stumm dies, Hannay says, "That was God's judgment on the man who sets himself above his kind." Since both men are German intelligence officers, Hannay's opposition counterparts, the judgments seem harsh. But if the men are seen as embodiments of evil and as agents of the devil and if England's cause is identified with that of *Christian* civilization, the words are appropriate. In *Greenmantle,* Hilda von Einem, who manipulates an Islamic prophet so that he will raise the Turks in a religious crusade to support Germany's power aims in the Middle East, is described as a "devil incarnate." Hannay's friend, Sandy Arbuthnot, says that "Her life is an infernal game of chess, and she plays with souls for pawns. She is evil—evil—evil." But when Arbuthnot assumes the green mantle and rides at the head of a mad charge against Erzerum, and the Turks sink by the roadside in awe, Hannay speaks of him reverently: "Then I knew that the prophecy had been true, and that their prophet had not failed them. The long-looked-for revelation had come. Greenmantle had appeared at last to an awaiting people." Arbuthnot's deception is unintentional; he is simply swept up by the course of the battle. The machinations of Germany are turned against her, and the hand of God, who struck down the prophet with cancer, raised in favor of England. The statement made by a German to an English spy in Le Carré's *The Spy Who Came in from the Cold,* "We're all the same, you know, that's the joke," is impossible in Buchan's world where a sharp moral dichotomy rules.

Nowhere is this clearer than in *Mr. Standfast* (1919) in which Hannay, now a Brigadier General serving on the Western Front, is recalled from active duty to pose as an advocate of a speedy peace, a task he finds humiliating and shameful. He first feels "bitter as sin" about his activities, but a letter from his old friend, Boer hunter Peter Pienaar who, with the help of *Pilgrim's Progress,* is bearing life in a German prison camp "like an early Christian martyr," provides a needed example, and he decides to "trust myself to Providence." Once he has done this, made the decisive choice symbolized by passage through the Wicket Gate (the title of the first chapter), Hannay finds a "new purpose in life" and has a revelation of the future. Standing, like Christian, on a hill gazing down upon the fields and streams of England, he feels his burden drop from him as he understands the meaning of his mission: "I had a vision of what I had been fighting for, what we all were fighting for . . . in that hour I had a prospect . . . which made all the present trouble of the road seem of no account . . . I seemed to see beyond the fog to a happy country." Hannay's vision is patriotic and his prospect peace in a quiet English countryside, but the language is Bunyan's and the experience unmistakably religious.

Buchan, of course, modified and adapted the plot of *Pilgrim's Progress* in order to write a secular adventure story, but the parallels are many and exact. In Biggleswick, the Village of Morality, Hannay meets numbers of people whose false beliefs and denigration of war efforts earn his condemnation. After a strenuous climb up his personal Hill Difficulty, Hannay discovers a hidden submarine anchorage and a way of feeding false information to Germany. When Moxon Ivery, the master spy whom he had been investigating, escapes just when Hannay has learned his real identity, he enters the Valley of Humiliation and learns that "fortitude was the thing a man must possess if he would save his soul." In the course of his running battle with Apollyon-Ivery, Hannay is tricked and imprisoned in a chateau in France. Here, in an episode resembling Christian's encounter with the Giant Despair, Hannay is overcome by apathy until he notices the position of Orion, realizes that Ivery has lied, and finds the key called Promise in his revolver. The first part of his journey through the Valley of the Shadow of Death is made alone, but the second, a hazardous climb on an icy mountain in the dead of night, is shared by Launcelot Wake.

Wake is one of four companions provided for Hannay; only one, Mary Lamington, has no counterpart in *Pilgrim's Progress.* Peter Pienaar, the Boer hunter who shared Hannay's adventures in *Greenmantle,* identifies himself with Mr. Standfast, and the novel concludes with a moving description of his death in aerial combat. John S. Blenkiron, an American "hard-shell Presbyterian," displays the cheerful optimism and intelligence characteristic of Hopeful, but Wake, as Faithful, is surely the most interesting of the group. A conscientious objector who is also a man of incredible spiritual and physical courage, Wake earns Hannay's respect and affection through consistent devotion to his principles. Although he eventually serves first in a non-combatant labor battalion in France and later as Hannay's personal messenger during the German breakthrough in 1918, Wake, like Faithful, is a "man of peace" whose last words are "A year ago I was preaching peace . . . I'm still preaching it . . . I'm not wrong." He was, says Hannay, "the best of the pilgrims."

Buchan's attitude towards war had matured considerably between *Greenmantle,* where it is presented as a glorious adventure in which Hannay and Arbuthnot ride off to battle like schoolboys on holiday and Arbuthnot shouts, "Well done, our side," and *Mr. Standfast* in which he attempts a serious description of conditions on the Western Front. He does not question the validity of England's cause and makes no overt criticism of British generals, but the inclusion of Wake as a major character reveals an ability to separate spiritual from political loyalty. Although the novel is not, like *Pilgrim's Progress,* an allegorical romance, its presentation of British agents actively engaged in espionage as pilgrims on the King's Highway creates a fusion of patriotism and morality which enabled Buchan to write an adventure story that is also a moral tract.

The concept of espionage as a redemptive activity reappears in *The Prince of the Captivity* (1933), and emphasis upon Christian duty in *The Three Hostages* (1924) and in the last Hannay novel, *The Man from the Norlands* (1936). Men like Hannay, Arbuthnot, and Sir Archie Roylance, whose incomes and social position are assured, are spared the difficulties of ordinary men. But difficulties are necessary: the good life must be earned and civilization protected from those who would destroy its foundations. The idea of a worldwide criminal conspiracy, first used in *The Power-House* (1913), is repeated in *The Three Hostages,* a novel that features one of Buchan's most fascinating villains, Dominick Medina. Extraordinarily handsome with "entrancing" eyes, Medina is a rising Member of Parliament who is secretly trying to gain control of men's minds and rule the world. The evil surface beneath the glamorous exterior is first recognized by Arbuthnot who realizes that he dabbles in the occult and then by Hannay when Medina attempts to hypnotize him. A magician and wizard whose mother is portrayed as a blind spinner, Medina is also a modern man who recognizes the importance of the unconscious and the effectiveness of propaganda in manipulating the masses. The dislocation and breakdown of traditional moral and social values which followed the Great War created an ideal climate for Medina's wizardry, but challenged by Hannay's solid common sense and lack of susceptibility to mind control and Arbuthnot's superior knowledge of Eastern mystical practices, he is defeated.

Mingling old themes in a new setting, *The Courts of the Morning* (1929) takes Arbuthnot, now Lord Clanroyden, Sir Archie Roylance, and Blenkiron to the Latin American republic of Olifa where they engineer a popular revolution. Filled with the stuff of melodrama and romance—a copper magnate intent on creating a docile world which he can rule with the aid of his assistants, all addicted to a powerful drug which enhances mental ability, a series of guerilla actions led by Clanroyden whom the Indians called El Obro, and a last-minute victory against the Oli-

fan army—the novel represents yet another mingling of the romantic and the religious. Castor, Gobernador of the Gran Seco, exploiter of Indian labor and manipulator of the Olifan government, is kidnapped by the group, who force him to serve as an unwilling leader of the rebellion. Clanroyden tells the Gobernador, "We think so highly of you that we're going to have a try at saving your soul." This, of course, is precisely what happens: living in the open without the luxuries to which he has been accustomed and in the almost constant presence of Janet Roylance, Archie's wife, he learns the limitations of his intellectual pride and the value of humility.

When they first reach Olifa, the Roylances are told, "You are unfortunate pilgrims . . . You come seeking romance, and I can only offer the prosaic." He was wrong. Buchan's fortunate pilgrims find the road filled with adventures, and because they are not mere adventure-seekers but genuine pilgrims, they find, too, the Delectable Mountains and look upon the gates of the Celestial City. Combining fairy tale and romance with stern Protestant morality, Buchan created a world in which patriotic men who adhere to traditional moral and religious beliefs are rewarded with both worldly success and the promise of salvation.

Morally simplistic though this world is, and however offensive contemporary readers may find Buchan's advocacy of nationalism and imperialism, it is both coherent and credible. The presentation of heroes who combine moral and physical superiority, the clear dichotomy between good and evil, and the absence of ambiguity recreate a familiar landscape: adventure stories which reaffirm traditional values are the typical fare of childhood. Buchan's espionage fiction presents a world from which the complexities and problems of adult life are missing, a world which offers readers—both sophisticated and naive—the chance to escape from the uncertain and ambiguous present into the safe and unshadowed past. To say that Buchan writes escapist fiction is not to denigrate his achievement; it is to acknowledge his obvious limitations and simultaneously to understand that the preceptions of a mind shaped by fairy tale and Calvinism are necessarily different from our own. (pp. 230-41)

*Jeanne F. Bedell, "Romance and Moral Certainty: The Espionage Fiction of John Buchan," in* The Midwest Quarterly, *Vol. XXII, No. 3, Spring, 1981, pp. 230-41.*

## Philip E. Ray   (essay date 1981)

[*In the following essay, Ray explores "both the aesthetic value and the historical significance of the typical Buchan villain."*]

Unlike the heroes, about whom everyone agrees, the villains in John Buchan's spy novels have aroused considerable critical discussion. In his "existential-phenomenological" study of the thriller genre [see Further Reading], Ralph Harper observes that "in John Buchan's world, evil is represented in a rather adolescent form" and that "the awareness of evil is sentimental, vague, telling more about the boy's sense of duty to kill the dragon than about the character of the dragon." Gertrude Himmelfarb, on the other hand, finds the dragon to be impressive in its own right. Her essay on the Victorianism of John Buchan [see essay dated 1968] contains the following account of the typical Buchan villain:

> He is not a fallen gentleman but a fallen man, the personification of evil. He dabbles in black magic rather than sex, seeks not money but power, and trafficks in the secrets of the soul as much as those of the nation. Compared with him, even the sadist of the contemporary thriller is frivolous, for instead of private sexual perversions, Buchan's villains are satisfied with nothing less than the subversion of society.

Far from embodying a "sentimental romanticism," Buchan's evil-doers reflect "a Gothic, almost apocalyptic vision of the dark, destructive forces contained in human beings and society."

The issue here is the villain's power to harm: Himmelfarb finds it to be credible, Harper does not. For example, when in *The Three Hostages* (1924) Sandy Arbuthnot tells Richard Hannay that their arch-foe, Dominick Medina, " 'aims at conquering the very heart, the very soundest part of our society' " and " 'wants to conquer in order to destroy, for destruction is the finest meat for his vanity,' " the reader may reasonably take either side. He may feel that Medina does indeed represent a threat to soul and society or that this sort of talk is just Buchan's way of getting his boys, who are normally reticent, to talk about the dragon.

Occupying the middle ground in this discussion is Francis Russell Hart, who, while dismissing the villain as a menace to society, believes in his capacity to work his evil upon the hero. In his comprehensive study of Scottish novelists from Tobias Smollett to Muriel Spark [see Further Reading], Hart argues that, when Buchan has a Dominick Medina encounter a Richard Hannay, "the combat has vitalistic roots deeper than those of conventional morality."

> This is why the moral and cultural stereotypes that give Buchan's adversaries their surface of melodrama and reactionary cliche matter little, and why the combat at its deepest level is against death or spiritual torpor. . . . The antagonist— beneath the nay-saying fanaticisms, the "incarnate devils" of history—is a spiritual torpor that is death, the sick heart.

This torpor, being a mere state of mind, threatens no one except the hero, and the villain himself begins to seem a projection of the hero's dark, unhealthy side. The danger to society meanwhile fades entirely away. But the reader can arrive at this view of things only by probing deeply: by ignoring the villain's "surface of melodrama and reactionary cliche" to seek out "the combat at its deepest level," by detecting "beneath the nay-saying fanaticisms" the figure of Death. Hart thus recommends that we discard the surface of a Dominick Medina before taking him seriously. Hart has some of Harper's skepticism but finally holds that the dragon matters just as much as the boy. Of course he differs more with Himmelfarb since she sees Medina's personality as a unified whole, without surface or

depth. She suggests that the reader take him seriously, from the start.

The question this essay attempts to answer now emerges: is there anything to be gained by reading Buchan's spy novels as Harper and Hart read them? This essay will argue that there is something very substantial to be lost; that, when the reader interprets Hannay's analysis of the foe as mere talk about duty or plunges beneath Medina's moral and cultural stereotypes to get at certain vitalistic roots, he loses sight of both the aesthetic value and the historical significance of the typical Buchan villain.

We can best begin the latter subject by sketching the situation of the spy novel in Britain before the appearance of Buchan's first two efforts, *The Power-House* (1913) and *The Thirty-Nine Steps* (1915). Two basic kinds of novels were being written: the villain's part went to agents of the German government in the first kind and to revolutionary anarchists in the second. Practitioners of the former include William LeQueux, E. Phillips Oppenheim, and Erskine Childers. Unlike Childers, who wrote only one novel and that a novel of considerable literary value, LeQueux and Oppenheim produced a great many (more or less) worthless books. Practitioners of the latter kind include Joseph Conrad, G. K. Chesterton, and Edgar Wallace. In

*Buchan's bookplate with the Latin motto "Following Nothing Base," which he later used in his coat of arms.*

this group, the quality tends to be very high indeed and the output proportionately low: Conrad produced two spy novels, *The Secret Agent* (1907) and *Under Western Eyes* (1911); Chesterton one, *The Man Who Was Thursday* (1908); and Wallace one, *The Council of Justice* (1908). Of course the advent of World War I was to doom, at least in the short run, the spy novel in which an anarchist figured as the villain; with real German agents to worry about, the British reading public could scarcely be expected to regard *him* as a threat. And it is precisely at this moment that John Buchan arrives as a spy novelist.

In retrospect, we can say that Buchan managed to save one element of the superior kind of spy novel just before the events of 1914 forced it to yield to the inferior. He did so by successfully transplanting that element into his own anti-German tale, the enormously popular and influential **Thirty-Nine Steps.** The element Buchan preserved is in fact the psychological motivation of the villain, which he took from Conrad's and Chesterton's anarchists and gave to his own Germans and, ultimately, to those of many other, later British spy novelists. Thus, if we refuse to take the Buchan villain seriously, we are certain to miss the single most important achievement in John Buchan's career as an author of spy novels.

That achievement, put quite simply, is the preservation of the best part of a newly emerging literary tradition. Had Buchan failed to transplant that element, all connection with Conrad and Chesterton would probably have been impossible for subsequent writers: the war and its aftermath would have drawn them irresistibly toward the examples of LeQueux, Oppenheim, and Childers. John Buchan performed his saving mission between 1913 and 1915, just before it ceased to be performable at all. And his achievement is such that it is even overrated, with Buchan given credit for starting the whole tradition single-handedly. For example, in a 1941 essay [see excerpt dated 1941] Graham Greene saw **The Thirty-Nine Steps** as providing the model for every future imitator:

> More than a quarter of a century has passed since Richard Hannay found the dead man in his flat and started that long flight and pursuit . . . that were to be a pattern for adventure-writers ever since.

This goes too far, but it seems undeniable that, without the achievement of John Buchan, there would have been a weaker tradition for later spy novelists to turn to and fewer spy novels of any literary merit.

Let us look now at the motives behind the villains in both the superior and inferior kinds of spy novel. For LeQueux, Oppenheim, and Childers, the German agent is a gentleman, a product of good breeding and the right background. In this way he resembles his adversary, an Englishman with the best that nature and nurture can supply. (His direct literary ancestor is the villain of late nineteenth-century Romance; the type is fairly represented by Anthony Hope's Ruritanian evil-doer, Rupert of Hentzau.) As a gentleman the villainous German is of course motivated by the desire to maintain his personal reputation and to keep faith with king and country. The heroic Englishman may approve of little that his opponent does

in the name of Honor and the Fatherland but at least understands how and why he does it. Since the hero frequently acquires great respect for his adversary by the close of the tale, it is not uncommon for a spy novel of this kind to end as Childers' *Riddle of the Sands* ends, with the bringing in of a rather affectionate verdict on the villainous German. Here Carruthers, the narrator-hero, offers the reader his last word on von Brüning, the naval officer whose plotting he has sought to uncover throughout the action of the book:

> It is a point I cannot and would not pursue, and thank Heaven, it does not matter now; yet, with fuller knowledge of the facts, and, I trust, a mellower judgment, I often return to the same debate, and, by I know not what illogical paths, always arrive at the same conclusion, that I liked the man and like him still.

For Conrad and Chesterton, on the other hand, the anarchist is a person—no matter what his nationality—with whom the hero cannot easily sympathize. He is a misguided idealist, a half-crazed visionary. His breeding and background provide no links or ties to other human beings but are mentioned only to explain his commitment to the theory and practice of anarchy. In his description of the bomb-carrying Professor in *The Secret Agent,* Joseph Conrad does precisely that:

> He considered himself entitled to undisputed success. His father, a delicate dark enthusiast with a sloping forehead, had been an itinerant and rousing preacher of some obscure but rigid Christian sect—a man supremely confident in the privileges of his righteousness. In the son, individualist by temperament, once the science of colleges had replaced thoroughly the faith of conventicles, this moral attitude translated itself into a frenzied puritanism of ambition. He nursed it as something secularly holy. To see it thwarted opened his eyes to the true nature of the world, whose mortality was artificial, corrupt, and blasphemous. The way of even the most justifiable revolutions is prepared by personal impulses disguised into creeds. The Professor's indignation found in itself a final cause that absolved him from the sin of turning to destruction as the agent of his ambition. To destroy public faith in legality was the imperfect formula of his pedantic fanaticism.

Here the last word is the key word: what motivates the Professor is his own fanaticism, clearly irrational to us and barely capable of being rationalized by him. Strikingly similar is Chesterton's account in *The Man Who Was Thursday* of Monday, the Secretary of the central anarchist council which the hero, Syme, attempts to infiltrate and subvert:

> His fine face was so emaciated, that Syme thought it must be wasted with some disease; yet somehow the very distress of his dark eyes denied this. It was no physical ill that troubled him. His eyes were alive with intellectual torture, as if pure thought was pain. . . . He spoke with casual civility, but in an utterly dead voice that contradicted the fanaticism of his face. It seemed almost as if all friendly words were to

him lifeless conveniences, and that his only life was hate.

When Syme later requires a description of Saturday (also known as Doctor Bull), his informant contrasts him with Monday:

> [Saturday] has not perhaps the white-hot enthusiasm unto death, the mad martyrdom for anarchy, which marks the Secretary. But then that very fanaticism in the Secretary has a human pathos, and is almost a redeeming trait. But the little Doctor has a brutal sanity that is more shocking than the Secretary's disease.

Both Conrad and Chesterton employ the same language—"enthusiast," "frenzied puritanism" and "enthusiasm," "mad martyrdom"—to define the psychological power behind the anarchist as sheer fanaticism.

Turning now to the villain of *The Thirty-Nine Steps,* we can examine him in relation to von Brüning as well as the Professor and Monday. First, neither Richard Hannay, the narrator-hero, nor the reader ever learns the villain's name. From start to finish he is identified only as "an old man with a young voice who could hood his eyes like a hawk," although this talismanic phrase grows shorter with the passage of time. When Scudder, the doomed agent, pronounces it, with fear and trembling, in the book's initial chapter, Hannay of course can make nothing of it. He does do a little better when he subsequently finds himself the prisoner of the hawk-eyed man:

> Then he looked steadily at me, and that was the hardest ordeal of all. There was something weird and devilish in those eyes, cold, malignant, unearthly, and most hellishly clever. They fascinated me like the bright eyes of a snake. I had a strong impulse to throw myself on his mercy and offer to join his side. . . . But I managed to stick it out and even to grin.

Windows of the soul, these eyes—"cold, malignant, unearthly, and most hellishly clever"—reveal the essential fanaticism of Hannay's adversary, which supplies the driving power for all his sinister actions. Our hero is still unable, however, to grasp the full significance of the eyes until the very end of the story, when they give away the villain's disguise.

> As I glanced at him, his eyelids fell in that hawk-like hood which fear had stamped on my memory. I blew my whistle. . . . The old man was looking at me with blazing eyes. . . . There was more in those eyes than any common triumph. They had been hooded like a bird of prey, and now they flamed with a hawk's pride. A white fanatic heat burned in them, and I realised for the first time the terrible thing I had been up against.

Hannay now sees "for the first time" that the quality that made his enemy hawk-like was in fact fanaticism, metaphorically identified here with fire. He also perceives that he has "been up against" more than a Carruthers (or any other hero of the inferior spy novel) has had to confront: this is no gentleman who just happens to be on "the other

side" but an enthusiast and mad martyr of the German cause.

Fanaticism is not, however, the only thing that links the hawk-eyed man to the anarchists of *The Secret Agent* and *The Man Who Was Thursday.* As the villain of Buchan's second spy novel, he resembles, not too surprisingly, the villain of the first: Mr. Andrew Lumley, who is not only a believer in anarchy and anarchism but also the leader of a dangerous anarchist organization always referred to as "The Power-House." (We should keep in mind that, written in 1915 and published in *Blackwood's* in December of that year, this novel is entirely a product of the pre-war atmosphere and thus much closer, in both form and content, to Conrad's and Chesterton's novels than anything written after 1914 could be.) Like Hannay, Edward Leithen, the narrator-hero of *The Power-House,* focuses from the start on the eyes of his adversary. At their very first meeting, Leithen perceives that "his eyes were paler than I had ever seen in a human head—pale, bright, and curiously wild" and that "they spoke of wisdom and power as well as of endless vitality." Later Leithen is puzzled by the failure of other people to notice this striking feature of Mr. Lumley's appearance: "I wondered why nobody realised, as I did, what was in his light wild eyes."

The fact of the matter is that Lumley's spectacles usually conceal them from view, functioning like one of the many disguises employed by the hawk-eyed man:

> I glanced up blinking to see my host smiling down on me, a most benevolent and courteous old gentleman. He had resumed his tinted glasses.

> He took off his glasses, and his light, wild eyes looked me straight in the face. All benevolence had gone, and something implacable and deadly burned in them.

The mask of benevolence itself is this villain's principal disguise, one which he manages to wear even in death. After Leithen's threat to expose his organization forces him to commit suicide, Lumley receives in the newspaper obituaries universal tribute as a great philanthropist. Here he differs from the hawk-eyed man whom Hannay publicly identifies as a German agent. But, strikingly enough, this villain attempts, in the climactic scene of *The Thirty-Nine Steps,* to elude detection precisely by putting on the mask of benevolence. As Hannay scrutinizes the appearance of the man he believes to be his enemy, he is puzzled by his own slowness:

> The old man was the pick of the lot. He was sheer brain, icy, cool, calculating, as ruthless as a steam hammer. Now that my eyes were opened I wondered where I had seen the benevolence. His jaw was like chilled steel, and his eyes had the inhuman luminosity of a bird's.

Benevolence is what the hero beholds in either villain so long as he is blind to the evil there; the hero can see that evil only when he sees *into* the eyes of the other. The difference between Lumley and the hawk-eyed man is that, while the latter's benevolent appearance finally takes in nobody, the former's deceives everyone but Edward Leithen.

The villain of John Buchan's highly successful anti-German spy novel, *The Thirty-Nine Steps,* can be linked, then, to the villains of earlier anti-anarchist spy novels by Joseph Conrad and G. K. Chesterton in two important ways: through the language Buchan uses to present fanaticism as the motivation of his villain and through the resemblance of that villain to Mr. Andrew Lumley, the anarchist evil-doer of Buchan's own earlier spy novel, *The Power-House.* If we miss these two links, we cannot understand the literary-historical significance of the Buchan villain in the development of the British spy novel; in particular, without knowledge of the first link, we cannot see how Buchan managed to preserve the best part of a newly emerging literary tradition by transplanting one element from the superior but doomed kind of spy novel.

Of course it is also possible to lose sight of the aesthetic value of the Buchan villain. This topic, however, we have already covered in part because of the greatest single strength of the figure of the villain in Buchan is the imagistic component of the language of fanaticism. We need now to recall, within the large patterns of eye imagery in both *The Power-House* and *The Thirty-Nine Steps,* the specific references in the latter work to the eyes of hawks and snakes. These references function throughout the novel to reinforce the reader's sense of danger and menace: he feels that Hannay's adversary is in fact someone to be feared. And Buchan beautifully manipulates this sense, especially in the final scene when he has the eyes themselves change from passively hawk-like to actively hawk-like: "They had been hooded like a bird of prey, and now they flamed with a hawk's pride." This transformation naturally coincides with the villain's throwing off of his disguise, which reveals his fanaticism as well as his intention to fight Hannay to the death.

If the aesthetic value of the hawk-eyed man is nowhere clearer than in this scene, nothing sharpens our appreciation of it more than a comparison with the final scene of *The Power-House.* Whereas the eyes of Hannay's adversary "blaze" and "flame," those of Mr. Andrew Lumley do not come into imagistic play at all. He, however, remains calm throughout Leithen's explanation of the scheme to expose him and his organization. In fact, as the threat unfolds, his only effort is directed toward keeping his spectacles firmly on: "he made a sudden, odd, nervous movement, pushing his glasses close back upon his eyes." This is logically consistent since the curtain comes down with Lumley still wearing the mask of benevolence:

> I remember that on my way he pointed out a set of Aldines and called my attention to their beauty. He shook hands quite cordially and remarked on the fineness of the weather. That was the last I saw of this amazing man.

Of course he is also permitted to wear the mask even after his suicide, which occurs shortly after Leithen's departure. But, precisely because of this consistency, Buchan's handling of Lumley in this scene is aesthetically weak.

From aesthetic weakness, however, in this, his first spy novel, John Buchan was able to go on to create highly successful villains in his later ones. And we need not stop here with the hawk-eyed man, although the value of this figure has been shown to be far from inconsiderable. The two greatest villains in all of Buchan are probably Dominick Medina and his mother in *The Three Hostages,* published eleven years after *The Power-House.* Let us examine briefly the physical description that introduces each: first the child—

> The eyes were the thing. They were of a startling blue, not the pale blue which is common enough and belongs to our Norse ancestry, but a deep dark blue, like the colour of a sapphire. . . . They would have made a plain-headed woman lovely, and in a man's face, which had not a touch of the feminine, they were startling. Startling—I stick to that word—but also entrancing.

and then the parent:

> And then I saw that the eyes which were looking at the fire were the most remarkable things of all. Even in the half-light I could see that they were brightly, vividly blue. There was no film or blearing to mar their glory. But I saw also that they were sightless. . . . These starlike things were turned inward. In most blind people the eyes are like marbles, dead windows in an empty house; but—how shall I describe it?—these were blinds drawn in a room which was full of light and movement, stage curtains behind which some great drama was always set. Blind though they were, they seemed to radiate an ardent vitality, to glow and flash like the soul within.

The Medinas represent a different sort of villainy: since they are neither anarchists nor agents of a foreign power, since they are of a mixed and mysterious ancestry, it is appropriate that their eyes project a threat both more vague and more spiritual than that of the hawk-eyed man. The metaphorical fire of fanaticism still burns, however, in the eyes of the parent. And, while the reader may find these descriptions strained and tedious compared with the rapidly sketched portraits of the hawk-eyed man, their eyes are no less grounded in the plot than his. For the evil that Dominick Medina and his mother practice is hypnotism, by means of which they hold hostage a trio of victims: the eyes themselves have become the source of the villain's power. But that is another story.

This essay has posed the following question: is there anything to be lost by reading John Buchan's spy novels as they have been read by some critics who cannot take the villains seriously? If we dismiss his villains altogether or dive too often beneath "their surface of melodrama and reactionary cliche," we can neither pay sufficient attention to Buchan's artistry in creating those villains nor recognize their place in the historical development of the British spy novel. (pp. 81-8)

*Philip E. Ray, "The Villain in the Spy Novels of John Buchan," in* English Literature in Transition: 1880-1920, *Vol. 24, No. 2, 1981, pp. 81-90.*

## Alistair McCleery    (essay date 1986)

[*In the following essay, McCleery discusses Buchan's portrayal of Scottish national identity in his fiction, focusing on his depiction of Scottish dialect, characters, and settings.*]

During the period from the death of Stevenson in 1894 to the outbreak of war in 1914, Scots were divided, Janus-like, between looking outward to the opportunities of the wider world and looking inward to a defensive reassessment of national identity. For some, fulfillment was found in the enterprise of Empire; for others, in challenging the stock image of the Scotsman perpetrated and perpetuated by the worst of the Kailyard [a group of nineteenth-century writers whose works present a sentimental and idealized depiction of rural Scotland]. The choice open to John Buchan may not have been between such polarised options but his fiction does demonstrate a tension between projecting a Scotland that need not conform to the Kailyard vision and acquiescing in the ideology of North Britain that excludes any sense of internal nationalism. The earlier work reveals an attempt to understand what it is like to be Scots at that time; the writing for which he is best known represents an accommodation with received views; and only with **Witch Wood** (1927) does there seem to be any resolution of the tension. Speculations are seldom more than just wistfulness but if John Buchan had not been caught up in the imperial adventure, he might have developed as a significant writer of the period rather than a notable and remarkable public servant.

Buchan's attitudes to the Scots language and the Scots character will perhaps help to define the path he took. In 1907, he acknowledged the plight, close to extinction, of Scots as a living speech:

> In parts of the country where penny papers and music-hall songs have not blighted the talk of the people you may still hear the Scots of our forefathers. We stand at a critical point, for in another generation not only the spoken word but the knowledge of the written word may be a thing of the past. [**"The Scots Tongue"**]

However, seventeen years later [in his introduction to *The Northern Muse*], he concluded in a more pessimistic mood: "To restore the Scots vernacular is beyond the power of any Act of Parliament, because the life on which it depended has gone. . . ." The same contrast over time is found in his own writing. Borders dialect is widely used in the short stories of **Grey Weather** (1899); two are composed entirely in dialect and another nine contain large elements of it. Its use adds authenticity to the portrayal of character and setting. However, in his later poetry [**Poems, Scots and English** (1917)], the use of Scots, although skilful, is redolent of a literary exercise rather than the record of a living tongue. As far as Scots character was concerned, Buchan condemned the contemporary caricature of the Scotsman "firmly fixed in English minds . . . You will find it in bad novels and stupid music-halls." This represented part of his reaction against the Kailyard. R. B. Cunninghame Graham shared Buchan's distaste when he wrote of the Kailyard: "England believed them, and their large sale and cheap editions clinched it, and

today [1899] a Scotchman stands confessed a sentimental fool." Yet Buchan attempted to substitute for this caricature the equally dubious notion of the two-sided Scotsman, the Caledonian Anti-Syzygy, to use the term coined by G. Gregory Smith in 1919. The Scot was to be sentimental and hard-headed. The term has all the advantages of a general label: it is convenient for those questioning their identity, Scotsman or North Briton, since it incorporates both; it preempts further analysis. The two master elements in the Scots character, according to Buchan, are " . . . hard-headedness on the one hand and romance on the other: commonsense and sentiment: practicality and poetry: business and idealism. The two are often thought to be incompatible, but this is wrong. Almost everybody has got a little of both. It is the peculiarity of the Scottish race that it has both in a high degree." This is in itself a caricature, however more acceptable to Scots themselves, and it mars Buchan's later work in which the Scots characters tend to be formulaic ciphers. Moreover, the order within each pairing in the quotation above reveals Buchan's own setting of priorities. It might be argued that Buchan's brother Alastair, who served with the Royal Scots Fusiliers and was killed during the First World War, personified the idealist, romantic element, while Buchan himself personified the realist, opportunist element. He chose the path of practicality and compromise, in life and fiction.

His short stories, some written before he left Scotland, coming at an early point in his career, reveal a sensitive awareness of the people, places and customs of the Borders and a sense of the distinctiveness of the Borders within Scotland. As has been noted, Scots is used extensively in these short stories, both in the dialogue and when the story is narrated in character. There are few attempts to dilute it to retain the attention of the non-Scots reader, but rather there is a positive effort to portray as realistically as possible within the short-story form the people and character of the Borders. They are not the homogenised Scots of the Kailyard. **"Streams of Water in the South,"** an early story collected in **Grey Weather** (1899), includes a character narration, the tale told by the shepherd of the Redswinehead of the death and burial of the mysterious central figure. The parallel is obvious between this tale and such as Scott's "Wandering Willie's Tale"; they are similar tours de force of dramatic story-telling. The central character of Buchan's tale possesses a strange affinity with the burns and rivers of the Borders. He is described in terms which suggest membership of an older people. He appears "like some Druid recalled of the gods to his ancient habitation of the moors." Despite these echoes of the "Celtic Twilight," suggesting the remnant of an older and wiser race, the impetus which gives the story its vitality is a desire to capture in prose Borders ways and people. The new customs of the Borders people alienate the central character and, one day, driven further away from the inland streams than he has ever travelled, he attempts to ford the Solway Firth, relying on his well-known ability to cross any stretch of water. He is buried on a hillside where his grave has been long prepared and where he can hear the source of many streams. More than the note of melancholic mystery which this summary might imply to dominate, the story is infused with a love of the Borders, the landscape and the people.

**"The Riding of Ninemileburn,"** in *The Moon Endureth* (1912), is concerned with the most notable period of Borders history, the period of the raids into England, of the reivers. It produces a more powerful effect than **"Streams of Water in the South."** History is portrayed with grim reality; this is no tale of valiant derring-do seen through the mists of romance. Success in the fight against the English, however, the glory and the exultation, make Sim, the central character, forgetful of his own famished wife and child. He swells with the pride of his own battle prowess and succumbs to the passions of the moment. "There would be ballads made about him," he thinks in the height of his conceit, forgetful now also of the dead Englishman who so resembled him. Buchan reveals the reality behind the romance of the Border Ballads and their heroic appeal; Border history is given a different complexion. The close of the story conveys absolute disenchantment: " 'The coo, Sim,' she said faintly. 'Hae ye brocht the coo:' The rush light dropped on the floor. Now he knew the price of his riding. He fell into a fit of coughing." Yet the irony of this ending is in itself reminiscent of the barb in the tail of many of the ballads which are not concerned with the Border feuds and ridings but rather with the sad realities of life.

Other stories, for example those included in the collection *The Watcher by the Threshold* (1902), are dominated by typical period themes often incongruously transferred from the world of "Fiona Macleod" to the Borders so that Buchan could exploit to the full his detailed local knowledge. As Buchan himself moved farther away from home territory in his public career, so too in his writings that territory became more and merely a background against which he set stories designed to appeal to a wider readership. **"No-Man's-Land"** involves the existence of a lost tribe of Picts stumbled upon by an English academic in the manner of Professor Challenger. The vision of **"The Far Island,"** also found in *The Watcher by the Threshold,* is transmitted from generation to generation of the same family from the original blessing bestowed upon its founder by Bran the Blessed. Colin Raden eventually finds the islands drawing nearer as death approaches and he reaches them as he is killed by a sniper's bullet. **"The Watcher by the Threshold"** which gives the collection its title, is a tale of demoniacal possession in which the narrator's complacent faith in modern rationalism and his rejection of the Calvinist doctrine of his background are questioned: "I had been pitchforked from our clear and cheerful modern life into the mists of old superstition. Old tragic stories of my Calvinist upbringing returned to haunt me. The man dwelt in by a devil was no new fancy; but I believed that Science had docketed and analysed and explained the Devil out of the world."

Yet an additional interest in this story and another in the same collection, **"The Outgoing of the Tide,"** is that they are the seeds which were to germinate into the work in which Buchan comes closest to establishing his own view of Scotland, *Witch Wood* (1927). The main characters in **"The Outgoing of the Tide"** are called Sempill. Only one

man worked on Old Alison Sempill's holding, "a doited lad who had long been a charge to the parish," a natural like Daft Gibbie in *Witch Wood.* A minor character in the story is "Simon Wauch in the Sheiling of Chasehope"; Chasehope was to be the chief hypocrite of *Witch Wood.*

The most obvious Scottish element in the series of thrillers which contain the adventures of Richard Hannay, and for which Buchan is best remembered, is the landscape. But Buchan also learned the features of strong adventure-writing from Stevenson—suspense, surprise, complication, in short, everything that leads to the need in the reader to read on and on. From Calvinism Buchan drew a concern with evil, that only order, not the discipline of Fascism but an inner self-control, can keep at bay. If that reads like a grandiose claim for his writings, then it must also be said that he exhibits the class-consciousness of the socially-mobile "lad o' pairts" who found his fortune in London and elsewhere. He demonstrates the aptness of the description of the Scots as butlers to the Empire; there is a modesty close to obsequiousness and an advocacy of self-help close to callousness.

If landscape is the primary Scottish element in the Hannay series, then it is not confined to one particular place or one particular region. It should also be noted that, although the depiction of landscape ranges from the bare moorlands of *The Thirty-Nine Steps* to the Cuillin of Skye in *Mr. Standfast,* it is always integral to the action of the plot. Buchan's landscapes are backgrounds against which we view man in isolation, against the overwhelming bleakness of his surroundings. Nor is bleakness a synonym for indifference. Often it is just these surroundings which determine the fate of the characters and act as their executioners. The landscape is seen through the eyes of the characters, normally through those of the narrator, Hannay himself. The stark, impassive and impressive backgrounds against which Hannay is dwarfed act, throughout the novels, as a testing ground for the individual, often stalked by his fellow-men, to try his courage and self-control. Two points, though, are worthy of reiteration. First, the vast wilderness lacks the specificity of his descriptions of the Borders in the earlier tales. Nor need it be Scottish at all. In his last novel, *Sick Heart River* (1941), it is the far north of Canada which supplies the background against which Leithen is seen "through the wrong end of a telescope." Secondly, Hannay is no neutral, like Edward Waverley, acting as a touchstone in his response to Scotland, fact and fanciful. Indeed, he is representative of a specific type of character, the colonial returning to the mother country and becoming more Anglicised than the English. This may be seen as both Buchan's desire for a closer integration of the Empire and its heart and also a paradigm for the "Unspeakable Scot's" progress on journeying south.

A secondary Scottish element in this series of novels consists of those minor characters who are more strongly differentiated as Scots. Andra Amos, for example, in *Mr. Standfast,* is a shop-steward in Glasgow, the "Red Clydeside," but he is no Bolshevik, rather, in Buchan's eyes, one of the last representatives of an old Border radicalism: "I'm for individual liberty and equal rights and chances for all men. I'll no more bow down before a Dagon of a Goavernment official than before the Baal of a feckless Tweedside laird." These are sentiments which no extreme Conservative would repudiate. Amos's values are those of a libertarian individualist and it is significant that Buchan places his and their origins in the Borders, not Glasgow. Historians can now tell us that "Red Clydeside" was never as scarlet as it was painted but at the time of writing (1919) Buchan found it necessary to attempt to modify through fiction, the received image of Clydeside, particularly in England. The function of Andra Amos is to alter the picture of Scotland projected by "Red Clydeside" and restore it to an acceptable Burnsian homeliness of democratic aspirations. The communists of the Clyde are seen as puppets of malevolent criminals whose final objectives are selfish and destructive. The communists are misguided, but the workers will rally to the war effort nonetheless:

> The men that are agitating for a rise in wages are not for peace. They're fighting for the lads overseas as much as for themselves. They're not yin in a thousand that wouldna sweat himself blind to beat the Germans. The Goavernment has made mistakes, and maun be made to pay for them . . . What for should the big man double his profits and the small man be ill set to get his ham and egg on Sabbath mornin'?

Buchan is writing for an English readership. His concern is to justify his fellow-countrymen in English eyes. He reduces the agitation in the shipyards, by use of couthy language and imagery, to the just demands of the ordinary man for what is his—"ham and egg on Sabbath mornin' "—unsullied by any doctrinaire rationale or wider conspiratorial aims.

Throughout the novels, Buchan propagates the "common humanity" theme. Fate may have placed us in widely-differing circumstances, but we are all brothers under the skin. Yet this too is based in the class-sensitivity of the man who has struggled to establish a position in another culture, and is still insecure in that position. Certainly, Hannay's sympathy with the Kaiser (in 1916!) is an extreme example of this recognition of common humanity which, on closer reading, can be seen to be founded on Hannay's (and Buchan's) class-consciousness. The few characters who stray beyond this pale of common humanity are those who display a total disregard for the ties of society, who are essentially anarchist in their criminality. Moxton Ivery (to use the first name we know him by) or Stumm are men who would rip apart the thin curtain between civilisation and savagery: "Civilisation anywhere is a very thin crust." Buchan is concerned with the nihilism which exists beneath that thin crust. He may have inherited from the background of the Free Church an awareness of the evil that lurks below surface in all men, tainted as we are by Original Sin, but his preoccupation with the stability, and essentially the fossilisation, of society derived from the experience of the Scot who had made good in London and wished to cling as tenaciously as possible to that achievement. This is Buchan becoming more like the Kailyard that he had earlier condemned. The other characteristic of the "Unspeakable Scot," his desire for camouflage, is demonstrated in Buchan's few other major Scot-

tish characters, for example Sandy Arbuthnot or Archie Royland, who are indistinguishable from their English or colonial counterparts. Complete integration has been achieved by the North Britons.

Hugh MacDiarmid (C. M. Grieve) wrote in 1926 that "Buchan's books abound in loving and delightful studies of Scottish landscape and shrewd analyses and subtle *aperçus* of Scottish character," but qualified that praise by insertion of an exasperated "Only—!" The praise may be due to *Huntingtower,* first of the Dickson McCunn series, published in 1922. The exasperation may be due to the Anglocentric perspective of most of Buchan's work and to its concern for promoting an acceptable image of Scotland, an image which took no account of Scotland's variety but was sanitised and deodorised for the non-Scots (and non-critical Scots) readership. *Huntingtower* is the best of the Dickson McCunn novels because this process is not so acutely visible. Its sequels, *Castle Gay* (1930) and *The House of the Four Winds* (1935), are bland and contain less insight or "*apercus*" of Scottish character." There is still the same craft in creating a gripping adventure, but the characters have been pressed into the mould of Hannay, Arbuthnot and company. In *The House of the Four Winds* the scene of action has shifted from Scotland altogether to a small European republic. In both novels Dickson McCunn loses his place at the centre of the narrative and his perspective is no longer the predominant one, thereby robbing him of a great deal of his individuality. More importantly perhaps in the context of the present argument, the Gorbals Diehards, or at least Dougal and Jaikie, whom McCunn has taken under his wing, have undergone a "civilising" process; the former is now assistant to a newspaper baron, the latter has just taken a course at Cambridge and been capped for Scotland in Rugby: "He [Jaikie] spoke with the slight sing-song which is ineradicable in one born in the west of Scotland, but otherwise he spoke English, for he had an imitative ear and unconsciously acquired the speech of a new environment." Even the little hooligans of Glasgow slums can, given a change of environment, become worthy members of society—that is English society. To do this, however, is to sacrifice identity. Dougal and Jaikie are no longer as individually Scots, or Glaswegian, as they were in *Huntingtower.* In the latter, there is much to differentiate and distinguish both the Diehards and McCunn, not only in speech, but in character and outlook, as Scots.

Dickson McCunn, in *Huntingtower,* oscillates between a dour realism and a literary-inspired romanticism, between, on the one hand, the humdrum life of the grocer in his sombre clothes and, on the other, the quest for adventure on the road. He finds a world of the imagination in the books he reads but follows a career rooted in the world of Glaswegian respectability: "He was a Jacobite not because he had any views on Divine Right, but because he had always before his eyes a picture of a knot of adventurers in cloaks, new landed from France, among the western heather." The novel, in essence, recounts his quest for adventure, his discovery that real adventure is more hazardous than that confined to the imagination, and his return to the solid middle-class ethos he had formerly inhabited. It is a different sort of new-landed adventurer he meets eventually, a type originating in the concerns of contemporary politics. But this is after the eventful day when, possessed by a Spring madness, he decides to cast off his old clothes and to set off on a journey without pre-determined destination. The gentle irony of the language—"the plump citizen was the eternal pilgrim"—is recaptured at the close of the novel in the comparison with the homecoming of Ulysses.

The analogy should rather be with Don Quixote, for in this irony is the conspiratorial invitation to the reader to share in the humour of McCunn's folly. Like Don Quixote, too, the ideal picture of life on the road which McCunn draws for himself conflicts with reality but is never entirely erased by disenchantment: "He pictured them [tramps] as philosophic vagabonds, full of quaint turns of speech, unconscious Borrovians." But he is seized by fear and disillusionment at the character of the "philosophic vagabonds." An old stonebreaker tells him: "awa' hame wi' ye . . . its idle scoondrels like you that maks work for honest folk like me." Yet throughout, although his eyes are opened to the discrepancies between dream and reality, he never loses the candour of approach to people and events that betokens an essential honesty and integrity. Significantly, the last book he had been reading before he set out was Scott's *Waverley:* "Romance, forsooth! This was not the mild goddess he had sought, but an awful harpy who battered on the souls of men." This is significant because it is Scott who is the originator of the formula of duality that Buchan tries, unsuccessfully, to squeeze the more rounded character of McCunn into. He has the strength of character to withstand being "torn between commonsense and a desire to be loyal to some vague whimsical standard." His concern for the plight of others overcomes his apprehensions (more readily than Sir Archie Roylance manages to surmount his pride and fear of humiliation), and he sees himself needed to bring his business acumen and commonsense to bear upon the difficulties encountered. McCunn has more individual life than any abstract conception of Scots character.

In short, this is a portrait of the Scottish bourgeois which tends towards a middle-class ideal rather than a sentimentalisation, but it is saved from being either by the light, ironic humour the author plays on it and by its accuracy in the essentials of individual character, virtues and inhibitions. It is a more striking portrait than any of Buchan's other Scottish characters, perhaps because written from a background, a social level in Scotland, with which Buchan was more intimately familiar. In his combination of the Calvinist attitude towards work and career, which makes it an ethical duty to succeed, and a romantic sensibility which finds an outlet in literature, until the line between reality and adventure is blurred, McCunn seems both to represent his own creator and more generally to embody but not to be limited by this view of the Scots character that Buchan is pressing on his readers.

If there is a distinctive, regional element which strengthens **Huntingtower** and makes it more successful than its sequels, then it is the Gorbals Diehards. The mixture of Scots in speech in the novel is an index of social standing. McCunn varies between several densities of dialect in his conversation depending on his respondent. The Diehards speak in a broad Scots that has assimilated elements from working-class culture, not distinctively Scottish, from war stories or from the "picters." But Buchan uses this for comic effect, a humour intended to dilute the significance (or threat) of the Diehards and their background. Jaikie sings the hymns which he has learnt at the Socialist Sunday School and calls on the "Proley Tarians" to rise against the "Boojoyzee" (which the Diehards think is a type of dragon) as he joins with McCunn, the retired grocer, to save the life of a Russian princess. Like Andra Amos, the portrayal is intended to mitigate a harsh reputation. The Diehards are shown to possess, despite the disadvantages of their background, courage, ingenuity and an unselfish willingness to help others. It is the Diehards, rather than Heritage, McCunn or the Russian prince, who decisively win the day. Buchan's message is clear: all Scots are with you in the battle against the forces of disorder, the clash of ignorant armies by night. The Diehards, in particular, are the raw material to be transformed in later books, as we have already seen, into the faithful but Anglicised servants of the status quo.

Whereas the earlier Buchan compromised with the market by blending distinctive Borders settings and characterisation with more commonplace themes, the expatriate Buchan, more conscious not only of a largely non-Scots readership but of imperial mission, presents a view of the homogenised Scot which attempts to portray him in the best light possible and, in particular, as a worthy and loyal participant in Empire. The question of Scottish identity is seen as meaningless in the case of those of superior rank and as a matter of surface features, often of a harmless, humorous nature, in the case of others. **Witch Wood** represents both a summation and a resolution.

C. S. Lewis has written: "For **Witch Wood** specially I am always grateful; all that the devilment sprouting out of a beginning like Galt's *Annals of the Parish.* That's the way to do it." There is its family tree: a small parish Scotland, the minister as central character, the evil that flaws all men, culminating in the picture of the dual poles of stern duty and uninhibited romance. Buchan himself wrote in his autobiography that of his novels, "The best I think, is **Witch Wood,** in which I wrote of the Tweedside parish of my youth at the time when the old Wood of Caledon has not wholly disappeared, and when the rigours of the new Calvinism were contending with the ancient secret rites of Diana. I believe that my picture is historically true, and I could have documented almost every sentence from my researches on Montrose." This seems familiar ground from the earlier short stories. Buchan is writing partially out of his own experience, particularly out of the memories of youth. He writes to underline the historical authenticity of his fiction. Familiar too is Buchan's portrayal of the claustrophobic atmosphere of the small village and the repressed emotions of its inhabitants which find an outlet not just in spite, as in George Douglas Brown's *The House with the Green Shutters* (1901), but also in the evil of devil-worship. The claustrophobia is given substance in the surrounding menace of the wood. David Sempill, the new minister, comes to the parish, like Barrie's "Little Minister," full of great hopes, an optimism which is reflected in his perceptions of the countryside. That these perceptions are false, he comes soon to realise. The wood dominates all: "But it was the meadows and the open spaces that had been his kingdom, and his recollection was of a bare sunny land where whaup and peewit cried and the burns fell headlong from windy moors. But now, as he gazed, he realised that the countryside was mainly forest."

Sempill has a charitable, humanistic conception of Christianity which is at odds with the prevailing opinion of the church. He is advised to "keep a Gospel walk on the narrow rigging of the truth," and this he tries to do, maintaining the truth as he sees it. His charity is shown in his aid for the wounded trooper, Mark Kerr, but more fully in his concern for the welfare, material as well as spiritual, of his flock during the storm and the plague. Other ministers are more concerned with politics or the religion of hellfire and damnation. Sempill walks the narrow rigging between the excesses of Calvinism and the excesses of devil-worship. Both are, in fact, aspects of the same thing. The central figure of Ephraim Caird of Chasehope is at once the staunch defender of the arid dogma, an upright elder in the Kirk, and also the high priest of Beltane, the leader of the village coven. As becomes apparent in the later episodes of the novel, he is possessed by the species of antinomianism portrayed by James Hogg in *The Private Memories and Confessions of a Justified Sinner.* It is heresy which leads to the split personality of the sinner and saint, Hyde and Jekyll, at worst or at best to the hypocrisy of

*Governor General Buchan and Canadian Prime Minister Mackenzie King with President Franklin D. Roosevelt and his son James in 1936.*

"Holy Willie." The life-denying strictures of Calvinism lead to the obscenities practiced in the forest.

In travelling the middle path in the struggle against the evils of both extremes, Sempill is helped by Katrine Yester. She embodies the good, life-giving forces of Nature. On the borders of the wood, Natura Maligna, she has created a paradise, Natura Benigna. She is an otherworldly character, identified by many villagers as the Queen of the Fairies; she is innocent joy dancing "on a Spring morn to the Glory of God." Montrose himself personifies for Sempill the moderate Presbyterianism he tries to follow, and it is Montrose's representative, Mark Kerr, who voices the strongest denunciation of the excesses of Calvinism: "I tell you the Cities of the Plain were less an offence to Almighty God than this demented twist of John Calvin that blasts and rots a man's heart." This liberal theology would have received ready assent in the Kailyard.

But the significance of **Witch Wood** here lies in David Sempill's response to the alternative courses of action open to him. Katrine Yester may, by the close of the novel, be dead, but her spirit moves Sempill to a more positive assertion of his role and it is he, rather than any *deus ex machina,* who brings Chasehope to his fate. Retribution is paid in full to this man who had straddled both extremes of devil-worship and Calvinism. Faced with a seeming choice between the instinctive, emotional drives that lead to the rites in the wood, and the disciplined, stern spiritual suffocation of the visible church, Sempill refuses to see a monopoly of good or evil held by either and he elects for exile. There is a kind of hopeless frustration, an admission of impotence, in his leaving behind a basically unchanged church and his election of enlistment in the service of foreigners as a preferable course. Buchan leaves some room for hope, however. The ministers may be still in power but Sempill himself has left a lasting impression on the hearts of his ex-parishioners. He may have left Scotland because of its bigotry but there is hope for the country which bred Montrose and Sempill himself. The children of the prologue who believe he was "a guid man and a kind man" outnumber those who believe him carried off by the devil.

There is an obvious parallel between Sempill's choice of exile and Buchan's own career. Buchan too left Scotland to enlist in the service of others; he too found room for his talents to develop outside the narrow confines of his native land. But, in so doing, Buchan directed his literary talents towards propagation of a vision of Scotland, promulgated by those looking outward to Empire, as if it were the expression of self-evident truth. (pp. 277-85)

*Alistair McCleery, "John Buchan and the Path of the Keen," in* English Literature in Transition: 1880-1920, *Vol. 29, No. 3, 1986, pp. 277-86.*

### John G. Cawelti   (essay date 1987)

[*Cawelti has written several studies of American popular culture and formula fiction, including* The Six-Gun Mystique *(1971),* Adventure, Mystery and Romance: Formula Stories as Art and Popular Culture *(1976), and he coauthored* The Spy Story *with Bruce A. Rosen-*

berg. *In the following essay, attributed to Cawelti in the latter work, he discusses the importance of Buchan's contribution to the development of the modern espionage story.*]

Toward the end of the nineteenth century, the secret agent adventure had begun to assume a definite shape in the work of writers like Kipling, Stevenson, and Conrad. A number of Doyle's Sherlock Holmes stories came close to being accounts of counterespionage activity, and on the eve of World War I, in "His Last Bow," Holmes came out of retirement in order to foil the plots of a German agent. But it was the generation which came of age in the early twentieth century that made the spy story a major literary archetype by producing masses of formulaic spy adventures (e.g., Rohmer's *Insidious Dr. Fu Manchu,* Le-Queux's *Secret Service,* Wallace's *Four Just Men*) as well as a number of more complex fictions involving espionage as a theme (e.g., Childer's *Riddle of the Sands,* Kipling's *Kim,* and Conrad's *Secret Agent*). The Richard Hannay stories of John Buchan span the distance between the popular spy adventure and the novel of espionage. Like the popular stories, Buchan's tales are deeply romantic; his hero is a gentleman amateur, definitely one of that breed later labeled "clubland heroes." His enemies are supervillains who represent the threat of non-British races and cultures to the English hegemony. Their complex criminal organizations, like the international criminal syndicate of Doyle's Professor Moriarty, threaten the very heart of the homeland. With the help of a few other gentlemen friends, however, Buchan's dauntless hero is invariably able to uncover and defeat the supervillain's plots, saving the empire for the time being. Though his hero and antagonists sometimes lapse into the manichean simplicities of Sax Rohmer's Fu Manchu and Sir Dennis Nayland Smyth, Buchan's moral earnestness, his sense of humor, and his concern for literary values make his Hannay stories the very model of the early twentieth-century spy story.

If we are to take his own word for it, John Buchan would probably have written his stories whether they were successful or not. In his autobiography **Memory Hold-the-Door,** he tells us,

> It was huge fun playing with my puppets, and to me they soon became very real flesh and blood. I never consciously invented with a pen in my hand; I waited until the story had told itself and then wrote it down, and, since it was already a finished thing, I wrote it fast. The books had a wide sale, both in English and in translations, and I have always felt a little ashamed that profit should accrue from what had given me so much amusement. I had no purpose in writing except to please myself, and even if my books had not found a single reader I would have felt amply repaid.

There seems little reason to doubt that Buchan's account is essentially correct, that the stories were for him a pleasant and relaxing mode of fantasy, a refreshing escape from a life filled with problems, tensions, and achievements of a very wide range. The interesting thing is that Buchan's fantasies, coupled with his ability to put them into words, became the ground for a rich and varied series of collective fantasies. Buchan, more than any other writer, assembled the formula for the modern secret agent story.

In general, the comparison between Rohmer and Buchan is somewhat analogous to that between Mickey Spillane and Dashiell Hammett: Buchan, like Hammett, was the chief creator of a formulaic tradition which proved capable of complex and various developments; Rohmer was, like Spillane, a prolific popular exponent of the formula in its simplest and most extreme form. Because of this, the study of Rohmer's writings can sometimes reveal to us in an exaggerated way the themes that lurk beneath the more balanced and controlled surface of Buchan's work. The terror of racial degeneration, for example, is clearly an aspect of Buchan's thinking, but never so obsessively as in Rohmer's portrayal of the threat of the "yellow peril" in Fu Manchu and his minions.

Buchan's spy stories used highly colorful villains, plots, and incidents, but he combined these with allegory, using characters to represent general moral and social traits, thereby suggesting that the whole fate of society was at stake. Generally, the most successful writers of spy thrillers have dealt in this sort of combination, though for some, such as Graham Greene, the sense of realism has been in tension with it. Few spy writers have used the formula without feeling the temptation to transmute fantasy into allegory, and Buchan seems to have had a remarkably clear perception of this aspect of his psyche. We noted above his frank statement that his tales were fantasy outlets strongly needed at certain periods of his life. Early in his autobiography, he notes that the first and strongest influences on his thought were the fairy tales his father loved and collected and the strong Calvinistic discipline that was also part of his parson father's way of life. These two influences came together for Buchan when he discovered and read what would become for him the basic literary work:

> *The Pilgrim's Progress* became my constant companion. Even today I think that, if the text were lost, I could restore most of it from memory. My delight in it came partly from the rhythms of its prose, which, save in King James's Bible, have not been equalled in our literature; there are passages, such as the death of Mr. Valiant-for-Truth, which all my life have made music in my ear. But its spell was largely due to its plain narrative, its picture of life as a pilgrimage over hill and dale, where surprising adventures lurked by the wayside, a hard road with now and then long views to cheer the traveller and a great brightness at the end of it. (**Memory**)

It is probably more revealing than exaggerated to suggest that Buchan created the modern spy story out of his need to construct a contemporaneous fantasy that might have for him something of the power of *The Pilgrim's Progress.* In any case, his stories are full of Bunyanesque allusions and devices. This is obvious in the case of **Mr. Standfast,** in which one of the hero figures reads Bunyan throughout the novel and attempts to pattern himself on a Bunyan character, finally going to his death in emulation of Bunyan's Mr. Valiant-for-Truth. But, in an even deeper sense than such explicit references to *The Pilgrim's Progress,* the fantasy world of Buchan's spy stories takes on the basic form of the pilgrim's quest. In each of the novels, a hero sets out on a quest that takes him from the comfort and security of the city into an increasingly jagged and dangerous landscape. As he proceeds on his quest, he becomes more and more isolated and alone. He confronts the agents and the plots of a diabolical conspiracy that threatens to overthrow the moral world. Finally, with the assistance of a few courageous friends, he succeeds in uncovering the enemy's conspiracy and overthrowing it.

Thus, Buchan was able to take the situations of modern international intrigue and to cast them in the form of romantic adventure, permeating them with the particular allegorical intensity of a Bunyanesque sense of the world. At his best, he was able to clothe this allegorical fantasy with enough verisimilitude to effectively disguise, at least from time to time, the weaknesses inherent in his obsessive symbolic machinery and his tendency toward a completely fantastic dependence on providential coincidence. Perhaps the most important contributors to this surface verisimilitude are not such insights into the workings of government which the novels offer us but the moments of social comedy. Though basically a very serious man, Buchan apparently had a larky delight in social eccentricities and his best books are enlivened with incidents and characters that add an earthy touch of reality to the fantastic proceedings and remind us that the intense moral allegorizing of the story is not to be taken too seriously. In fact, one of the weaknesses of Buchan's spy stories was his tendency to let the overinflated moral seriousness of his fantasy overpower these contrasting moments of eccentric humor.

Buchan usually achieved his most effective balance of fantasy, moral allegory, and humor in narrations of the pursuit across the landscape which always seemed to rouse him to his best efforts. His own insightful description of the peculiar narrative power of the chase reveals how compelled he was by it:

> I was especially fascinated by the notion of hurried journeys. In the great romances of literature they provide some of the chief dramatic moments, and since the theme is common to Homer and the penny reciter it must appeal to a very ancient instinct in human nature. We live our lives under the twin categories of time and space, and when the two come into conflict we get the great moment. Whether failure or success is the result, life is sharpened, intensified, idealized. A long journey, even with the most lofty purpose, may be a dull thing to read of if it is made at leisure; but a hundred yards may be a breathless business if only a few seconds are granted to complete it. For then it becomes a sporting event, a race; and the interest which makes millions read of the Derby is the same, in a grosser form, as when we follow an expedition straining to relieve a beleaguered fort or a man fleeing to sanctuary with the avenger behind him. (*Memory*)

It was above all through his elaboration of the structure of the hurried journey or flight and pursuit that Buchan developed the basic rhythms of the spy story. One need only think of Latimer's journey from Istanbul to Paris in Ambler's *Mask of Dimitrios*, the train trips in Hitchcock's

*The Lady Vanishes* and Greene's *Orient Express*, James Bond's stalking pursuit and desperate flights from his multifarious antagonists, and Alec Leamas's clandestine journey into East Germany in Le Carré's *Spy Who Came In from the Cold* to realize how important Buchan's example was for this formulaic tradition.

Only one of Buchan's spy stories was completely organized around a single, sustained, hurried journey. This was the first and best of the Richard Hannay stories, **The Thirty-Nine Steps.** By looking at this novel in greater detail we can see the reasons for the effectiveness of this kind of structure and the special and unique characteristics Buchan was able to give it.

The story begins on the eve of World War I in London and is narrated by the central figure, Richard Hannay, who introduces himself as a mature man who has made his fortune in South Africa. Now, returned to the comfort of London, he finds himself at loose ends:

> Here was I, thirty-seven years old, sound in wind and limb, with enough money to have a good time, yawning my head off all day. I had just about settled to clear out and get back to the veld, for I was the best-bored man in the United Kingdom. (**Thirty-Nine Steps**)

Fortunately for his peace of mind, if not his physical comfort and safety, Hannay is soon plunged into an adventure as exciting as he might have wished. Returning to his lodging one evening, Hannay meets another tenant of the building on the stairs. Though they are not acquainted, this man, acting strangely and furtively, begs to be let into Hannay's apartment. Bolting the door, he announces suddenly; "Pardon . . . I'm a bit rattled tonight. You see, I happen at this moment to be dead." This curious gentleman reveals to Hannay that he is one Franklin P. Scudder, an American newspaper correspondent who has become a sort of amateur secret agent. He explains to Hannay that "behind all the governments and the armies there was a big subterranean movement going on, engineered by very dangerous people." In a typically Buchanesque passage he reveals how he has come upon their secret and how he has since scurried about Europe in disguise to avoid the enemy's agents:

> "I got the first hint in an inn on the Achensee in Tyrol. That set me inquiring, and I collected my other clues in a fur-shop in the Galician quarter of Buda, in a Strangers' Club in Vienna, and in a little book-shop off the Racknitzstrasse in Leipsic. I completed my evidence ten days ago in Paris. I can't tell you the details now, for it's something of a history. When I was quite sure in my own mind I judged it my business to disappear, and I reached this city by a mighty queer circuit. I left Paris a dandified young French-American, and I sailed from Hamburg a Jew diamond merchant. In Norway I was an English student of Ibsen, collecting materials for lectures, but when I left Bergen I was a cinema man with special ski-films. And I came here from Leith with a lot of pulp-wood propositions in my pocket to put before the London newspapers. Till yesterday I thought I had muddied my trail some, and was feeling pretty happy. Then . . ."

The three motifs announced here, unravelling a mystery, the dangerous lone journey, and the series of disguises, become the basis of the development of *The Thirty-Nine Steps.* Scudder explains to Hannay that a plot is afoot to assassinate an important European statesman when he visits London and gives him tantalizing hints about the secret organization. He refers to a Black Stone, to a man who lisps, and to "an old man with a young voice who could hood his eyes like a hawk." But before he can get any further information, Hannay finds Scudder with a knife in his heart.

After this brisk opening, which Buchan accomplishes in a single chapter, Hannay's hurried journey begins. He realizes that if he waits for the police to arrive, he will certainly be arrested and probably convicted of Scudder's murder. Since he will not be able to do anything about the enemy plot if he is locked up in jail, he decides to elude the police by going to Scotland, where his Scots background will enable him to blend into the country and he can try to unravel the mystery of Scudder's death and the assassination plot. Disguised as a milkman, he leaves his apartment and boards a train for the North.

Hannay's arrival in Scotland marks the beginning of a series of narrow escapes from capture by both the police and the forces of the enemy conspiracy. The combination of these adventures is ineffably Buchanesque, a synthesis of moral allegory, fantastic scrapes, and social comedy which has never quite been duplicated by any other writer of spy adventures including, alas, Buchan himself. The chapter titles, with their reminiscent flavor of Sherlock Holmes's adventures, give a pretty good idea of the distinctive ambience of this major section of *The Thirty-Nine Steps:* "The Adventure of the Literary Innkeeper," "The Adventure of the Radical Candidate," "The Adventure of the Spectacled Roadman," "The Adventure of the Bald Archaeologist," and "The Dry-Fly Fisherman." Each "adventure" is a set of incidents that elaborate in a different way the same basic pattern: Hannay, isolated and alone, pursued by both police and enemy agents, must find someone he can trust in order to communicate his knowledge to the higher authorities. To find such a person and to elude his pursuers, he disguises himself in various ways, but his disguise is always given away by some unforeseen flaw. Moreover, many of the persons he meets turn out to be enemy agents. This patterning of the situation enables Buchan to generate a variety of suspense effects and sudden twists: Will Hannay's disguise be penetrated this time or will he get away? Will the friendly gentleman turn out to be a real friend or an enemy agent in disguise? Will the police capture Hannay before he locates the enemy? In addition, this complex of situation and setting leads Buchan to imagine a rather marvelous sequence of contrasting and paradoxical incidents which take on a special force because of their connection with the underlying moral allegory. Hannay passes through a striking series of disguises, from South African mining magnate in trouble with the diamond association, to a "trusted leader of Australian thought" addressing a local political rally on colonialism and free trade, to a dirty and drunken Scottish road mender. Despite their fantastic diversity, Buchan manages to make each of these impersonations a plausible thing for

Hannay to do in the light of his background and ability. Each situation of disguise involves some humorous incongruity as well as danger, and Buchan is thereby able to take advantage of the emotional effectiveness of our uncertainty about whether a given moment will lead to fear or laughter. Alfred Hitchcock would later display an even greater mastery of this kind of suspense effect, but Buchan certainly showed the way to make this type of incident an important part of the spy thriller.

The overall structure of these adventures also embodies Buchan's flair for paradox and allegory. Each character Hannay meets has a Bunyanesque flavor and represents some moral or social characteristic. Hannay's own disguises and the perils he encounters are also the embodiment of temptations and obstacles to the accomplishment of the mission which, it becomes increasingly clear, is basic to the security of England. Even coincidence, which Buchan depends on to an inordinate extent, takes on something of a moral quality in the allegorical world of Buchan's fantasy. Throughout his adventures in Scotland, Hannay's flight leads him closer and closer to the heart of the enemy's power. Finally, with his pursuers close behind, Hannay comes to the isolated country house of a "benevolent old gentleman" and amateur historian and archaeologist of the local countryside. Certain that such a distinguished gentleman can be trusted, Hannay quickly blurts out his plight and the old gentleman turns away the pursuers with a misleading story. Then . . .

> I emerged into the sunlight to find the master of the house sitting in a deep armchair in the room he called his study, and regarding me with curious eyes.
>
> "Have they gone?" I asked.
>
> "They have gone. I convinced them that you had crossed the hill. I do not choose that the police should come between me and one whom I am delighted to honour. This is a lucky morning for you, Mr. Richard Hannay."
>
> As he spoke his eyelids seemed to tremble and to fall a little over his keen grey eyes. In a flash the phrase of Scudder's came back to me when he had described the man he most dreaded in the world. He had said that he "could hood his eyes like a hawk." Then I saw that I had walked straight into the enemy's headquarters.

The way in which Hannay's seemingly random flight leads him unerringly to a direct confrontation with the enemy is a sign of Hannay's instrumentality as the agent of some higher moral power. In Buchan's world, there is really no coincidence or accident. What appears to be chance is actually the mysterious and enigmatic working of providence. As Hannay puts it in *The Three Hostages,* "then suddenly there happened one of those trivial things which look like accidents but I believe are part of the rational government of the universe."

By his tenacity, his willingness to embark on a moral quest without assistance, his ability to disguise himself, his courage in facing the technology of airplanes and motor cars which his pursuers send after him, and the skills in wilderness living with which he escapes alone across the desolate moors of Scotland, Hannay demonstrates his worthiness to serve the cause of goodness. Thus, providential action leads him to the heart of the evil conspiracy and then puts him in touch with what might be called the good underground, the only political force capable of overcoming the threats of the evil conspiracy. Though captured by the enemy agents, Hannay manages to escape and find his way to the cottage of Sir Walter Bullivant of the Foreign Office. Bullivant has already received a letter from the late Mr. Scudder outlining the plot to assassinate the Balkan statesman Constantine Karolides. When the assassination occurs, Sir Walter knows that Hannay has stumbled onto a dangerous plot. By this time, Hannay has managed to solve the mystery of Scudder's mysterious hints about the Black Stone, and he realizes that the enemy agents have more important plans. As Hannay characteristically put it, "the fifteenth day of June was going to be a day of destiny, a bigger destiny than the killing of Dago." The final plot is to steal Britain's secret naval plans from the Admiralty and to use them in a surprise attack that would cripple the British navy. The remainder of *The Thirty-Nine Steps* deals with Hannay's tracking down the Black Stone, the secret group of German agents, capturing their leaders just as they are about to turn over the stolen plans to an enemy submarine waiting off the British coast. The thirty-nine steps are finally revealed as the number of steps down to the sea from the coastal villa where the group of enemy agents is captured. This last section of the story is marred by the kind of implausibilities that Buchan often could not resist; for example, the naval plans are stolen by an enemy agent disguised as the first sea lord, who takes them from a meeting with a group of military leaders who have been in intimate contact with the real first sea lord for years. But it is, on the whole, an effective continuation of the suspenseful chase initiated in the first chapter.

None of the later Hannay books is as completely successful as *The Thirty-Nine Steps.* Works like *Greenmantle, Mr. Standfast,* and *The Three Hostages* come alive when Buchan deals with the hurried journey motif, but are generally more rambling and digressive narrative structures with too many subplots and different phases of action. Though these later novels have many striking incidents and characters, they seem increasingly clotted by an attempt at seriousness and moralism, as if Buchan were increasingly seeing his fantasy creations as a vehicle for important social and political opinions. This trend reached a peak in later novels of international intrigue like *A Prince of the Captivity,* which is far too full of apocalyptic warnings about the vast conspiracies threatening Western civilization to be a very effective tale of secret adventure. Political ideologies inevitably play an important role in the spy story because the agent's mission must be related to larger political conflicts in order to increase our sense of its importance and to heighten our feeling of suspense about its outcome. However, the presence of political or moral attitudes that later audiences find outdated or noxious invariably leads to a fairly rapid decline in the appeal of the stories that contain them. We cannot respond emotionally to the story's suspense without taking its worldview with some degree of seriousness. Buchan's popularity has thus declined rather precipitously since the 1930s. In fact, his work seems most likely to continue to appeal to wider audiences mainly in the form of the superb film that Alfred Hitchcock based on the novel. In his film version, Hitchcock retained Buchan's excellent suspense structure, but eliminated most of his ideological moralizing. At the same time he strengthened the comic and satirical aspects of Buchan's original by inventing a witty and sophisticated romance which he made one of the main lines of the film's plot.

Yet Buchan's fantasy vision of the world retains a considerable historical interest because of the degree to which it was shared by other popular writers of the time, men like Dornford Yates, H. C. McNeile (pseud. Sapper), E. Phillips Oppenheim, and Sax Rohmer. Moreover, it is this vision that a later generation of writers, men like Eric Ambler and Graham Greene, inherited and had to struggle with. These writers faced the problem not only of maintaining the effective structures of suspense and action, which Buchan's generation had created, but of expressing these structures in terms of a very different vision of the world. Thus, Buchan's view of the world provides us with some clues about dominant moral fantasies in the first part of the twentieth century, and it gives us a point from which to measure the extent to which a later generation departed from these fantasies.

Richard Usborne, in a fascinating study of the heroes of Buchan, Sapper, and Yates [see Further Reading], coined the rather nice term "clubland heroes" to describe Hannay and his compatriots Bulldog Drummond and Jonah Mansel. This characterization of the hero is an important aspect of Buchan's fantasy. Hannay is a clubman, which means that he is, above all, a gentleman and an amateur, a member of the upper classes with an independent income, and one who lives by a very strong moral and social code in which the ideals of honor, duty, and country play a primary role. He is not a professional agent, nor does he belong even temporarily to any formal secret service. Even during the height of the war, he does his spying while on brief leave from his main occupation, the traditional gentlemanly one of military officer. After the war, his great dream is to settle down in a lovely country house in the Cotswolds and serve happily as the local squire. In these respects, Hannay symbolizes the continuity of British social tradition, the vision of an ordered and hierarchical social world which has lasted from time immemorial. The search for reassurance that this tradition can go on is one basic impetus of Buchan's fantasy:

> Many of my pre-War interests revived, but, so to speak, on sufferance, for I felt that they had become terribly fragile. Would anything remain of the innocencies of old life? I was reassured by two short holidays. One was a tramp in the Cotswolds from which I returned with the conviction that the essential England could not perish. This field had sent bowmen to Agincourt; down that hill Rupert's men, swaying in their saddles, had fled after Naseby; this village had given Wellington a general; and from another the parson's son had helped to turn the tide in the Indian Mutiny. To-day the land was as quiet as in the beginning, and mowers were busy in the hay. A second holiday took me to my Tweedside Hills. There, up in the glens, I found a shepherd's wife who had

four sons serving. Jock, she told me cheerfully, was in France with the Royal Scots; Jamie was in "a bit ca'd Sammythrace", Tam was somewhere on the Artic shore and "sair troubled wi' his teeth"; and Davie was outside the walls of Jerusalem. Her kind old eyes were infinitely comforting. I felt that Jock and Jamie and Tam and David would return and would take up their shepherd's trade as dutifully as their father. Samothrace and Murmansk and Palestine would be absorbed, as Otterburn and Flodden had been, into the ageless world of pastoral. (*Memory*)

Though this statement would sound right in Richard Hannay's mouth, it was actually made by Buchan, himself, in his autobiography.

But if the clubman's image of the world as a place of unchanging and stable social tradition is the ideal, Buchan was well aware of its fragility. It is significant that his hero is not only a clubman, but a colonial and self-made man, accustomed to scenes of violence and at home in the wilderness, for only such a hero might be capable of coping with the manifold dangers which threaten "the innocencies of the old life." The traditional world is threatened both by external and by internal enemies. New forces of barbarism have arisen on the periphery of civilized society, that is, the British Empire. In addition, there are threats from within, for the average man's civilized restraints and his commitment to traditional social ethics are subverted by the increasing moral chaos of modern life:

> The barriers between the conscious and the subconscious have always been pretty stiff in the average man. But now with the general loosening of screws they are growing shaky and the two worlds are getting mixed. . . . That is why I say you can't any longer take the clear psychology of most civilized human beings for granted. Something is welling up from primeval deeps to muddy it. . . . The civilized is far simpler than the primeval. All history has been an effort to make definitions, clear rules of thought, clear rules of conduct, social sanctions, by which we can conduct our life. These are the work of the conscious self. The subconscious is an elementary and lawless thing. If it intrudes on life, two results must follow. There will be a weakening of the power of reasoning, which after all is the thing that brings men nearest to the Almighty. And there will be a failure of nerve. (*Three Hostages*)

External threats are most strikingly dramatized through the fantasy of a great racial drama which is being played out on the world stage. Buchan was by no means a virulent racist. As a man and a colonial administrator he appears to have been unshakably convinced of the superior virtues of the Anglo-Saxon, but there is little evidence that he was hostile to other races and cultures. Even in his stories he was no direct manipulator of the popular paranoia surrounding the "yellow peril," as Sax Rohmer was. Nevertheless, the adventures of Richard Hannay have an unmistakably racist tinge, as if in fantasy Buchan was able to give vent to feelings about racial good and evil which he would never have made the basis of calculated political action. Hannay's continual and automatic use of racial epithets like "dago," "nigger," and "wog," while doubtless a real enough characteristic of a colonial gentleman of his era, is one of those aspects of Buchan's work that most embarrassingly grates on the contemporary reader's ear, preventing us from accepting Hannay as a hero without serious reservations.

But, on a deeper level than that of racial epithet and the instinctive superiority of the Anglo-Saxon gentleman, Buchan's treatment of the drama of racial conflict reflects his sense that the English Christian social tradition is no longer able to cope with the larger social forces the twentieth century has unleashed in the world. Buchan presents these forces as spiritual and racial, rather than political and economic, and in a number of ways he seems rather ambiguously attracted by the enemy, though ostensibly his stories represent heroic victory over the enemy's conspiracy. Indeed, the Buchan hero is often strongly attracted by the racial or spiritual force represented by the opposing supervillain.

> There would be no mercy from Stumm. That large man was beginning to fascinate me, even though I hated him. Gaudian [another German agent] was clearly a good fellow, a white man and a gentleman. I could have worked with him, for he belonged to my own totem. But the other was an incarnation of all that makes Germany detestable, and yet he wasn't altogether the ordinary German and I couldn't help admiring him. I noticed he neither smoke nor drank. His grossness was apparently not in the way of fleshly appetites. Cruelty . . . was his hobby, but there were other things in him, some of them good, and he had that kind of crazy patriotism which becomes a religion. (*Greenmantle*)

In *The Three Hostages,* Hannay must use all his spiritual resources to overcome the psychological spell of supervillain Dominick Medina, one of whose powers involves the almost hypnotic control of others, the capacity to bring both followers and opponents under his complete spiritual domination.

On the surface these supervillains and the forces they represent are evil because they pose a basic threat to the good tradition of the clubland world. Yet, in Buchan's fantasy, the new forces have a way of seeming far more compelling and attractive than the ordered life for which the hero officially yearns. After all, who would actually fritter away his life in the routine pastoral joy when he might be dashing about the world exposing secret conspiracies which are, fortunately, everywhere? We recall that, at the very beginning of the Hannay saga, our hero had become so bored with civilized life in London that he was about to return to the African veldt. The murderous intervention of a German conspiracy saves him just in time. Later, in pursuit of the Islamic prophet Greenmantle, one of Hannay's friends regrets that the prophet's attractive message of primitive fanaticism should have become perverted to the evil ends of German imperialism:

> "Well, Greenmantle is the prophet of this great simplicity. He speaks straight to the heart of

Islam, and it's been twisted into part of this damned German propaganda. His unworldliness has been used for a cunning political move, and his creed of space and simplicity for the furtherance of the last word in human degeneracy. My God, Dick, it's like seeing St. Francis run by Messalina." (*Greenmantle*)

A similar ambivalence reveals itself in Hannay's romantic life. In the course of his adventures he meets and falls in love with the beautiful Mary Lamington, who is the very epitome of English womanhood. Hannay dreams of retiring with his beloved Mary, but the real intensity of their romance results from the fact that Mary is also a secret agent, one of the most daring members of the informal espionage group Hannay himself works with. Not surprisingly, the supervillain Graf von Schwabing also falls in love with her and wrecks his own conspiracy by attempting to take Mary back to Germany with him. Even before his first encounter with Mary, Hannay's own feelings about the opposite sex had been most strongly aroused by the German agent Hilda von Einem:

> I see I have written that I know nothing about women. But every man has in his bones a consciousness of sex. I was shy and perturbed, but horribly fascinated. This slim woman, poised exquisitely like some statue between the pillared lights, with her fair cloud of hair, her long delicate face, and her pale bright eyes, had the glamor of a wild dream. I hated her instinctively, hated her intensely, but I longed to arouse her interest. (*Greenmantle*)

When Hannay finally marries his perfect English lady spy and settles down to the life of a country squire, it is not long before he is drawn back into the fascinating world of new racial and spiritual forces. The comforts of the traditional life quickly pale when a visitor brings news of new forces at work in the East:

> That took him to Central Asia, and he observed that if he ever left England again he would make for those parts, since they were the refuge of all the superior rascality of creation. He had a notion that something very off might happen there in the long run. "Think of it!" he cried. "All the places with names like spells—Bokhara, Samarkand—run by seedy little gangs of Communist Jews. It won't go on forever. Some day a new Genghis Khan or a Timour will be thrown up out of the Maelstrom. Europe is confused enough, but Asia is ancient Chaos." (*Three Hostages*)

The way in which the basic spy themes of conspiracy and disguise are treated in Buchan's works also illustrates a curious ambivalence. Though the British countryside is explicitly presented as an ideal world and the values of the British social tradition as the apogee of the civilized world, this way of life is also shown to be riddled with weakness and conspiracy. Significantly, the arch conspirators typically wear the garb of representatives of the tradition. The evil German agent with eyes hooded like a hawk is disguised as a Scottish country gentleman and amateur historian. The Graf von Schwabing has passed for many years as Morgan Ivery, liberal politician and philanthropist.

And their agents seem to be average British citizens. English country life thus seems at once the epitome of human civilization and a base deception, riddled with enemy agents. Buchan's treatment of disguise is even more curious. His supervillains are, above all, men of many faces, and their skill at disguises is implicitly condemned by contrast with the honesty, openness, and integrity of the British character. Though Hannay's missions frequently force him to hide his identity, he usually feels extremely uncomfortable when he must pretend to act in a way contrary to his nature. Yet this moral contrast between honest pilgrim Hannay and the enemy agents who delight in their deceptions and disguises is undercut on numerous occasions by characters who reflect a fascination with the idea of the British identity swallowed up in some alien way of life. The most striking of these characters, Sandy Arbuthnot, was evidently based on the historical figure of T. E. Lawrence. The way in which Buchan develops this character suggests the profound ambivalence his generation felt toward the character and exploits of Lawrence. Sandy is as British as they come, the offspring of an aristocratic Scottish family with a long and brilliant tradition of political and social leadership. Yet he has the capacity to become so totally identified with an alien way of life that he ends up not merely as an effective agent, but a leader of some bizarre tribe or sect:

> "Billy Arbuthnot's boy? His father was at Harrow with me. I know the fellow—Harry used to bring him down to fish—tallish, with a lean, high-boned face and a pair of brown eyes like a pretty girl's. I know his record, too. There's a good deal about him in this office. He rode through Yemen, which no white man ever did before. The Arabs let him pass, for they thought him stark mad and argued that the hand of Allah was heavy enough on him without their efforts. He's blood-brother to every kind of Albanian bandit. Also he used to take a hand in Turkish politics, and got a huge reputation." (*Greenmantle*)

Sandy's extraordinary conduct seems to be the same kind of dissembling for which the villains are condemned, and yet for Buchan there is clearly an important difference. Here we encounter one of the prime virtues of the British race:

> Lean brown men from the ends of the earth may be seen on the London pavements now and then in creased clothes, walking with the light outland step, slinking into clubs as if they could not remember whether or not they belonged to them. From them you may get news of Sandy. Better still, you will hear of him at little forgotten fishing ports where the Albanian mountains dip to the Adriatic. If you struck a Mecca pilgrimage the odds are you would meet a dozen of Sandy's friends in it. In shepherds' huts in the Caucasus you will find bits of his cast-off clothing, for he has a knack of shedding garments as he goes. In the caravanserais of Bokhara and Samarkand he is known, and there are Shikaris in the Pamirs who still speak of him around their fires. If you were going to visit Petrograd or Rome or Cairo it would be no use asking him for

introductions; if he gave them, they would lead you into strange haunts. But if Fate compelled you to go to Lhasa or Yarkand or Seistan he could map out the roads for you and pass the word to potent friends. We call ourselves insular, but the truth is that we are the only race on earth that can produce men capable of getting inside the skin of remote peoples. Perhaps the Scotch are better than the English, but we're all a thousand per cent better than anybody else. Sandy was the wandering Scot carried to the pitch of genius. In old days he would have led a crusade or discovered a new road to the Indies. To-day he merely roamed as the spirit moved him, till the war swept him up and dumped him down in my battalion. (*Greenmantle*)

Richard Hannay, the muscular Christian squire who fights to protect the old stabilities of British social tradition from the dangerous forces which threaten it, represents one side of Buchan's fantasy. But there is an equally important side encapsulated in this description of Sandy: the lure of the exotic, the dream of casting off the burden of identity like a suit of old clothes and letting oneself be swallowed up in the mysterious spiritual worlds of alien peoples, the desire to escape from the dull routines of civilized life into a more primitive and daring world, the search for a crusade to deepen and intensify the sense of life, to get away from the orderly and civilized patterns of British life which seem so constrained and restrictive. In this area of his fantasy, Buchan reflected the same tensions that have been so characteristic of a stream of modern Western European literature. The quest for the exotic, the urge to cast aside the constraining roles of civilized man, the ambivalent fascination with colonial peoples—these are the same urges that were articulated more powerfully and tragically in the life of a *poète maudit* like Rimbaud or in later works of Joseph Conrad like *Heart of Darkness,* or in the life and paintings of Paul Gauguin. The social-psychological causes of these curious urges in modern European culture have been explored from many different perspectives. Freud argued in *Civilization and Its Discontents* that the development of civilized society inevitably brought with it a neurotic desire to escape and to destroy. His explanation seems compelling in many ways, though it does not completely account for one central feature of this cultural phenomenon, its relation to colonialism and imperialism. It would appear that at a certain point in the development of democratic imperialistic societies, there emerges a fascination with the idea of entering into the identity of the colonial peoples. One of the key features of this fascination is a lurking fear that these traditional cultures, which have been destroyed or transformed by imperialistic power, possessed some deeper insight into the meaning of life. While this feeling has been an important theme in the culture of Britain and France since the end of the nineteenth century, it has only recently become widespread in America, where it has particularly taken the form of a fascination with traditional American Indian cultures.

Important cultural themes or ambivalences like this are often explored on a conscious and articulate level in the work of philosophers, artists, and novelists. In twentieth-century English literature, for example, the theme of fascination with the traditional culture of colonial peoples was explored with great subtlety and insight in E. M. Forster's *Passage to India.* Popular literature, however, tends to work toward a resolution of value conflicts and a reaffirmation of conventional beliefs or perspectives. With this in view, we are in a better position to see why Buchan's fantasy world was widely enough shared by his generation to make his stories highly successful, and also why more recent generations have found that they cannot become easily identified with the network of assumptions and attitudes that rules this landscape of the imagination. Buchan's work represents a world in which the Anglo-Saxon Christian social tradition is under attack but is still strong enough in the minds of men not only to be victorious over its enemies but to be revealed as an expression of the underlying truth of the universe. This latter characteristic is especially important in defining the spy stories of Buchan and most of his contemporaries in comparison with more recent works, like those of Ian Fleming. There are, as we will see, many fundamental similarities between the epics of James Bond and Richard Hannay, but one of the most striking differences is the almost complete absence in Bond's world of the sense of providential governance which played such an important part in Buchan's. We have seen how the sense of Bunyanesque moral allegory pervades the Hannay stories and how coincidence takes on the meaning of an illustration of higher powers taking a hand in human affairs. While there is certainly enough moral melodrama and coincidence in the works of Ian Fleming, there is never a hint that the confrontation between our hero and his enemies is being shaped by the decrees of providence or that Bond and his allies are being tested by transcendent forces. It is probably the association Buchan makes between Hannay's beliefs and actions and the symbols of religious tradition that makes it most difficult for contemporary readers to enter imaginatively into his stories. While Hannay's casual racist slurs might be accepted as no more than tics of character, or melodramatic artifices, the way they are in Fleming, when we are asked to associate Hannay's obvious ideological limitations with the views of heaven, the delicate tissue of plausibility and emotional identification breaks down and we become too conscious of dated moral attitudes to suspend temporarily our own commitments and attitudes.

If Richard Hannay were only a typical clubland hero defending British social tradition with the help of higher powers, Buchan's work would doubtless have faded into the oblivion that has swallowed up most of his contemporaries and followers like Dornford Yates and Sapper. However, Buchan also responded in his fantasies to a more contemporary sense of ambivalence about the social and religious tradition. While he worked to resolve this ambivalence through characters like Sandy Arbuthnot, who remains a cool British aristocrat despite his total involvement in Eastern ways of life, the fascination with the new forces unleashed in the world remains an important undercurrent of Buchan's fantasy. Though his works of adventure are optimistic on the surface and he imagines a revitalized Christian social tradition able to overcome the threats of the twentieth century, his stories also reflect on a deeper level a sense of the critical failure of modern civilization and a yearning for a more glorious, simpler, and more mystical way of life. On this level, he still speaks to some of the major currents in the fantasy life of men in the twentieth century. The modern spy story, even in the cynical and despairing intrigues of John Le Carré and Len Deighton, has come to express this kind of feeling still more strongly. Thus Buchan was instrumental in giving both a model of form and an inner spirit to the story of espionage, giving it through his vision of the world a capacity to express in terms of contemporary international politics and intrigue the yearning for a lost world of fullness and heroism. In this respect it might be said of Buchan's fantasy vision what he himself said of one of his contemporaries:

> He was not quite of this world; or, rather he was of an earlier, fairer world that our civilization has overlaid. He lived close to the kindly earth, and then he discovered the kindlier air, and that pure exultant joy of living which he always sought. (*Memory*)

(pp. 79-100)

*John G. Cawelti, "The Joys of Buchaneering: John Buchan and the Heroic Spy Story," in* The Spy Story, *by John G. Cawelti and Bruce A. Rosenberg, The University of Chicago Press, 1987, pp. 79-100.*

---

## FURTHER READING

Adam Smith, Janet. *John Buchan: A Biography.* Boston: Little, Brown and Co., 1965, 524 p.
Extensive biography.

———. *John Buchan and His World.* New York: Charles Scribner's Sons, 1979, 128 p.
Details Buchan's life. The book is based in part on documents made available since Adam Smith's biography, cited above.

Adcock, A. St. John. "John Buchan." In his *Gods of Modern Grub Street: Impressions of Contemporary Authors,* pp. 43-50. London: Sampson, Low, Marston & Co., n.d.
Comments on Buchan's early career.

Bloomingdale, Lyman G. "John Buchan: Author, Statesman." *Books at Brown* 18, No. 3 (March 1958): 83-93.
Biographical sketch of Buchan by a collector of his works.

Buchan, Anna. *Unforgettable, Unforgotten.* London: Hodder and Stoughton, 1945, 247 p.
Autobiography by Buchan's sister that includes commentary on his life and works.

Buchan, William. *John Buchan: A Memoir.* London: Buchan & Enright, 1982, 272 p.
Memoir of Buchan by his son.

Camp, Jocelyn. "John Buchan and Alfred Hitchcock." *Literature/Film Quarterly* 6, No. 3 (Summer 1978): 230-40.
Compares Alfred Hitchcock's film *North by Northwest,* from the screenplay by Ernest Lehman, and his film adaptation of *The Thirty-Nine Steps.* Camp argues that "the two films bear some resemblance to each other, as many Hitchcock films do, but in many ways, interestingly enough, *North by Northwest* is closer to Buchan's novel than is the film, *The Thirty-Nine Steps.*"

Couzens, T. J. " 'The Old Africa of a Boy's Dream': Towards Interpreting Buchan's *Prester John.*" *English Studies in Africa* 24, No. 1 (March 1981): 1-24.
Examines stereotypical images of black people in Buchan's works.

Cox, J. Randolph. "The Genie and His Pen: The Fiction of John Buchan." *English Literature in Transition, 1880-1920* 9, No. 5 (1966): 236-40.
Provides biographical information and analyzes the major characteristics of Buchan's espionage fiction.

———. "John Buchan, Lord Tweedsmuir: An Annotated Bibliography of Writings about Him." *English Literature in Transition, 1880-1920* 9, No. 5 (1966): 241-91; 9, No. 6 (1966): 292-325; 10, No. 4 (1967): 209-11; 15, No. 1 (1972): 67-9.
Most comprehensive bibliography of secondary sources on Buchan.

Daniell, David. *The Interpreter's House: A Critical Assessment of John Buchan.* London: Nelson, 1975, 226 p.
Focuses on what Daniell considers are unjust condemnations of Buchan's works.

———. Introductions to *The Best Short Stories of John Buchan,* by John Buchan, edited by David Daniell, 2 vols., pp. 7-12, 7-14. London: Michael Joseph, 1980-82.
Daniell offers biographical information and highly favorable assessments of Buchan's literary technique.

———. "Buchan and 'The Black General'." In *The Black Presence in English Literature,* edited by David Dabydeen, pp. 135-53. Manchester, England: Manchester University Press, 1985.
Textual analysis of "The Black General," a serial adaptation of *Prester John.* Asserting that Buchan was probably not responsible for the revisions, Daniell argues that "the adaptation into 'The Black General' systematically removed both the detail of the hero's observation and his weakness and humanity. This has the effect of dehumanising everyone in the book, particularly the blacks."

Gray, W. Forbes. Introduction to *Comments and Characters,* by John Buchan, Lord Tweedsmuir, edited by W. Forbes Gray, pp. ix-xxv. 1940. Reprint. Freeport, N.Y.: Books for Libraries Press, 1970, 422 p.
Discussion of Buchan's work as the editor of the *Scottish Review* in 1907 and 1908, followed by selections from his contributions to that journal.

Hanna, Archibald, Jr. *John Buchan, 1875-1940: A Bibliography.* Hamden, Conn.: Shoe String Press, 1953, 135 p.
Lists Buchan's books, pamphlets, contributions to books and periodicals, and cites secondary sources.

Harper, Ralph. *The World of the Thriller.* Cleveland: Press of Case Western Reserve University, 1969, 139 p.
Contains frequent references to the protagonists of Buchan's espionage novels in a study exploring "a natu-

ral correlation between the existential categories in thriller plots and the existential concerns of the reader."

Hart, Francis Russell. "Stevenson, Munro, and Buchan." In his *The Scottish Novel: From Smollett to Spark,* pp. 154-81. Cambridge: Harvard University Press, 1978.

Discusses Buchan's novels as romance adventures and notes the influence of Robert Louis Stevenson's fiction on Buchan's works.

Kruse, Juanita. *John Buchan (1875-1940) and the Idea of Empire: Popular Literature and Political Ideology.* Studies in British History, vol. 7. Lewiston, N.Y.: Edwin Mellen Press, 1989, 219 p.

Examines Buchan's views on the British Empire as expressed in his correspondence, speeches, and published works. Kruse comments: "One of the fascinating ambiguities which colored his work was his attitude towards Western civilization. His characters spent much of their time defending it, some of their time spreading it, and the rest trying to escape from it."

Lambert, Gavin. "The Thin Protection." In his *The Dangerous Edge,* pp. 79-131. London: Barrie & Jenkins, 1975.

Contains a section discussing Buchan's life and elaborating on protagonists who combat international conspiracies in his espionage novels.

Masters, Anthony. "John Buchan: The Romantic Spy." In his *Literary Agents: The Novelist as Spy,* pp. 15-34. Oxford: Basil Blackwell, 1987.

Relates Buchan's involvement in British propaganda and intelligence activities to his fiction.

Namjoshi, S. "Ezra Pound: Letters to John Buchan, 1934-1935." *Paideuma* 8, No. 3 (Winter 1979) 461-83.

Reprints correspondence between Buchan and Pound on world events, providing historical and biographical background information.

Ridley, M. R. "A Misrated Author?" In his *Second Thoughts: More Studies in Literature,* pp. 1-44. London: J. M. Dent & Sons, 1965.

Argues that Buchan's novels have been seriously underrated by literary critics.

Sandison, Alan. "John Buchan: The Church of Empire." In his *The Wheel of Empire: A Study of the Imperial Idea in Some Late Nineteenth- and Early Twentieth-Century Fiction,* pp. 149-94. London: Macmillan, 1967.

Examines Buchan's fiction as an expression of his belief in the British Empire. Sandison states: "The 'philosophy' of the early Buchan hero reflects the creed of his author's 'Church of Empire': a creed which . . . turned out to be remarkably sterile."

Schubert, Leland. "Almost Real Reality: John Buchan's Visible World." *The Serif* 2, No. 3 (September 1965): 5-14.

Elaborates on the settings and use of fictional place names in Buchan's novels.

Stafford, David. "John Buchan's Tales of Espionage: A Pop-

ular Archive of British History." *Canadian Journal of History* 18, No. 1 (April 1983): 1-21.

Evaluates the popularity of Buchan's works and the attitudes toward world events expressed in them.

Swiggett, Howard. Introduction to *Mountain Meadow,* by John Buchan, Lord Tweedsmuir, pp. v-xlix. Boston: Houghton Mifflin Co., 1941.

Discusses the plots and protagonists of Buchan's espionage fiction.

Toynbee, Philip. "Philip Toynbee Tries to Account for the Fascination of *Greenmantle* by John Buchan." *Punch* 242, No. 6341 (21 March 1962): 462-64.

Explores the critic's differing reactions to reading *Greenmantle* as a child and as an adult.

Turnbaugh, Roy. "Images of Empire: George Alfred Henty and John Buchan." *Journal of Popular Culture* 9, No. 3 (Winter 1975): 734-40.

Contrasts the different views of the British empire expressed in the works of Buchan and Henty, a nineteenth-century English novelist, and notes the relationship between their values and the attitudes of their times.

Turner, Arthur C. *Mr. Buchan, Writer: A Life of the First Lord Tweedsmuir.* London: SCM Press, 1949, 114 p.

Biographical study.

Tweedsmuir, Susan. *John Buchan by His Wife and Friends.* London: Hodder and Stoughton, 1947, 303 p.

Discussion of Buchan's adult life by his wife. Lady Tweedsmuir includes a preface by George M. Trevelyan and essays by Catherine Carswell, A. L. Rowse, Leonard Brockington, and Alastair Buchan.

Usborne, Richard. "John Buchan," "Richard Hannay," "Sandy Arbuthnot and Others," and "Edward Leithen." In his *Clubland Heroes: A Nostalgic Study of Some Recurrent Characters in the Romantic Fiction of Dornford Yates, John Buchan and Sapper,* rev. ed., pp. 81-99, 100-10, 111-24, 125-30. London: Barrie & Jenkins, 1974.

Contains essays originally published in 1953 on major characters in Buchan's shockers. "John Buchan," a general discussion of Buchan's espionage novels, is excerpted above.

Voorhees, Richard J. "John Buchan Today: The Richard Hannay Novels." *The University of Windsor Review* 9, No. 2 (1974): 30-9.

Analyzes major figures in Buchan's espionage fiction, primarily focusing on Richard Hannay. Although Voorhees notes that Buchan's protagonists seem naive when considered in relation to later historical and literary events, he praises Hannay in particular as an embodiment of noble virtues.

Williams, Orlo. "John Buchan's Autobiography." *The National Review* 115, No. 692 (October 1940): 485-91.

Favorable review of *Memory Hold-the-Door.*

# Robert W. Chambers

## 1865-1933

(Full name Robert William Chambers) American novelist and short story writer.

Considered one of the most important authors of supernatural horror fiction since Edgar Allan Poe, Chambers is best remembered for his bizarre, imaginative tales of the supernatural, especially those collected in *The King in Yellow.* A prolific writer of best-selling romance novels, Chambers was accused of commercialism by many critics. While his once-popular novels are unread today, Chambers's supernatural stories are included among the classics of the genre.

Chambers was born in Brooklyn, New York, the son of a distinguished lawyer. Deciding to pursue a career as an artist, Chambers attended art school in New York and in 1886 traveled to Paris to study at the Ecole des beaux arts and later at the Académie Julien. On returning to New York in 1893, he worked as an illustrator for the magazines *Life, Truth,* and *Vogue,* and published his first book, *In the Quarter.* With the success of his second work, *The King in Yellow,* Chambers abandoned art for a literary career, a decision which proved extremely lucrative. Few of the society novels and historical romances that he subsequently produced are considered more than potboilers which catered to the market for love and adventure stories. Chambers's works—including *The Restless Sex, The Rake and the Hussy,* and *Love and the Lieutenant*—ensured his status as one of the most popular writers of his time. Chambers died in 1933.

Critical commentary on Chambers's work generally focuses on *The King in Yellow,* a collection comprising prose poems, sketches of Parisian life, and the five tales of the supernatural for which it is renowned. The title of the collection is taken from a fictitious play referred to in several of the stories. The nature of this play is intentionally obfuscated yet understood to be so appalling as to cause madness, even death, when read. Names and terms which Chambers invented, as well as those he borrowed from two horror stories by Ambrose Bierce, "An Inhabitant of Carcosa" and "Haita the Shepherd," recur in various tales. Both the play and the recurring terms serve to create a quasi-mythic background for his fiction. In what are considered his best horror stories, Chambers skillfully depicted a nightmarish world inhabited by such characters as the depraved dwarf from "The Repairer of Reputations," who, it is suggested, commands a secret army of adherents intent on national dominance, and the doomlike figure from "In the Court of the Dragon," who eventually overwhelms the narrator with a demonic vision of the world. Critics observe that what is most distinctive about these works is Chambers's ability to convey the sense of evil as a force that pervades all of existence. Chambers's later tales of the supernatural are generally considered less inventive.

*The King in Yellow* has been noted as an influence on later horror writers who have admired Chambers's creation of a unifying mythic background for stories. H. P. Lovecraft, who is similarly renowned for stories based on a fictitious mythology, praised Chambers's imagination while regretting his failure to "further develop a vein in which he could so easily have become a recognised master."

## PRINCIPAL WORKS

*In the Quarter* (novel) 1893
*The Red Republic* (novel) 1894
*The King in Yellow* (short stories) 1895
*The Maker of Moons* (short stories) 1895
*Lorraine* (novel) 1896
*The Mystery of Choice* (short stories) 1896
*Ashes of Empire* (novel) 1897
*The Haunts of Men* (short stories) 1898
*Outsiders* (novel) 1899
*Cardigan* (novel) 1901
*The Maid-at-Arms* (novel) 1902
*The Maids of Paradise* (novel) 1903
*A Young Man in a Hurry* (short stories) 1903

*In Search of the Unknown* (short stories) 1904
*The Fighting Chance* (novel) 1906
*The Tracer of Lost Persons* (short stories) 1906
*The Tree of Heaven* (short stories) 1907
*The Younger Set* (novel) 1907
*The Firing Line* (novel) 1908
*Some Ladies in Haste* (short stories) 1908
*The Danger Mark* (novel) 1909
*Ailsa Paige* (novel) 1910
*The Adventures of a Modest Man* (short stories) 1911
*The Common Law* (novel) 1911
*The Hidden Children* (novel) 1914
*Police!!!* (short stories) 1915
*The Better Man* (short stories) 1916
*The Restless Sex* (novel) 1917
*The Slayer of Souls* (novel) 1920
*The Little Red Foot* (novel) 1921
*The Talkers* (novel) 1923
*The Man They Hanged* (novel) 1926
*The Rake and the Hussy* (novel) 1930
*Love and the Lieutenant* (novel) 1935
*Smoke of Battle* (novel) 1938

---

### The Critic, New York   (essay date 1895)

[*In the following review, the critic relates* The King in Yellow *and to a lesser degree* In the Quarter *to the contemporary trend of Decadent literature.*]

A certain portion of the reading public must be in a sad way for lack of a little mystery and romance when it can seek these necessaries of life in the pages of *The Yellow Book* and **The King in Yellow.** The latter is a mixture of nightmare, Paul de Kock and modern journalism. Anybody can enter into the "sad, bad, mad world" of which it affords a glimpse, by reading three or four Sunday newspapers and three or four French novels, and "topping off" with canned lobster and American champagne. But, like a good many other experiences, this comes cheaper at second-hand; and, as it is best that one should suffer for all, we should, perhaps, acclaim Mr. Chambers a martyr to Degeneracy, especially as he seems to be possessed of a sort of ingenuity that might be turned to account in other directions. "The King in Yellow," we learn from the verses prefixed to his first story, is the title of a supposititious book. It is a book as bad as that which Mr. Grant Allen thought he could write, but could not. It is a drama such as Maeterlinck, Wilde and Ibsen, without the devil for a co-laborer, could hardly evolve between them. In it the depths of depravity are lifted up to the acme of art. It inverts all order. It reasons away reason. Whoever reads it goes mad. Half of the actual book is devoted to stories of these crazed readers, which are of a character to make us tremble for the author's intellect. There are a decomposed driver of an empty hearse; a fluid which turns fish and flesh and good red herring into cold, cold stone; a dwarf who is to lead the universal revolution, and who falls in a battle with his cat. The other half supplies the erotic element, for which the reader who has had any previous acquaintance with this sort of stuff will begin to look as soon as he has read the first few stories. There are tales of artists who do not paint, of students who do not study, of Americans whose conduct revolts yet charms the Quartier Latin, of repulsive Jews, of models, grisettes, cocottes and ladies whose exact position in society it takes many pages to define. There is no downright grossness; but the author accepts the Bohemian point of view with the enthusiasm of a convert.

**In the Quarter,** his other book, is of the same sort, but is artistically and morally better. The heroine having sinned once by mishap, sins again, it would almost appear, by good luck, since, this time, it is with an American who finally determines to marry her. But her dissolute sister and a couple of repulsive and utterly preposterous Jews prevent this consummation by drowning the hero, upon which the heroine promptly dies of a broken heart. Mr. Chambers has a facile pen. It is to be hoped that he has some versatility, and that he can turn in time to more wholesome themes. (pp. 379-80)

*"More Yellowness," in* The Critic, *New York, Vol. XXVI, No. 692, May 25, 1895, pp. 379-80.*

### The Bookman, London   (essay date 1895)

[*In the following review, the critic extols Chambers's talent as a writer of supernatural tales.*]

Mr. Chambers succeeds where so many try and fail. He makes our flesh creep. He has a gruesome ambition to torture us with mysterious horrors of the night and of madness, and the skill for it is not wanting in him. The book should be kept out of the way of all nervous and morbid persons, for even the healthy will dream miserably of his imaginings, and throw the volume aside with a shudder. But they will first have read it. He belongs to the school of his compatriot Poe, though his workmanship is of another stamp, and though he is perhaps a trifle more sensational. But he is not imitative. Within the suggestive covers of the little book there is an unusual amount of invention, and it is very rare that to nerve-assailing tales so much genuine talent is devoted. It is this talent that calls us to protest against some things. We feel doubtful of the right of anyone to invent such a tale as **"The Yellow Sign"**; the physical disgust that mingles with the mysterious horror condemns it. But yet we read that with the others, chained to them like a child to the fireside where ghost stories are circulating. Nevertheless, Mr. Chambers is so master of the power or trick of mysterious suggestion that he need never stoop to such means to cause a thrill. In **"The Demoiselle d'Ys"** he has landed us far more surely in a world of mystery by fine touches. His book divides itself into two parts. The first are stories of strange delirium, of characters subjugated and made mad by the influence of a book of evil genius, called *The King in Yellow.* The second contains mostly tamer stories of student life in the Latin quarter. The former are perhaps the more powerful and original, as well as the more sensational. But in them he is tempted to greater artistic sins—to force the note, whether of horror or of mystery, till it defeats its end, or to become self-conscious in his style, and to aim too much at fine writing. In the superficially less striking stories we see more promise, and, indeed, with respect to the beautiful Breton vision, **"The Demoiselle d'Ys,"** and the excellent description of the siege of Paris in **"The Street of the First Shell,"** it is too late to speak of promise. Self-conscious, rhetorical, sensational, Mr. Chambers may be; we name his faults not unkindly, feeling sure they will fall away from a writer of force and imagination, from one endowed with an unusual sense of beauty. (pp. 29-30)

> *A review of "The King in Yellow," in* The Bookman, *London, Vol. 9, No. 49, October, 1895, pp. 29-30.*

## Duffield Osborne  (essay date 1898)

[*Osborne was an American author and critic. In the following review, he praises many of Chambers's early works.*]

In view of the recent and almost simultaneous publications of **Lorraine** and **The Mystery of Choice,** the moment seems auspicious for a short resumé of Robert W. Chambers' work. To say that, all things considered, Mr. Chambers stands foremost among the American writers of fiction who are alive today, may occasion a stir of surprise among a certain great public that knows little of his claims,—may call up a sentiment of languid indignation among some half dozen authors who have gotten into the habit of patting each other on the back and assuming it as axiomatic that the best name lies somewhere within their little circle. Mr. Chambers may be fairly termed an outsider. He did not begin by writing down to the standard of magazine commonplace nor up (?) to the flattery of society complaisance. He was not unobjectionable from the standpoint of the young female person of North Shelby Center, nor did he fire the heart of the matinee girl with impossible pictures of her truly godlike though four-hundredesque hero. He just wrote what was in him to write; and the name and locale of his first publisher would have sufficed to cause the literary pharisees to lift up their hands and make the usual pharisaical comments, had not the aforesaid pharisees felt it quite impossible for them to notice a book bearing such an imprint.

Fortunately, however, we have in this country a small but ever widening class of readers who can recognize and enjoy what is really good; and **The King in Yellow** won at least a name for its author, where a name was best worth having. I maintain now, as I have maintained from the first, that there are no better short stories in the language than **"The Demoiselle d'Ys," "The Court of the Dragon," "The Street of the Four Winds,"** and **"Rue Barrée"**: nothing more weirdly imaginative, nothing finer in sentiment, nothing more finished in execution, and nothing more absorbing in interest. At times it has seemed to me as if Poe had come to life; but Poe with an added lightness of touch and shading, Poe with a newly developed sense of humor.

Previously to **The King in Yellow,** another book had been put out by the same publisher [**In the Quarter**]: a novel which, though showing unmistakable promise, had failed somewhat of fulfillment. Later appeared from a New York house a second collection of stories, called **The Maker of**

**Moons,** wherein was the same remarkable combination of weirdness, naturalness, and humor. Several of the tales, including the title story, **"The Silent Land"** and perhaps **"A Pleasant Evening,"** were fully up to the high standard of the earlier works. Then came two novels and they came like a fulfilled vaunt of triumphant versatility. In **A King and a Few Dukes,** Mr. Chambers sauntered over into Anthony Hope's home grounds and beat him handily at his own game; while in **The Red Republic** he wrote an historical romance of Paris under the Commune which is warranted to hold the interest of any living reader, not to mention a few who have not been too long deceased. I do not speak of Mr. Chambers' book of poems: **With the Band** because they hardly seem to be truly Mr. Chambers'. What he himself may do in poetry is better foreshadowed by some stray dedication or introduction or scraps here and there under the titles of his tales.

And now to open the new books. **The Mystery of Choice,** contains several stories that show their author at his best, such as **"Pompe Funebre," "The Messenger,"** and **"Passeur;"** while, if in two or three instances both here and in the **Maker of Moons,** he has revealed a trace of the blighting magazine impulse, it cannot be said that he has ever forgotten to be interesting, and it is perhaps his misfortune that the author of **"The Demoiselle d'Ys"** and **"Rue Barrée"** has condemned himself to be judged by a higher standard than most of us. As for **Lorraine,** it is another historical romance—a tale of the Franco-Prussian war, and unquestionably the best of Mr. Chambers' longer works—best in style, proportion, truth, and sustained interest.

And now a general word by way of conclusion. I have not ventured to use the term "great" in this paper. It is one that is used much too freely now-a-days. Nor do I feel that an individual critic is justified in applying it unless supported by a very general critical sentiment. Besides, I am a confessed adherent of the romantic cult and might fairly be said to have some measure of bias. I do not mean by this, that there are not realistic novels that have aroused my strongest enthusiasm and interest—but these novels are not by the professed, and if I may say so, professional realists. The latter parties may be pretty safely counted upon either to evolve some pitiful libel on humanity or to invite you to meet a lot of people who would bore you to death in the flesh and whom I find equally competent when translated into type. I do not affect such hosts whether they be social or literary. It is he who writes well what is known as romance, that tells me of things which, while they may not happen very generally, certainly ought to—if only to enliven life; who takes his guests away on short vacations—away from the sordid details of office and shop, away from the monotonous routine of domesticity and society, and who presents them to people they have perhaps never known—people very pleasant to meet— people whom, for the moment at least, you feel convinced you might have met had you only turned that last corner in the other direction. Is not this the highest art? To me the best realist is only a painter of portraits and landscapes; a man endowed with observation, judgment, taste, and skill. The best romanticist must be all of these but he must also be a creator of great compositions, a thinker of great thoughts. It is to Robert W. Chambers, the romanticist that I pay my respects. (pp. 86-7)

> *Duffield Osborne, "A Writer of Romance," in*
> Overland Monthly, *Vol. XXXI, No. 181, January, 1898, pp. 86-7.*

## Frederic Taber Cooper (essay date 1911)

[*An American educator, biographer, and editor, Cooper served for many years as literary critic for the* Bookman. *In the following essay, he presents an overview of Chambers's works.*]

There are certain novelists whose phenomenal popularity challenges us, almost like a blow in the face, and demands an explanation. Mr. Robert W. Chambers is a case in point. We have not at present a large number of writers who have made good their claim to a place among the born story tellers; but of these few, Mr. Chambers is one who, in the estimation of the big reading public, seems to have proved a clear title. For this reason it is distinctly worth while to examine the work of Mr. Chambers with an unsparing frankness that would seem unkind to a writer of less popular favor, and to ask ourselves, without prejudice or illusion, just what he has succeeded in accomplishing, wherein he has fallen short of his early promise, and why he has not attained that higher goal which has always seemed to lie so easily within his reach.

In the first place, it is worth while to rehearse briefly and to keep in mind just a few biographical details: that Mr. Chambers was born in Brooklyn, May 26, 1865; that he and Mr. Charles Dana Gibson were fellow-students at the Art Students' League in New York; that in 1886 he went to Paris and studied at the École des Beaux Arts and at Julian's for seven years, his paintings finding acceptance at the Salon when he was but twenty-four years of age. He returned to New York in 1893; and a glance over the old files of *Life, Truth* and *Vogue* reveals his activity at that time as an illustrator. But the story-writer's instinct, the riotous fertility of imagination that insisted on flashing endless motion pictures before his eyes at all times and in all places demanded a fuller and more rapid means of expression than that of palette and brush stroke. The tangible realities of his student's life in Paris formed the raw material for a first novel, ***In the Quarter;*** while the yet undisciplined extravagances of his imagination found outlet in the short stories of uncanny and haunting power that make up the volume entitled ***The King in Yellow.*** It was the cordial recognition accorded this second volume that decided Mr. Chambers's subsequent career.

To a critic attempting a conscientious and discriminating study of Mr. Chambers's work, the first and most salient feature is his productivity. In barely seventeen years he has produced thirty-six volumes, including four juvenile stories and a collection of verse. Furthermore, his uncommon versatility once found expression in a drama entitled ***The Witch of Ellangowan,*** written for Miss Ada Rehan and produced at Daly's Theater. It is neither practicable nor advantageous to study in detail more than a fraction of these works; singling out such as clearly mark the author's several periods of transition and stand as significant

landmarks of gain or loss in technique. But before taking up these separate volumes, it is well to get a general impression of Mr. Chambers's literary methods, his characteristic practice of the art he has chosen in preference to that for which he was trained.

The emphasis of position is deliberately laid upon the concluding phrase of the preceeding paragraph. The disadvantage under which the art of fiction has always suffered is that there is demanded of it no such long period of probation, no such definite apprenticeship as are exacted from all the other arts. It is true that many a beginner in story writing is condemned, usually with justice, to months and years of disappointment; an augmenting collection of rejection slips; and the consignment, one by one, of treasured manuscripts to the waste-paper basket. On the other hand, it happens every now and then that a new writer breaks into print like thunder out of a clear sky, with scarcely any preliminary training and by sheer force of an inborn talent. But the important point is that, whether premature or belated, the success of the story writer comes from self-tuition. There exists no Julian's to train the budding novelist, no salon to give a world-wide recognition to real genius. The case of Mr. Chambers himself is interesting and significant. Seven years seemed not too long a time to serve for the right to have a few sketches published in our illustrated magazines. But when one day it casually occurred to him to sit down at his desk and to turn the things he had seen into written pages, the result a few months later was the irrevocable black-and-white of a printed book. Of course, in one sense such an experience is high testimony to a writer's natural talent, and not merely justifies, but well-nigh demands his continuance along the same path. On the other hand, such an inborn and spontaneous vein of creative power is a handicap as well as an advantage. It minimizes the importance of self-discipline and of that mastery of technique which is to be acquired only at the price of many failures.

All this is by way of preface to the one obvious and all-pervading weakness in the writings of Mr. Chambers. For it is important to get this weakness clearly in mind before we recognize cordially his many distinctive talents. Some admirers of Mr. Chambers have spoken enthusiastically of his rare constructive ability and of the unerring instinct with which he brings his stories to the desired climax. To a great extent this is true, if only we place the principal accent upon the word "instinct." What Mr. Chambers's literary methods are, the present writer does not know in detail; but a careful analysis leaves the impression that he allows his stories very largely to construct themselves, relying upon that inborn faculty for narrative which we have already so cordially granted him. For instance, the elementary principle of Economy of Means is a rule for which Mr. Chambers seems to have no use. He has found by experience that the public likes to listen to him; and so long as they listen, he sees no reason for curtailing to fifty words a sentence which, left to itself, flows along to upward of a hundred. In his latest books, he no more sees the objection to interrupting the progress of a plot by a few pages of unnecessary dialogue than in his earlier period he saw the harm of delaying progress with superfluous paragraphs of quite vivid and wonderful description.

In other words, the impression left by Mr. Chambers's work as a whole is that he has not chosen to study carefully and to practice the best technique of the recognized masters of modern fiction. He prefers to begin and to end a story where he pleases, regardless of the question whether this beginning and end coincide with those dictated by the best art. In a measure, this is rather curious, because of all the arts none is so closely related to fiction as that of painting, none that should be a more unerring guide to the best methods of composition. And yet in his stories, Mr. Chambers over and over again interjects extraneous details which, if he had been thinking in terms of brush strokes and paint tubes, he would have known at once to lie far beyond the borders of his canvas. These criticisms of Mr. Chambers's methods are based not upon individual impressions but upon facts, easily to be demonstrated from the books themselves. Nevertheless, they are made hesitantly, because it is quite possible that Mr. Chambers has been wise in writing precisely as he does. It may be that his erratic, effervescent, irrepressible flow of invention would have become clogged and diverted under the trammels of a stricter technique. What he does possess and what must be acceded to him freely and generously are a graphic power of visualization that sets before you, with the lavishness of a glowing canvas, precisely the picture that he has in his mind's eye; an ability to handle crowds and give you the sense of the jostle and turmoil of busy streets, the tumult and uproar of angry throngs, the din and havoc of battle; and thirdly, he possesses to an exceptional degree the trick of conveying a sense of motion. You are caught, swept off your feet, and breathlessly carried onward by the irresistible rush and surge of his narrative. Many another writer has succeeded in describing speed; few of them have been able so intensely to make you feel it; few of them have given the impression of the inexorable rapidity with which the tragedies of life sometimes succeed each other.

And, furthermore, a quality which must be conceded to Mr. Chambers in common with such specialists in the outdoor life as Stewart Edward White or Charles G. D. Roberts, is an enthusiastic and all-pervading love of nature—of wood and field and water, of hunting and fishing, of all creatures of the earth and air, large and small. There is not a story but what has in it some furred or feathered creature that plays a more or less prominent part in the structure; not a chapter that is quite lacking in the song of birds or the fragrance of flowers or the flutter of insect wings. And with all this is the unmistakable imprint of authority. You feel that Mr. Chambers may blunder in the color of a man's hair or the motive for a woman's action; but he is too good a naturalist to mistake the species of a beetle or a butterfly, or misname a wayside weed or a woodland creeper. The great majority of our society novelists confine themselves so largely to the artificial life of drawing-room and boudoir that we ought to be grateful to Mr. Chambers if only for the sake of the breath of open air and song and sunshine that he never quite loses, even in the darkest and meanest of our city streets.

It will not be necessary, in order to arrive at a well-rounded estimate of Mr. Chambers's real value, to examine critically more than half a dozen of his books. An au-thor's first published volume usually possesses a peculiar significance as a standard of measurement for what comes after. Therefore, *In the Quarter* cannot be disregarded. One's first impression in reading it is that of astonishment at its vividness; it is so unmistakably a series of pen drawings, of things actually seen and lived, a pellmell gathering of the humor and pathos, the gladness and the pain of the modern art student's life. One's second thought is that, while essentially modern in material, the book is curiously old-fashioned in structure, almost as destitute of coherence as *La vie de bohême* itself. There is not an episode that you wish to prune away—they are so frankly enjoyable for their own sake; but as for plot, with the best intentions in the world, one fails to extract anything more definite than this: An American art student, who drifts into quite the usual entanglement with a young girl of a rather better sort than the average Parisian model; an estrangement brought about by the American's inheritance of a fortune, and the interference of the French girl's jealous sister; and finally the unjustifiable and melodramatic murder of the American by the sister just as all misunderstandings have been cleared up and the wedding is arranged. In this book, in spite of certain crudities, the following points are to be noticed: Here at the very start, Mr. Chambers showed a rare power of description, a distinct ability at portraiture of such types as he really knew; and because the book was written under French influences, the slight structure that it possessed was logical—even the melodramatic ending was foreshadowed and structurally justifiable.

Following this novel come a succession of volumes which, with the exception of one or two negligible efforts, consist of collections of short stories: *The King in Yellow, The Maker of Moons* and *The Mystery of Choice.* Mr. Chambers has, at intervals since then, published other volumes of tales, such as *The Tree of Heaven,* and *Some Ladies in Haste;* but unquestionably, his fame as a writer of the short story will rest upon these earlier volumes. Widely as they differ in character and quality, ranging from painfully sinister horror-stories to fantasies light as rainbow bubbles, they all of them have one quality in common: A wanton unreality, a defiance of everything that, in our sober senses, we are accustomed to believe, coupled with a certain assumption of seriousness, an insistence upon little realistic details that force us for the time being to accept as actual the most outrageous absurdities, and to vibrate, as responsively as a violin string, to the touch of the author's finger and the sweep of his imagination.

It would be easy to pick a dozen of these stories as characteristic examples of Mr. Chambers at the height of his fantastic mood. As a matter of personal preference, I would single out the story which gives its name to the volume entitled *The Maker of Moons,* for it runs the gamut of all the varied emotions that characterize these stories—the repulsion of tangible, physical ugliness, the dread of unguessed horror, the witchery of supernatural beauty, the pervading sense of invisible, warring forces of good and evil. We start with cold, prosaic details—a favorite trick of Mr. Chambers. The United States Treasury officials have reason to believe that an unscrupulous gang of counterfeiters have discovered a method of manufacturing gold, so adroitly that it defies chemical analysis, and they decide that these makers of "moonshine" gold must be suppressed. There is only one peculiarity about this gold—and herein lies the first suggestion of creepy repulsion—wherever a lump of the gold is found, there are pretty sure to be found also one or more curious, misshapen, crawling creatures, half-crab, half-spider, covered with long, thick, yellow hair, and suggestive of uncleanness and venom. The headquarters of these counterfeiters is somewhere in the northern woods, in a region of peaceful trees and still waters. And the whole effect of the story is obtained by the swift series of transitions between the physical violence of a ruthless man-hunt and the ineffable charm and beauty of a dream-lady, who appears to the hero repeatedly and without warning, standing beside a magic fountain and talking to him of a mystic city beyond the Seven Seas and the Great River, "the river and the thousand bridges, the white peak beyond, the sweet-scented gardens, the pleasant noise of the summer wind, laden with bee music and the music of bells." It is hard, in a clumsy retelling of such gossamer-spun tales, to give the impression of anything more than a jumble of mad folly. Yet the tale itself leaves an insistent memory of supernatural beauty, seen vaguely through moonlight, and of the fulsome opulence of demon gold, distilling foully into writhing, crawling horrors.

*Lorraine, Ashes of Empire, The Red Republic* and *The Maids of Paradise,* though appearing at irregular intervals, from 1894 to 1903, belong together, for the twofold reason that they all four have the Franco-Prussian War as a setting, and dashing young Americans for their heroes. Of these four, *Ashes of Empire* seems best adapted for analysis, since it shows, perhaps the best of any of them, the qualities and weaknesses of Mr. Chambers in this type of novel. It is essentially the type of the modern novel of adventure, the type made familiar by Stanley Weyman, Max Pemberton, Henry Seton Merriman and Richard Harding Davis—and on the whole, Mr. Chambers's treatment of the type may be compared not unfavorably with any one of these. He happens to know unusually well both the history and the topography of France during the period that he has chosen to treat; he attempts no ambitious character study, he takes no daring liberties with recorded facts; he is content to tell a series of rattling good stories that not only keep moving but keep you moving with them. And there is no doubt that he himself is having as much enjoyment in the writing as any of the readers have in the reading. And yet it is evident that this type of book is not what Mr. Chambers would have deliberately chosen as his favorite life work. One may venture to risk the conjecture that he would never have written these books at all had it not been for the sudden popularity, a decade ago, of the adventure novel, coupled with his own fatal facility for turning out pretty nearly any sort of story that he chooses to undertake. Had he cared more for his work, we should have had in these books characters less wooden and more like real people, and episodes more uniformly serious and less apt to approach the border-line of farce. *Ashes of Empire* is in this respect typical. It deals with the Empress Eugénie's flight, the siege and the surrender of Paris. There are two young American war correspondents, who happened to be outside the Tuileries at an opportune time to aid two unknown young women to hood-wink the crowd and effect the Empress's safe retreat. These two war correspondents, partly by design, partly by good luck, succeed in tracing the young women to their home, abutting on the city's fortifications, learn that the girls live there quite alone, renting the upper apartments to lodgers, and keeping a bird shop on the ground floor, in which parrots, jackdaws and a tame lioness harmlessly romp together. The war correspondents promptly fall in love with the two sisters, rescue them from the villainous machinations of two German-Americans (who turn out to be Prussian spies), and after undergoing the usual allotment of hair-breadth escapes, marry and live happily ever after. But while the characterization is weak, and the plot conventional, the background is really alive. We feel the tension of a national crisis, the dread of approaching disaster, the scream of shells, and the wails of starvation, the despair of a people who know that both from within and without they have been betrayed. To this extent, at least, the book is a worthy piece of work; and it is exasperating in the same way that so much of Mr. Chambers's work exasperates, because we feel that he might so easily have made it better.

Many a sincere friend of Mr. Chambers has frankly declared *Outsiders* to be his one great blunder. Yet it is a finer and more sincere piece of work than many of his successful volumes. Moreover, it throws some useful light upon his attitude, not so many years ago, toward publishers, critics and life in general in the city of New York. It is not surprising that the book failed to achieve popularity. He committed in it almost all the indiscretions which are supposed to bar the way to a big sale; he ridiculed American culture, American architecture and American social standing; and he rounded out the story with an ending which sinned doubly by being not only unhappy, but structurally unnecessary. Nevertheless, one cannot help liking the book; it is so vigorous, so cleverly satirical, and, in the main, so well written. The life of the self-styled Bohemian circles, the life of the petty artists, the minor poets, the second-rate scribblers of all sorts is, to be sure, largely done in caricature, but it is caricature of an easily recognized sort. And the background, though frankly painted by an outsider, and a hostile outsider at that, is vividly, unmistakably, aggressively New York. You cannot at a single moment of the story forget your whereabouts, or imagine yourself in any other city in the world.

> Far up the ravine of masonry and iron a beautiful spire, blue in the distance, rose from a Gothic church that seemed to close the great thoroughfare at its northern limit.
>
> "That's Grace Church," said Oliver, with a little catch in his voice.
>
> It was the first familiar landmark that he had found in the city of his boyhood—and he had been away only a dozen years. Suddenly he realized the difference between a city, in the Old World acceptance of the term, and the city before his eyes—this stupendous excrescence of naked iron, gaunt under its skin of paint, flimsily colossal, ludicrously sad—this half-begun, irrational, gaudy, dingy monstrosity—this temporary fair-ground, choked with tinsel, ill-paved,

ill-lighted, stark, treeless, swarming, crawling with humanity.

In the decade that has since passed, Mr. Chambers has learned to make his characters, even when they have long resided abroad, more uniformly courteous regarding their expressed opinions of American cities and American customs. One wonders a little whether this is because he has succeeded in acquiring a taste for our ugly buildings and our noisy streets, or whether it is simply a matter of expedient reticence. Be this as it may, one cannot read attentively his latest and most mature volumes, his present series of contemporary New York life, without observing that descriptive passages of city streets and buildings are conspicuously absent. The moment that he escapes from the city, the moment that he finds himself in the open once more, on the wide-spreading levels of Long Island, or the picturesque stretches of the Maine coast, or the Adirondacks, we get again that fertile vividness of landscape painting which was one of the great charms of his earlier books.

For the most part, however, one notices a great change in method in these later society novels that already include *The Fighting Chance, The Younger Set, The Firing Line* and *The Danger Mark.* He has begun to take himself much more seriously; he no longer gives you the impression of deliberately having fun with his characters and situations; he is trying quite sincerely to handle social and ethical problems of real importance—and what is more, to handle them in the only way that is worth while— namely, by using for his setting the present-day social life in the city and among the people that he best knows. And for these reasons, the recent work of Mr. Chambers must be judged more strictly than his earlier volumes. Because he has become more ambitious, he must be held more closely to account for his deficiencies.

These four novels have the following points in common: The action is divided between the social whirl of New York City and the country homes of the fashionable set; the central interest in each of the four volumes is due to certain hereditary instincts or impulses which make it either inexpedient or impossible for a certain man and woman to marry. In two of the volumes, namely, *The Younger Set* and *The Firing Line,* they unwisely have married and the story itself largely hinges on problems raised subsequently by divorce. In *The Fighting Chance* and *The Danger Mark,* the problem is that of unfitness to marry, the only difference between the two volumes being that the one is the reverse of the other—the former presenting a case where the man inherits a craving for alcohol and the woman an abnormal instinct for the flattery and attentions of men, while in the latter it is the woman who is intemperate and the man whose gallantries are uncontrolled. Now it cannot be denied that these themes are good enough in themselves; and that, if properly handled with adequate knowledge of life and sincerity of purpose, they might have given us something worthy of standing as an American substitute for the Continental type of analytical novel.

And it is precisely for reasons of this sort that one becomes every now and then distinctly exasperated with Mr. Chambers—not because his work is bad, but because one feels that it falls just short of being something a great deal better. *The Fighting Chance* and *The Danger Mark* are easily the best works of this later period—so much better than the two divorce problem novels that the latter may be left out of consideration. You read along in *The Fighting Chance,* rather skeptically perhaps at the start, because of a conviction that it has been much overpraised by the general public. Then, little by little, you find it taking hold upon you because it has much of Mr. Chambers's earlier qualities and something new in addition—it has his pictorial vividness, his skilful light and shade, his rapidity of action, his mesmeric trick of making even the improbable seem quite a matter of course; and at the same time it reveals a new power of delineating character, of presenting us with people who are not merely types but individuals as well, people whose inward struggles and anxieties we feel a keen and growing desire to share. And then, all at once, we run up against a paragraph or a chapter that gives us a shock, because it seems so out of keeping with the rest of the picture, so clearly the sort of thing that people do not say or do. One charitably minded reader, who is at the same time a sincere admirer of Mr. Chambers at his best, explains these occasional notable lapses, at least so far as the dialogue is concerned, on the ground that the author at such times has contented himself with merely giving, as it were, the bare scenario,—with telling what his characters said, without taking the time or trouble to work up the still more important question of just how they really said it. In other words, the simplest explanation of the unevenness of style in *The Fighting Chance* is that Mr. Chambers, to borrow one of his own titles, permits himself at times to be A Young Man in a Hurry.

But the real reason why Mr. Chambers's studies of American life at times strike a note that we feel to be off the key is this: His portraits of men are always a little stronger, surer, more convincing than those of his women. Study them all carefully from first to last, from his roughly blocked-in women of the Latin Quarter and the vaporous dream-maidens of his early fantasies, down to the designedly flesh-and-blood women of his latest book, and you feel that in varying degrees they all have one little defect; they are all of them what men like to think women to be, rather than the actual women themselves; in their actions they live up to man's expectation of what they are going to do next rather than to woman's inalienable right to do the unexpected and illogical thing. Take, for example, *The Fighting Chance;* in substance it amounts to this: A young woman already pledged to a man enjoying all the advantages of wealth and position, one day meets another man, under the shadow of a heavy disgrace due to his intemperate habits. They are guests at the same house party, they are thrown much together, and within forty-eight hours she falls, unresisting, into his arms, and yields her lips as readily as any servant girl. Heredity, says the author; the girl cannot help it; the women in her family have for generations been all that they ought not to be. Nevertheless, the reader retorts, the girl does not become "all that she ought not to be." During the weeks that follow there is many a venturesome scene, many a dialogue between the two that skirts the edge of impropriety; but in spite of heredity, the lady never quite loses her head; and after they separate at the close of the summer season, and the months slip by, and she knows quite well that the man she loves is drinking himself to death, when a word from her would stop him, she continues to wear the other man's large diamond ring and play her part in the social whirl; and only after the lapse of many months does it occur to her that she can effect the salvation of a human soul without in the least endangering her own reputation, by merely calling him up on the telephone and having a five minutes' chat. Now, this is not said with the object of belittling Mr. Chambers's work; the greater part of it is good—surprisingly good when one considers that he is a romanticist suddenly turned psychologue. Only it does not seem that a real woman could have acted in quite that way. She either would have flung discretion to the wind and done all sorts of mad things earlier in the game and thrown the blame upon heredity; or else she would, from the very beginning, have had sufficient self-control to keep her lips her own for somewhat longer than forty-eight hours.

It is always an interesting question—interesting largely because it is in a measure unanswerable—what position is going to be assigned by a later generation to any one of our contemporary novelists? As regards Mr. Chambers, there are just a few predictions which may be made without hesitation. As a writer of short stories, he has produced at least half a dozen that deserve to rank among the best that American writers have produced; and no future collection of representative short stories can claim to be complete if it happens to neglect his name. As a novelist, he has to face the handicap that must accompany too great an adaptability. With rare exceptions, the great names in fiction are those of writers whose work throughout has been fairly homogeneous—writers who have known from the beginning precisely what sort of books they wanted to write, and whose volumes have differed in degree and not in kind. Mr. Chambers has veered, and apparently with intention, in accordance with the breeze of popular demand: first to the French historical novel, then to the Civil War story, and finally, when the demand was sufficiently emphatic, to the contemporary society novel. In this last field, there is still a hope that Mr. Chambers will at length find himself: and the fact that the last of the four books is the best and most sustained and most honest piece of work that his later manner has produced affords solid ground for the hope that he may have still better and maturer volumes yet to come. Nevertheless, the accumulated experience of the ages has inculcated a wise distrust of the literary weathercock. (pp. 68-89)

> Frederic Taber Cooper, "Robert W. Chambers," in his Some American Story Tellers, 1911. Reprint by Books for Libraries Press, 1968, pp. 68-89.

## John Curtis Underwood    (essay date 1914)

[Underwood was an American poet and critic. In the following excerpt, he claims that Chambers's later books are superficial and the result of calculated commercialism.]

Very few of [Chambers's] best friends will pretend that his

later work shows a serious spirit of devotion to anything but record-breaking sales and the most obvious results of the same, and to the almighty dollar that inspires and creates them. (p. 447)

Here in America to-day, there is a growing tendency to question the educational value of fiction of the order of ostentatious mediocrity turned out wholesale by Mr. Chambers and his closest trade rivals, manufactured and sold in bargain-counter consignments over the counters of the largest dry goods stores of our largest cities at the uniform rate of $0.98 or $1.08 per volume, in editions that run regularly into the hundreds of thousands, at least once or twice a year.

If demand inevitably breeds supply, Mr. Chambers is less to be blamed perhaps for this state of things than his consumers, ultimate and parasitic.

If the Waldorf-Astoria was the first huge American hotel to provide exclusiveness for the masses; if it remains still without a rival as a palace of delight in rural communities, where the St. Regis and the Plaza are yet unknown, then Mr. Chambers enjoys the equally questionable distinction of having provided a sense of literary exclusiveness for the people who live in these hotels, and the people whose ambition centers there, both on Manhattan Island and in the outer darkness where the fame of Richard Harding Davis is already eclipsed.

If Mr. Chambers thoroughly deserves to be called the prince of wholesale and cheap illusion, of commercialized darkness and flippant immorality in American fiction; if he gets the highest current prices for literary lies and extravagant frivolity based on false social distinction and exclusively patrician ideals; if continually he assumes more than he proves, and alternately professes the most inconsequent triviality in his treatment of contemporary life and a pose of the social reformer of Society from the inside, who satirizes what he exploits; then it is small wonder that a comparatively large and unsophisticated section of the reading public, who still buy and read his books, are at a loss just where and how to place him. (pp. 447-49)

Mr. Chambers stands for more than the yellow peril of extreme commercialism in American literature; he is something less than the Great American Joke in the same field. It would be hardly fair to a greater man and truer American to call him the Phineas T. Barnum of American fiction; none the less, equally with Mr. Barnum, he is a man of his time and of the day and hour; and his rise to fame and Philistine prominence is quite as symptomatic of certain fundamental racial and human qualities that he shares, to our frequent sorrow and occasional diversion, with the rest of us. (p. 450)

Mr. Chambers studied art for more than seven years in New York and Paris, and had exposed paintings in the Salon before he returned to New York in 1893, at the age of twenty-eight, to attain an initial local prominence as an illustrator for Life, Truth and Vogue.

As a matter of fact, the career of Mr. Chambers, in art as well as in fiction, is an admirable instance of the application of the principle of the easiest way to the chase of the almighty dollar and social distinction.

It is an equally admirable example of the pressure of environment upon character or its absence.

The facts speak for themselves. Mr. Chambers comes back to New York, after seven years spent in Paris, at the culmination of his formative period. There is no evidence extant to show that he took himself seriously, with any lasting success, as a painter or illustrator. Naturally he wanted a wider recognition than that involved in contributions to the three most frivolous and ephemeral publications of any commercial standing that New York has ever known.

Naturally he went to work to transcribe the life that he had lived and seen in Paris, as a painter might work up sketches of any environment known to him, for publication. (p. 452)

On the whole, in contrast with much of his later work, *In the Quarter* is very well worth reading. So is much of *The King in Yellow,* his third book, published in 1895, and consisting in part of a series of short stories characterized by the same commercialized mingling of motives of curiosity and horror later treated with more success in *The Maker of Moons.* The latter half of the book—including **"The Demoiselle d'Ys,"** an exquisite bit of modern mediæval drama romance, and **"The Street of the Four Winds," "The Street of the First Shell," "The Street of Our Lady of the Fields"** and **"Rue Barée,"** wherein he reverts to the Latin Quarter at the time of the siege of Paris by the Prussians—contains much of the work that makes Mr. Cooper [see excerpt dated 1911] consider his early short stories better than his later ones, and claim that he is the author of at least half a dozen tales that deserve to rank among the very best that American writers have produced. *The Mystery of Choice* is classed by him in this series. (p. 453)

[*Cardigan*] which, like the rest of its series, Mr. Cooper disregards, . . . was the first of three historical novels dealing with our own Revolutionary and pre-Revolutionary period. There is a great deal of careful work in *Cardigan* and in *The Reckoning,* and not a little in *The Maid at Arms,* which is distinctly inferior to the other two, to justify Mr. Cooper's general conclusion that Mr. Chambers enjoys a graphic power of visualization, an ability to handle crowds and to give one a sense of the tumult and uproar of angry throngs and the din and havoc of battle, and that he possesses to an exceptional degree the trick of conveying a sense of motion.

At first reading *Cardigan* appears to be a brilliant bit of work. More careful analysis, however, reveals comparatively little except the conventional plot machinery of the commonplace historical novelist and the painter's trickery of massing effects picturesquely to confirm the reader's first impression.

*Cardigan* consists of a series of sufficiently vivid historical tableaux, a schoolroom scene at the home of Sir William Johnson, Commissioner for the Crown of Indian Affairs in North America in 1794, a fishing party in the woods near by, a dancing of the minuet, an incident on the trail

to Fort Pitt, a parley in the Long House of the Iroquois, a riot at Fort Pitt, a view of the interior of the debtors' prison in Boston, and finally another interior view of Buckman's Tavern at Lexington during the British attack on the town.

These pictures are most of them brilliantly executed. They dovetail into each other well enough, with a sufficiently accurate sense of historical perspective from the most obvious point of view. Through them the schoolboy who tells the story and the schoolgirl that is destined on the first page to be his wife on the last, in the conventional manner of historical novels and novelists for the last two hundred years, pass plausibly and develop sufficiently to hold the reader's attention for the time being and no longer. There is no effort, successful or unsuccessful, to represent the general temper or tendency of the times.

The whole Revolutionary agitation and uprising, in spite of the careful portraits of Jack Mount and one or two more incidental "Friends of Liberty," serves simply as a frame for the picture of the moment and an obscure background for the whole series of carefully posed and proportioned tableaux. None the less, *Cardigan,* conventional though it is in some respects, remains a fine and stirring historical romance, fit for comparison with all but the best of its type in English and American literature, and having a very perceptible intensity and charm of its own.

This intensity and charm is heightened and deepened in *The Reckoning.* Much the same method is followed as in *Cardigan,* but save in the first few chapters, where we have a picturesque account of affairs in New York City under British rule during the last year of the war, the artificiality of the treatment is less obvious. (pp. 455-57)

To say that in *Cardigan* and *The Reckoning* [Chambers] found himself on the frontier, for the time being; that here his natural facility and love for outdoor life, for adventure and picturesque description, might legitimately have satisfied itself; that he might have made the American frontier his own, working West and South for a hundred years or more, as neither Cooper nor any other American novelist had done, if he had seen fit to concentrate himself and serve a longer and more painful apprenticeship to the art that comes to him at second hand, is to deal with quantities unknown and comparatively unimportant at this moment.

The fact remains that Mr. Chambers, tempted by the facile versatility which has wrecked so many other and abler artists, or by the obvious increase in financial returns, has turned to other, less creditable fields; that the *Cardigan* series is still unfinished, and that the missing third volume is not the only loss to him and to us.

Taken as a whole, the method and purpose of the vast majority of Mr. Chambers' novels and stories of every type and period, is that of a man who is, by temperament and training alike, a painter of surfaces and very little more.

Mr. Cooper makes the most of the fact that there is one exception to prove this rule, in the course of seventeen years' work and an output of more than thirty volumes. He admits that many of Mr. Chambers' friends have declared *Outsiders* to be his one great failure. At the same time he calls it a better and more sincere piece of work than many of his more successful novels. He says it is not surprising that the book failed to achieve popularity; that in it the author has ridiculed American culture and American social standing; and has expressed freely and forcibly his attitude toward publishers, critics and life in general in New York. He admits that it is done largely in caricature; he says that it is caricature that is easily recognized; he fails to add that much of it is the caricature largely unconscious of a man whose chief use for sincerity seems to be to get back at the people and things that have rasped his own personal susceptibilities. He quotes as memorable the following passage:

> Suddenly he realized the difference between a city in the Old-World acceptance of the term, and the city before his eyes—this stupendous excrescence of naked iron, gaunt under its skin of paint, flimsily colossal, ludicrously sad—and this half-begun, irrational, gaudy, dingy monstrosity—this temporary fair-ground, choked with tinsel, ill-paved, ill-lighted, stark, treeless, swarming, crawling with humanity.

In one way this passage is memorable. It is a notable example of how English should not be written. It is obviously more superficial than discerning; it does not quite represent Mr. Chambers at his worst, but it is a fair sample of his modern descriptive style when he really tries to let himself out.

Needless to say, there is very little of it in his later series of lighter books calculated to please the public—including volumes of short stories and brief prose extravaganzas like *The Tree of Heaven, A Young Man in a Hurry, In Search of The Unknown, Some Ladies in Haste, A Tracer of Lost Persons, The Green Mouse, The Adventures of a Modest Man;* artistic and social satires like *Iole;* charming outdoor stories like *A Cambric Mask;* and Civil War novels and novelettes like *The Special Messenger* and *Ailsa Paige.*

Here and there in the series of four long novels of contemporary New York Society life beginning with *The Fighting Chance* and ending with *The Danger Mark,* in which Mr. Cooper thinks he has found himself at last, we do find a yielding to the natural tendency to hit out and hit back at the things that he doesn't like; and which, both by his long residence abroad and his social and professional associations ever since, he is incapable of appreciating at their exact and evolutionary value, either as novelist or wider critic of life.

Mr. Cooper thinks that *The Firing Line* and *The Younger Set* which have to do with divorce unconclusively and indifferently, are so much worse than *The Fighting Chance* and *The Danger Mark* that they may be left out of the discussion. In the last two books he admits that he becomes every now and then mildly exasperated with Mr. Chambers: "Not because his work is bad but because it falls just short of being something a great deal better."

Passages like the following suggest cause for exasperation more than mild:

> By January the complex social mechanism of the metropolis was whirling smoothly again. . . . The glittering machine, every part assembled, refurbished, repolished and connected, having been given preliminary speed tests at the Horse Show and a tuning up at the opera was now running under full velocity; and its steady subdued whir quickened the chattering pulse of the city, keying it to a sublimely syncopated ragtime. . . . Like a set piece of fire works spectacle after spectacle glittered, fizzed and was extinguished, only to give place to new and more splendid spectacles; separate circles, sets and groups belonging to the social solar system whizzed, revolved, rotated, with edifying effects on every one concerned, unconcerned and not at all concerned. . . . And the social arbiter of Bird Center was more of a facsimile of his New York confrère than that confrère could ever dream of in the most realistic of nightmares.

Such passages do not occur frequently enough to warrant Mr. Cooper's suggestion that the unevenness of style characteristic of *The Fighting Chance* is due to mere haste and oversight on the author's part. They appear to be inserted perversely, provocatively, to show how well Mr. Chambers sees through the Society that he is content to exploit, which he takes just about as seriously as he does any other financially available literary material; and to heighten the general spectacular effect of the book. (pp. 461-65)

[There] is no doubt whatever about his cleverness in building his book so as to capture at the start that section of the reading public whose taste in fiction is as degenerate as his own, and to hold their attention securely through the resulting pages at record prices per word.

He makes his two young degenerates, Stephen Siward and Sylvia Landis, meet at a railroad station chaperoned only by a dog which, together with other dogs and several square miles of shooting country, help to give a sporting turn to the story. Before they reach the house in the course of an hour's drive, he has them on terms of "the gayest understanding." Subsequently they meet and embrace in the corridor outside of their respective rooms, and on one occasion inside of hers, in order that the subsequent plot machinery of blackmail and the literary vivisection of three or four more degenerates in Society and out of it, may be started early in the game and the reader given the promise of a lot of this sort of thing to look forward to.

It is only fair to Mr. Chambers to say that, when he cares to do this sort of thing, he does it indifferently well. The cumulative degeneration of Leroy Mortimer, his relations with his wife, Beverley Plank, Harold Quarrier and Lydia Vyse, and the joint blackmailing of Quarrier by Mortimer and Lydia in the house where he has himself installed the girl, are portrayed with a realism that is as readable as it is rare in this part of the world.

This phase of the story, in which Mr. Chambers shows that he has a great deal to learn yet from the men who failed to teach him the art of novelizing the demi-monde during the seven years that he lived in Paris, is on the whole far from being the least conclusive, or artistically the least tolerable part of the book.

There is no indication that he has achieved a rigorously Parisian literary conscience, here or elsewhere. He handles vice that commercially justifies its existence, as he handles questionable virtue that spectacularly advertises his own cleverness, not with any clarifying or inspiring effect of getting at the vital problems of existence, but as literary material superficially ready to his hand.

With the single exception of Mortimer, his sinners, like his heroes and heroines, lack the breath of life. Harold Quarrier and the woman that he finally marries are sufficiently improbable to be quite at home in the pages of Lady Novelists of the caliber of Elinor Glyn and Marie Corelli.

The other characters compose well enough into the pictures that Mr. Chambers chooses to paint. Taken by themselves—with the exception of Beverly Plank who is rather a superior, good-natured, simple-minded, well-meaning snob among inferior snobs, and whose friendship for Siward is the one decent human interest of the book—they bear a curious resemblance to the rudimentary figures of a tragi-comedy of marionettes.

Stephen Siward, who inherits the curse of drink in order to make him interesting to Sylvia Landis and a sufficient quantity of Mr. Chambers' readers, is pictured like the majority of the author's heroes and heroines as young, handsome, clever, charming, socially eligible and sexually rather irresistible. We are assured in this case by a clubman and contemporary, that in one way, with women, he has always been singularly decent. (pp. 466-68)

Sylvia Landis is rather more of a marionette than Siward himself. Stripped of her superficial charm and her inherited sexual allure, she is simply a blind hunger for money and social position. She admits this to herself and to Siward. She binds Quarrier by the terms of a long engagement, and lets him do as he likes in the meantime, provided she is given the same liberty. (p. 470)

Books like *The Fighting Chance* not only help the idle rich to take a curiously perverted and imperfect view of their own insignificance: they tempt the idle poor to do the same. They induce thousands of empty-brained women of all classes, who waste their time over them, to sentimentalize falsely over the sham passion of Mr. Chambers' marionettes and to tell themselves truly in their commercialized heart of hearts that Sylvia Landis was a bigger fool than they ever would have been if they had had her chance to sell herself to her multi-millionaire.

Books like this advertise in wholesale the commercial possibilities of matrimony on a large financial scale; they concentrate feminine attention and appetite upon extravagance and irresponsibility; they crowd out other books and other ideals, and they have more to do with the tragedies of the divorce-court and the stock exchange than either Mr. Chambers or critics like Mr. Cooper are likely to imagine.

In this respect, in view of its large circulation and its trifling with truth from various points of view, *The Fighting Chance* may properly be considered one of the most immoral books ever published in America. (p. 472)

In *The Danger Mark,* Mr. Chambers' usual superficial fer-

tility in the evolution of his plots seems to have failed him. He has seen fit merely to reverse the mechanism of *The Fighting Chance.* We have the same country house, with its sporting side issues, bulking largely in the action of the book, full of the same irrelevant, unimportant and uninspiring minor characters. In this book the heroine is afflicted with the hereditary curse of drink aggravated in the course of her childhood by a habit of nibbling lumps of sugar drenched in cologne. (p. 473)

The hero, like other heroes of Mr. Chambers before and since, is a painter gifted with marvelous and quite unsubstantiated facility, as well as with money and social standing of his own, sufficient to render him eligible in the homes of the Best People on Manhattan Island in spite of a somewhat sultry past in Paris and other Continental centers. During the panic of 1907 he loses most of his money. By this time inspired by his sweetheart's heroic struggle against her besetting weakness—a large part of said struggle consisting of the shooting of wild boars on skiis, at her country estate and private preserve somewhere in Eastern Canada or near there—he has himself struggled sufficiently to have attained wealth and fame as a fashionable portrait painter in the city where he is most at home; and where we are given to understand, without any vast weight of testimony in favor of the author's assumption, that happiness awaits him.

To say that this book is about as true to life as *The Fighting Chance* is to slander the latter—slightly. At the time of its publication it met with a more immediate and outspoken effusion of parody and ridicule in New York and elsewhere than any book that has been prominently before the American public for many years.

Obviously, with the kind of reading public which takes Mr. Chambers seriously, a reception of this sort might have been considered an honor for some books and some authors. The only trouble about any theory of this sort is that the only reading public to which Mr. Chambers's books continue to appeal is the public which, through ignorance or perversity, puts a premium on shallowness, insincerity, pretentiousness, extravagance, and a lively sense of the spectacular that verges on vice where it does not cross the line in life and literature alike. (pp. 474-75)

There is a passage in *Ailsa Paige* that panders equally to the local pride of snobbery for snobbery's sake and to the *noblesse oblige* of commercialized pretense in the regions where his heroes and heroines find themselves most at home:

> To Ailsa Paige the Seventh was always The Guard, and now in the lurid obscurity of national disaster . . . out of the dust of catastrophe emerged its disciplined gray columns. Doubters no longer doubted, uncertainty became conviction; in a situation without a precedent, the precedent was established; the *corps d'elite* of all state soldiery was answering the national summons; and once more the associated states of North America understood that they were first of all a nation one and undivisible.—Above the terrible alarms of political confusion rolled the drums of the Seventh steadily beating the assembly.

It is possible that Mr. Chambers, who was born in Brooklyn, may be equally sincere in his patriotism and his local pride set forth spectacularly in the pages of *Ailsa Paige.* It is true that the Seventh Regiment of New York has a long and worthy record as a militia organization in the field, and as a training school for officers, sufficient to stand by itself without the sort of extravagant exploitation with which Mr. Chambers has seen fit to advertise it.

It is true that *Ailsa Paige* contains bits of spirited character drawing, pages of graphic and essentially readable descriptions and suggestions of commonplace manhood's and womanhood's capacity to rise to heights of heroism and devotion under the stress of war.

None the less the whole tendency of the book, as in the instance quoted above, is to remind us irresistibly of packages of popcorn, candy, cheap toilet soap and other non-essentials on which the American flag is displayed for commercial purposes in states where the practice is not forbidden by law.

As for *The Common Law,* whose "nude heroine" was not held in modest retirement by the absence of obvious press agent methods previous to and during its publication as a serial in the yellowest of our yellow magazines, too much has been said and written already about it and her, for the peace of mind of a long suffering public.

It is perhaps due to Mr. Chambers to say that, having decided to utilize the nude heroine aforesaid (who later develops into rather a model young lady in the conventional sense of the word) in the "altogether" in a fashionable New York studio in the first chapter or two, the initial scenes in the nude are staged with a discreet dexterity of exploitation which is either maddening or pitiable according to the temperament of the critic; and that any reader of a salacious turn of mind looking for more lurid pages later will be grievously disappointed.

The bareness of the artifice, the suggestiveness of the title, the way in which the reader of this order is cleverly strung along till he reaches the last pages and finds that which began as a rather highly-colored, near-Parisian romance subsiding into a New England Sunday School story, is doubtless highly diverting in its way. It also doubtless proved highly profitable to the original perpetrator, who has at least proved himself unmistakably the most adroit literary faker that America has ever produced. (pp. 477-79)

More briefly and mildly, in the words of a tabloid book review by Mr. J. D. Kerfoot in a recent copy of *Life,* we may characterize *The Common Law* as "a pseudo problem novel of New York studio life which gives a clever imitation of being serious while making much ado about nothing." (p. 479)

There is a certain class of readers in America to-day to which Mr. Chambers's books seem to appeal. There always will be as long as publishers of books and magazines are allowed to exploit unchecked the least sincere and inspiring phases and portrayals of American life. This class unfortunately is not confined to that section of Society which Mr. Chambers chooses, for reasons of his own, to satirize, to advertise, and to exploit.

Consequently, . . . he appears together with his readers, admirers, imitators and closest trade rivals, as a product of environment for which the American people is responsible; or as a by-product not altogether uncharacteristic of the trend of to-day.

Viewed in this light, he may be worth considerable study and detailed thought.

Otherwise, as a literary producer and poseur whose insincerity is notorious and inveterate, he reminds us irresistibly of Kipling's Tomlinson, for whose soul after death not even Satan himself could find either room or use. (p. 480)

> *John Curtis Underwood, "Robert W. Chambers and Commercialism," in his* Literature and Insurgency: Ten Studies in Racial Evolution, *Mitchell Kennerley, 1914, pp. 447-80.*

### Joyce Kilmer    (interview date 1917)

[*Kilmer was an American educator, journalist, and poet. Regarded as an accomplished editor and reviewer, he was internationally renowned for his poem "Trees," which begins "I think that I shall never see / A poem lovely as a tree." In the following excerpt from an interview, Kilmer questions Chambers about theories of writing.*]

[The] great predecessor in the relentless pursuit of the "right word" was, teachers of literature tell us, . . . Gustave Flaubert. But these academic gentlemen, who insist that the writer shall spend hours, even days, if necessary, in perfecting a single sentence, seldom produce any literature.

I asked Robert W. Chambers, who has written more "best sellers" than any other living writer, what he thought of Flaubert's method of work.

He looked at me rather quizzically. "I think," he said, with a smile, "that Flaubert was slow. What else is there to think? Of course he was a matchless workman. But if he spent half a day in hunting for one word, he was slow, that's all. He might have gone on writing and then have come back later for that inevitable word."

"But what do you think of Flaubert's method, as a method?" I asked. "Do you think that a writer who works with such laborious care is right?"

"It's not a question of right or wrong," said Mr. Chambers, "it's a question of the individual writer's ability and tendency. If a man can produce novels like those of Flaubert, by writing slowly and laboriously, by all means let him write that way. But it would not be fair to establish that as the only legitimate method of writing.

"Some authors always write slowly. With some of them it's like pulling teeth for them to get their ideas out on paper. It's the same way in painting. You may see half a dozen men drawing from the same model. One will make his sketch premier coup; another will devote an hour to his; another will work all day. They may be artists of equal ability. It is the result that counts, not the method or the time."

"And what is it that makes a man an artist, in pigments or in words?" I asked. "Do you believe in the old saying that the poet—the creative artist—is born and not made?"

"No," said Mr. Chambers, "I do not think that that is the truth. I think that with regard to the writer it is true to this extent, that there must exist, in the first place, the inclination to write, to express ideas in written words. Then the writer must have something to express really worthy of expression, and he must learn how to express it. These three things make the writer—the inclination to say something, the possession of something worth saying, and the knowledge of how to say it."

"And where does genius come in?" I asked.

"What is genius?" asked Mr. Chambers, in turn. "I don't know. Perhaps genius is the combination of these three qualities in the highest degree.

"Of course," he added, with a laugh, "I know that all this is contrary to the opinion of the public. People like to believe that writers depend entirely upon an inspiration. They like to think that we are a hazy lot, sitting around and posing and waiting for some sort of divine afflatus. They think that writers sit around like a Quaker meeting, waiting for the spirit to move them."

"But have there not been writers," I asked, "who seem to prove that there is some truth in the inspiration theory? There is William de Morgan, for example, beginning to write novels in his old age. He spent most of his life in working in ceramics, not with words."

"On the contrary," said Mr. Chambers, "I think that William de Morgan proves my theory. He really spent all his life in learning to write—he was in training for being a novelist all the while. The novelist's training may be unconscious. He must have—as William de Morgan surely always has had—keen interest in the world. That is the main thing for the writer to have—a vivid interest in life. If we are to devote ourselves to the production of pictures of humanity according to our own temperaments, we must have this vivid interest in life; we must have intense curiosity. The men who have counted in literature have had this intense, never-satiated curiosity about life.

"This is true for the romanticists as well as the realists. The most imaginative and fantastic romances must have their basis in real life.

"I know of no better examples of this truth than the gargoyles which one sees in Gothic architecture in Europe. These extraordinary creatures that thrust their heads from the sides of cathedrals, misshapen and grotesque, are nevertheless thoroughly logical. That is, no matter how fantastic they may be, they have backbones and ribs and tails, and these backbones and ribs and tails are logical—that is, they could do what backbones and ribs and tails are supposed to do.

"In real life there are no creatures like the gargoyles, but the important thing is that the gargoyles really could exist. This is a good example of the true method of construction.

The base of the construction must rest on real knowledge. The medieval sculptors knew the formation of existing animals; therefore they knew how to make gargoyles."

"How does this theory apply to poets?" I asked.

"I don't know," answered Mr. Chambers, "but it seems to me to apply to all creative work. The artist must know life before he can build even a travesty on life."

I called Mr. Chambers's attention to the work of certain ultra-modern poets who deliberately exclude life from their work. He was not inclined to take them seriously.

"There always have been aberrations," he said, "and there always will be. They're bound to exist. And there is bound to be, from time to time, attitudinizing and straining after effect on the part of prose writers as well as poets. And it is all based on one thing—self-consciousness. It is self-consciousness that spoils the work of some modern writers."

I asked Mr. Chambers to be more specific in his allusions. "I cannot mention names," he said, "but there are certain writers who are always conscious of the style in which they are writing. Sometimes they consciously write in the style of some other men. They are thinking all the while of their technique and equipment, and the result is that their work loses its effect. A writer should not be convinced all the while that he is a realist or a romanticist; he should not subject himself deliberately to some special school of writing, and certainly he should not be conscious of his own style. The less a writer thinks of his technique the sooner he arrives at self-expression.

"It's just like ordinary conversation. A man is known by the way in which he talks—that is his 'style.' But he is not all the while acutely conscious of his manner of talking—unless he has an impediment in his speech. So the writer should be known by his untrammeled and unembarrassed expression." (pp. 75-80)

[Have] you such a thing as a favorite author?" I asked.

"Yes," said Mr. Chambers. "Dumas." (p. 82)

Mr. Chambers, although he has intimate knowledge of the Quartier Latin, has little use for "Bohemia."

"What is Bohemia?" he asked. "If it is a place where a number of artists huddle together for the sake of animal warmth, I have nothing to say against it. But if it is a place where a number of artists come to scorn the world, then it is a dangerous thing. The artist should not separate himself from the world.

"These artistic and literary cults are wrong. I do not believe in professional clubs and cliques. If writers form a combination for business reasons, that is all right, but a writer should not associate exclusively with other writers; he should do his work and then go out and see and talk to people in other professions. We should sweep the cobwebs from the profession of writing and not try to fence it in from the public." (pp. 83-4)

I mentioned to Mr. Chambers the theory that literature is better as a staff than as a crutch, as an avocation than as a vocation. This, like the "inevitable word" theory, is greatly beloved by college professors. Mr. Chambers said:

> "I disagree utterly with that theory. Do you remember how Dr. Johnson wrote *Rasselas?* It was in order to raise the money to pay for his mother's funeral. I believe that the best work is done under pressure. Of course the work must be enjoyed; a man in choosing a profession should select that sort of work which he prefers to do in his leisure moments. Let him do for his lifework the task which he would select for his leisure—and let him not take himself too seriously!"

> (pp. 84-5)

*Joyce Kilmer, "What Is Genius? Robert W. Chambers," in his* Literature in the Making by Some of Its Makers, *1917. Reprint by Kennikat Press, Inc., 1968, pp. 75-85.*

## Grant Overton   (essay date 1922)

[*An American novelist and literary critic, Overton served as the editor of the book review section for the* New York Sun *and later as the fiction editor for* Collier's. *In the following excerpt, he relates Chambers's perspective on his own writing.*]

Once a man came to Robert W. Chambers and said words to this effect:

> You had a great gift as a literary artist and you spoiled it. For some reason or other, I don't know what, but I suppose there was more money in the other thing, you wrote down to a big audience. Don't you think, yourself, that your earlier work—those stories of Paris and those novels of the American revolution—had something that you have sacrificed in your novels of our modern day?

Mr. Chambers listened politely and attentively. When the man had finished, Chambers said to him words to this effect:

> You are mistaken. I have heard such talk. I am not to blame if some people entertain a false impression. I have sacrificed nothing, neither for money nor popularity nor anything else.

> Sir, I am a story-teller. I have no other gift. Those who imagine that they have seen in my earlier work some quality of literary distinction or some unrealised possibility as an artist missing from my later work, are wrong.

> They have read into those stories their own satisfaction in them and their first delight. I was new, then. In their pleasure, such as it was, they imagined the arrival of someone whom they styled a great literary artist. They imagined it all; it was not I.

> A story-teller I began, and a story-teller I remain. I do pride myself on being a good story-teller; if the verdict were overwhelmingly against me as a good story-teller that would cast me down. I have no reason to believe that the verdict is against me.

And that is the ground I myself have stood upon. I am not responsible for the delusion of those who put me on some other, unearthly pinnacle, only to realise, as the years went by, that I was not there at all. But they can find me now where they first found me—where I rather suspect they found me first with unalloyed delight.

This does not pretend to be an actual transcription of the conversation between Mr. Chambers and his visitor. I asked Mr. Chambers recently if he recalled this interview. He said at this date he did not distinctly recollect it and he added:

> Probably I said what is true, that I write the sort of stories which at the moment it amuses me to write; I trust to luck that it may also amuse the public.

> If a writer makes a hit with a story the public wants him to continue that sort of story. It does not like to follow the moods of a writer from gay to frivolous, from serious to grave, but I have always liked to change, to experiment—just as I used to like to change my medium in painting, aquarelle, oil, charcoal, wash, etc.

> Unless I had a good time writing I'd do something else. I suit myself first of all in choice of subject and treatment, and leave the rest to the gods.

> (pp. 366-68)

*Grant Overton, "Robert W. Chambers and the Whole Truth," in his* Authors of the Day: Studies in Contemporary Literature, *George H. Doran Company, 1924, pp. 366-79.*

## Fred Lewis Pattee   (essay date 1923)

[*An American literary historian, critic, poet, and novelist, Pattee was a pioneer in the study of American literature. He believed that literature is the popular expression of a people, rather than the work of an elite group. In the following excerpt, Pattee praises the dialogue in Chambers's works, citing it as representative of potential that was never realized.*]

The deadly sin, according to the editors of [the first decade of the twentieth century], was heaviness: the tale must move trippingly, with modernness in every sentence. A critical test was the dialogue: of all things it most clearly revealed the artisan. It must seem perfectly natural, inevitable, indeed, and yet it must be in reality the perfection of the artificial. It must be stripped to the barest essentials, relieved to the last possible degree of the childish "tags," of older days, like "said he" and "replied she," and it must move with brilliance and vivacity. In Robert W. Chambers, the most skillful exponent of the ultramodern methods, the dialogue often leaves the reader breathless. The characters talk cracklingly, in fragments of sentences often, in epigrams, exclamations, sudden dramatic thrusts and parries. It is rapier work. This for example:

> "I was in love with you once."

> She bent her head and looked down gravely at her slender hand, which lay across his.

"That was very dear of you," she murmured.

After a silence.

"And—you?" he asked.

"Do you mean, was I ever in love with you?"

"Yes."

"I—don't—know. I loved your letters. I adored you. I do now. Perhaps, if you had come back—"

"I wish I had!"

"Do you?" She lifted her eyes to him curiously. "You know, Jim, I must be honest with you. I never did love anybody—but, if you—had come home—and if you had told me that you cared for me—that way—"

"Yes."

"Well, I was just a girl. You had my affections. I could have been taught very easily, I think—to care—differently—"

"And—now?"

"What?"

"Is it too late to teach you, Steve?"

"Why, yes—isn't it?"

"Why?"

"I'm married."

Chambers had begun his work after a long residence as an art student "in the Quarter" at Paris. His second volume, **The King in Yellow,** shadowy unrealities, tales of weird terror treated with what seemed like dawning power, appeared in 1895. Remarkable facility he had and lightness of brush with a French quality of taste that promised well, but—read Mrs. Wharton's caustic tale "The Pot-Boiler." The girl wooed by the penniless genius Stanwell and by the unbelievably-paid panderer to vulgarians, Mungold, chose the latter, for Mungold was using the best that was in him:

> "I can take money earned in good faith—I can let Caspar live on it. I can marry Mr. Mungold because, though his pictures are bad, he does not prostitute his art."

(pp. 367-68)

*Fred Lewis Pattee, "O. Henry and the Handbooks," in his* The Development of the American Short Story: An Historical Survey, *Harper & Brothers Publishers, 1923, pp. 357-88.*

## H. P. Lovecraft   (essay date 1933-35)

[*Lovecraft is considered one of the foremost modern authors of supernatural horror fiction. Strongly influenced by Edgar Allan Poe, Lord Dunsany, and early science fiction writers, he developed a type of horror tale that combined occult motifs, modern science, and the regional folklore of his native New England to produce the personal mythology on which he based much of his work.*

*In the following excerpt, Lovecraft notes "The Yellow Sign" as perhaps the best of Chambers's horror tales.*]

Very genuine, though not without the typical mannered extravagance of the eighteen-nineties, is the strain of horror in the early work of Robert W. Chambers, since renowned for products of a very different quality. **The King in Yellow,** a series of vaguely connected short stories having as a background a monstrous and suppressed book whose perusal brings fright, madness, and spectral tragedy, really achieves notable heights of cosmic fear in spite of uneven interest and a somewhat trivial and affected cultivation of the Gallic studio atmosphere made popular by Du Maurier's *Trilby.* The most powerful of its tales, perhaps, is **"The Yellow Sign",** in which is introduced a silent and terrible churchyard watchman with a face like a puffy grave-worm's. A boy, describing a tussle he has had with this creature, shivers and sickens as he relates a certain detail. "Well, sir, it's Gawd's truth that when I 'it 'im 'e grabbed me wrists, sir, and when I twisted 'is soft, mushy fist one of 'is fingers come off in me 'and." An artist, who after seeing him has shared with another a strange dream of a nocturnal hearse, is shocked by the voice with which the watchman accosts him. The fellow emits a muttering sound that fills the head "like thick oily smoke from a fat-rendering vat or an odour of noisome decay." What he mumbles is merely this: "Have you found the Yellow Sign?" A weirdly hieroglyphed onyx talisman, picked up in the street by the sharer of his dream, is shortly given the artist; and after stumbling queerly upon the hellish and forbidden book of horrors the two learn, among other hideous things which no sane mortal should know, that this talisman is indeed the nameless Yellow Sign handed down from the accursed cult of Hastur—from primordial Carcosa, whereof the volume treats, and some nightmare memory of which seems to lurk latent and ominous at the back of all men's minds. Soon they hear the rumbling of the black-plumed hearse driven by the flabby and corpse-faced watchman. He enters the night-shrouded house in quest of the Yellow Sign, all bolts and bars rotting at his touch. And when the people rush in, drawn by a scream that no human throat could utter, they find three forms on the floor—two dead and one dying. One of the dead shapes is far gone in decay. It is the churchyard watchman, and the doctor exclaims, "That man must have been dead for months." It is worth observing that the author derives most of the names and allusions connected with his eldritch land of primal memory from the tales of Ambrose Bierce. Other early works of Mr. Chambers displaying the outré and macabre element are **The Maker of Moons** and **In Search of the Unknown.** One cannot help regretting that he did not further develop a vein in which he could so easily have become a recognised master. (pp. 409-10)

*H. P. Lovecraft, "Supernatural Horror in Literature (1925-27)," in his* Dagon and Other Macabre Tales, *edited by August Derleth, Arkham House Publishers, Inc., 1965, pp. 365-436.*

## E. F. Bleiler  (essay date 1970)

[*Bleiler is an American editor, biographer, and critic prominent for his work in the genres of science fiction, fantasy, supernatural horror, and detective fiction. In the following essay, he praises Chambers's early tales of the supernatural, most notably those in* The King in Yellow, *and provides a survey of related works by Chambers.*]

During the last decade or so of the nineteenth century, some forgotten impulse drove several unexpected persons into brief association with supernatural fiction. The architect Ralph Adams Cram wrote a collection of ghost stories entitled *Black Spirits and White* (1895). The historical novelist F. Marion Crawford wrote "The Upper Berth" (1894). The social worker Charlotte Perkins Gilman mixed psychology and supernatural adumbrations in "The Yellow Wallpaper" (1899). Two authors of somewhat saccharine children's books, Mrs. Nesbit and Mrs. Molesworth, wrote respectively *Grim Tales* (1893) and *Uncanny Tales* (1896). And Robert William Chambers— "the shopgirl Sheherezade," "the barker of the New York society side show"—wrote *The King in Yellow* (1895), one of the most important books in the literature of supernatural horror. (p. vii)

Chambers's fiction can be classified fairly easily. Many of his novels were historical. There was a series about the American Revolution, of which the best-remembered book is *Cardigan.* Four novels centered in the Franco-Prussian War, the best-known being *The Red Republic.* Others took place in the American Civil War. Perhaps most popular, however, were his society novels, which in a certain way were problem novels. Aimed at the shopgirl market and deliberately written on a trivial level, they were framed around such questions as social mésalliances, marriage and divorce, hereditary alcoholism in the upper crust, the morality of posing "in the altogether" for artists, and similar topics in the pre-Titanic social world of New York. These include *The Fighting Chance, The Danger Mark, The Younger Set,* and *The Firing Line.* He also touched briefly, with less financial success, the modern pastorale, the detective story, and other forms. (p. viii)

Today almost all Chambers's work is forgotten. It is doubtful if his novels are even read for period nostalgia. Indeed, their fate has taken a paradoxical turn. They were once so common and in so little demand that used-book stores discarded them or consigned them to the ten-cent bin. As a result they are now sometimes more difficult to find than many books that were once scarcer.

This rejection of Chambers is as it should be, for he wrote very consciously for his present, and wrote to the level where he could make the most money. He had no illusions about the quality or permanency of his writing, and candidly admitted that he was more interested in collecting antique furniture and restoring his ancestral home in the Appalachians than in literary reputation. His novels are bad from the point of view of craftsmanship: the American historical novels read like parodies of Stanley Weyman, the French novels are hysterical, and the society novels are simply incredible. In a certain sense, too, most of his work is immoral in implanting or reinforcing vulgar attitudes.

A contemporary attack on the grounds of immorality was made by John Curtis Underwood [see excerpt dated 1914]: "The prince of wholesale and cheap illusion . . . the highest current prices for literary lies and extravagant frivolity based on false social distinctions . . . he reminds us irresistibly of Kipling's Tomlinson, for whose soul after death not even Satan himself could find room or use."

Yet if all this verbiage is washed away, all six or seven million words of it, something of Robert W. Chambers remains that is still worthwhile. This is *The King in Yellow* and certain other early pieces that he wrote before commercialization set in. Perhaps he still had a youthful exuberance that was later overwhelmed by cynicism. Perhaps there was a thoughtfulness that was later brushed aside by the need for improvisation. Perhaps there was a feeling of work-conscience, a desire to produce the best, that somehow vanished later. Or, perhaps, there may have been outside assistance.

*The King in Yellow* appeared in 1895 as a rather attractive little book bound in light green cloth, with a salamander (or butterfly) printed on its cover. It was a member of Neely's Prismatic Library, a series of popular novels and short story collections, mostly by unknowns. In addition to several Parisian sketches, reprinted from an earlier publication, it contained five stories . . . . : **"The Yellow Sign," "The Repairer of Reputations," "The Mask," "The Court of the Dragon,"** and **"The Demoiselle d'Ys."**

Ambrose Bierce stands behind much of this book, with his "Inhabitant of Carcosa" furnishing a mythology within which Chambers worked. But there are also obvious differences between Bierce's work and Chambers's. The stories of *The King in Yellow* lack Bierce's tortuous craftsmanship and narrative complexity; they are more conventional in pattern. They have recognizable heroes and heroines, and what happens has a beginning, a middle, and an end. Gone, too, is Bierce's icy, macabre irony. Instead there are undercurrents of direct terror and (probably in compensation) oversweetness.

Chambers also wrote from an aesthetic of the supernatural that was quite different from Bierce's. For Bierce the supernatural had meaning of a sort, not in the literal terms of his stories, but in their psychological equivalents. The ideas within his stories were for him ideas of power that had motivated or wrecked much of his life. For Chambers, on the other hand, there is no evidence that the horrors he wrote about were personal in any profound way. With Bierce there is usually a question of psychological interpretation: how much of what is happening is taking place in the darknesses of the psyche and how much is objective? Or, is there anything really objective? For Chambers the imprecision is metaphysical rather than psychological, a matter of evil rather than of evil men. There are suggestions of other worlds of experience where there may really be a King in Yellow, where the Yellow Sign may exist. Like "The Mysterious Card" by Cleveland Moffett, *The King in Yellow* sets up a deliberate barrier to comprehension and solution.

The stories in this book have been very important in the developmental history of American fantastic literature.

All the major writers in the emergence period of the pulp story seem to have known the book. Its influence spread almost universally, even when it was out of print. Motives were lifted from it, story lines imitated and rechanneled, and, most of all, the new concepts of metaphysical-physical horror were taken over by a host of writers who were tired of stock ghosts, weary of occult phenomena, and unconcerned with mysticism or psychological probing. Indeed, one might even single out *The King in Yellow* as the most important book in American supernatural fiction between Poe and the moderns.

After *The King in Yellow* Chambers gradually drifted away from supernatural fiction, with only occasional stories in periodicals or collections. On the whole these show a decline from *The King in Yellow,* but an occasional story is still worth examining. (pp. ix-xi)

"The Maker of Moons," from the book of the same title first published in 1896, has long been one of Chambers's best-liked stories. In its blending of the Oriental menace, the Secret Service, black magic, adventure and love it anticipates a popular form of the 1920's, which Sax Rohmer practiced skillfully. To my mind, however, it is an unsuccessful venture into a subgenre, both undeveloped and too long, naive and sentimental. Still, it has exciting pictorial moments—as was often the case with Chambers's work—and the image of the Maker at work is likely to remain in the reader's memory long after the rest of the story has been forgotten. In the same collection appeared "A Pleasant Evening," a somewhat individual development of a common theme in fantastic fiction: the revenant who announces his own death. It is unusual in Chambers's work in having an occasional naturalistic touch.

"The Messenger," . . . from *The Mystery of Choice* (1897), is one of a series of stories set in the Breton countryside that Chambers seems to have loved. It is a material-horror story, possibly a little unsubtle, but it does have the characteristics of a nightmare with its disruptions of the time dimension, interlocked identities, and repetitive fate, which are all novel touches for the period. "The Key to Grief," from the same collection of stories, is basically a restatement of Bierce's "An Occurrence at Owl Creek Bridge," but sentimentalized, without Bierce's precision or hardness of prose. Also in *The Mystery of Choice* . . . is "The Purple Emperor," a rather interesting detective story with slight touches of the supernatural.

A persistent trend in Chambers's work was an attempt to achieve the "light touch." He tried to create a story that would be bright, cheerful, flippant, elegant, sophisticated and slightly cynical. In this he usually failed. Sometimes he resorted to the light manner in the wrong place, as in "The Maker of Moons," and became garrulous and diffuse. In one extended area, however, he was successful. This was a collection of biological science-fiction stories published under the title *In Search of the Unknown* (1904). Their hero, an Edwardian Archie Goodwin, is a little coy at times, but on the whole these biological fantasies are among the most successful science-fiction humor. (pp. xi-xii)

[Three stories from *In Search of the Unknown,* "The Har-

bor-Master," "In Quest of the Dingue," and "Is the Ux Extinct?"] carry obvious reminiscences of H. G. Wells and A. C. Doyle. It should be pointed out that Chambers's more scientifically minded contemporaries were more aware of the Prince of Monaco's (historical) interest in biology than modern readers are likely to be, and that the third story probably had humorous extensions that are now partly lost. (p. xii)

The four books [mentioned above] were not Chambers's only attempts at fantasy. Approximately another dozen books fall into the same category, although in several the fantastic element is slight and secondary. *The Tracer of Lost Persons* introduced Mr. Keene, the private detective. Mr. Keene, who used to be called Bayard Keene on the radio back in the 1930's, was still alive on television not too many years ago. His original adventures were a peculiarly sentimental detective form—which Bernard Capes handled better—in which occasional elements of the supernatural entered. *The Tree of Heaven* is a series of slight stories vaguely connected with the symbolism of an Oriental carpet. It is not worth reading. *Police!!!* continues the adventures of the young zoologist of *In Search of the Unknown,* in search of biological marvels and beautiful women. The individual stories are sometimes more fantastic than those of the earlier book, but are carelessly written and lack spontaneity and conviction. *The Talkers* is an occult novel, more distressing and unpleasant than terrifying. Much the most important of these secondary books is *The Slayer of Souls,* a novel set in the same milieu as "The Maker of Moons," which was a preparatory version of it: the Yellow Peril, German-Bolshevik plots, black magic from Central Asia, secret agents and romance. In it Chambers achieved a seacoast of Bohemia feat by bringing China into geographical contact with the devil-worshiping Yezidees of Kurdistan. *The Slayer of Souls* has its faults, but it is a real thriller with many memorable scenes.

At this moment it seems probable that Robert W. Chambers is going to end as a magnetic pattern in the memory tank of some bibliographic machine of the late twentieth century. The generation that once read his work is mostly gone, and in another decade or two Chambers will have been completely outlived except as a possible topic in social research. Yet there is one exception to this judgment: as long as there are readers of supernatural fiction, *The King in Yellow* will survive. (pp. xii-xiii)

> *E. F. Bleiler, in an introduction to* The King in Yellow, and Other Horror Stories, *by Robert W. Chambers, edited by E. F. Bleiler, Dover Publications, Inc., 1970, pp. vii-xiii.*

## Lee Weinstein    (essay date 1979)

[*In the following essay, Weinstein examines the nature, sources, and influence of the mythic background that unites the four central tales in* The King in Yellow.]

*The King in Yellow* has been referred to as the most important work in supernatural fiction between Poe and modern times, and at least one contemporary review compared the work to that of Poe. It has been reprinted many times in whole and in part . . . and the individual stories have enjoyed endless reprinting in magazines and anthologies.

One of the unique aspects of the book, and probably the major reason for its popularity and influence, is the central idea of having a number of seemingly unrelated stories tied together by a common mythical background, an idea which H. P. Lovecraft was later to develop independently, and much more fully. In none of the stories are we given a clear idea of what this mythical backdrop actually is, yet this gives the imagination a free reign, and provides another major reason for the book's popularity. As the book review column in the June, 1897 issue of *Godey's Magazine* put it, " . . . This group of stories, varied in idea, yet bound together by one subtle thread: the baleful influence upon the life of everyone that reads that mysterious volume, *The King in Yellow*. The spell of this wonderful book is wisely left unexplained and vague. It floats shapelessly and stealthily into the story . . . like the effluvia of a fatal marsh."

E. F. Bleiler [see excerpt dated 1970] refers to this obscurity as "a deliberate barrier to comprehension" comparable to that in "The Mysterious Card" by Cleveland Moffett. This may be exaggerated; we are made aware of the general intent of the mythical elements, although certainly the meanings of the specific elements from the play are deliberately kept vague.

The four stories that revolve about this obscure background are **"The Repairer of Reputations"**, **"The Mask"**, **"In the Court of the Dragon"**, and **"The Yellow Sign"**. The fifth fantasy story in the book, **"The Demoiselle d'Ys"**, is quite powerful in its own right, but is thematically unrelated to the others and will not be discussed here.

The central element of the mythos is *The King in Yellow*, itself a fictitious play in two acts, in which depravity is raised to the level of high art. The idea was apparently suggested to Chambers by *The Yellow Book*, a risque and daring periodical of the late 1890's. In a 1928 anthology of material from *The Yellow Book*, the introduction describes the periodical in terms very similar to those used by Chambers to describe his *King in Yellow*. Both are "poisonous" and "sinful". An unfavorable contemporary review bearing the title "More Yellowness" [see review dated 1895; *The Critic*] also stressed the comparison of Chambers's book with the scandalous periodical, calling Chambers a "martyr to degeneracy". As Marion Zimmer Bradley pointed out in her article "The (bastard) Children of Hastur" . . . , the word "yellowness", during the late 1890's, had . . . , connotation of wickedness, decadence, and spiritual danger. She also stressed the comparison of "The King in Yellow" with *The Yellow Book,* noting that both were credited with the ability to corrupt.

Since the four stories, as we shall see, are set in the future, perhaps Chambers was extrapolating what the *Yellow Book* concept would evolve into if it were to be taken to its absurd extreme.

The stories are introduced by a poem called "Cassilda's Song". This poem, supposedly from Act 1, Scene 2 of *The King in Yellow*, sets the mood by introducing us to the mysterious city of Carcosa, where black stars hang in the heavens, and twin suns rise and set. These and other related references form the mythical backdrop of the stories.

In the first story, **"The Repairer of Reputations,"** . . . we are introduced to the somewhat utopian atmosphere of the United States 25 years in the future. (The book was published in 1895: the story is set in 1920). All major political problems have been solved, bigotry and intolerance have been eliminated, suicide having been legalized, the first Government Lethal Chamber has been erected. This chamber, a symbol of purification, stands in contrast to *The King in Yellow,* which has "spread like an infectious disease from city to city, from continent to continent".

The plot centers around a madman named Castaigne, who, working under a deformed and insane dwarf named Wilde, hopes to become king of the United States. Castaigne, who narrates the story, tells us at the beginning that he has read *The King in Yellow* during the convalescent period following a fall from his horse. It is not made clear whether his ensuing madness is due to the injury to his head, or to his reading of the play, but it is the play that has motivated both him and Wilde in their lust for power.

"Cassilda's Song" introduced us to some of the mythical trappings of the play. In **"The Repairer of Reputations"** we find that these elements, plus several new ones, are integrally related to the mad lust for power that afflicts the two central characters. Thus Castaigne is pathologically fascinated by a manuscript of Wilde's, "The Imperial Dynasty of America", which opens with the words, "When from Carcosa, the Hyades, Hastur, and Aldebaran", and ends by naming him the new king. (The significance of these and other allusions to the play will be discussed later).

In his mad frame of reality, Castaigne believes that to become king, he must prevent his cousin Louis from marrying Constance Hawberk, Louis's fiancee. To accomplish this, Castaigne and Wilde send an assassin, another man haunted by the insidious play, to murder Constance. It is this that proves Castaigne's undoing, as foreshadowed by the assassin's self-destruction in the Government Lethal Chamber.

Yet there are strong hints that there is more to the nefarious schemes of Wilde and Castaigne than mere madness. Wilde seems to know about a secret past of Constance and her father. And he predicts correctly, where a certain piece of armor, missing for years, can be found. Obviously, he does possess certain knowledge that surpasses our plane of existence. As the epigram in French at the beginning of the story warns us, "Let us not scoff at madmen; their madness will outlast ours . . . " This possibility, that there may really be something behind their ravings, lends a certain edge of horror to their activities. Throughout the story, a deliberate ambiguity is set up regarding the reality of the narrator's delusions. In one scene, Wilde sends a Mr. Steylette from his door, who, he explains, is the Arnold Steylette, owner and editor-in-chief of a well-known newspaper. Wilde adds as the man leaves, "I pay him very badly, but he thinks it is a good bargain." Does

Wilde actually have a powerful newspaper editor under his control? The only tangible evidence we have been given is the knock at the door, and the voice claiming to be "Mr. Steylette". Yet somehow our disbelief is partially suspended. Wilde was telling the truth about the armor.

In a following scene, Wilde goes on to say that he is in communication with ten thousand men, and that within 48 hours he can have the state and country rise *en masse* excepting places that have not received the Yellow Sign. The fanciful dream of a madman. Or is it? Where, in the smooth transition of events, did reality leave off and sheer madness begin? There lies the true horror of the piece.

Again, later in the story, Castaigne is intruded upon by his cousin Louis as he is trying on what he describes as a gold diadem studded with diamonds, which he has removed from a steel safe equipped with a time lock, in his room. This is what he will wear when he is King, by his "right in Hastur" of America. Yet his cousin refers to his crown as being brass, and to the safe as a "biscuit box." Perhaps the crown is brass, except in the deluded mind of Castaigne, but there is the definite possibility that Louis merely assumes it to be brass because that is the more likely possibility. And is his reference to the safe as a biscuit box to be taken literally, or as sarcasm?

In addition to these elements of psychological horror, there are a few elements of real physical horror. The description of Wilde, with his flat, pointed head, his artificial ears, and his fingerless left hand is quite gruesome. Even more horrifying are the scenes in which he has been clawed to a bloody mess by the cat he perpetually teases, and in which he finally has his throat torn open by the creature. Chambers seems to associate cats with death, as can be seen in **"The Street of the Four Winds,"** also from *The King in Yellow,* and in **"The Man at the Next Table"** from *The Maker of Moons.*

From greed and lust for power, Chambers leads us to falsity and self-deceit in the second story, **"The Mask."** In **"The Mask",** we have a love story about artists in which the mythical *King in Yellow* elements fall into the background, while a science-fantasy element enters the forefront in the form of a liquid that turns living things to stone. Yet it is obvious that this story is taking place in the same *milieu* as the first one. The sculpture of "The fates" upon which Boris Yvain is working throughout is the same sculpture that is seen standing before the Government Lethal Chamber in **"The Repairer of Reputations".**

The story centers about the triangular love affair between Boris, the girl Genevieve, and the protagonist, Alec. Genevieve has professed her love for Boris, and Alec has withdrawn himself until, at the turning point, he discovers that she really loves him.

The horror in this piece is much more subtle than in the previous story, and works along two parallel tracks. The first track is built around Boris's chemical solution, and the horror gradually mounts as Boris progressively petrifies a lily, a goldfish, and a rabbit; the final outcome being the accidental petrifaction of Genevieve. The second track is based on horror of a more spiritual nature, as Alec gradually comes to realize the deceptions of Genevieve and himself.

*The King in Yellow,* which Alec chances upon at the turning point, seems to reflect symbolically his own condition as he falls ill. The quotation at the beginning of the story, (incidentally, the only quotation from the play besides "Cassilda's Song") illustrates this symbolic connection. In the quotation, Cassilda and Camilla are terrified to find that a stranger whom they have asked to unmask is wearing none. This seems to be reflected at the story's turning point, when Alec realizes that he has been wearing a mask of self-deception to hide his love for Genevieve from himself, as well as from her and Boris, and that this self-deception has become an inseparable part of him. When Alec's friend, Jack Scott, asks the doctor, "What ails Alec to wear a face like that?" as Alec succumbs to delirium, we know it is because of the two years of hiding the truth from himself and his friends. When Alec overhears the question, he immediately thinks of the Pallid Mask from the play. Assuming this to be the mask referred to in the opening quotation, it would seem that Alec has realized he is a personification of the stranger whose apparent mask is a part of him.

Again, in this story, we find the same type of ambiguity that was a keynote in **"The Repairer of Reputations".** When Boris calls Alec to come see the goldfish turned to stone in the magical fluid, there is "a feverish excitement in his voice." In the next sentence, Alec states, "a dull weight of fever lay on my limbs . . . " It is shortly thereafter that he reads *The King in Yellow.* Then, after Genevieve, who at this point actually is delirious with fever, reveals her love for Alec in front of Boris, Alec himself falls ill with fever and delirium. It is unclear what has caused his illness. Was his mention of "dull weight of fever" to be taken literally, or was it a reference to the "feverish excitement" in Boris's voice in the previous sentence? If we are to believe the latter, are we to assume it was the reading of the play that induced his fever? The play seems to have this sort of effect on characters in other stories. Or did he merely catch the fever from Genevieve, who also seems to have been stricken inexplicably? Here, too, her illness seems to be a symbolic externalization of her own hidden feelings. It was apparently triggered by a sprained ankle she sustained after Alec had startled her, as she was crying alone.

However, the ambiguity here does not add so much to the effect of the piece as the subtle blend of beauty and horror surrounding Boris's solution. The description of the beautiful play of colors during the transformation of lilies and goldfish into their exquisitely sculpted and tinted marble counterparts, perfectly counterpoints the disgust Alec feels at the thought of turning living things to stone. The beauty overtakes the horror at the end when the effects wear off, and Alec and Genevieve, masks removed, are free to begin anew.

In the third story, **"In the Court of the Dragon",** we finally lose the ambiguity of the sort used in the previous tales, and come into a direct confrontation with the realm of *The King in Yellow.*

The story is short, direct, and achieves considerable effect as the protagonist is pursued through the city by the pale-faced, black-garbed organist, only to awaken at the last instant before capture to confront the King in Yellow, himself.

For the first time, in this story, we see the actual effect of reading the play, without the vagueness of before. We are told by the narrator at the outset that he is in the church for healing after having "three nights of physical suffering and mental trouble" from reading the play.

Throughout the course of the story, we see two frames of reality superimposed on one another; the realm of *The King in Yellow* lurking beneath the apparent reality of the Parisian streets. As the protagnist sits in the church at the beginning, he thinks he sees the organist leave twice. This duality is reasserted at the end of the chase as he awakens and thinks, "I had slept through the sermon . . . Had I slept through the sermon?" and again with, I had escaped him . . . Had I escaped him?"

This dualism makes the story ambiguous, but on a higher level than we have seen so far. While in **"The Repairer of Reputations"** we were merely uncertain as to the reality of the protagonist's schemes in a concrete setting, here we are uncertain as to the concretcncss of the story as a whole, presented, as it is, as an internal fantasy. The King in Yellow has become real, but only in an unreal, or at least uncertain, setting. The hints of concrete reality, the indifference of the congregation to the organist's wild playing, and the race through the streets of Paris are later negated as they are revealed to be parts of a possible dream sequence.

In **"The Mask"** there were hints of the nature of *The King in Yellow*. In Alec's delirium of imagery from the play, the only sane thought that persisted was his own internal lie, persisting through the maddening ultimate truth of the play. **"In the Court of the Dragon"** now allows the nature of the play to emerge more fully. H. P. Lovecraft, in his essay, *Supernatural Horror in Literature* [see excerpt dated 1933-35] refers to "primordial Carcosa . . . some nightmare memory of which seeks to lurk latent and ominous at the back of all men's minds," and calls it an "eldritch land of primal memory." **"In the Court of the Dragon"** bears out this interpretation beautifully. The protagonist, after awakening in the church, realizes that he has always known who his pursuer really is. The primal memory has been awakened. He states (twice, significantly), "Death and the awful abode of lost souls, whither my weakness long ago had sent him, had changed him for every other eye but mine." It is significant that it was his *weakness* that had banished his strange pursuer. At the close the protagonist has gained the strength to realize the nature of these latent memories and to comprehend the ultimate Truth. It is only then that the church walls dissolve away to reveal the black stars and the towers of Carcosa in a dazzling example of the imagery that was Chambers's forte. Yet this is only the prelude to the final image as he sinks into the increasing waves of radiance and hears the King in Yellow whisper, "It is a fearful thing to fall into the hands of the living God!"

Thus we see that this play, the ultimate in "yellowness", is the key to unlock some unthinkably evil truth that we have long sought to suppress with decency and morality.

**"The Yellow Sign"** is the final story in the series, and is generally conceded to be the most powerful. Certainly, it has been the most frequently anthologized, probably due to its final combination of supernatural and spiritual horror with physical horror.

We have again returned to the real setting of **"The Repairer of Reputations"** and **"The Mask",** as the protagonist, Mr. Scott, tells us when he says of the play: "If I ever had had any curiosity to read it, the awful tragedy of young Castaigne, whom I knew, prevented me . . . " Yet the reality of the realm of *The King in Yellow* made apparent in the dream-like setting of **"In the Court of the Dragon,"** assumes tangibility in the concrete reality shared by the first two stories. There is no denying the common dreams shared by Scott and his model, Tessie. But the corpse-like watchman, and his fight with the newsboy, remove any doubt that supernatural events are occuring. A man whose fingers come off from his soft mushy fist is not a being of the natural world. Yet it is not until the story's climax that these events begin to tie in with the play. Scott and Tessie realize that the dreams are centered around a black onyx talisman, engraved with what they discover to be the Yellow Sign, when a copy of the play mysteriously turns up in his studio. It is then that they realize the watchman has come for his talisman, but it is too late; their doom has been sealed as prophesied in the dreams.

The fantasy elements in the story closely parallel the realistic ones. The first warnings of the supernatural are Tessie's dreams of Scott being driven in a hearse by the watchman. It is a direct result of these dreams that Tessie and Scott become romantically involved with each other. This culminates in Tessie's giving of the talisman to Scott as a token of her affection, thus sealing their fate. In their whole relationship their is a hint of sin; of "yellowness." Scott feels himself unworthy of Tessie and is distraught that he has kissed her. As a result of this "sin" she is no longer able to pose nude for him; they have tasted the forbidden fruit. This anticipates her reading the forbidden fruit of the play, resulting in his reading of it also, and their final departure from this life. But as the verse at the beginning of the story says: "Let the red dawn surmise / What we shall do / When this blue starlight dies / And all is through." With every death is the promise of rebirth. (pp. 51-4)

The mysterious Yellow Sign, about which the story revolves, is really the only tangible symbol of the play's content we are ever given. In **"The Repairer of Reputations,"** the only other story that mentions it, we are given a few clues to its significance. At one point, Wilde tells Castaigne that the portions of the country that do not follow when the revolution occurs, "might better never have been inhabited," for he would not send them the Yellow Sign. Thus we see that the Yellow Sign is intended as a tangible symbol of the other reality of the play, used in this first story to indicate allegiance to the King in Yellow.

In **"The Yellow Sign"** we see the effect of this unasked-for sign of allegiance on two unsuspecting people. They are gradually drawn into something they are at first unaware of, and later do not understand, until finally they have read the play. It is only then that the final revelation occurs. After they have read it, Scott tells us: "I knew that she knew and read my thoughts as I read hers, for we had understood the mystery of the Hyades, and the Phantom of Truth was laid." This last remark could be interpreted as saying that the thin veil of what we consider to be truth has been torn away.

Later, after the watchman has come for his talisman and Scott lies dying, he goes on to say: "I could tell more, but I cannot see what help it would be to the world . . . They of the outside world may send their creatures into wrecked homes and death-smitten firesides . . . but with me their spies must halt at the confessional." His reference to writers and reporters as "those of the outside world" is an important clue here. The implication is that the great Truth he has unwittingly discovered is internal. This rings true in all four of the stories. Castaigne and Wilde were dealing with what appeared to be their own mad fantasies; Alec's realization of his self-deception was, of course, internal, as was the protagonist's plight in **"In the Court of the Dragon."** And now here, in **"The Yellow Sign,"** we are told, despite the physical presence of the dead watchman, that again the ultimate revelation belongs to a subjective reality. Indeed, there is no physical reason for their deaths.

It is well known that Chambers got much of the mythical backdrop for his imaginary play from Ambrose Bierce. Two of Bierce's minor short stories provided him with material: "Haita the Shepherd" and "An Inhabitant of Carcosa."

"Haita the Shepherd" is a parable about a young shepherd boy and his fleeting moments with a beautiful and elusive girl named Happiness. In it we see him praying to the god of the shepherds; a nondescript god named Hastur. This is the first appearance of a name that was to survive, in a variety of incarnations, to present-day fantasy.

"An Inhabitant of Carcosa" is a short tale about a man who has been somehow resurrected as a spirit upon the ruins of Carcosa, the ancient city that had been his home during life. The story is introduced by a short quotation describing various types of death, ascribed to someone named Hali. (Another Bierce tale, "The Death of Halpin Frayser," also begins with a quotation from this fictitious personage). The story contains a reference to Aldebaran and The Hyades, and the spirit to whom the tale itself is ascribed is named Hoseib Alar Robardin (from which Chambers borrowed the Alar).

Although it has been said that Chambers built his *King in Yellow* mythology upon the background provided by Bierce, this is not really the case. True, he borrowed names from Bierce's tales, but the use he made of them corresponds in no way to that of the original. Carcosa was no longer an ancient city of the Middle East, but a strange and fabulous place under a double sun, whose towers can be seen rising behind the moon, and where black stars hang in the heavens. Hali no longer referred to an author

of mystical quotations about death, but rather to a lake whose waves are of cloud rather than water.

In "An Inhabitant of Carcosa," toward the end of the story, the narrator exclaims, "Looking upward, I saw through a sudden rift in the clouds Aldebaran and the Hyades!" He has just discovered that although it appears daylight to him, it is actually night, for the stars are visible. Compare this with a line from **"The Mask"** in which Alec describes his fevered delirium. "Aldebaran, The Hyades, Alar Hastur, glided through the cloud rifts which fluttered and flapped as they passed like scolloped tatters of The King in Yellow." The similarity is obvious, yet equally obvious is the change in meaning, import, and purpose that Chambers has brought about.

Special mention should be made of Chambers' use of the name Hastur, to clarify its later incorporation into the Cthulhu mythos. Although Bierce used it as the name of a benign shepherd god, Chambers merely sprinkled the name through his stories without ever explaining what it referred to. There are a few vague clues in **"The Repairer of Reputations"**. Castaigne says at one point, " . . . the people should know the son of Hastur," and later he raves, "I was King, King by my right in Hastur." One other grammatically ambiguous sentence mentions " . . . the establishment of the Dynasty in Carcosa, the lakes which connected Hastur, Aldebaran, and the mystery of the Hyades." Aside from these three vague references, the name Hastur, like the name Alar, only appears in groups of other names, some referring to places and some referring to people. Apparently, Chambers liked the sound of the name and merely threw it in where he thought it sounded good; he didn't have any particular meaning in mind. To illustrate this, the volume's fifth fantasy story, **"The Demoiselle d'Ys,"** although unconnected to the four King in Yellow stories, has a human character named Hastur. In his later works *The Maker of Moons* and *The Mystery of Choice,* he also plays around with names and meaningless words, carrying them from one story to another.

To the names he took from Bierce, he added a large measure of his own. In addition to the Yellow Sign, and the King in Yellow himself, there are the Pallid Mask, the Phantom of Truth, Cassilda, Camilla, Demhe, Uoht, Naotalba, Aldones, and so on. Some of these apparently have some import, as we have seen, while others seem to be meaningless. Cassilda and Camilla, as well as the King himself, are characters from the play, while Uoht, Thale, Naotalba and Aldones may or may not be. Demhe seems to refer to a lake like Hali. The Pallid Mask acts as a symbol of falsity in **"The Mask"**, while in **"The Repairer of Reputations"** it seems to represent the truth of the play (" . . . The state, the whole land were ready to rise and tremble before the Pallid Mask"). The Phantom of Truth seems to be a member of the Dynasty in **"The Repairer of Reputations"** (" . . . the ramifications of the Imperial family, to Uoht and Thale, from Naotalba and Phantom of Truth, to Aldones . . . "), while in **"The Yellow Sign"** the meaning, notwithstanding my earlier attempt at interpretation, is quite obscure (" . . . we had understood the mystery of the Hyades and the Phantom of Truth was laid.").

It seems likely that Chambers did not have any coherent mythical structure in mind, and no concrete concept of what constituted the play, aside from the generalities touched upon. Like an impressionistic painting it looks fine from a distance, but falls apart under close scrutiny.

Marion Zimmer Bradley makes some interesting observations about the possible origins of *King in Yellow* mythology in her article " . . . And Strange Sounding Names" in *The Conan Swordbook*. . . . She says that Chambers was influenced by a new school of impressionistic writing common at that time in France and Spain, and that most of the stories in *The King in Yellow* can be translated stylistically into Spanish without shifting a word, while the idioms are French. She theorizes, then, that Chambers, intentionally or otherwise, used names in the stories relating to the "ghosts of the Pyrenees, the endless war between Moorish pagan and sternly tenacious Spain." Thus, Mrs. Bradley concludes that Casilda [*sic*] is a common name among Spanish women; Hastur is a probable corruption of Asturias (a Spanish province that never surrendered to the Moors); Carcosa is a corruption of Carcasonne (an ancient French city formerly called Carcaso); and Hali is Arabic (Moorish influence on Spain) for the constellation of Taurus (which contains Aldebaran and the Hyades).

Of course what Mrs. Bradley fails to note in her article is that with the exception of 'Casilda', all of the aforementioned names were taken from Bierce. However, Bierce was contemporary with Chambers, and may himself have been subjected to Spanish influence.

After *The King in Yellow*, Chambers never did anything to further the mythology. There are only a few small hints in his later work of its existence. In **"The Silent Land"**, a borderline fantasy story in *The Maker of Moons*, there are two passing references to "a king in Carcosa" presented as snatches of a tale one of the characters is telling another. In *The Slayer of Souls*, a supernatural spy thriller written in 1920 (the year in which **"The Repairer of Reputations"** is set), we are confronted with disembodied souls indistinguishable from flesh and blood people, as in **"In the Court of the Dragon."** To make the point more obvious, Chambers worked into the dialogue of the novel the phrase, "It is a fearful thing to fall into the hands of the living God," the last line of **"In the Court of the Dragon."** There is also some background borrowed from **"The Maker of Moons"**, which E. F. Bleiler considers to have been a preliminary version of the novel.

The real longevity of the *King in Yellow* mythology was due to its incorporation by other fantasy writers, long after Chambers had dropped the idea. H. P. Lovecraft was the first of these. It is often thought, in fact, that he got his idea for the *Necronomicon* from *The King in Yellow*. This, however, is not the case. The fact is that Lovecraft's first mention of the *Necronomicon* was in "The Hound", written in 1922. He did not discover the existence of *The King in Yellow* until 1927, when he was finishing up his "Supernatural Horror in Literature," as is recorded in his letters. Moreover, there is really little resemblance between the two fictitious volumes. *The King in Yellow* is a futuristic play of such depraved beauty that it drives people mad. The *Necronomicon* is an ancient book of forbidden rites

and rituals, and no one in a Lovecraft story ever went mad from reading it.

But though he was not so obviously influenced by it, Lovecraft did revive interest in Chambers's work. He praised *The King in Yellow* in his *Supernatural Horror in Literature* (although I see no justification for his statement that the Yellow Sign was "handed down from the accursed cult of Hastur. . . . " Chambers tells of no such cult). He also incorporated some of Chambers's mythical names in his story "The Whisperer in Darkness" (1930). It is the only story in which he did so. Like Chambers, he did not attach any particular meaning to the names he borrowed, but merely included them in a hodge-podge of other Cthulhu Mythos names. Thus, in the story, the protagonist tells us that he found himself faced with names and terms he "had heard elsewhere in the most hideous of connections—Yuggoth . . . Azathoth, Hastur, Yian, Leng, the Lake of Hali, Bethmoora, the Yellow Sign . . ." Later in the story we are told in a letter to the protagonist from his friend who has become involved with alien beings from Yuggoth,

> . . . they [the beings from Yuggoth] have never knowingly harmed men . . . There is a whole secret cult of evil men (a man of your mystical erudition will understand me when I link them with Hastur and the Yellow Sign) devoted to the purpose of tracking them down and injuring them on behalf of monstrous powers from other dimensions.

It is obvious from the context of the story that the beings from Yuggoth are sinister creatures in league with the rest of Lovecraft's Cthulhoid pantheon. Since the second quotation turns out to be from one of the creatures, it is unclear whether it is true that they are at odds with the cults linked with Hastur and the Yellow Sign.

It was apparently this tangential reference to Hastur, however, that inspired August Derleth, Lovecraft's associate, to incorporate it into the Mythos as a relatively benign Great Old One constantly at battle with the rest of Lovecraft's pantheon. In 1932 Derleth, in collaboration with Mark Shorer, wrote "The Lair of the Star Spawn." It is in this tale that Hastur makes its first appearance as a definable entity in the Mythos. We are told that "Hastur the Unspeakable" is an evil being in league with Cthulhu *et al.* When these beings were banished by the Elder Gods, Cthulhu was imprisoned in the sunken city of R'lyeh, and Hastur was "exiled to Hali in the Hyades." In 1939, Derleth further expanded the idea in "The Return of Hastur." Here we find that Hastur is the half-brother of Cthulhu. The story tells us, "Hastur was hurled into outer space into that *place where the black stars hang,* which is indicated as Aldebaran of the Hyades, which is the place mentioned by Chambers, even as he repeats the Carcosa of Bierce." Derleth also throws in a few passing references to Aldones and Thale along the way, undoubtedly to help tie together the two mythologies.

Derleth was not the only one to take a liking to the name Hastur. Marion Zimmer Bradley, herself a Chambers fan, created her own concept of Hastur, unaware of what Derleth had been doing. In 1961, *The Sword of Aldones,* the first of her Darkover novels appeared, having as its hero a young man by the name of Regis Hastur. His family, the Hasturs, were "members of a ruling caste of telepathic families . . . ethical, serious, (and) virtuous," as Mrs. Bradley puts it herself . . . (pp. 54-6)

In *The Spawn of Cthulhu, . . .* Lin Carter dredged up another example of Chambers's influence, from a 1938 issue of *Weird Tales.* It is a short poem by the journalist Vincent Starrett, entitled "Cordelia's Song (from *The King in Yellow*)." It is not a bad poem, and has an eerie atmosphere about it, but aside from the title there seems to be no connection to *The King in Yellow.* In the same volume, however, Carter himself has written a sonnet sequence emulating Lovecraft's "Fungi from Yuggoth," entitled "Litany to Hastur." Carter is quite adept at imitating the styles of others, and in this sonnet sequence has achieved a subtly brilliant blend of the ideas and images of Chambers, Lovecraft, and Derleth, in an atmosphere of unworldly horror.

The influence of *The King in Yellow* lives on. In 1967, Robert Silverberg opened his science fiction novel *Thorns* with the quotation from the beginning of **"The Mask."** And in 1973, Manly Wade Wellman's collection, *Worse Things Waiting,* was published by a new specialty press called, simply, Carcosa House. Its colophon shows a weird skyline in front of the moon. The ultimate in tributes to Chambers, however, must be conceded to James Blish. His short story "More Light" in Anne McCaffrey's anthology *Alchemy and Academe* is a framework in which he presents us with the entire play *The King in Yellow* as supposedly written by Chambers himself. Allegedly, Chambers actually wrote the play he had hinted at in his stories and sent a copy to Lovecraft, who in turn sent a copy to a young fan named Bill Atheling (Blish's pseudonym). The gist of the story is that for some mysterious reasons, no one can read the entire play through.

The Blish version of the play is quite clever, and manages to include a good bit from Chambers's stories, although it does fall short on a few important points. What we are presented with is a story of a pair of stagnating cities in the midst of an interminable siege. They are the cities of Hastur and Alar, and lie on the banks of the lakes Hali and Dehme [*sic*], respectively. With the exception of Carcosa, they are the only cities in Godwanaland (the theoretical land mass that broke apart to form our present continents). Carcosa is a strange ghostly city that seems to float by the far shore of Hali; it is the home of the King in Yellow. Into Hastur comes a strange figure in a pallid mask and wearing the Yellow Sign; he is Yhtill, the Phantom of Truth. He entices Cassilda, queen of Hastur, to end the siege by having the entire kingdom attend a masque, all wearing a pallid mask to hide themselves from the King. The King retaliates by disintegrating Yhtill and permanently fixing the masks upon the faces of the people. The last lines echo Chambers in **"The Mask"**: "Not upon us, Oh King, not upon us," which Alec remembers Cassilda crying, in his delirium.

Although he includes many such references and allusions throughout the body of the play, Blish seems to have over-

looked the most obvious ones. "Cassilda's Song" and the opening quotation from **"The Mask"** are both cited by Chambers as being from Act 1, Scene 2 of the play, but Blish includes both in Act 2 of his version. And he totally disregards the line in **"The Repairer of Reputations"** that tells us of "Camilla's agonized scream and the awful words echoing through the dim streets of Carcosa . . . the last lines in the first act . . ." No such thing happens at the end of Blish's first act, or anywhere else, for Chambers has made it plain in this line that the play is set in Carcosa, not Hastur.

However, it is all in good fun. Blish has even managed to include the Walt Whitman quotation Chambers used at the beginning of **"The Maker of Moons."** And of course when the King himself appears, he advises the people of Hastur, "It is a fearful thing to fall into the hands of the Living God!"

We have now had a close look at *The King in Yellow,* itself, traced its origins, and followed its varied influences to the present day. No doubt even if Chambers himself is someday forgotten, Hastur will still be around in one form or another to haunt the pages of fantasy. (pp. 56-7)

*Lee Weinstein, "Chambers and 'The King in Yellow'," in* The Romantist, *No. 3, 1979, pp. 51-7.*

## David Punter   (essay date 1980)

[*In the following excerpt, Punter finds that* The King in Yellow *differs from American horror fiction of its time in not being derivative of the tales of Edgar Allan Poe.*]

In the same year as [Ambrose] Bierce's *Can Such Things Be?* [(1893)], another volume of horror stories was published in America, *The King in Yellow* by Robert W. Chambers. Chambers went on to become a successful writer of magazine potboilers, alternating between historical romance and 'tales of fashionable life' set in and around New York; he never followed in the direction in which *The King in Yellow* pointed. What is perhaps chiefly remarkable about the book is that it actually demonstrated the possibility of an American writing horror fiction which was *not* obviously derivative from Poe, and this was all the stranger in that Chambers had spent several of his youthful years in Europe studying art, and was even more aware than Bierce of the decadent interest in Poe. Those stories which were most clearly influenced by this aspect of his experience are couched in a lush, incantatory prose which is directly connected with the Bierce of 'An Inhabitant of Carcosa', though not at all with the morbid and cynical Bierce of 'Halpin Frayser' or the Civil War stories; connected both mythologically and stylistically, as one can see from the very brief **'In the Court of the Dragon'.** Here the narrator is inexplicably pursued by a figure of doom. His endeavours to escape are hampered by dreamlike immobility but eventually take him to a church, where he again perceives the same figure; the story concludes with the hero's perception of the real world being overwhelmed by the alternative diabolic vision offered by the pursuer.

I crept to the door; the organ broke out overhead with a blare. A dazzling light filled the church, blotting the altar from my eyes. The people faded away, the arches, the vaulted roof vanished. I raised my seared eyes to the fathomless glare, and I saw the black stars hanging in the heavens: and the wet winds from the Lake of Hali chilled my face.

And now, far away, over leagues of tossing cloud-waves, I saw the moon dripping with spray; and beyond, the towers of Carcosa rose behind the moon.

Death and the awful abode of lost souls, whither my weakness long ago had sent him, had changed him for every other eye but mine. And now I heard *his voice,* rising, swelling, thundering through the flaring light, and as I fell, the radiance increasing, increasing, poured over me in waves in flame. Then I sank into the depths, and I heard the King in Yellow whispering to my soul: 'It is a fearful thing to fall into the hands of the living God!'

The vices and virtues of Chambers's style are difficult to separate: the ornateness, and the attempt at poetic rhythm, are only partly achieved, and Chambers's seemingly adolescent pride in 'literariness' can be hard to take, yet behind this lies a singular attempt to recreate a type of horror which flows not directly from psychological obsession in the manner of Poe or Bierce but from blasphemy. Chambers, it is true, is very concerned with the workings of the mind at the point of breakdown, but his best effects come from connecting observation of mental operations with a sub-Baudelairean diabolism.

A good example, and one of the best of the stories, is **'The Repairer of Reputations'.** This is an internal study of megalomaniac insanity, but its interest lies less in the process of mental disintegration which it depicts than in its creation of a decadent mythology, with a devil-figure to match, whose name, not accidentally chosen, is Wilde. It is set thirty years into the future (1920), in an America curiously transformed into a place of security and beauty: 'everywhere good architecture was replacing bad and even in New York, a sudden craving for decency had swept away a great portion of the existing horrors'; this brave new world has also repealed 'the laws prohibiting suicide', and Government Lethal Chambers provide a conveniently unembarrassing point of exit for those for whom American world domination and consequent national self-confidence are too much to take. The first-person narrator, Castaigne, who has ominously suffered from a serious accident which, he informs us, has 'fortunately left no evil results'—except an increased ambitiousness—comes across the book *The King in Yellow,* which is both a symbolic work of blasphemy and also, clearly, an apotheosis of 'yellow-bookery', and is so affected by it as to believe in the predictions about his own glorious future made to him by Wilde. Wilde himself is, in a certain sense, laughable; the terror comes through in Castaigne's cheerful acceptance of him as a prophet and semi-divinity:

> When he had double-locked the door and pushed a heavy chest against it, he came and sat down beside me, peering up into my face with his little light-coloured eyes. Half a dozen new scratches covered his nose and cheeks, and the silver wires which supported his artificial ears had become displaced. I thought I had never seen him so hideously fascinating. He had no ears. The artificial ones, which now stood out at an angle from the fine wire, were his one weakness. They were made of wax and painted a shell pink, but the rest of his face was yellow. He might better have revelled in the luxury of some artificial fingers for his left hand, which was absolutely fingerless, but it seemed to cause him no inconvenience, and he was satisfied with his wax ears. He was very small, scarcely higher than a child of ten, but his arms were magnificently developed, and his thighs as thick as any athlete's. Still, the most remarkable thing about Mr Wilde was that a man of his marvellous intelligence and knowledge should have such a head. It was flat and pointed, like the heads of many of those unfortunates whom people imprison in asylums for the weak-minded. Many called him insane but I knew him to be as sane as I was.

Chambers's little joke in the last sentence is one of the many points at which he alerts the reader to the discrepancy between the narrator's view of the world and those of the other people with whom he comes into contact; the scratches on Wilde's face are caused by his persistent habit of fighting murderous duels with his cat, but Castaigne puts this down to harmless eccentricity. He is convinced that Wilde has at his command a secret army of adherents who are going to reinstate him (Castaigne) to his rightful position at the head of 'the Imperial Dynasty of America', and has as token of his eventual success a collection of crown jewels. The adherents, however, are no less psychologically suspect than Wilde, and the 'jewels' are 'theatrical tinsel'; Castaigne's eventual attempt to appear in all his promised glory is thwarted by the efforts of his relatives, and by the simultaneous and bloody defeat of Wilde by his remarkable cat.

> Mr Wilde lay on the floor with his throat torn open. At first I thought he was dead, but as I looked, a green sparkle came into his sunken eyes, his mutilated hand trembled, and then a spasm stretched his mouth from ear to ear. For a moment my terror and despair gave place to hope, but as I bent over him his eyeballs rolled clean around in his head, and he died. Then while I stood, transfixed with rage and despair, seeing my crown, my empire, every hope and every ambition, my very life, lying prostrate there with the dead master, *they* came, seized me from behind, and bound me until my veins stood out like cords, and my voice failed with the paroxysms of my frenzied screams. But I still raged, bleeding and infuriated among them, and more than one policeman felt my sharp teeth. Then when I could no longer move they came nearer . . .

The reactionary revolution which Wilde and Castaigne have intended comes to nothing; it is revealed as a thing of dream and madness by those forces (policemen, soldiers, an 'armourer') devoted to the perpetuation and protection of a grotesquely caricatured welfare state. Chambers's displaced aristocrats lack the self-destructive grandeur of Poe's, or of Dracula, who would not have sullied his teeth with the blood of policemen.

In **'The Demoiselle d'Ys'**, the American hero, travelling in a bleak part of Finistère, loses himself, tries to sleep and awakens to find that 'a great bird hung quivering in the air above my face'. He encounters a lady who talks mainly of falconry, in terms long outmoded, and accompanies her hunting. He is taken to her chateau, falls in love with her, and is invited to 'win her'. At the climactic moment,

> as she lay trembling on my breast, something struck my foot in the grass below, but I did not heed it. Then again something struck my ankle, and a sharp pain shot through me. I looked into the sweet face of Jeanne d'Ys and kissed her, and with all my strength lifted her in my arms and flung her from me. Then bending, I tore the viper from my ankle and set my heel upon its head. I remember feeling weak and numb,—I remember falling to the ground.

When he awakes a second time, the crushed viper is still there, but apart from that there is only a heap of mouldering ruins. He gets up, dragging his 'numbed foot', and falls 'before a crumbling shrine carved in stone for our Mother of Sorrows'. It is a memorial to Jeanne d'Ys, who died in 1573; upon it lies 'a woman's glove still warm and fragrant'.

To mention just one further story, **'The Mask'** begins with a successful experiment to perpetuate living beauty:

> Although I knew nothing of chemistry, I listened fascinated. He picked up an Easter lily which Geneviève had brought that morning from Notre Dame and dropped it into the basin. Instantly the liquid lost its crystalline clearness. For a second the lily was enveloped in a milk-white foam, which disappeared, leaving the fluid opalescent. Changing tints of orange and crimson played over the surface, and then what seemed to be a ray of pure sunlight struck through from the bottom where the lily was resting. At the same instant he plunged his hand into the basin and drew out the flower. 'There is no danger', he explained, 'if you choose the right moment. That golden ray is the signal.'
>
> He held the lily toward me and I took it in my hand. It had turned to stone, to the purest marble.

The story turns on the relationships between the sculptor, Boris, his wife Geneviève and Alec the narrator. Geneviève reveals under the influence of fever that she really loves Alec, upon which he, with the weakness endemic in decadent heroes, goes into a decline. He pulls out of it to discover that Geneviève, stricken to the soul by her revelation, her removal of the mask, has plunged herself into a pool of the magic fluid, upon which Boris has shot himself. The marble Geneviève is placed in an unfinished sculptural group of Boris's, along with a figure of the Madonna. Alec does the decent thing and boards the 'Orient express for Constantinople', but after two years he is drawn back to the sculptor's abandoned house, to find that strange things are happening: two goldfish and a rabbit which Boris had petrified come back to life. Alec sees the Easter lily, and goes to pick it up:

> But the flower I lifted from the table was fresh and fragile and filled the air with perfume.
>
> Then suddenly I comprehended and sprang through the hall-way to the marble room. The doors flew open, the sunlight streamed into my face and through it, in a heavenly glory, the Madonna smiled, as Geneviève lifted her flushed face from the marble couch, and opened her sleepy eyes.

The implication of the smile on the face of the *Madonna* is an example of Chambers's technique at its most economical.

His French and American exquisites have a touch of life— and of humour—quite foreign to the Poe tradition; terror comes to them not in the blackness of underground passages and dungeons but in the blindness of too much streaming sunlight, the 'scalloped tatters of the King in Yellow'. Where Poe looked back to Coleridge and to the romantic versions of the 'long night of the soul', Chambers found his inspiration in the fatal ambivalence of beauty which preoccupied Keats and Shelley. Yet what Chambers does have in common with Poe is a particular relation to 'modernism': to put it simply, his stories do not feel like complete wholes but like assembled fragments, in the course of which questions are deliberately left open. Vague pieces of mythology are introduced and fade out of sight; at the end of **'The Yellow Sign'**, a figure appears 'and the bolts rotted at his touch', but the doctor who is called to explain 'a horrible decomposed heap on the floor' has 'no theory, no explanation'. The stories are themselves 'tatters', one of Chambers's favourite words, fragmentary manifestations of evil which are not *produced* by dislocation of sensibility, although that dislocation tears gaps in the world through which evil may come—and through which may also come, simultaneously, a beauty which it is death or madness to behold.

Chambers's stories also mark a curious point in the transmutation of horror fiction into 'pulp'; Lewis Pattee refers to his 'fineness', 'finesse', 'deftness and lightness of touch', and H. L. Mencken assents to 'a fundamental earnestness and a high degree of skill', but Mencken also and in the same breath talks of 'the shoddiness in Chambers, the leaning toward "profitable pot-boiling" ' [see Fred Lewis Pattee, *The New American Literature, 1890-1930*]. One way of looking at these contradictory judgements is by saying that Chambers had in his horror stories very little to express but a high awareness of the elliptical techniques which terror fiction invites, techniques which he was to go on to waste on the weary dialogue of upper-class New York alcoholics. His literary devices are polished but unrooted; at least, however, he, like the earlier writers of terror-fiction, regarded the genre, if only briefly, as worthy of effort and poise, as a fit field in which to practice that evasion of crudity and naturalism which was a linchpin of the decadent aesthetic. His stories are not obviously concerned with any of the great themes of decadence except that of the Medusa, but their style is at times more truly decadent than anything to be found in Wilde; where Wilde tries to use paradox to overturn a rationalist framework, Chambers works obliquely, always suggesting a wider dominance of evil and decay without being drawn into portraying the dimensions of that dominance. (pp. 275-81)

*David Punter, "Later American Gothic," in his* The Literature of Terror: A History of Gothic Fictions from 1765 to the Present Day, *Longman, 1980, pp. 268-90.*

## Martha Banta   (essay date 1983)

[*Banta is an American educator and critic. In the following excerpt, she discusses* The Common Law.]

Robert Chambers' best seller of 1911, **The Common Law,** [was] illustrated . . . by Charles Dana Gibson to whom Chambers dedicated his novel.

Chambers' hero, Louis Neville, is most art students' fantasy of the successful painter. Still in his handsome twenties, Neville has already achieved fame, honors, and wealth. "Thousands" have stood in awe before his paintings hung in major New York museums. His current commissions include the decorations for a palatial new theatre and murals for the state capitol. A Harvard man, with an impeccable old-eastern family whose countryhouse graces the area near the city, he runs an unending salon in a studio whose dimensions are so immense it can be filled with guests while he paints—perched high on a ladder—winged creatures on a vast canvas. When someone plays a baby grand piano in one corner, others gather around tea-things in another. He can serve intimate little breakfasts there, too, to lovely models—repasts that consist of "chilled grapefruit, African melon, fragrant coffee, toast, and pidgeon's eggs poached on astrakan caviar." Neville's studio, enhanced by a few extravagant details of *luxe,* is uncommonly like those that excited the readers of the Sunday supplements: the famous Tenth Street establishment run by William Merritt Chase or the equally well-known studio of Howard Chandler Christy on West 67th Street. All this, and (as the illustrations make clear) the looks of the Gibson Man. As Neville admits, fortune is his mistress, one who has perhaps been too faithful to him. (p. 26)

Neville is too dedicated to his art, too fond of his male companions, and too pre-adolescent to have much interest in women. They are dimly in the background, adding fillip to studio life. All this leaves the story wide open for Valerie West to walk through the door and ask if she may be his model.

In the parlance of Hollywood, Neville and Valerie "meet cute." He mistakenly thinks she is a seasoned professional and brusquely tells her to disrobe since he wishes to use her as the type of a nymph-on-a-cloud he is in the midst of painting. In fact, she is a blushing virgin and this is her first time out as a model; therefore, the agonies she suffers over removing her clothes go quite past him when she emerges from behind the dressing-screen to stand before him in naked splendor. Neville is properly businesslike. He writes down her name and physical description in his

notebook (not the proverbial bachelor's little black book): "Height, medium; eyes, a dark brown; hair, thick, lustrous, and brown; head, unusually beautiful; throat and neck, perfect." (pp. 26-7)

Neville has no interest in hiring beautiful souls; he simply wants a highly professional model whose figure and face he can use as the guide to his trained hand and instructed imagination. He certainly does not want to think of her as someone he might have to give thought to. . . . Still, Neville finds himself listening as Valerie reports shyly that prostitution is the only other emotional outlet for a lonely, attractive young woman with her way to make in the city.

Like all proper heroes of this genre, Neville is obtuse when it comes to the human heart. He admits, however, that he has been told he needs to experience suffering and its consequence—love. Otherwise, he will never gain the warm sympathy for humanity that could transform his fatal facility as a painter into true genius. Valerie will be the undoing of Neville's smug male conventionality of heart and mind and the making of him as an artist and a man. For she is Chambers' version of the type, New Woman, and the sub-type, Professional Model. Even more, she is meant to be the "model" for a bracingly realistic view of the relationship between art, life, and love. The novel's title indicates the intellectual and emotional conundrums that Valerie must solve for herself before finding the way to tutor Neville in the truths she has discovered.

As a statement of plot, the question **The Common Law** raises is whether a nice orphan girl (who has passed the entrance examinations to Barnard College, although too poor to matriculate) can find happiness with a handsome Harvard man bound to society's conventions about marriage (deemed a stay against social chaos) and illicit liaisons (declared the destruction of civilization). As a statement of the narrative's "intellectual" commitment, "the common law" has to be redefined. It must be taken beyond the usual notions of free-love relationships between unmarried persons whereby Neville and Valerie would live out the public's expectations of what happens in the demi-monde of artists and models who take to the bed. Further, the basic source of "the law" has to be determined in order to see whether individual conduct arises from social needs and the head or from nature and the heart.

This best seller, which draws upon all the conventions of the romance genre, takes as its philosophical impetus two matters of high concern that attempt to break past the boundaries of genre altogether: *art* defined as more than the techniques that take its practitioners toward skillfully executed generalizations, because art requires the heart's overflow that enables one to particularize individual motives, desires, and principles; *love* viewed as more than social convention, because love necessitates each person to define his or her relations to other people in terms of nature's law of emotional response. It is these two areas of education through which Louis Neville, type of the Handsome Artist, must progress toward knowledge, guided by Valerie, type of the Beautiful American Girl as New Woman and Model.

But true love and a proper education cannot run smoothly

(as Henry Adams was currently in the process of noting in his big book on the subject). Not when Neville has everything yet to learn about what loving and art actually consist of, as well as how the "real things" Valerie represents are different from the stereotypes he and his class hold as preconceived judgments against professional models.

From the start Neville labors under the fact that he comes of a particularly stuffy family. The time comes when his sister faces Valerie and tells her . . . that she must give up her hold on Neville in order to save him from social ruin. Nor is Neville helped by the presence of his parents, depicted in 1911 as tottering relics from a by-gone age of innocence. His mother wears a lace cap and a long black ante-bellum gown; his father is bearded, eats bread and milk from a bowl with a large spoon, reads outmoded literary journals such as the *Atlantic,* appreciates Bierstadt, Hiram Powers, and Herbert Spencer, and angrily sends his son from the room for saying the word "seraglio" in his mother's presence.

But Neville has a further difficulty to overcome before he can become more than a type flawed in its lack of completed identity. Chambers follows out the fictional theme of the split self that had been in vogue for several decades by showing Neville as an uneasy patching together of two subtypes: he is "Louis" (worried, conventional, very human) and he is also "Kelly" (the nickname by which friends indicate his godlike, supremely assured self). Although Valerie tells him she loves both these personalities, he will have to merge the two before he can attain to full recognition of what his own "real thingness" consists. He will have to do this for his own sake, but also so that he does not enforce destructive splits upon others. . . . (pp. 27-9)

Since Valerie is the figure of saving grace in Chambers' novel, she . . . is meant to represent wholeness and completed self-identity. Within her type she contains all that is pure, intelligent, amusing, serious, frolicsome, tender, questioning, knowing, beautiful: the qualities currently exacted of the American Girl in general when approached by author, illustrator, and reading public.

Neville and his friends keep discovering new aspects of her unity-in-multiplicity, which is what makes her such a successful artist's model (and which made, as Henry Adams was just then writing, such a splendid form of Virgin-and-Venus, that consummate type that American society had long since rejected out of its fears of complex simplicity). (p. 29)

Neville immediately paints Valerie in a variety of forms. He sees her as a radiant allegorical nude for the Byzantine Theatre mural, but also as "just a girl in street clothes." . . . His male friends like to escort her around after hours because she can, as they note, "impersonate" anyone. "Castless" and "placeless," she is fun to be with. She is also safe. If they encounter relatives, she can "pass" as a lady even though she *is* a model. (They have not yet *recognized* her; they are still looking at the superficial type that disguises the real thing and true type.) As they see it, this very adaptability of the young woman who has no

proper place in proper society means that she is *out of* the world that Neville possesses by right of birth and success. If she ever gave herself to him in common-law marriage, he would have *come down* to her debased level.

When Neville suggests ways for Valerie to raise herself socially, she rejects them. Not for her one of those "respectable" jobs open to self-supporting women: as a typewriter, milliner, or store-clerk. She wants to prove she can be "free" and "pure," while doing it *as a model.* Valerie has already become a "personality," her beauty is so great. . . . Her image as a celebrity appears everywhere: on the back advertising covers of leading magazines and in Sunday supplement photos. But she continues to insist she will retain her "private" life as one who lives virginally in a small white room as spotless and tidy as a nun's cell. . . . (pp. 29-30)

Valerie wants to have it both ways. She makes as her demand upon society that it let her and all young women have an identity so "right" they can go anywhere and do anything because committed to the antinomian belief in their authority to choose the kind of "real thing" they are. Chambers, as novelist, also wishes to have it both ways—to a point. Contemporary readers were given the enjoyment of seeing this lovely young woman of twenty-two take down social convention and Neville's ingrown snobbery several pegs; but they were still protected from any radical revolt against the proprieties. Valerie could be allowed to seem to shape her identity as she willed, but since she never "sins," all her little freedoms were kept this side of the dangerous. The threat of her "modernity" and her "realism" as the type of the New Woman was carefully contained by the fact that Chambers guided the plot and kept her pure.

Immersed as Neville is *within* the narrative, he cannot realize how safe it is for him to love Valerie. Chambers provides a rousing confrontation. . . . It is New Year's Eve. Neville is morosely in the company of friends and a woman named Maizie, obviously the type of the prostitute. (Chambers' readers could readily identify this by means of his words and Gibson's illustration.) Suddenly he looks up and sees Valerie. She is with a rival artist, standing on top of a table pelting the revelers with rose buds, her gown torn loose from her beautiful shoulder. Neville is outraged, but cannot understand that he is feeling jealousy and desire. All he knows is that he instantly *doubts*. Her appearance, which previously had brought him delight over the innocence it represented for him, is now that of a loose woman: a model. All along, Neville has been written up very much after the manner of Edith Wharton's Newland Archer and Lawrence Selden. Just like them, he is quick to cast Valerie (as Archer and Selden do to Ellen Olenska and Lily Bart) into the shadows. After this incident, he returns to his studio to brood before a painting he has recently completed of Valerie as the type of The Bride. It is the work everyone says is the most brilliant thing he has ever done. It is the sign that he is at last learning how to suffer—a fact that that night's events have confirmed.

This very long novel winds to its close when Valerie comes to offer herself to him, with or without a wedding ring, as a "bride" who is—she insists—"all new." Before she presents herself, she prepares for this sacrificial act of love by kneeling to pray beside her little white bed. Her prayer that she know how to interpret "the law" is answered by the one "god" she has to counsel her—her heart's intuitions.

If Chambers' readers *had* been afraid (and simultaneously titillated by) the thought that "the common law" might be interpreted in terms of "situational morality" that flies in the face of social law, their fears were laid to rest (and their expectations dashed). In her own way, Valerie comes around to the position earlier argued by Neville's sister: that marriage is the only safety a woman has and that women need limitations in order to enjoy the social freedoms that being married allows them. But to give Valerie-as-written-by-Chambers credit, she goes a little way past this self-serving stance. At the basis of her decision is the fresh new discovery of the biological fact that, if she and Neville came together, there might be children, and it is *they* she must protect. (Babies getting born is something that had never occurred to her until that night.) As the result of this startling piece of knowledge, she concludes that marriage is indeed right; it blends nature's laws (biology and birth) with man's laws (society and order).

All ends happily for the artist and his model. Aided by the impact his painting of her as a bride has upon his family, her true identity as a "soul" is finally made clear. The "sacred" quality of the painted image, inspired as it was by "the real thing" of her selfhood that lay within the physical form of Valerie as model, has been exposed. Not only is Valerie to be taken up into Neville's social world, he has risen into the realm of her free and natural spirit where real things always dwell. Through the penance he suffers and the reward he gains by learning to love, he has found his own realness as a painter. She has had the wholeness of her identity recognized by the outside world; he has had the breach between "Louis" and "Kelly" healed within himself. Marriage, art, love: all are made safe by the conclusion of Chambers' novel. The appearances are saved because they are finally matched with what is actually there.

At this point, in the face of the obvious fudging and compromises Chambers' novel reveals at its ending, it is imperative to realize that it is not the type of the New Woman as Professional Model that defaults on the possibilities that Valerie's story started to set loose. It is Chambers' final timidities that do this. Instead of throwing caution to the winds, what he throws away is the opportunity to push type to the edges of realism and romance, and beyond. (pp. 30-1)

*Martha Banta, "Artists, Models, Real Things, and Recognizable Types," in* Studies in the Literary Imagination, *Vol. XVI, No. 2, Fall, 1983, pp. 7-34.*

## S. T. Joshi   (essay date 1984)

[*An American editor and critic, Joshi has written extensively on authors of weird fiction and is the leading figure in the field of H. P. Lovecraft scholarship and criticism. In the following excerpt, Joshi discusses Chambers's tales of the supernatural that were written after* The King in Yellow.]

[Chambers's] *The Mystery of Choice* is an undeservedly forgotten collection, and—in its more refined and controlled prose style, greater unity of theme, and exquisite pathos—may well be a generally better work than *The King in Yellow.* The first five stories are linked by a common setting—Brittany—and some recurring characters; and although the first ("The Purple Emperor") is a rather amusing parody on the detective story, the rest of the collection contains fine tales of fantasy and even science-fiction. Here again Chambers can, when he chooses, create moments of heart-rending exquisiteness, and his powers of description are unexcelled:

> Then the daily repeated miracle of the coming of dawn was wrought before our eyes. The heavens glowed in rainbow tints; the shredded mist rising along the river was touched with purple and gold, and acres of meadow and pasture dripped precious stones. Shreds of the fading night-mist drifted among the tree tops, now tipped with fire, while in the forest depths faint sparkles came from some lost ray of morning light falling on wet leaves. Then of a sudden upshot the sun, and against it, black and gigantic, a peasant towered, leaning upon his spade.
> ("The White Shadow")

This is the art not only of the painter but of the etcher or engraver, and holds us breathless while it lasts; but it all too frequently does not last long.

*In Search of the Unknown* reveals a disastrous falling off of quality, and shows that while Chambers' conceptions are as fertile as ever (we are here concerned with a series of tales depicting successive searches for lost species of animals, including a loathsome half-man and half-amphibian called "the harbormaster," a group of invisible creatures apparently in the shape of beautiful women, and the like), they are marred by a mechanical and adventitious love-element which in its flippancy and pseudo-sophistication nearly destroys all the horror which Chambers can so easily create. In every tale the narrator tries to flirt with a pretty girl but ultimately loses her at the last moment to some rival. Chambers oddly chose to reprint **"A Matter of Interest"** (from *The Mystery of Choice*) in this volume; a work which, though labeled a novel, is in fact a string of tales (actually published separately in journals) very bunglingly stitched together into a continuous narrative. Indeed, so many of Chambers' "novels" are of this sort that few can be termed other than episodic. A pseudo-sequel to this volume is *Police!!!,* a collection of tales where further searches are made into lost species—including mammoths in the glaciers of Canada, a group of "cave-ladies" in the Everglades, and the like. This book is even further injured by frivolity than its predecessor (although, in justice to Chambers, several of the tales are intentionally parodic and actually quite amusing), and also shows a decline in the fertility of invention which alone lends some merit to Chambers' work: the amphibian man in **"The Third Eye"** too closely resembles the harbormaster, while in **"Un Peu d'Amour"** we encounter an irascible character very obviously reminiscent of a similar character in the first segment of *In Search of the Unknown.* But even here there are some gripping moments: "Un Peu d'Amour" presents some horrifying glimpses of a gigantic worm burrowing beneath the fields of upstate New York, while a previous tale ("The Ladies of the Lake") discloses a school of huge minnows the size of Pullman cars.

With *The Slayer of Souls*—a novel which has gained inexplicable popularity amongst modern aficionadoes of fantasy—Chambers reaches the nadir of his career. Even if we could swallow the appallingly tasteless premise—that "Anarchists, terrorists, Bolshevists, Reds of all shades and degrees, are now believed to represent in modern times" the descendants of the devil-worshipping Yezidi sect of inner Asia, which is poisoning the minds of misguided leftists and labor unionists (the IWW is specifically mentioned) for the overthrow of good and the establishment of evil, whatever that means—there is no escaping the tedium of the whole work, which is concerned with the efforts of the U. S. Secret Service, along with a young girl who, although having lived for years with these evil Chinese, has now defected and converted to Christianity, to hunt down the eight leading figures of the sect and exterminate them. They succeed in their task with mechanical regularity, and it is no surprise that civilization is saved in the end for God-fearing Americans. The novel—an elaboration of the title story of *The Maker of Moons,* although that tale is handled far better and contains some delicate moments of shimmering fantasy—is further crippled by a ponderous and entirely humorless style, and with characters so moronic that they cannot reconcile themselves to the supernatural even after repeated exposure to it. And the crowning absurdity is that the origin of all these evils is a "black planet . . . not a hundred miles" from the earth! There is not a single redeeming element in this novel.

*The Tree of Heaven,* although not exclusively fantastic, actually contains some very fine moments. The construction of the "novel" is ingenious: at the outset an odd mystic utters prophecies to a group of his friends, and the subsequent episodes are concerned with their fulfillment. For once the love-element is not extrinsic to the plot, and in several of these tales love is simply given a supernatural dimension which creates a profundity not often found in Chambers; even the non-fantastic romantic tales are handled with a seriousness and depth completely absent in other of Chambers' works. The superb atmosphere of delicate pathos and dream-fantasy maintained in some of these tales may place this volume only behind *The King in Yellow* and *The Mystery of Choice* as Chambers' finest.

Some general remarks can now be made on Chambers' fantastic work. One of its most interesting features is a proto-science-fictional element which emerges in some works cheek-by-jowl with the overt supernaturalism of other tales—a supernaturalism which finds greatest expression in the incoherent series of fantastic episodes in *The Slayer of Souls.* . . . "The Repairer of Reputations" is set in the future, but "The Mask" actually makes greater use of a science-fictional principle of great importance: the scientific justification for a fantastic event. Chambers

never precisely explains the nature of the petrifying fluid used in the story, but we are led to believe that it would not be beyond the bounds of chemistry to encompass it. Similarly, in "A Matter of Interest" elaborate attempts are made at the outset to establish the veracity and accuracy of the narrative, which concerns the discovery of the last living dinosaur (the "thermosaurus"). *In Search of the Unknown* is even more emphatic on the point, and one of the characters vigorously denies the supernatural character of the harbor-master: " 'I don't think that the harbor-master is a spirit or a sprite or a hobgoblin, or any sort of damned rot. Neither do I believe it to be an optical illusion.' " Less scientific justification is presented for the creatures in *Police!!!,* but even here few strain credulity beyond the breaking-point. Even *The Slayer of Souls* enunciates the principle: " 'We're up against something absolutely new. Of course, it isn't magic. It can, of course, be explained by natural laws about which we happen to know nothing at present' "; unfortunately, in this case little effort is made to coordinate the bizarre events into a plausibly scientific framework.

The detective element in Chambers emerges in such parodies as "The Purple Emperor" and "The Eggs of the Silver Moon" (in *Police!!!* ), but most concentratedly in the episodic novel *The Tracer of Lost Persons.* The central character is an enigmatic and seemingly omniscient figure who presents himself much in the model of Sherlock Holmes; although perhaps the parallel to Poe's C. Auguste Dupin would be closer, since one segment of the novel involves the decoding of an ingenious cipher derived very obviously from "The Gold Bug." This novel in addition contains a magnificently haunting tale involving the revival of an ancient Egyptian girl suspended in a state of hypnosis for thousands of years, and reveals the same aura of *fin-de-siècle* beauty that makes *The Mystery of Choice* so exquisite.

Finally, we have had frequent occasion to remark upon interrelations between Chambers' tales. Many of the short-story collections use the same characters and setting, and are not much different from his episodic novels. Interrelations between entire works exist: *The King in Yellow* derives some of its characters from *In the Quarter*; some characters in *In Search of the Unknown* return in *Police!!!*; in *The Tree of Heaven* there is passing allusion to the central character of *The Tracer of Lost Persons.* Much of this seems to have been done in a spirit of fun, and need imply no serious thematic connection. (pp. 30-3)

Robert W. Chambers is a decidedly frustrating writer—a man for whom writing seems to have come as easily as (on a far higher level) composition seems to have come for Telemann or Mozart. He could draw literary substance from his own experiences: as a painter in France, as a hunter and fisher in New York state, as a collector of butterflies and general dabbler in science—but who marred so many of his creations with flippancy, pseudo-sophistication, and catch-penny sentimentality; whose descriptive and imaginative powers were of a high order but who was too lulled by the favor of the mob to use them consistently and effectively; who has left us some immortal tales of horror and fantasy which must be laboriously sifted out from a plethora of trash appalling in its scope. Chambers was an intellectual dilettante, and wrote whatever came to mind; we are fortunate that he now and again turned his careless and free-flowing pen to the creation of a few weird tales of transcendent beauty and horror. (p. 33)

*S. T. Joshi, "Robert W. Chambers," in* Crypt of Cthulhu, *Vol. 3, No. 6, Roodmas, 1984, pp. 26-33, 17.*

## FURTHER READING

Baldwin, Charles C. "Robert W. Chambers." In his *The Men Who Make Our Novels,* pp. 89-96. New York: Dodd, Mead and Company, 1924.

> Prefaces a harsh analysis of Chambers's works by saying, "Had I my choice I'd take the first three or four and let the rest go hang."

A review of "The Maker of Moons." *The Critic* n.s. 27 (15 May 1897): 337.

> Questions the merit of *The Maker of Moons* as horror fiction.

Daniels, Les. "Robert W. Chambers: 'The Yellow Sign.'" In his *Dying of Fright: Masterpieces of the Macabre,* pp. 79-91. New York: Charles Scribner's Sons, 1976.

> Cites Chambers's tales of horror as the best of his literary works.

Harkins, E. F. "Little Pilgrimages among Men Who Have Written Famous Books: No. 13." *The Literary World* 35, No. 7 (July 1904): 189-91.

> Discusses Chambers's life and provides an admiring appraisal of his literary career.

Hughes, Rupert. "The Art of Robert W. Chambers." *Cosmopolitan* 65, No. 1 (June 1918): 80-1, 116.

> Writes appreciatively of Chambers's works, which are described as "written with expert skill, with a determined eagerness for beauty, color, vivacity, variety and charm."

Sharp, William. "Robert W. Chambers: An Appreciation." *The Academy* 51, No. 1289 (16 January 1897): 71-2.

> Commends Chambers for his early works, especially *The King in Yellow* and *The Red Republic.*

Sullivan, Jack. "Psychological, Antiquarian, and Cosmic Horror." *Horror Literature: A Core Collection and Reference Guide,* edited by Marshall B. Tymn, pp. 221-75. New York: R. R. Bowker Company, 1981.

> Reference guide which includes brief entries commenting on Chambers's horror fiction. Sullivan calls Chambers "one of the most exotic and powerful of American horror writers."

Weinstein, Lee. "Robert W. Chambers." In *Supernatural Fiction Writers: Fantasy and Horror,* edited by E. F. Bleiler, pp. 739-45. New York: Charles Scribner's Sons, 1985.

> Overview of Chambers's stories of the supernatural. Weinstein notes that *The King in Yellow* "is one of the most important works of supernatural horror between Edgar Allan Poe and modern horror fiction."

Williams, Blanche Colton. "Robert W. Chambers." In her *Our Short Story Writers,* pp. 55-72. New York: Dodd, Mead and Company, 1941.

> Defends the artistic merit of Chambers's works, adding that "his best stories, of rare beauty and spirituality, are those of the supernatural."

# Elizabeth

## 1866-1941

(Pseudonym of Mary Annette Beauchamp Russell; also wrote under the pseudonyms "Author of *Elizabeth and Her German Garden*" and Alice Cholmondeley) English novelist, biographer, and author of children's books.

Russell is best remembered for autobiographical novels written early in her career that recount the events of her life in rural Pomerania, a region in Central Europe now divided between Poland and Germany. Her best-known work, *Elizabeth and Her German Garden,* was published anonymously and Russell came to be known by the name of her literary persona, "Elizabeth," the narrator of her early novels. Both these works and such later novels as *The Pastor's Wife* and *Mr. Skeffington* are esteemed for their charming wit and satiric yet sensitive characterizations.

Russell, a cousin of New Zealand short story writer Katherine Mansfield, was born into a wealthy Australian family. She spent most of her childhood and early adulthood in London, England. In 1889 Russell traveled on the continent with her father, and while in Italy she met Henning August von Arnim-Schlagenthin, a German count twenty-five years her senior. They married in 1891, moved to Berlin, and later raised five children. In 1896 Russell convinced von Arnim that they should take up residence at his family's country estate, Nassenheide, in Pomerania. Inspired by the solitude and beauty of the region, Russell began to write and publish her first literary works, each of which became a highly praised best-seller. In 1908 the von Arnims moved to England, where von Arnim died a few years later. Afterward Russell made plans for a chalet to be built in Switzerland and settled there with her children in 1912. At her Swiss home Russell welcomed numerous guests, including such notable figures as the novelists H. G. Wells and Hugh Walpole. She also met and was courted by Lord Francis Russell, the brother of the philosopher Bertrand Russell. The couple were married in 1916 and resided in London. The marriage lasted only three years; a revealing fictional portrait of her second husband appears in Russell's novel *Vera* as the character Everard Wemyss, called by some critics "the meanest man in fiction." Russell moved between England and the continent, continuing to write best-selling novels, until the Second World War, when she fled to the United States to escape the hardships of wartime Europe. She died in Charleston, South Carolina, in 1941.

Russell's first work, *Elizabeth and Her German Garden,* attracted immediate critical and popular attention for the whimsical and discursive style in which she depicted life in provincial Germany. The narrator, Elizabeth, is an English woman married to a German count, whom she affectionately calls the "Man of Wrath." Elizabeth exalts in nature, solitude, and the tasks of gardening, although her efforts are nearly always thwarted by those around her be-

cause, as a woman of the upper class, she is not allowed to attend to the gardening herself. Russell satirically contrasts Elizabeth's eccentricities and spontaneous nature with the conventional and rigid lives of her German neighbors. This comic situation recurs in several of Russell's later works, including *The Solitary Summer* and *The Adventures of Elizabeth in Rügen,* in which she continued to write fictionalized accounts of her life. Russell's more traditional novels are praised for their controlled irony and detached narrative perspective. In *The Pastor's Wife,* for example, Russell objectively portrays the tragicomic tale of Ingeborg, the English wife of a taciturn German pastor. The narrative centers on Ingeborg's sense of isolation from her husband and children and her subsequent naive involvement with an English painter, whose flagrant attempts to seduce her are completely ignored by her husband. Considered one of Russell's highest artistic achievements, *The Pastor's Wife* is noted for its verisimilitude in depicting the lives of German peasants.

While Russell frequently wrote about peaceful settings and charming people, she employed satire to expose underlying tensions amid tranquility and to reveal the shortcomings of her characters. Russell applies this method in

*The Caravaners* in representing the overly patriotic German narrator; George Lanning has referred to this novel as "a high comedy that was nevertheless a chilling forecast of Germany's intention to conquer England." Relationships between women and men also became the object of irony in many of her novels. *Mr. Skeffington* features Fanny Skeffington, a character considered to resemble Russell in her later years: once quite beautiful, she appears in the story as "striking and ravaged." The novel traces Fanny's attempts to attain self-sufficiency when she realizes that her husband and many admirers have little importance for her and that her life is essentially empty. Katherine Woods praised the sensitive characterization of Fanny as well as minor characters in the novel, stating that Russell "is light without triviality, her bright malice is never careless or gratuitous, her values are as clear and sure as her wit. Hers is a sword which thrusts the deeper for being highly polished."

While Russell was an exceptionally popular author during her lifetime, she expressed the belief that her works would not endure. Today her writings are still admired, and Elizabeth Jane Howard has asserted that the idyllic portrait of Elizabeth in *Elizabeth and Her German Garden,* wherein Russell charmingly delineated a woman who sought solitude from marriage and motherhood, prefigured the works of later women writers in its "interesting and original exposition of the conflict between liberty and oppression that in [Elizabeth's] day it was taken for granted was the lot of women."

## PRINCIPAL WORKS

*Elizabeth and Her German Garden* (novel) 1898
*The Solitary Summer* (novel) 1899
*The April Baby's Book of Tunes* (children's book) 1900
*The Benefactress* (novel) 1901
*Adventures of Elizabeth in Rügen* (novel) 1904
*The Princess Priscilla's Fortnight* (novel) 1905
*Fräulein Schmidt and Mr. Anstruther* (novel) 1907
*The Caravaners* (novel) 1909
*The Pastor's Wife* (novel) 1914
*Christine* [as Alice Cholmondeley] (novel) 1917
*Christopher and Columbus* (novel) 1919
*Vera* (novel) 1921
*The Enchanted April* (novel) 1922
*Love* (novel) 1925
*Introduction to Sally* (novel) 1926
*Expiation* (novel) 1929
*Father* (novel) 1931
*The Jasmine Farm* (novel) 1934
*All the Dogs of My Life* (autobiography) 1936
*Mr. Skeffington* (novel) 1940
*The Blessings of a Good Thick Skirt: Women Travellers and Their World* (biography) 1986

## The Athenaeum (essay date 1898)

[*In the following review, the critic offers a favorable assessment of* Elizabeth and Her German Garden.]

The writer of *Elizabeth and Her German Garden* does not disclose her identity, but she appears to be an Englishwoman married to a German. From internal evidence we imagine that she is *une originale qui ne se désoriginalisera jamais,* one of those rare beings whose companionship is curiously interesting and satisfying. The book is not a novel—it is apparently a soliloquy. The fascinating Elizabeth sits in the garden she has made and talks about everything and nothing—herself, her husband (whom she persistently styles the "Man of Wrath"), her children, her visitors, and, above all, her garden. She lives in the north of the Fatherland, almost on the shores of the Baltic, and her garden is "surrounded by cornfields and meadows, and beyond are great stretches of sandy heath and pine forests, and where the forests leave off the bare heath begins again." The garden was a desolate waste till Elizabeth took it in hand, and it pleased this eccentric young woman to make every step an experiment and to work by the light of nature, ignoring all the gardening wisdom of past generations—a plan which afforded her immense satisfaction and furnished her with many good stories for our delectation. The fair Elizabeth is by no means all sweetness; she has a stout will of her own, and we do not quarrel with her on that account, though we think she was a little too summary in her methods with Miss Jones, the nursery governess. A keen sense of humour is another characteristic of this gardening lady, and her account of her stolid neighbours is really delightful. To these good Germans she is a downtrodden wife, exiled from town delights by her stern husband. Of course, she is not downtrodden; she lives in the country because it is her wish. We wonder why she chooses to see so little of her husband, for she is evidently fond of him, and the Man of Wrath seems to be altogether friendly and pleasant, though his tirade against nurses is unjust and wholly unfair. However, in spite of our liking for the deserted husband, we hope that Elizabeth will desert him a little longer and write more rambling and delightful books.

*A review of "Elizabeth and Her German Garden," in* The Athenaeum, *Vol. 112, No. 3708, November 19, 1898, p. 711.*

## The Spectator (essay date 1899)

[*In the following review of* The Solitary Summer, *the critic focuses on the character of Elizabeth.*]

The author of ***Elizabeth and Her German Garden*** has written a second book of the same description which is even more charming than the first. Unlike so many of its kind, it is not written to instruct, nor, indeed, for any apparent purpose beyond the wish to talk to sympathetic listeners about her garden, her neighbours, or herself. After reading it we are as ignorant of the nature and growth of plants as, we suspect, she is, and the mysteries of domestic economy have not been made any clearer. But in her company we have never been dull, no pages have to be skipped, and the only regret is that there are not more to read.

Those who remember Elizabeth in the ***German Garden*** will find her grown more mellow in ***The Solitary Summer.*** "The Man of Wrath," too, appears in far more attractive colours. His sarcasm is less biting, and we begin to suspect that in real life he is much less "superior" and priggish than he was made to appear in the first book. Even her neighbours, too, are treated more tolerantly; but as those of her own class are somewhat conspicuous by their absence, it is probable that they may have come to realise that she is a strange bird not quite suited to a German aviary, and one best left to itself. To the ordinary German, or indeed English, county society, Elizabeth may well present a problem difficult to reconcile with any conventional teaching on the ways of woman, and the perveristy which makes her wholly charming in the pages of *The Solitary Summer* cannot fail to be trying to the conventional mind. Then, too, a large sunny estate on the shores of the Baltic, with streams and forests of its own, is not vouchsafed to all. Sordid circumstances in the shape of children clamouring for careers, husbands or wives demanding constant attention, not to speak of the grovelling necessity of making money wherewith to feed them, is unfortunately a far more common lot. Should Elizabeth's exclamation—"I want to be alone for a whole summer and get to the very dregs of life. I want to be as idle as I can, so that my soul may have time to grow"—escape the lips of one of these unhappy toilers, it is far more likely to be answered by a score of voices: "We too would have life all our own way," than by a kindly "Man of Wrath" saying: "Very well, my dear, only do not grumble afterwards when you find it dull." Still it is a great gain to weary workers that Elizabeths exist who can command a season of leisure. To those struggling with the anxieties of, say, a country parsonage and ten children, or immersed in the busy life of the successful money-making classes, *The Solitary Summer* will speak of beauty and repose as still existing as part of earth's heritage. With Elizabeth we can "sit amidst the pine-needles of those noble forests which the rain never penetrates, or lie on the heath and see how the broom flares against the clouds." We can go with her to the dip in the ryefields where there is "a little round hollow like a dimple, with water and reeds at the bottom, and a few water-loving trees and bushes on the shelving ground around." Here with Thoreau as her companion she lies upon the grass, and looking down "can see the reeds glistening greenly in the water," and looking up "can see the rye-fringe brushing the sky." Even Thoreau himself could ask for no better spot wherein to "dream away the profitable morning hours to the accompaniment of the amorous croakings of innumerable frogs." In these pages she teaches us the positive value of intercourse with Nature, and the untold mischief of coming to love the fuss and turmoil of which our lives are perhaps inevitably full. We realise that the only attitude which can make such lives noble is patient endurance born of the hope that one day we shall be free to lead the life of Nature,—free to be idle for long hours and not ashamed, free to listen and not to talk, while the voice of wind and water, bird and beast, carries us back to the days of our birthright, and we hear once more the still small voice of our own heart. Again, in *The Solitary Summer* we find Elizabeth more human than in the *German Garden.* She has realised that the best of intentions does not always produce success. She has "studied diligently all the gardening books" she could lay hands on, but discovers that "if an ordinarily intelligent person devotes his whole time to studying a subject he

loves," healthy lilies and roses do not of necessity follow. The pathetic cry, "The failure of the first two summers had been regarded with philosophy, but that third summer I used to go into my garden sometimes and cry," must endear her to all would-be gardeners. All garden-lovers know that wild despair of having lost another summer when summers are growing all too few, and that maddening certainty that the next summer will be no better. Mistakes will again occur, and frost and wind, drought and insects, will fill up the measure of our woe. And yet summer will bring again most of our plant-children, and mistakes are buried in the unexpected, which is more delightful in a garden than anywhere else.

The picture she draws of the peasantry in these far-off Baltic provinces is most unattractive. Not only is their morality of the laxest description, but their ignorance and prejudice is extraordinary. Health and conduct are alike a matter of the simplest animal instincts. Self-will is their sole motive for either living or dying. The orders of doctors are construed into nostrums that gain in proportion to the amount consumed. Consequently, when a bottle of opium with explicit directions as to its use in drops is sent to a poor woman, she takes it all at once, on the ground that "if it had been any good and able to cure me, the more I took the quicker I ought to have been cured." Naturally, the result was such that no power on earth could persuade her to open her door to any doctor again. The social standing of the inhabitants of the cottages is settled by the size and plumpness of their feather-beds, while fresh air and washing are only suitable to the children of those who have "accumulated vast strength during years of eating only possible to the rich." Their customs, too, are funny in the extreme. It is *de rigueur* that the German Frau, be she gentle or simple, should be provided with suitable burial apparel. Even for the humblest cottager this should not consist of less than "a very good black silk dress . . . and everything to match in goodness, nice leather shoes, good stockings, and under-things all trimmed with crochet; real whalebone corsets, and a quite new pair of white kid gloves." Elizabeth herself, should she die among her retainers, must not hope to escape the custom. "Nothing but a shroud is to be put upon me," she protests; but "such a thing would never be permitted," is the reply. "The gracious lady may be quite certain that . . . she will have on her most beautiful ball dress and finest linen, and that the whole neighbourhood shall see for themselves how well Herrschaften know what is due to them."

With such aspirations around her we are not surprised that Elizabeth knows "of no objects of love that give such substantial and unfailing returns as books and a garden." "How easy," she says, "it would have been to have come into the world without this, and possessed instead of an all-consuming passion, say, for hats, perpetually raging round my empty soul." Books are to her more than human friends in suiting every need and answering every call:—

> "My morning friend," she says, "turns his back on me when I re-enter the library, nor do I ever touch him in the afternoon. Books have their idiosyncrasies as well as people, and will not show me their full beauties unless the place and time in which they are read suits them. If, for in-

stance, I cannot read Thoreau in a drawing-room, how much less would I ever dream of reading Boswell in the grass by the pond! Imagine carrying him off in company with his great friend to a lonely dell in a rye-field and expecting them to be entertaining. 'Nay, my dear lady,' the great man would say in mighty tones of rebuke, 'this will never do. Lie in a rye-field? What folly is that? And who would converse in a damp hollow that can help it?'"

In the afternoon she wanders with Goethe, and sheds "invariable tears over *Werther*," and sits "in amazement before the complications of the *Wahlverwandschaften.*" In the evening, "when everything is tired and quiet," she is with Walt Whitman by the rose-beds, listening "to what that lonely and beautiful spirit has to tell of night, sleep, death, and the stars." Keats goes with her to the forest, and while with Spenser on the Baltic shores the blue waves become to her the "ripples of the Idle Lake." With such friends as these, and a score more, even a hermit's cell would be peopled with spirits choice and rare. Then there are gardening books of all kinds to turn winter into summer, and she can "wander in fancy down the paths of certain specially charming gardens in Lancashire, Berkshire, and Surrey." Such is her love for England and English culture that we must take her with a grain when she calls herself a German. Surely the Fatherland does not boast any one so piquant and full of open-air thought.

Elizabeth, too, is fortunate to have a house which she has evidently taught to run by itself. She has as well three charming babes who also run by themselves, full of amusing curiosity for what happened long ago, and what will follow after. The German village schoolmaster called in to wrestle with their active intelligence over Bible history is greeted daily with laughter and posies, and information upon the washing of their heads and the matching of their hair-ribbons:—

> "Herr Schenk told us to-day about Moses," began the April baby, making a rush at me.— "Oh?"—"Yes, and a *böser, böser König,* who said every boy must be deaded, and Moses was the *allerliebster.*"—"Talk English, my *dear* baby, and not such a dreadful mixture," I besought.—"He wasn't a cat."—"A cat?"—"Yes, he wasn't a cat, that Moses—a boy was he."— "But of course he wasn't a cat," I said with some severity; "no one ever supposed he was."—"Yes, but mummy," she explained eagerly, with much appropriate hand-action, "the cook's Moses *is* a cat."—"Oh, I see. Well?"—"And he was put in a basket in the water, and that did swim. And then one time they comed, and she said—"— "Who came? And who said?"—"Why, the ladies; and the *Königstochter* said, 'Ach Hörmal, da schreit so etwas.'"—"In German?"—"Yes; and then they went near, and one must take off her shoes and stockings and go in the water and fetch that tiny basket, and then they made it open, and that *kind* did cry and cry and *strampel* so"—here both the babies gave such a vivid illustration of the *strampeln* that the verandah shook—"and see! it is a tiny baby. And they fetched somebody to give it to eat; and the

*Königstochter* can keep that boy, and further it doesn't go."

And further we must not go in the sayings of the three babes, though their conversation is very instructive and wholly delightful, except to express a hope that it may be long before they learn to chatter French, or even English, fluently, or have to walk upon "the stony road that leads to *Himmel.*" Long, too, may they hold their own theories of *der lieber Gott,* and look for angel wings where feathers never grow. But we hope it will not be long before Elizabeth tells us more about herself and them, and reveals more secrets as to the "art of life" in far-off German lands. (pp. 863-64)

> *A review of "The Solitary Summer," in* The Spectator, *Vol. 82, No. 3703, June 17, 1899, pp. 863-64.*

## The Spectator   (essay date 1914)

[*In the following review, the critic considers* The Pastor's Wife *to be Russell's most noteworthy work.*]

The reader's usually unmixed delight in acclaiming a new book by Elizabeth of the German Garden will be modified by a certain mixture of feeling at finding that the scene of the greater part of [*The Pastor's Wife*] is laid in Germany. It is difficult to regard with the detachment proper to the contemplation of a work of art names which stand out in letters of fire in our daily newspapers—East Prussia, Königsberg, Berlin. Perhaps we may take the story as a wholesome reminder that life is not all war, and that behind the barbarities of the German Army stands the German people, full of zeal for matters of intellect and science, and as vitally concerned as we are with the domestic drama of everyday life. Another lesson, too, may be learnt from the portrait of Pastor Dremmel—the unremitting, unrelenting energy with which the intellectual German pursues his object. The object of Pastor Dremmel is by no means the spiritual progress of his flock, but, as he frankly tells the heroine, "manure." In his laboratory Pastor Dremmel forgets the rest of the world in the infinite combinations of chemical manure, and his rhapsodies on the subject are eloquent:—

> "Its infinite varieties! Kali, Kainit, Chilisaltpetre, Superphosphates"—he rolled out the words as though they were the verse of a psalm. "When I shut the door on myself in the little laboratory I have constructed I shut in with me all life, all science, every possibility. I analyse, I synthesize, I separate, reduce, combine. I touch the stars. I stir the depths. The daily world is forgotten. I forget, indeed, everything, except my research. And invariably at the most profound, the most exalted moments someone knocks and tells me it is Sunday again, and will I come out and preach."

It may be useful not to forget that the destruction of England is the ultimate object of the whole people of Germany, military and intellectual, and that this object will be pursued with the enthusiasm and determination shown by Robert Dremmel in his endeavour to improve the soil of

East Prussia. Nothing but chemical manure signifies to Pastor Dremmel. Nothing but the destruction of the Allies signifies to the people of Germany.

If we essay the difficult task of trying to forget the war in the artistic achievement of "Elizabeth," we shall have to acknowledge that this book is, on the whole, her most notable. She has abandoned her usual reticences, and makes no bones this time of calling a spade a spade, and, indeed, the whole of Part II. of the book might be labelled "Hints to a Wife," or "Mother, Nurse, and Baby," so full is it of obstetric details concerning the generation about to be born. But none of the medical authorities consulted in such a tremulous flutter by successive brides has one word to say as to the psychological situation which exists between the woman and the unborn. "Elizabeth," on the contrary, concerns herself with very little else. She calmly writes of nauseating physical details, but they are interesting to her only from their effect on the physical, moral, and intellectual well-being of Ingeborg, her heroine. Ingeborg, we should explain, is the daughter of an English Bishop, who, like the young man of Jamaica in the *Nonsense Book,* "casually married," not a Quaker, but a pastor. Her hard fate is the *raison d'être* of this tragi-comedy. If all children were like the Dremmel babies, the situation to the expectant mother would be one of unrelieved gloom. Indeed, the extraordinarily exasperating quality of their stolid goodness is unnatural; that is, unless we believe in a remark made by a character in one of "Elizabeth's" earlier works, that German children are quite unlike their English contemporaries. What can surpass in unattractiveness children who take no advantage of being left to themselves?—

> Robertlet did not turn on Ditti and seize her dinner because she was a girl; Ditti did not conceal more than her share of pudding in her pocket for comfort during the empty afternoon hours. They sat in silence working through the meal, using their knives to eat with instead of their forks, for knives rather than forks were in their blood, and unmoved by the way in which bits they had carefully stalked round and round their plates ended by tumbling over the edge on to the tablecloth. They were patient children, and when that happened they made no comment, but dropping their knives also on the tablecloth picked up the bits in their fingers and ate them. At the end Ditti said the closing grace as her mother had taught her, Robertlet having officiated at the opening one, and they both stood behind their chairs with their eyes shut while she expressed gratitude in German to the dear Saviour who had had the friendliness to be their guest on that occasion, and having reached the Amen, in which Robertlet joined, they did not fall upon each other and fight, as other unshepherded children filled with meat and pudding might have done, but left the room in a sober file and went to the kitchen and requested the servant Rosa, who was the one who would have been their nurse if they had had one, to accompany them to their bedroom and see that they cleansed their teeth. They spent the afternoons in not being naughty.

One cannot but accuse the malicious sprite who often guides "Elizabeth's" pen of exaggeration. Remembering Philip of *Struwwelpeter* fame, it is impossible to suppose that all German children are as good as this.

The first section of the book, which is concerned with Ingeborg's father, the English Bishop, is full of delightful pictures drawn from the author's peculiar point of view. That extremely good-looking dignitary of the Church is represented as a personage not too easy to get on with. Here is a description of how the heroine's mother solves the situation.—

> Ingeborg's mother had found the sofa as other people find salvation. She was not ill. She had simply discovered in it a refuge and a very present help in all the troubles and turmoil of life, and in especial a shield and buckler when it came to dealing with the Bishop. It is not easy for the married, she had found when first casting about for one, to hit on a refuge from each other that shall be honourable to both. In a moment of insight she perceived the sofa. Here was a blameless object that would separate her entirely from duties and responsibilities of every sort. It was respectable; it was unassailably effective; it was not included in the Commandments. All she had to do was to cling to it, and nobody could make her do or be anything. She accordingly got on to it and had stayed there ever since, mysteriously frail, an object of solicitude and sympathy, a being before whose helplessness the most aggressive or aggrieved husband must needs be helpless too. And she had gradually acquired the sofa look, and was now very definitely a slightly plaintive but persistently patient Christian lady.

The account of the beautiful Juliet and her marriage to the master of Ananias is also full of delight for the reader; and altogether the portion of the book which passes in the Cathedral Close at Redchester is as entertaining as anything which "Elizabeth" has ever written.

It cannot be said, however, that Part III. of the book is convincing. In it, Ingeborg, refusing her wifely duties, runs away with Edward Ingram, a celebrated painter, in order that he shall make an immortal portrait of her. The extreme *naïveté* of her attitude is really quite incredible, and although these chapters are charged with solitary pieces of illuminating intuition, they cannot be said to be successful as a whole. In detail, indeed, nothing could be more brilliant, witness this account of the effect of Milan on Ingeborg's mind:—

> The shop windows, the behaviour and foreign faces of dogs, the behaviour of children, the Italian eyes all turned to her, all staring at her,— they fascinated and absorbed her like the development of a vivid dream. Who were these people? What would they all do next? What were they feeling, thinking, saying? Where were they going, what had they had for breakfast, what were the rooms like they had just come out of, what sorts of things did they keep in their cupboards? "If one of them would lend me a cupboard," she exclaimed to Ingram, "and leave me alone with what it has got inside it, I believe I'd know all Italy by the time I'd done with it. Ev-

erything, everything—the desires of its soul and its body, and what it works at and plays at and eats, and what it hopes is going to happen to it after it is dead."

If Ingeborg had known Italian furniture at all intimately, she would have realized that what is usually inside Italian cupboards is immense patches of glue which stick them together. But perhaps artistic pieces of furniture are not what in this context she means.

It is impossible to go on for ever with quotations from the book. Whether it is suitable for the reading of the "young person" may be very greatly doubted. Or, rather, it is undoubted that for young women the reading of Part II. might prove as dangerous as would an account of the possible results of wounds by shrapnel to the recruits of "Kitchener's Army." We beg their pardons for this suggestion. Probably the descriptions of the wounds would merely double their determination to go and face them.

Quite another matter is the abstract question whether the early years of married life can be made bearable when the union is founded on nothing but physical passion on one side and calm friendship on the other. At any rate, the novel, even if we must pronounce it in some ways faulty in design, is brilliantly faultless in literary detail and execution. There is a touch of virile originality in "Elizabeth's" style which is often amazing. One wonders where she acquired this clarity, this power of subtle suggestion which yet never makes for obscurity, this intellectual detachment which is never a non-conductor. There is no padding in her books. What a rare, what a delightful gift. (pp. 566-67)

> *A review of "The Pastor's Wife," in* The Spectator, *Vol. 113, No. 4504, October 24, 1914, pp. 566-67.*

## Anice Page Cooper   (essay date 1927)

*[In the following essay, Cooper surveys Russell's novels up to the publication of* Introduction to Sally *in 1926.]*

A wise publisher once said that every so often in the cycle of literary fashions comes the appropriate moment for an anonymous novel. Perhaps so, but to us the lure of the unknown has no season. There is never a day when those bold or tender or wistful little lyrics marked "anon" in our anthologies do not stir a feeling of gentle curiosity about the unnamed writers whose moods are thus crystalized for our delight. And the anonymous authors of novels are even more interesting, for one likes to speculate about the environment, the circumstances of life, and the habits of mind that have produced the story. Almost always, if a book wins wide popularity, the name of the author becomes common knowledge, even though it is not announced in print. Such feats as that of Ray Stannard Baker, who lived for more than a score of years a double life as himself and David Grayson, the rustic philosopher of Hempfield; and that of "Elizabeth," who wrote a dozen widely read books under the cumbersome *nom de plume* "the author of *Elizabeth and Her German Garden,*" before she was identified as the Countess Russell, are rare in contemporary history. Yet "Elizabeth" is so warmly per-

sonal and subjective a writer that her refusal to give interviews and talk about the details of her private life for publication does not really affect our knowledge of her. Such books as *Elizabeth and Her German Garden* are as distinctly autobiographical as *Marbacka,* and much more vividly pictorial than many a serious *Life and Works.* (pp. 1-2)

Most of us made our acquaintance with "Elizabeth" when *Elizabeth and Her German Garden* was first published in 1898. It was written in the blithe spirit of the early twenties, when not even the arrival of the April, May, and June babies could entirely occupy her attention. Those first years as a German Countess, spent in maintaining the formal dignity and mediæval state of her position as the mistress of her husband's estate of sixty thousand acres, were a continual adventure to the gay-hearted, bright-haired young English girl, who delighted in spading the flowers when the gardener was not looking and lunching on salads under the lilac bushes when the "Man of Wrath" was away, instead of sitting alone in state in the lofty dining room.

"Elizabeth" was a schoolgirl in her teens when she met Count von Arnim. She was spending a holiday with her father in Italy, playing among the picture galleries and the pagan ruins, and going to tea in the dim old palaces of Roman high society. Von Arnim was twenty-five years older than she; very blond and tall and German, but, curiously enough, a liberal, although he belonged to one of the famous old Junker families to whom their nationalist caste was as sacred as their religion. He was the only son of the Ambassador Count Henry von Arnim, who was broken politically by the Iron Chancellor.

He married this flamelike young girl with her gold hair and romantic notions of love, and carried her away to an estate in East Prussia, where she spent most of the next twenty years.

Von Arnim was, as the Southern planters phrase it, "land poor." He was the master of great estates, a huge patriarchal system of tenants, crops, barns, cattle, a charming old château with numberless servants, nurses, governesses, which had to be maintained in mediæval state; and not much actual cash. The house stood in the middle of a vast Pomeranian plain, a rambling building of gray stone and many gables. The vaulted hall, with its worn brick floor, was once the chapel of a convent, but during the Thirty Years' War, Gustavus Adolphus passed through and turned the nuns out on to the plain to find some other shelter. There was one neighbour ten miles away with whom the Von Arnims exchanged yearly calls. "Elizabeth" asked this pleasant Junker and his wife to dinner at Nassenheide in the winter, and they invited the Von Arnims to dinner in the summer. "Elizabeth" looked with something of awe at this energetic country lady who managed her troop of flaxen-haired children; superintended the feeding of the stock, the butter and sausage-making; drove around in her pony carriage to oversee the tenant farms; and boxed the careless dairymaid's ears. But the young mistress of Nassenheide, whose days were filled with the delights of her babies, her garden, and her books, could never quite see the necessity of cooking, sewing, and sausage-making, when the cooks and the maids did it all so much better and there was not half enough time in the world to be completely happy with the dandelions and the daisies.

When she and the April, May, and June babies were first transplanted to the estate in Pomerania, "Elizabeth" found a wilderness that would challenge the heart of any gardener. The paths were effaced by exuberant grass, periwinkles, and Solomon's Seal, and the neglected lawns were glowing with bird cherries, lilacs, and Virginia creeper. Discovering this abandoned garden was the beginning of her real life, she says. "It was my coming of age, as it were, and entering into my kingdom." That first summer was occupied with pansies and roses and dwarf mignonette; making beds about the sundials; comparing the virtues of Duke of Teck, Cheshunt Scarlet, and Prefet de Limburg; and learning, as every gardener learns, by mistakes. But there were also pleasant hours of writing on the verandah, for "Elizabeth" did not retire behind locked doors to shut out interruption. One little picture of such a morning we remember in her diary:

> The three babies, more persistent than mosquitoes, are raging around me, and already several of the thirty fingers have been in the ink pot and the owners consoled when duty pointed to rebukes. But who can rebuke such penitent and drooping sunbonnets? I can see nothing but sunbonnets and pinafores and nimble black legs.

As the years slipped away, "Elizabeth" never took her household solemnly, never outgrew a secret amusement at the servants in their scarlet liveries; the formal dinners with her husband; the babies; and the silent tutors and governesses who, according to custom, did not speak until the Count or Countess spoke; the cooks and maids and gardeners who were horrified if she pruned a bush or touched a spade. During these years, the April, May, and June babies grew taller and the garden more beautiful. During these years the books by "Elizabeth" also grew in number and brought wide recognition for the witty and charming unknown, although she was scarcely aware of it, for fame found it hard to penetrate the fastnesses of Pomerania. Nine books belong to this period, the first two garden volumes: *Elizabeth and Her German Garden* and *The Solitary Summer;* and in succession, *April Baby's Book of Tunes, Adventures of Elizabeth in Rügen, The Princess Priscilla's Fortnight, Fräulein Schmidt and Mr. Anstruther, The Benefactress, The Caravaners,* and *The Pastor's Wife.* Of these the garden diary, although it was published nearly thirty years ago, still retains its lead in popularity and goes into new editions season after season.

*The Solitary Summer* is, in a sense, a continuation of *Elizabeth and Her German Garden.* Remembering her dream of a cottage at the edge of a little wood of silver birches by an amiable meandering stream, starred with yellow flags, a pathless place just big enough to hold herself and a baby, "Elizabeth" began to think how delightful a summer would be entirely by herself. "Two paradises 'twere

*The von Arnims' estate, Nassenheide, where Russell planted her garden.*

in one, to live in Paradise alone" was a true song, she thought, but hardly the argument to quote to the "Man of Wrath." On May Day evening, in the garden full of stars and scents of sweet wallflowers and pansies, she asked him for a whole summer alone to idle and loaf with her soul. Although he could not understand her whim, the "Man of Wrath" was indulgent.

"Very well, my dear," he consented, "only don't grumble afterward if you find it dull. It is always best to allow a woman to do as she likes if you can, and it saves a good deal of bother. To have what she desires is generally an effective punishment."

This second garden book has the charm of the first, but one misses the babies, the "Man of Wrath" himself, and some of the gay, humorous touches that make "Elizabeth's" people, even the most casual of the governesses, amusingly human.

*Adventures of Elizabeth in Rügen* is the last book in which the young Grafin wrote of her own experiences in the first person. In this story of her trip around Rügen, Germany's big island in the Baltic Sea, "Elizabeth" indulges in her rollicking sense of the ridiculous, which was to reappear with a more satirical edge in such books as *The Caravaners* and *The Pastor's Wife.* To walk around the island was an alluring project, but the women of her acquaintance were appalled at the suggestion and could not be persuaded, not even by the argument that the exercise would be excellent for the German nation, especially those portions of it that were not yet to come. So "Elizabeth" drove in a light victoria behind a pair of horses "esteemed at home for their meekness." Accompanied by August, the coachman; Gertrud, the maid; August's wet weather hat; the tea basket; innumerable bundles; and the inevitable shiny yellow wooden bandbox, "into which every decent German woman put her best hat," she spent a diverting holiday, getting lost on the road and floating with the beautiful jellyfish in the sandy coves along the way.

"Elizabeth's" next book was a venture in pure fiction, *The Princess Priscilla's Fortnight,* the tale of her Grand Ducal Highness the Princess Priscilla of Lothen-Kunitz, a vivacious young lady with red-gold hair and a nose that was not quite straight. Having spent twenty-one years at the top of the social ladder, she decided to spend the next twenty-one at the bottom of it, and as the nicest place to live at the bottom was England, she ran away. Abetted by the Ducal Librarian, she spent a glorious holiday at Creeper Cottage, but ended by marrying the very prince from whom she had fled a fortnight earlier.

Two years later "Elizabeth" adventured in a new literary form, a comedy of manners in letters. *Fräulein Schmidt and Mr. Anstruther* records the progress of a romance between Fräulein Rose-Marie and her "Dear Roger." The letters are Rose-Marie's. At least, they started as letters, reams and reams of them, but after she decided that she would be a sister to him, the correspondence languished. Wounded that he did not prove a faithful lover, indeed not even a faithful friend after she told him about her helpful sisterly attitude, she made her communications brief, finally limiting her last five letters to one sentence each, in this order:

> It would be useless.
>
> I would not see you.
>
> I do not love you.
>
> I will never marry you.
>
> I shall not write again.

In this history of a blighted romance, "Elizabeth" indulges in gentle irony, but in *The Caravaners,* her gift for satire is for the first time fully employed. One cannot remember a more devastating picture of a Prussian army officer than this self-drawn portrait of the lazy, pompous, miserly Baron von Ottringel, yet withal so stupid and childlike that he wins the reader's grudging sympathy. But even in her most biting moods, "Elizabeth's" merriment cannot be suppressed. There is something so irresistibly funny about Edelgard's rebellion, abetted by the attractive Frau von Eckthum, with the scandalously small feet and the dark eyelashes; not to mention Jellaby, the unspeakable socialist; and Browne, who turned out to be not plain Browne at all, but Lord Sigismund Brown, the youngest son of The Duke of Hereford and the nephew of the Princess of Grossburg-Niederhausen.

It has been said sometimes that perhaps the Baron von Ottringel was a portrait of the Count von Arnim, but we have "Elizabeth's" word for it that he was not. Her husband appeared in none of her works except the two garden books, and it is evident that she had a very deep affection and admiration for the "Man of Wrath."

In 1910, "Elizabeth's" pleasant, isolated life in Pomerania came to an end. The husband, who loved her devotedly, died, and without him she began to feel the differences of opinion and the racial hostilities that separated her from his countrymen and his kin. There is another book, however, that belongs to this German period, one of the most wistful and potentially tragic stories that she has done, yet at the same time one of her most amusing both in character drawing and situations: *The Pastor's Wife.* Ingeborg, the plain young daughter of the Bishop of Redchester, who in one mad moment of escape from the Bishop's gaiter buttons, the Bishop's speeches, his correspondence, and his tea parties, got carried away by a scientific German pastor, who forgot his fertilizers long enough to fall in love with her, is just such a direct, romantic, ignorant young creature as "Elizabeth" was herself when she set off for Prussia years ago. Her eagerness to adjust her joyous, pliable little self to the stiff and formal customs of her Prussian neighbours, her cheerful abandonment to bearing little Prussians, her final rebellion and readjustment to a bewildering solitude, shut out from her husband's thoughts, is a story of such poignancy that the diverting episode of Edward Ingram, the great artist, who wanted to capture her soul, is just so much whipped cream on a rich pastry.

*The Pastor's Wife* is the last of "Elizabeth's" books that has a German setting, and its appearance marked the end of her own life in Germany. It had been Count von

Arnim's wish that his children be educated in England, so their mother joined them there and sent her son to Eton. When the war broke out, the youngest daughter, the June baby, was in Germany and was unable to get away. She married a Bavarian and remained German in sympathies, but it happens that "Elizabeth" and her son-in-law like each other, so there is no discord in the family. Early in the war, "Elizabeth" regained her English citizenship through her marriage to Earl Russell. After three years, there was a separation, and now "Elizabeth" has returned to her writing and her friends and her children. During these later years, her reputation as a writer has steadily increased, and with it her fame as one of the wittiest and most popular of London's hostesses. Her April and May babies, who were not entirely happy in England during the war, came to the United States and have since married Americans. Their adventures are the basis, very much altered as to fact, of that amazing odyssey, *Christopher and Columbus.* In the story "Elizabeth" names the April and May babies Anna-Rose and Anna-Felicitas, and makes them seventeen-year-old twins; Anna-Rose the elder by twenty minutes. Although they were very German outside with their fair hair and blue eyes, they were very English inside. But this was something which a British uncle, who did not like orphaned alien nieces, could never understand, so he shipped them to some vaguely remembered friends in America with a letter of introduction and five hundred pounds. On the boat, as they were looking disconsolately at a vast deal of dreadfully wet sea and pretending to be thoroughly happy, they named themselves Christopher and Columbus, setting sail to discover America. Instead, it was Mr. Twist who discovered them. Mr. Twist was an American engineer with ample means and, being a "disciplined son and brother," he thought much in his cabin—one with a private bathroom—about those two defenseless children who were being set adrift in a strange and none too hospitable land. So it happened that Mr. Twist appointed himself their guardian, took them to California, invested in a tea room which Anna-Rose and Anna-Felicitas furnished with sea-blue cushions and flower pots and a canary, and found himself and the twins involved in such ludicrous and compromising situations that there was nothing else to do but marry one of them.

With her two daughters and her son married in America, and her June baby married in Germany, "Elizabeth" found more time to devote to her writing than she had ever known. Consequently, the past few years have been her most productive ones. After the separation from Lord Russell, she spent long summers in Switzerland at her "Chalet Soleil," perched high on a green shoulder of the Alps. Here much of the next book, *Vera,* was written, the book in which "Elizabeth" reaches the heights of her power as a satirist. To begin with, Vera, the heroine, if one may call her such, is dead when the story opens, but her spirit so pervades the tale that in the end her successor, Lucy, the gentle, simple, pretty young second wife of Wemyss, begins to wonder if perhaps Vera's fall from the second-story window was not suicide after all. And Wemyss himself is a character etched in such sharp clear lines that he immediately becomes one of the unforgettable fiction people. The meanest man in fiction, the critics called him, and it would be difficult to think of a competi-

tor for the title. *Vera* was the book which led Mrs. Meynell to call "Elizabeth" one "of the three finest wits of our day," and there is ample justification for her choice. "Elizabeth's" metaphors have an aptness and a whimsical quality that give a distinct fillip to her style. Lucy's Everard, for instance, was so comfortable to lean on mentally. "Bodily, on the few occasions on which her aunt was out of the room, he was comfortable, too; he reminded her of the very nicest of sofas—expensive ones, all cushions. But mentally he was more than comfortable, he was positively luxurious. Such perfect rest listening to him talk." Miss Entwhistle, the intrepid little aunt, who dared to tell Everard that Lucy had not the staying powers of Vera, before she was turned out into the night without a hat, is one of the most likable and human women that "Elizabeth" has done. Although *Vera* is written in a sardonic mood, there are many lighter humorous touches, reminiscent of the earlier *Christopher and Columbus* and *The Pastor's Wife.*

After expressing her devastating opinion of the *genus homo,* "Elizabeth" turned to happier things, to wisteria and sunshine and the miracle that scenic loveliness works on tired humans. Her next book, *The Enchanted April,* is rivalled by none of her others except perhaps *Elizabeth and Her German Garden.* It contains also some of the most sparkling examples of her wit. Of Frederick, Mrs. Arbuthnot's errant husband, she gives fleeting pictures, sketches with a certain tolerant delight. He "had been the kind of husband whose wife betakes herself early to the feet of God. From him to them had been a short, though painful, step. From her passionately loved bridegroom, from her worshipped young husband, he had become second only to God on her list of duties and forbearances." And again, "Her very nest egg was the fruit, posthumously ripened, of ancient sin." The way Frederick made his living was one of the standing distresses of her life. He wrote immensely popular memoirs, regularly every year, of the mistresses of Kings.

> There were in history numerous Kings who had mistresses, and there were still more numerous mistresses who had had Kings, so that he had been able to publish a book of memoirs during each year of his married life, and even so there were great further piles of these ladies waiting to be dealt with. The more the memoired lady had forgotten herself, the more his book about her was read and the more free-handed he was to his wife. The parish flourished because, to take a handful at random, of the ill behaviour of the ladies Du Barry, Montespan, Pompadour, Ninon de l'Enclos and even of the learned Maintenon. The poor were the filter through which the money was passed, to come out, Mrs. Arbuthnot hopes, purified. Their very boots were stout with sins.

In this tale of the four runaway ladies in the Italian castle, "Elizabeth" breaks occasionally into hilarity that borders on farce. The bathroom scene, in which the eccentric Italian water heater explodes and ejects the dignified solicitor Mellersh Wilkins, clad in a bath towel, into the presence of the lovely Lady Caroline Dexter, none other than the daughter of the Droitwiches, needs very little dramatization to transform it into an excellent vaudeville sketch.

But, above all, the book breathes the beauty of gardens and sea and sky and the happiness that one may find in shaking himself free of mundane affairs and very simply enjoying the blessings of being alive. It is the old "Elizabeth" who danced for joy among the blue hepaticas and celandines of that far-away Pomeranian garden, but an "Elizabeth" with a freer spirit. Then, being very young, she danced behind a bush, mindful of her "years and children and having due regard for the decencies." In *The Enchanted April* she dances again for joy, but, being older and wiser, more conscious of the preciousness and rarity of joy, she dances gloriously in the centre of the lawn.

Like all of "Elizabeth's" books, *The Enchanted April* is the picture of a place which she knows well. The original of the castle of the wisteria and the lilacs is the Castello of Portofino, a gracious old group of towers, dating from the Crusades. It is on the Gulf of Rapallo and looks down over the little village of Portofino, in whose church rest the relics of St. George of the dragon fame.

From the Puck-like delights of *The Enchanted April,* "Elizabeth" touches in her next book, *Love,* a theme that is essentially tragic: the love of a young man and an older woman. Carried away by the impetuosity of his wooing, Catherine married Christopher, in spite of the fact that she had a married daughter who was almost as old as he. "Elizabeth's" picture of this charming, sensible, middle-aged woman, who from loving fell in love, is one of the most poignant character studies that she has done. Catherine's grotesque efforts to stay young for him, and her final decision that she could no longer live a deception when the shock of her daughter's death revealed suddenly the marks of years, are among the unspoken tragedies that are too painful to read with enjoyment. Nor is Christopher's plight any the more happy, for he loved her with a genuine devotion.

> "Good God, Catherine," he pleads, "do you think a man wants his wife to scrub herself with yellow soap as if she were the kitchen table, and then come all shiny to him and say, 'See, I am the Truth'? And she isn't the Truth. She's no more the truth shiny than powdered. She's only appearance anyway. She's only a symbol—the symbol of the spirit in her which is what one is loving the whole time."

But the fact remains between them, and "Elizabeth" offers no solution. She leaves them trying to laugh, "but it was a shaky, uncertain laughter, for they were both afraid."

As a comic relief, "Elizabeth" is on a glorious holiday in her hilarious *Introduction to Sally,* a tale in which she laughs at love and beauty and misplaced "h's," culture and elderly suitors, and all the other amusing ingredients of this decorous world. The innocent cause of her amusement is Sally Pinner, whose beauty is so bright that the customers of her father's little shop never notice her lapses in grammar. On her serene and devastating way, Sally meets and subdues a garage mechanic with a bucket of Irish stew, a marquis with an untouched glacial heart, a deaf old duke whose eyesight is unimpaired, not to mention a prospective father-in-law and all the casual passers-by who chanced to see her glory. It is an odyssey of amusing episodes done in the countess's most impish humour.

*Sally* brings "Elizabeth's" literary history to date, fifteen books in almost as many moods, and, it is rumoured by those who know her, at least two others published entirely anonymously. What she will do next, one cannot prophesy, for she is still in her prime. One's only safe conjecture is that her next book will be unlike her last. Although she is a grandmother, "Elizabeth" looks and is surprisingly young. She has retained the delicate colouring and flowery grace of a Dresden china figure, but with all her gracious femininity, there is a boldness and keen mental alertness, both in her writings and her conversation, that justify Alice Meynell's choosing her as one of the three great wits among our contemporaries. (pp. 2-18)

*Anice Page Cooper, " 'Elizabeth',' " in her Authors and Others, 1927. Reprint by Books for Libraries Press, 1970, pp. 1-18.*

### Margaret Lawrence (essay date 1936)

[*In the following excerpt, Lawrence offers a characterization of the literary persona of Elizabeth, contrasting her early and later works.*]

The sophisticated lady is feminine but with reservations. The reservations have to do with her emotions. These she contains cleverly within her technique. She is engaged always with the picture she presents of herself.

She goes back in her history, whether she chooses to make the admission or not, to the ancient courtesans. She uses, whether she knows it or not, the technique of the trained courtesan, which was a technique of the concealment of the emotions and of the presentation of an art of the senses. (p. 281)

There are two types of sophisticate among women.

There are the simple personal sophisticate and the intellectual sophisticate.

The simple personal sophisticate is a lady who shrewdly estimates the world as still a place, for all the radicals may wish it to be different, wherein all the plums go to the best showman, and wherein women only get such bites out of the plums as they can inveigle men to give them. The best way to get a plum from a man is to flatter him. That is sound thinking, things being as they are. It is practical. Such a woman is distinctly a man's woman. She has no use for women because women do not usually have the plums, or if they do have them, are cagy about sharing them. So she gets herself ready for the men. And the plums. The plums may not be necessarily in checks or bank-notes. They often are merely jobs and chances of jobs. Such a woman puts paint on her face, a wave in her hair, lipstick on her lips and lacquer on her nails. She buys the clothes that she thinks will hit men in the eyes. She uses her figure so it will be noticed. She adds perfume. She trains her eyes to look admiringly upon the lords of creation. She thinks of appropriate remarks. She watches for the best moments to bring them out. She cultivates personality plus. It is no wonder. All the magazines tell her to. The advertisers insist that she have a success appearance philosophy. She cannot possibly interest any man unless she uses a mouth wash and a fine-grained peach-bloom powder. She must have long lashes; she is well advised to have thin arched eyebrows. It is to be hoped that she will have pearly teeth. This is a deliberate appeal to the remnant of the courtesan that is in every woman, as the advertisers suppose. The films take up the insistent story and feature women of exotic personalities. They set the styles, and every woman tries to look and act like some star of the screen. They dress for business carefully, and the women in the homes are reminded how much the women in offices do care for their persons, and are cautioned to follow their example. So we find an era of women playing the part in appearance at least of the very sophisticated ladies of the past. Even though there are those among them who have no idea whatever of what they are doing. But those who do know play themselves off assiduously.

Their tricks are quite obvious. They brighten when a man enters the room. They overlook the women. They enjoy conquest. Usually they feature their conquests. The world as it still is to-day is comparatively an easy place for these women so long as they have their youth. Some of them get along very well indeed. Men can still be taken for rides and the sophisticated lady of simple designs upon men has lots of opportunities for getting away with her designs.

The intellectual sophisticate is quite another woman. Her designs upon men are not tangible. It is a matter of admiration. She is like the second type of helpmeet, an image-builder, but the image is built around herself and not around a man. Therefore she is, all things being equal, likely to be happier than the helpmeet. The image is comfortably attached to herself. She is under no necessity, therefore, to go hunting for some being to whom to fasten it.

She is self-contained, and it is in this self-containment that the reservations of her femininity lie. Much as she likes, and to an extent needs, admiration, she is never entirely intent upon getting it. She always has herself upon which to fall back. She realizes her own self-sufficiency. Admiration is a pleasant tribute and is always graciously accepted, but she will never go unduly out of her way to get it, and because she does not go out for it, she usually gets it.

These women are never capable of love as the helpmeet is capable of it, and certainly not as the priestess. They cannot become engrossed with a man. The image of no man ever completely fills their imaginations. They treat such men as they take to themselves as audiences. As soon as any man in relation to a sophisticated lady begins to take her for granted, she begins automatically to look around for his successor. Though very often the little look around is all that is necessary to put an end to the casual acceptance of her. She holds her man by the very fact that he is not absolutely necessary to her. Her attitude is psychologically one of self-assurance. Because she is ready to lose him, the sophisticated lady rarely loses her man. Except when she wants to.

She is a woman who through incapability of love for a man is able technically to promote an atmosphere of *amour*

which is far more satisfying to the normal male than intense love. He feels more at home with it. The man never knows her mind though he may know her body. For the woman who is really intellectually sophisticated, and adept at *amour,* is mysterious. Da Vinci painted her once and for eternity in the Mona Lisa, with her still sensuousness and her secretive withdrawal into her own personality.

The withdrawal of the sophisticate is an outcome of judiciously cultivated skepticism, and the skepticism is the outcome of a desire for self-preservation.

The helpmeet in love is helpless. Everything she has is open to the inspection of the man she loves. Her hands are held out to him. The sophisticate controls her hands. She keeps them quietly folded within her sleeves.

The attitude of the sophisticate is not natural to a woman, for neither the desire for self-preservation and its corollary, skepticism, is innate in the normal woman. The very existence of the womb within a woman denotes instinctive belief. For to take life within the body is to believe in life, and to nourish it there is to imply a permanent acceptance of that belief, and a corresponding indifference to self-preservation.

It is possible that there are women who started out as natural loving women, and as helpmeets, with an image in their minds, and finding no man to fit the image, gradually became skeptical about men and the habit of expecting image fulfilment from them. In other words, the helpmeet sometimes becomes a sophisticate because she has suffered through some man, or through men. If this is so, she puts herself under some manner of discipline planned to eradicate from her system the inclination to lay herself open to the wounding of men. Such a woman from then on plays at love with men. All the ardor she may want to feel she will deliberately divert into some other form of expression. All the glamour of which she may be aware in the presence of a man she will gather into herself to make her the more glamorous. She will never permit her lover to touch her soul. She will preserve inviolate some center of her being. Because of this inviolability she is free to play with love as no other woman is free to play with it. It preserves her sight. She comes under no more illusions. If she does meet an illusion she raises her eyebrow skeptically and reminds herself cryptically that she herself is all that counts. So she remains in control of her emotions, and therefore can use them. She knows when to be moved, and when to be unmoved. She becomes a complete technician. She knows when to be tentatively conversational and when to be tantalizingly silent. She knows when to come to the edge of tears and when to be casually amused. She keeps an eye on the responses of the man, and always remembers that in every love affair she must be the gainer, if not in actual cash, certainly in her own opinion of herself. So she sets out according to the particular status of the affair to be the sophisticated lady, whether as wife, or mistress, or little girl pal, by the way. She is under no illusion that the man is hers by destiny. She takes him as a matter of biological course, but knows that he is hers only so long as the mood will last, and she makes it her vocation to sustain the mood by whatever means she has, and all the time she herself remains mysteriously aloof.

The sophisticated lady in writing surveys the scene skeptically. She does not believe altogether in what she sees. She looks for the thing which if understood would change the whole aspect. Therefore she never is emotional about what seems to be seen, and is never surprised when something else comes to the surface. If what comes to the surface is something that is quite upsetting, she is never upset. She is faintly amused. And out of her amusement she writes. She makes delicate entertainment out of it for her readers. Her own deft aloof mind controls the story. She tells it with a side glance.

Whether she deals with a sophisticated situation or a simple one, does not matter at all. It is how she presents the situation that counts. The presentation is always ironical, but never obviously ironical. The irony lies not in the story itself but in the slant she gives it in her writing. The story she tells never quite gets her. She does not allow it to get her. She is never riotously funny as some of the little girl pals are. She is never completely objective as others of them are. She is never enterprising in her search for new material, as some of the go-getters are. She is never bored as others of them are. She is never tragic as many of the helpmeets are. Nor is she ecstatic in her emotionalism. Neither is she serious about the plan of life as the matriarchs seem on the whole to be. She is merely interested in seeing what there is to be seen easily, and in what is not so easily seen. In some cases she is close to being an artiste, but in most cases she willingly sacrifices art for the ironical effect. She is in all things an emotional dilettante. (pp. 286-90)

***Elizabeth and Her German Garden*** is the study of an English woman living in Germany, the wife of a German aristocrat prior to the war. It is a story-book atmosphere, but there is no story. The man is a shadowy background. The woman herself is a ghostlike personality, wandering among her gardens, watching for the first lilacs, catching their rain-drenched fragrance, watching the glint of the sun on the grass, taking books of poems down to read by particular spots. The world of the garden, with a man in the background and three babies.

This again is the self-sufficient feminine mind. The man might as well not be there, except that with precision he comes forward occasionally with this law or that law concerning the estate. He was Lord of the Manor, and unquestionably it was what his wife wanted him to be. The woman assumes his happiness and his comfort and withdraws into her own pleasure with the garden and her thoughts. The picture of the woman is entrancing. She is a woman with peculiar balm in her spirit, a quiet woman aware of beauty, and drawing the man and the reader to her by presenting a banquet of sweetness. Along with the sweetness there is a touch of gentle irony. It is a mind which, though encased for the time within the walls of a garden, is a mind that belongs to the world. It has the aloofness which only comes to the completely sophisticated. It has the impersonality which only comes from much cogitation upon life in all its aspects.

"Elizabeth" carried her German garden through a sequence, and through the studies the same woman glides mysteriously, showing a thought here, and a feeling there, appreciating the fine taste of things, the perfumes and the delicate underplay of psychic atmosphere.

When later she turned to straight fiction, she was not quite so happy. The irony which was well controlled in her early studies got rather too much force in the later books. She moved into a less aristocratic setting. The woman she drew in *Love* was a baffled woman to whom love came too late. She was a widow, who in her maturity attracted the devotion of a young man. She married him, and found it increasingly difficult to keep pace with him in passion. She had longed all through her first matter-of-fact marriage to know the great emotion, and when it came she could not stand it. She spent her days in beauty parlors struggling with the lines left upon her face. It was useless. Until her second marriage she had remained youthful in her appearance. She had not really lived. Life had put nothing, therefore, upon her face to tell her story. With the second marriage life got at her, and told the story on her face.

She has followed in this the pattern of the sophisticate's familiar thesis, which was summed up in the wise-crack of Anita Loos' famous Blonde, "Love never did any girl any good." She has followed it in other books of this period, and for all that she is following a pattern that is tragic to the women involved, she carries it through with the ironical shrug. Love is, as far as the woman herself is concerned, something from which to steer meticulously clear. The technician cannot afford it. It gets into the mind and muddles one's technical mastery of a situation. So long as the woman does not love she has control of herself and the relationship. If she loves she is helpless and she loses sight of the salient little points upon which every sustained relationship is built and maintained. So she paints a woman losing her beauty and consequently her dignity and her essentially feminine prestige over an incalculable emotion for a man, who after all is only one man out of many men. It is all so futile. It is the sophisticate laughing up her long mysterious sleeves behind her hidden hands at women who let themselves go. Far better is it to read poetry in particular spots in a lovely garden, and to watch the flowers as they come out in their seasons. Only with the emotion cleared of devastating fixations can a woman be free to enjoy what goes on round about her, and be in a position of feminine invulnerability in the relations of the sexes. What if she does long for the grand sweep of what might be? The point conceivably may be that enjoyment may be utterly in the longing and not in the realization. And it is just possible that the woman who longs to love and will not let herself love does exude from her own personality the perfume of that longing, and with far greater aphrodisiacal effect upon her associates than any perfume there is among all the flowers in the garden. (pp. 303-05)

*Margaret Lawrence, "Sophisticated Ladies," in her* The School of Femininity: A Book for and about Women as They Are Interpreted through Feminine Writers of Yesterday and Today, *Frederick A. Stokes Company, 1936, pp. 281-310.*

*Russell's first husband, Henning von Arnim (the "Man of Wrath"), oversees farm work.*

## Orlo Williams   (essay date 1941)

[*Williams was an English critic. In the following essay, he offers a personal tribute to Russell and her work.*]

Mary, Countess Russell was her proper style, but she was known to all her friends as Elizabeth—the fictitious name that she gave herself when, as Gräfin von Arnim, she wrote her first book and won immediate fame. And now to the already portentous account against Hitler is to be added this, that death has arrested that witty and charming pen, expressive of all its holder's personality, stilled that small, high voice so apt, with its willow-warbler cadence, for unexpected remarks, and removed for ever from her friends, her adoring dogs and her appropriate setting a most original and delightful person. I add it to Hitler's account because, had it not been for the war, she would not have fled to the United States from her *Mas des Roses* with its lovely garden. It was here that she meant to end her days. Elizabeth had no illusions, except, perhaps, about dogs; but none certainly about human beings, singly or in the aggregate, none about the French, and most certainly none about the Germans. She knew what would happen and uprooted herself; and I suppose that she was wise, for what could have pleased a German more than to have made life uncomfortable for the author of *The Solitary Summer* and *The Caravaners?* Had things been oth-

erwise, she would still, under Providence, have been with us and with the things she loved. I can imagine her now, rejoicing in the rich, early promise of a Riviera spring, firmly rooted herself but uprooting plants and flower-clumps for their eventual benefit, or giving directions to her jobbing gardener in fluent French uttered with that half-gay, half-plaintive cadence which she never altered to suit her language but which gave that language a new and original cachet. The almond trees would be in bloom, the peaches and prunuses would follow, and she would exult in each—for the beauty of Nature made her exult as she walked in the morning to her garden study, for the wall of which I once wrote a Latin couplet, or returned from it for lunch, or lingered in the sunset after exercising her dogs. I can imagine, too, getting before long a letter in her sprawling hand suggesting that it was once more time for me to take an early aeroplane and arrive at Mandelieu by tea-time. That can never happen again, nor shall I ever sit under the shade of that medlar tree sipping coffee after lunch and tempting Elizabeth to say something mildly outrageous in revenge for having been tempted by her to tell things about myself only known—I hope—to the recording angel. One didn't confess to Elizabeth, no, it was not that. She was anything but the amply sympathetic comforting mother-superior kind of person who elicits; still less was she the companion-cynic with whom to swap sneers at the weaknesses of humanity. I doubt if she was a proficient comforter, but she certainly hated cynicism. The enchanting thing was that, combined with genuine humanity and emotions, not to speak of acute intelligence and a great stock of literary knowledge, she had a sprite-like mind which simply provoked one into defying the censors—one's own censor, be it understood. And then, if one met her mood, conversation could become unbelievably gay and comic, as in one of those marvellous dreams from which one wakes up laughing. As for sadness, she could join in a little agreeable melancholy too, with quotations from the poets and philosophers—I remember once that we talked of death all one evening after the ritual game of chess—but the cheerfulness broke in before long; for she had a natural optimism, more delicate than Pippa's, but as fervent, which could be illustrated from almost all her books, from the **German Garden** to **The Jasmine Farm,** and particularly from **The Enchanted April.** It was an infectious optimism, only failing a trifle in contagion when she was driving one in a fast *coupé* round the sharp curves of the *grasse* road with two hefty terriers sprawling and wheedling off one's knee on to, or under, the steering wheel. It was then a little difficult to share her assurance that all was right with the world, particularly at the corners. But the apprehension was unjustified, and nothing untoward happened: indeed, everything came off brilliantly when one stayed at the *Mas des Roses,* from the deliciously arranged morning tray that was brought to her guest's room to the first meeting in the garden after the morning's work, the picnic tea on the beach towards La Napoule followed by a bathe and the evening hours when, sharing a sofa with her sleepy dogs, she cleverly managed to convey that her guest was providing all the entertainment. She was as good a hostess as she was a gardener, and that is to say all. Flowers grew for her because she loved them: and how she loved them was as magnificently shown by her roses and zinnias at Mougins as, doubtless, by all the flowers she tended in her Pomeranian countryhouse and described in her first book many years before I came to be one of her guests. Always to love human beings in spite of disappointment needs the quality of a saint, which she would not have claimed: but the things that never disappoint—the sun and the stars, trees and the flowers of earth, great poetry and great music—she loved without reserve, and with a response of gladness, fresh and youthful, that was a perpetual reproof to those who had allowed custom to stale their appreciation.

Elizabeth, unlike the general run of writers, seldom spoke of her books, and never of her work in hand. Praise of them gave her great pleasure, and I do not know that she cared to have praise tempered by criticism: but literary vanity had, I feel, nothing to do with this attitude. Indeed, more than once she said to me: "my dear Orlo, I can't *write*"; and if I observed that her books proved the contrary, she would only agree that she had "a little way of saying things." This, I believe, was a genuine modesty. Being herself extremely well-read and having a reverence for great literature, she looked on her own works not so much as literature, to be discussed and compared, as a contribution made by herself to the amenity of existence, her own life included. Therefore, she preferred that they should be treated as bits of herself, which permitted open compliments but not cold-blooded dissection. Besides, she naturally preferred the positive, warmth-giving attitudes to the negative, warmth-arresting ones: although she made no little capital out of it in her books, she sincerely mourned that people in general loved each other so little and bored or loathed each other so much, and still more that people were so blind to the real secret of happiness. Mrs. Wilkins, in **The Enchanted April,** is a complete expression of this propensity. Some people have found Mrs. Wilkins a little overpowering in her insistence that happiness, true happiness, produces immense outputs of love, for instance, in the conversation between her and Mrs. Arbuthnot after the first radiant day in the Mediterranean *castello.* The latter thinks it odd that her friend, having deliberately stolen away from her husband, has immediately written to invite him to come. Mrs. Wilkins says: "It's quite true. It seems idiotically illogical. But I'm so happy, I'm so well, I feel so fearfully wholesome. This place— why, it makes me feel *flooded* with love."

And, on Mrs. Arbuthnot's inquiring whether she thought it would have the same effect upon Mr. Wilkins, she goes on: "I don't know, but even if it doesn't, there's enough love about to flood fifty Mr. Wilkinses, as you call him. The great is to have lots of love *about.*"

An earlier page describes what had happened to Mrs. Wilkins; she had looked out of a window at the radiance of Italy in April (Mezzago was really Porto Fino) and felt happy without being good.

> How beautiful, how beautiful. Not to have died before this . . . to have been allowed to see, breathe, feel this . . . Happy? Poor, ordinary, everyday word. But what could one say, how could one describe it? It was as though she could hardly stay inside herself, it was as though she were too small to hold so much of joy, it was as though she were washed through with light. And how astonishing to feel this sheer bliss, for here she was, not doing and not going to do a single unselfish thing, not going to do a thing she didn't want to do. According to everybody she had ever come across she ought at least to have twinges. She had not one twinge. Something was wrong somewhere. Wonderful that at home she should have been so good, so terribly good, and merely felt tormented . . . Now she had taken off all her goodness and left it behind her like a heap of rain-sodden clothes, and she only felt joy.

Whatever comment the saints and philosophers might make on that passage and on the moral of **This Enchanted April,** there is much truth in both; moreover, this capacity for moral and physical elation at the sight of beauty was a capacity of Elizabeth's, and one which gave half the colour to her books.

But, of course, another capacity of hers, as an author, was that of expressing, because she realised with such comic certitude, how exquisitely men and women get upon each other's nerves, and how they suffer from each other's egoism. There is no book of hers from which one could not illustrate this. The reform of Mrs. Fisher in **The Enchanted April** is one instance; and others can be found in that extremely amusing novel, *Father,* which has never had all the appreciation it deserves. Miss Alice Ollier, who tyrannizes over her brother, the vicar, in that book is a masterly piece of delineation; and who could forget the account of James Ollier's sufferings in the Swiss hotel whither he had been wafted by his sister's sense of danger to him and injury to herself through the intrusion of a young woman into the village, and the culminating scene in which James and Alice, goaded by wholly different impulses, seek to elude each other in a secret dash for England, meet on the lake steamer, and spend the whole night standing in the corridor of a Continental express, vociferously wrangling to the misapprehension and discomfort of sleepy French passengers?

> "Dare to say God to me," gasped Alice, beside herself at his calling the woman Jennifer. "You swearing—you, a clergyman——"
>
> "Oh, damn being a clergyman!" cried James very loud; so loud that, had there been any English or Americans in that coach, the train being at a standstill they must have heard him.
>
> And the French passengers, their eyes heavy from want of sleep, watching the uncontrolled and formidable pair still at it in the corridor even though it was now another day, supposing them to be husband and wife, and marvelling at the sorts of persons the natives of Britain married, groaned in profound disgust, *"Quel ménage!"*

Of the monumental, all-embracing, breezy but terrible egoist portrayed in *Vera* I need hardly speak; as a piece of sustained tragi-comedy it is, from a literary point of view, the most finished and complete of her works. Nevertheless, there is an element of bitterness in it which all her other books belie and which was not part of the real Elizabeth.

I say "the real Elizabeth," but, after all, it was only comparatively late in her life that I knew her, in the 'twenties of this century. She was living alone, and all her children—the "babies" of her early book—were married, most of them in the United States. So that the charming hostess of the Châlet Soleil below Moutana and of the *Mas des Roses* at Mougins was not, in all respects, the original Elizabeth, the wife of a Pomeranian Junker, who, in books that were half fiction, half autobiographical essays, drew a lightly fanciful picture of herself, of the "Man of Wrath," of babies, governesses and stray visitors, in a setting of country life and garden-gossip that was something quite new to a generation slightly older than mine. Those books, *Elizabeth and Her German Garden, The Benefactress, The Solitary Summer* and *Elizabeth in Rügen* are still delightful, more delightful even than that very amusing, rather cruel—but who shall say unjustified?—farewell to the German scene in *The Caravaners.* They described her life at Nassenheide—that was the house's name—without much fictitious embroidery. The opening pages of *Elizabeth and Her German Garden* describe the house and surrounding landscape, while *The Solitary Summer* fills in many of the details. The picture is that of a young English wife of a kindly, and certainly older, German husband, a happy mother, a conscientious if not very enthusi-

astic housekeeper and mistress of many servants, a passionate gardener, with a taste for solitude in a green shade, a tolerable performer of a *châtelaine*'s duties to the countryside, but mutinously critical of German ways and habits and uncontrollably independent in thought and speech. On the testimony of one who knew her then and was her guest in Pomerania, it was a delightful home animated by the enchanting spirit of Elizabeth, and made additionally agreeable by the extremely amiable manners of the "Man of Wrath," Count von Arnim. A certain amount of ceremony and routine there had to be; there were many maids, none very well trained, and many rather loutish menservants handing dishes in white gloves at the all-important *Mittagessen* to which the whole family of children, governess and tutors assembled. Elizabeth hated hearty eating, witness her remarks on German holidaymakers' habits in the description of Rügen, and she was never tired of tilting at German guzzling: but she could not, in her own house, completely undermine German institutions, she could only reduce some of their grossness. But best of all—so I am told—was the inexhaustible spirit of laughter and gaiety which Elizabeth exercised upon her guests and upon her household. So it is not surprising that these are happy books, for her's, German by marriage though she was, was a happy spirit even amid the ignorance, dirt and grossness which she saw among the country-folk, and the combination of servility, arrogance, narrow-mindedness, intolerance and grasping selfishness which she plainly descried among her *hochwohlgeborene* relations and acquaintances. Those were the days when German philosophy ruled in our Universities, when to speak of music meant German music and German players, the high days of Hegelianism at Oxford, of Joachim and the Saturday Pops and of ecstatic pilgrimages to Bayreuth. To us who have suffered so much from Germanity since then, it is doubly interesting to see how Elizabeth understood the Germans among whom, married to an intelligent, courteous German Liberal, she had accepted her lot with content. The content did not last, as the discomfitures of the unpleasant husband in *The Caravaners* bear witness. When it came to the test, a spirit such as Elizabeth's could only stand for freedom, as her nation alone interpret it. Freedom to live, to think, to enjoy, to be yourself was, in her mind, the whole secret of living. She had the secret, and that is why her books, even the earliest, are still so fresh. (pp. 482-88)

*Orlo Williams, " 'Elizabeth' and Her Novels,"* in The National Review, *London, Vol. CXVI, No. 698, April, 1941, pp. 482-88.*

**George Lanning   (essay date 1971)**

[*Lanning is an American novelist and short story writer. In the following excerpt, he presents a biographical portrait of Russell and summary discussion of* The Pastor's Wife, *highlighting autobiographical elements in the novel.*]

In the latter part of the 1940s, I spent an evening in Cambridge, Massachusetts, with Pamela Frankau and her husband—a tall, pale man, somewhat her junior, I think—named Dill. (p. 210)

I had just been lent *The Merry Wives of Westminster,* the latest in a series of reminiscences that Mrs. Belloc Lowndes was then publishing. A part of it dealt with Gilbert Frankau, Pamela Dill's novelist father; her grandmother, who had written successfully under the pseudonym "Frank Danby"; and the great Frankau house in Belgravia—right on the square, if memory serves me. Coincidentally, I had recently managed to buy a copy of **Christine,** that notorious best seller of World War I which, though it was signed "Alice Cholmondeley," was widely considered to be the work of "Elizabeth"— Countess Russell in private life and before that the Gräfin von Arnim-Schlagenthin of the vast Schloss at Nassenheide and later and more briefly tenant of the Gutshaus on the estate at Schlagenthin, both in Pomerania. *The Merry Wives of Westminster* contained an unflattering but fascinating portrait of Elizabeth and in addition much material on the Frankaus.

With Mrs. Belloc Lowndes's comments about Elizabeth Russell fresh in my mind, I asked Pamela Frankau whether she and the Countess had met. They had, although once only, and only briefly. But the image was sharp, if unexpected in the context of what I then knew about Elizabeth. The encounter had taken place on a street in one of those hilly villages along the Italian Riviera. "We were walking up and she was coming down one blistering, sunny afternoon," Pamela Frankau said. "I'd never have recognized her, though I must have seen pictures, but my friend had been introduced to her somewhere. She was a little old lady covered over in dusty black, and she had a face like a crumpled football."

That was all, but for contrast it was enough. How could one reconcile this unprepossessing, solitary woman with the famous London hostess, the austere beauty, the femme fatale whose liaisons were almost as notorious as her ill-fated second marriage? This was the woman who had employed E. M. Forster and Hugh Walpole as tutors to her children, who had created at Nassenheide a German garden which became so world famous that Forster privately circulated a pamphlet denying that any garden existed. This was the celebrated novelist who became a best seller with her first book about that garden and by and large remained one through **Mr. Skeffington** (1940), her triumphant last. Though she had begun sweetly (or seemingly so), writing about flowers and books and her husband, the Man of Wrath, and the April, May, and June babies, she had gone on to startle her readers with such novels as **The Caravaners** (1910), a high comedy that was nevertheless a chilling forecast of Germany's intention to conquer England, and **Vera,** a *roman à clef* at least on the psychological level, about her disastrous marriage to Francis Russell. And possibly her intimates blinked a bit when she published **Love.** There was also the unsigned **In the Mountains,** a rather oblique description of her slow recovery from her second marriage.

I am trying to suggest that this elderly person in dusty black, encountered in an Italian village, didn't accord at all with the common impression of a glamorous woman who moved comfortably through international social and literary circles, was mistress of H. G. Wells, sister-in-law to Bertrand Russell, cousin of Katherine Mansfield (they were both born Beauchamps), and friend of statesmen, writers, scholars, and the aristocarcy of several countries.

It wasn't until years later, when I read Leslie de Charms's biography [see Further Reading], that the two disparate images came tentatively together. But that is a partisan work, at least where the life is concerned (one suspects the pseudonymous author is a daughter of Elizabeth's), and blurred otherwise by a zealous amateurism that simply does not always know where to omit or condense and where to expand. It is the best reference to date, however, and almost all we have except for scattered comment in Frank Swinnerton's volumes of literary essays, Rupert Hart-Davis's biography of Hugh Walpole, some letters of Katherine Mansfield's, a few lines in Bertrand Russell's autobiography, Mrs. Belloc Lowndes's comment, and Elizabeth's own, severely restricted autobiography, **All the Dogs of My Life** (1936). She is a minor writer, but it continues to surprise me that references to her should be few when she knew well so many articulate and often indiscreet people. On the whole, Swinnerton serves her best. In *Figures in the Foreground* [see Further Reading] he writes: "She was extremely kind. Her judgments of men and women, however, being unsentimental, were often destructive. . . . The lucid ridicule of dullness and brutality that quickens nearly all her books was what produced for every hearer an awful delight in her more intimate conversations. I have never known any woman with the same *comic* detachment of mind." He goes on (with some unintentional horticultural imagery): "Perhaps because of this characteristic, she had loyal admirers rather than a great literary reputation. It was as long ago as the eighteennineties that she first set a fashion of 'garden' books and drew to her side, whenever she was in England, so many of the cultivated people of her day."

By way of summary comment Swinnerton says:

> Now a literary life of nearly fifty years is long enough to allow any reputation to wax and wane. Whether there is any other example of a writer who scored such tremendous successes of delight with her first and last books as Lady Russell did with **Elizabeth and Her German Garden** and **Mr. Skeffington** I cannot say. In her case the progress was from demure comedy to rueful hilarity. It was from the young wife pitilessly regarding the idiosyncrasies of a Man of Wrath to the ageing flirt who discovers that, one by one, she has lost her adorers, and that while charm may be perpetual, allure inevitably dies. . . .
>
> Her style did not change. She unobtrusively depicted herself as she was or had been, surrounded by husbands or friends seen with what Jane Austen called "open pleasantry". Her talent lay in fun, satirical portraiture, and farcical comedy, qualities which are scorned by those obsessed by what a correspondent describes to me as "the modern dilemma". Her fame has therefore sunk. If it ever recovers, as I hope it will do, she may find a place below the highest but in a discreet jostle with Fanny Burney, Emily Eden, and Rhoda Broughton.

Comedy in fiction has been supplanted in our time by scatological joking, a form of alienation and life-denial that seems to suit our present temper better than a literature of affirmation, which is what comedy traditionally has been. But Elizabeth has more than her attitude toward human life working against her now. As Swinnerton notes, her style didn't change—except, perhaps, to become slightly more baroque as she grew older. We now admire a demotic style, or what passes as such. Perhaps we think of it as writing with no style at all (although some examples seem to me as consciously mannered and artificial as anything Lyly ever came up with). It is possible to read Elizabeth for her punctuation alone, a statement that would probably enrage any contemporary writer to whom it was applied. I have never read a study of the evolution of English punctuation, but my impression is that in early fictions—at least from the pens of serious writers—it follows the rhythms of speech. Where, to our eyes, irrational or irrelevant punctuation occurs, I have assumed that we were to think of the speaker as pausing, perhaps in midgust, to catch his breath or rephrase his thought, or to emphasize what would come next. I will say arbitrarily, and with the freedom that total ignorance confers, that this engaging disorder reaches its peak and its splendid apotheosis in Jane Austen. After her, as the century moves along, punctuation becomes more orderly, though no author of my reading has ever subscribed consistently to common rules. Elizabeth lived until 1941, but she grew up in what might be called the period of High Punctuation, when, for instance, conjunctions were preceded and often followed by commas, when interpolations required both a comma and a one-em dash, and prepositional phrases and introductory adverbs and even short appositives were usually set off by themselves. Here, from the opening of *Mr. Skeffington,* is a characteristic example of Elizabeth's style and her copious punctuation:

> Fanny, who had married a Mr. Skeffington, and long ago, for reasons she considered compelling, divorced him, after not having given him a thought for years began, to her surprise, to think of him a great deal. If she shut her eyes, she could see him behind the fish-dish at breakfast; and presently, even if she didn't shut her eyes, she could see him behind almost anything.
>
> What particularly disturbed her was that there was no fish. Only during Mr. Skeffington's not very long reign as a husband had there been any at breakfast, he having been a man tenacious of tradition, and liking to see what he had seen in his youth still continuing on his table. With his disappearance, the fish-dish, of solid silver, kept hot by electricity, disappeared too,—not that he took it with him, for he was much too miserable to think of dishes, but because Fanny's breakfast, from the date of his departure to the time she had got to now, was half a grapefruit.

Contemporary readers either like this style and habit—believing that it possesses a clarity and is capable of a subtlety that the demotic headlong tumble cannot achieve—or else they are entirely put off. Obviously, I like the way Elizabeth writes. But it is a kind of writing that can become unbearably arch if control isn't maintained, and

most of Elizabeth's books are flawed by passages that make even the most ardent reader flinch. Worse still, like many satirists she possesses (in her books if not, as Swinnerton suggests, in her life) a vein of gush, often sentimental in its origins, which sometimes spoils what might be her best effects. This is most evident in her early works until we come to one of the last, *The Jasmine Farm,* the only novel of hers that requires an act of will to get through.

Nevertheless, the quality of most of her work is generally good. I'm especially fond of *The Adventures of Elizabeth in Rügen, Fräulein Schmidt and Mr. Anstruther, The Enchanted April, Father,* and *Mr. Skeffington.* I've selected *The Pastor's Wife* rather than any of these others because in several ways it is uncharacteristic of her fiction. It is, to begin with, a detailed study of lower-class Prussian society in the years preceding the First World War. All Elizabeth's books, even the nonfiction ones, might roughly be termed comedies of bad manners, bad temper, or neglect, and the particular society is sketched in sparingly, no more being given than is necessary for an understanding of the action. Another reason for my choice is that *The Pastor's Wife* is the most naturalistic of Elizabeth's novels—a quality that will not, of course, recommend it to today's more sophisticated readers. But to me it is interesting to see how a comedic writer can work successfully within the form without sacrificing her special gifts. *The Pastor's Wife* is sad, funny, rueful; the reader is less a spectator than a participant in the action because he is given such a thorough experience of the pastor's household and community. (pp. 210-16)

The narrative starts when Ingeborg, the heroine, comes up to London to have a tooth pulled and on impulse, instead of going straight home again, takes a conducted tour to Switzerland. (This unlikely name for an English girl is due to the fact that her maternal grandmother was a Swede.) It is on this tour that she meets her German husband. Within fifty pages she is betrothed, and by page 119 she has faced the wrath of her family and been married. That suggests a novel that is moving along at a respectable rate, but my impression persists that the story doesn't really begin to quicken—in both senses of the word—until the scene shifts to East Prussia and to the village of Kökensee, where Ingeborg will spend the rest of her life except for one other impulsive excursion. (Though I should add, in fairness, that there are some splendid scenes in Redchester, her home, when she returns to break the news of her engagement to her father, the most eminent of Anglican bishops, and her mother, who long ago "had found the sofa as other people find salvation.")

Elizabeth—at least in her work—often took a dim view of Germans, but this never seems to have affected her response to the German countryside, especially to those areas near or bordering the Baltic. That flat land of murmuring pine forests and lakes and vast fields of rye evoked a lyricism that is almost unique in her writing (I say "almost" because on occasion she also wrote lovingly of Italy and Switzerland). It is against the immensity and under the sunlight of this lonely landscape that Ingeborg and Robert Dremmel, her pastor husband, finally emerge as individuals, and that their problems become more than those to be found in any amusing, skillful romance about unlikely partners. Ingeborg, dominated all her life by her father, ignored by her mother, eclipsed in the family by the rare beauty of her sister, has until now lived submissively. When, for instance, she faces her parents with the news of her engagement, it is with "the real courage found only in the entirely terrified." In Kökensee, she believes that an altogether new and different life will open before her: "spacious untouched canvases on which she was presently going to paint the picture of her life."

On the tour to Switzerland, it is the immense amount that Ingeborg and Herr Dremmel find to say to one another that first draws them together. The delight turns out largely to be Ingeborg's, though. Herr Dremmel's real passion is that of the experimental farmer. Once the couple marries, the pastor resumes his taciturnity. Ingeborg "seemed to sit in his mind on the top of a slope up which he occasionally clambored and caressed her. Eagerly on these visits she would buttonhole him with talk and ask him questions so that he might linger, but even as she buttonholed his gaze would become abstracted and off he slid." (I suspect the sexual imagery is unintended.)

Ingeborg takes long walks, exploring forest paths, or with picnic provisions paddles a punt down the lake adjoining Kökensee, tying the punt where the forests begin. "The forests were quite out of the beat of tourists or foreigners, and the indigenous ladies were too properly occupied by indoor duties to wander, even if they liked forests, away from their home anchorage."

The parish is well satisfied with its pastor: he has trained his parishioners to be "unobtrusive in return for his own unobtrusiveness." Herr Dremmel spends almost all his time in his experimental fields or in his laboratory. He has no need to prepare a weekly sermon, having years before worked up twenty-six of them which he regularly repeats. The most popular is the Advent sermon on "Isaiah lxv., part of the 4th verse, *Swine's flesh:* This sermon filled the church. In spite of the poor opinion of pigs in both the Old and New Testaments . . . in his parishioners' lives they provided the nearest, indeed the only, approach to the finer emotions, to gratitude, love, wonder. . . . Herr Dremmel on pigs was full of intimacy and local warmth."

During the six months which her idyll lasts, Ingeborg's life is marred by only three people: her disapproving mother-in-law, her daily servant (known as Müller's Ilse), and Herr Dremmel's patron, the Baron Glambeck. Baron Glambeck knows that nothing can be done in the face of the parish's opposition to a change in pastors and has ceased to attend divine services at the church. "Until Herr Dremmel brought Ingeborg to make his wedding call he [the Baron] had had no word with [Herr Dremmel] for three years." Müller's Ilse has "surprisingly" thick legs but persists in wearing short skirts and no stockings. When Ingeborg gently protests, "Ilse raised her voice and said that she had no money to get a husband with but at least . . . she had these two fine legs."

Ingeborg's rapturous happiness does not last long. By Christmas Eve she learns she is pregnant—and none too

soon according to local views. Becoming pregnant is the first popular thing she's done since her arrival. "She could not if she had planned it out with all her care and wits have achieved anything more dramatically ingratiating [this is because she collapses during the Christmas Eve service, and has to be carried from the church]. The day was the most appropriate day in the whole year." But the pregnancy is a particularly difficult one, and when the child (a boy) is born, Ingeborg at first can feel no interest in it—or in anything else. Later, she is brought to some form of affection, but the child is too grave.

Five more children are born in the next six years, although only the first and second (a daughter) survive, and the glorious canvas that Ingeborg has planned to make of life grows steadily more somber. The daughter of an eminent churchman, the friend of the rich and influential, she finds that in East Prussia a pastor's wife has no more social status than a peasant. Quite literally, she has no one to talk to (not even Robert), no one to invite to her house or to visit. Even parish calls are frowned on.

During these years, a single event, touching in its briefness and casualness, brightens Ingeborg's life. The famous British portrait painter Edward Ingram comes as a house guest to the Glambecks, and one day Ingeborg encounters him in the road when he is returning from a day of sketching. He is intrigued with her because, though an Englishwoman of obvious breeding, she is a pastor's wife living in a village nearly on the border of Russia. But he is even more intrigued—or provoked—when he learns that she has no idea of his international reputation as an artist. Perhaps largely from pique, he admonishes her to enlarge her plainly limited outlook. " 'Read, read, read—everything you can lay your hands on. . . . Get some notion of people and ideas.' "

Inspired by this advice, as severely as it has been worded, Ingeborg quickly subscribes to a number of British reviews, and "whatever books she read about she immediately bought." Unhappily, her continued pregnancies exhaust her cultural intentions. "Gradually sinking away more and more from energy as one child after the other sapped her up, she left off reading, dropping the more difficult things first." Instead, she takes to a kind of private religion. "The more anaemic she grew the easier religion seemed to be. It was much the least difficult thing to be passive, to yield, not to think, not to decide, never to want explanations." But after her sixth child is born dead, it occurs to Herr Dremmel that "an atmosphere of *chapelle ardente*" is pervading his house, and he consults the local doctor. As a result, Ingeborg is sent off with a nurse to the seaside resort of Zoppot, near Danzig, in the hope that fresh air and freedom from household cares and further pregnancies will restore her health and diminish somewhat her inclination to be religious.

Two and a half months later, on the day when Ingeborg, outwardly much restored, returns, her husband gives up his afternoon in the fields and in his laboratory to meet her train, waiting "on the platform with an impatient expectancy he had not felt for years." She arrives sunburned, freckled, very youthful and rounded, and in Herr Dremmel arises the expectation of many more children. But Ingeborg's doctor is less pleased with her progress, despite the seeming physical improvement, and forbids further sexual encounters. At first, Ingeborg "spilt over like a brimming chalice of gratefulness for the great common things of life—sleep, hunger, power to move about, freedom from fear, freedom from pain." But this new freedom soon palls: "She hovered uncertainly round the edges of life, fingering them, trying to feel the point where she could best catch hold and climb into its fulness again." Worse still is Robert's indifferent attitude toward her. "He had loved her. She knew he had. . . . Now nothing fetched him up. He was quite unresponsive. . . . She had never felt so far away from him. He was not angry evidently; he was quite kind. She could not guess that this steady unenthusiastic kindness was the natural expression of a fraternal regard."

In the chill that settles over her life, Ingeborg turns to the children for solace and occupation, but they are as phlegmatic as their grandmother. "What would make Robertlet and Ditti lissom, quick, interested, and gay?" She decides on a spirited combination of education and play, and spends hours over the *Encyclopaedia Britannica* in search of information that may interest the little boy and girl. She becomes "heavy with facts" about flies and stars and distances, but she alone ends up possessing the information. She tries dancing and gymnastic classes, and a conversational hour at bedtime that quickly transforms itself into a monologue. " 'What are you thinking of?' she would ask them sometimes, disturbing their dreamless dream, their happy freedom from thought. And then together they would answer, 'Nothing.' " On the whole, they are immensely patient with their mother. "When . . . in spite of discouragements [Ingeborg] went bravely on, so did they. When out of doors she snowballed them they stood patiently till she had done. She showed them how to make a snow man, and they did not complain." Eventually, reaching school age, the children are removed from their parents' care and settle with their grandmother, who lives near the school they are to attend, and at this point in the narrative the children fade away.

Utterly deserted now, Ingeborg wakes to the fact that "after all, there's still me. . . . Nobody can take that away. . . . Whatever happens, I've still got my own inside." She takes up the sort of reading that Ingram had recommended to her long before. By the end of the following year she has read a mass of unrelated books sent her from London by a news agent who is evidently in his dotage, for what she mostly gets from him is "mid, early, and pre-Victorian literature" which rubs shoulders oddly with the books she sends for on her own. "Ruskin jostled Mr. Roger Fry and Shelley lingered, as it were, in the lap of Mr. Masefield." One day she is in the "placid arms of the Lake Poets," and on another "caught in the exquisite intricacies of Mr. Henry James."

But her enthusiasms focus increasingly on the literature of travel. She, who has been almost no place at all, begins to dream of the cathedrals of France, of the lagoons of Venice and all of Italy. In these empty days of reading and dreaming she achieves a measure of solitary happiness, and it is at this point that Ingram reenters her life, having

returned to the Glambecks for a few days in the futile hope of escaping the boredom that everywhere pursues him.

There can be little doubt that Edward Ingram is a thinly disguised portrait of H. G. Wells. Lovat Dickson, in his recent book *H. G. Wells: His Turbulent Life and Times*, remarks that in 1912 Wells was infatuated with Elizabeth, who was by then a widow and living in England. She "was an attractive woman with a sharp wit and a very wide circle of friends in the literary and social worlds. She had taken a house in London, and here she entertained a great deal, flirted furiously, wrote busily, and was the centre of a little maelstrom of activity." Dickson adds:

> Wells fell under her spell, and one sees why. She represented the aristocratic disdain—which can be melted, and then what fire!—discernible in Beatrice in *Tono-Bungay* and the girl on the wall who captivated Mr. Polly's imagination; as a type, she reappears under one name or another in many of the novels he was to write long after the painful episode of his experiences in 1912. . . . He bombarded her with letters, telegrams and protestations of love; she seems to have enjoyed humiliating him and using him for her own convenience.

Wells was later to portray her more or less literally as Mrs. Harrowdean in *Mr. Britling Sees It Through*, but that book was not begun until 1915 and not published until 1916. In the meantime, Elizabeth had got in her own licks (*The Pastor's Wife* came out in 1914 and presumably must have been started at least a year earlier). Why, when in her relationship with Wells she was so clearly the victor, she draws a rather severe picture of him in her novel isn't clear, unless, as Swinnerton says, it is because her judgments of people were always unsentimental. There is one other possible reason, however. When, in 1911-1912, she built the Châlet Soleil and moved there in October of the latter year, Wells must have been one of her first visitors. They then began an affair in earnest. At some point Wells told Swinnerton, "when you've had her for a week you want to bash her head through the wall." He may have conveyed this feeling to her, and in addition told others besides Swinnerton.

Edward Ingram encounters Ingeborg one day when she is out in her punt and he is sketching on the shore. Later he speaks of her Scandinavian coloring, and determines to do her portrait. He deserts the Glambecks, to their rage, and to their humiliation takes a room in the squalid Kökensee inn, "to paint the hair of the pastor's wife." A portrait will have to be prefaced by a series of sketches, and soon Ingeborg and Edward are together every day. "Hardly ever did he do more than her head and throat, and sometimes the delicate descent to her shoulder. The day she saw his idea of her neck she flushed with pleasure, it was such a beautiful thing." For Ingram, at first, these are blissful days.

> From this remoteness . . . he looked at his usual life as at something entirely foolish, hurried, noisy, and tiresome. All those women . . . who collected and coagulated about his path, what terrible things they seemed from here! . . . Women who had claims on him—claims on him! on him who belonged only to art and the uni-

verse. And there was his wife—good heavens, yes, his wife.

Ingram's seduction is unsuccessful. At first he finds Ingeborg's naïveté charming, "but to persist in it was tiresome. Nothing he could say . . . brought the faintest trace of self-consciousness into her eyes." To Ingeborg, part of the delight of Ingram's company lies in the fact that he talks to her. "She was interested in Ingram . . . and she was not interested in Robert. Perfect love . . . cast out a lot of things besides fear. It cast out, for instance, conversation. And interest, which one couldn't very well have without conversation."

After the third week of sketching, when the weather changes and becomes wretched, Ingram tells Ingeborg that she must come with him to his studio in Venice, so that the portrait can be done. "She laughed. 'How I wish I could!' she said. 'I ache and ache to see things, to go to Italy—'" (This penultimate movement of the narrative may have been inspired by Wells's once having almost persuaded Elizabeth to go to Ireland with him, and to the fact that later they did go to Italy together. "It was," says Elizabeth's biographer, "his excessively trying behavior on one of those journeys that decided her to break away at last.")

Ingram finally convinces Ingeborg that it's outrageous she should be stuck in Kökensee for the rest of her life, and that the portrait, plus the coming and going, will take at most ten days. When it becomes clear to the startled lady that Herr Dremmel is not to be of their company, Ingram talks to her "of the folly of conventions."

It is "wonderful," Ingram thinks with some impatience, how much trouble a man takes at the beginning over a woman. He also thinks—indeed, it's seemed obvious to him all his life—

> that when it came to the supremest things not only did one give up everything oneself for them but other people were bound to give up everything, too. The world and the centuries were to be enriched—he had a magnificent faith in his position as a creator—and it was the duty of those persons who were needful to the process to deliver themselves, their souls and bodies, up to him in what he was convinced was an entirely reasonable sacrifice.

Still Ingeborg, unconvinced, hovers on the edge of decision until Ingram reminds her of her one other impulsive adventure—that which brought her, eventually, to Kökensee. She can tell her husband that she has some long-delayed shopping to do in Berlin; he need never know of the Italian trip. She is finally persuaded, but at the last moment she is invaded by conscience and leaves a note for Robert confessing the truth.

The trip south is a leisurely one—the ten days indeed seem to be passing without much progress toward Venice and the great portrait. But Ingram's expectation of an affair still fails to materialize. "The first step, the process of the actual removal from Kökensee to Berlin, from legality to illicitness, had in its smoothness been positively glib; and he had supposed that, once alone together, lovemaking,

which was the very marrow of running away—else why run?—would follow with similar glibness." But Ingeborg continues to consider her trip a holiday filled with "frank companionship" and much conversation and sightseeing. At last, in despair, Ingram determines to take her somewhere ugly—to Milan (for "who would not be galled by the discovery that he has become a background?"). Another threat to further sightseeing is that when they finally get to Venice Ingeborg will find the city enchanting, as she has found every other place enchanting, unless she has learned "to blot out everything in the world with his image alone. This blotting out, he perceived, would have to be achieved in Milan, and quickly."

Milan is, in every sense, Ingram's ultimate mistake. Ingeborg adores looking at its buildings—all the worst ones, in Ingram's view—and she is indifferent to the awful food. What finally rouses her sense of guilt is the realization that the ten days are passing; that this kind, thoughtful man has devoted a large number of them merely to giving her a view of Italy. "Why, of course—the picture. Why—incredible, but she had forgotten it. Actually forgotten it in the wild excitement of travelling."

Encouraged by her penitence, Ingram at last declares his love. He compares Ingeborg to "'the light on crystals'" and "'the clear shining after rain,'" and she interprets his declaration in an innocent fashion. Robert couldn't possibly mind her being "loved" in this wholesome way. But as Ingram continues she finds her response "tinged with a faint uneasiness. . . . Pastors' wives didn't give love except to their pastors. Friendship, yes . . . but love? She had supposed love was reserved for lovers. Well, if he liked to call it love . . . one must not be missish . . . it was very kind of him." But before the day is over it at last becomes clear to her that in Ingram's view she has "'completely and gloriously burned [her] ships. . . . Little worshipful thing . . . did you really think you could go back? . . . After that letter [Robert] couldn't [let you]. And Kökensee wouldn't and couldn't. And Glambeck wouldn't and couldn't. And Germany, if you like, wouldn't and couldn't. The whole world gives you to me. You're my mate now for ever.'"

Ingeborg realizes she must run away—that very night, even though Ingram has taken all her money for safekeeping. There is no alternative, however vigorous the rejection of her both by Robert and by Kökensee. Yet she also knows, miserably, that she is leaving "something she would never find again . . . a light and a warmth, however fitful, and a greatness." She is now, if belatedly, becoming an adult, feeling "the acute desolation of life, the inevitable hurtings, the eternal impossibility, whatever steps one took, of not treading to death something that, too, was living and beautiful."

When she believes that Ingram is asleep that night, she slips into his room to retrieve some of her money. There is a train to Berlin at 1:30. She finds his wallet in the drawer of a table—"Italian notes, the first she found, a handful of them"—but when she turns to leave the room she finds that Ingram is looking at her. "'Ingeborg?' he said in a sleepy wonder, still half in the deep dreams he had come up out of. 'You? My little angel love—you? You've come?' " With the ingenuity of panic, she assures him that she has indeed come to share his bed, but must return briefly to her own room. " 'I—I've forgotten my toothbrush—' "

Two days later, minus luggage, she is almost home, exhausted, dirty, and dilapidated. Penniless, she walks the distance from the railway station to Kökensee, observed by many disapproving people, including her own children, her mother-in-law, and the Baroness Glambeck. To all of them, the explanation for this creature in tatters is *"Engländerin."* By the time she has reached the steep part of the road just before the village she is crawling "like a hurt insect," and she is in tears. "It was the thought of having ruined Robert that clove her heart in two. To have ruined him, when all her ambition and all her hope had been to make him so happy. . . . "

Inexplicably, Robert is not in his fields but in his laboratory—"still going on doggedly among the ruins she had created." As she enters his room, he doesn't look up, and when he does he expresses no surprise at her appearance. He merely inquires whether she has managed to obtain the boots for which, ostensibly, she went to Berlin. At first Ingeborg believes he is playing a particularly cruel cat-and-mouse game with her, but then, to her incredulity, she discovers that he has never got round to reading her letter. When she refers to it, "Herr Dremmel wore a slight air of apology. 'One omits, occasionally, to notice,' he said." He then asks for his tea, and bending over his work begins to write again. Ingeborg retrieves the unopened letter, and then hovers uncertainly. "Tradition, copious imbibing of the precepts of bishops," impel her to persuade him to read the letter now, but her voice fails, as do "the precepts of a lifetime." As she goes slowly toward the door, she hesitates and looks back. " 'I—I'd *like* to kiss you,' she faltered. But Herr Dremmel went on writing. He had forgotten Ingeborg."

And so, with these words, Ingeborg's story reaches its finish. Some readers will feel that Elizabeth has abdicated responsibility with this wryly "happy" ending, but my own feeling is that the unread letter is entirely consistent with all we have seen of Robert's conduct since his return to Kökensee after the wedding. A more valid criticism, I think, is that his character throughout the narrative, except for the courtship period and the unlikely fact of his being on a conducted tour at all, is too unvarying. He is not quite a Forsterian "flat" creation, but except when he relegates Ingeborg to the role of sister we see little of his inner workings.

Ingeborg is a far more completely realized character (the story is, after all, about the pastor's *wife*). But it is a bit difficult to believe that even a girl as thoroughly sheltered as she could be so entirely unaware of Ingram's real intentions. Still, one must, I suppose, remember that the action takes place prior to 1914—no dates are ever given—and women, even married women of at least a certain class, were far more ignorant then than they would be today. And that would be especially true of a bishop's daughter in whose home neither love nor marriage was ever mentioned.

We all know that many authors, especially best-selling ones (Edna Ferber is perhaps our prize American example), "get up" a book by saturating themselves in a particular background or way of life. A situation, usually not very interesting, is then imposed on the material. It has always seemed to me a sad thing that John Marquand, whose early (nondetective) novels have genuine literary quality, ran out of material after, let's say, *Wickford Point*— or, at a pinch, *H. M. Pulham, Esq.*— and subsequently had to dig around not just for theme and subject but for backgrounds to put them in. A remarkable thing about *The Pastor's Wife* is that one has no sense of a writer desperately consulting notes about an unfamiliar or alien way of life, and then sticking details willy-nilly into the manuscript. Yet, Elizabeth lived most of her life among the rich or at least the prosperous famous. Nor had she married above her station, since her father, Henry Beauchamp, was a rich man, and Elizabeth had grown up in Australia with all the amenities. No doubt as a result of all this she usually wrote about the rich, or the well-to-do, or the more prosperous clergy—and on one occasion about royalty. When she decided before the First World War to move from England to Switzerland, she constructed the Châlet Soleil near Randogne-sur-Sierre in the southwest corner of Switzerland because the site, according to her biographer, had a "truly glorious view across the Rhône Valley to the Pennine Alps, the Weisshorn, Rothorn, and the Mont Blanc range and to the east to the Simplon." On the first page of *In the Mountains,* which as I have indicated is an account of her recovery from her marriage to Francis Russell, Elizabeth writes: "I crawled up here this morning from the valley like a sick ant, struggled up to the *little house* on the mountain side that I haven't seen since the first August of the war." She adds: "Here I am once more, come back alone to the house that used to be so full of happy life that its *little wooden sides* nearly burst with the sound of it." (All italics mine.) Yet Hugh Walpole, while visiting the châlet in 1914, wrote Henry James of the house's "splendour" and added that the experience there was "like staying with Queen Mary at Windsor." James, in his reply, says that Walpole's letter "presents little Elizabeth to me . . . like some small shining quartz-crystal set in the rock to which she is kindred and yet hard enough to break by her firm edge the most geological hammer." Elizabeth's biographer calls these references to a "little" house "an inaccurate endearment," and this is nothing if not a spectacular understatement. The châlet had sixteen bedrooms on its two top floors; passing travelers, charmed by the house and the site, often mistook it for a hotel. In her autobiography, Elizabeth herself wrote ruefully of what social constrictions life in the Schloss at Nassenheide imposed on both her and her husband.

Elizabeth's biographer gives us some idea of how she came by the material she used in *The Pastor's Wife.* In doing research for that earlier novel, already referred to (*Fraülein Schmidt and Mr. Anstruther*), she hired herself out in 1905 to a university professor in Jena. She called herself "Miss Armstrong," explained that she was a governess in the Arnim household, and that during her vacation she wanted to improve her German. In return for her lessons, she would help the lady of the house with domestic tasks.

The arrangement didn't last long. According to Fräulein Backe, a governess who remained a friend of Elizabeth and her children long after the Nassenheide years had come to an end: "To her consternation she found that she was not only expected to live in an unheated attic room, but that she had to do the marketing—herself carrying her purchases home and up many flights of stairs—to brush the family's clothes and do the household mending." So ended, rather rapidly, what could be called Elizabeth's "descent to the lower-middle classes," resulting, writes her biographer, "in some unexpected physical disciplines that she often spoke of with amusement, much insight into lives very different from her own that would come in handily not only for the contemplated book, but for a later one, *The Pastor's Wife.*"

As to the amount of farming information in the latter book, one assumes that Elizabeth picked this up from her husband. Henning von Arnim had been an urban dweller all his life until Elizabeth persuaded him to move to Nassenheide, but once there he became a passionate farmer until his health failed him.

In her journal, only a few months before her death, Elizabeth wrote: "Read Hugh Walpole's *Roman Fountain.* The archness and gush and female skittishness of it! Mixed up with the most uncomfortable-making elementary philosophising. And also a great gift for slap-dash journalism. Poor Hugh. He so longs to be a great writer. I blushed for him, reading the stuff."

As I've said, Elizabeth herself is not entirely free of "archness and gush and female skittishness," but as a philosopher, at least of the mentality and sensibility of a certain class of woman, she has few peers. And because she had, I suspect, no profound ambition to see her books last beyond their time, they may have a better chance of doing so than any of Walpole's. At the end of her autobiography, speaking of one of her pets, she says, "Wise and sensible dog; making the most of what he has, rather than worrying over what he hasn't. . . . Ruminating . . . it occurred to me that it would be very shameful if I were less sensible, less wholesome, and less sturdy of refusal to go down before blows, than Chunkie." She concludes, "So I made another vow."

It seems to have been a vow, despite the misfortunes of her life that included exile, illness, and death in [the United States] during the Second War, that she kept. (pp. 216-31)

*George Lanning, "On Elizabeth's 'The Pastor's Wife',"* in Rediscoveries: Informal Essays in Which Well-Known Novelists Rediscover Neglected Works of Fiction by One of Their Favorite Authors, *edited by David Madden, Crown Publishers, Inc., 1971, pp. 209-31.*

### The Times Literary Supplement (essay date 1973)

[*In the following review of a reissued edition of* The Enchanted April, *the critic favorably evaluates the novel.*]

In answer to a seductive advertisement a down-trodden wife, Mrs Wilkins, and a wife who has alienated her husband by the excess of her good works, Mrs Arbuthnot, unite to rent a small castle smothered in flowers and with a view over the Gulf of Spezia. To spread the rent they acquire two more co-tenants, who might symbolize Youth and Crabbed Age, the dazzlingly beautiful Lady Caroline Dester and the frozen-hearted crone Mrs Fisher. The year is 1922, but Fascisti are only a disquieting background presence, briefly mentioned when Mrs Wilkins and Mrs Arbuthnot arrive belatedly by a train service which had not yet bowed to Mussolini. Under the spell of San Salvatore itself, backed up by Mrs Wilkins's determination that love shall be the only emotion allowed within its battlements, cold hearts melt, new understandings are achieved by those who seem to have lost each other for ever, and a new love blossoms between those who meet for the first time among the lilies and acacias.

Summarized thus [*The Enchanted April*] sounds as if it would be an appallingly cloying cream puff of a fairy tale, but that would be to ignore that the author habitually kept a pot of lemon juice mixed with vinegar beside her ink-pot. With this bracing element there is additionally what can only be called a feast of flowers, hanging from every ancient wall and pouring scent over the company.

It is the horror of the everyday which has driven Mrs Wilkins to snatch a holiday apart from her husband, and the author leaves the reader in little doubt about exactly how horrible the everyday is, passed in the society of Mr Wilkins. The "Author of Elizabeth, etc" had been married to a German Count and an English Earl. Her first marriage had many trials, and her second, to the disreputable elder brother of Bertrand Russell, was a cosmic disaster. With this material to work on, her portraits of husbands as a category may have played no small part in her success as a writer, bringing for different reasons consolation both to wives and to spinsters. Her portrait of Mr Wilkins, a solicitor to whom each new acquaintance is a prospective client, either as someone destined for tangles in this world or likely to leave an estate on passing to the next, is a picture both savage and comic.

It is with an eye to the owner of what may turn out to be a satisfyingly large estate when probated that Mr Wilkins makes himself agreeable to Mrs Fisher, who in her turn appreciates the solid boringness of his conversation on public affairs. Mrs Fisher has lived for years on the memory of the great Victorians who had taken kindly notice of her when a child, nursing her souvenirs in a house of inherited Stygian gloom. "Death", wrote the author, "had furnished it for her." In the general mellowing Mrs Fisher has farthest to go and mellows the most, progressing from building ingenious barricades to reserve the nicest sitting-room for herself to beaming over the love-happiness round her.

Having, as it were, tested the temperature of the water, it is to be hoped that the publishers will make available further novels by this remarkable writer. *Vera* and *Love,* harrowing studies of marriages between those of different ages, certainly deserve to be reprinted.

*"Lilies and Lemon Juice," in* The Times Literary Supplement, *No. 3734, September 28, 1973, p. 1136.*

## Elizabeth Jane Howard   (essay date 1985)

[*Howard is an English novelist, short story writer, and editor. In the following introduction to a new edition of* Elizabeth and Her German Garden, *she assesses the merits of Russell's first literary work.*]

[*Elizabeth and Her German Garden*], published anonymously, was an instant success, reprinting eleven times in the first year, and with twenty-one editions printed by May 1899. It received a good press on the whole, although one reviewer grumbled that "even the amateur gardener will be disappointed, for he will find therein no tips as to the best methods of grafting apples, or of destroying vermin . . . " and the *Spectator,* in the person of Quiller-Couch, complained that he found her "not only selfish, but quite inhumanly so and her mind . . . of that order which finds a smart self-satisfaction in proclaiming how thoroughly it is dominated by self." The *Derby Mercury* felt sure that the anonymous author was a gentleman, "betraying his sex by more than one sign" but on the whole *The Times*—in spite of its rather patronising attitude—conveys the most general contemporary response to the book.

> The anonymous author of *Elizabeth and Her German Garden* has written a very bright little book—genial, humorous, perhaps a little fantastic and wayward here and there, but full of bright glimpses of nature and sprightly criticisms of life. Elizabeth is the English wife of a German husband, who finds and makes for herself a delightful retreat from the banalities of life in a German provincial town by occupying and beautifying a deserted convent, the property of her husband, in one of the Baltic provinces. Her gardening experiences are somewhat primitive and unsophisticated, but this is, no doubt, only a harmless literary artifice, for the charm of the book lies not in its horticultural record, but in its personal atmosphere, its individuality of sentiment, its healthy sympathy with nature and outdoor life, its shrewd but kindly appreciations of character and social circumstance. There is a pleasant sub-acid flavour in some of Elizabeth's pages which show that she could do better if she chose; but she is seldom ungenerous except in the remarks about nurses and their ways which she puts into the mouth of her husband, and is never dull.

The book—described rather loosely as a novel—*is* an extraordinary piece of work. It has an idyllic quality; Elizabeth's joy and excitement about transforming a wilderness into a garden is seconded only by her desire simply to revel in the place—to become part of a great and continuing pastoral romance—of the seasons, the times of the day, of the weather, of all the amazing machinery of nature that provided such infinite variation. Her enthusiasm is matched by her self-confessed ignorance: she buys *ten pounds* of ipomaea seed—sows it in eleven beds and "round nearly every tree, and waited in great agitation for the promised paradise to appear. It did not, and I learned my first lesson." It did not matter, she had the wild flowers—the old lawns that had become meadows filled with "every pretty sort of weed". The opening of the book contains the ecstasy of a release that every woman who has experienced marriage and motherhood will recognise and many will envy: the opportunity to be alone, to have space and privacy with no demands made upon her, to eat and sleep and read when she pleased, to have silence and solitude and the time to be with herself—all things that no doubt people like Quiller-Couch would regard as infra dig, selfish, unbecoming and unnecessary for a woman. But a singular aspect of this book is the author's determination to be something more than a good German wife and mother, and it is this quality, set against the more traditionally romantic hymn to nature that gives the work its unique flavour.

In the midst of the first few weeks of this solitary paradise, her husband arrives to rebuke her for not having written. She says that she has been too happy to think of writing. This, unsurprisingly, does not reassure him—he thinks it extraordinary that she should be happy in his absence and the absence of the children. She shows him her beloved lilacs and he remarks that they badly need pruning, she offers him her salad and toast supper "but nothing appeased the Man of Wrath, and he said he would go straight back to the neglected family". Henceforward, in her book, he is known as the Man of Wrath, and her relationship with him (she was in conflict with his private as well as his formal demands) adds an original dimension to the book. There seems to be no doubt but that he was devoted to her—found her fascinating and rewarding company, and was only occasionally put out by her eccentricities—her spending her pin money on artificial manure, for instance. Her portrait of the Man of Wrath is affectionately satirical—she teases him, but he comes well out of it—she feeds the liberal, eccentric aspect of his nature, but she has the rest of him to contend with, and this she does throughout with a most daring tact.

Her children, called throughout the April, May and June baby respectively, make welcome appearances. Here is Elizabeth about the April baby and a governess.

> . . . Miss Jones cast down her eyes. She is always perpetually scenting a scene, and is always ready to bring whole batteries of discretion and tact and good taste to bear on us . . . I would take my courage in both hands and ask her to go . . . but unfortunately the April baby adores her and is sure that never was anyone so beautiful before. She comes every day with fresh accounts of the splendours of her wardrobe, and feeling descriptions of her umbrellas and hats. In common with most governesses she has a little dark down on her upper lip, and the April baby appeared one day at dinner with her own decorated in faithful imitation, having achieved it after much struggling with the aid of a lead pencil and much love. Miss Jones put her in a corner for impertinence. I wonder why governesses are so unpleasant? The Man of Wrath says it is because they are not married. I would add that the strain of continually having to set an example must surely be very great. It is much easier, and often more pleasant, to be a warning than an example . . .

The garden is her escape from domestic duties; indeed,

with the exception of the "white and yellow library", the house is hardly described at all. It is the garden that is her element—the place where she can breathe and live, meditate, dream, plan and above all, read. Elizabeth was a voracious reader. Books accompanied her everywhere, and it would seem that during those early years at Nassenheide she was, perhaps unconsciously, preparing herself for her subsequent career as a writer (by the end of her life she had published twenty-two books). But even her dauntless spirit was sometimes circumscribed by the rules of her society.

> I wish with all my heart I were a man, for of course the first thing I should do would be to buy a spade and go and garden, and then I should have the delight of doing everything for my flowers with my own hands, and need not waste time explaining what I want done to somebody else. It is dull work giving orders and trying to describe the bright visions of one's brain to a person who has no visions and no brain, and who thinks a yellow bed should be calceolarias edged with blue.

And again . . .

> In the first ecstasy of having a garden all my own, and in my burning impatience to make the waste places blossom like a rose, I did one warm Sunday in last year's April during the servants' dinner hour, double secure from the gardener by the day and the dinner, slink out with a spade and a rake and feverishly dig a little piece of ground and break it up and sow surreptitious ipomæa and run back very hot and guilty into the house and get into a chair and behind a book and look languid just in time to save my reputation. And why not? It is not graceful, and it makes one hot; but it is a blessed sort of work, and if Eve had had a spade in Paradise and known what to do with it, we should not have had all that sad business with the apple.

When we consider all the skilled and fulfilled women gardeners who have flourished in this century, the frustration for poor Elizabeth is poignant.

Elizabeth was ahead of her time in that she envisaged an English garden, and what she meant by that was *not* the vast elaborate geometry of bedding plants en parterre, but rather a merging of cultivated plants with the wild—a blending of garden to park—an apparent carelessness that was none the less artful. E. M. Forster, who stayed at Nassenheide in 1904 as tutor to her children, in complaining about the garden unconsciously describes it rather well:

> I couldn't find it. The house appeared to be surrounded by paddock and shrubberies. Later on, some flowers—mostly pansies—came into bloom. Also rose-trees in the little whirligig of laid-out beds. But there was nothing of a show—only the lilacs effected that, and the white flowering faulbaum by which the dykes were edged. Nor did Elizabeth take any interest in flowers. The garden merged in the "park" which was sylvan in tendency and consisted of small copses . . . There was also a field in the park, over whose long grass, at the end of July, a canopy of butterflies kept waving.

And Hugh Walpole, also a tutor remarked in 1907: "the garden is becoming beautiful in a wild rather uncouth kind of way, but it is a garden of trees rather than flowers". These two may have been highly educated in some respects, but their expectations of a garden were fashionably commonplace compared to Elizabeth's.

She went on to write some very good novels, but *Elizabeth and Her German Garden,* its more rhapsodic passages nicely balanced by her acute and sometimes very funny perceptions about her family and friends, has a freshness, a freakish charm, an irrepressible energy that springs straight from the very source of her personality. It has also the seeds of an interesting and original exposition of the conflict between liberty and oppression that in her day it was taken for granted was the lot of women—a theme that was to occupy her in her writing life for many years to come. (pp. vii-xii)

> *Elizabeth Jane Howard, in an introduction to* Elizabeth and Her German Garden, *by Elizabeth Von Arnim, Virago, 1985, pp. v-xii.*

---

# FURTHER READING

*The Bookman* 21, No. 122 (November 1901): 68.
Review of *The Benefactress* in which the critic commends Russell's portrait of German life and characters.

de Charms, Leslie. *Elizabeth of the German Garden: A Biography.* London: Heinemann, 1958, 429 p.
Biography that includes numerous excerpts from Russell's correspondence with family and friends as well as her journal entries.

Marble, Annie Russell. " 'Elizabeth'." In her *A Study of the Modern Novel: British and American since 1900,* pp. 209-11. New York: D. Appleton and Co., 1928.
Sketch of Russell's life and literary career.

Sidgwick, Cecily. Review of *Elizabeth in Rügen,* by the author of *Elizabeth and Her German Garden. The Bookman* 25, No. 150 (March 1904): 258.
Admires the humorous adventures of Elizabeth and her optimistic outlook.

*The Spectator* 81, No. 3667 (8 October 1898): 467.
Negative review of *Elizabeth and Her German Garden,* finding much of the book tedious.

———. 95, No. 4042 (16 December 1905): 1039-40.
Positive review of *The Princess Priscilla's Fortnight,* praising Russell's humor and narrative technique.

———. 98, No. 4115 (11 May 1907): 763.
Review of *Fräulein Schmidt and Mr. Anstruther* in which the critic praises Russell's innovations in the form of the epistolary novel and commends her delineation of characters entirely through the one-sided correspondence of the protagonist.

Swinnerton, Frank. "Elizabeth and Katherine." In his *Figures in the Foreground: Literary Reminiscences, 1917-1940,* pp. 47-62. Garden City, N. Y.: Doubleday & Co., 1964.

Recollections of Russell in her later years, with comments on her work. Swinnerton maintains that Russell's "style did not change. . . . Her talent lay in fun, satirical portraiture, and farcical comedy, qualities which are scorned by those obsessed by what a correspondent describes to me as 'the modern dilemma'."

Ure, John. "Taking to the Hills." *The Times Literary Supplement,* No. 4367 (12 December 1986): 1398.

Review of Russell's nonfiction book *The Blessings of a Good Thick Skirt: Women Travellers and Their World,* appraising Russell's "impressive compendium of female achievement."

Woods, Katherine. "'Elizabeth's' Brilliant Comedy." *The New York Times Book Review* (7 April 1940): 1, 16.

Applauds Russell's satiric though sympathetic delineation of characters in *Mr. Skeffington.*

# Paul Eluard

## 1895-1952

(Pseudonym of Eugène Grindel; also wrote under the pseudonyms Jean du Hault and Maurice Hervent) French poet and essayist.

For further information on Eluard's career, see *TCLC*, Volume 7.

One of the most admired French poets of the twentieth century, Eluard was a prominent figure of the French Surrealist movement. Influenced by the psychological theories of Sigmund Freud, the Surrealists sought to give expression to the subconscious through such techniques as automatic writing, in which they would transcribe freely associated images into poems. Many critics consider Eluard the most direct and accessible of the Surrealist poets, and his work has been praised for its lyricism and imagistic beauty. He was popularly known both for his love poems and for his political poems on behalf of the Communist party and the French Resistance movement of World War II. Eluard's personal and political writings share a concern with the need for human unity and the expression of hope in spite of adversity.

Eluard was born in an industrial suburb of Paris. At the age of sixteen he suffered a respiratory illness and was sent to a Swiss sanatorium, where he remained until 1914. During this time he developed an interest in poetry, particularly the works of Guillaume Apollinaire and Arthur Rimbaud. He also met Elena Dmitrievna Diakonova, or "Gala," whom he later married and who provided the inspiration for many of his most renowned love poems. Soon after his discharge from the sanatorium, Eluard enlisted in the French army and during World War I sustained lung damage in a poison gas attack. This injury affected his health for life and images of the suffering he witnessed in battle surface repeatedly in his poetry. After the war he published *Le devoir et l'inquiétude* and *Poèmes pour la paix,* and joined the newly formed movement of writers and artists known as Dada. Dadaists saw the war as proof of the failure of civilization and reacted by creating deliberately nonsensical, primitivistic art that mocked authority, rationality, and art itself; in one Dada performance, Eluard and a friend rang bells loudly while the poet Tristan Tzara read from a newspaper. In the early 1920s Eluard, along with André Breton, Louis Aragon, and Benjamin Péret, abandoned the fundamentally nihilistic movement of Dada and founded Surrealism, which desired to rehabilitate art and society rather than simply mock them. Both in their lives and in their works, the Surrealists attempted to eradicate what they considered the false artistic and social values of the past, seeking means for spontaneous action and expression unmediated by convention.

Eluard's poems became more despondent as his marriage grew strained in the late 1920s, climaxing in 1929 when Gala left him for the artist Salvador Dalí. This period is reflected in the worshipful and agonized tone of his love

poems, in particular works collected in *Capitale de la douleur* (*Capital of Pain*). With his odes to Gala and to his second wife, Maria Benz ("Nusch"), whom he married in 1934, Eluard developed a reputation as a love poet. He was also passionately involved in politics, joining the Communist party in 1926. With the advent of fascism, Eluard recognized the threat to European civilization and began to write ideological poetry; the bombing of Guernica during the Spanish Civil War prompted one of his best-known poems, "La victoire de Guernica." In the essay "L'évidence poétique" he wrote, "The time has come for poets to proclaim their right and duty to maintain that they are deeply involved in the life of other men, in communal life." Eluard's increasingly strong affiliation with the Communist party led to his break in 1938 with Breton and the Surrealists, who favored greater political independence. Although Eluard continued to utilize Surrealist techniques, his later poetry became more traditional. During World War II he wrote poems for the French Resistance, including the famous "Liberté," copies of which were dropped from airplanes throughout France. Following the war, he released the acclaimed collection *Poésie ininterrompue,* which many critics consider the most artistically successful statement of his poetic themes, and emerged as a preeminent literary spokesperson for communism. Eluard continued to write prolifically until his death in 1952.

Eluard's writing during and immediately after World War I was highly influenced by Romantic and Symbolist poets, including John Keats, Charles Baudelaire, and Rimbaud. With his 1921 volume *Les nécessités de la vie et les conséquences des rêves,* he began to employ the dreamlike imagery and Freudian psychological associations that characterized Surrealism, while retaining romantic love as a dominant subject in such poems as "L'amoureuse" ("Woman in Love") and "Celle de toujours, toute" ("She Who Is of All Time, All"). During the 1920s, Eluard practiced such Surrealist literary techniques as automatic writing in an effort to reproduce the spontaneity and enigmatic associations of the subconscious. "In the end," he wrote, "nothing is as beautiful as an involuntary similarity." In 1930 Eluard and Breton published *L'immaculée conception,* a collection of poems in which the authors attempted to replicate various states of psychosis. Eluard's poetic style typified the Surrealist reaction against rationality and the conventional use of language and metaphor, which Surrealists believed to be intellectually repressive. A highly imagistic writer who befriended and collaborated with many painters, including Pablo Picasso, Max Ernst, and Joan Miró, Eluard borrowed from the aesthetics of visual art, emphasizing in his poetry the association of often disparate images to communicate his ideal of the harmony of existence and his belief that elements of all things could be found in all other things; one of his most-quoted lines reads "la terre c'est bleue, comme une orange" ("the earth is blue like an orange").

The problem of human isolation and the desire for companionship and community were Eluard's predominant poetic themes throughout his career. For Eluard, romantic love was the only means through which life could be experienced and understood fully, and through which humans could overcome existential isolation and despair. Eluard's love poems are noted for their erotic and highly symbolic descriptions of the female body, and he represented his lover as a redeeming force in which such contradictory concepts as good and evil are reconciled. As critic Robert Nugent wrote, "Woman represents for Eluard the welding of opposites: She is the fog, the sea, the mystery of darkness. She is also light, the sun, the paths." When Eluard began to write increasingly political works in the 1930s, he continued to emphasize the human need for unity and love. In "Sisters of Hope," Eluard sketched an optimistic vision of a future commonwealth of humanity in which "every face will have a right to kisses." Critic Max Adereth observed, "Both [Eluard's] Surrealism and his communism must be seen as attempts to be at one with other people," and the enmeshment of Eluard's personal life with his politics is underscored by the fact that "Liberté," which addresses liberty as a lover whose name the poet writes, "On my schoolboy's copy-books / On my desk and on the trees," was originally intended as a love poem to his second wife.

Critics consistently rank Eluard among the foremost of the Surrealist poets, but some perceive a tension in his po-

etry between his lyricism and sensitivity and the calculated irrationality of the Surrealist aesthetic, arguing that Eluard practiced Surrealism only in order to thrive in a poetic climate that demanded innovation. However, critics also acknowledge his proficiency with Surrealist compositional techniques; he has also been highly praised for the clarity and precision of his images. Commentators have occasionally criticized Eluard's political poetry, particularly that written for the Resistance, as simplistic, but others have argued that the exigencies of war forced him to sacrifice stylistic complexity to reach a wider audience. A consistently inventive poet whose work is marked by lyricism and depth of feeling, Eluard established himself as an exemplar of experimental technique, a champion of liberty and human rights, and one of the most admired love poets of his time.

(See also *Contemporary Authors,* Vol. 104.)

## PRINCIPAL WORKS

*Le devoir et l'inquiétude* (poetry) 1917
*Poèmes pour la paix* (poetry) 1918
*Les nécessités de la vie et les conséquences des rêves* (poetry) 1921
*Les malheurs des immortels* [with Max Ernst] (poetry) 1922
*Répétitions* (poetry) 1922
*Mourir de ne pas mourir* (poetry) 1924
*Capitale de la douleur* (poetry) 1926
 [*Capital of Pain,* 1973]
*L'amour la poésie* (poetry) 1929
*A toute épreuve* (poetry) 1930
*L'immaculée conception* [with André Breton] (poetry) 1930
*La vie immédiate* (poetry) 1932
*La rose publique* (poetry) 1934
*Facile* (poetry) 1935
*Les yeux fertiles* (poetry) 1936
*Cours naturel* (poetry) 1938
*Chanson complète* (poetry) 1939
*Donner à voir* (poetry) 1939
*Le livre ouvert, 1938-1940.* 2 vols. (poetry) 1940-42
*Poésie et vérité* (poetry) 1942
 [*Poetry and Truth,* 1942]
*Au rendez-vous allemande* (poetry) 1944
*Le lit, la table* (poetry) 1944
*Le dur désir de durer* (poetry) 1946
 [*Le dur désir de durer,* 1950]
*Poésie ininterrompue* (poetry) 1946
*Poèmes politiques* (poetry) 1948
*Premiers poèmes, 1913-1921* (poetry) 1948
*Une leçon de morale* (poetry) 1949
*Selected Writings of Paul Eluard* (poetry) 1951; also published as *Uninterrupted Poetry,* 1975
*Le phénix* (poetry) 1952
*Les sentiers et les routes de la poésie* (lectures and poetry) 1952
*Anthologie des écrits sur l'art.* 3 vols. (criticism) 1952-54
*Oeuvres complètes.* 2 vols. (poetry) 1968
*Last Love Poems of Paul Eluard* (poetry) 1980

*Selected Poems*   (poetry)   1987
*Letters to Gala*   (letters and poetry)   1989

---

## S. A. Rhodes   (essay date 1933)

[*In the following excerpt, Rhodes recounts meeting and discussing the philosophy of Surrealism with Eluard.*]

The room in which Paul Eluard received me had all the aspects of housing a man who lives in a world of his own inner vision. The walls had vanished behind huge canvasses by Dali, Chirico, others. His desk, bookshelves, sidetables were covered with objects of surrealist conception of a nature to nonplus the sedate spirit. "My mother thinks I am crazy", he said. "The way I live, the things I do, are beyond her. I come from common people, workmen, or let us say, small bourgeois". I recalled Rimbaud's mother. "No", he remarked. "My mother is not so harsh. I live in a world that is not her own: that is all".

Eluard showed me the manuscript of an anthology in which he had planned to include selections ranging from Petrus Borel and Aloysius Bertrand, through Nerval, Baudelaire, Rimbaud, Lautréamont, Charles Cros, Maeterlinck, Apollinaire, down to the present surrealist poets. His aim was to show the evolution of the poetry of to-day, a kind of apologia for the school. I asked him to mention the ancestors of the surrealists among the prose writers. He placed Huysmans first. He declared himself sympathetic to Zola. He admired the violence, anti-rationalism, and pure romanticism of Petrus Borel. He stopped finally in the eighteenth century, at Diderot, D'Holbach, Condillac. I did not ask him to bridge the gap between the encyclopedists and Borel. A certain element of paradoxical humour is found at the bottom of every serious thought; it is found mixed to the very essence of surrealism.

Eluard showed much less enthusiasm than I expected for the immediate predecessors of the new poetry: Rimbaud, Laforgue, Mallarmé. He regretted the vantage position given to reason in their creative acts. With logic in control of the uncontrollable forces of the subconscious, the poet is deprived of all his inner liberty of action, he thought. The result is that, as with Mallarmé, he is ultimately bound and gagged by his own servants: words and their forms.

Eluard admitted that he made a clear distinction between his poetical activity, and his adhesion to the latest communistic tenets of surrealism. Giving voice to what, I feel sure, was but one side of the creative artist in him, he declared that he looked upon poetry merely as an interesting exercise for the mind. He liked a poetic image while he was elaborating it. He was not insensible to poetic visions; but they interested him only as long as they required the services of the poetic mechanism within him. Once it was composed, he insisted, a poem lost its interest for him; he re-read with pleasure only certain naïve, simple, almost child-like expressions in his poems. This poet who stands to-day as one of the finest representatives of pure poetry, insisted that purely poetic images, once they were created,

annoyed him. It was as if he wanted to escape always, even from a world of his own creation. This, I thought, was precisely the case with the greatest poets.

We joined André Breton and we went to a near-by *brasserie*. There, sure enough, was the whole group, the surrealist *cénacle*. I met Benjamin Péret, Salvador Dali, René Crevel, whom I already knew, and a dozen others.

I don't remember what the subject of our conversation was, but I observed to Eluard that I saw no musician within the surrealist phalanx. I was more surprised at his answer than he at my question. "Never", he said. "There is no room for a composer within our group. We have banished music from our midst. We deny its place and importance". And as I looked more and more puzzled, Eluard added: "I do not mean I do not like music. I like Mozart, for example. But that is a prejudice from the culture I have received. Music appeals to the senses, to the instincts in man, and not to the pure intelligence; and we hold that only what can be comprehended, what expresses a clear idea, is worth investigating and expressing". I saw a great deal of contradiction between this view and other doctrines of surrealism. Eluard shook his head. "Music", he went on, "is an elaboration of noise, it has no moral or spiritual background". I spoke of the close connection between poetry and music. "Not in my case", insisted Eluard. "I strive to free my verse from whatever musical qualities the words I employ may contain". "This fact notwithstanding", I observed, "most of your poetry is truly and subtly musical, and many of your poems have been put to music". "I know", he replied, "but I cannot help that. I cannot prevent certain musical elements from entering unconsciously into my poetry. I strive to use only what is susceptible of general, universal comprehension, and music is not". This sounded paradoxical to me. I said that music had been regarded until now, and was still regarded, as a sort of universal language. "It is the language of universal confusion", he retorted. At this point, Breton joined in our conversation. I asked him if he agreed with Eluard. The question was superfluous. "Only Tristan Tzara likes music in our group", he declared. (And yet, I thought, Tzara's poetry is less musical than either Eluard's or Breton's). "I never go to a concert. The day when they admit a composer in their midst, I shall have ceased to belong to the surrealist group".

It was time to go. I realized now what had been a mystery to me; the reason for certain plastic, angular, somewhat objective and unlyrical qualities in surrealist poetry. But this is true in partial cases only. Especially with Breton and Eluard, their unconscious and emotive artistry constantly submerges the barriers of their doctrinal principles. What better proof could be invoked of their inherent and essential sincerity? (pp. 298-300)

> S. A. Rhodes, "*Imagist of the Absolute Reality: Paul Eluard,*" in The Sewanee Review, *Vol. XLI, No. 3, July-September, 1933, pp. 298-300.*

## Paul Eluard   (lecture date 1936)

[*In the following lecture, which was later published as*

*the essay "L'evidence poetique" ("Poetic Evidence"), Eluard defends the political intent of his poetry and of the Surrealist movement.*]

The time has come for poets to proclaim their right and duty to maintain that they are deeply involved in the life of other men, in communal life.

On the high peaks!—yes, I know there have always been a few to try and delude us with that sort of nonsense; but, as they were not there, they have not been able to tell us that it was raining there, that it was dark and bitterly cold, that there one was still aware of man and of his misery; that there one was still aware and had to be aware of vile stupidity, and still hear muddy laughter and the words of death. On the high peaks, as elsewhere, more than elsewhere perhaps, for him who sees, for the visionary, misery undoes and remakes incessantly a world, drab, vulgar, unbearable and impossible.

No greatness exists for him that would grow. There is no model for him that seeks what he has never seen. We all belong to the same rank. Let us do away with the others.

Employing contradictions purely as a means to equality, and unwilling to please and be self-satisfied, poetry has always *applied itself,* in spite of all sorts of persecutions, to refusing to serve other than its own ends, an undesirable fame and the various advantages bestowed upon conformity and prudence.

And what of pure poetry? Poetry's absolute power will purify men, all men. 'Poetry must be made by all. Not by one.' So said Lautréamont. All the ivory towers will be demolished, all speech will be holy, and, having at last come into the reality which is his, man will need only to shut his eyes to see the gates of wonder opening.

Bread is more useful than poetry. But love, in the full, human sense of the word, the passion of love is not more useful than poetry. Since man puts himself at the top of the scale of living things, he cannot deny value to his feelings, however non-productive they may be. 'Man', says Feuerbach, 'has the same senses as the animals, but in man sensation is not relative and subordinated to life's lower needs—it is an absolute being, having its own end and its own enjoyment.' This brings us back to necessity. Man has constantly to be aware of his supremacy over nature in order to guard himself against it and conquer it.

In his adolescence man is obsessed by the nostalgia of his childhood; in his maturity, by the nostalgia of his youth; in old age, by the bitterness of having lived. The poet's images grow out of something to be forgotten and something to be remembered. Wearily he projects his prophecies into the past. Everything he creates vanishes with the man he was yesterday. Tomorrow holds out the promise of novelty. But there is no today in his present.

Imagination lacks the imitative instinct. It is the spring and torrent which we do not re-ascend. Out of this living sleep daylight is ever born and ever dying it returns there. It is a universe without association, a universe which is not a part of a greater universe, a godless universe, since it never lies, since it never confuses what will be with what has been. It is the truth, the whole truth, the wandering palace of the imagination. Truth is quickly told, unreflectingly, plainly; and for it, sadness, rage, gravity and joy are but changes of the weather and seductions of the skies.

The poet is he who inspires more than he who is inspired. Poems always have great white margins, great margins of silence where eager memory consumes itself in order to re-create an ecstasy without a past. Their principal quality is, I insist again, not to invoke but to inspire. So many love poems without an immediate object will, one fine day, bring lovers together. One ponders over a poem as one does over a human being. Understanding, like desire, like hatred, is composed of the relationship between the thing to be understood and the other things, either understood or not understood.

It is his hope or his despair which will determine for the watchful dreamer—for the poet—the workings of his imagination. Let him formulate this hope or despair and his relationship with the world will immediately change. For the poet everything is the object of sensations and, consequently, of sentiments. Everything concrete becomes food for his imagination, and the motives of hope and despair, together with their sensations and sentiments, are resolved into concrete form.

I have called [this lecture] **'Poetic Evidence'**. For if words are often the medium of the poetry of which I speak, neither can any other form of expression be denied it. (pp. 171-74)

For a long time degraded to the status of scribes, painters used to copy apples and become virtuosos. Their vanity, which is immense, has almost always urged them to settle down in front of a landscape, an object, an image, a text, as in front of a wall, in order to reproduce it. They did not hunger for themselves. But surrealist painters, who are poets, always think of something else. The unprecedented is familiar to them, premeditation unknown. They are aware that the relationships between things fade as soon as they are established, to give place to other relationships just as fugitive. They know that no description is adequate, that nothing can be reproduced literally. They are all animated by the same striving to liberate the vision, to unite imagination and nature, to consider all possibilities a reality, to prove to us that no dualism exists between the imagination and reality, that everything the human spirit can conceive and create springs from the same vein, is made of the same matter as his flesh and blood, and the world around him. They know that communication is the only link between that which sees and that which is seen, the striving to understand and to relate—and, sometimes, that of determining and creating. To see is to understand, to judge, to deform, to forget or forget oneself, to be or to cease to be.

Those who come here to laugh or give vent to their indignation, those who, when confronted with surrealist poesy, either written or painted, talk of snobbism in order to hide their lack of understanding, their fear or their hatred, are like those who tortured Galileo, burned Rousseau's books, defamed William Blake, condemned Baudelaire, Swinburne and Flaubert, declared that Goya or Courbet did not know how to paint, whistled down Wagner and Stravinsky, imprisoned Sade. They claim to be on the side of good sense, wisdom and order, the better to satisfy their ignoble appetites, exploit men, prevent them from liberating themselves—that they may the better degrade and destroy men by means of ignorance, poverty and war.

The genealogical tree painted upon one of the walls of the dining-room of the old house in the north of France, inhabited by the present counts de Sade, has only one blank leaf, that of Donatien Alphonse François de Sade, who was imprisoned in turn by Louis XV, Louis XVI, the Convention and Napoleon. Interned for thirty years, he died in a madhouse, more lucid and pure than any of his contemporaries.

In 1789, he who had indeed deserved the title of the 'Divine Marquis' bestowed upon him in mockery, called upon the people from his cell in the Bastille to come to the rescue of the prisoners: in 1793, though devoted body and soul to the revolution, and a member of the *Section des Piques,* he protested against the death penalty, and reproved the crimes perpetrated without passion: he remained an atheist when Robespierre introduced his new cult of the Supreme Being; he dared to pit his genius against that of the whole people just beginning to feel its new freedom. No sooner out of prison than he sent the First Consul the first copy of a pamphlet attacking him.

Sade wished to give back to civilised man the force of his primitive instincts, he wished to liberate the amorous imagination from its fixations. He believed that in this way, and only in this way, would true equality be born.

Since virtue is its own reward, he strove, in the name of all suffering, to abase and humiliate it; he strove to impose upon it the supreme law of unhappiness, that it might help all those it incites to build a world befitting man's immense stature. Christian morality, which, as we often have to admit to our despair and shame, is not yet done with, is no more than a mockery. All the appetites of the imaginative body revolt against it. How much longer must we clamour, struggle and weep before the figures of love become those of facility and freedom?

Let us now listen to Sade and his profound unhappiness: 'To love and to enjoy are two very different things: the proof is that we love daily without enjoyment, and more often still we enjoy without loving.' And he concludes: 'Moments of isolated enjoyment thus have their charms, they may even possess them to a greater degree than other moments; yes, and if it were not so, how would so many old men, so many dissemblers and people full of blemishes, enjoy themselves? They are sure of not being loved; they are certain that it is impossible to share their experience. But is their pleasure any the less for that?'

And justifying those men who introduce some singularity into the things of love, Sade rises up against those who regard love as proper only to the perpetuation of their miserable race. . . . 'Pedants, executioners, turnkeys, legislators, tonsured rabble, what will become of you when we shall have reached that point? What will become of your laws, of your morality, of your religion, of your gallows, of your paradise, of your gods, of your hell, when it shall be demonstrated that such and such a flow of liquids, such

a kind of fibre, such a degree of acidity in the blood or in the animal spirits, is sufficient to make a man the object of your penalties or of your rewards?'

It is his perfect pessimism which gives his words their sober truth. Surrealist poetry, the poetry of always, has never achieved more. These are sombre truths which appear in the works of true poets, but they are truths, and almost all the rest is false. And let us not be accused of contradiction when we say this! Let them not try to bring against us our revolutionary materialism! Let them not tell us that man must live first of all by bread! The maddest and the most solitary of the poets we love have perhaps put food in its proper place, but that place is the highest of all because it is both symbolical and total. For everything is re-absorbed in it.

There is no portrait of the Marquis de Sade in existence. It is significant that there is none of Lautréamont either. The faces of these two fantastic and revolutionary writers, the most desperately audacious that ever were, are lost in the night of the ages.

They both fought fiercely against all artifices, whether vulgar or subtle, against all traps laid for us by that false and importunate reality which degrades man. To the formula: *'You are what you are,'* they have added: *'You can be something else.'*

By their violence Sade and Lautréamont strip solitude of all its adornments. In solitude each being, each object, each convention, each image also, premeditates a return to its own non-becoming reality, to have no longer a secret to reveal, to lie hatching peacefully and uselessly in the atmosphere it creates.

Sade and Lautréamont, who were solitary to the last degree, have revenged themselves by mastering the miserable world imposed upon them. In their hands they held earth, fire and water, the arid enjoyment of privation, and also weapons; and anger was in their eyes. They demolish, they impose, they outrage, they ravish. The doors of love and hate are open to let in violence. Inhuman, it will arouse man, really arouse him, and will not withhold from him, a mere accident on earth, the possibility of an end. Man will emerge from his hiding-places and, faced with the vain array of charms and disenchantments, he will be drunk with the power of his ecstasy.

He will then no longer be a stranger either to himself or to others. Surrealism, which is an instrument of knowledge, and therefore an instrument of conquest as well as of defence, strives to bring to light man's profound consciousness. Surrealism strives to demonstrate that thought is common to all, it strives to reduce the differences existing between men, and, with this end in view, it refuses to serve an absurd order based upon inequality, deceit and cowardice.

Let man discover himself, know himself, and he will at once feel himself capable of mastering all the treasures of which he is almost entirely deprived—all the treasures, material as well as spiritual, which he has accumulated throughout time, at the price of the most terrible sufferings, for the benefit of a small number of privileged persons who are blind and deaf to everything that constitutes human greatness.

Today the solitude of poets is breaking down. They are now men among other men, they have brothers.

There is a word which exalts me, a word I have never heard without a tremor, without feeling a great hope, the greatest of all, that of vanquishing the power of the ruin and death afflicting men—that word is fraternisation.

In February 1917, the surrealist painter Max Ernst and I were at the front, hardly a mile away from each other. The German gunner, Max Ernst, was bombarding the trenches where I, a French infantryman, was on the lookout. Three years later, we were the best of friends, and ever since we have fought fiercely side by side for one and the same cause, that of the total emancipation of man.

In 1925, at the time of the Moroccan war, Max Ernst upheld with me the watchword of fraternisation of the French Communist Party. I affirm that he was then attending to a matter which concerned him, just as he had been obliged, in my sector in 1917, to attend to a matter which did not concern him. If only it had been possible for us, during the war, to meet and join hands, violently and spontaneously, against our common enemy: THE INTERNATIONAL OF PROFIT.

'O, you who are my brothers because I have enemies!" said Benjamin Péret.

Even in the extremity of discouragement and pessimism, we have never been completely alone. In present-day society everything conspires at every step we take to humiliate us, to constrain us, to enchain us and to make us turn back and retreat. But we do not overlook the fact that that is so because we ourselves are the evil, the evil in the sense in which Engels meant it; that is so because, with our fellow men, we are conspiring in our turn to overthrow the bourgeoisie, and its ideal of goodness and beauty.

That goodness and that beauty are in bondage to the ideas of property, family, religion and country—all of which we repudiate. Poets worthy of the name refuse, like proletarians, to be exploited. True poetry is present in everything that does not conform to that morality which, to uphold its order and prestige, has nothing better to offer us than banks, barracks, prisons, churches, and brothels. True poetry is present in everything that liberates man from that terrible ideal which has the face of death. It is present in the work of Sade, or Marx, or of Picasso, as well as in that of Rimbaud, Lautréamont or of Freud. It is present in the invention of the wireless, in the Tcheliouskin exploit, in the revolt of the Asturias, in the strikes of France and Belgium. It may be present in chill necessity, that of knowing or of eating better, as well as in a predilection for the marvellous. It is over a hundred years since the poets have descended from the peaks upon which they believed themselves to be established. They have gone out into the streets, they have insulted their masters, they have no gods any longer, they have dared to kiss beauty and love on the mouth, they have learned the songs of revolt sung by the unhappy masses and, without being disheartened, they try to teach them their own.

They pay little heed to sarcasms and laughter, they are accustomed to these; but now they have the certainty of speaking in the name of all men. They are masters of their own conscience. (pp. 174-83)

> *Paul Eluard, "Poetic Evidence," translated by George Reavey, in* Surrealism, *edited by Herbert Read, 1936. Reprint by Faber & Faber Limited, 1971, pp. 169-83.*

## Neal Oxenhandler    (essay date 1948)

[*Oxenhandler is an American critic, essayist, and novelist. In the following excerpt, he describes the importance of the imagination in Eluard's poetry.*]

Paul Eluard . . . is a contemporary French poet little known in this country. He was one of the founders of the Surrealist movement in its early years after the First World War and with his friend Andre Breton performed experiments in dream symbolism, simulated madness, and automatic writing. Recently published in this country is a collection of observations and poems by Eluard on Pablo Picasso who is the poet's close friend.

During the last War, at which time Eluard was active in the French Underground, much of his work concerned itself with the theme of liberty and heroism under Nazi oppession. These fervent poems were circulated surreptitiously among patriotic Frenchmen; and the poet who had earlier been the champion of liberty in art now became the champion of political liberty. For freedom has always been a pre-condition for art and for what Eluard has called *the Truth, with its endless procession of childish evidence.*

Surrealism was an experiment with words, an adventure of the poet armed only with his dazzling vocabulary, by which he hoped to recapture that truth which Eluard has characterized above as the property of children.

A child never sees the objects at which he looks in any practical sense. Instead he sees them as the symbols of his own dream or desires, his other or real life as Rimbaud has told us.

It is the practice of imagination, which the poet has remembered from his childhood, which transforms empty and dissociated symbols into the poem. Wallace Stevens has told us that drama played constantly in the mind of man which he calls the drama between "imagination" and the "pressure of reality."

The poet begins with an emotion for which there is no means of expression possible other than the names and associations of his real or object world. It is his ability to present this emotion as a symbol, that is a name or an association, and to seal it there in all its essence as an emotion that we recognize imagination. It is the power to reconstruct, out of second-hand, banal, or familiar materials, the startling pattern of an emotion.

Yet what about this world of real objects which the poem transforms? Does the poet, for instance, ever talk about women as tax-deductible entities or of flowers as cellular structures that serve to lessen the carbon-dioxide in the atmosphere? He never does and he never will as long as he is a poet, for as a poet he is not practical and he is not interested in the fashions of speech of the practical world. And yet, as a citizen of this world he is a victim of its fashions and unavoidably corrupted by them. This is "the pressure of reality" of which Mr. Stevens speaks and it is with it that the poet engages to cause the drama of his poem. Eluard desires simply:

> To have speech
> Be as generous
> As embracing.

But if we remember that in the embrace restraints are broken down, personality is diffused and lost, and sympathy flows from man to woman without regard for decorum, we see that Eluard's wish is a large order. He depicts for us the slow corruption of men and beasts under the pressure of the real world: *animals are domesticated; Children attain the age of "reason"; savages become civilized; madmen are cured; poets forget.* All of which brings about that lessening of the imaginative form, or myth, which it is the poet's duty to rediscover and intensify. There is too much of the *drama of seeing when there is nothing to see save oneself and what is like oneself;* for oneself is a name, a height, a face, a personality, in short, that which is inimical to the imaginative response to myth and the immersion in myth which is man's emotional function.

The Surrealist is characterized by the force and vitality of his imagination. The world therefore is transformed by him. It becomes what Eluard has called *a spotless mirror* in which the poet sees the reflection of his own face. Many of Eluard's poems, of which **"First in the World"** and **"She Who Is of Always, All"** are examples, are an adoration of woman. She is the occasion and the inspiration for the poet's glance into the mirror from which the poem results. With the creation of the poem the myth of the poet becomes possible; and by this myth the chaotic world becomes an ordered cosmos around the principle of man. (pp. 128-29)

I have chosen **"We Are"** to analyze for some further insight into Eluard's themes and methods. It will be convenient to discuss this poem in three parts as this seems to me the rise and fall of the main conceptions.

The first six stanzas are a depiction of scenes as the moving eye, at sunset, briefly characterizes what it sees. Suddenly the forest gives way to the city and we are aware of the presence of man in his two antithetical states of being: love and solitude. We see the animals yoked together; they look up slyly with their white eyes, aware of the guilt of man who has subjugated a part of himself in their domestication.

Then there is a child, after the vision of *a desert of blood,* whom we visualize with wonder:

> He is much smaller
> Than the little bird on the tip of the branches!

Balanced against the man the city characterized by love and solitude, and pivotal between him and the animal's degradation of the next stanza, is the child who is at once man's innocence and his renewal or hope of immortality. Therefore it is proper that by the Biblical symbols of oil

and water, used when divine blessing is to be invoked, the sixth stanza emerges from the drama of man to reaffirm the earth's fertility.

The stanza which follows, part two in my framework, is at once a continuation of the preceeding themes and a statement of the special mission of the poet. In a previous poem [**"She Who Is of Always, All"**] Eluard has said:

> I sing the great joy of singing you . . .
> I sing only to sing, I love you that I may sing
> The mystery where love creates me in delivering
>  himself.

The world is like a mirror where the poet may see only what he feels. Love, the motive to sing, must be present to move the poet to look into the mirror. It is woman, that absolute before whom he is humble, who at once is the motive and the subject of the poet's song. Thus it is woman, visualized as fecundating all the historical past, who demonstrates to the poet his youth and his power. Finally it is the poet's beloved, *one whose clarity is your sail,* who permits the final purification of his vision and *shows you secretly the world without you.*

>  It is with us that all will live.

This line like the stroke of a bell begins the third section in which a pattern of life is laid down. It achieves the unification of the diverse aspects of life portrayed earlier in the poem. There have been animals, cities, and the fertility of the earth; now by the power of imagination the poet transforms these into his own happiness. He demonstrates how it is that all will live:

> Beasts my true standards of gold
> Plains my unexpected luck
> Useful verdure sensible cities

This is the cryptic lesson in the use of imagination by whose powers objects not logically related to one another come together on a different level than logic and are woven into the pattern of the whole. Whatever the poet sees he sees with sympathy; and what he sees with sympathy is transformed into his happiness, which arises, from this interaction, as the whole. The poet attains unity because of the feelings inspired by his vision of the world; the world attains unity because it is seen sympathetically by a poet. Life itself seems no burden to him. Even though sweat, blows, and tears come, he will be able to cull all his dreams. With that power he may lie down in some open place, and free from fear or remorse, go to sleep in the noise of the sun. (p. 129)

> *Neal Oxenhandler, "Paul Eluard," in* Chicago Review, *Vol. II, No. 3, Fall-Winter, 1948, pp. 128-29.*

## Anne Fessenden   (essay date 1962)

[*In the following essay, Fessenden discusses Eluard's interest in painting and painters, and his application of visual aesthetics to his poetry.*]

Every artist reaches up with his mind to a world where disturbed and broken energy moves around—perhaps backward in time—a world which, without the artist as intermediary, comes to men only as silence or chaos. The true reality of this world, of its depth and vitality, is best revealed in a poem or a painting or a musical composition. Some still strange force inhabiting the artist (which has to do with his love of earth and his love of heaven) enables him to give aesthetic form to this primitive energy. The force, the impact, the charm, the exquisiteness and the deeply meditative quality of vision vary according to the artist and the medium in which they are expressed. Some untold conjuncture of forces, of stresses and strains or simply of talents and temperaments (never forgetting that the world into which one is born is the cocoon a butterfly never leaves) determines the medium an artist will use to express most satisfyingly the presence of that world which is always beating away on the shore of his mind.

The temperaments of two artists may be similar while their talents differ, leading one to become a painter, another a poet. At such times there exists an affinity of expression in works of different media.

Paul Eluard was drawn to painting throughout his life. His truly poetic imagination was always sensitive to the expression in pigment of those forces toward which all aspire and to which the artist gives an intense aesthetic order. For Eluard painting was a ceremony, a mystique. The studio became a cathedral, the easel an altar, the canvas an ostensory containing infinity. The artist was a priest invoking the gods. The paint and the way it was placed on the canvas was the ritual, one which each time expressed a new vision. There is a tangibility to the ceremonial symbols of painting which appealed to the artistic and sensual nature of Eluard.

This is not a unique conception of painting nor of art in general at this time. Wallace Stevens expresses a similar idea:

> The theory of poetry, that is to say, the total of the theories of poetry, often seems to become in time a mystical theology or, more simply, a mystique. The reason for this must by now be clear. The reason is the same reason why the pictures in a museum of modern art often seem to become in a time a mystical aesthetic, a prodigious search of appearance, as if to find a way of saying and of establishing that all things whether below or above appearance, are one and that it is only through reality, in which they are reflected or, it may be, joined together, that we can reach them.

Eluard's temperament conceived of art in still more deeply mystical terms than is generally done today. His mysticism could never deny the physical manifestation in beauty, be it of art or of action. The life blood of his spiritual and mental existence depended on this. His enthusiasm for a life of creative adventure overflows in every word with a generosity found only in those who have exposed their deepest sensitivities to the joys and sorrows of the world.

Eluard was enchanted throughout his life by painting as the expression of a spiritual, poetic world. Through it and around it he saw and constructed a microcosm, a set of meaningful symbols. It was for him an expression of existence, open and sensitive to all the vibrating realities of the world, which its opposite, living-death, conceals.

The central theme which radiates outward in all directions is vision. It is the seed, it is the deeply aromatic fruit and also the beautiful skin around it. And as with the fruit, all parts are forever dependent one upon the other. The vision of some reaches only the outer skin and its truth is limited. One must constantly try to penetrate to the richer truth and beauty of the fruit and then to the seed which is the inexhaustible source of life itself.

For Eluard all of life finds its balance and meaning in the constant extension of vision. To have vision is to have a heightened awareness of the world. It constantly challenges, excites and penetrates our dearest sense—eyesight. By some still unknown and very complicated law of optics the placement of totally personal (which is to say very universal) forms on a canvas through color and shapes, so shakes up the world of the viewer's mind that it is caused to spin and rise in such a manner as to behold a "vision," be it of the deepest realities of this world or of some transcendental one.

Eluard's highly attuned sensual nature reacted with magical perceptiveness to the physical world which surrounded him. Every object he approached took on a proportion far beyond its limited physical presence, or rather, revealed its true proportion, and at the same time retained the concreteness which its poetry insists upon. The wonder of Eluard's seemingly elusive perceptivity is its very concreteness. This is perhaps the secret to his truly poetic charm with all that the original meaning of this word suggests of incantation. This charm always transparent yet always apparent delighted and excited the painters he knew, as they, Eluard affirmed it constantly, delighted, excited and nourished him.

Liberty is a word Paul Eluard used often. The most popular poem of the French Resistance was his **"Liberty."** (Good poems too can be popular). But it is not simply the word he used.

There is an inner glow of freedom throughout his poetry, which was in him and which is bound to grow in the reader sensitive to his work. This spirit he brought to painting.

Here are a few prose, but never prosey, lines of the poet which suggest liberty:

"The joy of building in order not to die."

"And I oppose to love the ready-made image instead of images still to be made."

"I trust my sense of orientation, the attraction that leads me to others in order to bring me back to myself."

"I regret nothing, I advance."

"I speak of what helps me to live, of what is good. I am not of those who seek to lose themselves, forget themselves by loving nothing, by reducing their needs, their tastes, their desires, by leading their life which is to say life, to the repugnant conclusion of their death. I don't insist on submitting the world by the virtual power of intelligence alone, I want everything to be sensible to me, real, useful, for it is only from there that I conceive my existence. Man can exist only in his own reality. He must be conscious of it. Otherwise he exists for others only as a dead man, as a stone, as dung."

The poet's surrender to every day, every person, every experience enabled him to receive. One feels in Eluard more than in most poets an effortlessness, as though no barriers existed between him and the accomplishment of his act. This very "facilité" (a word Max Ernst said is "très Eluard") is both a source of the poet's charm and a trap which limits him.

Tantalizing paradoxes and contradictions occur constantly in Eluard's writing. Inconsistencies never concerned him. When two sides of a paradox meet, they decide they can occupy the same space after all. He cried "down with art" and his most enchanting poems were born.

The idea of perfection, the belief in it and the aspiration toward it always remained with him. He wrote: "I endure to perfect myself." And then he set down the proposition and deduction: "There is only one life, therefore it is perfect."

One does not progress on this road to perfection without forgetfulness. "The poetics of Eluard is as his poetry, founded on forgetfulness. The object is metamorphocized providing we forget what it was." Forgetting implies the ability to see again for the first time, which accounts for the persistence of Eluard's pristine freshness and also for a certain lack of development in him. He wrote: "To see, is to understand, to judge, to transform, to imagine, to forget or forget oneself, to be or to disappear." Eluard had no shadow, left no wake.

Paul Eluard has been called the "Great white voice of this century." In **"The Face of Peace"** he speaks of "The white illumination of believing all the good possible."

He was even able to bring this incandescent life to the "principles of faithfulness." In **"Shared Nights"** he wrote:

"Principles of faithfulness—Because principles do not depend always on rules dryly inscribed on the white wood of ancestors, but on lively charms, glances, attitudes, on words and signs of youth, of purity, of passion. Nothing of all that is erased."

Eluard's connection with painting and painters took many forms. He kept an *Anthology of Writings on Art,* of which 3 volumes have been published, and wrote many prose-poems concerned with painting.

Nearly all of his poems were at some time in some edition accompanied by illustrations. In an article entitled **"Physique of Poetry"** published in *Minotaure 6* in the winter of 1935 Eluard considers the question of illustration.

> In 1910, a painter, Picasso, discovered in the work of a poet a new mode of inspiration. Since then painters have not ceased to depart from description, from imitation of subjects which were proposed to them: images accompany a poem only in order to enlarge its meaning, unravel its form. In order to collaborate painters and poets want each other to be free. Dependence denigrates, prevents understanding and loving.

> There is no model for him who seeks what he has never seen. In the end nothing is as beautiful as an involuntary similarity.

Eluard worked directly with painters such as Max Ernst and Pablo Picasso, writing poems which were extended by illustrations and at times extending drawings with poems. His poetry has inspired many of the greatest contemporary painters to illustrate them. One of the most beautiful is Miró's interpretation of **"Fool-Proof."** There seem to be qualities in the imagery and instantaneous mood of Eluard's poetry which is particularly suggestive and sympathetic to painters. A publication entitled "A poem in each book," appeared in 1956 with original engravings and lithographs accompanying poems by Eluard. The artists contributing to this include Jean Arp, Georges Braque, Marc Chagall, Max Ernst, Albert Giacometti, Fernand Léger, Joan Miró and Pablo Picasso.

But all the artists associated with Eluard are not of such consummate ability. Often he seemed to esteem artists of inferior talent. Still the prevailing mood a person brings to the world establishes his quality and is more important than the number of right choices made from it.

Throughout his creative life Eluard wrote poems devoted to and inspired by paintings and painters. These poems which suggest the artistic transparency, the instantaneous quality of painters and paintings, collected in a volume entitled **"Seeing"**, are the antithesis of rigid and worldly. They exist in a realm beyond psychology where the painter is left free to roam in his own world—a world whose poetry Eluard so often senses. He does not "capture" it in a poem, but rather, by giving it unbounded form, frees it for further flight. Here is a free-flying poem: **"Joan Miró."**

> Sun of prey prisoner of my head
> Take away the hill, take away the forest.
> The sky is more beautiful than ever
> Dragonflies around the grapes
> Give it precise forms
> Which I resolve in one gesture
> Cloud of the first day
> Insensible clouds that nothing authorizes
> Their seeds burn
> In the straw fire of my glances
> Finally to cover oneself with dawn
> The sky will have to be as pure as night.

With freedom, or liberty, we are back at the beginning—at the only beginning and the only end which for life must be without either. (pp. 85-92)

*Anne Fessenden, "Paul Eluard: Poet in the World of Painters," in* Wagner Literary Magazine, *No. 3, 1962, pp. 85-92.*

### Times Literary Supplement   (essay date 1969)

*[The following is an excerpt from a critical overview of Eluard's poetry, relating Eluard's works to events in his life.]*

The most vital factor in [Eluard's] life was the need to love and be loved, and this is the dominant theme of his work from first to last. His earliest poems were written in his mid-teens while he was being treated for tuberculosis in a Swiss sanatorium and they were inspired by a Russian fellow patient, Hélène Diakonova ("Gala"). Eluard's persona in these poems is that of an idealistic and bookish young lover, dreaming impossible dreams, scarcely daring to act and masking his discomfiture with self-deprecating light irony. There is little self-pity, no high-flown rhetoric and the most successful of them, a Pierrot sequence and **"Les cinq rondels du tout jeune homme"** read like accomplished pastiches of Laforgue.

Eluard married "Gala" in 1917 and her presence dominated his poetry from then until the early 1930s. The early years of the marriage were happy, and in **Poèmes pour la paix** (1918), which won for Eluard the crucial patronage of the prominent pundit, Jean Paulhan, he voices the demobilized soldier's contentment with the simpler pleasures of family life, daily chores and pride in paternity. But as early as 1922 with **Répétitions,** a discordant note is sounded and "Gala" begins to emerge as a tantalizing and enigmatic figure, withholding consolation, or even conversation, when her husband is in need of it, and saving her gaiety for the company of other people.

Eluard's unhappiness is obviously much more acute in **Mourir de ne pas mourir** (1924). He was, in fact, so distressed at this period, because of differences with his father as well as with his wife, that he announced the book would be his last and, the day before its publication, he set off on a Rimbaud-type flight to the Far East where he spent the next seven months. The major theme of this collection, as indeed of all his poetry of the 1920s, is the gulf between ideal and reality, between the woman he thought he had married and the real "Gala". . . .

The original title of **Capitale de la douleur** (1926) was *L'art d'être malheureux,* and nearly all the poems are . . . shot through with a despairing awareness of vanished purity and lost light. Through most of the 1920s, in fact, the private world evoked in Eluard's poetry is essentially lonely and desolate; the images of domestic calm give way to images of squalor and violence, and what was luminous and transparent becomes dark and opaque. The more everyday life proved intolerable, the more persistently Eluard sought refuge in dreams: inevitably, as is made poignantly clear in the prose-poems of **Les dessous d'une vie ou la pyramide humaine** (1926), the result was nightmare more terrifying than reality or beauty so perfect that his discontent with the waking world was acutely intensified; "Gala" can still provide the inspiration of happy poems, as in the "Premièrement" sequence of **L'amour la poésie** (1929) but, significantly, in the work of a writer who normally eschewed nostalgia, the joys are those of recollection.

Eluard's emotional conflict was at its most acute at the beginning of the 1930s, just before and just after "Gala" left him to marry Salvador Dali. The poems in **A toute épreuve** (1930) painfully convey his sense of loneliness and the world's hostility, and "Gala's" stubborn passivity is starkly contrasted with memories of love-making when their marriage was young and passionate. The following volume, **La vie immédiate** (1932) captures further memories of "Gala" in the section "Nuits partagées", and expresses

his growing realization that no abiding satisfaction can be found in a world of dreams. What is most striking, in fact, is the new note of confident expectation that erotic consolation can be provided in the reality of the present and the future. . . . (p. 1095)

In his next volume, **Comme deux gouttes d'eau** (1933) Eluard declared that he had wasted too much of his life on self-pity and that he had resolved henceforth to seek more determinedly for happiness; the title of the collection proclaimed that he had found his ideal mate or twin soul. She was an Alsatian girl, Maria Benz ("Nusch") whom he first met in 1929 and finally married in 1933. From Eluard's point of view, she had all the qualities that "Gala" conspicuously lacked: she was gentle, passionate, gay, generous, refreshingly uncomplicated, and in love with Eluard. His sense of ecstatic happiness found lyrical expression in a flowing succession of poems produced in the 1930s: in **La rose publique** (1934), he claimed that "Nusch" was so much a part of him that she even shared his dreams: **Facile** (1935) and **Médieuses** express the exaltation of an ardent lover, at long last fulfilled, delighting in the infinite variety of his partner. "Nusch" is endowed with Protean qualities and is transformed into the landscape, the sky, shimmering water or the very consciousness of the Universe. Nature, so black and hostile in the poems of the 1920s, now echoes the words and the gestures of the happy lovers.

The triumphant solution of his private problems enabled Eluard to involve himself with those of his fellow-men and the poems of the later 1930s express a direct concern with

*Eluard and Nusch (far right) with Louis Aragon, Elsa Triolet, and André Breton in 1931.*

the major public issues of the day. He had never been a-political but until he married "Nusch" the role played by politics in his poetry had been faint and sporadic. His political outlook was for the most part fashioned during the First World War in which, apart from a brief period of front-line experience in the infantry, he served as a hospital orderly. His close friendship with a number of anarchists from 1916 onwards but, most of all, his close contact with the maimed and the dying, filled him with compassion for his fellow-men and an abiding sense of disgust with a society which not only made war possible but actually condoned it.

It was an active mood of revulsion which first led him to participate in the most notorious of the Dada manifestations of 1920 and to join the Communist Party in 1926. The causes which aroused his intensest feelings were social injustice, poverty, the degradation of the individual, and the collective folly of war. He remained implacably opposed to individuals or institutions who seemed to him to have a vested interest in preserving such phenomena and, in his view, these were the bourgeoisie, the capitalist state and the church. He attacked these intermittently all his life, but his most succinct and scathing indictment remains **"Critique de la poésie"**, the short poem which serves as epilogue to *La vie immédiate* (1932). . . . (pp. 1095-96)

The killing of Lorca and the murderous air-raid on Guernica crystallized Eluard's left-wing hostility and inspired one of his most notable pieces of polemic, **"La victoire de Guernica"** (1936), the more effective for being less shrill. From this time on, both in his theoretical writings and in his poetry, he proclaimed the need to establish closer links with his fellow men. To translate this theory into practice did not, however, prove quite so easy, and from the mid-1930s onward, a major new theme emerged in Eluard's poetry, the tension between an all-too satisfying private love and social and political responsibility.

The rival claims of love and duty were particularly acute during the German occupation. Eluard was sometimes tempted to take refuge in a world of pure poetry, as is clear from the *Blason des fleurs et des fruits* (1940) and the richly illustrated anthology, *Poésie involontaire et poésie intentionnelle,* published in 1942, one of the darkest years of the war. But his main commitment was to the French resistance movement, a cause which enlisted his sense of poetic mission, his considerable gifts of invective, his profound humanity and his real love of France. In his poetry of this period his resolve to inspire his comrades-in-arms is expressed through the use of a number of devices common to most traditional forms of popular verse: emphasis through heavily accentuated rhythms, through a recurrent refrain or near-repetition, and through short and easily memorable lines. There is greater directness in his use of language, but at its best it remains characteristically elusive. . . .

["Liberte"] was originally conceived as a private tribute to "Nusch", and it is indicative of Eluard's keen sense of wartime priorities that he chose eventually to transform it into a hymn to freedom. Yet Eluard remained particularly sensitive to the competing demands of his private and public roles. This is nowhere expressed more vividly than in **"Poésie ininterrompue I"** (1946), his longest poem and, by common consent, the greatest work of his maturity. He takes full stock of his life's experiences and rejects the past in favour of the present; any lingering temptation to take refuge in erotic complacency is dispelled by the embittered reminder of bourgeois iniquities, and the poem ends as a hymn to hope and to fraternity.

Only when the Second World War had ended did he judge it seemly to publish any further collection of poems exclusively devoted to love, and these, *Lingères légères* and *Une longue réflexion amoureuse* (1945) together with *Le dur désir de durer* (1946), convey once again how enduring was the happiness "Nusch" provided and how much he depended on her. This was brutally brought home to him in November, 1946, when she died of a cerebral haemorrhage at the age of forty. He mourned her in *Le temps débordé* (1946), short and spontaneous forms of grief which, like Hugo's famous *Demain dès l'aube* are all the more poignant for being quite unrhetorical:

> Nous ne vieillirons pas ensemble
> Voici le jour
>    En trop! le temps débordé

Eluard was for a time so overcome that he more than once contemplated suicide. He was won back to life by his friends, in particular by Jacqueline Trutat to whom he dedicated *Corps mémorable* (1948), which contains the most overtly erotic poems he ever wrote, and also *Une leçon de morale* (1950), a balance sheet of moods and reactions in which a remarkable series of linked texts express first a pessimistic and then an optimistic reaction to the same set of experiences. As a further act of homage to "Nusch" he dedicated himself anew to the class struggle in *Poèmes politiques* (1948), secure in the conviction that this is what she would have wanted of him.

For the remaining years of his life, Eluard acted as a poet laureate for the communist cause: he was as ever ready to denounce capitalist atrocities as to eulogize a hero of the revolution or to hail the opening of a party congress. He travelled extensively throughout eastern Europe as well as to America, and it was in Mexico in 1949 that he met Dominique Lemor, whom he married in 1951. To Dominique he dedicated the poems of *Le phénix* (1951), expressing his resolve to live for the present moment and his faith in the indestructibility of love. The most characteristic mood expressed in these final love poems is like that of Ronsard's odes to Hélène or Baudelaire's poems to Marie Daubrun: a deep feeling of tenderness and of gratitude for a companionship he had not dared to hope for, counter-pointed with an autumnal melancholy and sense of finality. . . .

The dominant mood of Eluard's last poems was, however, guardedly optimistic. He remained remarkably unembittered by the long years of unhappiness with "Gala", by the traumatically sudden death of "Nusch" or by the atrocities committed during the Spanish Civil War and the Nazi Occupation. His persistent refusal to accept defeat as final, which eventually shines through even the darkest periods of his life, is affirmed yet again in *Le château des pauvres,* his poetic testament completed at an old farm-house in the

Périgord a few months before his death. It expresses a tender love for Dominique, and beyond her, for his fellowmen, and it proclaims his faith in ultimate victory. . . .

What distinguishes Eluard from all other twentieth-century French poets is his insistence on the paramount need to communicate, the rationalization in practical linguistic terms of his lifelong fear of loneliness; "Vivre c'est partager", he wrote in 1948, "je hais la solitude". The need to communicate with the reader runs like a refrain through all Eluard's theoretical writings, from the preface to *Les animaux et leurs hommes* in 1920, repeatedly in his public lectures and *arts poétiques* of the 1930s, and again in the collection of poems published in 1951 and significantly entitled *Pouvoir tout dire.* The period when his language is most opaque, during his involvement with Dada and the early years of the Surrealist movement, can be seen as his linguistic apprenticeship. His enthusiasm for proverb-making and for all manner of plays on words, from old-fashioned puns to ultra-modern *cadavres exquis,* were so many *exercises du style* in which he explored the resources of the French language. Throughout his career, however, he never sought to bedazzle or to alienate the reader with recondite allusions, and his vocabulary remained essentially simple.

The words Eluard employs nearly always designate things or attributes within the normal reader's experience: the parts of the human body, human activities like laughing, weeping, kissing or caressing, and the sights and sounds of landscape and of the domesticated animal world. What constitutes both the chief difficulty and the chief attraction of his poetry is how his words, so simple in themselves, are combined to form highly charged and very often elliptical images.

Eluard derived from the Surrealists his belief in the poetic importance of images and confidence in his continuing ability to make them. . . . In his poetic practice, he only briefly coined images illogically and haphazardly in the approved Surrealist manner and, significantly, these are to be found almost exclusively in works of which he was only part-author, in *L'immaculée conception* (1930), written in collaboration with André Breton, or in *Ralentir travaux* (1930), written with Breton and René Char. In the poetry which was wholly his own, the images are carefully disciplined, organically linked and, as is true of all poets, they reveal his particular preoccupations.

He is specially fond of images of fire and water, and frequently interchanges their qualities so that fire is said to liquefy and flow like water while water burns and glows like fire; to light a fire or to plunge into water are two of his favourite analogies for the act of love. Fire, indeed, is the most constant and the most potent of his symbols, representing the rejuvenating powers of life and love: it sustains the whole of his first wholly successful poem, "Pour vivre ici" (1918). . . . And it dominates his last major collection of love-poems, *Le phénix,* in which he explains that the Phoenix is Adam and Eve forever being born anew in the fire of love.

But what emerges most clearly of all from Eluard's work is his obsessive reliance on visual imagery. Sight was, to Eluard, by far the most vital of all the senses. With their power to reflect and to multiply images, the eyes have traditionally been linked by poetic analogy with mirrors or with water. Eluard goes much further. Eyes, in his poems, have the power to dispel darkness, to engender life and to liberate from time; they are likened to the sun, with power to create and to illumine. His characteristic analogues for euphoria are objects or surfaces which reflect or transmit light: the sun, the stars, mirrors or pools of water. Conversely, when he wishes to convey a sense of despair, the qualities he invokes are darkness, heaviness and opacity.

For Eluard, the act of seeing is intimately linked with the act of loving. Eyes are important to the lover not so much because they enable him to see but because they permit him to be seen. To be seen by the beloved is to be made aware that one exists, and lovers' eyes become mirrors in which they watch themselves seeing each other. Yet intense though the pleasures of contemplation may be—and Eluard's love-poems are more frequently litanies of praise to the body of his beloved than incitements to or memories of love-making—his ideal is the conventional one of union so complete that the lovers' individual senses are wholly obliterated.

Yet it was not only as a lover that Eluard prized the faculty of sight. For him, it provided infinite enrichment to the very quality of living: "Voir c'est comprendre et agir: c'est unir le monde à l'homme et l'homme à l'homme." His confirmed belief in such an adage is expressed not merely in his image-making but in the particular sympathy he always felt for painters; he numbered among his greatest friends Picasso, Max Ernst, and the art-critic and collector Sir Roland Penrose; he compiled three remarkable anthologies of *Ecrits sur l'art* (1952-54) and, over the course of his career, he wrote a large number of poems on a wide range of twentieth-century painters which take the form of subtle analyses of single paintings or lyrical tributes to the particular painter's art.

Just as Eluard's images were determined and disciplined by his preoccupations, so his poems were shaped and ordered by his keen sense of form, a sense that was partly innate and partly developed through extremely extensive reading. During his years of maturity, he produced a highly distinctive series of poetry anthologies which, he claimed, were the result of a lifetime's study: *Premières vues anciennes* (1937), *Poésie involontaire et poésie intentionnelle* (1942), *Le meilleur choix de poèmes est celui que l'on fait pour soi* (1947), *Première anthologie vivante de la poésie du passé* (1951) and *Les sentiers et la route de la poésie* (1952). These reveal Eluard's lasting love for pre-classical French poetry, for striking imagery from any age, and for folk-lore, children's counting rhymes, and the unconsciously poetic utterances of ordinary people. They also reveal how proudly conscious he was of being part of an unbroken poetic tradition. (pp. 1096-97)

In practical terms, the consequences of his sense of kinship with France's poetic past meant the borrowing of a number of strictly disciplined forms: *ballades* and *rondeaux* are to be found among his very earliest poems and Renaissance-type *blasons* among the works of his maturity; in "Couvre-feu," one of the most celebrated of his Resistance poems, he takes over a rhythm schema from the *Grands Rhétoriqueurs,* while one of the last poems he ever wrote, **"Ailleurs ici partout,"** is consciously modelled on the "Fortunes et adversitez" of the fifteenth-century poet Jehan Régnier; in a striking number of poems which are not modelled on any pre-existing fixed form, he reveals a fondness for enumeration and for near-repetition which is markedly liturgical.

Because of his conscious indebtedness to French poetic tradition, Eluard was never at ease in the role of iconoclast demanded by avant-garde doctrine. He was faithful to the Surrealist movement after his fashion and was for a time as fanatical as any. He played an active part in all the noisiest demonstrations of the inter-war years, engaged in such joint enterprises as the *152 proverbes mis au goût du jour* (1925) with Benjamin Péret and the *Dictionnaire abrégé du Surréalisme* (1938) with André Breton. Yet Breton, the "Pope" of the Surrealists, came to look upon Eluard as a heretic, not so much because of his faint praise of "automatic writing" or because of his lingering fondness for the alexandrine, but because he committed the cardinal sin of preferring poetry itself to Surrealism.

Eluard's continued participation in the movement was motivated partly out of deep personal loyalty to Breton, partly out of his indelible sense of outrage with the social and cultural establishment of his day, but most of all because Surrealism seemed to hold out the promise of self-knowledge and instant integration when his private life was riven with tensions. Significantly, it was in the 1920s, when his personal problems were most acute, that he was most militant in his behaviour and his pronouncements. Equally significant is the attraction he found in the Surrealists' keen interest in dreams, and his best poems of the 1920s are the renderings of dream-sequences or have an authentically dream-like quality. When his emotional problems were solved through marriage to "Nusch", and when he came to believe that the Communist Party was likely to prove a more efficient instrument of social change, his enthusiasm for Surrealism dwindled away.

Some of the poems Eluard wrote in this later period are conspicuously successful: **"Poésie ininterrompue"**, and the poems mourning "Nusch" in *Le temps déborde,* are to be ranked among the finest French poems produced this century. On the other hand, other poems of this period widely hailed as successes have not worn at all well: the Resistance poems now seem too direct a commentary on the age for which they were so necessary, and the "Hommages" to communist heroes are embarrassing as much for their poetical as for their political misjudgment. Eluard's genius was not for polemic nor for invective; it was to sing of private rather than public moments. His best role was as the Verlaine of his age not, as he sometimes imagined, as its Hugo. He was most consistently successful as a poet in the 1920s when he was particularly unhappy and when his language, though fresh and simple, was most musical and most subtly evocative. His collected works demonstrate beyond dispute that oblique suggestion in poetry is more effective than direct statement and that, for the artist, deprivation is more fruitful than fulfilment. (p. 1097)

*"The Need for Love: The Poetry of Paul Eluard," in* The Times Literary Supplement, *No. 3526, September 25, 1969, pp. 1095-1097.*

## Robert Nugent   (essay date 1974)

[*An American critic, poet, and biographer, Nugent is the author of the biographical and critical study* Paul Eluard. *In the following excerpt from that work, he comments on imagery in Eluard's poems.*]

The primary question a poet must ask himself is how he is going to see reality and to define reality in terms of that vision. The real can be moral or religious, a conviction of a truth that informs his entire poetic outlook (as is the case of a religious poet like Claudel); it can be a notion of things about him (tables, animals, roses) into whose life he must enter (as with Rilke). It can be the very profound awareness of his own life, of his own aloneness, as it touches that of others and of the external world. Eluard, in the title of a collection of poems published in 1921, *Les nécessités de la vie et les conséquences des rêves,* gives a clue to his concept of reality, or of how he conceives reality. He is preoccupied with living in the world, with being a part of its activities, meeting its demands; at the same time, his own personal inwardness, defined in terms of that aloneness, has to be recognized and given expression. These preoccupations were already evident in earlier volumes of verse published before 1921: *Le devoir et l'inquiétude* (*Duty and Anguish* ), 1917; *Poèmes pour la paix* (published separately in 1918); *Les animaux et leurs hommes, les hommes et leurs animaux* (*Animals and their Masters, Masters and their Animals*), 1920. In the poetry of this period, Eluard's concern is with a contrast between the "living reality" of dreams and the "pure image" of the external world, between an inner purity of one's own solitude and a necessity of finding a corresponding purity in the outside world.

Since Baudelaire, especially, French poets had tried to find a pure image in the outside world; a poet then can refine from this discovery all dross of secondary considerations, either didactic or philosophic. The Romantics had first sought a pure reality, distilled in an inner world of the psyche, in an effort to seize the image in itself, existing in itself and not dependent for its meaning on the relationships to external interests. Nerval, for example, had written of the secrets of the reality of the mind; Baudelaire had tried to seize the image as the key to the meaning of the refined existence, this purified reality. Rimbaud and Mallarmé continued and deepened the two streams of "refinement" and "purification." It is in Eluard's early poetry that he brings together these two tendencies.

In the early collection *Poèmes* (1914), in the poem beginning **"Le coeur sur l'arbre"**, Eluard gives a series of moments of dream (*rêve*) where the inner vision makes clear the pureness of an image. In the first stanza, Eluard speaks of "the heart of the tree" where *le coeur* depends on the inner world. He associates this inner world, where he dreams of love, with the fulfillment of love. (The two themes become the principal subjects of his poetry around 1924.) The significance of the image *arbre* is that it indicates the focal point to which the inner concerns become attached: The act of thus narrowing the association be-tween *coeur* and *arbre* (heart and tree) gives to the total image a stronger effect and therefore greater significance. The fusion of the two aspects of experience in a single phrase is *poesis,* the writing of the poem in itself. Eluard considers love in the light of the other person's action, *vous n'aviez qu'à le cueillir* ("You had only to pick it"). In other words, his solitude depends on another, experience is de-fined as two people alone who try to reach out to one an-other. Eluard also speaks of the pleasures and exaltations of love: *Sourire et rire, rire et douceur d'outre-sens* ("Smil-ing and laughing, laughter and sweetness beyond sense"). The duality and purity of love—*Vaincu, vainqueur et lu-mineux, pur comme un ange* ("Conquered, conquering and shining, pure as an angel")—gain meaning through identification of the experience of love with that quality of *arbre* which is most characteristic, its elevation: *Haut vers le ciel, avec les arbres* ("High towards the sky, with the trees"). The image *arbre,* moreover, takes on the purity of the experience of love.

In the second stanza of the same poem, Eluard again fuses the reality of his vision of the woman ( . . .*une belle qui voudrait lutter / Et qui ne peut, couchée de la colline,* "a beautful woman who would want to struggle / And who cannot, woman asleep at the foot of the hill"), with the dual quality of the sky which Eluard describes as *miséra-ble* or *transparent.* The concept of his love takes on the pu-rified meaning of the sky; the sky, which cannot struggle against itself and cannot become other than it is, empha-sizes the inevitable nature of the poet's love. In the third stanza, Eluard speaks of "days" (*jours*): The furthest ex-tension of reality includes the added dimension of time; the sense of time is existential, in that it is the experience itself that time itself brings. Eluard equates the duality of experience, taken in an almost moral sense of good and evil, with the duality of the seasons (*Les fleurs sont dessé-chées, les graines sont perdues, / La canicule attend les grandes gelées blanches,* "The flowers are withered, the seeds are lost, / The heat of summer is waiting for the great white frosts"). Again the psychic reality of his expe-rience becomes meaningful through the perception of the pureness of his vision of the world as it has a beginning in his solitude.

In the fourth stanza, Eluard speaks of death, which, like love or experience itself, has a dual nature. On the one hand, Eluard emphasizes the blindness of death; to consid-er it otherwise is, in one way, to no avail and "decorative" (*peindre des porcelaines,* "to paint china"). In another way, death has a terrible beauty, like music, like *bras blancs tout nus* ("completely bare arms") which can rise towards the sky or stretch out to embrace the poet. An un-derstanding of death underlies the vision of the world where opposites (*les vents et les oiseaux,* "the winds and the birds"), become one (*s'unissent* ) and yet where change is possible or even a necessary part of the world (*le ciel change,* "the sky changes"). Yet in his working towards a poetic image workable on all levels—present experi-ences, their inherent dilemmas and solutions—Eluard is looking for common denominators in experience which give a classic universality and timelessness to his images and which help him to bear his aloneness.

Even in the most heartrending of experiences, war—with the separation it brings about, the solitude, the memories of love—peace, its opposite, becomes possible. The real-ization of peace, in **Poèmes pour la paix,** is understood again, in terms of the pure significance of images. The sol-dier-husband returning from war brings warmth as does the morning sun (*revient du soleil* ); the images of war (*fusil, bidon,* "rifle, jerry can") are contrasted with the splendidness of the curving breast of the wife, the human face gains an importance through love and the happiness of love; the moon is associated with the beauty of the woman; a garden is like the poet's solitude, the poet works in this orchard and the source of life—the sun—burns also on the poet's hand, which in turn brings about the poem.

Again the consideration of reality is thus extended to in-clude more than private association and private anguish. These emotions are in a constant state of tension because they can be dealt with only by means of an awareness of others. This awareness is seemingly impossible, because a poet writes from his aloneness. Reality, to be fully under-stood and adequately dealt with—even in a consideration of the nature of poetry—must include a preoccupation with fraternity; the enlargement of private concerns must expand towards a larger concept of fraternal love. In the collection **Pour vivre ici (In Order to Live on this Earth ),** in the poem by the same title, Eluard again speaks from a viewpoint of solitude, of his aloneness (*l'azur m'ayant abandonné,* "the sky having abandoned me"). The poet makes a fire in order to have a kind of friendship and com-panionship; he shares with the fire the total experience of the day. Then he can say, *je vécus* ("I lived"); he experi-ences a feeling of containment, of oneness, of comfort within himself:

> *J'étais comme un bateau coulant dans l'eau fer-*
> *   mée,*
> *Comme un mort je n'avais qu'un unique élément.*
>
> (I was like a boat flowing in closed water, / Like
> a person dead I had only a single element.)

Further, the kind of reality in Eluard is a "seen" one, seen in the sense of capturing images and juxtaposing one against the other. He follows in this technique the Surreal-ist doctrine of free-association, not only for the primary purpose of aesthetics, but also for the purpose of getting hold of reality. From such control of the external real the poem grows, is itself creative, and reality takes on a depth—an extension into time—that relieves the poem from remaining on a single level of descriptive reality. El-uard is the most poetic of poets because his is a visual art or—more correctly—a visionary art. He perceives the *cor-respondances* between images. In **"L'amoureuse"** (**Mourir de ne pas mourir**), for example, a "real" image is superim-posed on a visionary one: *Elle est debout sur mes paupières* ("She is standing on my eyelids"). The image of the woman standing is a real image; the idea, however, that she might stand upon his eyelids, though real, is imagined. Throughout the poem the real image is thus amalgamated with the poet's proper self, the poetic self for whom the imagined is the real. In this fashion, the reality of the ex-ternal world is made one with the reality of the poet's self, and the inner reality of his emotions becomes evident. Eluard, unlike Baudelaire, very rarely uses the adverb *comme* (like) and then only to reinforce the texture of an image:

> *Elle s'engloutit dans mon ombre*
> *Comme une pierre sur le ciel*

> (She was engulfed in my shadow / Like a stone against the sky.)

The noun *pierre* gives a density to the verb, underscores the plunging notion of the verb; the noun *ciel* gives a dimension of depth and distance.

Eluard has defined a poem in the poem **"Le miroir d'un moment"** (*Capitale de la douleur*). Poetry is a mirror, certainly. Yet Eluard's doctrine of the imagined real differs profoundly from the imitation of nature of neoclassical aesthetics. For the neoclassicists, following Horace, art was still a mirror, still an imitation, a refabricating as closely knit as possible on the original model. For Eluard, the use of the mirror is far more intimate; the reader sees into the mirror, the mirror is the image itself which holds, as does the mirror, truth. . . . The essence of Surrealist doctrine is the truth of the mirror itself; a kind of reversal is operative: not the holding up of the mirror to nature by the poet, but the image in itself constitutes a mirror. In **"Le miroir d'un moment,"** the mirror has several functions: It breaks up light, the light that might distort (*il dissipe le jour*, "it dissipates the light"); it shows the unconnected images of appearances, those images which are implicitly joined but appear to be unjoined (*il montre aux hommes les images déliées de l'apparence*, "it shows men images which are freed from appearance"). The image is deprived of softness: *dur comme la pierre, / La pierre informe, / La pierre du mouvement et de la vue* ("hard as stone, shapeless stone, The stone of movement and of sight"). The image shows up truth, takes away hypocrisy; it has thus a very definite moral function, a kind of moral pragmatism which underlies Eluard's constant anguish over the nature of man's relationship with others, which relationship should be one of truth and forthrightness, even though everyone stands alone. This pragmatism, moreover, helps to overcome feelings of anguish and solitude.

Eluard's intent, however, is never moralistic; the value of the experience of an image resides in the image itself: *Ce que la main a pris dédaigne même de prendre la forme de la main* ("That which the hand took even disdains to take on the form of the hand"). The image exists purely, with no intellectualization, only the living reality of the image itself:

> *Ce qui a été compris n'existe plus,*
> *L'oiseau s'est confondu avec le, vent,*
> *Le ciel avec sa vérité,*
> *L'homme avec sa réalité.*

> (That which had been understood no longer exists, / The bird has become one with the wind, / The sky and its truth, / Man and his reality.)

Eluard thus reaches a definition of his solitude through a definition of the image. Solitude is simply the reality which is man himself, just as any part of nature is defined by itself. The real self, for Eluard, is his being alone.

The reader then wonders, in reading and studying the poems, what part does reality of the imagination play in a poet's life. In **"Nuits partagées"** (*La vie immédiate*) he writes: *Je m'obstine à mêler des fictions aux redoutables réalités* ("I insist on mixing fictions with fearful realities"). He populates *maisons inhabitées* ("empty houses") with *femmes exceptionnelles* ("exceptional women"). He defends such imaginative fiction by a reason which is similar to Valéry's *charme*. In order to sing of objects, in order for them to be poetic, Eluard must discover them again in a kind of poetic invention: *Objets inutiles, même la sottise qui procéda à votre fabrication me fut une source d'enchantement* ("useless objects, even the stupidity which preceeded the making of you, was a source of enchantment for me"). He conquers the indifferences of *êtres indifférents* and seems to force a recognition of his solitude. Like Baudelaire, Eluard discovers in a world of poetic fancy a habit of poetry: *J'ai pris l'habitude des images les plus inhabituelles. Je les ai vues où elles n'étaient pas* ("I got into the habit of the most unaccustomed images. I saw them where they were not"). All that surrounds us is reinvented through such magic—streets, squares, women. In a way, such reinvention is a protest against reason: *La raison, la tête haute, son carcan d'indifférence, lanterne à tête de fourmi, la raison pauvre mât de fortune pour un homme affolé, le mât de fortune du bateau* ("Reason, with its head high, with its iron collar of indifference, ant-headed lantern, reason poor mast of fortune for a maddened man, mast of fortune of the boat"). Reason often misdirects awareness towards another end than understanding. Reason cannot give understanding, although it can help explain to others what is understood intuitively.

Poetic fancy, moreover, depends on the compulsiveness of any word or words which come to mind. The role of reason, in the perception of reality, is to seize upon the verbal situation which imposes itself upon the poet. The reader might compare Eluard's practice with Valéry's. Valéry writes of inspiration as follows:

> The poet is awakened in man by an unforeseen event, an incident outside or within himself: a tree, a face, a "topic," an emotion, a word. At times, it is a desire for expression (*volonté d'expression*) which begins the game, a need to translate that which is felt; at other times, it is, on the contrary, an element of form, a sketch of an expression (*esquisse d'une expression*) which seeks its cause, which seeks a direction in the space of my soul. . . . Observe this possible duality beginning the action: sometimes some means of expression wants something that it can serve.

In Eluard's poetics, however, this distinction is not made. The *volonté d'expression* is identical with the *esquisse d'une expression*. Both arise from the same kind of thinking about, or reasoning with, the image in itself; the image wills the expression and the expression, which is itself the image, wills the image. Much more is involved than inspiration, much more than Ronsard's possession by poetic madness (*je suis troublé de fureur*, "Ode à la Reine," 1550), much more than the melancholy Musset experiences in writing verse ( . . . *quelle singulière et triste impression / Produit un manuscrit*, "Dédicace" to *La coupe et les lèvres*), much more even than Valéry's inescapable fatalism of purity:

> Je touchais à la nuit pure,
> Je ne savais plus mourir,
> Car un fleuve sans coupure
> Me semblait me parcourir . . .
> ("Poésie," *Charmes*)

(I touched upon the fine night, / I was no longer able to die, / Because a seamless river seemed to run through me.)

For Eluard there exists both an aspect of intellectual discovery—poetic rationalization—and the surprise of the action itself. The poem **"L'univers solitude" (*A toute épreuve* [*Holding Fast*]),** though concerning the experience of love, uses a comparable notion of the experience of poetry as a means of expression; the two experiences are eventually welded together. Eluard writes:

> Le corps et les honneurs profanes
> Incroyable conspiration
> Des angles doux comme des ailes
> —Mais la main qui me caresse
> C'est mon rire qui l'ouvre
> C'est ma gorge qui la retient
> Qui la surprise
> Incroyable conspiration
> Des découvertes et des surprises.

(The body and profane honors / Unbelievable conspiracy / Of angles sweet as wings. / —But the hand which caresses me / It is my laughter which opens it / It is my throat which holds it / Which quells it / Unbelievable conspiracy / Of discoveries and surprises.)

The element of poetic inspiration is similarly dual: both *découvertes* (acts of the reason of the will) and *surprises* (the given moment of pleasure forced upon one when the will is in abeyance).

The underlying theory of the identification of the two roles of images is given in **"Identités" (*Cours naturel* ).** For Eluard all life has a unity which constitutes the basic unity of his work. All aspects of reality, the subjects of images, are seen in the same light:

> Je vois les champs la mer couverte d'un jour égale
> Il n'y a pas de différence
> Entre le sable au bord qui sommeille
> La hache au bord de la blessure
> Le corps en gerbe déployé
> Et le volcan de la santé.

(I see the expanse of the sea covered by an even light / There is no difference / Between the sand which sleeps / The axe on the edge of the wound / The body unfolded as a sheaf of corn / And the volcano of well-being.)

Basically Eluard's approach is moral:

> Les fêtes sans reflets les douleurs sans écho
> Des fronts des yeux en proie aux ombres
> Des rires comme des carrefours
> Les champs la mer l'ennui tours silencieuses tours
>      sans fin.

(Holidays without gleams of light sufferings

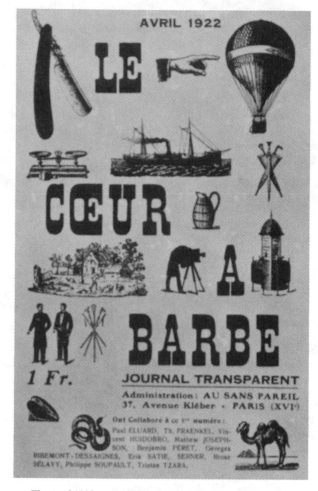

*The April 1922 issue of Tristan Tzara's* Le cœur à barbe, *featuring poetry by Eluard.*

without echo / Foreheads eyes which are prey to shadows / Sound of laughter like city squares / The fields the sea boredom silent towers endless towers.)

The enlargement of a purely aesthetic notion becomes a moral preoccupation. This enlargement reflects a distress over personal solitude, the ultimate world where the poet must operate. Eluard continues (in **"Identités"**) a tradition of the nineteenth century, that of romantic solitude:

> Je vois je lis j'oublie
> Le livre ouvert de volets fermés.

(I see I read I forget / The open book of my closed shutters.)

In **"Blason des fleurs et des fruits" (*Le livre ouvert* [*The Open Book* ], II)** Eluard takes up an older poetic form, the *blason,* and uses it for his own purposes. The poem begins with the statement:

> A mi-chemin de fruit tendre
> Que l'aube entoure de chair jeune
> Abandonnée
> De lumière indéfinie
> La fleur ouvre ses portes d'or.

(Half-way on the tender fruit / That the dawn surrounds with young flesh / Abandoned / By the undefined light / The flower opens its golden gates.)

The poem is structured musically, with refrains that amplify the connection with his own solitude; the idea of the death of love (*Poème plein de frondaison / Perle morte au temps du désir,* "Poem full of foliage / Pearl dead at the time of desire"); the passing of pleasure (*Marguérite l'écho faiblit / Un sourire accueillant s'effeuille,* "Daisy the echo weakens / A welcoming smile sheds its petals"); the oneness, akin to worship, of the life force that informs all characteristics of nature that are available for poetry (*Dans le filet des violettes / La fraise adore le soleil,* "in the net of violets / The strawberry worships the sun"); the harshness of life, which is the necessary counterpoint to the adoration of life (*Mure fuyant entre les ronces / Aster tout saupoudré de guêpes,* "The blackberry fleeing among the brambles / The aster all powdery with wasps"). In all of these *blasons,* however, the poet is forever tied, bound, to his own solitude:

> *J'ai beau vous unir vous mêler*
> *Aux choses que je sais par coeur*
> *Je vous perds le temps est passé*
> *De penser en dehors des murs.*

> (To no avail I bind you / To the things I know by heart / I am losing you the time is past / To think beyond the walls.)

The impossibility of external attributes corresponding to an absolute reality of the images parallels the impossibility of the poet's attributing to these images his own escape from solitude.

The problem lies in understanding reality and in appreciating reality; it is essentially one of communication. In **"La halte des heures"** (*Le livre ouvert,* II), Eluard writes: *Immenses mots dits doucement* ("Immense words spoken quietly"), and describes the quiet power of these words:

> *Grand soleil les volets fermés*
> *Un grand navire au fil de l'eau*
> *Ses voiles partageant le vent.*

> (Bright sun closed shutters / A big ship going with the current / Its sails sharing the wind.)

They have the qualities of dream; their capacity is to bring opposites together:

> *Et les saisons à l'unisson*
> *Colorant de neige et de feu—*
> *Une foule enfin réunie.*

> (And the seasons in unison / Staining with snow and fire— / A crowd brought together at last.)

For it is within the structure of imagery that the poet lives. The structure is, moreover, not only an internal one of private feeling, but also one of a visual experience. It therefore has, at the same time, a reality with two possibilities of poetic expression, the visual and the emotional. In **"Le cinquième poème visible"** (*A l'intérieur de la vie* [*Within Life's Limits*]), Eluard writes: *Je vis dans les images nombreuses des saisons / Et des années* ("I live in the numerous images of the seasons / And the years"). Within time the poet weaves the fabric of his poem from the variety of images time produces. He sees all around him sources of poetic imagery: *Je vis dans les images innombrables de la vie / Dans la dentelle / Des formes des couleurs des gestes et des paroles* ("I live in the innumerable images of life / In the lace / Of forms, colors, gestures, words"). Again the intention is moral: *Je vis dans la misère et la tristesse et je résiste / Je vis malgré la mort* ("I live in misery and sadness and I hold out / I live in spite of death").

The poem constitutes a series of images, each corresponding to an emotional quality. Eluard does not attempt to equate his emotional state with the image; he refuses to give way to the pathetic fallacy. Rather he uses images, words, which stand as kinds of symbols for qualities. He is surrounded by people who are looking for, seeking out, answers. He employs the image of a river:

> *Je vis dans la rivière atténuée et flamboyante*
> *Sombre et limpide*
> *Rivière d'yeux et de paupières.*

> (I live in the river which is diminished and blazing / Dark and limpid / River of eyes and eyelids.)

To indicate the dual quality of his existence, Eluard uses contrasting images:

> *Je vis en même temps dans la famine et*
> *l'abondance*
> *Dans le déarroi du jour et dans l'ombre des ténè-*
> *bres.*

> (I live at the same time in famine and abundance / In the disarray of light and in the order of shadows.)

Though summoned by images, which speak to him (as do images in Baudelaire's "Les correspondances") Eluard still accepts what we may call day-to-day life:

> *Malgré la mort malgré la terre moins réelle*
> *Que les images innombrables de la mort*
> *Je suis sur terre et tout est sur terre avec moi*
> *Les étoiles sont dans mes yeux j'enfante les*
> *mystères*
> *A la mesure de la terre suffisante.*

> (In spite of death in spite of the earth less real / Than innumerable images of death / I am on earth and all is on earth with me / The stars are in my eyes and I give birth to mysteries / In tempo with the adequate earth.)

Within the real structure of images in Eluard there is a kind of *élan vital,* a giving of life to the image as the image gives life to the poet. He does not achieve this by comparison. He does so, rather, in the fashion of Baudelaire, by seizing upon one aspect of nature (a person, a thing, an animal even) which has the inherent qualities that the poetic emotion of the poetic situation demands. This structure, moreover, is physical. In **"Tout dire"** (*Tout dire* [*To Tell Everything*]), to express the quality of freedom, Eluard uses the most homely and the most physical of objects:

> *Pourrai-je dire enfin la porte s'est ouverte*
> *De la cave où les fûts mettaient leur masse som-*
> *bre*

*Sur la vigne où le vin captive le soleil
En employant les mots du vigneron lui-même.*

(Will I be able, then, finally, to say that the door has opened / From the cellar where the casks placed their somber mass / On the vine where the wine makes captive the sun / By using the words of the wine-grower himself.)

The idea of the cellar, the casks, the labor of the vineyard and the growth of the vines, all suggest the acquiring of growth, of something solid being achieved. It is not a question, I believe, of Eliot's objective correlative, which would make of the poem a duality, saying one thing on the verbal level, and implying another on the moral. There is far more feeling and emotive implication in Eluard, the objects correlated constitute not only the poetic situation but also make up a part of the poet's life itself. In other words, Eluard's poetry is far less intellectualized, far more natural, and, in this sense, direct, than, for example, is the poetry of Eliot. There is far more, in Eluard, of movement, of life, of actual *présence* of the image. In the passage just quoted, the image of the door opened is much more an *image vécue;* the notion of captivity (with so many memories of the past), is here construed in the sense of the vine capturing the sun, so that a sense of physical presence is experienced. It is this capacity of association, of tying together—in a living and organic whole—that gives strength to Eluard's poetry. In **"Printemps"** (*Le phénix*) [*The Phoenix*], the reader perceives a deepening of the emotional significance of a commonplace poetic notion, the idea of the rebirth of spring. Eluard begins with an enumeration of the qualities of spring:

*Il y a sur la plage quelques flaques d'eau
Il y a dans les bois des arbres d'oiseaux
La neige fond dans la montagne
Les branches des pommiers brillent de tant de
    fleurs
Que le pâle soleil recule.*

(There are on the beach several pools of water / There are in the woods trees sweet with birds / The snow is melting on the mountain / The branches of the apple trees sparkle from too many flowers / That the pale sun drags back.)

The significance of images, for Eluard, lies in his ability to create reality visually and to attribute such a recreated and reappreciated reality to the woman he loves (*je vis ce printemps près de toi l'innocente,* "I live this spring near to you, woman of innocence"); Eluard enlarges the visual capture of spring to include a statement of value (*Rien de ce qui périt n'a de prises sur toi,* "Nothing which perishes has hold over you"). The capability to revive the image, in the etymological sense of reliving the image, is the basis of Eluard's poetic choice of image. He has entitled a volume of poetry, *La vie immédiate,* and it is this urgency of an immediacy of perception that allows an image to function organically in a poem. In the prose poem **"Nuits partagées"** (from *La vie immédiate*), Eluard writes:

*Quand j'arrive, toutes les barques s'en vont,
    l'orage
recule devant elles. Une ondée délivre les fleurs
obscures, leur éclat recommence et frappe de nou-
    veau*

*les murs de laine.*

(Whenever I arrive, all the boats leave, the storm draws back before them. A wave delivers the dark flowers, their brilliance begins again and strikes anew the walls of wool.)

The verbs are in the present tense, giving both an immediacy and an eternity to the actions. The maritime image, as in Baudelaire, gives an impression of vastness, of *voyage*. There is also a feeling of calmness and tenderness. Parallel with the maritime image is that of a shower which causes the flowers to shine against "the fuzzy garden walls." Both are organic images, dealing with natural phenomena. Both, moreover, are essential to the feeling tone the poet wishes to establish. They are, additionally, delivered from a kind of monotony of tone, of flatness of expression, not only by their liaison with the feeling, but more especially through a kind of "aesthetic distance" or *élévation* that is found in Baudelaire. The poet looks at these images, the poet's eye inspects them, as from above, almost omnisciently. The peculiar combination of intimacy of feeling and aloofness reminds the reader of Baudelaire.

The poem in Eluard's work is relieved from a static quality of mere description by the verbs, which are—for the most part—verbs of action. In **"Nous sommes"** (*Chanson complète* [*Total Song*]), Eluard gives the image visually, calls upon the reader to participate in the movement of the image: *Tu vois le feu du soir qui sort de sa coquille / Et tu vois la forêt enfouie dans ta fraîcheur* ("You see the fire of evening which comes out from its shell / And you see the forest hidden in your freshness"). The contrast between the verb *sort* and the past participle *enfouie* gives an impression of action, both past and present. This invitation to the reader to participate visually and actively in the poem expands the reader's vision; not only is it a momentum or surface participation, but one in depth, one which calls upon the reader to restate to himself the use of images and their significance and to reevaluate for himself a kind of moral grandeur:

*Tu vois la plaine nue aux flancs du ciel traînard
La neige haute comme la mer
Et la mer dans l'azur.*

(You see the bare plain with the sides of the laggard sky / The snow high as the sea / And the sea high in the blue heavens.)

It is a kind of discovery, a kind of transformation of reality. Frequently the reality of the image is based on physical, bodily, characteristics. It is a poetry of physical concreteness: *Des hommes de dessous les sueurs les corps les larmes / Mais qui vont cueillir tous leurs songes* ("Men are underneath sweat bodies tears / But who are going to gather all their dreams").

As in Baudelaire, the preoccupation with the physical is associated with the spiritual. Eluard is obviously not a Catholic poet the way Baudelaire is. Nor does Eluard tend towards Manichaeism, especially in his view of love, as does Baudelaire. Eluard accepts both the spiritual and the physical sensitivity; the two feelings are linked by chains of concerns for the woman he loves, for mankind. Together, they lead towards an understanding of suffering, loneliness, spiritual anguish, and desolation. Eluard, as does Baudelaire, discovers in the physical presence of the person loved a true beauty, profound and moving, one that he would not willingly discard in favor of another; the reader asks himself if this beauty is a step, as on the Platonic ladder, towards a supernatural beauty. The function of the image is to imply such a function:

> *Au son d'un chant prémédité*
> *Tout son corps passe en reflets en éclats*
> *Son corps pavé de pluie armé de parfums tendres*
> *Démêlé le fuseau matinal de sa vie.* (**"Médieuses,"** *Médieuses*)

> (At the sound of a premeditated song / All her body passes in reflections in outbursts / Her body paved with rain armed with tender perfumes / Unwound the matinal distaff of her life.)

The appeal to all the senses is in the *lignée* of Baudelaire and Valéry. There is the auditive (*chant* ); visual (*reflets, éclats*); olfactory (*parfums tendres*); touch (the image of the unwinding distaff, an action performed by hands); even, in a way, taste (the moisture implied in *pluie* associated with *corps*). Eluard's imagery, as does Baudelaire's, works on all these levels. The total impression is one, in Baudelaire's phrase, of *luxe, calme* et *volupté*.

In a total envisioning of reality, a problem arises: Where does a poet fit into this scheme of universal beauty based on the immediate sensations? Eluard places himself in the middle of the universe he has thus created; he tries to identify himself by placing himself visually in the center of the image. In the poem **"Médieuses,"** Eluard writes:

> *Près de l'aigrette du grand pont*
> *L'orgueil au large*
> *J'attends tout ce que j'ai connu*
> *Comblée d'espace scintillant*
> *Ma mémoire est immense.*

> (Near the crest of the big bridge / Pride spread wide / I await all that I have known / Filled with shining space / My memory is immense.)

Eluard speaks here through the figure of the *médieuse,* or a myth of woman; in a Valéryean sense, as does Valéry in *La jeune parque,* Eluard describes himself. In the midst of his own solitude, in a complete *dénuement* of all other accompanying emotions, the poet waits. He is "filled with shining space," he has become one with the world which is the real source of his poetic imagery. It is the *je universel* that Pierre Emmanuel finds in Eluard. The poet's memory thus becomes the memory of the universe, and this memory, in turn, informs the imagery of the world. The imagery in the poems contains a perception of universality. Although Eluard does not attempt to teach he does wish to know some kind of reason why the world was created. Eluard does not think as does Valéry. Eluard's images always try to prove an affirmation of the principle of such knowledge. His poetry many times can be read and understood as the story of how a poet seeks knowledge. Underneath the surface of the images, the reader comes upon a biographical element of Eluard's search in this respect, which is related to *mémoire,* but is closer to *souvenir.* In **"Vivre"** (**Le livre ouvert,** I), Eluard writes:

> *Ah le garçon lucide que je fus et que je suis*
> *Devant la blancheur des faibles filles aveugles*
> *Plus belles que la lune blonde fine usée*
> *Par le reflet des chemins de la vie.*

> (Ah the clear-minded boy I was and am / In front of the whiteness of the weak blind girls / More beautiful than the blond delicate moon worn out / By the reflection of the roads of life.)

The implicit humanity of the image is typical of Eluard, his participation in the human condition that is a constant theme of his verse. The creation of an image, according to Surrealist belief, is a product of the mind, a completely private image, pure in its spontaneity, oneiric in its origin. True Surrealist doctrine would deny, as had André Breton, that poetry—as imagery founded on the reality of the world—served a function beyond its own adventure. In the poem just quoted, Eluard, I think, goes beyond true Surrealism and shows a deep desire to help men by his example and his courage. It is true that many poems by Eluard exist only as a kind of spontaneous illustrations of what the poet is feeling at the moment, the more or less confirmed "picture" in the mind. Much Surrealist art is in this vein; Picasso and Dali illustrated books for the Surrealist writers. Yet I am convinced there is a deeper belief in Eluard. While maintaining the mystery of the image, Eluard refuses to create literature (especially in the sense of Romantic, poetic pose) and wishes always to be a part of others' lives. In **"Vivre"** Eluard writes:

> *Présence ma vertu dans chaque main visible*
> *La seule mort c'est solitude*
> *Du délice en furie de furie en clarté*
> *Je me construis entier à travers tous les êtres*
> *A travers tous les temps au sol et dans les nues*
> *Saisons passantes je suis jeune*
> *Et fort à force d'avoir vécu*
> *Je suis jeune et mon sang s'élève sur mes ruines.*

> (Presence my virtue in each visible hand / The only death is solitude / From delight to madness from madness to light / I build myself anew complete through all beings / Through all times on the ground and in the clouds / Passing seasons I am young / And strong by dint of having lived / I am young and my blood rises as from my ruins.)

Thus Eluard's poetry does not end up in nihilism as was true of the Dadaist experiments. His effort is not to destroy, but to build up. It is true that he reduces the appearance of things, objects, nature, even people in a kind of process of volatilization. The earlier experiment called pure poetry was a purification in that it was similar to a chemical reduction to the purest essence of the thing, as in Mallarmé, or to the purest intellectual perception, as in Valéry. In Eluard, however, *le mot pulvérisé* ("the pulverized word") is reconstructed: *je me construis entier,* through all the experiences of others, of time, of nature. So that Eluard can say, *Saisons passantes je suis . . . ,* so that he can also say that his *sang s'élève sur ses ruines.*

The employment of imagery is the process of reducing the visible world to a fine powder, as the ore is crushed to remake, from the elements, an enduring structure; in this structure, his own inner vision is sensitized and the external world takes on the purity of light. Critics frequently refer to this process as poetic alchemy. In a way it is a search for the original world the *recherche de l'enfance perdue* of Rimbaud. But whereas Rimbaud's world ended in flight, Eluard's world ends in a restatement of personal sincerity and moral integrity which lies at the basis of his choice of imagery. Further, this world is made one, integrated into a complete and whole statement. The reader is reminded, in reading Eluard, of Baudelaire's appreciation of Hugo in *L'art romantique:*

> Victor Hugo was, from the beginning, the man best endowed, the most visibly chosen to express, through poetry, that which I will call the *mystery of life*. Nature which places before us, whichever way we turn, and which envelops us like a mystery, shows herself under several simultaneous states, each one of which, according to the extent it reacts in us, our intelligence and our sensitivity, is reflected more acutely in our hearts: form, attitude and movement, light and color, sound and harmony.

In the eighteenth stanza of **"Règnes"** (*Le livre ouvert,* I), for example, the reader can see a similar organization of materials into a single integrated view of reality:

> *Les fleurs les feuilles les épines*
> *Redevinrent visibles*
> *Les bourgeons et la rosée*
> *Virent le jour*
> *Sous le fleuve de mai*
> *Une voile écarlate*
> *Fit battre le pouls du vent*
> *Sous couleurs de vie et d'espace*
> *Sous forme de légers nuages*
> *Sans un frisson*
> *Le sein de l'aube consentait.*

> (The flowers the leaves the thorns / Became visible again / The birds and the dew saw the day / Under the river of May / A scarlet sail / Caused the pulse of the wind to beat / Under the color of life and space / Under the form of light clouds / Without a shudder / The breast of the dawn gave its consent.)

The form of the verse reflects the flowing quality of the images of the poem (opening buds, flowers, rivers, clouds), which tend towards a fixed state reflected in the simple literary past tense of the verbs. The attitude towards these phenomena of the world is both acceptance of the image itself, the *don du poème,* as well as a simultaneous refusal to hold on to what is given, a kind of consent, as *le sein de l'aube consentait.* There is light: The entire poem has to do with light in all of its density (*jour,* the heavy light of *écarlate*) and opacity (*nuages*). The *harmonie du vers* is apparent: the repetition of the consonants *f* and *v.* The poem expresses through such a combination, as Baudelaire finds in Hugo, *le mystère de la vie,* which is the secret of Eluard's understanding of the reality of the world as he brings it over into the poem and redefines both the unwilling from his subconscious and also the image reticent to be captured, in a very moving statement of the necessity of acknowledging the real. And from this acknowledgment, Eluard can proceed to an understanding of his own solitude and how this understanding makes the real more

meaningful. The way is one of images; the functioning of the images, in turn, makes possible a constant awareness of both oneself and the world. (pp. 29-49)

> *Robert Nugent, in his* Paul Eluard, *Twayne Publishers, Inc., 1974, 153 p.*

## Max Adereth    (essay date 1987)

[*In the following excerpt from his introduction to Eluard's* Selected Poems, *Adereth outlines the major characteristics of Eluard's poetry.*]

A great poet does not really need lengthy introductions or sophisticated commentaries in order to be appreciated. This is especially true of Eluard, whose poetry is that of the real world. To anyone who has but a drop of 'the milk of human kindness', i.e. to anyone who feels a sense of kinship in the world of fellow human beings, the voice of Eluard will sound like the voice of a close friend. All the same, a few words concerning his versification, his imagery and his main themes may help to add to our enjoyment by providing a number of simple, easily recognisable guidelines. The chief characteristic of Eluard's poetic technique is the great variety of metres he uses; some are fairly common among French poets, others less so. He refuses to be the slave of any one metre, always choosing a rhythmic structure which is adapted to the content of his poem and which relies on the positioning of key words in order to emphasise or clarify the meaning. It is often assumed that Eluard spurns the alexandrine on principle as being too formal and too traditional, but this is not really true. Apart from the fact that in the twenties, his surrealist friends used to chaff him for his 'unorthodox' interest in the alexandrine, it so happens that this particular metre occurs time and again in his poems, from the 1924 **"L'égalité des sexes"**(**"The Equality of the Sexes"**) in *Mourir de ne pas mourir,* which is made up of three quatrains in alexandrines, to the 1951 poem, **"Tout dire,"** which is made up of twenty-three quatrains and uses no other metre throughout. To Eluard, the alexandrine was neither a must nor a taboo, it was, like all other metres, a metre to be used when the occasion required it. Neither is it quite correct to regard Eluard as opposed to rhymes as such, even though he once told Yves Sandre that 'the rhyme is dangerous because it lulls you to sleep.' For here again, it is the content which decides whether rhymes would add to or detract from the overall idea which the poet wishes to convey.

Another important feature of Eluard's poetry is that he never, or very seldom, uses punctuation. Here he merely follows Apollinaire, and for the same reason, believing that in a poem, punctuation is unnecessary, because the rhythm and the sense create their own natural punctuation. Unlike Apollinaire, however, Eluard does not rely on the lack of punctuation to make his verse ambiguous and capable of more than one interpretation, but rather to increase the self-evident meaning of what he is trying to say. A number of students who read Eluard for the first time were somewhat surprised to be told that he does not use punctuation—they themselves had not even noticed it, so compelling was the inner logic and the structure of what the poet had to say. One device which helps to forget the absence of punctuation is the skilful use of repetition. Sometimes, an expression regularly occurs at the beginning of each line, such as the "Que voulez-vous" in **"Couvre-feu,"** sometimes, it is found, no less regularly, at the end of each stanza, as is the case with "J'écris ton nom" in **"Liberté."** These repetitions carry the reader or the hearer away and create their own atmosphere, an atmosphere which varies with each poem; it ranges from incantation to strking antithesis, from the music of a soothing lullaby to the indignation at the sight of injustice and cruelty.

With regard to imagery, it is characterised by its appeal to the senses and the importance of concrete objects and of everyday things. For Eluard, to be wholly part of the world, the world of matter and the world of men, meant above all to experience the former to the full, and to share with the inhabitants of the latter the most natural, most commonplace sensations and feelings. This explains why he was able to invest almost anything with a poetic quality. In this respect, the poem, **"Gabriel Péri,"** is not only a tribute to a martyr of the Resistance, it is also in part a kind of *Ars Poetica,* of which the golden rule is that the simplest of words are those which are the real texture of life, and consequently of poetry:

> Il y a des mots qui font vivre
> Et ce sont des mots innocents

It was once said of Racine that the secret of his effective imagery was that he almost did away with images. The same might be said of Eluard, for his images are the very opposite of refined metaphors, they belong to life as we know it. No wonder that Gaston Bachelard was able to say that in Eluard's poetry, 'images are right': they do not take us away from reality, they rather plunge us straight into it. It is significant that the poet seldom uses similes: to him, happiness is not *like* the light, it *is* the light:

> Que le bonheur soit la lumière

It is equally significant that he is so fond of personification. He speaks, for example, of

> Une tranquille rue rouillée
> Qui n'a jamais été jeune

> A quiet rusty street
> That was never young

thus endowing the street with character, colour and old age. Eluard's favourite images are drawn from the human body, from nature, and from familiar surroundings. A good illustration of the 'basic' character of his poetry is the importance of the four elements, fire and water in the first place, and air and earth to a lesser extent. Sometimes, an image is quite unexpected, as is the case in the line,

> La terre est bleue comme une orange

> The earth is blue like an orange

but this is neither gratuitous nor a piece of utter nonsense: the earth is indeed like an orange because it is round, and an orange can turn blue when it is mouldy.

A clue to Eluard's approach to poetic style and imagery is provided by what he says in *Les sentiers et les routes de la poésie* (*The Paths and the Roads of Poetry*), a book which came out in 1952 and is made up of five radio talks he gave he gave in 1949. Two statements stand out. The first one asserts that 'nothing is more horrible than poeticised language, than words which are too nice and are gracefully linked to other pearls. Genuine poetry includes coarse nudity, anchors which are not the sheet-anchors of last hope, tears which are not rainbow-hued . . . *For poetry is in life.*' In the second one, we read that the real poet eagerly listens to the 'obscure news of the world' which is supplied by 'grass, pebbles, dirt, splendours', and that his task is to convey all the delights of language, the language of 'the man in the street' and 'the sage', the language 'of a woman, a child, a lunatic'. The man who uttered these words was no longer a surrealist, yet as he spoke in this vein, he was truer than ever to the ideals of his youth. For it was one of the surrealists' ambitions to give poetry the aim and the content which Lautréamont had in mind when he said that the goal of poetry was practical truth ('La poésie doit avoir pour but la vérité practique') and that it should be made by all, not by one person ('La poésie doit être faite par tous, non par un').

Finally, the main themes which are found in Eluard's poetry are love, brotherhood and kindness. The first one is to be expected from most poets. Eluard's originality, which he shares with Aragon, is that he is the poet of the couple. In this respect, his sense of genuine love and his sense of human solidarity are complementary, for the couple is the first step towards a society of brotherhood. When he took part in a surrealist questionnaire in the twenties, one of the questions that was put to him was: what do you think of a man who betrays his beliefs in order to please the woman he loves? This is what he replied: 'The cause which I defend is also the cause of love. To demand such a token from an honest man can only destroy his love or lead to his death.' Eluard looked upon love as providing physical pleasure and human warmth, and above all as the antidote to loneliness. In the following lines, which succinctly sum up his approach, love and commitment are inextricably linked (the lines come from **"Notre vie,"** the last poem in *Le temps déborde*):

> Nous n'irons plus au but un par un mais par
>    deux
> Nous connaissant par deux nous nous con-
>    naîtrons tous
> Nous nous aimerons tous et nos enfants riront
> Da la légende noire où pleure un solitaire

> We shall not reach the goal one by one but in
>    twos
> Knowing each other in twos we shall all know
>    one another
> We shall all love one another and our children
>    will laugh
> At the sombre legend in which a lonely man is
>    weeping

The couple being the embryonic form of humanity reconciled with itself, Eluard could declare in 1947 that 'to love is our only reason for living.' One can distinguish three love cycles in his life and in his poetry: the Gala cycle (1913-1929), in which love is youthful, pure, idealised and self-absorbing; the Nusch cycle (1929-1946), in which love gradually takes on the form of the highest form of human communication, a fact eloquently illustrated by the increasing use of 'nous' (we, us) instead of 'je' (I); and the Dominique cycle (1949-1952) in which the love of the elderly poet for a young woman restores both his confidence and his resolve to contribute to the happiness of others.

The theme of brotherhood is an extension of love. Loving a woman and loving his fellow human beings were to Eluard part of the same process of overcoming solitude. In the 1948 preface to the **Poèmes politiques,** he summed up his own personal and intellectual development as an evolution:

> De l'horizon d'un seul à l'horizon de tous

> From the horizon of a single man to the horizon
> of all

Both his surrealism and his communism must be seen as attempts to be at one with other people, to share their dreams and their yearnings for happiness. One of his favourite images was the use of the intimate pronoun 'tu' in order to express kinship, as this is reserved for close friends. The highest tribute he could pay Péri was to call him a friend, 'tutoyons-le', and the supreme lesson of the martyr's death in his eyes was that all men should be friends, 'tutoyons-nous'. Some people may regret the fact that his ideal of brotherhood should have led him to political involvement, but this must be seen as part of Eluard's realism: he knew that mere declarations were not enough, that purely individual gestures were limited, and that it was by reorganising society that one could lay the basis for genuine human solidarity. One need not share his political beliefs in order to respect the sincerity of his commitment and the humanitarian motives which were responsible for it.

The last theme which deserves a brief mention is kindness. This makes him almost unique among poets, at any rate among his contemporaries, if one excepts Bertolt Brecht. The other surrealists and the other committed writers of his generation were more violent, more impatient, more intolerant than he. Although in the great majority of cases, their love for humanity was genuine and deep, it was not accompanied by the gentleness which characterises Eluard. Aragon, for example, wrote movingly about the French women who had been tortured in the Auschwitz concentration camp; could he also have written the poem in which Eluard expressed his sorrow at the sight of a woman ill-treated by an angry crowd because she had slept with German soldiers? He might have agreed with his friend that she was far less guilty than the real 'collaborators', but only Eluard could have found it in his heart to call her a victim who was unaware of what she was doing. Although far from being a Christian, the poet could have paraphased Christ and told his countrymen: 'Forgive her, for she knows not what she does.' All the same, again like Christ, and indeed like all great moral reformers, he never allowed his kindness to extend to the tyrants, the executioners and the torturers. His kindness was allied to a great sense of justice, and without any trace of petty vindictiveness, he could calmly assert that

> Il n'y a pas de matin plus éclatant
> Que le matin où les traitres succombent
> Il n'y a pas de salut sur la terre
> Tant que l'on peut pardonner aux bourreaux

> There is no dawn more glorious
> Than the dawn when traitors fall
> There is no salvation on earth
> So long as torturers are forgiven

One of the most revealing signs of his evolution as a man and as a poet is provided by the three *Critique de la poésie* which he wrote. The first one, which is part of the 1932 **La vie immédiate,** aggressively asserts that the finest poems are those which denounce 'the reign of the bourgeois, the reign of coppers and priests'; the second one, included in the 1942 **Poésie et vérité,** and still called a 'critique' of poetry, is neither aggressive nor polemical: it contrasts all that is good and beautiful in life with the cruelty that led to the killing and torture of great artists—Garcia Lorca, Saint-Pol Roux and Decour—; the final one, entitled **"La poésie doit avoir pour but la vérité pratique,"** and included in the **Poèmes politiques,** represents the final 'critique' of poetry: in it, Eluard replies to his 'exacting friends' who are unwilling and unable to follow him whenever he sings of his 'whole street'; he tells them that he, for his part, has discovered that the great secret of genuine poetry is the knowledge that men

> Ont besoin d'être unis d'espérer de lutter
> Pour expliquer le monde et pour le transformer

> Need to be united to hope to struggle
> In order to explain the world and to change it
> (pp. 20-7)

> *Max Adereth, in an introduction to* Paul Eluard: Selected Poems, *edited and translated by Gilbert Bowen, John Calder, 1987, pp. 9-27.*

## Jean-Jacques Thomas (essay date 1987)

[*In the following excerpt, Thomas compares Eluard's poetic rendering of the massacre at Guernica during the Spanish Civil War in "La victoire de Guernica" with his later essay, "Guernica." The unmarked prose quotations within the text of the excerpt are taken from the essay "Guernica."*]

Of all the military atrocities perpetrated between the two world wars, the bombing of Guernica probably had the greatest impact upon the writers and artists of that era. Fixed in time:

> *Le 26 avril 1937, jour de marché, dans les premières heures de l'après-midi, les avions allemands au service de Franco bombardèrent Guernica durant trois heures et demie par escadrilles se relevant tour à tour;*

> (In the early afternoon of April 26th [market day] Guernica was bombed for three and a half hours by relays of German Air Squadrons under General Franco's orders;)

and in space:

> *Guernica. C'est une petite ville de Biscaye, capi-*

*tale traditionnelle du Pays basque. C'est là que s'élevait le chêne, symbole sacré des traditions et des libertés basques. Guernica n'a qu'une importance historique et sentimentale.*

(Guernica: a small town and the traditional capital of the Basque country. It was here that grew the oak of Guernica, sacred symbol of Basque traditions and Basque freedom. Guernica's importance is purely historical and sentimental.)

the reality of this event was bound to attract the attention of the author of **Yeux fertiles** and **Donner à voir** who held that poetry should first and foremost reveal "le visage de la vérité" (the face of truth). The event obviously lent itself to journalistic writing and was reported in great detail. Nonetheless it was to this same event (perhaps better suited to the epic form since it so magnified reality) that the poet turned for material he later exploited to symbolic effect [in **"La victoire de Guernica"**]. While depleting the events of their referential value, this symbolic effect progressively drains them of their reality, transposing them into a system founded on language universals and totally independent of the mimetic event which originally triggered production of the poem's verbal system.

The mere name *Guernica* binds the text to reality since, as Derrida points out, it acts on a "monumémoire" or "monumemory" and constitutes a whole store of information related to this particular event.

Now, for there to be reference, the referent (the sign's third element and its only non-symbolic one—contingent on objective reality and thus "parasitic"), must figure explicitly in the text so that its textual presence can act as an extra-linguistic shifter, as something which speaks about reality while acting as a support for the other purely symbolic constituents of the verbal sign.

The name *Guernica* constitutes the poem's only historical emblem: it indicates the constraints and imperatives of time and space, imposed by history, and acts both as milestone and textual boundary. Against this background of reality the text constructs an autonomous sign system of its own. Thus from the title onwards, the exclusively referential value of the name *Guernica* is negated since, though primarily designating an atrocious massacre, the effect is counterbalanced by its link with "victoire"—"victory" being a term which contradicts what "we know" about events in Guernica as reported in the press.

This system of bipolar opposition provides a preliminary model for the entire text in that it is based on the principle of contradiction. Thus the referential presence underlined by *Guernica* exists for the sole purpose of allowing the opposite pole (signaled by *victoire*) to be developed. *Guernica*'s denotation and connotations have no value *per se*, since here Eluard is not concerned with pseudomimesis of the type found in the Annals of History.

Inevitably, though, one must recognize the proper name's particular function in this system. As Benveniste points out, the proper name's distinguishing linguistic feature is that, by its very nature, it incorporates its own actualization and self-determination, these being intrinsic components of any proper name. Whence the special referential

status of a text engendered by a verbal component of this type. In an utterance such as *la victoire du génocide* (the victory of the genocide) one could recognize a contradiction similar to the one expressed in *la Victoire de Guernica*. There is, however, a fundamental difference between the two: "genocide" refers to an atopical and, alas, universal reality, while *Guernica* implies the reader's encyclopedic knowledge—knowledge which cannot possibly be anhistoric. The poem's contradiction, that is to say its *meaning*, is, of course, clear without referring to the event. But the event's importance (it justifies the text in relation to a particular system of meaning) in no way diminishes it as a referential anchor, one which functions as a *trigger* rather than a matrix. This is demonstrated by the fact that when Eluard wanted to commemorate the actual historic event, its site and meaning, he eliminated *victory* from the title (and consequently the principle of contradiction the word provided), keeping only "Guernica." This transformation in turn alters the way the text is treated: its meaning fades and what was elliptic, paratactic, and antithetical in the poem becomes direct, explanatory, and justificatory in the commemorative discourse:

*On a tout lu dans les journaux en buvant son café; quelque part en Europe, une légion d'assassins écrase la fourmilière humaine. On se représente mal un enfant éventré, une femme décapitée, un homme vomissant tout son sang d'un seul coup.*

(People read all about it in the newspaper over coffee at breakfast: somewhere in Europe a legion of murderers had crushed a human anthill. It is hard to imagine a child disembowelled, a woman beheaded, or a man suddenly vomiting all his blood.)

Whereas the poem only exists by virtue of the tension created between deceptively vague reference on the one hand, and a system of symbols that refer to a highly specific context on the other, the commemorative discourse refers only to the specific event. If one compares the two versions, written fourteen years apart, the differences between the two modes of writing are quite obvious from the very first verse.

Beau monde des masures
De la mine et des champs

(Beautiful world of hovels
mines and fields)

becomes, in the second version,

*Les gens de Guernica sont de petites gens. Ils vivent dans leur ville depuis bien longtemps. Leur vie est composée d'une goutte de richesse; et d'un flot de misère.*

(The people of Guernica are humble folk. They have been living in their town for a very long time. Their life is made up of a drop of wealth and a flood of poverty.)

Although in 1919 Eluard wrote in *Littérature* "Let us reduce, transform the displeasing language which satisfies mere talkers, language as dead as the crowns which sit upon our equally dead brows," and goes on to propose an aesthetics "aiming at an immediate rapport between the object and the person who sees it" (**Physique de la Poésie** [Physics of Poetry]), when he speaks of the event itself, he cannot help developing an explanatory, metadiscursive level of discourse. Even when interpolating fragments of the original poem in the prose commentary, he feels it necessary to modify them so that the gap between the two not be too obvious.

Thus:

> Ils vous ont fait payer le pain
> Le ciel la terre l'eau le sommeil
> Et la misère
> De votre vie
>
> (They made you pay for the bread
> the sky the earth the water the sleep
> and the misery
> of your life with your life)

becomes

> *Ils vous ont fait payer le pain*
> *De votre vie*
> *Ils vous ont fait payer le ciel la terre l'eau le som-*
>     *meil*
> *Et même la misère noire*
> *De votre vie.*
>
> (They made you pay for the bread
> of your life with your life
> they made you pay for the sky the earth the
>     water the sleep
> and even the black misery
> of your life with your life.)

The repetition of *De votre vie* and the interpolation of

*Eluard (kneeling) with Philippe Soupault, André Breton, and Théodore Fraenkel in a performance of Breton and Soupault's play,* Vous m'oublierez.

*même* introduce a hierarchical distinction, whereas originally the mere juxtaposition and accumulation of words suggested equivalent, similar components, all equally essential to the life of the *beau monde*. "Bread" becomes something one acquires, the result of work; "sky," "earth," "water," and "sleep" are something given. *Même* is the author's intervention and a comment since the adverb hails both a reiteration and an amplification, so that *misère* becomes a sort of superlative in relation to the other terms, as is further underlined by the addition of *noire*. Or, if one were to use the terminology of traditional rhetoric, one might say that whereas a metabole suffices in **"La victoire de Guernica," "Guernica"** is more explicit and takes the reader from one step to the next. And in case the reader or listener did not notice these distinctions, the prose commentary points them out quite unequivocally:

> *Leur vie est composée de tout petits bonheurs et d'un très grand souci: celui du lendemain. Demain il faut manger et demain il faut vivre. Aujourd'hui, l'on espère. Aujourd'hui, l'on travaille.*
>
> (Their life is composed of small joys and one great worry: that of tomorrow. Tomorrow they must eat and tomorrow they must live. Today they hope. Today they work.)

This type of discourse is quite foreign to that of our poem, since, as Nicole Charbois notes, in the poem

> "Eluard makes an utterance, then remains silent: no comment whatsoever. . . . Picasso conveyed the violence by the shrieking and convulsed colours and shapes he used, but Eluard chose silence to make us aware of this violence. He holds in his cry, masters his language—but he says all."

There is no need for further demonstration since examples so far given abundantly prove the difference between the way the poem and the commemorative text treat the referential given. The didascalic inscription differs too: in the poem the symbolism generated by the referential trigger leads one to the meaning without there being any need for circumstantial reference. In the commemorative text, reference is the force which maintains the legitimate meaning, controlling and producing it by the discourse's underlying naturalism.

Thus a study of **"La victoire de Guernica"** is also a study of a language system whose only postulate is to negate precise reference and endow it with a symbolic importance which transcends any *mimesis* of the specific, transposing it into a universal and anhistoric mode.

In our introduction, we pointed out the *antithetical* character of the title and, to that end, emphasized that the antithesis was not founded solely on the semantic qualities of *Guernica,* since this word, being a proper name, retains its essential designatory quality and implies, in the process of perception, the actualization of a set of extra-linguistic connotations that are indissociable from its denotative function. Indeed it is this aspect which creates the poem's special status, and leads me to place it in the category of *topological poetics,* since the fundamental trigger of the poem's system appears as a sign-signal. This process is distinct from the poetic practice of opposing two verbal signs in such a way that each is deprived of its complete sign status. For example, when Leiris writes *Étrusques aux frusques étriquées* (Etruscans in tight togs), *Étrusques* is only used so that it can appear as a reverse contraction (or porte-manteau word) of *frusques étriquées* and vice versa: *étr*(iquées fr)*usques*. Here language is only fighting itself: no extratextual reference is ever involved in this type of game which never goes beyond the simple sign's specific properties—that of the meeting of signifier and signified.

It would not be rash to claim that once the title's emblematic effect and its value as a referential trigger are established, the poem's significance and its role as a "universal and atemporal monument" are created in a language which brings into play an exclusively verbal system. Extratextual reference plays only a minor role in relation to the poem's main preoccupation, which is to show language pitted against itself. Thus in topological poetics, the status of reference is that of a pretext which legitimizes and justifies the creation of a complex sign whose referent is the excluded third component. Nonetheless its impact is felt marginally all along the symbolic chain, since, within the framework of the co-presence of an encyclopedic knowledge in each linguistic element's field, an allusion to the name *Guernica*—and, by the same token, to its referential context—can be attributed to each element.

This explains how, in the first stanza, *masures, mine,* and *champs* (hovels, mine, and fields) can be seen as offering a precise description of the lifestyle of Guernica's inhabitants; though one would have to be sufficiently well-informed to assess the accuracy of such a statement—a geographer's or sociologist's task rather than a literary commentator's. In fact, *masures, mine,* and *champs* all serve as general signs for a hard and laborious life; they are used in order to contrast with *beau monde,* a fixed expression which in French usually designates the idle, elegant world of the privileged. The sole purpose of this antithetical disjunction is to herald a theme which runs through the entire poem: namely, that the little these people possessed was a "treasure" compared to their plight after the disaster. This theme of life seen as a treasure as long as there is hope returns covertly in stanzas V, VIII, IX, XII and overtly in stanza XIII in a paradoxical formulation accentuated by the homophony of the two rhyming words:

> Hommes réels pour qui le désespoir
> Alimente le feu dévorant de l'espoir
>
> (Real men for whom despair
> feeds the devouring fire of hope.)

The importance given here to *espoir*—and it is of some intertextual comfort that Malraux was later to choose it as the title of his own account of the Spanish Civil War—brings to the text a set of variants such as: *feuilles vertes* (green leaves), green being associated with hope in French; *de printemps* (of spring), the season of germination; and *lait pur* (pure milk), *milk* is a metonym for motherhood, for promise, and *pure* contributes the image's meliorative value by connoting natural innocence and fragility.

The thematic pole opposing this *beau monde* is obviously *mort* [dead] and *vide* (empty), lines 6-7, which transform *feuilles vertes . . . dans les yeux* (green leaves in their eyes), line 20, into *roses rouges dans les yeux* (red roses in their eyes), lines 26-27. For here "red" is doubly overdetermined, first by *sang* (blood), line 28, which follows it, introducing violence into the field of utterance, and, second, by the fact that *rose rouge* is a metonym for extreme intensity and also the very end of a cycle. A metaphoric extension of this opposition between foliage and flower is embodied in the formula which contains the poem's exhortation: *ouvrons ensemble le dernier bourgeon de l'avenir* (let us open the future's last leaf bud together). *Bourgeon* (bud) refers directly to "leaf," to "green" and thus to "hope," whereas in the flower system the precise term for bud would be *bouton* rather than *bourgeon*.

The asyndetic construction of the third stanza and of its first line introduces a new cumulative series of notations which are presented as a figurative description not of a lifestyle, this time, but of the inhabitants themselves—though the description's "naturalist" flavor is again transformed into a negative value by an exclusively verbal semantic artifice. However, unlike the first stanza where the semantic opposition to the "beautiful world" was direct, disjunction now occurs within the syntactic framework implying the restitution of the fixed expression "bon à quelque chose" (good for something) and indicates a positive value, good for action or a particular state. Here *feu* (fire) and *froid* (cold) represent the entire paradigm of climatic conditions since they evoke its two extremes. *Bons au feu . . . bons au froid* (good for the fire good for the cold) is thus the interchangeable equivalent of "good for all weather" as far as meaning is concerned, but adds a certain concreteness to the utterance. The accumulation which follows it brings together a group of negative elements: *refus, injures, coups* (refusals, insults, blows) which, through analogical contamination, give *nuit* (night) (an *a priori* neutral element) a similar pejorative value that it retains from this first context when it recurs a second time in *la couleur monotone de notre nuit* (the monotonous color of our night); "monotonous," usually laden with negative presuppositions, confirms this value. Thus the effect of semantic contrast relies upon the opposition between "good," considered as positive, and the negative value of the elements to which this term is structurally attached and which all indicate the natural or man-made atrocities these people suffered.

This type of syntactic dislocation of a fixed structure is used again in stanza V, since the syntagm *de votre vie* (of your life) can be linked equally well to both the preceding nouns (*le pain, le ciel . . . la misère de votre vie* [the bread, the sky . . . the misery of your life]), and to the verb if one allows for a stylistic inversion such as *Ils vous ont fait payer de votre vie le pain Le ciel . . .* (They made you pay with your life for the bread, the sky . . . ). In this case, the phrase would imply a simple *quid pro quo,* whereas the first structure would elaborate upon the idea of "treasure," by insinuating that "they" (*ils*) have so indulged in excess that they even put a price on the most complete destitution. This interpretation would concur with *ils exagèrent* (they exaggerate) in line 18. One should note, however, that any partial interpretation matters little here: for the dislocation of the syntactic structure creates ambiguity and, unlike what happens in the second stanza, where the ensuing disjunction concretizes the semantic opposition between the two poles (good/bad), in stanza five, dislocation reinforces meaning to the point of redundancy, since the co-presence of the two formulations serves to reinforce both of them and corroborate the notion of excess, being themselves a type of "overflow" of meaning.

In both cases, the use of syntactical possibilities forces language into a state of internal ambivalence and the resulting dichotomy removes any possibility of direct, unitary denoting: it produces a meaning which establishes either redundancy or opposition, as the case may be. It seems clear, then, that referential mimesis, always based on an utterance's direct meaning, is overshadowed by a symbolic process which introduces a certain number of exclusively verbal distinctions which then proceed to take over.

The asyntactic utterance in line 8, *La mort coeur renversé* (death heart overturned), derives its force from the encounter of verbal effects on different levels. The absence of an explicit grammatical or semantic link between the two parts is naturally perceived to be a case of symbolic disorder, the precise nature of their relation depending on how the reader construes it. Yet one cannot overlook the well-known expression *coeur renversé,* which adds to its physical meaning (upside down, upset, or even knocked over) a quite special psychological, figurative value making it the semantic equivalent of "emotionally upset" and "overwhelmed." Such an interpretation would create a consecutive link between "death" and "upset heart": it is death that upsets. But *renversé* is also a synonym of "changed to the exact opposite," which is precisely what death has done in relation to the victims' former state. In this case *renversé* would simply appear as an expansion of "death," with a more limited meaning focusing on the result of the latter. Naturally one would still have to explain its association with "heart" since, given this meaning, "upset" and "heart" cannot constitute a fixed expression. But one can envisage that the sequence *coeur renversé* (taken in the sense of upside-down heart), instead of being a pseudo-mimetic representation of the victims' situation, plays an emblematic role in relation to "death" and that both terms could be joined to make a heraldic description. If a "beating heart" is a symbol of life, *coeur renversé* is its opposite: the blazon of death. The structure *La mort coeur renversé* would thus introduce the bearer (the enemy) and his sign, his "speaking arms." This brings us back, indirectly, to the original context, war; and also introduces the adversary, an undefined *Ils* (They) mentioned in the fifth stanza. Here again meaning results from symbolic densification (compression) and cannot, therefore, be reduced to singular, unequivocal reference.

Just as the hovels, mine, and fields could be seen as referring directly to the real world of Guernica's inhabitants, so the characterization in the sixth stanza could make us think that these are fragments of description referring metonymically to the chronicle's "nazi pilots." In fact the undefined "They" marks the moment at which the poem breaks loose from its specific frame of reference and introduces a generic dimension devoid of any specific actualization. What appear are thus generic qualities—hypocrisy, vanity, avarice. The opacity of *Ils saluaient les cadavres*

(They saluted the corpses) hides a semantic short-cut which plays on the choice of a term indicative of finality instead of something in progress as expected. "Corpses" can refer just as well to "dead heroes" as to victims of military atrocities—but that is beside the point. What the expression "They saluted the corpses" does indicate is a fetishistic and ritualized (salute) taste for death, the complete opposite of "life" (fifth stanza) and thus of the positive pole presented here as the only remaining goods of (future) victims. So it is that the overall effect of these connotations is to establish a semantic field based on the notion of excess. This is confirmed semantically in line 18 by *Ils persévèrent ils exagèrent ils ne sont pas de notre monde* (They persevere they exaggerate they are not of our world). "They are not of our world" doubly defines the definition since, over and above the opposition life/death, the utterance also incorporates the opposition excess/destitution continued in the stanzas which follow. The "leaves," "spring," and "pure milk," in addition to their previously mentioned values, characterize women and children and so connote the victims' natural simplicity (these victims being "real men") in contrast, let us say, to *sou* in line 15; for a cent connotes a society which is organized, artificially based on monetary exchange (a society of conventions, just as the use of "salute" has already indicated).

The antithetical formulation of stanza XI

> La peur et le courage de vivre et de mourir
> La mort si difficile et si facile
>
> (The fear of living and dying and the courage to
>   do both
> death so difficult and so easy)

could be put anywhere in the poem, since it merely restates in an explicitly paradoxical and abstract formulation what the various concrete expressions have thus far sought to reveal: living out one's daily life is a continual and hard-won victory, so precarious that at any moment it may be interrupted. Similarly, death, always easy, within reach the moment one gives up, is nonetheless relentlessly deferred by effort and work. As it stands, this statement applies not just to the inhabitants of Guernica, but to many others, and this explains the way we interpret "pariahs" (line 36) in the final stanza: as a term used to generalize, it destroys once and for all the poem's specific meaning and gives it a collective dimension.

If it were still necessary to prove that stanzas VI, VII, XIII, and XIV lead us to read the poem as a generalization, it would suffice to note that they are the only ones which do not appear in **"Guernica"**; that is to say, the only ones excluded from the substance of the chronicle, since, necessarily, the latter was restricted to specific events in a particular place at a given time. But this demonstration provided by **"Guernica"** is not essential, merely a confirmation, since a careful reading will undoubtedly reveal that, through this *generalizing process,* the text frees itself of referential implications. And indeed in each of the poem's sections one notices a type of formulation which makes retroactive generalization a model of language function, thereby allowing the text to expel the real and the specific and attain the general and the universal. Thus each element of a paradigmatic series is picked up by a term which both resumes and contains the whole series. This term, then, can be regarded as a condensed version of the series and also appears, retrospectively, as a particularizing and redundant anticipatory expansion of the series' closing generic term. Thus *bons à tout* (good for everything), line 5, picks up *bon au feu, au froid, au refus, à la misère, aux injures, aux coups* (good for the fire, the cold, refusal, misery, swearing, blows). *Ils vous ont fait payer. . . la misère* (They made you pay for your misery) in line 11 picks up *ils vous ont fait payer le pain, le ciel, la terre, l'eau, le sommeil* (they made you pay for the bread, sky, earth, water, sleep) of lines 9 and 10; *les femmes les enfants ont le même trésor. . . de durée* (women and children have the same treasure of lasting), lines 19 and 21, picks up *de feuilles vertes de printemps de lait pur* (of green leaves of spring of pure milk) of line 20; finally *la couleur monotone de notre nuit* (the monotonous color of our night), line 38, picks up *la mort, la terre, la hideur de nos ennemis* (death, earth, the hideousness of our enemies) of lines 36 and 37.

The repetition of the process, coupled with the practice of adding juxtaposed terms, compounds, on a formal level, the semantic value of "monotonous" and gives the poem a canonic structure typical of the plaintive ballad traditionally used for the tragic poem. Here, however, instead of being based on a repeated refrain, the repetition is maintained by the reappearance of the same asyndetic syntactic structures and by the use of a general term to sum up the paradigmatic series. The ensuing monotony is only broken by the final line *Nous en aurons raison* (We will overcome them): a collective appeal with which the poet associates himself—something already anticipated by *notre monde* (our world), line 18, *ouvrons ensemble* (let us work together), line 35, and *nos ennemis* (our enemies), line 37, and which is another way of subverting Guernica's topical specificity "your life," "your death" (in lines 12 and 7) to give it a general and symbolic dimension. Moreover, one can hardly fail to notice that the exceptional quality of the last line conforms to the pattern of the *envoi* or *coda* which constitutes the traditional climactic ending of this type of poem.

Eluard concludes **"Guernica"** by extending the lesson of this particular agony to other grimly remembered landmarks: *"Guernica comme Oradour et comme Hiroshima sont les capitales de la paix vivante"* (Guernica like Oradour and like Hiroshima is the capital of living peace).

The subject then broadens, and Guernica returns as one of several examples of a pattern of conflict which transcends all particular circumstances: *"Guernica! l'innocence aura raison du crime"* (Guernica! innocence will overcome crime). From this standpoint the lessons of **"La victoire de Guernica"** and **"Guernica"** are similar. But in **"Guernica"** Eluard is forced to abandon the chronicle form so that he can proclaim the event's universal and perennial quality. The referential model is brutally stripped of its specific value and becomes confused with other Guernicas, thus losing its particularity and all the spatio-temporal characteristics which make it a unique place and subject. In **"La victoire de Guernica"** the pro-

cess is more closely linked to intrinsically symbolic procedures and it is language which, by exclusively verbal operations (opposition, expansion, condensing, etc.), strips specific extra-linguistic reference of its naturalistic identity, thus transforming what is said into a victorious song of hope which is both plural and universal.

### "La victoire de Guernica"

| | |
|---|---|
| I. | Beau monde des masures |
| | De la mine et des champs |
| II. | Visages bons au feu visages bons au froid |
| | Aux refus à la nuit aux injures aux coups |
| III. | Visages bons à tout          5 |
| | Voici le vide qui vous fixe |
| | Votre mort va servir d'exemple |
| IV. | La mort coeur renversé |
| V. | Ils vous ont fait payer le pain |
| | Le ciel la terre l'eau le sommeil    10 |
| | Et la misère |
| | De votre vie |
| VI. | Ils disaient désirer la bonne intelligence |
| | Ils rationnaient les forts jugeaient les fous |
| | Faisaient l'aumône partageaient un sou |
| |     en deux    15 |
| | Ils saluaient les cadavres |
| | Ils s'accablaient de politesses |
| VII. | Ils persévèrent ils exagèrent ils ne sont pas |
| |     de notre monde |
| VIII. | Les femmes les enfants ont le même trésor |
| | De feuilles vertes de printemps et de lait |
| |     pur    20 |
| | Et de durée |
| | Dans leurs yeux purs |
| IX. | Les femmes les enfants ont le même trésor |
| | Dans les yeux |
| | Les hommes le défendent comme ils peu |
| |     vent    25 |
| X. | Les femmes les enfants ont les mêmes |
| |     roses rouges |
| | Dans les yeux |
| | Chacun montre son sang |
| XI. | La peur et le courage de vivre et de |
| |     mourir |
| | La mort si difficile et si facile    30 |
| XII. | Hommes pour qui ce trésor fut chanté |
| | Hommes pour qui ce trésor fut gâché |
| XIII. | Hommes réels pour qui le désespoir |
| | Alimente le feu dévorant de l'espoir |
| | Ouvrons ensemble le dernier bourgeon de |
| |     l'avenir    35 |
| XIV. | Parias la mort la terre et la hideur |
| | De nos ennemis ont la couleur |
| | Monotone de notre nuit |
| | Nous en aurons raison. |

*Cours naturel*
Paul Eluard

### "The Victory of Guernica"

| | |
|---|---|
| I. | High life in hovels |
| | In mines and in fields |
| II. | Faces staunch in the fire staunch in the |
| |     cold |
| | Against denials the night insults blows |
| III. | Faces always staunch    5 |
| | Here is the void staring at you |
| | Your death shall be an example |
| IV. | Death heart overturned |
| V. | They made you pay for bread |

Sky earth water sleep            10
And the poverty
Of your life
VI.   They said they wanted agreement
      They checked the strong sentenced the
        mad
      Gave alms divided a farthing     15
      They greeted every corpse
      They overwhelmed each other with po-
        liteness
VII.  They insist they exaggerate they are not
        of our world
VIII. The women the children have the same
        treasure
      Of green leaves of spring and of pure milk
                                         20
      And of endurance
      In their pure eyes
IX.   The women the children have the same
        treasure
      In their eyes
      The men defend it as best they can   25
X.    The women the children have the same
        red roses
      In their eyes
      All show their blood
XI.   The fear and the courage of living and of
        dying
      Death so hard and so easy        30
XII.  Men for whom this treasure was extolled
      Men for whom this treasure was spoiled
XIII. Real men for whom despair
      Feeds the devouring fire of hope
      Let us open together the last bud of the
        future                         35
XIV.  Pariahs
      Death earth and the vileness of our ene-
        mies
      Have the monotonous colour of our night
      The day will be ours.
                  (Translated by Roland Penrose
                         and George Reavey)
                                   (pp. 57-68)

*Jean-Jacques Thomas, "Topological Poetics: Eluard's 'La victoire de Guernica,'" in his* On Referring in Literature, *edited by Anna Whiteside and Micheal Issacharoff, Indiana University Press, 1987, pp. 57-69.*

## Nicole Irving   (essay date 1988)

[*In the following excerpt from a review of* Selected Poems, *Irving comments on ambiguities in Eluard's poetry.*]

Paul Eluard's **"Liberté"**, written in Occupied Paris in 1941, must rank among the most widely read poems of our century—and deservedly so: few poems could be more limpid and fresh, and at the same time match it in impact. With its simple, repetitive pattern, **"Liberté"** charts the entire world, from jungle to desert, childhood to old age, happiness to solitude and despondency in its search for places where the poet might inscribe "your name"—a woman's, we assume:

Sur mes cahiers d'écolier

Sur mon pupitre et les arbres
Sur le sable sur la neige
J'écris ton nom

(On my schoolboy's copy-books
On my desk and on the trees
On sand and snow
I write your name)

But after nineteen such stanzas listing the places, real and abstract, which turn into repositories for this inscription, the poem delivers a surprise:

Et par le pouvoir d'un mot
Je recommence ma vie
Je suis né pour te connaître
Pour te nommer

Liberté

(And by the power of a word
I begin my life again
I was born to know you
To name you

Liberty)

Today the poem may still be pleasing, even uplifting, but it also seems a touch naive. It is easy to guess, however, the resonance of Eluard's assertion in the bleak times in which it appeared. Indeed the poem quietly changed hands as a message of hope, and thousands of copies were eventually dropped over Occupied France by the RAF.

Eluard's fame as a Resistance poet was well earned, for his output, although broadly in a similar popular vein, was considerable and varied. Abandoning the distanced approach of **"Liberté"**, poems such as **"Gabriel Péry"** or **"Les armes de la douleur"** were hard-hitting and accusatory, telling of specific individuals who were victims of the Nazis. Eluard also tapped a highly emotive, popular seam, virtually singing a romanticized Paris: **"Courage"** is a supremely effective example. Allied to Eluard's rare gift for working everyday words into simple but surprising patterns—a gift reinforced by his years as a leader of the Surrealist movement—the heroism and combative spirit in these poems undoubtedly still draws a broad readership. The period itself of course seduces too, with its image of a world neatly divided into bad/black and good/white; but then Eluard's spontaneous myth-making helped to create that image.

As **"Liberté"** shows, Eluard's public face is buoyant and confident: his words leave no space for self-doubt. Yet always there is a note of provocativeness or wilfulness that undermines the show of confidence. It is often to be found in the characteristically Eluardian, jauntily detached last line or word, and it is one strand in a web of contradictions at the heart of his poetry. For each light-footed image, warm-hearted sentiment or rousing assertion of love, comradeship, solidarity or goodwill, there is also its opposite. Eluard's human and political beliefs never alter, but he struggles to maintain the strength of his conviction. He builds up and nurtures the buoyant Eluard (beginning with the name which, light and airy as it is, is borrowed), but never rids himself of his lonely pessimistic, occasionally cruel or violent "sosie ténébreux" (dark double) whom perhaps Eluard was too essentially gentle to tolerate.

A much-read First World War poem ["**Pour vivre ici**"] sets out his strategy: "Je fis un feu, l'azur m'ayant abandonné" ["I made a fire, the sky having abandoned me"], and to keep at bay the darkness he will drown in, the poet feeds his life-giving-fire with "all that daytime had given me", which are the disparate but free and open things that make up Eluard's imagery. Much of his love poetry celebrates the power of words over the complexities and bitterness of actual love. In **"La terre est bleue comme une orange . . . "**, he writes: "Au tour des baisers de s'entendre", which could mean something like "words cannot lie, and I'd like to say the same about love".

*Nicole Irving, "Buoyant but Ambiguous," in* The Times Literary Supplement, *No. 4453, August 5-11, 1988, p. 856.*

---

## FURTHER READING

Caws, Mary Ann. " 'One in the Other': Communicating Images." In her *A Metapoetics of the Passage: Architextures in Surrealism and After,* pp. 36-46. Hanover: University Press of New England, 1981.

    Examination of Eluard's use of images of passage and metamorphosis.

Collier, Peter. "The Poetry of Protest: Auden, Aragon, and Eluard." In *Visions and Blueprints: Avant-garde Culture and Radical Politics in Early Twentieth-Century Europe,* edited by Edward Timms and Peter Collier, pp. 137-58. Manchester: Manchester University Press, 1988.

    Commentary on Eluard's political vision as expressed in the poem "La victoire de Guernica."

Gill, Brian S. "Eluard's Dadaist Poetry." *Essays in French Literature,* No. 18 (1981): 65-71.

    Examination of the physical and syntactic structure of Eluard's Dadaist poetry from 1917 to 1922.

Maranda, Pierre. "The Dialectic of Metaphor: An Anthropological Essay on Hermeneutics." In *The Reader in the Text: Essays on Audience and Interpretation,* edited by Susan R. Suleiman and Inge Crosman, pp. 183-204. Princeton, N. J.: Princeton University Press, 1980.

    Semiotic analysis of Eluard's line, "La terre est bleue comme une orange" ("the earth is blue like an orange").

Matthews, J. H. "Experimental Research." In his *Surrealism, Insanity, and Poetry,* pp. 113-28. Syracuse: Syracuse University Press, 1982.

    Discussion of Eluard's role in Surrealist psychological experiments involving spontaneous association.

Mounin, Georges. "Paul Eluard's Forbidden Words." *Forum for Modern Language Studies* 18, No. 2 (April 1982): 97-107.

    Examination of the Eluard poem "Quelques-uns des mots qui, jusqu'ici, m'étaient mystérieusement interdits" using a variety of different critical approaches.

Rhodes, S. A. "Aspects of Paul Eluard." *The French Review* 30, No. 2 (December 1956): 115-20.

    Laudatory overview of Eluard's career.

Riffaterre, Michael. "Text Production." In his *Semiotics of Poetry,* pp. 47-80. Bloomington: Indiana University Press, 1978.

    Analysis of Eluard's line, "the earth is blue like an orange."

Rivas, Daniel E. "Eluard's 'L'amoureuse': Mimesis and Semiosis." *The French Review* 55, No. 4 (March 1982): 489-96.

    Semiotic analysis of the use of incongruous images in Eluard's poem "L'amoureuse."

Soupault, Phillippe. "Paul Eluard." *Broom* 3, No. 3 (October 1922): 197.

    Poem written to Eluard.

Winspur, Steven. "Reading a Poem's Typographical Form: The Case of Paul Eluard." *Teaching Language through Literature* 23, No. 1 (December 1983): 38-46.

    Discussion of Eluard's concept of "donner à voir" ("rendering visible" or "making things seen"): the idea that the role of a work of art is to enable the reader or viewer to see the world in a different manner.

# Marcus Garvey

## 1887-1940

(Full name Marcus Moziah Garvey) Jamaican essayist, editor, journalist, and poet.

Garvey was a racial activist who founded the "back to Africa," or Garveyist, political and social movement among African and West Indian Americans at the end of the First World War. In his essays, poems, and speeches Garvey advocated racial separatism, encouraging African Americans and others of African heritage to achieve economic and cultural unity and to form an independent nation in Africa. A highly controversial, flamboyant, and charismatic figure, Garvey drew the scorn of many prominent black intellectuals, most notably W. E. B. Du Bois, who saw him as an antagonistic demagogue. Nevertheless, Garvey attracted an immense following among the disaffected working class, who rallied behind his calls for racial pride and African home rule, and he is today remembered as one of the most important black political theorists of the twentieth century.

Garvey was born into a working-class family in St. Ann's Bay, Jamaica, in 1887. His family's financial difficulties forced Garvey to leave school and find work at the age of fourteen. He became a printer's apprentice in the Jamaican capital of Kingston, and involved himself in political oratory and labor politics. In 1907 he led a printer's union strike, and in 1910 he founded his first periodical, *Garvey's Watchman*. After this venture failed, Garvey spent the next two years traveling in Central America, where he developed several radical journals and tried unsuccessfully to lobby white business owners to improve the working conditions of black laborers; this embittering episode hardened his desire to agitate for black rights on an international level. In 1912, while traveling in Great Britain, he read *Up from Slavery* by Booker T. Washington, whose philosophy of black economic and social self-reliance inspired Garvey to found a black nationalist movement. In Garvey's words, "My doom—if I may so call it—of being a race leader dawned upon me. . . . I asked: 'Where is the black man's Government?' 'Where is his King and his kingdom?' 'Where is his President, his country, and his ambassador, his army, his navy, his men of big affairs?' I could not find them, and then I declared, 'I will help to make them.' "

Returning to Jamaica, Garvey unsuccessfully attempted to found a school modeled on Washington's Tuskegee Institute. He subsequently traveled to New York in 1916, hoping to find a more receptive audience for his ideas. Within three years Garvey was well known as a lecturer, and had sufficient financial backing and contacts to establish the Universal Negro Improvement Association (UNIA) and its journalistic organ, the weekly *Negro World* newspaper. Garvey wrote editorials for the periodical and gave speeches on the need for an independent African state, which he said was the only way black people

worldwide could gain the power needed to win social equality. In 1919, to further African nationhood, he organized the Black Star Line, a fleet of ships owned and managed by black Americans. Operating between New York and Africa, the ships carried many passengers who were seeking repatriation in Africa. Garvey envisioned colonies of African Americans bringing Western technology to help native Africans gain self-sufficiency and eventually independence from European colonial powers. Having gained popular and financial support from around the world, Garvey negotiated with the government of Liberia for land grants to settlers, and was elected provisional president of Africa by the 25,000 delegates at the international UNIA convention in 1920. He also began to formalize the political, theological, economic, and aesthetic aspects of his pan-Africanist philosophy in essays and manifestos collected in *The Philosophy and Opinions of Marcus Garvey; or, Africa for the Africans.*

In spite of the successful sales of stock in the Black Star Line, the company suffered a series of financial and nautical setbacks that proved a crippling drain on UNIA resources. After an attempt to raise money through a mail-soliciting campaign, Garvey was arrested for postal fraud in 1922. He represented himself, staging a dramatic and eloquent but legally inept defense, and was convicted. In 1927 Garvey was released from prison and deported to Jamaica, where he established the periodical *Black Man,* began a mail-correspondence school of African philosophy, and ran an unsuccessful campaign for a seat in the Jamaican legislature. With his reputation tarnished by his imprisonment, and pan-African activism dampened by the more immediate concerns of the Great Depression, Garvey's influence steadily decreased until his death in London in 1940.

Garvey's most highly regarded statements of his ideals and social philosophy are contained in his speeches and essays, particularly those collected in *Philosophy and Opinions.* Garvey's separatist philosophy represented a radical break from previous civil rights movements, which had advocated equality with whites socially, politically, and financially within the same milieus. Such integrationist groups as W. E. B. Du Bois's National Association for the Advancement of Colored People (NAACP) criticized Garvey's ideas as counterproductive and his business plans as foolish. Garvey, however, argued that no race would willingly relinquish power, and that black citizens who attempted integration were doomed to second-class status. He maintained that only the existence of a separate, free, and powerful African state could ensure rights and security for black people living outside of Africa. He further charged that the African-American intelligentsia was elitist and dominated by mulattoes who sought preeminence for those with light complexions rather than dark. Garvey frequently maligned Du Bois's racially mixed heritage and quipped that NAACP stood for the "National Association for the Advancement of Certain People." Critics have suggested that Garvey thus needlessly alienated black leaders who might have helped him.

Paralleling Garvey's call for African political nationalism was his development of a black theology and aesthetic. Garvey argued that black people had been cowed into submission by such institutionalized propaganda of white superiority as the anthropomorphism of God as white and the slight attention paid to black historical achievements. He called on black people to reject the white aesthetic and to adopt African standards of physical and artistic beauty instead. However, he also rejected as elitist the literature of the Harlem Renaissance, much of which contained lyrical celebration of the black body and drew on images of Africa as a spiritual touchstone. Instead, he used the *Negro World* as a vehicle for black authors whose work he believed more relevant to the masses. In the mid-1920s Garvey's advocacy of separatism and racial purity grew more radical, and he endorsed the aims of white supremacist groups including the Ku Klux Klan; Garvey asserted that these organizations opposed miscegenation, as the UNIA did, and he stated that he regarded "the Klan, the Anglo-Saxon Clubs, and White American Societies . . . as better friends of the [black] race than all other groups of hypocritical whites put together."

Scholars generally agree that, although Garvey's concrete contributions to civil rights were few, his ideological impact was tremendous. Garvey's calls for Afrocentric scholarship and the rediscovery of a black aesthetic are believed to have strongly influenced such groups as the Black Arts movement of the 1960s. Garvey's development of a black theosophy and ideology of separatism presaged the efforts of subsequent black nationalist and Black Muslim leaders, including Elijah Muhammad and Malcolm X. Critics also credit Garvey's pan-Africanist political thinking for increasing the scope of the American civil rights movement, which had been largely isolationist, and also for influencing such African liberation leaders as Jomo Kenyatta. While many critics fault Garvey for the impractibility of some of his goals and for allying with white racist groups, others argue that the novelty and audacity of his methods were precisely what helped him fire the imagination of the greater public; even Garvey's detractors have conceded that Garveyism succeeded as few other movements have in galvanizing and restoring racial pride to African Americans. An editorial in the integrationist *Messenger* magazine in 1922 conceded that, as much as he proved a scourge to the black intellectual mainstream, "Garvey has done much good work in putting into many Negroes a backbone where for years they have only had a wishbone."

(See also *Contemporary Authors,* Vols. 120 and 124.)

## PRINCIPAL WORKS

*The Philosophy and Opinions of Marcus Garvey; or, Africa for the Africans.* 2 vols.  (essays)  1923-25
*The Tragedy of White Injustice*  (poetry)  1927
*The Poetical Works of Marcus Garvey*  (poetry)  1983
*The Marcus Garvey and Universal Negro Improvement Association Papers.* 6 vols.  (essays and journalism) 1983-87

---

### John Edward Bruce  (essay date 1922)

[*An American journalist, essayist, and short story writer, Bruce was a vocal and witty proponent of black nationalism, and in his newspaper columns written under the pseudonym "Bruce Grit" he argued for black pride and racial purity. During the 1920s Bruce was one of the most prominent intellectuals in the Garveyist movement. In the following essay, he praises Garvey's social philosophy and defends Garvey's integrity as a leader.*]

I have been studying Marcus Garvey for the past four years, and I have studied some of his opponents for thirty or forty years, and find that my estimate of Marcus Garvey is much higher than it is of many of those whom I have personally known in all these years. To me, two of the tests of true leadership are the absence of the love of money and a desire to help the masses to get on and up. I haven't discovered such altruism in the ethics of many of these leaders whom Mr. Garvey is putting out of business by his straightforward methods and bull-dog tenacity.

When Mr. Garvey first came to this country from his island home in Jamaica, B.W.I., I was one among the first

American Negroes, on whom he called. I was then residing in Yonkers on the Hudson, New York. He was a little sawed-off and hammered-down Black Man, with *determination* written all over his face, and an engaging smile that caught you and compelled you to listen to his story. Like all other Negroes who feel deeply the injustices of the White Man, whether they are committed by individuals or by the State, he had a grievance, and I listened with interest to its recital, which is much too long to repeat here, but the substance of which was, that the Negroes in the West Indian Island, from which he came, were not receiving fair play at the hands of the Whites, either in the matter of education or in the industries, in that the school facilities were inadequate, and that the workers were underpaid, thus preventing them from doing for themselves what they would like to do to improve their educational and economic condition. All they needed was a fair opportunity and the Organization which he was then endeavoring to form, he believed would give them, in some slight measure, this opportunity, if the Negroes on this side of the World would lend a helping hand.

Mr. Garvey is a rapid-fire talker, and two reporters are necessary to keep up with him at his meetings here in Liberty Hall on Sunday Nights, when he speaks to audiences of 5000 or more; I was able to catch enough from his rapidly spoken story, however, to convince me that he had a real mission, and I promised him such aid in the furtherance of his plans as I could give him, morally and substantially. We parted the best of friends. I had given him a list of the names of our leading men in New York and other cities, who, I felt, would encourage and assist him. Some of them were Clergymen; some professional men; and some of then private citizens. He called on some of these, and among them, Prof. Du Bois, who did not think well of his plan, but he kept on.

The Jamaica Club of New York City hired St. Mark's Hall on 138th Street, near Lenox Avenue, for a public meeting and announced that Mr. Garvey would speak on his favorite subject. He spoke with so much vigor and earnestness that he stepped off the platform to the floor. The tickets were $5.00 and I gladly purchased one and went to hear him. Since I had seen him in Yonkers, he had been *seeing things* in and around New York, and his vision had become enlarged. His address in St. Mark's Hall indicated, from its tenor, that his plan for Racial uplift was not to be wholly confined to his Island Home. The problems which it embraced were universal, because the Negro in the United States of America was but little better off than the Negro in the West Indies. Later on, he *reasoned* that the Negroes throughout the World had as much to complain of as those of Jamaica, and to prove that he was right, he made a trip into our *Southern Shambles,* and mingled freely with the humble and lowly classes, "who, in the Halcyon days of politics, served as 'meal tickets,'" for the scalawags of the White Race, seeking office and power through their Black accomplices, in the dirty game of American politics, which has at last come to a period in that section of the Country, and left the Negro political leader on the outside looking in.

Among these leaders were many men calling themselves ambassadors of God, who made a good living out of the political game, by using their Congregations as weavers use a shuttle-cock, for their personal gain. Garvey saw all the rottenness and deceptions of both White and Black leaders. He saw his Race being used as a plaything by these men, who had no other aim than to advance themselves politically at the expense of these Blacks, and then to pose as their Champions and defenders. Their hollow pretensions, their mock heroics, their false zeal and their rank hypocrisy set him to thinking, and after months of travel in the West Indies and the United States, where he used his eyes and kept his own counsel, he finally changed his plans, and began a vigorous soapbox campaign in Negro Harlem, out of which grew the Universal Negro Improvement Association, the original membership of which was thirteen (13), and which now numbers four millions in the United States, with 800 Divisions throughout the United States and the World which include Africa, the West Indies, and South and Central America. The Divisions which are established are growing by leaps and bounds in every part of the World where Negroes are to be found.

In the incipiency of this newer Movement of Garvey, the old leaders paused, and snorted; the preachers, who found their Congregations thinning out and slipping away from them, and the Professional leaders for Revenue only, discovering that majorities for the candidates who had paid them to get results in Negro districts were growing more and more uncertain, combined and united in a campaign of slander and abuse of the Garvey Movement, and threw all sorts of obstacles in the way, to prevent the accomplishment of his plans. But they continued to develop, despite these handicaps, and, like the proverbial steamroller of the G.O.P., they will all of them be flattened out, if they wait long enough.

Mr. Garvey is very busy now working out the larger details of his plan, jailing crooks who have robbed his Association, and finding and fitting men to take up the work of spreading the Gospel of the U.N.I.A., among those who sit in darkness.

I was among those who opposed him at the start and who wrote against him, and I tried my best to defeat his aims, which, I confess, I did not then thoroughly understand. They seemed to me wild, chimerical and impossible of accomplishment. I stood, one night, at a corner of Lenox Avenue and 135th Street, when Garvey, standing on an especially built platform—a step ladder—with which he could take liberties without falling, unfolded, in part, the plan of his Organization, which was to draw all Negroes throughout the World together, to make one big brotherhood of the Black Race for its common good, for mutual protection, for commercial and industrial development, and for the fostering of business enterprises. This sounded not only good to me, but practical. The things he proposed were easy of accomplishment under a leader as full of his subject as he, and, "Why not?" I said to myself, "let him try out his plan; since no one else has submitted a better one, why oppose him?" and from that cold night, in October, I ceased writing and talking against Garvey.

His street corner audiences were larger than those of the

Socialist Orators on the other corners a few blocks away, and they stayed longer. The people hung upon his words, drank in his messages to them, and were as enthusiastic and earnest about this business as their doughty little Black Orator. To me, this connoted that Marcus Garvey was more than the average Street Corner Orator and that his work and mission had more than an ordinary significance. The people to whom he spoke heard him gladly, pondered his words, and acted wisely by organizing what is today the most powerful Negro Organization in the World. There is absolutely no corner of the earth where there is a Black or Brown or Yellow face, where there is not a Branch of the U.N.I.A. There are branches in Germany, London, Wales, Scotland, and recently, I saw a letter from far off Peru, requesting the literature of the Organization. What does this mean? It means clearly, that Mr. Garvey has caught the vision, that the people of Color, throughout the World, believe in his leadership and want him to lead them. Nothing could be plainer.

The old leaders were not able or were too lazy or indifferent or both, to work out a plan for the redemption and regeneration of the Race, as attractive and practical from any angle in which it is viewed, as that of Marcus Garvey. It has progressed too far now for any of them singly or all of them combined to stop it, and it will be a hazardous undertaking for those who think they are powerful enough to do so. They have had their chance and failed, and the wisdom of prudence suggests that they let Garvey alone. Let him carry on the work to which he has put his hands and to which he, in the greatness and bigness of his heart, is inviting them now to put their hands, their brains, and their money to make the Big Negro World Brotherhood, the accomplished *fact* that he intends it to be, with or without the consent of any Negro leader or leaders who now think they are IT.

Garvey is neither a rum drinker, a user of tobacco in any form, a social bug, nor a grafter. He is scrupulously honest in the handling of the funds of the Organization, and exacts the strictest accounting of its funds from those holding subordinate positions in the Organization, and through whose hands its money passes. "His spear knows no brother." The man caught stealing the people's money is promptly cut off the payroll and headed for jail, if the offense is sufficient to justify such action. He is branded a thief in the "Negro World," and must change his name and complexion to do business elsewhere. Garvey is relentless with crooks and fakers, and he is the idol of the masses of the common people, of whom he is one. (pp. 167-70)

> *John Edward Bruce, "Marcus Garvey and the U.N.I.A.," in his* The Selected Writings of John Edward Bruce: Militant Black Journalist, *edited by Peter Gilbert, Arno Press, 1971, pp. 167-70.*

## Elliott M. Rudwick   (essay date 1959)

[*An American educator and critic, Rudwick wrote several books on African-American history and civil rights movements. In the following excerpt, he delineates the conflict and rivalry between Garvey and W. E. B. Du Bois and their respective publications, the* Negro World *and the* Crisis.]

After World War I, large numbers of Negroes were stirred by race pride and demanded a "spiritual emancipation." They were encouraged to seek improvement of their own living conditions and work for the betterment of the natives on the African continent. During this post-war decade two prominent leaders, W. E. B. DuBois and Marcus Garvey, clashed in their separate plans to establish an African state and an international organization of Negroes. Both men were propagandists. DuBois was editor of the *Crisis,* the official magazine of the N.A.A.C.P. and Garvey owned the *Negro World.* (The Jamaican regularly wrote articles for his newspaper and the editorial writers he hired adopted his tone.) The present article is based primarily on a study of these two publications and seeks to examine the DuBois-Garvey debate which—especially from Garveyite quarters—was abusive and acrimonious.

In 1917, DuBois, favored the formation of a "great free central African state" (the amalgamation of German East Africa and the Belgian Congo); later, he declared that the state should be enlarged to include Uganda, French Equatorial Africa, German Southwest Africa, and the Portuguese territories of Angola and Mozanbique. In his conception, a "Brain Trust" of Negro administrators were to be responsible for the establishment of an "industrial democracy," *i.e.,* a socialized system of production and distribution. In 1919, through the help of Blaise Diagne, a Negro Senegalese representative in the French Chamber of Deputies, DuBois received permission from Prime Minister Clemenceau to organize the First Pan-African Congress in Paris. The delegates (from the United States, West Indies, Europe, and Africa) asked the League of Nations to guarantee political, social, and economic rights to the African natives and set up a legal code for the "international protection" of these people. The League was requested to consider the Africans in "international labor legislation" and to provide for native representation within the organization.

According to the Pan-African Congress, "Negroes of the world demand" that the natives should hold title to all African land which they could "profitably" cultivate. The conclave petitioned for effective controls upon the white capitalists in order to prevent further economic exploitation. The conferees also maintained that the Africans should receive assurances that elementary, vocational, and college education would be available to them. To create international racial unity, DuBois proposed to found the *Black Review* (with English, French, and perhaps Spanish and Portuguese editions). He hoped that American Negroes would learn to speak French and Spanish and he was certain that Negro literature and art would thereby gain momentum in all nations. He suggested that U.S. Negroes should travel to Europe on *"personal rencontres* for information and propaganda." The League paid little attention to DuBois's Pan-African Congress, nor did any other group consider the conclave as "representative of the Negro race." The convention had no real grass roots organizational support; only on paper was the N.A.A.C.P. headquarters concerned and the N.A.A.C.P.

branches simply ignored the Pan-African Congress. However, DuBois seemed undaunted and continued to grind out propaganda which was moderate in tone and intellectual in approach.

Unlike DuBois, Marcus Garvey was able to gain mass support and his propaganda had a tremendous emotional appeal. He established the Universal Negro Improvement Association in New York (with branches in many U.S. cities and several foreign countries). The aim of the organization was the liberation of Africa. By 1919, he set up the Black Star Line and the Negro Factories Corporation. In August, 1920, Garvey called a month-long convention of the U.N.I.A. in New York City. In the name of "400,000,000 Negroes of the World," he declared that Africa must be free. He did not bother to display the restraint which characterized Pan-African leaders and many of his remarks were inflammatory. He warned that his race was prepared to shed its blood to remove the whites from the natives' rightful land in Africa. His convention delegates and members paraded through Harlem. Tens of thousands of Negroes were excited by the massed units of the African Legion in blue and red uniforms and the white-attired contingents of the Black Cross Nurses. Garvey's followers sang the new U.N.I.A. anthem, "Ethiopa, Thou Land of Our Fathers" and they proudly waved the Association's flag (black for Negro skin, green for Negro hopes, and red for Negro blood). Never again was the race to have a leader who could produce such a wonderful show.

DuBois publicly ignored Garvey until December of 1920 [see Further Reading] and this tardiness of editorial recognition was probably due to the *Crisis* editor's ambivalence toward him. DuBois was profoundly impressed by "this extraordinary leader of men," and he acknowledged that Garvey was "essentially an honest and sincere man with a tremendous vision, great dynamic force, stubborn determination and unselfish desire to serve." However, the *Crisis* editor also considered him to be

> dictatorial, domineering, inordinately vain and very suspicious. . . . The great difficulty with him is that he has absolutely no business sense, no *flair* for real organization and his general objects are so shot through with bombast and exaggeration that it is difficult to pin them down for careful examination.

The following month, after DuBois had requested (and failed to receive) a financial statement from the Jamaican on the Negro Improvement Association and the Black Star Line, the *Crisis* editor wrote [see Further Reading]:

> When it comes to Mr. Garvey's industrial and commercial enterprises there is more ground for doubt and misgiving than in the matter of his character.

Originally, DuBois believed that his own hopes for Africa's reclamation and an international black economy could be achieved through Garvey's mass appeal. He concluded that the failure of the Garvey Movement, which had generated so much "spiritual" potential, might seriously damage racial self-confidence. He was impressed by the "bold effort and some success" of the Jamaican, who, after all, had sent ships ("owned by black men") to sea.

However, the editor of the *Crisis* announced that Garvey was expending funds for current expenses instead of using the money for capital improvements. (The flamboyant Garvey seemed more interested in public relations than in buying ships.) (pp. 421-23)

DuBois's comments showed remarkable temperateness in view of the fact that the Garvey Movement had been attacking him for more than a year. Just before the Pan-African Congress in 1919, Garvey alleged that DuBois talked so mildly and equivocally to French reporters about American race relations, that the Jamaican's "High Commissioner" abroad found his own work sabotaged. DuBois denied the accusation. The *Negro World* instructed its readers that the *Crisis* was basically reactionary and was published from an "aristocratic Fifth Avenue" office. After a *Crisis* editorial on Woodrow Wilson's faithlessness, and following a DuBois comment on the post-war imperialist resurgence in England, the *Negro World* reminded the N.A.A.C.P. propagandist that Garvey had forseen these developments as early as 1918, when the editor was counseling cooperation with the United States Government. DuBois was pictured as a fallen old warrior whose contributions to the race were at an end. With relish the *Negro World* also took up the cry of A. Philip Randolph's *Messenger* that DuBois was "controlled" by white capitalists on the N.A.A.C.P. board. When the *Crisis* editor was awarded the Spingarn Medal in 1920 for "founding" the First Pan-African Congress, Garvey's paper charged that the entire affair was "a discreditable fraud." (The N.A.A.C.P. citation ignored a 1900 Pan-African conclave. By juggling words, DuBois had "founded" the first Congress because he argued that the 1900 organization was called the Pan-African *"Conference."*) As far as Garvey was concerned, the 1919 Pan-African Congress had accomplished little and he asserted that William Monroe Trotter's National Equal Rights League had contributed more to the race when it presented its petition to the Peace Conference in Paris:

> But perhaps Mr. Villard [one-time N.A.A.C.P. board chairman] and the other gentlemen of the Committee on award regard Mr. Trotter as too radical, perhaps they do not regard him from a white man's point of view as safe and sane a leader as Dr. DuBois.

At the 1920 U.N.I.A. convention, Garvey called the *Crisis* editor "the associate of an alien race," and his remark received "the most enthusiastic applause" of the session. The *Negro World's* editorial reaction to DuBois lengthy critique was typical: "subtle, shrewd, untruthful in its professed sincerity, cunning and adroit in its attempt to blow hot and cold at the same time." The N.A.A.C.P. propagandist was accused of petty jealousy and of being quite possibly "more of a white man than a Negro and [he] seems to be only a professional Negro at that." Garvey mounted the platform to chide DuBois for ignoring the masses and believing in a "bastard aristocracy." In contrast, the Jamaican recalled how he "always walked among [his own] ordinary humble people . . . (cheers)." Garvey provided his ability to write demagogic propaganda:

Where did he [DuBois] get this aristocracy from? He picked it up on the streets of Great Barrington, Mass. He just got it into his head that he should be an aristocrat and ever since that time he has been keeping his very beard as an aristocrat; he has been trying to be everything else but a Negro. Sometimes we hear he is a Frenchman and another time he is Dutch and when it is convenient he is a Negro (Derisive cheers and laughter). Now I have no Dutch. I have no French, I have no Anglo-Saxon in me, but I am but a Negro now and always (thunderous applause). I have no Frenchmen to imitate, I have no Anglo-Saxon to imitate; I have but the ancient glories of Ethiopia to imitate. (Great applause.) The men who built the Pyramids looked like me, and I think the best thing I can do is to keep looking like them. Anyone you hear always talking about the kind of blood he has in him other than the blood you can see, he is dissatisfied with something, and I feel sure that many of the Negroes of the United States of America know that if there is a man who is most dissatisfied with himself, it is Dr. DuBois.

In order to demonstrate that displeasure with DuBois was mounting in various quarters of the race, the *Negro World* reprinted several comments and editorials from other Negro papers. The Richmond *Planet* believed that DuBois was much out of his element for having the audacity to reproach Garvey, the "man of action." The Oakland *Sunshine* expressed similar sentiments: "DuBois is talking big things and Garvey is doing big things. We rather admire the man that does rather than talks." According to this newspaper, the N.A.A.C.P. propagandist was hurting the Association by his anti-Garvey campaign. The *Sunshine's* editor contended that the Garvey organization was larger and more powerful than the N.A.A.C.P. and was dedicated to DuBois's principles of improving the status of Negroes in the United States. The *National Review* took DuBois to task for editorializing on Pan-African movements and omitting the U.N.I.A. For this incompleteness, DuBois was dubbed, "king of journalistic jugglers."

The *Negro World* was resentful because of the *Crisis*'s tone of superiority and public omniscience. DuBois was castigated for thinking that Negroes who wanted to start race enterprises were obliged to appear before his inquisition. A Garveyite published a pamphlet in 1921 entitled, *The Mistakes of Dr. W. E. B. DuBois,* which was designed to show its victim's feet of clay:

> Garvey's old, unseaworthy wooden ships are still plowing through the turbulent waters of old Father Neptune's salty domains. Unlike the wreck of the Niagara Movement, they are not lying high and dry upon the weather-beaten shores of Disaster.

Such remarks brought forth DuBoisian retaliation, and he blasted the Garveyites as "scoundrels and bubble-blowers" who were causing havoc within the race. He denounced them for damning all whites and exploiting the Negro masses. (He claimed that the white supremacists were retreating and that the N.A.A.C.P. would liberate the Negroes in another quarter of a century. In the past, DuBois had also condemned whites in wholesale fashion,

but in fighting Garvey, he undoubtedly tried to appear more optimistic about interracial relations than he actually was.)

During the early months of 1921, DuBois was preparing for the Second Pan-African Congress which he announced for the fall. He promised to invite not only the Negro Governments, but "all Negro organizations interested in the peoples of African descent." He also mentioned that colonial powers would be encouraged to send delegates to the conclave which was to be held in Europe again. Realizing that his organization would be confused with and compared with the Garveyites, he stressed that the Second Pan-African Congress was not convening to prepare a "scheme of migration." Shortly before the Congress, the *Negro World* reminded DuBois that only about one-fourth of the delegates to his first Congress were from Africa, and since the ratio had been so small, the term "Pan-African" was unrealistic. The N.A.A.C.P. propagandist had only recently printed a letter from the Liberian President, and the note was intended to rebuke the Garveyites. (The Liberian chief of state warned that his country would not allow itself to serve as a base of operations from which the Garvey Movement could harass other governments in Africa.)

DuBois found it necessary to make a public statement after it became known that Garvey had not been invited to the coming conclave, and the *Crisis* editor announced that the U.N.I.A. leader was ignored because his movement was "dangerous" and "impracticable." The *Negro World* told its readers that such studied neglect was all that could be expected of DuBois, who directed his Pan-African Congress like "an exclusive college function." The newspaper followed up this criticism with another entitled, "Is Dr. DuBois Misled or Is He Misleading?" In this piece, DuBois was advised to join forces against the "white beasts." (Garvey predicted a race war, and he asserted that DuBois and the old-time leaders were not really preparing for it.) The *Crisis* editor was invited to attend the second convention of the U.N.I.A.

Strategically, Garvey decided to call his own international conclave in New York a few weeks before the Pan-African Congress. Unanimously, the U.N.I.A. delegates condemned DuBois's movement (and they dispatched their caustic comments to European newspapers.) Garvey considered it an absurdity for the Pan-African Congress leaders to ask white representatives of the imperialists to attend their meetings:

> Just imagine that! It reminds me of the conference of rats endeavoring to legislate against the cats and the secretary of the rats convention invites the cat to preside over the convention.

The Jamaican tried to create the impression that DuBois represented "the antithesis" of the U.N.I.A.—on the alleged grounds that the *Crisis* editor's policy was racial amalgamation. Contending that the whites would always hold firmly to their racism, Garvey suggested that the Negro develop

> a distinct racial type of civilization of his own and . . . work out his salvation in his mother-

land, all to be accomplished under the stimulus and influence of the slogan, "Africa for the Africans, at home and abroad!"

His speech was delivered at a special meeting "called unexpectedly" after press dispatches of the Second Pan-African Congress (condemning the U.N.I.A.) arrived from Europe.

The Second Pan-African Congress met in London, Brussels, and Paris, in late August and early September of 1921. As in 1919, the conclave promulgated its belief in the physical, social, and political equality of all races. The Negroes were to be guaranteed "the ancient common ownership of the land and its natural fruits and defence against the unrestrained greed of invested capital." The League of Nations was asked again to set up one agency to study Negro problems and another to insure that native labor was not exploited. England, Belgium, and France were accused of taking advantage of the natives. However, within the Pan-African movement itself there was a rupture between the American-British delegations who favored a critical approach to colonialism and the French-Belgian delegates, who desired an accommodation to the status quo. (pp. 423-26)

After the Second Pan-African Congress, Marcus Garvey challenged DuBois's group "to fight to a finish (applause)." He laughed at those who argued that they owed their primary allegiance to the nations in which they lived. When one Pan-African leader said that he would "lose everything" if he returned permanently to Africa, Garvey jibed that "everything" meant Parisian white women. Garvey charged that the American whites were encouraging European immigration in order to replace the Negro "and cause him to die by starvation." The Jamaican argued that it was only a matter of time before the whites would exile Negroes from all countries. However, he declared that some members of the race would remain in the United States for another hundred years; he announced that they would occupy a higher status because their welfare would be guaranteed by the prestige of the African Republic.

Although he excoriated N.A.A.C.P. leaders, Garvey denied that he hoped for the demise of the organization. He announced that he would not "originate an attack" on the Association, but that he was prepared to defend the race against "our bitterest enemies [who] are not so much those from without as within; men who will continue to find faults where there are no faults." He asked the N.A.A.C.P. to send its representatives to the third convention of the U.N.I.A. and to permit "the real leadership" to assume command of the race. The Jamaican wanted his followers to believe that DuBois lived in fear of being dropped by the Association—"the National Association for the Advancement of (Certain) Colored People."

During all of this time, DuBois was still requesting the U.N.I.A. to issue a financial statement of its activities, and the *Negro World's* reply was that this interloper had no right "to say what people should do with their money and what other organizations should do." The Garveyites declared that their leader supplied jobs to twelve hundred

Negroes, when one included such enterprises as the U.N.I.A., the *Negro World,* the *Negro Times,* a printing plant, the Negro Factories Corporation, a hotel, restaurant, steam laundry, and a doll factory.

In sharp contrast to the Garveyite hysterics, DuBois's comments about the Jamaican's program were usually calmly delivered and based on objective data. Since he viewed the Black Star Line as crucial in a consideration of the leader's fame and influence, DuBois examined the development of this business venture. He proceeded to recount the history of Garvey's mismanagement of the enterprise. DuBois described the unseaworthy *Yarmouth*'s voyage to the West Indies. The ship carried a cargo of whiskey, much of which was stolen; the American Government fined the vessel's owners. Since the ship was old, much money was spent on repair bills, and the *Yarmouth* was finally sold in order to pay off the creditors. Another vessel, the *Antonio Maceo,* was also lost to the Black Star Line after it was beached in Cuba because it required extensive repairs. A third ship, the *Shady-side,* suffered the same ignominious fate, after it served a short propaganda stint as an excursion boat up the Hudson. In early 1921, the Jamaican said he purchased the *Phyllis Wheatley* in order to handle the African trade, and later he stated that some of his associates had absconded with funds which had been designated as a deposit for the ship. Since Garvey had announced sailings and sold passage on the *Phyllis Wheatley,* he was indicted for fraud. In 1922, after the Black Star Line collapsed, DuBois wrote feelingly, "Here then is the collapse of the only thing in the Garvey Movement which was original or promising" [see Further Reading].

The *Crisis* editor also attempted to learn how many members of the U.N.I.A. there actually were. Garvey claimed four million by August of 1920 and for 1921 he listed two figures. (During the early part of the year he stated that there were still four million members, but two years later, he recalled that there were six million members in 1921.) The year after Garvey's indictment, DuBois estimated the membership in the U.N.I.A. for the period of September, 1920 to July, 1921. (He divided the annual dues into the total sum which was collected.) The *Crisis* editor calculated that there were fewer than ten thousand "paid up members," between ten and twenty thousand "active members," and very much less than a hundred thousand "nominal members."

DuBois reached a white public when he analyzed the Garvey Movement in *Century* magazine, and while he made no attempt to mask his disapproval of the organization, he did try to account for it. He viewed Garvey as a disoriented victim of the color line:

> All his life whites have laughed and sneered at him, and torn his soul. All his life he has hated the half-whites, who rejecting their darker blood have gloried in their pale shame.

DuBois referred to the Jamaican as a "little, fat, black man; ugly, but with intelligent eyes and a big head." Garvey made the most of this description, replying that his physiognomy was "typical of the African:"

Anything that is black, to him [DuBois] is ugly, is hideous, is monstrous, and this is why in 1917 he had but the lightest of colored people in his office, when one could hardly tell whether it was a white show or a colored vaudeville he was running at Fifth Avenue [the offices of the N.A.A.C.P.].

The *Crisis* editor was labeled as an apostle of "social equality," which in Garvey's thinking represented the kind of person who demanded to squire a white woman to a dance at the Waldorf-Astoria Hotel. The Jamaican said that the U.N.I.A. was the only agency which was able to protect the darker-skinned Negro masses against the DuBois-led "caste aristocracy" of light mulattoes many of whom were "intellectuals." Paradoxically, Garvey denied that he was prejudiced against mulattoes, and he argued that all men had equal opportunity in the U.N.I.A.

In 1923, Garvey was convicted of mail fraud. After the trial, DuBois reprinted an editorial from a West Indies newspaper, wherein the U.N.I.A. leader was termed a "transparent charlatan." Frustratedly, DuBois declared once again that his own attempt to settle the race problem on an international scale through "cooperation" with the whites) was "harmed by the tragedy and comedy of Marcus Garvey." The Jamaican refused to accept his defeat. In his prison cell, he continued to write diatribes, and DuBois angrily denounced him as "the most dangerous enemy of the Negro race in America and in the world. He is either a lunatic or a traitor."

Since DuBois had been his chief critic, Garvey charged that the *Crisis* editor was responsible for his indictment and conviction. He blamed the N.A.A.C.P. propagandist for all of his difficulties and he asserted that the editor's malevolence had prevented the Black Star Line from sending "dozens" of ships to sea. During the summer of 1924, the U.N.I.A. exiled DuBois from the Negro race. However, such sentiments were only the last breaths of the movement. The Liberian Government announced that no members of the Garvey organization were welcome in the country. In January, 1925, President King remarked that his administration would not support any organization which dedicated itself to stirring up racial animosity. (pp. 427-29)

This article has examined the intraracial battles between DuBois and Garvey. During the 1920's, in the pages of the *Crisis* and the *Negro World*, they employed the same propaganda style and approach in their attacks on each other as they used in their organizational pronouncements on Africa. Garvey's expressions were explosive, irrational, and flamboyant. Their emotional appeal attracted large numbers of frustrated, uneducated blacks. DuBois's remarks were usually moderate, thoughtful, and analytical and were directed to a minority within the minority. (p. 429)

*Elliott M. Rudwick, "DuBois Versus Garvey: Race Propagandists at War," in* The Journal of Negro Education, *Vol. XXVIII, No. 4, Fall, 1959, pp. 421-29.*

## Robert H. Brisbane    (essay date 1970)

[*An American educator, Brisbane is the author of* The Black Vanguard: Origins of the Negro Social Revolution, 1900-1960. *In the following excerpt from that book, he discusses the impact of Garveyism on intellectual and social trends among black Americans.*]

To a great many white people in America who knew anything at all about him, Marcus Garvey was simply a clown, a combination of Negro Baptist minister and minstrel. When Garvey was arrested, a prominent New York newspaper columnist commented that to hold him was "equivalent to 'jailing a rainbow.' " Far more substantially, however, Garveyism was the first genuine mass movement to take place among American Negroes. Unlike the Black Power movement that was to shake up America some two generations later, Garveyism did not really create Negro militancy—it merely channelized an activism that had previously been generated by such black irreconcilables as [William Monroe Trotter, W. E. B. Du Bois], A. Philip Randolph, and Robert S. Abbott, and which had already exploded in the race war of 1919. However, Garveyism did produce its own isolated incidents of violent black militancy. Such an incident occurred on June 20, 1920, when two hundred Garveyites burned two American flags in a bonfire on East Thirty-Fifth Street in Chicago. Two white men were killed and a Negro policeman was wounded in the uproar that followed. This was very probably the first desecration of the American flag during this century and certainly the first by Negroes.

What has become known as the Negro Renaissance reached its full flowering during the high tide of the Garvey movement. In the field of literature young Negro writers and poets turned to the Dark Continent for the subjects of new verses. Thus, Langston Hughes chanted in his "The Weary Blues":

> All the tom-toms of the jungle beat in my blood.
> And all the wild hot moons of the jungles shine
>     in my soul.
> I am afraid of this civilization—
>     So hard,
>     So strong,
>     So cold.

And Countee Cullen queried:

> What is Africa to me:
> Copper sun or scarlet sea,
> Jungle star or jungle track,
> Strong bronzed men, or regal black. . . .
> *One three centuries removed*
> *From the scenes his fathers loved,*
> *Spicy grove, cinnamon tree.*
> *What is Africa to me?*

The serious study of the Negro's past begun in 1915 by Carter G. Woodson won several brilliant young recruits during the Garvey era. Such men as J. A. Rogers and Arthur Schomburg rummaged through libraries and collections the world over in search of material dealing with the Negro's history. The new outlook was manifested also in the realms of music and art. The importation of African art, barely a trickle before World War I, swelled to a virtual torrent during the early twenties. African sculptures in clay, wood, ebony, and ivory became prized and eagerly sought for. Also Negro composers devoted a new interest to African themes and rhythms. To summarize the new trends, in May, 1924, *Opportunity,* a Negro periodical edited by Charles S. Johnson, produced an African art issue containing African-inspired poems by Claude McKay, Langston Hughes, and Lewis Alexander. The publication featured other African art numbers in 1926 and 1928. The new pride in things black and things African fathered a drive on the part of the Negro press to substitute the term "black men" for "colored men" and "Afro-American" for "American Negro." Gradually, Negroes learned to refer to their African ancestry and heavy pigmentation less self-consciously.

In the realm of politics Garveyism accelerated the shift of the Negro electorate from the Republican to the Democratic Party. Among other things the new Negro considered himself a radical. He was beginning to distrust the hidebound traditionalism of Republican political leaders and specifically the Negro element in this group. The new self-confidence and spirit of independence among the black masses in the Northern and Eastern metropolises was manifested in new allegiances between the black electorate and Democratic political machines. On the economic front, the teachings of Garvey ran parallel to those of Booker T. Washington. Both men were interested in the establishment of a sound and thriving Negro bourgeoisie. Garvey particularly hammered away at the necessity for the building of Negro factories, the organizing of cooperative markets among American Negroes, and the establishment of international trade among the world's black population. During his heyday numerous attempts were made by his followers to establish Negro enterprises. In general, however, Garvey's economic doctrine produced little of lasting benefit to the race. In passing, perhaps it should be mentioned that the followers of Garvey were among the leaders of the Jobs for Negroes Campaign which blossomed in Northern cities during the early 1930's. Some Garveyites were to be found among the early recruits of the Black Muslims.

In the long run, however, the meteoric flash of Garvey's rise awed even his bitterest enemies, and some of the more thoughtful among them eventually paid him the high tribute of emulation. As to his attempts to translate his dreams into reality, no more poignant words were spoken of Garvey than those of Henry Lincoln Johnson:

> If every Negro could have put every dime, every penny into the sea, and if he might get in exchange the knowledge that he was somebody,

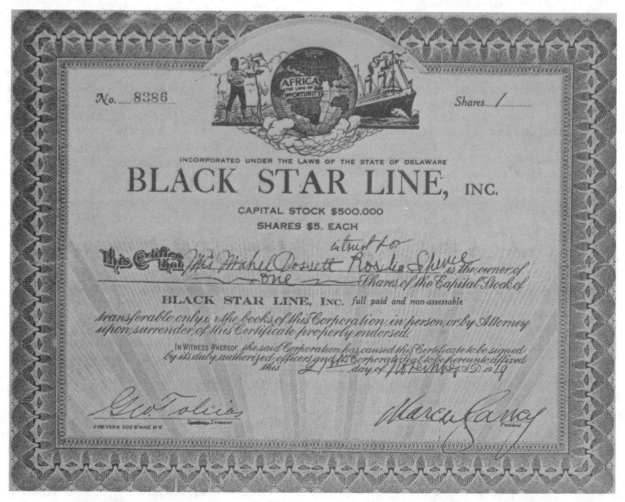

*A certificate of stock in the Black Star Line, the shipping company Garvey founded to repatriate African Americans.*

that he meant something in the world, he would gladly do it. . . . The Black Star Line was a loss in money but a gain in soul!

(pp. 97-9)

> Robert H. Brisbane, "The Era of Marcus Garvey," in his The Black Vanguard: Origins of the Negro Social Revolution, 1900-1960, *Judson Press, 1970, pp. 81-99.*

## Oliver C. Cox   (essay date 1976)

[*A West Indian–born American educator and critic, Cox wrote several books on capitalism and on civil rights activism. In the following excerpt, he refutes Garvey's philosophy of black empowerment through racial separatism.*]

The most persuasive black nationalist and racist, Marcus Garvey, came to the fore during World War I, the period of the great universal efforescence of nationalism when racism in general was first brought into serious contention. He encouraged whites to be racist so that his own black racism might be justified and accepted by American Negroes. "No real race-loving white man," he argued, "wants to destroy the purity of his race, and no real Negro, conscious of himself, wants to die, hence there is room for an understanding and an adjustment, and that is just what we seek." Apparently, Garvey believed racism on both sides could be made to offset each other.

Although the idea of returning to Africa was never completely abandoned by Negroes, it was not until about 1920, with the advent of the dynamic Garvey, that Negro nationalism received definitive formulation. More recently Garvey was followed by such advocates as Elijah Muhammad, Malcolm X, Stokely Carmichael, and others. Let us, however, briefly examine the strategy of the prototype. Garvey's program was contrived particularly for American Negroes and it was here that it enjoyed overwhelming success. West Indians and Africans were true colonials—they were already at home—hence the Negro nationalists of those areas would come into possession of their country merely through a normal grant of independence from the mother country. A black exodus differs from a black accession to power; hence the two groups' politics were not interchangeable. Garvey planned to lead an emigration movement, and he did this in the guise of a black savior. He never gave up his contention that a "repatriated" black population in a nationalized African continent was the only hope of Negro Americans. He declared:

> Until the Negro reaches this point of national independence, all he does as a race will count for naught. . . . If the Negro were to live in this Western Hemisphere for another five hundred years he will still be outnumbered by other races who are prejudiced against him. He cannot resort to the government for protection for government will be in the hands of the majority of the people who are prejudiced against him, hence for the Negro to depend on the ballot and his industrial progress alone, will be hopeless as it does not help him when he is lynched, burned, jim-crowed and segregated. The future of the

Negro therefore, outside of Africa, spells ruin and disaster.

Garvey's pamphlet, ***An Appeal to the Soul of White America,*** had two principal objectives: to point out to Negroes the futility of efforts to secure civil rights in America, and to ask the United States *not* to grant the civil rights demanded by "Negroes in positions of honor" but to help all Negroes to leave the United States for Africa. He said: "Let foolish Negro agitators and so-called reformers, encouraged by deceptive and unthinking white associates, stop preaching and advocating the doctrine of 'social equality' meaning thereby the social intermingling of both races, intermarriage, and general social co-relationship." Then, turning to the United States government he made this supplication: "The Negro must have a country, and a nation of his own. . . . We have found a place, it is Africa; and, as black men for three centuries have helped white men build America, surely generous and grateful white men will help black men build Africa."

It was no paradox, therefore, that Garvey should find in the attitude and actions of the Ku Klux Klan an effective counterpart to his own designs. He praised the activities of that organization as "an honest expression of the white man's attitude toward the Negro; [which] prepares him to help himself." In 1921 Garvey actually visited the Imperial Wizard of the Klan in Atlanta, Georgia, and came away seemingly further convinced that "the Ku Klux Klan had [no] other desire than to preserve their race from suicide through miscegenation and to keep it pure, which to me is not a crime but a commendable desire and [does] not supply the reason why Negroes should attack them. . . . I believe in the purity, honor, and pride, and integrity of each and every race."

It was precisely on this point that the charismatic Garvey was able to drive home his nationalistic theories. As the *Amsterdam News,* a Negro weekly, declared in 1925: "In a world where black is despised, he taught them that black is beautiful." Garvey would say to his audiences: "Negroes, teach your children that they are the direct descendants of the greatest and proudest race who ever peopled the earth . . . it is because of the fear of our return to *power,* in a civilization of our own, that may outshine others, [that] we are hated and kept down by a jealous and prejudiced contemporary world."

It probably seemed obvious to Garvey that any demagogue who proclaimed the racial superiority of his group would have a large, fanatic following. Garvey would have had little to say to blacks had he not dangled the lure of power. "The Japanese," he pointed out, "would receive very little courtesy or fair play in any country if they had not a nation of their own to back them up in case of persecution. The Negro desires to have a nation of his own for identical reasons." As soon as it became clear that he could not carry out his plans, Garveyism simply withered away.

More specifically, there seem to have been three immediate reasons for Garvey's decline: (a) He was dealing with an essentially fictitious world. The retarded Negro nations—Liberia, Haiti, Ethiopia—were not impressed by his declarations that blacks are descendants of the greatest powers on earth. Africa, in other words, rejected him.

(b) He apparently misunderstood the nature of the culture with which he was dealing. The British imperial system that he proposed to duplicate among African blacks—in his colorful street parades he usually dressed like a colonial governor—was not built by Marcus Garvey states but by private enterprise.

And (c) his exaltation of blackness, regarded as his residual contribution, had to be skin deep. In reality, "black is beautiful" (indeed, black can be beautiful) only insofar as black behaves beautifully; and blacks or whites can behave beautifully only to the extent that they are culturally prepared to do so. On the whole, the culture of the ghetto does not prepare blacks to behave beautifully; and the ultimate remedy seems hardly the blatant repetition of the slogan.

Moreover, his glorification of physical blackness was clearly a direct reaction to white racists in exactly their terms. As we should expect, therefore, the latter were more than a match for the black racist. The late Tom Mboya, in an article offering no comfort to American Negro nationalists, observed: "The objective of the black American must be the achievement of full and unqualified equality within American society. . . . The Black American should . . . not look to Africa for escape. He must merge his blackness with his citizenship as an American, and the result will be dignity and liberation."

If, for example, the black tenant farmer tells his children that they are descendants of a mighty black race of historic African preeminence and, conversely, the white plantation owner tells his children that they are descendants of Aryans, the originators of the greatest culture known to mankind, the black children will, at most, still remain in their relative position. But then Negroes will have helped whites to concentrate on biological differences as determinants of cultural differences. Probably Negro achievers such as Benjamin Banneker and Frederick Douglass and white educators such as General O. O. Howard and the post-Civil War white missionaries in the South did incalculably more to impress permanently upon Negroes and upon the world that "black is beautiful" than the ideology of black nationalists. The "magnificence of Africa's ancient civilizations" is largely irrelevant to Africa's current problems of development. Preoccupation with it could even be a serious intertribal distraction.

The pride which Negro nationalists seem to experience in response to Garveyite exhortations emanates from psychological absorption in a more responsive mythical culture. They seem to turn their backs on the sophisticated culture in which they must inevitably live, the only culture from which they can derive pride of achievement, and thus they merely postpone the day of reckoning. Some of the same groups that castigate the Negro middle class, the "black bourgeoisie," for its middle-class behavior praise the Black Muslims for their advocacy of certain middle-class practices among their members—with the difference that the Muslim social structure has been devised peripherally by and for the societally underprivileged. (pp. 229-33)

*Oliver C. Cox, "The Projections of Nationalist Leadership," in his* Race Relations: Elements and Social Dynamics, *Wayne State University Press, 1976, pp. 226-41.*

### Randall K. Burkett   (essay date 1978)

[*An American educator and critic, Burkett is the author of* Garveyism as a Religious Movement: The Institutionalization of a Black Civil Religion. *In the following excerpt from that book, he examines the religious concepts expressed in Garvey's essays and speeches.*]

Garveyites frequently commented on the importance of religion to the work of the Universal Negro Improvement Association and on the imperative need to rewrite the theology which had been taught to most of its members. The remarks of the Reverend John Dawson Gordon, Assistant President-General of the UNIA, offer a typical example of this concern. In a speech to a Boston audience Gordon "compared the U.N.I.A. with religious organizations and acclaimed that the white man's religion had met its Waterloo and that the Hon. Marcus Garvey and the Universal Negro Improvement Association have found the missing link in the Christian Church." The UNIA would not simply be content with new organizational forms, Gordon declared, for "the Negro people of the world will have to reconstruct the theology of the church in order to hasten the building up of the morale of the Negroes of the world."

Garvey himself frequently stated that "our theologians" are at work rewriting (white) theology so as to make it pertinent to the needs and experience of the Black man. He rarely specified who was included in this group of theologians and never explicitly included himself among them. On the contrary, he repeatedly insisted that he was neither a preacher nor a theologian nor any manner of religious leader. In spite of his denials, however, it is my contention that Marcus Garvey was the UNIA's most shrewd and perspicacious theologian.

This conclusion is based on the examination of annual UNIA convention debates concerning religious questions, in which Garvey invariably took a leading role, and on a careful reading of his countless speeches and editorials, which are replete with discussion of theological issues. Garvey was by no means a systematic theologian, in the sense of carefully setting forth a unified or definitive statement concerning his doctrine of God, of Christ, of man, and of man's destiny. By imposing the categories of systematic theology upon his disparate speeches and writings, however, I hope to demonstrate that there is a palpable unity to Garvey's thought, and that he self-consciously sought to interpret the Christian faith which was his heritage, in the light both of his people's experience and of the latest scientific information available.

If Garvey's theology was by temperament unsystematic, it was also by principle nondogmatic. He insisted that religion was a phenomenon universally experienced, and that no man ought to criticize another either for holding to religion in general or for believing in a particular conception of the deity. Speaking at the Sixth International UNIA Convention (1929) he declared,

> Man is a religious being, that is to say, he must have some kind of belief—call it superstition or what not. Man who has started to think traces his origin beyond man; and as such has been groping in the dark to find out the source from whence he came, and by our own intuition we have attributed that source to something beyond us; and in so believing we accept the idea of a religion. Some make our God the God of Fire; some make our God the God of water; some make our God the God of the Elements and others of us accept the Christian belief. Man's religion is something we cannot eliminate from his system or destroy in him; therefore, it is folly for any man to go about attacking another man's religion, because to him it is fundamental. You may be a Christian; you may be a Mohammedan; that is your religion. We are all entitled to our own religious belief. Some of us are Catholics, some of us are Presbyterians, some of us are Baptists, and we deem it a right to adhere to our particular belief.

While Garvey was thus content to have his followers remain within any (Black-led) religious organization, whether Protestant or Catholic, Christian or non-Christian, he was not willing for them to retain the religious ideals or conceptualizations of another race. In the first place, he specifically and emphatically rejected the conceptualization of God as white. As he declared on one occasion,

> If the white man has the idea of a white God, let him worship his God as he desires. . . . We, as Negroes, have found a new ideal. Whilst our God has no color, yet it is human to see everything through one's own spectacles, and since the white people have seen their God through white spectacles, we have only now started out (late though it be) to see our God through our own spectacles. . . . We Negroes believe in the God of Ethiopia, the everlasting God—God the Father, God the Son and God the Holy Ghost, the one God of all ages. That is the God in whom we believe, but we shall worship Him through the spectacles of Ethiopia.

As Biblical warrant for rejection of the white God, Garvey cited not only the Psalmist's prophecy concerning Ethiopia, but also the Mosaic prohibition against idolatry. God has declared that He made man in His own image, and since "Every man is a pattern of God . . . and all of God's creatures go to make God" (all men being part of God), thus Black men must see that it is idolatrous to make God white. "When you bow to a graven image, when you bow to the god of another species, you dishonor the God that is in you, and you . . . abase the God of your existence and commit a sin against the Holy Ghost. . . . Therefore, the U.N.I.A. desires every Negro to destroy the image of the white God that you have been taught to bow to."

Garvey had much more to say about God, however, than that He must not be conceived by Black men to be white. In the confidential Lesson Guides written for his School

of African Philosophy, for instance, he sought to characterize the attributes of God. God must first be understood, Garvey wrote, as *Universal Intelligence:*

> There is a God and we believe in Him. He is not a person nor a physical being. He is a spirit and He is universal intelligence. Never deny that there is a God. God being universal intelligence created the universe out of that intelligence. It is intelligence that creates. Man is a part of the creation of universal intelligence and man was created in the image and likeness of God only by his intelligence. It is the intelligence of man that is like God, but man's intelligence is only a unitary particle of God's universal intelligence.

God is thus absolute mind, the sum of all intelligence of which man can see only a part. But as He has the capacity to create and control, He must also be characterized as *absolute power*. This is a power which no man has the ability to deny.

> There is a God.
>
> No man can say there is no God, because no man is like God. Man is limited in his intelligence at the most and man knows how insufficient he is between life and death—that he is born without his knowledge and dies without his will or wish; when his birth and death [occur] must logically and naturally be controlled by somebody else.
>
> It could not be man because man is always man whether he be a big man or small man. So power that gives birth and causes death must be greater than man's power. Whatsoever that power is, it must be an absolute power.
>
> Some men call it by different names but all mean the same thing and it is *God*.

Now the perennial problem with which all theologians have had to deal, having posited an all-knowing and all-powerful God, is to explain the source of suffering and misery to which man is subjected. To Garvey that question took a particular poignancy for the Black man, who had endured more than his share of suffering. As he forthrightly queried, "If God is God, and He is God, if He is the God of love and of justice, how can He permanently permit these men [who oppress us] to rule the destiny of all mankind?" In the various answers which Garvey offered to this question he identified several other attributes of God. On the one hand, God had to be a God of absolute impartiality and fairness, which was the meaning of the oft-repeated phrase, *God is no respecter of persons*. In an extended explication of this theme Garvey observed,

> There can be no God if there be inequality in the creation or in the creative purpose of God. And there could be no God that would create a race to be a race of slaves and another to be one of Masters. That race, this race of slaves, would reject such a God.
>
> There is no God who would create me a black man, to be a hewer of wood and a drawer of water. It is a lie! It is a damned lie.
>
> If there is such a God, then I would have to look for another God. But there is no such God. The

God that exists, the God that I love, the God that you also love and adore, is a God of love, a God of Mercy, a God of Charity and a God that is no respecter of persons. Such a God I worship; such a God I adore; and such a God I know would never place me here especially to be a hewer of wood, a drawer of water, a picker of cotton and a laborer in a cane field. He placed me here AS MY SOVEREIGN LORD to make of life whatsoever I desire to do. If I want to be an industrial captain, it is all left to my selection. God has no plantation; He is not an economist; He has nothing to do with the affairs of men or the economic arrangements of humanity. Otherwise he would be an unfair God.

From the premise that God is absolutely impartial and is not a respecter of persons, Garvey at various times offered two different and perhaps finally irreconcilable lines of argumentation. On the one hand, he insisted that whereas God is not responsible for a race's being in or out of slavery, the responsibility and the fault had to be placed squarely on the enslaved race itself. "You take *yourselves* into slavery," he insisted, "and you will remain in that state so long as you lack human will."

> Some of us flatter ourselves to believe that God is with us and God is a being who is taking care of us in this serfdom and peonage and slavery that we are enduring. God is vexed with you because you are subordinating the powers that He gave you.
>
> (pp. 45-9)

For the most part Garvey argued this line consistently, insisting that as absolute impartiality, God does not side for or against one race or another; that each group and each individual receives its just desserts; and thus that one ought not to sit around and pray to God for the help one could best give oneself. On the other hand, Garvey occasionally argued that *since* God is just and fair and *since* one particular race has suffered so much, a time is coming when retribution will be paid. Indeed, the trials through which God had put the Negro race must reflect a special purpose for which He is preparing them:

> If humanity is regarded as made up of the children of God, and God loves all humanity—we all know that—then God will be more pleased with that race that protects all humanity than with that race that outrages all humanity. Up to now, we have found no race in power that has held out a helping hand and protection to all humanity, and it is apparent that that position is left for the new Ethiopia. Let us, therefore, continue our journey, man. I believe when we reach the goal we shall reign forever, because *we shall be the elect of God.* He must have had His purpose when He took us through the rigors of slavery for more than two hundred and fifty years. . . . [T]here must be some wonderful purpose of God in bringing us through all we had to endure in the past three hundred years, down to the present, and I attribute it to that prophecy of God that His children shall one day stretch forth their hands again unto Him.
>
> (pp. 50-2)

Garvey was adamant in his insistence on the indisputability of the existence of God, regardless of how He might be conceptualized. It is interesting to discover, however, that he was much less certain as to the historicity of Jesus and to claims that He was the Christ. Thus, in the chapter of the confidential Lesson Guides devoted to the topic of "Christ," Garvey began with the observation that "Christ is *supposed* to be the begotten Son of God," whose special mission was to take the form of man in order "to teach man how to lift himself back to God." He even found it necessary to offer a defense of the very idea of a Christ, declaring that "If Christ as man never existed, but was only an assumption it would have been a glorious assumption to set man a spiritual high example of how he should live." Just as one does not doubt the existence of one's great-grandfather, though never having seen him, so one ought not to doubt the existence of Christ. Garvey thus advised his students to "Deny that positively which you know of, and not that which you do not know of."

It is difficult to ascertain whether Garvey's doubts about the historical Jesus as Christ were a reaction against the "Jesus, meek and mild," whose turned cheek was the model preached by white Christians to Blacks, or whether he simply could not accept as intellectually tenable the risen Christ of orthodox Christianity which the then-flourishing "higher criticism" was bringing into question. In any case, Garvey never discussed the question in public; and he had no difficulty in accepting as the highest ideal for all of mankind both the central teaching of Jesus, which was love, and Jesus as the model of the moral life.

It was imperative, of course, that the doctrine of Christ be properly understood. Just as was the case in his discussion of the nature of God, this meant first of all that He had to be conceived historically as a Black man. One of the most spectacular ceremonies which took place under UNIA auspices, and the event which probably caused more comment throughout the United States in both the white and the Black press than any other in Liberty Hall, was the divine service for "the canonization of the Lord Jesus Christ as the Black Man of Sorrows, and also the canonization of the Blessed Virgin Mary as a black woman." It is in the Lesson Guides, however, where one finds Garvey's private assessment as to the paramount themes which would be emphasized concerning the doctrine of Christ:

> In reading Christian Literature and accepting the doctrine of Jesus Christ lay special claim to your association with Jesus and the Son of God. Show that whilst the white and yellow worlds, that is to say—the worlds of Europe and Asia Minor persecuted and crucified Jesus the Son of God, it was the black race through Simon the black Cirenian [sic] who befriended the Son of God and took up the Cross and bore it alongside of Him up to the heights of Calvary. The Roman Catholics, therefore, have no rightful claim to the Cross nor is any other professing Christian before the Negro. The Cross is the property of the Negro in his religion because it was he who bore it.
>
> Never admit that Jesus Christ was a white man,

otherwise he could not be the Son of God and God to redeem all mankind. Jesus Christ had the blood of all races in his veins, and tracing the Jewish race back to Abraham and to Moses, from which Jesus sprang through the line of Jesse, you will find Negro blood everywhere, so Jesus had much of Negro blood in him.

Implicit in the latter portion of this statement is a principled universalism in Christ, for Garvey's claim was not that Jesus Christ was of pure African descent, but that He "had the blood of all races in his veins," and on this depended His capacity to redeem all of mankind. The overall impact of the remarks, however, was to reinforce a particularistic interpretation of Christ's significance. This was accomplished primarily through emphasis on the centrality of Simon the Cyrenian, the Black man who had been forced to bear Jesus' Cross up Calvary Hill. By virtue of this unique deed Garvey argued that the Negro race stood in a special relationship to Jesus; and on occasion this special act of Simon's was publicly contrasted with the act of betrayal by the white men who, he suggested, had to bear responsibility for Christ's crucifixion:

> Give us the standard bearer of Christ; let him lead and we shall follow, Christ the crucified, Christ the despised, we appeal to you from the great memories of the past; we appeal to you for help, for succor and for leadership. . . . Oh Jesus the Christ, oh Jesus the Redeemer, when white men scorned you, when white men spurned you, when white men spat upon you, when white men pierced your side out of which blood and water gushed forth, it was a black man in the person of Simon the Cyrenian who took the cross and bore it on heights of calvary. As he bore it in the past to lighten your burden as you climbed your Calvary, so now, when we are climbing our calvary and the burden being heavy—Jesus we ask you to help us on the journey up the heights.

In terms of Garvey's use of Jesus as a model for the present world, this passage also points to one aspect of His life on earth, namely, Jesus the despised, the rejected, the one who bears undeserved suffering, and who thereby has a special affection for those who are despised, rejected, and forced to bear unmerited suffering. This model of Jesus as suffering servant was always balanced, however, with the model of Jesus as great reformer or as "the greatest radical," who suffers unto death, it is true, but who does not do so meekly. In one Easter sermon Garvey characterized Jesus as having met the same resistance to His message to which "all reformers and reform movements" are subject when they cease to preach a strictly spiritual message and demand that existing social and economic relationships be transformed. When it became clear that Jesus' message was both spiritual and temporal, He was quickly declared to be an impostor, a dangerous individual who must be destroyed.

> When Jesus came the privileged few were taking advantage of the unfortunate masses. Because the teaching of Jesus sought to equalize the spiritual *and even the temporal rights of man,* those who held authority, sway and dominion sought His liberty by prosecution, sought His life by

death. He was called to yield up that life for the cause He loved—because He was indeed a great reformer.

One another occasion Christ was characterized, like "all great reformers," to be a radical—one who was rough, unyielding, uncompromising, fearing only God. "All true warriors know no fear. Our friends are fainthearted, but Jesus Christ was the greatest radical the world ever saw. Jesus opposed wrong. His program was to lift up humanity and save mankind." And on still another occasion the theme of Christ, the One who suffers, and Christ, the Greatest Reformer, were conflated as parts of a whole:

> If we could see the sufferings of Christ, if we could see the patience of Christ, if we could see the very crucifixion of Christ, then we would see the creature, the being spiritual that God would have us to be; and knowing ourselves as we do, we could well realize how far we are from God. . . . [T]he world derided Him; the world scoffed at Him; they called Him all kinds of names. He was an imposter; He was a disturber of the public peace; He was not fit to be among good society; He was an outcast; He was a traitor to the king. . . .

> Christ was the first great reformer. . . . [T]here is one lesson we can learn from the teachings of Christ. . . . [T]he spiritual doctrines of Jesus were righteous; the doctrines of Jesus were just, and even though He died nearly nineteen hundred years ago, what has happened? After the lapse of nineteen hundred years His religion is the greatest moving force in the world today, morally and spiritually. It shows you, therefore, the power of a righteous cause.

For Garvey, as for most theologians, there are analogues between one's doctrine of God and one's conception of man. This was the point, after all, of Garvey's insistence that God had in some sense to be Black, for it affirmed that Black men were fully men, that they were coequal sons of God with all other of His sons, and that they too would share in the divine inheritance. Garvey made explicit the inter-connection between the doctrines of God and of man, in a speech to a UNIA audience in Cincinnati.

> Do you know what it is to be a man? To be a man is to bear the semblance of my Creator, the image of my Creator. If you are conscious of the fact that you were created in the image of your Creator, then you realize that you are a man. Man is the supreme lord, the supreme master of the world.

The most definitive public statement of Garvey's doctrine of man was published in a front page editorial of the *Negro World* and was entitled **"Dissertation on Man."** In this statement (reproduced here only in part) one can discern several key elements in his conception of the nature of man.

> *Man* is the individual who is able to shape his own character, master his own will, direct his own life and shape his own ends.

> When God breathed into the nostrils of man the breath of life, made him a living soul, and be-

stowed upon him the authority of Lord of Creation, He never intended that that individual should descend to the level of a peon, a serf, or a slave, but that he should be always *man* in the fullest possession of his senses, and with the truest knowledge of himself.

But how changed has *man* become since creation? We find him today divided into different classes—the helpless imbecile class, the sycophantic class, the slave class, the servant class and the master class. These different classes God never created. He created Man. But this individual has so retrograded, as to make it impossible to find him. It is so difficult to find a real man.

As far as our race goes, I hardly believe that we can find one hundred real men who are able to measure up to the higher purpose of the creation. It is because of this lack of manhood in us as a race why [*sic*] we have stagnated for several centuries and now find ourselves at the foot of the great human ladder. . . .

After the creation, and after *man* was given possession of the world, the Creator relinquished all authority to his lord, except that which was spiritual. All that authority which meant the regulation of human affairs, human society, and human happiness was given to man by the Creator, and man, therefore, became master of his own destiny, and architect of his own fate.

Man is here understood above all else as a creature whose will is free to act as he chooses; he is a lord over creation in his own right, who was made by the supreme Lord of Creation to serve no other man. Distinctions of class or intelligence are not indelible distinctions bestowed by God, but are the manifestations of the failure to realize the potential for which man is intended. The Creator has stepped back from his creation to see how and what man can accomplish with his God-given powers, and man must depend upon his own resources to achieve what he will.

The attributes of God which Garvey describes in their infinity are characteristic of man in his finitude. Thus, in the passage cited earlier describing God as Universal Intelligence, Garvey observed that it was precisely in man's intelligence that he shared the likeness of God, though of course that intelligence was only partial and incomplete. Whereas God was characterized as absolute power in his capacity as Lord of Creation, man has also been given dominion as a lord of creation to utilize physical, material power for his own benefit and for the benefit of his fellow man. And whereas God is understood as absolute impartiality, so man must recognize that he is created equal to all other men, with no group being divinely intended to reign over the other.

While man has the capacity, then, as a free agent to act with benevolence and charity toward his fellow man, inasmuch as he is created in the image of an impartial God, the cruel and harsh fact is that for the most part he does not so behave. The dark side of man's nature, his capacity for evil, was by no means neglected in Garvey's theology. This theme is elaborated in the eleventh of his Lesson

Guides written for the School of African Philosophy, in the chapter entitled "Man."

> Man because of his sin which caused him to have fallen from his high estate of spiritual cleanliness to the level of a creature, who acts only for his own satisfaction by the gift of free will, must be regarded as a dangerous creature of life. When he wants he can be good, otherwise he is generally bad. If dealing with him you must calculate for his vices and his damnable evils. He is apt to disappoint you at any time therefore you cannot wholly rely on him as an individual. Always try to touch him with the hope of bringing out that which is good, but be ever on your guard to experience the worst that is in him, because he is always in conflict with himself as between good and evil.
>
> When he can profit from evil he will do it and forget goodness. This has been his behaviour ever since the first record of his existence and his first contact with his fellows.

(pp. 52-8)

Just as there is a two-fold aspect to the nature of man, namely, man's capacity for evil on the one hand and his creation as a free agent in the likeness of God on the other; so there is a dual aspect to Garvey's doctrine of salvation. The persistent self-reliance which was at the heart of his social philosophy meant that salvation had to lie within man's own grasp and could not rest solely on the salvific act of another. Salvation would be achieved not by faith alone, but by the persistent work of every man. In the previous chapter, reference was made to Garvey's "beatitude of bread and butter," in which he had declared, "this is the time for our salvation. Prayer alone will not save us; sentiment alone will not save us. We have to work and work and work if we are to be saved." A corollary to this salvation by work was his adamant rejection of "fatalism," which he repeatedly characterized as the bane of the race's existence. In his powerful Easter sermon entitled **"The Resurrection of the Negro,"** Garvey declared,

> Some of us seem to accept the fatalist position, the fatalist attitude, that God accorded to us a certain position and condition, and therefore there is no need trying to be otherwise. The moment you accept such an attitude, the moment you accept such an opinion, the moment you harbor such an idea, you hurl an insult at the great God who created you, because you question Him for His love, you question Him for His mercy. . . . All that you see in creation, all that you see in the world, was created by God for the use of man, and you four hundred million black souls have as much right to your possession in this world as any other man.
>
> Created in the image of the same God we have the same common future, and tonight I trust that there will be a spiritual and material and a temporal resurrection among Negroes everywhere.

If one side of Garvey's doctrine of salvation was emphasis upon work, individual self-reliance, and a rejection of fatalism, the other (social) side of his concept of salvation

was his admonition to secure *power.* As would be anticipated, given his basically Arian Christology, Jesus was not
himself the instrument or vehicle of salvation. As the great
reformer or the "greatest radical," He empowered man to
act for his own and his people's salvation. The demand for
power was argued most persuasively in one of Garvey's
*Negro World* editorials:

> Gradually, even though slowly, we are getting to
> realize that the fight is now or never. We have
> to fight for a place in the world if we must exist;
> that place is not going to be yielded up to us by
> philanthropy, by charity, but only through that
> stronger power that will compel others to give
> us that which is our due. I say POWER because
> it is necessary. Except the individual, the race or
> the nation has *power* that is exclusive; it means
> that that individual, that race or that nation will
> be bound by the will of the other who possesses
> this great qualification. It was the physical and
> pugilistic *power* of Jack Johnson that kept him
> in the ring. It was the industrial and scientific
> *power* of the Teutonic race that kept them for
> years as the dictators of the economic and scien-
> tific policies of Europe. It is the military, naval,
> and political *power* of Great Britain that keeps
> her mistress of the world; hence it is advisable
> for the Negro to get *power;* get *power* of every
> kind, *power* in education, in science, in industry,
> in politics, in higher government, and physical-
> ly. We want that kind of *power* that will stand
> out signally so that other races and nations can
> see, and if they won't see, feel. POWER is the
> only argument that satisfies man. Man is not sat-
> isfied; neither is he moved by prayers, by peti-
> tions, but every man is moved by that *power* of
> authority which forces him to do, even against
> his will. . . . The only advice I can give the
> Negro is to get *power.*

In the final analysis it must be said that the salvation Garvey most earnestly sought was both social and this-
worldly. He shared with the proponents of the Social Gospel who were his contemporaries a rejection both of the
overemphasis on salvation of the individual soul and of an
other-worldly orientation which led to neglect of man's
physical and social needs. In his passionate demand for social justice, however, he had no illusion that the Kingdom
was nearly at hand. In fact, a fair reading of the times indicated that things were getting worse, not better, in the
present world. As Garvey remarked at the conclusion of
his survey of international events during the previous year,
"Those of us who lead the Universal Negro Improvement
Association can interpret the signs of the times. We foresee the time when the great white race in America will
have grown numerically to the point of selfish race exclusion, when no common appeal to humanity will save our
competitive race from their prejudice and injustice, hence
the Universal Negro Improvement Association warns the
Negro of America as well as of the western world of the
dangers of the future, and advises that the best effort of
today should be that concentrated on the building up of
a national home of our own in Africa." With this pessimistic forecast of the course of racial relations, Garvey insisted that justice could be achieved only by a fair distribution
of power. "Why does the white man act today as he does

towards you and me?" he queried, and then answered his
own question: "It is not because there is a difference between us in religion or in color, but because there is a difference between us in power."

In keeping with his insistent demand that attention be focused on the present world, Garvey rarely spoke of life
after death and he never spoke of it in compensatory terms
so as to suggest that injustices of the present would be rec-
tified on the other side of the grave. Death was not something to be feared but was to be welcomed, especially if it
came as a consequence of fighting for the freedom of Africa. A note of apocalypticism frequently crept into his language as he spoke of the impending world conflagration
that he insisted (only a year or two after the end of World
War I) was bound to come.

> Keep your eyes steadfast on the object, and what
> is it? It is the emancipation of four hundred mil-
> lion souls. It is the freeing of our own country
> Africa and the making of it of a great United
> States, a powerful government, not to be con-
> trolled by alien races, but to be dominated by
> ourselves. This is the object, this is the vision, for
> this we live, and for this we will die. . . .
>
> As the war clouds gather let us gird our loins
> and in greater numbers and stronger determina-
> tion hold fast until the hour comes, and come it
> surely will. . . . [F]our hundred million Ne-
> groes [are] ready for the march toward African
> redemption.

This apocalyptic element was made even more explicit in
Garvey's long poem, ***The Tragedy of White Injustice.*** He
regarded this poem as of crucial importance in revealing
the true character of the white man's behavior and the opportunity that his avarice would present to the Black man:

> The white man now enjoys his "Vanity Fair";
> He thinks of self and not of others care—
> Fratricidal course, that to hell doth Fratricidal
> course, that to hell doth lead—
> This is poison upon which the gentry feed. . . .
>
> Out of the clear of God's Eternity
> Shall rise a kingdom of Black Fraternity;
> There shall be conquests o'er militant forces;
> For as man proposes, God disposes.
> Signs of retribution are on every hand:
> Be ready, black men, like Gideon's band.
> They may scoff and mock at you today,
> But get you ready for the awful fray.

While Garvey repeatedly denounced those who called for
renunciation of the present world and its vale of woes in
favor of a life to come, this is by no means to suggest that
he did not articulate a vision of the future towards which
his people could look with expectation and hope. This vision was embodied in the powerful image of the "Redemption of Africa," one of the most enduring and potent motivating myths in Black American religious history. As St.
Clair Drake has demonstrated, the image of the "redemption of Africa" had served throughout the nineteenth century as "one important focus of meaningful activity
among New World Negroes," and as "an energizing myth
in both the New World and in Africa itself for those pre-
political movements that arose while the powerless were

gathering their strength for realistic and rewarding political activity." It was revitalized in the twentieth century by Marcus Garvey, who seemed to want to make it a legitimate political goal as the specific objective of the UNIA. Even for Garvey, however, the "redemption of Africa" functioned primarily in a religious sense as the eschatological goal toward which all of history was leading, and for the realization of which all one's efforts ought to be directed. In one of his many eloquent statements of this theme, Garvey illustrated how the vision of Africa redeemed could empower one to act on his own behalf for the uplift of the race:

> I have a vision of the future, and I see before me a picture of a redeemed Africa, with her dotted cities, with her beautiful civilization, with her millions of happy children, going to and fro. Why should I lose hope, why should I give up and take a back place in this age of progress? Remember that you are men, that God created you Lords of this creation. Lift up yourselves, men, take yourselves out of the mire and hitch your hopes to the stars; yes, rise as high as the very stars themselves. Let no man pull you down, let no man destroy your ambition, because man is but your companion, your equal; man is your brother; he is not your lord; he is not your sovereign master.

Even when denying that his "vision of the future" was anything more than a careful analysis of political realities, his prophetic self-consciousness was never far from the surface. This was evident in a speech Garvey delivered to a midwestern audience that had gathered to hear the political program of the UNIA.

> I am sounding this second warning, and I want you to take it from a man who feels the consciousness of what he says. I am not pretending to be a prophet; I am not pretending to be a sage or a philosopher. I am but an ordinary man with ordinary common sense *who can see where the wind blows,* and the man who is so foolish as not to be able to see and understand where the wind blows, I am sorry for him. . . . I can see where the wind is blowing, and it is because of what I see that I am talking to you like this.

The wind only bloweth, however, as the gospel writer tells us, where it listeth, and the one who can discern where it blows is surely a man of God. Garvey knew which way the wind was moving, and, as he declared in one of his most celebrated passages, its object was Africa:

> No one knows when the hour of Africa's Redemption cometh. It is in the wind. It is coming. One day, like a storm, it will be here. When that day comes all Africa will stand together.

The proper way in which to conceptualize the UNIA as a religious or quasi-religious organization was a matter of considerable concern to Marcus Garvey. Given the fragmentation of the Black churches and the tenacity of denominational loyalties among both clergy and laity, it was clear that the UNIA could never succeed as simply one more denomination or sect from which one might choose one's religious affiliation. (pp. 60-6)

An unsigned article appearing in the *Negro World* in August 1923 stated the goal for which Garvey was striving in terms of his ecclesiology:

> The churches were not doing the work undertaken by Marcus Garvey, yet some preachers are among the crusaders. A full explanation of their attitude might be pretty hard to arrive at and harder to state without entering on contentious matter. It is enough simply to point out the obvious fact that Negro churches are divided, in some cases forbidden to work together with other movements, and they furnish no convenient meeting-ground for united work. *Only a movement that welcomes all people of all denominations and is officially attached to none while having its own assembly halls can spread its net wide enough to gather in all people desiring to identify with it.*

The last quoted statement is as close as we are likely to come to an explicit formulation of the all-embracing role into which Garvey sought to cast the UNIA. What he was struggling to institutionalize can most accurately be described as a species of civil religion, or more specifically, a Black civil religion. It provided a common set of shared beliefs and value commitments which sought to bind its adherents—all those men and women of African descent who proudly took the name Negro—into a collectivity which was divinely called to a special task in the world. The movement possessed its own meeting halls, its own order of worship as set forth in the *Ritual,* its distinctive set of beliefs, and even special holidays of its own creation. The beliefs and rituals of the UNIA, however, were of a sufficiently high level of generality so that in assenting to them one could continue to adhere to particular doctrines and practices of the separate Black denominations; and one could still attend those churches on Sunday mornings while participating in UNIA activities on Sunday evenings.

The symbols, rituals, and beliefs which constituted the inchoate Black civil religion were, of course, not new to Garvey's audience; indeed, had they been new they would not have found a responsive hearing. They rather grew out of and built upon a shared experience of slavery and of racial discrimination, as that experience was interpreted in the light of a transcendent goal: the uplift of the Negro race and the Redemption of Africa. They stood as symbols of national solidarity, binding all men who willingly accepted the hitherto opprobrious term "Negro" into a single people whom God had specially chosen for the task of building up a nation in Africa—a nation capable, first, of securing that continent's freedom and, second, of ensuring the rights of Negroes wherever they might reside in the world.

It should be evident that the characterization of Marcus Garvey as Black theologian is one that is being made not simply by virtue of the fact that a considerable number of Garvey's speeches took up the subject matter of religion; nor is it being made as a result of his insistence that God must be painted Black. The point is rather that in an unsystematic but nevertheless consistent manner Garvey was persistently about the business of interpreting the world and its travails in an ultimately meaningful way. Though rejecting any dogmatic claim concerning the finality of his own perceptions, Garvey was convinced of the indelibly religious nature of man. It was precisely his relativism, coupled with his ineradicable belief in the transcendent, which permitted Garvey to have no qualms about defining God, man, Christ, and Providence, in the light of the historical experiences and needs of his own people. God was never the God only of men and women of African descent; yet He was uniquely the God of Ethiopia who had promised that princes would be brought forth out of Egypt and into their own inheritance. The themes were by no means new to the tradition of the Black church; what was distinctive was the uncompromising this-worldly context in which they were interpreted, and the supra-institutional structure into which Garvey sought to organize them. (pp. 66-8)

> *Randall K. Burkett, "Garvey as Black Theologian," in his* Garveyism as a Religious Movement: The Institutionalization of a Black Civil Religion, *The Scarecrow Press, Inc., 1978, pp. 45-70.*

## Robert M. Kahn   (essay date 1983)

[*In the following excerpt, Kahn analyzes Garvey's political and social ideology as expressed in* The Philosophy and Opinions of Marcus Garvey.]

Marcus Garvey's strong advocacy of separatism for the American black community reflects his understanding of the fundamental principles which govern economic and political development. African nationalism is not an adventure for Garvey; it is a necessity. He concludes from his knowledge of history that there is literally no future for blacks in the United States: ultimately blacks face, as a minority race in a white nation, the certainty of economic displacement, starvation, and genocide. Garvey confidently forecasts the coming of black genocide—avoidable only if African nationalism is pursued—because of three interlocking principles of social survival which are operant in the world: (1) the world is increasingly subjected to population pressures; (2) human races are engaged in the Darwinian struggle for the survival of the fittest; (3) majority rule always places political power in the hands of a racially prejudiced majority.

Espousing the dismal lesson of Malthus and Ricardo, Marcus Garvey posits world overpopulation as the root cause of racial and national antagonism. Mankind is plagued with an increasingly unfavorable ratio between land mass and population: "the world is small and humanity in the many and various race groups, is growing larger every day" (***Philosophy and Opinions of Marcus Garvey***). Garvey indicates that, as increasing numbers of people depend on a fixed amount of land, food shortages are imminent; indeed, he argues that humanity has already outstripped its food supply. Moreover, the hungry victims of economic imbalances will create a Hobbesian world of disorder: "Hungry men have no respect for law, authority or human life." Not only is the world already experiencing tangible harm, but the land-rich United States will not be

*Garvey, pictured in the scholar's robe he often wore when giving speeches.*

spared the ravages of over-population in the future. Garvey predicts that eventually the American scramble for food will result in racial competition and antagonism:

> In another one hundred years white America will have doubled its population; in another two hundred years it will have trebled itself. The keen student must realize that the centuries ahead will bring us an over-crowded country; opportunities, as the population grows larger, will be fewer; the competition for bread between the people of their own class will become keener, and so much more so will there be no room for two competitive races, the one strong, and the other weak.

For Garvey, the spectre of overpopulation has an immediate ideological significance for the black community. The preeminent concern of the black community must be physical survival.

In isolation, the problem of world overpopulation is as liable to inspire cooperation as to inspire antagonistic efforts. Yet, for Garvey, overcrowding is not an isolated principle of world reality; the convergence of other conditions forces a separatist response upon the black community. In Garvey's view, human history is firmly channeled along the path of antagonistic self-interest:

The world is not in the disposition to divide the spoils of materialism, but on the contrary every group is seeking the aggrandizement of self at the expense of those who have lost or who ignore the trend of human effort in the direction of self-preservation.

Man is not selfish because of a defect in his character or reason; man acts selfishly because the laws of nature dictate that only the strongest races and nations will survive.

Garvey's belief in the Darwinian survival of the fittest, it must be emphasized, is a critical element in the appreciation of Garvey's ideology. Garvey's proclivity for the bumptious pose, bombastic declarations of African glory, and the chauvinistic touting of black nationhood must be viewed in the context of Garvey's overriding and most serious objective: black survival. It is not racial glory and prestige which form the proximate goals of Marcus Garvey. It is survival. Garvey's arousal of the black masses is a preparatory step; the American black community must be prepared and strengthened before the struggle for survival intensifies. The alternative is extinction.

In concrete terms, Garvey asserts that the struggle for survival has already arrived on American shores. In a short essay entitled **"White Man's Solution for the Negro Problem in America,"** Garvey reveals the white man's genocidal plan for America:

> A hearty welcome is extended to white people from all parts of the world to come to and settle in America. They come in by the thousands every month. Why? The idea is to build up a vast white population in America, so as to make the white people independent of Negro labor; thereby depriving them of the means of livelihood, the wherewithal to buy bread, which means that in a short while they will die of starvation.

In effect, Garvey argues that massive white immigration represents the effort of American whites to prepare for an intense struggle of survival; as the result of such preparation, when food shortages do occur in America, the black community will succumb to mass starvation. To the skeptic who questions the genocidal capacity of the American white community, Garvey offers the example of American Indians as an unprepared weaker race which was exterminated by American whites. To the skeptic who cites years of black progress within the United States as evidence that American whites are not predisposed toward a policy of black extermination, Garvey replies that such progress is illusory and that such a liberal spirit on the part of whites is only temporary:

> What progress have we made when everything we do is done through the good will and grace of the liberal white man of the present day? But can he always afford to be liberal? Do you not realize that in another few decades he will have on his hands a problem of his own—a problem to feed his own children, to take care of his own flesh and blood? In the midst of that crisis, when he finds not even enough to feed himself, what will become of the Negro? The Negro naturally must die to give way, and make room for others who are better prepared to live.

Finally, to the skeptic who would attack this revelation of an extermination plan by attacking Garvey's personal integrity, Garvey responds by recalling that the whites whom he is attempting to thwart are the original critics of his character:

> because I love my race to the point of objecting to his secret and cunning policy of destruction and extermination, he claims that I am a "Bad Nigger." I would rather die than be good, if being good in this respect means that I must acquiesce to the extermination of my race, like the American Indian and other native peoples.

Garvey's basic point is that American whites, in light of nature's rule for choosing survivors in a teeming world, are preparing for the extermination of blacks in the long run.

However, even conceding both that whites are capable of exterminating the black community and that blacks possess few instruments of self-protection, the inevitability of black genocide within the American political system is still not a closed question. An additional ingredient must be added to this combustible mixture before it becomes undeniable that the American political community offers death, rather than a safe haven, to its black minority. Given that the United States has a democratic regime which boasts of constitutional protections for minorities lacking the tools of self-protection, it can be hypothesized that those whites who would exterminate blacks either constitute a minority or are effectively constrained by constitutional bulwarks. Garvey dismisses both possibilities. First, races are intrinsically prejudiced against each other: "No race in the world is so just as to give others, for the asking, a square deal in things economic, political and social." Indeed, Garvey is so certain of universal prejudice and suspicion that he is an open admirer of the Ku Klux Klan for its honesty and lack of hypocrisy. Ultimately, "the strong hand of prejudice" will exterminate the black community which lacks organization and preparation. Thus, racial prejudice among whites is inescapable, universal, and, when unopposed by blacks, impelled toward extermination.

Marcus Garvey is equally convinced that a democratic constitution provides no protection against the exterminationist tendencies of a prejudiced majority:

> the majority of the people dictate the policy of governments, and if the majority are against a measure, a thing, or a race, then the government is impotent to protect that measure, thing or race.

> If the Negro were to live in this Western Hemisphere for another five hundred years he would still be outnumbered by other races who are prejudiced against him.

Garvey, in effect, identifies himself as an absolute majoritarian in his general conception of democracy and his specific description of the American political regime. Because a democratic regime expresses the will of a majority without impediment, the American regime places no obstacle before the prejudice of its white majority; government-level and regime-level protections for the black minority yield in the presence of that prejudice.

Whether persuasive to the modern reader or not, it must be acknowledged that, given Garvey's premises, his advocacy of black separatism represents a thoughtful conclusion for a man whose principal concern is the universal improvement of his race. In this context, black separatism is the denouement of a systematic political analysis and a consistent ideological position. Even if introduced with semi-mystical oratorical embellishments or flourishes of gaudy salesmanship, Garvey's proposal of a separatist solution cannot be dismissed as a superficial *deus ex machina* or delusory *non sequitur*. Marcus Garvey perceives a world population explosion for which he discerns no solution. He perceives a Darwinian scramble of survival among nations and races for which he discerns no surcease. Finally, apropos the specific dilemma of the minority black community within the United States, he discerns no democratic remedy for black genocide in a regime which, by its very nature, is controlled by a prejudiced white majority.

Garvey proposes the establishment of a separate black nation—rejecting participation in the American government, regime, and political community—because, ultimately, nationhood offers the only effective protection for the black community:

> NATIONHOOD is the only means by which modern civilization can completely protect itself.
>
> Independence of nationality, independence of government, is the means of protecting not only the individual, but the group.
>
> Nationhood is the highest ideal of all peoples.

For the black people of the world, the abstract appreciation of nationhood translates into a concrete pursuit of African nationalism. Maintaining that "Africa is the legitimate, moral and righteous home of all Negroes," Garvey characterizes his effort as an attempt at "repatriation." Surrounding his program with Christian symbolism and the spirit of righteousness, Garvey also frequently characterizes his purpose as that of "African Redemption."

In the short run, African nationalism provides an escape from the genocidal intent of a prejudiced majority; in the long run, however, successful nation-building can diminish that prejudice which is the engine of black destruction:

> Prejudice of the white race against the black race is not so much because of color as of condition; because as a race, to them, we have accomplished nothing; we have built no nation, no government; because we are dependent for our economic and political existence.

Thus, while color prejudice may remain relatively intractable in the relations between races, that component of prejudice which represents the snobbish contempt of the strong toward the weak can be lessened.

In order to avoid the inevitability of genocidal slaughter, Garvey proposes black nationalism as the salvation of the black community. Yet, a proposed solution to the predicament of the black commuity is only valuable to the extent that there is a realistic prospect of its achievement. Garvey is no utopian. The avoidance of future ravages through repatriation is possible, he reasons, because of the convergence of certain favorable circumstances which are immediately exploitable. Specifically, three existing circumstances foretell the achievement of black nationhood by American blacks: (1) the emergence of nationalism as an increasingly legitimate principle for justifying conduct within the international community; (2) a growing awareness and appreciation of the mutual advantages which are possible when blacks and whites join together in the cause of black nationalism; and, (3) the progress in preparing the black community for separatism which has been effected since the Garvey movement became the foremost organizational and planning instrument of African repatriation.

Marcus Garvey discerns abundant evidence that he is witnessing an era of triumphant nationalism, promising opportunity and hope for the black community. Garvey proclaims the validity of nationalism as both an intellectual and an historical force within the international political system. On the intellectual plane, the principle of self-determination appears as a hard-learned lesson of World War I and the only legitimate starting point for any discussion of international political evolution. For Garvey, the proper vehicle for securing liberty is the racial group as it pursues national independence:

> If liberty is good for certain sets of humanity it is good for all. Black men, Colored men, Negroes have as much right to be free as any other race that God Almighty ever created, and we desire freedom that is unfettered, freedom that is unlimited, freedom that will give us a chance and opportunity to rise to the fullest of our ambition and that we cannot get in countries where other men rule and dominate.

In effect, liberty is filtered through the territorial claim of each and every group: "The world is the property of all mankind, and each and every group is entitled to a portion." Garvey's major premise becomes that the liberty of the black community will be secured when the world is properly partitioned.

Garvey's optimism on this point springs from his beliefs that the principle of self-determination permeates geopolitical thought and, more importantly, that the actual partitioning of the world has accelerated. Amid this international land rush, Garvey stakes a claim for the black community:

> Now that the world is readjusting itself and political changes and distributions are being made of the earth's surface, there is absolutely no reason why certain parts of Africa should not be set aside absolutely for the Negro race as our claim and heritage.

If pessimistic conclusions about the future of the American black community impelled Garvey toward embracing black separatism, optimistic themes now emerge which help to explain the enthusiasm with which Garvey advocates black separatism. Given that the principle of national self-determination is in vogue and that a trend toward world partitioning seems to exist, Garvey could expect a favorable reception for his oft-proclaimed doctrine of "Africa for the Africans." In this atmosphere, Garvey could conclude that the eventual success of his program for African nationalism depended only on the enlistment of sufficient white support and on the adequate preparation of the black community for its role as nation-builder; with his customary exuberance, Garvey could also conclude that there was considerable justification for the optimistic view that white support and black preparation would soon be forthcoming.

Marcus Garvey often expresses his confidence that a significant segment of the American white community will come to the assistance of Africa-bound black separatists. White allies will, above all else, recognize that African nationalists are not destructive haters of the white race, but basically benevolent in their intentions. In order to dispel the image of seething racial hatred within the black separatist movement, Garvey provides effusive disclaimers. The race as a whole is defended: "At no time within the last five hundred years can one point to a single instance of the Negro as a race of haters." Referring to himself in the third person, Garvey also defends his own equanimity:

> At no time has the President of the Universal Negro Improvement Association preached hatred of the white people. That in itself is a violation of the constitution of the organization, which teaches all its members to love and respect the rights of all races, believing that by so doing, others will in turn love and respect our rights.

Once denuded of false fears, there are, Garvey contends, myriad reasons for whites to make positive contributions to the cause of African redemption. Initially, it is possible to tap a reservoir of white sympathy for the subordinate black community:

> there is a deep feeling of human sympathy that touches the soul of white America, upon which the unfortunate and sorrowful can always depend for sympathy, help and action.

In Garvey's estimation, the sympathetic assistance of whites is readily obtainable because the black community is putting forth a just claim. Garvey argues that whites who possess a sense of justice will honor the debt which has accrued to the black community during its generations of productive labor in the service of the American economy.

If, however, white Americans falter in their commitment to justice and lose their penchant for a sympathetic response, white assistance to black separatism will nevertheless flow from calculations of white community self-interest. Not only does Garvey hold out the prospect of a thriving trade between black-controlled Africa and white nations but he also reminds whites that a settlement of just claims through the racial partitioning of the world is a two-sided proposition. As American blacks achieve repatriation and national independence, American whites stand to gain undisputed possession of their homeland, eschewing in the process the rigors of racial competition with its attendant antagonism and insecurity.

When Garvey surveys the established record of white support for black separatism, he derives additional encouragement. Garvey recalls, in laudatory terms, the contribution of the nineteenth-century American Colonization Society in the founding of Liberia. Garvey also cites openly and without shame the ideological and political comradeship which he feels for white supremacist organizations such as the Ku Klux Klan and the Anglo-Saxon Clubs of America. Garvey not only praises white supremacist organizations, but even met with an official of the Ku Klux Klan and established friendly contacts with the Anglo-Saxon Clubs; indeed, these efforts culminated in a speech by a white supremacist to Garvey's followers in Liberty Hall and the printing of that speech in both the *Negro World* and the ***Philosophy and Opinions of Marcus Garvey.*** These and similar actions were seen as outrageous by all American black leaders who did not share Garvey's brand of separatism.

Because of the manner in which Garvey's position served as a lightning rod for the anger of more moderate black leaders and because of the controversy it engendered, Garvey's willingness to associate with white supremacist organizations merits further consideration. In final analysis, to understand Garvey's exculpation of the most virulent embodiments of white supremacy is to understand the essential nature of Garvey's separatist ideology.

First, the Klan and other supremacist groups are supportive because their threats, warnings, and atrocities lend weight to Garvey's prediction of a genocidal future. Since genocide is rooted in impersonal forces (overpopulation and so forth), one's personal loathing of white supremacist organizations is a misappropriation of energy. White supremacists, following the laws of nature and survival, will only cease pressing their advantage when the black community is strong; such strength depends on national independence.

Second, Garvey argues more generally that white supremacists benefit the black community by presenting an unadulterated and unobstructed view of the indelible racial prejudice of white Americans:

> I regard the Klan, the Anglo-Saxon Clubs and White America Societies, as far as the Negro is concerned, as better friends of the race than all other groups of hypocritical whites put together. I like honesty and fair play. You may call me a Klansman if you will, but, potentially, every whiteman is a Klansman, as far as the Negro in competition with whites socially, economically and politically is concerned, and there is no use lying about it.

It bears repeating: potentially, every whiteman is a Klansman. Given that the white supremacist appears to Garvey, not as a special and different kind of white person, but as the prototypal white without disguise, the enemies of the black community are clearly identified as those whites and blacks who cling to illusions of white liberality and who are, therefore, incapable of dealing with white supremacist organizations. Garvey believes that, if blacks desire African redemption, they must be able to talk and bargain with even the most transparently prejudiced of whites.

Finally, it must be understood that Garvey's ability to ally himself with vicious extremists who are shunned by more moderate blacks and whites is intimately related to the nature of a separatist ideology. The Ku Klux Klan and other white supremacist organizations in America are acceptable partners for Garvey because he can find no evidence that these groups are seeking an international (i.e., extranational) role to play. Totally engrossed in reshaping their own political community, these supremacist organizations are ultimately of little consequence for the dedicated separatist whose rejection of the American political community for an African homeland is complete. It is hardly surprising, therefore, that those black accommodationists, activists, and militants who are determined to pursue their goals within the American political community would take sharp exception to Garvey's tolerance of perennial enemies.

Ultimately Garvey places the responsibility for securing his separatist goals in the hands of the American black community. Garvey is convinced that American whites, destined to act from multiple motives of justice, sympathy, and self-interest, will provide material assistance for the cause of African nationalism. Yet, no external factor can succeed without the utmost effort and preparation of the black community. It is Garvey's dictum that the principle of self-determination only functions as a real and vital force for those groups which demonstrate the depth of their determination. Garvey trusts that his organization, the U.N.I.A., is well-suited for the important mission of instilling such determination in the black community:

> The mission of the Universal Negro Improvement Association is to arouse the sleeping consciousness of Negroes everywhere to the point where we will, as one concerted body, act for our own preservation.

As head of the U.N.I.A., Garvey himself delivers both pedagogical and prophetic messages designed to hasten the preparations of the American black community.

The activation of American blacks begins for Garvey with general appeals (i.e., appeals that are not only appropriate for the black separatist, but familiar to the black activist and the black militant as well). Reflecting his early absorption with the teachings of Booker T. Washington, Garvey prescribes heavy doses of racial self-help. Garvey proves a stalwart foe of fatalism:

> Some of us seem to accept the fatalist position, the fatalist attitude, that God accorded to us a certain position and condition, and therefore there is no need trying to be otherwise. The moment you accept such an attitude, the moment you accept such an opinion, the moment you harbor such an idea, you hurl an insult at the great God who created you.

In opposing religious fatalism, Garvey does not strike out at all religious belief; instead, he articulates a spiritually-based humanism which emphasizes God's desire for man to assume direct and personal responsibility for his own condition:

> All that authority which meant the regulation of human affairs, human society, and human hap-

piness was given to man by the Creator, and man, therefore, became master of his own destiny, and architect of his own fate.

Claiming that the white world has always tried to rob the black community of its history, Garvey also educes black pride and determination by recalling the glories of past black civilizations and the primitiveness of early white history.

Once the enervated and impassive are energized by broad appeals to unity and racial pride, the mobilization efforts of Garvey and the U.N.I.A. channel such energies into organized separatist activities. Garvey argues that, in final analysis, the strength which allows a race or nation to survive is closely dependent on organization:

> If we must have justice, we must be strong; if we must be strong, we must come together; if we must come together, we can only do so through the system of organization.

> The wonderful force of organization is today making itself felt in every branch of human effort. Whether in industry, society, politics or war it is the force of organization that tells; hence, I can advise no better step toward racial salvation than organization among us.

Garvey argues, in general terms, that a group's strength is maximized through organization and that the nation represents the highest and most potent form of organization available to groups. It follows that, in the specific case of American blacks, power is maximized when the organization of a separate nation is adopted as the black community's primary purpose.

As a planner, promoter, and organizer of black separatism, Garvey exhibits two chief concerns: (1) the physical transfer of the American black community to its African homeland, and (2) the establishment of political authority for the incipient black nation.

Marcus Garvey is promoting a mass—indeed, total—colonization effort which envisions the transfer of all blacks to their African homeland. His negotiations with the government of Liberia and the founding of the Black Star shipping line presuppose an interest in a massive exodus of the American black community. Yet some discussion of his advocacy of large-scale repatriation is necessary because of the controversy surrounding Garvey's designation as the leader of a "wholesale" Back-to-Africa movement. Indeed, in prefaces to the **Philosophy and Opinions of Marcus Garvey** written over forty years apart, two authors make the almost identical assertion that Garvey does not advocate mass colonization. In 1925, the author of the preface to the original edition of Garvey's second volume writes, "They [newspaper reporters] intentionally or unintentionally hailed him as the Moses of a wholesale 'Back-to-Africa' pilgrimage, a scheme which Mr. Garvey has never advocated nor planned." In 1968, the author of a new preface to the latest edition of Garvey's **Philosophy** writes, "Garvey never advocated or intended a wholesale 'repatriation.' " Both authors are quite incorrect.

Predicating his program of land acquisition and colonization on an outpouring of assistance from whites, Garvey reveals territorial aspirations of sweeping proportions:

> This plan when properly undertaken and prosecuted will solve the race problem in America in fifty years. Africa affords a wonderful opportunity at the present time for colonization by the Negroes of the Western world. There is Liberia, already established as an independent Negro government. Let white America assist Afro-Americans to go there and help develop the country. Then, there are the late German colonies; let white sentiment force England and France to turn the mover to the American and West Indian Negroes who fought for the Allies in the World's War. Then, France, England and Belgium owe America billions of dollars which they claim they cannot afford to repay immediately. Let them compromise by turning over Sierra Leone and the Ivory Coast on the West Coast of Africa and add them to Liberia and help make Liberia a state worthy of her history.

In another lengthy passage, Marcus Garvey outlines the principal reason for a fifty-year timetable:

> if a plebiscite of or a referendum to the masses of people were to be taken it would show an overwhelming majority in favor of the plan of returning the race to Africa by careful and proper arrangements and methods, whereby the somewhat settled national equilibrium industrially and generally, would not be disturbed, but by a gradual system of release, and replacement, at the same time, by assimilable duplicates, continue the migration until in the course of probably a half century the problem adjusts itself by the friendly and peaceful removal and by the return to the race of its native home, and the assimilating into the body politic of America those members of the majority race who would have replaced the Negro industrially and generally in the South and other sections of the Country that now depend on Negro labor.

In effect, Garvey attempts to strike a bargain with the white community. The whites in America will forgo monetary payments and accept African territories as settlement of the wartime debts of her allies. In return for title to these territories, the black community would promise an orderly withdrawal from the United States. Whites would gain, not only full possession of America, but the luxury of a half-century period of gradually effecting the internal migration of white labor to areas of the country where precipitous black departure would disrupt the economy. Clearly, this kind of concern for the destabilizing effects of sudden black emigration is only intelligible within the context of a plan for mass colonization.

Garvey, the separatist, evidences interest in the development of authoritative political structures which could serve the repatriated black community. However, it must be stated that Garvey only possesses rudimentary plans for the internal organization of an African political system. Garvey even fails to clarify whether he seeks a single African nation, a number of nations, or a political entity which transcends the conventional definition of nation. Thus, at various points, Garvey refers to a black republic,

a black empire, a collection of "African Communities," and a "political superstate;" indeed, one statement outlining the objectives of the U.N.I.A. schizophrenically pledges that the association will develop "Independent Negro Nations and Communities" and establish "a central nation for the race."

Beyond a wealth of smaller discoveries, the student of Marcus Garvey's ideology is finally left with two general impressions. First, Garvey's specific formula for black separatism illustrates some of the pervasive problems of political separatism in general. For example, separatism is, by its very nature, incessantly and insistently provocative; the separatist movement finds itself constantly buffeted by a churning sea of controversy. In opposing all levels of the political system, separatism calls down upon itself the ire of all other ideologues. Thus, Garvey stands alone, supported only by the *bons mots* of apartheid-minded whites, against the gentler spirits in the white community and the full panoply of black accommodationists, black activists, and black militants. Moreover, by staking a claim on Africa, Garvey also saddles himself with the responsibility for simultaneously securing: (1) recognition from the international community, (2) allegiance from the black political establishment of Africa, (3) political favors from the white American power-holders, (4) broad-based support from the American black community, and (5) the overthrow of European imperialism.

Garvey's relative neglect of regime-level phenomena is another characteristic problem of black separatism. Separatism, like all other types of political ideology, tends to concentrate its thought and action on that level of the political system which it identifies as critical. Separatism differs from its ideological competitors by emphasizing the importance of dissolving the existing political community; thus, separatist ideology addresses the merits of a new and separate nation, with insufficient regard for the nature of the new regime which it would establish concomitantly. Naive dissertations by Garvey on democracy and putting an end to official corruption illustrate this tendency.

There is a second general impression which remains when one completes a detailed examination of Garvey's thought: how easy it would be to underestimate the quality of Garvey's political ideology amid accounts of the legal difficulties, political indiscretions, and blustering style which characterized his life. Though all is not strength, there is remarkable ideological coherence in Garvey's analyses of why the black community suffers and how separatism is both a logical necessity and a practical possibility. If the contemporary student of black politics is sometimes distracted from the importance of political ideology, Marcus Garvey himself has no such problem; he recognizes that the continuing vitality of thought can surpass the importance of life itself. Prophesying that "the world shall hear from my principles even two thousand years hence," Garvey, the political ideologist and visionary thinker, writes:

> The time has come for those of us who have a vision of the future to inspire our people to a closer kinship, to a closer love of self, because it is only through this appreciation of self will we

be able to rise to that higher life that will make us not an extinct race in the future, but a race of men fit to survive.

Though it has only been fifty years thus far, it can be reported that the black community's struggle for survival still continues and that his people are still listening. (pp. 119-37)

> Robert M. Kahn, "The Political Ideology of Marcus Garvey," in The Midwest Quarterly, Vol. XXIV, No. 2, Winter, 1983, pp. 117-37.

## John Runcie (essay date 1986)

[*In the following excerpt, Runcie traces the mutual hostility between Garvey and writers of the Harlem Renaissance.*]

During the 1920s Afro-American history was dominated by two developments. Black intellectuals, who believed that a display of cultural achievements by black writers and artists would foster pride within the black community and win respect and other more tangible benefits from white America, launched the Harlem Renaissance. Meanwhile, Marcus Garvey organized and led a very different type of movement. His Universal Negro Improvement Association attracted a large following, especially among the black masses of the urban north. Both these movements contributed to the idea of the "New Negro" which flourished during the 1920s. They seemed to have much in common in their attitudes to race pride and the African past and yet the relationship between them was frequently characterized by mutual hostility or indifference.

Antagonism towards black intellectuals was certainly a recurring theme in Garvey's speeches and writings during the 1920s. In the early years of the decade his attacks were not directed at the Harlem Renaissance as such but at intellectuals in general and at such individuals as W. E. B. DuBois and James Weldon Johnson in particular. DuBois and Johnson incurred Garvey's enmity because they were among his principal rivals for leadership within the black community; their status as important figures in the Renaissance movement was largely coincidental. However, though it may not have been deliberate, Garvey's criticism of these "rogues and vagabonds" effectively contradicted one of the central tenets of the Renaissance—that cultural achievement would pave the way for black social and political equality. In a speech delivered during July 1924 at Liberty Hall in New York, Garvey scorned the idea that "the solution of the race problem depends upon our development in music, in art, in literature . . . and in poetry." Over a year earlier in the course of a U.N.I.A. meeting in Carnegie Hall, Garvey had identified himself with a quite different set of priorities. "You talk about music and art and literature, as such men like DuBois and Weldon Johnson take pride in doing. A nation was not founded first of all on literature or on writing books, it is first founded upon the effort of real workers." Clearly sensitive to the charge that his followers were "rude, ignorant and illiterate," Garvey argued that "Philosophy and the ability to write books were not going to bring to the Negro the recognition for which he was looking." Instead he empha-

sized the value of the practical knowledge and skills of the ordinary worker which could be translated into industrial and commercial progress for the black race. "They call us the common people," Garvey sneered, "They say we are illiterate. Let us see if they can live without the so-called illiterates." On another occasion he stressed that "when we can provide employment for ourselves, when we can feed ourselves, then we can . . . find time to indulge in the fine arts."

By the late 1920s Garvey's criticisms of the Harlem Renaissance had changed direction and become more specific. His skeptical dismissal of intellectuals in general and his particular dislike of the older upper-middle class elitist wing of the Renaissance gave way to a virulent attack on the movement's younger, more radical writers, who sought to exploit the folk culture of the black lower class and the primitive exotica of the black experience.

The publication in 1928 of Claude McKay's controversial novel *Home to Harlem* furnished Garvey with the occasion for an attack on this trend, but his bitter comments were clearly directed at the Harlem Renaissance movement and not just at McKay. In a front page *Negro World* editorial Garvey contended that "It is my duty to bring to your attention this week a grave evil that afflicts us as a people at this time. Our race, within recent years, has developed a new group of writers who have been prostituting their intelligence, under the direction of the white man, to bring out and show up the worse (sic) traits of our people. . . . They have been writing books, novels and poems under the advice of white publishers, to portray to the world the looseness, laxity and immorality that are peculiar to our group. . . . "

There was nothing particularly original in Garvey's remarks. Many other blacks had attacked this trend in the race's literature from a variety of political and cultural perspectives. Writers like Claude McKay and Langston Hughes had been widely criticized for pandering to depraved white tastes, succumbing to the demands of white publishers, and publicizing everything that was coarse, brutal and grotesque in the lives of the superstitious, illiterate dregs of black society. Garvey's criticisms were inaccurate and uninformed as well as unoriginal. To link the short story writer Eric Walrond with Claude McKay was perhaps not inappropriate, but to include DuBois, Johnson and Walter White in the same group of writers suggests that Garvey had personal rivalries and political propaganda in mind, as much as objective literary criticism. The work of writers like Hughes and McKay did not always conform to the "high art" expectations of this older generation and indeed DuBois had been just as critical of the direction of the Harlem Renaissance as Garvey. However, none of this detracts from the significance of Garvey's position. In the space of four years he had progressed from an unfocused tirade against all black intellectuals to a much more specific attack on some of the principal luminaries of the Harlem Renaissance in which he denounced them as "literary prostitutes" and demanded a boycott of their works.

Garvey's hostility to the intellectuals of the Harlem Renaissance is more easily described than explained. It was the product of a complex combination of circumstances and influences. One would, for example, hardly have expected Garvey to endorse a movement whose very existence was so dependent on the approval and support of white patrons, publishers, critics and readers.

White involvement in the Harlem Renaissance was complemented by the support, encouragement and publicity given to the movement by such black magazines as the *Crisis, Opportunity,* and the *Messenger.* These were the mouthpieces of organizations and individuals who were vying with Garvey for influence in the black community and who were critical of his policies and his personality. Support for the Renaissance by magazines whose editors dismissed Garvey as a "monumental monkey," an "unquestioned fool and ignoramus," "the most dangerous enemy of the Negro race in America and in the world," was unlikely to dispose Garvey favorably towards it. It was also partly as a result of their connection with these magazines and the organizations they represented that some of the Renaissance intellectuals identified the movement with the kind of integrationist interracial philosophy which was incompatible with Garvey's separatist black nationalism. This in turn helps to explain why the writers of the Renaissance, whose work appeared so frequently in other black publications, rarely submitted any material to the *Negro World.*

Another vital clue to Garvey's apparent anti-intellectualism lies in the dramatic contrast between his comparatively deprived educational background and the high level of formal education enjoyed by virtually all the participants in the Harlem Renaissance. The educational attainments of the Renaissance artists were remarkable by any standards. By those applicable to the black community in the 1920s their record was positively astonishing. DuBois and Alain Locke both held Ph.D.s from Harvard University. Countee Cullen and Sterling Brown had earned their Master's degree from the same university. James Weldon Johnson, John Matheus, Zora Neale Hurston and Jessie Fauset had also completed their M.A.; while Rudolph Fisher held both an M.A. from Brown University and an M.D. from Howard. Most of the others had completed their first degree and many of them had spent some time as graduate students. Someone like George Schuyler who never attended any university or college was a rare exception to this characteristic pattern.

Garvey enjoyed none of these advantages. Most of his formal education was acquired at an elementary school in Jamaica which he was forced to leave at the age of fourteen as a result of his father's financial difficulties. Garvey's enemies frequently contended that the U.N.I.A. attracted only ignorant and illiterate blacks and they did not allow Garvey to forget his own educational deficiencies. DuBois, in particular, placed considerable emphasis on this fact. Garvey, he contended, was " . . . a poor black boy . . . He received little training in the Church of England grammar school . . . he had no chance for a university education. . . . Garvey had no grasp of high education and a very hazy idea of the technic of civilization."

Garvey reacted to this situation in a number of fairly predictable ways. He claimed to be better educated than he was; he evolved a pretentious pseudo-intellectual style of speaking and writing; he frequently addressed his audiences wearing the cap and gown of the academic, and he invented degrees as well as impressive-sounding titles for himself. Garvey's attempts to compensate for the inadequacies of his formal education also led him to question the value of this kind of training. In his ***Philosophy and Opinions*** he wrote, "Many a man was educated outside the school room." "Develop your mind," he argued, "and you become as great and full of knowledge as the other fellow without even entering the class room." Education according to Garvey was "not so much the school that one has passed through, but the use one makes of that which he has learned." Garvey did not approve of the use which many of the Harlem Renaissance intellectuals were making of their many formal qualifications. His attack on them was another form of compensation for his own shortcomings and those of his followers.

Color prejudice further widened the gulf between Garvey and the Negro intellectuals. Garvey viewed the American racial situation from a West Indian perspective and insisted on dismissing light-skinned mulattoes as a separate and hostile caste. He repeatedly denounced racial amalgamation and called for "pride and purity of race." Hitherto, light-skinned Negroes had enjoyed certain advantages in America and there was a disproportionate number of them in the better educated upper strata of Afro-American society. This fact is at least partially reflected in the membership of the Harlem Renaissance. The point should not be exaggerated. The physical appearance of Claude McKay, Wallace Thurman, and Countee Cullen could hardly have offended Garvey's inverted racial prejudices. However, the fact remains that the movement did attract a significant percentage of light-skinned Negroes. Langston Hughes had so much white blood in him that native Africans did not even recognize him as a negro. Nella Larsen had a Danish mother. The appropriately named Walter White was blond-haired, blue-eyed and could very easily have passed for white. Jean Toomer was a very pale-skinned mulatto who twice married white women, and for whom color was so unimportant that he once declared, "I am of no particular race. I am of the human race." Finally, two of the leading figures in the Renaissance, DuBois and Weldon Johnson clearly belonged to the mulatto group.

Garvey exploited the possibilities of this situation. He dismissed Walter White as someone "whom we can hardly tell from a Southern gentleman . . . ," and referred scathingly to DuBois as "This unfortunate mulatto," "this near white or colored man." According to Garvey, DuBois represented a group that hates the Negro blood in its veins . . . " This was a charge which was clearly inapplicable to many of the extremely race-conscious Renaissance artists, but for reasons of ignorance or expediency Garvey showed no understanding of the complexities of this movement. Without any attempt to distinguish between one artist and another he accused all the authors and poets of the Renaissance of being unworthy of their race and of feeling no pride in their color. Instead, said Garvey, "they are prostituting their intelligence and ability as authors and writers against their race for the satisfaction of white people."

Garvey's hostility towards the Harlem Renaissance was reciprocated in full. To the more politically involved members of the movement Garvey represented a threat to their leadership which had to be met, and they responded with a stream of critical essays, articles and editorials. Many of the important figures in the Renaissance were not politically active. Their lives and their correspondence were often dominated by literary and cultural concerns and reveal little interest in Garvey or his Universal Negro Improvement Association. However, Garvey was too important a figure to be ignored even by the most apolitical of writers. He provided a rich source of subject matter for light-hearted satire as well as for serious analysis. The Renaissance reaction to Garvey was expressed in novels by Countee Cullen, Claude McKay and George Schuyler, in essay and short story form by Zora Neale Hurston, Rudolph Fisher and Eric Walrond, and in Wallace Thurman's unpublished play *Jeremiah the Magnificent,* just as effectively as in the critical analyses of W. E. B. DuBois and James Weldon Johnson.

The intellectuals of the Harlem Renaissance attacked Garvey in many different ways and on many different le-

vels. His aims and objectives, his policies and programmes were all subjected to critical scrutiny. Assessments of Garvey's character and personality and references to his physical appearance were particularly abusive. In his satirical novel *Black No More,* George Schuyler depicts Santop Licorice, head of the Back to Africa Society, and clearly a fictional version of Garvey, as "250 pounds, five-feet-six inches of black blubber." Schuyler's description of the real-life Garvey in his autobiography as "a short, smooth, black, pig-eyed, corpulent West Indian," was scarcely less offensive. Garvey, according to Schuyler, was an "ignorant mountebank," a rabble rouser and a megalomaniac who in many respects "anticipated Hitler." These views were shared to a greater or lesser degree by many other members of the Renaissance. DuBois, himself the subject of so much of Garvey's contempt, retaliated by describing his tormentor as "A little, fat black man, ugly, but with intelligent eyes and big head." In DuBois' eyes Garvey was a dangerous demagogue, "dictatorial, domineering, inordinately vain and very suspicious." DuBois also referred to Garvey's penchant for "bombast and exaggeration," identified an element of paranoia in his behavior and dismissed him as "either a lunatic or a traitor." To Wallace Thurman, Garvey was in certain respects like "a primitive child, arrogant, egotistical and lacking any real

*Garvey (in military dress) appears in a parade during the August 1920 UNIA convention in New York.*

mental depth." Claude McKay was less restrained. He described Garvey as a "West Indian charlatan" who cowed his audiences with "his huge ugly bulk," and who "wasn't worth no more than the good boot in his bahind that he don got."

Garvey's success in the early 1920s owed much to his realization that policies had to be supplemented by the colorful pageantry of massive parades, gaudy uniforms, marching bands, banners, ostentatious titles and "court receptions." This dimension of Garveyism attracted mass support to the U.N.I.A. It also attracted the attention of several members of the Harlem Renaissance. Claude McKay referred to Garvey's activities as a form of "stupendous vaudeville", while James Weldon Johnson saw them as "the apotheosis of the ridiculous." Even the normally sober DuBois saw the humor in the knighting of U.N.I.A. members at a specially organized reception. "A casual observer," he said of the ceremony, "might have mistaken it for the . . . rehearsal of a new comic opera . . . " Characteristically, George Schuyler went further. His satirical "Shafts and Darts" column in the *Messenger* frequently poked fun at Garvey. To Schuyler, Garvey was a suitable candidate for the "Nobel Mirth Prize. Certainly no man or woman living today has contributed more to the mirth of the world than the little octoroon admiral. He has outdistanced Falstaff, Don Quixote and Bert Williams in the production of guffaws."

This resort to humor in dealing with everything that was most ostentatious and pretentious in Garvey's behavior is also apparent in some of the literature of the Renaissance. In his only novel, *One Way to Heaven,* Countee Cullen gently mocks the elevation of an undistinguished elocution teacher to the rank of Duchess of Uganda in Garvey's self-created nobility. The much more abrasive Zora Neale Hurston dealt less gently with Garvey's conceited arrogance in an unpublished essay titled appropriately, "The Emperor Effaces Himself." Using the language of exaggerated irony, Hurston argued that "Self-effacement was typical of Mr. Garvey and his organization. He would have no fuss nor bluster—a few thousand pennants strung across the street overhead, eight or nine bands, a regiment or two, a few floats, a dozen or so titled officials and he was ready for his annual parade." Hurston also directed her irony at Garvey's weakness for bestowing the most grandiloquent-sounding titles on himself. Garvey, she suggested, granted titles to others "till it hurt them to carry all that he gave them. . . . For himself he kept almost nothing. He was merely Managing Editor of the *Negro World,* President of the Black Star Steamship and Navigation Line, President-General of the Universal Negro Improvement Association, Supreme Ruler of the Sublime Order of the Nile, Provisional President of Africa and Commander in Chief of the African Legions."

Garvey was attacked in a similar vein in the unpublished satirical play *Jeremiah the Magnificient,* co-authored by the white writer William Jourdan Rapp and the important Harlem Renaissance figure, Wallace Thurman. The central character in the play, Jeremiah Saunders, is very obviously based on Garvey and nowhere is this more apparent than when the authors describe their hero's exaggerated

sense of his own importance. Jeremiah strikes poses before a mirror and practices his oratory with such modest statements as "The Jews had their Moses, the Italians their Caesar, the French their Joan of Arc, the Americans their George Washington . . . the Russians their Lenin, and now the black man has Jeremiah." Jeremiah also shared with Garvey a weakness for ostentatious and colorful costumes. He addresses his followers wearing "a purple robe lined with red and trimmed with imitation ermine." In his lavishly furnished private office the walls "are literally covered with flag draped full length pictures of Jeremiah in his various costumes of state; one in an emporor's robes, another in an admiral's regalia, another in a general's outfit, and another in a religious habiliment worthy of a high priest." It was left to Claude McKay to deflate Garvey's pretentions completely and to see the man from an altogether different perspective. The hero of McKay's novel, *Banjo,* says of Garvey, "I guess he thought . . . that he was Moses or Napoleon or Frederick Douglass, but he was nothing but a fool, big-mouf nigger."

Treating Garvey as a buffoon, as someone to be mocked and ridiculed, was one way of reacting to the excesses of the man and his organization, but Garvey was a source of concern and embarassment as well as of amusement to the Renaissance intellectuals. Eric Walrond grasped the fact that Garvey's use of pageantry, of colorful parades, and impressive-sounding titles was enabling him to manipulate increasing numbers of the repressed black proletariat, by bringing an element of excitement into their otherwise drab lives. Both Cullen and Johnson saw sinister implications behind the creation of Garvey's nobility. If he ever fulfilled his African ambitions, the government he would establish there would be based upon the hereditary class distinctions which he had experienced as a colonial in the British West Indies and far removed from the democratic republican system favored in America. Finally, to the more conservative wing of the Renaissance in particular, Garvey's antics were intolerable. He threatened their power and status in the black community, and at a time when they were seeking to prove something to white society through their artistic achievements, Garvey's excesses seemed likely to confirm many of the contemptuous white prejudices and stereotypes about blacks. At one point in Thurman and Rapp's play, Jeremiah is visited by a group of leaders of other black organizations. One of the characters, clearly based on DuBois, expressed precisely these anxieties when he complained that "We feel that your organization is a detriment to the whole race. It holds the Negro up to ridicule. Because of you, the world is laughing at us." (pp. 7-14)

Africa was another bone of contention between Garvey and the intellectuals of the Harlem Renaissance. Garvey argued that America was a white man's country and that Afro-Americans should seek to establish an independent nation in Africa, their ancestral homeland. To many of the period's black intellectuals Garvey's ideas on African redemption, his creation of the U.N.I.A.'s African Legion, and his pretentious styling of himself as "Provisional President of Africa," constituted another of his wild fantasies. During the 1920s many black creative artists were interested in and influenced by their African heritage. They extolled Africa's culture and its contribution to civilization and this sensitivity to their racial past was reflected in their poetry, novels, essays and graphic art. Africa was important in more immediate ways. Unlike Garvey, George Schuyler, W. E. B. DuBois and Langston Hughes all visited Africa and were much moved by the experience. However, the intellectual of the Renaissance was primarily interested in the aesthetic meaning of Africa and in the idea of Africa as a symbol of primitivism, and this kind of interest, which was in any case not shared by all the Renaissance writers, was far removed from the back-to-Africa activities of Marcus Garvey. This central part of the U.N.I.A. program was criticized by many different members of the Renaissance for a wide variety of reasons.

Claude McKay, for example, emphasized just how naive and ill-informed Garvey's understanding of the African situation really was. "He talks of Africa as if it were a little island in the Caribbean Sea. Ignoring all geographical and political divisions, he gives his followers the idea that that vast continent of diverse tribes consists of a large homogenous nation of natives struggling for freedom and waiting for the Western Negroes to come and help them drive out the European exploiters." Some of McKay's points were taken up by George Schuyler and Wallace Thurman. Schuyler pointed out that the whites who controlled most of Africa would prevent any large scale immigration of American or West Indian Negroes, and that there was no reason to anticipate that native Africans would be any more enthusiastic about it. According to Schuyler, "The experience of the American Negro colonists in Liberia who have had to fight off the natives for almost a century proves that." Thurman also had something to say about the Liberian situation. He made the point that Abyssinia and Liberia were the only independent states in Africa. The former excluded foreign blacks and the latter "was too much in debt to America and American financiers to risk incurring their displeasure by becoming a colonization center for empire building Garveyites." The failure of Garvey's negotiations with the Liberian government partly affirmed the accuracy of Thurman's analysis.

Events also confirmed that Afro-Americans were no more interested in emigrating to Africa than the native Africans were in having them there. Garvey's African vision received as little popular support as its various nineteenth century incarnations. Rudolph Fisher got to the root of this problem in his short story, "Ringtail," in which a group of West Indians living in Harlem discuss the merits of African emigration. One of them argues the U.N.I.A. line of America as a white man's country and Garvey as the "Moses of his people," but the response of one of the others, a naturalized American, is more convincing. " 'Back to Africa!' snorted Payner. . . . I stay right here! . . . How de hell I'm goin' back where I never been?" (pp. 15-16)

W. E. B. DuBois had his own particular reasons for opposing Garvey's African policies. Of all the intellectuals identified with the Harlem Renaissance he was the one most interested in Africa. DuBois' interest was not confined to the complex history and sophisticated cultures of Africa. He was also a leading figure in the Pan-African movement during the 1920s. Pan-Africanism shared with Garveyism an interest in the idea of redeeming Africa for the African people but it hoped to accomplish this through the efforts of black leaders on an international basis. The idea of international cooperation working for gradual reforms which would lead to independence and self-determination for the countries of Africa was incompatible with the separatist fantasies of the Provisional President of Africa. It annoyed DuBois that the U.N.I.A. attracted much more support than the Pan-African movement, and that foreigners sometimes confused the two. He felt that Pan-Africanism had been "seriously harmed by the tragedy and comedy of Marcus Garvey." In this area as in others, DuBois was clearly embarrassed by Garvey's behaviour and by the impracticability of his schemes.

Garvey's African policies have to be seen in the context of his belief in the importance of racial solidarity and his exaltation of everything black. This emphasis on race and color, and Garvey's West Indian way of viewing these matters were further sources of annoyance to some of the Renaissance intellectuals. For someone with socialist sympathies, like Claude McKay in the early 1920s, Garvey's emphasis on race rather than class stood in the way of cooperation between black and white workers in their struggle against the capitalist system. McKay complained that Garvey had "never urged Negroes to organize in industrial unions." From a totally different conservative, middle-class, perspective George Schuyler made a similar point when he argued that racial differences between blacks and whites were less important than cultural and class differences which cut across racial boundaries. According to Schuyler, blacks and whites in America shared a common culture and a common language and consequently "the Aframerican is just a lamp-blacked Anglo-Saxon." When Garvey's preoccupations with racial purity and black separatism led him into dealings with the Ku Klux Klan, Schuyler used similar terminology to express a distaste which was shared by other black intellectuals. He dismissed the Garveyites as "nothing more than lamp-blacked Ku Klux Klansmen, leading their followers astray with absurd doctrines of fanatical racialism. . . . "

The fact that Garvey and many of his supporters in America were West Indian was a further source of annoyance. The level of black West Indian migration to America was high in the early 1920s and this generated various nativist prejudices and resentments among the Afro-American group. Without in any way identifying himself with these feelings, Rudolph Fisher described them in one of his short stories. Having expressed the hope that Garvey would take all the West Indian "monkey-chasers" back to Africa with him, one of Fisher's characters justifies this hope on the grounds that the foreigners are "too damn conceited. They're too agressive. They talk funny. They look funny. . . . An' there's too many of 'em here." There is no evidence that the intellectuals of the Harlem Renaissance ever held prejudices quite as blatant as this, but many of them valued their American identity, and their descriptions of Garvey as a "West Indian Charlatan," a "black, pig-eyed, corpulent West Indian from Jamaica," and a "West Indian agitator," suggest that his foreign birth contributed to their hostility towards him. This was certainly true in the case of Johnson and DuBois both of whom resented Garvey's influence and dwelt on the fact that he was not an American citizen, and that his followers, in DuBois' words were "the lowest type of Negroes, mostly from the Indies."

The enmity between Marcus Garvey and the intellectuals of the Harlem Renaissance was deep rooted and mutual, but it was far from absolute. To interpret the relationship between the two purely in terms of their hostility and indifference towards each other fails to recognize the complexity and subtlety of the situation. To some members of the Renaissance, Garvey was more than simply a figure of fun, a source of embarrassment or a target for criticism. Garvey was equally ambivalent in his attitudes to culture and his opinions of intellectuals.

Garvey's scathing comments on black intellectuals must be off-set by the clear understanding of the potential importance of this group to the success of the U.N.I.A., which he and other members of his organization occasionally displayed. In October 1924, for example, the *Negro World* carried **"An Appeal to the Intelligentsia"** on its front page. "I appeal," wrote Garvey, "to the higher intelligence as well as to the illiterate groups of our race. We must work together . . . for the higher development of the entire race." The reasoning behind this appeal is clear enough. When it suited him to do so Garvey sang the praises of the illiterate common people and the ordinary workers but he understood with T. Thomas Fortune, the editor of the *Negro World* from 1923 until 1928, that "No movement that amounts to anything can get anywhere without intelligent leadership."

In the light of these opinions it is not surprising to find that in its heyday the U.N.I.A. attracted a diverse group of individuals who clearly qualify as members of the black intelligentsia, and who in some instances had important connections with the Harlem Renaissance.

This group included such people as William Ferris who held Masters degrees from both Yale and Harvard, who served for a year as Assistant President General of the U.N.I.A. and who was literary editor of the *Negro World* from 1919 to 1923. During this same period the paper was edited by the orator and lecturer, Hubert Harrison, described by one of his contemporaries as "perhaps the foremost Afro-American intellect of his time." Also identified with the *Negro World* and hence with Garvey were T. Thomas Fortune who edited the paper from 1923-1928, and the essayist, short story writer and important Harlem Renaissance figure, Eric Walrond, who was one of the paper's associate editors from 1921-1923. The most committed of Garvey's supporters among the black intellectuals was the journalist, historian and co-founder of the Negro Society for Historical Research, John E. Bruce. Other black intellectuals of the period enjoyed a much looser relationship with the Garvey movement. Without actually joining the U.N.I.A. respected figures like Carter G. Woodson, Joel Rogers, and Arthur Schomburg contributed to the *Negro World* and lectured to meetings of Garvey followers.

The implications of this situation should not be exaggerated. For all their qualities people like Bruce and Harrison had enjoyed little formal education. They and the mildly eccentric Ferris were not part of the intellectual mainstream represented by the Harlem Renaissance. Renaissance writers who did have something to do with Garvey, like Eric Walrond, who wrote short stories and book reviews as well as editorials for the *Negro World*, Claude McKay who contributed a series of articles to the *Negro World* in 1919, and Zora Neale Hurston, three of whose earliest poems were published in successive April 1922 editions of the paper, were motivated by considerations other than a belief in Garveyism. McKay admitted this when he noted that by 1920 "I had stopped writing for the *Negro World* because it had not paid for contributions." For Hurston the *Negro World* offered an opportunity to have some of her poems published. There is no evidence that she was interested in or influenced by Garvey's ideas and in different circumstances she was perfectly willing to ridicule the man and his movement. Walrond's involvement with Garveyism went deeper and lasted longer but in the end he too displayed a similar lack of commitment and consistency. He joined the ranks of Garvey's critics and within a year of leaving the *Negro World* had become business manager of *Opportunity*, the magazine issued by the Urban League, which was a rival organization to the U.N.I.A.

However, the fact remains that men of intelligence did participate in Garvey's movement in a variety of different ways, and this in turn meant that Garvey and the Harlem Renaissance were not two totally unrelated phenomena. (pp. 17-20)

[U.N.I.A.-sponsored] cultural activities helped to reduce the distance between Garvey and the Harlem Renaissance, but they also reveal how different the two movements really were. Culture in the context of the U.N.I.A. was frequently quite different in content, quality and motivation from the efforts of the Renaissance. Artists like Professor Packer Ramsey, "the celebrated Bassoprofunda," and Miss Carolina Reed, the "song bird of the East," could captivate audiences in New York's Liberty Hall, but it is unlikely that they would have been as well received by more discerning audiences as were Roland Hayes or Marian Anderson. Similarly, although the Renaissance produced more than its share of inferior, derivative literature, its artists rarely sank to the depths of cultural ineptitude regularly reached by contributors to the *Negro World*. It is hardly surprising that Ethel Trew Dunlap, "the poetess-laureate" of African redemption, appears in no anthologies of Afro-American poetry from this period, though her efforts were superior to those of many others including Garvey himself. Garvey in his ***Poetic Meditations*** and in lengthy works like ***The Tragedy of White Injustice*** vacillated between the bombastic pretention which characterized so many of his speeches and a kind of banal saccharine naivete. Thomas Fortune could claim that Garvey was "a poet of high order," but his wife showed more insight when she conceded that "he never learned versification." This fact was everywhere apparent in Garvey's poetry, for example in a poem like **"Love's Morning Star,"** which contained the immortal lines

I've waited patiently for you,
And now you come to make me glad
I shall be ever good and true
And be the dearest sweetest dad.

The motives underlying Garvey's encouragement of cultural activities were fairly complex. They were both similar to and quite different from the purposes of the Harlem Renaissance. Both groups shared a common interest in fostering race pride among blacks through artistic achievement and by glorifying African history and culture. Garvey's motives also coincided with those of at least a faction of the Renaissance in one other respect. Although their objectives were totally different, Garvey shared with the elitist conservatives of the Renaissance the belief that art could prove the black man's worth and further his cause. As he put it on one occasion, "let us build up a culture of our own, and then the whole world will fall down in appreciation and respect before the black man." This objective required a certain kind of art, and the Renaissance conservatives would certainly have endorsed the suggestion that the best way to educate white public opinion was by promoting "such songs, plays, paintings, motion pictures and literature as will fully interpret the true ideals and aspirations of the Negro." Garvey had similar considerations in mind in 1928 when he attacked Claude McKay's *Home to Harlem* for its misrepresentation of black life, and insisted that "We must encourage our own black authors . . . who are loyal to their race, who feel proud to be black. . . . " These were the people who would "advance our race through healthy and decent literature." There was more than a little irony in the fact that Garvey's position on these matters should have aligned him with his arch-enemy DuBois in opposition to those Renaissance writers who were seeking to explore the culture and life-style of the black proletariat, so well represented in Garvey's own movement.

The element of irony and confusion in the relationship between Garvey and the Harlem Renaissance was reinforced by another part of Garvey's cultural philosophy—his belief that culture should reach and influence a mass audience. This belief differentiated Garvey from the bourgeois elitists of the Renaissance who were committed to the concept of "high" culture, and took him closer to artists like Claude McKay and especially Langston Hughes. Hughes was certainly active in trying to take his poetry to a larger black audience by means of poetry readings and by making available special cheap editions of his poems, which he claimed on one occasion "sold like reefers on 131st Street." However, on the subject of culture and the black masses the priorities of Garvey and Hughes were quite different. Hughes was primarily interested in utilizing and legitimizing in his poetry the language and folk culture of the black ghetto, and in providing blacks with an alternative to the middle-class consciousness which permeated so much of the Renaissance. Garvey was primarily interested in capturing and manipulating a mass audience in the interests of the U.N.I.A. This objective was not immediately reconcilable with Garvey's hopes of advancing the race by artistic achievement, but he overcame this problem skillfully. Garvey's bid for respect combined with his British West Indian background to encourage the kind of art which strove to be impeccably "decent," Europeanized and middle-class. This is reflected, for example, in Garvey's own poetry, and in the kind of music invariably performed at U.N.I.A. functions. There was little trace of the colloquial speech, or of the jazz and blues, so dear to Langston Hughes. At the same time, however, Garvey catered to the masses by exploiting a different more popular kind of culture, in the form of mass meetings, political rhetoric, colorful parades, marching bands, banners, uniforms and impressive-sounding titles.

One final motive remains to be considered. It can be discerned in much of the cultural activity of the U.N.I.A. and it is totally absent in the work of the Harlem Renaissance. It was the degree to which art was deliberately used as propaganda on behalf of Marcus Garvey and his organization. The propaganda value of U.N.I.A. pageantry is obvious enough, but the manipulation of culture went much further than this. When the *Negro World* urged its readers to "Read Good Books During the Vacation," it was Garvey's *Philosophy and Opinions* which was recommended. When the *Negro World* sponsored its "Great Literary Contest" in 1926 it stipulated that all entries were to be essays on the subject of "Why I Am a Garveyite," and when the winning entries were subsequently published in the paper they all emphasized Garvey's important role in arousing race pride and race consciousness. The 1927 contest offered more choice. Entrants were to select what they felt to be the most forceful passage from Garvey's *Philosophy and Opinions,* and to explain their choice. In similar vein, songs were sung in praise of Garvey at U.N.I.A. meetings and he was defended and applauded in poems and plays written by U.N.I.A. members. John Bruce's work was typical in this respect. In his short play *Soundings,* one of the characters describes Garvey as "one of the common people. . . . He is honest, brave hearted and true blue to his race. . . . "

No member of the Harlem Renaissance ever expressed sentiments of this kind. Neither the ambivalence of Garvey's attitudes towards intellectuals and black culture, nor the cultural activities of the U.N.I.A.'s own intellectuals and artists were enough to resolve the considerable differences and mutual hostility between the two movements. However, the cultural dimension of Garveyism, plus the limited interests and objectives which it shared with the Renaissance, did have some influence on the relationship between the two. Occasionally the abuse which they hurled at each other was qualified by an element of mutual recognition and respect. (pp. 21-4)

Even Garvey's most bitter critics occasionally paid him compliments. George Schuyler described him as a "charismatic character," and Claude McKay conceded that he possessed "a very energetic and quick-witted mind." Both of them recognized Garvey's abilities as propagandist, orator and organizer, and so too did men like James Weldon Johnson and W. E. B. DuBois who admired and envied the great influence which Garvey enjoyed among the black masses. In 1920 DuBois referred to Garvey's "tremendous vision" and "great dynamic force," and even some years later when the relationship between the two men was one of almost unrelieved hostility he conceded that his enemy's "plan to unite Negrodom by a line of steamships was a brilliant suggestion and Garvey's only original contribution to the race problem. Alain Locke also recognized the significant implications of Garvey's African policy. He emphasized how important and potentially constructive it was that Garvey had "stirred the race mind to the depths with the idea of large-scale cooperation between the variously separated branches of the Negro peoples." The Garvey movement in Locke's view had served to arouse a serious interest in Africa among American and West Indian Negroes and had effectively "built bridges of communication for the future."

Alain Locke was also a perceptive enough observer of the Afro-American scene during the 1920s to grasp the fact that for some of the period's artists these "bridges of communication" were related parts of the phenomenon which he identified as the "New Negro." Although he never mentioned Garvey by name, Locke clearly had him in mind when in his analysis of the background to the Renaissance he emphasized the importance of the current upsurge of race-pride, race-consciousness and race-solidarity in the black community. "The younger generation," Locke wrote, "is vibrant with a new psychology; the new spirit is awake in the masses."

What Locke had implied about the relationship between Garvey and the Harlem Renaissance was much more forcefully stated by Wallace Thurman. Thurman had been among the most articulate of Garvey's Renaissance critics and had condemned most aspects of the U.N.I.A. leader's personality and policies. One of the characters in Thurman's novel *Infants of the Spring* describes Garvey as "a great man with obvious limitations," and although Thurman himself found the limitations much more obvious than the greatness he was objective enough to recognize the importance of Garvey's role. For Thurman, Garvey's "one great contribution to the American Negro" was his insistence that Negroes should reject white standards and be "proud of their black skins, thick features, and kinky hair." It was precisely this issue which formed the core of Thurman's novel *The Blacker the Berry* in which the central character Emma Lou Brown suffers much pain and humiliation until she comes to terms with her color. Thus Thurman drew on his own experience as an artist as well as on his familiarity with the work of his contemporaries when he summed up the relationship between Garvey and the Harlem Renaissance in this way: "Garvey did much to awaken 'race consciousness' among Negroes . . . The alleged Negro renaissance which has been responsible for the great number of suddenly articulate Negro poets, novelists, etc. (sic), owes much to Garvey and to his movement. He laid its foundation and aroused the need for its inception." (pp. 24-5)

*John Runcie, "Marcus Garvey and the Harlem Renaissance," in* Afro-Americans in New York Life and History, *Vol. 10, No. 2, July, 1986, pp. 7-28.*

## FURTHER READING

Akpan, M. B. "Liberia and the Universal Negro Improvement Association: The Background to the Abortion of Garvey's Scheme for African Colonization." *Journal of African History* 14, No. 1 (1973): 105-27.
    Extensive analysis of the failed relations between the UNIA and the government of Liberia, concluding that a major factor in the breakup was the Liberian ruling class's perception of the potential immigrants as a threat to their status.

Boulware, Marcus H. "The Marcus Garvey Period, 1916-1927." In his *The Oratory of Negro Leaders, 1900-1968,* pp. 54-62. Westport, Conn.: Negro Universities Press, 1969.
    Discusses the oratory of Garvey and of other black leaders prominent during his lifetime within the context of the Garvey movement.

Brisbane, Robert H. "His Excellency: The Provincial President of Africa." *Phylon* 10, No. 3 (Third Quarter 1949): 257-64.
    History of Garvey and his movement, concluding that Garvey "adversely affected the slow but definite integration of the Negro into American society."

———. "Some New Light on the Garvey Movement." *The Journal of Negro History* 36, No. 1 (January 1951): 53-62.
    Outlines Garvey's rise to prominence and examines his impact on subsequent black intellectuals. Brisbane credits Garvey with revitalizing black racial consciousness but concludes that his economic ideas had little benefit.

Chaka, Oba. "Marcus Garvey: The Father of Revolutionary Black Nationalism." *Journal of Black Poetry* 1, No. 14 (1970-1971): 82-96.
    Provides a history of the Garvey movement and discusses its influence on later black nationalist movements and leaders.

Clarke, John Henrik, ed. *Marcus Garvey and the Vision of Africa.* New York: Random House, 1973, 496 p.
    Offers a broad sample of essays on Garveyism, including several by Garvey.

Cronon, E. David. *Black Moses: The Story of Marcus Garvey and the Universal Negro Improvement Association.* Madison: University of Wisconsin Press, 1955, 278 p.
    Highly regarded biography of Garvey.

"A Black Moses and His Dream of a Promised Land." *Current Opinion* 70, No. 3 (March 1921): 328-31.
    Profile of Garvey and the UNIA.

Du Bois, W. E. B. "Marcus Garvey." *The Crisis* 21, Nos. 2, 3 (December 1920; January 1921): 58-60, 112-15.
    Questions the feasibility of Garvey's economic plans and the desirability of his nationalist objectives, but commends him for creating a black business initiative.

———. "The Black Star Line." *The Crisis* 24, No. 5 (September 1922): 210-14.
    Account of Garvey's trial for fraud, implicitly criticizing his business practices and organizational methods.

Edwards, William A. "Racial Purity in Black and White: The Case of Marcus Garvey and Earnest Cox." *The Journal of Ethnic Studies* 15, No. 1 (Spring 1987): 117-42.
    Examines Garvey's intellectual collaboration with Ear-

nest Sevier Cox, a white supremacist theorist, on the basis that both opposed racial assimilation and miscegenation.

Fierce, Milfred C. "Economic Aspects of the Marcus Garvey Movement." *The Black Scholar* 3, Nos. 7, 8 (March-April 1972): 50-61.
Discusses Garvey's philosophy of black economic independence.

Frazier, E. Franklin. "Break with the Traditional Background: The Renaissance That Failed." In his *Black Bourgeoisie: The Rise of a New Middle Class in the United States,* pp. 103-07. 1957. Reprint. New York: Collier Books, 1962.
Briefly examines the Garvey movement and notes its lack of support among the rising black bourgeoisie of his time.

Garvey, Amy Jacques. *Garvey and Garveyism.* New York: Octagon, 1978, 336 p.
Biography of Garvey by his wife.

Graves, John L. "The Social Ideas of Marcus Garvey." *The Journal of Negro Education* 31, No. 1 (Winter 1962): 65-74.
Discusses Garvey's social theory and conjectures as to how he would view contemporary racial issues.

Hart, Richard. "The Life and Resurrection of Marcus Garvey." *Race* 9, No. 2 (October 1967): 217-37.
Outlines Garvey's life and philosophy, concluding that he had a major impact on modern black civil rights movements in that "he successfully challenged the imperialist doctrine of Negro inferiority which millions of Negroes in the Western world had come to accept."

Hill, Robert A. " 'The Foremost Radical among His Race': Marcus Garvey and the Black Scare, 1918-1921." *Prologue* 16, No. 4 (Winter 1984): 215-31.
Elaborates on the efforts by the U.S. Federal Bureau of Investigation to suppress the political activities of Garvey and the UNIA.

Langley, Jabez Ayodele. "Garveyism and African Nationalism." *Race* 11, No. 2 (October 1969): 157-72.
Examines the influence of Garveyism on nationalist politics in Africa during the 1920s.

Levine, Lawrence W. "Marcus Garvey and the Politics of Revitalization." In *Black Leaders of the Twentieth Century,* edited by John Hope Franklin and August Meier, pp. 105-38. Urbana: University of Illinois Press, 1982.
Includes biographical discussion of Garvey and describes his political and social theories.

——. "Marcus Garvey's Moment." *The New Republic* 191, No. 18 (29 October 1984): 26-31.
Surveys Garvey's career and evaluates *The Marcus Garvey and Universal Negro Improvement Association Papers.*

Lewis, Rupert. *Marcus Garvey: Anti-Colonial Champion.* Trenton, N.J.: Africa World Press, 1988, 301 p.
Study of Garvey's philosophy, stressing its opposition to European colonialism in the third world.

Martin, Tony. *Race First: The Ideological and Organizational Struggles of Marcus Garvey and the Universal Negro Improve-ment Association.* Westport, Conn.: Greenwood Press, 1976, 422 p.
Provides an extensive analysis of Garvey's ideology and describes the struggles of the UNIA against such political opponents as the Communist party, the black integrationist movement, and the governments of the United States and the European colonial powers.

——. "The Economic Programs of Marcus Garvey." *The Black Collegian* 9, No. 1 (September-October 1978): 12, 14, 16.
Outlines the business ventures of the UNIA, particularly the Black Star Line enterprise.

——. *Literary Garveyism: Garvey, Black Arts and the Harlem Renaissance.* Dover, Mass.: Majority Press, 1983, 204 p.
In-depth examination of Garvey's literary aesthetics and of the writers whose work Garvey endorsed through his periodical the *Negro World.* Martin argues that Garvey's work strongly affected the racial consciousness of later black literary movements.

Matthews, Mark D. "Perspective on Marcus Garvey." *Black World* 25, No. 4 (February 1976): 36-48.
Asserts that Garvey incorporated much Marxist-Leninist analysis into his philosophy.

Okonkwo, R. L. "The Garvey Movement in British West Africa." *The Journal of African History* 21, No. 1 (1980): 105-17.
Examines the UNIA's influence on nationalist movements in British West Africa during the early 1900s.

Padmore, George. "Black Zionism or Garveyism." In his *Pan-Africanism or Communism,* pp. 65-82. Garden City, N.Y.: Doubleday and Co., 1971.
Describes Garvey's career and elaborates on the UNIA's failed dealings with the government of Liberia.

Rogers, J. A. "Marcus Garvey: 'Provisional President of Africa' and Messiah, 1887-1940." In his *World's Great Men of Color,* Vol. II, edited by John Henrik Clarke, pp. 415-31. New York: Collier Books, 1947.
Offers a biographical survey of Garvey's career.

Simmons, Charles Willis. "The Negro Intellectual's Criticism of Garveyism." *The Negro History Bulletin* 25, No. 1 (October 1961): 33-5.
Summarizes criticism of Garveyism by black intellectuals, concluding that Garvey was taken more seriously by his contemporaries than some critics have suggested.

Weber, Shirley N. "Black Nationalism and Garveyist Influences." *The Western Journal of Black Studies* 3, No. 4 (Winter 1979): 263-66.
Assesses various black nationalist movements, asserting that Garveyism was one of the most successful at integrating economic, social, and political aspects of black empowerment.

Weisbord, Robert G. "Marcus Garvey, Pan-Negroist: The View from Whitehall." *Race* 11, No. 4 (April 1970): 419-29.
Examines the British government's reaction to Garvey and the UNIA in relation to black nationalist movements within British colonies in Africa and the West Indies.

# Louise Imogen Guiney

## 1861-1920

American poet, essayist, biographer, editor, and short story writer.

Guiney is known for her lyrical, Old English–style poems that often recall the literary conventions of seventeenth-century English poetry. Informed by her religious faith, Guiney's works reflect her concern with the Catholic tradition in literature and often emphasize moral rectitude and heroic gallantry. Today Guiney is praised for her scholarship in both her poetry and in her numerous literary and historical studies.

Guiney was born in Boston, the daughter of an Irish-Catholic immigrant who was a general in the Union Army during the Civil War. Critics frequently note the role of Guiney's father in establishing the ideal of chivalric heroism later presented in her poetry. Pursuing a liberal arts curriculum at the Elmhurst Academy in Providence, Rhode Island, Guiney graduated in 1879, two years after her father's death. Throughout most of the next two decades she resided with her mother and aunt in Boston and Auburndale, Massachusetts. Guiney began writing poems and essays in the early 1880s that were published in New England periodicals. Her first collection of poetry, *Songs at the Start,* appeared in 1884 to critical approval; her first volume of essays, *Goose-Quill Papers,* was published the next year to a similar reception. During the late 1880s Guiney produced essays, fairy tales, and a second volume of poetry, *The White Sail, and Other Poems.* She lived in England from 1889 to 1891, meeting several writers and antiquarians whose work encouraged her interest in the Catholic tradition in English literature. After returning to Massachusetts, Guiney completed her first biography, *"Monsieur Henri": A Foot-Note to French History,* a work that details the life of the eighteenth-century French military figure Henri du Vergier, Comte de la Rochejaquelein, and in 1893 her most renowned volume of poems, *A Roadside Harp,* was published. While *A Roadside Harp* garnered much critical commendation, Guiney was not able to subsist financially on her literary earnings at this time, and she worked at several jobs during the 1890s, including a position as a postal official in Auburndale.

In 1901 Guiney moved to Oxford, England, where she devoted herself to writing essays and works of criticism that she contributed to English journals. Throughout the following decade she also completed several biographies and was engaged in editing the works of various authors, especially those associated with the Catholic literary tradition in England and Ireland. Her last collection of poetry, *Happy Ending: The Collected Lyrics of Louise Imogen Guiney,* was published in 1909 and includes selections from her previous works as well as unpublished poems. During the succeeding decade Guiney suffered frequent health problems that significantly interfered with her literary endeavors. She died of arteriosclerosis in 1920.

Criticism of Guiney's works generally focuses on her poetry, particularly emphasizing her use of archaic poetic structures and themes. Her first two collections, *Songs at the Start* and *The White Sail,* are similar in content and style. Both present subject matter derived from classical legend and tales of medieval gallantry, as well as from the natural world, employing strong rhythms and imagery to convey concepts of valor and moral fortitude that resonate the concerns of English literature of the 1600s. Commentators occasionally fault Guiney's early poetry for a derivative style and overly condensed diction. Her poetic voice was established, critics contend, with *A Roadside Harp,* a collection of works marked by finely attuned rhythms and rigorous attention to form. The volume includes such sonnets and lyrical ballads as "The Vigil-at-Arms" expressing a chivalric ethos, as well as those including "The Kings" that mark Guiney's use of pagan themes and motifs derived from Greek mythology in the collection. The works in her later volumes, *"England and Yesterday"* and *The Martyr's Idyl, and Shorter Poems,* are deemed less successful than her previous poems.

Guiney's literary studies and editions of other poets' works are credited with establishing several little known authors as valid subjects of further critical study, most notably nineteenth-century Irish poet James Clarence Mangan. Guiney is also praised for the posthumously published *Recusant Poets,* an anthology of poetry by Catholic authors from the sixteenth, seventeenth, and eighteenth centuries that she coedited with Geoffrey Bliss. Guiney's essays and biographies generally deal with minor figures in English and Irish history, and include works on English Jesuit martyr Edmund Campion and Irish nationalist Robert Emmet. While at the turn of the century Guiney was regarded as a major contributor to American literature, her reputation during the late twentieth century has largely declined. Critics today generally view her poetry as aesthetically dated, especially in light of modernist poetry, although her works continue to earn respect for their craft and moral concerns.

(See also *Dictionary of Literary Biography,* Vol. 54.)

## PRINCIPAL WORKS

*Songs at the Start*   (poetry)   1884
*Goose-Quill Papers*   (essays)   1885
*The White Sail, and Other Poems*   (poetry)   1887
*Brownies and Bogles*   (fairy tales)   1888
*"Monsieur Henri": A Foot-Note to French History*   (biography)   1892
*A Roadside Harp*   (poetry)   1893
*A Little English Gallery*   (essays)   1894
*Lovers' Saint Ruth's, and Three Other Tales*   (short stories)   1895
*Nine Sonnets Written at Oxford*   (poetry)   1895
*\*James Clarence Mangan: His Selected Poems* [editor] (poetry)   1897
*Patrins, to Which Is Added an Inquirendo into the Wit & Other Good Parts of His Late Majesty King Charles the Second*   (essays)   1897
*"England and Yesterday"*   (poetry)   1898
*The Martyr's Idyl, and Shorter Poems*   (poetry)   1899
*Robert Emmet: A Survey of His Rebellion and of His Romance*   (biography)   1904
*Blessed Edmund Campion*   (biography)   1908
*Happy Ending: The Collected Lyrics of Louise Imogen Guiney*   (poetry)   1909; revised and enlarged, 1927
*Letters.* 2 vols.   (letters)   1926
*Recusant Poets* [editor; with Geoffrey Bliss]   (poetry) 1939

*This work also contains an introductory study by Guiney.

---

**Bliss Carman**   (essay date 1894)

[*Carman was considered Canada's leading poet during the early twentieth century and was honored by the Canadian Parliament as the nation's poet laureate in 1928. His early collections especially gained admirers for their lyrical, moody descriptions of nature and for a free-spirited bohemianism found particularly in the popular "Vagabondia" series (1894-1901), which he coauthored*

*with Richard Hovey. In the following excerpt, Carman commends the lyric quality of Guiney's poems in* Songs at the Start, The White Sail, *and* A Roadside Harp.]

> North from the beautiful islands,
> North from the headlands and highlands,
>     The long sea-wall,
> The white ships flee with the swallow;
> The day-beams follow and follow,
>     Glitter and fall.
>
> The brown ruddy children that fear not,
> Lean over the quay, and they hear not
>     Warnings of lips;
> For their hearts go a-sailing, a-sailing,
> Out from the wharves and the wailing
>     After the ships.

Such are the first lines of the first page of a little volume of poems, called **Songs at the Start,** published in Boston ten years ago. It is not a particularly original or characteristic poem, this **"Gloucester Harbor,"** yet it is smooth and sweet with a charm reminiscent of Longfellow in his sea verse. It repeats his cadences and the color of his peaceful reverie just touched with pathos.

> Woe, woe, for the old fascination!
> The women make deep lamentation
>     In starts and in slips;
> Here always is hope unavailing,
> Here always the dreamers are sailing
>     After the ships!

This might easily have been written of the gentle poet of the Charles, who has indeed laid so many young writers under his spell. The volume as a whole, however, hardly keeps up our delight of these opening lines and contains little else, I fancy, that its author will care to preserve, with the exception of one brief lyric.

> **"Spring"**
> Again the bloom, the northward flight,
> The fount freed at its silver height,
> And down the deep woods to the lowest,
> The fragrant shadows scarred with light.
>
> O inescapeable joy of spring!
> For thee the world shall leap and sing;
> But by her darkened door thou goest
> Forever as a spectral thing.

There is in these verses alone any hint of the racy and wonderful style Miss Guiney was soon to develop. But her second venture in the sea of letters, **The White Sail,** published some three years later, shows a marked advance upon the first and contains a number of distinctly original and notable poems. It is full of that delightful freshness of health which lends her words their inspiring quality. The joy of her lyric mood is as clear and inevitable as the "inescapeable joy of spring." Absolute sincerity and health possess her lines and bear them with a rush beyond the commonplace monotony of minor chords. She is never dolorous and never dull. Even natural sorrow is so infused with the perennial gladness of this beautiful world as to become scarcely more poignant than an ancient tale of pathos.

> The young Sun rides the mist anew; his cohorts
>     follow from the sea.

Let Aztec children shout and sue, the Persian
    bend a thankful knee:
Those glad Auroral eyes shall beam not any-
    where henceforth on me.

Up with the banners on the height, set every
    matin bell astir!
The tree-top choirs carouse in light; the dew's on
    phlox and lavender;
Ah, mockery! for, worlds away, the heart of
    morning beats with her.

The exquisite touch is here, the lightness of hand, the perfection of temper. Not to be overborne by the turbulence
of our days, nor too much moved by any sadness, is the
first lesson of art,—art, that helper and continual solace
of the world's life. So that the great artist must be first of
all joyous, then assured, then fervent, then unrestrained
and out of all bounds save those of his own conscience and
contriving. His only patent is originality. And while he
says something new about all the facts of experience, he
brings them all to the touchstone of his unjaded spirit. He
must not merely see Homer's world with an eye trained
to minuter vision and wider sweep, he must bring to its appreciation a zest as wholly unspoiled as that of a savage.
If the revelations of knowledge mean for him the dissolution of old faiths and historic creeds, he must not despond;
he must have merely so much faith the more, believing
that what has come safely so far may be trusted to journey
to the end without any anxiety of his. He must know that
while dogma, which is only fossilized creed, can never be
anything more than a curiosity, the need of worship is a
craving of the human heart, a living desire neither to be
ridiculed nor overthrown. If the discoveries of science
seem for the time to overshadow the achievements of art,
he must only rejoice, remembering that art has been the
mother of science, and that all science has returned the
benefits of its parent a thousand fold. When he hears on
every side the detractors of art belauding science and decrying the work of the artist as a thing long past use to the
world, he will recall similar periods of history and smile
to think how art has always been entirely equal to the task
of absorbing whatever innovations science might unfold.
He will keep in mind forever and ever the necessary place
of art in the general economy of the state, and no temporary dethronement of his mistress will cause his loyalty to
swerve. While the artist, then, ponders the word of God
in the wind through the tree, he will be glad and brave before all other men.

But the artist will be the gladdest and bravest of men only
if he is great. For the same sensitiveness of inward vision
which makes the great artist the happiest of his kind will
make a lesser spirit the most miserable. Revelation will
come to him as a burden too heavy to be borne, not as a
rapture too keen to be expressed. So you will find all the
minor poets of a nation piping in a minor key, while their
greater and robuster brothers are bearing up the eternal
chorus of the world, refrain after refrain, to the final triumph of right and love and beauty and goodness, to the
final assurance of gladness and the contentedness of peace.

The true artist, therefore, in these qualities of courage and
hope must be distinctly the most manly of his fellows, and
there is no more manly note in American letters to-day
than that which rings through the lyrics of the little lady
of Auburndale, [Massachusetts]. She can put more valor
in a single line than one can squeeze from our periodical
poets in a twelve month. For it is a sorry but certain fact
that our magazines are fast becoming the nincompoopiana
of literature. And this not because they are ill-conducted,
but because their practical success depends upon it. We
must always make allowance in any art for the influence
of popular demand. When we consider the circulation necessary to make a book or a magazine a practical success,
the wonder is, not that contemporary letters are so poor,
but that they are so good.

A ballad like **"Tarpeia"** or a single lyric like **"The Wild
Ride,"** has virility enough to furnish the ordinary minor
poet with lyric passion ten times over. I am permitted to
quote a version of the latter lyric, longer by two stanzas
than that contained in *The White Sail.*

I hear in my heart, I hear in its ominous pulses
All day, the commotion of sinewy mane-tossing
    horses;
All night, from their cells, the importunate
    tramping and neighing.

Let cowards and laggards fall back; but alert to
    the saddle,
Straight, grim and abreast, vault our weather-
    worn galloping legion,
With a stirrup-cup each to the one gracious
    woman that loves him.

The road is thro' dolor and dread, over crags and
    morasses;
There are shapes by the way, there are things
    that appal or entice us:
What odds? We are knights, and our souls are
    but bent on the riding!

Thought's self is a vanishing wing, and joy is a
    cobweb,
And friendship a flower in the dust, and glory a
    sunbeam:
Nor here is our prize, nor, alas! after these our
    pursuing.

A dipping of plumes, a tear, a shake of the bridle,
A passing salute to this world, and her pitiful
    beauty!
We hurry with never a word in the track of our
    fathers.

I hear in my heart, I hear in its ominous pulses,
All day the commotion of sinewy mane-tossing
    horses,
All night, from their cells, the importunate
    tramping and neighing.

We spur to a land of no name, out-racing the
    storm-wind;
We leap to the infinite dark, like the sparks from
    the anvil.
Thou leadest, O God! All's well with thy troop-
    ers that follow.

To find just such another dauntless note, the very elation
of courage, we must go to Miss Guiney's own new volume,
*A Roadside Harp,* a particularly pleasing piece of book-
making, by the way. There in **"The Kings,"** and in the fol-

lowing extract from **"The Knight Errant,"** we are touched in the same strain.

> Spirits of old that bore me,
> And set me, meek of mind,
> Between great dreams before me,
> And deeds as great behind,
> Knowing humanity my star
> As first abroad I ride,
> Shall help me wear, with every scar,
> Honor at eventide.
>
> . . . . .
>
> O give my youth, my faith, my sword,
> Choice of the heart's desire:
> A short life in the saddle, Lord!
> Not long life by the fire.
>
> Forethought and recollection
> Rivet mine armor gay!
> The passion for perfection
> Redeem my failing way!

"The passion for perfection," that is so characteristic of our time! Indeed all our artistic activity may be said to be distributed among two classes, those who have a passion for perfection, and those who have a madness for reform. While the latter are running with socialism, realism, "veritism," the New Ethic, the New Education, the New Granny's Nightcap, and all sorts of feather toppery whatever, the former are frittering away their efforts in symbolism and the deceptive sound. In matters of faith, too, the latter are devoured by a thousand untried notions and nostrums for the betterment of this precious race of pigmies, while the former have turned back to a paganism older than Athens, a paganism on which the shadow of the time has passed as a cloud on the sea. **"To a Dog's Memory," "Open Time," "Athassel Abbey," "A Friend's Song for Limdisius,"** there is no more gracious and winning and impassioned note in English letters to-day than rings through these beautiful and pagan, perfectly pagan, lyrics. Listen to the opening of the last:

> The breath of dew, and twilight's grace,
> Be on the lonely battle place;
> And to so young, so kind a face,
> The long protecting grasses cling!
> (Alas, alas,
> The one inexorable thing!)
>
> In rocky hollows cool and deep,
> The bees our boyhood hunted sleep;
> The early moon from Ida's steep
> Comes to the empty wrestling-ring.
> (Alas, alas,
> The one inexorable thing!)
>
> Upon the widowed wind recede
> No echoes of the shepherd's reed,
> And children without laughter lead
> The war-horse to the watering.
> (Alas, alas,
> The one inexorable thing!)
>
> (pp. 27-33)

It is given to few poets to write so. And if such lines are not unmistakable proof of genius of the very finest lyric quality, one must be sadly deluded as to what is good and bad in English poetry. While this writer is thus so worthy

a follower of the masters of song, she is in her serene unvexed temper at one with that eternal paganism which lies like the deep sea calms far below all passing storms of faction and fashion and the virulence of creed.

There are, it seems to me, two characteristics in Miss Guiney's work, either one of which would render her most worthy of distinction as a poet. The first is this pagan quality of joy, which she must inherit from our New England saint, Emerson; the second is a rich and anything but modern quality of style entirely her own, yet one whose seeds must have been sown by those robust and individual poets of the Elizabethan times. I find none of the verse-makers of to-day whose product is so markedly original and at the same time so free from affectation. It is easy to adopt this or that sort of originality at will,—to acquire a mannerism. But real style is an attitude of the heart, a frame of mind, quite impossible to imitate. When suffused by an abundant wholesome imagination, as in the author of *A Roadside Harp*, such an attitude of spirit, such a power of style, becomes capable of the rarest self-revelation and expression in art. Take for instance that lovely **"Ballad of Kenelm."** So absolutely fresh and unhackneyed in every line, yet so free from any taint of affectation, it could only have been born of the most genuine poetic impulse working through the sincerest and most unconscious style.

> They travelled down the lane,
> An hour's dust they made.
>
> But once I hear the blackbird in Leighlin
> hedges call,
> The foolishness is on me, and the wild tears
> fall
>
> He has done with roofs and men,
> Open, Time, and let him pass.
>
> The gusty morns are here,
> When all the reeds ride low with level spear.

These are the things, so simple in their loveliness, which look so easy to do, and which none but a master ever achieves. Like Browning, Miss Guiney has often a too curious and irresponsible fancy which leads her through perplexities of speech; she wreaks expression upon some thought too trivial or vague or remote to be worth the while; and yet like the great Victorian of "Pippa Passes" or "Home Thoughts from Abroad," she has at command a golden unmarred deliciousness of cadence and a smooth sufficiency of utterance, that make all rival effort toil in vain. (pp. 34-5)

And so we lay aside this thin little volume of exquisite poetry, reassured that it is only the blind who can believe that the poets are all dead to-day, while there walks among us a very child of the old Greek spirit,

> Whose random hand
> Struck from the dark whole scenes like these,
> Archaic beauty, never planned
> Nor reared by wan degrees,
>
> Which leaves an artist poor, and art
> An earldom richer all her years;

We lay it aside with one quotation more, summing up in a single couplet, itself worthy of the Greek Anthology, the light-hearted philosophy of that elder paganism, a hundred times overthrown by the casuistries of the schools, yet always returning with its unobtrusive solace, dauntless and unperturbed, to our human need at last. How large and sweet a benediction of farewell within the small compass of a score of words!

> Praise thou the Mighty Mother for what is
>     wrought, not me,
> A nameless nothing-caring head asleep against
>     her knee.

(p. 36)

Bliss Carman, "Louise Imogen Guiney," in *The Chap-Book, Vol. II, No. 1, November 15, 1894, pp. 27-36.*

## Helen Tracy Porter   (essay date 1901)

[*In the following excerpt, Porter examines characteristics of style and theme in Guiney's poetry and prose.*]

It is an interesting comment upon American letters, and so one already often made, that but few of our poets have confined themselves to a single chosen form of expression. Born to be the artists, the "makers-see" of their time and country, they have large liberty to speak their message in any tongue they will. Your true poet, it appears, can also be the keenest, wisest, and happiest of essayists; he can, though this is more rare, turn his hand to the building of romance, or the somewhat lighter structure of the short-story architect; he can even hold sway as the man of affairs, and use his pen to guide the policies of state. All these things have been; and not only so, but increasingly in our day do poets choose, when they list, other forms of expression besides their native tongue of measured melody.

Among our singers who have taken this larger liberty is Miss Guiney. Her work, if bulk be considered, is thus far more largely a prose than a poetic expression; and there is much that may be said of the former. But, since therein the poet-temper also reveals itself, we naturally turn first to the volumes where it finds fullest expression. The first to come is the book of short poems, whose title, **Songs at the Start,** so aptly suits the content, since they both give confident, high-hearted promise of what shall follow. The poems are not of many moods. Most, like **'Gloucester Harbor,'** have a minor key:—

> Woe, woe for the old fascination,
> The women make deep lamentation
> In starts and in slips;
> Here always is hope unavailing,
> Here always the dreamers are sailing
>     After the ships!

Even in the first volume do the poems give evidence of a characteristic still more observable in the later ones,—an instinctive seizure of the picturesque moment. It does not result in drama. Miss Guiney has but once given herself dramatic expression, and that under certain limitations to be spoken of. But it results in a picture, the salient features of which leap out and challenge you, so that you cannot but see it as its painter did. Such poems are **'A Ballad of

Metz,' 'The Rival Singers,'** and **'Charondas.'** A touch of humor in the volume is the whimsical little **'Lover Loquitur.'** For the most part, Miss Guiney's humor, so far as her poetry is concerned, is over the border line and into the pathetic.

**The White Sail** was published in 1887, acknowledging its inspiration, as the dedication shows, to Keats,—nay, not to him, but to that same virgin passion after the perfectness of beauty which is the outcry of the elder poet's soul. That such was the inspiration of many of the poems in **The White Sail** is clear both from their matter and their manner. The poem which gives the book its title is the story of the hero Theseus. It is the Greek theme, with all the Greek passion of beauty which the choice of it implies, that Miss Guiney is interpreting in her version. But there is a something more,—an admixture of a different and un-Greek motive, if we may use the word; for to Miss Guiney's mind the tragedy of the sombre sail turns upon an ethical pivot,—namely, the moral lack in Theseus's character.

> Remorse, and irremediable ache,
> And ruin, following him whose manhood
>     swerves
> To the eased by-ways of forgetfulness.

In her rendering such is the aspect which the legend takes. Yet one could not say that the theme is modernized: it does not cry "forward" to the sense of to-day any more than does [Keats's] *Endymion,* and so is like it, not a message, but an absorption of beauties seen by the poet, and witnessing themselves again, having been given tongue by her. As for the manner, it is perhaps the conscious or unconscious mixture of motive above suggested that takes just a thought from smooth inevitableness throughout. There are lines of haunting beauty and suggestive witchery, pure exquisiteness of sound, such as that of the ship when

> Forward she sobbed on black unwilling wing,

and Rhodalus's reply to the king's appeal for music to heal his soul:—

> "Our strings are jangled, wrested
> From their discreet and silvern vassalage,
> Snapped quite with languishment for Theseus'
>     sake.
> I cannot sing."

Many of the other poems in the volume typify the same mood as that of Theseus, or another facet of the same. One of the finest, most ethereal to soul and sense, most blended together, of fancy and spirit is **'The Wooing Pine,'** in which the lady, "star-shine in her look," suggests Keats' own Madeline, but is still more herself, a being "from feud and uproar dewily distraught," compact of fancies and desires whose yearning feels no thrall of sense. The story of the maiden and her mystic wonderful tree-lover illustrates well another characteristic of Miss Guiney's poetry. I mean her penchant for those realms of legend, of fancy, of the whimsical, upon which to dwell most lightly, most by means of skilled and delicate suggestion, is to dwell most lovingly and best. The characteristic is shown to its height in 'The Wooing Pine.' It is visible in 'The Last Faun,' 'The Rise of the Tide,' and 'The Serpent's Crown.'

We learn from this volume, too, that Miss Guiney, like Chaucer's knight, 'loves chivalrye,' and finds with Stevenson, whom she quotes in her preface to *'Monsieur Henri,'* that "the finest action is the better for a piece of purple." Accordingly, in such poems as 'Chaluz Castle,' 'A Chouan,' and 'Tarpeia,' the splendid rash deeds flaunt in lavish martial color. 'Tarpeia,' in particular, is noteworthy for its perfection in choice of rhythm: one hears as in music the sound of the clanging brazen shields on the guilty head of her who betrayed her trust. In natural beauties, however, Miss Guiney is again for the minor key,— the timid reluctant spring, the lingering mournful autumn of the year. One of her finest nature poems is '**Garden Chidings**,' with a delicate significance, which, indeed, pervades most of Miss Guiney's interpretations of nature with a subjective tinge:—

> The spring being at her blessed carpentry,
> This morning makes a stem, this noon a leaf,
> And jewels her sparse greenery with a bud:
> Fostress of happy growth is she. But thou,
> O too disdainful spirit, or too shy!
> Passive dost thou inhabit, like a mole,
> The porch elect of darkness; for thy trade
> Is underground, a barren industry,
> Shivering true ardor on the nether air,
> Shaping the thousandth tendril, and all year
> Webbing the silver nothings to and fro.
> What wonder if the gardener think thee dead,
> When every punctual neighbor-root now goes
> Adventurously skyward for a flower?
> Up, laggard! climb thine inch; thyself fulfil;
> Thou only hast no sign, no pageantry,
> Save these fine gropings; soon from thy small
>   plot
> The seasonable sunshine steals away.

If it is as the seer of beauty in its more ethereal and pensive guise that Miss Guiney appears in *The White Sail*, her next volume, *A Roadside Harp,* has some pages of a robuster tone. '**Peter Rugg the Bostonian**' is strong and virile, and still has that flavor of the fanciful that was to be noticed in the earlier books. '**The Ballad of Kenelm**' and '**Tryste Noël**' have a wonderful power of simplicity; and the two Irish peasant songs, '**In Leinster**' and '**In Ulster**,' something more than the wild lilt of Irish melody, though they have that, too. The first is wholly feminine, a plaint of the heart unrest that comes with the spring, and a mourning, rebellious refrain,—

> The foolishness is on me, and the wild tears fall.

The second is the rollicking masculine mood that finds an added pleasure in the glint of a pretty Irish eye when it reflects the budding year in its laugh. Thus are *das ewig Weibliche* and *das ewig Männliche* ["the eternal feminine" and "the eternal masculine"] playfully contrasted. From '**A Foot-Note to a Famous Lyric,**' as well as from some of the descriptive sonnets in *A Roadside Harp,* we begin to gain the shrewd suspicion that Miss Guiney, like Sir Walter Scott, is a reverencer of admired authority, and much of a loyalist at heart. That she draws poetic inspiration from such a fount becomes more certain in later volumes.

A deeper interest than animates these scattered poems I have mentioned for some special mood or skill that each betrays is found in certain others, such as '**Vergniaud in the Tumbril,**' '**The Kings,**' and '**Summum Bonum.**' They contain more outspokenly what is faintly suggested now and again in poems of quite a different turn: Miss Guiney's philosophy, her forward look, her creed. It has a stoic hint: it is more a gospel of despair than of hope, though Vergniaud in the tumbril, stancher than the others, hopes beyond and above despair, in a brave recognizance of the truth that

> Manhood has a wider span
> And larger privilege of life than man.

On death's threshold he knows his failure but as a condition of ultimate success:—

> Out of the human shoots the divine:
> Be the Republic our only sign,
> For whose life's glory our lives have been
>
> Ambassadors on a noble way
> Tempest-driven and sent astray
> The first and the final good between.
>
> Close to the vision undestroyed,
> The hope not compassed and yet not void,
> We perish so; but the world shall mark
>
> On the hilltop of our work we died,
> With joy of the groom before the bride,
> With a dawn-cry through the battle's dark.

The human is here encompassed with the divine, time with eternity. The complement to '**Vergniaud in the Tumbril**' is '**The Kings,**' with its splendid reassertion of the individual. Naught matters it whether man wins or loses, says his angel. The event is not in his hands. His part is but

> To fear not sensible failure,
> Nor covet the game at all,
> But fighting, fighting, fighting,
> Die, driven against the wall!

After this, what a surprise it is to turn to the last of the three poems I have selected as striking the deepest notes of Miss Guiney's song! '**The Kings**' is bravely pagan, acknowledging the unequal struggle, yet lifting the slughorn dauntlessly to blow defiance to the end. '**Summum Bonum**' is an expression not of defiance, but of submission. There is, to be sure, the same unregardfulness of the outcome which is part of the creed of '**The Kings**'; but it is rooted not in faith in God in the individual, but in the Supreme Being of expressed religion. One guesses that the two views are not irreconcilable, that they perhaps express rather conditions than convictions, and differ from the artistic necessity of their composition. By referring, however, to Miss Guiney's latest published volume of poetry, one may find reasserted the view with which she finds herself in the greater sympathy. The poem called '**Four Colloquies,**' in *The Martyrs' Idyl, and Shorter Poems,* is subdivided into '**The Search,**' '**Fact and the Mystic,**' '**The Poet's Chart,**' and '**Of the Golden Age.**' All four, in their form of question and answer, have a virile, objective treatment; but '**The Poet's Chart**' seems to contain the gist of the matter:—

"Where shall I find my light?"
"Turn from another's track:
Whether for gain or lack,
Love but thy natal right."

. . . . .

"Whence shall I take my law?"

"Neither from sires nor sons,
Nor the delivered ones,
Holy, invoked with awe.
Rather, *dredge the divine*
*Out of thine own poor dust,*
Feebly to speak and shine."

The italics are mine, as comprehending in a new reassertion of the divine in humanity itself, Miss Guiney's last word thus far on the subject of her poet-creed.

We have wandered somewhat away from the chronological track; but, after all, clearer understanding of her significance as a poet is to be gained rather from a consideration of subjects than of times and places. To return: she has published two volumes of poetry since the *Roadside Harp.* The first, *'England and Yesterday,'* is in part a reprint of the *Roadside Harp,* containing, in addition to the beautiful series of sonnets on London printed in the former, a second series on Oxford. *'England and Yesterday,'* is truly yesterday in England,—the poet's yesterday, drawing new visions from the storied spots where was wrought a splendid past, and showing yet more clearly than the former volumes that Miss Guiney is, indeed, a poet of the backward glance, that to her times gone are glorified with a glamour which the present lacks, and even the future. The exquisite lines **'On Leaving Winchester'** illustrate well this native sympathy of hers, as also the gift of descriptive imagery which pervades the sonnets and lyrics of the whole volume:—

A palmer's kiss on thy familiar marge,
My oriel city, whence the soul has sight
Of passional yesterdays, all gold and large,
Arising to enrich our narrow night:
Though others bless thee, who so blest before
Hath pastured from the violent time apart,
And laved in supersensual light the heart
Alone with thy magnificent No More?

. . . . .

Bright fins against thy lucid water leap,
And nigh thy towers the nesting wood-doves
    dwell.
Be lenient winter, and long moons, and sleep
Upon thee, but on me the sharp Farewell.
Happy the shepherd (would that I were he!)
Whose early way is step for step with thee,
Whose old brow fades on thine immortal breast.

Miss Guiney's one piece of work in dramatic form, barring some translations of the work of others which need not here concern us, is a Dramatic Idyl, in the volume of poems to which it gives a name [*The Martyr's Idyl*], published in 1899. This Dramatic Idyl is founded on a narrative of early Christian persecution, taken from the 'Acta Sanctorum,' wherein Didymus, the Cappadocian soldier of Rome, learns, just at the hour when the spirit in him upwakes to an immortal thirst, that the Christian maiden Theodora is persecuted, doomed first to foul disgrace and then to kindlier death, because she persists in faith to the

Christ whom Didymus, but now enlightened, dimly yearns also to serve. He saves her by exchanging garments: she, having consecrated him to her religion, goes forth in his centurion's armor, and he remains behind. Interrogated by the prefect when the truth is discovered, he refuses, as had Theodora, to sacrifice to Roman gods; and, being led forth to die, he and his captors are met on the hill of death by Theodora, retaken by her persecutors. The twain die together, joyful of spirit, uplifted beyond mortal pangs to the clear dawn of perfected faith.

Miss Guiney has chosen to call this dramatic work an 'Idyl,' and fittingly so, for the material in its simplicity of development is largely narrative; but, with that same appreciation by which in her shorter poems we perceived her seizing the vital moment of legend or history, she adds much dramatic strength to the dramatic form in which the narrative is clothed, and makes the whole convincing. Throughout the 'Idyl,' long narrative speeches are a necessity of the material: this were a flaw in the dramatic effect; but therein are some of the best of all Miss Guiney's powers displayed,—her skill of distinctive subtle imagery, of inevitable epithet, of wooing pathetic fancy.

It would be amiss as yet to sum up the value of Miss Guiney's poetry, to cast up accounts when the page is not full. But before speaking of her prose the threads that have been gathered from a survey of her published verse may well be examined, that we may recognize them again if they are used in the warp or woof of another weaving. They are then, briefly, a passion of beauty, in form and spirit; an intermingling of imagination and fancy in deft proportion; an æsthetic pleasure in the pathetic; instant sympathy with the richness, the large beauty of tradition; a poetic sureness of touch and phrase, showing itself by skill to paint a mood, a battle, or a dying flower. In expression her art has been chiefly lyric,—a violin melody of a pensive unforgettable strain. She has walked but lightly in that province which is of the poet even more than of the prose-writer, and seldom cares to teach whom she gladdens the way to self-inspiration. The credo of **'The Kings'** and **'The Poet's Chart'** is rare, perhaps the more emphasized on that account.

I am tempted to quote, as the best introduction to her prose, some words prefixed to one of the most perfectly artistic and sympathetic of biographical writings, *'Monsieur Henri.'* They are a guiding principle by which she has reached such a refinement of results as much of her prose writing witnesses:—

I do not plead for pardon in treating an all-but-hallowed theme in a rather high-handed fashion, since every grain here has been painfully sifted and weighed, and the material, if not the proportioning of it, as true as truth. But, in so treating it, I bore in mind that excision is the best safeguard against decay, that time throws away as rag and bob-tail the political specifications thought to be precious, and that we must at once, and in the nobler sense, romanticize such dry facts as we mean shall live.

In all her prose, of which the most important separate volumes are the charming *Little English Gallery, 'Monsieur*

*Henri,'* the *Memoir of Prosper Mérimée; Patrins,* a collection of essays on various subjects, together with the half-whimsical **'Inquirendo,'** a glorification of his Majesty Charles the Second; and, lastly, the volume containing four short stories [*Lovers' Saint Ruth's, and Three Other Tales*], Miss Guiney's only published fiction,—in all these she has remembered to romanticize, and in the nobler sense, what she means shall live. But, more than this, she has chosen her facts by that instinct for the picturesque, for the chivalric, which we noticed in her poetry. That brave championing of a lost hope, called the Vendean insurrection, is all to her mind; and the lovable boy who led the van and foremost fighting fell has his story fitly told by one whom we feel might have ridden with the Vendean women, had she lived in those stirring years.

Miss Guiney's literary sympathies, judged from the critical biographies in the *English Gallery* and from allusions in *Patrins,* as well as from some two or three pages in *'England and Yesterday,'* entitled **'Lines on Various Fly-Leaves,'** are, as one might expect, for certain choice spirits among her kindred of the pen,—not the most famous nor even the most deserving of fame, which is a wide difference, but chary writers, who lived, as it were, a notch above the finest they could say, and had a gentlemanly indifference for results. Your true humorist is he who can include himself in the sorry jest with all humanity, instead of standing out to make quips at the rest of the world. And with all true humorists, even if they be unconscious ones, Miss Guiney has such comradeship that to see them through her eyes, to know them by her introduction, is to form lifelong friendships, for which you thank her ever after. Her sketch of Topham Beauclerk and Bennett Langton, gallant scapegraces after her own heart, belongs by right of its innate sympathy abreast of two other books on the robustious Johnsonian period,—namely, Fanny Burney's *Letters* and Irving's *Life of Goldsmith,*—and makes one feel that for pure deliciousness of emotion this is the scene of all others in England's literary past to be set down in at a moment's notice: "When the Turk's Head is ajar in Gerrard Street, when the unclubable Hawkins strides over the threshold, when Goldsmith poses in purple silk small-clothes, Sir Joshua fingers his trumpet, and the king of the hour is rolling about in his chair of state, saying something prodigiously humorous and wise."

The same quality which in Miss Guiney's poetry manifested itself as an æsthetic pleasure in the pathetic has in her prose put on the laughing mask, and is a faculty and appreciation of humor. The two volumes of essays, *Goose-Quill Papers* and *Patrins,* display this faculty abundantly. They are full of delicate fooling, of coquetting with their themes; of airy and flashing play of rapier, yet of sufficient strength for every now and then a keen thrust into the heart of the matter. Their range of subjects is not great, nor are their moods many. Chiefly they impress one as of a person wandering abroad of a pleasant day,—say, perhaps, in the late spring or early fall, for there is a warmth of atmosphere about them,—and reflecting lightly, but broadly, on whatsoever falls within his ken. They have a perambulatory spirit of meditation about them, and the wanderer is pleasantly philosophical over such fanciful slight adventures as **'An Encounter with a Pickpocket'**

and **'The Delights of an Incognito.'** Other like whimsicalities of thought and expression are **'On Dying Considered as a Dramatic Situation,' 'On Teaching One's Grandmother How to Suck Eggs.'** As for the **'Inquirendo,'** one would consider that, too, a delightful piece of foolery, yet may not altogether stop at such a view; for there is both interior and exterior evidence to prove that Miss Guiney is picturesquely-minded still to hedge about with divinity the house of Stuart, and bid hodden morality stand aside for the artistic temperament. The Restoration period had, along with its dashing vice, some not inconsiderable virtue; and the two scowled not at each other after the inartistic Puritan fashion, but walked arm in arm and cheek by jowl, finding much amusement in companionship. It is this picturesque juxtaposition, one cannot but think, which induces Miss Guiney ingeniously to beg the question and enter her brief for that engaging ne'er-do-well, Carolus Rex.

*Lovers' Saint Ruth's* is the title of Miss Guiney's only book of fiction, published in 1895. It contains four short stories, spoken of in a prefatory note as "my apprentice work in fiction"; but one takes issue with the term. As a whole, they speak the practised hand. They are strong. They are human. They have narrative excellence, more marked than in her poetry, though we observed it in the latter, also. In return, her poetry, has lent something of its richness, its effect of background, to her narrative prose. The literary workmanship of the four stories is on a lofty plane, higher than that of the essays, because achieved, apparently, in more serious and consistent spirit. They are artistic in showing not their art; yet a sort of fine polish which each character has, as also each event, each development of plot, shows them to be well-considered, careful studies. The plots of two turn upon incidents of human frailty, with their ever-widening ripples of consequence. The other two portray the crushing pitifulness of circumstance. Thus all four are in essence pathetic, yet not crudely so nor inartistically heart-rending; for their mellowness includes a restraint and balance of effect. Of the four, **'The Provider,'** a mournful tale of unchildlike childhood, with its tragically peaceful close, probably strikes the most universal key.

There is, finally, yet another quality which Miss Guiney's prose and verse have in common,—a quality so obvious that it scarcely needs mention; namely, the fine flavor of letters pervading the whole, whether poem, essay, or fiction. This is an old-fashioned literary virtue, somewhat gone out of frequent use. One wonders whether the reason is that modern conditions of composition rarely give leisure for the assimilation of by-gone culture, or that with the proud sterility of a new shoot, the infant literature of the century to come chooses to grow unsupported by the parent stock. At all events, this modern bareness of adornment, be it a sign of progress or degeneration, is not to be found in Miss Guiney's work. She revels in all the richness of the literary past, having made it her own beyond peradventure. To read her is much of an education in the paths—particularly in the choice and least-frequented paths—of English letters.

Miss Guiney is a poet wayfarer who sings as she journeys,

like a minstrel of old. In this errant spirit her books are named: *Songs at the Start; A Roadside Harp;* and, finally, *Patrins,* which latter signifies, she says, "handfuls of leaves or grass cast by the Gypsies on the road, to denote, to those behind, the way which they have taken." This is Miss Guiney's own interpretation of her work, and should be ours. . . . (pp. 287-99)

> Helen Tracy Porter, "Characteristics of the Work of Louise Imogen Guiney," in Poet Lore, *Vol. XIII, No. 2, April, May, June, 1901, pp. 287-99.*

## Alice Brown (essay date 1921)

[*An American short story writer, novelist, and dramatist, Brown is best known for her regional fiction set in New England. These works, which characteristically portray rural female protagonists through realistic detail and local dialect, have earned comparison with the those of Sarah Orne Jewett and Mary Wilkins Freeman. Brown was also a close friend of Guiney's; the two collaborated on several literary projects and Brown authored* Louise Imogen Guiney, *the first full-length study of Guiney's life and career. In the following excerpt from that work, Brown surveys Guiney's literary career.*]

[Guiney's] first book was *Songs at the Start* (1884) and the first collected essays *Goose-Quill Papers* (1885). The essays, despite a wilful archaism, an armored stiffness of light attack learned out of library shelves, are astonishingly mature for a pen so young—if by youth or age we mean the mere cumulative sum of time passed. Indeed, the author thought well enough of the scintillant little papers to include two of them, **"An Open Letter to the Moon,"** and **"On Teaching One's Grandmother to Suck Eggs,"** in her later *Patrins.* You have but to love Louise Guiney to find *Goose-Quill Papers* a jovial self-betraying little book to recur to when you long for her whimsical face again or the cascading gamut of her laugh. It is spiced with playfulness, a learned playfulness, it must be owned, and yet, if you know her, you know also how much learning was waiting in her teeming mind, eager to get into the book and cram it, cover to cover, and you are grateful for the sense of just values that let you off so gently. For she had one of those fructifying minds which absorb like a sponge; everything they draw in breeds something else, and the two, fact and mother wit, breed again until you are swept along on a stream of rushing lineage. And over her happy selection of topics quaint and gay, her own illuminating humor plays like a thread of gold in tapestry moved lightly by a wind. We may not, of course, actually assume, so objective is she even then, that her whimsies of the first person are literally self-betraying; but they do sometimes open a window upon her as we know her, the gay relish of life that was hers, the ardor for the great game of chasing a happy fancy to its born destiny of an ultimate end, and stroking it into the gentle complaisance of the willing captive; the healthy, untrammeled revolt against bugaboos "nature itself cannot endure"—notably mathematics when she "roars you" like any lion (albeit smiling behind his whiskers as begging to remind you he has no idea of resorting to the argument of claws).

When she has mounted her gaily caparisoned jennet of unforced humor, she takes the world by inversion; you shall follow her circumspectly, or her steed will throw up his heels in your face and gallop off in the dust of his own making. "My novitiate page," she ruefully confesses, invoking the influence of Hazlitt, "smelled hard of that dear name, likewise of Browne, Taylor, and Cowley, and Lamb, and of one R. L. S., a Romany chal then utterly unknown, whom I had found in secret and in secret worshiped." It was a brave beginning, this slender book of little essays, and it was dedicated to Oliver Wendell Holmes. How charmingly, with what engaging gallantry he must have taken it!

To leap the fecund years to the *Patrins* of her later youth is to follow the same whimsical and reflective vein. This book, deriving its fortunate title from patrin, "a Gypsy trail: handfuls of leaves or grass cast by the Gypsies on the road, to denote, to those behind, the way which they have taken," is primarily for him whom reading "maketh a full man." The style, with a scholarship better tempered and easier to carry, being, as it were, woven into chain mail, not the armor of her earliest adventuring, is the despair of the less agile and instructed mind. It is tinctured with her personal quality, and is incredibly rich, the richer when you return to it after absence and intercourse with more immediate things, to find fruits of her commerce with far off civilisations and loving sentience to the "hills of home." Like the buyer in Goblin Market, she drips with juices from the very fruits of life, antidote for our dull ambitions: the years "wasted in prison on casuist industries." It is full of a not too quaint and bookish but an altogether delicious persiflage. She praises the scholar's right to "fall back with delight upon a choice assortment of ignorances." Yet, with whatever innocent suavity she puts it, you suspect her of having few scholarly ignorances of her own to fall back upon. So absolutely four-square was her tower of recondite knowledge that you imagine her as having some ado to prevent its shadow from falling on the reader less equipped and terrifying him into escaping her spell altogether. It is a book of praise. Most of all does she advertise the great narcotic of out-of-doors: the enchanting diversion of walking until the rhythm of the first arduous stretch dulls into the monotony of muscles settling into their slowly apprehended task. She betrays an unimpeachable bodily sanity. Though urban by birth, she is also, through adoptive kinship of Pan and all the nymphs, a sylvan, to her "a dear Elizabethan word." You may find her beside the sea until conscious response to it ebbs into that trance of wonder which is the withdrawal of the soul into ultimate chambers, the inviolable retreat whence it comes forth washed clean of the injuries time has dealt it. She sings a remorseful dirge over the "defeated days" of captive animals. She quickens her pace, at moments, to the measures of a hilarious mind. Throughout that mischievous "encourager of hesitancy," the Harmless Scholar, she all but dances.

"The main business of the scholar," she informs you, with a wicked twinkle behind her spectacles, "is to live gracefully, without mental passion, and to get off alone into a corner for an affectionate view of creation."

This she concedes you as an egg warranted to hatch into something you don't expect, or a bomb likely to burst harmlessly, if disconcertingly, under your chair. For she knows, by diabolic instinct, just what your idea of the scholar is: the conserver of chronologies and sapient conclusions fit chiefly to be waved in pedagogical celebrations or trumpeted at authors' readings. No such sterile destiny as this for her, as she shall presently "fructify unto you."

"Few can be trusted with an education." This she tells you with a prodigious lightness of self-assurance.

> The true scholar's sign-manual is not the midnight lamp on a folio. He knows; he is baked through; all superfluous effort and energy are over for him. To converse consumedly upon the weather, and compare notes as to "whether it is likely to hold up tomorrow,"—this, says Hazlitt, "is the end and privilege of a life of study."

Mark you how humbly she proceeds, this multi-millionaire of the mind. Her intellectual barns are bursting with fatness, her cattle are on a thousand hills; yet she spares you not only the inventory of her acquisitions but any hint of her respect for them. (pp. 26-32)

This book, *Patrins,* smiles all through. It informs you, chiefly by an innocently indirect implication, that the phenomenon of being, while it may be taken by schoolmen and moralists for a balance between good and ill, is a whimsical business, and the more you see of it the more firmly you will determine to view it aslant, with an eye to pleasing paradox.

As the tree of [Guiney's] mental life grew and broadened into wider air, it cast a shade not even her votaries were always zealous to penetrate. She tended more and more to the obscure, the far-off and dimly seen. In her biographical work she was the champion of lost causes, the restorer of names dropped out of rubricated calendars through sheer inattention of an unlearned world, or rusted by time in chantries no longer visited. She would sail, not for those known islands on every map where harbors are charted and the smallest craft can coal and water, but for some lost Atlantis, even if she might only moor in its guessed neighborhood and hear, at least, the plash of ripples over it. She was always listening, the generous hand to the responsive ear, to echoes from "forgotten or infrequent lyres."

"Apollo," she says,

> has a class of might-have-beens whom he loves: poets bred in melancholy places, under disabilities, with thwarted growth and thinned voices; poets compounded of everything magical and fair, like an elixir which is the outcome of knowledge and patience, and which wants, in the end, even as common water would, the essence of immortality.

It is not quite easy to tell why she delighted so absolutely in digging for ore in spots of incredible difficulty. It was not that she was ill-grounded in the greater, more entirely accepted cults. Shakespeare was hers and Milton, and in Dante she did authoritative work. And it is idle to wonder whether, so many of the big critical jobs being done, she had a keen eye to the market value of such unconsidered

trifles as were left. The practical worth of a task would never have been an incentive; it might have been a deterrent. Like [Irish poet James Clarence] Mangan, there was that in her which bade her not to cross the street to advance her own interests; it persuaded her to what seemed even wilful adoption of the losing cause. . . . Nor was her attachment to the imperfectly known by any means the pleasure of the chase, the exhilaration of the hunt when dates and genealogical and critical sequences had "gone away" from her hounds of scent and swiftness. It was simply true that she had an inextinguishable love for the souls "ordained to fail." As it made no difference to her whether a lasting line of verse were hers or another's, so she had the patience of the born annalist in picking up and conserving every least coin of the realm of letters or of manly and romantic deeds.

One of the floating bits of wreckage she gave a hand to confirming in the illustrious place given him by a few discerning minds, was Mangan, the uniquely brilliant author of an authoritative version of "My Dark Rosaleen," a perverse and suffering soul, prey to a blackness of mind and the Nemesis of his own wandering will. There were "two Mangans," she quotes from a previous biographer, "one well known to the Muses, the other to the police; one soared through the empyrean and sought the stars, the

*Guiney in 1887.*

other lay too often in the gutters of Peter Street and Bride Street."

He was a worshipper of that which is above us, and prey to what is below, the body's slave, the poor brain's mistaken ministrant, striving alternately to fire it to new apprehensions and drug it with a despair of its own possibilities. In [her introductory study to *James Clarence Mangan: His Selected Poems* (1897)] Louise Guiney says:

> One can think of no other, in the long disastrous annals of English literature, cursed with so monotonous a misery, so much hopelessness and stagnant grief. He had no public; he was poor, infirm, homeless, loveless; travel and adventure were cut off from him, and he had no minor risks to run; the cruel necessities of labor sapped his dreams from a boy; morbid fancies mastered him as the rider masters his horse; the demon of opium, then the demon of alcohol, pulled him under, body and soul, despite a persistent and heart-breaking struggle, and he perished ignobly in his prime.

Could a combination of evils have been imagined more poignantly appealing to this young champion of shipwrecked souls? "My Dark Rosaleen" alone was enough to enlist her generous pen. As Mangan himself rescued it from the indifferent fame of an archaic fragment, a norm of beauty, and clothed it with the flying draperies of a glorifying fancy, so she unfolds its history and holds it up to new appreciation in a world not given to dwell upon the historically obscure. (pp. 36-41)

This Study of hers reflects, with an especial clarity, the form and color of her own critical genius. In the comparison of masterpieces and the measurement of values by accepted standards, she was at ease in a large activity. If we would understand her method, we may look on it here. The shallow conception of the critic's task, as an expression of personal preference, was not even germane to the richness of preparation she brought to even the most inconsiderable reviewing. Here are no snap judgments, ingenuous betrayal of temperamental likings. The genesis of criticism is the tool in her hands. Lead her to the slenderest rill of poetry and, out of her witchhazel magic, she locates the spring that fed it. She bows before "the few whose senses are quick at literary divination." In this Study learning ran, not wild, but at a splendid even pace over the road of past achievement, saluting guideposts by the way. Literary resemblances, the least intentional, are rarest joys to her. She is enchanted to find some of Mangan's lighter verse rattling on like a Gilbertian libretto.

Behold the exhumed precursor of *The Mikado!*

Nothing rewards her more indubitably than the discovery of even a quasi-lineage, a shadow of likeness not to be developed into the actual relationship supported by time and place. She does not often floor you with unimpeachability of dates, but she knows the very complexion of her time, "his form and color." She remembers what wings beat the air of fortunate decades, dropping pinions more than one imitator snatched in falling and wore brazenly in his cap. She can rehearse the unbroken descent of metres. Her parallel between Mangan and Poe, their dependence on the

haunting adjunct of the refrain, does revolve about chronology; but chiefly she relies upon the convictions of her divining mind. She compares the "neck and neck achievements of Mangan and Poe." She traces both back to the colossus Coleridge, with his wells of color. His was the spring of youth, and they bore away full flagons. It is hardly possible to overrate her value to the student of literature in these learned but uncharted flights all over the visible sky of the periods where her subjects moved. Literature, she knows, is a species of royal descent. The Titans may not live to see the faces of their own children, yet out of those rich fecundities of authentic utterance children are born and show trace of august lineage. And it is hers, the "abstract and brief chronicler" of values, to find it.

To Louise Guiney, there were two transcending realities: poetry and what men call, with varying accent, religion. She believed in poetry as, in the old sense, an ecstasy. She loved archaic phrases and grieved because fit words should perish, mourning them as men would mourn if, believing there were children of immortal lineage among them, they discovered these could die. To her there were archetypes of beauty, the living heavenly substance we have, with an unshaken prescience, learned to call undying. Wandering evanescences, we persuade them down to us or snatch at them and cage them in our heavier atmosphere with the hope, sometimes bewilderingly justified, of their singing on and on. One condition of our even hearing the beat of those wings bending their swallow flight to the responsive mind, is the high vibration in ourselves, the intense activity of what we call imagination. . . . To [Guiney], poetry is an unspoken allegiance to the very essence of mysticism, magic, glamourie. It is the echo from far hills of space. It is never without the witchery of the unknown, the guessed-at, the adored but never seen. Not all its dances are woven under the sky we scan chiefly for the weather, but in the elusive gleaming where not we but our dreams are denizens. It is perpetually looking from "magic casements." It brings the twilight feeling. It may not be melancholy, yet it inspires melancholy. It may not be joyous, yet the pleasure it awakens is more exquisite than it has words to celebrate. These are matters far from the market where we buy and sell and measure our worth by cleverness in exploiting it. These are courts where our poet's "shy foot" dared penetrate with the confidence of a daughter of the house.

From *Songs at the Start* to *Happy Ending* (1909), this last bearing her stamp as comprising "the less faulty half of all the author's published verse," her work hardly varies in a certain cool, limpid, sometimes austere content. *Songs at the Start* is distinctly unlike the familiar books of perfervid and unbridled youth. Almost childlike, in some instances, the songs are always restrained within due measure. The gusts of a too tempestuous heart, the revolt of youth against a world ready made for it, are not hers. She might be the child of a pagan ardency of simple joy, singing to the echo in some waking spring. These are the dewy recognitions of a world "not realized." The faults she showed in this first printing are the ones that plagued her throughout, though she recognized them with a rueful self-dispraise and mock extravagance of remorse. They are the infrequent lapses of a not invariably musical ear. To the end, she would, from stanza to stanza, unconsciously change her cadence. It might be a fault for her to redress; but who among her lovers would complain of it now? It was an individual flaw, the little human imperfection like a mole on beauty's cheek; the too studied reverse of it might have been something not only "icily regular" but "splendidly null."

**The White Sail,** part legend and part lyric, with an academic ballast of sonnets, sang out in fuller tone, though with no less individual a measure. The legends ring curiously scholastic in these days when the industrious versifier celebrates the small beer of his own "home town" in untrained eccentricities all too faithful to his villageous mood. Her legends were the tall pines of the fairy grove she wandered in. There were pillared aisles and porticos, not New England dooryards, tapestries shaken by winds of the past, not leaves, red and gold, blown her from the swamps and hills she knew. Yet her bookish fetters were straining from within, and in **"Daybreak"** she sings out with a more individual note, a faint far music, as if some young chorister dared part the antiphonal ranks of ordered service and try the song he heard that morning when he and the lark together saluted the hills of dawn.

> The young sun rides the mists anew; his cohorts
>     follow from the sea.
> Let Aztec children shout and sue, the Persian
>     lend a thankful knee:
> Those glad Auroral eyes shall beam not any-
>     where henceforth on me.
>
> Up with the banners on the height, set every
>     matin bell astir!
> The tree-top choirs carouse in light; the dew's
>     on phlox and lavender:
> Ah, mockery! for, worlds away, the heart of
>     morning beats with her.

This she did not reclaim for the authorized last printing, and none can say whether she would let us snatch it out of its young obscurity. But it is so unmistakably one of the first trial flights of the pure lyric in her, it sings so melodiously, that the mere chronology of her work demands it. In the same book beats the haunting refrain:

> Youth is slipping, dripping, pearl on pearl,
>     away.

And as you are about to close the door on this virginal chamber of April airs and cloistral moonlight, of ordered books breathing not leather only but the scent of "daffodilean days," your heart rises up, for here is **"The Wild Ride,"** a poem which first beat out its galloping measure in a dream, and continued, with the consent of her own critical mind, to the last book of all. The beginning and the end are like nothing so much as the call of youth and the answer of undaunted age. It was, one may guess, her earliest lyric runaway, the first time she lost herself in the galloping rush of a stanza's trampling feet. (pp. 41-50)

In **The Roadside Harp** (1893) (and this she calls, as late as 1911, "my best book") she is in full swing of that individual color and form of verse that were hers thenceforth, hall-marked, inimitable, of a delicate yet imperishable fragility of loveliness, unique as the hand they were written in. Here sounds her own true note. Here were more plainly distinguishable the defined colors of the braided strands of destiny that made her so rare a nature and were perhaps—it is well to put it softly, this question—to hinder her in robustness and variety of performance. Irish by birth, she had not to the full, what she finds in Mangan, that "racial luxuriance and fluency." And, like him, her "genius is happier on Saxon than on Celtic ground." She was too subject to varied impulses to be the exponent of one. Her love in letters ran passionately to the Anglo-Saxon; the seventeenth century was her home. She was devoutly Catholic, yet living fibres in her knew the earth as it was in its unsymbolized freshness before the Great Deliverer came.

"You are a natural Christian," she wrote once to a friend poor in the consolations of belief, "with a birthright of gladness and peace, whether you seize it or not; whereas I am the other fellow, a bed-rock pagan, never able to live up to the inestimable spiritual conditions to which I was born."

This was humility only, no wavering from her transcending faith. Yet the wholesome natural man in her was acutely sensitive to that earth which saw the immortal gods. You find her listening, responsive, to the far heard echoes of Greek harmony. She was ready with her cock to Æsculapius, the tribute of her gentle allegiance to those kingly pagans who loved the light of the sun and shrank from the "dishonor of the grave," who knew the face of Nemesis and were, above all, disciples of the law of Aidôs, the negation of excess. In the rich exposition of Gilbert Murray:

> Aidôs implies that, from some subtle emotion inside you, some ruth or shame or reflection, some feeling perhaps of the comparative smallness of your own rights and wrongs in the presence of the great things of the world, the gods and men's souls and the portals of life and death, from this emotion and from no other cause, amid your ordinary animal career of desire or anger or ambition, you do, every now and then, at certain places, stop.

Now this, of course, concerns emotion, conduct. But the same sense of just limit concerns also art. Your emotion must be "recollected in tranquillity" lest it drag the hysteric Muse into frenzied measures. We must—stop. Louise Guiney knew this through a flawless intuition, but she went pace by pace with the Greeks while they counselled her anew. It is not merely her choice of Attic subjects, like Simoisius, or the Alexandriana that are, we are told, so faithful in spirit, though she had no Greek. It is that in this book we are renewedly conscious of the oneness of mortal longing and earth loveliness, so tightly are they entwined. Here is a sentience to the throes of that earth which is not solely the earth set to man's uses, but mysteriously made and mysteriously continued, with its uncomprehended language of light and dark and its ebb and flux eternally in sway. Christian in belief, she was pagan in her listening nerves. And her harp, hung in the window opening on what we call eternity, thrilled to many breezes. Being Christian, she was, as in her life, all devotion, all pure obedience, rapt celebrant of the story of the Birth and the

Cross, a vowed Eremite to the belief that counts all things loss, save One. Hands of diverse angels reached out of the sky and touched her harp to song or Litany. There was the spirit of an assured immortality. There was, too, the voice of Erda, the Earth, crooning from the root caverns in abysses of time past. The pagan heart of her, the heart that was still immovably centred in the gentle certainties of Christ, is embedded in **"The Still of the Year."** She knows the earth, because she has entered into the very spirit of created things and her mortal part suffers the pang of awakening which, to the earth, is spring. But what is it to the soul?

> Up from the willow-root
> Subduing agonies leap;
> The field-mouse and the purple moth
> Turn over amid their sleep;
> The icicled rocks aloft
> Burn saffron and blue alway,
> And trickling and tinkling
> The snows of the drift decay.
> Oh, mine is the head must hang
> And share the immortal pang!
> Winter or spring is fair;
> Thaw's hard to bear.
> Heigho! my heart's sick.

Some of the verse from this middle period is so fragile and austerely tremulous, like bare boughs moved by a not unkindly wind, that you are aware of what has, in another sense, been called "scantness." Not only does she adventure delicately in her shallop, she is fain of archaic brevity and pauses that do unquestionably halt the accompanying voyager, to his discomfiture. **"A Ballad of Kenelm"** was such as they chanted "on a May morning" in other days than ours. It has the consonance of prose trembling into verse. We are too luxurious for it. We want to be borne along on a lilting wave, we who have not found it possible to accommodate ourselves to the peg-leg-to-market of free verse (what our poet herself once called, in a mischievous snapshot of judgment, "the rag-tag of *vers libres*"). Even the loving apostrophe to Izaak Walton is more chant than song, justified rather by the spirit than the form. One who knew her unceasing pains with verse and prose, how a stanza could never count itself finished beyond possibility of being smashed into unrecognizable fragments and remade, remembers this as an instance of her ruthlessness to her children even after they had grown up and gone their ways into the ultimate stronghold of the printed page. Here the opening lines run:

> What trout shall coax the rod of yore
> In Itchen stream to dip?

Months after printing, the incorrigible dissonance of the two opening words struck her and, having no smallest modicum of professional vanity, she must needs admit a friend immediate to her to the excellent fooling of the discovery, and went about shouting, between gusts of mirth: "What trout! what trout!"

The harsher the discord she could lend the unfortunate twain, the more gustily she laughed, and in *Happy Ending* the choppy sea subsided into unimpeachable cadence:

> Can trout allure the rod of yore
> In Itchen stream to dip?

But in *The Roadside Harp,* though her metres were sometimes inhospitable to the ear unprepared, she did attain the topmost reaches of the hills of words' delight. The **"Two Irish Peasant Songs"** ran with a light step, and a breath as sweet as the whispers over Ireland's harp. Here also is an imperishable beauty of a lyric, fit for some ecstatic anthology, so rare in form and color that the listening ear scarce cares for the meaning, so its music may go on and on. (pp. 51-7)

*The Martyr's Idyl* (1899) [Guiney] wrote with a fervor of devotional conviction, and in the same volume, a fringe upon the hem of its brocaded stateliness, is **"An Outdoor Litany,"** a cry full of earth's blood and tears, and more immediate to earth's children who also suffer than the high counsels of the abstinent:

> The spur is red upon the briar,
> The sea-kelp whips the wave ashore;
> The wind shakes out the colored fire
> From lamps a-row on the sycamore;
> The bluebird, with his flitting note,
> Shows to wild heaven his wedding-coat;
> The mink is busy; herds again
> Go hillward in the honeyed rain;
> The midges meet. I cry to Thee
> Whose heart
> Remembers each of these: Thou art
> My God who hast forgotten me!

Here are beauties dear to the mortal mind to which an anguish of discontent is comprehensible because "it is common." Here is the sum and circle of nature, tagged with the everlasting paradox: the mindlessness and indifference of the beauty wherewith we are surrounded and our hunger to which it will not, because it cannot, minister. This is great writing: for here the soul walks unabashed, articulate, impassioned, the finite crying to the infinite, the perishing atom appealing to the sky of the universal over him. Perhaps there can be nothing greater in a dramatic sense, in our prison-house under the encircling sky, than the accusatory or challenging voice of the creature, through the unanswering framework of his mortal destiny, to the God Who created both him and it. Lear, in the storm that was unmindful of him, set his breath against its blast. When the cry breaks into hysteria, then the man is mad. The merciful reaction that lies in nature's anodynes sets in to counteract and dull. But our poet, though she can write:

> Help me endure the Pit, until
> Thou wilt not have forgotten me,

never challenges her God with mad interrogation. It is not His justice she assails; she but beseeches the quickening of His will to save. There is an immeasurable distance between entire overthrow and the sanity of the creature who, though sorely wounded, has lost no jot of faith in divine medicaments. Her plea is only that she may share the wholesome life of His birds and trees. (pp. 64-6)

But the actual crown of the book is in the two stanzas called **"Borderlands."** Within the small circle of recurrent rhythm this poem holds the ineffable. It is a softly drawn and haunting melody on the night wind of our thoughts, it hints at the nameless ecstasies that may be of the rhythm of the body or the soul—but we know not!—it is of the texture of the veil between sense and the unapprehended spirit.

> Through all the evening,
> All the virginal long evening,
> Down the blossomed aisle of April it is dread
>     to walk alone;
> For there the intangible is nigh, the lost is
>     ever-during;
> And who would suffer again beneath a too
>     divine alluring,
> Keen as the ancient drift of sleep on dying faces
>     blown?
>
> Yet in the valley,
> At a turn of the orchard alley,
> When a wild aroma touched me in the moist
>     and moveless air,
> Like breath indeed from out Thee, or as airy
>     vesture round Thee,
> Then was it I went faintly, for fear I had
>     nearly found Thee,
> O Hidden, O Perfect, O Desired! O first and
>     final Fair!"

The line:

> Keen as the ancient drift of sleep on dying faces
>     blown,

is one of those pervasive beauties which, though in a perfect simplicity, invoke the universal that is beauty's self. You see in it—or you fancy, for it falls on the sensitive plate of emotion that far outranks your intellect—all the faces of all the dead from the shepherd slain outside Eden past the Pharaohs and queens that "died young and fair" to him "that died o' Wednesday."

*Happy Ending* is her renewed hail and her farewell. Here are some of the old beauties and, gathered up with them, the later buds of a more sparsely blossoming fancy, snowed under time and yesterday. It is a sad book, for all its nobility; it breathes the accent of farewells. To a friend who challenged the appositeness of the title she said, smiling, it was, on the contrary, exact, for her life of verse was done. In 1917, she wrote:

> The Muse, base baggage that she is, fled long
> ago. (I knew what I was up to when I called it
> *Happy Ending.*)

The additions of this later period are slightly more involved, much more austere. The world does not call to her now in the manifold voices of that vernal time when she and her dog went field-faring. It is a spot, though still dearly loved, to leave. In **"Beati Mortui"** she celebrates the "dead in spirit" who, having renounced the trappings of a delusive day, are henceforth like angel visitants in a world where they hold no foot of vain desire. The sonnet **"Astræa,"** her actual farewell, has the poignant sestette:

> Are ye unwise who would not let me love
>     you?
> Or must too bold desires be quieted?
> Only to ease you, never to reprove you,
> I will go back to heaven with heart unfed:
> Yet sisterly I turn, I bend above you,
> To kiss (ah, with what sorrow!) all my dead.

Next to the Golden City of belief she had, as she began, continued to love poetry, the making of it, the "love of lovely words." And though an initiate world had hailed her, when, like a young shepherd wandered into town, a bewildering "strayed reveller," she came "singing along the way," man had been finding out many inventions and kept no ear for strains out of Arcady or long notes prophetically echoed from the New Jerusalem. He was laying the foundations of a taste which was to flower in jazz and the movies and the whirling of wheels on great white ways. She had her own small public always. To these, her books were cool colonnades with the sea at the end. But she had learned, now with no shadow of doubt, that there would never be any wider response from the world of the printed word. She was not, in the modern sense, "magazinable." Editors were not laying up treasure in the safety deposits of the immortalities; they were nursing their subscription lists. If she had kept on singing, it would have been into that silence whence the poet's voice echoes back to him with a loneliness terrifying to hear. Need that dull his fancy and mute his tongue? Not in youth, perhaps. When the blood flows boundingly, you write your verses on green leaves, so they are written, and if nobody wants the woven chaplet of them, you laugh and cast it on the stream. Through the middle years it is different. You must be quickened by an unquenchable self-belief or warmed at the fire of men's responsive sympathy to write at all. There is something in the hurt an unheeding world can deal you that, besides draining the wounded heart, stiffens the brain and hand. And Atalanta's pace may be slackened by the misadventures of the way. Her sandal may come loose, or she slips on a pebble and strains the tendon of that flying foot.

For poetry is a matter of the mounting blood as well as the tempered mind. It has, in spite of those who have suffered the horrible disaster of physical overthrow and yet have kept on singing, something intimately dependent on the actual coursing of the blood, the beat of the physical heart. The only verse Louise Guiney prized, was the verse with wings, spontaneous as the gestures of childhood or the oriole's song. She could knock her lines into a wild ruin and rebuild, but that was after the first swift assembling of stone on stone. Any idea of verse soberly and slowly evolved, as an intellectual feat, was afar from her. "Our best things," she said, "are the easiest. They're no trouble." They did cost, in the last sweet pangs of intent consideration, of rearranging, polishing, and hunting down the best and only word. When the poetic impulse seized her, she bent to it in obedient delight. She never coaxed or beckoned. Only into the living spring did she dip her cup: no thrifty piping it to the house in forethought of the day when the frost creeps and "no birds sing." The greatest beauties in her verse were as spontaneous as they dropped from the skies and she set them in their chaste enduring gold. Though she was so unwearied in polishing and changing, in their general scope and temper the poems came as from the hand of God, and when her own hand fell too laxly to receive them, they did not come. Her resultant loneliness of mind she accepted with a decorum due the gods who give and take away again; you might almost have called it unconcern. For she was not greedy of life: only grateful for its temperate dole. She might own, under anxious accusation, to having "no luck, no leisure, no liberty," but that was only for the intimates who inevitably "knew."

"As to the Muse," (this in 1916) "she has given me the go by. No matter: this dog has most hugely enjoyed his day, which was Stevenson's day, and Lionel Johnson's, and Herbert Clarke's, and Philip Savage's." (pp. 68-74)

Alice Brown, in her Louise Imogen Guiney,
*The Macmillan Company, 1921, 111 p.*

## Horace Gregory and Marya Zaturenska   (essay date 1942)

[*Gregory was an American poet, translator, biographer, and editor who was respected for the erudition and classicism of his poetry, most notably the volume* Collected Poems *(1964), which won the 1965 Bollingen Prize. His wife, Zaturenska, was a Russian-born American poet who achieved renown for finely crafted poetry that often reflects the conventions of English Decadent verse of the 1890s. Her collection* Cold Morning Sky *(1937) won the Pulitzer Prize in poetry in 1938. Together Gregory and Zaturenska edited and coauthored several poetry anthologies and surveys, including* A History of American Poetry, 1900-1940. *In the following excerpt from that work, they emphasize the influence of seventeenth-century English authors on Guiney's writing.*]

"Damn the age," Charles Lamb is reputed to have said as someone warned him that his work was out of tone with his own time; "if the age cannot take me, I shall write for antiquity." And today it seems as if Louise Imogen Guiney wrote for antiquity thirty-six years of her life, or rather, for the England of Lord Clarendon's *Rebellion* in which she had found her deepest inspiration. She was one who had turned to the poetry of Herbert and of Vaughan long before the generation that matured in 1920 had heard of the "metaphysicals." Born in Boston, Massachusetts, in 1861, her first book, ***Songs at the Start,*** was published in 1884. Within the fastnesses of the seventeenth century Louise Guiney had discovered a congenial and secure vantage ground; she had an "original" temperament, and a feeling for excellence in poetry in the work of others that was by no means neglible. Near the end of her life (she died in 1920) she was one of the first to praise Gerard Manley Hopkins, and she was one of the few Americans, Ezra Pound among them, to respect the fine gifts of the often neglected British poet, Lionel Johnson. But her soul was with the minor Caroline poets, "my men," she called them—Cartwright, Quarles, Habington, Stanley, Fanshawe, Rochester, and lesser figures, "those golden lyricists who have not come . . . into their inheritance." Something of their grace, wit, delicate precision, and elegant wildness—and for her, there is no other word but "wildness" for it—entered her verse; and with the "wildness" she took their virtues to her heart:

> Take temperance to thy breast,
> While yet is the hour of choosing,
> An arbitress exquisite
> Of all that shall thee betide.
> For better than fortune's best
> Is mastery in the using,

> And sweeter than any thing sweet
> The art to lay it aside.

[**"A Talisman"**]

In prose as well as in verse her models were of the various styles of her favorite century: Sir Thomas Browne, Jeremy Taylor, and Lord Clarendon; and it is said that she once absentmindedly dated a letter to a friend, "March 12th, 1667." Among her more "modern" masters were Lamb, Hazlitt, and, since she, too, was a devout Roman Catholic, Cardinal Newman; and when she turned to the century that followed the seventeenth, it was to the prose of Burke and to the poetry of Christopher Smart, whose phrase, "the quick, peculiar quince," had caught her eye and became the touchstone of her appreciation in reading poetry. The search for things that were "peculiar," romantic, and quaint both spurred and lightened her literary enthusiasms and her learning. She wrote of her passion for an age, a century other than her own, with all the eloquence of her Irish ancestry, and never did she betray that ancestry more clearly than when she wrote of an England whose supernatural beauty could have existed only in her imagination:

> . . . the soul hath sight
> Of passionate yesterdays, all gold and large,
> Arisen to enrich our narrow night.

[**"On Leaving Winchester"**]

Nor did she forget in writing of a time other than her own the figure of Robert Emmet and his love for Sarah Curran; and some of the most moving and eloquent passages of her prose are to be found in her study of James Clarence Mangan, the temperamentally unhappy and unfortunate Irish poet. The sublime failure and the gallant and royal martyr held her interest equally; and her extraordinary enthusiasm, which offered the contradictions of well-controlled hysteria, was also reserved for such figures as the Earl of Surrey, poet and soldier, who died on the block during the reign of King Henry VIII and the learned and saintly Edmund Campion, the Jesuit priest who suffered martyrdom for his faith in England under the rule of Queen Elizabeth.

In 1901 Louise Guiney left Boston for the British Isles where she spent the rest of her life, and there, as she walked London's streets, she saw the shade of William Hazlitt who also aroused her romantic sensibilities.

> Between the wet trees and the sorry steeple,
> Keep, Time, in dark Soho, what once was Hazlitt,
> Seeker of Truth, and finder oft of Beauty.

[**"Beside Hazlitt's Grave"**]

After a visit to the neighborhood of a seventeenth-century battlefield Louise Guiney wrote:

> I didn't see the battlefield as it happened. . . .
> Nothing more personal ever got hold of me than
> that war. . . . I can bear any grief of my own
> better than I can King Charles's.

It was to celebrate this veritable King Charles's head that she wrote in her copy of Lord Clarendon's *History of the*

*Rebellion* one of her most characteristic poems ["**Writ in My Lord Clarendon, *His History of the Rebellion*"**]:

> How life hath cheapen'd, and how blank
> The Worlde is! like a fen
> Where long ago unstained sank
> The starrie gentlemen:
> Since Marston Moor and Newbury drank
> King Charles his gentlemen.
>
> If Fate in any aire accords
> What Fate deny'd, Oh, then
> I ask to be among your Swordes,
> My joyous gentlemen;
> Towards Honours heaven to goe, and towards
> King Charles his gentlemen!

When this poem first appeared in a magazine, young H. G. Wells (who even in his youth had been properly insulated from poetic flights and fancies) clipped it for quotation in one of his lesser-known "scientific" novels; the poem in its new setting reappeared as evidence of the queer modes of thinking and writing that Wells's Utopians of the Millennium looked back upon with horror. But kindly H. G. Wells could have spared himself that trouble: the poem was as uncommon to the day that he discovered it as it was to the seventeenth century; its spirit and its spelling were Louise Guiney's contributions to her own enthusiasms, and it is probable that the poem would have puzzled her favorite, Lord Falkland, and certainly John Wilmot, Earl of Rochester, as much as it charmed and bewildered her contemporaries. For many years, it had been her ambition to compile the wealth of her singular "discoveries" among the poets of the sixteenth and seventeenth century, and when the anthology at last appeared under the title of ***Recusant Poets*** (1919) it was more a tribute to her Celtic imagination, her lively and perceptive wit, and her deceptively artless charm than an example of anything that remotely resembled scholarship. Not since Chatterton's day had anyone attempted a resurrection of the past with so marked a gift of poetic discernment and fervor. If one of Louise Guiney's friends, Sir Edmund Gosse, brushed the book aside and could not read it (he was no great scholar himself), another friend, Alice Meynell, who had more seriousness than he, was delighted by it.

Louise Guiney's versions of seventeenth-century spelling often produced mildly exciting and not unpleasant effects; if they were artless, which is to be doubted, they were remarkably consistent in their waywardness, and if they were not, they created an atmosphere, which she undoubtedly desired, of writing poems from a world that had escaped the limitations of time and space:

> The Ox he openeth wide the Doore,
> And from the Snowe he calls her inne,
> And he hath seen her Smile therefor,
> Our Ladye without Sinne.
> Now soone from Sleep
> A Starre shall leap,
> And soone arrive both King and Hinde:
>     Amen, Amen:
> But O, the Place co'd I but finde!
>         . . . . .
> The Ox is host in Judah stall

> And Host of more than onelie one,
> For close she gathereth withal
> Our Lorde her littel Sonne.
> Glad Hinde and King
> Their Gyfte may bring,
> But wo'd to-night my Teares were there,
>     Amen, Amen:
> Between her Bosom and His hayre!

["**Five Cards for Christmastide**"]

Louise Guiney wrote a number of "cavalier rhymes," but the true image of what she saw was neither Prince Rupert nor his men, but the image of her father, the Irish-born General Patrick Guiney of whom Van Wyck Brooks wrote:

> [He was] an Irish lawyer who had commanded a regiment in the American Civil War. Brevetted a brigadier-general . . . he had been hopelessly wounded; and one day in Boston, twelve years later, he suddenly stopped in the street, removed his hat, knelt, crossed himself and died. Miss Guiney's spirit rode forward in her father's stirrups [see Further Reading entry dated 1940].

His portrait shows an attractive and intelligent face, one that seems well suited to the son and grandson of men who had been out in "the '98," and "the '45." "My preux chevalier of a father," Louise Guiney called him, and perhaps it was—and that likeliness seems very clear—in loyal deference to his memory that her verses were filled with gallant soldiers who rode forth to battle during which, of course, they always fell:

> A dipping of plumes, a tear, a shake of the bridle,
> A passing salute to this world and her pitiful
>     beauty:
> We hurry with never a word in the track of our
>     fathers.
>             . . . . .
> We spur to a land of no name, out-racing the
>     storm-wind;
> We leap to the infinite dark like sparks from the
>     anvil.
> Thou leadest, O God! All's well with Thy troopers that follow.

["**The Wild Ride**"]

It was in England that Louise Guiney, possessed by the very daemon of antiquarian research, did her most characteristic work, and became "a Bodleian mole." Many years of her life were spent in searching for and at last discovering the grave of her beloved Vaughan. As a friend once wrote of her, "a half-effaced inscription was more dear to her than whole broadsides of modern paeans to success." In 1903 and of America Miss Guiney herself had written:

> I can't go home. It gives me the most genuine and involuntary fit of trembling. . . . The pace at which everything goes there, the noise, the publicity, the icicles, the mosquitoes, the extreme climatic conditions, I am not equal to them any more.

Her remarks were not unlike those in another letter, written by Mrs. Church, in New York, to Madame Galopin, at Geneva, dated October 17, 1880, in Henry James's "The Point of View":

> We have found a refuge in a boarding-house which has been highly recommended to me, and where the arrangements partake of that barbarous magnificence which in this country is the only alternative from primitive rudeness. . . . There is no wine given at dinner, and I have vainly requested the person who conducts the establishment to garnish her table more liberally. She says I may have all the wine I want if I will order it at the merchant's, and settle the matter with him. But I have never, as you know, consented to regard our modest allowance of *eau rougie* as an extra. . . . In this country the people have rights, but the person has none.

It was her "person" that Louise Guiney wished to retain, and with it the right to live in her own world, "that green and growing England" where "the gracious parks, the clean-cut hedges, the old abbeys" were "the evidences everywhere of nature controlled and enjoyed to the full." And unlike Mrs. Church, Louise Guiney had of course no daughter to marry off, and she had none of Mrs. Church's concern for the material advantages of those who on a small income found sufficient means to live away from home; living in England was her means of preserving an individuality, of fulfilling the particular nature of her gifts. Her antiquarian researches and her devotions to her faith kept her mind employed and her talents fresh and young; in her chosen environment, she held the motto of her saint, St. Francis de Sales, before her eyes: "In the royal galley of Divine Love there are no galley slaves; all the rowers are volunteers."

> In loneliness, in quaint
> Perpetual constraint

### ["Planting the Poplar"]

she wrote her essays and her verses, and within them she preserved the quality of seeming to live in pastures above the earth which is the secret of their charm:

> Hither felicity
> Doth climb to me,
> And bank me in with turf and marjoram
> Such as bees lip, or the new-weanèd lamb . . .

### ["Sanctuary"]

Through the eyes of her early friends in Boston, she was remembered as "a slight, blue-eyed girl, delicate as a wild rose, elusive as thistledown," which was perhaps another way of saying that she was both reserved and shy. A few of her verses will always speak to the initiate who share an interest in her favorite themes; however willful and extravagant her fancies became, she rarely wrote a shoddy line of verse—and she was the author of one extraordinary poem, **"A Friend's Song for Simoisius."** . . . (pp. 83-90)

[In this poem, the] expression of classical imagery in . . . fresh, clean diction reminds one of what an early critic of her work had written—that it was often felt in reading it as if one had suddenly encountered a Greek temple, standing alone, in an American woodland. In her **"Song for Simoisius"** Miss Guiney as early as 1893 seems to have an-

ticipated the spirit of a finer poet, who followed her exactly a decade later to London and who wrote memorable poems out of her private vision of another age, H. D. (p. 91)

> *Horace Gregory and Marya Zaturenska, "Four Women of the 'Twilight Interval': Reese, Guiney, Crapsey, and Teasdale," in their* A History of American Poetry, 1900-1940, *Harcourt Brace Jovanovich, Inc., 1946, pp. 79-106.*

## Henry G. Fairbanks   (essay date 1973)

[*Fairbanks is the author of two major studies of Guiney's life and career,* Louise Imogen Guiney: Laureate of the Lost *(see Further Reading) and* Louise Imogen Guiney. *In the following excerpt from the latter work, Fairbanks notes the influence of Guiney's Catholicism on her works written during the last two decades of her life.*]

[Guiney's] writing had always been religious in tone, infused with a Christian humanism; and, after her departure for England in 1901, it had become increasingly Catholic in focus as was apparent in her handling of Royalist-Cavalier poets. John Donne, for example, was "A Lost Catholic Poet"; and the Restoration had revived Catholic culture, but only secretly had it edged toward reunion with Rome.

Even [Robert] Emmet, the ill-starred Irish patriot, exercised more than the appeal of doomed youth and Hibernian hopes. His execution in 1804 had undermined any bridge of reconciliation between Old and New Orders. Like most advocates of Irish nationalism, he had been Protestant. His execution for "treason" was only an episode, historically, in the evolution of Irish independence culminating in 1922. But, because he had seemed a symbol of the burial of ancient divisions, she had rushed her biography of 1904 [***Robert Emmet: A Survey of His Rebellion and of His Romance***] into publication to coincide with the hundredth anniversary of his death.

Although the work manifested her persistent fascination with young and brilliant failures, it also demonstrated that, proximity to Ireland notwithstanding, she was still unseduced by the myth of the Irish Question. Actually, she anticipated James Joyce's indictment of Ireland as "the old sow that eats her farrow." She conceded that the story of starry-eyed Emmet reflected "a great unwritten chapter of perfidy behind his lonely ineffectual blow struck for national freedom." She frankly acknowledged the irony of Protestant leadership and the fickleness of the Catholic rabble in Emmet's futile seizure of Dublin Castle. He was less Irish and less denominational than universal as a hero: "To be unbiased and Irish is to love Robert Emmet; to be generously English is to love him; to be American is to love him anyhow."

Her interpretation was not surprising. She had consistently rejected the role of Hiberian or Catholic polemicist. But, in the love story of Emmet and his sweetheart, Sarah Curran, which was resolved after his death by Sarah's marriage to the English Captain Sturgeon who served with Wellington at Waterloo, Louise envisioned the burial of ancient animus. (pp. 113-14)

On her personal annotated copy of *Hurrell Froude: Memoranda and Comments,* Louise had linked in an epigraph from Isaias: "He has made me a chosen arrow." Froude had all the ingredients of the Guiney hero formula—youth, idealism, pugnacity, and early death. That he had lived so briefly or accomplished so little visibly only confirmed her summation of [Henri du Vergier, Comte de la Rochejaquelein's] *raison d'être:* "Vital and unexhausted spirits, under no subjection to results, can afford . . . to die anonymous. . . . He was a mere man of genius." Yet, if Froude, the fighting Anglican, had little lasting influence ascribable to his works, he was "the lost Pleiad of the Oxford Movement." She quoted Principal Fairbairn's epigram: "Hurrell Froude lives in Newman." She concluded that Froude, a close companion of [Cardinal John Henry] Newman at Oxford, had given the cardinal "every single one of his theories."

Publication of *Hurrell Froude* had been attended by disappointments. Longmans had contracted for and then rejected it. The division of contents, understandably, had jeopardized acceptance; for the presentation of material was almost as modern as today's cinema with its interweaving of multiple viewpoints. The long preface was her own, and the "Comments" refracted the opinions of Froude's contemporaries. Together, they challenged the reader to form his own estimate of a phenomenon as complex as *Rashomon,* through "the unfolding of a soul."

If *Hurrell Froude* was Anglo-Catholic, ***Blessed Edmund Campion*** was Roman Catholic, *à l'outrance.* (pp. 114-15)

Louise's biography of the heroic proctor of St. John's College was published in 1908, both in London and New York; and it was dedicated to "Campion's Brothers of the English Province of the Society of Jesus." With ***Patrins*** and ***Happy Ending,*** it was one of only three of her books to go into a second edition (1914). For the facts of Campion's story, her work leaned heavily on earlier studies by Robert Parsons, William Allen, Richard Simpson, and John Pollen. It successfully avoided the inherent melodrama of Campion's career, exploited by Robert Hugh Benson in *Come Rack, Come Rope.* By focusing on the perplexing confusions of religious loyalties in Elizabethan England, she eliminated incredible villains and instant-infallible heroes. Even Campion, the steadfast recusant who endured the hanging, drawing, and quartering at Tyburn, gains credibility by an earlier temporizing; for the doubts of his Oxford days become in the book a heavier interior cross than the barbarous public torture of the last hours. He emerges as a gentle but brilliant humanist and a promising successor to scholarly John Colet and William Grocyn, whom ironic circumstance propelled more brutally toward the fate of Thomas More. Such humanization enabled Guiney to transcend her usual difficulties with narrative, and she added a tragic note not often associated with martyrdom. For the irresistible eloquence which had skyrocketed his early career to acclaim and office trapped him at Lyford Grange when his pursuers were closing in on the secret mass-house. He had yielded, fatal-ly, to the entreaties of the recusant congregation for one last sermon.

His eloquence never deserted him subsequently, whether on the rack in the Tower of London, in private interrogation with Elizabeth and Leicester, or on trial, after torture, in Westminster Hall. Campion's was an authentic Renaissance style, one radiating the vision which George Chapman's vigorous translation of Homer had imparted to the young Keats. In Louise's own sensitive response to the felicity of Campion's language, she anticipated by forty years Evelyn Waugh's praise of the style that distinguished Campion's early *History of Ireland.* Though the *History* is hardly more than a brochure, "the melodious phrases fall into place" effortlessly, thereby convincing the reader that Lord Burghley and Sir Francis Walsingham killed a book, as well as a man, when they sent Campion to Tyburn. For just as Father Robert Parsons, Campion's Jesuit partner in the covert English mission, had confirmed the recusant John Shakespeare in the Old Faith, Campion himself had supplied, through Holinshed's edition of *History of Ireland,* the dramatic description of Wolsey's fall which son William, almost verbatim, incorporated into the second scene of Act IV of *Henry VIII.*

Campion kept his eloquence to the end. Like More at the block confessing himself "the King's good servant" (if God's, first), Campion's last words to the mob, before the hurdle was pulled from under him, invoked a blessing on the Elizabeth who might have saved him (and, privately, wished to): "to your Queen and my Queen, unto whom I wish a long, quiet reign, with all prosperity."

> No remote mystic was Edmund Campion, but a man of his age, with much endearing circumstance about and in him. . . . But in his kinship with his place and time, his peculiar greatness, his scholarship lightly worn, . . . he was a great Elizabethan too. He had sacrificed his fame and changed his career. He had spent himself for a cause the world can never love, and by doing so he has courted the ill-will of what passed for history, up to our day. But no serious student now mistakes the reason why his own England found no use for her "diamond" other than the strange use to which she put him. He is sure at last of justice . . .

As Louise's visit to Boston in 1906 had involved her in an apologia for her preference for living in England, her expanded circle of Catholic friends at Oxford led her to make comparisons between English and American Catholics. (pp. 116-18)

The English Catholics increasingly in her company edified her by their zeal and intelligence; and she attempted, accordingly, to explain them to their American co-religionists because she wanted to share what she had found admirable in English Catholicism. Her first attempt was rejected by the Reverend Herman J. Heuser, editor of *The American Ecclesiastical Review,* on the venerable principle that all comparisons are odious and that this particular one was bound to rub American Catholic sensibilities the wrong way. A more daring American editor, the Reverend Daniel E. Hudson, C.S.C., accepted it for *Ave Maria,* but with some revisions, as **"Catholicism in En-**

gland: A Non-Scientific Survey." He published it in 1909 in four installments to challenge reader reactions which, not long delayed, were approving or disapproving strongly.

In 1910, the astute Jesuit editors of *America* capitalized on the stir this article had created by printing her bolder criticism: **"What American Catholics Lack."** Louise did not spare the rod of chastisement: American churches were esthetic nightmares; cemeteries were atrociously pagan; money was overstressed; pews, too speedily vacated after mass. American Catholics had little private recollection and no interior life. The drama of the liturgy had been reduced to the dumb shows of private devotions. The "Hail Mary" had become "a drudge of work" for all occasions. Whereas the English priest remained "quite free of class and caste," at ease alike with squire or charwoman, the American pastors, too frequently, divided their attentions according to the social cleavage of the railroad tracks.

On the other hand, Guiney conceded that English Catholics lacked that free access to Protestant circles open to their American counterparts; and, contrary to a widespread supposition, she noted that the strength of twentieth-century English Catholicism derived more from converts than from either aristocratic old county families or new Irish immigrants. The handicaps of the Catholic writer, as a member of a subculture, applied to both English and American authors. In Louise's balanced assessment, these derived from limited talent rather than, as defensively alleged, from the obstacles of bias.

If Louise's candor forfeited some popularity with Irish-Catholic readers back home, it neither strained her personal devotion to Catholic cultural tradition nor curtailed her friendship with Catholic clergymen. Between the leading American editors with whom she corresponded regularly and the British intellectuals frequenting her Oxford chambers, one might have compiled a "Catholic Who's Who." Catholics and intellectuals continued to consume a high proportion of her time and interests, and the former led her into a maze of pious research, combing ancient records for misty legendary figures like St. Frideswide, ninth-century princess-patron of the City of Oxford.

Among the titles of her articles during this period, a selection suffices to attest her absorption: **"The Shrine of St. Edward the Confessor"** (*American Catholic Quarterly Review,* 1906); **"Newman's Littlemore: A Few Addenda"** (*Catholic World,* 1906); **"St. Frideswide's Day in Oxford"** (*Tablet,* 1907); **"A Notable Collection of Relics for Oxford"** (*Ecclesiastical Review,* 1907). . . . (pp. 118-19)

As Louise's friendship with priests multiplied, in person and in correspondents, they prompted her to considerable composition also on the nature of their sacerdotal office. Her verse tribute to Father Arthur Day (**"To One Who Would Not Spare Himself "**) was such, incomparably superior as a poem to the somewhat forced **"To an Unknown Priest."** The essay **"Flavian: A Clerical Portrait"** did not fail to show her sincere admiration for the priesthood, but it suffered from overwriting. **"On the Loneliness of Priests,"** however, her best and longest essay in this vein, is still a classic pre-Vatican II conception of the dignity of the pastor and of his unique relationship to his flock. She compressed her theme into an opening quotation from Lionel Johnson's paraphrase of Plotinus: "Lonely unto the Lone I go; / Divine, to the Divinity." Her insights are tender; her respect, absolute. Without sentimentality, she focused on the priest's life of entailed sacrifice:

> a demonstration which is all abstinence, a nearness without approach, an all-affectionate friendship which has dropped its personality upon the threshold . . . (to use a fine and abused word advisedly) the most romantic relationship under heaven.

> Yet he lives along borderlands. . . . Long ago he faced that possibility, weighed the loss, took the leap, and chose in his youth a work like no other, as in its delight, so in its pain. . . . Cooperation of the most availing kind can never go so far as to cheat a priest of his sacred loneliness. . . . Since he will not shirk it, neither shall we.

Nor was her promotion of priests confined to her poems and essays, though these were the best contributions within her means. Ceaselessly, she tried to secure their advantage in other ways. She introduced editor Heuser to the fiction of Monsignor Robert Hugh Benson and obtained serialization of Benson's *Mirror of Shalott* in *The American Ecclesiastical Review* (April-December, 1906). She wangled an invitation from Father Gasson of Boston College for Father Arthur Day's needed rest in America. She importuned the Reverend Henry Shandelle, S.J., to intercede with his Jesuit provincial for an English assignment for a brilliant contributor to *America* who could profit from exposure to Oxford. All priests were her brothers, as hers was an unfailing sisterly solicitude for them.

Louise's feelings toward Lionel Johnson were certainly sisterly. Their natural kinship was evident in familial features that confirmed their origin from the same Muse: Anglo-Irish both, Catholic-humanist to the core, gentle and obscure. Interestingly, even their handwriting and grammatical idiosyncrasies asserted the propinquity: "a slender, close slant, very odd, but not illegible; a true script of the old time, without a flaw" which seemed to whisper, "Behold in me the inveterate foe of haste and discourtesy, of typewriters, telegrams, and secretaries." So, too, their common penchant for use of the colon, which each jocularly bemoaned to the other would be friendless after their demise. When she had met Johnson in London in 1895, she had recorded that "He is not noticeably human. . . . But you know that I have a kindness for inhumanity." Her affection ripened with acquaintance, and the mutual admiration never slackened. She dedicated **Robert Emmet** to Johnson, whose baronet grandfather had suppressed the Irish rebellion at New Ross in 1798; Johnson, who had previously acknowledged her as "the American poetess" in his 1896 *Chronicle* review of "Henry Vaughan, Silurist," dedicated his *"De Profundis"* to her in 1897. She knew the rumored weakness for drink alleged to explain his periodic, and ever longer, withdrawals from London society; but she valued his patent virtue more.

When Johnson died suddenly in 1902 after a London street accident, she suffocated any personal judgment of his frailty in a single line: "In the bitter pathos of his end he was not with Keats, but with Poe." More to her point, however, she also noted that he had died, appropriately, on the feast of St. Francis of Assisi. Her best memorial to his brief-breathing genius was her introduction to *Some Poems of Lionel Johnson, Newly Selected* (1912); and her solid, if unsigned, contributions which she made in editing the *Catholic World* reprints of his articles (1910-1912) and also Professor Thomas Whittemore's *Post-Liminium: Essays and Critical Papers by Lionel Johnson* (1911).

Louise, a literary critic of integrity, as well as a loving friend, acknowledged that "The shortcomings of his verse lie in its Latin strictness and asceticism, somewhat repellent to any readers but those of his own [Classical] temper. Its emotional glow is a shade too moral, and it is only after a league of stately pacing that fancy is let go with a looser rein" [Introduction to *Some Poems of Lionel Johnson*]. The poems which she selected represented a distillation of Johnson's best, compressed into fifty-plus pages: "Winchester," "Oxford," "In Falmouth Harbor," "The Dark Angel" (so like her own **"Kings"**), "By the Statue of King Charles at Charing Cross" (which, in its salute to "the fair and fatal king," could not fail to evoke sympathy from Jacobite Louise), and Johnson's very last poem, perhaps the finest verse tribute from a student to his teacher, "Walter Pater."

Johnson's loyalty to persons, so like her own, extended also to his art, for it, too, was like hers: a nonprofessional concept of the man of letters; a disinclination to acknowledge work by signature; a sustained passion in vocation; a culture integrated beyond miscellaneous information; and a faith that was his treasure and an abiding peace and compensation. "At ten years old, or at the impossible sixty, he must equally have gone on, in a sort of beautiful vital stubbornness, being a unit, being himself." Accordingly, Louise guarded his reputation protectively. As late as 1915, she was still fretting about the misplacement of Johnson's papers in the hands of Mr. Arthur Galton, who had neither published nor returned them since 1903. Still later, hardly a year before her death, she forgot her own failing health to rejoice at the news that Robert Shafer of Annapolis had announced his forthcoming edition of Johnson's *Academy* essays: "The circle of Lionel's lovers is certainly growing, as it was bound to do!" Christian humanists were precious because rare; and young bridge-builders, like Emmet and Johnson, were rarer.

Louise . . . briefly enjoyed the personal resurrection brought about by a slender leaflet compiled by a Johnson-like admirer in the *Pathfinder*. Edward J. O'Brien, in whom Guiney had discerned a resemblance to her "Lionel," had been actively engaged in honoring her own neglected achievement. His slight paper-covered tribute of 1911, prefaced by some verses of Clinton Scollard "On the Lyrics of Louise Imogen Guiney," featured her familiar anthologized pieces: **"The Kings," "The Knight Errant," "The Vigil-at-Arms," "Sanctuary," "To a Dog's Memory,"** and others. Sensitively, O'Brien's appreciation focused on the gaiety and faith which had made her "one of the few who go singing through the land." More importantly, it consolidated the devotion of O'Brien who, after

Louise's death, collaborated perseveringly with Grace Guiney in editing Louise's masses of notes for belated posthumous edition of one volume of *Recusant Poets* in 1938.

Nor did Louise depend wholly upon others to establish her in the land of the living. Though now acclimated to the damp tunnels of the past, she emerged, periodically, to comment upon the contemporary scene. In two such poems, she touched sensitively upon problems still regarded as current . . . : war and pollution. **"Despotisms"** protested, for example, the inane brutality of imperialist overreach in World War I:

> Lost on the wind is holy Belgia's cry,
>     And Poland's hope shrinks underground
>     again,
> And France is singing to her wounds, where lie
>     The golden English heads like harvest grain.

**"The Motor,"** in retrospect, seems to anticipate the modern pollution of rampant technology:

> Vast intimate tyranny! Nature dispossessed
>     Helplessly hates thee, whose symbolic flare
> Lights up (with what reiterance unblest!)
>     Entrails of horror in a world thought fair.
> False God of pastime thou, vampire of rest,
>     Augur of what pollution, what despair?

Greater than speculative reassurance that Louise's residual powers survived these years of blight is derived from **"To an Ideal,"** originally published in *McClure's Magazine*. It proves not only Louise's retention of poetic inspiration but her conversion of it to the service of her overriding concern with her search for God:

> That I have tracked you from afar, my crown
>     I call it and my height:
> All hail, O dear and difficult star! All hail,
>     O heart of light!
> No pleasure born of time for me,
> Who in you touch eternity.
> If I have found you where you are, I win my
>     mortal fight.
>
> You flee the plain: I therefore choose summit
>     and solitude for mine,
> The high air where I cannot lose
>     our comradeship divine.
> More lovely here, to wakened blood,
> Sparse leaf and hesitating bud,
> Than gardens in the dewy vale for which the
>     dryads pine.
>
> Spirit austere! lend aid: I walk along
>     inclement ridges too,
> Disowning toys of sense, to baulk my soul
>     of ends untrue.
> Because man's cry, by night and day,
> Cried not for God, I broke away.
> On, at your ruthless pace! I'll stalk a hill-top
>     ghost with you.

Louise had always been spiritually oriented, as evident in such early poems as **"Summum Bonum"** and **"When on the Marge of Evening"** (both written in 1892) and in **"Sanctuary"** and **"Borderlands,"** written, respectively, in 1895 and 1896. The subsequent years of toil, disappoint-

*Guiney's study in her house in Auburndale, Massachusetts.*

ment, and refuge in Oxford as anchoress editor and scholar had purged her spirit of ambitions once fondly cherished; and, as a result, they had deepened her spirituality
with a new sense of unchanging verities beyond the tran-
siency of worldly praise. The period 1906-8, when she
composed **"Astræa"** and **"To an Ideal,"** reflects this religious maturity in a submerging of the self in submission
to God in exchange for a new-found peace that was to sustain her, largely, through the years of trial ahead. In its
frank communication of struggle partly won, **"To an
Ideal"** expresses the paradoxical freedom found in resignation, avoiding alike the conventional constrictions of
her favorite sonnet form and the imitations of Wordsworth and Tennyson that had shadowed her early verse.
Unlike Francis Thompson who had pictured God as "The
Hound of Heaven" relentlessly pursuing the fleeing soul,
Louise identified herself as the hunter tracking the course,
if falteringly, toward the Unchanging. Even so, she does
not exult in a quarry caught as much as in a vision
glimpsed from afar; for she conditions the goal (like
Dante's light seen on the distant summit from the "Dark
Wood" opening on the Inferno): "If I have found you
where you are, I win my mortal flight." Her discovery is
tentative, not terminal. For the fight for genuine fulfillment must still be carried to "inclement ridges" where

only the humblest beauty can survive, purer there in its essential simplicity than in the opulent gardens cultivated in
the lowlands.

One couplet of **"To an Ideal"** offers a personal explanation
of her withdrawal from earlier preoccupations and former
ambitions: "Because man's cry, by night and day, / Cried
not for God, I broke away." And the last line bravely acknowledges the uncertainties still to be met in the mystic's
unending ascent, even after the dazzling epiphany of a
flash of reassurance: "On, at your ruthless pace! / I'll stalk
a hill-top ghost with you." The realism which closes the
poem recalls the spirit of St. Theresa of Avila returning
from a comparable transfiguration to the routine of super-
vising her Order's far-flung, and often turbulent, convents.
That Louise, too, was not to dwell uninterruptedly on the
heights of serenity or ecstasy is patent in the fact that soon,
in 1910, she was to write one of her most disturbing
poems, **"The Kings."** . . . Here her vision evokes dark images of the Four Horsemen of the Apocalypse rather than
of the exploding illumination of Dante's *Paradiso*. But this
momentary relapse only authenticates **"To an Ideal's"**
embodiment of the universal truth discoverable in every
man's spiritual odyssey; whereas the earlier **"Sanctuary"**
and **"Borderlands"** . . . give wider scope to the purely
personal-subjective and, less chastened by experience, as-

sume a permanence not truly to be found in the illusory security of momentary inspiration. There the victory is too easy. On the other hand, the diction of **"To an Ideal,"** like life itself, conveys the agony inseparable from the mystic's ecstasy: "crown," "light," "hail," and "height" are juxtaposed against the austerer "track," "inclement," "ruthless," and "ridge." The same tension of opposites complicating the ceaseless struggle toward spiritual perfection expresses itself in the beckoning vision of the distant goal which she hails as "dear and difficult star." "Hill-top ghost" in the final line also sustains her appreciation of the unavoidable ambiguities confusing the quest for spiritual fulfillment. On one level of meaning it suggests her retreat from the secular mainstream; and, as coupled with God, it recognizes the fading of religion in her society. On another level of meaning the word "ghost" suggests the creative spirit "disowning toys of sense" for a liberation which releases the soul to ascend toward union with the eternal. As a Catholic, knowledgeable in pre-Vatican II theology and liturgy, Louise was quite familiar with this traditional equation of "ghost" with "spirit," particularly in the common usage of "Holy Ghost" as "Holy Spirit" or as "Creator Spirit." Whatever, the vision of "the glory and the dream" beheld "apparelled in celestial light" enabled her to persevere throughout the lonely, grinding years to follow. (pp. 119-25)

The final seven years of Louise Guiney's life guaranteed the "austerity" and the "inclement ridges, too." The pace, indeed, was ruthless: the dislocations plaguing England during the Great War; the bouts with illness, increasingly frequent and serious. Throughout this period, she labored on her major scholarly work, **Recusant Poets.** Years before, in the jesting conclusion of a letter to Van Allen, she had written with ironic prophecy: "I am to be hanged, drawn and qu—no, only drawn, for a Copeland and Day Christmas catalogue; so, as I await the executioner, I send you my last words, and the assurance that I die fairly bookish and as 'recusant' as Campion of St. John's Oxford." Her prophecy had all come true: Oxford, Campion, recusancy, martyrdom. By stepping aside from the mainstream, she had herself become the last of the recusants.

"Recusant" had been the term applied during the reign of Elizabeth to religious holdouts who repudiated subscription to the Act of 1559 by refusing to attend the Reformed Church services. Recusancy entailed devastating fines and civic disabilities that were intended to break the back of resistance to the union of church and state. More even than the disappropriation of church and monastic holdings, the Recusant Act consolidated Protestant conformity and the dissolution of the Old Faith. (p. 126)

From the rolls of such recusants, Louise and her Jesuit collaborator, the Reverend Geoffrey Bliss, assembled the evidence of the strangled culture of Old England.

To do this research was exhausting. Bliss had extra-Oxford duties assigned that allowed him few weekends for exchange and conference, and Louise had to interrupt her researches for the release of periodic, extraneous "potboilers" to sustain her throughout the project. Moreover, the penal laws against recusants had been so strictly enforced that many of the records had been consumed in public book burnings. A few manor attics still held the tattered, legally tainted documents; the libraries of England, even fewer. Yet, together, the collaborators accumulated an overwhelming testimony and, stubbornly, set about reducing it to a pattern. (p. 127)

[Eighteen years] after Louise's death—Grace Guiney, aided by Edward J. O'Brien who had compiled the *Pathfinder*'s Guiney tribute in 1911, succeeded in assembling one volume [of **Recusant Poets**] for publication. This Sheed and Ward edition of 1938 had been made possible by advance subscriptions raised by Dr. James A. Magner of Chicago. The materials for a second volume remain unedited, but they are in the custody of Professor Thomas Birrell of Nijmegen University who still plans to complete the work begun by Grace Guiney and O'Brien.

The dates 1535-1745, setting the scope of Louise's plan for **Recusant Poets,** indicated her intention to begin with Thomas More (1478–1535) and to end with the Battle of Culloden, 1745. The plan would have covered the period from the first Tudor persecutions to the defeat of Bonnie Prince Charlie, after which all hopes of any Stuart restoration had been extinguished. The first, as released, covers only from Thomas More to Ben Jonson; and, as the editors explained, new bibliographical and textual knowledge appearing in the interval between Louise's death and 1938 required revision of several chapters, such as those on Thomas Lodge, Henry Constable, William Alabaster, and Ben Jonson.

Louise's criteria for admission to the anthology were strict: where selected contributors were converts, only in exceptional instances had verse from their pre-Catholic days been included; and such inclusions had to be supported by "spiritual foreshadowings plain in the extreme." If a Jonson or an Alabaster relapsed in public profession of his creed, only the verified work of his Catholic period was used. Although some familiar lines win instant recognition (such as "Mortality, behold and fear" and "The glories of our birth and state"), many of the selections are undistinguished, for they lack any compelling literary artistry. Others, as Guiney duly noted, had become lyrical mainly by excision from longer narrative texts like "The Pilgrimage of Grace." The crushing onus of the penal laws militated against the freedom indispensable to creativity; as a result, the historical value of the collection outweighed its literary significance.

Louise was less interested in proving that Catholics were poets, or better poets because they were Catholic, than in showing not only the considerable number of Catholic authors who had continued to write despite the threat of punishment but also the distinctive features of their works as compared to Protestant contemporaries who were often superior from a purely literary standpoint:

> It need be no surprise if the distinction between Catholic and Protestant religious poetry is not immediately obvious. The Reformers retained far more of Christian truth than they threw away. . . . The differences, however, are perceptible to a Catholic reader, be he never so great a lover of Herbert and Vaughan and Giles Fletcher. . . . and yet what worlds asunder, to

take an extreme instance, are those two splendid poems, the Nativity Odes of Milton and Crashaw! In the first, a stately reverence, cold almost to formalism; in the other simplicity, confiding tenderness, an abandon of delight, a reckless ardor and happy daring born of the sense that exaggeration is here impossible.

Though often minor, literary quality was far from negligible. Surrey's sonnets are here; and Southwell's "A Child of My Choice," which Louise preferred to the better-known "Burning Babe." So is Thomas Lodge's "Of Rosalynde," bequeathed for reinvestment to William Shakespeare, just as Lord Vaux of Harrowden's "The Image of Death," included here, was to supply the original of the three stanzas spoken by the First Gravedigger in *Hamlet.* Side by side with Henry Howard, one finds that quaint man of letters, Nicholas Grimald, whose *Christus Redivivus* (possibly written in Cologne in 1543) became the direct ancestor of the Oberammergau Passion Play.

With Louise's consistent sympathy for "the great meanings in minor things," she could not have overlooked the importance of recusant culture; for she had uncovered a treasure trove of social significance in the priest-holes of England. Historians, as well as literary scholars, remain in her debt whenever they reassess extraofficial records between 1535 and 1745. For she did much to reconstruct the underground life of England which persecuting governments and Whiggish apologists had buried when they could not extirpate it. Her study does not refute the record, so much as sets it in a fuller perspective allowing a clearer understanding of religious changes antecedent to the development of modern industrialism and capitalism. Where Max Weber, Richard Tawney, and Amintore Fanfani took the high road of economics to illumine the relationship of Protestantism to industrial capitalism, Louise, characteristically, took the low road of obscure singers. What might have become an antiquarian's rummaging became an estimable insight, obliquely, into the spiritual and social history of Great Britain.

Although Louise, the born hero worshiper, took pride in the recusant record of independence in the face of oppression, she kept her sense of humor and light touch to the end. Some in her company of recusants were incongruously grotesque and were born to be martyred in any society. Myles Hogarde's doughty polemics, for example, she describes as "loud, verbose efficiency." Jasper Heywood, a Jesuit priest and the son of John Heywood the epigrammatist, is spared neither his native contentiousness nor the predisposition to mental unbalance that clouded his last years after deportation to the Continent. Nor is *Recusant Poets* clerically dominated; much less is it a priest-ridden work. Long before the age of ecumenism and the emergence of the layman, she credited lay leadership with its influence in preserving the faith among the recusants: Francis Tregian, the wealthy landowner who impoverished himself in the care of refugees at home and abroad; Richard Verstegan, exiled printer and publisher.

Her exhaustive researches have already enriched scholars by a pathfinder's trail to neglected writers like Henry Constable and Sir Edward Sherburne. Her probes have provided thesis materials on the period for graduate students yet

to come. Her style, in both introductory biographies and in footnotes even, evidences the unlost sparkle that, from the very start, had made her incapable of a bad phrase, though she might mar a sentence or two and miff a meter now and then. It makes one look forward to the issue of volume two of *Recusant Poets,* especially for her treatment of Dryden and Pope. Assuredly, her exhaustive researches enable us to understand the fitness of the inscription on her gravestone in Oxford: DELASSATA ("Worn-out"). (pp. 128-31)

> *Henry G. Fairbanks, in his* Louise Imogen Guiney, *Twayne Publishers, Inc., 1973, 170 p.*

## Cheryl Walker    (essay date 1982)

[*Walker is an American critic and educator who specializes in the work of American women poets. In the following excerpt from her* The Nightingale's Burden: Women Poets and American Culture before 1900, *she considers Guiney's poetry in relation to that of other women poets in turn-of-the-century America.*]

By the time the first volume of Emily Dickinson's poems had gone through eleven editions, that is by the end of 1892, the "gentle lady" whose "dimity convictions" Dickinson had scorned no longer presided unopposed over the social scene. The theory of separate spheres was on the wane and the "new woman" had arrived, expressing herself with a new frankness and invading traditionally masculine enclaves. Genteel magazines were beginning to publish women in great numbers. Often the poems published in *Scribner's, Century,* and the *Atlantic* were unidentifiable as to gender. In this brief transitional period male and female poets were almost indistinguishable, which is why critics like George Santayana, Thomas Beer, and Fred Lewis Pattee were dissatisfied with the verse and called it effeminate, gutless, dainty.

One observer summarized the new situation in which women found themselves in the following way:

> Their volumes, bound in creamy vellum and daintily tinted cloth, began more and more to fill the book tables, until reviewers no longer could give separate notice to them, but must consider the poets of a month in groups of ten or twelve. The quality of the feminine product was high enough to find place in the most exclusive monthlies, and the quantity published was surprising. The *Atlantic Monthly,* for instance, during the decade from 1870 published 108 poems by Longfellow, Whittier, Holmes, Lowell, Aldrich, and 450 other poems, and of the latter 201 were by women.

No longer were women praised for their effusiveness and men for their control of the language. In the introduction to his famous *American Anthology,* Edmund Clarence Stedman half-seriously called this period "the woman's age." Unlike his predecessor, Rufus Griswold, Stedman did not relegate women poets to a separate volume. Women were still not the mainstay of American verse, he felt, but at least they were competing in the same league.

In spite of changing conditions, however, women's poems

were not substantially different in attitude from their predecessors'. Birds winging their way into the ether still symbolically expressed missed or rejected opportunities. The sanctuary motif remained a constant; both Lizette Woodworth Reese and Louise Imogen Guiney—among the most highly respected women poets of the day—wrote poems titled **"Sanctuary."** Furthermore, women of the 1890s continued to use poetry to create fantasies of power, only to end by rejecting their implications. Martyrdom persisted as a haunting strain in their work. To inhabit a purely spiritualized world seemed preferable than to bid for this one. (pp. 117-18)

Hardly for the first time but with a new boldness, women poets took up the theme of passion. Ella Wheeler Wilcox's *Poems of Passion* (1883) created a scandal and became a sensation. The burning kiss, so offensive to some members of the Victorian world, grew to be a stock feature in women's poems. However, more than ever before, sexuality and romantic love in general became hyphenated with an equally old theme, death. Helen Hunt Jackson's ghostly lovers flit through the poems of many *fin-de-siècle* females. Death itself is eroticized and erotic love is made morbid. Emily Dickinson, with her "wild nights" and deflowering bees, could write provocatively, even frankly, about sex; one is sometimes unsure whether the experience a poem describes is love or death. But nowhere in her work does one find the morbid ecstasy of her niece, Martha Gilbert Dickinson, who wrote:

> Deep down in the dusk of passion-haunted ways,
> Lost in the dreaming alchemies of tone,—
> Drenched in the dew no other wings frequent,
> —Our thirsting hearts drank in the breath
> Of violets and love in death.—

> ["Her Music"]

The times seemed to inspire such poems, for men were writing them, too. (pp. 118-19)

Among male poets there were those, like Thomas Hornsby Ferril and Richard Hovey, who defied such tendencies in American poetry and wrote rugged nature poems, fierce accolades of Walt Whitman, or, like Hamlin Garland, stirring lyrics drawn from the American West. Among women, however, even a supposedly "virile" poet like Louise Imogen Guiney seems less hardy, less death-defying, than death-enamored.

In point of fact, women poets of this period were still more fully engaged in the drama of life's disappointments than were their male counterparts. Not completely at home with their recent past, they were still not quite attuned to their future. Femininity seemed too fragile, masculinity too alien to them. Their work dramatizes the development of preoccupations traditionally feminine into lyric expressions surprisingly modern. They were poets of the transition, wearing new fashions to do traditional work.

In an article entitled "The Transitional American Woman" published in the *Atlantic Monthly* in December 1880, Kate Gannett Wells describes the woman of the day in these terms:

> Women do not care for their home as they did;

it is no longer the focus of *all* their endeavors; nor is the mother the involuntary nucleus of the adult children. Daughters must have art studios outside their home; authoresses must have a study near by; and aspirants to culture must attend classes or readings in some semi-public place. Professional women have found that, however dear the home is, they can exist without it.

When we remember Emily Dickinson's feverish proclamations about her blessed home, when we recall Mary Hewitt's "Hearth of Home" and Lydia Sigourney's enthusiasm for the functions of housewife and mother, it seems we have come very far from them. Still, these new women could hardly be called liberated in the sense in which we understand the word today or even in the sense in which the 1920s might have used it. Poets and professional women may have been more self-sufficient than their mothers. They still lived in a world where many occupations were closed to them. Lizette Woodworth Reese had to support herself by being a schoolteacher for 48 years. Louise Guiney went from being postmistress of the Auburndale, Massachusetts, post office to becoming a cataloguer in the Boston Public Library. These were rather new jobs for women to hold but still low-paying and not nearly as glamorous as being a college professor or the editor of an important magazine, jobs held by her friends Oliver Wendell Holmes and Richard Watson Gilder. Furthermore, none of these women was sexually aggressive. They would have been horrified by Edna St. Vincent Millay. Ella Wheeler Wilcox was horrified by Amy Lowell. Although she was pro-suffrage, Louise Guiney was dismayed by America's overly eager "gynaecocracy." She preferred women who were sturdier and more reticent.

In this Guiney shared with a number of other successful women a profound suspicion about "the new woman" and the social changes inevitable in her wake. To Richard Watson Gilder she wrote in 1894: "I am not in the least given to any violent interest in womankind, such as has addled the country's brains of late. Give me a man-and-woman world: 'tis good enough!" (pp. 119-21)

The lives of Wilcox, Guiney, and Reese inform us in numerous ways that they were women of their generation. While the *Atlantic, Century,* and *North American Review* published articles like "Are Women to Blame?" "Our Foolish Virgins," "The Change in the Feminine Ideal," and "The Steel-Engraving Lady and the Gibson Girl," these women poets were themselves embodiments of the transition so interesting to the press. (p. 121)

Caroline Ticknor, writing in 1901, characterized the Gibson Girl as wearing "a short skirt and heavy square toed shoes, a mannish collar, cravat, and vest, and a broad-brimmed felt hat tipped jauntily upon one side." She imagined her saying: "I can do everything my brothers do; and do it rather better, I fancy. I am an athlete and a college graduate, with a wide, universal outlook. My point of view is free from narrow influences, and quite outside of the home boundaries."

Louise Guiney was not a Gibson Girl. None of the innocent impishness of this person could have been hers, and yet she was in her own way a rebel against Victorian prudery. Her contempt for Victoria was violent:

> That money-saving, gillie-adoring, etiquette-blinded, pudgy, plodding, unspiritual, unliterary, mercantile, dowdy, sparkless, befogged, continuous Teuton lady is not, in one's line of life, a Necessary. How could Van Dyke have posed her? What could Falkland have said to her which would have been comprehended?

Fuming over Victoria's Diamond Jubilee, she wrote to a friend: "As the godly Mr. Wilfrid Meynell said in his pious paper . . . when reviewing a bookful of virtuous gentlewoman *circa* 1670, who were of a punless cast of mind— 'O for an hour of Nell Gwynne!' "

Like the Gibson Girl, Guiney had a healthy taste for outdoor activities, particularly for brisk walking. She once remarked: "If ever I get to Paradise, I have a stipulation: that I shall play games in the open air, for ever and ever." In 1895 she took a walking tour of England and Wales with her friend Alice Brown. They were unchaperoned and they dressed unconventionally, in gaiters. She wrote: "Divided skirts are my horror. Gimme kilts to the knee, or trousers outright." Most women were still wearing dresses that swept the ground. Encountering bewildered Englishmen, the strangely clad Guiney and Brown would inquire with perfectly straight faces if the gentleman had seen ten other women dressed just as they were.

In spite of her proclaimed lack of interest in womankind, Guiney spent a great deal of her time with women. Among her female literary friends were Louise Chandler Moulton, Sarah Orne Jewett, Annie Fields, and Alice Brown. She corresponded with Lizette Reese. Long before the advent of current interest in Katherine Phillips, she wrote a book about the "Matchless Orinda," which she published in 1904. Although her assessment of Phillips mixed praise and blame she was particularly sympathetic with the independence of this seventeenth-century woman poet. In essence, Guiney (and many others like her) did not wish to be lumped together with what Thomas Beer called "the Titaness," a stern, aggressive female reformer who abhorred strong passions and strong drink and whose power was clearly being felt in the 1890s. Nevertheless, Guiney favored women's suffrage and she admired other women poets. To Herbert E. Clarke she wrote enthusiastically in 1896: "There is a new volume coming from Miss Reese, Lizette Woodworth Reese, whom I have always 'ighly hadmired. The women over here are regular Atalantas in the poetic race." To her credit, she did not resent other women on their way up.

With all Guiney's adventurous spirit and hard-headedness, it comes as something of a shock to find her as deeply attracted to martyrs as her early nineteenth-century sister poets like Elizabeth Oakes-Smith. She once wrote: "Thwarted growths always have an attraction for me, and the might-have-beens are more interesting than Sarah Lynches." Her elegy to Thomas Parsons could have been written by any nineteenth-century woman poet early or late.

> Look not on fame, but Peace; and in a bower
> Receive at last her fulness and her power:

> Not wholly, pure of heart!
> Forget thy few, who would be where thou art.

The renunciation of ambition and worldly power in favor of peace, and ultimately death, is all too familiar among women of this tradition. Her sense of her own failure at the end of her life was intense. She wrote: "I am a rounded and perfect Failure, so far as getting on in this world is concerned." Two years before her death, she complained in a letter:

> I've been heading up against the wind very unnaturally for some six years now. Some sort of break-up is immenent, for I'm not getting any younger. I'm like a galvanized corpse kept alive by [others]; but in myself I have no weapon to fight the world with. And my mind is like the "walking-stick" insect, so infernally sensitive that if touched or breathed upon, it can only hang lifeless, instead of scuttling away.

For a woman who had "hungered for a largeness like the sea, / For space, for freedom, scope, infinity," this is a sad confession, though a familiar one.

Although much had changed for women poets, underneath the bravado much had remained the same. This is particularly obvious if we analyze the poems of these women. They may have allowed themselves a new frankness in using the language of passion, but behind this bold display lay many of the same fears and hesitations we recognize earlier in the century. (pp. 124-26)

Poems in which sex, or passion, appear threatening are rare among men, even in this relatively androgynous period. Women, on the other hand, have often written such poems. Christina Rossetti's "Goblin Market" stands as the paradigm. (p. 127)

For some reason the prospect of satisfaction and self-indulgence filled these women with horror, and this at a time when essayists in the magazines were writing about "the general idleness and self-centredness of the average American woman." Quite possibly, at a subconscious level, guilt was still associated in their minds with ambition. The common wisdom of the day was that the past ethic of self-sacrifice had been replaced by women with a new ethic of self-fulfillment. "Formerly," wrote Kate Wells, "to be a good housekeeper, an anxious mother, an obedient wife, was the *ne plus ultra* of female endeavor,— to be all this *for others' sakes*. Now, it is to be more than one is, for *one's own sake*" (her emphasis).

However, at a deeper level the ideal of renunciation and self-sacrifice did not lose its appeal for women so quickly. Much of the poignancy of Lizette Reese's poetry depends upon our recognition of woman's presumed need to serve. (p. 128)

Sometimes one can hear in the heart of this self-denial a hint of masochism, "the pleasure of despair" as Wilcox calls it. Elinor Wylie was to become an expert at it. Lizette Reese suggests it in "To Life":

> Unpetal the flower of me,
> And cast it to the gust;
> Betray me if you will;
> Trample me to dust.

But that I should go bare,
But that I should go free
Of any hurt at all—
Do not this thing to me!

Obviously this conjunction of pain and pleasure has something to do with the ecstatic rendering of love as an image of death or of death as love. "Cruel and sweet," Louise Guiney's pairing, make up the quintessential 1890s' expression of deathly lust or lustful death. Guiney is probably the most interesting of the turn-of-the-century poets, less of a hack than Wilcox and more vibrant than Reese, but even she is not immune to the love/death union, as we can see by this poem called **"Borderlands"**:

Through all the evening,
All the virginal long evening,
Down the blossomed aisle of April it is dread to
    walk alone;
For there the intangible is nigh, the lost is ever-
    during;
And who would suffer again beneath a too divine
    alluring,
Keen as the ancient drift of sleep on dying faces
    blown?

Yet in the valley,
At a turn of the orchard alley,
When a wild aroma touched me in the moist and
    moveless air,
Like a breath indeed from out Thee, or as airy
    vesture round Thee,
Then was it I went faintly, for fear I had nearly
    found Thee,
O Hidden, O Perfect, O Desired! O first and final
    Fair!

This poem seems to me intentionally ambiguous. Are we meant to conclude that the terrifying yet longed-for figure is God? Whoever the "Thee" is, the "too divine alluring" is a threat to the "virginal long evening." We recognize the diction of sexual desire here but it is a passion "keen as the ancient drift of sleep on dying faces blown." Is the valley, the valley of the shadow of death? Fear and desire combine to make this "first and final Fair" a haunting presence seemingly amoral, certainly not traditionally Christian. Yet even when Guiney is at her most vibrant and militaristic, as in **"The Knight Errant,"** death is presented invitingly:

The passion for perfection
Redeem my failing way!
The arrows of the upper slope
From sudden ambush cast,
Rain quick and true, with one to ope
My Paradise at last!

Although she did not reprint it in later editions, Guiney wrote one extraordinary ballad that must be of interest to those concerned with women's poetry as female expression. **"Tarpeia"** has unfortunately been omitted from women's anthologies. Though its subject is overtly classical, and part of the revival of classicism in which Guiney participated with male poets like Trumbull Stickney and William Vaughn Moody, the handling of the theme is characteristically feminine.

Woe: lightly to part with one's soul as the sea
    with its foam!
Woe to Tarpeia, Tarpeia, daughter of Rome!

Lo, now it was night, with the moon looking
    chill as she went:
It was morn when the innocent stranger strayed
    into the tent.

The hostile Sabini were pleased, as one meshing
    a bird;
She sang for them there in the ambush: they
    smiled as they heard.

Her sombre hair purpled in gleams, as she
    leaned to the light;
All day she had idled and feasted, and now it
    was night.

The chief sat apart, heavy-browed, brooding
    elbow on knee;
The armlets he wore were thrice royal, and won-
    drous to see:

Exquisite artifice, whorls of barbaric design,
Frost's fixèd mimicry; orbic imaginings fine

In sevenfold coils: and in orient glimmer from
    them,
The variform voluble swinging of gem upon
    gem.

And the glory thereof sent fever and fire to her
    eye.
'I had never such trinkets!' she sighed,—like a
    lute was her sigh.

'Were they mine at the plea, were they mine for
    the token, all told,
Now the citadel sleeps, now my father the keep-
    er is old,'

'If I go by the way that I know, and thou follo-
    west hard,
If yet at the touch of Tarpeia the gates be un-
    barred?'

The chief trembled sharply for joy, then drew
    rein on his soul:
'Of all this arm beareth I swear I will cede thee
    the whole,'

And up from the nooks of the camp, with hoarse
    plaudit outdealt,
The bearded Sabini glanced hotly, and vowed as
    they knelt,

Bare-stretching the wrists that bore also the
    glowing great boon:
'Yea! surely as over us shineth the lurid low
    moon,'

'Not alone of our lord, but of each of us take
    what he hath!
Too poor is the guerdon, if thou wilt but show
    us the path.'

Her nostril upraised, like a fawn's on the arrowy
    air,
She sped; in a serpentine gleam to the precipice
    stair,

They climbed in her traces, they closed on their
    evil swift star:
She bent to the latches, and swung the huge por-
    tal ajar.

Repulsed where they passed her, half-tearful for
    wounded belief,
'The bracelets!' she pleaded. Then faced her the
    leonine chief,

And answered her: 'Even as I promised, maid-
    merchant, I do.'
Down from his dark shoulder the baubles he sul-
    lenly drew.

'This left arm shall nothing begrudge thee. Ac-
    cept. Find it sweet.
Give, too, O my brothers!' The jewels he flung
    at her feet,

The jewels hard, heavy; she stooped to them,
    flushing with dread,
But the shield he flung after: it clanged on her
    beautiful head.

Like the Apennine bells when the villagers'
    warnings begin,
Athwart the first lull broke the ominous din
    upon din;

With a 'Hail, benefactress!' upon her they
    heaped in their zeal
Death: agate and iron; death: chrysoprase, beryl
    and steel.

'Neath the outcry of scorn, 'neath the sinewy
    tension and hurl,
The moaning died slowly, and still they massed
    over the girl

A mountain of shields! and the gemmy bright
    tangle in links,
A torrent-like gush, pouring out on the grass
    from the chinks,

Pyramidical gold! the sumptuous monument
    won
By the deed they had loved her for, doing, and
    loathed her for, done.

Such was the wage that they paid her, such the
    acclaim:
All Rome was aroused with the thunder that
    buried her shame.

On surged the Sabini to battle. O you that aspire!
Tarpeia the traitor had fill of her woman's de-
    sire.

Woe: lightly to part with one's soul as the sea
    with its foam!
Woe to Tarpeia, Tarpeia, daughter of Rome!

At the heart of this poem, so thrilling and yet so disturb-ing, is an unresolved tension between the judgment ex-pressed against Tarpeia and the injustice at a human level of her fate. If we assume, for a moment, that the poem is about what it claims to be about, that is, the betrayal of a great city, then Tarpeia is a villain deserving of her fate. Yet the poem refuses to consider the assault of the city se-riously. It leaves off where the battle begins, and the re-frain informs us that the real issue is lightly parting with

one's soul. Of primary importance is not the betrayal of the city but the betrayal of the self. To make us despise Tarpeia, the poet need only have dwelt on the havoc she created or the defects of her character. Clues in terms of the imagery associated with her might have convinced us. However, her mercenary desires seem utterly childish rather than deeply wicked. She is characterized at the be-ginning of the poem as "innocent." She strays into the tent like a young animal who has lost her way. The Sabini are "pleased, as one meshing a bird." In the actual accom-plishment of her traitorous act, the only description given is of her "nostril upraised, like a fawn's on the arrowy air." Why did the poet choose such a simile? The fawn is a young animal, relatively helpless, concerned merely with self-preservation in a dangerous environment, "the ar-rowy air." What's more, Guiney intensifies the description of Tarpeia's death to make the Sabine warriors seem far more barbaric than she. Theirs is a vengeful, adult de-structiveness; hers merely a short-sighted, puerile selfish-ness. If we take her "woman's desire" to be one of merce-nary self-interest, we might consider Guiney's warning in light of the endless reprimands of women for marrying for money which were published in the magazines, usually by women themselves. Commentators often described such marriages as a betrayal of the citadel, the home, resulting from women's immature and selfish desires. In suggesting such an interpretation, we have already stepped outside the intentional boundaries of the poem, but to deal ade-quately with it, it seems we must do so.

At a deeper level the poem is not about treason but prosti-tution; it is about sexual rather than national politics. It is useful to remember that prostitution was a live issue in this period, and one over which women were divided be-tween feeling that prostitutes were utterly degraded and that they were innocent victims of male lust. Some of this conflict of attitudes is evoked in us by the poem's handling of Tarpeia. How are we to see her as a sexual figure?

To begin with, the image of a lone maiden in a campful of soldiers immediately suggests sexual danger. The struc-ture of the bargain is further suggestive: the girl agrees to sell her favors for a material reward. The moon is "lurid," the men glance "hotly." However, the unmistakable clue that we are concerned with lust comes at the point where the Sabini take revenge on Tarpeia for "the deed they had loved her for, doing, and loathed her for, done." At this point her betrayal seems secondary to the betrayal of human trust that she suffers. Furthermore, the city is roused to action by the noise of her murder. Guiney's final words are deeply ambiguous: "O you that aspire! / Tar-peia the traitor had fill of her woman's desire."

It is probable that Louise Imogen Guiney was not fully aware of the issues she was raising. Consciously she seems to have had a healthy appreciation for sexual life. In the Tudor Exposition she found herself dissatisfied because the paintings so completely avoided what she called "the mystery of sex." However, at a deeper level she was as un-nerved by woman's sexual vulnerability in a patriarchal society as her less liberated, earlier nineteenth-century sis-ters. The clear message is that what men will love you for doing at the moment, they will hate you for afterward.

(One might compare Emily Dickinson's poems 213 and 1339.) In **"Tarpeia"** passion and death merge, with the gravest implications. Aspiration itself is guilty and must be punished. The traitor Tarpeia becomes through a curious inversion one of Guiney's martyrs.

Perhaps the unresolved tension in this poem was what led Guiney not to reprint it. Among serious women poets at the turn of the century, it is hard to find a poem that celebrates a woman for her aggressiveness or her success at doing "unwomanly" things. (pp. 129-33)

In general, women poets at the turn of the century sounded a mournful note, as non-controversial as Ina Coolbrith's "Fruitionless":

> Ah, little flower, upspringing, azure-eyed,
>           . . . . .
> Living and blooming thy brief summer-day:
>       So, wiser far than I,
>       That only dream and sigh,
> And, sighing, dream my listless life away.

The mournful note might have been sounded for the passing away of a world in which women at least had well-defined roles. Yet, beneath the listlessness of the 1890s was a restless hunger which surfaced at moments only to be subsumed under a philosophy of renunciation. As Louise Guiney wrote of Pascal in *Happy Ending:*

> Spirit so abstinent, in thy deeps lay
> What passion of possession?

Ambivalence continued to be for women poets their primary attitude toward engaging in the struggle for power—sexual, literary, or political. (pp. 134-35)

What the poetry of women like Guiney and Reese shows is that aspiration and success still made them uneasy. Even the feminists suffered from doubts; Christopher Lasch refers to "the suspicion that obsessed the feminist imagination: that in pursuing a masculine ideal she had betrayed her own femininity." Despite her bravado, the Gibson Girl's self-confidence was only skin-deep.

In **"Astræa"** Louise Guiney's speaker asks of the men she is leaving behind:

> Are ye unwise, who would not let me love you?
> Or must too bold desires be quieted?
> Only to ease you, never to reprove you,
> I will go back to heaven with heart unfed:
> Yet sisterly I turn, I bend above you,
> To kiss (ah, with what sorrow!) all my dead.

In 1900 the question still hung in the air: Must too bold desires be quieted? Those like Victoria Woodhull, advocate of free love, who answered "no" were outcasts. Most tried in the best way they could to negotiate their own peace. In this atmosphere of compromise and self-denial, it is no wonder that the most highly respected women poets like Guiney and Reese were attracted to an aesthetic of self-restraint. In **"Planting the Poplar"** Guiney describes her sense of her own craft.

> In loneliness, in quaint
> Perpetual constraint,
> In gallant poverty,
> A girt and hooded tree,

> See if against the gale
> Our leafage can avail.

Reese, for her part, added:

> If you dig a well,
> If you sing a song,
> By what you do without,
> You make it strong.

Both poets shared an eerie sense of martyrdom about their professions. "Bargain," from Reese's last book *Pastures,* expresses it most directly:

> A rose will cost you more
> Than its gathering;
> A song be such a price
> You dare not sing.

> What must you pay for each,
> Else loveliness fare amiss?
> Yourself nailed to a Tree—
> This.

Wilcox, Reese, and Guiney all shared a high degree of popularity in their time, although they are mostly forgotten today. Wilcox remained a poet of fireside sentiment, the author of "Laugh, and the world laughs with you; / Weep, and you weep alone." William Randolph Hearst was her champion. H. L. Mencken thought Reese had written some of the greatest sonnets in the language and he continued to praise her work after her death. Willa Cather remarked that during her time at *McClure's Magazine* no verse "passed from hand to hand with so much excitement" as Guiney's.

Still, these women ended their lives feeling unfulfilled. Wilcox and Guiney both had nervous breakdowns in their last years. Reese's poem is eloquent concerning the "bargain" she felt she had made. They had gained a certain degree of recognition and independence but at a great price. Wilcox's comments in "An Open Letter to Literary Aspirants" may serve as a characteristically ambivalent summary for them all:

> Seen from a distance, fame may seem to a
> woman like a sea bathed in tropical suns, where
> in she longs to sail. Let fame once be hers, she
> finds it a prairie fire consuming or scorching all
> that is dearest in life to her. Be careful before you
> light these fires with your own hands.
>
>                                        (pp. 135-37)

*Cheryl Walker, "One Brief, Transitory Hour: Ella Wheeler Wilcox, Lizette Woodworth Reese, and Louise Guiney," in her* The Nightingale's Burden: Women Poets and American Culture before 1900, *Indiana University Press, 1982, pp. 117-37.*

---

## FURTHER READING

Alexander, Calvert. "Fin de Siècle in America." In his *The*

*Catholic Literary Revival: Three Phases in Its Development from 1845 to the Present,* pp. 201-30. 1935. Reprint. Port Washington, N.Y.: Kennikat Press, 1968.

> Includes discussion of Guiney's life and work, noting her role in the development of Catholic literature in the United States at the turn of the century.

Berrigan, Daniel J. "Forgotten Splendor." *America* 70, No. 22 (4 March 1944): 605-06.

> Applauds Guiney's moral vision in *Happy Ending* and asserts that the volume contains "some of the truest lyrical bursts in the history of American poetry."

Brégy, Katherine. "Louise Imogen Guiney." In her *Poets and Pilgrims: From Geoffrey Chaucer to Paul Claudel,* pp. 169-90. New York: Benziger Brothers, 1925.

> Celebrates Guiney's life and literary career.

Brooks, Van Wyck. *New England: Indian Summer, 1865-1915,* 412ff. New York: E. P. Dutton & Co., 1940.

> Offers brief discussion of Guiney's life and poetry within the context of the literature of New England at the turn of the century.

———. *The Confident Years: 1885-1915,* 243ff. New York: E. P. Dutton, 1952.

> Discussion similar to that cited above.

Fairbanks, Henry G. *Louise Imogen Guiney: Laureate of the Lost.* Albany, N.Y.: Magi Books, 1972, 315 p.

> Examines Guiney's literary career, stressing her championing of generally overlooked authors and historical figures in her poetry, biographies, and editions of collections by other poets.

Gosse, Edmund. "A Belated Cavalier." In his *Silhouettes,* pp. 365-71. London: William Heinemann, 1925.

> Reprint of an earlier essay that commends the emphasis in Guiney's works on both chivalric gallantry and Catholicism.

Greene, Graham. "Poetry from Limbo." In his *Collected Essays,* pp. 249-52. London: The Bodley Head, 1969.

> Praises Guiney's selection of poetry in the posthumously published anthology *Recusant Poets.*

Gundy, H. Pearson. "Flourishes and Cadences: Letters of Bliss Carman and Louise Imogen Guiney." *Dalhousie Review* 55, No. 2 (Summer 1975): 205-26.

> Provides excerpts from correspondence between Guiney and the Canadian poet, and examines their friendship and literary interaction.

Kurth, Paula. "The Sonnets of Louise Imogen Guiney." *America* 43, No. 18 (9 August 1930): 430-31.

> Asserts that Guiney's "muse was particularly at home with the sonnet."

Lucey, William L. "Louise Imogen Guiney and Her *Songs at the Start." Records of the American Catholic Historical Society of Philadelphia* 66, No. 1 (March 1955): 53-63.

> Discusses the significance of Guiney's previously unpublished letters written during the development and publication of her first volume of poetry.

———. "Louise Imogen Guiney and the *American Ecclesiastical Review." The American Ecclesiastical Review* 136, No. 6 (June 1957): 364-70.

> Elaborates on Guiney's contributions of poetry and essays to the Catholic journal and on her correspondence with the editor, Father Herman J. Heuser.

———. " 'We New Englanders . . . ': Letters of Sarah Orne Jewett to Louise Imogen Guiney." *Records of the American Catholic Historical Society of Philadelphia* 70, Nos. 1-2 (March-June 1959): 58-64.

> Reprints several letters to Guiney from the American short story writer and novelist.

Payne, William Morton. "Recent Books of Poetry." *The Dial* 15, No. 177 (1 November 1893): 265-69.

> Contains a brief review of *A Roadside Harp.* Payne concludes, "In quality it is compact and exquisite, while imitative in but slight degree."

Reilly, Joseph J. "The Case for Louise Imogen Guiney." In his *Of Books and Men,* pp. 137-51. New York: Julian Messner, 1942.

> Describes Guiney's career, noting biographical influences on her poetry: "her race, her faith, her feeling for her father, and the absence from her life of one of the most vital and universal of emotional experiences."

Rittenhouse, Jessie B. "Louise Imogen Guiney." In his *The Young American Poets,* pp. 75-93. Boston: Little, Brown, and Co., 1904.

> Commends the classicism and expressive strength of Guiney's poetry.

———. "The Charm of Louise Imogen Guiney." *The Bookman,* New York LII, No. 6 (February 1921): 515-20.

> Sketch of Guiney's literary career offering recollections of visits with the poet.

Tenison, E. M. *Louise Imogen Guiney: Her Life and Works, 1861-1920.* London: Macmillan & Co., 1923, 348 p.

> Biographical and critical study, with a descriptive bibliography of primary sources.

Tully, Sheila A. "Heroic Failures and the Literary Career of Louise Imogen Guiney." *The American Transcendental Quarterly: A Journal of New England Writers,* Nos. 47-8 (Summer-Fall 1980): 171-86.

> Investigates "the possible connections between Guiney's life-long desire to live a heroic life, molded on the life of her father, and her career as a writer."

# William Dean Howells

## 1837-1920

American novelist, critic, essayist, travel writer, short story writer, autobiographer, dramatist, poet, and biographer.

The following entry presents criticism of Howells's novel *The Rise of Silas Lapham* (1885). For information on Howells's complete career, see *TCLC*, Volumes 7 and 17.

*The Rise of Silas Lapham* is Howells's best-known novel and is considered his fullest rendering in fiction of the Realist literary theory he advocated as one of the most influential American critics of his time. Decrying Victorian romanticism in favor of true-to-life depictions of commonplace characters and situations, Howells presented in *Silas Lapham* the story of a provincial businessman's unsuccessful attempt to gain recognition in Boston society. Concluding with the protagonist's financial ruin and his moral "rise," *Silas Lapham* evidences Howells's concern with the ethics of capitalism and refutes such common themes in fiction of the Gilded Age as the happiness of self-made millionaires and the nobility of self-sacrifice in the name of love.

Howells's long career as a novelist is generally divided into three overlapping phases, and *The Rise of Silas Lapham* is seen as representative of the second, transitional phase between his early novels of manners and his later economic novels which attack laissez-faire capitalism. In the mid-1880s, just as the Ohio-born Howells was reaching the apex of his literary, financial, and social success, he was becoming increasingly disaffected with the American class system and Boston aristocracy. In a letter to his father dated 10 August 1884, Howells remarked on the inequitable distribution of wealth in American society and noted that the mansions of his Boston neighborhood sat empty while their owners summered elsewhere. Howells commented: "[How] unequally things are divided in this world. While these beautiful, airy, wholesome houses are uninhabited, thousands upon thousands of poor creatures are stifling in wretched barracks in the city. . . . I wonder that men are so patient with society as they are." His growing alienation from wealthy society, coupled with personal problems, including the severe illness of his daughter, led to his emotional collapse during the writing of *Silas Lapham* in late 1884. Many critics believe Howells's personal circumstances influenced the harsh social criticism in the novel, as well as the characterization of Silas Lapham as a provincial man seeking respectability in Boston.

*The Rise of Silas Lapham* consists of two central and closely related plots which critics generally term the "business," or "moral," plot and the "romantic," or "social," plot. The former centers on the rise and fall of Lapham's business. The son of a New England farmer, Lapham is a self-made millionaire who has gained sole possession of his paint-manufacturing business by forcing

out his inept partner, Milton K. Rogers, a move with far-reaching moral ramifications that eventually precipitates Lapham's financial ruin. The second plot focuses on the efforts of Lapham's nouveau riche family to ingratiate themselves into Boston society by cultivating a relationship with the aristocratic Corey family. Lapham builds a mansion in the Coreys' fashionable neighborhood and takes young Tom Corey into his business in the erroneous belief that Tom wants to marry Lapham's beautiful but shallow daughter Irene.

Unacquainted with the conventions of Boston society, Lapham seeks status through garish displays of wealth that only further mark his lack of breeding. In a pivotal scene, Lapham gets drunk and humiliates himself at a dinner party hosted by the Coreys; later, Tom declares his love for Lapham's plain-featured but intelligent daughter Penelope, causing a crisis within the Lapham household. When Penelope refuses to marry the man her sister loves, the Laphams' pastor, Reverend Sewell, denounces the decision as the product of a foolish moral code propagated by romance novels, and Tom and Penelope wed. Meanwhile, Lapham discovers that his business is on the brink of failure, owing to foolish investments and a substantial unpaid loan that he made to Rogers in an effort to appease his conscience. As Lapham struggles to save his business, Rogers offers him a legal but unethical means of avoiding bankruptcy: a charitable organization wants to buy property owned by Lapham, not knowing that under the terms of the deed the property can be claimed by a railroad company, and is thus worthless. Lapham refuses to sell, ensuring his own bankruptcy but exhibiting the moral "rise" for which Howells titled the novel.

An artistic representation of Howells's literary theory, *The Rise of Silas Lapham* attacks romantic ideals of love and morality not only in the embroilment of the love triangle, but also through a fictitious romantic novel, *Tears, Idle Tears,* which several characters have read and which provides the inspiration for Penelope's proposed self-sacrifice. In a discussion of that book, Reverend Sewell comments: "The novelists might be the greatest possible help to us if they painted life as it is . . . but for the most part they have been and are altogether noxious." Furthermore, the character of Lapham himself is a refutation of the rags-to-riches hero common in much of nineteenth-century fiction, particularly in the novels of Horatio Alger. Critics have said that Howells debunked the Alger-type storyline by extending it past its usual conclusion in which a hard-working protagonist attains social and material success. Contrary to this romantic idea, Howells argued that under the American class system a man of humble origins cannot live "happily ever after" simply by becoming wealthy because he will always be marked by the stigma of his birth.

Early critics of *The Rise of Silas Lapham* were divided in their appraisals of the novel. Some were shocked by Howells's characterization of Lapham, whom they considered an inappropriate and vulgar hero; others argued that Howells's attention to lifelike detail caused him to overwrite mundane scenes, diminishing the effectiveness of the plot. However, Howells was also lauded for his engaging portrayal of ordinary characters and his creation of dramatic tension from commonplace events, and the novel was acclaimed by several eminent contemporaries, including William James and Mark Twain. In the early twentieth century Howells's brand of realism was eclipsed by the more stark and bitter works of such authors as Theodore Dreiser and Sinclair Lewis. Consequently, *Silas Lapham* was largely disregarded by critics who considered its themes trivial and who charged that Howells avoided confrontation with the more disturbing aspects of American society. With the New Deal economic reforms of the 1930s came renewed interest in Howells as a social novelist, and critics began to view *Silas Lapham* as a creditable study of ethics in the Gilded Age. Later critical examinations focused on the effectiveness with which Howells thematically and stylistically combined the novel's two plots. Some have maintained that the love story was an afterthought, added only to satisfy public demand for romance. However, admirers of the novel's construction praise the manner in which Howells gave balanced attention to both plots and related them to many of the same moral themes, in particular the theme of self-sacrifice. In recent years many critics have accorded new levels of meaning to the work, examining its sexual symbolism and use of architec-

tural metaphor, and such studies have served to enhance the reputation of *Silas Lapham* as one of the strongest literary representations of Gilded Age society and a significant contribution to the development of American Realism.

(See also *Contemporary Authors,* Vol. 104; *Dictionary of Literary Biography,* Vols. 12, 64, 74, and 79; and *Concise Dictionary of American Literary Biography 1865-1917.*)

---

### *The Atlantic Monthly*   (essay date 1885)

[*In the following excerpt, the critic maintains that* Silas Lapham *is flawed by overattention to character development at the expense of plot.*]

While a novelist is living and at work, his growth in power is more interesting to critics than the expression of that power in any one piece of work. ***The Rise of Silas Lapham*** would probably affect a reader who should make Mr. Howells's acquaintance through it, in a different manner from what it does one who has followed Mr. Howells, as so many have, step by step, ever since he put forth his tentative sketches in fiction. We do not think that Mr. Howells has kept back the exercise of certain functions until he should have perfected his faculty of art by means of lighter essays, but that, in the process of his art, he has partly discovered, at any rate has convinced himself of the higher value to be found in a creation which discloses morals as well as manners. An art which busies itself with the trivial or the spectacular may be ever so charming and attractive, but it falls short of the art which builds upon foundations of a more enduring sort. A pasteboard triumphal-arch that serves the end of a merry masque is scarcely more ephemeral than the masque itself in literature.

The novel before us offers a capital example of the difference between the permanent and the transient in art. Had Mr. Howells amused himself and us with a light study of the rise of Silas Lapham in Boston society, what a clever book he might have made of it! We should have chuckled to ourselves over the dismay of the hero at the failure of the etiquette man to solve his problems, and have enjoyed a series of such interior views as we get in the glimpse of Irene "trailing up and down before the long mirror in *her* new dress [Mr. Howells never seems quite sure that we shall put the emphasis where it belongs without his gentle assistance], followed by the seamstress on her knees; the woman had her mouth full of pins, and from time to time she made Irene stop till she could put one of the pins into her train;" we should have followed the fluctuations of pride and affection and fastidiousness in the Corey family, and have sent a final shuddering thought down the vista of endless dinner parties which should await the union of the two houses. All this and much more offered materials for the handling of which we could have trusted Mr. Howells's sense of humor without fear that he would disappoint us.

But all this is in the story; only it occupies the subordinate, not the primary place, and by and by the reader, who has followed the story with delight in the playful art, discovers that Mr. Howells never intended to waste his art on so shallow a scheme, that he was using all this realism of Boston society as a relief to the heavier mass contained in the war which was waged within the conscience of the hero. When in the final sentence he reads: "I don't know as I should always say it paid; but if I done it, and the thing was to do over again, right in the same way, I guess I should have to do it," he recognizes, in this verdict of the faithfully illiterate Colonel, the triumphant because unconscious attainment of a victory which justifies the title of the story. No mere vulgar rise in society through the marriage of a daughter to a son of a social prince, or the possession of a house on the water side of Beacon Street, would serve as a real conclusion to the history of a character like that of Silas Lapham; as if to flout such an idea, the marriage when it comes is stripped of all possible social consequences, and the house is burned to the ground. In place of so trivial an end there is a fine subjection of the mean and ignoble, and as in Balzac's *César Birotteau,* a man of accidental vulgarity discloses his essential nobility; it is with this added virtue in the case of Mr. Howells's hero, that we see the achievement of moral solvency unglorified by any material prosperity, and the whole history of the rise unadorned by any decoration of sentiment.

We have intimated that this bottoming of art on ethical foundations is a late development in Mr. Howells's work. In truth, this is but the second important example. *An Undiscovered Country* hinted at the possibility of there being other things than were dreamt of in the philosophy of light-minded young women, but it has always seemed to us that the book suffered from its use of an essentially ignoble parody of human far-sightedness. The real break which Mr. Howells made in his continuity of fiction was in *A Modern Instance.* That book suffered from too violent an effort at change of base. With all our respect for the underlying thought . . . , we think that the author's habit of fine discrimination misled him into giving too much value in his art to the moral intention and too little to the overt act. (pp. 554-55)

[Though] there can be no mistaking Mr. Howells's intention in this novel, and though he uses his material with a firmer hand, we confess, now that we are out of the immediate circle of its charm, that *The Rise of Silas Lapham* suffers from the same defect as *A Modern Instance.* The defect is not so obvious, but it arises from the same super-refinement of art. In brief, Silas Lapham, a man of coarse grain and excessive egotism, is, in the crucial scenes, treated as a man of subtlety of thought and feeling. We do not say that the turnings and windings of his conscience, and his sudden encounters with that delicious Mephistopheles, Milton K. Rogers, are not possible and even reasonable; but we complain that the author of his being, instead of preserving him as a rustic piece of Vermont limestone with the soil clinging to it, has insisted upon our seeing into the possibilities of a fine marble statue which reside in the bulk. Moreover, when one comes to think of it, how little the rise of this hero is really connected with the circumstances which make up the main incidents of the story. The relations with Rogers, out of which the moral struggle springs, are scarcely complicated at all by the personal relations with the Corey family arising from the love of young Corey for Penelope Lapham. The Colonel goes through the valley of tribulation almost independently of the fact that he and his are sojourning meanwhile in another half grotesque vale of tears.

This same over-refinement of motive, as supposed in natures which are not presumably subtle, impresses us in the whole history of Penelope's love affair. We feel, rather than are able to say why we feel it, that there is something abnormal in the desolation which falls upon the entire Lapham family in consequence of Irene's blindness and Penelope's over-acuteness. We frankly confess that when reading the scenes, it seemed all right, and we gave ourselves up to the luxury of woe without a doubt as to its reality. But when *thinking* about them (forgive the italics), it seems an exaggeration, a pressing of the relations between these interesting people beyond the bounds of a charitable nature.

But when all is said, we come back with satisfaction to the recollection that Mr. Howells has distinctly set before himself in this book a problem worth solving, and if his statement and solution are presented with an art which has heretofore been so cunning as quite to reconcile one to the fragility of the object under the artist's hand, and this art still seems sometimes to imply the former baselessness, we can at least thank our stars that when we criticise such a book as *The Rise of Silas Lapham,* we are dealing with a real piece of literature, which surely will not lose its charm when the distinctions of Nankeen Square and Beacon Street have become merely antiquarian nonsense. (p. 556)

> *A review of "The Rise of Silas Lapham," in* The Atlantic Monthly, *Vol. 56, No. 336, October, 1885, pp. 554-56.*

### Hamilton Wright Mabie   (essay date 1885)

[*In the following excerpt from a review of* The Rise of Silas Lapham, *Mabie evaluates the emotional power of Howells's novel and the aesthetic value of Realistic fiction in general.*]

In *The Rise of Silas Lapham* Mr. Howells has given us his best and his most characteristic work; none of his earlier stories discloses so clearly the quality and resources of his gift or his conception of the novelist's art. As an expression of personal power and as a type of the dominant school of contemporary fiction in this country and in France, whence the special impulse of recent realism has come, this latest work of a very accomplished and conscientious writer deserves the most careful and dispassionate study. If Mr. Howells's work possessed no higher claim upon attention, its evident fidelity to a constantly advancing ideal of workmanship would command genuine respect and admiration; whatever else one misses in it, there is no lack of the earnestness which concentrates a man's full power on the thing in hand, nor of the sensitive literary conscience which permits no relaxation of strength on subordinate parts, but exacts in every detail the skill and care which are lavished on the most critical unfoldings of plot or disclosures of character. Mr. Howells evidently leaves nothing to the chance suggestion of an inspired moment, and takes nothing for granted; he verifies every insight by observation, fortifies every general statement by careful study of facts, and puts his whole force into every detail of his work. In spite of its evident danger in any save the strongest hands, there is a tonic quality in this exacting conscientiousness which writers of a different school often lack, and the absence of which is betrayed by hasty, unbalanced, and incomplete workmanship. It is this quality which discovers itself more and more distinctly in Mr. Howells's novels in a constant development of native gifts, a stronger grasp of facts, and a more comprehensive dealing with the problems of character and social life to which he has given attention. In fact, this popular novelist is giving thoughtful readers of his books a kind of inspiration in the quiet but resolute progress of his gift and his art; a progress stimulated, no doubt, by success, but made possible and constant by fidelity to a high and disinterested ideal.

Nor has Mr. Howells spent his whole force on mere workmanship; he has made a no less strenuous endeavor to enlarge his knowledge of life, his grasp of its complicated problems, his insight into the forces and impulses which are the sources of action and character. If he has failed to touch the deepest issues, and to lay bare the more obscure and subtle movements of passion and purpose, it has been through no intellectual willfulness or lassitude; he has patiently and unweariedly followed such clews as he has been able to discover, and he has resolutely held himself open to the claims of new themes and the revelations of fresh contacts with life. The limitations of his work are also the limitations of his insight and his imagination, and this fact, fully understood in all its bearings, makes any effort to point out those limitations ungracious in appearance and distasteful in performance; if personal feeling were to control in such matters, one would content himself with an expression of hearty admiration for work so full of character, and of sincere gratitude for a delicate intellectual pleasure so varied and so sustained. The evidence of a deepened movement of thought is obvious to the most hasty backward glance from *The Rise of Silas Lapham* and *A Modern Instance* to *Their Wedding Journey* and *A Chance Acquaintance.* In the early stories there is the lightness of touch, the diffused and delicate humor, which have never yet failed Mr. Howells; but there is little depth of sentiment, and almost no attempt to strike below the surface. These slight but very delightful tales discover the easy and graceful play of a force which deals with trifles as seriously as if it were handling the deepest and most significant problems of life. Seriousness is, indeed, the habitual mood of this novelist, and in his early stories it was the one prophetic element which they contained. There is a progressive evolution of power through *The Lady of the Aroostook, The Undiscovered Country, Dr. Breen's Practice,* and *A Modern Instance*; each story in turn shows the novelist more intent upon his work, more resolute to hold his gift to its largest uses, more determined to see widely and deeply. His purpose grows steadily more serious, and his work gains correspondingly in substance and solidity. The problems of character which he sets before himself for solution become more complex and difficult, and, while there is nowhere a really decisive closing with life in a determined struggle to wring from it its secret, there is an evident purpose to grapple with realities and to keep in sympathy and touch with vital experiences.

In *The Rise of Silas Lapham* Mr. Howells has made a study of social conditions and contrasts everywhere present in society in this country; not, perhaps, so sharply defined elsewhere as in Boston, but to be discovered with more or less definiteness of outline in all our older communities. His quick instinct has fastened upon a stage of social evolution with which every body is familiar and in which everybody is interested. The aspect of social life presented in this story is well-nigh universal; it is real, it is vital, and it is not without deep significance; in dealing with it Mr. Howells has approached actual life more nearly, touched it more deeply, and expressed it more strongly than in any of his previous stories. The skill of his earliest work loses nothing in his latest; it is less evident because it is more unconscious and, therefore, more genuine and effective. There is the same humor, restrained and held in check by the major interests of the story, but touching here and there an idiosyncrasy, an inconsistency, a weakness, with all the old pungency and charm; a humor which is, in fact, the most real and the most distinctive of all Mr. Howells's gifts. There is, also, stronger grasp of situations, bolder portraiture of character, more rapid and dramatic movement of narrative. Still more important is the fact that in this novel life is presented with more of dramatic dignity and completeness than in any of Mr. Howells's other stories; there is a truer and nobler movement of human nature in it; and the characters are far less superficial, inconsequential, and unimportant than their predecessors; if not the highest types, they have a certain force and dignity which make us respect them, and make it worth while to write about them. Add to these characterizations of *The Rise of Silas Lapham* the statement that Mr. Howells has never shown more complete mastery of his art in dealing with his materials; that his style has never had more simplicity and directness, more solidity and substance, and it will be conceded that the sum total of excellence which even a reader who dissents from its underlying conception and method discovers in this story is by no means inconsiderable; is, indeed, such as to entitle it to very high praise, and to give added permanence and expansion to a literary reputation which, from the standpoint of popularity at least, stood in small need of these things.

And yet, when all this has been said, and said heartily, it must be added that *The Rise of Silas Lapham* is an unsatisfactory story; defective in power, in reality, and in the vitalizing atmosphere of imagination. No one is absorbed by it, nor moved by it; one takes it up with pleasure, reads it with interest, and lays it down without regret. It throws no spell over us; creates no illusion for us, leaves us indifferent spectators of an entertaining drama of social life. The novelist wrote it in a cool, deliberate mood, and it leaves the reader cold when he has finished it. The appearance and action of life are in it, but not the warmth; the frame, the organism, are admirable, but the divine inbreathing which would have given the body a soul has been withheld. Everything that art could do hs been done, but the vital spark has not been transmitted. Mr. Howells never identifies himself with his characters; never becomes one with them in the vital fellowship and communion of the imagination; he constructs them with infinite patience and skill, but he never, for a moment, loses consciousness of his own individuality. He is cool and collected in all the emotional crises of his stories; indeed, it is often at such moments that one feels the presence of a diffused satire, as if the weakness of the men and women whom he is describing excited a little scorn in the critical mind of the novelist. The severest penalty of the persistent analytic mood is borne by the writer in the slight paralysis of feeling which comes upon him at the very moment when the pulse should beat a little faster of its own motion; in the subtle skepticism which pervades his work, unconsciously to himself, and like a slight frost takes the bloom off all fine emotions and actions. There are passages in Mr. Howells's stories in reading which one cannot repress a feeling of honest indignation at what is nothing more nor less than a refined parody of genuine feeling, sometimes of the most pathetic experience. Is Mr. Howells ashamed of life in its outcries of pain and regret? Does he shrink from these unpremeditated and unconventional revelations of character as vulgar, provincial, inartistic; or does he fail to comprehend them? Certainly the cool, skillful hand which lifts the curtain upon Silas Lapham's weakness and sorrows does not tremble for an instant with any contagious emotion; and whenever the reader begins to warm a little, a slight turn of satire, a cool phrase or two of analysis, a faint suggestion that the writer doubts whether it is worth while, clears the air again. Perhaps nothing more decisive on this point could be said of Mr. Howells's stories than that one can read them aloud without faltering at the most pathetic passages; the latent distrust of all strong feeling in them makes one a little shy of his own emotion.

This failure to close with the facts of life, to press one's heart against them as well as to pursue and penetrate them with one's thought; this lack of unforced and triumphant faith in the worth, the dignity, and the significance for art of human experience in its whole range; this failure of the imagination to bridge the chasm between the real and the fictitious reproduction of it, are simply fatal to all great and abiding work. Without faith, which is the very ground upon which the true artist stands; without love, which is both inspiration and revelation to him, a true art is impossible. Without faith there would never have come out of the world of the imagination such figures as Jeanie Deans, Colonel Newcome, Eugénie Grandet, Père Goriot, and Hester Prynne; without love—large, warm, generous sympathy with all that life is and means—the secret of these noble creations would never have been disclosed. Mr. Howells and Daudet practice alike the art of a refined realism, but what a distance separates the Nabob from Silas Lapham! Daudet is false to his theory and true to his art; life touches him deeply, fills him with reverence, and he can no more rid himself of the imagination than he can part the light from the flower upon which it falls. The Nabob might have suggested a similar treatment of Silas Lapham. How tenderly, how reverently, with what a sense of pathos, through what a mist of tears, Daudet uncovers to us the weakness and sorrows of Jansoulet! The Nabob is always touched by a soft light from the novelist's heart;

poor Silas Lapham shivers in a perpetual east wind. Imagine the "Vicar of Wakefield" treated in the same spirit, and the fatal defect of Mr. Howells's attitude towards life is apparent at a glance.

The disposition to treat life lightly and skeptically, to doubt its capacity for real and lasting achievement, to stand apart from it and study it coolly and in detail with dispassionate and scientific impartiality, is at bottom decisive evidence of lack of power; that is, of the dramatic power which alone is able to reproduce life in noble dramatic forms. A refined realism strives to make up in patience what it lacks in genius; to make observation do the work of insight; to make analysis take the place of synthesis of character, and "a more analytic consideration of the appearance of things"—to quote Mr. James—the place of a resolute and masterly grasp of characters and situations. The method of the realism illustrated in *The Rise of Silas Lapham* is external, and, so far as any strong grasp of life is concerned, necessarily superficial. It is an endeavor to enter into the recesses of character, and learn its secret, not by insight, the method of the imagination, but by observation, the method of science; and it is an endeavor to reproduce that character under the forms of art, not by identification with it, and the genuine and almost unconscious evolution which follows, but by skillful adjustment of traits, emotions, passions, and activities which are the result of studies more or less conscientiously carried on. The patience and work involved in the making of some novels constructed on this method are beyond praise; but they must not make us blind to the fact that no method can take the place of original power, and that genius in some form—faith, sympathy, insight, imagination—is absolutely essential in all true art. The hesitation, the repression of emotion, the absence of color, are significant, not of a noble restraint of power, a wise husbanding of resources for the critical moment and situation, but of a lack of the spontaneity and overflow of a great force. Ruskin finely says that when we stand before a true work of art we feel ourselves in the presence, not of a great effort, but of a great force. In most of the novels of realism it is the effort which impresses us, and not the power. In Turgénieff and Björnson, masters of the art of realism, and yet always superior to it, the repression and restraint are charged with power; one feels behind them an intensity of thought and feeling that is at times absolutely painful. No such sensation overtakes one in reading *The Rise of Silas Lapham* or *The Bostonians*; there is no throb of life here; the pulse of feeling, if it beats at all, is imperceptible; and of the free and joyous play of that supreme force which we call genius there is absolutely not one gleam. If either novelist possessed it, no method, however rigidly practiced, could wholly confine it; it would flame like lightning, as in Björnson, or suffuse and penetrate all things with latent heat, as in Turgénieff, or touch all life with a soft, poetic radiance, as in Daudet.

Mr. Howells has said, in substance, that realism is the only literary movement of the day which has any vitality in it, and certainly no one represents this tendency on its finer side more perfectly than himself. Its virtues and its defects are very clearly brought out in his work: its clearness of sight, its fixed adherence to fact, its reliance upon honest work; and, on the other hand, its hardness, its lack of vitality, its paralysis of the finer feelings and higher aspirations, its fundamental defect on the side of the imagination. Realism is crowding the world of fiction with commonplace people; people whom one would positively avoid coming in contact with in real life; people without native sweetness or strength, without acquired culture or accomplishment, without that touch of the ideal which makes the commonplace significant and worthy of study. To the large, typical characters of the older novels has succeeded a generation of feeble, irresolute, unimportant men and women whose careers are of no moment to themselves, and wholly destitute of interest to us. The analysis of motives that were never worth an hour's serious study, the grave portraiture of frivolous, superficial, and often vulgar conceptions of life, the careful scrutiny of characters without force, beauty, aspiration, or any of the elements which touch and teach men, has become wearisome, and will sooner or later set in motion a powerful reaction. One cannot but regret such a comparative waste of delicate, and often genuine, art; it is as if Michael Angelo had given us the meaningless faces of the Roman fops of his time instead of the heads of Moses and Hercules. (pp. 417-23)

> *Hamilton Wright Mabie, "A Typical Novel," in* The Andover Review, *Vol. IV, No. XXIII, November, 1885, pp. 417-29.*

## The Catholic World (essay date 1885)

[*In the following excerpt, the reviewer characterizes* The Rise of Silas Lapham *as morally bankrupt.*]

[In *The Rise of Silas Lapham*] Mr. Howells has produced the most scientifically realistic novel that has yet been written. M. Zola's books are as the awkward gropings of an amateur compared with this finished treatise. The field that Mr. Howells takes for his investigation is, he tells us, "the commonplace." By studying "the common feelings of common people" he believes he "solves the riddle of the painful earth."

Silas Lapham is a type of the self-made American. He has grown rich through the instrumentality of a mineral paint of which he is the proprietor. He lives in Boston and entertains social ambitions for his wife and two daughters. Bromfield Corey is a Boston aristocrat with a wife, two daughters, and a son. The Laphams and the Coreys are thrown together in consequence of a contemplated misalliance between young Corey and one of the Lapham daughters; and in the contrasts and developments that appear among all these "types" is supposed to consist the main interest of the story. There are no incidents that are not sternly commonplace, but everything connected with these incidents and their psychological effect on the actors is analyzed and detailed with microscopic accuracy. (pp. 276-77)

[Howells] studies men and women as a naturalist does insects. We read his book on the manners, habits, sensations, nerves of a certain set of people as we might a treatise on the coleoptera. And he investigates and expounds his theme with the same soullessness and absence of all emotion. Even Mr. Henry James, beside this chilly *savant,* appears quite a child of sentiment. He is capable of receiving "impressions"—which, in Mr. Howells' eyes, would be a most unscientific weakness—and he manages to retain some smack of art about the work he does.

Is this kind of novel-writing an elevating pursuit? and is the reading of it beneficial? To these two queries the answer must be emphatically, No.

Novels like *Silas Lapham* mark a descent, a degradation. Of course art is debased when it has fallen so low into realism. Art is ever pointing upward, and the influence of true art upon man is to make him look upward, too, to that vast where his Ideal sits,

> —pinnacled in the lofty ether dim,

where all is beautiful, but where all is immeasurable by him until he beholds it with his glorified intelligence. Science points downward, and when science is unguided by religion it leads its followers lower and lower into the mud beneath their feet. And even as we see some scientists making a distinct "progress" downward from the study of the higher to that of the lower forms of animal life, so in the novel-writing of Mr. Howells we can already mark this scientific decadence. He began with people who were not quite commonplace, whose motives and acts and ideas were a little bit above the common. He now declares that nothing is worthy to be studied but the common feelings of common people; and having begun *Silas Lapham* with people who were inoffensively commonplace, he was unable to finish the book without falling a stage lower. Towards the end he introduces a young woman who speaks thus of her husband: "If I could get rid of Hen I could manage well enough with mother. Mr. Wemmel would marry me if I could get the divorce. He said so over and over again." He introduces a scene in which this young woman, her tipsy sailor-husband, her drunken mother, and Silas Lapham as the family benefactor, figure—a scene that, for hopeless depravity both in the author and subject, out-Zolas Zola. The old woman, who has a bottle in her hand, complains of her son-in-law not giving the daughter an opportunity to obtain a divorce. " 'Why don't you go off on some them long v'y'ges?' s'd I. It's pretty hard when Mr. Wemmel stands ready to marry Z'rilla and provide a comfortable home for us both—I han't got a great many years more to live, and I *should* like to get more satisfaction out of 'em and not be beholden and dependent all my days—to have Hen, here, blockin' the way. I tell him there'd be more money for him in the end; but he can't seem to make up his mind to it." Again says this old harridan: "Say, Colonel, what should you advise Z'rilla do about Mr. Wemmel? I tell her there an't any use goin' to the trouble to git a divorce without she's sure about him. Don't you think we'd ought to git him to sign a paper, or something, that he'll marry her if she gits it? I don't like to have things goin' at loose ends the way they are. It an't sense. It an't right." Before Mr. Howells reaches the end of the book he makes even the worthy Mrs. Lapham suspect her husband of infidelity and make a scene, accusing him, in the hearing of her children. It has seldom been our duty to read a book whose moral tone was so unpleasantly, so hopelessly bad; it is a book without heart or soul, neither illumined by religion nor warmed by human sympathy. This is all the more astonishing that

Mr. Howells seems convinced that he is fulfilling a high moral purpose in writing it. It might be explicable on the theory that it was the legitimate outcome of the doctrine of total depravity; but it is more probably the logic of the downward progress of godless science. We shall not be surprised if the next book of Mr. Howells deal with characters and feelings that shall be so far below the commonplace from which he has already fallen that even M. de Goncourt will not enjoy reading about them. It is the progress from man to the apes, from the apes to the worms, from the worms to bacteria, from bacteria to— mud. It is the descent to dirt. (pp. 277-79)

*"Novel-Writing as a Science," in* The Catholic World, *Vol. XLII, No. 248, November, 1885, pp. 274-80.*

## Alexander Harvey   (essay date 1917)

[*An American editor and short story writer, Harvey was the author of* William Dean Howells: A Study of the Achievement of a Literary Artist. *In the following excerpt from that work, Harvey proclaims* The Rise of Silas Lapham *"the greatest novel ever written."*]

The most effective scene in fiction to me occurs in *The Rise of Silas Lapham.* There is, I know, a tremendous episode in *Ivanhoe,* and more than one judicious critic has pronounced it the supreme thing. Nor can the thrill of Robinson Crusoe's discovery of that footprint in the sand be passed by in any compilation of the triumphs of narrative art. A certain swimming scene in Meredith has its champions, and they can, as the lawyers say, make out a case. Anthony Trollope deserves very honorable mention for the manner in which Mr. Slope is set turning around and around during one infatuated hour in the presence of Bertie's lame sister. What scene shall be chosen out of all fiction as its greatest is no question to answer pontifically. It implies, too, a wider knowledge of all the world's novels than most of us gain time to acquire.

I must risk all, nevertheless, upon my own judgment and make what terms I can with the champions of the British literary superstition. The most thrilling scene in fiction reveals Irene Lapham in the bedroom of her sister Penelope. Irene has just been told that young Corey never loved her. There had been a terrible blunder from the beginning. Young Corey loved Penelope only. Rallying at once from the shock of the disclosure, Irene went with those poor trinkets of hers to Penelope. One by one she handed them over—the pin she got that very day because it was so like the one his sister wore, a newspaper account of that ranch he visited in Texas, the buttonhole bouquet he left beside his plate and which she stole, and finally the pine shaving fantastically tied up with a knot of ribbon. Irene's surrender of these trophies, the words she speaks to poor Penelope and the circumstances attending her mother's participation in the tragedy of it all render this chapter in the history of the Lapham family the great event in my career of adventure among the world's novels. I have panted after d'Artagnan, too, and sat in agony at the head of old Goriot's bed.

Not that this exhausts my praise. From the standpoint of

literature regarded as a fine art, I consider *The Rise of Silas Lapham* the greatest novel ever written. In structure, that is to say in its form as distinguished from its content, it surpasses *The Egoist* of Meredith, and it is, of course, immeasurably better written. Of the pair, Howells is the best stylist. In the matter of form, structure, style, whatever we choose to call that part of the novelist's equipment which reveals him as an artist, this tale of the Laphams is more finished than the masterpieces of Flaubert. If the suggestion were not so misleading, one might liken the art with which *The Rise of Silas Lapham* is written to the art of the great French novelists generally, or to the art displayed in the tragic drama of the Greeks. There is something of the ease of de Maupassant or of Daudet and much of the beauty of Euripides in the manner of Howells throughout this masterpiece of his.

The cunning of the master hand is manifest in the very first chapter. We must know all about Silas Lapham from the start, who he is, what he is, his temperament and his financial and family affairs. Balzac is deplorably heavy in his masterpiece itself when he has to cope with a difficulty of this sort. Thackeray has a fashion of postponing this task until we get beyond his opening chapter. Trollope is frankly heavy and British as he fatigues us with detail respecting everybody's private affairs. In *The Rise of Silas Lapham* we are afforded all the light essential to the clarification of his mystery by that expedient of Bartley Hubbard's call at the millionaire's place of business. The journalist wants material for a character sketch. The skill with which this expedient is utilized to turn Silas Lapham inside out before our eyes is possible in a master of the art of narrative and in a master only.

The essential quality of *The Rise of Silas Lapham,* however, is poetical. *Romeo and Juliet* itself is not more deliciously pervaded, saturated with love's essence. It is a tale of the love of Irene for Tom and of Tom for Penelope, every development of the plot being critical to us because it bears, in a manner near or remote, upon that intense affair. I have been unable to call to mind a novel in which the sentiment, indeed, the passion of love has been steeped in so unsparing a realism with such an intimate knowledge of the subject matter. We are all familiar with the practice of the purveyors of the excessively romantic in the line of fiction. They insist upon talking about a thrilling story of a young girl's love. Well, *The Rise of Silas Lapham* is the most thrilling story of a young girl's love since that affair between a certain Capulet and a certain Montague.

The ease with which Howells transfers our sympathy from Irene to Penelope is uncanny. Theoretically, she wrings our withers. She is in the most humiliating of all the dilemmas imaginable as that of any heroine. Then, too, she is beautiful, distractingly beautiful. The realization of this beauty for our benefit is so adequate that Scott himself has no young lady in all his collection who conveys so vivid, so ravishing an effect of feminine loveliness as Irene Lapham. Sweetness, too, is hers and it neither cloys nor is insipid, and still how good she is, how like nothing so much as her own perfect and imperishable self!

The most remarkable feature of *The Rise of Silas Lapham* is that it has two heroines. Irene is the heroine of the story until Corey has disclosed his love. Then that trying part of heroine is allotted to Penelope. Nothing could be more delicate than the task the novelist has undertaken here and the success that rewards it is without a parallel in the annals of imaginative literature. Apart from the qualities of Howells as a writer, this success must be ascribed to his amazing insight into the heart of woman. In this detail alone his superiority to Meredith has not won any recognition only because Howells is an American. He brings Penelope forward and he draws Irene back with a subtlety that transfers our sympathy from one to the other completely. The tragedy of it all is exposed without compunction, especially as it affects the mother of these girls. The words of the mother as she makes Irene understand, accompanied by that harshness of manner, acquire a poignancy, a control over a reader of which only the masters of the written word possess the key.

Howells has revealed the heart of woman with all his cunning throughout this work—Mrs. Corey, for instance. Her dinner to the Laphams serves incidentally to reveal the superiority of the humor of Howells to that of Meredith. In the American, as the greater literary artist, we have a more intimate relation between an episode like that Corey dinner, for instance, and the structure of his tale as a whole. *The Rise of Silas Lapham* is a model of structure. It is such easy reading from beginning to end. The humor, mainly at the expense of the Laphams, is eternal. Pericles and Aspasia could have enjoyed it and Aristophanes might have written it. There is that passage, for instance, between Penelope and the father of the youth she was to marry. He said he hoped they parted friends if not quite acquaintances. Penelope told her future father-in-law that she hoped they would be able to recognize each other if they ever met again.

In its revelation of American family life, this Howells masterpiece is a permanent historical document. The sweetness, the purity of the atmosphere disclosed and the simplicity of all the characters make me think of *The Vicar of Wakefield*. A striking point of resemblance between them has relation to the sense of humor. It is universal, Shakespearean. The sense of humor as exploited in the tale of the Lapham family is not "American" in the terribly vulgar implication of the travestied word. The American sense of humor is refined, spiritualized, at the opposite pole from the heavy British idea of it. Howells and Goldsmith are alike in the freshness, the spontaneity of their humor. I think the American is far more sophisticated. The two tales are typically Anglo-Saxon in turning upon and about the snobbishness of the race. They are alike in being models of style. I think the American has given us the best writing. The poetical quality of *The Vicar of Wakefield* and the poetical quality of *The Rise of Silas Lapham* indicate an element in common between the genius of Howells and that of Goldsmith. Each is a great humorist and a great stylist and versatile, but there is a gravity, a ballast, a sophistication in the American, an intellectuality not discoverable in the other. This difference suggests as anything else could not the significance of the "realism" with which the work of Howells is associated in some minds, as distinguished from the "romanticism"

which underlies the type of fiction so roundly censured in some of the Bostonian masterpieces of Howells.

His study of the career and the character of Silas Lapham is the most successful treatment the native American has ever received in fiction. If we are to deem the red Indian the native American, Cooper has a monopoly of the glory to be derived from his revelation in imaginative aspects according to modes of realism. I have thought of the noble Chingachgook while following with the closest scrutiny the vicissitudes of that still nobler savage, Silas Lapham. He is a true native American of Anglo-Saxon origin, this Silas, reared in all the terrible "arrivism" for which our country has come to stand. Like the breed to which he belongs, Silas Lapham is destitute of the combination of psychological insight with imagination and fancy. Incarnate in him is the unredeemed ugliness of the material prosperity of his type and of his race. He is the characteristic product of a people without genius. The emptiness, the forlornness, the dreariness and the dullness of the domestic life of the "successful" American are vividly experienced for us vicariously through the ordeals of Silas Lapham. He is a typical American in his ignorance of human nature, of beauty, of ideas. His conception of life takes the form of an enthusiasm for the paint he sells. Everything should be coated with that. As far as he can be said to have a theory or conception of culture at all, it is a coat of paint.

In this aspect of him, Silas Lapham is the most American thing imaginable. No inspiration could be more authentic than that which decided Howells to involve his greatest character in paint. Paint symbolizes the Silas Lapham attitude to life. Silas Lapham in his essence is the realization of the merit of the "coat of paint" policy. Put a coat of paint upon despotism and the effect is liberty. Art is a coat of paint upon the hideousness of American life. "I believe in my paint." Silas Lapham is made to say. "I believe it's a blessing to the world." The American attitude exactly! Lapham's notion that a pig pen covered with paint must be all right is natural enough. Never was there such a painted world as this American world. Pig pens certainly look better after a coat of paint and there wasn't a board fence nor a bridge girder nor the face of a cliff nor a bold prospect in nature without Silas Lapham's advertisement in huge flaming letters. He began life as a bare footed boy, too, without a cent to his name and he is worth a million dollars!

I never rise from a perusal of *The Rise of Silas Lapham,* and I have read it many times, without a vivid realization of the inadequacy of the native American head to ideas. Howells in all his books has a tendency to expose our intellectual poverty. In his account of Silas Lapham he renders very obvious the inaccessibility of the native American to what may be called the artistic conduct of life. As I follow the agonies of Silas Lapham at the dinner table of the Coreys I can see why the beauty of our republican institutions is buried beneath the growth of legal technicalities, hidden by coat upon coat of the Lapham paint. Our institutions are too beautiful for a people to whom the poetry of politics is meaningless. In any reference to the artistic conduct of life at the Corey table, we find Lapham staring from one to another of the guests, blankly. The attitude he affects to all artists, especially to the artist who built that house for him, is the most American thing in all Howells. I associate it with the shock received by Lemuel Barker at sight of that nude in a Boston park. To Lapham, in fact, as to the native Americans one encounters in the world of Howells generally, there is something meretricious in the whole artistic attitude to life. Art in the native American mind enjoys the dubious importance attached to the devil in the medieval mind. Art may be very well in its way, when subservient to the police, but in its protest against a landscape vivified with Lapham's paint, the thing is an obstacle to legitimate business.

The lesson of Silas Lapham's career, then, is that the native Americans of Anglo-Saxon origin are the last survivors of the barbarian world of which the ancient Greeks left us their profound impressions. As I think I said before, the Laphams are haunted by an uneasy suspicion of what they really are—a tribe of savages. Silas Lapham spurns the suggestion with fury and with high words. He's as good as anybody! Silas Lapham!

All native Americans of Anglo-Saxon origin are like Silas Lapham. They know how to deal with all the British aristocrats in the peerage. They have been taught how to treat a waiter. They do not know how to deal with an artist. They can make nothing of the artistic attitude to life. For this reason the native American is a bigot, intolerant, disposed to suspect ideas. The fact that artists are the conspicuous victims of native American bigotry—I use the word artist in its true sense—is the reason our country remains a great stronghold of barbarism, despite the passing of Chingachgook. Silas Lapham is all over the place.

The Silas Lapham of Howells is thus to be regarded as a companion portrait to the Chingachgook of Cooper. They are the two types of savages our country has produced. We have seen the last of the Mohicans, but the native Americans of Anglo-Saxon origin are still with us and the contract has been given the place as well as the importance of the tomahawk. The American savage has come in from the wilderness to the board of directors. He has put off his feathers and his paint for a straw hat and a business suit. He has lost the buffalo and the forest primeval but he has got hold of painting and the arts. They flourish with us only when they comply with the standards of Silas Lapham. They are those of Chingachgook—for in all things we are the heirs of the Mohicans, the land of the barbarian. And precisely as Silas Lapham is the reincarnation of Chingachgook, the dominant American is a contemporary version of Silas Lapham, a noble savage, a fine barbarian, with not a trace of self-consciousness to mar the simplicity of his effect. By liberty, freedom, art, democracy and the like, the American means what Chingachgook meant by such things after they had passed through the crucible of Silas Lapham's mind. Chingachgook streaked his face with the colors he got from the earth. Lapham sold them. That is all. The Howells masterpiece depicts this barbarism. (pp. 145-60)

> *Alexander Harvey, in his* William Dean Howells: A Study of the Achievement of a Literary Artist, *B. W. Huebsch, 1917, 267 p.*

## Howard Mumford Jones   (essay date 1947)

[*A distinguished twentieth-century American critic, Jones was noted for his illuminating commentary on American culture and literature. Awarded the Pulitzer Prize for his study of the formation of American culture in* O Strange New World *(1964), he was also acclaimed for his criticism in* The Theory of American Literature *(1948) and similar works in which he examined the relationship between America's literary and cultural development. In the following excerpt, Jones discusses Howells's presentation of Boston society in* The Rise of Silas Lapham, *focusing on the values and points of view embodied by the Coreys and the Laphams.*]

[The] place to begin one's study of **The Rise of Silas Lapham** is where the novel begins—in Boston. In one sense the theme of the book is universal. In another sense no one can fully understand either the substructure or the nuances of the novel unless he has steeped himself in the history of Boston, particularly after the Civil War. No book by Howells is more thoroughly rooted in St. Botolph's town. Not only is the action principally conducted in the Massachusetts capital and its nearby suburbs—across the Mill Dam to Brookline or by steamer to Nahant—but the names and local references have a flavour and vitality that have special meaning to Bostonians.

The obvious and exportable Boston problem is of course the conflict in values and points of view between the Corey family and the Laphams. We are to take Bromfield Corey as representative of the Brahmin class first amusingly described by Oliver Wendell Holmes in the first chapter of *Elsie Venner* in 1861. The suave culture of pre-Civil War Boston, after the termination of that struggle, was confronted even in the Hub of the Universe by a rising, untutored, wealthy group. In one sense this conflict is general in the nineteenth century and may be followed in Balzac and Stendhal. In another sense the very localism of Howells, who, if not a Bostonian by birth, was at least Boston-plated, gives this conflict special significance. The accuracy of his picture is borne out in this description of the change in Boston business habits by a writer who lived through it:

> Before 'Appomatox' the banker and merchant appeared upon State Street, the business center, about ten o'clock in the morning, conventionally dressed, precise in movement and habituated to archaic methods. Within six months after the fall of the Confederacy the financial centers of the 'Hub' vitalized by the inflow of new and very red blood, had taken on the aspect which is familiar to this generation. Everything that interfered with serviceable activity was set aside. Tall hats and long coats disappeared. Office doors swung open in the early hours. Young faces were found on 'Change', in the street, everywhere. New names appeared at the head of great industrial enterprises. Boys who had gone to the War as junior officers had brought back honorable titles which vouched for responsibility, character and daring. . . . You can't, if you will, hold down a Captain, a Colonel, a General, who has earned and won the admiration of the public, and who has tested his own worth.

So it is in the novel that the Boston of culture embodied in Bromfield Corey confronted the aggressive wealth and coarser values of Silas Lapham. Howells, a kindly man, resolved the conflict by discovering business ability in young Tom Corey and native refinement in Penelope Lapham. The solution does credit to the novelist's heart, but one wonders why he wrote no sequel, which might have revealed much.

A Boston fact less obvious is Lapham's new house. This was rising on the 'New Land' and on the water side of Beacon Street when it was destroyed. As the book opens the Laphams have been living comfortably in Nankeen Square in the South End, and only Silas wants to move. The social significance of this matter may escape the casual reader, for it refers to a Bostonian phenomenon. When Beacon Hill filled up, Bostonian gentry developed what is known as the South End into a second socially acceptable area. To this day the lovely little squares suggestive of London, the rows of 'swell front' brick houses, the iron balconies, the trees, and the platting of this part of Boston show how charming the Victorian world could be. But at the opening of the eighties, for inexplicable reasons, the tide of fashion turned from the South End to the filled-in lands known as Back Bay; and it is to this district on the banks of the Charles River that the Colonel wishes to go, thinking (as Bromfield Corey once stipulates) that the gates of Society, if they cannot open on golden hinges, may perhaps be crashed. The burning of the new house is therefore both material and symbolical, representing Lapham's growing awareness that the kingdom of heaven is not to be seized by violence.

The Corey family next deserves our comment. There are in Howells's handling of them a good many loose ends. In the first place, Bromfield Corey is too passive to be effective except as a commentator; and Howells apparently sought to embody the vitality of old Boston in his son. In the second place, the Corey fortunes shrink, we are told; yet nothing effective follows from what would appear to be a plot datum of significance. In the third place, there are two Corey daughters who, wraiths that they are, hover on the edge of the story. Did Howells intend some parallel between the bankruptcy of Lapham and the dwindling Corey income? Did he intend to show that Bromfield Corey had a principle of action in him as Lapham grew more and more ineffective? And why two Corey sisters, unless some undeveloped parallel was intended with the Lapham girls?

There are no loose ends in the character of Mrs. Corey, a matron who frightens me. In her Howells incarnated the Boston matriarchate, a powerful and sometimes a divisive force in Brahmin society. So far as he dislikes anybody, Howells dislikes Mrs. Corey, whose calls upon the Laphams are etched in acid. But what did he intend the relations of mother and son to be? Mrs. Corey yields with suspicious readiness to a matrimonial prospect she dislikes; and I, for one, do not feel the battle is over when Penelope marries Tom. As Howells says at the end of the book, our manners and customs go for more in life than our qualities. Did he mean that Penelope was not educable in the Corey sense?

No novelist can be made to write what he does not want to write; but it must be said that Howells's Boston is an entirely Anglo-Saxon Boston. The fact that the greater part of its population was Irish, Italian, Jewish, and the like newer Americans could never be guessed from the novel. Our only glimpse into the life of the poor is a visit to 'Miss Dewey's' home, and it would appear that Howells was unaware of what Boston slums were in reality, just as he was unaware of the racial and religious tensions in his beloved town. And there are no politicians in *The Rise of Silas Lapham.*

If we turn from the Corey family to the Lapham household we face the true glory of the tale. The Colonel remains to this day the best portrait in American letters of an up-state New Englander. His nearest rival is David Harum of New York state [in Edward Noyes Wescott's *David Harum*], but there is little tragic strength in Harum, whereas Lapham is as solid as the granite of the Vermont from which he comes. Whether in his conversation or in his silences, in prosperity or adversity, flushed with wine at the Corey dinner table (that painful, yet deliciously comic scene) or humbly consulting the minister after Tom's proposal to Penelope is known, Lapham is essentially himself, three-dimensional and foursquare. And it is a mark of the real greatness of Howells that, creating Silas, he was also able to create his wife, who lives in her own right as a powerful, uneducated person, and whose relation to her husband is instinctively understood by the novelist and presented as a profound value, silent and enduring. It is sometimes said that to create a good woman in fiction who is also interesting is impossible; if this be so, Howells triumphs over an impossibility.

Controversy over the Lapham girls has continued ever since the novel first appeared. Howells is generally unsurpassed among American novelists in portraying the *jeune fille* of his period. In *The Rise of Silas Lapham* he has in some sense triumphed with the well-worn device of two contrasting sisters in love with the same man. These sisters are seen in isolation from their own generation of youth, so that we are made aware of them only in the family relationship. They have no friends and no admirers except Tom Corey. Howells may have deliberately intended this as a fictional device to make the resulting complication more serious, but it threw upon him a responsibility he sought, as it were, to avoid. Novelists and dramatists are ill-advised in most cases to keep an important plot secret from the reader; and close reading will show that Howells drops a good many hints about the state of Tom Corey's affections before they are made known to the Laphams. But most readers do not see the significance of these hints and rather feel that Howells has taken an unfair advantage of them for the cheap satisfaction of springing a surprise on everybody. Keeping this secret down, so to speak, means that Howells is unable to show any clear reason why Penelope rather than Irene should attract Corey because, through dramatizing the Irene-Tom relationship, he wishes to make the surprise more drastic and the tension more powerful. But this in turn induces a second difficulty, which is that since Irene rather than Penelope has been mostly in our eyes, it is hard to believe in Tom's continuing attachment to Penelope through a series of events, emotions, and messages that make no sense to him. It is fortunate that the novel preceded the common use of the telephone; but even so, one wonders why an ardent lover does not storm the fortress, or at least write in more burning terms than a Corey can manage. In truth, once Howells has got Tom down to Nahant, the conditions of the plot compel him to lose interest in the hero as a person; he becomes merely the occasion of tension in the Lapham family and quite fades out at the end.

The management of the plot is, I think, the real weakness here, and not, as hasty contemporary critics allege, that too much fuss is made over a trivial incident. Uninformed readers sometimes grow impatient with the emotional and ethical nuances in the Lapham family and, if they knew the word, would dismiss these as so much *marivaudage*. But the modern reader is not invariably to be trusted. Matrimony is not precisely a trivial matter even now; and even in the most advanced circles Irene's misinterpretation of Corey's friendliness would, one suspects, lead to very similar scenes. How much more, then, would complexities pile up in the isolated Lapham circle! How much deeper the hurt in that forgotten world of the eighties, where 'young ladies' expected young men to ask permission to 'correspond'! Possibly Howells tries to hold the situation too long, squeezing every ounce of value out of it; possibly his two plots interfere with each other, but does not the very truth to life in his study of Irene and Penelope still have power to hurt and irritate those who are put off by it? And is not this a tribute to his success?

In one sense **The Rise of Silas Lapham** is the old, old tale humanity never tires of, though it never follows precept by example. It is a delicate preachment on the text not to lay up treasures on earth. Howells in this respect is one with Thackeray, Trollope, George Eliot, and the other great Victorians. His characters grow or fail in moral grace as characters rarely do in contemporary fiction. His kindly morality gave him measure and value; and measure is precisely what is mainly to seek in recent novels. He is therefore in American fiction what Trollope is to English literature; and precisely as there has been a return to Trollope in order to rediscover a world we have lost, so there will yet be a return to Howells in order to revaluate American society and American family life. (pp. v-xi)

> *Howard Mumford Jones, in an introduction to* The Rise of Silas Lapham, *by William Dean Howells, Oxford University Press, 1948, pp. v-xi.*

## George Arms  (essay date 1949)

[*An American critic and educator, Arms compiled* A Bibliography of William Dean Howells *(1948) and has edited a number of Howells's works. In the following excerpt, he presents a favorable overview of* The Rise of Silas Lapham.]

Before publication **The Rise of Silas Lapham** appeared serially in the *Century Magazine,* where, in keeping with the leisurely reading habits of the time, it came out in ten monthly installments (November, 1884, to August, 1885). It was successful from the start. But perhaps because of

its favorable reception and because of the headway that its author seemed to be making in his program for realism, many reviewers did not take kindly to the novel when it was published as a book in the late summer of 1885.

At first glance we may smile at some of the early antipathies expressed by reviewers. Special points of attack were the choice of vulgar characters and the cynical tone. The *Catholic World* went a little further than other reviews when it remarked that one scene "for hopeless depravity both in author and subject, out-Zolas Zola" [see excerpt dated 1885], but it only overstated what was elsewhere being said. In the *Andover Review* there was essential agreement, with attention directed more to manner than matter. Its reviewer was troubled by "the subtle skepticism which pervades [Howells's] work, unconsciously to himself, and like a slight frost takes the bloom off all fine emotions and actions" [see Mabie excerpt dated 1885].

Though these quotations are from Catholic and Protestant journals, their counterparts occurred in many reviews of the lay press. But more significantly we also find counterparts of this type of attack today, though with certain twists appropriate to our modern temper. Lapham has, for instance, been objected to as a businessman not at all representative of the period after the Civil War, as lacking the ruthless energy and money-mad amoralism of a Vanderbilt, a Drew, or a Fisk. He is commonplace (to use a favorite word of Howells's), but commonplace because he is superficially bourgeois and not, as the first readers had it, because he is vulgar. Again, though no one now advances skepticism against Howells, his contemporaries in using that word were making a judgment which not only in class but in degree comes close to what is today's most damning indictment of Howells. Our critics charge that he lacks emotional density, that he does not impart the vital quality to his novels which is the *sine qua non* of permanent literature.

Thus the terms of disparagement have shifted, but the grounds remain much the same: Howells falls short in his choice of people and in his handling of them. Since *The Bostonians* and parts of *Huckleberry Finn* were serialized in the *Century* at the same time as **The Rise of Silas Lapham,** it is worth comparing the reputations of the three authors for a moment. In 1885 criticisms were being made of Henry James and Mark Twain that were much like those being made of Howells, a natural result of these two authors largely subscribing to the same tenets that their friend and former editor held. But the bad people in James and Twain have become interesting people, and their realistic handling has proved to have depth. Since no such metamorphosis has blessed Howells, are we to conclude that a critical tradition of more than a half century has indisputably fixed his place as a novelist whose modest merit is only a certain importance in literary history?

The question is of course asked in such a way that it would be hard to reply with a positive "yes." Admittedly, a book that after sixty years of familiarity has not at least drawn to itself an elite of enthusiasts stands little chance of ever achieving the status of a major classic. But **The Rise of Silas Lapham** has always had, if not the enthusiastic backing of a few, a widespread group of well-wishers. Because it continues to be read in this fashion, it is right to reconsider the two main objections that have been made against it, and to go over some other matters as well.

Tone and character are not entirely separable; in so far as they can be distinguished, Howells's tone may surely be the more justly impeached. But though the tone of *The Rise of Silas Lapham* constitutes its greatest weakness, the fault is less deplorable than it has sometimes appeared to those who approach Howells with expectations other than they ought to hold.

Without attempting to urge that Howells conveys emotional feeling of the deepest sort, we can suggest that he does not wholly lack vitality. His art is a restricted art. Instead of violent explosions he provides a series of minor tremors, from which he hopes that his reader may derive an image of life that is more true because it is more restrained. Unfortunately he sometimes seems to insist that the explosions do not exist, but to a large extent he expects his readers to become aware of something greater than the tremors themselves. His description within this novel of the passengers to Nantasket hints at both his potential superficiality and depth: "In face they were commonplace, with nothing but the American poetry of vivid purpose to light them up, where they did not wholly lack fire." His interest in men is rational and polite, but it does not follow that it is belittling or false. It is incomplete; but by restriction Howells makes gains, even though he suffers losses.

In nearly every one of his novels, Howells was writing a comedy of manners. Since he deals with men and their actions in a social rather than in a deeply ethical fashion, we must not try to read him as an author with a tragic sense partially realized. To do so will cause us to turn from him with as great disappointment as we might turn from Jane Austen or Anthony Trollope if we had gone to them with such expectation. Simply stated, comedy trusts in the triumph of common sense over false emotion, whereas tragedy deals with the conflict of emotions that are good and of sense that is false. With both Lapham's conduct and with his daughter's, this novel follows the comic mood. Howells accepts the goodness of life, as indeed most of us do in our everyday living. But in so doing, he is neither passive nor blind, for he joys in the proper and mocks the false. This he does largely within his medium.

Largely, but not consistently. As almost invariably happens, the comedy of manners makes a natural expansion of its boundaries into morals. *The Rise of Silas Lapham* does this too. Howells is aware of his problem when he says, " . . . Our manners and customs go for more in life than our qualities. The price that we pay for civilisation is the fine yet impassable differentiation of these." Yet at the same time Howells's control of his medium seems to slip. The joyous acceptance and mischievous mockery that we find in the Hubbard-Lapham interview or at the Corey's dinner are largely lost toward the end of the novel. The author becomes more sober than he can afford to be without offering us something that will more seriously occupy us. Nearly everyone who reads the novel feels that the story lags in the latter third. There are various reasons, but perhaps the principal one is that Howells becomes too preoccupied with his characters as potentially tragic figures.

Howells's discussion of *Daisy Miller* in his 1882 essay on Henry James is pertinent to the handling of the novel. He noted that James's treatment of his heroine had caused most readers to misunderstand her. Yet he favored this ambiguity of effect; James's method, which was one of impartiality rather than confidential treatment, made it inevitable. Howells further asserted that impartiality was one of the most valuable qualities of art, and he hinted that it resulted in a richer sympathy than was otherwise possible. Applying this same approach to *The Rise of Silas Lapham,* we see that when Howells keeps his impartiality, we feel a profound and understanding sympathy. But when, as too frequently happens, Howells becomes confidential, the sympathy blurs off into silliness. Again, it is in the latter third of the novel that these faults are most evident.

The mistaken identity of the love affair is also apt to annoy the reader who insists upon regarding it as serious stuff rather than as what it is, the situation of a farce. As a love affair it marks a concession to audience, a concession which Howells continued to make throughout his career, in spite of his doubt at one point that he should "ever write another story in which mating and marrying plays an important part." But as farce the mix-up is good farce, and its solution proposes a useful rule of conduct, the "economy of pain." All members of a lovers' triangle should not suffer when circumstances require the suffering of only one. As with most rules, this one is too simple, but by hinting such other concepts as complicity, atonement, and fate, the author recognizes that it merely shares in the truth and is not the whole truth.

The surprise plot is pleasant enough, and by careful preparation in the characters' talk about literature Howells effects a neat satirization of morbid self-sacrifice in the popular novel of the period. Yet there is some doubt that the author *always* limits the mood to farce and satire. He seems to want to make somewhat more of it, and is yet unable to observe the irony that could evolve from his attempt. He does not achieve a richly satisfying relationship between the daughter's conduct in love and the father's in business. If Lapham had used so worldly a standard as "economy of pain" in his business dealings, he might easily have argued himself out of the self-sacrifice that his honesty demanded. Here perhaps we come to the heart of the trouble in the novel. Howells does not fully comprehend the function of the comic writer; when he expands into essentially moral situations he cannot continue his comedy on every level. The inability is not complete nor entirely disabling, for in great part Howells does show aesthetic control; but it is marked enough to keep the work short of achieving an ideal perfection and to provide basis for the main stricture against the novel.

Though the novel has a major shortcoming in tone, it has none in characterization. We no longer condemn Silas Lapham as vulgar, and we should not condemn him as commonplace, nor as faultily incomplete. We can properly wish that Howells could have seen his way to making Lapham still more complex. For instance, the author might at least have canvassed the possibility that Lapham's righteous conduct was caused by desire to fail (from his inability to cope with the social demands of his financial position) as well as by rational moral code. Such a wish is certainly more justifiable than to demand, as so many have, that Lapham should have been made more representative of his time. In the novel there is recognition of Lapham as an ante-bellum type when his meeting with the English agents is described. Theirs was a "deeper game than Lapham was used to." Given his method, Howells could not treat a Vanderbilt as he does Lapham; and it is enough to see him aware that a robber baron type of financier exists.

Though Lapham is not as comlex as he might be, he is sufficiently complex if we judge him upon his own terms and those of the novel. The book shows understanding of the intricacy of Lapham's sensibility and grossness, for it not merely attaches sensibility to his morals and grossness to his manners, but presents both these qualities as mutually involved in all aspects of his being. Howells plays constantly upon these contrasts from the opening interview with its reference to Lapham's great hairy fist, its allusions to the virtues of the Old Testament and *Poor Richard's Almanac,* and its use of Hubbard as a foil. Summing up this episode, Hubbard calls Lapham "the old fool," but his wife Marcia exclaims, "Oh, what a good man!" At the end of the novel Lapham is presented as a rustic Vermonter, shaggy, slovenly, and unkempt, still bragging, yet realizing finally a social and moral repose. Elsewhere Howells condemns him for his "thick imagination," fills his mouth with clichés, and ridicules his bourgeois nature (" 'It's the best paint in God's universe,' he said, with the solemnity of prayer."). Yet Lapham, anticipating Sewell, comes out with the right answer on what to do about Tom's proposal to Penelope, as he does in his own affairs. A fine epitomization of his character is given through the Coreys' dinner, where he develops from the shy blunderer of the first courses into a rough but dignified conversationalist over the coffee cups—and at the end of the evening is led away a drunken ranter.

Our feeling for Lapham's moral character is achieved mostly through its comparison with his wife's. The first scene of the novel, when the author drops in a comment about wives, starts an extremely interesting line of development, which ends with Mrs. Lapham's paint—the Persis brand—effecting her husband's modest recovery from failure. In much of this, particularly in her concern for Rogers and in her opposition to Lapham's social ambitions, she is a good influence. Indeed, Howells first uses the word "rise" in writing of Lapham's marriage. Yet the social rise and the building of the house do not leave her stainless; she is only smarter than her husband, and pays her way with checks of one hundred dollars instead of five hundred. The extent of her own contamination is made plain by her inward cringing when Mrs. Corey calls the second time. With all her urging of justice to Rogers, and even because of it, she forsakes her husband when he most needs her moral backing and makes his trial greater by foolishly suspecting him of having a mistress. The very virtue upon which she prides herself plays her false. Hers is a legalistic morality, made morbid by her longing "to have someone specifically suffer for the evil in the world." But her husband recognizes the essence of moral law, both in acting on it and in refusing to be proud of his action.

As the moral side of Lapham is developed largely through his wife, the social side comes to us through Bromfield Corey. Through an ambivalent attitude toward Corey, Howells gains our sympathy and makes one of the most moving portraits in the book. Howells is fair to the elder Corey; he underlines the propriety of his relations with Lapham and at one place gives him a speech sympathetic to the Boston poor that had come from one of Howells's own letters to his father. Yet always the doubt of decadence intrudes. In his acceptance of Lapham does Corey show a spirit safe in humility or one triply armed in pride? "This is a thing that can't be done by halves!" says Corey when he resolves to call on Penelope with his wife. To this generous protest Howells then adds the stage direction: "He cut his orange in the Neopolitan manner, and ate it in quarters."

If Howells is ambivalent toward Corey, Lapham is simply nonplused by his aristocratic acquaintance. Corey personifies the great social world that Lapham longs to enter, and in Corey he sees all graces that he lacks. Yet always there is "the struggle of stalwart achievement not to feel flattered at the notice of sterile elegance." Lapham is too much a part of the situation to comprehend it; he can never realize, as does Mrs. Corey, the real repugnance that exists in her husband's self-satire. But in the scene when Lapham apologizes for his drunkenness young Tom Corey recognizes the quality that raises his employer above blind conflict. There the young man perceives Lapham in all his stupid arrogance, yet with a saving humility that comes from a sense of wrong.

One of the rewards of the novel is that the reader will retain his impression of these people, and of several lesser characters. But equally memorable should be the style and form. Here certainly is a book that is *written,* a book that bears the mark of heightened pleasure in words that one finds in all Howells. When Mark Twain wrote an essay about his friend, he confined himself altogether to the subject of diction; and though the exclusiveness of that concern reflects a shortcoming in Twain's critical outlook, it properly recognizes the importance of Howells's urbane colloquialism. Howells had the new American tone, which may well be the most generous contribution of this early realist to his national literature. It works from the ground up, beginning in Lapham's rustic directness ("What's the matter?"—"Trouble's the matter") and in his more ponderous middle-class locutions ("But what I say is, a thing has got to be born in a man. . . . "). It flowers in Howells's easy geniality, with sentence after sentence striking one as the almost perfect realization of stylistic grace.

It is hard to separate Howells's scenes from language because scene after scene is speech, depending little upon action or setting. There are of course the big scenes, such as the interview or the dinner party, which have become almost synonymous with the novel. But an even greater delicacy enlivens the slighter scenes—the parasol-and-pine-shaving game played by Irene and Tom, with its undertone of sexual symbolism so perfectly though unconsciously rendered; the domestic conference between Mrs. Corey and her husband that ends in her despairing permission for him to read and smoke. Or there are passages like that of the prayerful meditation on paint between Lapham and young Corey or of Mrs. Lapham's unexpected discovery of a pretty secretary in her husband's office. In such passages and scenes and in the occasional settings which the author sketches, we get a sense of the story as a part of its people and environment, and as always a sense of the author's discriminating portrayal of them.

Another of the important, though slighter, techniques of the novel that should not go unnoticed is cross reference. Details are seldom given for their sake alone, but in anticipation and retrospect. The technique is common enough in any well-written novel, but here it is practiced with a greater pervasiveness than is ordinary. Every critic has had something to say about the introduction of anticipatory detail in the first episode, and perhaps in those beginning chapters cross reference is a little too much done. But when this technique occurs more subtly and easily throughout the whole novel, it creates a desirable tension in effect.

This effect is the more needed because the novel breaks un-

*The Beacon Street house in which Howells wrote* The Rise of Silas Lapham.

happily at its closing chapters. As Firkins, one of the best of Howells's critics, has written, there is "an ataxia or paralysis of the limbs, which arrests motion and slackens enterprise." If Howells were an inexperienced or frugal artist, one might conclude that he had simply become tired. But rather, as has been earlier argued, the real difficulty lies in Howells's inability to maintain his comic tone. The suggestion may also be made that Howells intended to spread out his sequence of actions in the later pages (for this is what he frequently did in other novels), but with too much story left to tell the amount of summary narrative is relatively too great for the book to hold.

In spite of this defect, one does get a sense of form in *The Rise of Silas Lapham* that is notably fine and in last analysis renders the novel a work of art. The form is not simple, but allows a number of variations which, as in a painting, play about the central design. The essential movement of the novel divides into three parts: growth toward success (Chapters 1-10), the failure of social ambitions (Chapters 11-19), and the failure in business (Chapters 20-27). In the first part are four main sequences, with a slight loosening of chronological limits in the last of these. The second part consists of one highly concentrated sequence, the dinner party and the events anticipating and following it. In the third part (with time picking up a week later and extending through winter and spring to several years), the business failure occurs—not the quick catastrophe that is expected but a series of hopes and disappointments.

The love affair, the relation of the Coreys in general, and the dealings with Rogers follow this movement. Most of all do Lapham's rises, in which his business failure is only a means to the end. The real rise is the moral one: but this is preceded by other rises, from which the final rise receives its dramatic force. Recurring to the essential movement, we have in the first part the rise in fortune with the promise (particularly after the easy payment of the debt to Rogers) of the happiness and honor it will bring. But in the next rise, into Boston aristocracy, Lapham suffers defeat. When in the third part he is struck down again, this time in business, he begins to climb toward final triumph.

The moral rise that follows is in two steps: Lapham does not gain the real, the ultimate rise by his resistance to the several temptations with which he is confronted. Rather, that rise comes in the testing of his sensibility by Sewell—an episode that stands in pleasing symmetry with the Hubbard interview of the first pages. Now at last he refuses to indulge in overweening righteousness, a type of which had been suggested by the earlier conduct of his wife. "I don't know as I should always say it paid; but if I done it, and the thing was to do over again, right in the same way, I guess I should have to do it."

It remains to be said that the house on Beacon Street functions as the major symbol. The house rises with Lapham's hopes, it seems to survive his social failure (though Irene realizes it has not), and in its ashes lies one of the last hopes of salvaging his business. But since Lapham's rise is not social but moral, the house is always a false image for him, "his pride and glory, his success, his triumphant life's work which was fading into failure in his helpless hands." Early in the novel, Mrs. Lapham recognized the place as accursed: "I shan't live in it. There's blood on it." As the trysting spot of Tom and Irene, it furnished what was to become the true measure of his love for her, a wood shaving. Much as Lapham had come to feel that the house was his own creation, Howells again and again holds up that feeling as delusion. It may represent Lapham's aesthetic potential, but nothing more, for he knew the house only as the unlearned might know an exquisite bit of harmony. But the Vermont farmhouse belonged to Lapham in a way that the Beacon Street house never could; and regardless of his earlier association with an architect, when he returned to Vermont his plans for improvement were limited to steam heat and naptha gas. "There were certainly all the necessaries, but no luxuries, unless the statues of Prayer and Faith might be so considered." Only with a house like that might Lapham have his triumph.

We cannot call *The Rise of Silas Lapham* a great novel. It is not that for our generation and probably not for any generation to come. But the total effect—in spite of its several faults, even in spite of the lapse in tone which does so much harm—is touched by greatness. We can properly consider the novel a work of competence and illumination. It offers refreshment and insight, which may be renewed and deepened each time one returns to it. (pp. v-xvi)

> George Arms, in an introduction to The Rise of Silas Lapham, *by William Dean Howells, Rinehart & Co., Inc., 1949, pp. v-xvi.*

## George N. Bennett    (essay date 1959)

[*A scholar of Howells's life and works, Bennett is the author of* William Dean Howells: The Development of a Novelist *and* The Realism of William Dean Howells, 1889-1920 *(1973). In the following excerpt from the former work, Bennett focuses on structure and theme in* The Rise of Silas Lapham.]

[*The Rise of Silas Lapham*] is a novel which deals with the potential moral corruption of a man by money. The outward signs of Silas Lapham's corruption are his attempts to buy his way into social acceptance with a costly house and to buy his way out of moral responsibility through a deliberately unwise loan to a former partner and victim. The loan is made with money which his wife prevented him from spending on the house, a complication which is neither accidental nor trivial. His eventual "rise" is the moral one resulting from the rejection of a legally sound but purely materialistic standard. It is accompanied by a corresponding adjustment in his understanding of the meaning of social differences, and a return to the "tradition" which had given his own family life solidity and dignity.

This initial oversimplification of the issues and method of *The Rise of Silas Lapham* is a necessary step to perspective. It is not necessary to compress the novel into narrow limitations, to regard it as dealing merely with social life. It need not be viewed simply as a comedy of manners which somehow comes to be involved with a moral problem. There have been many variations of such readings, and they would seem to be based on the assumption that the story of the triangular love affair and the story of

Lapham's business fortunes have only incidental or accidental kinship. But if the story belongs to Lapham, as every indication including the title insists, it seems just to ask that he bear some significant relationship to both sets of events. Put to this test, *The Rise of Silas Lapham* scores high. Lapham's conduct in relation to the love affair and his conduct in business issue from the same set of values—of which the famous and much abused principle "economy of pain" is merely a part. His reaction to the plight of his daughters is a vital factor in revealing to his consciousness the true factors which had been governing his attitudes and in restoring him to an active sense of his original purposes in acquiring material gains: the well-being and happiness of his family.

One sign that the demand for this kind of artistic control in *The Rise of Silas Lapham* is not presumptuous is the fact that the comment which the novel makes on the broad sweep of American life and society is grounded firmly in the individual characterizations—particularly, of course, in the portrait of Lapham himself. Howells was so sure of his subject he felt no need to make explicit generalizations. He had so long meditated on the average American—"the man who has risen" in some fashion or another—that he could interweave the comic richness of Lapham's immediate social situation not only with the ethics of his business relations but with the ethics of that same social situation. There is an organic development from a deeply perceived ethical situation to the fullest reaches of its effects, which may include comedy. Again Howells' imagination may be seen functioning freely and creatively as it works outward from a given instance to generalizations about society and the economic structure. Howells' article on Twain explaining the appeal of his friend's humor is clear evidence that he was so convinced of the essential "parity in the experience of Americans" that there was no necessity to establish Lapham's typicality. Howells was aware then, as he was aware a couple of years later, when he wrote the novel, that this condition might change, but in understanding and presenting Lapham he was sure that he was understanding and presenting America. Fortunately, there is further evidence, too, that the original conception of the story was based on Lapham's moral rise and that the questions of Lapham's relation to Boston society and of the entangled love affair were subordinate. An unpublished synopsis of the original plan removes all doubt of the respective emphases on ethics and social comedy as the novel grew in Howells' mind.

But the evidence merely supports what is, after all, apparent in the novel itself. The opening and closing scenes provide a clearly defined framework within which the related structure of Lapham's social rise and moral decline followed by his social decline and moral rise are thoroughly explored. The opening interview with Bartley Hubbard is in itself a sign of social position as well as business success, although it is not the kind of sign which Bromfield Corey would ever recognize. Moreover, the interview is more than just a device of exposition by which something of Lapham's past is revealed and certain details of the plot are anticipated: it sets the stops for the contrapuntal arrangement which will follow. The themes are lightly fingered but they are unmistakable. Lapham is insistently modest about his success, but he is obviously pleased with his rise from humble beginnings and is instinctively resentful of Bartley's unimpressed irreverence. Bartley soon beguiles him into talking again, and Lapham's later mention of the interview to Bromfield Corey is not as casual as it appears. Similarly, reference to the new house he is building occurs naturally enough in the course of the interview, but Lapham is hardly unaware that it will receive prominent mention in Bartley's article. In themselves these signs indicate no more than a normal amount of pride in accomplishment. In the light of later developments, however, they are controlled hints that Lapham is losing the objectivity necessary to prevent not only the disease of empty social ambition but the more serious corruption of materialism. And the one is a symptom of the other. Mrs. Lapham merely sighs when he responds to the problem of their daughters' social status with a reference to their wealth and its purchasing power. But on the day of the interview with Hubbard, when they visit the house which that money is building and meet Rogers, the man who has been sacrificed to it along the way, she is more explicit. Upon Lapham's refusal to admit his moral guilt, she exclaims " 'I sha'n't live in it. There's blood on it.' " Lapham's fit of temper which occasions this reprisal from his wife is to be explained not merely because this is an old argument. Bartley Hubbard's own materialism had already that day given the reporter an insight into the relationship between Lapham and his former partner. Lapham's pleasure in the interview emblematic of his ascent to public position had been momentarily marred by the abrasion of his memory by Bartley's questioning, and he is thus doubly sensitive to his wife's recriminations.

The initial episode of the novel succeeds in sounding, also, a positive note. It begins to play on the recurring theme of the simple and unself-conscious dignity of Lapham's own family tradition, which will be of vital importance to the preservation of his integrity. It is a tradition that is easily mocked, as Bartley glibly proves by his questioning: " 'Worked in the fields summers and went to school winters: regulation thing? . . . Parents poor, of course. . . . Any barefoot business? Early deprivations of any kind, that would encourage the youthful reader to go and do likewise?' " In his conventional reverence for motherhood, his pride in his paint, his philistine justification of landscape advertising, and his willingness to talk about himself, Lapham is easy prey for Bartley's clever cynicism. It is Bartley, though, who finally suffers from a comparison, particularly when Lapham momentarily touches on one of the deepest forces of his life—touches only momentarily because, significantly, this is one point at least on which he will not allow himself to brag: " 'All my brothers went West, and took up land; but I hung on to the old farm, not because the paint-mine was on it, but because the old house was—and the graves.' " This firm sense of continuity and of the values of love and devotion to be found in the family unit has been for Lapham and his wife a link with the past and a justification of the future. For their children it has created an atmosphere which not only protects them from the outside world but makes any other world largely superfluous. It is, in fact, the very strength of the mutual affection uniting the family in self-sufficiency which contributes to their social ignorance,

and one of the complications of theme is the disruption of this solidarity.

The intrusion of Tom Corey is a disturbing element not merely because he represents a different tradition, but because, innocently, he causes the members of the Lapham family to act toward him from motives which are no longer wholly frank and open. It is Lapham, of course, who is particularly devious, and it is his refusal to admit his real motives which provides a measure of his surrender of values. In taking Tom Corey into his business, he insists that he is acting purely from business motives; he is obviously delighted at the invitation to dinner with the Coreys but claims he is acting only in Irene's interest. Neither evasion really deceives Mrs. Lapham, who knows, that "in his simple, brutal way, he had long hated their name as a symbol of splendour which, unless he should live to see at least three generations of his descendants gilded with mineral paint, he could not hope to realize in his own."

Howells functions at the peak of his powers in treating the Coreys. Bromfield Corey in particular, charmingly aristocratic and useless, is a labor of love from Howells' pen. Yet it is chiefly by his treatment of Bromfield Corey that Howells introduces the comic aspects of his theme. Having established Corey as the aristocratic dilettante who has deliberately withdrawn from the active commitments of life, Howells permits him to be gracefully witty at the expense of those who take life seriously. The note of indulgence is important: Howells can gain comic relief without abandoning the seriousness of his position. It is for this reason that he resists the patent temptations to farce offered by the famous dinner party at which Lapham makes a drunken fool of himself. Similarly he refuses to enlarge on the ludicrous aspects of the general mistake concerning Tom Corey's intentions toward the Lapham girls, but maintains a firm artistic control over his characterizations by showing Penelope's initial resentment over her secondary role and by indicating that there is no real doubt about how the situation will be resolved.

The spectacle of a man making a fool of himself is, after all, essentially painful rather than comic. It is comic only as it is enclosed in some larger view of human nature—a view which derides the folly of all human action, for example, or, as in Howells' case, a view which includes an awareness of the essential soundness of the victim which will eventually redeem him from his foolishness. A certain amount of comedy arises from Lapham's social ineptitudes, but it is finally the gentlemanliness of Tom and Bromfield Corey that suffers by comparison. They suffer diminution because Lapham's social failure promotes an action from him which is more than social, an act of character possible only to a person who has the moral courage to see himself honestly and to accept the consequences of the knowledge. His apology to Tom Corey is in one sense as excessive as the conduct that necessitated it, but it has its roots in a renewed sense of humility, a renewed sense of distinction between himself and his money.

Lapham's conduct at the dinner party serves to confirm the opinion of Bromfield Corey and his wife that social intercourse with the Laphams is impossible, and the most that Lapham's subsequent apology can produce is a letter of praise from Bromfield. Tom Corey is not unaffected, however, and the experience has more than social meaning for him. Having realized that he was guilty of adding to Lapham's humiliation by remaining aloof from motives of mere gentility, Tom is forced to a revaluation of his whole position in relation to the Laphams. He owns up to the fact that social conduct—at least such relations as his to the Laphams—involves ethical responsibilities and that the possibility of injury is not entirely confined to his family and himself. His proposal to Penelope follows, and the family crisis within the Lapham household results.

It is at this point that the bankruptcy theme (which quantitatively has been in abeyance for seven chapters of 135 pages) begins to reassert itself. It is typical of Howells' quiet irony, moreover, that the minor theme should continue for a time to overshadow the major, for it is Mrs. Lapham's insistence on revealing this latest complication between the Coreys and the Laphams which prevents Silas from telling her of his increasing difficulties with Rogers. But the two themes merge in even more subtle fashion. With a sincerity which has been lacking for some time, Lapham can now state the only terms on which it is possible to resolve the situation: they must act from the motive on which their life together had been predicated—for the good of the children. It is on this basis that he decides that the marriage between Penelope and Tom must be allowed, and his reaction to Mrs. Lapham's suspicion that he may still be acting from unworthy motives—that he is allowing his judgment to be controlled by his desire to have Tom Corey for a son-in-law—dispels any doubt of his sincerity.

Lapham's renewed sense of the values and purposes which had been his before material success clouded his vision is part of the process which enables him to rise to the highest and best that is in him in deciding the business situation from which a legal escape is possible. The standard of "economy of pain" which he had used to decide what would be best for his children cannot be applied to himself. That standard applies to special conditions: when it is to be determined who must suffer when no one is at fault. Penelope's greatest fault remained merely "potential," and in contrast to her father's active guilt even her potential blame is largely forced upon her. Lapham's guilt in his original relation to Rogers is clear from the start and is finally acknowledged by him. Although the whole family must pay for Lapham's original fault, the payment is the loss of their material wealth. Only strict honor can finally redeem Lapham's sin, and redemption brings spiritual compensations not only to him but to the whole family. (pp. 150-57)

The novel is brought to a close in a scene which, as George Arms has pointed out, "stands in pleasing symmetry with the Hubbard interview of the first pages" [see excerpt dated 1949]. Sewell, the minister who had been consulted by the Laphams in solving the dilemma caused by Tom Corey and who had confirmed Lapham's solution, visits their Vermont homestead. Sewell's interest in the moral lesson of Lapham's story enables Howells to give final emphasis to his theme and allows Lapham to state in his own words his reflections upon the meaning of the experience which brought him back where he started. Gone is the

bragging Lapham of the opening interview; gone is the Lapham who could ease his conscience with a loan whose loss he never expected to matter; gone even is the Lapham who somehow expected that his virtue in refusing Tom Corey's offer of a loan would be recognized by further insistence that it be accepted. The morality which Mrs. Lapham has been preaching throughout the novel, but which she has in a sense been denying by tacitly accepting the benefits of its rejection, is now really Lapham's. And because it has become his through struggle and temptation, it is free from any exaggerated sense of righteousness and heroics. To Sewell's question about regrets, he replies: " 'Seems sometimes as if it was a hole opened for me, and I crept out of it. . . . I don't know as I should always say it paid; but if I done it, and the thing was to do over again, right in the same way, I guess I should have to do it again.' "

The mention of Mrs. Lapham suggests another way in which Howells binds his theme of Lapham's moral rise to the family unit. Howells plays on the word *rise* from the start. He describes Lapham's marriage as a "rise in life for him" and continues the same discussion with an account of the relationship with Rogers in which his wife had assumed the role of his conscience. But in this affair Lapham could not "choose the ideal, the unselfish part," he "could not rise to it." Yet it is finally he who achieves moral stature and his wife who fails. She is taught a moral lesson by her husband, and it is because he has risen beyond her that he can administer the lesson without rancor or triumph. During the course of Lapham's business troubles, Mrs. Lapham is led by Rogers to suspect her husband of keeping a mistress. When she discovers her mistake, she draws the same kind of moral application for herself which she has been preaching to her husband: " 'If we're brought back to the day of small things, I guess it's a lesson for me, Silas.' " But the real lesson is in Lapham's explanation of Rogers' motives: " 'Mebbe he believed it,' said Lapham, with patience that cut her more keenly than any reproach. '*You* did.' " This is what Howells had in mind when he opened the whole discussion of the rise in Lapham's life through marriage by commenting that the "silken texture of the marriage tie bears a daily strain of wrong and insult to which no other human relation can be subjected without lesion." It is not irrelevant to remark that Lapham exhibits precisely the kind of character which was beyond the young reporter who introduces his story and whose own story was told in *A Modern Instance.*

Howells' achievement in *The Rise of Silas Lapham* was to embody a permanently interesting statement of human conduct in an esthetically satisfying form. The broad pattern of that form as it divides into Lapham's social ambition, his social failure, and his moral rise is easily recognizable. It is the skill with which Howells weaves the related implications of social and moral conduct into the whole fabric, however, that makes the novel a finished artistic product. As Mrs. Lapham herself remarks, Rogers "always manages to appear just at the moment when he seems to have gone fairly out of our lives." The house, too, the symbol of the success in which Lapham takes inordinate pride, has a way of associating itself with decisive moments: it is there that Tom Corey renews his acquaintance with the Laphams; it is there that the mistaken notion of Corey's love for Irene takes definite shape in the minds of the Laphams; and it is to the house that Lapham turns in despair because "his pride and glory, his success, his triumphant life's work . . . was fading into failure in his helpless hands."

And in almost the mathematical center of the novel is the dinner party. Almost every critic has his word of censure because of its length or because nothing decisive occurs during it. Yet it is far more than the quantitative center of the novel: it draws together the strands of Howells' story and spins them out again. Aside from Lapham's social inadequacies, it focuses attention once more on the house; it reveals the background of Lapham's relation to Zerilla Dewey and prepares for Mrs. Lapham's instance of moral failure; it prepares, also, through the discussion of the novelists' sentimental doctrine of self-sacrifice, for the actual situation to be faced by Penelope and Irene; it precipitates Lapham's apology to Tom Corey and Corey's subsequent proposal to Penelope. The general critical as well as popular favor which *The Rise of Silas Lapham* continues to enjoy after seventy years of existence is clearly merited and may well be inadequate to its deserts. (pp. 158-60)

> *George N. Bennett, in his* William Dean Howells: The Development of a Novelist, *University of Oklahoma Press, 1959, 220 p.*

## John E. Hart   (essay date 1963)

[*An American critic, educator, and poet, Hart has written extensively on Stephen Crane and other American novelists. In the following essay, Hart examines Howells's artistic treatment of commonplace characters and circumstances in* The Rise of Silas Lapham.]

What gives *The Rise of Silas Lapham* significance in the history of the American novel is not Howells' "faithful treatment of material"—all writers strive for an accuracy of statement. His originality of vision lies, rather, in his ability to recognize and convey the heroic in "poor Real life." Although Howells made much of the doctrine of writing what "his fleshly eyes have seen," he insisted that an artist's duty was to interpret human nature: the novelist, he wrote, should "seek the universal in the individual rather than the social interests." Clearly he draws his material from common, ordinary life, but his interpretation in *The Rise of Silas Lapham* follows the form and pattern long used for the hero of myth and romance: heroism is a discovery of self that involves the hero in an unmistakable ordeal that amounts to a symbolic dying and rebirth. Howells makes the intent of his method clear in the question Silas puts to Bartley Hubbard. Silas asks, " . . . so you want my life, death, and Christian sufferings . . . ?" In depicting the motives and passions, the moral and spiritual sufferings of his hero, Howells shows how the inner vision of truth that is the discovery of self is recreated out of ordinary events and commonplace happenings. It is this vision of the heroic in the commonplace and Howells' particular portrayal of it that bear critical exploration.

Silas' life is actually the story of self-deception and self-discovery that begins in innocence and ends in wisdom. In one sense the pattern of his life is circular. Silas comes from a Vermont farm and returns to it. But within the circle of wandering, there are two lines of development, one of conquest and one of quest. If conquest is a matter of will, a matter of conscious planning made manifest through overt action, quest is more the inward shaping of character through circumstance and growing awareness. Both the overt action and the inward shaping take place simultaneously. As Silas' conquest takes him from bucolic innocence into the intricate world of Boston, so his success in business shows his awkward failure in the world of personal and social prestige. Yet the very events that bring destruction serve as the series of tests and trials that enable him to recognize the nature of pride and greed, and to understand that real values come, not from external possession, but from moral and spiritual resources that lie within man's nature. Howells did not, of course, discover the pattern of regeneration, but his use of it in portraying the common average business man of his day was both new and startling.

As a way of making the symbolic fall and rise integral to the structure of the novel, Howells uses two major symbols: paint and houses. Both carry a burden of aesthetic, moral, and social meaning, and while they are inextricably linked with the lives of the characters, paint is, in its various stages of manufacture, most closely related to Silas, Mrs. Lapham, and Bromfield Corey. To Silas paint is a matter of commodity. As he says, "the landscape was made for man, and not man for the landscape." Paint is material, money. It has become his passion, his "heart's blood," the driving force behind his way to wealth and power. As symbolic agent, paint is both energy and matter; it can both destroy and create. It makes his financial rise possible, but as Silas grows greedy and ambitious, his greed and pride entangle him in both moral and economic destruction. Yet the paint-mine, like the landscape, remains as a gift freely given, an endless source of moral and creative life to which he can return with renewed understanding after his ordeal in Boston. It is a credit to Silas' moral insight, however, that he names his best grade of paint—the Persis brand—after his wife, whose values and actions, though warped by Puritanical righteousness, are more refined and honest than his own. And in the end, it is the Persis brand that is salvaged from the financial collapse as worthy to compete in a highly competitive market. To Bromfield Corey, paint is hardly a commodity at all, but the medium by which he has once expressed artistic sensibilities as a painter of portraits. If his dilettante interests suggest a loss of vital energy, his indifference to material values accentuates an aesthetic appreciation of life, a cultivated objectivity, a devotion to form and manners. Like the artist or the poet, he is refined, fragile, durable, but he has hardly become involved in the actuality of life. Once he painted it. Now he merely observes it.

The second major symbol is that of houses, and there are four of them. They function not as agent, but as agency. The old farm house in Vermont contains both beginning and end, both source and sanctuary: "I hung on to the old farm, not because the paint-mine was on it, but because the old house was—and the graves." And just as the farm house implies a native innocence, an honesty and uprightness, so the house on Nankeen Square reflects the wealth and greed, the vulgarity and artificiality, the social, moral, and aesthetic poverty which conquest brings. Even the statues of Faith and Prayer become decorative bric-a-brac rather than visual guides of moral attitudes. But the half-built house on Beacon Street perhaps best symbolizes Silas' partially realized aims and aspirations in the social world. It is to be the monument to success and personal aggrandizement. But the classical simplicity of its form and decoration reflects not so much Silas' acquired good taste as his illusory belief that extravagance and hired experts can endow him with taste and position. Similarly, the Corey mansion, inherited from Mrs. Corey's family, not only reflects the air of "aristocratic seclusion," the inherited taste of the new sterile and enervated Corey family, but as scene of Lapham's initiatory ordeal into a world of grace and refinement, it also illustrates the social and aesthetic distance which Silas must travel in order to achieve his goal. Of the four houses the farm house and the Corey mansion suggest real and abiding values in a post Civil War America that found many a rising middle-class hero trying to pass through the Nankeen Squares to the rarefied atmosphere of a Beacon Street. The four houses contain the symbolic movement of the novel: the departure and return, the rise and fall, the destruction and renewal. In a sense, the life, death, and suffering of Silas is a story of paint and houses, a story of energy and matter shaping the destiny of modern man.

In the conquest that moves him from Vermont to Boston, Silas has worked with boundless energy to turn paint into money and property. Two essential ingredients in his success have not come from him at all. He inherited the paint-mine from his father; his wife's "zeal and courage formed the spring of his enterprise." In these early days, the "blunt, outspoken" Laphams have worked toward success together. As Silas says, he mixed paint "with *Faith*" and "the best quality of boiled linseed oil that money will buy." But as success comes, Silas relies less and less on faith, less and less on the old resources. Although Mrs. Lapham warns that he has made paint his god and cannot "bear to let anybody else share in its blessings," she has gradually "abandoned herself to a blind confidence in her husband's judgment, which she had hitherto felt needed her revision." Silas bows easily to his false material gods. He forces his business partner out of the firm, rationalizes his guilt as smart business tactics, and retreats, however uneasily, into his greed for more. Having cut himself off from the familiar moral sources, the strength of his inheritance, the moral wisdom of his guides, he is motivated, not by self-sacrifice, but self-gain, not by inner resourcefulness, but external display. The decaying Nankeen Square district is visual index to the Laphams' social poverty: in spite of the clothes and fine horses, the summers at expensive resorts, the gifts "with both hands" to church and charity, they have acquired neither gesture nor form that insures acceptance in a cultured society. They remain isolated and alone, gaining whatever strength they can from "mutual affection."

Silas' attempt at social conquest demonstrates his inability to realize that acceptance into the world of the Bromfield Coreys demands "something more besides money." Inspired by the apparent interest of Tom Corey in one of the Lapham daughters, Silas envisions himself as the social success that a fine house on Beacon Street may bring. And as he relies on a house to create position for him, so he relies on someone else to conceive it, to bridge, as it were, the aesthetic and intellectual differences between Laphams and the Coreys. His own knowledge is limited. He basks in the architect's tendency towards extravagance and experimentation. Of the architect's talk of permanent art forms, the classical simplicity of design, he understands nothing. He finds greatest pleasure in seeing the piles driven for the foundation, as if he comprehended only the crude, if essential beginnings. He is appalled to think a builder would prefer painted woodwork to the more expensive and fashionable black walnut. While Mrs. Lapham inspects the decoration, he sits ill at ease in what will be the reception room and whittles, dreaming, like a man bewitched, of his new social role and of his daughter's marriage into an aristocratic family. As Mrs. Lapham warns: "You've lost your head, Silas Lapham, and if you don't look out you'll lose your money too."

As Silas' guide and conscience, Mrs. Lapham, for all her righteous warning, hardly understands the nature of Silas' guilt. She senses danger in the sudden appearance of Rogers, the old business partner: "he always manages to appear at the moment when he seems to have gone fairly out of our lives, and blight everything." Yet she believes that Silas, in lending money to him, has now atoned for the initial fraud: "You've taken the one spot—the one *speck*—off you that was ever there, and I'm satisfied." She does not see that in trying to buy redemption, Silas has only piled sin on sin; unwittingly she has helped to plot his social and financial downfall.

Thus, for all his success in business, Silas knows little of the true nature of self. He has told Bartley Hubbard that man should keep his conscience "as free from paint as you can, if you want much use of it," but has done just the reverse: his passion has made paint his god and increased his greed for personal gain. Holding fast to those values which gratify his pride and inflate his ego, Silas has not yet learned that man's real strength derives from the inner self, from a moral and spiritual concept of life that is in harmony with the inexhaustible and unseen sources in man and nature. Acting as if such strength were his own, he has broken the vitalizing connectives and made his quest merely parody, the pursuit of a delusion. In the language of Emerson, he has become but partial man, a fragment of the total image, a man disunited within himself. Although, finally, Silas must realize these truths for himself, he now needs someone to guide him on the way. As much as anyone else, that guide turns out to be Bromfield Corey.

Although the Corey family is a name that Silas has long hated "as a symbol of splendour which . . . he could not hope to realize in his own," he is awed and elated to have young Tom Corey as an employee in the paint factory, as a guest in his house, as a suitor to his daughter. Actually Tom is the connecting link in the social struggle of which the Laphams and Coreys are only symbols, for Tom is of a new generation, and can combine old idealism with new energy. He has inherited the nose and energy of his forefathers, and he is attracted to paint as an opportunity that honestly interests him for the first time in his life. Since he honors neither social prestige nor family prejudice, he can look on Silas, not as vulgar rich, but as "simple-hearted and rather wholesome." But the backgrounds of the Lapham and Corey families reflect great differences that a mutual interest in paint and houses can hardly unite.

Bromfield Corey, a man who never whittles, is a study in "sterile elegance." He has dabbled in oil painting, in culture, and in life; his judgment has more objectivity than passion. For all his social position, he has long ago discovered that he is not "some sort of porcelain," but "common clay, after all." With values firmly built on moral, aesthetic, and intellectual standards, he has gained the social knowledge and self-insight that prevent a violent sympathy for old certainty or new fashion. Although he acknowledges that money is now "the romance, the poetry of our age," the thing "that chiefly strikes the imagination," he clings to the decayed splendour of a "faded tradition," to the belief in "good sense and right ideas," in the mentality and manners that make up the "airy, graceful, winning superstructure" of a society. He sees the Laphams as "rude, native flavours," but without the "sauce piquante." As his reading of the *Revue des deux mondes* suggests, he is a man of two worlds; indeed, he is a man of many attitudes and sympathies and understandings.

It is through Bromfield Corey, then, that Silas comes to understand something of the nature of society and self. On a visit to the paint office, Corey acts with courtesy and kindness; he is neither arrogant nor condescending. He is, Silas thinks, "about the pleasantest man I ever did see." Howells spells out the interpretation: where once Silas "could not have imagined any worldly splendour which his dollars could not buy," he now has a "cloudy vision of something unpurchasable," a vision that comes to him "in spite of the burly resistance of his pride." In this moment Silas has caught a glimpse of that impalpable world of being that lies beyond the visible world of matter. But one glimpse is not a gleam of truth, and before Silas can overcome his egotism, his attachment to self, he must be shown the way again and again.

The dinner party at the Coreys, which begins as a tribal masquerade and ends as an unmasked confessional, is an unmistakable ordeal of discovery. Actually, the whole dinner scene is an ironic comedy of manners that exposes both Laphams and Coreys. The invitation is a calculated move: by exposing the Laphams, the Coreys hope to save themselves from an alliance with a family that neither speaks grammatically nor has the habit of wine at the table. For Silas it is the realization of social ambition. There are losses and gains on both sides. A family alliance is achieved; Silas fails miserably to achieve social sanction. But as a result of undergoing what amounts to an initiatory ritual, Silas realizes something of self. Except for Bromfield Corey, the members of the Corey clan, despite the timeless qualities of good taste and form which the house

suggests, have much to learn also. Mrs. Corey addresses Silas as General instead of Colonel. At the table Bellingham tucks his napkin in his collar. There are jokes about money and charities. They are, in reality, clannish and vulgar and given to improprieties. They try to dazzle their unsuspecting guests; they lure Silas into a shameful exhibition of bravado. Under the influence of too much wine, Silas monopolizes the conversation, brags of his war experiences, tells how Jim Million's "hard" death saved his own. The listeners are stunned. They see Silas as a man of "gross appetites, . . . blunt sense, . . . purblind ambition, stupid arrogance." Although Silas feels successful at the time, he realizes next morning that he has disgraced both himself and his family. But in catching this long glimpse of self, he has acquired, as Howells says, a "sense of wrong."

Humility is not easily acquired. Before Silas is able to relinquish the deluding dreams which have fed his ego, he must pass three major crises in his life: the mix-up in the love affair between Irene, Tom Corey, and Penelope; the burning of his new house; and the series of financial disasters. His final rise and reformation are not, as with heroes of romance, a matter of sudden consequence. As Howells says, in real life "the theory of disaster" is not "incessant." Although the direction of Silas' life spells inevitable failure, his reverses are punctuated with hope. The difficult quest of the inner vision is tedious and awesome.

The discovery that Tom Corey loves Penelope, not Irene, forces Silas into the moral sphere for his answers. As he says to Mrs. Lapham, "We don't either of us want anything but the children's good. What's . . . [money] . . . for, if it ain't for that?" It is Silas who senses their inadequacy: "Suppose we don't want Pen to have him; will that help Irene any, if he don't want her?" And it is Silas, not Mrs. Lapham, who sees that they need help in making a decision: Mr. Sewell advises that better one should suffer than all three. It is Silas, too, who understands that in her suffering Irene will be strong as iron and that Penelope will accept her responsibility to Tom without faltering. In this family crisis, Silas proves himself to be gentle, kind, understanding.

As the financial disasters mount, Silas must reckon with the loss of that very foundation on which his idea of success has been based. Money and paint have been his life, and now with the mishandling of funds, the loans to Rogers, the purchase of bad stock, a rising competitive market which can undersell him, he loses the very means on which conquest has been built. Beset by destruction from without and from within—Mrs. Lapham hears of Zerilla and suspects him of supporting another woman—Silas, in silence and alone, must examine the position to which his corrupted conscience and enfeebled sensibilities have brought him. In his agony he sees that he has been a fool. He tells Mrs. Lapham: "I haven't hurt anybody but myself—and you and the children."

Silas' full shock of recognition comes, however, with the destruction of the new house. As symbol of financial success and hope for social privileges, it is his "pride and glory," "his triumphant life's work." Yet just as his grandiose social schemes remain unrealized, so the house is but partly completed. Having resolved to sell it, Silas journeys to it in despair. Alone with his sorrow in the silence, he recalls his long talks with the architect: now he seems to have a feeling for the "simplicity of the whole design and the delicacy of its detail." As Howells interprets, using sound imagery: "It appealed to him as an exquisite bit of harmony appeals to the unlearned ear, and he recognised the difference between this fine work and the obstreperous pretentiousness of the many overloaded housefronts . . . on the Back Bay." He even detects the "peculiar odour of his own paint," and following a whim, decides to test the chimney. The success of having made the fire inspires him: he feels that he, too, can rise above his adversity. Then as the fire turns into destruction, he knows that with the burning of the house, his last hope for economic and social success has been destroyed. It is ironic that people cannot gossip, as Mrs. Lapham fears, that he has set it on fire himself in order to collect the insurance, for there is no insurance. Completely broken, Silas falls "into the deep sleep which sometimes follows a great moral shock." It is the symbolic sleep of death. When he awakes, he knows that he can neither sell his paint business, nor raise enough money to buy out his competitors. If he sells the worthless mill and stocks, he will be dishonest; if he does not, he will fail. Emerging from the "isolation to which adversity so often seems to bring men," from the trials and tests that have brought material defeat but moral strength, Silas knows that he can and must stand "firm for right and justice."

If, then, Silas' adventure in Boston began as a conquest for financial and social aggrandizement, it has come to serve as a series of ordeals through which he recognizes the need for moral rectitude. Recognition has come, however, not as a matter of triumph over society, but as a by-product of the battle against it. His return to Vermont is a return to the "necessaries" of life, "to the day of small things," to country ways and plain living, to the paint-mine and the old house, to the source of inspiration, which has both led him astray and brought new faith and understanding. Silas' return was, as Howells writes, "as much the end of his proud, prosperous life as death itself could have been. He was returning to begin life anew, but he knew as well as he knew that he should not find his vanished youth in his native hills, that it could never again be the triumph that it had been." Yet, out of his greed and pride, out of the evil generated by social ambition has sprung an understanding of moral self. As Howells says: "Adversity had so far been his friend that it had taken from him all hope of the social success for which people crawl and truckle, and restored him, through failure and doubt and heartache, the manhood which his prosperity had so nearly stolen from him." To be restored to manhood is to discover the nature of self, the native and primal stuff of inner being. Just as a passion for paint and money has nearly destroyed Silas' sense of values, so the return to the paint-mine has aided the redemption.

*The Rise of Silas Lapham* begins and ends with an interview. The interview with Bartley Hubbard, which forms the opening chapter, reveals Silas at his boasting best and makes Hubbard a kind of malign helper to our hero's fortunate fall. At the end, the interview with Mr. Sewell,

whose role of chance acquaintance and willing guide has helped Lapham atone for his mistakes, reveals the scope of Silas' moral and spiritual growth. Without actually admitting that he ever wronged his partner, Silas owns "that he had made mistakes." Yet, he can also say that "he had been no man's enemy but his own; every dollar, every cent had gone to pay his debts; he had come out with clean hands." Silas has achieved more than clean hands. He has undergone a rebirth that points the way to symbolic ascension. As he says: "Seems sometimes as if it was a hole opened for me, and I crept out of it." The hole is, of course, the still center of creative realization that constitutes self-scrutiny. Having achieved an awareness and conception of self that enables him to overcome the attachment to his pride and greed, having become a man of integrity, Silas can look at himself and his relation to others with the confidence of humility that is truly heroic. Ennobled by the ordeal of experience and "Christian suffering," he can speak freely of his failure with an understanding that bespeaks wisdom.

Howells is not the first to portray the heroic in the commonplace. Such writers as Stendhal, Dickens, Balzac, Irving, Emerson, and Melville had already worked "understandably [at] bestowing form upon reality as given," at depicting a true reflection of the common, the familiar, the low in human life. In a sense, then, Howells is only continuing a literary tradition that had come to focus on real conditions and events. For all his middle-class morality, he is able to attach conditions and events to their roots, to inform them with an inner essence, to illumine and interpret them, to shape them through archetypal pattern and allegorical movement that avoids the stock-types of the romantic novel or morality play. The reality of his vision shows an informed and accurate knowledge of the social, economic, and moral thought of his time; his representation of events, colored as they are in *The Rise of Silas Lapham* by Christian ethics and Greek moderation, is based on rationalistic and empirical points of view, rather than philosophical and historical dogma. It is Howells' major strength that his program of artistic purpose helped him to see the heroic in the "smiling aspects" of "poor Real life." (pp. 375-83)

*John E. Hart, "The Commonplace as Heroic in 'The Rise of Silas Lapham',"* in Modern Fiction Studies, *Vol. VIII, No. 4, Winter, 1962-63, pp. 375-83.*

## William Wasserstrom   (essay date 1965)

[*An American educator and critic, Wasserstrom has written extensively on American fiction. In the following excerpt, he argues that critics have overrated* The Rise of Silas Lapham.]

During the last twenty years considerable groups of university scholars have addressed themselves or led their students to the problem of William Dean Howells. All have been drawn to the work which seemed best suited either to repay or reprove their devotions, *The Rise of Silas Lapham,* a novel which has puzzled Howells' audience from the time, 1884, when it first appeared. Today, we have shifted the ground both of satisfaction and discontent but the work itself, despite steadfast and energetic labor by apologists for Howells' art, continues to tease us. What this novel presents us with, what we inherit from our predecessors is an unsolved problem in literary taste and literary history: how is it that Howells, whom F. O. Matthiessen called the "most disconcerting figure in the American past," continues to defy death even as he manages to evade celebrity.

Today, reading books and essays by the newest generation of Howellsians, one is told that this problem does not exist. Howells, formerly estranged, is now quite reintegrated within the main schemes of modern thought. Only men of capricious mind or recalcitrant taste, his partisans say, perversely withhold acclaim. Indeed the final essay in the latest book, *Howells: A Century of Criticism,* edited by Kenneth Eble, maintains that the business of criticism has passed through a cycle of bust and come to a state of permanent boom. Howells is suddenly a kind of "growth stock," traded "briskly by the most finicky critics." He is a "major author."

Aside from this vulgarity of image, the claim itself is untrue. What is true is that some devotees, dazzled by the splendor of Howells' career as a man of letters in an unlettered society, polish up and then polish off certain classic dilemmas of Howells' art. The more thoroughly they studied the man's career, the more lustrous they found the novelist to be. Because this state of affairs displays a confusion about the value of fealty and the uses of fact it is again necessary to retrace the history and redefine the quality of Howells' reputation. In this way, more or less unobtrusively, I shall evoke certain perplexities in *Lapham* itself—from the time when William James "squealed" with pleasure over every word until the time when H. L. Mencken said that it alone, of all Howells' books, might survive: "but go read it if you would tumble downstairs" [see excerpt dated 1917 in *TCLC,* Vol. 7, pp. 369-70]. Then, coming from the late 20's to the late 50's, when random Howellsians were in full career—when, as Everett Carter said, Silas' Beacon Street house offers the key "symbol on which the structure of the novel is erected"—I shall turn to this as the prototypical issue on which the case for Howells rests.

Right off the proper thing to say is that Howells' adherents have succeeded in reclaiming a segment of that audience which, by 1929, had fallen away, dispelled in part by the journalist, Mencken, who most clearly mirrored national prejudices in the 1920's. Dismissing Howells as a clever stylist who compiled a long row of "uninspired and hollow books," Mencken decided that the truth "about Howells is that he really has nothing to say." This opinion, though not unanimous, had been current since 1917 when another literary journalist, Francis Hackett, had rebuked his colleagues for neglect of that "master . . . from whose large intentions and richly freighted performances too few national writers have renewed themselves." The rebuke had no noticeable effect until 1937. Then Howells' disciple, Booth Tarkington, reflecting how his teacher, alone in the American nineteenth century, had sought to "make true things," recalling that Howells single-handed had led

younger writers out of a wilderness of fantasy and falsehood—Tarkington reminded a new generation of critics that their disdain of this writer's work was a serious loss to fiction.

Inherent in Tarkington's impassioned piety, inside Hackett's thick prose, there was a sharp point. The period of decline in Howells' fame coincided with the time when critics, suddenly rediscovering James and Melville, undertook to restore these distinguished but unappreciated writers to proper eminence in our literature. That labor of rediscovery did not rest on the ruin of Howells' fame. But its most compelling claims were in fact designed to undermine esteem for the work of a novelist whose language and subject were, unlike theirs, ordinary. For Melville, James, even Hawthorne exploit moods of imagination alien to the mood which shapes Howells' best fiction. They are intent to intuit inner reality whereas Howells is content to imitate external life. Their minds turned to allegory and epic, symbol and myth. His mind treated profundities too, but rejected queer plots and exotic actions and stressed the utility, for art, of simple acts by familiar people.

A half century earlier his realism had represented to the general audience a triumph of mind and brilliance of art glittering enough to eclipse all but one of his colleagues: Mark Twain alone was better loved. And although many readers were puzzled rather than dazzled by his art, nevertheless they cherished a man who lived so prodigious a life, who had made a career miraculous for a person of his breeding. (pp. 366-67)

During the 1920's and 30's he retained no audience to speak of among critics who, having learned to prize James and Melville, wondered what could be salvaged from the 200 books or items in books, the thousand or so periodical pieces written during Dean Howells' sixty years of work. Then in the 1940's beginning with Alfred Kazin's *On Native Grounds,* historians undertook to stress Howells' worth as a literary figure. Here was the one native writer who had portrayed the American nineteenth century at large and in small. Here too was a utopian of the old and new order, a perfectibilitarian who fused Jeffersonian democracy with Tolstoian socialism. More bumpkin than Brahmin but no more uneasy on Beacon Street than on Broadway and no less at home in Florence than on the frontier, in his own day Howells had a devout national public and an appreciative international following. Here, therefore, was a home-bred and self-made man of letters, phenomenal less for the uniqueness of his powers than for the range and authority of his labors as a novelist, editor and critic.

Despite this range, none of his works successfully contained its action within any single coherent system of structure. No one fiction, said Edwin A. Cady in 1948, was indisputably first rate. "Even in *The Rise of Silas Lapham,* where the parallel plots are much more firmly joined" than in *A Modern Instance*— Howells' first effort to make a major novel—"one sometimes has the feeling of watching two simultaneous tennis matches on neighboring courts." These gradually merge as "Silas's business problems and the Lapham-Corey romance gradually blend. Defensible if sometimes dizzying as that is, what shall we do with the hiatus devoted to the building of Silas's house?"

By 1956, after two volumes of biography which brought to an end eight years of study, Cady decided that the structure of *Lapham* presents problems only to the rude not the keen mind [see essay dated 1956 in *TCLC*, Vol. 7, pp. 381-84]. The origins of our modern age, the 1870's and 80's, coincide with the time Howells himself came to maturity. Eager to record the effects on society of problems new to American life, in *Lapham* he recreated the process by which decent people permitted the control of culture to pass to indecent people, the barbarians of business. Among the many aims of this novel is a portrayal of the ways each of the Laphams resist one or another kind of blandishment. Irene rebels against the cliché of innocent genteel American girlhood; Mrs. Lapham purges herself of cheap ambition; Silas of course in the end refuses to pay the cost of fortune; and Penelope rejects the attractions of a purity so exacting it would immobilize not enliven her virtue. Observing these acts of decency, we know that our civilization will continue to flourish even among men reared to cherish the gospel of cash, among women intimidated by the cult of conscience.

"*The Rise of Silas Lapham* is the testament of a realist who wishes his readers to see directly the moral confusion into which the new times have fallen." Observing too that this "drama of the moral imagination" is performed in a succession of homes (the Lapham farmhouse in Vermont, the house on Nankeen Square, the house on Beacon Street, the Corey house), Cady decided that the novel, properly read, was itself a great edifice erected on plots roomy enough to accommodate all Howells' projects and people. Devised according to a tongue and groove of the imagination, *Lapham* is built to the scale of the culture it is supposed to symbolize.

Surely the novel is made to stand so. Clearly Howells planned to achieve this kind of confluence and effect. For Silas himself says that his first wrong act of business, the Rogers affair, is best conceived as the first brick in a row of bricks which tumble one after another. "It wasn't in the nature of things that they could be stopped till the last brick went." But no one has managed to say precisely how Howells' art itself manifests the design of national life in the gilded age. Instead, having contracted to show why *Lapham* is a sturdy novel, scholars industriously modify the novelist's plans a little. Refurbished here and there, in their hands *Lapham* becomes a palatial book written by a prince of a man. Monumental in the life of its creator, it must be restored, they believe, to a capital place in the life of letters. I exaggerate a little. But I must underline the fact that nobody has contrived to show how each of its components—the great scene of drunkenness, the coincidences of love and discontinuities of time, the stagy business of Zerilla—merge in faultless or even formidable union.

Despite two decades of sustained and hard work, therefore, neither Howells' reputation nor *Lapham's* is very much altered. Both the novel and the man are far better understood. But, despite all ingenuity of argument and zeal, neither has recovered fame of really high order. Sure-

ly, it is time to suspend debate: Howells is after all no more disconcreting a figure than Irving or Cooper. A notable writer not a masterly one, he need not be reviled or worshipped. And surely there is no unfathomable problem in *The Rise of Silas Lapham,* best of Howells' fictions but clearly no masterpiece. The writer's gifts are demonstrable everywhere but incontrovertible nowhere in a novel, first of its kind in America, which manifests the real speech, true wants, and grand actions within the inner lives of representative persons in all spheres of national life during an historic time. Its value as a major document of culture is indisputable. A marvelous artifact it surely is, as Cady claims, but its quality as a work of literary realism must be measured against similar works by European masters, Flaubert and Balzac and Zola. American critics have preferred to avoid such tasks of measurement because they are accustomed to reserve for our nineteenth-century writers a special generosity of judgment. And Howells' critics are peculiarly generous.

*Lapham* is not a novel of the highest order because it does not achieve a coalescence of image and idea. In spite of extraordinary skills of invention, Howells never made a fiction in which there is an absorbing fusion and interplay of figure and theme. His themes are obscure but not, as Mencken thought, hollow. The speech is always plain but invariably unclear not because Howells was uninspired but because he was unconvinced by the system of ideas to which presumably he had given his full assent. Balzac, for example, really believed that Napoleon had seized on a prime truth of moral life: tyrants impose their wills on civilization and shape it to suit their tastes. Taking Napoleon as his model, portraying the uses of tyranny, of sheer selfishness, in the daily lives of people whatever their station or calling, Balzac sought to make himself an emperor of letters. Zola's art—I compress into one sentence a vast enterprise—stylized his desire to test some key propositions in the new physical, social, and biological sciences. And Flaubert, who knew that the duty of imagination is to appear guileless but to be above all artful, naturally chose those details of passion and politics, of legend and history, which substantiated his views on the nature of Being: existence, a disease which foolish people think can be cured, turns wise men and women into martyrs who accept with grace the only certain balm, death. Howells, who pegged his art to an ideology of the heart, wrote no naturalistic or realistic or scientific novels. He wrote "realitistic" novels: he struggled to prove that his countrymen were heirs to an American constitution strong enough to sustain a healthy and selfless national life, heartening enough to inspire and shape any honest writer's art.

But because he was a very intelligent man, he never quite believed in the future of his own illusions. Indeed mind and myth were in permanent conflict. The public person, the man who had come from an Ohio boyhood to the first Presidency of the Academy, had started as a printer's devil, self-taught in languages and literature, and ended with offers of professorships in literature at Union College, at Johns Hopkins and Yale and Harvard. From *My Year in a Log Cabin* to *The Rise of Silas Lapham,* this Horatio Alger of American letters fashioned a career far more substantial than any one of his plots. And although the career itself was no illusion, what principles of social or moral order did it embody?

It is this question, rooted deep in his own life, he hoped to resolve in his work. The more closely we study the rise of William Dean Howells, the more obvious it is that the man, unlike the character, Silas, could not decide where to live or what to live for. I introduce this echo of *Walden* because I suspect that Howells, despite the year in the log cabin, throughout his life was obsessed by Thoreau's questions. We know that he was plagued by episodes of personal stress, of distress seeing the sorrows of friends and countrymen whose American virtue should have been rewarded but was instead punished. Knowing, it is now fair to say, that Howells was periodically distraught because he could neither accept Thoreau's admonitions nor assent to Alger's creed, we are led back to *Lapham.* There, no single house, no cluster of homes symbolize the drama as a whole. What is symbolized is Howells' own obsession. For this homely Midwestern boy had made an elegant Eastern marriage to Elinor Mead, sister of a leading partner in the chic architectural firm of McKim, Mead and White, itself famed for having established the fashion of grandeur along Fifth Avenue and elsewhere in New York City. In 1877, seven years before *Lapham* appeared, Howells' brother-in-law built him a house outside Boston, in Belmont, about which Henry James's father said he had never seen a place that "took my fancy more captive."

In Howells' own fancy, it was merely another in a succession of dwelling places in which he never felt thoroughly at home. Doubtless there are deep reasons why Howells lived in almost permanent discomfort, but these are still unknown. More visible clues to the state of his mind, and to the structural problems of *Lapham,* are available in his thoughts on that master-builder, Thoreau, whom the young Howells on his first Eastern visit had come to see and to "revere." Although it was Thoreau's views on the Abolitionist John Brown that Howells particularly prized, what stayed with him was Thoreau's "clear . . . vision of the falsity and folly of society." Deriving from this vision a permanent lesson both in morals and mathematics, Howells learned to compute the cost of a house according to Thoreau's arithmetic. Its cost, said Thoreau in *Walden,* the cost of anything, is "the amount of what I will call life which is required to be exchanged for it, immediately or in the long run." Although Silas decided that the cost of his house demanded life in amounts he was not prepared to pay, Howells himself was unable to resist doing precisely what Thoreau condemned: he built "for this world a family mansion and for the next a family tomb." Precisely because the official, public person was unable either to condemn or to cherish the house of national culture, the private man, the artist, was unable to build a literary work tight from subcellar to attic. "When I consider how our houses are built and paid for," said Thoreau, unremitting in contempt, "I wonder that the floor does not give way under the visitor."

For many years visitors, wondering how *Lapham* is built, have miscalculated the price Howells paid for its most pleasing adornments. And they have tried to jack up a floor that continues to give way. Only when critics stop trying to justify his art, stop trying to find some figure of speech which presides over and distinguishes the novel as a whole—only then will his readers learn why he is a man of extraordinary worth. In itself *Lapham* is a disjointed novel because it labors to present, at once, those two contradictory lines of action which Thoreau selected for praise and blame. Because most men hope to build mansions and tombs, he said, "the best works of art are the expression of man's struggle to free himself" from this general taste for monuments. The chief effect of American writing, however, is to sanctify such monumentally bad taste: American art strives "merely to make this low state comfortable." The first line culminates in Silas' heroism; the second in the merger of Tom and Penelope, that triumphant marriage of culture and cash. And the novel itself reveals Howells to us as a man determined to exploit Thoreau's symbol in behalf of a system to which he devoted all his art but only half his heart.

Because Howells sought both to discredit and to certify the national taste for mansions, an adoring audience "hung on every issue of the splendid and fortunate magazine," *Century,* in which *The Rise of Silas Lapham* (Silas Needham, he was called then) was first serialized. For Howells' dual-mindedness mirrored a conflict of consciousness inherent in society at large during a period when most Americans realized that their way of national life contradicted the national ideology. Today, we seldom dream of utopia. And we no longer require the kind of solace, the comfort, Howells felt impelled to offer. Reading about the activities of Bernard Goldfine or Billie Sol Estes, about tampering and fixing, we do not despair because such behavior and such men seem to represent a failure of the American Dream. Rather we recall that our literature long ago imagined that another kind of choice was available to a similar sort of man. And we re-read Howells' novel in order to remind ourselves of Silas' ill-informed but radical inquiry into the virtues of responsibility at a time when willfulness, immeasurably better-paid then than now, was full-fledged among self-made men of American business. What people everywhere continue to require each day is the example of Silas' choice. (pp. 368-72)

The case of Silas Lapham remains open because Silas, himself a figure of the first order, engages a moral issue of abiding concern among us. But *The Rise of Silas Lapham* continues to resist neglect mainly because Howells, inspirited by what Kazin called a "shy moral splendor," continues to evade oblivion. Not the other way around. (p. 372)

*William Wasserstrom, "Howells' Mansion and Thoreau's Cabin," in* College English, *Vol. 26, No. 5, February, 1965, pp. 366-72.*

## Robert Lee Hough    (essay date 1965)

[*In the following excerpt, Hough discusses the strengths and weaknesses of Howells's antiromantic approach in* The Rise of Silas Lapham.]

It is often difficult today, when the battle for realism seems so assuredly won, to appreciate the position that romantic fiction held in America in the late nineteenth century. One gains some idea of its public favor by looking at the list of best-selling novels for some of the years of the controversy. In 1884 Robert Louis Stevenson's *Treasure Island* was the year's best seller; in 1886 Frances Hodgson Burnett's *Little Lord Fauntleroy* and H. Rider Haggard's *King Solomon's Mines* were the two leading sellers, and Haggard repeated his triumph in 1887 with *She: A History of Adventure.*

Moreover, one gains a real appreciation of the conflict between romance and realism by looking at the periodicals of the time, which were often filled with charge and counter-charge. On one side were the defenders of the older idealistic-romantic tradition—men like Stevenson, Haggard, F. Marion Crawford, and Andrew Lang. Their attack on realism was many-pronged, but basically it came down to a question of purpose. Literature, these men felt, was to entertain, to refresh, and to instruct, and it did this best, not by giving a photographic picture of life, but by taking the reader out of the real world and placing him in an imaginary one where love and adventure and morality could all be intensified. Literature provided escape, and the romantic genre best lifted man out of his workaday world and gave him glimpses of eternal truth.

Howells objected to such a theory because it contaminated so easily. He agreed with most romantic writers that the finest effect of literature was ethical, not aesthetic, and felt that Hawthorne was one of the finest novelists that America had ever produced. But most romantic writers, Howells found, were not really interested in morality at all; they were interested in effect, in "bouncing" the reader, in "awakening at all cost . . . vivid and violent emotions, which [supposedly] do credit to the invention and originality of the writer." In this way romantic fiction was actually immoral. In *Criticism and Fiction,* Howells wrote:

> Romantic novels hurt because they are not true—not because they are malevolent, but because they are idle lies about human nature and the social fabric, which it behooves us to know and to understand, that we may deal justly with ourselves and with one another.

This concept of literary truth was central to Howells' beliefs. What he wanted literature to become was a kind of artistic mirror by which men saw and understood something about themselves and their environment; this created a more vital, more significant literature than could ever be created by writers who dealt with pirates and princes and "moral pap," as Louisa May Alcott once called romantic novels. What Howells did, in effect, was to expand the concept of what was "moral" to include the true, the probable. This tack, of course, was the one taken by early American authors to combat the Puritan charge that the novel was simply a pack of lies, but Howells buttressed his argument more pragmatically than did Mrs. Rowson. If something was importantly true, it could not be immoral because it informed man on something that he should know. He maintained that:

> We must ask ourselves before we ask anything else, Is it [the novel] true?—true to the motives, the impulses, the principles that shape the life of actual men and women? This truth, which nec-

essarily includes the highest morality and the highest artistry—this truth given, the book cannot be wicked and cannot be weak. . . .

With this statement, with this theory, Howells provided the critical rationale for Stephen Crane's *Maggie: A Girl of the Streets,* Frank Norris's *McTeague,* and Theodore Dreiser's *Sister Carrie;* he swung open the gates to the twentieth century.

Perhaps the best way to begin a study of **The Rise of Silas Lapham** is to consider it as an antiromance. The story concerns a common man become millionaire, a massive, middle-aged Vermont farmer whose father, forty years before, had discovered a mineral paint mine and thus provided the opportunity which his son's energy and resourcefulness have turned into wealth and a paint company in Boston. The skillful opening chapter, in which Silas is interviewed for the "Solid Men of Boston" series, gives a clear-cut exposition of his qualities: he is vulgar, bragging, and sentimental, yet along with these qualities he has a self-respect, an integrity, and kindness that are endearing. As the chapter ends, Silas sends the reporter's young bride a complete set of his best-grade paint. What an "old fool," the cynical reporter says; "What a good man," the girl exclaims, and this contrast sums up and projects Silas's character in the novel.

His goodness, of course, triumphs, and the book is Howells' supreme eulogy to the integrity of the common man. But Howells was determined that Silas should not be the conventional hero. He wanted a true-to-life, believable American man, and he insisted on Silas' "grayness." In several scenes Lapham is crude and pathetic in his ignorance of the social gap that exists between Lumberville, Vermont, and Boston, Massachusetts. In the scene following the Coreys' dinner party for the Laphams, for example, a party at which Silas becomes drunk and eventually patronizing to Back Bay society, Silas realizes how he must have appeared and compounds his error. "Will you tell your father," he gasps out to young Tom Corey, "I don't want him to notice me if we ever meet [again]?" The same treatment, though subdued, is accorded Silas' wife, Persis, his two daughters, Penelope and Irene, the young lover, Tom Corey, and Tom's parents, Mr. and Mrs. Bromfield Corey. These characters have admirable traits, but they are meant to resemble real people and thus they all have their foibles and weaknesses. Howells does not gild the lily; in fact the most frequent contemporary criticism of the novel was that the Laphams were too common. They were the kind of people, a critic wrote, that one avoided in real life. Howells was always pleased by this kind of recognition of the reality of his characters. He was once told that he seemed interested only in the real and was asked when he was going to create an Ideal Woman. Howells replied happily that he was waiting for the Almighty to begin.

The title of the book suggests the anti-Horatio Alger nature of the main plot. Silas' rise is a moral one and it is this rise that causes his financial ruin. Howells is careful to keep the paradox before the reader: Silas rises as he falls, he is saved morally as he is doomed financially. Actually Silas has three chances to recoup his fortune. He can re-establish himself by selling his now completely devalued Western property either to the rascally Englishmen or to the slippery Rogers, or he can take in the innocent New Yorker who is willing to put money in the paint company without knowing of the ruinous West Virginia competition. Though tempted almost beyond endurance (Silas wrestles with temptation as Jacob wrestled with the angel), he rejects each chance. He has accidentally burned down his new Beacon Street home, the symbol of his social rise; now he deliberately refuses the money which would allow him to maintain his financial position. In a muted variation of the opening scene, Howells closes the book with a conversation between Reverend Sewell and Silas on the farmstead in Vermont, where the Laphams have come back to live. Here Howells makes no romantic concessions; Sewell finds Silas more countrified than ever, even "rather shabby and slovenly in dress." Though quieter, Silas still brags in the old way, but now there is some moral justification for his pride. "One thing he could say: he had been no man's enemy but his own: every dollar, every cent had gone to pay his debts; he had come out with clean hands." Sewell, who realizes what his fortune and pride in being a self-made man have meant to Lapham, asks him if he has any regrets. Silas says, "I don't know as I should always say it paid; but if I done it, and the thing was to do over again, right in the same way, I guess I should have to do it." It is sad but true, Howells comments in his own person, that the price of civilization is nothing less than that our manners and customs count more in life than our qualities.

Howells' antiromantic feelings are most clearly evident in the secondary strand of action, the Irene-Pen-Tom triangle. Here, in plot and in phrase, Howells re-echoes the dangers of romantic sentiment that he had pointed out in *Criticism and Fiction.* Irene, the younger Lapham girl, falls deeply in love with Tom Corey, and Silas and Persis suppose the affection returned because of Tom's frequent visits to the house. In reality, however, Tom is in love with Penelope, the older sister, and when he reveals this fact, everyone is thunderstruck. Pen, crushed for her sister and guilt-stricken because she feels she may have done something to win him away from Irene, refuses to listen to Tom and sends him away. Up to this point the plot suggests that of a typical romantic novel of the time, one which Howells calls *Tears, Idle Tears* (from Tennyson's poem) and inserts into the conversation at the Coreys' dinner party. There, after Miss Kingsbury has expressed tentative approval of the "wildly satisfying" self-sacrifice of the hero and heroine, the antiromantics take over. Nanny Corey renames the book, *Slop, Silly Slop,* and Reverend Sewell calls such novels "psychical suicide." "The novelists," he explains, "might be the greatest possible help to us if they painted life as it is, and human feelings in their true proportion and relation, but for the most part they have been and are altogether noxious." Later, when the Laphams come to him for advice, the Reverend gets the bit in his teeth:

> We are all blinded, we are all weakened by a false ideal of self-sacrifice. . . . I don't know where this false ideal comes from, unless it comes from the novels that befool and debauch almost every intelligence in some degree. . . . Your daughter believes, in spite of her common sense, that she ought to make herself and the man who loves her unhappy, in order to assure the life-long wretchedness of her sister, whom he doesn't love, simply because her sister saw him and fancied him first. And I'm sorry to say that ninety-nine young people out of a hundred . . . would consider that noble and beautiful and heroic; whereas you know at the bottom of your hearts that it would be foolish and cruel and revolting. You know what marriage is! And what it must be without love on both sides.

Howells knew that self-sacrifice proceeded from romantic pride and egomania and was doubly dangerous because its springs were hidden under conviction of nobility. He was fascinated by its emotional hold on people and by its literary possibilities; in *Letters Home, Indian Summer,* and *The Minister's Charge,* as well as in *The Rise of Silas Lapham,* he deals with virtually the same plot: a triangle in which one member considers sacrificing herself. Pen comments on the silliness of *Tears, Idle Tears,* but when faced with the same situation in her own life she is unable to shake off the tenacity of the ideal. Eventually, of course, she accepts Tom, but only because her love proves stronger than her other feelings. Even Mrs. Sewell takes a sentimental view of the situation and feels contempt for Pen because of the misery she has caused Irene, and her shocked husband is able to wring only a partial retraction from her.

The weaknesses of the book too, at least in part, stem from Howells' literary philosophy. The big "bow-wow," he said, anyone can do; all you have to know is the trick of the thing. But the little "bow-wow," that was something different, that required consummate skill, and Howells was forever trying to bring it off. Howells' insistence on the average, the commonplace, the usual gives *The Rise of Silas Lapham* its realism, but it also gives it an evenness that keeps the novel from rising to heights. Howells' dislike of the melodramatic or sensational often undercuts the legitimately dramatic. There is, for example, no highly charged, "big" scene in the novel though Howells had opportunities both in Silas' story and the love plot. The longer scenes all tend to be expository, such as the opening interview, or comic, such as the Coreys' dinner party. The genuinely dramatic moments are rendered in short scenes or in narration. Tom's revelation of his love for Pen, for instance, is given in four pages, and the awful significance of his avowal—the fact that everyone has supposed him in love with Irene—is not explained to him until forty pages later, where in another scene of four pages Pen discloses the reason for her reaction. Narratively, there is no reason that the two events could not go together, and if handled properly, they might form a highly effective emotional scene. But Howells chooses to split them, and it is this kind of fragmenting of sensation which gives the book its levelness and which has caused some later realists to agree with Frank Norris that Howells' brand of realism is generally as exciting as "a cup of tea" or "a walk around the block."

There is no doubt that the last fourth of the book is less successful than the earlier portions, and though on the whole Howells is extremely skillful in his plotting, there is a general slackening of pace in the last six or seven chapters. George Arms, one of Howells' best critics, attributes the letdown to the author's inability to maintain his comic tone. "Howells," he says [see excerpt dated 1949], "becomes too preoccupied with his characters as potentially tragic figures." This is true, but as Arms suggests without elaborating, the matter is more complex than this. Howells apparently decided, for sound artistic reasons, that the two strands of the plot should end together, but that Lapham's rise-fall should occupy the major part of the last one hundred pages. Accordingly, all the major complications of the love story are unraveled by Chapter 19 and action almost ceases in this part of the story, with Pen unable to make up her mind whether to accept or reject Tom. Thus the stage is clear for Silas, and here the author's low-key realism fails him. Howells decided against building toward a climactic financial collapse which might have been dramatically effective but apparently was not sufficiently probable. Instead Lapham's ruin becomes a slow disintegration with his speculation in stocks, his glutting of the paint market, his dealings with Rogers, the destruction of the Beacon Street house, and the competition from the West Virginia company all combining to bring him down. Though these matters are simplified by Howells, they clog the momentum of the action and the fact that Howells is forced to narrate many of the business involvements and to deal with them so summarily robs the story of its earlier density.

The long delay also undermines the earlier character portrait of Pen, who is forced to wait in the wings so long that the reader begins to wonder about her. Before Tom's proposal, she is shown to be the most perceptive of the Laphams and in some ways the most independent and mature. But after Tom's offer, because Howells needs the stage for the financial story, Pen simply wrings her hands and mopes in her room. Her willy-nilly attitude and her inability to decide in the only rational way possible make her seem like quite another girl. Paradoxically, Howells' realism for Silas results in a kind of unreality for Penelope.

Thus, in both its weaknesses and strengths, ***The Rise of Silas Lapham*** reveals a moral or literary attack on the romance, but were the book no more than this, it would have long since been relegated to grandmother's trunk in the attic. That it is more is due, in the first place, to Howells' craftsmanship. Though there are lapses, the book, on the whole, is masterfully put together. Signposts lead somewhere; details anticipate situations. Bartley Hubbard's notice of the pretty girl in Lapham's anteroom and his comment that she is the kind of a girl that wives do not like to see in their husbands' offices has significance later in the novel. So does the early mention of Silas' dabbling in stocks, the Persis Brand, and Tom's interest in the foreign distribution of Lapham's paint. The point of view is skillfully handled. Howells is almost always where he should be: in Silas' mind during the comic ordeal of the dinner party, in Tom's mind for the Back Bay judgment on Lapham's behavior, in Mrs. Corey's mind for the Brahmin reaction to Tom and Pen's marriage. (pp. 75-82)

Howells' craftsmanship is perhaps best displayed in his handling of scene. One is surprised on examining the novel

*Cartoon captioned "Men of the Day—W. D. Howells: Demonstrator of the American Girl" in the 1 May 1886 issue of* Tid-Bits.

to find how much of the story is told in dialogue, particularly in the first three-fourths of the book. One chapter after another is simply a series of scenes, occurring usually between two people (Howells felt that all really dramatic encounters occurred between two people) and serving both to explore character and advance the action without the author's narrative intervention. Howells was much impressed by James's "scenic method," partly, perhaps, because it allowed such scope for his own gift of recording conversation. Here Howells combines his own word sense and his ear for dialect to run the range from the blunt Vermont twang of the Laphams to the proper Bostonian accents of Bromfield Corey. As with all good dialogue, one can visualize the characters from it. Silas says:

> Well, then, the fellow set down and told me, "You've got a paint here," says he, "that's going to drive every other mineral paint out of the market. Why," says he, "it'll drive 'em right into the Back Bay!" . . . Then he went into a lot of particulars, and I begun to think he was drawing a long-bow . . . young chap, and pretty easy; but every word he said was gospel. Well, I ain't a-going to brag up my paint. . . .

As befits an author who wrote over twenty light farces in addition to his novels, Howells uses his dialogue to produce most of the droll, witty humor of the book. Bromfield Corey, who is a dilettante and an amateur painter, tells his son Tom, who wishes to join Lapham's paint firm:

> It's a consolation to think that while I've been spending and enjoying, I've been preparing the noblest future for you—a future of industry and self-reliance. You never could draw, but this scheme of going into the mineral-paint business shows that you have inherited something of my feeling for color.

Howells' ability in handling scene goes beyond a talent for dialogue; it has to do with the motivation of character, the revealing of the right fact at the right time, and the relationship between one scene and another. In many ways the novel is a story of social gaps, and one can gain some appreciation of Howells' talent by studying the alternation of scenes that occur in the Corey and Lapham houses at various times throughout the novel.

Beyond these aspects of Howells' technical skill, the book has the *sine qua non* of realistic fiction: the texture of life. This quality is cumulative; it comes to the reader through detail, speech, incident, and characterization. At the end most readers feel that they can accept Howells' characters as "real" people and that the author is seriously interested in what happens to real people. Howells may be weak in places, but he does not cheat. In fact, if Howells, in a few passages, seems to us overly concerned about the morality of literature, it reveals that we have lost something of the idealism and high purpose that he held for fiction. In America, Bromfield Corey says, all civilization comes through literature:

> A Greek got his civilization by talking and looking, and in some measure a Parisian may still do it. But we, who live remote from history and monuments, we must read or we must barbarize.

The great tragedy, Howells says in *Criticism and Fiction,* comes when one reads and barbarizes.

In the final accounting, *The Rise of Silas Lapham* has not proven itself a classic. It is not alive today in the same way that *Huckleberry Finn* and *The Red Badge of Courage* are. Nonetheless, in its artistry, its quality of "felt" life, and in its theme, which is nothing less than the Biblical question, "What shall it profit a man, if he shall gain the whole world, and lose his own soul," it is a novel that a writer and a literature can take pride in. And if the book does fall short of total greatness, its failure is partly due to the goal that Howells set for himself. In the book Charles Bellingham calls for the novel of the commonplace. He says:

> The commonplace is just that light, impalpable, aerial essence which [writers] have never got into their confounded books yet. The novelist who could interpret the common feelings of commonplace people would have the answer to "the riddle of the painful earth" on his tongue.

Howells was willing to settle for nothing else. (pp. 83-5)

> *Robert Lee Hough, "William Dean Howells,*
> *'The Rise of Silas Lapham'," in* The American

Novel: From James Fenimore Cooper to William Faulkner, *edited by Wallace Stegner, Basic Books, Inc., Publishers, 1965, pp. 73-85.*

## Margaret Mead, Norman Holmes Pearson, and Lyman Bryson (essay date 1966)

[*An American anthropologist and essayist, Mead helped popularize the field of anthropology through her stylistically accessible writings on human sexuality, gender relationships, and American and South Pacific cultures. Her anthropological studies were important for their multidisciplinary approach and for stressing the role of cultural shaping of individuals over biological determinism, and her writings on the role of women in society gained her the sobriquet "a general in the army of feminism." Pearson is an American critic and educator; Bryson is an American educator, poet, and critic who has written extensively on education. In the following excerpt, the three critics discuss* The Rise of Silas Lapham *in relation to the evolution of American culture.*]

BRYSON: I was surprised in rereading **The Rise of Silas Lapham** to discover that, although the book is now almost seventy years old and was written to be contemporary history, it is dated so little.

MEAD: It's extraordinarily modern. And at the same time, it gives me the sense of the world that my grandmother lived in, because Howells was her favorite novelist.

PEARSON: That's one of the extraordinary things about the novel that struck me as well: it's not only a history of a time, a period of our life at the emergence of modern America, but it's a pattern of life and a problem of life that seems to be still with us. We haven't changed as much, I think, as we sometimes like to imagine we have; and it's a good thing for all of us to go back in time to see how much like our grandmothers and grandfathers we actually are. It's a humbling experience, I find, for myself.

BRYSON: Being a grandfather myself, I don't feel that the world has changed very much in my lifetime. As a matter of fact, I'm very much amused that the younger generation is always discovering old things and thinking that they couldn't have existed when you were young.

MEAD: The thing that made me almost jump out of my chair, though, was a conversation in the book between the mother and the daughter, when they were facing exactly the same thing that I've been describing as very post-World War II.

BRYSON: What was that?

MEAD: " 'Well, we must stand it anyway,' says Mrs. Lapham, with a grim, antique Yankee submission." (Now we just call it a Puritan sense of moral duty, you know.) " 'Oh, yes, we've got to stand it,' said Penelope, with a quaint, modern American fatalism." Now, what we'd say today is that the older generation is still appealing to morals, the younger generation to necessity; but it's the same conflict, just slightly different words.

BRYSON: The "ought's" have gone out, but the "have to's" are still there. Is that right?

MEAD: The "ought" is still in the parents and the "have to" in the children today.

BRYSON: Well, what's the machinery of this? How did Howells undertake to tell the story of his own time? You know, he was not only a very conscious craftsman, but a thinker. He thought of himself as depicting American life as it really was.

PEARSON: I think he placed his story, Mr. Bryson, at the very center of concern. That is, how was man, as an individual, to act in what we would call "this new industrial age"? What were the ethical problems concerned with it? How was his desire—that is, I mean Silas Lapham's desire—to improve the lot of himself and his children to be squared with his methods for acquiring the free capital that is so essentially a part of our American scheme of life, and, along with it, the idealism that is always a part of American life? Because Americans are idealists, even when for a moment they forget it, just as Silas Lapham so often forgot it.

BRYSON: Typically American, I should say, is the fact, that American artists (at least they used to do this; perhaps they don't any more) believed that a man could be a businessman and still be an idealist, which is a notion that Europeans don't find very easy to understand.

MEAD: And it's beautifully stated here, really, in this story of a man who marries the girl who'd been his schoolteacher and who, as was so often the case, is slightly more educated than he is; and then he discovers the paint on his old farm and builds up the paint with another man's money; then the other man hasn't any imagination and has to be squeezed out; and then he "rises" and paints his paint all over the landscape.

BRYSON: So that the first rise is making money out of paint?

MEAD: The first rise is making money out of paint, which is his life's blood. And that's said over and over again; you have to care about the thing you're making your money out of with real idealism, or it won't work. I think he does that very convincingly, don't you?

PEARSON: Beautifully and very effectively, from the American point of view. Because the American loves business, not to the exclusion of other things, but as a full and accepted part of his life. And this is something that very few of our novelists and very few non-American novelists have ever attempted.

BRYSON: Almost no novelists outside of a few Americans, and far too few of them, Mr. Pearson, have ever depicted a businessman as having any right to care about his business.

MEAD: And that, of course, is one of the pretty things that's dramatized here in the story of Lapham, when he is a successful man in Boston, ready to build a house on the "right" street, or the street that's *going* to be the right one (that's very nicely done, I think, too—not the old right street, but the new right street). Then there's the young son of a dilettante, wanting to live in Rome and living on an income, who is a grandson of a businessman. And you get the renaissance of the old business sense coming back.

PEARSON: And may I mention, too, the ending of **The Rise of Silas Lapham,** where the business is taken over by a younger generation of West Virginians, and where Howells says, "They were young fellows and country persons, like Lapham, by origin." This is a story that continues in America. The question is, can we learn from the past, our own past?

BRYSON: **The Rise of Silas Lapham** involves a fall, too, because Silas Lapham not only lost his money, but came very close to losing his character—at least, you have the fear that he's going to lose his character.

MEAD: And today do you think this would be called **The Rise of Silas Lapham,** or would it have to be called *The Rise and Fall of Silas Lapham?* Because he goes down materially: he loses his money, his house burns down, he has to move back to the country, and his paint business goes to people who've got natural gas next door. Now that really is a pretty sad story, isn't it? But he keeps his character.

PEARSON: The mere fact that you can ask whether we would call it something different today is the very problem that existed in Howells' own day and made the novel possible for his time and, it seems to me, makes it possible for our own.

BRYSON: Is he saying, Mr. Pearson, that the real rise of Silas Lapham was not when the country boy married the schoolteacher and borrowed the money and squeezed out his partner and got control of the paint business, but when, under the pressure of misfortune and some mistakes, he lost his money, but kept his honesty? Is that the real rise, then?

PEARSON: He kept two things: his own integrity, which had gone into a kind of shadow, and—I think this was very important for Howells—he learned that no man can live alone. He had his responsibility to his family; he had a responsibility to the man he had harmed in the past; and he had a responsibility to people he had never even met, whom he could trick without any greater effort than a little sophistry in ethics, and thereby recover all that he had lost.

BRYSON: He didn't do it.

PEARSON: But he could have, with the Englishmen who wanted to buy the land and to whom he refused to sell. This is what you would call later a social, in addition to a personal, ethic.

MEAD: And the fascinating thing, of course, is that these were Englishmen who were wiser and shrewder than we were, the same notion you still get today that the European or the Englishman can always pull the wool over our eyes. You have a double-take here: this homespun American integrity is set against European business, which is dramatized as totally evil, whereas American business has all this idealism in it.

BRYSON: Of course, we think of European business as "totally evil" because, generally speaking, European writers make it so.

MEAD: Exactly! Because they isolate business from the other aspects of life more than we do.

PEARSON: And yet, in a sense, Howells shows the dangers that business can have when it thinks of itself alone—that is, one businessman out for his own gain, with the devil taking the hindmost. (pp. 253-56)

BRYSON: . . . [*Silas Lapham* is] a novel of manners. But what of it as a plot, as a comedy? Is this still a live idea in America?

MEAD: Well, that was another thing that fascinated me. You know there's been a recent book on the movies, comparing our principal plots with the English and French plots that keep recurring. You can speak of them as popular American fables that are deep in our moral consciousness. Now, one of the things that happens in this popular American fable—you find it in popular writing today, too—is that the hero is always really good. He's falsely suspected, you think he's going to fall, you think he's going to do dreadful things, but he doesn't. In the end he turns out to be a hundred per cent good. And that's what we've got here.

BRYSON: What about the heroine?

MEAD: The heroine, too. She's met under very peculiar circumstances, but in the end she's good.

BRYSON: She looks like a toughie and turns out to be really an angel.

MEAD: Yes. The good-bad girl, as we've sometimes called it. Now, this book is just filled with this. You even have a slight episode of the pretty typist in the office. Mr. Lapham is the sort of man who is suspected of being interested in pretty typists; but then, in the end, she turns out to be the daughter of a buddy of his who was killed in the war. You couldn't have a better plot in which virtue triumphs, in which integrity is more important than money, in which human kindness is more important than snobbery, more heavily emphasized. I think that's one reason it was a popular book—because it appealed to some of our very deeply felt American ideals.

PEARSON: Do you think, then, that there's a great difference between this book and Dreiser's *Sister Carrie,* where you can't say there is any optimism in regard to the possibilities of reason triumphing over passion?

MEAD: Yes. I think that Howells is close to the American myth and is not contrapuntal to it to the same extent that Dreiser is.

BRYSON: Are we taking this man merely as social history—"merely" is a bad word here—as social history only? After all, what he tried to do was to write a novel as well as to write the history of his time. Did he write a novel? Is it a novel today? You say it has a familiar plot that we get all the time out of Hollywood, Miss Mead, and the Rinehart people have just put out this new paper edition of it. Could you expect this thing to be read now? Would you tell people to read this book now?

MEAD: Yes, I think they could read it with great enjoyment, because it is so well written.

PEARSON: Well written in the sense of an extraordinary ear that Howells had for people's speech—as a New Englander I can recognize the cadences of it from the page—and because of the craft in arranging it. Just think how skillfully he gives us this popular picture of Silas Lapham at the beginning, where he is being interviewed by a newspaperman, as the typical successful, honest, and certain-of-himself businessman. Now this is rather a trick, in a sense, but we have presented to us the myth that we then have to explore throughout the rest of the book.

BRYSON: By starting out with the newspaper interview and the way in which the newspaper exploits the idea of this successful, honest businessman, is Howells making a little bit of fun of the American attitude toward the businessman?

PEARSON: Why, certainly! Because he's saying that the picture that Bartley Hubbard presents to the public is not the true picture; and the purpose of his novel is to give you the true picture, even if the true picture is in itself partly falsified by the artist's arrangement.

BRYSON: But I was disturbed, Mr. Pearson, by something Miss Mead spoke of before. In the beginning Howells seems to say, "No, this is not the truth about the businessman," he pokes fun at him a little bit. But in the end the virtue of his own hero overcomes even him, and in the latter half of the book Howells is on Lapham's side. Now, which was his real attitude? Or is it just a craftsman's trick on himself?

PEARSON: I would say it's a craftsman's trick on himself and on his audience. Having been presented with Silas Lapham in the opening chapter as an almost perfect person, we then come to know him as one knows friends. And as this happens, bit by bit, we see his uncertainties, we see the way his wife acts on him as his conscience. This symbolic arrangement of a man's conscience as a projection through his wife is very skillfully done. Then at the end we are prepared—or, at least, Howells hopes we are prepared—for the redemption of the man, a redemption that was always possible, a redemption that is sometimes worked out by comic means, but is nonetheless there when it is finished.

MEAD: There's something that I'm not quite certain about: is this all artistry, or did Howells get caught a little bit himself? Didn't he start this novel being a little gayer, a little more satiric? It's almost as if Lapham grew on him and he decided, after all, "There is more in this myth that was presented by the reporter, at the beginning, than I quite recognize myself."

PEARSON: I suspect that you may be right, Miss Mead, at least in part. We might remember, perhaps, the experience of Sinclair Lewis in writing *Babbitt,* which is in the same family of novels about the American businessman. Sinclair Lewis started out making Babbitt foolish; by the time he has finished we become, I think, if we read the book correctly, sympathetic to Babbitt, realizing what goes on within him.

MEAD: So that one starts with the snobbery of treating culture as a mark of class (what kind of books do people read, and how crass are they, and do they know how to sign a letter), and ends with the seduction of the over-intellectualized writer by the character of his hero.

BRYSON: Because, of course, Howells was himself a good person, of integrity, from Ohio; and that veneer of Bostonian culture didn't go too deep in him. He had to reassert his own Puritanism. I'm interested in his attitude toward women. After all, there's a love story in this book.

MEAD: Yes, but you'd hardly know it.

BRYSON: A most charming one at times.

MEAD: And also a love story that would be very difficult for people to accept today—this situation where the young scion of the Boston family is thought to be in love with the pretty, feminine, domestic, brainless younger sister, and is really in love with the older one. No one thought that he could be in love with the older one; she is brainy and not pretty and not domestic. What were you going to say, Mr. Pearson?

PEARSON: I was going to say that I think you're too kind to Penelope Lapham. If I had to criticize the novel, I would say that Penelope was never very convincing to me. In the first place, we talked about snobbery. Remember that she's always at her wittiest when she is making fun of her family and everyone else.

BRYSON: That's because she's defending.

PEARSON: She's defending. Hers is a position that, it seems to me, she never quite resolves in the end. And when they go off to Mexico, you have the feeling that perhaps that's the best place for them to stay.

BRYSON: He doesn't like Penelope.

MEAD: Well, I didn't like her especially, either, because I thought that part of the plot was so extraordinarily overdone—this refusal to marry a man who everybody had thought was in love with your younger sister. He *hadn't* been in love with her.

BRYSON: No, and never said so.

MEAD: He wasn't engaged to her. It almost looked as if Howells was trying to put into this love story a kind of thematic echo of what was going on in Lapham's head, and didn't succeed in doing it. There's a certain amount of contrivance in it.

PEARSON: He obviously gets deeper into Silas Lapham himself than he does into any other character, with the exception of Lapham's wife, Persis. I think those two are worked out pretty well. Bromfield Corey, Tom Corey's father, is witty, urbane, European—we might call him today a kind of Marquand character—but rather thin, rather shallow.

BRYSON: Of course, I think Howells has one disadvantage as a novelist, Mr. Pearson. A man with his marvelous limpidity of style betrays his own faults of structure more than the ponderous and obscure writers do. There are some writers, as you know—I think Dreiser is one of them—who can make all kinds of mistakes in plot and character, but their style is so thick that you're not quite sure whether they've made the mistake or not. Howells had the disadvantage of having an absolutely pellucid style, one of the clearest styles of any novelist we've ever had.

PEARSON: In this particular book, Mr. Bryson, he wrote with extreme economy as well as lucidity; or perhaps we ought to say, in the good novel those two often go hand in hand. Howells used them to describe the life he knew, the life he had lived, with not only the external but the internal drives. And when an author succeeds in conveying that, he has given us something priceless.

MEAD: And even if you do find faults in the structure—where the character doesn't quite come through, where the two girls aren't completely convincing; and also this terrific rush at the end of the book, where everything gets settled in the last forty pages—we can take this not only as a novel, very beautifully written, but as an extraordinarily good picture of the struggle of a commentator on American life at this period, using his own skill and not quite certain, it seems to me, how he's going to come out.

BRYSON: Because, of course, like every other person who is really a child of his age and an artist of considerable magnitude, Howells reflected in himself a lot of the things that he wanted to comment on. And I'm not quite sure that he didn't actually produce here just the kind of plot that on other occasions he himself tried to satirize, which makes it all the better reading. (pp. 258-61)

*Margaret Mead, Norman Holmes Pearson, and Lyman Bryson, "William Dean Howells: 'The Rise of Silas Lapham'," in* Invitation to Learning: English & American Novels, *edited by George D. Crothers, Basic Books, Inc., Publishers, 1966, pp. 252-61.*

## Kermit Vanderbilt   (essay date 1968)

[*In the following excerpt, Vanderbilt analyzes revisions Howells made to the serialized version of* The Rise of Silas Lapham *before book publication, arguing that the revisions reveal Howells's concerns about Boston society during the Gilded Age.*]

During the autumn of 1884 and into the winter months of 1885, Howells was writing hard to keep ahead of the serialized chapters of **The Rise of Silas Lapham** appearing each month in *Century* magazine. Some time during this period he suffered a psychic impasse. In the next decade, after **A Traveler from Altruria** had appeared, Howells recalled that he had felt at the time as though "the bottom dropped out" of his world. He was talking with an acquaintance who shortly afterward reported the conversation in *Harper's Weekly*. **A Traveler from Altruria,** Howells had said, was an attempt to resolve some of his conflicts about American society.

> They made their demand—these questions and problems—when Mr. Howells was writing *Silas Lapham.* His affairs prospering, his work marching as well as heart could wish, suddenly, and

without apparent cause, the status seemed wholly wrong. His own expression, in speaking with me about that time, was, "The bottom dropped out!"

Later commentators on Howells, though aware of a deepening in his concern with social questions in America after *A Modern Instance,* have not speculated at any length on what matters, public and private, may have profoundly upset him. Critics of the 1920s and 1930s generally ignored the question, more bent as they were on making sport of Howells the timid, prissy novelist, the quiet man and captive dupe of the Boston literary giants before whom he bowed in constantly fawning acquiescence. More recently, a better informed and more sophisticated view has had it that Howells was, instead, a disengaged observer during his twenty-year apprenticeship in Boston. In this revised portrait, Howells appears a dispassionate satirist-with-scalpel, coolly dissecting Proper Boston society in the period before and during *Silas Lapham.* Neither of these diverging estimates of Howells as a social critic has lent itself to an inquiry into Howells' apparently anguished soul-searching over the problem of "status"—of social and economic inequality—during the writing of *Silas Lapham.* From both of these opposing critical camps, however, the novel itself has received proper attention and praise for the art with which Howells traced the moral fall and rise of a back-country paint millionaire in postwar Boston. And indeed, there is much here to praise. (pp. 96-7)

But why, then, should Howells while writing this enjoyable novel have felt that the bottom had dropped out of his world because of unresolved problems of American democracy? Perhaps something is present in the novel that has been missed. Perhaps even more, what is *not* present in the novel may be in some ways as important as what does appear. Precisely what were Howells' feelings, for example, toward the newly rich businessman in Boston? Or the older Brahmins? Or the new immigrant laboring classes? And if one finds in Howells' correspondence that he discussed these matters of status in a democracy, how can one determine the precise meanings? A Howells letter to Charles Eliot Norton may be harder to interpret than a letter to Mark Twain. What were his relations to each man—early and late? When was he being ironic, or wearing a mask, and why? "With whom is one really and truly intimate?" Howells once asked Norton. "I am pretty frank, and I seem to say myself out to more than one, now and again, but only in this sort to one, and that sort to another." When the literary scholar has refined and polished the biographical detail, his labors have hardly begun. The way that a writer's life issues in literary creation is, in general, still a mystery; and the mystery is unique in the career of each writer. And it might be added, the conversion of life into art is to some extent unique in each work of an author. Just as his craft may grow and change, moreover, so may his previous attitudes toward morality, art, and society. That is, fifteen years before *Silas Lapham,* Howells was writing about social snobbery in Boston, but he suffered no grievous conflict over what he saw. In fact, he had treated the Boston scene several times in the period immediately preceding *Silas Lapham* without undue harm to his social conscience.

The literary scholar, lost in this welter of contradictory and sometimes intractable biographical data, may liken his task to a version of the quest for the Grail, wherein the knight can free the waters and restore the land if only he ask the right question. Among the materials which may point one to the fruitful question about an author's feelings and intentions is the record of his prior revisions of the work. Here he can be studied in the very process of literary creation. Fortunately, with *The Rise of Silas Lapham,* one can trace a fairly satisfactory history of Howells' conception and composition of the work in the evidence of how he revised the novel. First, he submitted a short prospectus; second, he wrote the serialized version which appeared each month in *Century* magazine; and finally, he revised certain passages for the final copy of the novel as it now stands. The way the novel grew and changed can next be related to certain biographical evidence of the urgency and conflict with which Howells wrote and revised. Because these data are somewhat meager and difficult to interpret does not necessarily mean that one is foolhardy to try to use them.

In considering three of the most important of these revisions, one receives intimations that Howells in Boston was casting worried glances upward on the social ladder (the Proper Bostonian of Back Bay), downward (the immigrant slum-dweller), and alongside (the rising Jew). A fourth matter of revision (an anachronism which Howells refused to change) suggests the conflict between his social aspiration and his defiance of the good people of Boston who were opponents of his literary modernism. Finally, in moving from the synopsis through the main revisions of the serial, one discovers that in the Corey-Lapham "subplot" resides a set of conflicts together with a final resolution which may have been more crucial for Howells than the more celebrated dilemma of his businessman-hero. Taken together, these revisions suggest that *The Rise of Silas Lapham* is a novel ultimately concerned with social eruption in a new Boston, leaderless and morally adrift in the Gilded Age.

In the first installment of *The Rise of Silas Lapham* in the *Century* (November 1884), Silas and Mrs. Lapham are discussing the projected new Back Bay residence which will presumably bring them into the orbit of respectable Boston society:

> [Mrs. Lapham]: "Where is your lot? In the Diphtheria District?"
> [Silas]: "No, it ain't in the Diphtheria District . . . and I guess there's more diphtheria in the name than anything else, anyway."

Howells modified the passage to read in the novel the next year:

> [Mrs. Lapham]: "Where is your lot? They say it's unhealthy over there. . . . "
> [Silas]: "It ain't unhealthy where I've bought . . . , and I guess it's about as healthy on the Back Bay as it is here, anyway."

The revised passage obviously removed the sting of sarcasm from the serial version. Small though it is, why did Howells make the change? Had Back Bay readers of the *Century* been annoyed at Howells' repeating what appears to have become a well-worn gibe at the status issuing, or oozing, from an address on the "New Land" in the "Diphtheria District"? And if they had resented the passage, why should Howells have been concerned? Nothing approaching a complete explanation of Howells' motives for easing his thrust at Back Bay society can ever be set down, but speculation at least can begin.

We shall start with what is known—and it will be necessary to summarize a fair amount of familiar Howells biography from time to time to reinterpret Howells' state of mind. After *A Modern Instance,* he had removed his family to Europe for a year of travel, convalescence, and, for Howells himself, the hard work of a self-supporting writer. (Among other tasks, he completed *A Woman's Reason,* germinating since the late 1870s, and gathered the materials for *Tuscan Cities* which would serve as well his last international novel *Indian Summer.*) When he returned to Boston in late summer of 1883, Howells took up temporary residence in a rented house at 4 Louisburg Square. Then in August of 1884 he bought the house at 302 Beacon Street and became a resident of Back Bay. He wrote to Henry James soon after and described his proud view from the new house:

> The sun goes down over Cambridge with as much apparent interest as if he were a Harvard graduate; possibly he is; and he spreads a glory over the Back Bay that is not to be equalled by the blush of a Boston Independent for such of us Republicans as are going to vote for Blaine. Sometimes I feel it an extraordinary thing that I should have been able to buy a house on Beacon str.

(pp. 99-103)

A far more significant and deeply personal motive may have caused Howells to play down his sarcasm about Back Bay. His daughter Winny, during this crucial time, figured in Howells' anxiety on more counts than her mysteriously failing health. Some years earlier, he had written Charles Eliot Norton that he hoped the play *A Counterfeit Presentment* would bring forth enough proceeds to allow Winny to attend a private school in Boston—a well-known preliminary step necessary to establish a young lady in the proper circles of the Boston social world. Again, when the Howellses made their new home on the water side of Beacon Street, they hoped the prestige address would help their ailing daughter to make her debut in Boston society. The ambition was entertained especially by Mrs. Howells. But the Back Bay investment took a fearful toll from the outset. "I have had a frightful year of work," Howells wrote in March 1885. "I must give my daughter her chance in this dispicable world . . . ," he explained. In addition to making his payments on a $21,000 home, he was also paying to get his son through school and then to college. To cover these mounting expenses, Howells had to rely chiefly on his earnings as a professional writer. Here, then, may have been the strongest reason of all to question, on second thought, the wisdom of belittling the exclusive district from which the Laphams, like the Howellses, were planning to launch their daughters into the company of the sons and daughters of Proper Boston.

A second revision further illuminates Howells' attitude toward Boston in the Gilded Age and also helps to make the reasons for his personal crisis somewhat more knowable. A passage which never reached the pages of the *Century* involved Howells' surprisingly bold allusion to current anarchist violence on the American scene. In February 1885, the editor of the *Century,* Richard Watson Gilder, was reading the proofs of the Corey-Lapham dinner episode. To Gilder's horror, Howells had allowed the Brahmin host, Bromfield Corey, to raise the terrifying spectre of anarchist revolution on Beacon Street. What restraint, Corey wryly asks, has kept the poor laborers of Boston from coming out of their stifling slums in summer with dynamite to blow up the spacious mansions standing empty on Beacon Street while their owners are away for the season at their Newports and Saratogas? Howells was here plagiarizing from two passages he had previously written in concern over this threat to the safety of well-to-do Americans. Isabel and Basil March, wandering through the oppressive heat of New York in *Their Wedding Journey,*

> morbidly wondered what that day's murder would be, and in what swarming tenement-house, or den of the assassin streets by the riversides,—if indeed it did not befall in some such high, close-shuttered, handsome dwelling as those they passed, in whose twilight it would be so easy to strike down the master and leave him, undiscovered and unmourned by the family ignorantly absent at the mountains or the seaside.

This possibility of burglary and murder became far more real to Howells shortly after he had moved into Back Bay. "There are miles of empty houses all round me," he wrote to his father in late summer of 1884. "And how unequally things are divided in this world. While these beautiful, airy, wholesome houses are uninhabited, thousands upon thousands of poor creatures are stifling in wretched barracks in the city here, whole families in one room. I wonder that men are so patient with society as they are."

But Howells had added something new this third time— the reminder that American laborers had grown less patient in recent years. The dread word was "dynamite." Gilder and publisher Roswell Smith panicked. Both men wrote letters to Howells imploring him to revise the passage. Howells complied, whether with some reluctance or not we do not know. The conversation that appears in serial and novel versions goes like this (Bromfield Corey is speaking):

> "If I were a poor man, with a sick child pining in some garret or cellar at the North End, I should break into one of [those close-shuttered, handsome, brutally insensible houses], and camp out on the grand piano."
>
> "Surely, Bromfield," said his wife, "you don't consider what havoc such people would make with the furniture of a nice house."
>
> "That is true," answered Corey, with meek conviction. "I never thought of that."

This second instance of a bold first writing again changing to rather insipid tameness leads us further toward a definition of Howells' private ordeal during these months. How deeply was Howells troubled by this second aspect of status in the literally explosive period before and during *Silas Lapham,* when labor strikes were already numbering into the hundreds each year?

Howells' attitudes toward the status of the workingman in America, which involve also his opinions about race, can be traced from his early years in Ohio, a generally unhappy boyhood, as Professor Cady has ably shown in his biography. The grandfather, Joseph Howells, had engendered in his family a sense of their Welsh superiority to other mill hands in Steubenville. Howells later made sport of his Welsh "pedigree," inherited from the "royal blood" of the ninth-century Hywel Dha, but the fact was important enough for him to repeat with undisguised pleasure. The father, William Cooper Howells, was a socially respectable printer and a Whig, a member of the "employing class." True, for a brief period at Eureka Mills he was a utopian—to the despair of his comfort- and status-conscious wife—but a utopian of a rather exclusive brand. What he mainly passed on to his son William Dean was not a practical commitment to an egalitarian society. "My convictions were all democratic," Howells recalled many years later, "but at heart I am afraid I was a snob. . . . " Olov W. Fryckstedt notes that Howells, arriving in Europe as Lincoln's consul to Venice, was first alarmed at the poverty that resulted from a caste-ridden aristocracy, but presently discovered it to be "picturesque." Nor did the abolitionist idealism of his youth dispose Howells, after the war, to welcome the new influx of urban laborers. His early *Atlantic* sketches and reviews, for all their irony, do not disguise his concern over the numbers of Chinese, Irish, and free Negroes on the national scene. (pp. 104-07)

So one has his work cut out in trying to make Howells into a democratic champion of the village commoner and a satirical "observer" of cultivated Boston society. Indeed, a stronger case can perhaps be made for Howells' disengagement from Western "democracy" than from Boston aristocracy. When he came to Boston to live after the Civil War, Howells was, in spirit, virtually an insider, with four years of marriage to a daughter of New England as practical apprenticeship. Up to then, he had never been closely identified for an extended period, intellectually or socially, with any group. The Boston and Cambridge community, not Ohio, was the logical home for the maturing Howells. He was received with civility by the most revered of the elder Brahmins, and greeted with affectionate cordiality and invaluable help by Lowell, Norton, and Fields. For the first time in his life, Howells could enjoy a stimulating intellectual and social milieu. In his earliest months there, he admitted to "an undercurrent of homesickness" after a three-day holiday by the sea. He was homesick not for the Western village but for his new home in Cambridge. "I don't believe that when I am rich as I one day intend to be," he wrote Norton, "I shall ever leave Cambridge at all." (p. 109)

During his rise to a position among the leading citizens of Boston and Cambridge, Howells was quite aware, however, that the peerage had come through hard work rather than inheritance. The feelings of a natural aristocrat were not identical to those of the hereditary aristocrat. Lowell prodded Howells for appearing to be constantly on the alert for a snub from the first families. Howells' sensitive awareness that he had not been permitted by birth to feel a secure identity inside the closed circle of Boston "cousinships" stands revealed in a passage of *Silas Lapham.* He described the Corey ladies pondering their selection of dinner guests from among "one of the most comprehensive of those cousinships which form the admiration and terror of the adventurer in Boston society." Even while he lightly satirized an undemocratic exclusiveness based on the accident of birth, Howells would not have destroyed these distinctions which characterize a stable, stratified society. For although a fluid society is necessary to allow a family to rise, some semblance of a stratified division of classes must be maintained to make the rise meaningful—and the debut of one's own daughter possible.

The leveling power of dynamite could not have been comfortably entertained by Howells. Indeed, one can see in the Lapham-Corey dinner conversation an extremely revealing attitude toward social revolution. Silas the rising man in America, in his concern over the safety of his hard-won property holdings, has become even more conservative than the aristocratic Corey, who has taken his own inheritance for granted. During the dinner-table talk about labor discontent, Howells gives us Silas's reassuring thoughts about the essential conservatism of the laboring classes, apparently without heavy irony.

> Lapham wanted to speak up and say that he had been there himself, and knew how such a man felt. He wanted to tell them that generally a poor man was satisfied if he could make both ends meet; that he didn't envy anyone his good luck, if he had earned it, so long as he wasn't running under himself.

(pp. 110-11)

Howells' developing conflict over the problem of status in an increasingly fluid and complex American society took still a third direction. The serialized version includes references to newly rich Jews rising in Boston society. In the second chapter published in the *Century,* Mrs. Lapham has heard at the summer resort that wealthy Jewish outsiders are invading the fashionable residential districts of Boston, including Nankeen Square where the Laphams live. Is it true that the property of the established owners is worth less than they paid? Silas the businessman can answer with authority, "It's worth a good deal less. You see, they *have* got in—and pretty thick, too—it's no use denying it. And when they get in, they send down the price of property." Though he claims to deplore the housing discrimination against Jews, Silas still feels moved to reaffirm that "prices begin to shade when the first one gets in." Several pages later, Mrs. Lapham returns to the same topic, and says "thoughtfully" that a prosperous "Mr. Liliengarten has bought the Gordon house across the square." She then "sighs" as she announces, "They've all got money." To assess fully what Howells is suggesting here, we need to recall, first, who is the original source of Mrs. Lapham's information about the Jewish menace. It is Tom Corey, the young Boston aristocrat. (The extent of Brahmin apprehensions about Jews will deserve a hard look in just a moment.) Further, Howells apparently was trying to present the Laphams' rural-parvenu attitudes toward the Jews. Mrs. Lapham, forgetting that they are as yet really outsiders from Vermont trying to rise in Boston society, has rapidly adopted the attitude of an established Bostonian toward the aspiring Jew. Silas does offer his religious objections to anti-Semitism. The Savior, after all, was a Jew, and Silas believes that Adam must have been one, too. But for all this comic confusion, Silas clearly has his own strain of racial bigotry. Howells, in fact, allows Silas to repeat his forceful misgivings over the economic and social disorder created by the newly rich Jew in Boston. In short, Howells was again tapping one of the vital nerve centers of Boston society in the Gilded Age. It may have been also, in a quite painful and ambivalent way, a nerve center of Howells himself.

Anti-Semitism in this period was an attitude which Howells had many chances to experience at first hand. Virtually every old-guard Bostonian of his acquaintance harbored suspicions and fears of the rising Jew in America. In the early 1880s, the professional Anglo-Saxon was beginning to take arms against a sea of immigrants. Among them were Fiske, Parkman, Shaler, Hart, and Barrett Wendell. In 1881, the British historian Freeman lectured to a Boston audience on the appalling decline of the Anglo-Saxon, and in private conversations could be heard to advocate elimination of the Irishman, Negro, and Jew from the entire English-speaking world. In his visit in 1881, Herbert Spencer warned Americans that the immigrant races were undermining the pure Anglo-Saxon development of America.

Among his closer acquaintances, Howells knew the personal anti-Semitic fears of Henry Adams, Charles Eliot Norton, and, most paranoiacally, James Russell Lowell. (pp. 116-17)

Howells, then, was hitting close to the heart of one of the most threatening aspects of the rising man in that age when he presented the Anglo-Saxon fear of the growing status of the Jew in Boston. As could be expected, Jewish readers of the *Century* studied carefully the implications of Silas's and Mrs. Lapham's comments. Three of these readers wrote to Howells and accused him of actually encouraging a rise of anti-Semitism in America. To repeat, without dispelling it, the vicious rumor that Jewish neighbors lowered the value of property was, in fact, an indirect way of feeding the prejudice. Howells defended the ironic intention of the passages, but he deleted them forthwith. He explained in his reply to one of the readers, Cyrus L. Sulzberger, editor of the *American Hebrew:*

> I supposed that I was writing in reprobation of the prejudice of which you justly complain, but my irony seems to have fallen short of the mark—so far short that you are not the first Hebrew to accuse me of "pandering" to the stupid and cruel feeling against your race and religion. . . . In that passage I merely recognized to rebuke it, the existence of a feeling which civilized men should be ashamed of. But perhaps it is better not to recognize all the facts.

The final sentence surely moves us closer to the heart of Howells' conflict. Had he been able to recognize all the facts regarding this unlovely aspect of the Brahmin mentality, he might well have felt a strong disengagement from his Boston acquaintances, the tough-minded attitude which has sometimes been attributed to him. Instead, what startles one here is the very frank self-irony with which Howells defined his own dilemma. Though he recognized the strain of racism in these eminent colleagues, and allegedly meant to satirize and rebuke it, he felt himself tied to Lowell, Norton, and the rest on too many other counts to allow him to "recognize all the facts" about these "civilized men."

But there is more. What of Howells' own private feelings about the Jews? Deleting these passages out of sympathy for Jewish feeling, since his irony had misfired, was one thing. But one strongly suspects that Howells may have been willing to avoid, thereby, an issue on which his own feelings were probably not clear to himself. Why, for example, did he not rewrite the passages to make the "stupid and cruel feeling" more apparent to the victims of it, the audience with whom he professed his sympathy? Anti-Semitism could easily have been made a bit less vague. Tom Corey as the indoctrinator of Irene and Mrs. Lapham had been identified only as a "young man" in the original passage. And if Silas's remarks actually were meant to portray him as unwittingly anti-Semitic, surely Howells' artistic subtlety would not have suffered greatly by a slight elaboration of the comic portrait. Irony has literary uses, to be sure, but it can also provide a convenient shield for hiding one's personal, ambivalent feelings. By recasting the passage, Howells could also have alleviated whatever residual guilt he may have felt for once writing in the *Atlantic* that the "dread advance of the Irish" was at that time lowering the value of homes. Or if an ironic Howells was then recognizing to rebuke anti-Irish prejudice and panic selling, still he had written to Norton in the same month:

> Our Sacramento Street has lately become much less desirable than it was: Irish have moved in, and I think it would be the part of prudence to sell the house if I could find a good purchaser. I'm afraid it will depreciate on my hands.

Howells' sympathetic letter to Mr. Sulzberger indicates that by 1885 these early sentiments about race had grown perhaps more complex and divided. No conclusive proof has come to light that Howells ever was able to resolve these feelings.

Indeed, to the extent that he retained his village reflexes, why should we expect Howells to discover within himself, as he did not in his rural Silas Lapham, clearly pro-Semitic feelings? In *A Modern Instance,* Howells had posed Kinney, the vulnerable and faded pioneer of the West, in opposition to the unscrupulous new pioneer of business—the Jew. Not once but twice, Howells indicated that Kinney travelled into the city only to be victimized by the "cheap clothier" Jew. In this period, the Jew rather widely called to mind, also, the financial tyranny of a fixed gold standard emanating from the House of Rothschild in England. It may be worth speculating whether this fact helps to explain why it should be English money in search of Silas's Western property that threatens to corrupt him during his moral crisis in the book. In the year after ***Silas Lapham,*** Susy Clemens wrote that one evening at Hartford Howells had alluded to the matter we have been discussing: "After he received letters from 'two or three Jews' objecting to 'a sentence about a Jew' " in the serialized novel, he had deleted it. This is skimpy evidence, to be sure. But assuming that Susy, then in her early teens, was quoting Howells accurately, one cannot help noticing the casual underplaying of the actual passages and the intensity of feeling they had occasioned. (pp. 121-25)

One more passage in the serial gives us a further glimpse into Howells' troubled spirit in 1884. At this point we begin to sense how his incipient social conflict over status was being complicated and intensified by his literary conflict with Boston and Cambridge, including some of his closest acquaintances. The revealing passage I have in mind occurs in chapter one during Bartley Hubbard's "Solid Men of Boston" interview with Silas Lapham. Silas is proudly recounting his self-made rise to riches, while Bartley amuses himself by jotting down sardonic phrases in his notebook. Silas reminds himself momentarily that brave Mrs. Lapham must share at least partial credit for the Laphams' first million. The tribute obviously tickles Bartley, and he describes Mrs. Lapham as "one of those women who, in whatever walk of life, seem born to honour the name of American Woman, and to redeem it from the national reproach of Daisy Millerism." Howells was probably not aware that he had just committed a four-year anachronism (the parallel action in ***A Modern Instance,*** chapter nineteen, dates roughly at August 1874; *Daisy Miller* first appeared in *Cornhill Magazine* in June-July 1878). Presumably he was embarrassed when an alert reader promptly informed him of his error. Yet Howells, with surprising stubbornness, maintained that the allusion to *Daisy Miller* was indispensable and could not be deleted. It suggested "the complexion of the period," he argued, and added even more cryptically that it gave "a characteristic tint in the portraiture." What important revelation of the period and the characters was Howells claiming for the tiny anachronism in this reference to the fiction of Henry James?

Howells and James had met in 1866. The two seem to have dismissed all formality and engaged at once in long talks on the art of the novel. Howells launched his younger friend on a successful literary career in the seventies, publishing James as often as he could in the pages of the *Atlantic.* They reviewed each other's work, and drew mutual courage from a shared encounter against proponents of an older theory of fiction. The friendship continued fifty years to James's death in 1916. In an unfinished essay four years later, Howells was still discussing, in the year of his own death, one of his favorite subjects—**"The American James."**

One important period in this relationship concerns us here—the years between *Daisy Miller* and ***Silas Lapham.*** During the months after James's novella appeared, Howells watched in dismay the popular misreading of his friend's ambiguous but essentially sympathetic study of the American girl. Howells summed up for Lowell in Spain the American reaction to James's heroine:

> Harry James waked up all the women with *Daisy Miller,* the inventions of which they misconceived, and there has been a vast discussion in which nobody felt very deeply, and everybody talked very loudly. The thing went so far that society almost divided itself in Daisy Millerites and anti-Daisy Millerites.

In the same year, Howells gave implicit support to James's characterization of the American girl by presenting readers with Lydia Blood in ***The Lady of the Aroostook*** (1879). And he made more direct his campaign for lifelike heroines in fiction through explicit dialog in ***A Modern Instance.*** Ben Halleck remarks during one conversation with Atherton, " 'I wonder the novelists don't take a hint from [real life], and stop giving us those scaly heroines they've been running lately.' " And later, the two bachelors realize why they cannot understand or predict the behavior of a Marcia Gaylord. As he closes the novel he is reading, Atherton observes that " 'we bachelors get most of our doctrine about women from [the novelists]. We don't go to nature for our impressions; but neither do the novelists, for that matter.' " (pp. 126-28)

So in 1884, as his co-warrior James was bringing together his defense of the new novel in "The Art of Fiction," Howells was preparing his in the pages of ***Silas Lapham.*** Indeed, in his zeal to strike back at his opponents, Howells seemed at times in the novel to be asking the reader to side with the character who displayed the best taste in literature. Irene Lapham reveals her shallowness by telling a comically indulgent Tom Corey that the library in the Lapham's new Back Bay home will need to have the right books and the right bindings. Shakespeare aside, she is certain only of two names—Scott and Cooper. She has not read their novels, however, and thereby is innocently admitting that she has been influenced by what is obviously the popular "romantic" taste of the day. In the love triangle that develops, she loses out. Her more perceptive sister Penelope, on the other hand, does read sentimental fiction, and complains of the currently popular novel, *Tears, Idle Tears,* "Why can't they let people have a chance to behave reasonably in stories?" At the Corey dinner, however, Clara Kingsbury describes the same novel as "perfectly heartbreaking." At that point, the Reverend Mr. Sewell intercedes to bring logical and perhaps, by implication, supernatural support to Howells' and James's concept of the novel. He considers sentimental fiction dangerous and "noxious" to a sane view of life, and adds, "The novelists might be the greatest possible help to us if they painted life as it is. . . . " Again, when the Reverend Mr. Sewell meets with the elder Laphams and recommends the "economy of pain" as the solution to the romantic triangle of Irene, Penelope, and Tom (the same practical formula, incidentally, which will solve Silas's own ethical dilemma with Rogers and the English financial agents), the minister suspects why so much moral confusion prevails in the world: "It comes from the novels that befool and debauch almost every intelligence in some degree."

All of these passages (the novel contains more) help to explain why Howells refused to delete even the brief, ironic defense of Henry James. If both he and James were out of step with the literary spirit of Boston, they could at least enjoy their private laugh together. Moreover, in a relationship marked by a fair amount of mutual banter and gentle prodding, we have reason to believe that James responded to the joke. In his essay on Howells the following year, in fact, he specifically praised the "admirable, humorous image" of that "ineffectual sinner," Bartley Hubbard. And more pointedly regarding heroines of fiction, the Daisy Millers of Howells' novel, James added, "Everything in *Silas Lapham* is superior—nothing more so than the whole picture of casual female youth. . . . "

Howells' growing warfare against the sentimental and improbable in fiction led him to the obtrusive literary polemics in *Silas Lapham.* And yet for all his jibes against the old-fashioned novel, Howells appears not to have greatly offended the romantic-idealists among his older friends. Indeed, some of them were highly pleased with this dramatic study of new Boston. What was the essential meaning they had discovered in the book?

In the original five-page synopsis, actually a prospectus, entitled **"The Rise of Silas Needham,"** Howells devoted nearly the entire sketch to his intended portrayal of Silas. He buried in two short sentences the subject of a closely related subplot:

> His family and its social status in Boston is depicted in a series of incidents all bearing on the main story. The romance of his daughter's love-story, and her marriage against his liking is told.

One suspects, then, that crucial conflicts troubling Howells during the composition of the novel after he had submitted his synopsis to the *Century* can rightly be predicated from the enlarged subplot.

Keeping the synopsis in mind, one realizes how fully Howells shifted his conception of the novel from the central moral dilemma of a blustering and uncultivated new millionaire to a more general inquiry into the social structure of a new era in America. The problem was specifically a Boston changing from the Brahmin certainties of Bromfield Corey's youth to a more fluid social order in the Boston of the seventies and eighties. In the early serialized chapters Howells was prepared to go into some of the most critical problems confronting new Boston, including the anti-Semitism of Tom Corey (willingly adopted by Mrs. Lapham and echoed by Silas) and, augmenting the threat of the new immigrant plutocracy, the threat also of the impoverished radical workingman in Boston's slums. But if he had been forced to modify and delete some of this bold first writing, he could still project the *solution* to this complex problem of "status."

As the novel developed, Howells apparently meant to keep the families Lapham and Corey in balance. He was not going to satirize the Coreys to the advantage of the ambitious, newly status-conscious Laphams. The elder Coreys have, unarguably, the prior claim to Boston by virtue of birthright—and are rather haughtily aware of it—while the elder Laphams have earned a rightful place in the new Boston, albeit insecure as yet, through solid achievement. But we soon come to know that the elder Laphams are not being groomed for the leadership of new Boston. In the opening chapter, Bartley Hubbard, for all his cynical humor about the yokel-on-the-rise, provides us with some correct intuitions about the Laphams. Silas *is* a humorless bore about his not quite self-made millions. Mrs. Lapham, with her moral angularities and her ludicrous jealousy of Zerilla Dewey late in the novel, *is* rightly contrasted to James's Daisy Miller. Similarly, Howells can admire the civilized virtues of Bromfield Corey, while allowing that the suave Corey gentility and prim social correctness cannot give the city the new leadership it needs in a rugged era of industrial enterprise. The Bromfield Coreys have a theoretical sympathy for the poor, but their practical acquaintance with the masses of society, who must soon be reckoned with, is seen to be too slight. Bromfield Corey moves, an alien figure, through the commercial streets of new Boston, and transacts (in Italian) the business of buying an apple (only to hold it) from a "swarthy fruiterer." And we easily see through the self-congratulatory charity work of a Clara Kingsbury, who knows her Italian slum dwellers even less well. What, then, is Boston of the future to do for leadership? Howells answered the question by developing and interweaving the subplot.

The story of Silas's business rise and his conflict between moral integrity and the gospel of wealth is proportionally much shorter in the novel than the reader may at first realize. The Corey-Lapham "subplot" interweaves roughly eighty per cent of the novel and frequently dominates the first twenty of the novel's twenty-seven chapters. It is, in other words, a *co-plot*. In developing this social conflict, Howells also struck on the happy notion of creating a love triangle for the "Penelope's romance" of the synopsis. The advantages were important. Howells was able to establish an effective contrast between the Lapham daughters. Irene is the predictable heroine of romantic fiction, slight and pretty. Everyone assumes from the beginning that Tom Corey must be in love with her. But he displays his responsible taste by choosing the less stunning sister, a William Dean Howells heroine with character and good sense. Penelope has a third quality that makes her the more suitable wife for Tom Corey. Through self-education she has become a cultivated, natural aristocrat. Here Howells was covertly making his heroine somewhat palatable to his reading audience in Boston. The romantic triangle, then, had enabled Howells to develop the full significance of his earlier notebook jotting, "the young trees growing out of the fallen logs in the forest—the new life out of the old. Apply to Lapham's fall."

The crucial issues begin to merge in chapters twelve to fifteen, the heart of the novel which brings the Laphams and Coreys together at the Corey dinner party. The episode turns out to be an elimination ceremony for the Laphams—save for Penelope, who is conveniently absent from the socially complex affair. On the other hand, it is no victory for the Corey's and their "sterile elegance." What happens during and immediately after the dinner chapters becomes highly significant, and one is tempted to locate the moment when the bottom dropped out at just that point. Themes of Proper Boston smugness, new immigration and lower-class discontent, parvenu crudity, and Daisy Miller "realism" converge here. At the very least, the dinner scene forced upon Howells a crucial moment of truth early in the novel. With what one suspects to have been strong personal feelings of self-identity, Howells had described the dissimilar backgrounds of the Boston Laphams and the Boston Coreys. Yet his integrity had forced Howells to delineate the shortcomings of social and moral vision in both families. What hope then remained for Boston in the mid-seventies? Who was to lead the city in the turbulent era just ahead? Even the casual student of political democracy in 1884 could observe one of the signs; an Irish mayor had just been installed in city hall by a mass electorate of nineteenth-century immigrants.

In *The Rise of Silas Lapham* Howells tried to restore hope after the Corey dinner fiasco by turning in the next five chapters to the love triangle. Esthetically, too, he was trying to restore tension to the novel after the near-climactic scene which foreshadows the elder Laphams' exodus from Boston. This dramatic tension now depended on his developing and bringing to a successful resolution what had begun to comprise the important underlying theme of the novel, the forces of new Boston in conflict with the old, and an implicit struggle for the power to guide the future destinies of the city. Neither the elder Coreys nor the elder Laphams can provide the leadership which combines the moral and intellectual values of the past with the energy and vision necessary to forge a conservative path into the future. This happy blend does exist, however, in mingling the best of the Laphams (Penelope—a mixture of new native vigor with the old respect for intellect and morality) with the best of the Coreys (Tom—a mixture of the old culture and the new enterprise). Be it noted also, we are given subtle assurance that sentimental-romantic fiction will find no place in this ideal marriage.

So at the end, Silas, with chastened moral vision, gives up his aspirations for a status Back Bay address and, it is to be hoped as well, his sinful love of fast horses. He has refused to allow the devilish mischief of his ex-partner Milton Rogers and English gold to corrupt him and his America. He returns to a village America and the agrarian virtues that have managed to survive the roadway advertising of "Lapham's Mineral Paint" in the Vermont hills. At the same time, Howells provides us with the wedding of a streamlined Brahminism and a de-provincialized agrarian America. In the marriage of Tom and Penelope, he projected a vision of an ideal Boston of the future that his closest friends could not help but feel was a comforting prospect. The novel gave Lowell and Norton, both advocates of romantic idealism in fiction, a high degree of satisfaction. Lowell liked *Silas Lapham* immensely, and Norton read and reread the novel. Aside from their undoubted pleasure in the moral allegory of Silas's fall and rise, their approval must have come from the heartening prospect that Boston society, through impeccable young gentlemen like Tom Corey, might remain essentially intact despite the Silas Laphams, Bartley Hubbards, and a mounting population of immigrants. But Howells' *dramatic* problem of setting the prospect into actuality was harder, and he avoided it. Instead, he sent the couple to Mexico, where Tom will complete his apprenticeship as a Boston businessman. The hopeful possibility for the future was unmistakable, current political and economic realities of the

Gilded Age notwithstanding. In the fullness of time, Lowell and Norton could feel, the counterparts of Tom Corey and Penelope Lapham would reappear to provide traditional Anglo-Saxon leadership for a new Boston. Perhaps it was to keep this brave hope alive that in his next novel, *The Minister's Charge* (earlier set aside for the more urgent *Silas Lapham*), Howells would include that the Coreys had grown rich once again "due to a piece of luck, and . . . the young Mr. Corey, whom they expected in the summer, had brought it about."

Reading *The Rise of Silas Lapham* in the light of biographical evidence that Howells was less than encouraged by the progress of democracy in Boston and in America—this is clearly a difficult and even treacherous method of adding to the insights one has gained from a close internal reading of the text itself. Yet given Howells' own admission that he suddenly had awakened to the mounting dangers of social inequality at this time, how does one escape the biographical approach to Howells' meaning within the novel? The present reinterpretation of *The Rise of Silas Lapham* has indicated that Howells seems a more complicated and troubled man during his residence in Boston than his critics, old and new, have fully conceded. The profound impasse that caused the psychic crisis during this intensive study of Boston in the Gilded Age demands an explanation that moves beyond the premise that Howells was either a servile captive or a detached critic of the city that had become his first long-time home. Howells appears to have resisted, unsuccessfully, a number of painful questionings about the inequities of Boston, and American, society during the writing of *The Rise of Silas Lapham.* These questions brought him certain identifiable conflicts which he could not resolve. While he was opposed to the undemocratic snobbery of Bostonians—both the Proper New and the Proper Old—he was more than dimly aware at this time that he did not welcome a new Boston electorate, or leadership, dominated by Italians, Irish, and Jews. A theoretical friend of an increasingly restive laboring class, he also aspired to the safe comforts of a residence in aristocratic Back Bay. (pp. 131-39)

Howells had gravitated to his spiritual home in Boston during the years of some of the most radical changes in our national life. His reactions toward urbanism were Brahmin even to the degree to which they contained the perspective of Western agrarianism. His Boston friends may have quarreled with Howells' portraying a "commonplace" America in fiction. But in actuality they had long cherished the Jeffersonian dream of an agrarian and village America. The yearning was never felt more strongly than after mid-century, as they began to watch the dreaded rise of the city and the mongrelization of Cambridge and Boston. Norton moved his summer residence from Newport to rural Ashfield in western Massachusetts in 1864. There only one Irish family tainted the purity of the village. And in the year of *Silas Lapham* Norton informed an audience in England that "The Great West [is] peopled by the children of New England"—so that Western agrarian virtues were closely linked with the pure Anglo-Saxon. As a transplanted Westerner in Norton's Boston, Howells could fully understand his friends' playing down the role of "foreigners" in the winning of the

West. More openly than Norton, Howells had remarked to his own countrymen, in the *Atlantic Monthly,* that the descendants of the Puritans had moved to the West. Unfortunately, foreign races had then moved into the vacuum created in New England. And while the context cannot be established here, a comment by the Reverend Mr. Waters in *Indian Summer,* written just before (but published after) *Silas Lapham,* repeats the historical observation Norton also was expressing at the time. The pure New England, Howells' minister remarks, had migrated to " 'the great middle West and the Pacific Coast.' "

Howells' sentiment toward the average man in America was perhaps most like Lowell's (as Howells himself was able to recognize it in his friend)—a democracy of the head but not profoundly of the heart. His life and career both before and after *Silas Lapham* reveal the continuing lack of resolution in the mind of a natural conservative with a humanitarian conscience who was trying, but ultimately was unable, to respond to the radical democracy of the new industrialism in the East. What Tolstoy's Christian brotherhood would do for Howells soon after *Silas Lapham* would be to provide him with a non-violent ideological formula for bridging the chasm between the haves and have-nots in America. He rebuked the capitalists for having failed to practice the Christian virtue of brotherly love toward the laboring classes. And he deplored in equal degree the violence which characterized the labor movement in its desperate early struggle for a share of the nation's wealth. Why could the laborers not quell the monster of industrial capitalism by just choking it to death quietly with votes?

After *The Rise of Silas Lapham,* Howells successfully negotiated with publishers from year to year for his own share of the nation's wealth, to become, with Mark Twain, one of our wealthiest authors. His net worth in 1890 had risen to $60,000; in 1892, to $68,000; and (despite the panic of 1893) to $84,000 in 1894. In the midst of this plenty, he admitted privately to his father the difficulty of finding a creed of social and economic democracy to live by:

> [Mark Twain] and his wife and Elinor and I are all of accord in our way of thinking: that is, we are theoretical socialists, and practical aristocrats. But it is a comfort to be right theoretically, and to be ashamed of one's self practically.

So by 1890, neither Tolstoy nor the writing of *The Minister's Charge* (1887), *Annie Kilburn* (1889), and *A Hazard of New Fortunes* (1890) had brought for Howells a satisfying articulation of the problems of social brotherhood, status, and privilege in America. Nor had he discovered it by 1894, after *A Traveler from Altruria.* In Paris to see his son in June of that year, he told Jonathan Sturges (as James remembered Sturges' account):

> "Live all you can: it's a mistake not to. . . . I see it now. I haven't done so—and now I'm old. It's too late. It has gone past me—I've lost it."

The remark gave to James the germ of *The Ambassadors;* does it not also furnish us with one more glimpse into a life of unresolved definition? Howells' concern over the inequalities of American society, during and after *The Rise of Silas Lapham,* had enlarged to become at times both courageous and profound. It was also confused. The theoretical socialist in him continued to be ashamed of the practical aristocrat. These conflicting sympathies led to irresolution of spirit and, at least once, during the writing of *Silas Lapham,* to some form of psychic desolation. Out of this returning ordeal of indecision in the years to come, he would create the novels which might yet advance the good and the true in human life, a fictional world which embraced, but never would solve, Howells' "riddle of our painful earth." (pp. 141-43)

> *Kermit Vanderbilt, in his* The Achievement of William Dean Howells: A Reinterpretation, *Princeton University Press, 1968, 226 p.*

## Elizabeth Stevens Prioleau     (essay date 1983)

[*Prioleau is an American critic who has written extensively on nineteenth-century English and American literature. In her study* The Circle of Eros: Sexuality in the Work of William Dean Howells, *she offers a predominantly Freudian examination of Howells's novels, focusing on their reflection of the author's personal background. "A strangely fearful child who suffered phobias and nightmares," she writes, "Howells endured three psychological collapses during his adolescence and early youth. Thereafter and to progressively lesser degrees, he was plagued by various neurotic ailments." From this starting point, Prioleau chronicles the psychological development of Howells, who, she says, "began as a priggish young editor of the* Atlantic Monthly, *with an early neurotic terror of sexuality, and ended as one of the leading exponents of frankness in literature. He grew lenient to the point of advocating 'scandalous' reforms like divorce and trial marriages, and his fiction moved from filigree indirection to bold erotic allegory." In the following excerpt, Prioleau examines the sexual subtext in* The Rise of Silas Lapham.]

While Howells was planning *The Rise of Silas Lapham* and jotting ideas in a "savings bank diary," he wrote R. W. Gilder: "It [the book] will involve more interest, I find, and be more of a love story than I expected." This "love story" element—including the other sexual "interests" in the novel—has aroused more controversy than any other aspect of the book. At the time [see excerpts dated 1885], reviewers accused Howells of "depravity," of "out Zola[ing] Zola," of promoting an aesthetic of skin—"very dirty skin." After his death, critics complained about the imperfect fusion of the love plot with the rest of the drama and charged that it was an embellishment for his female readers.

Now such dispute has long since subsided. Several recent articles defend the intrinsic unity of the two plots, and the excitement over the "shocking" physicality has so far abated as to be almost inconceivable. Except for quasi-Freudian speculations on the pine-shaving scene, in which Irene Lapham pokes the curls with her parasol, the novel is thought to be tame, blandly Victorian, and devoid of sexuality.

Yet, the question arises: might there not be an unexplored

level of sexual meaning that explains the old controversy? A reexamination of **Silas Lapham** suggests that there is indeed a sumberged erotic subtext which Howells's audience may have read and the next generation missed. By reconstructing this sexual dimension, the novel appears to be even more closely, intricately structured than is thought. To be sure, the sexual "story" is not the major story, but it provides a rich undertheme that deepens the texture, restores the vitality, and binds the book more tightly. At the same time, it offers a possible further explanation of Howells's breakdown in the middle of Silas's "fall" and shows how he began to work out of the deadlock he encountered in **A Modern Instance.**

Besides the obvious triangular "love story," in **Silas Lapham** a penumbra of sexual suggestion surrounds Silas's drama. Each of his overt "sins"—his egotism, greed, aggression, and intemperance—contains an implicit libidinal component which Hamlin Garland pinpointed when he called Silas the victim of "bad blood." Instinctually, he is not only dissociated; he is immature, a "primitive" whose ordeal resembles a *rite de passage* as much as a spiritual death and rebirth. This tacit dimension to his career has an external dramatization in the erotic complications in his family. Persis, Irene, and Penelope provide specific sexual illustrations of his flaws, reflecting, amplifying, and clarifying them. Their tests, moreover, duplicate his and predict his final fate.

"Barbaric" and "vulgar" recur repeatedly in discussions of Silas's character. Silas supports the sexual sense of these terms through speech, gesture, and appearance. The impression he creates in the first chapter is one of rough-hewn, elemental virility. Personifying his namesake, Silenus the Satyr, he rises up out of his chair like "one of nature's noblemen," pounds an envelope with a "great hairy fist," and slams the door with his "huge foot." Bartley Hubbard, the reporter, reinforces this sense of his sensuality. While he is ostensibly Silas's foil, there are libidinous similarities between them, which the readers of **A Modern Instance** would have picked up. Both have tell-tale red hair, physical intimacy in conversation, a passion for fast horses, and a "bond" that causes Silas to see "himself a young man again" in Bartley.

In addition to his sexual exuberance, Silas's immaturity and dissociation also appear in the opening interview. He disproportionally dwells on his childhood (harping on his mother as Bartley yawns), and suggests an inner head-heart division when he talks about his "passion," his paint. You should "keep [your conscience] as free from paint as you can," he tells Bartley, and then praises his wife's "supernal" virtue, as though he has displaced his moral maintenance to her. Bartley's similar view of *his* wife both establishes another parallel between them, and strikes a note of foreboding. The chapter closes on a quarrel between the Hubbards, sparked by Marcia's jealousy.

On his visit to Nantasket, Tom Corey notices that Silas only has three topics of conversation: paint, horse, and house. All are central symbols in the novel, and as such, give off a wide spectrum of meanings, one of which is libidinal. His paint is the most suggestive. Discovered in a hole in the earth caked to the roots of a fallen tree, it has the attributes of a life symbol, a procreative essence. To Silas it is his "heart's blood," his "poetry," and when he enters the scented, twilit storeroom, he puts a hand on a keg "as if it were the head of a child." The supporting characters corroborate the sensual significance of the paint; Marcia, by mistaking the "crimson mass" for "jam," and Bromfield Corey, by calling it "delicious"—the same adjective used for Irene's sexual allure.

The paint also mirrors Silas's psychosexual adjustment. His bragging, hoarding, driving competitors from the market, and rash over-stocking reflect the sexual modalities of childhood. Buried in the psyche are impulses to narcissism, greed, aggression, and reckless gratification, which he has not yet subdued. Yet, in the main, he is eminently normal; his richest, fanciest brand of paint is named for his wife.

Silas's horse has sexual overtones as well. In the same way that Bartley's wild colt personifies his undisciplined appetites in **A Modern Instance,** so Silas's high-blooded mare symbolizes his libidinal élan. Similarly, his horse gauges his immaturity. When he eulogizes his mare (his family calls his boasting getting up "on his high horse"), hogs the Milldam, and "lets out" with abandon, he exemplifies the untamed, presocialized id. Ecstatic with predatory glee, his "gaiety" perverted into "grim, almost fierce alertness," he becomes a model of unalloyed infantile aggressiveness. Still, his orientation is fundamentally adult and average, for he rides best, with a "pretty tight fit" with his wife. Her warning that his horse is a "fool" and will "kill" him is another crucial omen, adumbrating his downfall.

The house he is building, likewise, is more than just a visible manifestation of his material-social rise. With Spenser's "house of Pryde" in *The Faerie Queene,* it, too, contains a sexual dimension. Mythically and psychoanalytically, houses signify the bodily self, and in that context, Silas is both richly sensual and undeveloped. Luxurious as his new mansion is, it nonetheless remains half-finished, crude, and rudimentary, with his passion for pile driving suggesting primitive, phallic propensities. Even the fetid smell, which emanates from the foundations, is libidinally significant, since Swedenborg, Howells's family prophet, equated putrid odors with sexual maladjustments. Like the paint and mare, his house becomes a vehicle for expressing them. Incessantly bragging about it, he squanders on decoration and design, and greedily, belligerently builds "not [to be] outdone." The "normal" alloy is his equally strong desire to build for his daughters, and especially, his wife.

Money is a fourth index of his psychosexuality, and perhaps the most telling to a nineteenth-century audience. From a modern standpoint Silas's use of wealth—his irrational splurging, paint smearing, and sublimation of enjoyment into moneymaking, is a classic case of anality. But he is better understood within the Victorian "spermatic economy." According to this doctrine, sperm and money were synonymous; wealth accrued through mature, stringent repression; bankruptcy, through immature, undisciplined indulgence. Silas's prodigal spending and overextending, therefore, was indicative of sexual incontinence, and his financial boasting, avarice, and competitive "crowd[ing]" were symptoms of unwholesome, dangerous child's play.

These symbolic registers of Silas's unschooled, dissociated libido are supported by his actions in the first part of the book and presage his tragedy. Unable to feel anything but an "easy" conscience about edging Rogers out of his business, he atones by appropriating his wife's superego, and making an extravagant, quixotic reparation.

In Tom Corey, his "symbol of splendor," his whole primitive disposition comes to a focus. He swells with vanity over him, challenges his superior social position, and overconfidently, rashly lets things ride when his calls begin. As they take the ferry together to Nantasket, Silas's psychosexual immaturity rises to the fore. Looking at the couples on board, he tells Tom that he can't "make any sort of guess" about whether they're engaged, just as he will not be able to divine Tom's romantic intentions. It is here the narrator interjects: "We are no more imposing than a crowd of boys." When the ferry docks, Silas's callow obtuseness grows portentous. While he watches Penelope, the source of so much future discord, he imagines an "impending calamity" on the pier "as if it could not possibly include him."

At the Corey dinner, the precise center of the book, his libidinous immaturity reaches a peak of expression, and comes into collision with the reality principle, Proper Boston. His anxiety beforehand resembles the "mounting panic" of Susanne Langer's "caveman" before "the toils" of civilization—the essence of manners' comedy [*Feeling and Form*, 1953]. Nothing illustrates this better than Silas's anguish about his gloves, and the final image of his huge, hairy hands trussed up like "canvassed hams" before the party. During the first half of the dinner, his terror effectively obliterates his personality. He cannot "hold up his end of the line" and relapses into torpid silence. However, as he drinks and eats "everything," his fear dissolves, destroying his reserves. Recalling that inebriation and gluttony signalled licentiousness to Victorian Americans, Silas's after-dinner performance is freighted with implied sexuality. In one condensed period, he narcissistically touts his horse, house, paint, money, and Tom Corey, and crows over his "charity," Jim Millon. "Profoundly flattered" by the attention, he describes Millon's sacrifice for him, conscious only of "having talked very well." The other three strands of his untamed, primitive libido also converge in his drunken monologue. Greedily securing "the talk altogether to himself," he aggressively hammers his chair, goads Corey about his loss of four hundred dollars, and assures Mr. Sewell he has "more money than he [knows] what to do with." But the end of Silas's psychic "letting out" is the same as his anxious "holding in" earlier; when he steps in the cab after his "supreme triumph," he feels suffocated, his tongue "stop[s]," and he sinks into unconsciousness.

The dinner party marks a turning point in Silas's affairs. The phallic swelling, pounding, seizing, and spending cease and reverse. He begins a descent back into the hole from which the paint sprang—the disorganized irrational subconscious—and the predominant imagery changes to deflation, flaccidity, slippage, and contraction. Psychosex-

ually, his ordeal corresponds to a maturity trial, a passage through primal chaos to self-integration.

Irene's and Penelope's erotic crisis foreshadows and prepares him for his own. After his overatonement to Tom for his drunkenness he learns about the romantic misunderstanding and his chastening-in-miniature begins. During his daughters' ordeals, Silas suffers a forecast of what will befall him in the second half of the novel. His horse has an accident, he hears that Irene will "never live in" his new house, and his bearing sags so badly that the druggist presciently thinks the sleep potion is for him. The predicament, he says, "is a perfect snarl," like the tangle that will soon enmesh him. Without equating his semirobbery of Rogers with Penelope's, of her sister's, he assures her with an ominous lack of self-application that she "hasn't stolen anything" and that "whatever [she's] got belongs to [her]."

Rogers, like the repressed unconscious itself, though, comes back to haunt Silas and pursues him back to the hole. If he is a devil figure, as Richard Coanda suggests [see Further Reading], he is a Mephistophelean version, a "spirit that negates," a nonvital principle, who avenges Silas's exuberant, regressive sexuality. He bleeds him—to use Silas's term—of his very life essence. As soon as he reappears, images of entrapment, suffocation, curtailment, shrinkage, and flaccidity accrue. Telling Persis that he "can take care of [himself]," he embarks alone on his slow, tedious downward passage. His initial aggressive defenses, his threats of "squeezing" Rogers, gradually erode. With a "drownin' man's grip" on him, Rogers leads him to an underworld that is the reverse image of his former one. Instead of expanding, his paint and money begin an "awful shrinkage," and he withdraws, morose and humiliated, to "his own den." He rejects the food he had gorged before, his posture and features flag, his mare breaks down, and the "net" steadily closes about him.

As the meshes tighten, he confronts the underside of his charitable devotion to Jim Millon. Seen in the light of Howells's condemnation of charity, Silas's encounter with the drunken Moll Millon represents the "debauch[ing]" effects of self-sacrifice that Sewell warned him about. In any case, what filled him with vanity at the Corey dinner, now transports him downward to the most sordid recesses of alcoholism. From this, he is cast upon the necessity of selling his house and enters the "depths of gloom." Afraid of proving he was a "fool in some way," he turns into a true "fool"—the embodiment of the powers of unreason. Against his better judgment, he resists the sale of his "pride and glory" and goes to Beacon Street where he indulges in one last bout of infantilism. He inhales "the peculiar odor of his own paint," impulsively lights a fire in the fireplace, and decides—in a spasm of greed—that he can't part with the house. Among other things fire is a standard emblem of libido; therefore, as it builds, Silas "lets out" more and more. He angrily challenges a policeman who mistakes him for a tramp, exults in his fantasized preeminence, and consigns the buyers "to the devil." He achieves the same "perfect success" of the dinner party and the result is identical: annihilation. With the house, which is reduced to a human skull in the flames, Silas is physically eviscerated by the fire. Still, broken as he is, he persists in his regression and, like a "perversely proud and obstinate child," tries to save himself by buying out the West Virginia company.

When this fails, he finds himself "driven to the wall" and faced with his severest test. His narcissism wounded, aware that "he was not so rich and not so wise as he had seemed," he begins his deepest descent. His moorings start to drift, and he follows the sinister Rogers through the night to an amoral subworld where the Englishmen tempt him with their unethical offer. He responds in the archetypal way of the sexual initiate: he refuses the alcohol he had consumed so voraciously before, and barricades himself alone in his study without wife or family, for an all-night vigil. Surmounting his narcissism, "swallowing" his "self-pity," he wrestles with his tempter, the demonic, until daybreak. Afterwards, after the railroad squeezes him out, he can at last "feel like a thief " towards Rogers. But he does not emerge victorious from his *rite de passage*. Unlike the classic pattern of growth from "savagery" through chaos to an integrated body and mind, he comes out physically defeated if spiritually redeemed. A reversal has taken place; the dissociation remains. He has incorporated a civilized, adult conscience at the expense of his body; his "spring" has weakened, his "animal strength," ebbed. He returns to the ground of childhood without surmounting division or attaining full psychosexual maturity. Although he overcomes his narcissism, greed, aggression, and extravagance, he loses his fleshly vitality and appropriately moves into a "plain" house without central heating or "luxuries . . . [except] . . . statues of Prayer and Faith." All that remains of his paint is the monogamic Persis Brand, pursued on a "smaller scale." He bows to the next generation, and exchanges his horse for a frisky "immature" colt behind which he drives a buggy "long past its prime." As he tells Sewell, he has "crept" out of the hole. If he attains "manhood" through his ethical rise, it is a partial, disembodied manhood, bought at too high a price. This very likely is what Howells meant in his synopsis, when he emphasized that Silas *does not recover* from his bankruptcy.

The openly sexual "stories" in the novel repeat and elucidate the covert libidinal themes in Silas's. Persis, Irene, and Penelope each offer specific erotic examples of his sins and pass through the same maturity ordeals. Nor are they any more successful, despite the sexual ethic Mr. Sewell provides. Although Persis seems to be Silas's exact opposite, as wholly superego as he is id, she, too, falls prey to the very greed and foolishness she accuses him of. Her earthy remark about getting remarried if Silas were killed in the war, and the richness of her Brand, suggest an innate warmbloodedness. However, with her husband's material rise, she has become dissociated like him; her bodily life, severed from her moral life; her conscience, hypertrophied and hidebound. She warns Silas that he is "greedy," that he is "bewitched" and "los[ing] his head," but through her over-control, she is ambushed by these same lower impulses.

After inspiring his ruinous, surplus atonement to Rogers, her virtue begins to play "her false." Her sexual greed, the destructive lust for possession in Eros, starts to build as soon as she sees the mysterious "Mrs. M" on a scrap of paper. While her moral sermons mount, she oscillates between bitter suspicion and "sweet[ness]" until her conscience reaches a pitch of severity during Silas's crisis, and she breaks down. As the immature, tyrannical superego always does, it reduces her to "helpless[ness]" and exposes her to the influx of real evil. Trying for still higher virtuousness, she goes to Silas's office to atone, sees Zerilla, and is engulfed by jealousy. She herself plays the fool. Unable to "fight the madness off," she succumbs to the forces of unreason, and becomes so "demoniacal[ly]" possessed that she reels and faints. During her seizure, she plumes herself on her worth and lusts for revenge, tapping the veins of narcissism and aggression in her own psyche. When she discovers her mistake, she enters the deepest level of her ordeal and wrestles with "shame and self-reproach" in her darkened, shuttered room.

Yet, despite her chastening, her initiation is no more satisfactory than Silas's. Although she and Silas return to "their old united life," she cannot help relapsing into her former severity. Back in Lapham, her "satisfaction [is] not so constant." She lectures Silas about his former prodigality, and with a hint of still-unresolved jealousy, jibes that if he'd treated his paint as well as he treated the Millon women, he'd never have been ruined.

Irene, Silas's beautiful, headstrong daughter, sexually dramatizes his egotism and recklessness. High-pulsed like him, she has his red hair and a complexion that radiates her sensuality: "There is no word," says the narrator for her coloring, "but delicious . . . the tints of her cheeks and temples were such as suggest May-flowers and apple blossoms and peaches." With her father, though, she is psychosexually dissociated and immature. Throughout she is called a "child," and Bromfield Corey equates her with savages: girls like Irene, he exclaims, "ought to have been clothed in the skins of wild beasts and gone about barefoot with clubs over their shoulders."

In her pursuit of his son, Tom, she supports the Victorian association of savages with unregulated passion. On the slim evidence of a newspaper clipping, she deduces his interest in her, and rashly sets her cap on him. That her infatuation is largely hormonal, Howells insinuates through her choice of Tom's attractions. After she sees him at the building site, she ticks off all of his bodily endowments for her sister's admiration, dwelling particularly on his nose, his phallic icon. With Tom she is equally physical and precipitant. During the famous pine shaving scene, she first maneuvers him onto a trestle beside her; then mimes the act of intercourse, taking the masculine role with her parasol, while Tom passively holds the wood curls in place.

Besides embodying her father's extravagance in her love affair, she sexually mirrors his egotism as well. Although the introductory chapters insist that she is not conscious of her beauty, the image of her before her looking glass runs like a Narcissus leitmotif through the book. She devotes herself exclusively to preening and identifies with the arch-narcissist, Rosamond Vincy of *Middlemarch*, whom Howells accused of "deadly and deadening egotism." So self-absorbed is she that she doesn't notice Tom's unresponsiveness, and after his visit to Nantasket, in which he talks about her sister all night, she congratulates herself on the "splendid call," and selfishly pushes Penelope's "things aside on the dressing case to rest her elbow and talk at ease."

Both her immoderacy and narcissism come to a head at the Corey dinner. When she makes her eye-stopping entrance, she beams with the "knowledge of success" and reigns in "triumph" through the meal, unaware that she has not met Boston's sartorial or conversational standards. Self-intoxicated, she, too, believes it was a "perfect time." At a fever pitch of passion the next day, begging for flattery, and "giv[ing] [her]self up" to her imaginary romance, she encounters the same end of instinctual uncontrol as Silas. She learns the tragic news that Tom loves Penelope, and grows suddenly inanimate. Her floral complexion turns "snow-white"; her feelings, rock-like; her voice, icy. After her first angry thrust at Penelope, she locks herself in the kitchen, and paces out her agony like her father. Her parents comment that it is as though someone "died" in the house. Her ritual death, however, brings only partial rebirth. Although she returns from Lapham (the source of her being) with new altruism and self-discipline, she has acquired "the cutting edge of iron" and the accents of an "old maid." For her spiritual salvation, she has sacrificed her sexuality, which, like her beauty was "very great." "It had been a life and death struggle with her; she had conquered, but she had also necessarily lost much. Perhaps what she had lost was not worth keeping; but at any rate she had lost it."

Penelope provides a subtler, but no less dramatic sexual expression of Silas's sins. Secretly, "sly[ly]" (to use Mrs. Corey's term), she "squeezes" Irene, just as her father squeezes Rogers. The dark, competitive underside of Eros, the aggressive propensities Silas releases on the Milldam, Penelope vents on her sister through her "innocuous" funning. Warmblooded like the rest of her family, with her husky voice, brunette coloring, and demonstrative gestures, she is also immature and dissociated. If Irene illustrates the classic id-tyranny of adolescence, Penelope exemplifies the second maladjustment—the displacement of the impulses into self-betterment. Unaware of her sexual feelings, she expresses them semiconsciously through Freud's favorite defense mechanism, humor. Her comedy is not only another measure of her sexual élan; it is also a veiled, legitimate outlet for her rivalry with her sister and attraction to Tom. Her incessant teasing teeters on the edge of sadism, as the "cat and mouse" scene with Irene demonstrates. After Tom pays a surprise visit, she dangles the fact in front of her, snatches it away, and threatens to entertain Corey herself while her sister, "the mouse, moaned and writhed upon the bed." On two other occasions, she jokes, only half-humorously, that she is edging her out with Tom.

During his calls, she enacts this tabooed wish in the subtlest, most imperceptible way. Instead of promoting her sister, Penelope upstages her, through the same strategy of comedy. When she first meets Tom, she makes a jest so that he "looked at her," and she serenades him later at Nantasket with her wit and charm. While the three sit in the moonlight (always a dangerous omen in Howells's love stories), she leans forward and "croon[s]" to him, softly "clucking" as he laughs, and "funning" until he reels away "fascinate[d]."

Concealed in the text are clues that point to Penelope's half-knowledge of her "squeezing." When her mother asks her if Tom loves Irene, she cannot meet her eyes, and replies acidly that he should perhaps find out whether her sister can "interest him alone." Mrs. Corey's visit, as well, throws her into a suspiciously excited state. However, with a willed blindness to her impulses, she brags like Silas: "*I* don't intend to do anything wrong; but if I do, I promise not to be sorry for it."

Tom's visit after the dinner party triggers Penelope's boldest, most blatant seduction attempt. She ties a coquettish red ribbon on her throat, and escorts him to a "cozier" room, where she sits beneath him on a low stool in a flattering drop light. Her first joke, aimed at his missing her, is succeeded by a series of provocative maneuvers: she blushes at the sight of his hat, laughs wildly, flirts her fan, and as much as forces his love-confession. She asks him how she should reform, which predictably prompts his declaration and her self-awakening. All of her passion for Tom—so long buried and subversively expressed—suddenly surges up, and she faces her underself. She turns "white" though the blood rushes "to her heart," and she springs away despite her "potential complicity." She afterwards exaggerates what she had suppressed before, and dismisses Tom in a crescendo of contradiction: she forbids him to see her, seizing him in a tight embrace.

The ordeal that follows duplicates those of her family. She retreats without food to her darkened room and toils until daybreak with her demon, the repressed unconscious. Instead of integrating and mastering it, though, she segments herself further by adopting a suprapunitive infantile superego. At the same time that she admits her pursuit of Tom and resentment of Irene, she decides to punish herself and begins to rave about self-sacrifice. Her inner fragmentation worsens, until she regresses into a "fool"—the soul of incoherence. She grows emotionally labile, redoubles her pleas for martyrdom, and feeling pushed against the "wall" like Silas, thinks she is going "crazy." Only when she awakens to her father's cries does she recognize—in unison with his confessions and in the same language, that she has been at fault—an egotistical martyr.

Yet, despite her recognition, her passage to maturity is only minimally more successful than the others. She cannot wholly incorporate her libido into her adult identity. When she meets Tom's parents a year later, she behaves with "piteous distraction" instead of her old pluck, and seems no nearer the resolution of her conflict. During her final interview with Tom, she vacillates between acceptance and self-repudiation until she takes him in a fit of indecision. By default, she chooses Sewell's "economy of pain," the less punitive morality, but still does not fully recover. It is true that her humor (a gauge of her sexuality) is enough intact after a week with Tom's parents for her to quip that she won't "feel strange among the Mexicans." And she has also achieved enough intimacy with Tom to be honest emotionally. But in the final frame, as they drive off to Mexico, she has been psychically unhinged by his family. Neither able to accept their genteel ethic nor reach an integrated one of her own, she weeps on Tom's shoulder, and lets her competitiveness flare one last time. Explaining her tears, she whimpers "I only meant I should have you all to myself."

It is at this point that the narrator makes the famous observation about the price of civilization being "too much." Each of the Laphams has been unable to pleasurably assimilate value with passion; each has been libidinally lamed by "conscience," each left—fundamentally "normal" as they are—immature and dissociated. If their unmonitored passions lead to the Victorian "house of death," their mature accommodations are Victorian, too: they "kill" their sexual energy through overrepression. (pp. 70-81)

The real "hope" of the novel centers on Tom Corey. "Sweet," prudent, and moderate, he embodies Sewell's sober ethic, while at the same time, exhibiting Silas's libidinous élan. He recapitulates Silas's career, investing it with affirmation and renewal. He is the inspiration of Howells's note in his savings bank diary: "The young trees growing out of the fallen logs in the forest—the new life out of the old." In striking contrast to rigid, sterile Boston, Tom is warm and virile, an *homme sensuel* whose stylish clothes seem to "peel away" from his body and whose prominent nose, so pointedly emphasized, advertises his phallic drive. Unlike his mother who restrains the corseted Silas on the way to dinner, Tom, with his easy physicality, pulls a chair closer to him when they meet, and doffs his jacket. Silas's "instant pleasure" at this highlights their compatibility, and, in fact, Tom bears a marked likeness to his mentor. Like him, he has sought a fortune in Texas and returned home a prodigal, and is energetic, decent, and innovative. However, he corrects Silas's tragic flaws. Free of narcissism, he is not interested in "shin[ing]" and supplies "prudence" for rashness. When Silas says his paint is the "best in God's universe," Tom quickly amends it to "the best on the market." Having "nothing predatory" in his nature, he takes a dim interest in Silas's aggressive driving on the Milldam, and is so lacking in greed that he offers to work for nothing.

On the other hand, he is not without faults, chief of which is his innocence. The same sexual naiveté that makes him recoil in disbelief from Walker's hint of a liaison between Silas and Zerilla, plagues his courtship of Penelope and helps promote the triangle tangle. By densely overlooking Irene's infatuation (to the point of assuring his parents that she is "transparent"), by "dangl[ing]" after Penelope and sanctioning the dinner party, he assures the tragic dénouement.

His erotic immaturity, though, comes in for a ritual harrowing. In miniature, and on a lower frequency, he repeats Silas's night passage. After the dinner party debacle, he is overwhelmed by his repressed, irrational self, his own impulses to "shine," and struggles with his snobbishness through the night. For three hours, he paces up and down, his pride "wounded" like Silas's, his "savage" propensities rioting within him. Before his "chaos" ends, he also finds himself psychically trapped, combating a "blight" he can't "escape."

Of all the *rites de passage*, Tom's is the most superficially successful. He surmounts his prejudice through an inner, moral "girl's voice," faithfully meets Penelope's tests, and gains courage from his trial. "I'm not afraid, and I'm not guilty," he is able to say afterwards. As Silas sinks towards his material ruin, Tom's material-sexual rise begins: "a broad light of hope flashed upon him. It came from Lapham's potential ruin." Yet, he remains disturbingly naive, portending difficulties for his future, and perpetuating his psychosexual immaturity. Almost as imperceptive as before, he mistakes Penelope's masochistic histrionics for "nobility," and fatuously, "less judicially" assures her that she and his mother will be friends. When she collapses on his neck after a grueling week in his home, he cannot imagine what is wrong and begins his married life with a "puzzled smile." As they head off to Mexico, the narrator comments: "[He] ought to have known better." He is, then, an embryonic hero, at best, the core (as his name suggests) rather than the fruit of erotic hope. Despite his positive recapitulation of Silas's career, despite the apparent union of opposites in his personality—sweetness and force, sense and sensuality—he is still a boy, the colt behind Silas's buggy "which [has] not yet come of age."

Of Howells's novels, *The Rise of Silas Lapham* was uniquely autobiographical. He told Henry James that he had used "all of his experiences down to the quick," and the writing grew so intense that he suffered a breakdown somewhere in the middle of the book. Suddenly, with no apparent reason "the bottom dropped out." It is generally believed that the novel represented a crucial juncture in his career, an ethical-sociological moment of reckoning. Having just moved to the water side of Beacon, the argument runs, Howells faced a critical, ultimately debilitating conflict between Proper Boston and his social conscience, a contest that ended in the next decade in favor of his conscience. However, the sexual subtext suggests that the conflict went much deeper, beyond the moral question to the neurosis at the crux of his personality. This neurosis involved the psychosexual tug of war, the love and terror of the flesh, that caused three breakdowns in his youth and sporadic, milder relapses throughout his life. The tense prudery of his early prose was the visible scar. Yet, beneath the overt squeamishness was an aggressive exploration of sexuality—his conflict especially—via his fiction. According to Ernst Kris and others, creative work has the advantage of providing access to unconscious tensions while simultaneously permitting ego control and the possibility of resolution. Through the oblique route of narrative art, then, Howells imaginatively revived his neurotic difficulty over and over, gradually unknotting it.

*Silas Lapham* both illumines the difficulty more clearly than his previous novels and registers a breakthrough. The Laphams, named significantly for a family in Howells's first hometown, are a locus of his intrapsychic tension. Embodying the instinctual attraction and fear, they are equally sensuous and self-destructive. Their "tremendously good" living, country informality, and "funning" duplicate Howells's own boyhood home, and Irene's coloring, mirrors his earliest memory of beauty. "All his [the author's] life," he recalls in *A Boy's Town,* "he has never seen a peach tree in bloom without a swelling of the heart, without some fleeting sense that 'Heaven lies about us in our infancy'." But Silas most intimately registers the sensuous pleasure of his youth. The childhood idyll Silas paints for Bartley—the barefoot country rambles, the mother who doted on him, the kind father—echoes, sometimes verbatim, Howells's reminiscences of his Ohio boy-life.

But if Silas and his family contain the pleasure-pull of his psyche, they also project the competing terror with that gratification. Their infantile, lawless libido leads them to the very horrors that haunted Howells during his breakdowns: "death," darkness, insanity, vertigo, and suffocation. Again, Silas captures the sex fear in an intensely autobiographical way. He is a composite of the bad boy self in *A Boy's Town*—egotistical, acquisitive, combative, and extravagantly uncurbed—and he experiences Howells's neurotic symptoms most acutely. Before they assail him, at the floodtide of his "savagery" at the dinner party, Howells is supposed to have suffered his "vastation." Since the party is the pivotal point in the book, when libidinal excess and the available ethical options meet head-on for the first time, this is a tempting hypothesis. There, the Corey women are at their frigid worst, and the other guests, still without their redemptive proposals. Bromfield Corey's armchair liberalities wilt under the prospect of damage to his possessions, Tom fades into snobbish passivity, and Mr. Sewell provides only negative criticisms of

sentimentality, rather than a positive alternative. There are, then, no viable ethical checks to contain Silas's runaway instinctuality, no ego controls to prevent a resurgence of the conflict Howells had tapped so directly. When the bottom began to drop out for Silas, when Rogers got his "drownin' man's grip" on him, the bottom may also have dropped out for Howells, and plunged him back in his old, asphyxiating, terrible neurosis.

If something like this did happen, as it had happened before in *A Modern Instance,* the rest of the novel signals a psychic as well as an artistic advance. He was able to strike a partial accord with his demon, to bring up from his "vastation" the materials for a compromise between the engulfing fear and secret ambition for pleasure. Although Sewell's nonpunitive ethos cannot be implemented, although Bromfield's insights are dilettantish, Tom is still a naif at the end. Howells had found the raw data of a sexual affirmation. Out of Silas's psychosexual and financial destruction, which the age and Howells's excessive qualms demanded, arise the shoots, the "young trees" of a new stage in the resolution of his neurosis.

It is perhaps such a deep, inner shift rather than a sociopolitical or esthetic change of heart which prompted the upheavals of the next decade. Ironically, just when Howells moved to his Beacon Street home, he began to drift away from the dominant beliefs of the society he had been so anxious to join. The submerged longing for equality, moderation, and gratification apparently broke into his Boston idyll in the same way that the sexual theme had unexpectedly taken over his business novel. He turned to Christian socialism and realism—effectively alienating himself from the "right people." To be sure, the break was not entirely clean and a prudery seeps into his early realism credos, as though his critical thinking had not caught up with his imaginative discoveries. But his allegiance to the "red tides of reality" had been released in *The Rise of Silas Lapham,* never to be completely suppressed again. (pp. 82-6)

> *Elizabeth Stevens Prioleau, in her* The Circle of Eros: Sexuality in the Work of William Dean Howells, *Duke University Press, 1983, 226 p.*

*Howells in later life.*

### Irene C. Goldman     (essay date 1986)

[*In the following essay, Goldman examines economic issues and the portrayal of women in* The Rise of Silas Lapham, *commenting particularly on the character of Persis Lapham.*]

Critics have long agreed that William Dean Howells's *The Rise of Silas Lapham* is the first good, serious novel about an American businessman, one that treats a businessman realistically rather than exalting him as a Horatio Alger hero or denouncing him as a greedy, corrupt villain. While they may disagree as to how and how well Howells resolves the issues he raises, most critics now point to Howells's concern for business ethics as a major focus of the book. Interestingly, however, no critic to date has examined closely the essential business-related moral dilemma of the novel, the one preceding Lapham's economic fall:

his early partnership with Milton Rogers. George Bennett, one of the earliest Howells scholars [see excerpt dated 1959], states categorically, "Lapham's guilt in his original relation to Rogers is clear from the start and is finally acknowledged by him." Paul Eschholz, writing thirteen years later [in "The Moral World of Silas Lapham: Howells's Romantic Vision of America in the 1880's," *Research Studies of Washington State University,* 1972] still takes for granted Lapham was unfair, or worse, with Rogers: "Howells's irritable moral consciousness could not let this evil go unpunished." Wayne Westbrook suggests [in his *Wall Street in the American Novel,* 1971] that Rogers is the devil (Old Roger) bent on destroying Lapham after being forced out of the business and, most recently, Elizabeth Prioleau calls it Lapham's "semirobbery of Rogers" [see excerpt dated 1983]. Other critics make the same assumption, but such a reading may be simplistic. Until we have a thorough understanding of the relationship between the two business partners, particularly of Lapham's behavior towards Rogers during the building of his business, we cannot have a full appreciation of the view of business that emerges in the novel or of the reflection of the complex moral climate within a capitalist society.

As we know, Howells's work presents an interesting blend of the genteel tradition and desire to break from it, to eschew the sentimentality that he and his friends, particularly Samuel Clemens and Henry James, saw as having risen from it. As William Wasserstrom has recently pointed out . . . [in "Howells and the High Cost of Junk," *Old Northwest,* 1984], Howells presents "an arresting case of resolve and irresolution in the era of progress." In this novel alone we see him struggling with the contradictions: on the one hand he wishes us to admire Silas for his energy, his abilities, and his moral stature, on the other we must do so only from afar—Silas is not fit to be in the drawing room of the gentlemanly Bromfield Corey. Although we are meant to see Silas's underlying decency and dignity, the narrator cannot help poking subtle fun at him for being overweight, ungrammatical, and uncultured; and Howells ultimately can end the book only by banishing Silas, Persis, and Irene to Vermont and Penelope to Mexico. Further, while he criticizes the sentimentality of popular novels in his attack on *Tears, Idle Tears* or, as one of the characters calls it, *Slop, Silly Slop,* nevertheless he quite seriously portrays Silas's mother as a saint, kneeling at the foot of each of her children's beds each night to wash their feet.

In fact much of his ambivalence about gentility versus realism appears in the depiction of women. Because of this, as several critics have pointed out, Persis Lapham acts as her husband's conscience throughout most of the novel. I suggest that a reading of the novel concentrating on both economic issues and the portrayal of women in the novel, particularly of Persis, is in order. For several reasons which I will discuss, Persis serves as an unsettling presence in the book, always threatening to upset whatever balance is achieved. This can be read both as a product of Howells's ambivalence towards women and as an indication of his intuition of the impossibility of making moral choices in a world irrevocably changed by capitalist expansion. I therefore will begin my argument by setting

some context for the economic and sociological position of women like Persis Lapham at the time, then I will look at Howells's personal ambivalence about women, and finally examine more carefully Persis's role in the business and moral dilemmas of the novel.

I have said that Howells seems at once to critique the sentimental tradition and to affirm its gentility, and this ambivalence seems to me related to the ambivalence about capitalist enterprise critics have noticed in the novel. Ann Douglas, in *The Feminization of American Culture,* offers insight into this relationship. Women, she argues, during the period of 1820-1875, when the country was moving from agrarianism to industrialism, were "disestablished" from a direct role in the economic and intellectual development of their country. No longer the managers of a home/business where clothing and food were produced, women were relegated to various "claustrophobically cramped, if sacred" roles, including utter unselfishness in the guise of Christian virtue and discreet ignorance of all money matters. "Feminine," that is, passive virtues— piety, obedience, unselfishness, patience—were sentimentalized to the saccharine or bathetic. Her explanation of the instrumentality of such sentimentalization of qualities in themselves admirable is cogent:

> Sentimentalism is a complex phenomenon. It asserts that the values a society's activity denies are precisely the ones it cherishes; it attempts to deal with the phenomenon of cultural bifurcation by the manipulation of nostalgia. Sentimentalism provides a way to protest a power to which one has already in part capitulated. It is a form of dragging one's heels. It always borders on dishonesty but it is a dishonesty for which there is no known substitute in a capitalist country. Many nineteenth-century Americans in the Northeast acted every day as if they believed that economic expansion, urbanization, and industrialization represented the greatest good. It is to their credit that they indirectly acknowledged that the pursuit of these "masculine" goals meant damaging, perhaps losing, another good, one they increasingly included under the "feminine" ideal. Yet the fact remains that their regret was calculated not to interfere with their actions. . . .
>
> The sentimentalization of theological and secular culture was an inevitable part of the self-evasion of a society both committed to laissez-faire industrial expansion and disturbed by its consequences.

What Douglas observes is the investing of the "other"— that which was not capitalist man—with qualities he felt he could not or did not wish to possess himself, resulting in the sentimental tradition: Little Eva and the myriad of soft, sweet, virtuous heroines who ministered to their families in perfect Christian homes. While Howells was one of the earliest writers to break out of this sentimental tradition, he retained in his portraits of women some of the same assumptions and expectations pervading the sentimental novels, as well as some of his own more personal attitudes towards women. Persis Lapham, as the other half of Silas (and we note their similar names, much like

Howells's other Boston couple, Basil and Isabel March), becomes the receptacle for many of the qualities that Howells does not wish to ascribe to Silas, and as such she becomes a key figure in our understanding of Howells's complex moral vision.

Most critics give a rather simple reading to this story. They see Lapham, grown successful, get boastful and greedy and try to go too far into society. They argue that, as his success was founded on a faulty link—the selfish dumping of his partner, Rogers, just when the business was about to take off—it was doomed to failure. In atonement for that act Lapham is presented with a choice that will either save his business at the expense of his soul or his soul at the expense of his wealth; one cannot serve both God and mammon. Hence, his "rise" comes when he chooses the morally correct, though financially devastating, path; and the Laphams's move back to Vermont at the end is seen as either a nice pastoral retreat into the Jeffersonian ideal, or simply somewhat weak. And, in fact, there is reason to believe that Howells himself viewed the story this way. But on closer look certain intriguing inconsistencies and ambiguities arise which, I would argue, point to a deeper intuition on Howells's part about capitalist enterprise. The instability of the ending results from these unresolved underlying issues.

The book begins with an interview of Lapham by Bartley Hubbard, the clever but distasteful journalist who was the protagonist and villain of Howells's earlier novel, *A Modern Instance* (1882) and who is himself a self-made man. In that interview, Howells not only conveys the necessary information about Lapham's family and business background, but makes a statement about his feelings for the rags-to-riches fables then abounding as biographies, autobiographies, and fictional accounts of businessmen. From the first sentence we are asked to consider the relative worth of the genre. Every bit of information Silas offers in all sincerity about his family, Bartley takes with cynicism and records as formulaic sentimental pap. By having Bartley represent the two falsely simplistic versions of the businessman myth, Howells places Silas in the middle, thus enabling him to flesh out a more realistic portrait.

But the realism falters when it comes to the women in Silas's life. Lapham paints his mother as a saint, frail and small as a schoolgirl, working all day to feed, clothe, and watch over a husband and six sons, getting them to church and kneeling at night at each one's feet to wash them before they go to bed. Lapham chokes up at the memory (though Bartley yawns discreetly). "I tell you," Lapham adds, "when I hear women complaining nowadays that their lives are stunted and empty, I want to tell'em about my *mother's* life. *I* could paint it out for 'em." Persis, at this point, he admires as being the same kind of hardworking, morally firm helpmate, though that will soon change.

The phenomenon Lapham observes, without really understanding, is the disestablishment of women as important contributors to home economy, precisely the change that Ann Douglas described as happening over the nineteenth century. Contemporary women, relieved of the need to work so hard, found themselves with no purpose to their lives, no role except a decorative one. This phenomenon

occurs in the novel as well. Silas values Persis for her contribution to their lives, but her value gradually drops as he takes from her the need to work and places on her instead the burden of their social and moral lives. Thus Persis emerges as a woman in transition, no longer asked to perform her old role and unequipped for the new one. But Howells did not possess the insight into her character and situation that he did into her husband's, something he admitted himself years later in a letter to William Strunk: "I was fond of Lapham and fonder still of his wife; though I did not realize her so distinctly from life. . . . " Persis will not conform to her role as "angel of the house" any more than Silas will conform to the role of an Alger hero, but there is a significant difference in the nature of their non-conformity. In both cases we are given "realistic" characters rather than sentimental ideals, but, while Silas's realistic nature is praiseworthy, Persis's is seen as inadequate precisely because she does not retain all the virtues of the sentimental ideal. Lapham is coarse, and occasionally a buffoon, but ultimately we know him as strong, kind, competent, and dignified. Persis, on the other hand, goes from being a helpful business partner to a misguided, foolish woman who essentially causes both her husband's business failure and her daughters' near disaster in love.

Let me digress here to briefly describe Howells's attitudes towards women, which we know to be highly ambivalent. Kenneth Lynn, John Crowley, and Elizabeth Prioleau have all demonstrated how, as a boy and young man, Howells was intensely attached to his mother, to the point of being unable to leave her for more than a day without debilitating fits of anxiety and homesickness. At the same time he felt restricted by the closeness of life at home in a small town, and he and his sister Victoria yearned to leave and see the world. When he did finally leave to go to Columbus in 1858, his trips home grew gradually fewer and his letters, though expressing homesickness and sorrow for the pain he caused his mother by his absence, continually excused him from going home to visit. Once he received his consulship to Venice the break was made. His letters again expressed sorrow and guilt, but when he returned home to America with his new wife it was to Boston that he returned, and he never helped Victoria to escape as they had so often planned.

Of sexual subjects we know Howells was at best shy, at worst, as Crowley and Prioleau have demonstrated, severely neurotic. He is said, for instance, as a young boy to have refused to speak to or even to take a dish from the hand of a woman when he learned that she had been seduced and abandoned by a man. And these attitudes affected his notions of literature. In *Heroines of Fiction* (1901) he said that he could not consider in print, because of his audience of women, the heroines of Daniel Defoe, because Defoe was, "frankly, of the day before we began to dwell in decencies. . . . " Clearly overt sexuality, especially outside of marriage, was indecent. Although he consistently argued that realism should be "nothing more and nothing less than the truthful treatment of material," and he admired Balzac and Flaubert, for him certain material was taboo, most of it sexual, and must, like the heroines of Defoe, "remain under lock and key, and cannot be so much as named in mixed companies." His ideal heroines were those of Jane Austen, Maria Edgeworth, and Fanny Burney, who, "as women . . . were faithful to their charge of the chaste mind; and as artists they taught the reading world to be in love with the sort of heroines who knew how not only to win the wandering hearts of men, but to keep their homes inviolable."

Yet, in an article for *Harper's Bazaar* only one year later, he espoused a different opinion. Since women's "good and their evil are the good and the evil of men; there is not one law for women and another for men. They inherit their fathers as well as their mothers . . . they mirror their father's minds in quite surprising measure. . . . " So, he concludes, one could almost let them read anything. Purity cannot be tainted by a book, he says, "The innocent remain scatheless from DeFoe, Swift, Sterne, Byron himself," and he ends his essay by remarking coyly that, though it was at the time considered shocking for a woman to read the daily newspaper, the only part of it that could harm her was the Woman's Page. His words here, while in keeping with his strong dislike for sentimental fiction, express an opinion exactly opposite to the one he gave a year earlier. Are women so pure as to be incorruptible, or are they fragile vessels who must be protected from knowledge of sex and other evils? The question remained for him unresolvable.

His relations with his wife, while generally happy, were not without problems. Both she and Howells suffered from nervous disorders, and their daughter, Winnie, died tragically young from an ambiguous combination of emotional and physical illness. Elinor Howells was an even stricter moralist than her husband and, like Olivia Clemens, a stern critic of her husband's work. John Crowley sums up what he labels Howells's "lifelong ambivalence toward women" by saying:

> Howells masochistically courted women's domination. He sought emotional support from the women he feared, and this need prevailed over his concealed misogyny by means of a compensatory reaction-formation. That is, Howells defended against his repressed rage towards threatening women by consciously stressing their benevolence, by proclaiming "the fact of woman's moral and spiritual superiority" over man.

Thus, while Howells protects women, revered their putative sensibilities, often supported women writers and the cause of women's suffrage, there was an undertone of anxiety and fear in his relations with them, and these feelings come out in his characterization of Persis Lapham. He simultaneously sets her up as the book's moral standard and undercuts that position. Ultimately the question of Persis's reliability as moral arbiter is intricately connected with the issue of business ethics and with Silas's moral growth.

As I have said, the knottiest ethical dilemma in the book is Silas's dealings with his former partner Rogers. In order to make amends for buying Rogers out just before a boom in business, Lapham made substantial loans to Rogers which Rogers could not repay, and took as collateral some worthless stock and a mill made equally worthless by the

GL&P railroad's intention to deny it rail service unless the owner sold the land cheaply to the railroad. Most readers would agree that Silas made the right choice in refusing to sell the mill at a high price to some unscrupulous agents who were acting on behalf of a charitable organization in England. The organization was unaware that the property was about to be rendered worthless, although the agents knew and were hiding it because they stood to earn a high commission for their work. Thus if Silas sold to the agents, he and Rogers would both come out clean, the agents would make their commission, and the paint business would be able to weather the temporary depression in the market. All would gain by cheating the Englishmen and the charitable organization they represented. Clearly the morally correct decision for Silas was to absorb the loss made by his own blindness to Roger's lies rather than to cheat an innocent party. The same is true for Silas's decision to tell the full truth about his financial difficulties to some potential investors whose investment would have provided another way out of the impending disaster. The difficulty for Silas rests, not in discerning the right course, for the choices are clear, but in having the courage to choose the good act when he stands to lose all he has gained over years of hard work. That he can choose the hard way, and then bear its consequences, is proof of his moral stature.

The interesting question, however, precedes this dilemma. Given his good business sense and his insistence on being fair, how did Silas get in the position to lose everything in the first place? What made him become involved with Rogers a second time? As I have said, most critics agree that the entire Lapham success was built on a faulty link—forcing Rogers out of the business early on—and that his guilt for this act is what made him vulnerable to Rogers's scheme. Certainly Persis believes this to be true. But such a conclusion is by no means self-evident, and a careful examination of the text provides grounds for a more ambivalent interpretation.

We first meet Rogers in Chapter 3, at the sight of the Lapham's new house, on the same day of Silas's interview with Bartley. This is how we see him:

> As the colonel turned from casting anchor at the mare's head with the hitching-weight, after helping his wife to alight, he encountered a man to whom he could not help speaking, though the man seemed to share his hesitation if not his reluctance at the necessity. He was a tallish, thin man, with a dust-colored face, and a dead, clerical air, which somehow suggested at once feebleness and tenacity.

The image suggests that here stands a dangerous figure. In his feebleness Rogers seems near death, his face the color of the dust to which it must return, yet the air of tenacity suggests that he will pull down with him all who might be in reach of his grasping hand.

Mrs. Lapham is cordial to him, and we learn that Rogers has not been successful since parting with the Lapham paint company. Persis feels this to be her husband's fault, and when the man departs Silas and Persis argue, Persis insisting that Rogers blights everything, and Silas demanding why she lets Rogers blight everything. Persis claims that Lapham ruined Rogers by forcing him out of the business; Lapham asserts "it was a perfectly square thing. . . . My conscience is easy as far as he's concerned, and it always was."

The facts of the relationship were as follows: at a time when the business was just stretching its wings after the Civil War, it needed money to take flight. Despite his desire to keep the paint all to himself, Silas took Persis's advice and got a partner with money to invest. The business took off, but the partnership was not successful, and after a year or two Silas gave Rogers the option of buying him out or being bought out. Rogers could not buy, so he sold, receiving considerably more for his share than he had invested. Such a buy/sell arrangement is quite a common way of dissolving partnerships.

Persis's view of the situation was that Silas ruined Rogers by making use of his money, then forcing him out just when the business became successful. Silas contends that Rogers "was a drag and a brake on me from the word go. You say he saved me. Well, if I hadn't got him out he'd a' ruined me sooner or later. So it's an even thing, as far forth as that goes." Persis contends that Rogers's business life, and thus the comforts of Mrs. Rogers, were ruined by the transaction. But why should that be so? Why has Rogers not been successful; what happened to all the money he made on the sale of this share of the paint business? Rogers's fall from wealth would seem to indicate that Silas's assessment of him was correct.

These questions suggest the need to take a more considered view of the buy-out. Persis sees it as a moral issue in which Silas took the selfish part. Silas sees it as a business transaction in which he behaved fairly, even generously. The narrator has this to say:

> In that affair of the partnership she had tried to be his conscience, but perhaps she would have defended him if he had accused himself; it was one of those things in this life which seem destined to await justice, or at least judgment, in the next. As he said, Lapham had dealt fairly by his partner in money; he had let Rogers take more money out of the business than he put into it; he had, as he said, simply forced out of it a timid and inefficient participant in advantages which he had created. But Lapham had not created them all. He had been dependent at one time on his partner's capital. It was a moment of terrible trial. Happy is the man forever after who can choose the ideal, the unselfish part in such an exigency! Lapham could not rise to it. He did what he could maintain to be perfectly fair. The wrong, if any, seemed to be condoned to him, except when from time to time his wife brought it up. Then all the question stung and burned anew, and had to be reasoned out and put away once more. It seemed to have an inextinguishable vitality. It slept, but it did not die.

The narrator's view is ambiguous. On the one hand, he sees it as an incident which cannot be judged on Earth, beyond human justice. On the other hand, he says that Lapham "could not rise" to the ideal, unselfish act, thus passing implicit judgment on Silas's selfishness. He agrees

that Lapham was fair in terms of money, but implies that there is another unstated arena in which he was not fair, and he hedges yet again by saying "the wrong, if any," in a neat, Hawthornian dodge. To Silas it never seems wrong unless Persis brings it up; presumably the question would in fact die if Persis never mentioned it. But Persis is here designated the "other"—she will take whichever side of a moral debate that Silas does not take, and in so doing point out the instability of the concepts "right" and "wrong." Because of the narrative evasions and the impasse between husband and wife, we can never be sure whether a wrong was committed.

But Persis has her opinion, and her opinion carries weight. She believes that Lapham failed in his moral duty towards Rogers, and most readers are inclined to take her view of the matter. From the very beginning of the book we are shown how much influence Persis has over her husband and how close they are in marriage. We are prepared in the opening interview for Silas's reverential attitude towards her by his vivid deification of his mother. We are not disappointed; Silas refers to Persis often and proudly, and we learn that he has named the best line of his paint the Persis Brand. He credits much of the success of the business to her efforts, declaring that "it wasn't the seventy-five percent of purr-ox-eyed of iron in the *ore* that made that paint go; it was the seventy-five percent of purr-ox-eyed of iron in *her.*" Because we know that Persis was a schoolteacher and a good household manager, we feel secure in her intelligence and judgment. Silas is said to have risen in the world when he married her and clearly he feels it to be so. Up until chapter three, when we first encounter Rogers and the question of the partnership, the reader seems to have no reason to doubt her role as moral standard.

But there are other clues, and we find later in the book that hindsight gives us several criteria on which to judge Lapham's behavior to Rogers as a partner and hence to judge Persis's competence. First, of course, we learn just how unscrupulous Rogers is when we see him urge Lapham to cheat the Englishmen. Before that he had coerced Lapham, under false pretenses and with collateral that he knew to be worthless, to lend him large sums of money for a project that failed. In short, Rogers is a thorough scoundrel, and to see him merely as a tempter figure for Silas is to ignore Howells's commitment to realism. Lapham's business intuitions about Rogers were correct; it seems likely that Rogers would have harmed in some way the future of the paint company had he remained a partner.

From a business viewpoint, then, Lapham's decision to dissolve the partnership was good one. It was also fair, even generous, in terms of money. Morally it was unable to be judged. Why then did Lapham allow himself to get involved again with Rogers? The answer can provide the key to the unease we feel with the ending of the book. Silas was acting, not on his own guilt, but rather against his better judgment on the impulse of Persis, just as he had in taking a partner in the first place and just as he does in accepting Tom Corey as a suitor to the pretty but thoughtless Irene instead of to the more appropriate wry, sensible

Penelope. At Persis's prompting Silas made a misguided, sentimental gesture which brought about his financial ruin.

I have said that in the beginning both the reader and Silas perceive Persis as superior in moral judgment. But even while setting her up as the presumed moral standard of the novel, Howells begins to undercut her. He casts doubt upon her ability to help Silas any further in his business, which in turn makes the reader wonder about her capacity in other ways.

> Up to a certain point in their prosperity Mrs. Lapham had kept strict account of all her husband's affairs; but as they expanded, and ceased to be of the retail nature with which women successfully grapple, the intimate knowledge of them made her nervous.

Here is where Howells's personal beliefs about the limitations of women come to affect his story. This broad and inaccurate generalization about women softens the blow to Persis by making it seem as if she could not be expected to be any wiser or more competent than she is. Women are, after all, like Elinor and Winnie Howells, apt to be nervous. Furthermore, their province is the home, not the office. But while the remark seems not to blame Persis, in reality it lays open to question her intelligence and judgment in complex, worldly matters.

And these qualities continue to be undercut throughout the book by varying generalizations about the nature of women: In regard to the move from Nankeen Square, "She felt the trouble a woman knows in view of any great change." As to stocks, she disapproves "with the conservatism of her sex." In talking about Penelope, she demands her husband's attention, "yielding to the necessity a wife feels of making her husband pay for her suffering, even if he has not inflicted it." How could we help but question the wisdom of such a frightened, irrational creature?

The growing relationship between the Coreys, a Boston Brahmin family, and the Laphams, offers another arena in which to view Persis's judgment and to compare it to Silas's. Both are uncomfortable with the Coreys socially and aware of their own social inferiority. Persis is as much at a loss as her husband about how to return a call, how to respond to a dinner invitation, and what to wear to someone's home. But Silas can recoup his social losses with business competence, whereas Persis is left seeming inadequate in a realm that is her family responsibility. And her *faux pas* extends beyond the social and into both business and moral realms.

First, Persis does not believe that Tom Corey would enter the paint business and accuses Lapham when he suggests it of having "mineral paint on the brain" (as opposed to on the conscience, as Bartley jokingly suggests in the beginning interview). When Tom comes of his own volition to Lapham to seek employment, his request discredits Persis's judgment. She is also wrong about Tom's affection for Irene. Blinded by her own preference for her beautiful younger daughter, Persis cannot see that Penelope is the object of Tom's attention, not Irene. In fact, she insists on

this interpretation in the face of her own doubts and encourages Irene in her happy daydreams. Her error causes as much havoc, and more pain, to the family than Lapham's business failure.

These events prepare us for Persis's two major failures: her mistrust of Silas with Zerilla Millon and her collapse at the moment Silas must decide to cheat someone or lose his business. The story of Silas's typist, Zerilla, serves several functions in the book, including providing an opportunity for Howells to make some observations about social conditions in Boston. But its implications for Persis and her ability to judge are the most important. First it indicates how fallible she is when she believes the anonymous, salacious note about Silas and his typist. More importantly it shows us that she was, in fact, an inadequate moral accountant long before the action of the novel occurs. Jim Millon had died saving Lapham's life in the Civil War and Silas felt responsible for his widow and daughter, Zerilla, whom he now employed as a typist. Persis, however, had told Silas not to give them more money, that his debt to them was paid. The fact that Lapham continued to help the family despite Persis's objection illustrates that he was able to recognize a moral obligation and act upon it even if it meant crossing his wife. She, however, felt the debt discharged, in a kind of reversal of attitudes from her position on the question of Rogers.

This in turn prepares us for her inevitable failure at Silas's critical moment. Rogers has confronted the Laphams with his scheme for recouping their losses, which entails the legally correct but ethically dubious sale of the mill:

> Lapham glanced again at his wife; her head had fallen; he could see that she was so rooted in her old remorse for that questionable act of his, amply and more than fully atoned for since, that she was helpless, now in the crucial moment, when he had the utmost need of her insight. He had counted upon her; he perceived now that when he had thought it was for him alone to decide, he had counted upon her just spirit to stay his own in its struggle to be just.

Silas is forced to order her gently to bed and proceed through the evening, and in a sense, through the rest of his life, alone. Silas's moral rise is complete; he has cut all ties and made the final judgment for himself. Here is where the aesthetic demands of the text require Persis to be foolish and helpless: for Silas to achieve his rise, it was essential that Persis be unavailable to choose for him.

Thus Persis's portrayal provides chiastic structure to the plot. As Silas (and the reader) gradually realizes she is benighted, he becomes aware of the strength of his own moral vision. Formerly he had exalted his wife and assumed, along with everyone else, it had been a rise for him when he married her. By the close of the novel he discovers he's not the country bumpkin whose father discovered a paint mine, but rather a good, strong man capable of making some very hard decisions. His rise is as much a rise in self-esteem as in moral judgment. The reader learns, along with Silas, that the rules in "real life" are different from those in sentimental fiction. Business decisions must be made on the basis of fairness, not sentiment. The love plot here functions to reinforce the lessons of the business story: Irene's failed relations with Tom break the expectations of traditional sentimental fiction just as does Silas's business failure.

Donald Pizer has shown us how the two plots of the novel are tied in the way they resolve their ethical dilemmas by means of a utilitarian, "economy of pain" solution. (Even moral questions take on the rhetoric of business.) That is, the decision that Penelope should marry Tom and the decision that Silas cannot cheat the Englishmen or the investors are both made on the basis of hurting the fewest people. In both cases Persis acts as the voice of sentimentality which must be corrected. When Rogers pleads that his wife needs her comforts, Persis must be ordered out of the room so that Silas can make the right choice. She finds it equally difficult to accept Penelope's decision to marry Tom, even after repeated counsel from both her husband and the Reverend Mr. Sewell.

> Again and again Mrs. Lapham said she did not see how she could go through it. "I can't make it seem right," she said.
>
> "It *is* right," steadily answered the Colonel.
>
> "Yes, I know. But it don't *seem* so."

Persis's feelings about Penelope's marriage are as misguided and sentimental as *Tears, Idle Tears,* and as misguided as her feelings for Rogers and his family. Silas, now the stronger and wiser of the two, declares what is right. While we know it is right for Penelope and Tom to marry, and we agree that Persis is being foolish in expecting them to sacrifice their happiness, we can also see that she is voicing an understandable critique of the imperfect nature of moral choice.

How, then, are we to interpret the ending of the book? We, like the Reverend Mr. Sewell, are interested in the "moral spectacle" that Silas presents. Is his life in Vermont the happy pastoral resolution that most critics call it? Has Silas returned to live peacefully with nature on his farm? No, for that would be just as sentimental as if Irene and Tom married and lived happily ever after on the water side of Beacon. Rather, Silas's life in Vermont is a temporary stasis for him, and not a wholly satisfactory one. He still rides after a fast horse and, although he has pared his business down to one product, the Persis Brand, he is indeed working to rebuild his paint empire. He also has a share in the Kanawha Paint Co., owned by the West Virginians who bought out much of the old Lapham Works, and their success is helping Lapham by paying him dividends. He plans improvements to the house, and one wonders if he might not wish some day to move back to the city. He is "unkempt, after the fashion of the country," and the reader must be uncomfortable with this because of the narrator's obvious note of patrician superiority.

We see in this small remark another of Howells's genteel prejudices, one which may be responsible for the relegation of the Laphams to northernmost Vermont. From the beginning we are reminded they are unfit for Boston society. The Colonel is ungrammatical; neither he nor the Lapham women know how to behave in proper company. Silas reads the wrong paper and does not know when to wear gloves; Persis makes her own (inferior) tea and cakes and does her own wash. While Howells presents their awkwardness sympathetically, we sense that to establish the Laphams comfortably on the water side of Beacon, to have the Coreys forced to entertain them as intimate connections, would be as distasteful to the author as to his Brahmin counterparts in the novel. One of the less happy results of capitalist expansion seems for him to be the creation of a new class that threatens to infiltrate society. The best Howells can do is to let Tom and Penelope marry, giving the vague suggestions of a new generation with the Lapham energy infusing Corey taste. But even then he must take the young couple away to Mexico for he cannot quite imagine them together at a proper dinner party.

Another, perhaps more important, cause of the unease we feel with the ending is the break in the Laphams's perfect understanding. Sadly Silas tells the Reverend Mr. Sewell that he and his wife no longer talk about the moral implications of their experience; finally the subject of Rogers has died and, with it, some important tie between husband and wife. We realize that when, in the last full scene in which we see them together, Silas tells her of his ruin, and together they look at the note sent to Persis to "warn" her about Silas and the typist.

> "I guess I know who it's from," he said, giving it back to her, "and I guess you do, too, Persis."
>
> "But how—how could he—"
>
> "Mebbe he believed it," said Lapham, with patience that cut her more keenly than any reproach. "*You* did."

This has been a marriage filled with conversation, but the dialogue has ended. In order for Silas to be morally certain he must silence the voice that threatens disruption.

Left finally unresolved is the question of judgment of Silas's first act with Rogers, the dissolution of the partnership. The matter comes up again in the end, but without resolution. It would be easy to say that guilt for the original act prompted Silas's financial collapse, but Silas still does not admit to doing any wrong in the transaction. The truth is his mistaken reliance on Persis's sentimental judgment led him to resume dealings with a scoundrel. Thus, one could argue, his entire moral trial becomes unnecessary—he already knew how to recognize duty and to act on it as he did with Jim Millon's family, and his "prompt comprehensiveness and never-failing business sagacity" warned him correctly of the threat Rogers posed to his business. Had he relied on his own judgment in the beginning he would not have had to return to Vermont a bankrupt. And yet the issue of fairness remains. Perhaps Lapham was unfair to Rogers; perhaps the very nature of the dilemma prevents it from being resolved in economic terms. Rogers's timely infusion of capital made Lapham's success possible. What dollar figure could one put on that that would call the account even? But what way other than economically can fairness in business be practiced? The nature of moral debate in this context tends itself to instability; Persis serves as catalyst.

And the ending, too, is unstable. Howells may temporarily have resolved the dilemma of new business practices and manners by sending the Laphams to Vermont, but Silas is too smart, too likeable, too powerful simply to accept relegation to the country when his story is over. He may not fit the Back Bay, but he can no longer be contained in the backwoods of Vermont. The Persis Brand will sell; he will come back. (pp. 419-38)

> Irene C. Goldman, "Business Made Her Nervous: The Fall of Persis Lapham," in The Old Northwest, *Vol. 13, No. 4, Winter, 1986, pp. 419-38.*

## Brenda Murphy    (essay date 1989)

[*Murphy is an American educator and critic whose works reflect her interest in American Realism and its effect on American culture. In the following excerpt, Murphy discusses from a structuralist perspective Howells's approach to the Victorian paradigms of the self-made millionaire and the romantic act of self-sacrifice in* The Rise of Silas Lapham.]

In the two decades since Roland Barthes' "Introduction to the Structural Analysis of Narratives" (1966) appeared, the distinction between story *(histoire)* and narrative or text *(discours)* has become a standard assumption in the critical analysis of narrative. "In simple terms," as Seymour Chatman says, "the story is the *what* in a narrative that is depicted, discourse the *how.*" The relationship of this theoretical point to literary criticism, or analysis of specific texts, becomes clear in what Barthes had to say about structuralist analysis in *S/Z.* The first analysts of narrative were attempting, he wrote, "to see all the world's stories . . . within a single structure: we shall, they thought, extract from each tale its model, then out of these models we shall make a great narrative structure, which we shall reapply (for verification) to any one narrative." The problem with the project thus defined is that it really is a useless activity for those who are interested in literary criticism, the elucidation of texts. To the literary critic, the story, the sequence of events, is of interest precisely insofar as it affects the meaning of the text, and the discovery of a paradigm for stories is interesting primarily insofar as it affects the syntagmatic study of texts.

Barthes has provided a beginning for the literary study of story with his reading of the "proairetic code" in *S/Z.* He named the code after the Aristotelian concept of *proairesis,* or "the ability rationally to determine the result of an action," and he defined it loosely as the "code of actions and behavior." Like the other four codes by which meaning is construed, this code of action, or "empirics," as he sometimes calls it, is "one of the voices out of which the text is woven," and can be read as effectively as any of them. It is this code of action, story in narrative, story inseparable from its telling, that will be the focus for this reading.

*Silas Lapham*'s structure is fundamentally a "correction" of two popular nineteenth-century story paradigms, the rags-to-riches "success myth" and the sentimental novel of self-sacrifice, two story paradigms which the realist Howells rejected as false representations of reality. The overwhelming import of the novel's proairetic code is that the truth, the representation of reality the novel embodies, is only to be found in disruption of the conventional story paradigm, and that the false representation prevailing in popular literature not only is simple-minded and silly, but is cynically manipulated by its purveyors for their own profit, to the deep injury of its audience. Reading the proairetic code in *The Rise of Silas Lapham* brings Howells' polemic opposition to the falsity of contemporary popular narratives into sharper focus than has occurred with previous analysis and adds one more "voice," as Barthes would say, to the articulation of meaning in *Silas Lapham.*

The most significant cultural paradigm that Howells addresses in *Silas Lapham* is, of course, the success myth, a universal popular property since Benjamin Franklin's formulation of it in his autobiography and *Poor Richard's Almanac,* revised slightly by Horatio Alger during the eighteen-sixties, seventies, and eighties. In Kenneth Lynn's estimation, "the Alger hero represents a triumphant combination—and reduction to the lowest common denominator—of the most widely accepted concepts in nineteenth-century American society. The belief in the potential greatness of the common man, the glorification of individual effort and accomplishment, the equation of the pursuit of money with the pursuit of happiness and of business success with spiritual grace." While more recent scholarship on Alger has modified the view of the pursuit of money as the endpoint of a single-minded life of striving that Lynn's analysis implies, it is consistent with Michael Zuckerman's formulation of Alger's version of business success: "As Alger would have it . . . success follows dependability and a desire to serve others. It attends those who obey orders cheerfully and serve others willingly. And it is available to all, for Alger posited no pinnacle of preeminence for which many compete and few prove fit." The paradigm for the American success story pervaded Howells' culture, and it does not take much investigation to see the forms in which he encountered it.

The romance of the millionaire abounds in the newspapers of the eighteen-eighties. When John C. Eno was exposed as an embezzler during the financial panic that began in May of 1884 and continued into the summer (as Howells was composing *Silas Lapham*), the Boston *Herald* went back to his self-made father to create a story that fit the popular paradigm. The headline tells the story:

> A RISE TO MILLIONS
> Followed by a Fall to Criminal Disgrace
> The Career of the Young Embezzler John C.
> Eno
> Facts with the Romantic Interest of Fiction

The reporter begins his narrative with the heroic struggle of Eno's father, a self-made man who sounds very much like Silas Lapham:

> In 1857, when I owned as much ground as I do now, and this hotel was about half finished, it looked for a few days as though I didn't have a dollar's worth. It was the time of the great panic, you know. I had a lot of paper out, and all my resources were tied up in this enterprise. Money got awfully tight, and the banks put the screws

on me with a vengeance. I had to stop work, and for a while it seemed sure pop that everything would be swept clean. I held on like the bark to a tree, though, and never had any trouble again, and I guess I'm beyond any further danger. What I've got I'll keep clear through.

Here is the popular version of the story of Lapham and his paint business: the heroism of hard work wins out and comfortable success is its reward. Howells' refusal to acquiesce in that version of reality is his correction of the romantic popular paradigm. Of course, Eno's son does turn out to be an embezzler, but that is put down to the weakness of character caused by the lack of early privation and hard work in the second generation's upbringing. The rich boy is bound to fail, even in Alger's stories. The newspaper story's point is that the elder Eno comes out unscathed, in fortune and in honor. (pp. 21-3)

In *The Self-Made Man in America,* Irvin Wylie laid out the five sequences of events in the biography of a self-made man that were necessary to the success cult's ideology: origin in poverty, a rural childhood, migration to the city, a mother's moral influence that lasted for a lifetime, and marriage to a good woman who was an unfailing support to her husband. Howells' understanding of the rags-to-riches story paradigm and the cultural forces that manipulated it is abundantly clear in the opening of the novel. In the narrative of the interview between Bartley Hubbard and Silas Lapham, Howells carefully interweaves four distinct levels of discourse which articulate four levels of cultural awareness about the success myth. The first is the discourse of Silas' ingenuously egotistical narrative, delivered in his own language and in his own style. To him his story is personal and unique, a simple narration of what happened in his life. The second is the discourse of the newspaper article, Bartley's public reformulation of Lapham's story in accord with the cultural paradigm. The third is Bartley's cynical commentary on the story, reflecting his awareness that he is dealing in the culture's popular fictions rather than reality, and his willingness to manipulate both the story and Lapham for his own profit. The fourth is the narrator's commentary, the moral voice that represents Bartley to the reader as the "potential reprobate," weak and amoral.

All four of these levels are at work in the presentation of Lapham's early rural poverty. Lapham has been told to begin at the beginning:

> "Well, say I'm fifty-five years old; and I've *lived* 'em too; not an hour of waste time about *me,* anywheres! I was born on a farm, and—" [1]

> "Worked in the fields summers and went to school winters: regulation thing?" [3] Bartley cut in. [4]

> "Regulation thing," [1] said Lapham, accepting this irreverent version of his history somewhat dryly. [4]

> "Parents poor, of course," [3] suggested the journalist. [4] "Any barefoot business? Early deprivations of any kind, that would encourage the youthful reader to go and do likewise? Orphan

myself, you know," [3] said Bartley, with a smile of cynical good-comradery. [4]

Lapham looked at him silently, and then said with quiet self-respect, [4] "I guess if you see these things as a joke, my life won't interest you." [1]

Thus the first and third levels of awareness are set up for the reader: Silas' straightforward belief in the "real" events of his life, and the reporter's sense of them as material he can manipulate in order to fulfill the public's expectation of a familiar and satisfying story-line. Demonstrating the extent of this manipulation, and of Bartley's cynicism, Howells juxtaposes the second level, the text of the newspaper interview, with the conversation:

> Mr. Lapham . . . passed rapidly over the story of his early life, its poverty and its hardships, sweetened, however, by the recollections of a devoted mother, and a father who, if somewhat her inferior in education, was no less ambitious for the advancement of his children. They were quiet, unpretentious people, religious, after the fashion of that time, and of sterling morality, and they taught their children the simple virtues of the Old Testament and Poor Richard's Almanac.

Finally, the voice of the narrator comes in, revealing in its commentary a knowledge of Silas' simplicity, the public's acquiescence in the newspaper's formulaic discourse, the falsity of the formula's representation of reality, and the cynicism with which the reporter presents it: "Bartley could not deny himself this gibe; but he trusted to Lapham's unliterary habit of mind for his security in making it, and most other people would consider it sincere reporter's rhetoric."

By manipulating these four levels of discourse, Howells maintains a triple irony in the narrative. It is of course Bartley whose amoral cynicism comes under sharpest attack. Being shown a picture of Irene Lapham, for example, " 'She's a good-looking chap,' said Bartley, with prompt irreverence. He hastened to add, at the frown which gathered between Lapham's eyes, 'What a beautiful creature she is! What a lovely, refined sensitive face! And she looks *good,* too . . . And, after all, that's about the best thing in a woman,' said the potential reprobate." But the narrative treatment of both the formula's bland hypocrisy and Lapham's egotistical naiveté is ironic as well. The passage from Bartley's newspaper piece shows Howells' ironic treatment of the formula's hypocritical pretense of morality. As if the juxtaposition of the Old Testament and *Poor Richard's Almanac* were not enough, the glaring absence of the New Testament in the moral life of these supposed Christians sharply defines the limits of the success myth's morality. Lapham's inability to see "where the joke comes in" in his painting "Lapham's Mineral Paint—Specimen" on every available board-fence, bridge girder, dead wall, barn, or face of rock is a good example of the narrative irony with which he is treated. "I say the landscape was made for man, and not man for the landscape," he says. Whereupon Bartley replies, "Yes . . . it was made for the stove-polish man and the kidney-cure man," and Silas remains "insensible to Bartley's irony."

The pervasive irony of this opening chapter has an unsettling effect on the reader, who has not been directed clearly by its multi-level discourse into what perspective to take on Silas Lapham and his story. Howells settles this doubt in Chapter II, with a long narrative passage about the Laphams, and the truth about the lives of "successful" Americans. He takes up the "reality" of their lives where the paradigm for the success story ends, with the achievement of wealth and ease. What do these simple, hardworking and virtuous rural people do with their money after they've earned it? This, Howells suggests, is where the formula fails.

> Suddenly the money began to come so abundantly that [Mrs. Lapham] need not save; and then they did not know what to do with it. A certain amount could be spent on horses, and Lapham spent it; his wife spent in rich and rather ugly clothes and a luxury of household appointments. Lapham had not yet reached the picture-buying stage of the rich man's development, but they decorated their house with the costliest and most abominable frescoes; they went upon journeys, and lavished upon cars and hotels; they gave with both hands to their church and to all the charities it brought them acquainted with; but they did not know how to spend on society.

And this is the rub in their so-called success, for the Laphams find that they have put themselves in a social no-man's land where it will be impossible to find husbands for their daughters. They are too wealthy to seek out friends and acquaintances in the simple country fashion that is the only way the elder Laphams know, and in their ignorance they have violated the rigid codes of the society they hope to enter by sending their daughters to the "wrong" schools and not introducing them as children to the complexities of Boston social connections. The picture Howells paints is that of a family left completely to itself because its money has thrust it out of the class it belongs to but has not been sufficient to impel it into another. In social terms, Howells implies, success is a disaster. This is the part of the story that the success myth of the previous chapter omits.

The introduction of the Lapham family provides the link to the second major story-line in the novel, the action involving the Lapham sisters and Tom Corey that is Howells' treatment of the self-sacrifice paradigm in nineteenth-century popular fiction. Howells was never shy about showing the disgust with which he encountered the "gaudy hero and heroine" of popular sentimental fiction. He especially berated the heroine who "taught by example, if not precept, that Love, or the passion or fancy she mistook for it, was the chief interest of a life, which is really concerned with a great many other things. . . . More lately she has begun to idolize and illustrate Duty, and she is hardly less mischievous in this new role, opposing duty, as she did love, to prudence, obedience, and reason" [*Criticism and Fiction,* 1891]. His *bete noire* in this idolization of Duty was the cult of self-sacrifice, and his attack on it in his fiction has received cogent analysis, most recently by Alfred Habegger, who has argued [in "The Autistic Tyrant: Howells' Self-Sacrificial Woman and Jamesian Renunciation," *Novel* (Fall 1976)] that "in attacking the ideal of self-sacrifice Howells was aiming at the dead center of American life—the negative, passive, self-denying life that women were expected to lead."

In [*Gender, Fantasy, and Realism*], his study of the sentimental popular paradigm for what he calls loosely "women's fiction," Habegger has put his finger on precisely the aspect of these sentimentally idealized fantasies about self-sacrifice that Howells represents as so destructive to their readers. "Ultimately, the reason why novels encouraged the reader to identify herself with an altogether superior heroine was to make possible the intensely pleasurable pay-off at the end, a climax not considered successful unless it produced a physical effect—happy tears." The danger came precisely with this sense of identity, for "this gender identity was at one and the same time very private and very public—private because it formed the individual's goal or idealized self or wished-for image; public, because it was after all a kind of copy of cultural norms. Fantasy, then, was nothing less than a private drama in which one put oneself into the ideal gender role. And the popular novel was a prop for standard fantasies."

In foregrounding his presentation of the popular version of self-sacrifice, the imaginary novel *Tears, Idle Tears,* Howells was attempting to expose these standard fantasies to his readers for what they were, and in the story-line depicting Penelope's behavior in her dilemma, he was correcting the popular story paradigm, first by showing that romantic self-sacrifice was not heroic but silly and hurtful, and second by showing that the reality of human behavior was a good deal more complicated than the popular paradigm suggested.

Howells introduces the issue by presenting the paradigm and the standard reaction to it that Habegger describes. At the dinner party, the good-hearted but rather silly and emotional Clara Kingsbury brings up *Tears, Idle Tears* as a topic of conversation: "It's perfectly heart-breaking, as you'll imagine from the name; but there's such a dear old-fashioned hero and heroine in it, who keep dying for each other all the way through, and making the most wildly satisfactory and unnecessary sacrifices for each other. You feel as if you'd done them yourself." At this point, the narrative confronts the popular sentiment directly, with Nanny Corey's comment that the novel ought to have been called *Slop, Silly Slop* and the Reverend Mr. Sewall's condemnation: "The self-sacrifice painted in most novels like this . . . is nothing but physical suicide, and is as wholly immoral as the spectacle of a man falling on his sword." The crucial foregrounding of the conventional paradigm comes, however, in the discussion Tom and Penelope have of the book just before his proposal prompts her own struggle with self-sacrifice. Learning that Penelope has just read *Tears, Idle Tears,* Tom remarks:

> "It's a famous book with ladies. They break their hearts over it. Did it make you cry?"

> "Oh, it's pretty easy to cry over a book," said Penelope, laughing; "and that one *is* very natural till you come to the main point. Then the naturalness of all the rest makes that seem natural too; but I guess it's rather forced."

"Her giving him up to the other one?"

"Yes; simply because she happened to know that the other one had cared for him first. Why should she have done it? What right had she?"

"I don't know. I suppose that the self-sacrifice—"

"But it *wasn't* self-sacrifice—or not self-sacrifice alone. She was sacrificing him too; and for someone who couldn't appreciate him half as much as she could. I'm provoked with myself when I think how I cried over that book—for I did cry. It's silly—it's wicked for anyone to do what that girl did. Why can't they let people have a chance to behave reasonably in stories?"

"Perhaps they couldn't make it so attractive," suggested Corey, with a smile.

Foregrounding the story paradigm in this way, Howells was sure of at least getting his readers to think about the falseness of the ideal that it preached and of the harm that identification with the heroine could do to the readers of sentimental popular fiction. It also prepared his readers for the realistic correction he was about to offer, the sequence of events portraying 1) the pain that not only Penelope and Tom, but Irene, the elder Laphams, and even the Coreys had to endure; 2) the gradual conviction, largely through Sewall's agency, in all of them that Penelope could only do wrong to give Tom up because Irene had fancied him first; 3) the slow recovery of Irene from the pain of her rejection; and 4) the more or less happy union of Tom and Penelope. The "more or less" is important here, for Howells was representing real life. Penelope's final course is far from the noble and selfless decision of the sentimental heroine in her world of simple black-and-white choices. At the end of her year of trial, she complains, " 'There's no more reason now and no less than ever there was . . . why I should say Yes, or why I should say No. . . . if I could be *sentenced* to be married, or somebody would up and forbid the banns! *I* don't know what to do about it.' "

In the end, Penelope marries Tom because she loves him and he loves her and they want to be married, but she still feels guilty because, Howells has strongly implied, of that fantastic and silly popular ideal. Nor does Howells allow the romantic implication that all will be happy-ever-after romantic bliss following the wedding trip to slip into his love story.

> It would be easy to point out traits in Penelope's character which finally reconciled all her husband's family and endeared her to them. These things continually happen in novels; and the Coreys, as they had always promised themselves to do, made the best, and not the worst of Tom's marriage. . . . But the differences remained uneffaced, if not uneffaceable, between the Coreys and Tom Corey's wife. . . . That was the end of their son and brother for them; they felt that; and they were not mean or unamiable people.

Howells' correction of the popular sentimental story paradigm implies a new, "truer" one based on the faithful representation of what he saw in the world rather than on the

confirmation of the prevailing popular fantasy. The primary characteristic of this new narrative structure is that its impelling logic, the logic of human behavior, is not simple and one-dimensional, but complex, not ideally heroic but human.

Howells makes a similar correction of the conventional paradigm with the business story-line. Not only is success not what it's cracked up to be in the popular fantasy, as he demonstrates in depicting the Laphams' relations with the Coreys, but business success is neither the assured reward of hard work nor a synonym for virtue. Lapham, of course, loses his wealth and most of his business, partly through human frailty, partly through virtue, and partly through chance. He lends more money than he should to Rogers to ease his conscience about ill-treating him, and he spends more on his house than he should, mostly out of vanity. It is partly greed, partly excitement over an early gain, partly bad judgment that makes for his heavy losses in the stock market, and it is a combination of vanity and Yankee closeness about his affairs that keeps him from seeking expert help when his financial dealings get too complicated for him. It is a combination of chance and his own carelessness that causes the fire which destroys his house, a week after the insurance has expired. Finally, it is his conscience and his wife's that keeps him from taking the business chance that might save him by either deceiving the prospective buyers of his mill properties or helping Rogers to do so.

Again the novel's proairetic logic is no less complex than that which impels the events in life, although Howells isolates one strand of it in the telling. Silas has risen morally at the end of this sequence of events. He has learned from his earlier mistreatment of Rogers that morality does have force in business dealings, and he will have to square his behavior with both his conscience and his wife's. This knowledge leads him to behave morally, even when he is sorely tested, and he comes out of the trial with an easy conscience, though a considerably reduced fortune.

What does Howells' realistic correction of these two popular story paradigms amount to? Essentially, his narrative structure conveys the same message that he transmits in every other way in his fiction—that life is not as simple as sentimental popular fiction would have it; that moral behavior and moral decisions are immensely complicated; that the actions of people are governed neither by nobly heroic virtue nor by simple malevolence, but by a complex congeries of forces, internal and external; that fiction which seeks to represent truth cannot be satisfied with the quick fix of emotional satisfaction provided by the reinforcement of popular fantasies in popular novels; that these popular lies are harmful and need to be corrected. The action of *Silas Lapham,* like the action of Howells' other novels, is primarily a disruption of conventional expectations and assumptions, a statement that the action of life is not so simple as novelists who live off these expectations and assumptions, and readers who escape to them, would like to make it.

In short, Howells was engaged in the production of a new story paradigm for fiction, based on disruption of the conventional popular paradigms. From the rather bleak prospect for the ensuing marriage at the end of **April Hopes** to the less than easy road to success that the prospective rags-to-riches heroes of **The Minister's Charge** and **The Landlord at Lion's Head** encounter to the cold water of sense dashed on the impossible May-December romance in **Indian Summer**, Howells made a point of disappointing conventional expectations about the sequences of events his novels relate. In doing so, he was creating a realistic story paradigm based on the antithesis of convention, a disruption of the expected sequence of events. It represents a correction of what he considered the distorted popular notions about the logic underlying the events in life. By foregrounding the false, this realist managed to convey to his readers that he replaced it with the true. (pp. 25-31)

> Brenda Murphy, "Howells and the Popular Story Paradigm: Reading 'Silas Lapham's' Proairetic Code," in American Literary Realism 1870-1910, *Vol. 21, No. 2, Winter, 1989, pp. 21-33.*

---

## FURTHER READING

Arms, George, and Gibson, William M. "*Silas Lapham, Daisy Miller,* and the Jews." *The New England Quarterly* 16, No. 1 (March 1943): 118-22.
  Delineates contemporary controversies arising from an anachronistic reference to *Daisy Miller* and unflattering references to Jewish people in *The Rise of Silas Lapham.*

Berces, Francis Albert. "Mimesis, Morality, and *The Rise of Silas Lapham.*" *American Quarterly* 22, No. 2 (Summer 1970): 190-202.
  Relates Howells's theory of realism and its application in *The Rise of Silas Lapham* to Platonic and Aristotelian ideals of mimesis.

Bowden, Edwin T. "The Commonplace and the Grotesque." In his *The Dungeon of the Heart: Human Isolation and the American Novel,* pp. 103-49. New York: Macmillan Co., 1961.
  Treats Lapham's isolation from others in facing his ethical dilemmas.

Brown, Maurice F. "The Rise of Lapham: The Fall of Howells." *Journal of American Culture* 6, No. 2 (Summer 1983): 39-43.
  Criticizes *Lapham* as a flawed novel, charging that although Howells carefully presented detail of character and action, he addressed its implicit ethical issues timidly and inadequately.

Bucco, Martin. "*The Rise of Silas Lapham:* The Western Dimension." *Western American Literature* 23, No. 4 (Winter 1989): 291-310.
  Discusses Howells's thematic use of the West and frontier imagery in *The Rise of Silas Lapham.*

Cady, Edwin H. Introduction to *The Rise of Silas Lapham,* by William Dean Howells, edited by Edwin H. Cady, pp. v-xviii. Boston: Houghton Mifflin Co., 1957.

Credits the novel with being a superior example of American Realism, and concludes that the novel's greatest strength lies in its moral response to "the pressures of our way of life to lie and cheat and steal."

Clark, Harry Hayden. Introduction to *The Rise of Silas Lapham,* by William Dean Howells, pp. v-xix. New York: Modern Library, 1951.
  Presents a general overview of the novel, including discussion of the role of its two plots in characterizing American society of the era.

Coanda, Richard. "Howells' *The Rise of Silas Lapham.*" *The Explicator* 22, No. 3 (November 1963): 1, 3.
  Considers Rogers a diabolic figure in *The Rise of Silas Lapham.*

Crowley, John W. "Howells in the Eighties: A Review of Criticism, Part II." *ESQ* 33, No. 1 (1st Quarter 1987): 45-65.
  Summarizes critical opinion of several of Howells's works written in the 1880s, including *The Rise of Silas Lapham.*

Edwards, Herbert. "The Dramatization of *The Rise of Silas Lapham.*" *The New England Quarterly* 30, No. 2 (June 1957): 235-43.
  Describes Howells's failed attempt to adapt *The Rise of Silas Lapham* for the stage.

Elliott, Gary D. "Howells' Ideal Man: Theme in *The Rise of Silas Lapham.*" *Wascana Review* 16, No. 2 (Fall 1981): 80-6.
  Analyzes Howells's conception of the ideal male through his treatment of the characters Lapham, Tom Corey, and Bromfield Corey.

Hedges, Elaine R. "*César Birotteau* and *The Rise of Silas Lapham:* A Study in Parallels." *Nineteenth-Century Fiction* 17, No. 2 (September 1962): 163-74.
  Examines parallels between *The Rise of Silas Lapham* and Balzac's *César Birotteau.*

Jackson, Fleda Brown. "A Sermon without Exegesis: The Achievement of Stasis in *The Rise of Silas Lapham.*" *The Journal of Narrative Technique* 16, No. 2 (Spring 1986): 131-47.
  Maintains that Howells employed ambivalent language in *Silas Lapham* to represent a paralyzing conflict between emotional life and rationality.

Kirk, Clara Marburg. "Taste and Class in Boston." In her *W. D. Howells and Art in His Time,* pp. 99-116. New Brunswick, N.J.: Rutgers University Press, 1965.
  Discusses Howells's opinions on the art of his time and relates them to his thematic use of architecture in *The Rise of Silas Lapham.*

Liptzin, Sol. "Legend and Reality." In his *The Jew in American Literature,* pp. 68-90. New York: Bloch Publishing Co., 1966.
  Addresses Howells's removal of unflattering references to Jews in *The Rise of Silas Lapham* after receiving letters of protest from Jewish readers.

Macauley, Robie. " 'Let Me Tell You about the Rich . . . '." *The Kenyon Review* 27, No. 4 (Autumn 1965): 645-71.
  Assesses the portrayal of the wealthy in several novels, including *The Rise of Silas Lapham,* and concludes that Lapham, despite Howells's realistic approach to literature, remains more a character of fiction than an accu-

rate portrait of an American business millionaire of the late nineteenth century.

Manierre, William R., II. "*The Rise of Silas Lapham:* Retrospective Discussion as Dramatic Technique." *College English* 23, No. 5 (February 1962): 357-61.
Discusses Howells's presentation of events in *The Rise of Silas Lapham* through retrospective dialogue rather than direct description.

McMurray, William. "*The Rise of Silas Lapham.*" In his *The Literary Realism of William Dean Howells,* pp. 43-54. Carbondale and Edwardsville: Southern Illinois University Press, 1967.
Traces Lapham's moral development in *The Rise of Silas Lapham.*

Solomon, Eric. "Howells, Houses, and Realism." *American Literary Realism* 1, No. 4 (Fall 1968): 89-93.
Discusses the symbolic importance of Lapham's house in *The Rise of Silas Lapham.*

Tanselle, G. Thomas. "The Architecture of *The Rise of Silas Lapham.*" *American Literature* 37, No. 4 (January 1966): 430-57.
Relates the symbolism of architecture in *The Rise of Silas Lapham* to the symmetrical arrangement of chapters dealing with its two plots.

——. "The Boston Seasons of *Silas Lapham.*" *Studies in the Novel* 1, No. 1 (Spring 1969): 60-6.
Examines the changes of season within *The Rise of Silas Lapham* in relation to the novel's theme of fall and renewal.

Van Nostrand, Albert D. "Fiction's Flagging Man of Commerce." *The English Journal* 48, No. 1 (January 1959): 1-11.
Presents *The Rise of Silas Lapham* as one example of the treatment of the capitalist in American fiction.

# Johannes V. Jensen

## 1873-1950

(Full name Johannes Vilhelm Jensen; also wrote under the pseudonym Ivar Lykke) Danish novelist, short story writer, poet, dramatist, essayist, travel writer, biographer, critic, journalist, and memoirist.

Jensen was one of the foremost Danish writers during the first half of the twentieth century and the winner of the Nobel Prize for literature in 1944. His best-known work, the novel cycle *Den lange Rejse (The Long Journey),* traces the history of humanity from the emergence of the species to the discovery of America and reflects his interest in biological science and the evolutionary theories of Charles Darwin. Jensen wrote in a variety of genres, including poetry, drama, and short story, and the best of these works are noted for their sensitive characterizations and adept presentations of the natural landscape, as well as for expressing Jensen's wide-ranging travel experiences and his enthusiastic promotion of the technological advancements of modern civilization.

Born in Farsø, in north Jutland, Jensen was educated at home until the age of eleven when he entered the Viborg Cathedral School. He began medical studies at the University of Copenhagen in 1893 and supported himself during his studies by writing a number of serial novels for a popular magazine under the pseudonym Ivar Lykke. A competent but restless student, Jensen began a succession of travels to the United States, France, and Spain in 1896 as a reporter for the Danish newspaper *Politiken.* He subsequently withdrew from the university without completing his degree, intending instead to pursue a career as a journalist. In the mid-1890s he published the novels *Danskere* and *Einar Elkær,* as well as the short story collection *Himmerlandsfolk,* which is considered his most important work from this period. Maintaining a professional association with *Politiken* throughout his life, Jensen continued a series of international travels, visiting the Far East, Africa, and the United States, a country which he counted among his favorite travel destinations. Greatly inspired by the vitality of American life at the turn of the century, Jensen celebrated American inventiveness and vigor in the companion novels *Madame d'Ora* and *Hjulet,* which are set in Chicago and New York. With the publication of *Kongens Fald (The Fall of the King)* in 1901, Jensen turned from journalistic travel essays and novels with contemporary settings to historical works centered on evolutionary theory. His subsequent novels comprising *The Long Journey* amplify his views on the development of civilization. A popular lecturer and well-known cultural figure within Denmark, Jensen received little international attention before the English edition of *The Long Journey* was published in the early 1920s. He was later awarded the Nobel Prize in recognition of his numerous contributions to national and world literature. For the remainder of his life he continued to travel extensively and contribut-

ed essays, short stories, and poems to Danish journals. Jensen died in 1950.

Jensen's early novels *Danskere* and *Einar Elkær,* which reflect a youthful aestheticism and fin de siècle disillusion, are representative of the introspective literature prominent in Denmark at the close of the nineteenth century. Later renouncing these works, Jensen stated, "I myself do not have copies of them, and I would read them again only with reluctance." The first work to bring him acclaim, *Himmerlandsfolk,* and subsequent volumes of stories set in the Himmerland are largely based on Jensen's recollections of the region surrounding his childhood home in Farsø. These works are praised for their skillful delineation of landscape and local cultural traditions as well as for the combination of irony and sensitivity that distinguishes Jensen's character portraits.

Jensen's fondness for the Himmerland region greatly influenced his outlook on the evolution of human civilization, which formed the chief focus of many of his mature works. Beginning with *Den gotiske Renaissance,* a collection of newspaper articles written in Spain and France, Jensen praised the achievements and spirit of the "Gothic," or Anglo-Saxon, people, a race he believed had developed from the prehistoric inhabitants of Scandinavia, and he sought to revitalize the spirit of innovation in the descendants of this race by emphasizing the technological accomplishments of modern industrial nations. *The Long Journey,* an epic work presenting his view of civilization from its beginnings in Scandinavia to Christopher Columbus's discovery of America, depicts the struggle against nature as the impetus for human cultural progress and intellectual development. While the cycle combines elements from the Bible, ancient mythology, and the Icelandic sagas, it also evidences Jensen's knowledge of geography and anthropology, as well as the evolutionary theories of Charles Darwin. Applying Darwin's theory of natural selection to intellectual history, Jensen celebrated in *The Long Journey* the originators of such significant developments in human history as the discovery of fire, the invention of tools and modes of transportation, the emergence of art and architectural styles, and the undertaking of important human migrations. Considered Jensen's greatest achievement, *The Long Journey* has been described as a scientific counterpart to the Old Testament, and it remains the work for which he is principally known outside Denmark.

Jensen's prolific output also included writings in such various genres as drama, poetry, short story, essay, and what he termed "myth," or a brief work focusing on a moment of historical significance and combining literary characteristics of the short story, fable, and essay. His concept of myth—"short flashes of the essence of things that illumine man and time"—has been compared to James Joyce's idea of epiphany, and Jensen's mythological stories are considered innovative and significant literary achievements. Also a respected poet, Jensen published his works regularly in Danish periodicals, and a number of his lyrical poems on patriotic subjects became well-known in Denmark during his lifetime when they were set to music. The themes of Jensen's poems reflect those of his prose writings and include the celebration of nature, the advancement of time, and the achievements of human progress. Greatly influenced by the American poet Walt Whitman, Jensen wrote predominantly in free verse, and his works have been praised as powerfully expressive, yet he is not widely known as a poet outside Denmark, a situation that commentators suggest is due to the difficulty of translating his works for a wider audience. Within Denmark, however, he remains a highly esteemed contributor to Danish culture and national identity. Aage Marcus has commented: "Jensen has more than any other Danish writer become the interpreter of his race and his nation. He has once for all given conscious expression to the mentality of the Nordic race, and has enabled his people to find themselves by obtaining a foothold in that Denmark which, unaffected by political changes, goes back to the dawn of time."

## PRINCIPAL WORKS

*Danskere* (novel) 1896
*Einar Elkær* (novel) 1898
*Himmerlandsfolk* (short stories) 1898
*Intermezzo* (short stories and travel essays) 1899
*Den gotiske Renaissance* (travel essays) 1901

*Kongens Fald* (novel) 1901
 [*The Fall of the King,* 1933]
*Madame d'Ora* (travel essays) 1904
*Nye Himmerlandshistorier* (short stories) 1904
*Skovene* (travel essays) 1904
*Hjulet* (novel) 1905
*Digte* (poetry) 1906
*Myter og Jagter* (fables and short stories) 1907
*Den ny Verden* (essays) 1907
*Nye Myter* (fables) 1908
*†Bræen* (novel) 1909
*Himmerlandshistorier: Tredie Samling* (short stories) 1910
*Myter: Ny Samling* (fables) 1910
*Nordisk Aand* (essays) 1911
*Myter: Fjerde Samling* (fables) 1912
*Rudyard Kipling* (biography) 1912
*Skibet* (novel) 1912
*Introduktion til vor Tidsalder* (travel essays) 1915
*Olivia Marianne* (short stories) 1915
*Norne-Gæst* (novel) 1919
*†Det tabte Land* (novel) 1919
*Christofer Columbus* (novel) 1921
 [*Christopher Columbus,* 1922; published in novel *The Long Journey*]
*Digte: Tredie Udgave* (poetry) 1921
*Cimbrernes Tog* (novel) 1922
 [*The Cimbrians,* 1923; published in novel *The Long Journey*]
*The Long Journey.* 3 vols. (novel) 1922-24
*Aarstiderne* (poetry) 1923
*Aestetik og Udvikling* (essays) 1923
*Evolution og Moral* (essays) 1925
*Verdens Lys* (poetry) 1926
*Dyrenes Forvandling* (essays) 1927
*Aandens Stadier* (essays) 1928
*Den jydske Blæst* (poetry) 1931
*Kornmarken* (short stories) 1932
*Dr. Renaults Fristelser* (novel) 1935
*Paaskebadet* (poetry) 1937
*Mollen* (fables) 1944
*The Waving Rye* (essays and short stories) 1958

*These works comprise the novel cycle *Den lange Rejse,* published in English in three volumes as *The Long Journey.*

†These works were translated as *Fire and Ice,* 1922, the first volume of *The Long Journey.*

---

## Paul Rosenfeld (essay date 1917)

[*Rosenfeld was an American music and literary critic whose work is noted for its sensitivity and discernment. In the following excerpt, he evaluates Jensen's importance as an interpreter of contemporary society.*]

There is a moment when for the first time we truly see the light of the world. It is when there comes over us, in all its naturalness, the beauty of our own day. At that moment only do we commence living. Before, we have been sunk into ourselves, riveted to the past in each of us that will not let us free. We have been unable to lay hold on the world, to employ to the full our energy, to create life anew. The vision of the beauty of our own time comes with the power of liberation. It is as if the very sluices of our being opened. For we have glimpsed in what hitherto seemed a hostile, malevolent unreality, the blood-brother of our dreams, the likeness of ourselves. We are set free to create, to be created. There is scarcely a boon more to be desired than the vision of the proportions of the world in which we live. There is scarcely anything more necessary.

That vision comes to us in the works of the Danish author, Johannes V. Jensen. Not that other writers have not attempted similar revelations. What sets Jensen apart from H. G. Wells and the many others is the quality of a profound artistry. For Jensen is pre-eminently an artist. The strength and freshness of his genius, the deep richness and nervousness of his style, the boldness and originality of his ideas, place him among the dominant literary figures of the hour. There is another trait that sets him above the rest of those who have taken it upon themselves to interpret our day to us. Jensen's ideas are not the result of an intellectual process. They came to him as experiences. In them breathes all the warmth of a profound vitality. The manner in which he came by them recalls nothing so much as the story of Faust's salvation as Goethe tells it. Jensen, too, had his Gothic laboratory; turned with loathing from culture coupled with ignorance of reality. In the late nineties, fresh from the university, he was scribbling dime novels and literary reviews in Copenhagen. And there came over him a hatred of himself, of his world, the world "for which he was neither bad enough nor vulgar enough." "Sick with the northern sickness, an incurable longing," he wandered forth, and tramped and shipped about the globe. . . . And for years, Jensen wandered over the globe, disappearing and ducking up again in Seville, in China, in the Malay archipelago, in Chicago. Where Jensen actually went, is of secondary importance. Of primary, is the fact that his pilgrimage made Jensen anew. It is as if the age had entered into him and transformed him in its proper image. It was Whitman who first announced the coming of a race of men for whom no past existed, whose dreams were drawn to no sunken ages, who were wholeheartedly alive and whole-heartedly a part of their own time. Such a one is Jensen. And so it is given him to reveal to his day its grand proportions.

He does more than reassure us that it has proportions of its own. He comes to tell us that we are living in a Renaissance. For Jensen, all great ages have sought either to turn human energy from the world, or to restore it fully to it. Characteristic of the first direction were the Christianizing centuries. The Renaissance, the Reformation, the French Revolution, on the other hand, sought to bring human energy back to the battles of reality. But they were unsuccessful. The impulse of the Humanistic revival went into the heaping up of erudition for its own sake, and ended as philology in the library. The Reformation substituted one bond for another. The Revolution attempted to transform human beings into ideas. Not so our day. It alone has succeeded in ridding itself of all the theories and conceptions that divert man from his earthly existence. It alone has come again to the consciousness, so characteristic of the youth of the race, of the self-sufficiency of existence, the supreme importance of life itself. The stream of the *libido* has returned from theories, from hopes of extra-mundane heavens, to the one reality, the struggle with nature. And so, with the re-employment of man's force in the outer world, the dreams that have been humanity's since the cave-man in his cave dreamt of flying, have begun to be realized. Other ages had dreamt, too, of power over nature, of defiance of natural laws. They had been content to find satisfaction in myths, in realizing their wishes as gods. Ours has begun to turn the stuff of dreams into actuality. The imagination of man has returned from the cloud confines. The new man, fixed on the living of life, on the realization of his dreams on earth, has appeared. The world is young once more. And Jensen tells us, how while gazing out over Paris, he pitied Nietzsche, who had lived into himself, instead of out into a world that was far better than he.

Jensen's book of essays *The New World,* tells us how that vision came to him. It was while he was at the Paris World's Fair, before the machinery exhibited there. In the machines, he saw that man's imagination and strength, instead of wandering off in theories and systems, had returned to the world as energy. In them, he saw the type of the new beauty that was coming to be, the beauty that follows strength, and results from an economy of means based on practicality. And that beauty he finds in all human creations made for use, in steamships and locomotives, in bridges and steel constructed buildings. Nay, he tells us that steel-construction is the natural classic style, since it combines greatest strength with greatest economy. He tells us that the architecture of America, the skyscrapers, the grain-elevators, the collieries, embody the essential architectural style, and will one day be considered beautiful. For Jensen, Memphis, Tennessee, is far lovelier than the ruins of Egyptian Memphis. It is in America, in the teeming American cities, that he finds nature in the glory of her energy. He loves our crudity, the lushness and extravagance of our life. "What stories of mythological wonders," he cries, "can compare with the narration of the life that goes on in America today?" He tells us of the romance of our existence, of the poetry of our big business, of the young sound strength of it all. He wants no better story of magic than the rebuilding of San Francisco after the earthquake. For in America, nature has the strength to make life anew.

If *The New World* is Jensen's most brilliant book, *The Glacier* and its sequel *The Ship,* are his best. In them, his genius has most fully, most permanently, realized itself. Every generation of men produces a few works of art that symbolize for future ages its *Weltanschauung,* its aspiration, its self-justification. Such a work, in our own day, is [Leonid] Andreyev's *Life of Man.* Such a work is Jensen's double masterpiece. It is one of the actual accomplishments of our time. Into it has gone something of the struggle of our own day, its break with the dicta of past ages, its faith in work as the revealer of life. Into it has gone the glorification of the virtues cardinal to our own day— energy, strength, courage, self-expression. Waxing throughout Jensen's eighteen odd volumes, his poetic vision at last wholly realizes itself in those two books. The earlier Jensen, the man one visualizes as a surface of *n-th* power sensitivity, registering with delicacy and precision whatever of sight and sound and smell presented itself, is still here. He is still the writer who can transfer, brilliantly, economically, unmatchably, a landscape, a city, colorful and exotic nature, to the printed page. Only, he has become a deep romantic poet, who expresses himself in a form that unites a science based on the most recent Freudian contributions to anthropology with all the lyric wonder of the old myths. He has produced a perfect piece of work.

Jensen calls his story a "myth," the "Myth of the First Man." It is the fable of the birth of Jensen's own Gothic race, in prehistoric times, when the glacier came down over Scandinavia and overwhelmed the tropical forest that once flourished there. But in this fable, Jensen has symbolized the life of every man who, breaking with the past in him, returns to the giant realities, and is created anew out of his very struggle with nature for livelihood. Dreng, the hero of *The Glacier,* is the first anarchist. Driven from his tribe, which is flying south before hardship and winter, he turns north and combats the cold. In the bitter struggle, he adapts himself to the needs of existence. Human will is born. Human will is victor. Dreng maintains his life. He learns to make fire. On an island in the midst of the glacier, he rears sons and daughters. And, one night, in his cave, the First Man dreams. First, he seems swimming through a tropical sea, rising toward the steaming shore. Then, he is in a mighty city. It is Chicago, alive with noise and machinery and the brilliance of the combat for existence. And last, Dreng dreams of a forest of living trees, rocks of bone, an earth of breathing flesh. Over it floats "the sign of eternal resurgence." And, looking eagerly ahead into the land where his wife has preceded him, the First Man dies.

*The Ship* sings in accents differing little from those of the old Norse ballads, the day of a race that had the power to destroy life and create it new again. It is the story of the Danes who conquered Normandy and England, and gave the world an impulse that, after many centuries, comes to life again in the hard-headed practicality of America. Again, the story is but a symbol for the life of our time. One episode might stand as the epitome of Jensen's thought. A band of famished lads in search of food have broken into a Norse temple. "For a moment they stood rooted. In the glow of their torches, the Gods, misshapen figures, covered with crusts of dried blood, seemed to step out of the blackness and stand staring at them. For an instant, the young marauders trembled. It was so silent here. The dread Gods seemed to gaze at them from all parts of their forms. But at last Germund came to himself. Shaking the sparks from his torch, he stepped forward, and boldly said 'Is there any corn hidden here?' "

So Jensen sees our day. In the picture he has made of it for us lies his genius. One has to go far to find another writer so dynamic. From him there radiates an energy, a freshness, an encouragement otherwheres almost unmatchable. One cannot read Jensen statically. The stimulus is too powerful. The lust of life, the love of the hour, is infectious. There comes over us, too, the desire to live, to feel, to do, to betake ourselves into the world of reality, and learn for ourselves the glory of creation. So beautifully has Johannes V. Jensen told us of the day that awaits us. (pp. 281-86)

> *Paul Rosenfeld, "Our Day," in* The Seven Arts, *Vol. 1, No. 3, January, 1917, pp. 281-86.*

## Allen W. Porterfield   (essay date 1923)

[*Porterfield was an American educator and critic who specialized in Germanic languages and literature. In the following excerpt, he assesses* The Long Journey, *comparing it favorably to the Norwegian novelist Knut Hamsun's* Growth of the Soil.]

And still they come—these Scandinavians. Leif Ericsson was the first. But he came, by accident, a thousand years ago, christened the point he touched "Vinland," and then went back home, taking with him some samples of grass, probably also some maple syrup, and a sufficient batch of memories to make sagas flourish and the home folks envious. The last is Johannes V. Jensen. He comes now, in spirit, as the author of this gigantic novel in six volumes, entitled *The Long Journey,* two volumes of which are . . . translated under the collective subtitle of *Fire and Ice.* It is another "outline." It is an epic on the genesis of man and the world. But it is not Genesis; it is Darwin.

When those who are endowed with agile imagination, and who are not concerned one way or the other with Chautauqua dogma, lay this much aside, they are going to call for the rest; for this is captivating, and the rest is to be published shortly. When the others, the silver-tongued fundamentalists now so merrily engaged in dumbelling evolution out of the schools, churches, jails and cemeteries, lay it down, they are going to chant in unison: "Why, the fellow is not orthodox."

This is not Hr. Jensen's first appearance in the United States. On Oct. 25, 1902—he has been around the world three times—he arrived in San Francisco direct from the Orient. On that same day Frank Norris died. Hr. Jensen returned to his native Denmark and immediately set about the task he then felt called upon to perform, the making of Frank Norris known to the Scandinavian peoples. He himself translated the *Octopus* and persuaded others to translate other works by the man who made wheat famous in literature. Having succeeded in this, he took up Jack London and made him as popular in the North as he is in the sole country that could have produced him. Moreover, a number of his own works, including *Madame d'Ora* (1904) and *The Wheel* (1905), are based on conditions and experiences in the United States.

By reason of his unique and singular distinction as a creative writer Johannes V. Jensen should be given as cordial a welcome as any Scandinavian who has ever come to this country since that other great Dane, Jens Bronck, found and founded the Bronx in the early seventeenth century. By virtue of his appreciative and intelligent relation to us he has as much claim to our spiritual attention as any Scandinavian has had since the Swedes settled Delaware in 1625, or since those original Norwegians settled down at Kendall, Orleans County, N. Y., in 1825. . . .

On the occasion of [Jensen's] fiftieth birthday, a few weeks ago, Fritz Johansen and Aage Marcus brought out a gloriously got-up but limited edition (150 copies) of a study entitled *A Catalogue of the Works of Johannes V. Jensen.* It consists of no fewer than 570 titles (he is also editor of the Danish Forum), some of which are not even known in Denmark. There is, for example, his drama entitled **Trods (Defiance)**, which was given a private but gala performance at Chicago in 1903. It should be of interest, too, to American readers to know that Hr. Jensen really made his début with, or at least his first impression on, the more mature Danes by two articles he sent home from Madrid in May, 1898. The one is written under the caption, **"After the Defeat at Manilla,"** the other **"The Bull Fight."** These it was that proved that he had in him even then that Kipling-Norris-London ability to immortalize the open with its human, all-too-human events, and its natural phenomena that constitute both score and text of what is popularly known as the call of the wild. (p. 3)

And **The Long Journey?** Hardly had it appeared when the word was passed around that it is comparable to [Norwegian writer Knut] Hamsun's *Growth of the Soil.* There is some justification for the remark, the simile. Both novels go back to a primitive state of affairs, both deal with elemental traits in man, both show a civilization in the making, and both rise at times to truly grandiose heights as epic portrayals of the workings of the human heart. But here the similarity stops: the dissimilarity between the two novels is indeed nothing short of impressive. Hamsun's Isak "sowed the seed in Jesus' name," Jensen's Gunung Api stands in airy solitude in the third paragraph of **The Long Journey,** chewing the fire within him. That is, there was no fire, no ice; there was nothing but unreckoned time, and that time was a few million years before the beginning of the Christian era. When Jensen is through, Christopher Columbus, made to appear, incidentally, as a direct descendent of the Vikings—quite a jolt to Genoa—has discovered America. When Hamsun is through, the sons of Isak and Inger have grown up, and even Barbro, the once citified lady, has married and settled down. In reality, Hamsun covers the period from about 1916 to about 1950. Jensen notes not time except by its passing, and it passes exceeding slow.

Moreover—and this is the difference that is bound to give the American reader, and Jensen's discriminating publisher, some concern—to write **The Long Journey** necessitated at least a running familiarity with the leading "ologies," archaeology, geology, ethnology, and mythology. Knut Hamsun is thoroughly unstudied, unschooled, and unburdened with the erudition that annoys the club, straphanging, and commuting reader, however much of a success it may have at a meeting of the Scientific Society of the States. Even the names of Jensen's characters remind either of an old play à la *Everyman,* or they are forbidding in appearance. There is Gunung Api himself, a name which conjures up, at least in the mind of the writer, otherwise happily remote memories of Genung's treatise on rhetoric, a disagreeable book.

But apart from this difference, **The Long Journey** is a greater work in every way than *The Growth of the Soil.* It is greater in fancy, in vision, in thought, in construction, and especially in the unfolding of that particular idea, and the delineation of that particular theory of origin, growth and development which constitutes its basic merit. Of course, to the reader who is of the settled conviction that the account of the world given in the first five books of the Bible is literally true, word for word, and that God dictated these five books to Moses, naturally in English, Jensen's story will appeal as a wild phantasia, a maddened phantasmagoria, a Witches' Sabbath, of disjointed foolery and continental idiocy. But the world as it stands, with its three kingdoms, has to be explained. How did it attain to its present shape, and how did the animals, from amoeba to man, that use it as a habitat arrive at their present status? Had there been no growth, no development, no evolution? Jensen regards evolution (he is silent about it so far as direct statements are concerned) as merely another and obvious argument in favor of a supernatural divinity, as altogether the one principle of life that makes homage to God obligatory. What a dumb, if not despicable, bit of handiwork the world and its inhabitants would be if there had been no progress, no evolution, within the most recent thousands of years!

And lest any one fancy that this is a novel exclusively of prehistoric, if not proto-historic, times, that it deals only with non-human personages, and that it smells of soviet conceits, let us lose no time in adding that the beginning of monogamy is duly and favorably set forth; that Chicago is given real and honorable mention by way of explaining how Carl felt when he first struck fire; that Darwin is brought in as one of Carl's descendants, and for a reason which only fractional brains can controvert; that God, Heaven and Hell are made an integral part of this immortal scheme of things sublime; that the power of tradition, and the autocracy of heresy are commented on with the intelligence that makes men better, or proves that they are hopeless; that Gothic architecture is alleged to have made a propitious start when White Bear hauled his ship on land, canted it keel upward and built underneath for a hall, which is about as sensible as the contention that the Gothic arch was copied from the ant hill or the bent boughs of the forest; and that Denmark, Russia, indeed, the whole of Europe, with liberal attention to the Mediterranean countries, are given the place and space that are theirs by right of location. And the story closes with a hymn in prose to the lark that is as good as Shelley. **The Long Journey** is as fanciful a book, to have a scientific basis as has come out of Europe since the first man rode something. It is scientific fiction, just as Gertrude Atherton's *Conqueror* is historical fiction.

The plot? That is given at the beginning of the translation—five pages, in italics. It is diverting, though it reminds the writer of those "arguments" that preceded the creations of Horace and Virgil, Livy and Ovid, as once published in the black-lidded editions of Chase and Stuart. The best feature of it is that it shows how the forest became a ship, and the ship became a church until men like Columbus, seeking the Kingdom of Heaven, found the savages of Guanahani, whereupon the church changed back into a ship, the ship reverted to the forest, the ring was complete: "And with the life of a work of art, which lasts only until the mind has created new ones—within this circle *The Long Journey* is to be read." Thus ends the author's plot.

The reviewer's is different: The first part of *The Long Journey* shows how Gunung Api tamed the shrew of shrews, Fire. It was done through his son, Fyr by name, who, a graduate of the hard school of experience, learned a lot of useful things by memory, and introduced them through the medium of worship, art, poetry and roofs into the lives of his contemporaries. He rose to the position of a god, and was worshipped as such. But one day his own roof fell in; he was frightened. "Ah, ha," thought they, "if he be a god, why did he not avert this catastrophe?" (the quotation marks are the writer's), and they threw him on his own fire and burned him to death, instantaneous though the repentance for their haste was. After Fyr's death Gunung Api became silent, for the Ice Age followed thereupon.

Carl, the hero of the second part, a warrior of the fire tribe whose business it is to mind the fire while all the rest of them slumber and sleep, is hard put to it; for there is no fire; it is the Ice Age. Necessity is the mother of invention. Carl soon learned that a bearskin will make warm, where a stove is as cold as an icebox if there be no fuel. He met Mam (another name that fills with dismay. Why not "Mammy" and have done with it? Or the original and fascinating Danish, Moa?) and married her, for, though he saw at once that she was peculiar, he felt that she was relatively like himself, and two could fight their way through life better than one. They did. They bore children; invention followed on invention; the ice receded; the animals were subdued; sleds, boats, tools, weapons, skirts, trousers, cooked food, rivalry, hate and ambition were so many drugs on the market. There were unwritten laws of the sun, the moon, and the stars that made it possible to anticipate the seasons. The Vikings abandoned the creeks that gave them their name and took to more pretentious waters; the migration of the nations began; Denmark was settled (and let us add that there are philologists of repute who regard Denmark as the cradle of the Indo-Germanic peoples).

No normal human being is going to contend that Johannes V. Jensen wrote this novel to refute the Bible, or that he has refuted it unconsciously. And no man endowed with a shred of imagination or blessed with a sliver of reason is going to deny that it is of Old Testament grandeur; that it is something new in the world of literature, something similar in its effect, however dissimilar in reality, to the *Divine Comedy,* to *Gulliver's Travels,* to any of those creative works that appear about once a century, stake off an epoch in the evolution of creative literature, and are read by succeeding generations, first with the delight that comes from chancing upon something new, and then with the interest that is born of the desire to familiarize ourselves with works the world loved long since and then lost a while because superseded. That a work of art lasts until the human mind creates a new one is a truth that needs no proof; it

has already been proved as often as unqualified masterpieces have appeared.

This is typed in cold ink, despite the fact that there are parts of *The Long Journey* which are dull; other parts which are irritating, because they make the appeal neither of science nor of literature; and other parts of unctuous seriousness when they might have been relieved by a glint of humor, or omitted altogether in patience's name.

The day Hr. Jensen was 50 years old—Jan. 20, 1923—there appeared in Denmark a whole book of poems addressed to him. These we must omit; it is hard to be a just critic in rhymed verse when the objective is a live, young poet. Another book, in prose, appeared, entitled "Greetings to Johannes V. Jensen." With the exception of Georg Brandes, who admires Jensen, it contains the names of all the leading Danish intellectuals, including that of the venerable Professor Emeritus of Philosophy, Harald Höffding. Citations from this must also be omitted, for brevity's sake, and because the Danes celebrate the birthday of everybody, as a matter of hardened habit, from the delicatessen dealer around the corner to the king on the throne. There were wires to Jensen from Germany which stated unequivocally that he was the greatest living master of Danish prose, and that, in the matter of technique and Weltanschauung, he had a whole school of disciples among the younger writers of the Fatherland. There were other messages from other parts of the country, including France, England and the United States. There is room for but two of these congratulatory statements, Johan Bojer wrote:

> By the side of Hamsun stands Johannes V. Jensen as the greatest artist in language of the North. He has, like a second Columbus, discovered a new land for poetry, and over his works hovers a personality which—as was the case with Björnson—will some fine day be metamorphosed into a myth.

Selma Lagerlöf wrote from Stockholm:

> Johannes V. Jensen is the real Knight of St. George in Danish literature. He never fails to see beauty as a princess held captive by the manyheaded and detestable dragon known as the dull realities of life, against which he wages war unrelenting, he himself attired in the glittering canonicals of poetry. He fights with zest and courage. He has won, too, some glorious victories, as in the case of *The Fall of the King* and *Ice.* But as soon as he wins one victory, he sees another head arise, project itself over beauty, and call for decapitation. He sees that his work is never done; that his princess is never freed. That he may never lack the courage to keep up the brilliant fight is my fervent wish on this his fiftieth birthday.
>
> (pp. 3, 24)

It is passing strange that a country like little Denmark, flat as a pancake, with one wholly negligible exception, from Skagen to Gjedsery, steeped in the orthodoxy which, if it saves souls, does it despite itself, and living on co-operative farming, should be able to create a winner of this genre. (p. 24)

Allen W. Porterfield, "Creative Genius of a Scandinavian Novelist," in The New York Times Book Review, February 25, 1923, pp. 3, 24.

## Aage Marcus (essay date 1932)

[*Marcus was a Danish writer and editor who specialized in art history and produced an extensive bibliography of Jensen's works in 1933. In the following excerpt, Marcus presents a favorable overview of Jensen's works.*]

Johannes V. Jensen has more than any other Danish writer become the interpreter of his race and his nation. He has once for all given conscious expression to the mentality of the Nordic race, and has enabled his people to find themselves by obtaining a foothold in that Denmark which, unaffected by political changes, goes back to the dawn of time. (p. 339)

And though he is only in the fifties, and still in a mill of work, he has already behind him a vast production. He began to write towards the close of the 'nineties. He broke once for all with the literary traditions of his time by his *Himmerlandshistorier (Tales from Himmerland)* and by his novel *Kongens Fald (The Fall of the King)*. In the former book, which was based on impressions received in his childhood, peasants are seen and described in a setting of nature with a mastery rarely achieved before. In the latter the whole history of Denmark is gathered to a tragic focus in the fate of King Christian II, and interpreted in the light of internal events in a way so that it becomes a grand epic on youth and the passing of youth. These two books were the introduction to Johannes V. Jensen's real authorship. Since then his outlook has broadened; his ability to find the underlying unity has developed, and he has attained an unequaled power of communicating his own vision to others.

Johannes V. Jensen has written poems, novels, short stories, plays, satires, travel books, biographies, art-historical works, essays on nature, history, and philosophy, and last but not least a great number of *myths*. The myth is a literary form which he himself has evolved and developed to perfection. It is neither a prose poem nor an essay, nor yet a short story, but has something of the nature of all these. He himself has described it as follows:

> The novel is slow, more suited to the time of the mail coach than to our hurrying epoch. Besides, it keeps to the surface and does not go to the root of things; it is a mirror of society rather than of nature. Whenever you return to a novel which you have laboriously read through before, it is in order to pick out certain passages that have remained in your memory; the characters and the plot do not hold your attention more than once. Leave out the plot, concentrate on those short flashes of the essence of things that illumine man and time, and you have the myth, the name by which the present writer designates his shorter prose works. They are not short stories in the ordinary sense of the word, nor fairy tales; they have something of the essay and something

of the quality of a musical theme, an attempt to focus the essence of life in a dream.

*Eksotiske Noveller (Exotic Tales)* are a special form of the myths, more similar to the short story, but distinguished by a certain universal quality. Here human fates are snapshotted in the form of the myth so as to be indelibly impressed on our memory, such as A-Koy and Olivia Marianne, Little Ahasuerus of New York, and the wretched Chinamen. Each of the figures drawn in these works becomes a living reality to the reader like some intimate friend whom he knows to the core and now sees in perspective, and perhaps for that reason understands for the first time.

Simultaneously with the myths Johannes V. Jensen wrote purely lyrical poems, usually expressing some thought or mood the intensity of which necessitated the lyrical form. The world is reflected in his poetry; not only has the Northern landscape been as it were newly created for us in his verse, but our whole impression of life has been changed and made richer. For he sings not only of nature, but of life and death and the flight of time, with a strength and purity of feeling and a fullness and restraint of expression which are incomparable. *The Book of the Seasons (Aarstiderne)* in which each month is treated in a poem by Johannes V. Jensen, and illustrated with drawings by Johannes Larsen, is to many a young Dane what the family book of devotion was to the people of an earlier generation. Not a few of his songs have been set to music by Danish composers and are frequently sung at meetings and festivals.

It is not only in his myths and poems, however, that he spans the extremes of time and space. In *The Long Journey* as also in another book, *Aandens Stadier (The Stages of the Mind)*, he has described the whole history of mankind. The latter has justly been called a mighty prose epic of the world; and as a longitudinal section is supplemented by a transverse section, so it is supplemented by the magnificent *Introduktion til vor Tidsalder (Introduction to Our Epoch)*. Again and again, Johannes V. Jensen has treated the doctrine of Evolution; it forms the backbone of his production, and just as Goethe anticipated Darwin on certain points, so there is now every reason to follow with the greatest interest Johannes V. Jensen's attempt to apply the theory of Evolution to all the domains of intellectual history. The wonderful book *Dyrenes Forvandling (The Transformation of the Animals)* forms in a way an introduction to *The Stages of the Mind* which deals with the transformation of man; and the author's sympathetic understanding of even the lowest animals in the scale seems more magic than ever when we consider that this is the same man who has described highly complex modern individuals, both in his novels—as for instance *Madame d'Ora* and *Hjulet (The Wheel)* which take place in New York and Chicago—and in his penetrating portraits of great men that have attracted him, as Darwin, Björnson, Roosevelt.

I shall attempt a brief survey of the contents of what may be regarded as his chief work, *The Long Journey*. This work, which appeared in 1908-23, comprises seven volumes, *Det tabte Land (The Lost Land)*, *Bræn (The Gla-*

*cier), Norne-Gæst, Cimbrernes Tog (The Raids of the Cimbri), Skibet (The Ship), Christopher Columbus* and, as a kind of epilogue, a volume entitled *Æstetik og Udvikling* (*Esthetics and Evolution*), in which Johannes V. Jensen gives an account of his various hypotheses and sources, in other words, makes his own comments on the work.

The cycle opens in a remote primeval age when the earth was still a single steaming tropical forest. The first primitive attempts at forming a community are described, a stage so slightly removed from that of the animal that animal instincts predominate. A single man rises above the herd, a kind of primitive Prometheus, who is duly punished by being sacrificed to man's first deity, the fire, which throughout the book sheds its lurid glare from the volcano, Gunung Api. While, therefore, *Fire* has become the name of the English edition of the book, the next volume bears the English title *Ice.* Gradually, as the cooling of the earth progresses and the great ice ages set in, it is naturally the Northern regions that first become the scene of conditions rendering possible any kind of civilization. For, while life in the tropical forest is too easy, the cold becomes the factor which requires a strong antagonist to conquer it, and this antagonist becomes the first real human being, Dreng, the principal character in *Ice.* As the sequel to this book, whose descriptions of the Arctic and Northern landscape have never been surpassed, follows a volume called *Norne-Gæst* in which the prospect is widened to include all the ancient world. With a mythical Old Norse figure as our leader we travel down the wide rivers, the ancient ways of communication between the North and the South. But the book also gives us a beautiful picture of children of nature in innocence and love. While Norne-Gæst always returns from his journeys, the result of the great raids forming the subject of the fourth volume, *Cimbrernes Tog,* is more tragic. Here it is shown how the unrest and urge to travel which have always possessed the Northern peoples were nourished by the years of scarcity and distress at home, and how they set out on the ill-fated expeditions against Rome. The contrast between the Germanic and the Roman mentality is sharply emphasized, a contrast which often reappears in Johannes V. Jensen's books.

While the Cimbri went over land, the first vikings almost at the same time started on their cruises. These are described in the following volume, *Skibet,* of which, unfortunately, there exists no English edition. The theme, however, is the same: the roving spirit of the Northmen which urges the seafarers to go south. Here, in their longing for home, they first become conscious of their own nature, which is the nature of the North.

Finally, in the sixth volume entitled *Christopher Columbus,* we have come down to a time which forms the transition from the Middle Ages to the Renaissance. As we saw in the preceding volume, Northern blood had been carried southward, and in the Genoese seafarer we meet with a descendant of the Northmen. His unrest and longing to travel take him to the New World, as it has carried countless people from the North the same way in our own time. This work contains much more than the mere description of Columbus and his cruise. In the grand myth with which

it opens, nature and love, longing and happiness, time that passes, and the mortality of all things, have been woven together into a texture of a poetic beauty which has hardly been equaled in literature. The essence of all religion is shown to be the eternal yearning which finds an outlet in the long cruises, and is expressed in the Gothic of the North whether manifested in cathedrals or in ships. After a brilliant description of the conquistadores and their feats, the book, and with it the whole work, concludes with a mighty vision: a meeting on the sea between Columbus's ship, the *Santa Maria,* and Darwin's *Beagle* on its circumnavigation of the world. The long journey is not yet ended, will never end, as surely as we have, in the doctrine of Evolution, a key to the understanding of that long and continued ascent from the animal world through the lost land, the infancy of mankind, onward through struggle and defiance to the human apex of our own time which, again, represents only a stage in the development.

These brief lines can merely indicate the theme of *The Long Journey.* An account can give no idea of the wealth of thought and imagery, descriptions and characters of the work, and much less of the mode of writing, of Johannes V. Jensen's own distinctive and powerful style.

A keynote of Johannes V. Jensen's work is the longing for continuity which pervades all his books, and though he takes us through many epochs and continents, this does not denote that his mind is divided. It is merely the natural result of the fact that, once started on the path into which his genius had led him, he has worked steadily to cover the entire field of knowledge of his time. In this respect he shows a striking similarity to the two great eminently positive writers, Holberg and Goethe. The old man from Weimar, especially, may often be met with in Johannes V. Jensen. More and more his work shows evidence of the same serenity, the same warm harmony which covered the immense inner tension in Goethe, and which had not been attained without a struggle.

But actually it is the elements themselves that speak to us from Johannes V. Jensen's work, the elements in a wider sense: the sky, the sea, Nature through the changing seasons year after year, love and longing, the old enduring things. Hence the greater part of his work is timeless, even though he is planted in our own time, in the forefront of the present day. He has remained true to his origin in his taste for the simple and the genuine. His art of life is based on the healthy and simple instincts of the old peasantry, but he is not as earthbound as they. "Better soul than sun." The whole theme of *The Long Journey* is the struggle, the striving onward step by step, the evolution which is the inmost true essence of the spirit. (pp. 342-47)

*Aage Marcus, "Johannes V. Jensen," in* The American-Scandinavian Review, *Vol. XX, Nos. 6-7, June-July, 1932, pp. 339-47.*

## Jens Nyholm    (essay date 1945)

[*A Danish-born American educator and critic, Nyholm was a member of the editorial staff of* Scandinavian Studies *from 1945 to 1957. In the following excerpt from an essay written in observance of Jensen's Nobel award, Nyholm traces Jensen's development as a literary artist and praises his individualistic style.*]

The winner of the 1944 Nobel prize in literature, Johannes V. Jensen, has for years been recognized in his native Denmark as the foremost writer of the nation. By a curious twist of fate, his fame has spread to the English-speaking world more slowly than to other countries, although he has renewed the Anglo-American line in Danish literature. He broke definitely, in the nineties, with the French tradition dominant in Denmark. In his youth he was an admirer of Kipling, about whom he wrote a book. He translated Whitman, introduced Frank Norris to the Danish public, and has continued to keep in touch with American letters as testified by his interest in Hemingway.

Vitality, a phenomenal intuitiveness, and superb verbal powers are the characteristics that have made Jensen the leader of two generations of Danish writers. He began his literary career as an introverted, skeptical intellectual. He reached literary mastery as an extroverted, positive "naturalistic humanist," a firm believer in the destiny of man interpreted in the light of evolutionary philosophy. When as a young man he broke away from the psychological novel in whose web he was caught, he deliberately set out to discover the concrete world: the outdoors, nature, the machine, the actions of man. He became a confessed modernist. In this search for reality he used all the potentialities with which he was endowed. First and foremost among these were his five senses. Seldom, if ever, has a writer been able to see, hear, smell, taste, and touch, as does Jensen. . . . (p. 131)

Seen in retrospect, Johannes V. Jensen's authorship may be described in terms of a series of orientations on various levels, or as a series of self-identifications—first with his own ego, then, successively, with his forebears, his nation, his race, and finally, with man.

In his early youth Jensen identified himself with his own self. The result was two small novels, *Danskere* and *Ejnar Elkjær,* now by his own will excluded from his regularly listed publications. They bear evidence of subtle psychological insight and a trend toward self-analysis against which the author fought with an almost ruthless desperation.

Turning, as we have seen, to the outside world, he next identified himself, one might say, with the Jutlandic peasants from whose stock he came. The literary result was a series of stories, *Himmerlandshistorier,* begun in 1898 and concluded in 1910—virile descriptions, in concentrated form, of the tragedies and humor of as sturdy and stubborn peasants as have ever been depicted in literature. From intense interest in his forebears Jensen advanced to a deep concern for his nation. Being aware of its strength as well as its weaknesses, he symbolized its fate in the masterful historical novel, *The Fall of the King,* describing the tragic Renaissance king, Christian II, whose brilliance was undermined by a Hamlet-like doubt of his own destiny. This book, in a way, was Jensen's final farewell to the introversion of the nineties, to the Don Quixotesque fight with shadows which he had realized was one of the weaknesses of his people, whose realm had shrunk from a medi-

aeval empire to a very, very small kingdom. But he also realized that his people were only a small part of a race that had continued for centuries to exert itself as a vital element in the development of civilization. On the American continent he traced the steps of his Jutlandic peasants. His world expanded, and two new novels dealing with American civilization, *Madame d'Ora,* and *Hjulet (The Wheel )* followed.

Johannes V. Jensen was now identifying himself with his race. Out of this new orientation grew his six-volume epic, *The Long Journey* (1909-21), describing the rise and development of what he called the Cimbrians, from before the Ice Age through the tribal migrations and the exploits of the Vikings, to the discovery of America by Christopher Columbus. It is now generally conceded that a firm scientific and historical foundation for *The Long Journey* is often lacking. But the merit of a work of art is not determined by the scientific concept of its author. *The Long Journey* may well be conceived as an epic of mankind expressed in the symbols of late 19th century natural history, and as such it is a captivating work, sweeping in its visionary magnificence, electrifying in the suggestive power of its brilliant details.

While Jensen has obviously been directly concerned with the Nordic race as such, he has advanced beyond the stage of racial nationalism. Rightly interpreted, his *Long Journey* and succeeding works deal with man and with the potentialities of man who has not cut his ties with nature. In his travels he has been in touch with, studied, and gathered wisdom from a variety of races—primitive as well as highly civilized races. To Jensen, any type that is functional is a carrier of values. He has therefore never accepted Nietzsche's *Herrenmoral,* nor fallen prey to Hitler's perverted racial religion. He has opposed, directly and emphatically, the "wrong Darwinism" proclaiming the rule of brute force. The "good Darwinism," according to Jensen, leads ultimately to rule by controlled force. Because, like Whitman, he believes in the potentialities of the common man, unspoiled by an overdose of civilization, he believes that this controlled force can gain ascendance within a democracy, a democracy that must be strengthened by an intensification of its healthy elements, a purification of the stream of life.

Johannes V. Jensen admires greatness that is harmonious—*mens sana in corpore sano.* He once pictured the Norwegian poet, Bjørnstjerne Bjørnson, taking his morning shower, as the ideal of manhood. In seeking for the typical—"the norm" he calls it—he parallels Goethe whose *Typusidee* and endeavor to interpret life in its totality through a fusion of poetry and science seem to have been of great significance to him. If one understands the "norm" of nature and the "norm" of man, one has found, as it were, a place from which one may see things, at one time, in review and in preview—may embrace eternity. The finding of this place restores balance to the person haunted by that unquenchable quest for the unknown which Jensen found in the Viking spirit, in Christopher Columbus, in himself. Identifying himself finally with man—finding the "norm" of things—Jensen achieved maturity, attaining a placidity which seems classic, after a restless youth which, though concerned with a search for the real, seemed romantic.

"The purpose of my writing," Jensen once paradoxically said, "is to accustom people not to read." He wants people to live, to experience life directly. His style is admirably suited for this purpose. It transfers, as by magic, his own sensations, impressions, and observations, to his readers. In developing this style, he has learned from Hans Christian Andersen, from Hamsun, from Kipling, and probably from Whitman. Yet his style is entirely his own. It operates with a vocabulary that is charged with vitality, a syntax that is unconventional, permits of sudden contractions, of long expansions—with a pull as powerful as that of the tides. Such a style possesses an individuality that is lost if rendered into a foreign language with a differently shaded vocabulary and a different rhythm. And this, rather than fate, is perhaps after all the reason why in spite of Jensen's preference for the English, the English-speaking public has not fully appreciated him—could not fully appreciate him.

In Danish literature, Jensen succeeds a great master of prose, Jens Peter Jacobsen. Jacobsen's style was musical and rhythmical, but also adjectival and ornamental. Jensen's is verbal and direct. He does not describe a thing from without; he illumines it from within. His best writing is usually found in his smaller pieces: his "myths," and his poems. The "myth," a special art form he has created, is a brief prose piece, possessing elements of the short story, the fairy tale, the prose poem, and the essay, but endowed with a quality of its own. "Leave out the plot," Jensen has said in defining the myth, "concentrate on the short flashes of the essence of things that illumine man and time, and you have the myth." These "flashes of the essence" are characteristic also of his lyrical poetry, limited in amount, but qualitatively the best Denmark has produced since the turn of the century. His poems are not innately musical, but are so rich in suggestive power that they vibrate in the reader years after the actual words have been forgotten. In his youth, Jensen wrote chiefly free verse, the form of which was probably influenced by Heine's *Nordsee,* although it seems more akin to Whitman's prosody. In his maturity, he returned to more conventional forms into which he poured a weighty wisdom that stamps them with the impress of finality.

Johannes V. Jensen, through his individualistic style, has given a new tone to the Danish language. Through him, it has gained in power and expressiveness. Nature description has become nature revelation; the vigor of manhood, and the sweetness, the mellowness of womanhood, have been embodied in words as never before. There are people who have learned Danish in order to appreciate Kierkegaard and Jacobsen; it is entirely likely that there will be those who will learn it in order to catch those overtones which have escaped the translators trying to play Jensen's instruments in English.

Too much attention has probably been attached to Johannes V. Jensen's racial ideas, his glorification of progress, and his pseudo-science. Jensen is a confirmed evolutionist. However, in the last analysis it is not the ideas which have inspired him that matter, but the sparkle his genius pro-

duces in us. In all that he has written, he has really striven for one thing only, for catching the essence of things, the quintessence of living. If to say this is merely to say that Johannes V. Jensen is a poet, we may add that to be a poet who makes us experience the creation of the world is to be a poet worthy of the Nobel prize. (pp. 132-35)

> *Jens Nyholm, "The Nobel Prize Goes Nordic,"* in Books Abroad, *Vol. 19, No. 2, April, 1945, pp. 131-35.*

## Hamilton Basso    (essay date 1945)

[*An American novelist, biographer, and critic, Basso is best known for his novel* Sun in Capricorn *(1942), reportedly based, in part, on the career of politician Huey Long. Like much of his work, including* The View from Pompey's Head *(1954), this novel explores the social structure and cultural mores of the American South. In the following excerpt, Basso discusses the scope and imagination of* The Long Journey.]

Johannes V. Jensen's **The Long Journey,** a one-volume edition of the long and ambitious trilogy that won the Nobel Prize in 1944, is not a new novel. Mr. Jensen, a Danish writer whose position in his country is comparable to that of Sigrid Undset in hers and of Thomas Mann in pre-Nazi Germany, wrote it in the early part of this century. . . . [Upon its first publication in English *The Long Journey* was] received with a proper amount of respect, even with a burst of enthusiasm here and there, but that was about all. Americans don't go in much for epics, particularly an epic that sets out to tell the story of man's upward striving from the time of the cavemen to the discovery of this country, and Mr. Jensen was soon forgotten. Now that he has won the Nobel Prize, something his publishers will unquestionably let no one forget, he is not unlike a pitcher who, after a brief stay in the big leagues, drifts back to one of the provincial circuits and then is brought, with a great outcry, back to the majors as the hottest performer since Bob Feller or Dizzy Dean. Mr. Jensen isn't as good as that, prize or no prize, but it's obvious that he doesn't belong in the Buckeye League, either.

The author, in his trilogy, has turned out what must be the longest and most complicated story about a family ever written. Considering that his family is the human family, ranging all the way from a fellow called "The Man" to Daniel Boone, it could hardly be otherwise. It does make for a slightly crowded canvas, however, and the action, which manages to involve most of the major events in man's history from the coming of the Ice Age to Charles Darwin's voyage in the *Beagle,* also gets crowded at times. Mr. Jensen, a good storyteller, keeps things moving right along, though, and even those who usually get the trembles when exposed to an epic ought to be able to read this one without fidgeting too much.

Of the three books that make up Mr. Jensen's trilogy, the one I like best is **Fire and Ice.** The author, who plainly believes that the place to begin is the beginning, goes back to prehistoric times, when it was rather hard to tell the human animal from any of the other ones, and builds the drama of this book around man's terrible struggle with nature and his first great triumph over his physical environment—the discovery and domestication of fire. Cavemen are not my favorite people, and I'd rather have my evolution straight, but Mr. Jensen makes his gallery of fur-wearing primitives, as they go through the pangs of being the origin of the human species, considerably more creditable than a lot of recent fictional characters who have got far enough along in the evolutionary process to wear store clothes. The author has obviously been reading plenty of anthropological, geological, and evolutionary literature, including such standbys as Frazer's *The Golden Bough,* but his book is no mere recasting of facts in fictional form. Mr. Francis Hackett, in an appreciative preface for this new edition of Mr. Jensen's work, speaks of the author's great scientific knowledge and his "anthropological eye." Both are important, of course, but what strikes me as being more important is the author's imagination. Our scientific information about the social and family life of primitive man is relatively limited, and Mr. Jensen's eye as a novelist is much more valuable, for the business at hand, than his eye as an anthropologist. What Mr. Jensen is doing, since it is completely impossible to be altogether correct scientifically about things that were going on a few geological epochs ago, is offering his conception of what happened. Professional anthropologists, I feel sure, would want to quarrel with him on a hundred points, but I can't see that this matters. All that really counts in a novel is that we believe in it; the illusion of correctness is more important than correctness itself. What is called the "life" or "truth" of a novel derives not from a collection of fictionized facts but from the spinning of a web of imagined or remembered details that unites the actual existence of the reader with the pretended existence of the characters. And this, in *Fire and Ice,* is just what Mr. Jensen has done.

He isn't nearly so successful in his two other books in the trilogy. In both of them—*The Cimbrians,* which revolves about the Cimbrian invasion of Italy in the second century before Christ, and *Christopher Columbus,* which is about the explorer and a lot of other things—he depends more on facts and less on his imagination. Theoretically, and according to the rules that seem to govern the writing of the informed nonsense that constitutes the bulk of modern historical novels, this ought to bolster the illusion of correctness, but it does just the opposite. The fertility of Mr. Jensen's imagination is always evident, but *The Cimbrians,* persuasive though it is at times, often reads like a loose reworking of Plutarch and some of the Roman historians. Except for those passages that tell of the adventures of Norne Gaest, the central figure of Norse legend, who is used here as a symbol of the desperate hunger of man's mind and soul, it isn't very much better, on the whole, than *Ben Hur* or *Quo Vadis.*

Mr. Jensen, in the first part of *Christopher Columbus,* hits his stride again. We know considerably more about Columbus than we know about the cavemen, but since this knowledge is so fragmentary, particularly when it comes to the day-by-day details of his first voyage of discovery, the author can let his imagination go to work again. The result is that we get a wonderful picture of that voyage—the mounting fear of the men, the energy and singlemindedness of the explorer, the alternate periods of

hope and despair. It may or may not be historically correct, but I, for one, am quite prepared to believe that that was the way (or nearly the way) it happened. Not all of *Christopher Columbus,* unfortunately, is as good as that. I was more than a little surprised to find Norne Gaest turning up as Quetzalcoatl, the White God of the Aztecs, and I felt, on toward the end of the book, when I ran into Charles Darwin in the Beagle, that things were beginning to get quite out of hand. They don't often, however, and Mr. Jensen's trilogy, for all its sprawling six hundred and seventy-seven pages, is a reasonably disciplined book. Considering the sobriety of its theme, it is also a very readable one. It remains an epic, ornate at times and overreaching at others, but I certainly wouldn't let its being an epic frighten me off. (pp. 78, 81)

*Hamilton Basso, "Cavemen, Cimbrians, and Christopher Columbus," in* The New Yorker, *Vol. XXI, No. 11, April 28, 1945, pp. 78, 81.*

## Ralph Bates   (essay date 1945)

[*Bates was an American educator and critic. In the following review, he questions the historical validity of Jensen's* The Long Journey.]

Whether one refers to its form or content, *The Long Journey,* a trilogy that won for its Danish author the 1944 Nobel Prize for Literature, is about as difficult to describe as a late Beethoven quartet. It is not a symbolical novel, though symbols guide the course of the work, and its incident, except in the last volume of the trilogy, is wholly fictional. It is neither a connected history nor an allegorical drama of man's spiritual evolution, though both descriptions are in some measure appropriate. Something of the difficulty of writing about the book may be understood from this. The first volume deals with the pre-Ice Age conquest of fire (robbed from Gunung Api, a stupendous volcano of the Baltic region); the second volume treats principally of the Cimbrian invasion of Europe and the mingling of the nations just before the Dark Age; while the third deals with the discovery of the American continent by Columbus.

At first and even at second sight it is hard to conceive of a common denominator that might bring three such experiences within the boundaries of a single concept. And while having read the book with deep pleasure, I am still unconvinced that the attempted unification is wholly valid, though I am bound to accept the evidence of my wits that Mr. Jensen has been moved by it to write a massive and impressive work. His scheme is more or less as follows. When the Ice Age had razed the warm North European forests, a restless, fire-possessing folk still remained. Their restlessness invented the ship. The Forest becomes the ship and the northerners go in search of the Lost Land. Christianity, moving north from Asia Minor and from the Mediterranean, meets the northerners as they stream southward and the new faith again revives the old memory of a Lost Land. "From this union of south and north springs the most beautiful myth of the Middle Ages—the Virgin Mary, Goddess of Spring . . . the soul of the northerner and the arts of the Ancients in one." Another of the forest symbols is Ygdrasil, the World Tree, and this in the Middle Ages becomes the cathedral. Then, "a migration checked for the time leads to expansion in the domain of the soul; thus the aspiration of the northerner gathers and transforms memories of the youth of the race and Christian symbols into a work of art . . . the Forest and the Ship become the Church." Finally the age of voyages begins again and the Church changes back into the Ship. Columbus searches for Heaven and finds the savages of Guanahani. The impulse derived from memory of the Lost Land as primeval forest has met the Tropics. The Ship that was a Church has become the Forest. The cycle is complete.

The question cannot be evaded. Is there any validity in these concepts? Certainly *The Long Journey* cannot and does not claim to be either chronicle or history. And yet, if Man cannot comprehend his experience without a Myth, if he fails to organize his emotions without symbols, if he never brings his haunting conscience into relation with reality without a sense of a continuity of the race, then some such formulation as Jensen's is valid. As he says, "We cannot survey things that are dispersed in time and place" without such a plan. The world may be viewed in many other ways, through the organizing power of other concepts, but this is the myth by means of which this northerner will analyze the nature of Quest.

Understood in this fashion, many of the objections are removed. The most stubborn of those I felt in reading the book was Jensen's overestimate of the north. My glance kept straying to my bookshelves, to fall upon Toynbee, on Freud, on Breasted, Hall, on Fraser, with thoughts of Asia Minor, Egypt and Greece and the Mediterranean. Mr. Jensen, in asking me to imagine the medieval church as synthesized out of the racial forest memories of the north and the arts of the south, was asking me to make so great an effort that it was natural that I should fall back upon what he may consider mere prejudices. And indeed I do rebel when I am asked to believe that so great a part of Christianity came out of the north. The Church of the Middle Ages was not only a cathedral and not only a sacramental system. It was Augustine and Thomas Aquinas. And that remark, as well as anything, represents the real nature of my objection. The philosophies came out of the Mediterranean basin; particularly the Christian philosophy. There is nothing of all this in Mr. Jensen's plan. He makes the contribution of the south too exclusively artistic.

For my part, I have no objection to anti-rationalism as a temper, but I do resent anti-intellectualism. One may recognize the importance and universality of "Quest," but quest of what? A spiritual state, an impetus, a wholeness, a mode of being? If so, then more is required of Mr. Jensen than he has done. He has not adequately defined his mode, and he could not, within his terms, for he has too much neglected the intellect.

Yet there is a massive power in *The Long Journey.* There is something impressive about all such views as Mr. Jensen's, views which make man's fate a consequence at once of a causally determined process and of imaginative initiative. In this case the force of the suggestion is immense.

For the determinism itself springs from the primeval memory, the images of which are constantly recreated as symbols at ever higher levels of activity. One sees that the author's philosophy makes a bold effort to replace the dichotomy of matter and mind with the far more fruitful one of the Archaic and its recreation. In one sense he has drawn a rich prize from the Freudian revolution, though in the last account his anti-intellectualism has violated the true meaning of that revolution, which was intended to free man's mind from its excessive archaic burdens. Mr. Jensen is a man of courage, and though his cyclic conception at its close conveys a sense of defeat, this pessimism should not be exaggerated. The over-all effect is one of ascension and the conquest of dignity. And that, in these days, is reason for gratitude.

The demerits of the scheme from the purely literary standpoint are those inevitable in all imaginative efforts to reconstruct the archaic past. The reader must put up with too much bashing of skulls—too much gorging of raw meat. And he must read through much elementary material as context for the "Great Discoveries." There are other things to be set against these, however, such as the scenes of forest fire and the eruptions of Gunung Api. And in the second volume the incidental pleasures are numerous; the tour-de-force of the Baltic spring festival is surely unforgettable, as is the pervasive feeling of new life, of discovery and eagerness. For me, the high plateau of *The Long Journey* is not the one in which the Christian Cortes at last stands victorious over the horrible god Huitzilopochtli, but the Cimbrian march over the center of Europe. There is beauty in it. And this beauty, while it does not rise to splendor, transforms these simple incidents and at times quite redeems the coarse texture of the longplodding prose. When at last I put the book down I again found myself glancing at Toynbee's mighty work with desire to read in it. That is some little indication of Mr. Jensen's strength. (pp. 648-49)

*Ralph Bates, "Journey or Quest?" in* The New Republic, *Vol. 112, No. 19, May 7, 1945, pp. 648-49.*

### Niels Ingwersen (essay date 1971)

[*A Danish-born American educator and critic, Ingwersen is a contributor to a number of scholarly journals devoted to Scandinavian studies. In the following excerpt, Ingwersen examines America as a source of inspiration for Jensen. In an unexcerpted portion of the essay, Ingwersen recalls that Jensen visited the United States six times.*]

[Jensen's second stay in the United States (1902-03)] seems to have had a strong impact on him, for it resulted in two novels, a considerable number of short stories, sketches, and essays, and in what is normally considered to be one of his best poems. In all these works the setting is American, but the inspiration which JVJ gained from America made itself felt in other works as well, and JVJ was the first to admit that this was the case. (p. 272)

In the American experiment JVJ found an age-old pattern from the childhood of civilization repeated: man is confronted, once more, with nature. According to JVJ, the American emerges as being exceptionally fit for this battle. He is capable of doing battle because, in contrast to many decadent Europeans, he does not try to isolate himself from nature; because he does not interpret nature in terms of an ideal, higher reality; and because he consciously acts in a truly Darwinian spirit.

Since the emergence of a new healthy world became one of the cornerstones of JVJ's system, it is not surprising that the discovery of America and its discoverer, Christopher Columbus, achieve symbolic significance in his writings. Actually, in the works written during the first decade of the twentieth century, JVJ returns to this theme of the new world several times, either in identifying himself with, or in distancing himself from Columbus and his fate. In the novel **Madame d'Ora** (1904), the main setting of which is New York, there is a poem which interprets the discoverer as a man whose sense of reality has waned with the passing of years. He has become a man possessed by the dream of a new land—a world which is symbolic of everything man has lost or has desired for himself: " . . . den evige lykke, / som sjælen altid forfølger." He has set sail across the ocean and finally glimpsed land; but at the very moment of his sighting he loses his dream, for his longing has no longer any object, and his doom is forever to haunt the seas on his ghostly ship. As the poem closes we are informed that in the raging waves we will find *not* God, but the heart of Columbus, who through his yearning, man's universal torment, created a new and very real world for us.

The main theme of this poem is the longing which, according to JVJ, all men share. This longing may be simultaneously constructive and destructive: a new, glorious world is given to mankind in the very moment that the tragic individual, Columbus, becomes lost in utter unreality. (p. 273)

JVJ sees Columbus as a religious seeker who tried to satisfy his longing for paradise, but that central symbol for all religious quests faded away when he found land, and accordingly, man has had to accept this world as the only one possible. . . .

In the compassionate poem **"Christofer Columbus"** JVJ invokes the discoverer by saying, "Du gav os jorden igen." The discovery of America, which is Columbus' personal loss, is mankind's gain. Throughout the centuries man has been possessed by a longing which has been understood in metaphysical terms, and which, therefore, left him homeless in his world. The discovery of the new world finally redirected man's longing towards this earth; and he accepted his only home. In JVJ's writing this historical event figures as the symbol of man's healthy reaction against metaphysical dreaming. . . . (p. 274)

In numerous essays, particularly in the collection entitled **Den ny Verden** (1907), JVJ portrays America as a new beginning, as a new culture out of which a healthier and grander style of life is growing. Of this new style, of this new approach to the challenge of nature, he finds many examples in daily life in America: in man's close relationship to nature; in the effectiveness of American politics;

and in the vitality of the down-to-earth press and of the arts. He also sees aspects of life which he finds appalling, e.g. the squalor, the many broken destinies, the brutality, but he admits that a price must be paid by any new culture which would lead the world toward a brighter future. JVJ believes the reason for the American's success and unromantic view of life, e.g. his matter-of-fact attitude towards death, to be based upon his deep respect for facts, for the world around him, be it nature or the gigantic cities he himself has created. This appetite for reality as it is, has made him a stranger to metaphysical pondering and self-destructive introspection. . . . This unique quality of the American mind, which leaves it less prone to subjective fancies and, in general, less individualistically oriented than the European, enables the American to live in and to conquer a world in which he feels perfectly at home.

This view of America, in a somewhat sporadic fashion, appeared for the first time in **Den gotiske Renaissance** (1901), a travel-book in which JVJ collected the articles he had written in Spain during the Spanish-American War and in Paris during the World-Exhibition. Pondering the war, he found it inevitable that this Romance culture, which for centuries had been hallowed by Christianity, should lose to the Americans, a Gothic race which would be the next worldpower. JVJ predicted a Gothic renaissance which would sweep the earth because the Gothic race, made up of Anglo-Saxons, Germans, and Scandinavians, was finally rejecting those barren ideas which had kept the world trapped in metaphysics. Hitherto, no matter how many renaissances history had recorded, ideas that rejected the world as it is, for the sake of a higher reality, had always been victorious; but at last, not least due to *the machine,* modern technology, man had obtained powers which were earlier ascribed only to gods, and, thus, the gods had tumbled down from their heavens. Through machines, man had created a modern providence which would make everything possible. . . . (pp. 274-75)

Objectivity becomes the ideal for JVJ, and he repeatedly voices the deep conviction that, if man is to overcome his destructive passion for the subjective, i.e. unreal dreams of a higher reality, he must redirect his longing towards this earth and objectively register it on its own terms. . . . (pp. 275-76)

All in all, in this first attempt at formulating his new, healthy attitude, JVJ is taking on a formidable task: he is renouncing what he called . . . "inhuman individualism" and is attempting to establish a system that would eliminate the disharmony which, for centuries, has barred man from assuming a correct relationship to reality.

Much in **Den gotiske Renaissance** may seem preposterous, or at best, much in the book may strike one as being an inspired collection of postulates, but it must be kept in mind that, in his ensuing encounter with America, JVJ found a culture which seemed to him to prove that modern man, in his reliance on technology and in his objective approach to life, was perfectly capable of coping with life. In a sense, America became, for JVJ, the objective proof of the ideas set forth in **Den gotiske Renaissance.**

This outline of the young JVJ's views in general and of

America in particular, has hopefully suggested that, although he stubbornly insisted on seeing life as it is, he found symbols in, or projected them onto, the world. JVJ admitted as much himself, for even though he rejected religion, or rather theology, as being a destructive force, he was quite aware that man operates with symbols in his perennial battle with nature. JVJ has probably been one of Danish literature's staunchest Darwinists; but some years after the publication of *Den gotiske Renaissance,* he stated in *Den ny Verden* that a scientific view of nature should not be confused with any irreligious tendency. Religion, in its early stages, was man's first attempt to cope with nature, and the fact that science had now succeeded in giving more rational explanations, did not at all eliminate man's awe of nature. Although lightning might have been reduced to an electric spark, the thunderstorm, as well as Edison's lamp, remained a wonder of nature. In the place of religious awe, which might lead man to neglect this world, JVJ substituted, in his works, a tremendous awe for nature as it is.

JVJ's new attitude cannot be characterized as the giving up of the view that the world is deep, in favor a mere registration of the objects around him. JVJ thought of his development as being exactly the opposite; he escaped from the prison of his own reflective mind and found himself confronted with the world at large, a confrontation which gave him a deep insight into the workings of nature and of man fighting his age-old battle with nature. JVJ's new attitude furnished him with what can properly be called a *mythic consciousness,* which enabled him to sense not only how everything had been from the beginning of civilization, but how everything had developed—for good, or for bad—since that beginning. In the prose pieces, which he called *Myter,* this *Weltgefühl* dominates: one particular object is observed and, gradually, or abruptly, the perspective widens; the particular object, trivial as it may be, is seen in light of all time; its essence, so to speak, is brought out, and what the irreligious mind would consider to be just a fragment of reality is placed within the great order of nature. It should be added that the man of observant mind, who is capable of gaining this mythic perspective, simultaneously transcends his own individuality—his having been placed in a particular moment of time—and perceives that he is a link between passing and coming generations. In very simple terms, JVJ characterizes these experiences as "inspirerede øjeblikke, hvor naturen har rørt mig og jeg den."

America gave substance to JVJ's dreams of a Gothic renaissance. Figuratively speaking, he followed Columbus on the road west in order to satisfy his longing; but when he found the new world, he refused further identification with the old dreamer. JVJ's dream did not become unreal, but found its object in America where the Gothic race had finally accepted reality as it is. As has been previously mentioned, many of JVJ's essays testify to this view of American culture; and in several of these he took pains to praise American literature, especially the works of Walt Whitman, Mark Twain, and Frank Norris.

Since JVJ's praise is so abundant, it seems relevant to ask whether JVJ received—other than a general impression of

America—any specific impulses from these three authors. This question has received some treatment in Danish criticism, and it has been acknowledged that Whitman influenced the diction of some of JVJ's prose-poems, although JVJ admitted only that the American poet moulded his prose. It has also been shown that JVJ's colorful Chicago-novel *Hjulet* (1906) was basically patterned on Norris' *The Pit.* Danish critics have, otherwise, not dealt extensively with the possible influence of American literature on JVJ's works.

In his essay **"Whitmans Apoteosis,"** (1919) JVJ makes it clear that no poet could benefit from imitating Whitman's style, for mere imitation would actually not be in keeping with the American poet's own aesthetics. Whitman, in his enthusiasm for the facts of life which met his eye wherever he looked, was inspired to a poetry that was totally new. He jubilantly catalogued his observations of very real objects and created an anthology of facts, a temporary list of American realities, not by patching up earlier poetic diction, but by expressing his own age in the very language of that age. This is exactly the thing JVJ attempted to do when, after his return to Denmark, he published a collection of prose-poems (*Digte,* 1906) which broke drastically with the acknowledged poetic diction of the times.

One of the forces which helped Whitman to find a new mode of expression was, in JVJ's opinion, the American press and JVJ lavished it with praise. The reason for this enthusiasm was quite clearly founded upon JVJ's feeling a good deal of contempt for European literature, which he declared to have been written by people who had isolated themselves in their assorted ivory towers, from which they, nevertheless, exerted a stifling impact on an ever more literary and lifeless European press. In America, where literature received invigorating impulses from newspaper-reporting, both artist and journalist were in close contact with the immediate moment, and American literature seemed to read like long, well-structured, sparkling newspaper-articles. In this context JVJ was thinking, in particular, of Mark Twain, whom he praised several times, and some of whose writings can quite well be characterized as long well-structured, sparkling pieces of reporting, full of that freshness and tempo which is typical of the American mind and which conquers new material for American literature's epic appetite.

JVJ, who became increasingly preoccupied with the idea of spiritual health, was also attracted to Twain because he seemed to own that extraordinary American ability to overcome life's attempts to subdue man. Twain, asserted JVJ, had much in common with another great humorist, Heinrich Heine, for both shared an immense appetite for this life; but whereas Heine ultimately was destroyed, the healthier Twain reconciled himself to life. Twain, whom JVJ assumed to be of Jewish origin, seemed not only like a merry Ahasverus who had found a home, but also like a Job who had possessed the admirable strength to endure.

Both the examples of Whitman and Twain, or more precisely, their aesthetics as JVJ interpreted them, were undoubtedly important to him, but while he may have expressed himself somewhat vaguely on these two authors, he became much more specific when he turned to Frank

Norris. The affection which JVJ felt for the young American, whose obituary he read the very day he disembarked in America for the second time, may stem, to some degree, from the feeling that he had artistically much in common with and had shared the same development as the American. In Norris' early works JVJ found all the moods which possess the young man who is on the verge of exchanging his spiritual and aesthetic view of the world for a desire for the world itself; JVJ, in these works, also found the obsessive longing for happiness and the deep fear of death which haunted his own earlier works.

That which made JVJ Norris' admirer and translator seems, however, to be the fact that the American had managed to leave his earlier aestheticism behind and to write—in such works as *The Octopus* and *The Pit*—about the contemporary scene in a new way which transcended the naturalistic mode. JVJ's comments on Norris' road toward this achievement characterize the Dane as well as the American. JVJ is mildly critical of *McTeague* because it is slavishly written in the Zolaesque manner, but he finds in the unfinished *Trilogy of the Wheat* that Norris luckily frees himself from the naturalist's fatalism and "føjer Lykken til [Zola]." Both Zola and Norris portray this world, but the effects of their works vary greatly, and this must be so—asserts JVJ—because the one writes about a decaying culture, whereas the other has as subject matter the emergence of a new, healthy world.

While *The Octopus* and *The Pit* contain many tragedies, their ultimate effect is spiritually uplifting. Man is caught in a battle for survival, and even though the worthy may die, their deaths become meaningful within a larger perspective, for they are fighting against and ultimately defeat those who, in their inhuman individualism, have come to ignore the might of nature. The characters of these two novels are clearly divided into two groups—a grouping that can also be found in the Norris inspired novel *Hjulet:* the ordinary, anonymous citizens and farmers, who, in a sense, live in harmony with challenging nature, and the power-hungry individualists, who violate nature and who, as a punishment for their barren intentions, inevitably must and will be crushed. In JVJ's thinking Norris seems clearly to reject individualism; and no matter how much compassion he may feel for his characters, that which his two last novels reveal as being most essential is the awareness that man's struggle is to live in and from nature.

One may object to JVJ's reading of Norris, but curiously enough, in some of his own essays, Norris voices opinions that could very well have been JVJ's. In *The Responsibilities of the Novelist,* Norris delights in the revival of nature in American letters:

> The great wonder is this return to nature, this unerring groping backward toward the fundamentals, in order to take a renewed grip upon life.

Norris, like JVJ, is obsessed with mankind's history and sees it in a correspondingly racial light: the frontier has finally been eliminated, for America is settled; the world has been circled by the Anglo-Saxon race which has, thereby, fulfilled its destiny. This great achievement, of which the swift settlement of the American West was not its least important part, came about because the race had never been able to feel that the ultimate West had been reached; and indeed, the westward push was still continuing for American soldiers fought in Asia and American trade was conquering the old world. The globe was being encircled by the victorious Anglo-Saxon race.

Norris states that the literature which celebrates this eternal movement westwards is truly epic, but that many of the heroes of this conquest, and not least those of the American West, remain unsung. Norris insists that the hero to be remembered is not necessarily the striking individualist, but rather the ordinary, civilized man who brings justice and common sense with him. The hero is the good citizen who conveys and protects civilization.

Norris called for a new epic literature; but while he admitted that, for some time to come, such works would have to remain regional, for they could not yet encompass the whole of American experience, JVJ found Norris to be the only American author who had made an attempt in his works to encompass not only the culture of his own country, but also that of the old world. In a sense Norris had to consider the older traditions against which he turned.

Although JVJ never mentions Norris' essays on aesthetics, his own monumental history of civilization, **Den lange Rejse,** in which the Gothic race encircles the earth and in which many anonymous heroes are celebrated, has much in common with the epic of the Anglo-Saxon sweep westward which Norris had outlined.

Except in the few instances above, it is difficult to prove the existence of direct one-to-one influences on JVJ from the three American authors mentioned, and it is equally difficult to assess whether these authors opened new vistas to JVJ, or merely offered him techniques, thoughts, and attitudes which he recognized as being strikingly similar to his own. Since JVJ did not, however, hesitate to admit his debt to America and his admiration for these three American authors, it seems reasonable, at least, to suggest that for JVJ America became a catalyst in his search for a new mode of writing that would express the new outlook which he had newly gained.

It should be possible to categorize those aspects of Whitman's, Twain's and Norris' works which JVJ esteemed and which he made characteristic of his own works.

JVJ felt that, like the best American authors, he had made a conscious attempt to express his awe for this world in a new way. During these years, JVJ actually stressed that a new literature, which would express the twentieth century, was necessary.

JVJ was impressed, in particular, with these authors' new language because it seemed to him that it succeeded brilliantly in doing what it should do: it got much closer to and described more fully the objects, *tingene,* which were being observed. JVJ felt that he shared with these American authors the intention of depicting this earth on its own terms instead of utilizing inherited literary conventions.

JVJ felt that these authors' subject matter, as well as the attitude they took towards it, demonstrated their insight into the human condition. They could write passionately, humorously, or exuberantly about the single individual, but the fate of that individual was nevertheless seen in the light of ultimate truth: the necessity for mankind to meet nature's challenge, in a struggle that, turn out as it might for the individual, would reveal the harmony and grandeur of nature. JVJ consistently adhered to this view during his later career, which he devoted to depicting both the eternal that nature represents and the reality of the development of civilization that man's interaction with nature has caused. This view, which is both anti-individualistic and supra-individualistic, is at the core of all JVJ's later works.

It seems tempting, finally, to suggest that JVJ, who was definitely in search of a new mode of expression when he visited America, was impressed by those American authors who had already managed to solve the aesthetic problem of encompassing their vision—and to some extent his own—in artistically successful works.

Against the background of this examination of America as a source of inspiration for JVJ, it seems warranted briefly to consider a few of those texts in which the new world is the setting. A couple of the melodramatic novels which he had written in order to pay his way as a medical student take place in America, but the first work which deserves attention is the novel *Einar Elkær* (1898), which JVJ wrote shortly after his first trip to America in 1896, and whose protagonist lives for a brief time in New York. At the time this novel was written the new world had not yet become a positive symbol within JVJ's system, even though the hapless protagonist entertains vague notions of escaping his melancholy by becoming an American. Actually America, in this case New York, can hardly be called a setting, for the immense city does not really exist for Einar. Nothing is real for this sadly introspected, *fin de siècle* type, but his own dreams and moods, and these are perennially projected onto his surroundings no matter where he may be. Only momentarily are his fluctuating moods and reflections, which he cannot quiet, interrupted by outside forces that are strong enough to leave him in a moment of awe over life as it is. A blazing fire and a view from Brooklyn Bridge are brief intermezzos that seem to pull him out of the trap that is his own mind; but the trap always closes in on him again, and it remains a question as to whether, in these fleeting moments, Einar really succeeds in escaping from himself or merely in experiencing moods that are less ordinary to him. Although these moments reveal the protagonist's burning desire to escape from himself and into the world, they do not bring Einar one single step further towards experiencing the real world and seem to signify only that Einar's longing for escape is impossible. Einar Elkær leaves America as an unchanged and, spiritually speaking, unhealthy man headed for the inevitable destruction, which JVJ consistently allots to those who refuse to, or cannot, see this world.

If America can be called a symbol in this novel it remains a relative one—the private property of the protagonist's barely observant mind—for America does not encompass the universality which it assumed in JVJ's later works. At the turn of the century JVJ reacted strongly against the Einar Elkær mentality and maintained that the Gothic re-

naissance, of which JVJ claimed himself to be a member, was the cure for man's age-old, unhealthy inclination to futile reflection. America became his focal point, a place where the Nordic spirit seemed finally to have flowered without being blighted by ideas hostile to reality.

In some works, e.g. the novel *Madame d'Ora* (1904), America is hardly more than a backdrop for the action; but in many, the turbulent society of the turn of the century is an integral part of the action, and the American scenes, e.g. the bustle of New York's subway, the brassy bars of the Bowery, a snowbound Chicago, the prairie and the ever canyon-like streets, emerge clearly through JVJ's lively, matter-of-fact style. If one, however, compares these stories, **"Monsunen," "Et Møde," "Bonde-fangeren," "Lille Ahasverus," "Arbejderen,"** etc., with the America of *Den ny Verden,* it immediately becomes apparent that JVJ, the artist, differs in degree from JVJ, the essayist, or philosopher. When, in these stories, he keeps closer to the fates of individuals, he observes the squalor and the brutality of the new world more distinctly than his official attitude toward America would seem to allow. America seems to be, in fact, less of an allegorical symbol in his fiction than in his unambiguous essays. Although, like Norris, he may render an individual tragedy with deep compassion, these stories, as well as the novel *Hjulet,* nevertheless leave one with the impression that individual fates are of less significance than the American experiment as such. All these works are devoted, in reality, to a portrayal of the tempo and vitality of the new culture, which is progressing so fast that it is unavoidable that some individuals be crushed. A lust for seeing life as it is—be it sordid or beautiful—characterizes these works; and they, thereby, embody what JVJ saw as a prime feature of the American mind: an insatiable appetite for facts, *kendsgerninger.*

Although these works are realistic and realistically portray the American scene, the setting, nevertheless, takes on symbolic overtones, for the life observed becomes symbolic of the achievements, those accomplished and those to come, of the Gothic race. This is especially true of those works that depict city-life; and, in retrospect, these works may seem to be somewhat impersonal and superficial attempts to capture the vitality of the new world.

In those few works in which JVJ leaves for the American countryside and gets closer to nature, the transformation of setting into symbol—or rather a fluctuation between the setting as setting and as symbol—as the narrators' minds take in the scene around them, provides a profound insight into the attitude JVJ was assuming.

In the hunting-sketch, or *Myte* **"Potowatomis Datter"** (1905), an experience is rendered, which most accurately can be characterized as the expansion of an observing mind's consciousness to the point where the observed takes on mythic significance. As the hunter, JVJ, walks along the lakeshore in the twilight, he observes a dark figure in the lake. Since this experience repeats itself several times, it seems to transcend the accidental and to take on a special meaning: the dark figure becomes Potowatomi's daughter, the immortal woman who searches for the man who, in turn, has dreamt of her as his companion in life.

What JVJ experiences by this small lake in northern Illinois, has previously been characterized in this paper in very general terms. He is confronted with one of the wonders of nature, and he understands, during these particular spring days of 1903, that spring always has and always will remind man of his dream of the union between man and woman. The perspective has widened; the particular, trivial little incident has taken on universal significance and has revealed its essence. Through his contact with nature, a mythic moment has been granted him; the observer has become not just one particular hunter, but man longing for woman.

JVJ stresses emphatically that American literature has been unequaled in its descriptions of nature, and that America itself has simply meant a return to nature. "Potowatomis Datter" seems to reveal how strong a bond with and how profound an insight into nature man can obtain, if he allows himself to meet nature on its own terms.

The above analysis, which connects the text with the author's philosophy, may seem puzzling for it suggests that JVJ, in spite of his love for life as it is, tends to project his own mind into nature in a dreamlike, not to say romantic, fashion that negates his rejection of aesthetic subjectivism. Even though he postulates feeling *what always has been* and *what always will be* instead of a subjective projection of his own personal mood, the borderline between these two kinds of experience may seem very obscure indeed, even though it did not seem so at all to JVJ. In his system there was a distinct and absolute difference between the personal, and thus relative, projections of the individual's mind and the mythic, universal experience of how life has ever been.

In order to suggest that JVJ's mythic moment has a unique quality, it is, however, necessary to return to the text: the hunter's experience does not inspire him to passive dreams of a love between man and woman, but to the realization of nature's being an ever present challenge to him. He does not forget this world in order to turn his thoughts inwards, but faces nature with mounting excitement. He conceals himself at the shore, and when Potowatomi's daughter appears as usual, he fires his gun at her and kills her. The immortal female spirit proves to be a muskrat whose beautiful teeth he extracts and long keeps as a memento.

It is important to understand that this conclusion which brings us back to the setting after the mythic discourse does not reduce "Potowatomis Datter" to a hunting yarn, for JVJ, by firing his gun successfully, does not nullify his mythic insight. He actually confirms this insight by taking up the challenge of nature; and even if he finally has only a dead muskrat in hand, the timeless experience of man's longing for and meeting woman still remains with him as a perception into that which is true and universal. It is only in memory of these exalted moments of challenge that he keeps the muskrat's teeth. JVJ's deepest conviction, that man is simultaneously challenged by and lives in harmony with nature, speaks from the pages of "Potowatomis Datter."

This analysis should have suggested that it is necessary to distinguish between the various ways in which the American setting achieves symbolic significance in JVJ's works. When he focusses on the life of ordinary Americans and depicts the hustle and bustle of the big cities, American culture represents health and vigor in a manner that is so clear-cut that readers, familiar with his earlier works, may find his perception to be considerably restricted by the America he so fervently embraced. His rejection of so-called "inhuman individualism" led him to views so impersonal and chillingly robust that his prose seemed to suffer artistically. Fortunately, in some instances, JVJ allowed himself to speak about his own experience in America; and in such works—e.g. "Potowatomis Datter"—in which he is less preoccupied with the glory of the American nation, profounder aspects of his philosophy emerge. The setting, when it assumes symbolic significance, symbolizes challenging nature with which man is everywhere confronted and to which he must respond. The experience which "Potowatomis Datter" renders could just as well have taken place in Denmark; but if one can accept the celebrated poem "Paa Memphis Station" (1904) as supporting evidence, it would seem that, during his second stay in America, JVJ finally established and firmly accepted the view of the human condition which came to characterize his ensuring production.

It is necessary, finally, to discuss his only poem with an American setting, "Paa Memphis Station," which, being a highly personal, inner monologue, probably reveals, more than any other text, the essence of JVJ's American experience. In this poem one can again detect the fluctuation between setting and symbol, which is a distinguishing feature of much of JVJ's work, and which here enables the reader to grasp the decisive development which takes place in the mind of the poet.

As the poem opens the poet finds himself at Memphis Station, Tennessee, on one very early, very rainy morning. Stooped with his own discomfort and irritability, and still half-asleep with futile dreams, he can concentrate only on the ugly details that surround him, e.g. orange-peels, burned-out matches, and the witless, soaking rain. He does not, however, merely register his situation, but makes it symbolic of his fate: in Einar Elkær's style, he projects his mood onto the surroundings and sees them as a prison locking him away from the fulfillment of his dreams. His depression borders on the suicidal, for why should he chase around the world in an effort to escape meaninglessness only to find himself amidst this ugliness.

He then checks himself. By what seems to be an act of will, he turns his attention to the locomotive which is enveloped in steam. His tone now changes ever so slightly, for he describes the enormous machine for what it is and does not transform it into another depressing symbol of his own fate. This confrontation has, nevertheless, symbolic overtones, for he contrasts the locomotive's patience, as it stands ready to function, with his own destructive impatience. He then reacts against his former hopelessness by literally imitating the machine: he lights his pipe, curses God, swallows his pain, and puffing away, he, too, sends out smoke-clouds.

In spite of himself, he has assumed an attitude of patience, and although he sneers at life's shabbiness and his own waiting-room existence, the world around him is no longer just a mirror for himself. He can observe his surroundings, register them with a grudging humor, and conclude that, since life is this imperfect everywhere, he might just as well stay in Memphis. This thought fills him with sarcasm toward the gaudy town, but it also leads him to consider the happiness which life might have in store for him here, if he could cease his being impatient and his chasing about the world. Somewhere in this town a beautiful, young girl may be sleeping; they may meet; she may seem to recognize him; and she may be a part of the very happiness which life has set aside for him.

As he ponders this possibility, his tone becomes tender; and this new mood allows him to reconsider his earlier impressions. The falling rain now reveals that it is spring and reminds him of lovers quietly speaking to each other. The beginning dawn, which had earlier exposed only the general misery more distinctly, now seems to make even the rain beautiful. In spite of their negative aspects, his surroundings, as he considers the possibility of a purposeful life, take on a more positive meaning.

At this point, when he has begun to recognize the promises of nature for the return of spring, he is able to turn against his former desire to give up, and he is able to chide himself for not accepting life as the struggle it is. He is, so to speak, emotionally, slowly moving out from his inner dream-world and into the setting within which he has been physically placed; and that setting, the real world around him, seems to pose questions to him which he answers in a somewhat half-hearted, but affirmative way, which in turn, discloses his gradual acceptance of his situation. As his senses, thus, begin to embrace his surroundings, his formerly quite subjective associations become less personal and more universal. He concedes that there is fertility in the rain, that love exists, and that spring is foreshadowed in nature.

Being more open to impressions he now turns to view that immense river, the Mississippi. He delights in the beauty of the flooded landscape, ruled as it is by the mighty river; and his perception of this reality further widens his perspective. Whereas, earlier, he was concerned only with his momentary, personal situation, he now experiences the eternal Mississippi, and observes how healthily (*sundt*) the river flows through the flooded region under the pregnant clouds. His view is completely impersonal, for he now experiences eternity, the only eternity which exists, one which is of this earth. In this confrontation with nature, his consciousness has expanded beyond his actual situation and has grasped, in one incomparable moment— rendered without any accompanying irony or bitterness— the essence of existence.

Much calmer and much wiser, he returns to his own situation and outlines the only possible future course which can make his life sensible: he must forget all impatient, metaphysical dreams of eternal life; for if he does not do so, he will forsake this life and will never find any use for the love and gratitude toward life which he harbors.

In light of this attitude he can now reconsider his earlier

inclination to remain in Memphis, and he does so in a way that shows that his newly won attitude does not cause him to look at life through rose-colored glasses. He retains his earlier knowledge, that to become a representative citizen of the town is a far cry from the perfect, for daily life is a shabby affair asking compromises frustrating even for the one who has given up his lofty dreams. The prospects both of starting a saw-mill and of marrying the young girl he had earlier described so lyrically are rendered very soberly, for it is evident to him that this is the only kind of life offered him.

It has been pointed out earlier that JVJ's supra-individualistic view grants him harmony, but it is worth keeping in mind that harmony, to JVJ, does not denote the bliss of peaceful existence, but rather the waging of a healthy battle as man faces the challenge of nature. This battle, as JVJ's other works have shown, may be quite bitter, especially if—as in this poem—it is seen from the particular individual's point of view; but only by accepting and engaging in this battle, and thus by forsaking the dreams of another world, can the individual make his life meaningful.

Nature can never be a refuge in which man can shelter himself from this world, for besides granting man insight into his own role on earth, it promises him a continual struggle: the immense expanses of water, which has gone far beyond its normal boundaries, have caused destruction and death. The crossing riverboat is sailing on dangerous waters and is itself totally in the river's power.

The poet's reconciliation with his lot is interrupted by the arrival of the delayed train which has blocked the line. He is keenly aware of its wrecked carriages, and is abruptly struck by the sight of four bodies covered with bloody coats. The thought of death, which, in several ways, has been ever-present on this particular morning is suddenly and brutally brought home to him.

The track is, however, free at last, and he leaves Memphis to travel through the flooded forest in the pouring rain:

> Og vi rejser videre
> gennem de oversvømmede Skove
> under Regnens gabende Sluser.

This last stanza has caused some confusion on the part of the critics because the language is so utterly neutral. While the poet's attitudes clearly emerge through all the preceding stanzas, JVJ finally gives up either creating symbols of or finding symbols in his surroundings, and at last merely registers his setting. It is, however, possible to maintain that this very neutrality suggests the attitude which the poet finally reaches on this morning. The primary fact to be kept in mind is that the poet's reconciliation with this life, as represented by Memphis and by the Mississippi, has taken place before he is allowed to continue. If his experience is, thus, to be seen as something more than the overcoming of a bad case of morning jitters, he seems to be apt to bring his feeling of a reconciliation with him: he is leaving Memphis, only to reach some other Memphis, which may very well await him back in Denmark. The second important fact to be kept in mind is that the poet's sudden meeting with actual death must certainly have had both a shocking and sobering effect on him, but that it can hardly have changed his attitude, for at this point, he has realized that his own individual fate is quite insignificant and subject to a sudden termination. He has realized that ordinary, grubby, daily life must be lived and that nature, which grants beauty and insight, as well as havoc and death, always challenges man. His being confronted with the mutilated corpses may, then, be the final experience to confirm the truth of the insight into life that he has gained at Memphis station. The poem, thus, ends with the peculiar kind of harmony which seems to characterize JVJ's works after this period: by his unconditionally accepting the fact that life cannot be harmonious for the single, insignificant individual, who may even have understood that the challenge of eternal, healthy nature must ever be met, he achieves with regard to nature and within himself, a specific kind of harmony, which may not seem at all harmonious to others.

In order to understand the conclusion, that what JVJ called harmony has been achieved, it must be remembered that the protagonist of his poem goes through a development which JVJ always deemed positive. The protagonist started out in utter isolation; but as he gradually willed to gain a sense of reality, he rejected the homelessness to which his longing and dreams had banished him. Grudgingly, he has contemplated making Memphis, this unattractive and temporary reality, his home; and as his senses have expanded and allowed him to grasp eternity, as it exists in nature and, thus, on earth, he has transcended, for a moment, his own individuality. This insight, which "objectively" has shown him his role in life, has finally made him accept his life for what it is. This acceptance of reality signifies that he has broken out of his isolation from other men and from nature. His subjectivity has been replaced by a clear-sighted objectivity, which allows him, as his stay in Memphis is terminated, to register the human condition and the world around him exactly as they are. He has come back to this earth: a new world has been rediscovered.

This final summary of the poem's deeper structure has hopefully revealed that **"Paa Memphis Station"** contains not only all the attitudes which characterize the young JVJ's production, but the stand he took toward these attitudes as well. These years make up a transitional period which contains some fluctuation on JVJ's part: the dangerous metaphysical longing which he rejects still temptingly reveals itself in some of his works, but the healthy redirection of man's longing towards this earth is also firmly established there. Quite soon after his return to Denmark he started writing in a new vein, one that consistently eliminated the artistically fruitful tension, which such a novel as *Kongens Fald* and such a poem as **"Paa Memphis Station"** showed he harbored.

The question of JVJ's relationship to America warrants further investigation, but hopefully, this paper has succeeded in demonstrating that America was a determining influence on JVJ and in suggesting how this influence made itself felt in his works. As has been the case with many other authors, JVJ's exposure to a particular foreign culture came to figure prominently in his writings; and

since America came to mean more to him than a setting, it has seemed important to recognize it as possessing a certain symbolic quality and to characterize that quality. (pp. 276-91)

> *Niels Ingwersen, "America as Setting and Symbol in Johannes V. Jensen's Early Work,"* in American Norvegica, *Vol. III, 1971, pp. 272-93.*

### Sven H. Rossel    (essay date 1984)

[*A Danish educator and critic, Rossel specializes in Scandinavian languages and literature. In the following excerpt from his* Johannes V. Jensen, *he discusses Jensen's Himmerland stories.*]

Jensen's early self-analytical books have been subjected to divergent critical evaluation. His Himmerland stories, however, which begin the more extroverted phase of his work, have received universal critical acclaim. Jensen himself says: "My career as a writer starts with the Himmerland stories; there I began with the beginning." These stories mark the onset of a realistic trend which extends throughout Jensen's literary production, parallel with his mythic writing and essays.

Yet even this realistic aspect contains that introversion which was predominant in his earlier works, either concealed, as in several of the Himmerland stories, or the object of sharp attacks, as in the two America novels. Similarly the motif of longing is present here, although not so much directed toward distant lands as toward the land of his childhood: Himmerland. . . . In a way Himmerland is present in *all* of Jensen's books no matter the style or the motif he chooses.

Jensen's earliest Himmerland story, **"In the Darkness,"** was published in *Illustreret Tidende* on 2 May 1897. Jensen usually had his stories printed first in papers and later in almanacs, magazines, and other newspapers before they—with a few alterations—were issued in book form. The first collection, *Himmerland People,* was published in 1898 and the second, *New Himmerland Stories,* in 1904. A third volume came out in 1910, entitled *Himmerland Stories: Third Collection,* and in 1926 separately the novella *Jørgine.*

**"In the Darkness"** and **"Oktobernat"** (**"October Night"**), the first story in *Himmerland People,* are set in the distant past, whereas all the other stories take place in the years before industrialization. The common motif of all these stories, the tragic meaninglessness of death, is movingly represented in **"October Night"** by the young mercenary, who lies dying totally alone, far away on a desolate heath. This story seems like a sketch for *The Fall of the King.* In spite of his apparent vitality the main character possesses a sensitive mind, rather like Mikkel Thøgersen in the novel. . . . But otherwise the people who live in Himmerland, in and around Graabølle, the pseudonym of Farsø, are extremely robust characters. This is clearly illustrated in the thoroughly realistic **"Elses Bryllup"** (**"Else's Wedding"**), which tells of a young woman who is pierced by a hayfork—again a story about the meaninglessness of death—and in the somber murder story **"In the Darkness,"** about the murder of a tyrannical father who gets in the way of his daughter's happiness. The misdeed actually appeals to the reader's sympathy, but it only leads to the lifelong imprisonment of the girl and execution of her lover.

**"Thomas i Spanggaarden"** (**"Thomas of the Spang Farm"**) and **"Tre og tredive Aar"** (**"Three and Thirty Years"**) are stories about the meaninglessness of life and the absurdity of daily drudgery. The first portrays a quarrelsome, intemperate farmer who with deliberate malignity destroys his rival. In the latter Jensen tells of an entire family destroyed by tuberculosis, with the exception of the heroic wife, who ends up in an insane asylum. The title character of **"Cecil,"** on the other hand, is indomitable. Only dimly aware that she is acting out of defiance, she marries a drunkard who squanders their farm. In the equally brilliant story **"Den stille Mogens"** (**"Quiet Mogens"**), included in the second edition from 1905, Jensen for once lets the dramatic events find resolution in a happy ending.

Jensen's aptness at precise and well-formed character delineation is brilliantly shown in a colorful gallery of asocial eccentrics, such as the irrationally stubborn Vogn in **"En Beboer af Jorden"** (**"An Inhabitant of the Soil"**) and the epileptic fisherman and poacher in **"Lindby-Skytten"** (**"The Lindby Marksman"**) who is so intimately in touch with nature. The remaining four stories appear either as sketches or as pale afterglows of the texts mentioned above. They are partly anecdotal—one is simply an outright ghost story—and they fall apart because they lack tightness in their composition.

The volume of stories from 1904 is also of mixed quality. **"Tordenkalven"** is another outstanding, grotesque, and stirring portrait of one of Himmerland's many roving eccentrics:

> His body . . . was broader than it was long and of a yard's diameter from chest to back. His arms were so long that they almost touched the ground and as heavy as the legs of a normal person. . . . He walked with a short crutch under his arm and the stump from a heavy iron-clad stick in his right hand.

After this description of Tordenkalven's appearance, Jensen provides only a scant allusion to people's gossip about an unhappy love affair in his youth. On the other hand his talent as a poet is stressed: when he was given a coin he would sing a long ballad, "which was not satisfied with a mere glimpse into the land of obscenity, but even rendered a detailed topography of it."

Tordenkalven is fully accepted by his surroundings, but the title characters in **"Jens"** and particularly in **"Guldgraveren"** (**"The Golddigger"**) are outsiders. These stories tell of people's conflict with their environment. Jens, cheerful by nature, is an artless genius, and his meeting during his military service in Copenhagen with the natural sciences becomes "a huge source of light . . . a nourishing elixir which in a single moment permeated his entire thirsty interior." He decides to become an inventor, but the ignorance in his hometown—he is promptly dubbed

"the madman from Graabølle"—and a forced marriage put an end to his plans, and he dies soon after from tuberculosis—again an illustration of the meaninglessness of life. In **"The Golddigger"** Lavst Eriksen returns to Denmark after thirty years in the United States. But the parish and his son have passed judgment on him because he had left the family in order to find the work which had been denied him at home. His son's stubbornness and his own feelings of guilt prevent a reconciliation. In addition the people of the parish show only contemptuous irony and indignation when confronted with his American speed and effectivity, and he leaves his former home region in disillusion.

In **"Wombwell"**, the longest of the stories, Himmerland is again confronted with the outside world. Jensen presents a famous British menagerie which in a long train of carriages travels down through Jutland: first there is the excitement of anticipation and then confusion when the population, filled with suspicion, flocks to see "these tidings from the ferocious wide world." Finally Jensen tells of the complete but suppressed awe when the menagerie has been put on display, mixed with the peasants' spontaneous sympathy with the encaged animals. Jensen also manages to insert some evolutionary theories in this scene: " 'Isn't that our pussycat,' Erik said when he stood in front of the tiger cage. 'But it has become powerful, it has had too good a time.' The same man remarked about the elephant that it looked like a kind of big pig; it was the tapir that made him think like that."

**"Wombwell,"** a highpoint of descriptive prose, brings together all the characteristic elements in Jensen's art: excellent animal descriptions and brilliant, cinematic shots of the landscape, interspersed with sharply delineated portraits of the individual characters. Among these are three boys, one of them Einar Elkær, who spontaneously give themselves over to the enjoyment of the great fairy tale which the menagerie is to them. Finally mythic visions of the past are conjured up, together with omnipresent longing, when Einar on his way home suddenly catches a glimpse of the sea: "It lasted for only a few moments, then the shafts of light coming from the sea faded away. But Einar did not tell the others what he had seen. It couldn't be told. It was his fate that had called him in the silent dawn."

Great narrative art is present in the two totally dissimilar stories, **"Syvsoverne"** (**"The Sluggards"**) and **"Kirstens sidste Rejse"** (**"Kirsten's Last Journey"**). With baroque humor **"The Sluggards"** tells of the practical joke played by villagers one New Year's Day on the eternally sleepy people living at the Bak Farm. The second story is a brief account of a man's monumental struggle with the elements. When Kirsten, the farmer's wife from **"Three and Thirty Years,"** dies, a feeling of family solidarity emerges. With almost superhuman stubbornness—and helped by a liquor bottle—her nephew Christen brings the corpse back to Graabølle during a seventy-two-hour snow storm. While they are waiting for him to arrive, the villagers ponder the meaning of Christen's deed, and his figure grows in their minds to legendary proportions.

Also in this volume are found stories dominated by the episodic, exemplified by the strongly anticlerical satire **"Andreas Olufsen."** It begins as a picturesque description of a hypocritical upstart who, by means of his own revivalist movement, ends as a pillar of society. Unfortunately, the plot is developed rather erratically, and the story ends as little more than a sketch.

In the third volume, published in 1910, Jensen's narration swings between fable and essay. Pure fiction are **"Hr. Jesper"** (**"Sir Jesper"**), a tale of adultery, **"Bo'l,"** a love story with finely wrought detail, and **"Prangeren"** (**"The Horse Dealer"**), which continues **"The Sluggards"** from volume two. **"The Horse Dealer"** draws a tragicomic portrait of the oldest son of Bak Farm, Kresten, who wants to keep up with the times but is handicapped by lack of self-confidence and therefore brings the farm into great financial trouble. **"Bitte-Selgen"** returns to the somber atmosphere of volume one, with its account of the harsh fate of the peasantry and its lack of reconciliation. **"Hverres-tens-Ajes"** is another of Jensen's eccentrics, a crippled knife-grinder whose political ambitions give the author an opportunity to satirize harshly Danish politics.

The rest of the volume is devoted to a number of essays which contribute significantly to an understanding of Jensen's personality. **"The Emigrant"** is permeated with private memories of Jensen's schoolmates from Farsø who left the village and the peasant culture and went on to the United States. Using the difficult social and cultural change "from peasant to farmer" as a point of departure, he presents a penetrating picture of the feeling of homelessness, a feeling which was of particular poignancy for the author himself: They "were better off in America—but they felt a constant nostalgia for Denmark." In **"Graabølle"** we get a description of Jensen's native town and the surrounding countryside in the transitional period between the old peasant culture—of which Jensen gives a historical overview in **"Hedebonden"** (**"The Moorland Peasant"**)—and the modern industrial society. Progress is welcomed—with an undertone of resignation—when it relieves the peasant's harsh toil with the soil, but it is rejected when it brings about destruction of peasant traditions; we are far away from the enthusiastic and uncritical glorification of modern technology in *The Gothic Renaissance!*

**"Himmerlands Beskrivelse"** (**"A Description of Himmerland"**) is a topographical essay which in particular dwells on the region's many relics of the past. It concludes with some private remarks about the basis of Jensen's authorship. Thus Himmerland's nature serves as a symbol of the Jensen family history, indicating the source of tension in the author's works between the call of foreign places and homesickness:

> The outcroppings of scrubtrees, their growth broken by old age and storms through the centuries but still tenacious, made a deep impression on me in my childhood as the key to a happier, lost world. In the stately woods of Zealand I have since retrieved what those poor remnants of Jutland forest had called forth in my dreams—but, incidentally, it was a long time before I could *see* it; first I had to go around the world.

In the collected edition of the Himmerland stories from 1933 these essays are replaced with **"Vandmøllen"** (**"The Water Mill"**), a dramatic suicide story, **"Bakmandens Hund"** (**"The Dog of the Man from the Bak Farm"**), another story about the life on Bak Farm, this time with a subtle erotic point, and **"Jørgine,"** the most important of these texts, published separately in 1926. Here Jensen tells an apparently trite story about a crofter's frivolous daughter who is seduced and abandoned by the handsome and wealthy son of a peasant. Another man, the older and less attractive Anders Hansen, who is an incarnation of the industrious "Moorland Peasant," offers to marry her, and together they build up a life of wealth. In a factual, epic style Jensen incorporates this material into a brilliant presentation of older customs, culminating in a three-day-long wedding, but the traditional peasant society described is already moving toward a new epoch. With deep-felt admiration he depicts Anders's heroic battle with the heather and brush and his transformation of the barren land into thriving farmland—a Jutland counterpart to [Knut] Hamsun's Nobel Prize novel, *The Growth of the Soil.*

Like the other Himmerland stories **"Jørgine"** is to a large extent based on childhood memories. It is characteristic that as these memories gradually fade, a change takes place in the genre. The tragic-somber perspective—with death as the most frequently recurring motif—is replaced with a mood more dominated by reconciliation and humor. Stylistically there is a shift from the purely fictitious narrative toward the folkloristic essay; **"Jørgine"** fuses all these elements together in a splendid unity!

With the Himmerland stories Jensen has described a certain area and its inhabitants. The individual stories cannot be read and analyzed in isolation. A major character in one story appears as a minor character in another. Jensen does not simply depict individual persons, but rather a complete popular culture. The stories do not, however, have much in common with traditional regional literature: they are without the social and political propaganda found in the works of Aakjær, and they are completely devoid of the exaggerated local patriotism or idealization which frequently characterize this genre. They are written by a person from Himmerland who had been alienated and therefore was able to analyze the peasantry from the outside. From this fact stems Jensen's unsentimental, critical view of the peasantry: "Stubbornness and cantankerousness have always been part of the peasant; it has always amused him more to put an obstacle in a load's way than to help get it on an even keel when it has been overturned" (*New Himmerland Stories*).

Nevertheless, Jensen finds in Himmerland traces of the ancient culture, of the peasant world which to him was the sustaining element in this culture's history. The Himmerland stories form a memorial to those peasants whose spirit reflected the defiance of the Viking Age and the resilience of the peasant rebellions. These characters, portrayed in a realistic, strongly concentrated form, have something of the distance of the sagas, drawn on the background of the past, both what has been remembered and what has been forgotten. All the characters are therefore portrayed in the light of forgiveness. Their pugnacity, implacability, and malignity are balanced by a quiet resignation in the face of fate. The individual's tragedy is only a small detail in the course of generations; his life is regarded as half unconscious, governed by the heritage and the traditions of generations, and thereby elevated above a concrete, present milieu and epoch. The marksman from Lindby, "who carried the depth of nature and the ages deep within himself without knowing it" (*Himmerland People*), personifies this attitude, as does the tragic figure Cecil: "Cecil probably didn't know how everything was interrelated; her stubborn heart didn't know its own law. She didn't even know, Cecil, that she had defied and would continue to defy the whole of her life, beyond all happiness and completely counter to all reason" (*Himmerland People*). Here Jensen has succeeded in transcending the Himmerland horizon, the framework of concrete reality, and probing the distant, intangible forces of the human mind. (pp. 60-7)

> *Sven H. Rossel, in his* Johannes V. Jensen, *Twayne Publishers, 1984, 199 p.*

### Jorgen Steen Veisland (essay date 1989)

[*In the following excerpt, Veisland provides a detailed psychoanalytic interpretation of* Kongens Fald.]

The fact that Johannes V. Jensen's *Kongens Fald* (1900-01; *The Fall of the King,* 1933) is a highly poetic novel has often been overlooked, e.g., in classical Marxist and classical Freudian interpretations. This oversight has led to misinterpretations of the text; these misinterpretations reflect ideological and teleological preconceptions premised on the view that the subject (the subject as character and as text) is unified, i.e., hierarchical, nondialectical and nonprocessual. Traditional Marxist and Freudian analyses fall prey to what Jacques Derrida has called logocentrism; the novel is evaluated against a reference system external to the novel itself, and the result is that the characters are reduced to one-dimensional status and become separated from the aesthetic dimension of the text. For example, the Marxists claim that the King merely embodies despotism and imperialism; the Freudians claim that Axel is frozen at the pre-Oedipal stage. Both interpretations deny the validity of the poetry in the novel and disregard the interaction of the character, dream, and poetry that constitutes the dynamic open-endedness of the narrative and its complex ambiguities.

An opening up of the novel's aesthetic dimension—its images, symbols, and metaphors—will be facilitated by the implementation of concepts taken directly from Jensen's own definitions of *Myth* and *the Gothic,* and by the application of poststructuralist concepts, especially those of Jacques Lacan. This approach will focus on the deconstruction of logocentrism in *Kongens Fald* and on the structuring of desire by the absent or Symbolic Father. The structuring of desire by a pretextual Law of the Father produces the open-ended chain of signification to which the poetic imagery contributes and from which character and text derive a multiplicity of meaning.

From Jensen's *Den gotiske Renaissance* (1901), we may extract the following definition: the Gothic is a longing for the absolute, including beauty. This longing creates an imperfectly reproduced image of the absolute as it strives to reach it. Perfection is never possible, for the very striving for it always contains imperfection. The striving for the absolute is partly inhibited, constrained as it is by worldly conditions. Striving for the absolute is, however, an attempt at transcendence, and it is emancipatory in that its aim is for freedom. Jensen points to the duality of the Gothic; it contains two contradictory movements, a horizontal one and a vertical one. In spite of the fact that the Gothic artist is driven towards light and freedom, he remains crooked, lopsided, owing to his links with the horizontal aspect. But the vertical drive makes the best of, and is premised upon, human weakness and social restrictions, as it tries to transcend them and turn them into the opposite of what they are. Recognizing human weakness became, for Jensen himself, a revolt against bourgeois ideology, which tries to repress sexuality and hide its exploitation of the working class. The duality of weakness/strength is extended into a life/art duality, which become an insoluble dialectic in *Kongens Fald.* The Law of Gravity that governs the lives of the King, Mikkel, and Axel is transgressed, although not transcended, in the poetic discourse. The two conflicting laws, the Law of Gravity (the horizontal) and the Law of Poetry (the vertical), cannot be analyzed separately since they operate in unison and interact in the dialogue between the realistic and symbolic levels.

Like the Gothic, the Mythic contains an emancipatory aspect. Jensen, in his essay **"Myten som Kunstform"** (1916), writes that myth contains a joyous, free element that lifts the human mind out of its complex, anxiety-ridden existence. Myth is a short form that combines and condenses *sansning* ("sensory perception") and *forestilling* ("ideational representation") in an image produced by a sudden leap. Sensory perception is tied to the present, and ideational representation is a mass of memories extending into the past and history. The Mythical process is a hermeneutical process whereby memories are lifted into the present. Our senses select a few relevant ideas and memories, namely, those that are congruous with our experience of the present condition. Myth also forms the underlying principle of the author's theory of evolution. History tells us that we must fall; but according to Jensen, when and where we fall is determined by our striving. Each successive generation instigates its striving at a higher evolutionary stage, so that the fall is not an inevitable recurrence. Each fall generates a new force—psychological, cultural, and poetic—and this force, which is immanent in human nature, is forever striving upwards. The Mythical process is thus related to the Gothic. Both eliminate a weakness by turning it into a strength. The poetic image transforms anxiety into joy.

Using Lacanian terminology, we will translate Jensen's concepts of "force" and "joy" into the concept of *desire.* According to Lacan, the unconscious is structured like a language, and it comes into existence simultaneously with language. When words fail to fulfill their promise of satisfying a need, the unconscious breaks out and shows itself as a discrepancy between language and desire. The object of desire (the Mother or any love object) is forever suspended, deferred, absent. Desire, in its search for that absent object, invests the signifiers with meaning in order to fill the gap created by absence, i.e., the absence of what was originally signified. Desire causes the signifiers to slide. It also produces the aesthetic construct, the metaphoric and poetic complexity in literary discourse. Poetry, metaphor and symbol hint at the unconscious Other, which cannot be objectively signified in language. The unconscious Other comes about as the structure of desire, even though, paradoxically, desire evades structure and language. Terry Eagleton notes that for Lacan "our unconscious desire is directed towards this Other" but also "in some way always *received* from the Other too." The meanings invested in the signifiers by desire as it interferes with the signifying system are subjectively felt. They are "meant" but do not capture the substance of what was originally signified, the lost object. This object is deferred and different. When desire interferes with the language system, however, it partakes of what Lacan calls the Real.

The Other is that which provides unconscious desire with a residual structural imprint; or rather, since desire is directed towards the Other as well as received from the Other, structure comes about as an effect of the movement of desire towards the Other. We cannot define the Other as an origin, only as a difference, since it is always deferred. However, other Lacanian concepts are related to the Other—the Symbolic Order and the Law of the Father. Although we cannot speak of origins, we must conceive of the Other and of the Symbolic Order as somehow generative of structure. Desire is imprinted with structure, but also disrupts it. The disruption does not produce chaos (the opposite of structure). Rather, the disruption manifests itself as an alternative structure that we could characterize as a rhythmic pattern, a heterogeneous flow. Desire creates a new language through its interaction with the Other and with the Symbolic. Aesthetic law—poetry—is the product of the dialectical relation between desire and the Symbolic. The language of desire, initially repressed by the Law of the Father, follows an aesthetic law that is partly imprinted with the Father's Law, since desire is possible only as a result of repression.

We must understand that desire cannot be equated with Freud's unconscious chaos of needs and instinctual drives. The Freudian triangle mother/father/child is, in poststructuralist terms, a semiotic triad, and desire is defined as the structural relation between the three poles of the triad. Desire has a structure that might be called primal and fluctuating, since the relations in the triad shift in accordance with a primal scene. The structure of desire as a triadic relation is defined as the binding of desire to the Law, specifically the Law of the Father. The father lays down the Law as a prohibition against incest, to control the son's incestuous desire for the mother, which is a desire for the ultimate union. The Law of the Father also contains a threat of castration, designed to make the son passively submit to the Law. The threat of castration is meant to make the son passive (*passivus*, also meaning "suffering"), so that he may gain knowledge of the father. The son is seduced by the Symbolic Father who represents the laws of culture and civilization.

As Robert Con Davis points out, the question of the Father in fiction is one of absence; the text attempts to refind an absent Father, and the original Father is contained in the trace of his absence. Lacan states that the absence of the Father is a primordial "want-to-be" (*manque-à-être*), and this want-to-be is the precondition of structure and of discourse. The awareness of absence creates a need for the inauguration of discourse. The absence of the Father thus has a narrative function. Discourse fills a gap and is determined by a desire structured by the Symbolic Father (the son's deprivation of his biological father is only the initial step towards a recognition of a more pervasive absence). The absent Father becomes present as the trace of a law that governs discourse through the paternal "no," the prohibition against a static union with the Mother. Discourse is the dynamic dissolution of stasis. It is logical that in order for desire to become manifest in narrative discourse it must be preceded by the evocation of lack caused by the absence of the Father. Paradoxically, discourse signifies by being separated from an original signified—the subject is in constant flux as the *telos* of narrative is deferred. The term *absence* thus becomes abstract, symbolic, and even metaphysical, and it takes many forms, such as loss of power, anxiety, exile, and passivity. These forms accord with Lacan's axiom that essential links between the subject and the external world are established in a purely passive way.

This point is important for our evaluation of whether Mikkel Thøgersen succeeds or fails in mastering reality. Mikkel, the main character in **Kongens Fald,** is described as introverted, sexually frustrated, and alternately passive and aggressive in his relationship with other characters, especially women. He commits several acts of violence, including rape and murder, as his unreleased libido and his love turn into hate. His repressed sexuality is partly compensated for in dreams, however, as in the following passage: . . .

> And suddenly a fog evaporated, as it were, from Mikkel's eyes. He recalled his dream. He had been out on the distant sea, and there he had had a wonderful vision. Out on the horizon a radiant white column was shining, no taller than a finger; but he understood how high it must reach since it was so unfathomably distant. It stood out against the sky, brilliant as a snow-white silver top.

According to classical Freudian interpretation, the white column is a phallic symbol and a manifestation of a gigantic sexual potency in Mikkel. While it is true that Mikkel's inhibited nature warrants "phallic compensations," we will superimpose another layer of interpretation upon the Freudian one to avoid simplification. Given the Biblical implications of the white column (God appearing as a column of white smoke), it is tempting to see it as a symbol of desire less fixed than the Freudian libidinal theory would make it. The possibility of other symbolic meanings exists.

At the point in the narrative when the dream occurs (relatively early and in connection with Mikkel's infatuation with Susanna), a primal scene is staged in which the Law of the Father, symbolized by the column, binds Mikkel's desire. Mikkel unconsciously attempts to orient his desire by submitting himself to the column, which is so much larger than himself, larger than life. The dream is a signal from Mikkel's unconscious, admonishing him to navigate close to the column, just as Kirke advised Odysseus to "hug the rock" as he navigated between Skylla and Kharybdis. Unlike Odysseus, however, Mikkel's conscious mind does not heed the warning of his repressed sexuality, which erupts into violence several times throughout the narrative. It is not until the end that Mikkel becomes *passivus.* We contend, however, that this negative development in the narrative does not preclude an alternative discourse, as is amply testified to by the text itself. The image of Mikkel in the dream and his presentation as a "real" character are integrated, so that the text contains a preknowledge of itself and a set of values that are anything but nihilistic. They are, on the contrary, oriented towards the Law and towards the Symbolic Father, and while one might contend that the dream is an extension of the narrator's consciousness, it is indisputable that Mikkel is the author of the dream. The dream also highlights the text's own inherent aesthetic orientation (the Gothic or Mythic orientation), its desire for beauty and form. The Marxists and Freudians, more often than not, separate the characters from this aesthetic dimension, and this is a mistake. The beauty of the poetic discourse is due to the desire of the subject. Mikkel's defective orientation towards aggression and violence and his attraction to the King as the emblem of a unified, Imaginary subject (the Father as real and whole, rather than symbolic and traced) produce that negative force without which the complementary positive force (passivity and joy) could not come into being. In Lacan's scheme, the relation between the Imaginary and the Symbolic is dialectical. Through the characters, particularly Mikkel and Axel, Jensen performs a deconstruction of the Imaginary, unified subject, the Imaginary positioning of the subject that predates its social positioning. ***Kongens Fald*** points forward in time and becomes a critique of the aggressive, imperialistic type that Jensen worshipped superficially during the decade after 1900. In accordance with Jensen's own theory of the Gothic, Mikkel, Axel, and the King are partly twisted characters who must succumb to the harsh Law of Gravity, but who also strive towards the absolute and the Symbolic.

This statement can be further substantiated by analyzing a significant passage that illustrates Mikkel's progressive downfall and by interpreting Axel's death. Mikkel, after his dream of obtaining the love of Susanna has failed and after he has been dismissed from the university, ends up in the company of a scavenger, a knacker. The following passage describes the slaughter of a horse witnessed by Mikkel: . . .

> The knacker twisted Anders Grå's horse onto its back and started opening it up. The blood formed a large brown pool, melting its way down into the snow, and the pink froth quickly froze to ice. With each cut of the knife color would gush out from the steaming corpse, as the flesh was sparkling with lovely blue and red hues. And look, the shreds were still moving as they contracted and shivered in the icy air, and

the severed muscles shrank like worms in the stinging fire. The long windpipe saw the light of day; the back teeth became visible like four lines of mystical letters. A fine pink membrane appeared; it had a pattern of multiple blue veins, like a river landscape seen from up high. When the chest was cut open, it was like a cavern; large whitish-blue membranes were hanging down; brown and black blood oozed from small holes in the veined walls; yellow fat was standing there in long, wet clusters. The liver was more brown than all the brown in the world; the spleen came into sight, blue and moldy like the night and the Milky Way. And there were many more pure colors, blue and green entrails, brick-red and ochre-yellow parts.

Henrik Wivel points out in his Freudian analysis [*Den titaniske Eros,* 1982] that in the midst of death the libido flourishes in its raw, unmediated state. The passage shows that desire itself is living, beautiful, and kaleidoscopic, like a "river landscape" or like the "Milky Way," but at the same time the sexual drive is impure, dangerous, and even death-related. The slaughter of the horse is also a form of sacrifice—we can see it as an act of castration, a sacrifice of the id, a repression of animal nature, and a subsequent sexual renunciation. The attempt at renunciation is doomed to fail, however, because repression results in regression. Mikkel is trying to regress to a pre-Oedipal stage through a prenatal reunion with the Mother (the chest cavity of the horse is described in terms of the womb), and Mikkel has a vision of himself, shortly after this scene, as an infant growing and dying incredibly fast, obeying an accelerated Law of Gravity. The infant experiences knowledge of the world, as the womb also symbolizes the external world, and this knowledge is an awareness of a cruel and horrifying reality. The symbol of the horse, and the knowledge contained in the symbol, is therefore double: regression takes place and is blocked at the same time. The horse is both protective womb and demonic libido, and the butcher knife is both phallus and instrument of castration. The passage illustrates the brutal nature of the repressed libido and its inevitable link with time, and the symbolic experience serves as yet another warning to Mikkel that goes unheeded.

Wivel's analysis is interesting and plausible but remains limited because it neglects the positive aspect of the libido. As Wivel himself states, the libido creates an inner, organic landscape of great beauty, which appears only after the brutal opening up of the animal. Clearly the libido, in its raw state, is only a prelude to the transformation through which desire receives an aesthetic imprint and through which a symbolic space is evolved. We might say that character is sacrificed for text, closely related as they are in Jensen's Gothic scheme, which values psychological weakness as a precondition for aesthetic achievement. The symbolic space of the poetic discourse, which creates the kaleidoscopic river landscape, is desire bound to the Law of the Symbolic Father as aesthetic law. Mikkel's perverted libido must be interpreted as the inverse side of desire structured by absence. The narrative digression, the deflection of discourse throughout the central sections of ***Kongens Fald,*** forms a curve, the structural design governing the fluctuations of desire. This narrative digression can be understood only in relation to the overall function of the absent Symbolic Father, who makes up the superior consciousness of the novel. The characters are separated from this consciousness in terms of their digressions and their limited life experience, but they also become partly integrated with it owing to the interference of desire made manifest in euphoric visions and in poetic imagery. Through this interference, the underside of the characters' unconscious erupts into their consciousness, thus crossing the boundary of the Imaginary into the Symbolic. It is for this reason that we must attach value to the poetry in Jensen's novel, as indeed he did himself.

As noted above, castration is a significant event on the stage of the primal scene, since it instigates the passive suffering of the subject. We contend that Mikkel learns to suffer in the end. Castration is not just sexual renunciation, but a positive removal of aggressive libido and an initial structuring of desire, whereby absence (castration) turns into presence (orientation towards the Law of the Father), and Mikkel becomes *passivus* in this sense also. Thus, while it might be argued that Mikkel does not develop beyond the Oedipal Stage (he refuses to be a father to Ide, and his relationship to women is tragically immature), we must insist that the knowledge Mikkel gains through suffering initiates him into the Symbolic.

The tragic insight furnished by the novel is that the trace of the absent Father is searched for by the characters (especially by Mikkel and the King, who is himself a son, not a father) in the Imaginary manifestations of "real" fatherhood. This comes out in Mikkel's adoration of the King as father and in the loss of his own biological father, which is also the loss of a unified identity. During Mikkel's visit to his home, Thøger, his father, states that it is unhealthy to go out at night and warns Mikkel against *Jøven* (the Demon or Dragon). According to Wivel, Thøger's description of *Jøven* contains details and images that indicate a prohibition against masturbation and a general warning against the dangers of an uncontrolled libido. During Mikkel's visit a thunderstorm breaks out, and lightning strikes Thøger's anvil, an emblem of paternal power. After this incident Thøger weakens and rapidly deteriorates into old age. The thunderstorm has broken Old Thøger's libidinal prohibition as well as his status as a strong father figure. This decline of the biological father signals the beginning of a more profoundly felt deprivation and absence in Mikkel's life, exacerbated in the extreme by his doomed relationship with women. Mikkel fills the gap with libidinal outbursts, violence, and aggression, but also with visions of sovereignty and euphoric happiness. The Symbolic is attained only after Imaginary selfhood and fatherhood have been destroyed and dismembered.

Mikkel and the King are both defeated on the realistic level of the narrative because they fail to integrate sexuality and the drive for power and knowledge successfully. The King's downfall is absolute because he insists on a life in the Imaginary Mode; he embodies a language or a discourse based on homogeneity, exclusion, and negation—specifically, the negation of multiplicity and difference. The King strives to be a unified subject, as he strives to accomplish the enforced unification of the Scandinavian countries. His final debacle is the Stockholm Bloodbath, at which the decapitation of Swedish aristocrats symbolically becomes a castration scene. The King is both phallocentric, in his definition of himself as the sovereign personality, and logocentric, in his vision of himself as the center of the universe and as the embodiment of divine power and knowledge. The deconstruction of the unified human subject, as we see it in *Kongens Fald,* occurs at a time when a new view of character—the view that the subject is in process—is emerging. The traditional view of character still prevails, however. It is therefore logical that the dissolution of character in Jensen's novel will assume a tragic form—it will occur as an abrupt fall, at least in the King's case. The knowledge that the subject is in process and that it is "subjected to" suffering in its response to the demand of the Symbolic Father does not become completely integrated with the self-knowledge of the characters. However, the multiple and positive manifestations of desire are seen in that fluctuating, poetic discourse which is oriented towards the absent Father (who is also the aesthetic prerequisite of the pre-text) and which, paradoxically, creates life out of death by deconstructing the meaning of both. In this way Jensen's discourse abolishes the barrier between two ontological conditions; it also abolishes the barrier between psychology and aesthetics, thus accomplishing the dissolution of character in its own unique way. Character does not master reality in the tradition sense but is subtly and passively integrated with poetic experience. Desire communicates with reality despite the deflections of the libido in the digressions of narrative. In this manner form alters content, and the novel becomes much more positive and optimistic than it is assumed to be by most critics.

These contentions are also substantiated by the narrator's treatment of Axel. As mentioned above, traditional Freudian analysis would tend to see Axel as negatively fixed at the pre-Oedipal stage and see him as a projection of Mikkel's fantasizing ego. Axel would thus become Mikkel's ego-ideal, an active, sexually powerful person. It is certainly true that Axel, at one level, embodies Mikkel's sexual longings. Axel has many women, and for him all women are one woman; women have no separate, independent identity in his eyes. Axel's amulet contains the secret of love, and Mikkel kills Axel to obtain this secret. He finds the amulet empty, however. There is no ultimate secret, at least not for Mikkel. But the question remains whether Axel's death may not furnish us with part of that secret.

As we have seen, Axel is apparently a lover without depth of emotion, a Don Juan. He is active, but infinitely restless. He possesses an elemental force of nature, Eros, but has no integrated identity. Wivel argues that Axel's eroticism is finally judged to be negative through the symbolic figure of Zacharias, the doctor, whose hands and knife represent the same diseased, perverted sexuality as symbolized by the knife of the knacker.

Two passages will serve to illustrate and substantiate our claim that Axel's character partakes of the narrator's poetic experience. The first passage describes how Axel meets with his favorite love, Inger, after death: . . .

> Look towards the heavens, he said, laughing infinitely sweet and, yes, full of longing; he was exhausted with fatigue and with longing for the earth. You see how joyously the night goes by!

If Axel embodies only a pre-Oedipal lack of self-awareness and an immature eroticism, how can he express such deep longing? And how does he end up in the land of eternal summer after death? It is precisely the quality of his longing that endows him with another dimension.

The following passage describes Axel's death: . . .

> He died remembering all the little things, those forgotten things that ache like red-hot iron; but the cruelty of remembrance had become one with the joyous sensation of its ceasing. Thus Axel died, still living. Like snow that is melting. He entered death, living. . . .

Axel's death exemplifies the mythic process, which is the poetic transformation of the "cruelty of remembrance" into "the joyous sensation," the extension of the past into the present, which annihilates time in a moment of eternity, according to Jensen's own definition. The fact that Axel dies "like snow that is melting" substantiates our claim that character in *Kongens Fald* is not just psychological but poetic, blending with the discourse of the narrator. The function of character is extended into this second discourse and into the symbolic partaking of the Other. The poetic discourse structures desire so that the latter causes the signifiers to slide. This produces a deconstruction of logocentric meaning. To describe Axel's death in terms of "snow that is melting" is to reverse the meanings attached to life and death. The words "life" and "death" are no longer signifiers tied to specific signified contents but each becomes exchanged for the other. Axel's death is therefore not a union of subject and object, that union which we normally call death; it is a gradual dissolution, a melting, a process in time that follows the paternal formula first inscribed in Mikkel's vision of the white column. The white column as the Symbolic Father subsumes the subject by outlining the trajectory *in time* of the subject's desire for an end that is always deferred, postponed, and different.

The trajectory of the subject's desire also leads back to the pre-Oedipal Mother, and it is for this reason that the poetic language surrounding Axel (partly his own language, partly that of the narrator) has the rhythm and pulse that we associate with Julia Kristeva's "semiotic." This language stems from the infant's contact with the mother's body, so it is a feminized language. It is also an androgynous language, since it arises from a pre-Oedipal phase during which gender is indistinct. This explains why Axel also appears to have feminine and androgynous characteristics (his face, for example, is like a woman's or young girl's). Axel is, perhaps, truly liberated, since he is neither dominated by paternal nor by maternal power. He transcends both by synthesizing them.

In contrast to Axel's death, Mikkel's death is a complete blocking of desire: . . .

> . . . his mouth was closed in bitterness. The dead mouth was a universe of silenced pain. It was a mouth that had become quiet about its grief. It was like a mystical cipher hiding the key to secret sorrows.

The mouth as a "mystical cipher" echoes the "mystical letters" formed by the back teeth of the dead horse. Mikkel's death and the form his death takes is anticipated in the narrative, and as "mouth" stands for speech, discourse clearly becomes the articulation of desire through time. The final articulation of Mikkel's desire occurs in the Song of Fenja and Menja, which culminates in winter. But Mikkel also learns passivity and suffering before death (his final lesson is the meeting with the *Homunculus*), though his knowledge is bitterly earned and takes the form of total abnegation and progressive self-destruction, projected and intensified in an ever-increasing grinding noise, the noise of a universal interference.

The figure of Death itself is described in a passage that forms one of the myths interspersing the narrative: . . .

> But he goes on moaning, louder, he whimpers dry-eyed. He is lying there, his back arched up, resting on his neck and heels; he looks towards the ceiling in profound misery and screams, screams like a woman giving birth. In the end he collapses and moans only a little. Finally he lies still, forever silent.

The act of Death giving birth, thus participating in the temporal discourse, may serve as a final comment on Jensen's narrative, which, in the manner of both Myth and the Gothic, turns weakness into strength. The dialectic of verticality and horizontality deconstructs fixed signifieds. Death itself, the ultimate *telos* of narrative and the only sovereign ruler in life, becomes *passivus,* as he suffers through the pangs of childbirth. With a master-stroke Jensen reverses the "natural" order of life and death, subjecting death to life. (pp. 55-66)

> *Jorgen Steen Veisland, "The Absent Father and the Inauguration of Discourse in Johannes V. Jensen's 'Kongens Fald',"* in Scandinavian *Studies, Vol. 61, No. 1, Winter, 1989, pp. 55-67.*

---

## FURTHER READING

Allen, Gay Wilson. "Symbols of a Spiritual Rebirth." *New York Times Book Review* (15 April 1945): 4, 28.
    Favorable review of *The Long Journey.*

Brandt, Per Aage. " 'Oedipus in Memphis': Mythic Patterns in Jensen's Poem." In *The Nordic Mind: Current Trends in Scandinavian Literary Criticism,* edited by Frank Egholm Andersen and John Weinstock, pp. 37-49. New York: University Press of America, 1986.
    Analyzes the elements of Greek mythology evidenced in Jensen's poem "Oedipus in Memphis."

Friis, Oluf. "Johannes V. Jensen." *Scandinavica* 1, No. 1 (May 1962): 114-23.

Discusses Jensen's concept of "på bakken," ("on the hill") in relation to his life and works.

Hackett, Francis. Preface to *The Long Journey,* by Johannes V. Jensen, translated by A. G. Chater, pp. xi-xvii. New York: Alfred A. Knopf, 1945.

Introductory appreciation of Jensen's intellect, judgment, and imagination.

Heitmann, Annegret. "Search for the Self: Aesthetics and Sexual Identity in the Early Works of Johannes V. Jensen and Thit Jensen." *Scandinavica* 24, No. 1 (May 1985): 17-34.

Examines the extent to which gender determined the ideological differences in texts by Jensen and his younger sister Thit. According to Heitmann, "sex determined the different directions into which the literary talents of brother and sister were channelled."

Knaplund, Paul. "Johannes V. Jensen." *Sewanee Review* 33, No. 3 (July 1925): 331-34.

Approbatory overview discussing Jensen's life, work, and reputation.

Mortizen, Julius. "A Danish Novelist's Prose Epic of Mankind." *Literary Digest International Book Review* 1, No. 5 (April 1923): 18-19, 61.

Tribute to Jensen written on the occasion of his fiftieth birthday, declaring *The Long Journey* a masterpiece and praising Jensen's ability to chronicle the development of civilization in novel form.

"*The Fall of the King* and Some Other Recent Works of Fiction." *New York Times Book Review* (30 April 1933): 6.

Concludes that Jensen's "characters are pasteboard; his story never rushes us forward; his plots are specious and melodramatic. . . . What saves [*The Fall of the King*], what lures you on to the end is the power of its descriptions; what makes it distinguished at rare moments is the richness of its poetry."

Pritchett, V. S. "New Novels." *New Statesman and Nation* n.s. 5, No. 114 (29 April 1933): 535.

Briefly reviews *The Fall of the King.* According to Pritchett, Jensen "excels in evoking the raw animality, now shifty and now heroic, of Danish life, and one experiences this world with the skin. . . . There is a kind of clangorous poetry to this book, and there is happily no attempt to turn the early Middle Ages into nice, clean, skim milk for the Chestertonian babes."

Rosenfeld, Paul. "Johannes V. Jensen." In his *Men Seen: Twenty-Four Modern Authors,* pp. 313-22. New York: Dial Press, 1925.

Describes Jensen's outlook on modern society and discusses his treatment of the development of human civilization in *Den lange Rejse.*

Toksvig, Signe. "Johannes V. Jensen." *American-Scandinavian Review* 31, No. 4 (Winter 1943): 343-46.

Personal reminiscences and appreciative critical commentary written to commemorate Jensen's seventieth birthday.

Wiehl, Inga. "Johannes V. Jensen's 'Myte' and James Joyce's Epiphany: A Study of 'Potowatomi's Daughter'." *Orbis Litterarum* 23 (1968): 225-32.

Defines Jensen's concept of "myte" in terms of Joyce's concept of "epiphany."

# Claude McKay

## 1889-1948

(Born Festus Claudius McKay; also wrote under the pseudonym Eli Edwards) Jamaican-born American poet, novelist, short story writer, essayist, and autobiographer.

For further discussion of McKay's career, see *TCLC*, Volume 7.

McKay is often acknowledged as a seminal figure of the Harlem Renaissance, a period of unprecedented creativity among black artists and writers centered in Harlem, New York, and other urban areas of the United States during the 1920s. Like many writers of the Harlem Renaissance, McKay sought through his works to promulgate a heightened awareness of racial heritage. In his poetry and fiction, he challenged white authority in the United States and addressed the conflicts of black people throughout Western society. The publication in 1919 of his poem "If We Must Die" is considered by some to have been a major impetus behind the growing civil rights movement during the decade after the First World War.

McKay was born in Jamaica to peasant farmers whose strong sense of racial tradition was passed on to McKay through African folktales and stories of the enslavement of his African grandfather. Under the tutelage of his older brother, a schoolteacher and freethinker, McKay learned the importance of maintaining his intellectual independence from authority. In 1907 he left his rural home to become an apprentice woodworker in Brown's Town; there he met Walter Jekyll, an English linguist and specialist in Jamaican folklore. Jekyll introduced McKay to the works of such great English poets as John Milton, John Keats, and Percy Bysshe Shelley and also encouraged him to write poetry in his native dialect, a practice McKay later repudiated. In 1909 McKay moved to Kingston, Jamaica's capital, where he served in the local constabulary and for the first time witnessed the institutionalized racism of his country. Following the publication in 1912 of his poetry collections *Songs of Jamaica* and *Constab Ballads,* McKay moved to the United States. He briefly attended Tuskegee Institute and Kansas State College before moving in 1914 to New York City, where he entered into the literary circles and leftist politics of Greenwich Village.

Despite the racial discrimination McKay had known in Jamaica, he was unprepared for the extreme and overt racism he encountered in America. His first poetry collection published in the United States, *Harlem Shadows,* displays his anger and concern over the neglectful, abusive, and often criminal treatment of black Americans. Soon after the appearance of this volume in 1922, McKay left the United States, traveling during the next twelve years to the Soviet Union, Germany, France, Spain, and Morocco. While McKay was living in the Soviet Union, whose nascent communist society intrigued many writers of the time, he was extolled as a great poet, but he quickly grew disenchanted with the Communist party when it became

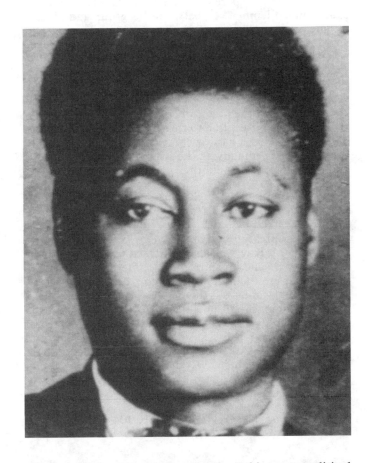

apparent he would have to subordinate his art to political aims. During the time McKay traveled outside the United States, American publishers continued to issue his new works: the novels *Home to Harlem, Banjo,* and *Banana Bottom,* and the short story collection *Gingertown.* While *Home to Harlem* was the first best-selling novel by a black author, McKay's subsequent works of fiction were almost wholly neglected by the reading public. When McKay returned to the United States in 1934, the country was in the midst of the Depression and the market for "black renaissance" literature had substantially declined. In the late 1930s McKay became active in Harlem's Friendship House, a Catholic community center, and he eventually converted to Roman Catholicism. None of the works he produced after his return to the United States was significant enough to revive the reputation he enjoyed in the 1920s. McKay died in 1948.

McKay reached his zenith as a poet with the publication of *Harlem Shadows.* Unlike the dialect poems of his first two collections, the poems in *Harlem Shadows* are based on conventional poetic forms, primarily the sonnet. Although his poetry often lapsed into an outdated Victorian style and tone, this shortcoming is considered to be balanced by the importance of his themes and the passion with which he developed them. Evident in McKay's poetry is the conflict he faced as a black poet writing within a white literary tradition. McKay wrote: "A Negro writer feeling the urge to write faithfully about the people he knows from real experiences and impartial observations is caught in a dilemma . . . between this group and his own artistic conscientiousness." Both as a poet and fiction writer McKay celebrated the life of the common people, whose vitality and spontaneity he contrasted with a restrictive and inhuman social order. McKay's works of fiction, however, are generally considered less successful than his poetry in terms of their artistry as well as their ability to convey the predicament of black people in Western society. An exception to this judgment is *Banana Bottom,* a novel in which the protagonist, a Jamaican peasant, is portrayed as embodying the strengths of both primitive and modern Western culture.

Critical opinion of McKay's work has never been as high as it was during the 1920s, and even then McKay was frequently attacked by black critics, including W. E. B. Du Bois, for his presentation of "low-life" black characters in his novels. McKay was also criticized for not sustaining a distinct style and for simple lack of literary skill. His poetic forms were thought to be too conventional for the expression of his ambitious themes; his prose was considered formless, unpolished, and spoiled by a shallow exoticism that obscured its basic seriousness. Nevertheless, in recent years critics have emphasized the intensity and ardor of McKay's poetry, praising his ability to convert social protest into art, while his novels are recognized as important efforts to articulate the problems and envision the possibilities for black people in Western society.

(See also *Contemporary Authors,* Vols. 104 and 124; *Poetry Criticism,* Vol. 2; and *Dictionary of Literary Biography,* Vols. 4, 45, and 51.)

## PRINCIPAL WORKS

*Constab Ballads*  (poetry)  1912
*Songs of Jamaica*  (poetry)  1912
*Spring in New Hampshire, and Other Poems*  (poetry)  1920
*Harlem Shadows*  (poetry)  1922
*Home to Harlem*  (novel)  1928
*Banjo*  (novel)  1929
*Gingertown*  (short stories)  1932
*Banana Bottom*  (novel)  1933
*A Long Way from Home*  (autobiography)  1937
*Harlem: Negro Metropolis*  (nonfiction)  1940
*The Passion of Claude McKay: Selected Poetry and Prose, 1912-1948*  (poetry, short stories, letters, essays, and journalism)  1973
*\*Trial by Lynching*  (short stories)  1977
*My Green Hills of Jamaica*  (essays and short stories)  1979
*\*The Negroes in America*  (nonfiction)  1979

\*These works were first published in Russian translation in 1923.

## Walter F. White   (essay date 1922)

[*An American novelist, nonfiction writer, and autobiographer, White was among the most important authors of the Harlem Renaissance. His novels* The Fire in the Flint *(1924) and* Flight *(1926) provided revolutionary depictions of middle-class African-Americans and the effects of racism on their lives. Also a civil rights activist and prominent member of the NAACP, White examined in his works such issues as the roots of mob violence and racial discrimination. In the following excerpt, he offers a favorable review of* Harlem Shadows.]

With the publication of **Harlem Shadows** by Claude McKay we are introduced to the work of a man who shows very genuine poetical promise. His work proves him to be a craftsman with keen perception of emotions, a lover of the colorful and dramatic, strongly sensuous yet never sensual, and an adept in the handling of his phrases to give the subtle variations of thought he seeks. He has mastered the forms of the lyric and the sonnet—in fact, there is in this volume perhaps too much sameness of form. Yet one can have no quarrel with a man who works in that medium in which he is most at home, and I do not quarrel with Mr. McKay for sticking to these modes of expression.

I wish that I had the ability to convey the sheer delight which this book of verse gives me. Keenly sensitive to color and beauty and tragedy and mirth, he does, as Max Eastman says in his introduction, cause us to "find our literature vividly enriched by a voice from this most alien race among us." Mr. McKay is most compelling when he voices his protest against the wrongs inflicted on his people, yet in his love lyrics there is a beauty and a charm that reveal the true poetic gift. Here is the title-poem with its feeling of tender pathos:

> I hear the halting footsteps of a lass
>   In Negro Harlem when the night lets fall
> Its veil. I see the shapes of girls who pass
>   To bend and barter at desire's call.
> Ah, little dark girls who in slippered feet
> Go prowling through the night from street to
>   street!
>
> Through the long night until the silver break
>   Of day the little gray feet know no rest;
> Through the lone night until the last snow-flake
>   Has dropped from heaven upon the earth's
>   white breast,
> The dusky, half-clad girls of tired feet
> Are trudging, thinly shod, from street to street.
>
> Ah, stern harsh world, that in the wretched way
>   Of poverty, dishonor, and disgrace,
> Has pushed the timid little feet of clay,
>   The sacred brown feet of my fallen race!
> Ah, heart of me, the weary, weary feet
> In Harlem wandering from street to street.

(pp. 694-95)

*Walter F. White, "Negro Poets," in* The Nation, *New York, Vol. CXIV, No. 2970, June 7, 1922, pp. 694-95.*

## Hugh M. Gloster   (essay date 1948)

*[Gloster is an American critic and educator. In the following excerpt from his book* Negro Voices in American Fiction, *he discusses* Home to Harlem, Banjo, *and* Gingertown.]

Claude McKay denies the influence of [Carl Van Vechten's novel] *Nigger Heaven* upon his first work of fiction, *Home to Harlem* (1928), which had greater popularity than any other novel of the Negro Renascence; but the fact remains that *Home to Harlem* capitalizes upon sex, the cabaret, atavism, and other selling points of the Van Vechten Vogue. The central character is Jake Brown, who deserts the American Army in Brest because he has to work in labor battalions rather than fight the enemy. Returning to the United States via London, he goes directly to Harlem, where he discovers sexual bliss in the arms of Felice, a beautiful brown girl. Losing her address and failing to locate her thereafter, Jake plunges into the fast life of Harlem, maintaining himself as a longshoreman and as a dining-car cook. We follow him to cabarets, pool rooms, chitterling joints, gambling dives, speakeasies, amusement basements, buffet flats, dance halls, prostitution houses, dining cars, and waiters' quarters. During this tour we observe streetwalkers, show girls, alcoholics, sweet men, scabs, loafers, loan sharks, and other characters of Harlem's underworld. Eventually Jake finds Felice and, in order to escape arrest as a military deserter, flees with her to Chicago.

Immediately after publication, *Home to Harlem* was censured by certain Negro intellectuals because it supposedly outstripped *Nigger Heaven* in magnifying licentious and promiscuous aspects of life in upper Manhattan. . . . While admitting certain merits of the novel, [W. E. B.] DuBois decries McKay's catering to "that prurient demand on the part of white folk for a portrayal in Negroes of that utter licentiousness which conventional civilization holds white folk back from enjoying" and protests that the book "for the most part nauseates me, and after the dirtier parts of its filth I feel distinctly like taking a bath" [see Further Reading]. It must be admitted that there is some basis for DuBois's objection to McKay's novel. Though rooted firmly in the author's experience, *Home to Harlem* is painted in exaggerated colors and saturated with libertinism. In his preoccupation with muck and sensual excesses McKay, like Van Vechten, fails to give a well-rounded picture of Negro life. This faddistic emphasis upon overpainting and overliving, this lack of balance, inevitably spelled the doom of the Van Vechten Vogue.

It would be unjust, however, to say that *Home to Harlem* is entirely a riot of exotic color and orgiastic indulgences. In the character of Ray, Jake's Haitian friend and the probable counterpart of the author, McKay portrays a sensitive, intelligent Negro who has a distaste and sometimes an aversion for his low-life environment. His dream is to be a writer. Upset in his thinking by World War I and the Russian Revolution, he stands as a confused black man in a social order dominated by whites. In his wide reading, which ranges from Sappho to Sherwood Anderson, he discovers no solution to his dilemma. He shrinks from marriage because he does not want to "become one of the contented hogs in the pigpen of Harlem, getting ready to litter little black piggies." Finding slight meaning in human existence, he cynically considers himself "a misfit" and sometimes wonders if he can abandon his education and lose himself "in some savage culture in the jungles of Africa." The obvious implication of *Home to Harlem,* then, is that a *carpe diem* philosophy gives unlettered Jake happiness, while knowledge of books brings thoughtful Ray disillusionment and despair.

Ray is the chief connecting link between *Home to Harlem* and McKay's second novel, *Banjo* (1929), an impressionistic kodaking of life among the colored boys of the Marseilles breakwater. A decided change, however, has taken place in Ray's outlook on life. In spite of poverty and introspection, he has made headway as a writer and is determined to tell his story regardless of the color prejudice of readers:

> If I am a real story-teller, I won't worry about the differences in complexion of those who listen and those who don't. I'll just identify myself with those who are really listening and tell my story.
>
> (pp. 163-65)

The main character of McKay's second novel is not Ray, however, but his friend Banjo, an irrepressible and irresponsible vagabond who—picking up odd jobs as seaman, longshoreman, farm hand, and factory worker—has wandered over much of North America and Western Europe. With Banjo and his companions we frequent bistros, bars, cabarets, eating sheds, and hovels of the Ditch, Marseilles's seaside slum district, and hear folk tales and racial discussions by colored men from all parts of the world. We note the evidence of first-hand knowledge in McKay's portraiture of tramps, seamen, soldiers, pimps, peddlers, gamblers, beachcombers, and prostitutes of the Mediterranean port; and we follow Banjo's casual and unashamed liaisons with Latnah, a mixed-breed girl from Aden, and Chère Blanche, a French prostitute of the Ditch. Late in the novel Jake of *Home to Harlem* meets Ray and the beach boys at a Marseilles bar. During a happy reunion Jake describes several years of family life with Felice in Chicago, the birth of a son named for Ray, a year in Harlem, a weariness of domesticity, employment as a seaman, and a current resolution to settle down to marriage upon his return to New York. At the close of the novel, the beach gang having dissolved, Ray zestfully sets forth on a vagabonding expedition with Banjo. (pp. 165-66)

To McKay's credit, *Banjo* is a fairly authentic depiction of life among those who dwell between the old port and the breakwater in the motley metropolis of Southern France. Though showing occasional proclivities for trumped-up exoticism and debauchery, the novel has social perspective, a quality lacking in *Home to Harlem,* and offers a well-rounded picture of the society with which it deals. Of documentary value are discussions of the Negro problem by individuals from various countries of the world. In *Banjo,* as DuBois has noted, "McKay has become an international Negro. He is a direct descendant from Africa. He knows the West Indies; he knows Harlem; he knows Europe; and he philosophizes about the whole thing" [Review of *Banjo, The Crisis* (1928)].

In six of the twelve stories of *Gingertown* (1932), his third volume of fiction, Claude McKay returns to the Harlem setting. A considerable part of the action takes place in cabarets, casinos, tonsorial parlors, and speakeasies; and once again cabaret entertainers, pimps, longshoremen, railroad men, bellhops, and chambermaids are leading characters. In contrast to *Home to Harlem,* however, the New York tales of *Gingertown* are largely concerned with intra- and inter-racial prejudice. (pp. 166-67)

Since McKay wrote *Home to Harlem, Banjo,* and *Gingertown* while abroad, he was not considered by a few critics as a participant in the Negro Renascence in New York. Nevertheless, *Home to Harlem* emphasized those aspects of Harlem low-life earlier stressed in *Nigger Heaven.* The Van Vechten approach is also evident in *Banjo* and *Gingertown,* but these two volumes are more faithful renderings of their milieus. Sex is a powerful motivating influence in most of McKay's work. The heroes of *Home to Harlem* and *Banjo* are spontaneously amoral in their sexual conquests; and Ray, the intellectual who is at first restrained by conventional rules and taboos, finally decides that the instinctive is preferable to the rational life. (pp. 167-68)

> *Hugh M. Gloster, "The Van Vechten Vogue," in his* Negro Voices in American Fiction, *1948. Reprint by Russell & Russell, Inc., 1965, pp. 157-73.*

## M. B. Tolson   (essay date 1954)

[*Tolson was an American poet, journalist, and dramatist. In his best-known work, the poetry collection* Harlem Gallery *(1965), he employed both standard and black English to illuminate the lives of African-Americans and to examine the role of the black artist in society. In the following review of* Selected Poems, *Tolson praises the universality of McKay's poems.*]

During the last world war, Sir Winston Churchill snatched Claude McKay's poem, **"If We Must Die,"** from the closet of the Harlem Renaissance, and paraded in it before the House of Commons, as if it were the talismanic uniform of His Majesty's field marshal.

The double signature of the role would not have gone undeciphered by the full-blooded African poet who could avouch, in spite of apartheid: "I have never regarded myself as a 'Negro' poet. I have always felt that my gift of song was something bigger than the narrow limits of any people and its problems."

And yet, in the sestet of **"The Negro's Tragedy,"** with its passive voice becoming an artery for an active idea, McKay declares the poetry "is urged out of my blood"; and then his raw, taut finality bristles in the monosyllables, "There is no white man who could write my book." In the moment of that milieu it was true, for the period discovered no one with the ethnic empathy of the genius who wrote "The Runaway Slave" and "The Wounded

Person", "The Drayman" and "Ethiopia Saluting the Colors": Walt Whitman was dead.

Professor Dewey, in his preface to [*Selected Poems*], singles out a line from the lyric, **"North and South"**: "A wonder to life's common places clings." The quotation revitalizes Yeats' observation that poets of the new idiom were "full of the unsatisfied hunger for the commonplace," since no manna fell, supposedly, from either the Temple or the Capitol. In this tradition, then, and out of a heterogeneity of experiences with an underlying unity, Claude McKay, as wheelwright, constable, agriculturist, porter, longshoreman, waiter, vagabond, rebel, and penitent, created his best poems.

Contrived seemingly as the plot of the Hardyesque is the triangle of a poet mythicized by Harlem, feted by Moscow, and haloed by Rome. His sensibility quick with image and idea, McKay explores the plurality of his world, inward and outward. He can etch, with a Dantean simplicity terrifying in detail, a picture of himself as surgeon in the grotto of the self.

> I plucked my soul out of its secret place,
> And held it to the mirror of my eye,
> To see it like a star against the sky,
> A twitching body quivering in space. . . .

McKay likes to explore the axis of day and night when he holds the looking glass to his ego, his race, his moment, his milieu; and sometimes what he sees shocks him, as in the case of his beloved Africa, bereft of her ancient honor and arrogance and glory, and he cries: "Thou art the harlot, now thy time is done, / Of all the mighty nations of the sun."

Although his odyssey took him into Temple and Capitol, his poems are without ideological vestiges. McKay's verse has interludes during which his "memory bears engraved the high-walled Kremlin" or his soul tingles in Tetuan from "Filigree marvels from Koranic lines." Often he cannot stay till dawn in a caravansary; some bedeviling urge drives him toward the rain of fluid rock. He is aware that his passions are "saturated with brine," and, leaving the crystal glass of lyricism, he can only cry, "O tender word! O melody so slender!"

McKay, like his contemporaries of the Negro Renaissance, was unaffected by the New Poetry and Criticism. The logic of facts proves Mr. [Allen] Tate's observation that this literary ghetto-ism "too often limited the Negro poet to a provincial mediocrity," from which he is just now escaping. Thus, in that era of ethnic mutation, McKay's radicalism was in content—not in form: the grammar of *The Souls of Black Folk* [by W. E. B. DuBois (1903)] demanded the seven league boots of the "huge Moor."

The Negro poet of the 20's and 30's broke the mold of the Dialect School and the Booker T. Washington Compromise. For the first time he stood upon a peak in Darien, but he was not silent. Like the Greeks of Professor Gilbert Murray, he had stumbled upon "the invention of habit breaking." It is aphoristic that he gave the "huge Moor" and Desdemona a shotgun wedding, minus the ceremony "Traditional, with all its symbols / Ancient as the metaphors in dreams" for the poet-rebel, whether in content or form, travels *his* hypotenuse and not the right angle, toward *his* reality.

In his most famous poem, ["If We Must Die"] Claude McKay's "if " reaches beyond this time and that place.

> If we must die, let us not die like hogs
> Hunted and penned in an inglorious spot,
> While round us bark the mad and hungry dogs,
> Making their mock at our accursed lot.
> If we must die, O let us nobly die,
> So that our precious blood may not be shed
> In vain; then even the monsters we defy
> Shall be constrained to honor us though dead!
> O kinsmen! we must meet the common foe!
> Though far outnumbered let us show us brave,
> And for their thousand blows deal one death-blow!
> What though before us lies the open grave?
> Like men we'll face the murderous, cowardly pack,
> Pressed to the wall, dying, but fighting back!

The mood of McKay's "must" is grammatical, psychological, and philosophical. The simile, "like hogs," packs both rhetorical and dialectical implication, as foreshadowed in the words "let us not die." The theme, ignobleness versus nobleness in man's tragedy, escapes, in this poem, from the abstract and the didactic into the reality of the imagination. McKay insures the catholicity of his theme in two ways: he does not reveal the ethnic identity of his protagonist, nor does he hog-tie the free will of the attacked by the imposition of an affirmative decision. This, then, is the poem, above all others in the *Selected Poems,* which, in the holocaustal year 1919, signalized Claude McKay as the symbol of the New Negro and the Harlem Renaissance. The poem is a pillar of fire by night in many lands. (pp. 287-90)

> *M. B. Tolson, "Claude McKay's Art," in* Poetry, *Vol. LXXXIII, No. 4, January, 1954, pp. 287-90.*

## Michael B. Stoff (essay date 1972)

[*In the following excerpt, Stoff discusses McKay's work within the context of the "cult of primitivism" in 1920s America, analyzing theme and structure in* Home to Harlem, Banjo, *and* Banana Bottom.]

The cult of primitivism which gripped many American intellectuals during the 1920s manifested itself in a number of ways. The rising interest in jazz, the study of African art forms, and the examination of tribal cultures were all variations on the theme of the primitive. The Negro as the uncorrupted remnant of preindustrial man became the central metaphor in this cult. Against the background of a tawdry culture stood the instinctive, sensual black man whose "dark laughter" represented a fundamental challenge to the effete civilization of white America. . . .

The primitivism in Claude McKay's art manifests itself even in his earliest efforts. As a Jamaican youth, McKay composed a series of dialect poems later published in two volumes: *Songs of Jamaica* (1912) and *Constab Ballads*

(1912). Both thematically, through their emphasis on everyday peasant life, and stylistically, through their use of native dialect, these poems reveal McKay's fascination with Jamaican folk culture. They capture the exotic and earthy qualities of the black peasantry with a lyrical sensitivity reminiscent of Robert Burns. (p. 127)

McKay's depiction of the Jamaican peasant is integrally related to a stereotyped image of the world's peasantry. His peasants have a universality of condition and reaction which allows them to be exchanged with peasants of any nationality. This conception is consistent with McKay's later claim: "As a child, I was never interested in different kinds of races or tribes. People were just people to me." In describing McKay's image of the Jamaican peasant, the French literary critic Jean Wagner [see Further Reading] has written:

> All things being equal, McKay's portrait of the Jamaican peasant is in substance that of the peasant the world over. Profoundly attached to the earth, he works the soil with a knowledge gained from age long habit; although a hard worker, the Jamaican, like his counterpart the world over, is condemned to exploitation.

This perception of common qualities among the world's masses later furnished McKay with a theoretical basis for his own peculiar vision of the ideal political state. At this early point in his life, the concept of a "universal peasantry" heightened his sensitivity to folk-art traditions of other cultures. That interest supplied him with a foundation for much of his work.

McKay emigrated from Jamaica in 1912 at the age of twenty-two. He carried with him not only a deep regard for the Jamaican peasantry but also a special vision of the island itself. He retained that vision until his death in 1948. The image of Jamaica as paradise permeates all his recollections of the island. In McKay's first American poems and in his later autobiographical material, Jamaica becomes the metaphorical equivalent of Eden. Its simplicity and freshness offered refuge from the complexities of a modern, industrialized world. Two stanzas from the poem **"North and South"** are typical of the nostalgic, pastoral strains found in McKay's early work:

> O sweet are the tropic lands for waking dreams!
> There time and life move lazily along,
> There by the banks of blue and silver streams
> Grass-sheltered crickets chirp incessant song;
> Gay-colored lizards loll all through the day,
> Their tongues outstretched for careless little flies.
>
> And swarthy children in the fields at play,
> Look upward, laughing at smiling skies.
> A breath of idleness is in the air
> That casts a subtle spell upon all things,
> And love and mating time are everywhere,
> And wonder to life's commonplaces clings.

The exotic setting and sensory images give a sensual flavor to the poem. These devices are re-employed in conjunction with themes of innocence and uncorruptibility in other Jamaican poems:

> What days our wine thrilled bodies pulsed with
>    joy
> Feasting upon blackberries in the copse?
> Oh some I know! I have embalmed the days,
> Even the sacred moments when we played,
> All innocent of passion, uncorrupt,
> At noon and evening in the flame-heart's shade.
> We were so happy, happy I remember,
> Beneath the poinsettia's red in warm December.

McKay did not lose the vision of Jamaica as an undefiled Eden where instinct and sensation reigned supreme. Although he never returned to his island home, he was forever swept back thematically to his preindustrial, peasant origins. In 1947, a year before his death, McKay wrote, "I think of a paradise as something of a primitive kind of place where there are plenty of nuts and fruits and flowers and milk and wild honey. Jamaica has all of this." Recapturing the lost innocence of that Eden provided one of the major themes in McKay's life.

McKay was also obsessed with describing the social role to be played by the intellectual. His membership in a visible and oppressed minority further complicated matters. In essence, the entire body of his art can be seen as a mechanism through which he sought to transform these personal problems into public issues. Such a transformation entailed an insistent reference to a recurring pattern of images. That pattern was the juxtapositioning of the instinctive black man and the educated Negro. These images defined, with increasing precision, McKay's own concepts and made them salient within a broader cultural context.

McKay's earliest use of this construction came in the first of his three novels, *Home to Harlem.* The book was published in 1928, the sixth year of McKay's expatriation from America. Its appearance initiated a violent debate among the black literati over the propriety of its theme and subject matter. Many of McKay's peers agreed with Langston Hughes's evaluation. Hughes argued [in a letter to McKay] that because it was so "vividly alive," *Home to Harlem* could legitimately be labeled, as "the first real flower of the Harlem Renaissance."

The elder black literary figures and much of the established Negro press were revolted by what they believed to be overtly crude allusions in McKay's book. Claiming the book was not representative of Negro life, this Old Guard expressed its shock and indignation at the lasciviousness of the novel. Its very existence, they suggested, was a calculated affront to the black community. W. E. B. Du Bois's reaction [see Further Reading] was typical of the initial reviews:

> *Home to Harlem* for the most part nauseates me, and after the dirtier parts of its filth I feel distinctly like taking a bath. . . . It looks as though McKay has set out to cater to that prurient demand on the part of white folk for a portrayal in Negroes of that utter licentiousness which convention holds white folk back from enjoying—if enjoyment it can be labeled.

The controversy enveloping *Home to Harlem* was merely the surfacing of an underlying tension engendered by conflicting visions of the Harlem Renaissance. The Old Guard saw the Renaissance as a vehicle for social amelioration. The Renaissance would not only demonstrate the intellectual achievements of the black man, but would also uplift the masses to some arbitrary level of social acceptability.

It was precisely this view of the Harlem Renaissance, this venture in cultural pretension, that McKay's work fundamentally challenged. His notion of a renaissance was an aggregation of ". . . talented persons of an ethnic or national group working individually or collectively in a common purpose and creating things that would be typical of their group." In 1929, McKay defined the problems one faced when speaking of a "racial renaissance." He delineated the tactics and sources to be employed in creating such a movement [in his novel *Banjo*]:

> We educated Negroes are talking a lot about a racial renaissance. And I wonder how we're going to get it. On one side we're up against the world's arrogance—a mighty cold hard white stone thing. On the other the great sweating army—our race. It's the common people, you know, who furnish the bone and sinew and salt of any race or nation. In the modern race of life we're merely beginners. If this renaissance is going to be more than a sporadic scabby thing, we'll have to get down to our racial roots to create it. . . . Getting down to our native roots and building up from our people is . . . culture.

For McKay, this meant the conscious and studied illumination of a black folk-art tradition whose central themes would be the indestructible vitality of the primitive black man and the inextricable dilemma of the educated Negro.

*Home to Harlem* is a vivid glimpse of the lower depths of black life in urban America. Its peripatetic plot and dialect-oriented style are consistent with its thematic emphasis on the black man as the unrestrained child of civilization. Set in New York's black ghetto, the novel establishes Harlem as a carnal jungle. Our senses are subjected to a barrage of erotic images: "Brown girls rouged and painted like dark pansies. Brown flesh draped in colorful clothes. Brown lips full and pouted for sweet kissing. Brown breasts throbbing with love." At the core of this physical world lies the cabaret Congo, "a real little Africa in New York." Forbidden to whites, the Congo is a distillation of Harlem life. Its atmosphere is filled with the "tenacious odors of service and the warm indigenous smells of Harlem." Its allusions to the unrepressed African culture provide an apt setting for the return of the novel's hero, Jake Brown.

Jake, an Army deserter, is introduced as the natural man whose actions are guided by intuition. He is the instinctive primitive, deeply rooted in the exotic mystique of Africa. As he walks down Lenox Avenue, he is overcome by the pulsations of Harlem life. "His flesh tingled," the narrator tells us, and "he felt as if his whole body was a flaming wave." Jake and Harlem are inexorably bound by a "contagious fever . . . burning everywhere," but burning most fervently in "Jake's sweet blood." That primitive passion sustains Jake and represents a profound threat to the cultural rigidity of modern society.

In contrast to Jake, McKay inserts himself as the Haitian

immigrant Ray. Ray represents the cultivated intellect, the civilized black whose education has sensitized his mind but paralyzed his body. Intellectually, Ray can comprehend the cluster of sensations and emotions about him, yet he lacks the naturalness of action and spontaneity of response that are the hallmarks of a Jake Brown. Although envious of Jake, Ray harbors the obsessive fear that "someday the urge of the flesh . . . might chase his high dreams out of him and deflate him to the contented animal that was the Harlem nigger strutting his stuff."

The result is a vision of the intellectual, and especially the black intellectual, as social misfit. Ray is capable of sensing and recording life, but he is unable to live it. "He drank in more of life," writes McKay, "than he could distill into active animal living." There is no outlet for his immense store of emotional energy. Robbed by his "white" education of the ability to act freely and impulsively, Ray remains little more than a "slave of the civilized tradition." Caught between two cultures, he is immobilized. "The fact is," he tells Jake as he flees to Europe,

> . . . I don't know what I'll do with my little education. I wonder sometimes if I could get rid of it and lose myself in some savage culture in the jungles of Africa. I am a misfit—as the doctors who dole out newspaper advice to the well-fit might say—a misfit with my little education and constant dreaming, when I should be getting the nightmare habit to hog in a lot of dough like everybody else in this country. . . . The more I learn the less I understand and love life.

The implications of Ray's final statement are not only applicable to McKay's personal problems but related to a broader cultural phenomenon. Notions of escape, alienation, and crude commercialism were by no means uniquely black images. They were embraced by intellectuals of varying hues in the twenties. McKay's use of these themes places the black experience into a larger cultural context. Blackness only added a further convolution to the already complex problem of the intellectual's social adaptability.

Ray's expatriation leaves the fundamental questions raised by the novel unresolved. The continuing focus on Jake, and his reunion with the "tantalizing brown" girl Felice, imply that only the instinctive primitive can survive happily in white civilization, its dehumanizing tendencies are irrelevant to his innately free existence. The intellectual, defiled by the process of civilization, is doomed to wander in search of that potency of action he has irrevocably lost.

McKay's second novel, *Banjo,* published in 1929, pursues the issues raised in *Home to Harlem.* Although the scene has shifted to Marseille's harbor district, the structural dualism characterizing *Home to Harlem* is present once more. Lincoln Agrippa Daily, familiarly known as Banjo, replaces Jake Brown while McKay again enters as Ray. The dichotomy is now expanded and more lucidly articulated.

In *Banjo* there is a sharpening of figurative focus and a widening of thematic scope. With the character Banjo, McKay adds a new dimension to the earthy black and pro-

vides a more concise definition of his own racial conceptions. At the same time, Ray's disposition has progressed from a confused uneasiness with American life to a coherent denunciation of western civilization. This increased clarity of imagery allows McKay to move toward a resolution to the quandary of the black intellectual.

The primitive black is given additional depth in *Banjo.* The loose plot, an account of the lives of a group of beach boys in the port city of Marseille, provides a background for the development of the protagonist, Banjo. He is the same intuitive vagabond originally described in *Home to Harlem*—with one significant difference. While Jake is nebulously characterized as a laborer, Banjo is depicted as an artist. He is a jazzman whose life is the embodiment of his art. Like the songs he plays, Banjo is unrestrained, free-spirited, and vibrantly alive. McKay immediately establishes the intimate relationships between Banjo and his music: "I never part with this instrument," Banjo says in the opening pages of the novel. "It is moh than a gal, moh than a pal; it's mahself."

After equating the protagonist with his instrument, McKay explains the aesthetic function of the banjo:

> The banjo dominates the other instruments; the charming, pretty sound of the ukelele, the filigree notes of the mandolin, the sensuous color of the guitar. And Banjo's face shows that he feels that his instrument is first. . . . The banjo is preeminently the musical instrument of the American Negro. The sharp, noisy notes of the banjo belong to the American Negro's loud music of life—an affirmation of his hardy existence in the midst of the biggest, the most tumultuous civilization of modern life.

The instrument is the cultural expression of American Negro folk-art, and Banjo represents the prototype black folk-artist lustily proclaiming the vitality of his race. His music, "the sharp, noisy notes of the banjo," is not derived from a pretentious adaptation of European culture. Drawing inspiration from the "common people," Banjo's art represents the truest expression of black culture.

Again juxtaposed to this earthy, intuitive black man is the intellectual Ray. Recently expatriated from America, Ray comes to Marseille in search of an artistic haven where he could "exist *en pension* prolitarian of a sort and try to create around him the necessary solitude to work with pencil and scraps of paper." Ray has not given up his earlier passion for writing, and although he is occasionally forced to work as a laborer, he never renounces his "dream of self-expression." Once in the Vieux Port, he finds, instead of solitude, a band of beach boys whose free and undisciplined lifestyle is particularly appealing to Ray's vagabond sensibilities. As a result, he immediately establishes an intimate relationship with the members of the group and especially with their leader, Banjo. At this point, the linear progression of the plot becomes of secondary importance, and the novel is reduced to a vehicle for the delineation of Ray's (*i.e.,* McKay's) brief against civilization and the formulation of a solution to his intellectual quandary.

McKay's condemnation of Western civilization in *Banjo*

is inexorably tied to the psychological problems arising from his blackness. In 1937 he wrote, "What, then, was my main psychological problem? It was the problem of color. Color-consciousness was the fundamental of my restlessness." And it is color-consciousness which is the fundamental of Ray's hatred for civilization. "Civilization is rotten," Ray proclaims, and in the following passage, McKay defines the sociological basis of Ray's sentiments:

> He hated civilization because its general attitude toward the colored man was such as to rob him of his warm human instincts and make him inhuman. Under it the thinking colored man could not function normally like his white brother, responsive and reacting spontaneously to the emotions of pleasure or pain, joy or sorrow, kindness or hardness, charity, anger, and forgiveness. . . . So soon as he entered the great white world, where of necessity he must work and roam and breathe the larger air to live, that entire world, high, low, middle, unclassed, all conspired to make him painfully conscious of color and race. . . . It was not easy for a Negro with an intellect standing watch over his native instincts to take his own way in this white man's civilization. But of one thing he was resolved: civilization would not take the love of color, joy, beauty, vitality and nobility out of *his* life and make him like one of the poor masses of its pale creatures.

Although the imagery utilized in the preceding passage is applied to the peculiar condition of the black man, this vision of a devitalizing, dehumanizing civilization is part of the larger, biracial indictment of American culture. While McKay's attack is rooted in color-consciousness, its targets remain remarkably similar to those of the general assault. McKay finds the fraudulence and duplicity of Western civilization in a multitude of situations beyond its psychological effect on individual black men. The arduous but profitable exercise of lifting the "white man's burden" was, for McKay, a particularly noxious undertaking of the civilized world. Under the guise of Judeo-Christian morality, Western civilization succeeded in its drive to commercialize and exploit the "uncivilized" masses of the earth. Furthermore, McKay saw the trend toward cultural standardization as effectively robbing the world of its "greatest charm"—ethnic diversity. The result was the creation of a sterile, monolithic culture in which "the grand mechanical march of civilization had leveled the world down to the point where it seemed treasonable for an advanced thinker to doubt that what was good for one nation or people was also good for another." Yet Ray does commit the "treasonous" act of disputing this conceptualization. And it is in his dissent that he arrives at an uneasy resolution of the problem which has plagued him through two novels.

In the closing pages of the novel, Ray explains that he has always wanted "to hold on to his intellectual acquirements without losing his instincts. The black gifts of laughter and melody and simple sensuous feelings and responses." It is in this rather untenable position that his problem lies. Given a world in which the terms intellect and instinct have been assigned opposing definitions, it seems improbable that one figure can plausibly synthesize both qualities.

Ray's attempt at such a synthesis is achieved through his decision to join Banjo in the vagabond life. Thematically, this decision represents a rejection of the standardized white civilization and an affirmation of the cultural diversity of the beach boys' existence.

Nevertheless, we are uneasy with the solution Ray has developed, and in his closing monologue, he unwittingly defines the source of our dissatisfaction. Although he hopes to learn from Banjo how to "exist as a black boy in a white world and rid his conscience of the used-up hussy of white morality," Ray realizes that "whether the educated man be white or brown or black, he cannot, if he has more than animal desires, be irresponsibly happy like the ignorant man who lives simply by his instincts and appetites." However, "irresponsible happiness" is the essence of a Jake or a Banjo. Ray's inability to adopt this posture precludes the possibility of his successfully embracing their lifestyle or their method of survival in the white world. Despite his delusions, Ray remains the same "misfit" at the conclusion of *Banjo* that he was when he expatriated from America in *Home to Harlem.*

In *Banana Bottom,* the third and last of his novels, McKay achieves an aesthetic structure which permits the formulation of a viable resolution to the predicament of the educated black man. This resolution is viable in that it does not contradict any of the definitions set forth in the novel, and it is consistent with McKay's affirmation of the primitive elements of black life. This new form is attained by abandoning the structural dualism of his earlier works in favor of a single protagonist. In this way, McKay frees himself from the limitations imposed by the rigid polarizations of instinct and intellect in separate characters. No longer constricted by Ray's inability to reject even a part of his cerebral existence, or Jake's (and by extension, Banjo's) static, unattainable sensuality, McKay now produces a novel in which the main character can credibly embody both instinct and intellect.

The plot of *Banana Bottom* is relatively simple. Set in the West Indies, the story commences with the rape of a young Jamaican peasant girl, Bita Plant. Following the incident, Bita becomes the ward of the Craigs, a white missionary couple who, with an air of condescension, take pity on the girl. In the best Anglo-Saxon missionary tradition, they see in her the golden opportunity for demonstrating to their peasant flock "what one such girl might become by careful training [and] . . . by God's help." As a result, they send her to a finishing school in England with the hope of "redeeming her from her past by a long period of education." After a six-year absence, Bita returns to Jamaica only to find that, for all her education, she is irrepressibly attracted to the island's peasant life. Despite the Craigs' insistence on her marriage to a black divinity student and on the devotion of her life to missionary work, Bita rejects their civilized world in favor of the simplicity of peasant life.

The novel derives its power from the dynamic tension established between the conflicting value systems of Anglo-Saxon civilization and the Jamaican folk culture. This thematic dichotomy first manifests itself in the contrasting reactions to Bita's rape. Priscilla Craig expresses her shock and indignation with an unveiled sanctimony. The "over-sexed" natives, she comments, are "apparently incapable of comprehending the opprobrium of breeding bastards in a Christian community." On the other hand, the village gossip, a peasant woman named Sister Phibby, reacts with a knowing smile indicating her "primitive satisfaction as in a good thing done early."

McKay expands and sustains the tension of contrary value systems through the ever-present antagonism between the civilized Christ-God of retribution and puritanical repression, and the African Obeah-God of freedom and primeval sensuality. Throughout the novel, the white missionaries and native ministers are constantly troubled with the problem of wandering flocks which "worship the Christian God-of-Good-and-Evil on Sunday and in the shadow of the night . . . invoke the power of the African God of Evil by the magic of the sorcerer. Obi [is] resorted to in sickness and feuds, love and elemental disasters." And although the missionaries struggle desperately to win the native populace, it is the Obeah-God who rules Jamaica, and it is the primitive African value system which is at the core of the peasant culture.

Of peasant origin and possessing a cultivated intellect, Bita Plant represents McKay's first successful synthesis of two cultures. When she finds it necessary to choose a lifestyle, it is a relatively easy decision. As opposed to Ray, she is not fraught with the vague uncertainties and questioning doubts over her ability to survive in either culture. Bita has readily internalized the concept of her blackness and willingly accepted her racial origins. Bearing no warping hatred for white civilization, she is characterized by an assertive self-confidence derived from a sense of her own innate worth:

> . . . a white person is just like another human being to me. I thank God that although I was brought up and educated among white people, I have never wanted to be anything but myself. I take pride in being colored and different, just as any intelligent white person does in being white. I can't imagine anything more tragic than people torturing themselves to be different from their natural, unchangeable selves.

For Bita, intellect and education are the handmaidens of instinct. Her return to peasant life provides a source of sustenance and vitality for her total existence: "Her music, her reading, her thinking were the flowers of her intelligence, and he [Bita's peasant husband] the root upon which she was grafted, both nourishing in the same soil."

In Bita Plant, McKay at last succeeds in framing an aesthetic solution to the black intellectual's problem of social incongruence. By rejecting not intellect nor education but rather the "civilized" value system in favor of the primitive values of a black folk culture, the intellectual can ultimately escape the stigma of "misfit." On the surface, this solution does not seem to differ from the one developed in **Banjo.** Yet in **Banana Bottom,** McKay makes an important distinction not present in his earlier work. For the first time, McKay distinguishes between education, or the cultivation of the intellect, and the necessary acceptance of the value system implied by that education. Ray's fail-

ure to make this distinction is the source of his problem. Believing, on the one hand, that a rejection of civilization implies a rejection of intellect, and at the same time, desiring desperately to hold his intellectual acquirements, Ray is immobilized. He can neither remain in a white world which denies his humanity, nor move into a black world which denies his intellect. However, once the distinction is made, the element of conflict between instinct and intellect is removed. Bita, who rejects the civilized value system but not her intellect, can move easily from one world to another without impairing either instinct or intellect. Unfortunately, it is one of McKay's personal tragedies that although he is capable of making this distinction in his art, he is unable to make it in his life. "My damned white education," he wrote in his autobiography, "has robbed me of much of the primitive vitality, the pure stamina, the simple unswaggering strength of the Jakes of the Negro race." (pp. 128-42)

Claude McKay was an integral part of the American literary movement of the 1920s. Responsive to metaphors embodied in the cult of the primitive, McKay's art served to reinforce the image of the Negro as the simple, liberated, uncorrupt man. At the same time, his work provided the means by which McKay made his personal problem of social incongruence part of the larger cultural phenomenon expressing itself in the white expatriate movement. His life represented a less successful effort. Forever seeking fulfillment of his desires to escape color-consciousness and recapture lost innocence, McKay was doomed to an existence directly opposed to the life he apotheosized in his art. It is McKay's special and tragic irony that although he clung tenaciously to the conception of himself as a "free spirit," his obsessions condemned him to a life of slavery. (p. 146)

*Michael B. Stoff, "Claude McKay and the Cult of Primitivism," in* The Harlem Renaissance Remembered, *edited by Arna Bontemps, Dodd, Mead & Company, 1972, pp. 126-46.*

### George E. Kent   (essay date 1974)

[*Kent is an American educator and critic who has written* Blackness and the Adventure of Western Culture *(1972; see Further Reading). In the following excerpt, he reassesses* Banana Bottom *within the context of other Harlem Renaissance novels in which a black protagonist seeks a racial identity and within McKay's own canon, finding fault in the novel's oversimplified characterizations and plot contrivances.*]

Those confronting [**Banana Bottom**] for the first time will find an interesting story and a relatively unified philosophy. Whatever its faults, the novel gives us a coherent sense of McKay's perspective on black identity, creates a portrait of a black woman conscious of her right to dispose independently of a possessed self, and provides something close to a life-sustaining alternative in a viable black community for one resisting violation of her roots. Thus it has, along with other worthwhile qualities, the obvious glow of relevance.

At first encounter, the novel would seem to have easy

*McKay during his sojourn in Paris in the 1920s.*

placement possibilities among other Renaissance novels focused upon identity: Jean Toomer's *Cane* (1923), Nella Larsen's *Quicksand* (1928), Wallace Thurman's *The Blacker the Berry* (1929), and Langston Hughes's *Not without Laughter* (1930). The two most prominent forces militating against easy placement are the tendency of the hard-driven American based novels to render tragic or near tragic conclusions, or, at best, in the case of Langston Hughes's *Not without Laughter,* to leave the situation open-ended; and the works' tendency to involve considerable forays into urban life. McKay's heroine, Bita Plant, attends an English university where she is to be "Englished" out of her Blackness, returns to make her adjustments in a Jamaican, overwhelmingly black rural community, where mainly strategic and opportunistic notice needs be taken of Whites's existence, and resolves her problems happily in her marriage to the peasant Jubban. Bita's experience takes place during the early part of the Twentieth Century.

Any number of differences, of course, can be found, but here we can be only a bit more suggestive. As I have suggested, the hard-driven black American novels of identity must confront powerful rhythms stemming from the massive and pervasive presence of Whites or white-induced conditions, in contrast to the symbolic presence of Whites in McKay's Jamaican novel. Further, *Cane's* women remain unfulfilled because ultimately neither the black nor white community provides adequate resources for self-definition and self-expression in either rural or urban areas. Kabnis, the most conscious male quester for identity, cannot absorb and regrasp the past, although the young woman Carry K. seems in touch with it and seems to represent hope for the future. *Quicksand's* Helga Crane, aside from the critically overemphasized concept of the tragic mulatto, soon moves in the large cities of America and abroad, runs into confusion concerning her selfhood and love life, and simply ruins herself through marriage to a folk preacher and attempts to live in a rural Southern folk community. *The Blacker the Berry's* Emma moves mainly in New York City, and ruins herself through her internalization of negative values associated with her black skin by both black and white communities, although at the end of the novel she vows to try anew. *Not Without Laughter's* Sandy, after being exposed to the spirituals and blues traditions in his upbring in a small Kansas town, ends in Chicago, vowing to incorporate both traditions within himself and to transform them.

Obviously, although differences are marked, relationships to *Banana Bottom* remain, since the characters are blacks confronting the Western World in a quest for identity. After allowing for a lower temperature of urgencies deriving from special Jamaican provincial conditions, one still finds the self threatened by the incursions of institutionalized Western rhythms and resulting inner divisions. But among black American novels of Renaissance spirit, perhaps Janie Starks of Zora Neale Hurston's *Their Eyes Were Watching God* (1937) comes closest to representing similar struggles for selfhood from a base in a somewhat self-contained and self-judging rural folk society. Despite significant differences, too numerous to go into at this point, Janie's struggle to express an essential self and an uncorrupted response to existence is also the core of Bita's strivings. But even with *Their Eyes Were Watching God* thrown into the equation, one would still finally have to place *Banana Bottom* within the Renaissance context by noting that the availability of an alternative community secure in its own self-definitions created the least frictioned identity struggle to be found in Renaissance novels.

To place *Banana Bottom* accurately within McKay's own works is first to confront inadequate criticism marred by overschematization and misleading terms. Thus the issues of McKay's novels are oversimplified and *Banana Bottom's* ability to resolve them, overpraised. The scheme is supposedly that of a conflict between instinct and reason or between primitivism and civilization. Rigid dichotomies follow both sets of categories: One character representing intellect, another, instinct or primitivism. McKay, himself, of course, is partly responsible. He used the term *primitivism,* and there are overtones of the idea in his sonnet, **"To the White Fiends."**

The first problem is that one can not find what is supposed to be represented by primitivism in McKay's works: happy, uncorrupted children of nature or malignant, undisciplined nature, or persons hardly differentiated from nature, unemerged. The second problem is that the term *primitivism* is, at best, a shaky, racialist concept, self-congratulatory, self-aggrandizing, filled with the white Westerner's pluming up of his own self-esteem. Hidden in the wings is the white Westerner's doctrine of progress and evolution as self-promoting polar opposites. Thus *primitivism* is more of an intellectualized and psychologized concept than a description of "simple" people's realities.

McKay's concern is preservation of human qualities of intrinsic worth and fostering a full expression of the human personality. Thus Western culture inspired McKay's ambivalence. He admired the energy and achievements, but their cost was registered in the West's drive to shave off portions of humanity inconvenient to its central rhythms, to standardize man as a product, to drain away vitality within the crucible of its puritan-machine culture, and thus to corrupt the deepest qualities of life. In the foregoing equation, the Blacks of Jamaica, Africa, and the black masses of America, are the symbol of the yet relatively unstandardized man.

Description of McKay's works in such terms evidences the fact that he tended to pose major symbols of the Black's dilemma in Western culture. He possibly had a greater grasp of the magnitude of that dilemma than that of any creative writer prior to the advent of Richard Wright. Earlier novels worked at the dilemma close to the central rhythms and high voltage wires of Western culture: *Home to Harlem,* involving New York City with Harlem as the recreation room; and *Banjo,* involving Marseilles with the "ditch" area as the recreation room. The results are mixed. Irreverence, exuberance, vitality, and rejection of soul-stealing standardization, are registered. In *Home to Harlem* are some of the most penetrating scenes McKay was to write—superior in penetration to those of either *Banjo* or the now highly praised *Banana Bottom.* And *Banjo* was suggestive and argumentative enough to exert influence upon the West Indian-African *negritude* movement.

But, alas! it is not McKay's highly celebrating Jakes and Banjos of less inhibited (selective) lower class vitality who possess even the vague outlines of the big picture, but the highly self-conscious Ray, whose tones are those of a merely rhetorical defiance within which his defeated position is ill-concealed. In the last pages of *Banjo,* Ray's doubts about Western culture contain the implications of defeat in his merely nomadic response to its tendency to fill the universe with its presence:

> He did not think the blacks would come very happily under the supermechanical Anglo-Saxon-controlled world society of Mr. H. G. Wells. They might shuffle along, but without much happiness in the world of Bernard Shaw. Perhaps they would have their best chance in a world influenced by the thought of Bertrand Russell, where brakes were clamped on the machine with a few screws loose and some nuts fallen off. But in this great age of science and super-invention was there any possibility of arresting the thing unless it stopped of its own exhaustion.

Feeling out Ray's situation, we can see also that his free spirit companions are only besporting themselves in Western culture's prison recreation rooms—closeable at any time the soul people's activities become inconvenient. Thus the earlier novels's issues, posed immediately adjacent to the high voltage room of Western culture, evasive of dialogue with the tragic muse, inevitably resolve themselves in some form of escapism: romantic bohemianism and vagabondage. The blight of such resolutions can be transcended. But what is required is that the life symbols (the Jakes, Banjos, etc.) impose themselves so powerfully that their beauty is their own excuse of being—a state in which the lost world is well lost. McKay does not infuse his symbols with such power. Interesting, entertaining, worthy of contemplation—yes! But our ultimate realization is that they constitute merely temporarily ignored or tolerated sideshows on the scene of the Western World. Coming to the foregoing realizations is also a process of acknowledging the threats to pure and simple *negritude* and *soul* in the fantasied demilitarized zones of the Western World.

The realizations also enable us more accurately to place *Banana Bottom* in the context of McKay's novels. It moves McKay's identity concerns away from adjacency to the high voltage room of Western culture in time and place. It moves to turn-of-the-century rural Jamaica, a place and time providing still the presence of voltage but a lower current with larger spaces between the fatal electric cables. Out of this move comes a more coherent philosophy and picture and the life sustaining alternative community already mentioned. We may now leave the contexts and turn to a closer examination of the novel, itself.

McKay's own comments upon *Banana Bottom* are most interesting in leading us into the conditions affecting its composition. He had been away from the intensities of the American color problem for many years. Seemingly, the novel was completed in Morocco where, in his autobiography, *A Long Way from Home,* he speaks of having "come to the point of a break-down." A year after its publication, December 3, 1934, he described his writing efforts and his novel in a letter to Max Eastman:

> Whether poetry or prose, my writing is always most striking and true when it is a little reminiscent and nostalgic. The vividness of *Home to Harlem* was due to my being removed just the right distance from the scene. Doing *Banjo* I was too close to it. *Banana Bottom* was a lazy dream, the images becoming blurred from overdoing long-distance photography.

McKay's comments should not be allowed to obscure the merits of the novel, but they do forewarn us concerning its easy-going chronicle form derived from nineteenth century fiction, and the disproportionate emphasis upon idyllic modes that we encounter.

The novel has a simple story line. Bita Plant, daughter of industrious peasant Jordan Plant, is raped by the nonconformist village musician Crazy Bow whom Bita, in carefree play, has unconsciously aroused sexually. The white missionary family adopt her: Malcolm Craig, the non-conformist minister, with the idea of continuing his family's traditionally close relationship to the Plant family; Priscilla, his very puritanical wife, with the idea of removing Bita from vicious surroundings and giving her an English university education which will make her English in everything but skin color. For the less restrained village girls, whose confrontation with womanhood and sex is often early and destructive, Bita is to be an exhibit and a model. "Many of the girls had had children," Bita finds upon her return, "one, two, three, some as many as five, without the benefit of a steady mate and were now heavy-footed and flabby-breasted and worried under the weight of motherhood."

Returned and redeemed, Bita finds new direction signals stirring faintly, confusedly, and slowly within. Appreciative of the Craigs's gift of education, she does not know whether she can fit into the mission's required patterns of respectability and religious piety. She seems at first to accept her impending marriage to Herald Newton Day, a redeemed Black designed for her by the Craigs, with unnatural passivity. She tells herself that the expected marriage is simply another part of the design for her improvement, and is to be accepted out of gratitude to her benefactors.

> It was while Herald Newton was preaching his sermon that Bita saw that she could not love him. But if she could just like him even, she thought, since it would please the Craigs for them to marry. And no doubt the families on both sides. But principally because it would please the Craigs she was inclined to do it, for they had made her what she was.

Also, she could not aspire higher than to marry a parson, since she lacked the light skin required in Jamaican society for capturing a law court functionary or a city manager of a business. The heart-breaking social climbing of the white girls at her English university had also repelled her. Here the Craigs would probably give her a dowry, if she married the man they approved. "And that was something to be reckoned on." Despite the fact that pleasing one's elders has firm roots in traditional societies, Bita's inner psychology seems distantly observed, barely adequate, her conflicts rather tentative.

Gradually, her inner rhythms draw her to her village roots. Squire Gensir, the English exile, helps her to put the values of village life into proper perspective. She enjoys the outings with young village friends, the sensations of her spontaneous self warming to the beauty of the countryside, to deeply rooted childhood experiences, and finally, to the fast village tea-parties to which the Craigs object. The clash intensifies when they also object to her attraction to Hopping Dick, the village lover. The Craigs reject her insistence upon his calling for her at the mission and are moved to arrange her ejection from the mission at Jubilee and her return home to Banana Bottom. Aunty Nommy, however, shrewdly gets rid of Hopping Dick, who is averse to marriage.

Although Bita has found the Reverend Herald Newton Day repulsive, it is really McKay who disposes of him in a rather poorly motivated episode by abruptly having him discovered cohabiting with a goat. It is one of McKay's uneasy resolutions in the novel.

The substance of Bita's character, however, develops into a charming, if not very searching, portrait, despite some improbabilities. McKay also touches the right fictional bases, in bringing forth a resolution to Bita's problems through her marriage to the peasant Jubban, but there is some serious clanking of manipulated machinery. He faces us with unsuitable wooers: Arthur Glengley, rapist and defamer of black-skinned girls; a dark brown preacher; a pharmacist; a schoolmaster; a black overseer of an estate. Earlier he had sharply satirized a "native gentleman," an owner of uncut and thus unread, but attractive books. None of the foregoing persons would have suited Bita who is determined that whatever she is, she will always be herself.

McKay also has Bita struck by a number of deaths affecting her emotional and psychological security: Her father, Jordan Plant, the Reverend Malcolm Craig and his wife Priscilla, then her mentor, Squire Gensir. Too many of the deaths occur in the same chapter, giving the feeling of a hurry-up setting of the stage for the happy outcome.

McKay is careful, in building the role of peasant Jubban. He mentions him several times in earlier sections of the novel and dramatizes his growing significance for Bita. Jubban takes care of her when she falls into a religious seizure, rescues her from the defaming Arthur Glengley, and pays the price to kiss her when she reigns as queen at one of the tea meetings. And McKay intensifies a celebration of peasant virtues and relationships to nature. In a moment which has long been germinating through the rhythms drawing Bita to her village roots, just before the burial of her father, Bita unites sexually with Jubban. The father is lifeless upon the dray where the lovers unite. A kind of transfer of roles is symbolized. Both Jubban and Bita, in the face of the father's death, had each begun to think of Jubban "as a kind of protector of the house." "Almost unconsciously Jubban's hands encircled her waist and spontaneously their mouths came together and a sweet shiver spread through her body against the impact of his warm passionate person." Bita experiences the union as a sacrament: "Her spirit was finely balanced between the delicate sadness of death and the subdued joy of love and over all was the glorious sensation of life triumphant in love over death."

Among other devices, the intensity built by the language forces us to pause, to hold back questioning whether the European education of Bita and its attendant Western rhythms would block a marriage between the university educated girl and the peasant. But what about subsequent marital experience outside the immediacy of the romantic glow provided by special circumstances and character? Well, three years after the marriage Bita finds that she is contented. Jubban is a silent man who returns from marketing trips, describes his experiences in a few monosyllables, peeps at the baby, goes to sleep. But Bita is undisturbed, since she "was not a talkative woman." Then, through his intimate relations with Bita and "mastership of the house," Jubban's qualities have flowered.

The land prospers more under his hands than it did under those of her father. The following long passage sums up the argument for Bita's fulfillment through Jubban:

> Thinking of Jubban and how her admiration for him had slowly developed into respect and love, Bita marvelled at the fact that they had never said "I love you" to each other. The thing had become a fact without the declaration.
>
> They lived their life upon a level entirely different from her early romantic conception of love. Once she had thought of love as a kind of mystical force, incomprehensible and uncontrollable. But gradually she had lost all that feeling of the quality of love, for it was a borrowed thing, an exotic imposition, not a real intrinsic thing that had flowered out of the mind of her race.
>
> She had no craving for Jubban to be other than what he was, experienced no hankering for that grace and refinement in him that the local soothsayers said was necessary to an educated person. She liked to play for him and he had a natural feeling for music and showed appreciation of even the most difficult things. But he was in no way a hindrance to the intellectual side of her. He accepted with natural grace the fact that she should excel in the things to which she had been educated as he should in the work to which he had been trained.
>
> Her music, her reading, her thinking were the flowers of her intelligence and he the root in the earth upon which she was grafted, both nourished by the same soil.

The above is good as authorial testimony. However, one need be neither a Conradian nor a Jamesian to feel that it is inadequate to enforce the happy resolution which it asserts, that McKay had huddled up an ending which would require imaginative dramatization and working out if it is to have binding force upon the reader. Today's novelist would probably settle for such a resolution as a necessary compromise, in the light of an inadequate supply of suitors, or as an open-ended situation. As a result of McKay's accepting the more difficult ending but failing to work it out dramatically, the ending lacks the conviction of inevitability and leaves the reader with a few hems and haws and doubts.

McKay also takes the easy path in other important matters. I've already indicated that two would-be important lovers are pushed out of the running by persons other than the heroine. Bita seems to have some light impingements of double-consciousness, which would cause her to devalue village life, but her natural instincts and some counseling by the romantic white English exile Squire Gensir quickly dispose of such obstacles. Finally, an open question is whether a village folk would allow one of its educated members to escape assumption of some public role. The iconoclasm of a Squire Gensir seems hardly the model for Bita, since he is not really needed in relationship to the basic welfare of his people.

The lack of firmness in McKay's grappling with his materials also gives an uneven quality to the interesting community of Banana Bottom. The portrait varies from the merely colorful and idyllic to some impression of penetration. He carefully describes village founders, events, customs, religious practices, entertainments, social layers, interracial relations, and the island's relationship to England. The more important white minor characters are well-drawn, and those of aristocratic claims are treated sympathetically even when satirized. Most sympathetically portrayed is, of course, Squire Gensir. Obviously, in real life, the philanthropic English exile Walter Jekyll who was important in McKay's own early appreciation of his native Jamaican background. In general, McKay feels that many of the Whites descended more from the abolitionist side of white pioneering groups than from the bigoted and exploiting side. Their mark, however inconsistently, is their commitment to universal human freedom.

The minor black characters, as a whole, give a sense of strength and flexibility within the folk culture, although the resolutions of their fates do not always seem probable. Aunty Nommy, Bita's stepmother, emerges as a model of village shrewdness and as the supreme arbitrator. Priscilla Craig's response to her handling and discouragement of Bita's suitor, Hopping Dick, registers something of her impact.

> . . . Priscilla's [face] relaxed its rigidity as she thought that Aunty Nommy was shrewder, after all, than she had guessed. They were a little baffling those dark folk. As a whole they seemed so insouciantly ignorant and unaware, yet as individuals they were sometimes capable of devilish ingenuity.

Aunt Phibby Patrol, midwife and servant of the Craigs, vigorous sexual sinner in her youth, triumphs now as the village tale bearer and woe-bringer to the lives of the warm-blooded young. However, Jordan Plant, though basic for our understanding of the shrewd, prosperous peasant, is a rather distant and vague image.

The common-sense accommodations of the folk culture are seen through its dealings with the young, although the portraits occasionally raise questions. Belle Black, village playgirl, is too free in her behavior for church membership, but her splendid voice makes her welcome in the church choir. The tea-parties allow good fun and much free behavior, but the village has its limits and areas affected by local notions of respectability. Gracie Hall's father slaps her off the carnival merry-go-round, because she has been trained in Kingston as a seamstress and should now reflect the status of nice people. Yoni Legge, a sewing teacher, loses her position with the mission and is also driven from home by her stepfather for being caught in her mission room with the dandy, Tack Tally. Crazy Bow, the village musician, has to express his secret soul in music and madness.

Unfortunately, McKay also tends to add to his tendency to make abrupt classifications and resolutions, in his dealings with some of the young. Even with Bita, he is startling by suddenly telling of the close relationship between her and her father near the end of the book when he has heretofore given us no evidence of it. And Tack Talley, it is suddenly announced is a bad man who has killed two people in Panama, but the author has given us only a sometimes amusing portrait of a blustering bully. Tally's suicide is unconvincing, and Yoni Legge's quick recovery from her passionate love for him is poorly handled.

This re-examination of **Banana Bottom** leads to several conclusions. Neither in the context of the identity novel of the Harlem Renaissance nor in that of McKay's own novels can the book really be said to be a searching analysis of the problem of identity. Even if we allow for the lower voltage of tensions provided by the rural Jamaican setting, it is clear that McKay stopped short of following up his available opportunities for close analysis. We must challenge then the usual pronouncement that the identity problems raised in his earlier novels receive satisfactory solution in **Banana Bottom.** The truth seems to be that McKay carried over his tendencies to whimsical iconoclasm, romanticism, and arbitrariness, into **Banana Bottom.** Added to the foregoing responses is a nostalgic emotion which leads to inconvenient emphasis upon the idyllic and abrupt, unprepared for resolutions.

More's the pity, because he did have the makings of a great novel and could probably have achieved it, despite shortcoming, had he given a truly searching portrait of Bita, alone. What makes the novel of continued interest is the relevance still of the issue of identity, its portrait of early twentieth century rural Jamaica, and its portrait of folkways and folk-laughter. Though too frequently careless and vague, they are rendered by an author who speaks from the inside and from their inner spirit. As a novel with an almost self-contained folk society, not yet conscious of all materialistic Western rhythms impinging upon it, **Banana Bottom** has a special place within our considerations of Renaissance aspiration. Second and third readings, however, begin to reveal the unsteadiness of many of its charms and the frequency of its flaws. (pp. 222-34)

> George E. Kent, "Claude McKay's 'Banana Bottom' Reappraised," in CLA Journal, Vol. XVIII, No. 2, December, 1974, pp. 222-34.

## Robert Bone    (essay date 1975)

[*Bone, an American critic and educator, is the author of the informative critical histories* The Negro Novel in America *(1958; rev. ed., 1965; see Further Reading) and* Down Home: A History of Afro-American Short Fiction from Its Beginnings to the End of the Harlem Renaissance. *A student of African-American, English, and American literature, Bone has said of himself: "A white man and critic of black literature, I try to demonstrate by the quality of my work that scholarship is not the same thing as identity." In the following excerpt from* Down Home, *Bone divides McKay's literary career into four phases—provincial, picaresque, pastoral, retrospective—and discusses the stories in* Gingertown *as marking a transitional phase from picaresque to pastoral.*]

McKay's literary career may be divided into four phases. The first, or provincial phase, encompasses his first two books of verse, **Songs of Jamaica** (1912) and **Constab Ballads** (1912). The second, or picaresque phase, includes a book of poems, **Harlem Shadows** (1922), and two novels,

**Home to Harlem** (1928) and **Banjo** (1929). The third, or pastoral phase, consists of a book of stories, **Gingertown** (1932) and a novel, **Banana Bottom** (1933). The fourth, or retrospective phase, includes an autobiography, **A Long Way from Home** (1937), and a sociological study, **Harlem: Negro Metropolis** (1940).

The stories of **Gingertown** mark a transition from the picaresque to the pastoral phase. The first six tales are concerned with Harlem life. They express McKay's ambivalent feelings toward the black metropolis which, despite its glamor and excitement, he comes to regard as a whited sepulcher. The last six represent the recoil of McKay's imagination from the polluted centers of occidental civilization. Four are set in Jamaica, one on the Marseilles waterfront, and one in North Africa. Their esthetic mode is pastoral; they celebrate the values of simplicity, community, harmony with nature, reconciliation with one's fellow man, and freedom from political or sexual repression.

The two halves of the book were written at different times and under strikingly different circumstances. The Harlem tales were written in France between 1923 and 1926. (pp. 162-63)

The second half of the collection was written in North Africa in 1930-1931. McKay had left Europe to escape "the white hound of Civilization." He had gone completely native in Morocco, whose landscape, people, and exotic customs reminded him of his Jamaican homeland. In the spring of 1931 he settled in Tangier to work on **Gingertown.** He was joined by an Afro-American woman of bohemian inclinations who was in flight from the stuffiness of bourgeois Harlem. After an idyllic "honeymoon" they quarreled, and she returned to Paris and her white lover. Wounded and resentful, McKay retreated to the mountains of Spanish Morocco, where he completed **Gingertown** and **Banana Bottom.**

This disastrous love affair compounded McKay's bitterness and increased his alienation from occidental values. The figure of his paramour, torn between her black and white lovers, became in his imagination an emblem of the Negro soul, torn between two hostile cultures and antagonistic ways of life. At the same time, his withdrawal to the mountains awakened memories of his Jamaican childhood. In surroundings reminiscent of his native village he made a valiant effort to repossess his peasant heritage. The pastoral impulse which inspired his early poems now became the source of McKay's most enduring fiction.

The Harlem tales of **Gingertown** are concerned with the cultural dilemma of blacks who are compelled to function in a white man's world. These tales reflect McKay's experience as an immigrant to the United States from the West Indies. They express his shock and dismay at being transplanted from a country which is 90 percent black to one where the opposite ratio obtains. The tension that results between the self and its environment, leading in turn to a divisiveness within the self, is McKay's essential theme. He is concerned not so much with the humiliations and inconveniences of segregation as with the breach they open in the black man's soul.

The classic formulation of the black American's dilemma

was made by W. E. B. DuBois in *The Souls of Black Folk* (1903): "One ever feels his twoness—an American, a Negro: two souls, two thoughts, two unreconciled strivings; two warring ideals in one dark body, whose dogged strength alone keeps it from being torn asunder." (pp. 163-64)

The protagonists of McKay's Harlem stories are men or women divided against themselves. Trying to escape their blackness, and the penalties imposed upon it by the white world, they expose themselves to psychological disaster. They may experience a brief moment of happiness while in pursuit of white ideals, but invariably it proves to be illusory. Sooner or later some racial trauma intervenes to remind them that the barriers of caste are insurmountable. What holds these tales together is the fantasy of playing white. McKay is trying to exorcise a certain kind of psychological infatuation.

The dangers and temptations of "white fever" are the focal point of these tales. Thus Bess of **"Brownskin Blues"** mutilates herself in a misguided effort to lighten her complexion. The heroine of **"Mattie and Her Sweetman"** is vulnerable to social and sexual humiliation by virtue of her passion for "yellow boys." Angie Dove of **"Near-White"** suffers a disastrous love affair with a white man symbolically named John West. The first half of *Gingertown,* in short, is part of a now familiar literature of extrication, whose aim is to liberate the blacks from psychological enslavement to a false cultural ideal.

Unfortunately the literary quality of McKay's Harlem stories is not high. These early tales, after all, were his first experiments with prose fiction. Their awkwardness of style, which is especially pronounced in the dialogue, suggests that the former poet, in shifting his major emphasis to prose, has not yet mastered his new medium. The widely anthologized **"Truant"** is hardly free of this defect, but by virtue of its summary position it merits more extensive treatment than the rest. This story, which concludes the Harlem section of *Gingertown,* illustrates McKay's dilemma as he tries to dramatize his disenchantment with the urban scene through the inappropriate conventions of the picaresque.

As the story opens, the hero and his wife are watching a vaudeville show from the "Nigger Heaven" of a Broadway theater. The curtain discloses a domestic scene in which a troupe of Irish actors personifies the happy family of American popular culture. The initial impact of the scene is idyllic, but its ultimate effect is ironic, for the Merry Mulligans possess the warmth, cohesiveness, and cultural integrity conspicuously lacking in the life of the black protagonist. The note of harmony on which the story opens thus serves as an ironic commentary on the disintegrating marriage of the two main characters.

Barclay Oram is an autobiographical creation closely related to the figure of Ray in *Home to Harlem* and *Banjo.* In a long flashback we learn that he has emigrated from the West Indies in pursuit of his dream of attending a Negro university. At Howard he meets and marries Rhoda, an Afro-American girl of middle-class background and assimilationist outlook. As the tale unfolds,

Rhoda emerges as a kind of enchantress who holds her man in thrall to the false values of an artificial civilization. Nor does fatherhood relieve Barclay's feeling of entrapment, for he envisions his daughter marrying a railroad waiter like himself and raising children "to carry on the great tradition of black servitude."

As the present action of the tale begins, Barclay is rousted out of bed at an early hour, in order to report for work on the Pennsylvania Railroad. It is a disastrous trip, and during the layover in Washington he gets drunk, thereby missing the return run. Savoring his truancy, he is not at all disturbed when he is laid off for ten days. Rhoda, however, reproaches him for irresponsibility, and her rebuke precipitates a crisis which is resolved by Barclay's desertion of his wife and child. Through the metaphor of truancy, McKay depicts the black man as a dropout from the Western world, a *picaro* who is condemned to a life of eternal wandering.

The trouble with **"Truant"** is a radical divergency of form and content. In his expansionist phase (Jamaica to New York), McKay gravitates instinctively toward the devices and conventions of the picaresque. The phase of recoil, however (New York to Jamaica), cannot be expressed through the same medium. The picaresque is a suitable instrument for the *celebration* of Harlem life (as in *Home to Harlem*), but it cannot be adapted to the theme of urban disenchantment. Pastoral is the appropriate vehicle for the expression of anti-urban sentiments. At this point in his career, McKay has made the emotional transition from expansion to recoil, but has not yet grasped its formal implications. He will do so in his stories of Jamaican peasant life.

Structurally speaking, **"Truant"** is the hinge of *Gingertown.* The last of the Harlem tales, it provides a logical transition to the counterstatement. For if **"Truant"** is a myth of disaffiliation, the Jamaican tales are parables of pastoral refreshment and renewal. As McKay's imagination turns from Harlem to Jamaica, a corresponding shift in tone occurs. Feelings of revulsion for the Western world are replaced by a vast affection for the Caribbean island and its people. (pp. 164-67)

To describe the latter half of *Gingertown* as McKay's "Jamaican tales" is only an approximation. Two of the weaker stories, **"Nigger Lover"** and **"Little Sheik,"** have Mediterranean rather than Caribbean settings. A third, **"When I Pounded the Pavement,"** is not in fact a story, but an autobiographical account of McKay's experience in the Kingston constabulary. The three remaining tales, which constitute the core of *Gingertown,* are set in the Jamaican highlands. **"Crazy Mary"** is an undistinguished piece, but **"The Agricultural Show"** and **"The Strange Burial of Sue"** are McKay's best stories.

**"The Agricultural Show"** is a pure specimen of Renaissance pastoral. The central characters are Bennie, an impressionable schoolboy, and his brother Matthew, the village pharmacist. Matthew, who is something of a local booster, undertakes to organize a country fair. There will be prizes for livestock and farm products, handicrafts and the domestic arts. Games and competitions will be held;

band concerts and political speeches given; and the Governor himself will address the assembled multitudes. The fair is a communal ritual in which all segments of society participate, and during which all petty barriers of caste or class are momentarily surmounted.

Matthew plays the role of mediator, who orchestrates and harmonizes the great event. Under his direction, lowlander and highlander mingle for a day; Baptist, Methodist, and Anglican rub elbows; village, town, and city folk are represented; black, white, and all shades in between take part. United in a common venture, the peasantry, gentry, and aristocracy transcend their traditional roles. Among the surging throngs, artificial distinctions of rank and status give way to a natural camaraderie, while on the speakers' platform a symbolic reconciliation of the classes and races is effected. The sign and seal of this communal harmony, and a scene that Bennie never will forget, is the presentation of his mother to the Governor.

To a modern sensibility, unacquainted with the pastoral tradition, **"The Agricultural Show"** will seem a sentimental fantasy. When the lion lies down with the lamb, our cynical century believes, only the lion gets up. We will mistake the author's purpose, however, if we read the story as a realistic social commentary. It is rather a poetic vision, an expression of an inner need. McKay's Jamaican pastoral, with its images of racial harmony and social peace, is an objective correlative of the inner harmony that he so desperately seeks. Split and shredded by his contact with the Western world, he returns in his imagination to Jamaica in order to reconstitute his soul.

What follows is a process of reduction. Tormented by his doubleness, McKay endeavors to achieve a psychic unity by exorcising his Western self. From the complexities of Negro experience in America, he turns to the simplicities of Jamaican peasant life. Intellectuality, which he has come to regard as a burden, is renounced in favor of instinct and emotion. The oneness of spirit that he craves necessitates a stripping away of the false veneer of white civilization and a closer accommodation to his primitive sources. The alien culture must be repudiated, and especially in its oppressive sexual forms. Such are the themes of McKay's most impressive story, **"The Strange Burial of Sue."**

The plot turns on a sexual triangle involving the title character, her husband, and an adolescent boy. Sue Turner is a peasant woman of free-loving ways, who is nonetheless universally respected and admired in her community. A hardworking field hand, volunteer nurse, and befriender of pregnant village girls, she conducts her private life in such a way as to threaten neither Turner nor the village wives. Her husband is a steady man, amiable, phlegmatic, and totally lacking the proprietary attitude toward sex: "One day an indiscreet relative was trying to broad-hint Turner about Sue's doings, and Turner remarked that he felt proud having a wife that was admired of other men."

Burskin is a shy and awkward youth, still a virgin at the outset of his liaison with Sue. After a passionate affair of several months' duration, she jilts him for a glamorous adventurer recently returned from Panama. Jealous and im-

portunate, Burskin makes a scene at the local grogshop which precipitates a public scandal. Turner, who has thus far been a model of patience and forbearance, now feels compelled to undertake a legal action against the youth who has abused his generosity. Before the case can come to trial, however, it is rendered moot by the sudden death of Sue, perhaps brought on (the facts are never clear) by an unsuccessful effort to abort Burskin's child.

The story gains a new dimension with the introduction of the brown-skinned village parson. A self-righteous busybody, he sees fit at one point to protect the public morals by expelling Sue from church. He represents, in short, the intrusion of Anglo-Saxon values on a world more African than European. Two rival codes of conduct, or concepts of goodness, are thus at issue in the tale. The permissive sexual code of the black peasantry, inherited from slavery times if not from Africa, is weighed against the missionary morals of the Baptist seminarian. As in **Banana Bottom,** McKay employs the metaphor of sexuality to dramatize the sharp divergencies of culture, lifestyle, and moral outlook that separate the colonizer from the colonized.

In **"The Strange Burial of Sue,"** the folk community rallies in defense of its immemorial customs. On the occasion of Sue's funeral, the whole mountain range turns out in tribute to her popularity. The parson makes the error, in his graveside sermon, of denouncing Sue as a backslider and a sinner. Outraged, Turner drives him off and invites the people to bear witness to his wife's goodness. In effect the folk community defrocks the village parson, rejecting him as the emissary of an alien culture. In defiant tribute to her passion—a value cherished by the black peasants—Turner plants two flaming dragon's bloods on his wife's grave.

Claude McKay's Jamaican pastorals, written in North Africa from 1930 to 1933, mark the outer limits of his flight from the West. The flight was doomed, as we can see in retrospect, because the fugitive was fleeing from himself. Within a year or two of the publication of **Gingertown** and **Banana Bottom,** McKay was back in the United States. In 1940 his last book appeared, a sympathetic portrait of urban life entitled **Harlem: Negro Metropolis.** His pastoral phase therefore must be seen as one polarity in a larger pattern of vacillation and ambivalence. It was a passing phase, expressive of a deep revulsion from the Western world, but incapable of sustaining an integrated moral vision.

McKay achieved this larger vision through conversion to the Catholic faith. Within its unifying framework, the intolerable tensions of duality could be resolved. The reductive strategy employed in the Jamaican pastorals did not prove permanently viable because it entailed a mutilation of the self. What was called for, McKay was later to discover, was not a mutilation but a synthesis. The oneness that he sought in a symbolic fusion with Jamaican peasant life he ultimately found in Roman Catholicism, which combined the simple faith and venerable customs of a peasant culture with the forms and rituals of a highly sophisticated and emphatically Western religion. (pp. 167-70)

Robert Bone, "Three Versions of Pastoral," in his Down Home: A History of Afro-American Short Fiction from Its Beginnings to the End of the Harlem Renaissance, G. P. Putnam's Sons, 1975, pp. 139-70.

## Marian B. McLeod   (essay date 1980)

[*In the following excerpt, McLeod discusses* The Negroes in America, *which was originally written and published during McKay's trip to Russia in 1923. Citing McKay's early efforts as a black artist assuming the role of social critic and polemicist, McLeod suggests that the work illuminates McKay's political and literary philosophy.*]

[Two] works, written at a critical period in [McKay's] literary and philosophical development, have recently been translated from the Russian in which they were published. **Trial by Lynching,** a booklet of three short stories that represents McKay's first experiment in prose fiction, reveals the author's anguish at the barbarity of Southern ways and his deep-felt sympathy for those deprived of self-respect, justice, and life itself. A longer work, **The Negroes in America,** provides us with fresh insights into McKay's subsequent works, reveals the strength of his criticism of American civilization, and states or implies the fundamen-

*Portrait of McKay in his later years.*

tal changes that he sought to help bring about, for in only a decade he had been greatly disillusioned. (pp. 336-37)

The race riots in the United States during 1919 were apparently the great catalyst for McKay; thereafter, he threw his lot in with the forces of reform, both socially and politically. He joined the staff of *The Liberator,* under Max Eastman; he worked for a time with Sylvia Pankhurst on *The Workers' Dreadnought* in London; and he associated with the members of the British Communist Party, eventually joining the American Workers' Party (the "legal" branch of the Communist movement) in New York. Following a contretemps at *The Liberator,* in which his stance for greater emphasis on the "Negro Problem" was rejected, he sailed for Russia at the end of 1922 to attend the Third International.

In Moscow he was feted: on 20 November he addressed the Fourth Congress; he met and corresponded with Trotsky; he was taken to Red Army barracks and generally treated with the greatest deference. As he later noted in his autobiography, "Never in my life did I feel prouder of being an African, a black; and make no mistake about it." The contrast between his reception and treatment in the Soviet Union and his recent American experience was clearly immense, and it was in this context that he was offered, and accepted, an invitation from the State Publishing House in Moscow to write a book "about the American Negro." This work, published towards the end of 1923, remained unknown to McKay scholars until 1973, when what appears to be the only copy in America was discovered in the Slavic section of the New York Public Library by Wayne Cooper.

Though it is a slim volume, **The Negroes in America** aids materially in understanding McKay's outlook on American society and culture and explains, in part at least, the reasons for his alienation from the black intelligentsia, from the liberal political movement, and ultimately from the left-wing groups through which he had long hoped to witness a fundamental change in the status of Negroes in the United States.

McKay shared a draft copy of his book's initial chapters with Eastman, who was also in Moscow for the meeting of the Comintern. Eastman recommended revisions, and McKay responded to him in these words:

> You assert that I say that the Negro problem is the chief problem of the Revolution in America. When you come to read my book, you will find that I have said no such thing. What I say is that the Negro problem is an integral part and one of the chief problems of the class struggle in America, and I stand by that declaration.

**The Negroes in America** is essentially a propagandist tract, but in McKay's view—as in Dr. DuBois's—such literature had the highest rank, since its goal was social transformation rather than merely the creation of a pleasing entertainment or the expression of inconsequential petulance. Furthermore, he was supported by Trotsky, who emphasized that "The training of black propagandists is the most imperative and extremely important revolutionary task of the present time." The whole work has the tone of didactic journalism, and at times it becomes rather less than cogent in its development of an argument or demolition of some popular shibboleth. It is repetitious of its central theme; the structure is not always wholly admirable; some chapters are little more than extended quotations strung together loosely by commentary that lacks penetration, and the final chapter is merely a reprint of a contribution to the October 1922 issue of *The Liberator*. Yet, notwithstanding these shortcomings, **The Negroes in America** provides one of the few examples of a genuinely thoughtful and committed black creative writer acting as social critic and polemicist.

"This book should have been written in America—for Americans," writes McKay in his Introduction, for

> There exist hundreds of books and brochures about the American Negro, but not one which has the aim of explaining to the black and white workers their close affinity, and of indicating to colored workers their true place in the class struggle and their role in the international workers' movement. . . . It was not my aim to please my Russian comrades: I have written with the aim of letting them know the truth about the American Negro . . . about his place in American society, and about the relationship of organized labor and American society to him.
>
> The Negro in America is not permitted for one minute to forget his color, his skin, or his race. The American Negro who was not imbued with race consciousness would constitute a strange phenomenon. If my words are harsh and unpleasant to some extent, one must not forget that they are the legitimate offspring of the social structure of America and are completely appropriate.

The harsh words do not appear in the Introduction itself, which gives a general view of the postwar condition of blacks in America that is noteworthy for being reasonably nonpartisan in its reconstruction of both social and political history and reprints an exchange of correspondence with Leon Trotsky—mainly on the role of black workers in the world-revolutionary movement and on the use of black troops in Germany. But this chapter does contain a succinct statement of the central tenet of McKay's thinking both then and for the remainder of his life: "The Negro question is at bottom a question of the working class, which is being used by the bourgeoisie for philanthropic purposes at the same time that the leaders of the class struggle ignore it."

Though he had earlier composed a paeon of praise for Booker T. Washington, by 1923 McKay had reconsidered the role of the Tuskegee president and attacked him for espousing "the false philosophy of meekness and gratitude" that, in retrospect, seems to have been its touchstone. At this time, just a generation after Washington's celebrated Cotton States Exposition speech in Atlanta, McKay's judgment must have appeared heretical to many of the mainstream black leaders, his words "harsh and unpleasant" indeed; but today it appears perspicacious, legitimate, and widespread. McKay saw the effect of Washington's philosophy as uniting Northern Democrats and Re-

publicans, the industrial North and the agrarian South "to shake hands with one another above the head of the Negro, who was fed on corn mush."

Irrepressible, apparently, McKay also took W. E. B. DuBois to task. He considered that DuBois's organization, the NAACP, wanted merely to substitute professional education for the technical and commercial education proposed by Booker T. Washington and to effect the "open shop" as a means of facilitating the entry of Negroes—still excluded from most trade unions—into the labor mainstream. He believed that the NAACP, the ACLU, and the Urban League all represented the reprehensible moderate social-welfare movement that proposed the gradual amelioration of the black workers' plight through legislative change, overt action, and the assumed goodwill of the "Northern oligarchy." He himself was less sanguine. He thought this *modus operandi* altogether too slow, predictably ineffective, and less desirable than some inchoate method that he enunciates only in the most vague of political and social terms. Nonetheless, he quotes with evident approval the observation of a North Carolina Negro that "Insofar as the vast majority of Negroes belong to the working class, their permanent interests are the same as the interests of other workers." And today few would gainsay him.

One weakness that McKay dwells on is the presumed DuBois hope that white society would "capitulate," and that blacks would be absorbed "on a class basis." This vain hope, he says, is disappearing as the intransigence of the dominant society is better appreciated, so that "the Negro intelligentsia is turning to the black workers" for leadership in the struggle against the entrenchment of a "two societies" system. What McKay perceived was what Gunnar Myrdal described in eloquent detail and what has apparently come to pass. Notwithstanding, he saw the social significance of the NAACP in its encouragement of higher education and of unionization (except for its "open shop" policy).

McKay's argument that the "open shop" principle is really a means for the emasculation and eventual elimination of trade unions is now generally recognised; his support for separate black unions (such as we still have in the building trades in some states) and professional organizations (such as the National Medical Association) was a tactical move intended to create a feeling of solidarity among workers and to prepare them for the time when the greater good—strong, united, nonracist unions—could be realized. But because of the notorious racism of the American Federation of Labor and its leaders, McKay favors "independent" unions—especially those that are in harmony with the Industrial Workers of the World, which he characterizes as "a revolutionary union in which not the slightest distinction is made on the basis of race." While many have opposed the creation of separate unions, organized on racial lines, McKay's advocacy was supported by the eminent French sociologist, Emile Durkheim, who advanced the belief that the act of joining a small group was a desirable means of preparing for the socialization necessary before large-group membership. Hence, the apparent paradox implicit in McKay's simultaneous advocacy of race-based independent unions and of the I.W.W. can be satisfactorily resolved.

From a consideration of labor organizations, McKay proceeds to a discussion of the role of blacks in the several aspects of American culture. Accurately gauging public priorities, he writes first on sports and opens the subject by quoting M. Diagne, the conservative Negro deputy from Senegal in the French Assembly who said, after the celebrated match between boxers Siki and Carpentier, "The white man refused to accept the idea that the black man can be equal to him physically and spiritually." Thereupon he abandons the ostensible subject and launches into a dissertation on the sociology of blacks in white societies, saying:

> The separate, individual black-skinned man from the West Indies or America receives much better treatment in London or Berlin than in New York or Kingston. He responds more quickly to the cordial atmosphere of Paris than to London. . . . Catholic countries, by tradition, treat Negroes tolerantly and in a friendly fashion. This can be explained by the fact that the Catholic church had more experience and contact with Blacks than the Protestant church, which from the very beginning of its existence was the concubine of the imperialist aggressors, while the Catholic church . . . was never a completely devoted ally in the imperialist adventures of European peoples. . . . Protestantism has become a kind of Roosevelt of imperialism; Catholicism has remained a sister of mercy.

To this he adds that "the black intelligentsia of America looks upon France as the foremost cultured nation of the world," but quickly reminds us that "American Negroes are beginning to believe that one imperialist exploiter can be better than another. . . . [T]hey are beginning to forget about the vile exploitation of Africans by the French."

Now, the general observations about Catholic and Protestant policy *via-à-vis* blacks is really just an echoing of Marx's well-known strictures, and thus an expression of communist orthodoxy; the first part of the quotation reveals McKay's own careful analysis of the difference between an *individual's* treatment and the application of imperialist policy to blacks *en masse*. And elsewhere he notes that perhaps the greatest hindrance to the progress of blacks derives from the so-called interest of the churches:

> The Negro question! Wherever it is posed, in Africa or in America, it is a question of the working class. And at the same time it has become a question of special attention on the part of the reformist bourgeoisie who divert it from its true path and obscure its proletarian character with Christian philanthropy. . . . [T]he leaders of the class struggle handed over a very important part of their work to the philanthropists.

Returning to the subject of sports, McKay says that Negroes are still effectively excluded from all except "the national American sport called Lynching," in which he is the featured performer, and that those few who have been tolerated in boxing, such as Jack Johnson, have been exploited by the white commercialists, who are the principal

beneficiaries. There are many today even who would concur in the general view that black athletes (while better remunerated than before) nonetheless provide handsome fortunes for the white lawyers, trainers, managers, and promoters who people the world of professional sports.

In his consideration of the several aspects of high culture, McKay makes some persuasive arguments, and the cogency of his reasoning is at times impressive, being based on argument from example; but again the substance of his chapter is less relevant to the role of blacks in American culture than to the general topic of the limitations of a Eurocentric high culture (with its concomitant antagonism to cultural plurality) and the hegemony of bourgeois taste. By way of illustrating the difference between British and French attitudes, however, McKay points out that while Queen Victoria surrounded herself with "the archaic apurtenances of a barbaric feudalism," and the British Museum stored its rare, beautiful Benin sculptures in the obscurity of its ethnological division, French artists,

> carried away by curiosity and a thirst for knowledge, followed the tricolor into the African jungles and returned to Paris with samples of Negro art, the influence of which it is clearly possible to trace in French Impressionist art. Primitive Negro art became the chief object of study of the industrious Teutonic scholars and the admirers of French art salons.

And Henry Tanner, the American Negro artist, he notes with obvious pleasure, became one of the cynosures of Parisian art circles.

Writing about the theater world, McKay notes that New York is less receptive to Negroes than London; in New York they are sought just for comic or supporting roles in which their race is caricatured. Now, this observation is not novel: it had been made with force by DuBois and was to be repeated by almost every other critic or commentator on American theatre thereafter, including several in *The New Negro* (1925). But McKay pointed out the cruelty of the dilemma in which the black actor and playwright were placed: they had to restrict their talents to farces for whites or serious work that could hope to attract only the limited audiences of the urban "black belts." And the problems of the actors were shared by the Negro musicians: the dominant white managers of the musical world severely circumscribed their participation to the presentation of jazz, spirituals, gospel or work songs. Oratorios, operas, recitals of the standard European repertoire, and symphonic orchestras were closed to the black artist. It is easy, then, to understand McKay's sorry conclusion that "In a capitalist society there is no slave equal to the artist. He is the greatest slave, because his instinctively revolutionary spirit is harnessed like a mechanical machine. And still the artist prides himself on the fact that he is free and stands above propaganda."

For his chapter on "Negroes in Literature," McKay uses as an epigraph Wordsworth's great sonnet "To Toussaint L'Ouverture" and, after a brief eulogy of that reknowned Haitian, considers the poetry of Phillis Wheatley. Though Thomas Jefferson thought her work beneath the dignity of criticism, some modern critics claim merit in it. In McKay's judgment,

> The verses of Phillis Wheatley occupy a prominent place in American literature of that time. They are distinguished by perfection of form, but they do not have any other merit. . . . They only prove to Christian slaveowners, in whose opinion the Negro was destined by God himself to be a slave, that a negro [sic] child brought from the African jungles can receive an education and become no worse than a child from the ruling white caste. Since the time of Phillis Wheatley many negro [sic] writers have written in English much better than she did.

What he is asserting here is that the black artist needs neither condescending special consideration nor the application of less rigorous critical criteria; that is, that his work should be judged, as the New Critics would later emphasize, only on the basis of the effectiveness of the language itself.

And on matters of language, McKay shows a greater awareness of linguistic principles than many other writers of his time: he suggests that the idiom of blacks has its own morphology and vocabulary, which are to be respected and subjected to scholarly analysis. Somewhat provocatively (though intended as a tongue-in-cheek aside, surely) he adds that "the dialect of the Islands is coarser and more poetic." Furthermore, he claims respect for the Negro literary heritage of "stories from the world of animals in the West Indies, field songs and house-servant games, the folk tales of Brer Rabbit, and the spirituals and slave songs of the southern states." In effect, he is advocating the change in attitude to the study of folklore that became the norm some forty years later. And he provides two important caveats: first, this traditional literature should not be mistaken for the extent and aspiration of contemporary black artistic aspirations; second, its great merit resides in its harmony with the life of the Negro workers of the time. For this reason he praises the dialect poems of Paul Lawrence Dunbar and depreciates his "literary language verse": the former represent "the very soul of the Negro during the period of emancipation. . . . They are full of optimism and contain more joyful notes than the plantation melodies of the slaves."

In this chapter there are few evaluations of specific authors; rather, McKay devotes his attention to theoretical matters, such as the possibility of full racial identification and expression in an essentially white society. But he comments at some length on the work of W. E. B. DuBois and his *The Souls of Black Folk* (1903) in terms that few today would endorse without some reserve:

> DuBois . . . deserves first place in the field of literature, unsurpassed by anyone else. There is no other Negro American writer who has such a clear, pure, and at the same time elevated and colorful language.

> Since the time of *Uncle Tom's Cabin,* no other American writer has taken the Negro as the subject of his writing, as real material in American life. The hypocritical puritan guardians try not to speak about the Negro in literature as a result

of which one can observe complete sterility in the literature of the South.

> All American novelists who depict negro [sic] types in their works write as biologists, anthropologists . . . but not as artists.

Expanding upon this last observation, he proposes that most white authors "stubbornly sacrifice the interests of artistic truth" by introducing to their works only stereotypes of Negroes: clowns, criminals, mammies, and devoted household servants. He argues for the exploitation of the immense range of black characters, a range that could people any legitimate creative work that attempts to capture the spirit of American society, and especially the newly enlarged and enriched urban segment. (Ironically, his own efforts to capture the vibrant life of Harlem in realist terms, as in *Home to Harlem,* 1928, were trenchantly denounced by Dr. DuBois for pandering to the prurient interests of white readers, for denigrating Negroes, and for squandering artistic talent for commercial gain [see Further Reading].) Instead of maintaining the traditional Southern agrarian milieu for black writing, McKay argues for an expansion to include the new life of the cities; instead of romanticism, he argues for social realism, for naturalism, for uncompromising verisimilitude. There are pimps and prostitutes as well as plantations; parties as well as prayer meetings.

From this general discussion, McKay develops what is perhaps his clearest statement of his personal philosophy of literature, especially as it affects the black writer:

> White writers who have Negroes as their themes serve the aims of the treacherously influential propaganda, which finds a much wider response and which has a much wider distribution than the direct, open propaganda of colored writers. The sphere of influence of the negro [sic] writer is limited to his own intelligentsia and to idealists from the ranks of the oppressor class. The wide masses of Negroes snicker upon reading the semi-artistic caricature of themselves in belletristic magazines, while the ideas of national propaganda being developed in the press of their own intelligentsia . . . do not reach them at all.

> In reality, of all negro [sic] literature the only literature that merits any attention is that which has the character of national propaganda. . . .

> There are only two paths by which American negro [sic] writers can go to attain their aim. The first path is to follow the direction of the decadent school of old critics who stubbornly cling to the old dialect which, in their opinion, must serve as the basis for creative work. The second path is to follow the direction of the new school of critics, chiefly Jews, who have a great heritage of racial community expression in literature and who appear inclined to strike definite racial notes in art rather than express general and universal ideas.

In this respect, McKay espouses "vivid poetry and prose of a more intimate and subjective character" than had earlier appeared and thus is at variance with the viewpoint later propagated by the influential critic Alain Locke, who saw greatest merit in "objective" literature by and about black writers. But both critics, though they frequently engaged in personal attacks, agreed on the necessity for widening the horizons of black writing and for inculcating a degree of race pride that was nothing short of revolutionary to those accustomed to sentiments of acquiescence, apology, and shame. For McKay, the goal was "a new spirit among the negro [sic] masses"; and this "new spirit" became manifest in the then nascent Harlem Renaissance. And when one considers the course of American literature in the half-century after his statement, particularly noting the characteristics of major Jewish and black writers, McKay's observations appear to have been particularly accurate.

McKay's final chapter in *The Negroes in America* is devoted to a consideration of "Sex and Economics." Here he makes the pertinent observation that "The Negro question is inseparably connected with the question of women's liberation"—even using that now familiar term—and demonstrates in the most lucid manner that both groups are notoriously underpaid, overworked, deprived of advancement, and restricted to the least prestigious employments, thus united in "poverty and humiliation." He repeats the sociological commonplaces about males' fear of Negroes raping white women and reminds us of the barbarities of lynching episodes that have been in large measure inspired by that fear, but he points to a common cause: both lynching and fear are the effects of an unjust economic system. In many ways, this chapter is a recapitulation of the opening chapters of the book. (pp. 339-49)

Despite its several and sometimes severe shortcomings, *The Negroes in America* does provide us with a rare opportunity to see an established black writer in the role of social analyst and critic. Furthermore, it provides us with a clear statement of his political and literary philosophy and thus the source of material that was subsequently incorporated in both poems and prose—for instance, the long section of *Banjo* (1929) that records Ray's discussion of the Negro Question with the Senegalese proprietor of a Marseilles bar who had made money in America and subsequently chose to leave it, and yet defended it against all criticism. More important, perhaps, it allows us to question the accuracy of some of the content of both *A Long Way from Home* (1937) and *Harlem: Negro Metropolis* (1940) and raises problems about McKay's relationship to the Harlem Renaissance, the black intelligentsia, and the left-wing political movement no less than about his latter-day conversion to Roman Catholicism. In sum, though it is a short work, it is important in the study of a major segment of black literature. (pp. 350-51)

*Marian B. McLeod, "Claude McKay's Russian Interpretation: 'The Negroes in America'," in CLA Journal, Vol. XXIII, No. 3, March, 1980, pp. 336-51.*

## Robert M. Greenberg (essay date 1981)

[*In the following excerpt, Greenberg examines idealism and realism in McKay's fiction.*]

Everywhere in the fiction of Claude McKay the impulse of the realist is fundamental. The centers of nightlife in *Home to Harlem* (1928), the savage and colorful waterfront district of Marseilles in *Banjo* (1929), the bright Jamaican countryside and pattern of peasant life in *Banana Bottom* (1933)—these physical and social settings are a genuine source of appeal in McKay's fiction. When first published, McKay's novels were noted and often criticized for their concentration on the lowly and sexual elements of black life. Today the impact of McKay's fiction continues to rest significantly on the success of its realism. Now, however, the sexual elements are not as striking, and it is largely the particularized and engrossing depiction of black worlds low on the social scale that engage us. In the foreground, McKay's realism manifests itself in its attention to the manners, morals, speech, and daily lives of its characters—in what Addison Gayle [in his *The Way of the World: The Black Novel in America*] describes as McKay's movement "toward a realistic appraisal of black life in all its existential trials and tribulations." And in the middle and background of his fiction, his realism manifests itself in its description and suggestion of societal forces, sometimes even international forces, framing and effecting the action—in what George E. Kent describes [see Further Reading] as McKay's "secure grasp of the big picture, the sheer magnitude of the problem of Black soul" in the West.

While in terms of style and attitude toward representation McKay is a realist, in his approach to his characters' inner lives he is a moral and philosophic idealist. As evidence of his moral or ethical idealism, we can note the importance he places on the lives of societally unimportant and undeveloped types in addition to his interest in the rebellion and quest for independence of more developed individuals. Regarding his philosophic idealism, that is, his belief in innate human qualities of mind that distinguish man's nature in a material and antagonistic world, we can note his occasional sympathy with the idea of incorruptible goodness, his belief in the reality and importance of ethnic identity, his belief in the critical powers of the mind, and his embrace of the pleasures of the body.

McKay's attraction to values grounded in subjectivity also plays a part in shaping the quality of the realism in at least one novel. In his autobiography, he says:

> Any critic who considers it important enough to take the trouble can trace in my stuff a clearly consistent emotional-realist thread, from the time I published my book of dialect verse (*Songs of Jamaica*) in 1912, through the period of my verse and prose in *The Liberator,* until the publication of *Home to Harlem.*

By "emotional-realist" McKay has in mind in his early writings the subjective lens through which the realities of existence are viewed. In the above passage, where he is responding to the charge that he is an imitator of Hemingway, he calls attention to his own "loose manner" (presumably of narration) and to the "subjective feeling in writing" (presumably of style). He contrasts this with Hemingway's "objective and carefully stylized form." The point he appears to want to make is that both he and Hemingway are realists; the difference lies in how the subjective element, the imaginative values, are fused with the objective report.

In calling his dialect verse "emotional-realist," McKay would seem to have in mind his adoption of the peasant point of view, the mellow tone of mind, out of which the pain of rural life is envisioned. As for his standard English poems of **Harlem Shadows** (1922) (many of which first appeared in *The Liberator*), he is thinking of the pastoral imagery, diction, and themes that fill these lyrics as the poet yearns for the lost Eden of his youth. Certainly he does not mean the taut, "chafing" sonnets of that volume, such as **"The White House"** or **"The White City."**

With regard to **Home to Harlem,** McKay's description of himself as an "emotional-realist" seems especially apt. In terms of selection of material and provision of a vivid picture of Harlem cabaret life, the work is indeed realistic; however, in terms of point of view, tone, even style, the work slides between realistic and highly Romantic and expressionistic effects. The narrator forgoes the detachment usually adopted in a third-person narration. Instead, the narrator identifies with the immediacies of the protagonist's experience and tries to render the pleasures and distresses of existence. He seeks to capture also the cumulative feeling of being in the swim of things, of being *with it.*

The reader may ask: Are not realism and idealism the ingredients of every novel? Are not a mimetic approach to subject matter and the presence of human beings' will some measure of self-consciousness and with the elements of most novels since Defoe? Clearly they are. My emphasis on these aspects, however, is intended to make explicit the qualities that distinguish McKay's fiction. McKay's effort at verisimilitude is not the reflex of a third-rate novelist who daubs in a mannerism or suggests a backdrop as a matter of narrative necessity. It is the expression of one of the primary factors of his artistic intelligence. With the exception of **Home to Harlem,** McKay's idea of what constitutes a simulacrum of the real world involves a totally delineated environment including racial, social, economic, religious, artistic, and political indices. To borrow a useful distinction from [Georg] Lukács, McKay's view of man's ontology is that it is as strongly social and historical as it is solitary and asocial.

In McKay's novels environment is an ever-present reality, cramping, loosening, coloring his characters' lives. In the Harlem stories in **Gingertown** (1932), environment is even determining and fatal. McKay is also a realist in the very simple sense that harkens back to the origin of the term "novel" from the French word for news, *novelle:* he brings us news about worlds where black men and women struggle to adapt to or transcend their situations in significant ways.

I have already mentioned several areas in McKay's fiction where we see the influence of his idealism on his conception of character. Let me step back a trifle from his fiction now and review the forms of radicalism McKay adhered to in his life, which directly or indirectly influenced his fiction and found further definition through it.

McKay was a political radical. From 1920, when he first studied Marxism in London, to nearly the end of his life, he was a socialist. His enthusiasm for the Russian experiment and for the American Communist Party dimmed earlier than that of most radicals, but his identification with the black proletariat never died. This was reinforced in the late thirties by a hope that "a new radical organization of Negroes along racial lines" would replace the traditional leftist idea that Negroes hadn't any problems different from the working class in general.

McKay was also a racial radical. Announced first in his sonnets, McKay's unusually firm racial pride was, as Kent points out, one of the advantages of his Jamaican origins. In the essay **"A Negro Writer to his Critics,"** McKay speaks explicitly of "racial attributes," stressing that the black man's birthright of bitterness in the New World was the seed for "his humor and ripe laughter and particular rhythm of life." From the time of McKay's arrival in New York at the age of twenty-five, he appears to have retained his appetite for the racial solidarity he knew when he "was forced down among the rough body of the great serving class of Negroes. . . ." The emotional liberation afforded him through contact with the "warm," "spontaneous," "loose" qualities of the black working class is noteworthy:

> I was perhaps then at the most impressionable adult age and the warm contact with my workmates, boys and girls, their spontaneous ways of acting on and living for the moment, the physical and sensuous delights, the loose freedom in contrast to the definite peasant patterns by which I had been raised—all served to . . . cut me finally adrift. . . . During the first years among Negroes my only object in working was to possess the means to live as they did.

Out of this contact he developed his belief that Afro-American culture in possession of its own psychological, spiritual, and artistic powers must percolate upward from the masses rather than downward from an educated minority.

Finally, McKay was a radical in terms of his manner of living and his view of art. He was influenced by the bohemianism and the belief in the authority of personal artistic vision that were typical attitudes of young writers after World War I. He was also influenced by a nondoctrinal view of the relationship between politics and art. Frederick J. Hoffman in *The Twenties* speaks of an "aesthetic radicalism" prevalent at the time and describes two variations: "One assumed that the aesthetic and the social conscience were the same; the other assumed there was no such thing as a social conscience, that there was no history but only persons." McKay, for the most part, belonged to the first group. He emphasized personal vision as the basis for social criticism or, as Hoffman puts it, as a "legitimate means of gaining insight and knowledge that are indispensable to our total view of a culture." But it would be inaccurate to deny that, like Hemingway, McKay condoned pleasurable personal experience as an end in itself and that he was even tempted at times by the idea that leaving society was—for the black man especially—entry to creative freedom.

As is quite obvious, McKay's political, racial, and aesthetic radicalism all fed into one another. His socialism enhanced his attraction to black folk culture and community experience; and his bohemianism helped gird his desire to describe the physical side of black life in positive terms. Taken together, socialism and bohemianism may even be said to have facilitated his rebellion against the genteel tradition in black fiction, for they encouraged him to write about lower-class individuals when "their primitive joys, their loves and hates, their work and play, their dialect" were an embarrassment to the black bourgeoisie.

The choice, then, of realism and idealism as the controlling terms of this analysis is not gratuitous. They locate the qualities of McKay's mind by which we can best grasp his novelistic motives and, through an understanding of these motives, best assess the nature of his successes and and failures.

McKay's idealism figures prominently in the characterization of Jake Brown, the protagonist of *Home to Harlem.* Jake is an anachronism. Born and raised in Virginia, a participant in the migration to the Northern cities that began before World War I, a veteran (and a deserter) from the Army in France, Jake, despite rootlessness, is a whole man. He is neither lonely for family, divided from himself by self-hate or education, nor contaminated by the "promiscuous thickness" of Harlem life. As the narrator puts it, "He, in his frame and atmosphere, was the Alpha and Omega himself."

Jake takes life easy. He falls naturally into the rhythm of new situations. Men and women like him. And, " 'young and pretty,' " he likes himself. Moreover, "his love nature was generous and warm without any vestige of the diabolical or sadistic." Uncoarsened, nonviolent, not addicted to a single object of passion, he is indeed a "unique type of humanity" when he is compared to the other men drifting through the swirling, centerless merry-go-round of Harlem night life.

But what does he embody? How are we to understand the significance of Jake's characteristics? His adequacy to his own needs and to his environment is clear enough; but less clear is the meaning—the historical origin or conceptual context—of the positive values he exemplifies. Does he embody the natural virtues of the common man which are concentrated in him in an uncommon degree? If so, then why are the other common men in his world fallen types and described with the animal imagery of a gorilla (Zeddy), a wolf (Billy Biasse), a rhino (the dining car chef)? And why are the women often prisoners of fixed passions or perverted needs—like Susie, who loves only yellow, or like Congo Rose, who craves sadistic men? Or if Jake is supposed to represent the undifferentiated virtues of a rural black, virtues that have survived transplantation to the northern Black Belt, then what is the reason he has remained intact while the others have been sucked down into the vortex?

The difficulty in interpreting Jake's significance stems from two related causes. One is that McKay has not yet mastered the technique to present a complete intellectual pattern, a coherent "argument," in fictional terms. Assume that he is trying to say that in the black men on the street—spontaneous, sensual, uneducated, upfront men—we will find the felicity, the malleability, and the physical appetite for living which is quintessential to the black soul. In that case he has not been completely successful, for we do not understand what produced a Jake other than the author's wishful thinking. Idealism in fiction, if it is to be compelling, must have its roots in a sense of reality that the reader feels to be valid; otherwise it races ahead of understanding. In a picaresque novel, where the protagonist is morally superior to the people he encounters and thereby reveals their corruptness, the hero's nature is explained often through his origins. He comes from the country rather than the city, or he turns out to be the son or the relative of a worthy individual. In *Home to Harlem* no such clarification exists.

The other reason that Jake falls short as an expression of the author's idealism is that, in the end, he does not signify an altogether happy ideal. McKay introduces the Haitian intellectual Ray in part II to serve as a foil. He and Jake are compared in terms of their ability to find enjoyment in daily life, their contentment with black working-class comradery, and their ability to think purposefully about themselves and the world. Ray is shown to be unable to find satisfaction "with the easy, simple things that sufficed for Jake." He experiences " 'those sensations that . . . turn you back in on yourself and make you isolated and helpless.' " Nevertheless, Ray, is shown as being able to confront "thought," even though it is "suffering" and pushes him toward the "precipice of imagination." And it is this characteristic of Ray, even though it exists in him in excess, that clarifies Jake's virtues as being essentially preindustrial ones, qualities that can only foster a marginal life for an individual in the urban North.

McKay suggests the pathos of Jake's limitations when Jake contracts syphilis. The doctor tells him to stay in bed and not drink, but Jake sends his landlady for several pails of beer a day. " ' . . . beer can't make me no harm,' " he reasons. " 'It's light.' " He complains to Ray that prophylactics are " 'kill-joy things,' " that they are " 'foh edjucated guys like you who lives in you' head.' " But Ray argues back: " 'They are for you, too. . . . This is a new age with new methods of living. You can't just go on like a crazy ram goat as if you were living in the Middle Ages.' " Some days later, when Jake's landlady fails to appear with his supper, he ventures onto the street, meets a buddy, begins drinking, and collapses.

Just as he is unable to conceive the reality of his own illness, he proves unable to grow from experience and understand the world. Admittedly, we are shown how from the inadequate use of black troops in the War he concludes, " 'Niggers am evah always such fools. . . . Always thinking they've got something to do with white folks' business.' " But despite this, in terms of day-to-day experience, Jake is a creature entirely of physical satisfactions and physical adaptations. If he has the same initials as Hemingway's Jake Barnes, he is Barnes's opposite: he is unaffected by his experience. After the War, he resumes the same pattern (though in a quickened tempo) that he followed before the War. Jake's inveterate health, impervious to larger problems, may have its charm, but the necessity for Ray to exist in the work and rescue it from Jake's mindlessness speaks for itself. As a hero, Jake is both dude and dud.

Jake and Ray seem to represent two halves of a whole that McKay could not reconcile. We might best think of them as extremes of heart and mind. The Ray in McKay sought to celebrate the warm feeling and spontaneity of the Jake Browns of his race. But the reader has difficulty sorting out the retrograde from the progressive elements of Jake's characterization. The contrast with the inhibited intellectual Ray reveals not only Jake's strengths but his limitations. The result is a confusing image that is not as attractive as McKay had hoped.

When one evaluates the adequacy of McKay's realism as a whole in *Home to Harlem,* one again confronts his failure to elucidate the causality in the material. Jake's immediate experience is drawn with fairly careful use of details. This is especially true in the railroad section, which is the most coherent portion of the book, and again in the speakeasy scenes, where there are passages about the clientele, the setting and decor, the women's clothing and make-up, the music, lyrics, and dancing. But this is only the foreground of the novel. The work's failure in terms of the larger subject of Harlem sporting life lies in the fact that it does not place the life in a meaningful context; it is allowed to glow in a void, unexplained. Robert Bone puts his finger on the problem when he observes that the novel has no antagonist or conflict; that Jake and Ray "acquire a broader significance only through their . . . relationship to contemporary society"; and that McKay fails to indicate the nature of that relationship [see Further Reading].

The broadened outlook of blacks that lived abroad during or after the War; the libertinism and material ostentation of the Jazz Age; the homeless, homesick rituals of a race twice uprooted from native soil; the flight from economic harshness and white hostility—all these separately or in any combination might have been the sort of influences adduced to explain the Harlem scene. But except for his slapdash effort at describing Jake's European sojourn, McKay defines no meaningful context. It is true that one of the cardinal virtues of *Home to Harlem,* indicative of the new pride we associate with the Renaissance, is that Harlem social life is *not* presented as a mere reflex of white oppression, as an escape valve from suffering. Rather, it is presented as an expression of intrinsic black qualities and cultural tendencies. Nonetheless it is not inconsistent to expect that a writer will be able to convey the inherent truths of a subject at the same time that he suggests formative influences. Only a naive mind sees the two as irreconcilable or discrete realms. With regard to this work, the incompleteness of McKay's realism seems to stem from just such an artistic naivety.

*Banjo* is far more successful in marshaling the fictional techniques and material for developing McKay's ideas about the wellspring, substance, and cultural potentialities of blackness—for giving fictional expression to his ethnic idealism. The strategy of his "argument" involves distinguishing a black identity from white Western characteristics; persuading us to accept the racial qualities of his outcasts as revealing a fundamentally different—an African—approach to life; and bringing about a reversal of values in which those socially and economically on top are shown to be low in human terms while those on the bottom are shown to be men of unexpected richness and potential value to civilization.

"I admire the man who responds to more 'gods' in himself than I do," says D. H. Lawrence; and McKay's emphasis, like Lawrence's on the passionate self over the rational ego and will, is the intellectual influence that animates his attack on the West. He attacks in *Banjo* the West's obsession with money and respectability, the increased standardization of man and mechanization of society as well as the cruelty, bawdiness, and racism that thrive beneath the surface of "enlightened" democracies.

*Banjo* is not a political novel in the sense of a novel about characters engaged in active political commitments. On the other hand, it is not a novel about private relationships or private emotions either. It is a novel concerned with ideas about culture and with defining an atmosphere of cultural antagonism. White civilization is presented as having the effect of an "ever-tightening" mechanism on the quality of life, while the band of black seamen comprises a subculture that argues for vitality, the pursuit of pleasure, self-expression, and brotherhood. Certainly *Banjo* is a novel intended to persuade the reader about a pan-African presence in the world and about the resources for a "racial renaissance" that tries " 'getting down to our native roots and building up from our own people . . . .' " In the figure of Ray, carried over from *Home to Harlem,* there is even an "advanced" character, a man of developed intellect, who exemplifies this ideological position put into practice.

Banjo occupies the same position in the novel as did Jake in the preceding one. He is an exemplary version of the common man and the vehicle for McKay's racial idealism. However, while the origin of Jake's special qualities is never clarified, the source of Banjo's uniqueness is clear. He is a product of experience, of worldliness: " 'I ain't one accident-made nigger. . . . Ise a true-blue traveling-bohn nigger and I know life . . . '." There are numerous similarities between Banjo and Jake. Like Jake, Banjo takes things easy or "nacheral"; he always lands on his feet; he avoids complications with women; and he will not live off them or panhandle. Like Jake also, he speaks in a "rich Dixie accent" and relies on great reserves of physical strength for his vagabond existence. Again, like his forerunner, he finds abstract thought uncongenial. Yet through experience Banjo has accrued a highly pragmatic philosophy that equips him to deal with all the problems of living, great and small, whereas Jake is without compass before the greater realities of life. Jake says to Ray rather pathetically in *Home to Harlem,* " 'Ef I was edjucated, I could understand things better . . . ' "; Banjo wouldn't make such a remark.

Banjo, to use Gayle's words, is a proletarian outsider, a black man who has turned his tenuous and largely negative status on the fringes of white society into a gambit for freedom and self-expression. Banjo has "worked at all the easily-picked-up jobs—longshoreman, porter, factory worker, farm hand, seaman." "His life was a dream of vagabondage that he was perpetually pursuing and realizing in odd ways, always incomplete but never unsatisfactory." As his nickname suggests, he sees himself as an artist; his dream is to form a black orchestra. His ethical philosophy also distinguishes him. The treacherous life of "the Ditch," the alley-ridden quarter of the old port, provides a benchmark in the novel for the nature of reality. Banjo's attitude toward this environment, which is full of touts, cocottes, derelicts, and seamen on shore leave, is rough, ready, and unsentimental: Avoid these who are going under. Take advantage of innocents; if you don't another will. Stay clear of police and government bureaucracy. And never allow political anger to move you to protest or righteous complaint. Keep things in proportion and they remain manageable.

Banjo is completely aware that " 'theah's a mighty mountain a white divilment on this heah Gawd's big ball,' " and that " 'niggers will find that mountain on every foot a land that the white man done step on.' " But he reminds his friends, " '. . . we niggers am no angels, neither.' " When he receives a severe beating at the police station, he can't help being aware that no one lives by the professed rules of society, neither the police nor the citizens, and that in the Ditch this was especially true. His reply, when Ray protests that " 'You fellows didn't do anything,' " is " 'But we *have*, though, pardner. Wese done a lot and didn't get caught.' " Even the lynching of his brother in the American South has not made Banjo willing to fight back. The powerless situation of the black man in France and America leads him to the conclusion that the problems of life can be solved, but only on *individual terms*— on what Kent would call "strategic" as opposed to "radical" or collective terms.

Of the beach boys in Marseilles—all of whom, white and black, were seamen deported from America as illegal immigrants—it is only the blacks who live in a "holiday spirit," siphoning casks of wine in freight yards, sunning, swimming, and washing on the breakwater, singing, dancing, and drinking in the bistros of the Ditch, or panhandling in "Bum Square." The white seamen, especially the Nordic ones, go to pieces from hard liquor and poor hygiene—victims of a romantic view of Marseilles. Hard pragmatic realism, along with a powerful appetite for physical enjoyment and self-expression, distinguishes the blacks.

Yet Banjo's gang, exemplifying differences of nationality, character, and opinion, is anything but homogeneous. Taloufa, a Nigerian taken from the bush to England at thirteen, is a Garveyite; the American Goosey calls himself a "race man" and is an advocate of the new Negro and uplift ideas of Locke and Du Bois. Bugsy, also American, is chronically aggressive; Ginger, a Jamaican, favors the line of least resistance and speaks with scholarly pomposity. Malty is another West Indian and is in jealous conflict with Banjo over Latnah, the olive-skinned Arab prostitute; and Dengel, a "shining anthracite" Senegalese, is always in a happy haze of wine. The frame of reference is entirely black, as they drift into the black-owned Café African or Antilles Restaurant, tell black folktales and racial jokes, argue about Back-to-Africa, intermarriage, and

whether or not the banjo is the "instrument of slavery." A pan-African vision of things, a clear basis for black solidarity, emerges from their gatherings. As Jacqueline Kaye has memorably put it, McKay "seeks to arrive at the common black denominator, the essential Negroness" as he exploits their "divergences."

The common denominator, besides their survival sense and earthly moral pragmatism, is their *joie de vivre*. In chapters such as " 'Jelly Roll' " and "A Carved Carrot" McKay creates an atmosphere of quintessential African soul-feeling and life-rhythm. Akin to the speakeasy scenes in *Home to Harlem,* the narration is saturated with the pulsation of dance, music, and sexuality. The stress is placed on the "gorgeous sublimation of the primitive African sex feeling" as they "Shake that thing!" McKay exalts the dancing, different in style for each individual, as an expression of the "eternal life-flow." Whether "savage, barbaric, refined," the African-influenced dance reveals the currents of the "divine dance of life."

As the characterization of the black beach boys stresses both their ability to deal with hardship and their *joie de vivre,* so does the general picture of reality in the novel emphasize a dualistic world where the harsh and the delightful regularly entwine. Given the close identity of viewpoint between the author and Ray, we can find a valuable clue to McKay's aesthetic goals for the novel by looking at Ray's statement of purpose for his life. For as Ray was resolved that "civilization would not take the love of color, joy, beauty, vitality, and nobility out of *his* life," so McKay appears resolved to use the subject matter of the black beach boys to infuse his picture of life with those same affirmative, vital qualities. Character and setting correspond in *Banjo.* They are an expression of the same imaginative standpoint on the author's part and reveal an image of man and things that is physical and resistant at the same time that it is sensuous and vibrant.

It is significant, however, that a prose—not a poetic—feeling for things affects the use of detail and narrative elaboration. The weight of meaninglessness competes with a meaningfully vivified world of experience in *Banjo.* Life is characterized, more than anything, in terms of the daily round, the quotidian sense of things, as the beach boys drift from one café to another, or as a sudden fight destroys a good group feeling, or the illness of one threatens the morale of all. Yet the readers should not take McKay's subtitle, "A Story Without a Plot," entirely at face value; it distorts what he has actually accomplished—perhaps out of lack of confidence. The action is not entirely plotless or random. There are "plots" within chapters and the arc of an overall development. These narrative elements, however, are minimal in nature. As in many Hemingway short stories, the fact that very little happens is central to the mimetic "message." It is the sudden shifts of mood or flashes of color as they rise from the grey everydayness of the drifters' lives that give the novel its distinctly modern quality—its mood of *ennui,* of repetition, of the burdensome weight of things.

Time and again we are also shown how the power of environment and circumstance buffets the black boys, in this way dramatizing the precariousness of their situation, their near-pariah status in the French city. A police sweep brings the danger of arrest or beating. The simultaneous docking of the American squadron and two English ships makes them *persona non grata* in the white tourist cafés. A change in the value of the franc affects their pitiable purchasing power. Such examples illustrate how comprehensively McKay describes his Port Vieux and Marseilles environment. The foreground of bistro, breakwater, and Bloody Lane, the middle ground of tourist locales, and the background of international events are all part of the total pattern, the "big picture."

Through the chapters that deal exclusively with Ray's viewpoint, McKay is able to subject the Marseilles material to harsh social criticism and to air his values in an expositional form. (This is, of course, only supplemental to the episodes that dramatize the elements of Occidental society which he is denouncing—episodes such as that about the sensation-seeking Englishman or the one about the French chauffeur who is working toward middle-class respectability through pimping.) The use of Ray as an authorial mouthpiece, moreover, does not split the novel in half, in terms of structure or sensibility, as was the case in *Home to Harlem.* For one, Ray's monologues and inner thoughts always concern the environment immediately at hand, not a distorted, abstract version of it in Ray's mind. Secondly, Ray is more reliable here as a critic of society because he is more comfortable with himself as a man.

The polarities of heart and mind have been closed considerably in this novel, so that there is not the sense of an insoluable divergence between intellect and instinct, the exceptional and the common man. A final argument for the coherence and unity of *Banjo* is found in the observation that the novel can be read as a portrait of the artist as a young man. The sensibility of the narration stands in direct relation to the experience it describes, and may be seen as the end product of Ray's time with the beach boys of Marseilles.

Only in McKay's third novel, *Banana Bottom,* does reconciliation with society achieve parity with the motive of criticizing it. This spirit of reconciliation stems primarily from the British West Indian subject matter rather than from a profound change on McKay's part. *Banjo,* because of its urban context and peripheral characters, is a novel forced to inhabit the realm of the problematical. On the other hand, *Banana Bottom,* with its confined rural setting, its female protagonist, and the influence of English literary models, is conceived in a manner that makes resolution of its tensions an intrinsic likelihood.

In *Banana Bottom,* for one, the schism between Westernized intellect and racial feeling has been narrowed yet again: the conflict occurs within a single character. Furthermore, when Bita Plant returns from England, she is still no more than a bright young woman with an *exceptional* education; she is not and will never be an iconoclastic intellectual like Ray. Secondly, while the burden of mobility is fundamental to the lives of the characters in *Banjo,* Bita Plant's acceptance of her homeland is a given in the novel; it puts an entirely new and different pressure on a McKay protagonist to reconcile self with society. Finally, where the main figures in *Banjo* are men with certain inherently masculine problems of labor and social identity, the protagonist of *Banana Bottom* is a woman for whom marriage can provide the necessary bond with the social order.

In *Banana Bottom* we are very close to the world of Jane Austen's fiction—a world where, as Dorothy Van Ghent says, the novelist seeks "to illuminate the difficult and delicate reconciliation of the sensitively developed individual with the terms of his social existence," and where, furthermore, the choice a woman makes in marriage often determines the nature of her accommodation. The facilitating ideal in *Banana Bottom,* as in the novels of Austen, is the neoclassical idea of measure and balance: of harmony between reason and feeling and of the self, not fleeing society, but willingly meeting it halfway.

When Bita Plant returns from England, her instinctive opposition to the plans conceived for her by the missionary couple, Priscilla and Malcolm Craig, is again an instance of McKay's idealism finding expression in characterization. The Craigs, especially Priscilla, wished to train Bita as an "exhibit" of how English "higher education and refinement" can lift a black peasant girl out of her native proclivities; how it can prepare her to marry an educated black man; and how it can make of husband and wife a "cultured native couple" able to replace the missionaries in their work. But Bita feels that in allowing herself to be "the subject of an experiment" she has "voluntarily conceded herself as one does to a mesmerist." "A latent hostility" to Mrs. Craig's will and ideals, "an old unconscious thing now manifesting itself," reveals the strength of Bita's drive for independence and the resentment she feels toward well-intentioned white people trying to improve blacks according to white ideals.

Still more central to the critical-idealist plane of *Banana Bottom* is the drama of what is taken to be "higher nature" in the novel struggling against "lower nature," the former, of course, associated with white Anglo-Protestant civilization, the latter with Jamaican peasant life and culture. Bita's early sexual awakening with Crazy Bow Adair typifies the peasant pattern the missionaries battle against. What happens to her at their hands is representative—on a somewhat dramatic scale—of how the natives become ensnared in the meshwork of white morality. In a rare authorial aside, McKay tries—not without sarcasm—to capture the flavor of this entrapment:

> Young Africa, expatriate, emancipated, turning out of barracoons and huts, pressing forward, eager eyes fixed upon the Light held *high* by a white hand, *tripping* and *falling* ingloriously in the sweet snare of the flesh.
>
> Bound on a preaching or a teaching way . . . and almost unawares dropping down in the pit, never to reach out and press on again. (stress mine)

Once Bita has fallen into "the profound pit that yawned between the plane of the peasantry and higher education," only the rigors of "higher breeding" and "higher education," only an understanding of the "high social significance" of all behavior can save her.

This outlook prevails not only with Priscilla and Malcolm Craig, but also with deluded blacks such as Herald Newton Day, Bita's intended, and with the Reverend Lambert and his family. Day, as a result of his condescension to "our common mountain people," is the victim of harsh satire and is ultimately tumbled from his perch of "high" development. The less Christianized backsliders, such as Sister Phibby Patroll and Yoni Legge, are treated with gentle humor, as though "their native philosophy was that in the enjoyment of life there must be constant sin and repentance."

The squelching of high potential in the lowly is also dramatized. Crazy Bow Adair is a precocious young musical talent—possibly a genius—whom the "peasants took . . . as a fine fiddler for the hill country, but laughed at the idea of greatness in him. Greatness could not exist. . . . anywhere in the colony. . . . greatness was a foreign thing." Crazy Bow is pushed by his family toward practical education and civil service work, but he is incapable of following the straight and narrow. His uncontrollable passion for music renders him a social deviant—at first harmlessly so, but with the Bita Plant incident, someone for local officials to arrest, try, and put into an asylum.

The black characters in **Banana Bottom** exist along a continuum. Those most identified with and perverted by the Anglo-Protestant viewpoint are at one end—Herald Day and the Lamberts; those unharmed by dual cultural pressures are in the middle—Yoni Legge, Belle Black, Teacher Fearon; the grogshop reprobates, Tack Tally and Hopping Dick, tend toward the other end; and at the extreme, perverted by primitivism and chicanery, is Wumba, the "Obeah man," who worships the African God of Evil, Obi. The underlying movement of the plot involves Bita's reaction against the "higher" values of God, Duty, and Breeding and her reversion to the things associated with the "lower nature" of peasant life: sexuality, emotionality, connection with the soil, and responsiveness to African resonances in the island folkways. There are points when she goes too far, such as when she wants to marry Hopping Dick out of rebellion; or when she slaps Rosyanna, the Craig's maid; or when she succumbs to the African fetish spirit at Evan Vaughan's revival meeting. But in the end she does not reject rationalism, white civilization, or her English education; she individualizes them; she brings them into balance with a life rooted in the soil.

The success of the "argument" of **Banana Bottom** depends considerably on its ability to show that the Christian life embodied by the Craigs and propagated among the peasantry is devoid of practical knowledge of human nature. The absence of psychological realism is illustrated, for one, in Mrs. Craig's own attitude toward sex. She conceals from her maid that her husband visits her bed. She decides Bita is "atavistic" because she attends night-time "tea-meetings" and that Bita must be a "nymphomaniac" because she wants to marry Hopping Dick. Her more general complaint, and the complaint of the other missionaries about the black peasantry, is that they lack the necessary sexual restraint to achieve "a higher and more complex social order." Judging from the prevalence of Obi worship and the evangelical revivals that periodically sweep the is-

land, another area where the mission fails to ground itself in a realistic perception of needs is in the nature of the religious service. The service, though we are never shown one, does not appear to successfully engage the peasants' sentiments. It lacks continuity with earlier African religious experience. Typifying the failure of the Christians to grant any positive spiritual value to the Jamaican's heritage, Reverend Lambert exhorts his congregation: "Throw the jungle out of your hearts and forget Africa."

Not only does the excessive valuation of Anglo-Protestant civilization lead to hypocrisy and ineffectiveness, but it seems to be responsible for the polarization of ideas in the local mentality. It results in all "evil" things—sex, superstition, social hostilities, vestiges of African ritual—beings relegated to the worship of the African God of Evil, because the Christian churches have too idealized and inflexible a view of human nature. For problems of "sickness and feuds, love and elemental disasters," Obi was resorted to, while the natives "worshipped the Christian God-of-Good-and-Evil on Sunday." When the exhibit of African masks causes Mrs. Craig's horrific vision of faces dancing around her, this is an instance of the repressed life of the mind returning with a vengeance. And when Herald Day copulates with a goat, this too illustrates the crippling effect of "higher" values that prevent him from integrating adult sexuality with his theological development.

A man who has apparently remained in what McKay describes as "whole contact with life" is Teacher Fearon. He is the only one who understands Day's startling reversion and tells Squire Gensir:

> "It's all in nature. If I should tell you about my experience with the kids. The curious little aberrations that crop out among them. . . . Playing with themselves just like toys in their hands. . . . The only thing strange about this is that one of Herald Day's toys may have remained with him and he growing up with it without being aware."

For the most part, Squire Gensir, the white collector of native folk tales and music, is a figure of enlightenment in the novel and the guide for Bita Plant's journey into native roots. Here is a portion of their discussion as he reveals to her his naturalistic ideas:

> ". . . when I speak of the freedom of your peasants, I mean that unconscious freedom in their common existence, their natural instincts. They don't know what repression is."

> "But that is so animal," said Bita. "Don't you think it would be better if they had a chance for finer living and education? You do believe in education, don't you?"

> "Yes, I do in the intrinsic sense. Education as a thing for individual cultural development. But I don't believe in the system of modern education. It grinds out certain fixed types . . . to fit into a preconceived plan."

Bita must adapt his ideas to her own situation. Nevertheless, this dialogue prefigures where Bita will wind up—married to a dignified man of the soil and pursuing "individual cultural development." In an ironic twist for a novel of manners, the heroine will resolve her problems by marrying "down."

The prose style of *Banana Bottom* is rather functional, the luxuriant floral descriptions notwithstanding. The immediacy of experience in *Banjo,* the grit and sensory freshness, have yielded here to the primacy of the total design. A sense of pastoral bounty neutralized by a recognition of social realities determines the quality of the narration in *Banana Bottom.* Kenneth Ramchand's phrase "the controlled idyllic tone of a distanced narrator" conveys nicely the diminished interest in working up close [see Further Reading]. McKay is concerned instead with the creation of a large and objective social picture with certain idyllic overtones.

On a first reading, the scope of the representation of reality, especially of the natural and social milieu, seems inordinately devoted to documentary ends. Like Melville's exposition of Polynesian life in *Typee,* there is in *Banana Bottom* a comprehensiveness of treatment that suggests informative rather than narrative goals. And certainly *Banana Bottom* is addressed to the *rest* of the English-speaking world, not to a Caribbean audience. Much, however, of what appears outside the frame of the story at first, on a second reading comes to seem a necessary part of the context. One example is the repeated explanations of the color-caste system. A rigid stratification of opportunity bears directly on the narrow options Bita Plant has. As a member of the dark-skinned group, she can marry a black minister or teacher—these are the only two professions permitted the dark group—or she can marry a peasant. . . . (pp. 237-58)

Still another function of the panorama of rural culture is that it enables us, as Ramchand suggests, to "credit . . . [Bita's] fictional process" through its depiction of a community with "spontaneous values of its own." Ramchand also provides the key insight to link more directly the function of the physical and social setting with the main story line concerning Bita's reversion to the folk. He speaks of several "images of immersion associated with constitutive elements of village life or with the landscape" that "impress her belonging to Banana Bottom." Bita's "immersion" or merging with certain external scenes and events that connote peasant experience are used to register the shift in her psychological orientation. Typical of a novel of manners whose medium is external behavior and the social milieu, *Banana Bottom* does not rely heavily on direct notation of its heroine's inner life. It depends on dramatic action to suggest conflict and change; and to suggest the substance of change, it depends on scenes that immerse her in the overtones and shadows of the peasant world—scenes such as the crowded market where she feels "a reservoir of familiar kindred humanity into which she had descended for baptism"; such as her return to her girlhood swimming hole where she drifts naked "in perfect confidence" over a "yawning depth"; and scenes such as the one in which she has the "glowing" discovery of Belle Black and Hopping Dick making love in a hollow tree during pimento picking.

Both the tendency for religious fervor and a less inhibited attitude about sex are aspects of personality Bita must face alone once she leaves the discipline of the Free Church. She also must find the means to continue her intellectual development along the lines of rational skepticism she knew in college. When after her father's death, Bita marries Jubban, a man of "sureness and firmness" in his realm but without education or social development, Reverend Lambert accuses her of "burying her talent and education in the mud." Really, her choice signals a flowering of independence and freedom of judgment, the emergence, in the words of Pascal quoted in the text, of "true morality."

A final perspective of the idealism in McKay's novels can be obtained by comparing them with the Harlem stories in *Gingertown.* These stories reveal an altogether different side of McKay. In them he is a painstaking technician, a detached observer, a cool moralist. These stories evidence little or no authorial idealism in their conception of character or in their plots. There is neither the embrace of a bohemian life-style nor the consolidation of positive ethnic qualities along with a criticism of white civilization. With the possible exception of **"Truant,"** these stories of Harlem are conceived in the vein of naturalism. They are analytic and fatalistic. They reveal an abstemious removal of the author's personality and an undeviating objectivity. If there is any moral outrage, it is implicit. It is not part of the narrator's attitude, though it may be part of the writer's expectation for the reader.

Interestingly, this absence of moral engagement has the effect of freeing McKay to achieve a degree of technical proficiency that exists nowhere else in his fiction. The best story, **"Hiball,"** moves with a precision and clarity of purpose that makes one think of the fluid artistry and poignantly defined social contexts of Fitzgerald. Yet these stories—with the possible exception of **"Hiball"**—are not memorable works. They are minor studies, atomistic presentations of the effects of racial self-hatred on individual lives. The neutral point of view with which they are narrated may even add to their marginality, their lack of moral force or significance.

Critics have complained about Ray's frequent lectures in *Banjo;* they have also questioned the marital harmony Bita Plant is supposed to have achieved in *Banana Bottom* [see excerpt dated 1974]. Such instances of excess or of failure at verisimilitude are, I suppose, the regrettable occasional consequences of intense idealism in a novelist. Yet when placed beside the moral chilliness of the Harlem stories in *Gingertown,* these lapses strike me as pardonable. It is better to have an occasional blemished fruit than a barren tree.

Ultimately, though, it is not McKay's moral engagement that distinguishes him as a novelist. It is the manner in which his idealism works through his powers as a realist. It is his selection of areas of experience where black men and women are living autonomously and with racial integrity in the world; and it is his impulse to describe wholeness, not only self-division. His forceful pictures of life in Harlem, Marseilles, and the British West Indies are an important step in the history of black fiction. They enlarge our sense of the world, both for what it is and what it can be. (pp. 259-61)

Robert M. Greenberg, "Idealism and Realism in the Fiction of Claude McKay," in CLA Journal, *Vol. XXIV*, No. 3, March, 1981, pp. 237-61.

## Geta J. LeSeur (essay date 1989)

[*In the following excerpt, LeSeur discusses aspects of romanticism in McKay's poetry.*]

When McKay says [in his autobiography *A Long Way from Home*] that he used [Robert] Burns as a model, he is also suggesting a silent rebellion on the part of a West Indian youth. When he wrote poetry in the Jamaican Scottish dialect, he used Burns' Scottish dialect as a model. His first poems published in the dialect were *Songs of Jamaica* (1912) and *Constab Ballads* (1912). This was only the beginning of the sturdy independence and faithful affection he was to exercise throughout his life and writing career.

Allegiances and coalitions were goals visualized by Claude McKay. They are present in his autobiography, as a specific statement of purpose, and in his verse. Although a radical, he was a conservative poet, for his verse forms were traditional. The sonnet was his favorite, and he actually wrote most of his poems on the time-honored subjects of love and nature. Regardless of the fact that the writing tradition adopted by McKay was that of the romantic "movement" from his school days in Jamaica, it was not until he came to the United States in 1912 at age twenty-three that his best poetry-writing began. Max Eastman, his lifelong friend and editor of the *Liberator,* which he coedited, later said this of him:

> It was not until he came to the United States that Claude McKay began to confront the deepest feelings in his heart and realize that a delicate syllabic music could not alone express them. Here his imagination awoke, and the colored imagery that is the language of all deep passion began to appear in his poetry [Introduction to *Harlem Shadows*].

(p. 297)

McKay has said that, of the English models and schools of writing he has been associated with, it is the classicists and romantics that he admires, but he owes "allegiance to no master." He adds that he has used only that which he considered to be the best of the poets of all ages. The language used in his poetry was that derived from the Jamaican dialect, archaic words, and figures of speech, which are then reshaped to suit his specific purposes. The introductory pages ("Author's Word") to *Harlem Shadows* has been cited repeatedly by scholars, critics, and McKay's readers to justify or support theories regarding his poetry. The important information given in that short essay is that McKay thinks the traditional should work best on "lawless and revolutionary passions and words," so as to give the feeling of the "highest degree of spontaneity and freedom." "For me," he says, "there is more quiet delight in 'The golden moon of heaven' than in 'The terra-cotta disc of cloud land.'" The last quoted line here is ironically from a poem by one of the best-known Harlem Renaissance poets, Langston Hughes.

It is no accident that Claude McKay felt uncomfortable with the poetry and lifestyle of the New Negro Movement of the 1920s. He was never really a part of that whole milieu. He disagreed with their involvement with "art for art's sake" and with their being self-appointed messiahs to uplift the privileged few. Theirs was a tightly knit circle which excluded many. Because McKay's tendencies were more akin to the European tradition and experience, he was a misfit at a time when blackness was being celebrated. First, McKay's reading was Byron, Shelley, Keats, and the late Victorians. Secondly, his friends, personal and literary, were the whites in New York's suburbs and its downtown Greenwich Village. Thirdly, he was older than most of the Renaissance writers—Hughes, Cullen, Toomer, and others. And fourthly, he lived in Europe during most of the key Renaissance years. Consequently, for these reasons and more, he was, as Frank Harris of *Pearson's Magazine* noted, "an oddity, . . . a noble black poet with romantic intentions."

McKay felt a great tension between black content and traditional white form, and this, for him, was perhaps the hardest problem to solve. He grappled with the two as to where the thrust of his writing should be. He had been praised for producing poems which gave no hint of color. . . . The problem became a personal one of how to keep his allegiance to the British models—whose poetry he truly felt and knew well—and be a black poet emotionally. Writing poetry was not difficult for him, but what was difficult was the personae in conflict, the paradox of self which mars some of the poems.

Consequently, while McKay constantly preferred to keep the West Indian identity and the British training, he was conscious that nothing could change the fact that he was a writer who also happened to be a Negro. When told to mask his identity, and when in his novel *Banana Bottom* (1933) certain words were changed into "Britishisms," he became extremely angry and replied to his publishers and friends in this way:

> Of all the poets I admire, major and minor, Byron, Shelley, Keats, Blake, Burns, Whitman, Heine, Baudelaire, Verlaine and Rimbaud and the rest—it seemed to me that when I read them—in their poetry I could feel their race, their class, their roots in the soil, growing into plants, spreading and forming the background against which they were silhouetted. I could not feel the reality of them without that. So likewise I could not realize myself writing without that conviction.

Again, the problem of allegiance and coalition were surfaced to deal with these constant attempts to subjugate color to content. The natural and the creative became problematic also. McKay, regardless of all the places to which he traveled, realized that the artist's faith had to be in his origins, a patriotism as one might find in Whitman's America and in Yeats' Ireland. Furthermore, McKay's best poetry and prose were about Jamaica; as for him, the artist being inseparable from his roots would be an alien thought.

The title of his autobiography, *A Long Way from Home,*

is from a Negro spiritual, the opening line of which is "Sometimes I feel like a motherless child, a long way from home." The title, however, is not coincidental, and even though McKay never returned to Jamaica but chose American citizenship instead, the title is a misnomer because Jamaican memories permeate his best later writings. The poetry looks romantically to Jamaica and prophetically to blackness. His prophecy for Jamaica as an independent, Third World nation, for example, was fulfilled in the last two decades. *Spring in New Hampshire* (1920) and *The Selected Poems* (1953) have in them mostly nostalgic lyrics about Jamaica and songs celebrating nature, and they reflect those themes found in the nineteenth-century Romantics.

McKay's romanticism exhibits itself in several ways but primarily in his writing and lifestyle. His literary heroes were writers of conventional works, the sonnet his favorite mode of expression, but some of his poems are done in freer style. An example of the combination of Jamaican remembrance and celebration of nature in the less conventional style is **"Flame-Heart."**

> So much I have forgotten in ten years,
> So much in ten brief years! I have forgot
> What time the purple apples come to juice,
> And what month brings the shy forget-me-not.
> I have forgot the special, startling season
> Of the pimento's flowering and fruiting;
> What time of year the ground doves drown the fields
> And fill the noonday with their curious fluting.
> I have forgotten much, but still remember
> The poinsettia's red, blood-red, in warm December.

Many critics have lingered over the meaning of the last line, which also closes stanza II, but the intention here is only to show the poems as examples of the different aspects of McKay's romanticism. He has forgotten the cycles of the seasons, but the emotion of the poem is rich in West Indian images.

In **"The Spanish Needle"** McKay uses a more conventional pattern to write about a very common and wild weed in Jamaica by the same name. It is a plant much like a dandelion in America, but the language and tone which he uses in the poem make the Spanish needle become a regal plant; thus the common and everyday in the hands of a romantic like McKay becomes uncommon. The following verses of that poem show the endearment which he feels for the ordinary:

> Lovely dainty Spanish needle
> With your yellow flower and white,
> Dew bedecked and softly sweeping,
> Do you think of me to-night?
>
> Shadowed by the spreading mango,
> Nodding o'er the rippling stream,
> Tell me, dear plant of my childhood,
> Do you of the exile dream?
>
> Do you see me by the brook's side
> Catching crayfish 'neath the stone,
> As you did the day you whispered:
> Leave the harmless dears alone? . . .

This poem is very much in the romantic tradition of Shelley and Keats and is probably one of the few poems by McKay that every Jamaican schoolchild must recite "by heart." **"Home-Thoughts"** is one of his better poems with the homeland theme:

> Oh something just now must be happening there!
> That suddenly and quiveringly here,
> Amid the city's noises, I must think
> Of mangoes leaning o'er the river's brink,
> And dexterous Davie climbing high above,
> The gold fruits ebon-speckled to remove,
> And toss them quickly in the tangled mass
> Of wis-wis twisted round the guinea grass;
> And Cyril coming through the bramble-track
> A Prize bunch of bananas on his back;
>                 . . . . .
> This is no daytime dream, there's something in it,
> Oh something's happening there this very minute!

The use of local words like *mango, wis-wis, guinea grass, bramble track, purple apple, ground dove, pimento, pingwing, rose apple, poinsettia,* and *banana* in **"Flame-Heart,"** **"The Spanish Needle,"** and **"Home-Thoughts"** are entire images in themselves, and even without notes to explain their meanings and connotations, the mood, tone and theme of the poems are obvious. These poems all go back to the West Indian scene, and in them are found the similar conflicts and opposing attractions which plagued McKay throughout his lifetime. In them, also, joy and sorrow are accepted with the stoic indifference which was part of the romantic passion.

**"The Snow Fairy," "Spring in New Hampshire,"** and **"After the Winter"** use the same American seasonal landscape as their background. They too are good, have a simplicity of diction and tone, and are full of longing and passion, but they by no means compare with the lilting, spontaneous yet deep emotion of **"Tropics in New York."** In comparing a few lines from **"Spring in New Hampshire"** with **"The Tropics in New York,"** one can see that the differences are very obvious, not only because of the subject, but because of McKay's involvement with the places closest to his heart:

> Too green the springing April grass,
> Too blue the silver-speckled sky,
> For me to linger here, alas,
> While happy winds go laughing by,
> Wasting the golden hours indoors,
> Washing windows and scrubbing floors.

The weariness and tedium of scrubbing floors in spring is felt, while outdoors the enjoyment of nature passes. Rather than being happy in nature, there is sorrow because the speaker is physically removed from it but is mentally aware of its presence. He is a prisoner of circumstance. **"The Tropics in New York"** finds the speaker a prisoner also in a foreign country, but the nostalgia, though sorrowful, is much more lyrical, and he seems closer to this subject, and the poem is richer:

> Bananas ripe and green, and ginger-root,
> Cocoa in pods and alligator pears,

And tangerines and Mangoes and grape fruit,
Fit for the highest prize at parish fairs,

Set in the window, bringing memories
Of fruit-trees laden by low-singing rills,
And dewy dawns, and mystical blue skies
In benediction over nun-like hills.

My eyes grew dim, and I could no more gaze;
A wave of longing through my body swept,
And, hungry for the old, familiar ways,
I turned aside and bowed my head and wept.

McKay obviously is the speaker in this poem, although he speaks for the hundreds of West Indians who became exiles away from their homeland primarily because of economic and diplomatic reasons. The poem, therefore, does have a oneness of feeling about it. The alienation felt is one of time and distance, and the consequence and helplessness is clearly felt in the last three lines. The progression is from glorious song to despair. It is one of his most moving poems on this theme, and the experience, as in **"If We Must Die,"** is the universal black experience.

It is not in the poems only that Claude McKay's romantic nature is exhibited, but in his lifestyle and relationship with people and the world. He traveled to Russia, England, Spain, Germany, and Morocco, and he had romances singularly with each of them. The flirting with Communism was short-lived, and in England he was just another West Indian. Both experiences were disappointing because of the romantic notions he held about them. Burns, Keats, Wordsworth, and Shelley were dead, and prejudice was alive. Learning from those two short "romances," he tried to savor the best in all of the other countries which he visited and in which he lived. In Spain it was the romanticism of the bullfight and the world of Hemingway; in Germany and France it was the beautiful art and architecture. The despairing moments were overshadowed by the glorious experiences of the people he met and the new countrysides to sing about. Again, some of McKay's better writings were done in Europe. His best works were not about the New York, Jamaica, or American scenes while he was living in these places but when he was away from them. In Tangiers, Morocco, he felt at home more than at any other time in his life. In a letter to Max Eastman (1 December 1930) he wrote, "There are things in the life of the natives, their customs and superstitions reminiscent of Jamaica." And in another letter (1 September 1932) he stated, "My attachment to Tangiers is sort of a spiritual looking backwards."

McKay, therefore, seemed to have done his best work when he maintained a distance between himself and his subject. This in itself was not true of all romantic writers, but it is true of the romantic spirit for nostalgia, mysticism and fascination. About life McKay wrote to Eastman (28 July 1919):

> . . . life fascinates me in its passions. It may survive when everything else is dead and fused into it. I revere all those spirits who in their little (bit?) way are helping the life force to attain its wonderful and beautiful communication.

In the same letter he says, "I love your life more than your poetry, more than your personality. This is my attitude toward all artists."

It is apparent that McKay believes strongly in the nationality, personal identity, and uniqueness that each writer brings to his art. It is that special uniqueness which makes each one different and reinforces the sturdy independence of each human's nature. It was in Europe and elsewhere that he missed America most and in America that he reminisced about Jamaica consistently.

All poetry, McKay thought, should be judged by its own merits, not by categories of race and nationality. The double standard was something which he opposed, and this too was carried over into his lifestyle. Because he was a "foreign" Negro with white friends, the reality of racial prejudice and the embarrassing moments he experienced from whites and blacks left him torn. He wanted to be accepted, but the pain which nonacceptance brought others plagued him. He was not accepted by the blacks of the Harlem Renaissance group, and his friends were the white literati, not the black "Niggerati," as he called them. It is no wonder, then, that the romantic modes and distances worked best for McKay. Some of the most personal poems are about those experiences such as **"To the White Fiends"** and **"The White House."** The militancy and anger are there and very uncompromising. Regardless of this, it was the realm of "literary truth" with which McKay was most preoccupied. He spoke of and "defined" it in a letter to Eastman:

> I think that if the intellectual idea of literary truth were analyzed, it would prove at bottom to be nothing more than "a wise saying" or a "beautiful phrase" delivered in a unique and startling manner—an addition to the sum of the universal wisdom of mankind. Such a wisdom exists telling of the passions, the folly and the sagacity, success and failure, pain and joy of life. It existed long before modern science and I believe it will continue to exist as vigorous and independent as ever as long as humanity retains the facilities of feeling, thinking—the inexhaustible source of which great and authentic literature springs whether it is cerebral or sentimental, realistic or romantic.

The essence of McKay's romanticism was not only in his poetry, but in the life he lived, the places he visited, and the people and ideas he encountered. His daily vocabulary was very interestingly sprinkled with romantic asides, as was his autobiography, *A Long Way from Home,* and his letters to Max Eastman of *The Liberator.* In *A Long Way from Home,* the Pankhurst secretary is a "romantic middle class woman"; his radical days on *The Liberator* were "rosy with romance"; "The Wondervogel had lost their romantic flavor"; he mentions "D. H. Lawrence's psychic and romantic groping for a way out"; and he comments on the fact that "it was grand and romantic to have a grant to write." It is obvious that McKay was completely immersed in a romantic style of life very similar to that of some of his British models and contemporaries. A vocabulary interspersed with words carrying the romantic notion means that he consciously draws attention to where his allegiances to nature, life, and self lie. All of these coalesced to create poetry which said yes to life by its explicit philosophy.

Claude McKay has been called "Jamaica's Bobbie Burns," although he gave up that citizenship some twenty-eight years later. The land of his birth, Jamaica, about which he wrote his best prose, verse, and lyrics, still claims him as its citizen. The comparison with the Scottish Burns is by no means superficial, however, as there are many similarities in their writing and points-of-view. The romantics—Keats, Shelley, Wordsworth, Whitman, and Yeats—were also his literary heroes, because of the content of their works and the lifestyles which they led. It was, and still is, unusual to have a black man writing in the mode of the romantics, using their themes, subject matter, and meter. The two natures of self and art, of allegiance and coalition, were things for which McKay worked throughout his life and career. Regardless of his thoroughly British orientation, emotionally and literarily he never forgot his blackness. For a modern poet, the sonnet was his favorite form, and he wrote most of his poems on the time-honored subjects of love and nature. The universality of his romanticism and poetry surpasses color or time lines. (pp. 298-308)

> *Geta J. LeSeur, "Claude McKay's Romanticism," in* CLA Journal, Vol. XXXII, No. 3, *March, 1989, pp. 296-308.*

---

## FURTHER READING

Bone, Robert. "The Harlem School." In his *The Negro Novel in America,* rev. ed., pp. 65-94. New Haven, Conn.: Yale University Press, 1965.

    Examines McKay's novels within a discussion of other Harlem Renaissance writers.

Condit, John Hillyer. "An Urge Toward Wholeness: Claude McKay and His Sonnets." *CLA Journal* 22, No. 4 (June 1979): 350-64.

    Views McKay's works as displaying a conflict between his "proud individuality" and his desire for unity with the world outside himself, concluding that these conflicting impulses are reflected in his use of the sonnet form. Condit explains: "McKay might have realized that the strong sense of structure afforded by the demanding nature of the sonnet's metrical pattern and rhyme scheme would allow him to be his most passionate self without running amok."

Conroy, Sister Mary. "The Vagabond Motif in the Writings of Claude McKay." *Negro American Literature Forum* 5, No. 1 (Spring 1971): 15-23.

    Examines characters in McKay's works who are vagabonds in both a literal and symbolic sense, relating these figures to the author himself, whose lifelong "vagabondage" ended with his conversion to Roman Catholicism.

Cooper, Wayne F. *Claude McKay: Rebel Sojourner in the Harlem Renaissance.* Baton Rouge: Louisiana State University Press, 1987, 441 p.

    Comprehensive biography.

Du Bois, W. E. B. "The Browsing Reader." *The Crisis* 35, No. 6 (June 1928): 202, 211.

    Review of McKay's novel *Home to Harlem.* Du Bois vehemently disapproves of McKay's passionate and unrestrained characterizations of Harlemites.

Giles, James R. *Claude McKay.* Boston: Twayne Publishers, 1976, 170 p.

    Critical biography.

Hansell, William H. "Some Themes in the Jamaican Poetry of Claude McKay." *PHYLON* 40, No. 2 (June 1979): 123-39.

    Analyzes poems in *Songs of Jamaica* and *Constab Ballads,* discerning four thematic categories that recur throughout McKay's later works: "poems on commonplace settings and activities, love poems, poems portraying the peasant mind, and poems with racial or social themes."

Kent, George E. "The Soulful Way of Claude McKay." In his *Blackness and the Adventure of Western Culture,* pp. 36-52. Chicago: Third World Press, 1972.

    Presents McKay's personal and artistic achievements as pioneering efforts toward developing a group consciousness among black individuals in Western culture.

Nicholl, Louise Townsend. "A Negro Poet." *The Measure,* No. 17 (July 1922): 16-18.

    Appreciative review of McKay's poetry collection *Harlem Shadows.*

Ramchand, Kenneth. "The Road to *Banana Bottom.*" In his *The West Indian Novel and Its Background,* pp. 239-73. London: Heinemann, 1983.

    Biographical and critical essay focusing on McKay's three novels.

Redding, J. Saunders. "Emergence of the New Negro." In his *To Make a Poet Black,* pp. 93-125. College Park, Md.: McGrath Publishing Co., 1939.

    Historical perspective on writers of the Harlem Renaissance, characterizing McKay's poems as demonstrating "the proud defiance and independence that were the very heart of the New Negro movement."

Story, Ralph D. "Patronage and the Harlem Renaissance: You Get What You Pay For." *CLA Journal* 32, No. 3 (March 1989): 284-95.

    Discusses McKay's position among other Harlem Renaissance figures, focusing on the role of white patrons in the careers of major artists and writers of the movement.

Wagner, Jean. "Claude McKay." In his *Black Poets of the United States: From Paul Laurence Dunbar to Langston Hughes,* translated by Kenneth Douglas, pp. 197-257. Urbana, Ill.: University of Illinois Press, 1962.

    Overview of McKay's poetry.

# Oscar Wilde

## 1854-1900

(Full name Oscar Fingal O'Flahertie Wills Wilde) Anglo-Irish dramatist, novelist, essayist, short story writer, critic, and poet.

The following entry presents criticism of Wilde's novel *The Picture of Dorian Gray,* first published in the periodical *Lippincott's Monthly Magazine* in 1890 and revised for book publication in 1891. For discussion of Wilde's complete career, see *TCLC,* Volumes 1 and 8; for discussion of his drama *The Importance of Being Earnest,* see *TCLC,* Volume 23.

Wilde was one of the foremost figures of late nineteenth-century literary Decadence, and *The Picture of Dorian Gray* is considered the most representative prose work of English Decadent literature. The English Decadents were a loosely affiliated coterie of writers and artists of the 1890s whose lives and works manifested a highly stylized, decorative manner, a fascination with morbidity and perversity, and adherence to the doctrine of "art for art's sake," which sought to eliminate moral, didactic, and social concerns in art. Exemplifying Decadent style and themes, *Dorian Gray* tells in elaborate, ornamental prose the story of a young man who becomes corrupt in his pursuit of experience. In evident fulfillment of his impulsive wish that he remain young and a painted portrait of himself grow old, Dorian retains his youthful attractiveness while signs of age and debauchery appear in the portrait. *Dorian Gray* created a sensation on its appearance, when it was widely interpreted as advocating the immoral behavior of its eponymous protagonist, and the relationship between morality and art—a topic of debate in English letters since the mid–nineteenth-century advent of a cult of aestheticism, promulgated by Algernon Swinburne, Walter Pater, and the Pre-Raphaelite painters and writers—was addressed with renewed fervor in the English literary press.

As a student at Trinity College in Dublin and later at Oxford University, Wilde had been influenced by the writings of Pater, who in his *Studies in the History of the Renaissance* (1873) urged indulgence of the senses, a search for sustained intensity of experience, and stylistic perfectionism in art. Wilde adopted such aestheticism as a way of life, cultivating an extravagant persona that was burlesqued in the popular press and music-hall entertainments, copied by other youthful iconoclasts, and indulged by the avant-garde literary and artistic circles of London wherein Wilde was renowned for intelligence, wit, and personal charm. *The Picture of Dorian Gray,* his only novel, was published during a period of great creativity and productivity for Wilde that extended from 1888 to 1895. Most of his highly regarded critical essays, later collected in *Intentions* (1891), as well as his best short fiction, subsequently gathered in *Lord Arthur Savile's Crime, and Other Stories* (1891), had already appeared. After *Dorian*

*Gray* was published to considerable controversy, Wilde attained the greatest critical and popular success of his lifetime with the plays *Lady Windermere's Fan* (1892), *A Woman of No Importance* (1893), *An Ideal Husband* (1895), and *The Importance of Being Earnest* (1895). These stylized, well-made comedies of manners, sparkling with wit and abounding with quotable epigrams, are considered his crowning achievement. *The Importance of Being Earnest* was in production at the time of Wilde's 1895 trial on charges of "gross indecency between male persons." His conviction and subsequent imprisonment led to ignominy for Wilde and obscurity for his works. At the time of his death in 1900 the scandal associated with Wilde led most commentators to discuss him diffidently, if at all. While critical response no longer focuses so persistently on questions of morality, Wilde's life and personality still arouse fascination. Biographical studies and biographically oriented criticism continue to dominate Wilde scholarship.

*The Picture of Dorian Gray* opens with the painter Basil Hallward completing a portrait of Dorian Gray, a young man of aristocratic background, engaging personality, and intellectual vapidity, to whom Hallward is devoted. Lord

Henry Wotton, a friend of Hallward, is also attracted to Dorian and persuades the youth to take up a life of sensual indulgence. On viewing the finished painting, Dorian for the first time recognizes his own physical appeal and, convinced by Wotton of the supremacy of corporeal beauty, expresses his longing to be spared the ravages of time. For the next eighteen years Dorian seeks pleasure and experience under Wotton's tutelage. He effects the unspecified "ruin" of a number of lives, acquires and revels in rare, beautiful, and costly objects, experiments with drugs and alcohol, and finally commits murder. During this time the portrait, hidden from view in Dorian's attic, mysteriously ages and becomes repulsive, reflecting the effects of Dorian's excesses, while Dorian himself remains unchanged. His ultimate attempt to destroy the painting results in his own death; the portrait then resumes its original appearance, and the hideous corpse found lying before it is only with difficulty identified as that of Dorian Gray.

Critical outrage greeted the initial appearance of *The Picture of Dorian Gray* in *Lippincott's Monthly Magazine*. Reviewers castigated the work and Wilde alike, questioning Wilde's motives in choosing such subject matter and attributing depravity to the novelist who portrayed transgressions and transgressors so alluringly. In letters to the publications that had reviewed *Dorian Gray*, Wilde responded to charges of immorality, correcting critical misapprehensions and offering explications of his work. He insisted that the novel had a moral: "All excess, as well as all renunciation, brings its punishment. . . . Yes, there is a terrible moral in *Dorian Gray*—a moral which the prurient will not be able to find in it, but which will be revealed to all whose minds are healthy." With characteristic paradox Wilde contended that the obviousness of the moral element of his novel was its only fault and announced that he intended to correct this perceived flaw when he revised the novel for book publication in 1891.

*The Picture of Dorian Gray* did not arouse wide critical notice on its appearance in book form, perhaps because reviewers were unaware that the novel had undergone significant change. For the 1891 edition Wilde rewrote portions of the story, added six chapters to the original fourteen, and appended a celebrated preface. These changes increase the scope and depth of the novel's second half, focusing on Dorian's mature experience, and de-emphasize the implication of homosexual relationships between the central characters. This aspect of the novel, portrayed fairly explicitly in the magazine version, probably accounted for some of the intensity of the initial reaction against it. The preface was composed of aphorisms on the role of art, the artist, and the critic. Such precepts as "Those who find ugly meanings in beautiful things are corrupt without being charming. This is a fault," and "All art is quite useless" were probably intended to provoke those who had condemned the novel on moral grounds. Wilde did not, however, alter the fate that befalls his protagonist and seemingly denotes a retributive moral to the story.

The passage of time and changes in conventional morality have led to more balanced critical assessments of Wilde than were possible during his lifetime and at the time of his death, when the scandal associated with him overshad-

owed other considerations. The subject of extensive analysis, *The Picture of Dorian Gray* has been assessed as a moral fable, a Gothic horror tale, a catalog of Decadent concerns owing much to Joris-Karl Huysmans's *A rebours* (1884; *Against the Grain*), a study of Victorian art movements, and a fictional dramatization of Paternian ideas about art and morality. It is often assumed to have an autobiographical base, and many biographical explications of the novel refer to Wilde's statement in a letter of February 1894 that *Dorian Gray* "contains much of me in it. Basil Hallward is what I think I am: Lord Henry what the world thinks me: Dorian what I would like to be—in other ages, perhaps." *Dorian Gray* continues to attract a wide range of readers and commentators who are drawn to the compelling story, the vivid evocation of fin de siècle London society, and the glittering demimonde in which Dorian moved, as well as Wilde's consummate narrative artistry.

(See also *Contemporary Authors*, Vols. 104 and 119; *Dictionary of Literary Biography*, Vols. 10, 19, 34, and 57; and *Something about the Author*, Vol. 24.)

---

## Daily Chronicle    (essay date 1890)

[*In the following review, which was originally published June 30, 1890, the critic condemns the perceived hedonistic moral of* The Picture of Dorian Gray.]

Dulness and dirt are the chief features of *Lippincott's* this month. The element in it that is unclean, though undeniably amusing, is furnished by Mr Oscar Wilde's story of **The Picture of Dorian Gray.** It is a tale spawned from the leprous literature of the French *Décadents*—a poisonous book, the atmosphere of which is heavy with the metaphitic odours of moral and spiritual putrefaction—a gloating study of the mental and physical corruption of a fresh, fair and golden youth, which might be horrible and fascinating but for its effeminate frivolity, its studied insincerity, its theatrical cynicism, its tawdry mysticism, its flippant philosophisings, and the contaminating trail of garish vulgarity which is over all Mr Wilde's elaborate Wardour Street æstheticism and obtrusively cheap scholarship.

Mr Wilde says his book has 'a moral.' The 'moral,' so far as we can collect it, is that man's chief end is to develop his nature to the fullest by 'always searching for new sensations,' that when the soul gets sick the way to cure it is to deny the senses nothing, for 'nothing,' says one of Mr Wilde's characters, Lord Henry Wotton, 'can cure the soul but the senses, just as nothing can cure the senses but the soul.' Man is half angel and half ape, and Mr Wilde's book has no real use if it be not to inculate the 'moral' that when you feel yourself becoming too angelic you cannot do better than rush out and make a beast of yourself. There is not a single good and holy impulse of human nature, scarcely a fine feeling or instinct that civilisation, art, and religion have developed throughout the ages as part of the barriers between Humanity and Animalism that is not held up to ridicule and contempt in **Dorian Gray,** if, indeed, such strong words can be fitly applied to the actual effect of Mr Wilde's airy levity and fluent impudence. His desperate effort to vamp up a 'moral' for the book at the end is, artistically speaking, coarse and crude, because the whole incident of Dorian Gray's death is, as they say on the stage, 'out of the picture.' Dorian's only regret is that unbridled indulgence in every form of secret and unspeakable vice, every resource of luxury and art, and sometimes still more piquant to the jaded young man of fashion, whose lives 'Dorian Gray' pretends to sketch, by every abomination of vulgarity and squalor is—what? Why, that it will leave traces of premature age and loathsome sensualness on his pretty face, rosy with the loveliness that endeared youth of his odious type to the paralytic patricians of the Lower Empire.

Dorian Gray prays that a portrait of himself which an artist, who raves about him as young men do about the women they love not wisely but too well, has painted may grow old instead of the original. This is what happens by some supernatural agency, the introduction of which seems purely farcical, so that Dorian goes on enjoying unfading youth year after year, and might go on for ever using his senses with impunity 'to cure his soul,' defiling English society with the moral pestilence which is incarnate in him, but for one thing. That is his sudden impulse not merely to murder the painter—which might be artistically defended on the plea that it is only a fresh development of his scheme for realising every phase of life-experience—but to rip up the canvas in a rage, merely because, though he had permitted himself to do one good action, it had not made his portrait less hideous. But all this is inconsistent with Dorian Gray's cool, calculating, conscienceless character, evolved logically enough by Mr Wilde's 'New Hedonism.'

Then Mr Wilde finishes his story by saying that on hearing a heavy fall Dorian Gray's servants rushed in, found the portrait on the wall as youthful looking as ever, its senile ugliness being transferred to the foul profligate himself, who is lying on the floor stabbed to the heart. This is a sham moral, as indeed everything in the book is a sham, except the one element in the book which will taint every young mind that comes in contact with it. That element is shockingly real, and it is the plausibly insinuated defence of the creed that appeals to the senses 'to cure the soul' whenever the spiritual nature of man suffers from too much purity and self-denial. (pp. 72-3)

*An excerpt from* Oscar Wilde: The Critical Heritage, *edited by Karl Beckson, Barnes & Noble, Inc., 1970, pp. 72-3.*

### Oscar Wilde    (essay date 1890)

[*In the following letter, Wilde replies to the anonymous* Daily Chronicle *review (see essay above), insisting that* The Picture of Dorian Gray *has an implied moral that was misunderstood by the reviewer: "that all excess, as well as all renunciation, brings its punishment."*]

Sir, Will you allow me to correct some errors into which your critic has fallen in his review of my story, **The Picture of Dorian Gray,** published in today's issue of your paper?

Your critic states, to begin with, that I make desperate attempts to "vamp up" a moral in my story. Now, I must candidly confess that I do not know what "vamping" is. I see, from time to time, mysterious advertisements in the newspapers about "How to Vamp," but what vamping really means remains a mystery to me—a mystery that, like all other mysteries, I hope some day to explore.

However, I do not propose to discuss the absurd terms used by modern journalism. What I want to say is that, so far from wishing to emphasise any moral in my story, the real trouble I experienced in writing the story was that of keeping the extremely obvious moral subordinate to the artistic and dramatic effect.

When I first conceived the idea of a young man selling his soul in exchange for eternal youth—an idea that is old in the history of literature, but to which I have given new form—I felt that, from an aesthetic point of view, it would be difficult to keep the moral in its proper secondary place; and even now I do not feel quite sure that I have been able to do so. I think the moral too apparent. When the book is published in a volume I hope to correct this defect.

As for what the moral is, your critic states that it is this— that when a man feels himself becoming "too angelic" he should rush out and make a "beast of himself!" I cannot say that I consider this a moral. The real moral of the story is that all excess, as well as all renunciation, brings its punishment, and this moral is so far artistically and deliberately suppressed that it does not enunciate its law as a general principle, but realises itself purely in the lives of individuals, and so becomes simply a dramatic element in a work of art, and not the object of the work of art itself.

Your critic also falls into error when he says that Dorian Gray, having a "cool, calculating, conscienceless character," was inconsistent when he destroyed the picture of his own soul, on the ground that the picture did not become less hideous after he had done what, in his vanity, he had considered his first good action. Dorian Gray has not got a cool, calculating, conscienceless character at all. On the contrary, he is extremely impulsive, absurdly romantic, and is haunted all through his life by an exaggerated sense of conscience which mars his pleasures for him and warns him that youth and enjoyment are not everything in the world. It is finally to get rid of the conscience that had dogged his steps from year to year that he destroys the picture; and thus in his attempt to kill conscience Dorian Gray kills himself.

Your critic then talks about "obtrusively cheap scholarship." Now, whatever a scholar writes is sure to display scholarship in the distinction of style and the fine use of language; but my story contains no learned or pseudo-learned discussions, and the only literary books that it alludes to are books that any fairly educated reader may be supposed to be acquainted with, such as the *Satyricon* of Petronius Arbiter, or Gautier's *Emaux et camées.* Such books as Alphonso's *Clericalis disciplina* belong not to culture, but to curiosity. Anybody may be excused for not knowing them.

Finally, let me say this—the aesthetic movement produced certain colours, subtle in their loveliness and fascinating in their almost mystical tone. They were, and are, our reaction against the crude primaries of a doubtless more respectable but certainly less cultivated age. My story is an essay on decorative art. It reacts against the crude brutality of plain realism. It is poisonous if you like, but you cannot deny that it is also perfect, and perfection is what we artists aim at. (pp. 263-64)

> Oscar Wilde, in a letter to the Editor of the Daily Chronicle on June 30, 1890, in his The Letters of Oscar Wilde, edited by Rupert Hart-Davis, Harcourt Brace Jovanovich, 1962, pp. 263-64.

## Julian Hawthorne    (essay date 1890)

[*Hawthorne, the son of the celebrated American author Nathaniel Hawthorne, was himself a journalist, critic, and author of popular romantic novels. He also wrote a highly respected biography of his father,* Nathaniel Hawthorne and His Wife *(1885). In the following excerpt from a review that originally appeared in* Lippincott's Monthly Magazine *in September 1890, Hawthorne commends the originality of* The Picture of Dorian Gray, *although he faults Wilde's portrayal of the title character.*]

Mr Oscar Wilde, the apostle of beauty, has in the July number of *Lippincott's Magazine* a novel or romance (it partakes of the qualities of both), which everybody will want to read. It is a story strange in conception, strong in interest, and fitted with a tragic and ghastly climax. Like many stories of its class, it is open to more than one interpretation; and there are, doubtless, critics who will deny that it has any meaning at all. It is, at all events, a salutary departure from the ordinary English novel, with the hero and heroine of different social stations, the predatory black sheep, the curate, the settlements, and Society. Mr Wilde, as we all know, is a gentleman of an original and audacious turn of mind, and the commonplace is scarcely possible to him. Besides, his advocacy of novel ideas in life, art, dress, and demeanour had led us to expect surprising things from him; and in this literary age it is agreed that a man may best show the best there is in him by writing a book. Those who read Mr Wilde's story in the hope of finding in it some compact and final statement of his theories of life and manners will be satisfied in some respects, and dissatisfied in others; but not many will deny that the book is a remarkable one, and would attract attention even had it appeared without the author's name on the title page.

*The Picture of Dorian Gray* begins to show its quality in the opening pages. Mr Wilde's writing has what is called 'colour,'—the quality that forms the mainstay of many of Ouïda's works,—and it appears in the sensuous descriptions of nature and of the decorations and environments of the artistic life. The general aspect of the characters and the tenor of their conversation remind one a little of *Vivian Gray* (sic) and a little of *Pelham,* but the resemblance does not go far: Mr Wilde's objects and philosophy are different from those of either Disraeli or Bulwer. Meanwhile his tal-

ent for aphorisms and epigrams may fairly be compared with theirs: some of his clever sayings are more than clever,—they show real insight and a comprehensive grasp. Their wit is generally cynical; but they are put into the mouth of one of the characters, Lord Harry, and Mr Wilde himself refrains from definitely committing himself to them; though one cannot help suspecting that Mr Wilde regards Lord Harry as being an uncommonly able fellow. Be that as it may, Lord Harry plays the part of Old Harry in the story, and lives to witness the destruction of every other person in it. He may be taken as an imaginative type of all that is most evil and most refined in modern civilisation,—a charming, gentle, witty, euphemistic Mephistopheles, who deprecates the vulgarity of goodness, and muses aloud about 'those renunciations that men have unwisely called virtue, and those natural rebellions that wise men still call sin.' Upon the whole, Lord Harry is the most ably portrayed character in the book, though not the most original in conception. Dorian Gray himself is as nearly a new idea in fiction as one has nowadays a right to expect. If he had been adequately realised and worked out, Mr Wilde's first novel would have been remembered after more meritorious ones were forgotten. But, even as 'nemo repente fuit turpissimus' ['no one ever became evil overnight'], so no one, or hardly any one, creates a thoroughly original figure at a first essay. Dorian never quite solidifies. In fact, his portrait is rather the more real thing of the two. . . . (pp. 79-80)

> Julian Hawthorne, in an extract from Oscar Wilde: The Critical Heritage, edited by Karl Beckson, Barnes & Noble, Inc., 1970, pp. 79-80.

## H. Montgomery Hyde    (essay date 1963)

[*Hyde, an Irish legislator, editor, and critic, has written extensively on legal matters and is the author of three books about Wilde:* The Trials of Oscar Wilde *(1948; rev. ed., 1963),* Oscar Wilde: The Aftermath *(1963), and* Oscar Wilde: A Biography *(1975). In April 1895 Wilde brought charges of libel against John Sholto Douglas, the Marquess of Queensberry, who had sought to prevent Wilde's association with his son, Lord Alfred Douglas. After a series of unpleasant encounters, Queensberry left a calling card for Wilde inscribed "For Oscar Wilde posing as somdomite" (sic). At Queensberry's trial, his leading counsel, Edward Henry Carson, quoted from Wilde's published works in an attempt to prove that Wilde had adopted a pose of homosexuality, rendering the charges of libel unfounded. Queensberry was acquitted, and Wilde was subsequently found guilty of "gross indecency between male persons" and sentenced to two years of hard labor. In the following excerpt from Hyde's account of Queensberry's trial, Carson offers an interpretation of* The Picture of Dorian Gray *as a perverted and immoral book and suggests that Wilde had experienced some of the situations and feelings of questionable morality portrayed in the novel.*]

Carson suggested that owing to certain criticisms which had been made [*The Picture of Dorian Gray*] was modified a good deal before its publication in book form. This was denied by Wilde, though he admitted that additions had been made. 'In one case', he said, 'it was pointed out to me—not in a newspaper or anything of that sort, but by the only critic of the century whose opinion I set high, Mr Walter Pater—that a certain passage was liable to misconstruction, and I made an addition.'

A characteristic piece of verbal sparring followed, which Carson began by reading a couple of short sentences from the Introduction to **Dorian Gray.**

' "There is no such thing as a moral or an immoral book. Books are well written or badly written." That expresses your view?'

'My view on art, yes.'

'Then I take it, no matter how immoral a book may be, if it is well written, it is, in your opinion, a good book?'

'Yes, if it were well written so as to produce a sense of beauty, which is the highest sense of which a human being can be capable. If it were badly written, it would produce a sense of disgust.'

'Then a well-written book putting forward perverted moral views may be a good book?'

'No work of art ever puts forward views. Views belong to people who are not artists.'

'A perverted novel might be a good book?' Carson persisted.

'I don't know what you mean by a "perverted" novel,' Wilde answered crisply.

This gave Carson the opening he sought. 'Then I will suggest **Dorian Gray** is open to the interpretation of being such a novel?'

Wilde brushed aside the suggestion with contempt. 'That could only be to brutes and illiterates,' he said. 'The views of Philistines on art are unaccountable.'

'An illiterate person reading **Dorian Gray** might consider it such a novel?'

'The views of illiterates on art are unaccountable. I am concerned only with my own view of art. I don't care twopence what other people think of it.'

'The majority of persons come under your definition of Philistines and illiterates?'

'I have found wonderful exceptions.'

'Do you think that the majority of people live up to the position you are giving us?'

'I am afraid they are not cultivated enough.'

'Not cultivated enough to draw the distinction between a good book and a bad book?' The note of sarcasm in Carson's voice was unmistakable.

'Certainly not,' Wilde replied blandly.

'The affection and love of the artist of **Dorian Gray** might lead an ordinary individual to believe that it might have a certain tendency?'

'I have no knowledge of the views of ordinary individuals.'

'You did not prevent the ordinary individual from buying your book?'

'I have never discouraged him!'

Counsel now proceeded to read out several lengthy passages from this work, which he put to the witness. He began with the description given by the painter, Basil Hallward, of his first meeting Dorian Gray and the impression the encounter made upon him.

> When our eyes met, I felt I was growing pale. A curious instinct of terror came over me. I knew that I had come face to face with someone whose mere personality was so fascinating that, if I allowed it to do so, it would absorb my whole nature, my whole soul, my very art itself. . . . He is all my art to me now. . . . You remember that landscape of mine, for which Agnew offered me such a huge price, but which I would not part with? It is one of the best things I have ever done. And why is it so? Because, while I was painting it, Dorian Gray sat beside me.

'Now I ask you, Mr Wilde, do you consider that that description of the feeling of one man towards a youth just grown-up was a proper or an improper feeling?'

'I think it is the most perfect description of what an artist would feel on meeting a beautiful personality that was in some way necessary to his art and life.'

'You think that is a feeling a young man should have towards another?'

'Yes, as an artist.'

The next passage was of a conversation between the painter and Dorian Gray, in which Basil Hallward declared his admiration for the younger man. When Carson began to read it, Wilde asked for a copy which he could follow, and he was given one of *Lippincott's*. 'I believe it was left out in the purged edition,' Carson remarked, in drawing Wilde's attention to the place.

'I do not call it purged.'

'Yes, I know that. But we will see.'

Carson continued reading:

> It is quite true that I have worshipped you with far more romance of feeling than a man usually gives to a friend. Somehow, I have never loved a woman. I suppose I never had time. . . . Well, from the moment I met you, your personality had the most extraordinary influence over me. I quite admit that I adored you madly, extravagantly, absurdly. I wanted to have you all to myself. I was only happy when I was with you. When I was away from you, you were still present in my art. It was all wrong and foolish. It is all wrong and foolish still. . . . One day I determined to paint a wonderful portrait of you. It was to have been my masterpiece. It is my masterpiece. But, as I worked at it, every flake and film of colour seemed to me to reveal my secret. I grew afraid that the world would know of my idolatry. . . .

'Do you mean to say that that passage describes the natural feeling of one man towards another?'

'It would be the influence produced by a beautiful personality.'

'A beautiful person?'

'I said "a beautiful personality". You can describe it as you like. Dorian Gray's was a most remarkable personality.'

'May I take it that you, as an artist, have never known the feeling described here?'

'I have never allowed any personality to dominate my art.'

'Then you have never known the feeling you described?'

'No. It is a work of fiction.'

'So far as you are concerned, you have no experience as to its being a natural feeling?'

'I think it is perfectly natural for any artist to admire intensely and love a young man. It is an incident in the life of almost any artist.'

'But let us go over it phrase by phrase,' said Carson, glancing down at the magazine in his hand. ' "I quite admit that I adored you madly." What do you say to that? Have you ever adored a young man madly?'

'No, not madly,' Wilde answered without thinking. 'I prefer love—that is, a higher form . . . '

'Never mind about that,' Carson interrupted. 'Let us keep down to the level we are at now.'

'I have never given adoration to anybody except myself.'

'I suppose you think that a very smart thing?' said Carson, when the laughter which greeted this sally had subsided.

'Not at all,' replied Wilde, who seemed to be almost enjoying this part of Carson's cross-examination.

'Then you have never had that feeling?'

'No. The whole idea was borrowed from Shakespeare, I regret to say—yes, from Shakespeare's sonnets.'

This answer immediately put Carson on to another line of questioning. 'I believe you have written an article to show that Shakespeare's sonnets were suggestive of unnatural vice?'

'On the contrary, I have written an article to show that they are not. I objected to such a perversion being put upon Shakespeare.'

This reply appeared to satisfy Carson, as he returned to his reading of **Dorian Gray.** ' " I have adored you extravagantly." ' He repeated the sentence in a tone of disgust.

'Do you mean financially?' Wilde queried.

'Oh, yes, financially! Do you think we are talking about finance?'

'I don't know what you are talking about,' said Wilde, attempting once more to be smart at Carson's expense.

'Don't you?' There was a grim look in Carson's face as he spoke to this irritating and self-assured witness. 'Well, I hope I shall make myself very plain before I have done.'

' "I was jealous of every one to whom you spoke." ' Carson went on reading. 'Have you ever been jealous of a young man?'

'Never in my life.'

' "I wanted to have you all to myself." Did you ever have that feeling?'

'No. I should consider it an intense nusiance, an intense bore.'

' "I grew afraid that the world would know of my idolatry." Why should he grow afraid that the world should know of it?'

'Because there are people in the world who cannot understand the intense devotion, affection, and admiration that an artist can feel for a wonderful and beautiful personality. These are the conditions under which we live. I regret them.'

'These unfortunate people, that have not the high understanding that you have, might put it down to something wrong?'

Carson's sarcasm left Wilde unmoved. 'Undoubtedly,' he agreed with his cross-examiner; 'to any point they chose. I am not concerned with the ignorance of others.'

Carson then mentioned a certain book in the story which Dorian Gray had received.

'Was the book to which you refer a moral book?'

'Not well written, but it gave me an idea.'

'Was the book you have in mind of a certain tendency?'

'I decline to be cross-examined upon the work of another artist. It is an impertinence and a vulgarity.'

On being further pressed on the point, Wilde admitted that the book he had in mind in the particular passage was a French novel by J. K. Huysmans, entitled *A rebours.* But when Carson persisted in his attempts to elicit the witness's view as to the morality of this work, Sir Edward Clarke appealed to the judge, who ruled against any further reference to it. [Hyde adds in a footnote that '*A rebours* was first published in 1884. "It was a novel without a plot," wrote Wilde in the passage alluded to by Carson, "and with only one character, being, indeed, simply a psychological study of a certain young Parisian, who spent his life trying to realize in the nineteenth century all the passions and modes of thought that belonged to every century except his own, and to sum up, as it were, in himself the various modes through which the world-spirit had ever passed, loving for their mere artificiality those renunciations that men have unwisely called virtue, as much as those natural rebellions that wise men call sin".']

The last passage which Carson read from Wilde's book described the painter's remonstration with Dorian Gray about his 'infamous reputation' and the fact that he had ruined the lives of several other men, including one who had committed suicide and another who had been obliged to leave England 'with a tarnished name'. Carson then asked Wilde whether this passage did not suggest a charge of 'unnatural vice'. Wilde admitted that it described Dorian Gray as a man of very corrupt influence, though there was no statement as to the nature of the influence, 'But as a matter of fact,' he added, 'I do not think that one person influences another, nor do I think there is any bad influence in the world.'

'A man never corrupts a youth?'

'I think not.'

'Nothing could corrupt him?'

'If you are talking of separate ages—'

'No, sir,' Carson broke in harshly. 'I am talking common sense.'

Wilde kept his temper, as he replied: 'I do not think one person influences another.'

'You don't think flattering a young man, making love to him, in fact, would be likely to corrupt him?'

'No,' Wilde replied emphatically. (pp. 109-15)

> *H. Montgomery Hyde, in his* The Trials of Oscar Wilde, *Dover Publications, Inc., 1973, 366 p.*

### Epifanio San Juan, Jr.   (essay date 1967)

[*San Juan is a Philippine-born American poet and critic. In the following excerpt, he considers the importance of the portrait as the central image in* The Picture of Dorian Gray.]

When *The Picture of Dorian Gray* appeared in 1891, the general reaction showed the widening split between the "nonconforming" artist and the reader. While Pater singled out the "really alive quality" of the dialogue, and Yeats praised it as "a wonderful book," the outraged comments in the newspapers vehemently decried the work's "immoral" message. The common reader was still addicted to the search for inspiring messages. And when he got something quite alien to his conventional expectations, his response naturally took a uniform crudeness:

> dulness and dirt . . . unclean. . . . It is a tale spawned from the leprous literature of the French Decadents—a poisonous book, the atmosphere of which is heavy with the mephitic odours of moral and spiritual putrefaction [see *Daily Chronicle* excerpt dated 1890].

Who were the French Decadents alluded to? Certainly not the chaste Mallarmé, who exulted in Wilde's novel: "une rêverie essentielle et des parfums d'âme les plus étranges s'est fait son orage. Redevenir poignant à travers l'inouï raffinement d'intellect, et humain, et unie pareille perverse atmosphère de beauté, est un miracle que vous accomplissez et selon quel emploi de tous les arts de l'écrivain! . . . Ce portrait en pied, inquiétant, d'un Dorian Gray, hantera, mais écrit, étant devenu livre lui-même." ["from an inner revery and the strangest perfumes of the soul it stirs up a storm. To make it poignant again, amid the outrageous refinement of intellect, and human as well, in so perverse an atmosphere of beauty, is a miracle that you bring about, and necessarily by all the writer's arts! . . . This full-length disquieting portrait of a Dorian Gray will haunt, but by virtue of being written, has itself become a book." The translation of the passage from Mallarmé is taken from Richard Ellmann's 1988 biography *Oscar Wilde* (see Further Reading).] Mallarmé gives us a clue toward a larger comprehension of the novel than has hitherto been accorded to it. This pertains to his conception of the central image of the story, Dorian's immutable portrait, as having become ultimately the whole book itself.

It is precisely through this picture of a permanent youth, an image objectifying the inner motivation of the major characters, that Wilde successfully integrates the formal elements of his narrative. His narrative acquires focus by a style which the picture itself announces. For at the end, the picture "the monstrous soul life," suffers a change only when Dorian himself, by an act of slaying what it embodies in idea, also renounces his fidelity to what it has always stood for.

The portrait, not Dorian Gray, emerges finally as the authentic hero. After all it is not life but art that inspires Dorian as well as Basil Hallward and, indirectly, Lord Henry. Just as Basil directs his passion from the flesh and blood youth to his painting, from person to artifice, so Dorian responds only to the actress in Sibyl rather than to her daylight personality. Dorian is enraptured by personae, by masks, and not by persons. Thus, when Sibyl forsakes acting and surrenders herself to emotional possession, she loses Dorian's love: his hate virtually kills her. (Similarly, Wilde in real life adored the "eternal feminine" as incarnated by actresses and acquaintances like Ellen Terry, Lily Langtry, Sarah Bernhardt, or by his fictitious women.) Dorian's decision to marry Sibyl is therefore a betrayal of his true nature; in the cult of immoralism, the good may be found by acting in harmony with one's innermost self.

When Dorian first beholds his portrait, "the sense of his own beauty came on him like a revelation." In Dorian's wish, a narcissistic motif appears for the first time: "If it were I who was to be always young, and the picture that was to grow old. For that—for that—I would give everything! . . . I would give my soul for that!" By grace of the omniscient point of view, Dorian's wish spins out its own realization. The novel is a fulfillment of this wish; it is the bridge that joins the conditional mood and the declarative mood. Dorian's wish functions as the germ of the plot; it impels episodes and invents details of scene, description, and summary. It lays out the background of the Dorian-Lord Henry-Basil Hallward complex. It indirectly causes Dorian's disillusionment with Sibyl. When Basil comes to see and borrow the picture, Dorian is tempted by some perverse imp of the unconscious to kill the painter. This murder leads to dissipation, opium dens, and the infernal labyrinth of the concluding chapters, until finally we attend Dorian's ascent to the chamber where the deeds of the past, memory, and the remorse of the present converge, pushing Dorian to affirm his will to reconciliation through death.

Such is the skeleton outline of the narrative. There are actually two parts to the basic action concerning the nature and destiny of Dorian's character: the first part before Chapter XI, which consists of the exposition (I-III) and the Sibyl-Dorian relation (IV-X); the second part after Chapter XI, which includes the climactic murder of Basil, Jim Vane's death, and the resolution (XII-XX). Despite the heavy rhetoric, the "purple" saturation, and the verbal embroidery in the manner of Huysmans' *A rebours* in Chapter XI, the plot as a sequence of beginning, middle, and end is clearly discernible.

Wilde himself calls this novel an "essay on decorative art," "all conversation and no action." He confesses: "I can't describe action. My people sit in chairs and chatter." These assertions render suspect the notion of **Dorian Gray** as a novel in the usual sense of a series of incidents arranged so as to produce a single concentrated effect. Chapter XI disrupts the sequence of the action since—notwithstanding the return of Jim Vane—it snaps the thread of Dorian's involvement with youthful love. It aborts the romance only to lead Dorian to incidents that play on "the note of Doom" which Wilde considers the cohesive ingredient in his work.

Taken literally as a melodrama of vengeance, **Dorian Gray** deals with Jim Vane's sentimental vow to avenge his sister's death in circumstances that are linked with the counterfeit atmosphere of his mother's sordid life. Indeed, the mother's "make-up" is revealing. Wilde portrays Jim with the gross, stilted diction reminiscent of his early plays, **The Duchess of Padua** and **Vera.** But Jim is, to an extent, functional: with his mannequin features, he enacts the role of the detective in pursuit of the guilty man. In contrast, Wilde's depiction of Sibyl's pathetic figure betrays his instinctive sympathy for his characters. Despite her immersion in theatrical life, Sibyl's nature displays a clean simplicity: she can only accept or deny love.

In this detective-novel stage, Dorian's role of "Prince Charming" provides the element of fantasy; the story as a romance figuratively presents the wager of good *versus* evil. What informs the theme of pride and downfall is the literal drama of return and pursuit, the rise and decline of Dorian. Dorian's existence preserves, and is itself preserved by, the picture. When he kills Hallward, he denies the creator of his beauty; for the painter is solely responsible for his preternatural beauty and his vanity. Just as Adam denies his Creator, so Dorian commits the "sin" of pride. The denial of authority foreshadows, and underlies, the murders of Basil, Campbell, and the death of Jim Vane. Dorian falls from an exquisite innocence into a haunted state of awareness. In exploiting Campbell's secret enormities, Dorian perverts science in order to get rid of his artistic creator.

Concern over genre, or the purely specific differentiae of **Dorian Gray,** is not an end in itself but a means toward defining its structure of values. One is reminded of Wilde's argument in emphasizing the primacy of the novel's existence as an imaginative work. He hopes here to demon-strate the value of renunciation as the moral poise gained from an intelligent discrimination of the issues involved in the hero's plight. Of course Wilde's pleading for his novel's positive qualities before a hostile audience must not be confused with the organic wholeness of the novel which is our primary interest.

Classified as "decadent," Wilde's novel pursues the attitude and style established by its main inspiration, Huysmans' *A rebours,* which Lord Henry's gift to Dorian vaguely resembles. On the surface, it illustrates the temper of the milieu that we meet later in Whistler, Beardsley, *The Yellow Book,* and *The Savoy.* It lays considerable stress on decoration, psychological experimentation, fantasy, abnormalities, the correspondence between odors and states of guilt and innocence; the purging of illusions by crude materialism; the contrast between consciously planned actions and instinctive drives—a variety of topics deriving from *Faust,* the Gothic novels, Pater's studies on the Renaissance, Gautier and the French Symbolists; and many other sources. Generalizations have indeed been made about the decadent novel and its subjects: the attenuation of emotion, the detailed analysis of ennui, moral disintegration, psychic alienation. In dealing with a rarefied atmosphere and the fetish of form and language, the decadent novel supposedly conveys a static condition in which time and space are fused in elaborate patterns. These patterns represent Axel's or Des Esseintes' mad pursuit of worldly pleasures and sensory hallucinations, their flair for the *outré* and the bizarre. How valid are these generalizations?

Called an escapist testament, a breviary of neo-hellenism, **Dorian Gray** bears indisputable affinities with aestheticism. But in truth the novel presents a spirit active and vivifying in its intellectual restlessness, with its adventurous energy seeking release in some fitting, viable form. One can interpret the scenes of dawn in the novel, when Dorian emerges from his nocturnal haunts, as prefiguring the consciousness rising from its dream to cast a defining light on the surrounding world. At this point, Wilde's handling of time and space, which has been so far overlooked, demands scrutiny. [In his *The Structure of the Novel,* 1954] Edwin Muir considers a novel dramatic when the progression and resolution of action figure in time. A character novel, on the other hand, has an action with a static nature; action is continuously reshuffled in space while the fixity and the circumference of the characters endow the parts with their proportion and meaning. Whereas the dramatic novel engages itself chiefly with time, the character novel is preoccupied with space as its field of action.

Now Wilde's novel, as the title suggests, revolves within a space definitely circumscribed, urban in locale, and urbane in taste. Within this field and at the center of it is the enigmatic canvas. Dorian's room, the idyllic garden, Lord Fermor's house in "a labyrinth of grinning streets and black, grassless squares," Piccadilly crowds and theaters, Sibyl's dressing room, a storeroom in the attic, innumerable dining-rooms, a secluded conservatory—all these comprise the physical setting in which eloquent gestures, decisive and expressive, bespeak more of spiritual crises than outright adventures. Even the hunt, a concrete analogue of Dorian's fugitive role, signifies a short interval which connects limited, enclosed spaces. This shrunken world, relatively speaking, is required by the aim of intensity. Since novelty and multiplicity of sensation, both of which Dorian elects as his dominating passions, abound more in the city than anywhere else, the city with its gorgeous courts and loathsome gutters assumes the function of a vast stage where life solidifies in the rigid shapes of an artwork. This is exactly the effect produced by the massive catalogue of jewels, treasures, bric-a-brac, in Chapter XI. Absolute stasis, caused by the enchantment over exotic wealth, tends to hold up the development of either physical or psychological action; that is, the novel tends toward lyrical condensation, not an epic sweep or dramatic mobility. Even the syntax of sentences sags with its excessive load of decorative epithets, substantives, phrasal units arranged in an endless procession.

It would be instructive to compare the dense texture of Chapter XI and the depiction of Dorian Gray's room or of Basil's studio with the shabby home of the Vane family, and the squalid slums of the London underworld. In all these descriptions, the same degree of skill and effort seems to have been expended. Consequently, whatever distortion may prevail in the extravagance of Dorian's life and the misery around him is restored to balance by the justice of narrative proportion. Each part receives the same painstaking treatment. To joyful outbursts on the glories of fashionable dandyism, Wilde counterpoints starkly realistic details which are either subtly insinuated or rendered in the process of accumulation. For example, juxtaposed with Dorian's raptures over Sibyl's voice with its "wild passion of violins" is the vulgarity of the "hideous Jew . . . smoking a vile cigar," who has "greasy ringlets, an enormous diamond blazed in the centre of a soiled shirt." Opposed to the slick glamor of Lord Henry and the blazing luxury of drawing rooms are the impressions of grotesque scenes, such as the dancing saloon with

> its tattered green curtain. . . . The floor was covered with ochre-coloured sawdust, trampled here and there into mud, and stained with rings of spilt liquor . . . [Dorian] looked round at the grotesque things that lay in such fantastic postures on the ragged mattresses. The twisted limbs, the gaping mouths, the staring lustreless eyes, fascinated him.

Restriction of space in the novel entails a corresponding withdrawal of characters into intense self-awareness which initially affects plot, diction, spectacle, and thought. This psychological trait prompts the unremitting attention paid to surfaces of objects, contours, masses, outlines of appearance that evoke the greatest density of sensations. This mode of treatment logically follows from such typical impulses as Dorian reveals ("I love beautiful things that one can touch and handle. . . . ") or from Lord Henry's preaching ("all experience is of value"). Organized around the vital process of Dorian's sensibility, the texture makes no pretense to detached objectivity. Wilde takes advantage of what E. M. Forster [in his *Aspects of the Novel,* 1927] considers the novelist's privilege of an unhampered point of view. Wilde uses a primitive version of

stream-of-consciousness technique in some sections, notably in Dorian's ponderings and reveries, to capture the character's unique apprehension of his inwardness and the "tone of things."

Wilde exploits visual and aural sensations to establish the moral correlatives of the psyche. A case in point is Jim Vane's despondency on the eve of his departure. The narrator projects his fate through the image of the flies buzzing around his "meagre meal," with the "loud rumble of omnibuses" and cacophony of the city as signs of the hostile pressure of an alien world. (Jim, symbol of the vengeful conscience, is slain by leisurely society: he is accidentally shot by hunters in a country retreat.) Sound and sight conspire in this situation:

> His mother was waiting for him below. She grumbled at his unpunctuality, as he entered. He made no answer, but sat down to his meagre meal. The flies buzzed round the table, and crawled over the stained cloth. Through the rumble of omnibuses, and the clatter of street-cabs, he could hear the droning voice devouring each minute that was left to him.

Wilde's analysis of subjective experience and the flux of feelings dictates a stylistic *ordonnance* of this kind. His style corresponds not only to the requirements of the individual natures he explores, but also to the ambience of cosmopolitan refinement, with its "thickness" of manners, intimations, rituals. Applied to other personages, like Campbell, Hallward, and Sibyl, this mode of presentation operates with efficient and telling economy.

Another example of concrete description serving a thematic purpose is the first two paragraphs of the novel, in which Wilde sketches deftly the landscape of Basil's studio:

> The studio was filled with the rich odour of roses, and when the light summer wind stirred amidst the trees of the garden there came through the open door the heavy scent of the lilac, or the more delicate perfume of the pink-flowering throne.
>
> From the corner of the divan of Persian saddle-bags on which he was lying, smoking, as was his custom, innumerable cigarettes, Lord Henry Wotton could just catch the gleam of the honey-sweet and honey-coloured blossoms of a laburnum, whose tremulous branches seemed hardly able to bear the burden of a beauty so flame-like as theirs; and now and then the fantastic shadows of birds in flight flitted across the long tussore-silk curtains that were stretched in front of the huge window, producing a kind of momentary Japanese effect, and making him think of those pallid jade-faced painters of Tokyo who, through the medium of an art that is necessarily immobile, seek to convey the sense of swiftness and motion. The sullen murmur of the bees shouldering their way through the long unmown grass, or circling with monotonous insistence round the dusty gilt horns of the struggling woodbine, seemed to make the stillness more oppressive. The dim roar of London was like the bourdon note of a distant organ.

Here the tonalities of surface and color in furniture, clothing, insects all appeal to an irrational stratum of awareness. Synesthesia furnishes one means of ordering things: the movement of scent and perfume coordinates distance and space, while visual, gustatory, and olfactory impressions coalesce in "the gleam of the honey-sweet and honey-coloured blossoms of a laburnum." One notes also the striking device whereby Wilde attributes life to inert artifacts. Opposites give rise to each other and are seen to be ultimately identical: "now and then the fantastic shadows of birds in flight flitted across the long tussore-silk curtains. . . . " Art souvenirs of antique civilizations combine with vivid tokens of spring and natural beauty to establish a world of half-fancy and half-reality. Under Wilde's touch, inanimate objects wake to life. Everything then breathes with organic energy and innocent charm.

Our knowledge of character in the world of this novel chiefly derives from the exposure in methodical sequence of typifying gestures or acts. They are disposed on strategic occasions: for example, when Jim Vane impulsively swears vengeance; or in the studied languor of Lord Henry's phrases and postures. Given the poses of the characters, we conceive of space here principally as the stage of behavior, with appropriate foreground, background, props, etc. Such actions as we see are executed for the sake of substantiating an idea which a character embodies. To this extent, Wilde's characters seem flat: we can always predict Lord Henry's opinions, Dorian's reactions, Basil's scruples. Granted Lord Henry's pervasive influence, which fills the book like a contagion, fixing the smell and shade and the whole panorama of every dramatic encounter in social exchange or in monologue, we can foretell probable consequences. From the moment the portrait registers a curve on its lips, we can intuitively forecast the limit to this magic, and the recognition and catastrophe that will soon follow.

One can easily demonstrate the affinities of the novel to a "well-made" play in its adroit management of the curve of incidents. But while Dorian may be a type in this play, he is still fluid in substance, as we see from his responsive liveliness, his energy of commitment, his impressionability. Up to the end, any move he determines to make seems urged on by shifting moods and spontaneous feelings. Take his deliberations to destroy the picture: the short sentences, with their staccato beat and jerky rhythm, suggest an actively scrupulous mind. Unlike Lord Henry's monolithic firmness of conviction, Dorian's susceptibility acquires depth in the choices and discriminations he makes. These discriminations embrace complex issues, antinomies in truth, perplexed by a profound sense of hovering retribution.

Since Dorian's awareness evolves in time, it is incorrect to classify *Dorian Gray* as a novel in which the element of space predominates. In the first place, the novel portrays the attempt of a young man to transcend the flux of temporal experience. This subject is handled by manipulating the concept of time which underlies the evolution of plot. Consequently we find that the factor of time governs the psychological experiences of the protagonist, and determines the states of his consciousness. Dorian's naive simplicity passes through stages of love, bitter disappointment, pride, ecstasy, solitary introspection, horror, humiliation, anguish, ennui, despair—the entire gamut, to be sure. These are manifold "events" within his consciousness. Each stage offers a problem that requires eventual resolution; each thesis generates an antithesis until, out of their conflict, a new synthesis is born. Such a dialectic seems to control the attraction and repulsion of characters among themselves, epitomized in Dorian's fluctuating love and hatred of his portrait.

In the anguished state of Dorian's life, the simple incidents that gradually entangle him come about with inexorable continuity. Realism becomes tempered by the remoteness of the supernatural picture from quotidian life. Unexposed, the portrait remains a mere artifact shrouded in mystery; exposed, it reflects the actuality that visible appearance and facts conceal. Could it be that Dorian, if he desires to know his true self, must ruin the good and beautiful? Wilde's narrative authority works through the changes of the portrait; thus, art becomes a vehicle of truth. The picture registers Dorian's acts in facial alterations, rendering the spiritual in concrete terms. This ironically fulfills Dorian's aim to unite the body and the spirit. Yet even his identity blurs in the end: Dorian's corpse, loathsome in decrepitude, can be identified only by means of his loathsome jewelry.

In the beginning Dorian accepts from Lord Henry a "poisonous" book which tells of men who tried to realize in their brief lifetimes all the passions found in the history of human experience. This fantastic record soon becomes a reality as Dorian imitates what it describes. Note that Dorian's lineage, his birth, childhood, and adolescence, all remain obscure, just as his name remains a secret to Sibyl and James Vane. His identity is never fully redeemed from its shadowy origin. London gossips about his debauchery, his association with drunken sailors and thieves, in a frantic quest for sensations; it is up to the reader to spell out the nature of his immoralism.

Although Dorian's immoralism, obscure throughout and obliquely referred to now and then, is never definitely compromised, still some primal urge drives him to hide and at the same time confess the secret of his total self. In a sense his fetish is not beauty but the need to know his integral self. And the talisman for this project is the portrait. Unlike other literary versions of the "double," e.g., Dr. Jekyll, William Wilson, the portrait functions less as a conscience than an emblem. It furnishes us the criterion of Dorian's growing lucidity as he follows the progress of his degeneration. It lays open the portentous disequilibrium that disturbs the spirit. Dorian's need to know indicates the absence of unity of being and sensibility. When he tries to break the cycle of corruption, the moral conflict ends; the novel ends, too. Somehow, for the fate-stricken Dorian, ideas and feelings lose their power. The ambiguity of Dorian's crimes affords an expansive field for the exercise of the reader's susceptibility, just as a kindred ambiguity of the specters in *The Turn of the Screw* provokes our curiosity. Wilde once defended himself by saying: "Each man sees his own sin in Dorian Gray. What Dorian Gray's sins are no one knows. He who finds them has brought them"—although we know that he is guilty of murder.

What then are the specific attributes that distinguish Wilde's work as a unique contribution to the genre of the novel?

In 1884 Henry James initiated a new period in aesthetic inquiry when he questioned the current orthodox practice of insisting on a moral message that can be directly drawn from the novel at a glance. He held the principle, later fully developed in "The Art of Fiction," that the task of the novelist is to grasp experience "which is an immense sensibility," "the very atmosphere of the mind." For James the novelist possesses "the power to guess the unseen from the seen, to trace the implications of things, to judge the whole piece by the pattern." Wilde assumed this vision of the artist when he affixed his witty preface to *Dorian Gray.* The preface no doubt is a synthesis of the ruling ideas that vitalized the creative instincts of a whole generation—Pater, Whistler, James, Yeats—and the tradition they gave rise to.

Despite Wilde's flippant ridicule of James' "elaborate subtlety" and "refined realism," his practice affirms James' dictum that the moral "sense of a work" immediately depends on the "amount of felt life concerned in producing it." Wilde likewise professed that "the moral life of man forms part of the subject matter of the artist, but the morality of art consists in the perfect use of an imperfect medium." Wilde disapproves of James' manner because it involves "analysis, not action" as its aim; it has more "psychology than passion." Unwittingly Wilde is characterizing the manner of *Dorian Gray.* We can justifiably say that because the narrative focus often isolates the spiritual struggle in Dorian's self, with the spotlight steadfastly thrown on the objective awareness that he exercises in moments of crisis, the primary issue in the novel is lucidity of discrimination; the secondary issue concerns itself with the antinomies of sense and soul, the clash of good and evil, and other opposites.

Analysis of psychological states figures in Wilde's fantasy to a considerable degree, chiefly as a response to the necessity of plot. Antagonisms among varying temperaments that surround Dorian do not happen in terms of overt hand-to-hand combat; rather, they occur as collision of wills, aims, likings, and the infinite ramifications of impulse and conscious intent. To Lord Henry's proposal of buying the picture, Basil says "no." To Dorian's passion over Sibyl, Lord Henry reacts with mocking shrewdness. Dorian's evasions, outright refusals, negative subterfuges, and shiftings of attitude all stem from his anxiety to keep faith to the vow he swore before his portrait. His gestures culminate in the supreme nihilism of murder, anticipated by Sibyl's suicide and followed by Jim Vane's accident, Campbell's slow wasting, and his death. Dorian's stab on the picture, a final assent to self-contradiction, comes with graceful inevitability.

Lord Henry, the presumed Mephistopheles of this Faustian drama, seems to have maneuvered everything from beginning to end. His cynical logic and the unflagging bravura of his sophistry are modulated by a tact that his entrances and exits indicate. Like the epigrammatic villains in the comedies, Lord Henry converts the traditional *raisonneur* into an incisive critic of manners. He caricatures people's faces and gestures in his private game of parody. He has Wilde's sharp, cruel eye for the hypocrisies of aristocratic society and the comic absurdities of life. Despite the fact that he does not act—he never practices what he preaches—Lord Henry gives us the strongest proof that Wilde, instead of being a dreamer, actually performs best as a satirist of mores and social behavior.

Although Lord Henry never does what he says, yet without him the novel could not exist. For he promotes the action at crucial points: (1) he reveals to Dorian the horror of growing old, thus inducing the youth to utter his fatal wish; (2) he buttresses Dorian's egoism when Dorian hears of Sibyl's death; (3) he convinces Dorian that all repentance is vain. Notwithstanding his influence, Lord Henry provides us not with merely a "satiric sketch," as Pater suggests, but a split personality. Professing subversive opinion, he does not however commit any malfeasance or give the slightest hint of scandal. Scorning action and cultivating exotic tastes, he nevertheless drives Dorian to a frenzied pursuit of active pleasure.

From a wider perspective, Lord Henry belongs in the deepest sense to a symbolic reality. His idiosyncrasies, his methodical incursions, awaken the real Dorian Gray embedded in the tissue of mundane superficialities. He is father to the Narcissus in Dorian that is caught within multiple contradictions; he affects radically the destiny of the novel's protagonist. But while he is the evangelist of sensuous perfectionism, his intelligence leaps forth with vigor, complementing Dorian's sensitivity. Dorian and Lord Henry together form an indivisible unity. From an allegorical standpoint, Dorian represents the experiencing self while Lord Henry represents the rationalizing self. Dorian acts, Lord Henry abstracts. It is possible also to discern in Lord Henry the intelligence of Wilde, in Dorian, his sensibility. At any rate, the dichotomy persists and pervades the whole work.

Compared with Lord Henry and Dorian, Basil Hallward, the other major figure, crystallizes the condition of a precarious self-sufficiency. Opposed to his secret passion for another man, the society of his time and its strict ethical code force Basil to conform to certain patterns of conduct. Consequently he acquires the status of spokesman of standard morality. He thus escapes his calling as an androgynous dandy by adopting the mask of collective conscience. At times he assumes the role of chorus to the tragic complications of Dorian's life. He sublimates his feelings in art, thus separating morality from nature. He insures himself from being a victim of perversion by always yielding to Dorian and Lord Henry. His middle class attitude, as shown in his compassion for Sibyl's mother, proves the counterpart to Lord Henry's distinction of birth and mind, to Dorian's fortuitous beauty. His death implies the defeat of sentiment when faced by an absolute faith in art. If Basil practically introduces the novel to us in his capacity as the maker of the miraculous portrait, he also concludes the novel as a victim of his own creation. His existence images the complete circuit of Dorian's action.

Using these typical traits and general outlines of the important characters, we can easily chart and diagram the conflicts and tensions that retard or accelerate the action of plot. However, their meaning within the thematic pattern—insofar as conflict is a function of character as given fact—must needs be defined. We must know the tenor of which the characters and their behavior are metaphoric vehicles. A handful of antitheses will subsume the topics of description and dialogue in the book, such as youth's magnificence, life's brevity, life as art, social corruption, and so forth.

At the heart of the narrative action, governing its pace and direction, is the irrational phenomenon of the portrait. This mystery is in turn contained within a form ordinarily given to a transcription of average, normal processes of thought and behavior. The reader shares Dorian's surprise at this inexplicable fact. The unexpected suddenly happens, upsetting all predictions of common sense: "Surely his wish had not been fulfilled? Such things were impossible. . . . And, yet, there was the picture before him, with the touch of cruelty in the mouth." Mirrorlike in effect, Dorian's picture participates in the life and fortunes of its original. Lord Henry's axiom that life has its elaborate masterpieces, that sometimes a "personality" assumes "the office of art," has been realized here without much ado. Wilde therefore begs at the outset the reader's willing suspension of disbelief. Grant the work its mystery and everything follows patly like clockwork. Given the dualism in Dorian of narcissistic pride and instinctive restraint that tends to discipline the libido, the novel's denouement follows with spontaneous naturalness.

Quite peculiar to the narrative substance is its position within a frame built from a miraculous phenomenon as *donnée*. The story proper hinges on the fulfillment of a wish that Dorian's youth be eternal; only when he violates the terms of the "contract" do the normal laws of life reassert themselves. From the suspension of normal law, the mood of uncanny artificiality emerges. Through the ingenuity of Campbell, guilty of sins we do not know, Basil's body disappears in a way we shall never know. We hear often the confused gossip of the London multitude. Dorian's sins are reported indirectly, and this poses a problem: if the novel "imitates" action, Wilde has to create some kind of conflict.

Conflict develops accordingly from the confrontation of characters. Dorian's character proves intriguing, when this *fin-de-siècle* Faust turns out to be an instrument of a didactic tale. Is he just a physiognomy designed for an illustration of a type? Or is he a created character with a palpable roundness of his own? By means of sustained interior dialogue, Wilde renders Dorian's most intimate confidences in set situations and tableaux. Dorian agonizes over Sibyl's suicide, he repents—but only for a while. He discovers himself invulnerable to pity; his cruelty soon mars the portrait. But he does not aspire to the status of a reality. He acts an ideal role in exemplifying a synthesis of sensibility and perversion, a rare yet plausible type. In other words, Dorian's character is a condition in which extremes meet; his acts signify the temporary triumph of one extreme over the other.

Lured by the siren of beauty in art, Dorian, however, succumbs to sensual dissipation. Rejecting good and bad, he yields nonetheless to an inner fatality, a passionate indifference which makes him incapable of feeling compassion for others. Becoming less perfect and even less human, he is also spiritually debased. Since pity and suffering ruin the sensitive enjoyment of voluptuous refinements, Wilde in actual life hated pain and suffering; only in **Reading Gaol** does he attempt to gain a sense of balance. Similarly, Dorian yields to the ravages of sensory delights. His case therefore bears a marked internal inconsistency. Opposing universality of taste to the relativity of awareness, he tries to unify soul and sense, passion and thought, by concentrating on limited aspects of experience. But such intensity suffers from narrowness of sympathy; and melancholy, ennui, desperation, and remorse are the result.

If we examine the logic behind Dorian's hopeless violence in demolishing the image of his conscience, an act itself prompted by the conscience within, the necessity of the act discloses itself. Dorian wanted to get rid of the guilt attached to his past so that he could relinquish all duties and obligations, and pursue freely his affections for Hetty Merton (Sibyl's ghost?). Could it be that he has forgotten his wish? Now he has become the portrait in his ageless glamor while the portrait has assumed the lineaments of his human self, human in the sense that its face grows more distorted whenever Dorian commits a vicious deed. How can one exist without the other? At the start, we have accepted the premise of imitation by the picture of the moral value of Dorian's conduct in terms of pictorial commentary. So far there has been no positive change. What this signifies is the failure of Dorian's nerve in endeavoring to arrive at an all-embracing reconciliation, a marriage of self and its appearances. Finally death lends the ultimate oneness.

Dorian's predicament exemplifies only one form, yet the most general, of the ordeal to attain unity of self. This theme, elaborately meditated upon in **De Profundis,** distinguishes one dominant strand in Wilde's literary compositions. Throughout the novel, opposing forces move within the stream of the plot. Antitheses between passion and spirit, consciousness and unconsciousness, feeling and artifice drive the characters to take up differing positions, differing judgments. Wilde gains a perspective on these conflicts by partly confining them within the range of Lord Henry's sophisticated survey; the latter's intellect delineates issues from a well-defined viewpoint. In Chapter IV, for example, Lord Henry constantly poses the disparity between soul and body. Yet he does not ignore the possibility of harmony between them: "There was animalism in the soul, and the body had its moments of spirituality. . . . Who could say where the fleshly impulse ceased, or the psychical impulse began?" Both logic and sentiment, pain and pleasure, have resemblances and differences. Lord Henry himself defines his mission: "To note the curious hard logic of passion, and the emotional coloured life of the intellect—to observe where they met, and where they separated, at what point they were in unison, and at what point they were at discord—."

We see now that Dorian's love for Sibyl is an attempt to

*Portrait of Wilde.*

abolish egoism and merge the self in empathic projection with the person of the beloved. But this love, being exclusive, fails. Love succumbs to the sin of self-consciousness, to its self-defeating fidelity to an art of transcendence. The obvious reason of course is the fact that Sibyl, no longer immersed in her act, becomes aware of her spectators: she loses unity of self as person and actress. She denies the imaginative, poetic detachment which, for Dorian, gave an ideal aura to her life. No doubt Dorian has mistaken dramatic illusion for the reality. Consequently, love fails to unify art and life—the art solidified in theaters, paintings, books; the life manifest in the hideous grin of Dorian's portrait, the dismal gutters, the filthy houses of lust.

Just as love, in Dorian's case, proves futile to unify warring forces, so does the willed dream of Huysmans' Des Esseintes fail to absorb all the possible experiences of mankind in a single moment. Dorian had hoped to partake of "that vivid life that lurks in all grotesques." He strove to spiritualize the senses. Likewise, Des Esseintes tried to "multiply personalities," being for Dorian that "wonderful young Parisian in whom the romantic and scientific temperaments were so strangely blended," who "became to him a prefiguring type of himself." Both these protagonists simply revolve within a circle of contradictions: desiring to transcend the flux of historical experience, they exploit experience itself to the extent that a mystical asceticism may grow out of self-titillation—strange dialectic, indeed! Dorian simply echoes Pater in theorizing that he

should never "accept any theory or system that would involve the sacrifice of any mode of passionate experience," experience being the obsessive goal. When Wilde, however, intrudes the information that Dorian "never fell into the error of arresting his intellectual development by a formal acceptance of creed or system," he is talking outside of the novel's context. Dorian's intellectual development remains circular in its fanatic adherence to epicureanism. Dorian descends to a lower type when he loses the sense of good and evil. He commits the cardinal error in practicing Lord Henry's hedonism, leading to the distortion of the beautiful portrait and his hopeless floundering. Instead of annihilating time, Dorian's unchanging youth shortens it; when his thirty-eighth year arrives, he finds himself still dissatisfied, restless, afflicted.

Paradoxically, Dorian's struggle to escape the laws of time and contingency restricts both his spatial and temporal reach. Spatial range, as we have seen, is limited. Duration in time means only a progression within a closed circuit; its terminal is the *cul de sac* of satiety and revulsion. Like Des Esseintes, who tormented himself between the extremes of sensuality and purity, Dorian staggers between ennui and flight from his nobler self. What is Jim Vane's vengeance but a form of nemesis? Character, then, is fate.

In his early fiction, Wilde examined the impulse of "duty" in **"Lord Arthur Savile's Crime,"** and showed his talent for producing clever, gratuitous mystifications; witness **"The Sphinx without a Secret," "The Model Millionaire,"** and **"The Canterville Ghost."** In **"Pen, Pencil and Poison,"** the artist's diabolic inspiration and morbid fatality convert sin into a sacramental act. In **"The Portrait of Mr. W. H.,"** the power of the "lie" quickens truth and self-knowledge. In ***Dorian Gray,*** Dorian's relation with his picture exemplifies duty counteracting self-indulgence: when he stabs the picture, Dorian commits a contradiction—he defies the power of time which ruins the portrait, but from which he himself is liberated. His remorse exists, curiously enough, in time. When he ceases to be a spectator of life and acts violently, he puts an end to the suspension of time; he destroys his beauty and the reason for his existence. The end products of Dorian's life are "a ruined body which is continuous with his personality and his society, and a work of art which will symbolize forever his power to explore the hell of reality" [Morse Peckham, *Beyond the Tragic Vision,* 1962].

It would be superfluous to make more explicit the battle between good and evil forces in Dorian's mind. Despite his resolve to shape his life into art, he still flinches and wavers under the piercing impact of life itself, life uncontrollably fertile and spontaneous. The organic vitality of life set over against the artifices of culture and fixed rituals; the vigor of desire and repugnance, of imagination against mechanical knowledge; of natural feeling and intuition against the reflexes of habitual and routine existence— these values, deducible from the interaction of characters and circumstances, helped to organize the luxuriance of rhetoric and imagery within a meaningful frame. They also endow the conventional cast of the plot with symbolic implications.

Wilde's triumph in the novel form consists in the careful

management of an interesting story as such, without sacrificing the virtue of style and the order of dramatic complications which express the judgment of the author. By manipulating situation, as when Dorian, the priest of beauty, is juxtaposed with ugly surroundings, Wilde achieves the end in which the judgment of experience upon character is objectively expressed. Choice of viewpoint exposes social foibles and individual absurdities. From this angle, *Dorian Gray* answers the requirements of a novel of social criticism. If fiction is sustained by entertainment value and justified by moral purpose, then Wilde's novel supplies both.

Assessed on the basis of literary and cultural history, *Dorian Gray* exemplifies the pervasive trend in the latter half of the Victorian period toward intense analysis of mental states. In the past the novel generally conceived of meaning and value as something imposed by an external authority, such as church, state, family. Gradually, however, the novel tended to view man as the sole creator of his own existence, thus relegating the myths of religion to a remote past. Symbolism gave rise to the technique of making the external world an outward analogue or extension of the psyche. Plunging into the mind and subconscious realm, Dickens, George Eliot, and others sought to transcribe the vicissitudes of the inner self as demanded by an outlook which decreed that what is significant is not truth in fact but truth in relationships; that is, not the statistics of Moll Flanders' world but the relationships of Middlemarch. This practice suggests the collapse of traditional norms of conduct, which is now almost a sociological platitude. The evolution of "terror" fiction, its changes of scope and emphasis, indicates the mutations of the novel form in the latter part of the century. Whereas Gothic romances showed us the success of naturalistic devices, occult lore, and ingenious contraptions, the ghost and mystery stories of Collins, Stevenson, Henry James, and others reveal the increasing ascendancy of a totally subjective viewpoint. Eventually the mind became the principal setting, while dreams and delusions became pivotal elements of narrative.

Parallel to this change is the heightened concern with the artist's predicament in an industrial, bourgeois civilization. Attention centered itself on biographical facts, on the ambiguities of art's connection with reality. The confession appeared as a favorite mode of self-expression. When the artist withdraws from social encounters to passive introspection, we find Beardsley and his "elegant" caricatures; we behold the estranged lives of poets, their exile or suicide. We discover Wilde in Reading Gaol; after his release, we see him descend into the squalid "pits" of Paris. Whatever commitment the artist had the courage to carry out into action was narrowed down to a dedication to his craft and the exaltation of the creative process to the realm of an absolute. Aesthetic experience fed on itself by being the paramount subject matter of fiction.

In the light of the development of the novel after Henry James, *The Picture of Dorian Gray* earns for itself a significant place in the tradition. In setting a portrait, a work of art, at the center of the action, Wilde effects the interplay of natural perception and moral judgment in the novel. From the reader's viewpoint, the picture suggests the treatment of angle and distance—the ways of telling and of showing—which make up the perennial issues of the aesthetics and criticism of fiction. (pp. 49-73)

*Epifanio San Juan, Jr., in his* The Art of Oscar Wilde, *Princeton University Press, 1967, 238 p.*

## Christopher S. Nassaar    (essay date 1974)

[*Nassaar is a Lebanese educator and critic who has stated that his "chief aim as a critic is to establish Oscar Wilde as a major literary figure and to show the importance of the Rossetti-Pater-Wilde line in nineteenth-century literature." In the following excerpt, Nassaar considers* The Picture of Dorian Gray *as a study of Victorian art movements and of the psychological traits of characteristic fin de siècle personalities.*]

It is doubtful that *The Picture of Dorian Gray* is "a great thing," but it has survived the test of time and is a deeper and more thoughtful novel than its critics have so far been willing to concede. The book is a strange one, a partly supernatural tale in which the characters are not individuals but symbols that move in a shadowy world of wit and terror. The novel is chiefly a study of various Victorian art movements corresponding to different stages in the development of Victorian human nature, and the main characters are meant to be personifications of these art movements and psychological states. Of central importance is the new art movement and type of person that was emerging in fin-de-siècle England. Dorian, as he degenerates, becomes a perfect example of the decadent, and his picture, as it grows more and more evil, a perfect type of decadent art.

The main difference between a morally committed aesthete and a decadent is that the latter, looking within and discovering not only purity but evil and corruption, yields to the corrupt impulse and tries to find joy and beauty in evil. Finally, the vision of evil becomes unbearable, the decadent has burned all his bridges, and he finds himself trapped in a dark underworld from which he cannot escape.

Lord Arthur Savile is an excellent example of the moral aesthete. Looking within, Arthur discovers not only the pure "Sybil" but also the corrupt and evil "Podgers." He rejects Podgers, however, and does everything in his power to marry Sybil. Finally, he is led by Providence to destroy Podgers and marry his love, thereby attaining a state of total purity.

*The Picture of Dorian Gray* is essentially a reversal of the situation in **"Lord Arthur Savile's Crime."** Sybil and Wotton represent the two opposing forces within Dorian, but Dorian, as soon as he becomes aware of the evil within himself, sells his soul in a fit of rebellion against the laws of God and nature. The determinism of *Dorian Gray,* moreover, contrasts with that of **"Lord Arthur Savile's Crime."** The idea of an external determining force is here abandoned in favor of a determinism whose springs well up from within the self:

There are moments, psychologists tell us, when the passion for sin, or what the world calls sin, so dominates a nature, that every fibre of the body, as every cell of the brain, seems to be instinct with fearful impulses. Men and women at such moments lose the freedom of their will. They move to their terrible end as automatons move. Choice is taken from them, and conscience is either killed, or, if it lives at all, lives but to give rebellion its fascination, and disobedience its charm. For all sins, as theologians weary not of reminding us, are sins of disobedience. When that high spirit, that morning-star of evil, fell from heaven, it was as a rebel that he fell.

Callous, concentrated on evil, with stained mind and soul hungry for rebellion, Dorian Gray hastened on, quickening his steps as he went.

A supernatural force does exist in the novel—it grants Dorian's demonic prayer—but that is its sole function. As it turns out, the devil Dorian sells his soul to is Lord Henry Wotton, who exists not only as something external to Dorian but also as a voice within him. *The Picture of Dorian Gray* is a psychological study of a nature—and an art movement—dominated by a passion for sin.

If we accept that Dorian died in 1890, the year in which *Dorian Gray* was mostly written and the earlier version published in *Lippincott's Magazine,* then the novel opens in the year 1873. We first meet Dorian shortly after he has passed the age of twenty, and he dies a few months after his thirty-eighth birthday, which he marks by murdering Basil. The novel thus traces Dorian's development over the span of approximately eighteen years, though Wilde's treatment of the passage of time in the novel is highly inadequate and is, perhaps, the book's most serious weak point.

The year 1873 was an important one for Oscar Wilde, for in that year Walter Pater published his *Studies in the History of the Renaissance* [revised in 1907 and published as *The Renaissance: Studies in Art and Poetry*]. Wilde is reported to have proclaimed during his first meeting with Yeats that *The Renaissance* "is my golden book; I never travel anywhere without it." Much later, in *De Profundis,* he broodingly referred to it as "that book which has had such a strange influence over my life." Indeed, *The Renaissance* casts a long, sinister shadow across *The Picture of Dorian Gray,* and the entire novel seems to be structured with Pater's book as its focal point.

*The Picture of Dorian Gray* begins in Basil Hallward's studio, with a conversation between Basil and Lord Henry Wotton. These are the two artists in the novel, Basil's art being his painting while Wotton's is his conversation. The two men are opposites: Basil is a largely pure man who yields to a streak of evil in his soul, while Wotton is a highly corrupt man who never commits an immoral action. Basil's attachment to Dorian has a homosexual dimension, and his disappearances are probably for the sake of homosexual relief. (This is clear in the earlier, shorter version of the novel, but Wilde toned it down considerably in the later version.) As for Wotton, Basil says to him: "You are an extraordinary fellow. You never say a moral thing, and you never do a wrong thing." Basil's purity is balanced against Wotton's corruption, while Basil's wrong actions stand opposed to Wotton's entirely moral existence.

Basil paints Dorian while Dorian is still in a state of innocence. "He seems to me little more than a lad, though he is really over twenty," Basil says; and Wotton, when he first sets eyes on Dorian, corroborates this view: "Lord Henry looked at him. . . . There was something in his face that made him trust him at once. All the candour of youth was there, as well as all youth's passionate purity. One felt that he had kept himself unspotted from the world." The painting is Basil's masterpiece because Dorian is the flawless manifestation of Basil's lost innocence. It is not until Dorian begins to respond to Wotton's poisonous sermon, however, that the picture becomes complete, for the faint flush of evil that comes across Dorian's face renders him the perfect embodiment of the painter's soul, and allows Basil to introduce the finishing touch to his masterpiece.

As I have said, the chief characters in *The Picture of Dorian Gray* are both human types and representatives of different art movements. This is clearest in Dorian, who exists both as a picture and as a human. This neat split allows us to separate decadence as an art movement from decadence as a mode of life, and to examine the two separately. Wilde clouds the issue, however, by making Wotton fasten on the live Dorian and, paradoxically, treat the breathing human being as a work of art. Basil expounds a theory of art straight out of Pater's essay on Leonardo in *The Renaissance.* The artist, Basil argues, searches in the outside world for the perfect manifestation of his own soul. When he finds this object, he can create masterpieces by painting it. Moreover, the proximity of this object can inspire the artist to trace his own soul in the forms of nature. Wotton muses on this theory, then reverses it by deciding to recreate Dorian the human until he becomes a perfect external manifestation of Wotton's own soul:

> He was a marvellous type, too, this lad, whom by so curious a chance he had met in Basil's studio, or could be fashioned into a marvellous type, at any rate. Grace was his, and the white purity of boyhood, and beauty such as old Greek marbles kept for us. There was nothing one could not do with him. He could be made a Titan or a toy. . . .
>
> Yes; he would try to be to Dorian Gray what, without knowing it, the lad had been to the painter who had fashioned the wonderful portrait. He would seek to dominate him—had already, indeed, done so. He would make that wonderful spirit his own.

That Wotton regards Dorian as an instrument for his art is clear from the way he thinks about him. In the above quotation, he seems to regard himself as a sculptor and Dorian's placid Greek soul as his clay. Here is another example of Wotton's thinking about Dorian: "Talking to him was like playing upon an exquisite violin. He answered to every touch and thrill of the bow."

The process of recreating Dorian begins in Basil's studio,

when Wotton preaches an invidious sermon based heavily on the Conclusion of Pater's *Renaissance.* There is an important difference between Pater and Wotton, however. Wotton, by substituting the word *sensations* for the word *impressions,* slightly but significantly modifies Pater's doctrine. Pater had written: "With this sense of the splendour of our experience and of its awful brevity, gathering all we are into one desperate effort to see and touch, we shall hardly have time to make theories about the things we see and touch. What we have to do is to be for ever curiously testing new opinions and courting new impressions." Wotton, on the other hand, preaches to Dorian: "Live! Live the wonderful life that is in you! Let nothing be lost upon you. Be always searching for new sensations."

The Conclusion to Pater's *Renaissance* was widely misinterpreted by the young men of his day, who understood it as a call to live a life of indiscriminate sensations—a fact that led Pater to suppress the Conclusion in the second edition of his book. Wilde was too intelligent to have misunderstood Pater's concluding chapter, but it was precisely this Conclusion that sparked the decadent movement in England. And since *The Picture of Dorian Gray* is primarily an examination of the decadent movement, it is proper that Wotton should present Pater's doctrine as it was understood by the decadents, not as Pater meant it to be understood.

There is more to the matter than that, however. In the third edition of *The Renaissance* (1888), Pater restored his Conclusion, but made "some slight changes which bring it closer to my original meaning." The changes are really insignificant, but it is possible, even probable, that Wilde also believed Pater's original meaning needed to be clearly brought out through some "slight changes." The modifications Wotton makes in Pater's Conclusion can therefore be seen as bringing it closer to what Wilde felt was Pater's original meaning. Wotton would then suggest—as Richard Ellmann believes—Walter Pater himself, but Pater as Wilde understood him. "In *The Picture of Dorian Gray*," Ellmann tells us [see Further Reading entry dated 1969],

> Pater is enclosed (like an unhappy dryad caught in a tree trunk) in Lord Henry Wotton. Lord Henry's chief sin is quoting without acknowledgment from the *Renaissance.* . . . Pater, who wrote a review of [*Dorian Gray*], was at great pains to distinguish Lord Henry's philosophy from his own. Wilde seems to have intended not to distinguish them, however, and to offer (through the disastrous effects of Lord Henry's influence upon Dorian) a criticism of Pater.

Wotton's demonic sermon destroys Dorian's state of innocence and plunges him into a state of experience. Paradoxically, Basil has already paved the way for Wotton by excessively worshiping Dorian's physical beauty and making Dorian aware of this beauty. The sermon begs the evil in Dorian to blossom forth, and he responds splendidly:

> He was dimly conscious that entirely fresh influences were at work within him. Yet they seemed to have come really from himself. The few words that Basil's friend had said to him—words spoken by chance, no doubt, and with wilful paradox in them—had touched some secret chord that had never been touched before, but that he felt was now vibrating and throbbing to curious pulses.
>
> Music had stirred him like that. Music had troubled him many times. But music was not articulate. It was not a new world, but rather another chaos, that it created in us. Mere words! How terrible they were! How clear, and vivid, and cruel! One could not escape from them. And yet what a subtle magic there was in them! They seemed to be able to give a plastic form to formless things, and to have a music of their own as sweet as that of viol or of lute.

Wotton's words are associated with music, which is an art. Basil is an artist who uses a brush, but Wotton is an artist who uses words. He is the decadent artist, who will recreate his evil soul in Dorian and derive pleasure from contemplating his demonic creation.

Wotton's words, however, seem to Dorian to come from within himself, for Wotton as artist is the external manifestation of the evil in Dorian. In Oscar Wilde's works, the movement of negative capability is often reversed, so that the main character seems to absorb the others into himself. Dorian, under the influence of Wotton's sermon, immediately sells his soul to the devil. Symbolically, what this means is that Dorian cannot and never will be able to resist the evil within himself—that is, the voice of Wotton. His passion for sin will be the governing principle of his life.

In his new thirst for sensations, Dorian's first action is to fall in love with Sybil Vane. The development of the decadent is a gradual process, and Dorian, newly emerged from a state of innocence, at first seeks pure sensations remote from evil. It is clear, though, that his love for Sybil Vane—in contrast to Lord Arthur's love for his Sybil—is Dorian's first decadent act. He says to Wotton:

> "It would never have happened if I had not met you. You filled me with a wild desire to know everything about life. For days after I met you, something seemed to throb in my veins. As I lounged in the Park, or strolled down Piccadilly, I used to look at everyone who passed me, and wonder, with a mad curiosity, what sort of lives they led. Some of them fascinated me. Others filled me with terror. There was an exquisite poison in the air. I had a passion for sensations."

Dorian spiritualizes his attachment to Sybil and deceives himself about its highly sensual nature, but Wotton is very aware that the attachment is Dorian's first step in his development as a decadent. This is Wotton's reaction as Dorian raves about Sybil's purity and divinity:

> Lord Henry watched him with a subtle sense of pleasure. How different he was now from the shy, frightened boy he had met in Basil Hallward's studio! His nature had blossomed like a flower, had borne blossoms of scarlet flame. Out of its secret hiding-place had crept his Soul, and Desire had come to meet it on the way.

Sybil is a character who knows nothing of evil. Unlike her counterpart in **"Lord Arthur Savile's Crime,"** however, she exists in a childlike world of innocence, and it is stressed over and over again that she is still immature. "There is something of a child about her," says Dorian, and goes on to say that when they first met they "stood looking at each other like children." Sybil, moreover, is presented not as an individual but as the embodiment of a state of the soul and an entire movement in Victorian art. Pater, in *The Renaissance,* wrote of the Mona Lisa that she is the symbol of modern human nature, "of what in the ways of a thousand years men had come to desire":

> Hers is the head upon which all "the ends of the world are come," and the eyelids are a little weary. It is a beauty wrought out from within upon the flesh, the deposit, little cell by cell, of strange thoughts and fantastic reveries and exquisite passions. Set it for a moment beside one of those white Greek goddesses or beautiful women of antiquity, and how would they be troubled by this beauty, into which the soul with all its maladies has passed! . . .

> The fancy of a perpetual life, sweeping together ten thousand experiences, is an old one; and modern thought has conceived the idea of humanity as wrought upon by, and summing up in itself, all modes of thought and life. Certainly Lady Lisa might stand as the embodiment of the old fancy, the symbol of the modern idea.

If the Mona Lisa is Pater's symbol of the modern idea, Sybil is Wilde's symbol of the old idea, gathering together ten thousand experiences and embodying in herself the world's purity. Dorian says of her: "I have seen her in every age and in every costume. Ordinary women never appeal to one's imagination. They are limited to their century." And again: "She is all the great heroines of the world in one. She is more than an individual." Pater had written of Greek art that it is too serene and undisturbed to satisfy us, for in ancient Greece the human race was still in its infancy, unaware of the seriousness and terror of evil and still uninfected by any spiritual sickness. Modern art, he held, must deal with the grotesque—with life, conflict, evil—for the evolution of the human spirit has made us terribly aware of the dark, evil caverns in human nature, and it is from this new situation that art must now try to wrest joy. The white Greek goddesses and beautiful women of antiquity no longer satisfy us.

Sybil, serene and untouched by any knowledge of evil, represents the Hellenic ideal. She has a "Greek head," and her name connects her with Greek mythology. When she appears in a play, it is invariably in the role of the spotless heroine—Juliet or Imogen or Rosalind—and Basil and Dorian see her purpose as that of spiritualizing the age. She is the visible symbol of an art and a state of the soul whose beauty is one of purity peculiar to the infancy of the race or of an age. Sybil exists in naturalistic surroundings—she acts in "an absurd little theatre, with great flaring gas-jets and gaudy play-bills," presided over by a "hideous Jew" who smokes "a vile cigar"—but her artistic imagination transforms her corrupt environment and renders it pure and spotless. Her imagination also transforms Dorian, for she sees him as entirely pure and untouched by evil at a time when he is already under Wotton's influ-

ence. For Sybil, Dorian is a fairy-tale prince out of the pages of literature:

> "She said quite simply to me, 'You look like a prince. I must call you Prince Charming.'"

> "Upon my word, Dorian, Miss Sybil knows how to pay compliments."

> "You don't understand her, Harry. She regarded me merely as a person in a play. She knows nothing of life."

Sybil, however, is a child who cannot come of age and survive. She exists in a protective world of art from which she cannot emerge without dying. Her projected marriage to Dorian coaxes her out of this world and causes her to come into contact with the demon universe. Pater, in the Conclusion to *The Renaissance,* maintained that success in life is to achieve a state of constant ecstasy, to burn always with a hard, gemlike flame, and ended his chapter thus:

> Great passions may give us this quickened sense of life, ecstasy and sorrow of love, the various forms of enthusiastic activity, disinterested or otherwise, which come naturally to many of us. Only be sure it is passion—that it does yield you this fruit of a quickened, multiplied consciousness. Of this wisdom, the poetic passion, the desire of beauty, the love of art for art's sake, has most; for art comes to you professing frankly to give nothing but the highest quality to your moments as they pass, and simply for those moments' sake.

It is art, then, that can give the highest quality to our moments, that can fire us with a constant flamelike ecstasy. Paradoxically, Sybil—in order to achieve this flamelike ecstasy—rejects art for life, for a great passion. After she gives her terrible performance in front of Basil and Wotton, Dorian rushes backstage to find that "the girl was standing there alone, with a look of triumph on her face. Her eyes were lit with an exquisite fire. There was a radiance about her. Her parted lips were smiling over some secret of their own." She says to him: "You have made me understand what love really is. My love! my love! Prince Charming! Prince of life! I have grown sick of shadows. You are more to me than all art can ever be." Prince Charming is no longer a character out of a play but is now the prince of life.

When Sybil's world of art is shattered, her imagination ceases to recreate the outside world and render it pure and spotless. As a consequence, she becomes aware of the sordid side of life:

> "To-night, for the first time in my life, I saw through the hollowness, the sham, the silliness of the empty pageant in which I had always played. To-night, for the first time, I became conscious that the Romeo was hideous, and old, and painted, that the moonlight in the orchard was false, that the scenery was vulgar, and that the words I had to speak were unreal, were not my words, were not what I wanted to say."

Sybil, however, is too fragile to confront the demonic and survive. The death blow falls when she becomes aware of the evil in Dorian. Dorian had loved her as an erotic symbol of purity, but when she rejects art for life, she loses her ability to isolate herself from "the stain of an age . . . at once sordid and sensual." Like the protagonists of the fairy tales, she moves from innocence into experience, but as soon as she enters the demonic world of the naturalists, she begins to have naturalistic experiences. Dorian callously walks out on her, and she dies by swallowing "some dreadful thing they use at theatres," with white lead or prussic acid in it. Her lonely suicide in a tawdry actress's dressing room is straight Zola. This is how people die in naturalist literature—not on the high seas or in Horatio's arms, but alone, in poverty and despair. Wotton reflects on her death, "The moment she touched actual life she marred it, and it marred her, and so she passed away."

Sybil's death has dimensions that far transcend her death as the result of a psychological state. "Without your art you are nothing," Dorian informs her, and indeed her death symbolizes the death of an entire movement in art. Sybil is inseparable from art. Dorian says:

> "On the first night I was at the theatre, the horrid old Jew came round to the box after the performance was over, and offered to take me behind the scenes and introduce me to her. I was furious with him, and told him that Juliet had been dead for hundreds of years, and that her body was lying in a marble tomb in Verona. I think, from his blank look of amazement, that he was under the impression that I had taken too much champagne, or something."

Pater saw the Mona Lisa as the supreme example of modern art, for modern art must encompass all of human nature, in all its evil and terror, and present it in a way that makes it beautiful. He saw the portrait of *La Gioconda* as combining in its chill beauty the pure and evil strains in human nature—as summing up human nature from a modern perspective. Humanity, for Pater, has developed beyond its initial state of innocence and can no longer be satisfied with an art that cannot deal with evil. Wilde, in **Dorian Gray,** modifies Pater's idea and applies it to the Victorian world as a separate entity, as though the human race had been born anew at the beginning of the Victorian period. [In his *Walter Pater,* 1959] Iain Fletcher has observed that "Pater's method, in *The Renaissance,*" is to explore "not so much a period as a movement of history through selected individuals." Wilde's method is the same, but he focuses instead on the movement of a single period, presenting the Victorians as having begun in placid innocence but developed beyond it.

Sybil is the symbol of the innocence of the Victorians, both in life and in art. She represents a movement in art that knows nothing of evil and dwells in a beautiful, private world. In this respect, she suggests Tennyson more than anyone else. The early Tennyson wrote poetry that was serenely unaware of evil and that advocated an isolated existence in a dazzling, beautiful world of art. It is precisely such a world that the poet seeks and finds in "Recollections of the Arabian Nights." The ivory tower of serene artistic delight is very much the message of Tennyson's early poetry. "The Palace of Art" and "The Lady of Shalott," however, reflect his growing dissatisfaction with this private world. And in *In Memoriam,* the beautiful art world crumbles and Tennyson confronts the demonic, mid-Victorian scientific universe.

Like Sybil, moreover, Tennyson tumbles from his ivory tower into the demon universe because of a great love. Unlike Sybil, though, he paradoxically survives to retreat into the world of Arthurian romance and to write about a virtuous king who is finally destroyed by evil forces outside himself. Interestingly, "The Last Tournament," one of the grimmest and darkest of the Idylls, was published in 1872, and Tennyson at the time meant it as the continuation and conclusion of *The Idylls of the King* ("The Passing of Arthur" had appeared earlier, in 1869). In 1885, he published another Idyll, "Balin and Balan," but that was to appear toward the middle of the sequence, not—like "The Passing of Arthur" and "The Last Tournament"—at the end. *The Idylls of the King* may be said to be Tennyson's last great work. Much of his time after 1872 was devoted to an unsuccessful attempt to storm the English stage with a series of historical tragedies, until in 1884 he gave up in despair! [In a footnote, Nassaar adds that "In 1884, Tennyson disclaimed any hope of 'meeting the exigencies of our modern theatre.' His attempt to storm the stage coincides with Sybil's rejection of it. Apart from Wilde's stylistic carelessness in **Dorian Gray** and his inadequate treatment of the passage of time, the book's chief fault is that it is far too heavily paradoxical."]

It is probably the art movement of Tennyson that Sybil is meant to represent. He looked to past ages and foreign lands in his poetry, and Sybil always appears in plays belonging to past centuries and set in foreign lands. Her relationship with Dorian, moreover, clearly suggests the Lady of Shalott, and she indeed echoes her when she rejects art and says to her lover, "I have grown sick of shadows." The art of an age can isolate itself from evil only during the infancy of that age. As the age matures, such art movements must collapse as evil presses in on them. Consequently, Sybil, the symbol of an innocent movement in Victorian art, dies. The Satanic Wotton reflects: "There is something to me quite beautiful about her death. I am glad I am living in a century when such wonders happen."

Sybil's mother and brother, like Sybil, represent a trend in art that belongs to the innocence of the Victorians, and they too are inseparable from the movement they symbolize. Wilde tells us of Jim Vane: "He was thick-set of figure, and his hands and feet were large, and somewhat clumsy in movement. He was not so finely bred as his sister. One would hardly have guessed the close relationship that existed between them." And yet a very close relationship does exist. Whereas Sybil represented the innocence of the Victorians at a very high artistic level, Jim represents the same thing at a much lower level. James Vane and his mother are straight out of Victorian melodrama, and Victorian melodrama, in its infantile treatment of evil, its lack of intellectual content, its presentation of heroes who always triumph and black villains who are always defeated, is a drama of childlike innocence. Jim Vane is not an individual but a type. To Sybil's artistic imagination, he is all the heroes of Victorian melodrama rolled into one. His future is envisioned by his sister:

He was to leave the vessel at Melbourne, bid a polite good-bye to the captain, and go off at once to the gold-fields. Before a week was over he was to come across a large nugget of pure gold, the largest nugget that had ever been discovered, and bring it down to the coast in a waggon guarded by six mounted policemen. The bush-rangers were to attack them three times, and be defeated with immense slaughter. Or, no. He was not to go to the gold-fields at all. They were horrid places, where men got intoxicated, and shot each other in bar-rooms, and used bad language. He was to be a nice sheep-farmer, and one evening, as he was riding home, he was to see the beautiful heiress being carried off by a robber on a black horse, and give chase, and rescue her. Of course she would fall in love with him, and he with her, and they would get married, and come home, and live in an immense house in London. Yes, there were delightful things in store for him.

The specific events in Jim's future are uncertain, but what is certain is that there are delightful, melodramatic things in store for him. And indeed, if he were acting in a melodrama there would be no question about that. Jim's tragedy, however, is similar to his sister's: he rejects art for life. Instead of joining the group, as his mother had wished, he decides to become a real-life sailor and says to his mother: "I should like to make some money to take you and Sybil off the stage. I hate it." By rejecting the stage, however, he becomes part of the terrible world of the naturalists. He continues to behave melodramatically in this world, making wild threats against Sybil's aristocratic lover, and Sybil says to him: "Oh, don't be so serious, Jim. You are like one of the heroes of those silly melodramas mother used to be so fond of acting in." When we meet Jim again, nearly eighteen years later, he is associated with loathsome dens, dark alleys, old hags, and the filth of port life. This is the world of the naturalists, but he continues to behave melodramatically in it. He is mistakenly shot and killed while hiding behind a bush—an unthinkable end for a stout-hearted British sailor in a proper melodrama, but a very usual end for a character in naturalist literature.

Sybil's mother is a secondary character, but she is a counterpoint to her son in that she is a melodramatic figure who clings on to the stage. She yearns for the days when melodrama was popular, and she compensates by trying to mold her life into a melodrama. This is how she reacts to Sybil:

> "Ah! mother, mother, let me be happy!"

> Mrs. Vane glanced at her, and with one of those false theatrical gestures that so often becomes a mode of second nature to a stage-player, clasped her in her arms.

And again:

> "Kiss me, mother," said the girl. Her flower-like lips touched the withered cheek, and warmed its frost.

> "My child! my child!" cried Mrs. Vane, looking up to the ceiling in search of an imaginary gallery.

Mrs. Vane absolutely must exist in a melodramatic atmosphere. She has outlived her time, however, and she suggests more than anything else a defeated character in a naturalistic novel. The "silly melodramas" she "used to be so fond of acting in" were probably of the *Black-Eyed Susan* and *Luke the Labourer* variety. As early as the 1860s, these crude melodramas were already on the decline. "By the 1860's melodramas were simply better written than they had been earlier. Characters remained types, but touches of subtlety and complexity appeared in characterization. Slapstick was replaced by witty repartee. Restrained sentiment now and then replaced tear-jerking sentimentality" [J. O. Bailey, *British Plays of the Nineteenth Century,* 1966]. The sordid world of the naturalists, moreover, infiltrated the melodrama in the 1860s and began to make appearances in the plays of Boucicault—in his famous melodrama, *After Dark,* for instance. By the 1890s, the old-fashioned branch of the melodrama had died out. The new and more vigorous branch had evolved into the new drama. Mrs. Vane dies after her daughter but before her son. Indeed, Wilde presents her as in a sense already dead, for she is old and withered and decayed. The Victorians having emerged from their state of innocence, melodrama is inevitably in a state of decay, moving toward certain death.

Sybil's rejection of art and her subsequent suicide constitute a further deliverance of Dorian into the hands of the devil. Dorian says to Wotton at one point, concerning Sybil:

> "And her voice—I never heard such a voice. It was very low at first, with deep mellow notes, that seemed to fall singly upon one's ear. Then it became a little louder, and sounded like a flute or a distant hautbois. In the garden-scene it had all the tremulous ecstasy that one hears just before dawn when nightingales are singing. There were moments, later on, when it had the wild passion of violins. You know how a voice can stir one. Your voice and the voice of Sybil Vane are two things I shall never forget. When I close my eyes, I hear them, and each of them says something different. I don't know which to follow."

The passage recalls an earlier one, already quoted, giving Dorian's reaction to Wotton's voice. Dorian's nature is gray: good and evil are locked in mortal combat within him. Wotton is the voice of evil, while Sybil, reinforced by Basil, is the voice of goodness. When Sybil dies, Basil becomes exclusively the voice of goodness for Dorian, but the voice comes primarily from within Dorian, and the murder of Basil, instead of silencing it, only intensifies it. It is Dorian's destiny, however, to yield to the evil voice within himself. He has, after all, sold his soul to the devil:

> "I wish now I had not told you about Sybil Vane."

> "You could not have helped telling me, Dorian. All through your life you will tell me everything you do."

> "Yes, Harry, I believe that is true. I cannot help telling you things. You have a curious influence over me."

At one point, Lord Henry Wotton says to Dorian: "A new Hedonism—that is what our century wants. You might be its visible symbol." It is Dorian's destiny to be the perfect embodiment of this new hedonism—of decadence.

Before Sybil's death, Dorian searches for pure sensations. After her death, the sensations he seeks become less and less pure. He falls heavily under the spell of a mysterious yellow book—usually identified as Huysmans's *A rebours*—and this is a crucial stage in his development as a decadent, although it is only chapter 11 and the final pages of chapter 10 that record the yellow book's evil influence. Since the yellow book forms such an important stage in Dorian's development, it is necessary to understand what Wilde meant it to suggest. Wilde wrote, in chapter 11, that one has "ancestors in literature, as well as in one's own race, nearer perhaps in type and temperament, many of them, and certainly with an influence of which one was more absolutely conscious."

The two major influences on the English decadent movement were Pater's *The Renaissance* (1873) and Joris-Karl Huysmans's *A rebours* (1884). The yellow book is a nonexistent combination of these two works, one English and the other French; Dorian, it will be recalled, was born of an English father and a French mother. Although chapter 11 mostly reflects *A rebours,* strong echoes of *The Renaissance* also occur, mostly toward the beginning. Dorian remains under the spell of the yellow book for eighteen years, moreover, and if we accept that he died in 1890— the year in which most of **The Picture of Dorian Gray** was written and the earlier version published—then it becomes impossible to see the yellow book as being simply *A rebours* and very easy to recognize it as also being partly *The Renaissance.*

Through the yellow book and because of it, the post-Sybil Dorian experiences the history of the entire human race, precisely as Huysmans's hero did, and learns everything that Pater asserted modern man already knows: "It seemed to him that in exquisite raiment, and to the delicate sound of flutes, the sins of the world were passing in dumb show before him. Things that he had dimly dreamed of were suddenly made real to him. Things of which he had never dreamed were gradually revealed." Finally, Dorian comes to feel that he has absorbed everything the human race has ever known, especially its evil passions and sensations:

> There were times when it seemed to Dorian Gray that the whole of history was merely the record of his own life, not as he had lived it in act and circumstance, but as his imagination had created it for him, as it had been in his brain and in his passions. He felt that he had known them all, those strange terrible figures that had passed across the stage of the world and made sin so marvellous and evil so full of subtlety. It seemed to him that in some mysterious way their lives had been his own.

Dorian, however, will go beyond anything the race— including Des Esseintes and the modern Paterian man— has yet known, and will become the visible symbol of Wotton's new hedonism. The yellow book teaches him an important lesson. Wilde ends chapter 11 thus: "Dorian Gray had been poisoned by a book. There were moments when he looked on evil simply as a mode through which he could realise his conception of the beautiful." The book teaches Dorian to seek beauty in evil, and as he comes to depend more and more on evil and evil sensations in his search for beauty, he becomes a full-blown decadent. Along with the detailed record in chapter 11 of Dorian's interest in jewels and perfumes, lengthy and mysterious absences are mentioned, after which he creeps back home, goes to the locked room and gazes with joy at his grinning, sin-scarred portrait, the mirror of his soul, gleefully comparing it with the beautiful mask that is his body: "He grew more and more enamoured of his own beauty, *more and more interested in the corruption of his own soul.* He would examine with minute care, and sometimes with a monstrous and terrible delight, the hideous lines that seared the wrinkling forehead or crawled around the heavy sensual mouth, wondering sometimes which were the more horrible, the signs of sin or the signs of age" (italics mine). The portrait is in the process of becoming a decadent work of art. The hideous, evil portrait, and Dorian's gleeful reaction to it, typifies a very important aspect of that art—the delighted recognition and celebration of the evil within the soul. We later learn—just before Basil's murder—that the portrait has "grinning lips." Decadent art, like aesthetic art, deals to a large extent with the world within, but while moral aesthetic art—Rossetti's is the major example—presents the soul as being essentially pure, decadent art sees it as being evil and derives pleasure from this evil. (pp. 37-57)

Dorian's grinning, evil portrait . . . and his delighted reaction to it, is typical of one very important aspect of decadent art—the gleeful recognition and celebration of a depravity whose wellsprings are within the soul.

The Pre-Raphaelite movement in England, dominated by the figure of Dante Gabriel Rossetti, began toward the middle of the nineteenth century and was on the wane by 1890. In **The Picture of Dorian Gray,** Basil Hallward is the representative of this movement. In his very photographic approach to painting, Basil suggests Holman Hunt, and perhaps also John Everett Millais, both members of the original Pre-Raphaelite Brotherhood. Jerome Buckley [in *The Pre-Raphaelites,* 1968] has observed of Hunt that "to perceive intensely and to paint with absolute 'truth to nature' were the first principles of his Pre-Raphaelite creed." In his paintings, Hunt strove for absolute authenticity in every last detail. For instance, *The Scapegoat* was "modelled by a real goat tethered in woebegone thirst by the actual shore of the Dead Sea." The background of *The Triumph of the Innocents,* moreover, was "drawn with photographic fidelity on the very road from Jerusalem to Bethlehem."

Basil, however, largely suggests Rossetti. Buckley has written of Rossetti: "Both as painter and as poet, Rossetti, though attentive always to detail, was more literary than literal, interested first of all in the psychology of moods, the analysis of states of soul, and eager to depict the life of an imagination nourished on books and private reverie." Far more anxiously than his disciples, however, "Rossetti sought to make the sharp sense impression the avenue to mystical revelation." In his paintings and writings, Rossetti presented women chiefly as sensuous manifestations of total spiritual purity—a purity he deeply yearned for and found personified in Elizabeth Siddal and Jane Morris. In Rossetti's early short story, "Hand and Soul," the beautiful, ethereal lady who appears in Chiaro's room and bids him serve God by painting her, identifies herself as his soul. There was a demonic streak in Rossetti's soul, however, and this is vividly expressed, for instance, in his portrait of Lilith. Basil, in painting and worshiping Dorian as the sensuous manifestation of his largely pure but tainted soul—the painting contains a tinge of evil—clearly suggests Rossetti, although he worships a beautiful boy instead of a beautiful lady.

In *The Renaissance,* however, Pater had presented the Victorian world with a new kind of artist, one who owed much to the Pre-Raphaelites but who could best be characterized as a decadent. Instead of painting and worshiping blessed, ethereal ladies, Pater's Leonardo—the type of the modern artist—had been fascinated, rather, by the head of the Medusa. Pater informs us of Leonardo's depiction of this terrible head: "The subject has been treated in various ways; Leonardo alone cuts to its centre; he alone realises it as the head of a corpse, exercising its powers through all the circumstances of death. What may be called the fascination of corruption penetrates in every touch its exquisitely finished beauty. About the dainty lines of the cheek the bat flits unheeded. The delicate snakes seem literally strangling each other in terrified struggle to escape from the Medusa brain." Leonardo plunged into the depths of "human personality and became above all a painter of portraits." In the bewitchingly evil, enigmatic, smiling face of the Mona Lisa, he found and captured on canvas the perfect expression of human personality as Pater felt the modern world has come to know it.

Insofar as one can generalize about the Pre-Raphaelite movement, it is possible to maintain that its fortunes after 1873 were on the decline. Rossetti, the chief Pre-Raphaelite, had two periods of intense creativity. The first occurred in the 1850s, the second around 1868. Most of the poems that comprise his masterpiece, *The House of Life,* were written between 1868 and 1870. However, Robert Buchanan's attack on him in "The Fleshly School of Poetry," which first appeared in the *Contemporary Review* in October, 1871, cut deep. Already "nervously debilitated, he now felt relentlessly persecuted by a whole Philistine world he had never cared to understand. Henceforth he was increasingly subject to delusive fears and more or less constant insomnia." He continued to write and paint until his death in 1882, and his reputation continued to spread as he attracted more and more disciples, but Rossetti himself was in a state of decline and no one of equal stature appeared to carry on the torch.

John Ruskin is another major figure one associates with the Pre-Raphaelites, though he was definitely separate from them. Ruskin was the chief promoter and defender of the early Pre-Raphaelites—Rossetti especially—and the author of the voluminous work, *Modern Painters*

(1843-60), upon which the original Pre-Raphaelites looked with admiration. He fervently believed, moreover, that art and morality are inseparable. Richard Ellmann has observed of Basil [see Further Reading entry dated 1969]:

> The painter Hallward has little of Ruskin at the beginning [of *Dorian Gray*], but gradually he moves closer to that pillar of esthetic taste and moral judgment upon which Wilde leaned, and after Hallward is safely murdered, Dorian with sudden fondness recollects a trip they had made to Venice together, when his friend was captured by Tintoretto's art. Ruskin was of course the English discoverer and champion of Tintoretto, so that the allusion is specific.

In 1882, however, the youthful Oscar Wilde himself, speaking in the name of the new, amoral aesthetes of the 1880s, wrote that "we of the younger school have made a departure from the teachings of Mr. Ruskin,—a departure definite and different and decisive. . . . In his art criticism, his estimate of the joyous element of art, his whole method of approaching art, we are no longer with him; for the keystone to his aesthetic system is ethical always. He would judge of a picture by the amount of noble moral ideas it expresses." In the same essay—titled **"L'envoi"**—Wilde declared that

> the ultimate expression of our artistic movement in painting has been, not in the spiritual visions of the Pre-Raphaelites, for all their marvel of Greek legend and their mystery of Italian song, but in the work of such men as Whistler and Albert Moore, who have raised design and colour to the ideal level of poetry and music (**Miscellanies**).

Wilde, in the essay, connects Ruskin with the Pre-Raphaelites and sees both as linking art with morality. Moreover, in 1878 Ruskin suffered the first of seven attacks of madness that culminated in 1889 with the most damaging one. Ruskin's recurring fits of insanity interfered seriously with his work, and after 1889 he wrote practically nothing and spent the rest of his life in mute retirement. As this was occurring, the decadent movement, sparked by *The Renaissance* and inspired from across the channel by writers such as Baudelaire, Verlaine, Mallarmé, and Huysmans, was gaining momentum. By 1890, it was clearly emerging as an important movement in literature, and the stage was set for the appearance of an Aubrey Beardsley in painting.

The steady deterioration of Basil Hallward as an artist between 1873 and the time of his death on a dark, foggy November night in 1889, is meant to symbolize the decline of Rossetti, Pre-Raphaelitism in general, and Ruskin's "Moral Aesthetic" [Nassaar cites Jerome Hamilton Buckley, "The Moral Aesthetic," in his *The Victorian Temper,* 1951, as "an excellent introduction to Ruskin"]. At the beginning of *Dorian Gray,* Basil had made a request of Wotton: "Don't take away from me the one person who gives to my art whatever charm it possesses: my life as an artist depends on him." Wotton did not heed the request, and Basil's art consistently deteriorated as Dorian—symbol incarnate of the painter's soul—drifted away from him. It is not until Dorian reveals his true soul to Basil in the sinister thirteenth chapter of the novel, however, that the painter is completely destroyed as an artist:

> Hallward turned again to the portrait, and gazed at it. "My God, if it is true," he exclaimed, "and this is what you have done with your life, why, you must be worse even than those who talk against you fancy you to be!" He held the light up again to the canvas, and examined it. The surface seemed to be quite undisturbed, and as he had left it. It was from within, apparently, that the foulness and horror had come. Through some strange quickening of inner life the leprosies of sin were slowly eating the thing away. The rotting of a corpse in a watery grave was not so fearful.
>
> His hand shook, and the candle fell from its socket on the floor, and lay there sputtering. He placed his foot on it and put it out. Then he flung himself into the rickety chair that was standing by the table and buried his face in his hands.

Basil represents an art movement that recognizes the evil within the self and deals seriously with it, but can accept it only in small doses. When the soul reveals itself as overwhelmingly evil, Ruskin, or the Pre-Raphaelite artist, can only shrink away in horror and yield to the decadent, who can accept this vision and wring satisfaction from it. Basil's murder is not only the murder of one human being by another but also the murder of Pre-Raphaelite art and the Ruskinian "Moral Aesthetic" by decadent art. The horror on the canvas is specifically presented as an accomplice in the murder:

> Dorian Gray glanced at the picture, and suddenly an uncontrollable feeling of hatred for Basil Hallward came over him, as though it had been suggested to him by the image on the canvas, whispered into his ear by those grinning lips. The mad passions of a hunted animal stirred within him, and he loathed the man who was seated at the table, more than in his whole life he had ever loathed anything. . . . He rushed at him, and dug the knife into the great vein that is behind the ear, crushing the man's head down on the table, and stabbing again and again.

Dorian murders Basil because of an uncontrollable passion for sin, an insane desire to destroy the man who is praying and asking him to go down on his knees and pray too. The murder is an attempt on Dorian's part to stifle the voice of goodness forever. The picture's complicity in the murder, however, gives the act an added dimension: decadent art, having replaced Pre-Raphaelite art on the canvas and destroyed—even inverted—the Ruskinian link between art and morality, now completes the job by murdering the Pre-Raphaelite artist who, Ruskin-like, is praying to God. Quite probably, Wilde must have seen Ruskin's serious and very damaging attack of madness in the autumn of 1889 as effectively marking the end of an entire movement in art—certainly the end of the idea that art and morality are somehow wedded, an idea found not only in Ruskin but "in the spiritual visions of the Pre-Raphaelites" as well.

The murder of Basil is the turning point for Dorian. The portrait records this evil act, and Dorian begins to lose his nerve. The sight of so much evil becomes intolerable even to him, and he finds himself unable to derive pleasure from his new sin:

> He felt that if he brooded on what he had gone through he would sicken or grow mad. There were sins whose fascination was more in the memory than in the doing of them, strange triumphs that gratified the pride more than the passions, and gave to the intellect a quickened sense of joy, greater than any joy they brought, or could ever bring, to the senses. But this was not one of them. It was a thing to be driven out of the mind, to be drugged with poppies, to be strangled lest it might strangle one itself.

"Poppies" fail to strangle Dorian's sense of horror, though, and his encounter with Jim Vane shatters his nerves. The voice of goodness wells up from within him, poisoning his existence. He decides to escape by retracing his steps, by becoming once again a pure, innocent being, and his first good action is to spare a country girl. Wotton, however, suggests to him that the action was simply an attempt to experience a new sensation, and the portrait corroborates this by becoming more hideous. Dorian examines his motives closely and decides that this was indeed the case. Dorian, in this respect, is a typical decadent. Having yielded to the evil in himself, he ultimately discovers, to his horror, that he can no longer derive pleasure from it and that the plunge into the demon universe has become an irreversible process. Trapped in this demonic underworld, he has only one road of escape left, and that is death.

It is a road that Alan Campbell before him had taken. Alan had been corrupted by Dorian, but withdrew from a life of sin and decided to give expression to his corrupt impulses only within the framework of science, cutting up corpses and experimenting on rotting bodies. Dorian, however, brings him to a terrible and unbearable confrontation with evil—a confrontation Alan could not have possibly avoided—and the result is Alan's suicide. This is the inevitable end of the decadent, and Alan's suicide presages Dorian's death. Dorian, unable to bear the sight of his hideous portrait any longer, and identifying it with his conscience, decides to destroy it. For Dorian, this is the ultimate evil act, the desire to rid himself of all moral sense. The attempt to escape through good actions having failed, he decides to escape by committing the most terrible of crimes. When he plunges the blade into his "monstrous soul-life," however, he kills himself—this is really his only way out.

Wotton remains alive, but his fate, paradoxically, is the worst in the novel and is foreshadowed when his wife deserts him. Wotton's wife is not an individual but a type. Wilde says of her: "She was usually in love with somebody, and, as her passion was never returned, she had kept all her illusions. She tried to look picturesque, but only succeeded in being untidy. Her name was Victoria, and she had a perfect mania for going to church." She is the Victorian world personified, and Wotton's marriage to her is as necessary to his well-being as the dinner parties he attends. The paradoxist must have a fixed standard of values if he is to create paradoxes. Wotton as paradoxist continually stands Victorian values on their heads, but his marriage to Victoria is necessary if he is to continue to do this.

Unfortunately for Wotton, the continual process of inverting Victorian values ultimately destroys those values, and Victoria finally commits the very un-Victorian act of eloping. This, however, merely foreshadows Wotton's loss of his artistic masterpiece, Dorian, into whom he had poured all his soul. Wotton's paradoxes were only the means to an end—they were the evil brush he used to refashion Dorian in the light of his own soul. It should be stressed that Wotton has entirely renounced evil in his life, and has given full expression to the evil within himself only in his art. When Dorian dies, Wotton, the Satan-figure of *The Picture of Dorian Gray,* suffers the very terrible fate of losing his soul. In their last meeting before Dorian's suicide, Wotton speaks:

> "By the way, Dorian," he said, after a pause, " 'what does it profit a man if he gain the whole world and lose—how does the quotation run?— his own soul?' "
>
> The music jarred and Dorian Gray started, and stared at his friend. "Why do you ask me that, Harry?"
>
> "My dear fellow," said Lord Henry, elevating his eyebrows in surprise, "I asked you because I thought you might be able to give me an answer. That is all. I was going through the Park last Sunday, and close by the Marble Arch there stood a little crowd of shabby-looking people listening to some vulgar street-preacher. As I passed by, I heard the man yelling out that question to his audience. It struck me as being rather dramatic. London is very rich in curious effects of that kind. A wet Sunday, an uncouth Christian in a mackintosh, a ring of sickly white faces under a broken roof of dripping umbrellas, and a wonderful phrase flung into the air by shrill, hysterical lips—it was really very good in its way, quite a suggestion. I thought of telling the prophet that Art had a soul, but that man had not. I am afraid, however, he would not have understood me."

What Wotton says is true primarily of himself. Lord Henry has placed his soul entirely in his art—in Dorian— and when Dorian dies he loses it. Wotton's terrible end is probably a jab at Pater, who was too timid to practice in any way what Wilde believed him to have preached.

*The Picture of Dorian Gray* is about the coming-of-age of Victorian art and attitudes. Wilde saw human nature in nineteenth-century England as rapidly plummeting from innocence into an awareness of the demon universe. Wotton is delighted by this. "The only people to whose opinions I listen with any respect," he says, "are people much younger than myself. They seem in front of me." Wilde's book mirrors this development, but it goes beyond that. The book contains a moral, as Wilde himself pointed out in a letter to the editor of the *St. James's Gazette* [excerpted in *TCLC,* Vol. 8, pp. 488-89]:

*Caricature of Wilde by English illustrator Aubrey Beardsley.*

The moral is this: All excess, as well as all renunciation, brings its own punishment. The painter, Basil Hallward, worshipping physical beauty far too much, as most painters do, dies by the hand of one in whose soul he has created a monstrous and absurd vanity. Dorian Gray, having led a life of mere sensation and pleasure, tries to kill conscience, and at that moment kills himself. Lord Henry Wotton seeks to be merely the spectator of life. He finds that those who reject the battle are more deeply wounded than those who take part in it. Yes; there is a terrible moral in *Dorian Gray.*

Basil's attachment to the figure of Dorian—to his physical beauty and the purity it reflects—is extreme, and it destroys him, while Dorian's attempt to yield entirely to evil leads to his death. Wotton's rejection of evil in life is total, and he loses his soul but remains physically alive to endure the agonies of his spiritual damnation. What is needed, then, is a point of balance. One must neither completely renounce evil in life nor yield entirely to it. Wilde is counseling moderation in *Dorian Gray:* the Victorians are now deep in the demon universe, and unless they maintain a balance between good and evil, renunciation and excess, they will be destroyed.

This is true of life but not of art. In a second letter on *Dorian Gray* to the editor of the *St. James's Gazette* [27 June 1890], Wilde wrote: "It is proper that limitations should be placed on action. It is not proper that limitations should be placed on art." In art, one can descend to the bottom of the demon universe and emerge unscathed. This is dramatized in the final pages of *The Picture of Dorian Gray.* Dorian's picture accompanies Dorian to the very depths of the demon universe, but it returns unharmed to its original state. Dorian, on the other hand, dies. The demonic, then, should be fully explored only in art, if the exploration is to remain a beautiful experience. *"The artist is the creator of beautiful things,"* Wilde wrote in the preface to *Dorian Gray,* and he also wrote that *"the artist can express everything."* An art that delves into the dark caverns of the soul and fully explores and celebrates the evil within can remain beautiful, but a way of life that seeks fully to translate inner evil into action will finally cease to be beautiful and become an inescapable nightmare. This is Wilde's position in *The Picture of Dorian Gray,* a position he never abandoned.

A biographical comment is inevitable at this point. Gone is the writer of fairy tales. Camelot is in ruins, and Wilde, now a habitual homosexual, is moving in the same direction as his protagonist, Dorian Gray. At the opening of the 1890s, Wilde was still convinced that he could escape disaster by maintaining a balance between renunciation and excess in his homosexual involvements. But in 1891 Lionel Johnson introduced him to Lord Alfred Douglas, soon to become the great passion of his life and for whose sake he was to abandon all restraint. It is fascinating that Dorian's fate prefigures Wilde's own: the novel suggests that Wilde probably had a presentiment of what the gods within had in store for him. (pp. 62-72)

> *Christopher S. Nassaar, in his* Into the Demon Universe: A Literary Exploration of Oscar Wilde, *Yale University Press, 1974, 191 p.*

### Jeffrey Meyers   (essay date 1977)

[*Meyers is an American critic and the author of biographical and critical studies of T. E. Lawrence, George Orwell, and Katherine Mansfield. In the following excerpt, he discusses* The Picture of Dorian Gray *as a homosexual novel that addresses the difficulties of attaining fulfillment as a homosexual in Victorian society because of attendant fear, guilt, and self-hatred. Meyers maintains that* Dorian Gray *fails as a novel because Wilde was himself unable to reconcile his homosexuality with his fears of moral censure. The excerpt by Claude J. Summers dated 1990 includes refutation of Meyers's interpretation.*]

Most critics of *The Picture of Dorian Gray* (1891) treat the book as a classical illustration of literary aestheticism and decadence or, like [Edouard Roditi, in his *Oscar Wilde,* 1947], concentrate on its heterogeneous sources, from the Gothic novel through Balzac and Poe to Pater and Huysmans. Despite the abundant evidence, both external and internal, no critic has discussed the work as a homosexual novel. But this interpretation defines more precisely the nature of its decadence and its relation to Baudelaire and *Against Nature;* reveals a coherence and consistency in the uneven, loosely structured, melodramatic and sometimes absurd work; and suggests that the real meaning of the novel, like so many others on this subject, is more complex and interesting than it appears to be.

It is really about the jealousy and pain, the fear and guilt of being a homosexual.

[In *The Unrecorded Life of Oscar Wilde,* 1972, and *Feasting with Panthers,* 1967, Rupert Croft-Cooke] writes that the models for two of the principal characters in the novel were notorious homosexuals. Basil Hallward was 'Charles Shannon, the artist who for many years lived in marital bliss with Charles Ricketts, and Lord Henry Wotton . . . was Lord Ronald Gower', whom Croft-Cooke calls 'a thorough-paced queer who liked rough trade and found time, in spite of a public career, to enjoy it prodigally'. Wilde himself emphasizes that the characters are also projections of his own personality and says that *Dorian Gray* 'contains much of me. Basil Hallward is what I think I am: Lord Henry what the world thinks of me: Dorian what I would like to be—in other ages, perhaps'. Wilde thinks he is an artist and an idealist who loves beauty and handsome young men, and wants to be inspired by them as Socrates was inspired by Alcibiades. The world, encouraged by his wicked *persona,* believes he is a posturing, dissolute cynic. Wilde would like to be a beautiful youth, and he would also like to enjoy homosexual love without the severe and repressive legal penalties of the late Victorian age. For as Dorian

> looked back upon man moving through History, he was haunted by a feeling of loss. So much had been surrendered! and to such little purpose! There had been mad wilful rejections, monstrous forms of self-torture and self-denial, whose origin was fear, and whose result was a degradation infinitely more terrible than that fancied degradation from which, in their ignorance, they had sought to escape.

Wilde's condemnation of the repression of homosexuals—who are not specifically mentioned though they are clearly the subject of this passage—anticipates Freud's ideas about the irremediable antagonism between the demands of instinct and the restrictions of civilization in *Civilization and Its Discontents* (1930). Wotton also believes that repression is evil and argues that 'the only way to get rid of a temptation is to yield to it. Resist it, and your soul grows sick with longing for the things it has forbidden to itself, with desire for what its monstrous laws have made monstrous and unlawful'. In the novel Hallward and Wotton, the artistic and cynical aspects of Wilde, personify Dorian's conscience and instinct, the irresolvable conflict between his superego and his id.

But this triple projection of Wilde's personality leads to a split between the characters and the ideas they are meant to represent. The kindly and optimistic Hallward seems to come closest to the ideal of the novel—'to teach man to concentrate himself upon the moments of a life that is itself but a moment . . . [and] find in the spiritualizing of the senses its highest realization'. But Hallward is killed by Dorian, whose descent into the 'vulgar profligacy' that dulls the senses and into the suicide that extinguishes them is the antithesis of the ideal that Wilde is trying to express through Hallward. The ideas of Wotton, who urges Dorian to realize his true nature and yield to temptation even though his passions might shame him, are discredited by Dorian's dissolute behaviour. Wotton epigrammatically expresses some fine and some bitter sentiments, but we cannot take him seriously because he is an essentially passive and negative character who vicariously experiences evil through Dorian and has no real life of his own. We are constantly told about the evil of Dorian, who also enjoys corrupting young men, but we never learn exactly what he has done because the theme cannot be overly expressed and the characters hide as much as they reveal.

The original inspiration for the novel also evolved from Wilde's personal experience:

> When the sitting was over and Mr Wilde had looked at his portrait, it occurred to him that a thing of beauty, when it takes the form of a middle-aged gentleman, is unhappily not a joy forever. 'What a tragic thing it is', he exclaimed. 'This portrait will never grow old, and I shall.' Then the passion of his soul sought refuge in prose composition, and the result was **Dorian Gray** [*St. James Gazette,* 24 September 1890].

This autobiographical incident is transposed directly into the novel when Dorian, staring at his finished portrait, remarks: 'How sad it is! I shall grow old, and horrible, and dreadful. But this picture will remain always young . . . If it were only the other way! If it were I who was to be always young, and the picture that was to grow old! . . . I would give my soul for that!' This fanciful yet fatal wish for eternal youth and beauty (since old age is horrible and dreadful), rather than for moral or intellectual or artistic qualities, is consummated by a devil's pact in which the face on the canvas bears the burdens of his passions and his sins in return for a final, Gothic retribution. This pact turns Dorian into an image without a soul and allows him to be loved by men (and women) without having to love them in return.

The opening paragraphs of the novel, with their evocation of opium-tainted cigarettes and Baudelairean *fleurs du mal* (an anodyne for pain that becomes a recurrent theme in the book, for Dorian sniffs a flower just before he murders Hallward), establishes an atmosphere of preciosity and corruption. And this ambience is reinforced by Hallward's description of his first meeting and subsequent relationships with Dorian:

> When our eyes first met I felt I was growing pale. A curious sensation of terror came over me. I knew that I had come face to face with someone whose mere personality was so fascinating that, if I allowed it to do so, it would absorb my whole nature, my whole *soul,* my very art itself . . . I have always been my own master; had at least always been so, till I met Dorian Gray. Then . . . something seemed to tell me that I was on the verge of a terrible crisis in my life. I had a strange feeling that Fate had in store for me exquisite joys and exquisite sorrows.

Though Dorian is young, innocent and beautiful—'a type that was to combine something of the real culture of the scholar with all the grace and distinction and perfect manner of a citizen of the world'—Hallward's first, intensely physical reaction, is of fear. And though Dorian's character has not yet come under Wotton's evil influence, Hallward immediately feels threatened, weak and subservient

as he enters the sexual crisis that provides far more sorrows than joys.

Hallward enjoys confessing his literal idolatry and admits, 'I couldn't be happy if I didn't see him every day. He is absolutely necessary to me'. He compares his love for Dorian to the love of Michelangelo, of Winckelmann (whom Pater discussed in *The Renaissance*), and of Shakespeare (whose passion for the young man of the Sonnets is described by Wilde in his story, **'The Portrait of Mr W. H.'**). Hallward needs Dorian not only as an artistic inspiration, but also as the dominant partner in their sado-masochistic relationship; and he explains that 'Dorian's whims are laws to everybody, except himself . . . He is horribly thoughtless, and seems to take a real delight in giving me pain'.

When Wotton (the corrupt homosexual) maliciously steals Dorian from Hallward (the idealistic homosexual), the latter is forced to make humiliating though ineffectual pleas for Dorian's company. As he had foreseen, his art declines as his passionate friendship ends, and as Dorian becomes weary of 'the painter's absurd fits of jealousy, his wild devotion, his extravagant panegyrics, his curious reticences'.

Lord Henry Wotton is supposed to represent cynical hedonism, but as Hallward justly remarks (paraphrasing Rochester's famous epigram on Charles II who 'never says a foolish thing, nor ever does a wise one'): 'You never say a moral thing, and you never do a wrong thing. Your cynicism is simply a pose.' If Hallward is the masochistic creator of Dorian's aesthetic glorification, Wotton (who manipulates the vanity stimulated by the portrait) is the sadistic catalyst of his moral degeneration.

Wotton is an extreme misogynist who intensifies the homosexual theme by insisting on the need to escape from the horrible *ennui* of fashionable society ('My dear fellow, she tried to found a *salon,* and only succeeded in opening a restaurant'), from the overwhelming dreariness of heterosexual relations, and from the tedium of marriage, a 'bad habit' whose one charm is that it 'makes a life of deception absolutely necessary for both parties'.

One of the subtlest scenes in the novel occurs when Wotton's wife first meets Dorian. Though she is a gauche and even ludicrous character, and an easy target for satire ('Her name was Victoria, and she had a perfect mania for going to church'), her awkward intrusion into her own library reveals her estrangement from Wotton and his intimacy with Dorian, whose photographs fill the house. Though Wilde writes, 'She was usually in love with somebody, and her passion was never returned', she causes a scandal by running away with her musical lover and divorcing Wotton. He deceives his wife with Dorian and appears indifferent to her infidelity; but she merely laughs at his affair, for his extreme passivity is the emotional equivalent of impotence.

Gray is inevitably compared to 'the perfection of the spirit that is Greek', to Greek marbles, a young Adonis and a Greek martyr (Hallward's masochistic projection) in order to create an aesthetic tradition for the homosexual ideal. Though he is more elaborately Corinthian than austerely Dorian, he takes his name from a race whom John Addington Symonds calls 'those martial founders of the institution of Greek love'.

The correspondence between Dorian's external beauty and internal corruption is a variation of a more important Greek idea. According to the Neoplatonic doctrine expressed, for example, in Sidney's *Astrophel and Stella* (1580), the face is the outward form of the soul. Because of the harmony between the body and the soul, a beautiful face reveals an inward spirituality and inspires 'those whom Dante describes as having sought to "make themselves perfect by the worship of beauty"'. This same connection exists in **Dorian Gray,** where one character states that 'wicked people were always very old and very ugly', and where the grotesque reflection of Dorian's spiritual state is transferred to the painting. Dorian's dualism is reflected in the attitudes of Hallward and Wotton. The former sees him as 'the visible incarnation of that unseen ideal whose memory haunts us artists like an exquisite dream', while the latter calls him the 'son of Love and Death'.

When Dorian attempts to love the young actress, Sibyl Vane, he ignores the warning in Juliet's speech: 'I have no joy of this contract tonight: / It is too rash, too unadvised, too sudden', and follows the pattern of Wotton's prediction: 'When one is in love, one always begins by deceiving oneself and one always ends by deceiving others'. Dorian deceives himself by believing that he is able to love a woman and that 'his unreal and selfish love would yield to some higher influence, would be *transformed* into some nobler passion'. He is attracted to Sibyl partly because she is an illusion who is idealized and distanced from him by the stage, and mainly because she is androgynous. For when she plays Rosalind in *As You Like It* she appeals to his homosexual tastes: 'she came out in her boy's clothes and was perfectly wonderful. She had never seemed to me more exquisite.'

Both Dorian and Sibyl have similarly sordid backgrounds which are meant to provide a melodramatic contrast to their youthful purity and to explain their bizarre behaviour. Both were children of a passionate but ill-considered love affair. When Dorian's father ran off with his mother, a beautiful heiress, he was forced into a duel and deliberately killed; and after the early death of Dorian's mother, the posthumous child was brought up by the same wicked grandfather who had arranged the duel and then replaced the man he had murdered. Sibyl was an illegitimate child whose father also died early in her life. His surrogate, at the time she meets Dorian, is a stereotyped 'hideous Jew' with greasy ringlets who has financial control over her and acts as her guardian and pander. The brief narration of their disturbed childhood attempts to account for their extreme sensitivity and vulnerability, their emotional instability, and their manic-depressive behaviour, for Dorian moves from adoration to hate and Sibyl from ecstasy to suicide. But none of these biographical details can make Dorian and Sibyl's relationship real, for the whole episode is merely symbolic.

Wilde suggests that Dorian rejects Sibyl when he discovers his preference for illusion to reality, and this polarity is similar to the art-life conflict expressed in Dorian's portrait. Hallward's early paintings of Dorian were 'unconscious, ideal and remote'; and when he first paints Dorian realistically, he reveals his love and Dorian's true nature, and destroys their friendship. Similarly, Dorian loves Sibyl as an actress, as an impersonator of romantic heroines in an unreal and artificial atmosphere. When her love for him freed her soul from her emotional prison and taught her to recognize reality, she saw the hollowness and sham of her empty performances. But when she began to 'live', she lost her ability to act and forced Dorian to accept her as a real woman, not as 'a dream or a phantom'. This change killed his 'love' because, in Huysmans' words, 'anyone who dreams of the ideal, prefers illusion to reality, and calls for veils to clothe the naked truth'.

Dorian is never really in love with Sibyl because he is too narcissistic to love anyone but himself. He tries to love her because he believes it will be good for him to love a woman, but recoils when confronted with a real woman who loves him. Wilde associates reality with heterosexuality and illusion with homosexuality, and expresses Dorian's confirmation of his homosexuality through these associations. The ferocity of Dorian's reaction to Sibyl's love reveals the conflict between what he really feels and what society thinks he ought to feel.

Wilde derived these sexual and aesthetic associations from *Against Nature,* for Huysmans connects reality with bourgeois respectability and conventional morality, and equates art with imagination, refinement, sensuality and immoral love. In Huysmans' and Wilde's scale of values homosexuality, which is anti-social and taboo, is related to art; and homosexuals surround themselves with rich and elaborate illusions to 'spiritualize the senses'.

Wotton completes his domination of Dorian by sending him a copy of *Against Nature* bound in yellow paper, for the 'whole book seemed to [Dorian] to contain the story of his own life, written before he had lived it'. Dorian responds passionately to Huysmans because he sanctifies the sensitive and *raffiné* mode of existence and provides an aesthetic justification of homosexuality. In view of Wilde's statement that **Dorian Gray** 'is a fantastic variation of Huysmans' over-realistic study of the artistic temperament in our unartistic age', it is significant that Des Esseintes and Dorian are not real artists but dilettantes who express their artistic temperaments through Dandyism, hedonism (that is, childish self-indulgence) and homosexuality. The whole of Chapter 11 is a weak imitation of Huysmans, with successive paragraphs appropriately devoted to the more *recherché* aspects of perfumes, music, jewels, embroideries and ecclesiastical vestments, all used by Dorian as an aesthetic means of escape from the guilt of his sexual perversity. Though Dorian, in another weak attempt to rationalize his outrageous conduct, complains that he was 'poisoned' by the book, it is clear that Huysmans' novel did not change Dorian's life but merely accentuated tendencies that already existed in him.

Auden observes in his review of Wilde's **Letters** that 'the artist and the homosexual are both characterized by a greater-than-normal amount of narcissism', and this trait is particularly prominent in the homosexual artist. Hallward rhapsodically tells Dorian: 'You had leant over the still pool of some Greek woodland, and seen in the water's silent silver the marvel of your own face'. And 'once, in boyish mockery of Narcissus', Dorian had kissed his portrait. But instead of falling in love, like Narcissus, with his own image, an aesthetic extension of himself, he comes to hate it and destroys himself as he attempts to destroy his portrait. In the modern age, the relation of the artist to society has been analogous to the relation of the homosexual to society, so that Dorian's image reflects his self-hatred as well as his self-love.

The numerous parallels between Hallward and Sibyl also emphasize Dorian's homosexuality. He tells Wotton about his adoration of Sibyl in the same way that Hallward told Wotton about his idealization of Dorian. And Sibyl assumes Hallward's self-abasing sexual posture, and expresses her love by flinging herself on her knees, trembling all over 'like a white narcissus' and sobbing at Dorian's feet. Hallward, who understands Dorian's true nature, finds his engagement to Sibyl 'Impossible'. But on reflection, though 'he could not bear this marriage, yet it seemed to him to be better than many other things that might have happened'. These other things could only refer to Dorian's liaison with another man. By contrast, Dorian's mad adoration of Sibyl did not cause Wotton the slightest pang of annoyance or jealousy because he knew that Dorian could never love a woman.

Dorian's rejection of Sibyl is as sudden and unexpected as his murder of Basil, and both crimes are inspired by the same motive. For Basil and Sibyl (both have Greek names, though he is not regal nor she prophetic) make a great emotional claim on Dorian who, because of the guilt about his homosexuality (the reason for his emphasis on purity), feels compelled to displace his self-hatred and to punish those who love him and attempt to redeem him. For Basil created the visible emblem of his conscience, and Sibyl's love might 'purify him, and shield him from those sins that seemed to be already stirring in spirit and in flesh—those curious *unpictured* sins whose very mystery lent them their subtlety and their charm'.

The irreconcilable conflict between art and life, between the homosexual and heterosexual modes of love, leads to the murder of Hallward just as it had led to the suicide of Sibyl and the corresponding signs of degeneration in Dorian's portrait. In the first chapter the artist says that he cannot exhibit the painting because 'I have put too much of myself into it', and he later adds that it would reveal the shameful secret of his idolatrous love for Dorian. The portrait also holds the secret of Dorian's life, for it teaches him to love his own beauty and to loathe his own soul, an impossible combination of homosexual narcissism and socially-conditioned self-hatred.

When Basil changes his mind and asks Dorian if he can exhibit the portrait, Dorian offers to exchange secrets about it. Though he discovers Hallward's secret, he never reveals his own until his friend visits him again on the night of the murder. Then, in response to the long sermon about his behaviour from Hallward, who has become an insufferable prig and a bore (and is killed, one suspects, partly for this reason), Dorian says, 'I shall show you my

soul . . . You are the one man in the world entitled to know everything about me'—though Hallward already knows virtually everything there is to know. After revealing the visual evidence to Hallward and hearing his horrified response, Dorian is madly inspired by the overt image of evil and, pursuing a false logic, kills 'the friend who had painted the fatal portrait to which all his misery had been due'. It is significant that Dorian impulsively kills Hallward by driving a knife into the great *vein* behind the ear (the play in the novel on vein, vain and Vane is a weak attempt to achieve unity), and that he blackmails one of his homosexual acquaintances (who later commits suicide) and forces him to destroy the corpse with acid, for Sybil had also used prussic acid to destroy herself.

Just as Basil haunts Dorian after his death through his portrait, so Sibyl posthumously pursues him through her brother James, who has sworn to kill her deceiver. James is motivated by jealousy as well as by revenge, for in the absence of their father, he developed an unusually close and protective relationship with his sister. When he left for Australia they parted like lovers: 'her arms were flung round his neck, and her fingers strayed through his hair, and he softened, and kissed her with real affection'. After James, like Dorian's father, is conveniently shot (during a hunting party), the way is clear for Dorian to kill himself, as he had killed Hallward, by stabbing.

The crimes of desertion and murder are the external manifestations of the inward corruption that is frequently hinted at but never defined, and Dorian's subsequent absorption in evil is essentially homosexual. He shares a house with Wotton in Algiers (where Wilde enjoyed the pleasures of pederasty without fear of the law), adopts (like Sibyl) the 'curious disguises' of a transvestite, frequents the low dens that cater to the perverse predilections of foreign sailors, and acquires an impressive list of male victims:

> There was that wretched boy in the Guards who committed suicide. You were his great friend. There was Sir Henry Ashton, who had to leave England, with a tarnished name. You and he were inseparable. What about Adrian Singleton, and his dreadful end? What about Lord Kent's only son, and his career? I met his father yesterday in St. James's Street. He seemed broken with shame and sorrow. What about the young Duke of Perth? What sort of life has he got now? What gentleman would associate with him?

All these male friendships are described in terms of strong moral opprobrium—they are shameful, vile and degraded—and though Kent's son married a whore and Singleton forged a bill, all these men obviously practised what Lord Alfred Douglas called 'the love that dare not speak its name'. Dorian has again punished a succession of well-born and promising young men for his own sin, which caused women who had wildly adored him 'to grow pallid with shame or horror if [he] entered the room'. These women felt shame for allowing themselves to be deceived by him, and horror of his vice. If Dorian were merely a libertine he would not be, as Hallward says, 'a man whom no pure-minded girl should be allowed to know, and whom no chaste woman should sit in the same room with'.

Though their purity and chastity would protect them from seduction, they could still be contaminated by his perversity.

Dorian's final, Faustian attempt to redeem himself as he slides from corruption to crime (and it is the crime that betrays the corruption) is a conscious repetition of his relationship with Sibyl. Dorian meets a working-class village girl named Hetty who 'was quite beautiful and wonderfully like Sibyl Vane. I think it was that which first attracted me to her'. He plans to run off with her but decides, suddenly and at the last moment, 'to leave her as flower-like as I had found her'. Wotton reinforces the parallel with Sibyl by insisting that Dorian's noble sacrifice has in fact broken her heart and possibly caused her to kill herself. And he compares her to Ophelia and Perdita just as Dorian had compared Sibyl to Juliet and Rosalind. Wotton quite rightly denies the morality of Dorian's renunciation, and his worldly and sophisticated analysis destroys the last flicker of idealism in Dorian and confirms his damnation. Though Dorian is more deliberately cruel to Sibyl, he treats both Sibyl and Hetty in the same way, commits the terrible Victorian crime of toying with a young girl's affections and ruins their lives. The greatest similarity in these two unconsummated affairs is, of course, Dorian's attempt to use a pure woman to rescue himself from homosexuality. In both cases, when he is forced to commit himself emotionally and sexually to a woman, he becomes frightened, abandons her and returns to his old way of life.

In *De Profundis* (1905) Wilde writes that homosexual love 'was like feasting with panthers. The danger was half the excitement'. But the legal danger cut both ways and diminished the pleasure at the same time that it intensified the excitement. This double aspect of ecstasy and fear is reflected in the many polarities that create a vital tension in Dorian, who keenly felt 'the terrible pleasure of a double life': the man and the portrait, youth and age, beauty and ugliness, body and soul, freedom and conscience, life and art. This ambivalence is also manifested in Dorian's intense emotions which lead both to his crimes and to his almost anaesthetic lack of feeling about them, in his extreme variation between ruthless behaviour and guilty repentance, and in his simultaneous desire to conceal his actions and to confess them.

The overt moral of *Dorian Gray* is not convincing. It is too heavy-handed, obvious and *de rigueur*, and too inconsistent with the defiant tone of the novel, which delights in the Baudelairean fascination of sin and authorization of evil. For as T. S. Eliot writes of Baudelaire [in "Baudelaire,' *Selected Essays, 1912-1932*, 1932], 'The recognition of the reality of Sin is a New Life; and the possibility of damnation is itself . . . an immediate form of Salvation— of Salvation from the ennui of modern life, because it gives some significance to living.'

Though Wilde insisted in his somewhat posturing Preface, 'There is no such thing as a moral or an immoral book', he felt obliged to emphasize the moral ending in his letters. He writes in 1890, the year the book was serialized, that Dorian Gray ('what I would like to be') 'is extremely impulsive, absurdly romantic, and is haunted all his life by

an exaggerated sense of conscience which mars his pleasures for him . . . In his attempt to kill conscience, Dorian Gray kills himself.' Though Dorian moves directly from renunciation of women to excess with men, Wilde's supposed 'moral is this: All excess as well as all renunciation brings its own punishment'. Wilde begins by pleading for sexual freedom and ends by equating homosexuality with undefined and pervasive evil.

*Dorian Gray* is a failure as a novel because Wilde was unable to resolve the conflict between his desire for homosexual freedom and his fear of social condemnation. Though the picture represents Dorian's conscience, it would be more accurate to say (despite Wilde's statement) that he is haunted by the fear that the visual evidence of the picture will lead to the *discovery* of his crimes and his corruption. As long as he feels the painting is securely hidden, he does exactly as he pleases. But when he feels threatened by exposure, he becomes convinced that if he kills the painting with the same knife he used to kill the painter, 'It would kill the past, and when that was dead he would be free'. But Dorian is already as free as it is possible to be—in the Victorian age—for he has regressed to a state of childish and narcissistic irresponsibility. The aesthetic point of the novel may be that if instinct overcomes restraint, it will destroy art. But the real subject of the book, where 'conscience' stands for law and 'soul' for body, is the impossibility of achieving homosexual pleasure without the inevitable accompaniment of fear, guilt and self-hatred. (pp. 20-31)

> *Jeffrey Meyers, "Wilde: 'The Picture of Dorian Gray' (1891)," in his* Homosexuality and Literature: 1890-1930, *McGill-Queen's University Press, 1977, pp. 20-31.*

## Rodney Shewan (essay date 1977)

[*In the following excerpt, Shewan considers the principal influences on* Dorian Gray *to be Wilde's own life, personality, and literary works.*]

Wilde's second 'imaginary portrait' is in many ways his most complex work. It may be, in part, 'a study of various Victorian art movements', a dramatisation of Ruskin's and Pater's tutelary influences, a rehash of Poe, a crib from Stevenson, a cento of *Vathek, Vivian Grey, Melmoth the Wanderer, Mademoiselle de Maupin, A rebours, Le peau de chagrin, Margery Merton's Girlhood*, Lefébure's *History of Lace*, and the handbook to the South Kensington Museum [Shewan cites, respectively, Christopher Nassaar (see excerpt dated 1974); Richard Ellmann (see Further Reading entry dated 1969); Edgar Allan Poe's 'William Wilson'; Andrew Lang's 'Literary Plagiarism,' *Contemporary Review*, June, 1887; and Isobel Murray's edition of *The Picture of Dorian Gray*, 1974, as well as Murray's 'Some Elements in the Composition of *The Picture of Dorian Gray*,' *Durham University Journal* 64, 1972, as sources for these interpretations]. Ultimately, Wilde is his own most important influence, and his multiple presence in the book effectively belies the simple tale with a moral, or simple lack of morals, dismissed by many early reviewers and certain later critics.

Central to the design is Dorian's portrait. Mallarmé thought that it became 'the book itself', but the book itself is really a triple portrait of the artist as a young man. In the relationships between the central trio we find Wilde's most serious statements. Something of this emerges in letters. In public, Wilde felt the need to defend himself against charges of immorality: 'The painter, Basil Hallward, worshipping physical beauty far too much, as most painters do, dies by the hand of one in whose soul he has created a monstrous and absurd vanity. Dorian Gray, having led a life of mere sensation and pleasure, tries to kill conscience, and at that moment kills himself. Lord Henry Wotton seeks to be merely the spectator of life. He finds that those who reject the battle are more deeply wounded than those who take part in it.' If the public requires a moral tag, Wilde will provide one: 'All excess, as well as all renunciation, brings its own punishment.' What the public will not have realised is the subjective significance of the proposition.

In the same statement, Wilde insisted on the novel's imaginary basis. 'Life by its realism is always spoiling the subject-matter of art. The supreme pleasure in literature is to realise the non-existent.' Such assertions have not prevented speculation about the original sitters for so provoking a 'picture'. There is an account, almost certainly apocryphal, of Wilde's visits during the 1880s to a studio where he supposedly conceived the idea for the story. John Gray and Alfred Douglas are obvious candidates for the hypothetical 'real' Dorian. Even Charles Ricketts and Charles Shannon might have posed as artist and sitter respectively: according to Rothenstein's double portrait they closely resembled Wilde's Basil and Dorian, and they shared an artistic establishment in Chelsea. There is, however, no definite evidence to support any of their claims, and the most obvious and most likely source for Wilde's experimental modern hero is the same as that for his idealised Elizabethan dramatic hero: his own wishful thinking. 'The supreme pleasure in literature is to realise the non-existent.' Another letter, to one Ralph Payne, supports this view: 'The book that poisoned, or made perfect, Dorian Gray', Wilde admitted, 'does not exist: it is a fancy of mine merely. I am so glad that you like that strange coloured book of mine; it contains much of me in it. Basil Hallward is what I think I am: Lord Henry what the world thinks me: Dorian what I would like to be—in other ages, perhaps.' This succinct account, to which surprisingly little attention has been paid, forms the basis of my argument.

The first version of **Dorian Gray,** published in 1890 in *Lippincott's Monthly,* differs from the 1891 volume as a longish short story generally differs from a novella: it concentrates on a single line of exposition and minimises incidentals. Apart from servants, waiters, and the like, there are only three characters besides the central trio, and none of the three—Sibyl Vane, Alan Campbell, and Lord Henry's wife—appears more than once. Wilde's 'art-decorator's' prose is also functional. As in **"The Birthday of the Infanta"**, it serves as an aid to characterisation. The notorious chapter about Dorian's collections is one of the few passages in the 1890 version to reveal something of the inner workings of his personality.

But the most publicised difference between the 1890 and 1891 texts concerns Basil's feelings for Dorian. [In a review cited in Stuart Mason's *Art and Morality* (see Further Reading)], Pater had observed that certain expressions were open to misinterpretation, and Wilde duly emended them; but his attitude seems to have been ambiguous from the start. Basil 'worships' Dorian. He is possessed by the image of him, and admits (in the 1890 version) that he had 'never loved a woman—I suppose I never had time'. Yet his love for Dorian—'for it was really love—had something noble and intellectual in it'. Wilde changed this to 'The love that he bore him—for it was really love—had nothing that was not noble and intellectual in it', continuing, 'It was such a love as Michael Angelo had known, and Montaigne, and Winckelmann, and Shakespeare himself. Yes, Basil could have saved him.' This change is significant beyond the obvious disclaimer. Dorian's list of intellectual lovers matches that which appears in the second **"Mr W. H."** (dating from 1893) though absent from the first (1889). (It also matches that given by Wilde during his third trial, after passages from **Dorian Gray** had been quoted to support the prosecution's allegations of immorality, in an attempt to justify 'the love that dares not speak its name' in the nineteenth century.) Moreover, the 1891 **Dorian Gray** anticipates the second **"Mr W. H."**, in which a section on neo-Platonism was introduced, by arguing, through Lord Henry, the application of Platonic theory to the modern artist, Basil:

> From a psychological point of view, how interesting he was! The new manner in art, the fresh mode of looking at life, suggested so strangely by the merely visible presence of one who was unconscious of it all; the silent spirit that dwelt in dim woodland, and walked unseen in open field, suddenly showing herself, Dryad-like and unafraid, because in his soul who sought for her there had been wakened that wonderful vision to which alone are wonderful things revealed; the mere shapes and patterns of things becoming, as it were, refined, and gaining a kind of symbolical value, as though they were themselves patterns of some other and more perfect form whose shadow they made real: how strange it all was! He remembered something like it in history. Was it not Plato, the artist in thought, who had first analysed it? Was it not Buonarotti who had carved it in the coloured marbles of a sonnet-sequence? But in our own century it was strange.

The one crucial parallel that Lord Henry understandably fails to draw is with Wilde's Shakespearean trio, though it is clear enough that Wilde associated them intimately in his own mind. Basil's love for Dorian and its capacity to 'save' him recalls Shakespeare's all-forgiving love for the fickle Mr W. H., and his faith in Dorian as an ideal could have negated, if Dorian had allowed it to, the terrible passions and evil dreams to which the influence of the artist's rival, Lord Henry, exposed him. Furthermore the power of the unconscious over Dorian, a theme elaborated in the 1891 version is analogous to the Dark Lady theory added to the second **"Mr W. H."**.

These details, however, are less important than the overall structural resemblances. Both works are based on all-male trios, and both are principally concerned with the relationship between art and life, theory and feeling. *Dorian Gray* not merely takes over the central situation of **"Mr W. H."**, but dramatises Wilde's current artistic and personal conflicts. Basil, Dorian, and Lord Henry embody Wilde's three most highly developed literary manners—romantic mythopoeia, social pastoral, and utopian criticism—but they also re-interpret the roles of Wilde's three Shakespearean protagonists: Basil being cast as the worshipping and idealising artist, Dorian as the capricious inspiring youth who involuntarily stimulates a fresh era in art, and Lord Henry as the 'rival poet' whose medium, with significant modification, is criticism, and whose working material is the personality of others.

This relationship is much clearer in the first version, and it seems likely that, quite apart from the details noted by Pater, Wilde shared Basil's anxiety that those who gazed at a portrait might spy out the artist's secret. Basil is unmistakably the artist (mentioned again in **"The Critic as Artist"**) to whom a rare personality suggests a new manner, and Lord Henry the critical swashbuckler, the proud sail of whose full paradox sweeps away the sitter towards a full awareness of himself as a being, not just a model. Basil's conventional medium is art; Lord Henry's rival and ultra-modern medium is life itself, and his subject is Dorian. He plays on Dorian as on 'an exquisite violin' (Shakespeare had so played on Willie Hughes) and his 'poisonous theories' which Dorian unwisely and uncritically puts into practice, 'just as I do everything that you say, Harry', make 'the lad . . . largely his own creation'. Lord Henry, a covetous sybarite fledged in the Paterian cloister, prefers the experimental or 'scientific' method, but the subject matter provided by science seems to him 'trivial and of no import'. 'Human life' is the one thing worth study; and so, like the 'true critic', but with none of his purity of motive, Lord Henry lives vicariously on the emotions and experiences of other people: 'One's own soul and the passions of one's friends—they were the two fascinating things in life.' Between Lord Henry and Basil, Dorian makes a more independent Willie Hughes, defining a new relationship between life and art. If Willie Hughes, who first suggested the identification of perfection with personality, was the first recognisable ancestor of the Romantic movement, as Wilde's narrator had suggested in **"Mr W. H."**, then Dorian articulates that movement's *dernier cri*. Basil sees in him the epitome of a new school which, like the 'English Renaissance' of Wilde's lecture, will combine 'all the passion of the Romantic spirit' with 'all the perfection of the spirit that is Greek.' But Lord Henry tells him later 'Life has been your art. Your days have been your sonnets,' and Dorian assents wearily. 'Yes, life has been exquisite.' He has devoted his life to the quasi-Paterian, or 'modern', aim of seeing (in Alfred Douglas' words) that 'the moment holds a madrigal', and his wish-fulfilment via the portrait enables such a life to continue without ethical or legal interference from others.

In his early dramas, Wilde had feared that even the briefest romantic ecstasies tended to cost too much. [In *The Duchess of Padua*] Guido may reassure the dying Duchess that he has no regrets: 'have I not / Stood face to face with beauty; that is enough / For one man's life'; 'Why, in this dull and common world of ours / Men have died looking for such moments as this / And have not found them'; but the dramatist still felt it necessary to place poetic justice on the side of those who venture. Ripeness may come too soon; adaptability, as Prince Paul shows, is all. In *Dorian Gray* the supernatural steps in and saves the hero from adapting. Lending his 'countenance' to 'fill up' Lord Henry's critical life-drama, he becomes 'the type that the age has been looking for, and is afraid that it has found'. Directly responsible for Hallward's new artistic vision, and thus for the furtherance of modern art as a whole, Dorian finally transcends art as 'Art' by establishing life as the quintessentially modern art form even though it is necessarily transitory, and even though, when the personal influence inevitably fades—as the actor must die—the formal works of 'Art' will remain, not merely as the actor's or model's epitaph but as the true and enduring record of the age. For the portrait does change back; and though it is unwise to press for too specific an allegorical pattern, the reinstatement of the artist's ideal matches, appropriately enough, Wilde's interpretation of the twelve-line sonnet (CXXVI) as Shakespeare's last word in the Willie Hughes story: 'An envoi . . . whose motive is the triumph of Beauty over Time and of Time over Beauty.'

Passing from Wilde's account of Shakespeare's sonnets to his account of his own novel, it is not difficult to fit the unadmitted trio to the admitted. Basil is 'what I think I am': the serious artist possessed by an ideal of beauty imperfectly understood until he sees its physical incarnation, but lifted by it into a wholly new phase in his art. While this influence is restricted to his art, the 'romance' is fruitful. As Basil, and Wilde himself in the Preface, insist: 'The artist can express everything'. As soon as Basil allows the feeling to impinge on his life, where it can find only incomplete expression, he is doomed by it. 'There was something tragic,' Dorian muses, 'in a friendship so coloured by romance.' Lord Henry is 'what the world thinks me': the dandiacal mental athlete, the sceptical voluptuary who finds cynicism (as Wilde said of it in *De Profundis*) 'fascinating from its intellectual side', and who is committed to nothing except remaining uncommitted—above all, uncommitted to serious passion. He has been seen as 'a jab at Pater', but there is no need to read in Lord Henry's philosophy of inaction any criticism of *The Renaissance* when the author of *Vera, The Duchess of Padua, The Happy Prince, A House of Pomegranates,* and **"The Critic as Artist"** saw such virtue in postponing self-commitment. Dorian, finally, is 'what I would like to be—in other ages, perhaps', Wilde's one serious romantic egotist in modern dress. Just as Basil had painted Dorian in all sorts of mythical and historical guises (including all of those admired by the Young King), so Wilde himself now faced the problem of embodying his own 'non-existent' ideal in a contemporary setting—the ultimate test of its dubious viability. Basil's contemporary portrait is 'one of the greatest things in modern art' and the artist's masterpiece; but it dislocates his sense of abstract beauty, destroys his artistic objectivity, and, by a curious reversal of the Pygmalion story, takes on a life of its own at the price of the artist's life.

Within this pattern, Wilde's enduring dilemma undergoes

definitive resolution. The egotistic romantic impulse, the impossible quest for the grail of self through art or through expressionistic action, is at odds with the sceptical critical faculty which refuses to accede to it, knowing such desires to be suicidal. Caught in the crossfire between these cohabiting antagonists is the artist, painted here as the worshipper and slave of beauty. But, in the words of the Wildean critic himself, 'There is nothing sane about the worship of beauty. It is too splendid to be sane. Those of whose lives it forms the dominant note will always seem to the world to be pure visionaries.' The visionary's world is a no man's land, doubly vulnerable from the theoretician and the man of action, as Basil learns. 'Sometimes,' Wilde wrote in 1886, before he had developed his critical stance, 'I think that the artist's life is a long and lovely suicide, and I am not sorry that it is so.' With a clearer view of the alternatives, he now took warning. After **Dorian Gray,** he moved back into the history-myth of **Salomé,** objectified through its woman hero; developed the autobiographical motive in the second **"Mr W. H.",** objectified by the conventions of aesthetic and textual criticism; and passed into the social compromise of stage comedy. Thus the novel stands at the crossroads, or more properly at the trivium, of personality—that fateful spot where the Muse-Sphinx must, and does, solve its own riddle.

Related to this motif of the tripartite personality is Dorian's development out of a state of pastoral self-ignorance. Pastoral images of countryside and garden are juxtaposed with dandiacal expositions of the 'new hedonism' and the novel fuses the symbolism of the fairy-tales with the philosophy of Wilde's utopian criticism. Beauty, however, not thought, is still the revelatory quality. For Dorian, as for the Young King, the Dwarf, and the Star-Child, personal beauty, present or absent, initiates the pastoral personality into the truth about itself.

This is the principal significance of the notorious book lent by Lord Henry, the hero of which attempted 'to realise in the nineteenth century all the passions and modes of thought that belonged to every century except his own, and to sum up, as it were, in himself the various moods through which the world-spirit had passed'. In a manuscript version Wilde gave the title of this book as 'Le Secret de Raoul' and its author as 'Catulle Sarrazin'. In the published versions it was untitled and anonymous. In public letters he insisted that the book did not exist, and in private he both denied a specific model and acknowledged the partial influence of *A rebours*. The influence is there, but Wilde's and Huysmans' heroes have little in common other than a set of elaborate artistic tastes. The above summary of the mysterious protagonist's life bears scant relation to the pathetic attempts of Des Esseintes to keep illness, the present, and the bourgeois at bay, though it does resemble the cultural ideal of Pater's Duke Carl or of **"The Critic as Artist"**: 'To realise the nineteenth century, one must realise every century that has preceded it and that has contributed to its making. To know anything about oneself one must know all about others. There must be no mood with which one cannot sympathise, no dead mode of life that one cannot make alive.' This is the creed that Dorian briefly embraces, and which makes him, for as long as he remains true to it, Wilde's only perfect speci-

men of the Marcusean Narcissist, whose 'life is beauty, whose existence is contemplation'.

Between the true critic and 'the type the age has been looking for', as defined by Lord Henry and exemplified by Dorian, there is, however, one crucial difference. The Wildean or neo-Hegelian critic was to relive history through his aesthetic sensibility, while the cultivated hedonistic egotist was to 'rewrite history' according to his own real or postulated appetites. The critic lives wholly in thought. For him the revelatory medium is 'imagination', the concentration of 'race-experience' in its purest form: 'The great events of the world take place in the brain. The great sins of the world take place in the brain also.' But the egotistical hedonist with his modern sensibility—'too intellectually subtle and too curious of exquisite pleasures to accept any speculations about life in exchange for life itself'—finds contemplation unsatisfying. Life is his only conceivable medium, and the 'experimental method' the only profitable way of exploring it.

Pater had outlined the 'experimental method' in the celebrated Conclusion to *The Renaissance* (1873), returning to it with more caution in *Marius the Epicurean* (1885), and *Gaston de Latour* (published serially, June-October 1889). In the third chapter of the unfinished romance (August 1889), entitled "Modernity", Pater had explored the prospect, for an impressionable youth of the sixteenth century, of 'the worship of physical beauty' becoming 'a religion, the proper faculty of which would be the bodily eye!' But Gaston feels reservations:

> Might that new religion be a religion not altogether of goodness, a profane religion, in spite of its poetic fervours? There were 'flowers of evil', among the rest. It came in part, avowedly, as a kind of consecration of evil, and seemed to give it the beauty of holiness. Rather, good and evil were distinctions inapplicable in proportion as these new interests made themselves felt. For a moment, amid casuistical questions as to one's indefeasible right to liberty of heart, he saw himself, somewhat wearily, very far gone from the choice, the consecration of his boyhood.

Gaston's boyhood state had been a dreamy, half-questioning absorption with the church around which his early years had been passed. A visit to Ronsard wakes him to life, but Montaigne's tutelage proves the formative influence. Although the school of Ronsard 'was soon to pay the penalty of that immediate acceptance, that intimate fitness to the mind of its own time, by sudden and profound neglect . . . like magic youth, or magic beauty, turned by magic's own last word into withered age', Gaston has genuinely loved the poet's lyrics. Even so, it is the philosopher's deliberate unpretentious egotism in which he recognises 'the pattern of the true intellectual life of everyone'. These successive influences at work upon Gaston operate simultaneously upon Dorian. Lord Henry's garden speech offers the instinctual and the philosophic approaches to life in one accessible creed, and Dorian's escape from the 'consecration of his boyhood' is accomplished within minutes.

The relationship between Dorian's development and Lord

Henry's influence was modified in the 1891 version. Originally, Lord Henry dilated on his theories only before Dorian and Basil. The trio could therefore be regarded as an eccentric clique, and the impetus for Dorian's backsliding—or for his climb out of the pastorally perfect state into 'modern' inclusive consciousness—could be supposed to come almost entirely from within himself. In the 1891 version, seeking to make the 'moral' less obtrusive, Wilde expanded the social setting so that Dorian's egotism in its everyday manifestation seems, if not 'the pattern of the true intellectual life of everyone', at least the norm of civilised contemporary life. Dorian's acceptance of Lord Henry's theories therefore appears little more than an exaggerated instance of the socialisation of the gifted individual. Only the artist remains an awkward anti-social exception.

Like **"The Birthday of the Infanta"**, the novel opens with a series of deliberate ambiguities. Entering the studio in which Basil works and Lord Henry lounges, we sense at once its interpenetration with the adjacent garden. The room brims with 'the rich odour of roses'; Lord Henry glimpses 'the gleam of the honey-sweet and honey-coloured blossoms of the laburnum' bowed with the Edenic burden of its beauty; 'the fantastic shadows' cast by moving birds against the curtains remind him of the paradox of arrested motion beloved of the 'pallid jade-faced painters of Tokio'. Even the 'dim roar' of the distant city resembles an organ's pedal note. Art and nature lie together here with incestuous freedom; and the intimacy of their mutual identification fixes the scope and manner of the novel.

As soon as the topic of Basil's absent sitter occurs, Lord Henry expounds a social satirist's view of the 'state of nature': 'Beauty, real beauty, ends where intellectual expression begins.' If Hegel could include in his *Bildungsgeschichte* a section devoted to phrenology, Wilde, not to be outdone, it seems, will include in his *Bildungsroman* a physiognomic corollary to the doctrine of the original lapse into thought:

> The moment one sits down to think, one becomes all nose, or all forehead, or something horrid. Look at the successful men in any of the learned professions. How perfectly hideous they are! Except, of course, in the Church. But then in the Church they don't think. A bishop keeps on saying at the age of eighty what he was told to say when he was a boy of eighteen, and as a natural consequence he always looks absolutely delightful.

Lord Henry is confident that Dorian will bear out his theory:

> Your mysterious young friend, whose name you have never told me, but whose picture really fascinates me, never thinks. I feel quite sure of that. He is some brainless, beautiful creature, who should be always here in winter when we have no flowers to look at, and always here in summer when we want something to chill our intelligence.

This calculated flippancy summarises the underlying premise of the novel and the visual metaphor by which it is expressed. Like the Star-Child, Dorian begins to lose his mysterious gift of beauty once his latent egotism is consciously developed; or rather, the loss is transferred to the portrait which, as long as Dorian lives, presents a sub-human figure, 'wrinkled and loathesome of visage', more repulsive even than the Star-Child's reptilian skin. This process begins as soon as Dorian stirs to Lord Henry's panegyric on youth and the physical world—as soon, in Lord Henry's terms, as Dorian begins to think.

The ambiguous relationship between art and nature is maintained throughout the early chapters. Basil makes his confession of Dorian's importance to him as 'a motive in art' in the garden, not in the studio. Upon re-entering the studio at the beginning of chapter 2, the men see Dorian sitting at the piano, leafing through Schumann's *Forest Scenes*, which he asks Basil to lend him. (Of these we hear no more. The next book with which Dorian is associated is *Manon Lescaut*, lying in Lord Henry's library.) Dorian's immaturity is pointedly exaggerated in this chapter, accentuating one of the ironies of Basil's portrait: the 'half-parted lips and the bright look in the eyes' (again recalling the Young King and the Narcissus of **"The Burden of Itys"**) are produced by the critic's persuasive invitation to self-knowledge. Wilde makes doubly sure of the point. While Basil stays inside to finish the picture, Dorian escapes into the garden from the 'stifling' air of the studio (as Salomé escapes, with analogous results, from the banquet). He buries his face in the 'great cool lilac-blossoms, feverishly drinking in their perfume as if it had been wine'. Lord Henry tells him:

> 'You are quite right to do that. Nothing can cure the soul but the senses, just as nothing can cure the senses but the soul.' . . .
>
> Dorian Gray listened, open-eyed and wondering. The spray of lilac fell from his hand upon the gravel. A furry bee came and buzzed round it for a moment. Then it began to scramble all over the oval stellated globe of the tiny blossoms. He watched it with that strange interest in trivial things that we try to develop when we are stirred by some new emotion for which we cannot find expression, or when some thought that terrifies us lays sudden siege to our brain and calls on us to yield. After a time the bee flew away. He saw it creeping into the stained trumpet of a Tyrian convolvulus. The flower seemed to quiver, and then swayed gently to and fro.

Later, both Basil and Dorian become convinced that Lord Henry's influence was pernicious, perhaps wilfully so; but here Wilde's imagery suggests that the instrument is less important than the moment, and that, while Lord Henry recognises the moment's psychological promise, the intellectual pollination that he effects is as inevitable to any complex personality as the simplest cyclical processes are to nature. Clearly, Lord Henry's assertion that the only nature that can be said to be spoiled is one whose development has been arrested can be countered by arguing that his hedonistic theory and his delight in playing upon 'the lad's unconscious egotism' leads to an *impasse* in Dorian's moral growth. But, at this first meeting between them, no such growth has yet begun. Dorian does not understand Basil's devotion, nor does he appear to care much for Basil's art or his own prominence in it. To the unfallen personality, the distinction between art and nature is either incomprehensible, as it was to the Dwarf, or has not yet acquired that intensity and clarity which are the consequence of regarding them as the polarities of civilised life. Wilde accordingly commences the 'fall' in the studio, pursues it in the garden, and completes it back in the studio. Basil's portrait is the instrument of revelation, but Lord Henry's seductive picture of the fruits awaiting youth and beauty is the immediate cause of Dorian's looking at his own likeness with new eyes. As a result of what he hears and sees, he wishes for a division between art and nature so extreme and so unnatural that it inevitably causes the total disintegration of personality. It is the fate of Basil's modern dress portrait to record, after the fashion of Pater's *Imaginary Portraits,* the crucial moment of cultural and psychological transition.

Only after the portrait has been hidden away, however, does Dorian's development enter its most interesting phase. As Nassaar has pointed out, Wilde deliberately consigns the corrupted picture to the scene of Dorian's boyhood innocence, the schoolroom at the top of the house [see excerpt dated 1974]. In the 1890 version, the housekeeper, Mrs Leaf, makes a point of calling her employer 'Master Dorian' although she feels that this is no longer appropriate, makes allusions to his boyish taste for jam, and provides further comic business of the kind. In the 1891 version the specifics were removed but the implicit contrast remained. While the image of his awakening ignorance festers obscenely in the surroundings where knowledge first touched him, its avatar lives out, in the adult apartments below, a life of sophisticated experimentation. The physical removal of the portrait, first from its creator, then from the presence of its owner and subject to a secret hiding-place, matches the increasing dichotomy within Dorian's personality. Basil saw in his Dorian-vision a potential re-incarnation of the harmony of soul and body, but Dorian, following Lord Henry's rival aesthetic, soon reaches the point at which he involuntarily rejoices in driving them further and further apart. Once more, physical and moral beauty appear incompatible. On the one hand,

> while he was but too ready to accept the position that was almost immediately offered to him on his coming of age, and found, indeed, a subtle pleasure in the thought that he might really become to the London of his own day what to Imperial Neronian Rome the author of the *Satyricon* once had been, yet in his inmost heart he desired to be something more than a mere *arbiter elegantiarum,* to be consulted on the wearing of a jewel, or the knotting of a necktie, or the conduct of a cane. He sought to elaborate some new scheme of life that would have its reasoned philosophy and its ordered principles, and find in the spiritualising of the senses its highest realisation.

On the other hand, he would

> creep upstairs to the locked room . . . and

stand, with a mirror, in front of the portrait that Basil Hallward had painted of him, looking now at the evil and ageing face on the canvas, and now at the fair young face that laughed at him from the polished glass. The very sharpness of the contrast used to quicken his sense of pleasure. He grew more and more enamoured of his own beauty, more and more interested in the corruption of his own soul.

The Young King's implied narcissism in an upper room of the palace here becomes explicit and perverse, as does the earlier suggestion of the influence of his ancestry. Indeed, Dorian speculates on the subject, walking past his ancestors' portraits and trying to determine the balance of their composite influences within him. He realises that literary forebears are 'nearer, perhaps, in type and temperament' than genetic ancestors, and that they act upon one 'certainly with an influence of which one was more absolutely conscious'. He appreciates also that 'Psychical environment is as important as physical: we cannot lay the ghosts of dead creeds'; but he feels that the uncertainty of mere genetic influence magnifies its grotesque potential:

> He used to wonder at the shallow psychology of those who conceive the Ego in man as a thing simple, permanent, reliable, and of one essence. To him, man was a being with myriad lives and myriad sensations, a complex multiform creature that bore within itself strange legacies of thought and passion. . . . Had the lover of Giovanna of Naples bequeathed to him some inheritance of sin and shame? Were his own actions merely the dreams that the dead man had not dared to realise?

Only a few months after publication of the first **Dorian Gray** Wilde suggested in **"The Critic as Artist"** that heredity, by annihilating the notion of free will, became 'as it were the warrant for the contemplative life'. Dorian, in so far as he consciously evaluates its role in his life, tends to regard it as the warrant for 'doing as one likes' in deed rather than merely in thought. In this, as in his choice of the schoolroom as soul-depository, there is a substantial degree of cultural rebellion. 'The pride of rebellion,' Wilde tells us, 'is half the fascination of sin', and he repeated in various contexts his conviction that disobedience is the first step in the growth of a man or a nation. Dorian's schoolroom was the place of his habitual banishment by an unsympathetic guardian; and whether or not Dorian's is one of those personalities half of whose strength 'is wasted in friction', his preference for the 'splendid sins' of history clearly stunts his growth towards inclusive culture. Those moments when he feels that 'history was merely the record of his own life . . . as it had been in his brain and in his passions' are firmly associated with wrong-doing.

Pater's warning against acquiescing 'in any facile orthodoxy of Comte or of Hegel or of our own' has its initial effect on Dorian—'of the asceticism that deadens the senses, as of the profligacy that dulls them' his philosophy was to know nothing. It was to 'teach man to concentrate himself on the moments of a life that is itself but a moment'. It was never to arrest his intellectual development. But Dorian avoids 'facile orthodoxy' only to fall into facile unorthodoxy. Like the Fisherman, he sees the possibility of a hedonistic ideal for the realisation of which the soul is an irrelevance or an embarrassment, and by a supernatural trick he cuts himself off from it. The portrait will bear the burden. But, as Wilde later wrote, 'To reject one's own experiences is to arrest one's own development. To deny one's own experiences is to put a lie into the lips of one's own life. It is no less than a denial of the Soul.' Dorian passes through Catholicism, mysticism, and Darwinism—a group of interests not unparalleled in Wilde's own career—but in wishing to create for himself worlds 'in which things would have fresh shapes and colours, . . . in which the past would have little or no place, or survive, at any rate, in no conscious form of obligation or regret', he denies the complexity of history and perverts its message. Eventually, suspended in time by the trick with the portrait, suspended in 'history'—in his own development—by wilful egocentricity, Dorian comes to regard the story of Tannhäuser as 'the presentation of the tragedy of his own soul'.

The recognition comes to him at the opera, but Wilde probably had Swinburne's version of the legend in mind as much as, if not more than, Wagner's. Elucidating his purpose in "Laus Veneris", Swinburne commented [in *Notes on Poems and Reviews,* 1866]:

> To me it seemed that the tragedy began with the knight's return to Venus—began at the point where hitherto it had seemed to leave off. The immortal agony of a man lost after all repentance—cast down from fearful hope into fearless despair—believing in Christ and bound to Venus—desirous of penitential pain, and damned to joyless pleasure—this, in my eyes, was the kernel and nucleus of the myth comparable only to that of the wise and foolish virgins, and bearing the same burden.

Dorian's uncritical pursuit of the 'new hedonism' propounded by Lord Henry matches Tannhäuser's imperfect religious dedication. Tannhäuser is 'Christ's knight, / No blinkard heathen stumbling for scant light'. Dorian also has his ideal, the ideal of perfect culture, the reintegration of 'sense' and 'soul', from which he is diverted into a false quest for the grail of self. The old schoolroom is his Venusberg, the portrait his Venus, self-consuming and all-consuming. The novel shows the romantic egotist's relation to that motto which was soon to become the quintessence of dandyism: 'To love oneself is the beginning of a lifelong romance.' Dorian's worship of the portrait turns to fascinated loathing. Beauty and youth are rejected (in the 1891 version) as 'a mask' and 'a mockery'. But his one 'real' attempt to repent of his sordid life—his conceited decision to 'spare' the rustic Hetty Merton—is as ineffectual as Tannhäuser's. Lord Henry, his lay-confessor, flippantly quotes from the Bible and mocks him for being absurdly 'boyish', and Dorian returns home to find the image of his soul looking even fouler than before.

The Sibyl Vane episode is the chief (in the 1890 text the only) instance of Dorian's self-destructive vanity at work beyond the central triangle. He wants 'to place her on a pedestal', he tells Lord Henry, 'and make the world worship the woman who is mine'. The prominent note of 'worship' throughout the 1890 version becomes the more interesting in the light of manuscript variations: Wilde veered between two forms of Sibyl's surname, 'Vane' and 'Fane'. Violet Fane was a character in *Vivian Grey* (1826), one of Wilde's putative sources, and he knew a Violet Fane as early as 1880. (Violet Fane was the pseudonym of Mrs Singleton, whose contributions to *The Woman's World* included, in 1888, a verse-confection entitled "The Mer-Baby".) 'Vane' is the name of the leading actor in Reade and Taylor's play *Masks and Faces* (dating from 1852), revived in 1885 in London and noticed in the newly established *Dramatic Review,* to which Wilde had contributed. A sentimental comedy set in eighteenth-century London, the piece relies for its main interest on the actress, Peg Woffington, who is being courted simultaneously by Sir Charles Pomander, donor of 'three hundred a year—house—coach—pin-money—my heart—and the et ceteras', and Ernest Vane, 'that pastoral youth who means to win a Woffington by agricultural courtship, who wants to take the star from its firmament and stick it in a cottage'. Woffington agrees to have her portrait painted by a pathetic incompetent jack-of-all-arts, and, when he despairs of his work and slashes it with a palette knife, she stands in for her image, placing her face behind the hole in the canvas and thus saving the painter's professional credit, besides discrediting the claptrap of visiting critics who pontificate on the differences between art and nature. Finally, Vane's wife, Mabel, seeking out her husband, sees what she takes to be the image of her rival and declares, 'Oh that she were here, as this wonderful portrait is; and then I would plead to her for my husband's heart!', whereupon, emulating Galatea, Hermione, and Walpole's Gothick statue of Alfonso, all combined, Woffington sheds a tear. Mabel is frightened, but Woffington steps down from the picture-frame, and being herself instead of merely playing herself, swears to relinquish all claim on Vane and break her influence over him. The strength and nature of this influence appear in the first scene:

> POMANDER. All this eloquence might be compressed into one word—you love Mrs Margaret Woffington.
>
> VANE. I glory in it.
>
> POMANDER. Why not, if it amuses you? We all love an actress once in our lives, and none of us twice.
>
> VANE. You are the slave of a word, Sir Charles Pomander. Would you confound black and white because they are both colours? Actress! Can you not see that she is a being like her fellows in nothing but name? Her voice is truth, told by music: theirs are jingling instruments of falsehood.
>
> POMANDER. No—they are all instruments; but hers is more skilfully tuned and played upon.
>
> VANE. She is a fountain of true feeling.
>
> POMANDER. No—a pipe that conveys it, without spilling or retaining a drop.
>
> VANE. She has a heart alive to every emotion.
>
> POMANDER. And influenced by none.

VANE. She is a divinity to worship.

POMANDER. And a woman to fight shy of. No—no—we all know Peg Woffington: she is a decent actress on the boards, and a great actress off them.

Wilde's susceptibility to names—the comedies, for instance, show name-changes in almost every draft—extended beyond his work, and he often dwelt on the names of recent acquaintances in his letters to them. Whatever the balance of emphasis—whether Sibyl is a sham temple to which men bring the text of their own false oracle, or whether she is merely a passive instrument swung by the changing wind of Dorian's favour—Wilde significantly used 'Fane' at three turning points in the manuscript: when Dorian first mentions her to Lord Henry; when Lord Henry reminds him that he had spoken of her as 'all the heroines of romance'; and in the newspaper report of the inquest. This suggestion of 'worship' is made plain in both the 1890 and the 1891 version when Lord Henry, like Pomander, deflates his friend's romantic bubble with a sceptical aphorism:

> 'Ordinary women never appeal to one's imagination. They are limited to their century. No glamour ever transfigures them. One knows their minds as easily as one knows their bonnets. One can always find them. There is no mystery in any of them. They ride in the Park in the morning, and chatter at tea-parties in the afternoon. They have their stereotyped smile, and their fashionable manner. They are quite obvious. But an actress! How different an actress is! Harry! why didn't you tell me that the only thing worth loving is an actress?'

> 'Because I have loved so many of them, Dorian.'

> 'Oh, yes, horrid people with dyed hair and painted faces.'

> 'Don't run down dyed hair and painted faces. There is an extraordinary charm in them, sometimes,' said Lord Henry.

> 'I wish now I had not told you about Sibyl Vane.'

> 'You could not have helped telling me, Dorian. All through your life you will tell me everything you do. . . . And now tell me—reach me the matches like a good boy: thanks—what are your actual relations with Sibyl Vane?'

> Dorian Gray leaped to his feet, with flushed cheeks and burning eyes. 'Harry! Sibyl Vane is sacred!'

> 'It is only the sacred things that are worth touching, Dorian,' said Lord Henry, with a strange touch of pathos in his voice.

In recounting Dorian's treatment of Sibyl, Wilde draws together several images from related works, notably **"Mr W. H."**, **"The Fisherman and his Soul"**, and **"The Critic as Artist"**. Like the Fisherman, Dorian has separated himself from his soul in order to follow a self-projecting myth. Filled with a new sense of his own beauty which has cast him in the fairy-tale role of 'Prince Charming', he an-ticipates joyfully his entry with Sibyl into a pastoral world of art—a realm unique in its combination of the richness of experience with the safety of innocence, lying within the bounds of knowledge but capable of being traversed repeatedly 'without hurt': 'I want the dead lovers of the world to hear our laughter and grow sad. I want a breath of our passion to stir their dust into consciousness, to wake their ashes into pain.' When Sibyl breaks from this world, in which she has always lived, and shows a preference for real life, of which she thinks Prince Charming a fine example, Dorian is bitterly disillusioned. Sibyl (the details of whose situation are a remarkable mirror image of the Dwarf's) accepted make-believe, like the Lady of Shalott, because spellbound by ignorance of anything else. Lancelot of stage-door-Johnnies, Dorian breaks the enchantment and makes the mirror look cracked and paltry. Wilde enlarged the sub-plot in the 1891 version by a chapter showing Sibyl's drab home and impossible mother, a tattered relic of 'the palmy days of the British Drama'. Extra grounds for her willing absorption in fantasy are hardly needed, however, and the reference to Tennyson is already explicit in the 1890 text:

> I believed in everything. . . . The painted scenes were my world. I knew nothing but shadows, and I thought them real. . . . You taught me what reality really is. To-night, for the first time in my life, I saw through the hollowness, the sham, the silliness of the empty pageant in which I had always played. . . . You brought me something higher, something of which art is but a reflection. You had made me understand what love really is. . . . I have grown sick of shadows.

'Shadows' also returns us to **"Mr W. H."**, in which Wilde had discussed the special theatrical meaning attached to the word in Shakespeare's day—'the best in this sort are but shadows'; 'Life's but a walking player, a poor shadow / That struts and frets his hour upon the stage'—as virtually a synonym for 'actor' or 'stage personage'. I have suggested that Basil reproduces something of Shakespeare's idolisation of Mr W. H., and that once Dorian awakes to his full personality he deserts the artist for his rival. Dorian follows a similar pattern with Sibyl. As Shakespeare had worshipped the interpreter of his timeless creations, so Dorian chooses to worship an actress as the human embodiment both of his romantic daydream and of his flirtation with 'history'. Interestingly enough, it is after her performance as Rosalind—in her boy's costume she had 'never looked lovelier'—that Dorian first kisses her. He watches her interpret 'all the heroines of romance' (his list is in fact wholly Shakespearean), and comes to grief, like Basil, once his ideal touches the modern and the actual and steps out of the frame of art. Like Basil's ideal (Dorian), like Shakespeare's ideal (Mr W. H.), Dorian's ideal (Sibyl) throws over art for life. However, 'the boy player of Rosalind had nothing to gain from marriage, or from the passions of real life'—so, at least, Wilde's Shakespearean critic had informed us. Lord Henry uses precisely the same argument to persuade Dorian that his egotistical indifference to Sibyl's suicide is natural and fitting to the occasion:

It often happens that the real tragedies of life occur in such an inartistic manner that they hurt us by their crude violence, their absolute incoherence, their absurd want of meaning, their entire lack of style. They affect us just as vulgarity affects us. They give us an impression of sheer brute force, and we revolt against that. Sometimes, however, a tragedy that possesses artistic elements crosses our lives. If these elements of beauty are real, the whole thing simply appeals to our sense of dramatic effect. Suddenly we find that we are no longer the actors, but the spectators of the play. Or rather, we are both. We watch ourselves, and the mere wonder of the spectacle enthralls us. . . . you must think of that lonely death in the tawdry dressing-room simply as a strange lurid fragment from some Jacobean tragedy, as a wonderful scene from Webster, or Ford, or Cyril Tourneur. The girl never really lived, and so she has never really died. To you, at least, she was always a dream. . . . The moment she touched actual life, she marred it, and it marred her, and so she passed away.

Dorian is reassured. He feels that Lord Henry has explained him to himself, and henceforth he concentrates on himself and becomes his own art-ideal.

*Still from the 1945 film version of Wilde's novel in which Hurd Hatfield, as Dorian Gray, looks at his portrait.*

In **"The Critic as Artist"**, Wilde had remarked of heredity: 'We may not watch it, for it is within us. We may not see it, save in a mirror that mirrors the soul'—an image taken from **"The Fisherman and His Soul"**. *Dorian Gray* combines the symbolism of the pastoral tale with the scientific pretensions of the critical dialogue. While the Fisherman disports himself with the Mermaid, his Soul returns to him periodically, at first tempting him with 'the Mirror of Wisdom' in which everything in the world is reflected except the beholder. Eventually, more experienced in the world's ways, the Soul successfully lures the Fisherman to land by other means, only to be rejected in its turn. Dorian's portrait becomes his soul-mirror of wisdom. When it shows him the evil in his nature, he cuts himself off from its presence, but decides to keep watch over it, like the solipsistic actor-spectator of Lord Henry's misleading exposition: he will become the modern or *sentimentalisch* artist-in-life. 'This portrait would be to him the most magical of mirrors. As it had revealed to him his own body, so it would reveal to him his own soul.' Meanwhile the public, the conscious, Dorian prefers the 'mirrors of opinion' in which nothing but the beholder is reflected, and his bargain with the portrait, like the Fisherman's undersea life, enables him to defy the true mirror's message—that truth offered by 'soul' to 'sense', or to the conscious by the unconscious. He stands 'with a mirror, in front of the portrait that Basil Hallward had painted of him, looking now at the evil and ageing face on the canvas, and now at the fair young face that laughed back at him from the polished glass. The very sharpness of the contrast used to quicken his sense of pleasure. . . . He mocked the misshapen body and the failing limbs.'

However, as Wilde commented in **"The Critic as Artist"**, when comparing the visual arts with literature,

> The statue is concentrated to one moment of perfection. The image stained upon the canvas possesses no spiritual element of growth or change. If they know nothing of death, it is because they know little of life, for the secrets of life and death belong to those, and those only, whom the sequence of time affects, and who possess not merely the present but the future, and can rise or fall from a past of glory or of shame.

The proper state for the portrait is the perfect representation of the crucial moment—time frozen—and the true balance is restored when Dorian, finding self-love and self-hate at last in equipoise ('For very love of self himself he slew'), decides to destroy it with a knife: 'As it had killed the painter, so it would kill the painter's work, and all that that had meant.' However, as Wilde has told us in the Preface, 'It is the spectator, and not life, that art really mirrors'. Only the self can destroy its self-projection. Wilde's final *tableau* reveals Dorian's self-portrait, his study in life, lying almost unrecognisable on the floor, while Basil's study from life, the real portrait, stands inviolate beside it.

The sudden and yet inevitable restitution has given rise to various ingenious interpretations, the most esoteric of which, perhaps, is that Dorian committed 'astral suicide'. Wilde's own version, taken from Poe—that 'when Dorian kills conscience he kills himself'—is the simplest. More recently, Christopher Nassaar has argued that the novel is a symbolic account of the decline of Aesthetic art at the hands of Decadence. Suggestive as this theory is in some particulars, especially in its interpretation of Sibyl Vane, it really applies only to the 1891 text, since much of the Naturalist material on which it depends was not present in the 1890 version. It is weakened, too, by overcircumstantial argument: Basil's resemblance, such as it is, to Nassaar's various Pre-Raphaelite contenders is diminished, not increased, by the little we are told of his ideals, subjects, and technique. But the real flaw in this interpretation lies in its definitions of Pre-Raphaelitism, Aestheticism, and Decadence—especially of the last, which leads to what I take to be a misunderstanding of the novel. To summarise: the portrait takes on, following Dorian's experiences, those qualities detected by Pater beneath the teasing mask of the *Mona Lisa* and defined by him as integral to the modern consciousness. It becomes, in other words, a modern Giocondo. Dorian rejects the 'Greek grace' of Sibyl Vane as Pater had rejected the 'white Greek goddesses and beautiful women of antiquity'. Only the evil embodied by Lord Henry can satisfy the modern sensibility, and through his spiritual ventriloquism—he projects 'his evil soul' into Dorian—his disciple becomes a Decadent masterpiece. As Leonardo had called mimes and fluteplayers to protract the subtle expression on his model's face (Pater records the story), so Lord Henry's surrogate talents serve the modern painter. Basil's admission that Dorian had been to him, before they had ever met, 'a dream of form in days of thought', matches Pater's account of Leonardo's preoccupation with 'the smiling of women', for 'From his childhood we see this image defining itself on the fabric of his dreams; and but for express historical testimony, we might fancy that this was but his ideal lady, embodied and beheld at last.'

However intriguing these parallels are, they do not account for the conclusion of the novel. Granted that Dorian learns to seek beauty in evil—granted even the premise that 'while aesthetic art . . . presents the soul as being essentially pure, decadent art sees it as being evil and derives pleasure from that evil'—it is plainly untrue that Decadent art sets out to be ugly. In so far as Decadent art had a unified and coherent aim, it might be defined in Baudelaire's phrase 'trouver le beau dans l'horrible', to find beauty in the ugliness of external or internal experience by subjecting it to the discipline of artistic form. Wilde himself, in public defence of his book, quoted Keats's remark that Shakespeare took as much delights in creating an Iago as an Imogen, and repeated it in other contexts. Dorian's portrait cannot fulfil both requirements at once. It cannot be both literally hideous, as we are encouraged to suppose it, and also a masterly distillation of the visual effects of vice. It is not, in fact, 'beautifully horrible' art, but beautiful art turning mysteriously, and temporarily, into horrible life. When the picture changes back again, the sitter's defacement of his soul-portrait amounts to no more than wilful graffiti scrawled over the artist's invulnerable Platonic dream.

The logical end of the 'demonic' theory is to project a terrible doom for Lord Henry, who 'has placed his soul entirely in his art—Dorian—and when Dorian dies he loses it'. Yet the fact remains that, however bleakly Lord Henry's future may stretch without his best friend and his uncompanionable wife, he, at least, survives—whereas the crusading egotist dies once he recognises the whole of himself; the sleeping-beauty actress dies once kissed to life; and the artist makes a third who dies when his human ideal defaces his imaginative ideal. But the critic, his rival, never confronts or knows the horror of the portrait—'the real Dorian'—and Wilde takes pains to make clear that Lord Henry thinks Dorian 'perfect' precisely because he has not changed. He sees him as 'the type of the age', but having once typecast him he becomes incapable of penetrating his character. He cannot credit that Dorian should have turned to crime. 'The wilful sunbeams of life' do not commit crimes and he treats Dorian's hint that he murdered Basil as mere affectation—'posing for a character that doesn't suit you'. To replace so unlikely a confession, he proposes for the disaffected lover a death both pseudo-romantic and full of arty pathos, an urban parody of the drowned Ophelia: 'I dare say he fell into the Seine off an omnibus, and that the conductor hushed up the scandal. Yes: I should fancy that was his end. I see him now, lying on his back under those dull-green waters, with the heavy barges floating over him, and the long weeds catching in his hair.' If these, too, are self-conscious pictorial echoes, then they could provide an amusing epitaph on the Victorian painter who confuses art with life. Has Basil's literal Pre-Raphaelite art died a natural death by misadventure in Symbolist Paris, picked off by 'one of the trammelling accidents of real life'? Has he gone there to finish 'a great picture that I have in my head', as he tells Dorian he intends to do, only to end up as an almost invisible component in a Whistlerian nocturne? Lord Henry's picture is perhaps most suggestive in parodying Wilde himself: it reminds us of the death of Little Hans, the affectionate masochist of **"The Devoted Friend"**, that least optimistic of Wilde's earliest set of ego-parables.

If, then, Lord Henry's soul is indeed as dead as the artist and his model, it must have perished from other causes. Though Dorian was 'largely his own creation' at first, 'the lad' emancipates himself from his mentor's influence and demonstrates the truth of Wilde's comforting critical doctrine that 'when a work is finished it has an independent life of its own, and may deliver a message far other than that which was put into its mouth to say'. Lord Henry never realises the irony of telling his 'creation' that he represents to him 'all the sins that you have never had the courage to commit'. The revelation of Dorian's full character would have shocked him no less than it shocked Basil. Perhaps this is why it never occurs. The real Muse-Sphinx of every conscientious egotist must be the enigma of his own personality, and, if the book is indeed built on a consciously autobiographical triangle, then one, at least, of the trio ought to survive. The likeliest candidate for this honour (or ignominy) is not the Platonising artist who cannot come to terms with life, nor the passionate egotist whose desires and attempts to gratify them overstep the bounds not only of the socially acceptable but also of the physically possible. The likeliest candidate is the critic, sceptical artist in modern life, who moves with the social tide and duly graduates into stage comedy—most refined of social metaphors—where romance and egotism are subjected to intellectual authority, where the riddling sphinx of personality, so mute or so menacing in private contexts, is teased into repartee by the chimera of dandiacal epigram, and where nobody dies at all. (pp. 112-30)

> *Rodney Shewan, in his* Oscar Wilde: Art and Egotism, *The Macmillan Press Ltd., 1977, 239 p.*

## Robert Keith Miller    (essay date 1982)

[*Miller is an American educator and critic. In the following excerpt, he discusses what he considers the thematic ambivalence of* Dorian Gray, *resulting from a discrepancy between the attractive portrayal of sensual pleasures in the novel and its abrupt moral conclusion.*]

Constructed around a series of highly theatrical scenes and enlivened by remarkably epigrammatic dialogue, *The Picture of Dorian Gray* remains a very readable novel. But it is much more than merely entertaining. Ever since its publication in 1891, many readers have found it to be deeply disturbing. For beneath its glittering surface, *The Picture of Dorian Gray* explores several serious subjects.

This is a story of moral corruption. When we first meet Dorian Gray, he is an attractive young man with all "the passionate purity of youth." He is innocent, if weak, until he looks upon a marvelous portrait that Basil Hallward, a great artist, has painted of him. Like Narcissus, Dorian becomes fascinated by his own beauty, and this prepares the way for his eventual destruction. He offers to sell his soul for eternal youth:

> I shall grow old, and horrible, and dreadful. But this picture will remain always young. . . . If it were only the other way! If it were I who was to be always young, and the picture that was to grow old! For that—for that—I would give everything! Yes, there is nothing in the whole world I would not give! I would give my soul for that!

Under the influence of Lord Henry Wotton, a worldly man about town, Dorian throws off all moral restraint and lives a life of passionate self-indulgence. But he has had his wish. He remains physically unchanged, his corruption recorded only upon the picture, which year after year becomes increasingly monstrous. When Dorian murders Basil Hallward, the portrait becomes evidence: "Loathsome red dew" appears on one of the hands "as though the canvas had sweated blood." Although he has always been careful to keep it concealed from public view, Dorian becomes haunted by the fear of the picture being used against him. Finally, he is driven to destroy it. Slashing the canvas with a knife, he destroys what is left of his soul, and thus destroys himself. When his servants enter the room, they find "a splendid portrait of their master as they had last seen him, in all the wonder of exquisite youth and beauty. Lying on the floor was a dead man, in evening dress, with a knife in his heart. He was withered, wrinkled, and loathsome of visage. It was not until they had examined the rings that they recognized who it was."

Although Wilde is often characterized as the vainest of men, it is clear that he recognized that vanity can lead to self-destruction. But *The Picture of Dorian Gray* is no simple moral tract in behalf of modesty. It is ultimately concerned with the nature of self-fulfillment. In particular, it explores the effect of experience upon character, in terms of both direct experience with life and the vicarious experience that is provided by art. In other words, to what extent are we shaped by what we do?

According to Lord Henry Wotton, experience leads to growth of character:

> The aim of life is self-development. To realize one's nature perfectly—that is what each of us is here for. . . . People have forgotten the highest of all duties, the duty one owes one's self.

Or:

> I believe that if one man were to live out his life fully and completely, were to give form to every feeling, expression to every thought, reality to every dream—I believe that the world would gain such a fresh impulse of joy that we would forget all the maladies of medievalism and return to the Hellenic ideal.

Of course, when Lord Henry calls upon us to forget "the maladies of medievalism," he is asking, in effect, for the rejection of Christianity and the restraints it has imposed. He argues that even sin can be ennobling:

> The body sins once, and it is done with its sin, for action is a mode of purification. . . . The only way to get rid of a temptation is to yield to it. . . . Resist it and your soul grows sick with longing . . .

In short, Lord Henry is an eloquent advocate of the contemporary notion that one should do whatever feels good. He is charming, like all great tempters, but his counsel is corrupting. When Dorian Gray abandons himself to the cult of experience, he discovers that vice can be addictive. So far from purging one's soul of longing, experience can stimulate one's appetite to the point at which satisfaction is no longer possible. Although we are told that "one could never pay too high a price for any sensation," it is evident that Dorian is forced to pay a high price indeed. Before long he is in the grip of desires he cannot control. His pursuit of experience leads not to "the Hellenic ideal" but to waterfront opium dens—and ultimately to death at the age of thirty-eight.

It might be argued, however, that Dorian Gray never really discovers experience so much as diversion—he flirts with life rather than engages with it. His goal, as he puts it, is "to become the spectator of one's own life." And eventually this goal becomes more desperate: "He wanted to escape from himself." Seen in this light, the modern belief in self-development has become grotesque. Whereas experience is traditionally defended as a means of emotional and intellectual growth, with Dorian Gray it becomes the means of dulling the senses and preventing the pain of self-awareness.

It would be a mistake, however, to see *The Picture of Dorian Gray* as necessarily opposed to all forms of experience. Wilde argues not so much against experience as the abuse of experience. An important distinction must be made between experience through which one might learn and grow and experience that serves no purpose beyond sensual gratification. Dorian's misfortune is not that he has lived deeply and well but that he loses the capacity to feel and with it the capacity to merge his life with others'. His life becomes a series of one-night stands, each encounter briefer than the last.

It is perhaps for this reason that Dorian Gray comes to prefer art to life. Although Wilde was very much influenced by the belief that humanity can find meaning in life through art, he was also skeptical of some of the more grandiose conceptions of art that are characteristic of modern culture. "All art is quite useless," he declares in the preface to **Dorian Gray,** and this idea is in sharp contrast to the values of both Basil Hallward and Dorian Gray.

Basil Hallward is an artist of great ambition. He believes that "there is nothing that Art cannot express." So far from settling for decorative effect, he seeks to found a new school, "a school that is to have in it all the passion of the romantic spirit, all the perfection of the spirit that is Greek." At first it seems that Wilde means us to accept this ideal as his own. But it is difficult to do so when we realize that the one painting that fulfills Hallward's conception of art is the picture of Dorian Gray, and it is for this picture that Dorian sells his soul. In effect, Dorian has sold his soul for art. Wilde reminds us that art can be valued to excess.

This reading is borne out by the story of Sibyl Vane, a great actress only because she has never experienced the reality of human love. When she falls in love with Dorian Gray, she loses her art. Because he values art more than love, Dorian then rejects her, and she dies. In telling this story, Wilde makes it clear that his sympathies are with Sibyl Vane. She is presented to us not simply as a clever actress but as a sensitive young woman who is devoted to her family and unsullied by the tawdry world in which she lives. Even Basil Hallward, who is appalled at first to think that Dorian might marry an actress, recognizes Sibyl's virtues when he sees her: "Through the crowd of ungainly, shabbily-dressed actors, Sibyl Vane moved like a creature from a finer world." And when Dorian begins to criticize her performance, Hallward reminds him, "Don't talk like that about anyone you love. . . . Love is a more wonderful thing than Art."

But the real love scene that is about to be played out at his feet holds less interest for Dorian than the romantic roles he has seen enacted upon the stage. Art is presented as an alternative to life; the two cannot coexist. "The moment she touched actual life," Lord Henry tells Dorian, "she marred it, and it marred her, and so she passed away. Mourn for Ophelia, if you like. Put ashes on your head because Cordelia was strangled. . . . But don't waste tears over Sibyl Vane. She was less real than they are." To this shallow counsel, Dorian responds: "You have explained me to myself, Harry. . . . I felt all that you have said but somehow I was afraid of it, and I could not express it to myself. How well you know me!"

Thus begins Dorian's withdrawal from life. He continues to pursue sexual pleasure, but he never again looks for love. His relationships become increasingly self-serving, and soon he is happiest only when he is fondling precious gems and fine brocades, for they make no demands upon him. There are moments, however, when even these pleasures become lost to him—they force him into awareness and inhibit the escape from reality that he ultimately finds in drugs.

A careful reading of **The Picture of Dorian Gray** suggests that Wilde had serious reservations about the modern celebration of art. So far from being an advocate of art for its own sake, Wilde showed that our real obligations lie elsewhere. Art, like experience, is good only so long as it contributes to self-development. When it is used as a luxurious means of passing time, it is no better than the drugs to which Dorian eventually falls victim.

By imposing upon the book a properly Victorian conclusion in which vice is roundly condemned, Wilde rejected the sensual self-indulgence with which he is often associated. If we see **Dorian Gray** strictly in terms of its plot, it becomes a proper nineteenth-century tale of what happens to young men who fall victim to temptation. Lose one's virginity, and it is only a question of time before one becomes an habitué of opium dens. The wages of sin are death.

It is impossible, however, not to feel that Wilde was strongly attracted to the temptations he condemned. Most readers are far more likely to remember the novel's lovingly detailed evocation of sensual pleasure than they are to ponder the rather abruptly moralistic conclusion. If **The Picture of Dorian Gray** tries to warn us against sin, the warning is obscured by the tantalizingly lush descriptions of the sins we are supposed to avoid.

It would be more accurate to recognize that **Dorian Gray** is highly ambivalent—the work of a man who was as yet uncertain of his own beliefs. Ultimately, it is best seen as a moral dialogue between conscience and temptation. It is as if two sides of Wilde's own nature are struggling for dominance. And the clearest sign of this is the way in which the principle characters continuously question their own sincerity. As early as the first chapter, we find Basil Hallward telling Lord Henry Wotton:

> I believe that you are really a very good husband, but that you are thoroughly ashamed of your own virtues. You are an extraordinary fellow. You never say a moral thing, and you never do a wrong thing. Your cynicism is simply a pose.

When Lord Henry persists in his argument, Hallward tells him: "I don't agree with a single word you have said, and what is more, Harry, I feel sure you don't either."

Hallward may be the most interesting character in the novel. He is in conflict not only with others but also with himself. He is torn between a fear of self-exposure and the public nature of the work he creates. Because he is a great artist, he reveals something of himself in his work. The realization of this makes him unwilling to exhibit his masterpiece, the picture of Dorian Gray, for the portrait reveals what Hallward delicately calls "a curious artistic idolatry"—pretty clearly a euphemism for what is, in effect, his passionate infatuation with a younger man. Although Lord Henry tells him that passion has commercial value—"Nowadays a broken heart will run to many editions"—Basil declares, "I will not bare my soul to shallow prying eyes. My heart shall never be put under their microscope."

If Basil Hallward represents the man who is dedicated to his work and committed to a private vision, Lord Henry Wotton represents the worldly life to which Wilde was fatally attracted. The conflict between hard work on the one hand and aristocratic ease on the other, between the ability to please and the determination to offend, were very real conflicts for Oscar Wilde. And it is the tension between these different values that makes *The Picture of Dorian Gray* so interesting. There is no clear victor within the book any more than there was within Wilde's own life, but the conflict between the moral and the immoral is nonetheless dramatic.

Hallward is important only in the first few chapters of the novel; thereafter he recedes, only to reemerge (for his own murder) in chapters 12 and 13. The Basil Hallward-Lord Henry Wotton conflict then becomes, out of necessity, a conflict between Lord Henry and Dorian Gray. Dorian, the professed voluptuary, is saddled with a role that Basil had filled much more appropriately—he tries to act as Lord Henry's better self, continually urging him to be less cynical. "You cut life to pieces with your epigrams," Dorian declares to Lord Henry, an accusation he frequently repeats as the novel draws to a close: "You would sacrifice anybody, Harry, for the sake of an epigram." And "I can't bear this, Harry! You mock at everything. . . ." These lines really belong to Basil Hallward, but he is dead by this point in the novel, and so they fall to Dorian Gray. It makes no sense, however, for Dorian to be shocked by Lord Henry's cynicism; his sins by now must surely outnumber his patron's. This leads one to suspect that it is not Dorian Gray but Oscar Wilde who is disturbed by the glib immorality that Lord Henry proclaims. Unwilling to allow Lord Henry to speak unopposed, Wilde forces upon Dorian Gray a role that is ridiculously inappropriate.

The conflicts behind *Dorian Gray* become clearer when we realize that no one character speaks for the author. Wilde merges his personality with those of Basil Hallward, Lord Henry Wotton, and even, at times, Dorian Gray. Wilde himself remarked in a letter that "Basil Hallward is what I think I am: Lord Henry what the world thinks of me: Dorian what I would like to be—in other ages, perhaps." The conflicts among these characters are conflicts that Wilde was trying to work out for himself. Ultimately, much of the novel can be seen as what Matthew Arnold called "the dialogue of the mind with itself"—the self-examination characteristic of modern literature.

Bearing this in mind, it is possible to understand the novel's most obvious flaw—the metamorphosis that Dorian Gray undergoes in the last fifty pages of the book. For most of the novel, Dorian has been presented as evil incarnate. When Sibyl Vane kills herself, Dorian successfully hardens himself to avoid the inconvenience of grief. Three years later, when we meet him again, he is the personification of sensuality, responsible, it seems, for corrupting half of London. Finally, when Basil Hallward beseeches Dorian to pray for salvation, the unrepentant sinner rushes at the unwelcome moralist "and dug the knife into the great vein that is behind the ear, crushing the man's head down on the table, and stabbing again and again."

Although Dorian is occasionally troubled by the fear of detection, he is never bothered by anything approaching the nature of guilt. This characterization remains consistent until the end of Chapter 18. James Vane, Sibyl's brother, has vowed to kill the man he holds accountable for his sister's death, and Dorian knows that Vane is finally on his track. Vane is accidently killed, however, and when Dorian views his body, "a cry of joy broke from his lips"—hardly the sort of response one would expect of a sinner on the eve of his conversion. Yet when we turn to the next chapter, we suddenly encounter a new Dorian Gray. Presumably, the accidental death of his worst enemy has moved Dorian to the remorse he could not feel after killing his own best friend. After rebuking Lord Henry for his cynicism, Dorian proclaims:

> The soul is a terrible reality. It can be bought, and sold, and bartered away. It can be poisoned or made perfect. There is a soul in each of us. I know it.

This discovery seems to come a little late in the day; the painting, after all, has been changing for almost twenty years. But now Dorian is filled with a new resolve:

> A new life! That is what he wanted. . . . He would never again tempt innocence. He would be good.

Unexpected though this resolve may be, it comes across as sincere; Wilde provides no evidence of hypocrisy. On the contrary, Dorian sounds genuinely troubled throughout his last conversation with Lord Henry. But however much Wilde may have wished to save Dorian Gray, he must have realized that his plot demanded that Dorian self-destruct. Therefore, the last chapter of the novel requires an abrupt shift in our point of view. Only pages after being led to believe that Dorian might yet manage to redeem himself, we are asked to see him as a sinner so hardened that he is compelled to destroy the last shreds of his conscience.

This shift suggests that Wilde used *Dorian Gray* not so much to advance a carefully defined set of beliefs but rather to explore conflicts he was unable to resolve. Although this uncertainty makes the resolution of the novel psychologically unconvincing, it contributes to the fascination of the work as a whole.

Among the unresolved conflicts of *Dorian Gray,* perhaps none is more striking than the way in which Wilde treats homosexuality. One of the most daring aspects of the book is its assumption that men can be in love with one another—hardly a new discovery in 1891, but nonetheless a relatively unexplored subject for English literature. Unfortunately, critics have often been too ready to interpret Wilde's work in light of what we know about his sexuality. And readers should be careful not to focus on this aspect of Wilde to the exclusion of all else. While it is impossible to overlook the implications of homosexuality that run throughout the book, we should view the subject as simply one of the many conflicts with which Wilde was struggling to come to terms.

Lord Henry Wotton's attraction to Dorian Gray is clearly physical; we hear a lot about the youth's "finely-curved scarlet lips," and before long, Lord Henry has filled his house with no less than eighteen pictures of Dorian and presented him with a mirror framed with "white-limbed" ivory cupids. During the early stages of his infatuation, Lord Henry rejoices in his sense of power over the younger man. Being with him was

> like playing upon an exquisite violin. He an-
> swered to every thrill of the bow. . . . There
> was nothing that one could not do with him.

If Dorian is unlikely to respond with equal ardor, he is certainly eager to engage in sexual experimentation. How else can one explain his mysterious hold over Alan Campbell? Or Basil Hallward's often-quoted plea:

> Why is your friendship so fatal to young men?
> There was that wretched boy in the Guards who
> committed suicide. You were his great friend.
> There was Sir Henry Ashton, who had to leave
> England, with a tarnished name. You and he
> were inseparable. What about Adam Singleton,
> and his dreadful end? What about Lord Kent's
> only son, and his career? . . . What about the
> young Duke of Perth? What sort of life has he
> got now?

Basil Hallward, of all people, should know the answer to the riddle he has posed, for he himself is passionately devoted to Dorian Gray. In a passage that prefigures Wilde's own feelings for Lord Alfred Douglas, Basil tells Lord Henry: "I knew I had come face to face with someone whose mere personality was so fascinating that, if I allowed it to do so, it would absorb my whole nature, my whole soul, my very art itself."

The implications of such passages were not lost on Wilde's audience. (Indeed, passages from *Dorian Gray* were read in court when Wilde was on trial.) Perhaps realizing that he had gone too far, Wilde goes through the motions of providing Dorian with at least one great passion for a woman, the seventeen-year-old Sibyl Vane. But even here there is a distinctly ambivalent note. Dorian proposes marriage to Sibyl Vane only after he has seen her perform as Rosalind in *As You Like It,* a role which demands male impersonation. "You should have seen her!" he declares, "When she came on in her boy's clothes she was perfectly wonderful."

Although Wilde was bold in approaching a subject that was seldom discussed in his time, he nevertheless brings himself to condemn it. All the young men associated with Dorian Gray meet unhappy ends, and Dorian's sexuality is presented as a problem—it leads to his confrontation with Basil Hallward, a confrontation that leads, in turn, to murder.

The question then arises, why did Wilde force his readers to confront the subject at all? Technically, one might argue that it relates to his determination to make Dorian

Gray experience everything that life has to offer. But homosexual love is not presented as a matter of casual experimentation. Clearly fascinated by the subject, Wilde constructed the entire novel around a triangle of three men. He used fiction as a means of exploring inner conflicts and forcing people to confront something that was about to become a public issue in his own life. In addition to many other concerns, Wilde used *The Picture of Dorian Gray* as a means of coming to terms with his own sexuality.

There is one additional conflict within this book: it is composed of radically conflicting styles. Half of the book consists of dialogue that remains, for the most part, engaging and original. When Lord Henry Wotton complains that a well known hostess "tried to found a *salon,* and only succeeded in opening a restaurant" or when he declares across a dinner table that "Nowadays people know the price of everything and the value of nothing" the novel prefigures Wilde's emergence as a dramatist in the years to come. Wilde can also be wonderfully clever in giving rapid sketches of his characters. An elderly woman is described as "a perfect saint among women, but so dreadfully dowdy that she reminded one of a badly bound hymn book." And the short paragraph devoted to describing Lady Henry Wotton is marvelously succinct:

> She was a curious woman, whose dresses always
> looked as if they had been designed in a rage and
> put on in a tempest. She was usually in love with
> somebody, and as her passion was never re-
> turned, she had kept her illusions. She tried to
> look picturesque, but only succeeded in being
> untidy. Her name was Victoria, and she had a
> perfect mania for going to church.

These lines are amusing, and one of the reasons why they are able to amuse is that they are easily digestible. They seem so clever, in fact, that some critics are led to dismiss them as glib. It is this aspect of Wilde that moved Jorge Luis Borges to conclude: "His perfection has been a disadvantage; his work is so harmonious that it may seem inevitable and even trite" [see *TCLC,* Vol. 1, pp. 498-99].

But if we can mine innumerable verbal gems from the pages of *The Picture of Dorian Gray,* we must labor through a good deal of sludge along the way. The novel often seems about to sink beneath the weight of an ornate prose style. The opening paragraphs are a case in point:

> The studio was filled with the rich odor of roses,
> and when the light summer wind stirred amid
> the trees of the garden there came through the
> open door the heavy scent of the lilac, or the
> more delicate perfume of the pink-flowering
> thorn.

> From the corner of the divan of Persian saddle-
> bags on which he was lying, smoking, as was his
> custom, innumerable cigarettes, Lord Henry
> Wotton could just catch the gleam of the honey-
> sweet and honey-colored blossoms of the labur-
> num, whose tremulous branches seemed hardly
> able to bear the burden of a beauty so flame-like
> as theirs; and now and then the fantastic shad-
> ows of birds in flight flitted across the long
> tussore-silk curtains that were stretched in front
> of the huge window, producing a kind of mo-

mentary Japanese effect, and making him think of those pallid jade-faced painters of Tokio who, through the medium of an art that is essentially immobile, seek to convey the sense of swiftness and motion. The sullen murmur of the bees shouldering their way through the long unmown grass, or circling with monotonous insistence round the dusty gilt horns of the straggling woodbine, seemed to make the stillness more oppressive. The dim roar of London was like the bourdon note of a distant organ.

Translated into contemporary English, this elaborate introduction might be condensed to read: "It was a summer afternoon, and the air smelled sweet. Lord Henry Wotton was chain smoking." Of course, this revision says very little. But when we look closely at Wilde's version, we must recognize that it does not say all that much more. And some of the things that it does say are questionable to say the least. Why would a painter have the curtains in his studio closed? And as cigarettes no longer seem as elegant as they did in 1891, one is left wondering how the laburnum could compete with all the tobacco.

Of the four sentences here, the average length is fifty-two words, with the second sentence weighing in at a whopping 119. Wilde would have defended himself by claiming that he was setting the scene, and the heaviness of the prose helps to suggest the rich and heavy atmosphere he is trying to evoke. But despite the wealth of detail we are given, we learn almost nothing which is relevant to the narrative. Does it matter, for example, that the woodbine in the garden was "straggling" or that the branches of the laburnum were "tremulous" or that the bees were "sullen"? Unfortunately not. The style of this passage has been arbitrarily applied, lacking any real connection with its subject. In pausing to describe the movement of a bee, another writer might manage to convey more than a decorative effect—to convey a parallel, somehow, between the observation of the natural world and the activities in which the story's characters are engaged. But Wilde seems unable to do this; his descriptions often seem as if they could be peeled off, leaving a stronger and more vigorous text behind.

The effect can be depressingly mechanical. One tremulous flamelike flower sounds very much like another—Wilde has an irritating tendency to re-use vocabulary. Within a relatively few pages, for example, we hear of "an exquisite violin," "exquisite knowledge," "exquisite disdain," "an exquisite day," "exquisite raiment," "exquisite taste," and "exquisite specimens." A similar predilection is shown for the words "graceful," "delicate," and "wonderful." Adjectives, in general, abound. Such prose as this is easily parodied.

In defending this style, Wilde argued that in prose "correctness should always be subordinated to artistic effect and musical cadence; and any peculiarities of syntax that may occur in *Dorian Gray* are deliberately intended, and are introduced to show the value of the artistic theory in question." The artistic theory to which he alludes rejected "modernity of form" as "vulgarizing" and argued that beauty can be found only in "the things that do not concern us." Certainly there is little in "the straggling wood-

bine" that concerns us. And there is no question about Wilde's belabored sentence structure having much in common with modernity of form. Contrived though this prose may now seem, it represents Wilde's attempt to emphasize the distinction between "art" and "the prison house of realism." He was determined to keep reality at bay through, in his own words, "the impenetrable barrier of beautiful style, of decorative or ideal treatment."

But there is more to conveying a sense of beauty than simply listing the tremulous flowers in a garden. As Lord Henry Wotton observes, "details are always vulgar"—a dictum Wilde would have done well to heed. As it is, he assaults his readers with great indigestible chunks of detail, a process that culminates in Chapter 11 in which Wilde lists, for the entire chapter, every scent, every song, every jewel, and every embroidery that Dorian Gray comes to admire. Reading this chapter is like reading the catalogue for an auction one will never attend.

Wilde is even unfaithful to his own aesthetic. Although he dismissed those novelists who write of "the sordid streets and hideous suburbs of our vile cities," he himself takes us—for no apparent reason—to the home of Sibyl Vane where we learn that "the flies buzzed round the table, and crawled over the stained cloth." Later we are brought into a waterfront tavern complete with "fly-blown mirrors" and "greasy reflectors of ribbed tin" illuminating a floor covered with mud and spilled liquor. And what are we to make of the description of Mr. Isaacs, the theater manager:

A hideous Jew, in the most amazing waistcoat I ever beheld in my life, was standing at the entrance smoking a vile cigar. He had greasy ringlets, and an enormous diamond blazed in the center of a soiled shirt.

Aside from its obvious anti-Semitism, this passage is coarse and melodramatic; it dates Wilde as surely as the would-be lyricism of the more decorative lines.

Thus in addition to faulting Wilde for being, at times, too precious, we must also charge him with occasionally slipping into the melodramatic. Could anyone have ever really spoken like Sibyl Vane:

He is called Prince Charming . . . Prince Charming, my wonderful lover, my god of graces. But I am poor beside him. Poor? What does that matter? When poverty creeps in at the door, love flies in through the window.

Of course, there's more to Wilde than lines like these. The conversation at Lady Agatha's luncheon, for example—or later at the house party at Selby Royal—is only a less-polished version of the brilliant dialogue that Wilde perfected in *The Importance of Being Earnest.* And, as we have seen, the novel is rich with ideas.

Nonetheless, in our final verdict on *The Picture of Dorian Gray,* we must conclude that interesting and enjoyable though it may be, it is very much the work of a writer who had yet to find himself. Both in its theme and in its style the book is marked by that inconsistency that springs from an inadequately defined purpose. It has plot, and it has wit. But it is intellectually and stylistically immature. (pp. 25-41)

Robert Keith Miller, in his Oscar Wilde, Frederick Ungar Publishing Co., 1982, 167 p.

## Robert K. Martin (essay date 1983)

[In the following essay, Martin discusses The Picture of Dorian Gray as Wilde's parody of and homage to Walter Pater.]

Artistic influence might often be called "the debt that will not speak its name." As Harold Bloom has reminded us [in The Anxiety of Influence: A Theory of Poetry, 1973], silence about the most important sources of a work of art may, paradoxically, serve almost as a confirmation of the importance of those sources. In other cases, an artist may follow quite closely on the heels of his aesthetic and intellectual mentors and yet, in Bloom's phrase, "swerve" at a crucial point away from the earlier artist. The "swerve" or "clinamen" is self-serving in the best sense; it is a necessary act of definition which enables the artist to establish at once his indebtedness, or filiation, and his independence, or self-paternity.

I propose that we examine the relationship between Walter Pater and Oscar Wilde in this light, in order to understand the complexity of Wilde's indebtedness to Pater and his simultaneous need to distance himself from the man whom he described during the first of his trials as "the only critic of the century whose opinion I set high" [quoted in H. Montgomery Hyde, The Trials of Oscar Wilde, 1973]. The Picture of Dorian Gray is at once an homage to the author of The Renaissance, which Wilde spoke of as "my golden book," echoing Pater's own description of the tale of Cupid and Psyche in Marius the Epicurean, and simultaneously a parody of Pater which draws specifically on what Wilde perceived as Pater's coy homosexuality.

The Picture of Dorian Gray has been considered, rightly, to be deeply indebted to Pater. In John Pick's words [see Further Reading], it "is largely a novelized form of the 'Conclusion' to the Renaissance . . . Lord Henry Wotton . . . represents the very voice—and indeed not infrequently the very words of—the 'Conclusion' and through him Dorian identifies his own acts with the philosophy of life presented there." The verbal echoes are so striking that there can be no doubt that Wilde was thinking of Pater as he wrote his novel. But what was he thinking? Granted that he was to make use of Pater, what was that use to be?

On this question there are two widely accepted answers. The first of these holds that Wilde simply cribbed his book from Pater. According to this school of thought, Wilde was a second-rate thinker who seized upon the ideas of the Oxford don and used them as if they were his own. Wilde is thus the popularizer and vulgarizer of Pater. The other school holds that Wilde misunderstood Pater. Those holding this position might agree that Wilde indeed vulgarized Pater, but they find in this vulgarization an act of misunderstanding and accidental distortion. Pater, they say, is far more subtle and intelligent than his crass admirer;

what is more, he clearly argued for a life of passion, but only while urging on his readers to "be sure it is passion—that it does yield you this fruit of a quickened, multiplied consciousness" whereas Wilde appears to celebrate a promiscuous indulgence in the senses.

Since according to the first of these interpretations, Wilde is little more than a plagiarizing thief, and according to the second, little more than a fool, anyone who takes Wilde's work seriously must wonder if there is not a third possible answer—that Wilde deliberately parodied Pater in Dorian Gray in order to demonstrate his own distance from a total committment to aesthetic or "eipcurean" values. This point has been briefly suggested by Richard Ellmann, who has written, "Wilde seems to have intended . . . to offer (through the disastrous effects of Lord Henry's influence upon Dorian) a criticism of Pater. [See Further Reading entry dated 1969. Martin adds in a footnote that "Ellmann is both witty and helpful. Pater, he writes, 'is enclosed (like an unhappy dryad caught in a tree trunk) in Lord Henry Wotton.' He concludes that 'In Dorian Gray the Pater side of Wilde's thought is routed, though not deprived of fascination', a very just assessment."] Ellmann's caution is unnecessary: Wilde's novel makes repeated use of Pater in a manner that should leave little doubt as to Wilde's ironic distance from his master.

Anyone who bears in mind the development of Wilde's career should find it difficult to imagine that Lord Henry functions, in any uncomplicated manner, as a spokesman for Wilde. Wilde's career underwent a significant alteration in the late 1880's, in part because of his recognition of his homosexuality (whether that recognition was sudden or gradual is still a matter of biographical debate). "The Happy Prince" is an important indication of Wilde's awareness of the way in which his homosexuality could function as a means to a deepening of his participation in humanity. Human love is placed above both aestheticism and utilitarianism, as a type of divine love. "The Portrait of Mr. W. H." is a work obviously indebted to Pater, but one which equally clearly offers a parody of Pater's method. In Wilde's story, works of art are used as a means to the discovery of personality, in the best Pater manner, but the portrait which is at its center is a fake. Do the characters, whose critical approach borrows from The Renaissance, deduce meaning from the artifact, or do they read back from their own lives into the works they purportedly read? By laying particular emphasis on the homosexual meaning of the sonnets, Wilde was engaging in a bit of fun at the expense of Pater, who hints repeatedly at the subject but always skirts it delicately.

Two major changes came about in Wilde's thinking in the years immediately preceding Dorian Gray: he came to a new understanding of the importance of personal love and increasingly defined that love in terms of sacrifice for the beloved, and he came to a new determination to speak and write openly of his own sexuality and to mock those who, like Pater, refused to express openly what was discussed fully throughout their works. These changes coincided with an artistic coming-of-age that produced an astonishing flurry of creativity. As Wilde became, in the years from 1888 to 1895, a major creative force producing works of lasting value in the theatre, fairy tale, novel, and essay, it became more and more important for him to establish his distance from his earliest mentors. Wilde's growing distance from Pater thus involved both a change of critical position and a need to assert his independence. By revealing the latent homosexuality of Pater's works, Wilde could simutaneously expose Pater and promote himself as the proper successor to Pater. In an act of what Harold Bloom might call "tessera" Wilde "misreads" Pater and then corrects him, offering his own work as the antithetical creation. **Dorian Gray** is an antithetical *Marius the Epicurean,* meant by Wilde as a way of reading, and then reducing, Pater.

The opening of Wilde's novel is the first indication of its ironic intent. The language of this section is a parody of Decadent style. The first paragraph is devoted entirely to the sense of smell, ranging from "the rich odour of roses" to "the heavy scent of the lilac" and "the more delicate perfume of the pink-flowering thorn." The second presents Lord Henry Wotton, looking like an "Odalisque": "From the corner of the divan of Persian saddlebags on which he was lying, smoking, as was his custom, innumerable cigarettes. . . ." In the almost parenthetical "as was his custom" and the precious "innumerable" there can be little doubt as to Wilde's comic intent. Following this parodic opening, the passage shifts to what is apparently its principal subject: the imaginary flight of the birds on the window-curtains and the noise of the bees in their sexual quest ("circling with monotonous insistence round the dusty gilt horns of the straggling woodbine"). The references are to time and eternity, and to the timeless quality of art, and above all to the dominating presence of sexual desire. The setting is thus an ironic representation of the novel's themes.

Lord Henry's words echo those of Pater in the "Conclusion" to *The Renaissance:* "You have only a few years in which to live really, perfectly, and fully. . . . Live! Live the wonderful life that is in you! Let nothing be lost upon you. Be always searching for new sensations." Pater wrote, "we have an interval, and then our place knows us no more . . . our one chance lies in expanding that interval, in getting as many pulsations as possible into the given time." Wilde quickly signals how we are to take this imitation of Pater, for in his next paragraph Dorian drops a sprig of lilac and a bee scrambles over it. Then the bee moves on: "he saw it moving into the stained trumpet of a Tyrian convolvulus. The flower seemed to quiver, and then swayed gently to and fro." The bee's contact with the flower mimes human sexual intercourse and reminds us that Dorian is being penetrated by Lord Henry's ideas, if not by his body. The abrupt sexuality is a deliberate undercutting of the previous passage, imitated from *The Renaissance:* for it makes Pater's message into a highly lascivious *carpe diem.* Wilde's use of the passage in this way would seem to suggest two things: first, that Wilde believed that Pater himself took "pulsations" to be at least partially sexual, so that Wilde is merely making explicit what Pater coyly left implicit and, second, that, in Wilde's review, Pater's theory of the value of ever-increasing sensations as a response to human mortality could lead to a violation of essential human relationships. Thus **Dorian Gray** is

both an exposure of the "secret" meaning of *The Renaissance,* and an illustration of its possible misapplication.

Lord Henry justifies his relationship to Dorian by a number of hardly concealed references to a homosexual tradition, similar to the references Pater makes in his criticism and his fiction. Thinking of the role of real objects in the development of ideal beauty, Lord Henry muses: "He remembered something like it in history. Was it not Plato, that artist in thought, who had first analyzed it? Was it not Buonarotti who had carved it in the coloured marbles of a sonnet-sequence? But in our own century, it was strange." (Wilde was to repeat the argument at his trial, when he spoke of a love "such as Plato made the very basis of his philosophy, and such as you find in the sonnets of Michelangelo and Shakespeare . . . It is in this century misunderstood, so much misunderstood that it may be described as the 'love that dare not speak its name,' and on account of it I am placed where I am now.") But in fact it is not Lord Henry who represents such love, as Dorian comes to recognize, but Basil:

> The love that he bore him—for it was really love—had nothing in it that was not noble and intellectual. It was not that mere physical admiration of beauty that is born of the senses, and that dies when the senses tire. It was such love as Michael Angelo had known, and Montaigne, and Winckelmann, and Shakespeare himself.

Lord Henry, as we have seen, responds to Dorian's physical beauty as a bee responds to a flower. For Basil Dorian represents something else, the integration of the physical and the spiritual: "he defines for me the lines of a fresh school, a school that is to have in it all the passion of the romantic spirit, all the perfection of the spirit that is Greek." By choosing to portray Dorian in a realistic mode, however, Basil betrays this insight. All of the principal characters of the novel are destroyed, as Wilde explained, Dorian and Basil for undue reliance on the senses, Lord Henry for his futile attempt to remain a spectator. It is simply wrong to see Lord Henry as the hero of the novel, as Edouard Roditi has done; to do so is to make the novel into a Decadent tract instead of a subtly moral work.

It is not only in his theorizing that Lord Henry imitates Pater, but also in his analysis of Dorian's development. Consider this passage: "How different he was now from the shy, frightened boy he had met in Basil Hallward's studio! His nature had developed like a flower, had borne blossoms of scarlet flame. Out of its secret hiding-place had crept his Soul, and Desire had come to meet it on the way." These cynical words have their source in Pater's luminous description of Florian Deleal's first sight of the flowering hawthorn: "a plumage of tender, crimson fire out of the heart of the dry wood." The sight is perhaps "some periodic moment in the expansion of soul" which brings him to a realization of "passionateness": "A touch of regret or desire mingled all night with the remembered presence of the red flowers." Wilde again uses Lord Henry's allegiance to a Paterian sensuality as a way of reproaching Pater for an undue emphasis on physical sensation. While the accusation is not just when applied to Pater's work as a whole and the context in which Pater clearly wanted it understood, it was important for Wilde as a way of asserting his own distance. Surprisingly, *Dorian Gray* served for Wilde to express the dangers inherent in the submission to sensation and to dramatize the difference between two modes of homosexual love, the physical and carnal love of Lord Henry, and the integrated physical and spiritual love of Basil. His "immoral" novel is in fact a highly moral work which traces the destruction wrought by the failure to acknowledge the spiritual element in sexuality.

One of the most astonishing of Wilde's parodies of Pater occurs in a speech of Basil's in which he laments his decision to attempt a realistic treatment of Dorian. He recounts the other works he has done: "I have drawn you as Paris in dainty armour, and as Adonis with huntsman's cloak and polished boat-spear. Crowned with heavy lotus blossoms you had sat on the prow of Adrian's barge, gazing across the green turbid Nile. You had leant over the still pool of some Greek woodland, and seen in the water's silent silver the marvel of your own face." Dorian is the expression of all history, like Leonardo's Mona Lisa as described by Pater:

> She is older than the rocks among which she sits; like the vampire, she has been dead many times, and learned the secrets of the grave; and has been a diver in deep seas, and keeps their fallen day about her; and trafficked for strange webs with eastern merchants: and, as Leda, was the mother of Helen of Troy, and, as Saint Anne, the mother of Mary . . .

We might even go so far as to call him the Eternal Masculine. By shifting Pater's references from women to men, Wilde provides a reading of the passage, and of Pater's regard for Leonardo. (Duchamp carried the process a step further when he gave the Mona Lisa a moustache.)

Wilde's parodies of Pater tell us only part of the story, however. Like all parodies they are rooted in deep admiration. Their mocking is designed in part as a way of realizing, of accomplishing that which is judged incomplete. Above all, *Dorian Gray* is Wilde's tribute, although, as we have seen, a hedged one, to Pater's concept of the "plotless novel," the novel as portrait. The source of that form is of course Marius, whose life forms the center of his novel as Dorian does that of Wilde's. In both cases the novel abandons traditional plot structure and substitutes a concern with a growth in consciousness (and so to some extent both may be thought of as more or less direct progenitors of *The Ambassadors,* whose cry, "Live all you can. It's a mistake not to. . . . Live!," . . . echoes both the "Conclusion" and Lord Henry's words). *Dorian Gray* is the story of a soul, far more than the story of a man. Dorian does almost nothing—and in fact many readers, from Pater on, have complained of the melodramatic intrusions when he does indeed act—what he *sees* remains the center of the novel's concern. Here again a divergence from Pater is evident. Marius' growth appears to be limitless. Only death may bring an end to his expanding perceptions, and to his accompanying spiritual growth (and there are strong suggestions that even death cannot arrest the expansion of consciousness). Dorian's growth is false from the beginning, since he is the means to Lord Henry's plea-

sure and not an end in himself. His curve of growth goes downward, not upward. His body and soul are split apart, and so his growth is an expansion of the ability to receive sensual pleasure without an accompanying increase in the ability for spiritual growth.

We recall that in Wilde's comment that *The Renaissance* was his "golden book" there was an echo of Pater's treatment of Marius' golden book, Apuleius' *Golden Ass,* and of Gaston de Latour's, Ronsard. Thus in the Dorian who is corrupted by a book there is something of Wilde's own self and his ambivalent response to his mentor. Wilde's use of the book is a deliberate inversion of Pater's motif: what was once a kind of epiphany leading the protagonist forward in a spiritual quest is now turned into a moment of poisoned perception, the kiss of the serpent.

Wilde's description of the celebrated "yellow book," Lord Henry's gift to Dorian, makes the relationship to Pater clear (although the book as described is an amalgam of both *Marius* and *A rebours,* and later references would also make it appear that the book is in fact *The Renaissance*).

> It was a novel without a plot, and with only one character, being, indeed, simply a psychological study of a certain young Parisian, who spent his life trying to realize in the nineteenth century all the passions and modes of thought that belonged to every century except his own, and to sum up, as it were, in himself the various moods through which the world-spirit had ever passed.

Like Pater, or Huysmans, Wilde sought in *Dorian* to create a psychological novel, through the study of a single personality. Like Pater Wilde considered such a study as a "portrait." Other models for such a title existed, of course—including James's *Portrait of a Lady*—but it was Pater who had most recently transformed fictional structure by creating a novel around a single portrait. Wilde terms his work a "picture," but the point is the same: the novel exists to depict the character of the hero. The ambiguity of the title's reference emphasizes Wilde's own role as yet another double. Each picture is, as the novel informs us, only a mirror.

Like *Marius,* too, *Dorian Gray* is a novel written out of the dramatization of criticism. Both Pater and Wilde began as critics, and when they turned to fiction, they helped to transform the nature of the novel (and the short story) by using that form to present in a fuller form the ideas already present in their critical works. All of Pater's subsequent work may be seen as an attempt to express more clearly, or more convincingly, the ideas of *The Renaissance.* In *Dorian Gray* Wilde also used his characters to represent critical points of view, even if, to some extent, all of the characters are self-portraits. Like Pater, he places his central character as a receiver of influences, one who learns from experience. The characters round him are ideas.

Wilde appears to have retained his interest in Pater even after his arrest. Among the books he arranged to receive in prison were *Greek Studies, Appreciations, Imaginary Portraits, Miscellaneous Essays,* and *Gaston de Latour.* (He had already received *Appreciations,* of course, and may have known other of the works as well.) But it is ***Dorian Gray*** which convincingly shows the deep influence of Pater on Wilde's ideas, charcters, themes, form and language. And it is ***Dorian Gray*** which attempts to convert the covert homosexuality of Pater into a more openly expressed homosexuality while at the same time exploring the morality of beauty and passion. It is astonishing to recognize that Wilde's depiction of Dorian, corrupted by a book, will become a portrait of himself, destroyed by his vanity and his insistence on confronting conventional morality.

Although many readers have been quick to dismiss Wilde's novel as the frivolous product of a moment, recent study of the manuscript changes should indicate that it was a work to which Wilde devoted considerable attention. He himself wrote of it in a letter, "I think it will be ultimately recognized as a real work of art with a strong ethical lesson in it." The complexity of his response to Pater that can be traced in the text is another element in defense of the novel's seriousness as a work of art. And the most serious objection to its ethical quality is removed when one realizes that the "Preface" is but one of the novel's voices, by no means that of the author speaking *in propria persona.* Pater himself, in his review of ***Dorian,*** acknowledged that Wilde "may . . . have intended Lord Henry as a satiric sketch." The urgency of his insistence that Lord Henry did not represent a properly understood Epicureanism testifies to his recognition that Lord Henry in particular, and ***Dorian Gray*** in general, was at once a parody and a tribute. (pp. 15-18)

> Robert K. Martin, "Parody and Homage: The Presence of Pater in 'Dorian Gray'," in The Victorian Newsletter, No. 63, Spring, 1983, pp. 15-18.

## Peter Raby   (essay date 1988)

[*In the following excerpt, Raby discusses the tension between life and art in* The Picture of Dorian Gray *and considers the narrative unified by dramatic form and mode.*]

Wilde's novel ***The Picture of Dorian Gray*** originated as a story for *Lippincott's Magazine,* where it was published in the July number, 1890. In this form, it consisted of fourteen chapters, which represented a sustained effort of concentration for Wilde: 'I have just finished my first long story, and am tired out. I am afraid it is rather like my own life—all conversation and no action. I can't describe action: my people sit in chairs and chatter.' The disclaimer is not strictly accurate. Even in the original version the story contains three deaths, including a suicide and a murder. Nevertheless, the limited space given to action, together with Wilde's abrupt, idiosyncratic handling of it, makes a noticeable feature of both versions, and raises questions as to the nature of the work, and how it was intended to be understood.

It was, inevitably, misunderstood, and Wilde turned his energies to constructing public replies to his critics, in particular those of the *St James's Gazette* and the *Scots Observer.* Wilde's first response included the declaration that he was 'quite incapable of understanding how any work of art can be criticised from a moral standpoint'. Such a statement, wholly to be expected from a writer such as Wilde, is none the less (and no doubt intentionally) ingenuous, given the form and subject matter of the book. The central idea consists of a beautiful young man 'selling his soul in exchange for eternal youth'; the portrait, which is the physical representation of his soul, reflects Dorian Gray's sins; Dorian Gray himself confesses that he has been 'poisoned' by a book. It would be hard to avoid a certain amount of moral inference; Wilde admitted as much in a letter to the Editor of the *Daily Chronicle:* 'I felt that, from an aesthetic point of view, it would be difficult to keep the moral in its proper secondary place; and even now I do not feel quite sure that I have been able to do so. I think the moral too apparent' [see excerpt dated 1890]. Wilde continued by defining the moral element:

> The real moral of the story is that all excess, as well as all renunciation, brings its punishment, and this moral is so far artistically and deliberately suppressed that it does not enunciate its law as a general principle, but realises itself purely in the lives of individuals, and so becomes simply a dramatic element in a work of art, and not the object of the work of art itself.

An excessively prominent moral element was one of the things Wilde hoped to correct in revising and expanding the *Lippincott's* version. His aim had been to keep the 'atmosphere of moral corruption' surrounding Dorian Gray 'vague and indeterminate and wonderful': 'Each man sees his own sin in Dorian Gray.' The indeterminate nature of Dorian's sins had already been assisted by J. M. Stoddart, the American publisher of *Lippincott's,* who had made numerous unauthorized deletions and substitutions. Wilde worked from the *Lippincott's* text, rather than from his original typescript, and only rarely reinstated his first version. One of his aims in the process of revision was to reduce the suggestions of homosexuality in the relationship between Basil Hallward and Dorian Gray, which he accomplished by stressing Dorian's importance for Hallward as artistic inspiration. At the same time, the inserted episodes such as Dorian's visit to the opium den in Chapter 16 have a greater specificity which runs counter to the claimed vagueness. In both versions the focus is not directed exclusively at either the aesthetic (Art) or the moral (Life), but at the tension between them.

The strength of ***The Picture of Dorian Gray*** derives primarily from the central and unifying idea of the picture itself. The artist Basil Hallward, obsessed and inspired by the youthful beauty of Dorian Gray, is about to complete his masterpiece, a full-length portrait. As Dorian poses, Lord Henry Wotton, the detached amoral observer, tempts him with words that stir him like music: 'Ah! realize your youth while you have it . . . Live the wonderful life that is in you! . . . Be always searching for new sensations.' Soon, the portrait is finished—'the finest portrait of modern times'—and when Dorian sees it, a look of joy comes into his eyes, 'as if he had recognised himself for the first time'. The sense of his own beauty comes on him like a revelation, and he expresses a fatal wish: 'If it were I who was to be always young, and the picture that was to grow old! . . . I would give my soul for that!'

The picture has become endued with terrible significance: Lord Henry offers to buy it at any price; to its creator Hallward, it represents his aesthetic ideal, though he secretly fears that it contains too much of himself; to Dorian, it reveals the transitory nature of his beauty so acutely that he is jealous of it, as though it had a life of its own. When Hallward takes up a palette knife to destroy the work which threatens to mar their relationships, Dorian tears the knife from his hand, crying out that it would be murder. The picture is preserved, and promised to Dorian. But the relationship between Dorian and Hallward has altered crucially. It is now Lord Henry who is to become Dorian's mentor.

This opening episode, contained in Chapters 1 and 2, establishes two patterns which are structurally important. The first involves the knife: Dorian tears the palette knife from Hallward's grasp, preventing a symbolic murder; he stabs Hallward to death in front of the portrait in Chapter 13; ultimately, he stabs the picture with the same knife— 'As it had killed the painter, so it would kill the painter's work'—and his own body is discovered with a knife in the heart. The second pattern is concerned with the relationship between Dorian's actions and the picture's appearance, which serves as a record of his soul's progress. The picture, initially, functions as a perfect image of his beauty, a beauty of soul as well as of feature. When Dorian rejects his love Sybil Vane—a rejection caused by her failure in the art of acting—and so precipitates her suicide, the picture's expression changes: 'One would have said that there was a touch of cruelty in the mouth'; after Hallward's murder, a 'loathsome red dew' 'gleamed, wet and glistening, on one of the hands, as though the canvas had sweated blood'; when Dorian commits a good action, by sparing the innocent Hetty Merton, he hopes the portrait may reflect his new life, but is horrified to find no change, 'save that in the eyes there was a look of cunning, and in the mouth the curved wrinkle of the hypocrite'. Finally, at Dorian's death, the youth and beauty which have been miraculously preserved in him are transferred back to the portrait, while he himself becomes 'withered, wrinkled, and loathsome of visage'.

Within the framework, and in addition to Dorian's relationships with Hallward and Lord Henry, who in places seem to function as good and evil angel to his Faustus, there are two major episodes. The first involves Dorian's passion for the actress Sibyl Vane. Sibyl, childlike and naive, acts 'all the great heroines of the world in one'; in a sordid little theatre, surrounded by third-rate players and grotesque scenery, she plays Juliet, Imogen, Rosalind, Ophelia, Desdemona. Dorian is entranced by her performance, and relates the nature of his happiness to Hallward and Lord Henry. (This act of confiding is frequently associated with danger in Wilde's writing, the process of convincing another leading to a failure of belief on the part of the speaker.) Sibyl was playing Rosalind, one of several glances at Gautier's Mademoiselle de Maupin, and a link also with Mr W. H. Significantly, Dorian defines Sibyl's qualities first in terms of art:

*Portrait of Wilde by Toulouse-Lautrec.*

She had never seemed to me more exquisite. She had all the delicate grace of that Tanagra figurine that you have in your studio, Basil. Her hair clustered round her face like dark leaves round a pale rose. As for her acting—well, you shall see her tonight. She is simply a born artist.

Next, he recounts the moment of ecstatic union:

As we were sitting together, suddenly there came into her eyes a look that I had never seen there before. My lips moved towards her. We kissed each other. I can't describe to you what I felt at that moment. It seemed to me that all my life had been narrowed to one perfect point of rose-coloured joy.

It is noteworthy that Wilde presents this moment as reported rather than direct action, so that the emphasis is placed upon Dorian's attempt to define the experience. As though to justify himself, he proceeds to seek assurance:

I have been right, Basil, haven't I, to take my love out of poetry, and to find my wife in Shakespeare's plays? Lips that Shakespeare taught to speak have whispered their secret in my ear. I have had the arms of Rosalind around me, and kissed Juliet on the mouth.

Hallward's response is tentative. Lord Henry, more deflationary, asks Dorian at what point he mentioned the word marriage. He proceeds to expand on the theme of Hedonism: 'When we are happy we are always good, but when we are good we are not always happy.' Ominously, Lord

Henry drives away to the theatre with Dorian, leaving the painter, silent and preoccupied, to follow in a hansom. The revelation which Dorian has promised his friends does not materialise. Sibyl Vane's beauty is as striking as ever, and when as Juliet she appears at her father Capulet's ball she is described in terms which seem to associate her with the perfected dancer, the human apotheosised in art, at once natural and artificial:

> Her body swayed as she danced, as a plant sways in the water. The curves of her throat were the curves of a white lily. Her hands seemed to be made of cool ivory.

But the revelation promised by her physical appearance proves misleading:

> The voice was exquisite, but from the point of view of tone it was absolutely false. It was wrong in colour. It took away all the life from the verse. It made the passion unreal.

The process of demythologising continues: 'The staginess of her acting was unbearable . . . Her gestures became absurdly artificial . . . ', until the final and laconic condemnation, 'It was simply bad art.'

The audience's reactions to the performance are interestingly differentiated. Wilde, somewhat unrealistically, makes even the 'common, uneducated audience of the pit and gallery' grow restless, and eventually tramp out. Hallward attempts to reassure Dorian by separating the girl from the actress, in one of those Wildean affirmations that carry scant conviction: 'Love is a more wonderful thing than Art.' Lord Henry delivers a dandiacal truth: 'It is not good for one's morals to see bad acting.' Dorian confesses that his heart is breaking. Backstage, after the performance, Sibyl is standing 'with a look of triumph on her face':

> When he entered, she looked at him, and an expression of infinite joy came over her. 'How badly I acted tonight, Dorian!' she cried.

Her explanation is the most significant speech Wilde gives to her. Before she meets Dorian, acting was the one reality of her life. She knew 'nothing but shadows', and thought them real. Dorian brought her 'something higher, something of which all art' was 'but a reflection'. She expected to be wonderful that night, found she could do nothing, and suddenly realised that it would be 'profanation' to 'play at being in love'.

However, just as Dorian's confession of love has stifled Sibyl's ability to act, so her withdrawal from art has killed Dorian's love: 'Without your art you are nothing.' He rejects her coldly, and tells her he can never see her again. Then, in a sequence closely modelled on Lord Arthur Savile's night-walking after Podgers's prophecy of murder, Dorian wanders through the dark London underworld before dawn breaks on a Covent Garden purified by pastoral overtones. It is on returning to his house that Dorian notices on his portrait lines of cruelty round the mouth. The next day he is full of remorse and resolves to make reparation to Sibyl:

> She could still be his wife. His unreal and selfish

love would yield to some higher influence, would be transformed into some nobler passion, and the portrait that Basil Hallward had painted of him would be a guide to him through life, would be to him what holiness is to some, and conscience to others, and the fear of God to us all.

As he finishes a passionate letter to Sibyl, imploring her forgiveness, Lord Henry arrives with the news of Sibyl's suicide, and consoles Dorian with the idea that her lonely death was simply an episode from art, 'a strange lurid fragment from some Jacobean tragedy': 'Mourn for Ophelia, if you like. Put ashes on your head because Cordelia was strangled . . . But don't waste your tears over Sibyl Vane. She was less real than they are.' Dorian thanks Lord Henry: 'You have explained me to myself.' An hour later 'and he was at the Opera, and Lord Henry was leaning over his chair'.

The Sibyl Vane relationship, which effectively occupies Chapters 4 to 9, forms the crucial action within the novel. It is the test which confirms Lord Henry's domination over Dorian: in terms of the choice with which Dorian is confronted, he instinctively chooses art rather than love, confirming in practice the poisonous theories which he first heard from Lord Henry in Basil Hallward's garden. Dorian's choice is analogous to Faustus's (and Faust's) first action of egotistical self-delight; and the Mephistophelean figure of Lord Henry is present to strengthen the protagonist's resolve. Dorian's action also prompts two self-destructive revelations. The first is that of Sibyl Vane herself, whose belief in art is destroyed by the declaration of Dorian's love, love which is itself presented as essentially ephemeral, an act of imagination, as suggested by her whimsical name for Dorian of 'Prince Charming'. The second comes from Basil Hallward, who calls on Dorian the day after Lord Henry's visit and is led into confessing his secret. Hallward defines the climactic moment when he drew Dorian not as Paris, Adonis, Antinous, but in his own dress and in his own time. Before, 'it had all been what art should be, unconscious, ideal, remote', but his wonderful portrait of Dorian in the method of realism would, he feared, reveal to others his idolatry. The interpenetration of personal feeling and the artistic process is presented as fatal. Dorian translated into art is lost to Basil Hallward; Sibyl Vane, translated out of art by Dorian, is lost to him. Wilde conveys vividly the extreme fragility and transitoriness of his images of perfection: the moment when the portrait is completed, which almost immediately informs Dorian of his mortality; the absorption of Sibyl Vane within her Shakespearean roles, which cannot be sustained within a context of reality. Against these exquisite but essentially tragic experiences Wilde sets the cool objectivity of Lord Henry, who remains a spectator, judging life by the standards of the connoisseur. For Dorian, once he has accepted as his mentor Lord Henry and his dictum—'to cure the soul by means of the senses, and the senses by means of the soul'—the portrait will become the living symbol of his Faustian choice:

> Eternal youth, infinite passion, pleasures subtle and secret, wild joys and wilder sins—he was to

have all these things. The portrait was to bear the burden of his shame: that was all.

The Sibyl Vane episode is handled more convincingly than the explanation of Basil Hallward's infatuation with Dorian, where Wilde seems, understandably, constrained by the need to suppress intimations of homosexuality. Absorption with the relationship between actress or dancer and her role is a prevalent theme in the nineteenth century, particularly since acting style became progressively more naturalistic. Wilde's choice of roles for Sibyl Vane—Juliet, Ophelia, Desdemona, Cordelia—recalls the Shakespearean characters in which Harriet Smithson appeared before Berlioz, who, like Dorian, imagined that by loving the transmitting actress he was somehow communing with Shakespeare himself. The descriptions of Sibyl as Rosalind owe something to *Mademoiselle de Maupin,* and perhaps to the open-air production of *As You Like It* produced by Lady Archibald Campbell and Godwin. There may also be an echo of Baudelaire's *La Fanfarlo,* in which the youthful Samuel Cramer, paying court to the actress in her boudoir, insists that she assume the make-up and costume of the stage role which she was portraying when he became infatuated with her, so recreating the artifice of the theatre within the context of reality.

For the extended version of **The Picture of Dorian Gray,** Wilde added a chapter (Chapter 5) which presents a number of difficulties. Its subject is Sibyl Vane and her family, her vulgarly melodramatic mother and her protective, morose brother James. The settings—their shabby lodging-house in Euston Road, the London streets, the park—have both a specificity and a shabby urban realism which contrast sharply with the decorated style which has dominated hitherto. This realism is continued in the descriptions of the tawdry theatre where Sibyl performs, and in Dorian's descent into the underworld in Chapter 16 (another addition to the original scheme). Chapter 5 is the only section in which Wilde focuses on a subject other than Dorian, who makes one brief appearance, driving past Sibyl and James as they sit in the park, but who is otherwise referred to only as Prince Charming. The change in focus is matched by an abrupt change in tone, or rather changes: the chapter contains the most uneven writing of the entire novel. In places, Wilde seems to be parodying the most banal examples of domestic melodrama:

> Mrs Vane winced, and put her thin bismuth-whitened hands on her daughter's head. 'Happy!' she echoed, 'I am only happy, Sibyl, when I see you act. You must not think of anything but your acting. Mr Isaacs has been very good to us, and we owe him money.'
>
> The girl looked up and pouted. 'Money, mother?' she cried. 'What does money matter? Love is more than money.'

Wilde signals awareness of the effect by imputing it to Mrs Vane:

> Mrs Vane glanced at her, and with one of those false theatrical gestures that so often become a mode of second nature to a stage-player, clasped her in her arms . . . a young lad with rough brown hair came into the room . . . Mrs Vane

fixed her eyes on him, and intensified her smile. She mentally elevated her son to the dignity of an audience. She felt sure that the *tableau* was interesting.

But in fact the melodramatic influence is pervasive, and even Sibyl's rebuke to James—'You are like one of the heroes of those silly melodramas mother used to be so fond of acting in'—does not justify or place securely the cumulative burden of derivative phrases. Wilde barely differentiates Sibyl's mode of expression from that of the rest of the family—or no more than the virtuous heroine is habitually differentiated from the rough-tongued, good-hearted brother or the vain mother. The plain and simple, unless within the artful context of a children's story, did not flow easily from Wilde. Wilde is, conceivably, presenting Sibyl's version of the romance as a fairy-tale—'Prince Charming rules life for us now'—and hence a counterpart to Dorian's equally transitory enchantment with the actress as Shakespearean heroine; but the narrative method is here too inconsistent to convey any clear structural purpose. The insertion forms a brief but disruptive interlude, compounded by its sequel, James Vane's attempted revenge and accidental death in Wilde's prefiguring of Isabel Colegate's *The Shooting Party.*

The second major episode in the novel concerns the 'poison' book, whose arrival is immediately preceded by the concealment of the picture in Dorian's former playroom. Returning to the library, Dorian finds two objects sent by Lord Henry: 'On a little table of dark perfumed wood thickly incrusted with nacre' was 'a book bound in yellow paper, the cover slightly torn and the edges soiled'; and, on the tea-tray, the *St James's Gazette.* In the newspaper paragraph Dorian reads of the ugly reality of Sibyl's death. Then, taking up the yellow book, he becomes absorbed:

> It was the strangest book that he had ever read. It seemed to him that in exquisite raiment, and to the delicate sounds of flutes, the sins of the world were passing in dumb show before him. Things that he had dimly dreamed of were suddenly made real to him. Things of which he had never dreamed were gradually revealed.

In function, the book serves a similar purpose to that of Apuleius's *Metamorphoses* in *Marius the Epicurean,* and to Ronsard's works in Pater's unfinished novel *Gaston de Latour,* which each exercised a powerful effect on the respective hero at a crucial stage of his development. (One might add the influence on Wilde himself of Pater's *The Renaissance*—'that book which has had such a strange influence over my life'.) For Dorian, however, the poison book is less a formative influence than a distraction once he has committed his self-defining act of objective cruelty towards Sibyl Vane, in something of the same way that the spectacle of the Seven Deadly Sins feeds Faustus's soul when he begins to waver. At the end of Chapter 11, Wilde summarises the novel's impact: 'Dorian Gray had been poisoned by a book. There were moments when he looked on evil simply as a mode through which he could realize his conception of the beautiful.' The book confirms Dorian in evil. The consequences of his cruelty towards Sibyl

Vane have been unforeseen. He now embarks upon a course of life which consciously embraces sin.

In Wilde's typescript for *Lippincott's,* the novel is called 'Le Secret de Raoul par Catulle Sarrazin' and it would seem that Wilde at one stage planned to create an imaginary book. In the event the poison novel bears, in spite of certain discrepancies, an unmistakable resemblance to Huysmans's *A rebours;* and Dorian shares a number of interests and enthusiams with Huysmans's hero Des Esseintes. These interests are described by Wilde in an astonishing sequence of economical transcriptions, drawing on books he had recently reviewed, or on sources like the South Kensington Museum Handbooks for Precious Stones or Textile Fabrics. The descriptions are not particularly memorable, relying for effect on sheer cumulative weight of example, rather than on any sensory finesse in the language.

As to Dorian's sins, Wilde offers no detail. Here, indeed, as later in **De Profundis,** he appears obsessed by the word sin itself, as though its use was self-explanatory. Instead of the particularity of Huysmans—Des Esseintes's encounters with Miss Urania the American acrobat, or the ventriloquist enacting Flaubert's Chimera and Sphinx—Wilde offers only the disconcerting tone of popular fiction:

> it was said that on one occasion, when he was brought into the smoking-room of the Churchill, the Duke of Berwick and another gentleman got up in a marked manner and went out. Curious stories became current about him after he had passed his twenty-fifth year. It was rumoured that he had been seen brawling with foreign sailors in a low den in the distant parts of Whitechapel, and that he consorted with thieves and coiners and knew the mysteries of their trade.

The style is reminiscent of the adventure fiction of John Buchan.

What holds the work together, here as throughout **The Picture of Dorian Gray,** is the sequence of passages which describe Dorian's relationship with his soul; the occasion when

> he himself would creep upstairs to the locked room, open the door with the key that never left him now, and stand, with a mirror, in front of the portrait that Basil Hallward had painted of him, looking at the evil and ageing face on the canvas, and now at the fair young face that laughed back at him from the polished glass. The very sharpness of the contrast used to quicken his sense of pleasure. He grew more and more enamoured of his own beauty, more and more interested in the corruption of his own soul. He would examine with minute care, and sometimes with a monstrous and terrible delight, the hideous lines that seared the wrinkling forehead or crawled around the heavy sensual mouth, wondering sometimes which were the more horrible, the signs of sin or the signs of age. He would place his white hands beside the coarse bloated hands of the picture, and smile. He mocked the misshapen body and the failing limbs.

This and similar passages convey a psychological convic-

tion that validates Dorian's experiments in Hedonism, and precipitates the final crushing of conscience expressed through the murder of Basil Hallward, who calls, good angel-like, to ask Dorian if the terrible rumours he has heard about him are true. The two chapters which describe this episode, Chapters 12 and 13, contain the full range of Gothic effects: damp odour of mildewed candles, cold current of air, exclamations of horror, and finally the drip, drip of blood on threadbare carpet, and the secret press in the wainscotting. Here Wilde strikes one as being wholly in command of the idiom, using it consciously for precise effect. In the following chapter, he has Dorian stretch out on the sofa reading poems from Gautier's *Emaux et camées* while he awaits the arrival of his scientist friend Campbell, whom he blackmails into disposing of Hallward's body. The contrast between the two frames of reference, the decadent and the Gothic, seems appropriate both in literary and psychological terms:

> When he had stretched himself on the sofa, he looked at the title-page of the book. It was Gautier's *Emaux et camées,* Charpentier's Japanese-paper edition, with the Jacquemart etching. The binding was of citron-green leather, with a design of gilt trellis-work and dotted pomegranates. It had been given to him by Adrian Singleton. As he turned over the pages his eye fell on the poem about the hand of Lacenaire, the cold yellow hand 'du supplice encore mal lavée', with its downy red hairs and its 'doigts de faune'. He glanced at his own white taper fingers, shuddering slightly in spite of himself, and passed on . . .

Lacenaire, the murderer executed by guillotine, with his 'cold yellow hand', is juxtaposed with Dorian, who has committed a comparable crime, with his white taper fingers. But even when Lacenaire is transmuted into art, the trace of reality is too disturbing, and Dorian moves on to Gautier's exquisite lines upon Venice:

> Devant une façade rose,
> Sur le marbre d'un escalier.

Dorian's memories of Venice, however, are haunted by the recollection that Basil Hallward had been with him for part of the time; and even Gautier's evocation of the Sphinx cannot distract him from the terror of what he has done.

In the novel's original scheme, the horror of the disposal of Hallward's body, and the corresponding reaction registered by the picture, an image of 'loathsome red dew that gleamed, wet and glistening, on one of the hands, as though the canvas had sweated blood', leads swiftly on to the final episode, Dorian's attempt to commit a good action, his terrible discovery that he is incapable of change and the culminating act of destruction with the knife. While the *Lippincott* version is shocking in its abruptness, the four chapters which Wilde inserted here flesh out the course of Dorian's life, intensify our sense of his suffering and clarify the persona of Lord Henry. There are two London episodes, a society dinner party at Lady Narborough's and Dorian's visit to the London underworld of dockland opium dens; and two contrasting sequences at Dorian's country house, Selby Royal, one in the conservatory, a setting for elegant conversation, and the other in the pine-woods, where James Vane is accidentally shot. Throughout these scenes there is a recurrent motif of death. While Dorian receives repeated reassurances that he is safe, both from events and from Lord Henry, the sense that he is damned becomes increasingly insistent.

These chapters contain numerous echoes of Wilde's other work. Lady Narborough seems like a preliminary sketch for Lady Hunstanton, and several of Lord Henry's conversational flourishes will be given to Lord Illingworth in *A Woman of No Importance,* while Madame de Ferrol, *décolletée* in Vienna, presages Mrs Cheveley in *An Ideal Husband.* The rhythms, and indeed some of the content, of the dialogue between Lord Henry and the Duchess of Monmouth recur in Lord Illingworth's verbal fencing with Mrs Allonby. The descriptions of the London underworld reflect similar images in **'Lord Arthur Savile's Crime'** and **'The Harlot's House':**

> Most of the windows were dark, but now and then fantastic shadows were silhouetted against some lamp-lit blind. He watched them curiously. They moved like monstrous marionettes, and made gestures like live things.

Such echoes and repetitions might be taken simply as the consequence of hasty writing; more probably, they indicate Wilde's attempts to create a satisfactory unity out of the ideas, images and styles which were his current concern. There are, too, passages which have more resonance when read in conjunction with **De Profundis,** and even **The Ballad of Reading Gaol:**

> There are moments, psychologists tell us, when the passion for sin, or for what the world calls sin, so dominates a nature, that every fibre of the body, as every cell of the brain, seems to be instinct with fearful impulses. Men and women at such moments lose the freedom of their will. They move to their terrible end as automatons move. Choice is taken from them, and conscience is either killed, or, if it lives at all, lives but to give rebellion its fascination, and disobedience its charm. For all sins, as theologians weary not of reminding us, are sins of disobedience. When that high spirit, that morning-star of evil, fell from heaven, it was as a rebel that he fell.

> Callous, concentrated on evil, with stained mind and soul hungry for rebellion, Dorian Gray hastened on, quickening his step as he went, but as he darted aside into a dim archway, that had served him often as a short cut to the ill-famed place where he was going, he felt himself suddenly seized from behind, and before he had time to defend himself he was thrust back against the wall, with a brutal hand round his throat.

In contexts such as this, Wilde gives indications that the novel is a portrait of the artist; James Joyce detected in it 'some wish to put himself before the world'.

If Wilde was intending to 'put himself before the world', he contrived to do it in a complex, multiple form. Pater, reviewing the novel, comments that Wilde is 'impersonal:

seems not to have identified himself with any one of his characters' [see excerpt in *TCLC,* Vol. 1, pp. 495-96]. Wilde himself wrote: 'Basil Hallward is what I think I am: Lord Henry what the world thinks me: Dorian what I would like to be—in other ages, perhaps.' In Wilde's myth, Basil Hallward is killed; Dorian, an image of perpetual youth, is spiritually dead; and Lord Henry refuses to acknowledge the existence of the soul. Earlier on the night of Dorian's death Lord Henry recounts to him how he heard a London street-preacher yelling out, 'what does it profit a man if he gain the whole world and lose—how does the quotation run?—his own soul':

> 'I thought of telling the prophet that Art had a soul, but that man had not. I am afraid, however, he would not have understood me.'

> 'Don't, Harry. The soul is a terrible reality. It can be bought, and sold, and bartered away. It can be poisoned, or made perfect. There is a soul in each one of us. I know it.'

> 'Do you feel quite sure of that, Dorian?'

> 'Quite sure.'

> 'Ah! then it must be an illusion. The things one feels absolutely certain about are never true. That is the fatality of Faith, and the lesson of Romance. How grave you are! Don't be so serious. What have you or I to do with the superstitions of our age? No: we have given up our belief in the soul. Play me something. Play me a nocturne, Dorian, and, as you play, tell me, in a low voice, how you have kept your youth. You must have some secret. I am only ten years older than you are, and I am wrinkled, and worn, and yellow. You are really wonderful, Dorian. You have never looked more charming than you do to-night.'

The ageing Lord Henry, distancing death and divorce with Chopin nocturnes, curing the soul by means of the sense, uses Dorian as the corner-stone of his philosophy, the perfect completed image:

> At present you are a perfect type. Don't make yourself incomplete. You are quite flawless now . . . I am so glad that you have never done anything, never carved a statue, or painted a picture, or produced anything outside of yourself! Life has been your art. You have set yourself to music. Your days are your sonnets.

It is significant that Wilde places the emphasis throughout the penultimate chapter on Lord Henry, while Dorian is shown retreating more and more into his renunciation of sin, and his resolution to be good. Lord Henry's affirmations become increasingly declamatory as the scene reaches its close—'Art has no influence upon action. It annihilates the desire to act. It is superbly sterile'—echoing the Preface which Wilde attached to the revised work. As Dorian leaves, he hesitates for a moment, 'as if he had something more to say. Then he sighed and went out'. The work's final image, the dead man 'withered, wrinkled, and loathsome of visage', recognisable only by his rings, is set against the previous chapter's farewell, and the plan to ride in the park to see the lilacs. (pp. 67-80)

*Peter Raby, in his* Oscar Wilde, *Cambridge University Press, 1988, 164 p.*

## Claude J. Summers   (essay date 1990)

[*In the following excerpt, Summers examines the homosexual subtext of* The Picture of Dorian Gray.]

Homosexuality is an important aspect of **The Picture of Dorian Gray,** and the novel deserves credit as a pioneering depiction of homosexual relationships in serious English fiction. The depiction of homosexuality in the book is undoubtedly—though perhaps unconsciously—shaped by Wilde's personal ambivalences toward his own sexuality, which found expression both in idealized love affairs and in liaisons with prostitutes. But it is important to stress that the novel's primary interest is literary rather than biographical, and that, especially in the final version, Wilde hints at homosexuality rather than expresses it directly. And it is necessary to insist that the work's homosexual subtext is far more complex and subtle than has frequently been acknowledged, complicated by the extreme difficulty of writing sympathetically about a taboo, though titillating, subject for a popular audience as well as by an unclear authorial vision. Homosexual readers would certainly have responded to the book's under current of gay feeling, and may have found the very name "Dorian" suggestive of Greek homosexuality, since it was Dorian tribesmen who allegedly introduced homosexuality into Greece as part of their military regimen; but Jeffrey Meyers's homophobic view of the novel as being "really about the jealousy and pain, the fear and guilt of being a homosexual" [see excerpt dated 1977] is simply wrong, a distortion based on egregious misinterpretations and on the *a priori* assumption that homosexuality is the root of all evil. Wilde purposely leaves the exact nature of the sins of Dorian Gray mysterious and vague, suggested but not defined. Characteristically playing hide-and-seek with his readers, he alternately exposes and conceals the homosexual dimension of the novel. In response to the attacks on the book, he remarked, with some justice if not complete candor, that "Each man sees his own sin in Dorian Gray." But whatever they may include, the dissipations of Dorian Gray are by no means exclusively or even primarily homosexual. Those that are specifically cited, in fact, are explicitly heterosexual. The evil in **The Picture of Dorian Gray** may encompass homosexual (as well as heterosexual) excesses, but it should by no means be identified with homosexuality per se.

Wilde's attitude toward homosexuality in the novel may best be seen in his portrayal of Basil Hallward. Hallward is the character most clearly delineated as homosexual, and it is significant that he is presented as the most morally sensitive character as well. So passive as to function largely as a choral figure, he nevertheless speaks as the voice of moderation. His love for Dorian seems altogether noble, especially in contrast to the blandishments of Lord Henry, his rival for the young man's affection. In the triangle formed by the competition of the two older men for the attention of the beautiful boy, Basil represents an idealized, platonized homosexuality, linked to a long tradition of art and philosophy. Indeed, he has been affected by Do-

rian in much the same way that the homosexual artists and thinkers celebrated in **"The Portrait of Mr. W. H."** have been affected by their lovers. Dominated by the beauty of the young man, Basil sees in Dorian "an entirely new mode of style." Actually, he is in love with him less as an individual than as the embodiment of a Hellenic ideal, the "harmony of soul and body." Tellingly, however, the idealized homosexual love that Basil feels for Dorian—"such love as Michael Angelo had known, and Montaigne, and Winckelmann, and Shakespeare"—is regarded by the artist as a shameful secret, a love that dare not speak its name.

The implied link between homosexual Eros and creativity is clear in Dorian's effect on Basil's art. Dorian's beauty and the ideal that he represents cause Basil to see the world afresh and inspire him to his greatest work as an artist. For this, Basil is profoundly grateful to Dorian, but at the same time he expresses ambivalence, for he sees his homosexually inspired art—indeed, his homosexuality itself—as both a gift and a curse. Declaring that "It is better not to be different from one's fellows," Basil early in the novel comments on the fatal aspect of the mark of difference. "Your rank and wealth, Harry; my brains, such as they are—my art, whatever it may be worth; Dorian Gray's good looks—we shall all suffer for what the gods have given us, suffer terribly," he remarks prophetically. Basil's ambivalence is apparent at the very beginning of his relationship with Dorian. When he first feels irresistibly attracted to the young man, whom he sees across the room at Lady Brandon's party, he literally attempts to escape. And however much he comes to appreciate the new vitality his love for Dorian gives to his art, he desperately fears exposure. His reluctance to exhibit the picture of Dorian, because "I have put too much of myself into it," indicates both his self-doubt and his fear of the world's contempt should it guess his secret.

Basil's ambivalence is evident in his guilty characterization of his love for Dorian as idolatry. "You became to me the visible incarnation of that unseen ideal whose memory haunts us artists like an exquisite dream," he explains to Dorian, confessing that "I worshipped you. I grew jealous of every one to whom you spoke. I wanted to have you all to myself. I was only happy when I was with you." This revelation is made after Basil's infatuation with Dorian has faded somewhat and he has overcome his inhibition against exhibiting the portrait; yet it is still permeated with guilt. Even the idealized homosexuality that Basil represents inspires shame and fear, and is condemned in theological terms as idolatry.

Tellingly, the confession of Basil's secret inspires only condescending pity in Dorian, for there "seemed to him to be something tragic in a friendship so coloured by romance." At the same time, the narcissistic youth characteristically wonders whether he might himself ever be so dominated by another. "Was that one of the things that life had in store?" he muses, as though Basil's love for him were simply another sensation to be tasted on his quest for experience. Later, however, he will wonder whether "Some love might come across his life, and purify him, and shield him from those sins that seemed to be already stirring in spirit and in flesh—those curious unpictured sins whose very mystery lent them their subtlety and their charm."

But Basil and Sibyl Vane, the young actress who commits suicide when Dorian rejects her, are the only characters in the novel capable of love for another, and the depth of their devotion serves to underline the shallowness of Dorian's addiction to pleasure and Lord Henry's devotion to emotional voyeurism. Interestingly, although the connection of each to Dorian involves art, both Sibyl and Basil value love before art. Early in the book, when Dorian laments the fact that the picture will mock him by remaining young as he grows old, Basil offers to destroy the painting. He is dissuaded from ripping up the canvas only by Dorian's revealing plea, "I am in love with it. . . . It is part of myself." Later, after the fiasco at the play when Sibyl performs poorly precisely because she has discovered the reality of love, Dorian complains bitterly but Basil remarks, "Love is more wonderful than Art." Basil's devotion to love is, in fact, the quality that ultimately redeems him.

Wilde conceives of Basil's homosexual love for Dorian as something positive but dangerous, an emotion that inspires guilt and fear: measures, respectively, of the internal and external condemnations brought to bear against homosexuality. Perhaps more pertinently, Basil's love is clearly, if imprecisely, implicated in the strange events that culminate in Dorian's loss of a moral sense and in his murder of the artist. When Basil confronts Dorian about the widespread tales of his corruption, pleading with him to deny the rumors, Dorian responds by offering to show him the picture, "the diary of my life from day to day," for "You are the one man in the world who is entitled to know everything about me. You have had more to do with my life than you think." Dorian unveils the portrait, and Basil shrinks in horror from the hideous face on the canvas, while Dorian observes the scene calmly, like an amused spectator, with merely a flicker of triumph in his eyes. The younger man blames his predicament on the artist, who taught him to be vain of his good looks. Although protesting that "There was nothing evil, nothing shameful" in his love, Basil nevertheless accepts responsibility. "I worshipped you too much. I am punished for it," he tells Dorian, adding: "You worshipped yourself too much." As he implores Dorian to pray for forgiveness, he is stabbed to death, Dorian receiving from the ugly portrait—his own debased conscience—a directive to murder.

The idealized homosexual love of Basil for Dorian, then, is presented ambiguously. On the one hand, it is repeatedly described as noble and its power is confirmed by the transformation of Basil's art that it effects. On the other hand, it is the source of guilt and fear, and the very art that it inspires is ominous, for that art culminates in the sinister portrait itself. By presenting the naive Dorian with a surprising image of himself (i.e., the artist's own image of him), by awakening him to his beauty and thereby encouraging his vanity, Basil may be said to initiate the entire tragedy. The diabolism of the painting may be dismissed as a gothic plot device, but Wilde's serious purpose in implicating Basil in the corruption of Dorian Gray is to underline the major theme of the work, the wickedness of using others. This theme is most clear in Dorian's heartless exploitation of others, and in the amused, detached voyeurism of Henry, but it is involved as well in Basil's reduction of Dorian to "simply a motive in art" found "in the curves of certain lines, in the loveliness and subtleties of certain colours." Although Basil is by no means the villain of the piece, he too partakes of the objectification of others that the novel most vehemently condemns. Yet his fault is not that of loving Dorian, for as Dorian himself recognizes, Basil's love might have saved him from his ugly fate. Rather, his fault is that of not loving him openly and disinterestedly, of appropriating his image as art. Basil's aestheticization of Dorian is analogous to Dorian's aestheticization of Sibyl Vane.

If Basil is to blame for objectifying Dorian, so too is Lord Henry Wotton. Whereas Basil reveals to Dorian a new image of himself, so Henry more deliberately attempts to shape Dorian and to experience through him sensations and emotions that he is too fearful and too detached from life to experience firsthand. Although Basil and Henry are at first glance extremely dissimilar—the one earnest and idealistic, the other cynical and disillusioned—the rivals share an artistic impulse. They both want to transform and re-present reality, a desire that may be a psychological compensation for their essential passivity. Basil's artistry finds expression in painting, Henry's in the exercise of influence. Tellingly, Henry's homoerotic attraction to Dorian is whetted voyeuristically by Basil's worship of the young man, and Henry is thereby roused from his characteristic languor to a desire to influence—that is, to shape—Dorian, a process that is itself a sublimated expression of homosexuality.

The rivalry of Henry and Basil centers in fact on the question of who will exert a shaping influence on the naive youth. Soon after meeting him, Henry determines to adopt Dorian as his protégé. "Talking to him," the aristocrat reflects, "was like playing upon an exquisite violin. He answered to every touch and thrill of the bow." This suggestive passage reveals the interconnection of art and sex, dominance and submission in Henry's response to Dorian, whom he regards as "a marvelous type" who "could be made a Titan or a toy." The worldly cynic undertakes as his goal the "making" of Dorian much as a poet or a sculptor might shape a work of art. "There was something terribly enthralling in the exercise of influence," he muses:

> To project one's soul into some gracious form, and let it tarry there for a moment; to hear one's own intellectual views echoed back to one with all the added music of passion and youth; to convey one's temperament into another as though it were a subtle fluid or a strange perfume: there was a real joy in that—perhaps the most satisfying joy left to us in an age so limited and vulgar as our own, an age grossly carnal in its pleasures, and grossly common in its aims.

Significantly, he later thinks of Dorian as "his own creation." The deliberate callousness of Henry's decision to influence Dorian is cast in relief by his early statement that "All influence is immoral" because it inhibits self-development, the perfect realization of one's nature.

Henry's agenda is to substitute for Dorian's unformed nature his own, which he is too timid to explore directly.

Interestingly, Henry's artistic aim in shaping Dorian is to create a harmony of matter and spirit, a synergistic balance of body and soul akin to Basil's Hellenic ideal. In a pivotal passage that profoundly affects the naive Dorian, Henry announces a credo that is strikingly congruent with Basil's idealistic vision, however divergent their ideas and means may appear. "I believe that if one man were to live out his life fully and completely, were to give form to every feeling, expression to every thought, reality to every dream," Henry asserts, "I believe that the world would gain such a fresh insight of joy that we would forget all the maladies of mediaevalism, and return to the Hellenic ideal." As Henry explains his "new Hedonism," a philosophy based clearly if tendentiously on Pater's (in)famous conclusion to *The Renaissance,* he tells Dorian that "The moment I met you I saw that you were quite unconscious of what you really are, of what you really might be."

Just as Basil's portrait offers Dorian a revelation of his own beauty as filtered through the artist's transforming vision, so Henry's belief in the mysterious interanimation of body and soul reveals to the youth a hitherto unsuspected potential. Dorian, in fact, murmurs his fatal prayer for unchanging beauty while Henry's suggestive words ring in his ear and Basil's instructive painting shines in his eyes. And just as Basil is fearful of the secret love for Dorian embedded in the portrait, so is Henry fearful of his own doctrine of self-realization. "People are afraid of themselves, nowadays," he remarks, and the comment is more applicable to himself than to anyone else.

Henry displaces Basil in the competition for Dorian's attention, yet his triumph is more illusory than real. Although the younger man accedes to Henry's statement that "All through your life you will tell me everything you do," in fact he tells Henry very little. "If I ever did a crime, I would come and confess it to you," Dorian tells him, but Henry naively believes his protégé incapable of crime. "People like you—the wilful sunbeams of life—don't commit crimes," he remarks. Blithely unaware of the extent of Dorian's depravity, he persists in believing that he represents to the youth all the sins that Dorian lacks the courage to commit, when precisely the opposite is true. Even when the younger man hints that he may have murdered Basil, the elder dismisses the suggestion: "It is not in you, Dorian, to commit a crime." And, unaware of the horror of his friend's existence, Henry admires Dorian's "exquisite life," telling him near the end of the book that "You have drunk deeply of everything. You have crushed the grapes against your palate. Nothing has been hidden from you. And it has all been to you no more than the sound of music. It has not marred you." The sentiments expressed here are, of course, mocked in the novel's final scene, just as during his life Dorian's unblemished appearance is mocked by the ugly visage of the portrait.

The central irony of *The Picture of Dorian Gray* is that the Hellenic ideal of "the harmony of soul and body" pursued by Basil and Henry alike, and localized in their separate visions of Dorian, is not realized largely because they project onto the young man their own unbalanced and fragmentary images. None of the three principal characters is complete or harmonious; hence, they appear mere caricatures. Each is fragmented, unable to achieve that wholeness of being implicit in Arnold's desire for a transcendent moment when "what we mean, we say, and what we would, we know." Basil says what he means in the homoerotic portrait he paints, but he is unable to act on what he knows. Similarly, Henry lives vicariously through Dorian, precisely because he too dares not act on what he feels. And in the corrupt and materialistic world of late-nineteenth-century London, Dorian's project of self-realization amounts simply to a self-indulgence that mocks both Basil's idealism and Henry's tendentious (mis)interpretation of Pateresque epicureanism. Rather than harmonizing, in the course of the novel Dorian's soul and body become increasingly disconnected and finally separated entirely, as symbolized in the increasing disjunction between the unaging beauty of Dorian's body and the hideous representation of his soul (i.e., the picture). This irony suggests that the Faustian theme is by no means confined to the gothic diabolism of Dorian's supernatural bargain for a youthful appearance. By assuming godlike powers of creation, Henry and Basil also partake in the Faustian desire to escape human limitations. Consequently, they too are implicated in the tragedy. In their unbalanced pursuit of the Hellenic "harmony of soul and body," they contribute to the disharmonious dualism represented by Dorian's external beauty and his internal ugliness.

The poignant tone of the novel derives from its conclusion that the romantic quest for wholeness and balance cannot be achieved either through the representation of an artistic ideal or through the vicarious realization of the new Hedonism. These defeats, rather than the gothic plot centered around the preternatural portrait, are at the heart of the book's haunting irresolution and the discrepancy between its tone and moral. Dorian's Faustian bargain can be dismissed as mere gothicism, and the novel's moralistic plot and retributive ending can be classified as melodrama. But the yearning for a new moral order, an escape from the "maladies of mediaevalism," and a return to the Hellenic ideal persist even after the contrived, conventionally moral conclusion. Dorian's recognition that mankind's distrust of the senses has led to a profound loss may be qualified by his own subsequent history of reckless abandon, but it nevertheless resonates with meaning:

> As he looked back upon man moving through History, he was haunted by a feeling of loss. So much had been surrendered! and to such little purpose! There had been mad wilful rejections, monstrous forms of self-torture and self-denial, whose origin was fear, and whose result was a degradation infinitely more terrible than that fancied degradation from which, in their ignorance, they had sought to escape, Nature, in her wonderful irony, driving out the anchorite to feed with the wild animals of the desert and giving to the hermit the beasts of the field as his companions.

In *The Picture of Dorian Gray,* homosexuality is a powerful and fatal attraction, guilt-inducing and dangerous, yet enormously creative and potentially salvific. The worship of Basil and the voyeurism of Henry are finally condemned for their objectification of Dorian and for their Faustian aspirations. Nevertheless, the romantic dream of an idealized harmony of soul and body—a dream that in the novel is clearly homoerotic in inspiration—survives the moralistic conclusion to protest against an unsatisfactory reality and a tragic history, linked to asceticism and medievalism. In this sense, the novel is a gay fiction, however ambivalent its depiction of homosexuality. **The Picture of Dorian Gray** is a text divided against itself, but its creative tensions yield both a poignant sense of loss that the world cannot be re-created and made whole and an implied vision of an imagined world at ease with homosexuality, a world in which sensual enjoyment has been made an element of "a new spirituality, of which a fine instinct for beauty was to be the dominant characteristic." Perhaps more responsible than any other single English work in forging the stereotypical link between art, decadence, and homosexuality, the novel—for all its moralistic posturing—mourns the loss of a golden age and art's inability to re-create that homoerotic harmony of flesh and spirit of which Hellenism is the nostalgically evoked *locus amoenus.* (pp. 45-51)

> *Claude J. Summers, "'In Such Surrender There May Be Gain': Oscar Wilde and the Beginnings of Gay Fiction," in his* Gay Fictions: Wilde to Stonewall, Studies in a Male Homosexual Literary Tradition, *Continuum, 1990, pp. 29-61.*

---

## FURTHER READING

Baker, Houston A. "A Tragedy of the Artist: *The Picture of Dorian Gray.*" *Nineteenth Century Fiction* 24, No. 3 (December 1969): 349-55.
Interprets *Dorian Gray* within the framework of Wilde's pronouncements on both art and the roles of artists and critics in society.

Beckson, Karl. "Wilde's Autobiographical Signature in *The Picture of Dorian Gray.*" *The Victorian Newsletter,* No. 69 (Spring 1986): 30-2.
Suggests that Wilde frequently used the adjective "wild," the comparative form "wilder," and the adverb "wildly" in the text of *Dorian Gray* deliberately to reinforce the novel's autobiographical nature.

Cervo, Nathan. "Wilde's Closet Self: A Solo at One Remove." *The Victorian Newsletter,* No. 67 (Spring 1985): 17-19.
Response to Kerry Powell's 1984 essay "The Mesmerizing of Dorian Gray" (cited below), suggesting that "far from being a mesmeric novel patterned after cheap thrillers, *The Picture of Dorian Gray* is a spiritual autobiography."

Cevasco, G. A. "The Breviary of the Decadence." *Research Studies* 49, No. 4 (December 1981): 193-203.
Discusses the influence of Joris-Karl Huysmans's *A rebours* on Wilde and its anonymous appearance in *The Picture of Dorian Gray* as the "poisonous" yellow-bound book that fascinates and corrupts Dorian Gray.

Charlesworth, Barbara. "Oscar Wilde." In her *Dark Passages: The Decadent Consciousness in Victorian Literature,* pp. 53-80. Madison: University of Wisconsin Press, 1965.
Biographical reading of *The Picture of Dorian Gray.*

Clark, Bruce B. "A Burnt Child Loves the Fire: Oscar Wilde's Search for Ultimate Meanings in Life." *Ultimate Reality and Meaning* 4, No. 3 (1981): 225-47.
Calls *Dorian Gray* the most important of Wilde's works in explicating his thoughts on reality and meaning.

Cohen, Ed. "Writing Gone Wilde: Homoerotic Desire in the Closet of Representation." *PMLA* 102, No. 5 (October 1987): 801-13.
Discusses Wilde's emergence as a homosexual writer in the late nineteenth century and his relationship to the sex and gender ideologies of his time.

Cohen, Philip K. "The Crucible: *The Picture of Dorian Gray* and *Intentions.*" In his *The Moral Vision of Oscar Wilde,* pp. 105-55. Rutherford, N.J.: Fairleigh Dickinson University Press, 1978.
Suggests that in *Dorian Gray* Wilde fully explored the potential tragedy that was circumvented in his satiric short story "Lord Arthur Savile's Crime," and maintains that in the essays in *Intentions* Wilde sought to establish a middle ground between the repression and hypocrisy portrayed in the story and the hedonistic abandon depicted in the novel.

Dickson, Donald R. "'In a Mirror That Mirrors the Soul': Masks and Mirrors in *Dorian Gray.*" *English Literature in Transition: 1880-1920* 26, No. 1 (1983): 5-15.
Considers the novel's "most significant structural device—the notion of mirror images that reflect the masks of the characters"—important to an understanding of the novel's subtle aesthetic design.

Doyle, Sir Arthur Conan. "My First Literary Success." In his *Memories and Adventures,* pp. 67-76. Boston: Little, Brown, and Co., 1924.
Reminisces about meeting Wilde on the occasion that Wilde was commissioned to write *The Picture of Dorian Gray* and Doyle to write the second Sherlock Holmes novel, *The Sign of Four.* Doyle reprints a portion of the text of a letter from Wilde in which Wilde wrote: "I cannot understand how they can treat *Dorian Gray* as immoral. My difficulty was to keep the inherent moral subordinate to the artistic and dramatic effect, and it still seems to me that the moral is too obvious."

Ellmann, Richard. "Overtures to *Salome.*" In *Oscar Wilde: A Collection of Critical Essays,* edited by Richard Ellmann, pp. 73-91. Englewood Cliffs, N.J.: Prentice-Hall, 1969.
Mentions the influence of Walter Pater and John Ruskin on *The Picture of Dorian Gray.*

——. *Oscar Wilde.* New York: Alfred A. Knopf, 1988, 680 p.
Excellent biography.

Ericksen, Donald H. "*The Picture of Dorian Gray.*" In his *Oscar Wilde,* pp. 96-117. Boston: Twayne Publishers, 1977.
Discusses sources, plot, critical reception, characterization, imagery, language, and setting.

Gordon, Jan B. " 'Parody as Initiation': The Sad Education of *Dorian Gray.*" *Criticism* 9 (1967): 355-71.
> Considers Wilde's novel in relation to the tradition of the *Entwicklungsroman,* or developmental novel, noting that Wilde inverted some of the characteristic features of this tradition in *Dorian Gray.*

Hart, John E. "Art as Hero: *The Picture of Dorian Gray.*" *Research Studies* 46, No. 1 (March 1978): 1-11.
> Suggests that *The Picture of Dorian Gray* is "essentially a treatise . . . on aesthetics, a dramatic narrative that examines the role of art and its relation to man at the end of the nineteenth century," as well as "a moral tract that shows how man's inability to prosper in time leads to the diminution of will and failure in self-achievement."

Keefe, Robert. "Artist and Model in *The Picture of Dorian Gray.*" *Studies in the Novel* 5, No. 1 (Spring 1973): 63-70.
> Considers the novel's moral "inescapable, but subordinate to its esthetic preoccupation."

Kohl, Norbert. "Culture and Corruption. *The Picture of Dorian Gray.*" In his *Oscar Wilde: The Works of a Conformist Rebel,* translated by David Henry Wilson, pp. 138-75. Cambridge: Cambridge University Press, 1989.
> Attempts to account for the "continued interest in and varied reception of *Dorian Gray*" through an examination of the novel's origins, structure, setting, themes, and characterization.

Lawler, Donald L., and Knott, Charles E. "The Context of Invention: Suggested Origins of *Dorian Gray.*" *Modern Philology* 73, No. 4, part 1 (May 1976): 389-98.
> Asserts that *The Picture of Dorian Gray* was derived primarily from themes and ideas drawn from two earlier works by Wilde, "The Portrait of Mr. W. H." and "The Fisherman and His Soul."

Manganiello, Dominic. "Through a Cracked Looking Glass: *The Picture of Dorian Gray* and *A Portrait of the Artist as a Young Man.*" In *James Joyce and His Contemporaries,* edited by Diana A. Ben-Merre and Maureen Murphy, pp. 89-96. New York: Greenwood Press, 1989.
> Comparison of the theme of distorted perception in the two novels.

Mason, Stuart [pseudonym of Christopher Millard]. *Oscar Wilde—Art & Morality: A Record of the Discussion Which Followed the Publication of "Dorian Gray."* 1907. Reprint. Haskell House Publishers, 1971, 325 p.
> Collects letters, reviews, and extended commentary pertaining to both the initial serial publication of *The Picture of Dorian Gray* and the later book publication.

Mikhail, E. H. *Oscar Wilde: An Annotated Bibliography of Criticism.* Totowa, N.J.: Rowman and Littlefield, 1978, 249 p.
> Lists book and play reviews, earlier bibliographies of criticism, and whole and partial books of criticism on Wilde.

———, ed. *Oscar Wilde: Interviews and Recollections,* Vol. I. New York: Barnes & Noble, 1979, 255 p.
> Includes reminiscences of Wilde by friends, acquaintances, relatives, and professional associates.

Oates, Joyce Carol. "*The Picture of Dorian Gray:* Wilde's Parable of the Fall." In her *Contraries: Essays,* pp. 3-16. New York: Oxford University Press, 1981.
> Contends that "Wilde's novel must be seen as a highly serious meditation upon the moral role of the artist" and its theme as "the Fall—the Fall of innocence and its consequences, the corruption of 'natural' life by a sudden irrevocable consciousness (symbolized by Dorian's infatuation with himself )."

Pappas, John J. "The Flower and the Beast: A Study of Oscar Wilde's Antithetical Attitudes toward Nature and Man in *The Picture of Dorian Gray.*" *English Literature in Transition* 15, No. 1 (1972): 37-48.
> Examines Wilde's novel for expressions of antithesis toward nature as well as toward the place of humans in the natural world.

Pearson, Hesketh. "The Artist." In his *Oscar Wilde: His Life and Wit,* pp. 117-43. New York: Harper & Brothers, 1946.
> Includes discussion of the circumstances surrounding the writing of *The Picture of Dorian Gray.* Pearson considers the novel a revelation of Wilde's essential nature.

Peckham, Morse. "Identity and Personality." In his *Beyond the Tragic Vision: The Quest for Identity in the Nineteenth Century,* pp. 307-25. New York: George Braziller, 1962.
> Mentions *The Picture of Dorian Gray* as an example of the "morally responsible" literature of the Decadents that "reveals the horror of eroticism."

Pick, John. "Divergent Disciples of Walter Pater." *Thought* 23, No. 88 (March 1948): 114-28.
> Calls *Dorian Gray* "largely a novelized form of the 'Conclusion' to *The Renaissance,*" and comments that Wilde espoused ideals in the 1890s that Pater had promulgated in the early 1870s.

Poteet, Lewis J. "*Dorian Gray* and the Gothic Novel." *Modern Fiction Studies* 17, No. 2 (Summer 1971): 239-48.
> Places Wilde's novel in the English Romantic literary tradition of the Gothic novel, in particular comparing it with Charles R. Maturin's *Melmoth the Wanderer* (1820).

Powell, Kerry. "Oscar Wilde 'Acting': The Medium as Message in *The Picture of Dorian Gray.*" *Dalhousie Review* 58, No. 1 (Spring 1978): 104-15.
> Considers the theatrical form and structure of Wilde's novel.

———. "The Mesmerizing of Dorian Gray." *The Victorian Newsletter,* No. 65 (Spring 1984): 10-15.
> Discusses *Dorian Gray* as part of a tradition of mesmerism in nineteenth-century literature in which characters act under the influence of a powerful mesmerist.

———. "Who Was Basil Hallward?" *English Language Notes* 24, No. 1 (September 1986): 84-91.
> Speculates about possible sources for the character of Basil Hallward in *The Picture of Dorian Gray.*

Ragland-Sullivan, Ellie. "The Phenomenon of Aging in Oscar Wilde's *Picture of Dorian Gray:* A Lacanian View." In *Memory and Desire: Aging—Literature—Psychoanalysis,* edited by Kathleen Woodward and Murray M. Schwartz, pp. 114-33. Bloomington: Indiana University Press, 1986.
> Applies principles of French psychoanalyst Jacques Lacan (1901-1981) to a discussion of themes of immortality and aging in Wilde's novel.

Robillard, Douglas, Jr. "Self-Reflexive Art and Wilde's *The*

*Picture of Dorian Gray." Essays in Arts and Sciences* 18 (May 1989): 29-38.

Contends that Wilde's message in his novel was that "the subject of a work of art provides the artist with an opportunity for self-reflection."

Smith, Philip E., II, and Helfand, Michael S. "Conscience as Tribal Self in *The Picture of Dorian Gray.*" In their *Oscar Wilde's Oxford Notebooks: A Portrait of Mind in the Making,* pp. 96-104. New York: Oxford University Press, 1989.

Consideration of the philosophical, scientific, and aesthetic ideas in *Dorian Gray* that were first developed in Wilde's Oxford notebooks.

Stokes, John. *Oscar Wilde.* Harlow, England: Longman Group, 1978, 56 p.

Biographical and critical essay that includes discussion of *The Picture of Dorian Gray* as "a symposium of opinions" about art and the role of the artist.

Sullivan, Kevin. *Oscar Wilde.* New York: Columbia University Press, 1972, 48 p.

Biographical and critical essay including discussion of *The Picture of Dorian Gray* as "an intensely imagined fantasy in which nothing really happens and there is only one character, a prescient author, who never appears."

Weissman, Judith. " 'The Castrating Gesture' in Wilde and the Post-Structuralists." *The Southern Review* 24, No. 3 (Summer 1988): 520-34.

Explores "the deep affinities" between Balzac's story "Sarrasine" and *The Picture of Dorian Gray.*

Ziolkowski, Theodore. "Image as Motif: The Haunted Portrait." In his *Disenchanted Images: A Literary Iconology,* pp. 78-148. Princeton, N.J.: Princeton University Press, 1977.

Includes commentary on Wilde's novel in a chapter about supernatural occurrences involving portraits in fiction.

# Emile Zola

## 1840-1902

French novelist, short story writer, critic, essayist, dramatist, poet, and journalist.

For further discussion of Zola's works, see *TCLC*, Volumes 1 and 6. For criticism focusing on Zola's novels *L'assommoir, Germinal,* and *Nana,* see *TCLC*, Volume 21.

Zola was the founder and principal theorist of the Naturalist movement in nineteenth-century literature. Naturalism is based on the principle that all phenomena can be understood by scientific examination and that human beings are most accurately represented in fiction as creatures whose lives are determined by environmental and internal forces which they can neither control nor fully understand. In his most important series of novels, "Les Rougon-Macquart," Zola drew on current theories of hereditary determinism and demonstrated in his depictions of characters how various genetic and environmental factors determine human psychology and behavior. The novels *L'assommoir, Nana,* and *Germinal,* generally regarded as the finest works in the series, are concerned with the misery and degradation of the French working class and have often been described as anatomies of disease, insanity, and perversion. While Zola did succeed in documenting a historical milieu with great detail and precision, commentators, nevertheless, find in the novels a highly personal vision expressed with emotion and artistry.

Born in Paris, Zola was raised in Aix-en-Provence, where his father was an engineer. When Zola was seven years old his father died, and, without his financial support, the family was plunged into poverty. Zola began his education at the local College Bourbon, where he became friends with Paul Cézanne. Considered a clever but indifferent student, Zola spent his leisure time wandering in the town and the countryside and reading and writing idyllic poetry. At eighteen he moved to Paris with his mother and attended the Lycée Saint-Louis; after twice failing his literature examinations, he left without a degree and for the next two years lived under financially straitened conditions. In 1864 he secured a position as a bookseller's clerk and the same year published *Contes à Ninon (Stories for Ninon),* which have more in common with medieval fables than with the strict realism of his later works. He also began developing his journalistic skills as a critic of art and music, and, with the publication of an article supporting the artists of the then controversial Impressionist school, to which his friend Cézanne belonged, Zola himself became a figure of controversy. His first novel, *La confession de Claude (Claude's Confession),* featured an unsentimentalized portrait of a prostitute, and when the book met with legal difficulties, Zola was accused of deliberately courting notoriety. With *Thérèse Raquin (The Devil's Compact)* and *Madeleine Férat (Magdalen Férat)* he began

to experiment with techniques that would lead to the Naturalism of the "Rougon-Macquart" cycle.

In 1873 Zola entered the circle of Realist writers that included Gustave Flaubert, Alphonse Daudet, and Edmond de Goncourt. After *L'assommoir,* the seventh novel in the "Rougon-Macquart" series, brought him critical and financial success in 1877, Zola himself was surrounded by disciples. Guy de Maupassant, Paul Alexis, Joris-Karl Huysmans, and others met at Zola's home in Paris and his villa in Médan on the Seine. Together they published *Les soirées de Médan,* to which Zola and the others each contributed one short story. The group broke up shortly after Huysmans split with Zola in 1884 because Huysmans wanted to create works that were more personal and artistic that the Naturalist credo would allow. By then the analyses of hereditary degeneracy in the "Rougon-Macquart" novels had earned Zola a reputation among his contemporaries as a pessimistic determinist. In 1887 a group of young novelists writing in *Le figaro* denounced *La terre (Earth)* as mercenary and pathogenic. Eventually Zola turned from the scientific analysis of the "Rougon-Macquart" cycle to the social pamphleteering of later novels such as *Fécondité (Fruitfulness).*

Zola's most famous example of social advocacy came in 1898 with his involvement in the notorious Dreyfus case. *"J'accuse"* (*"The Dreyfus Case"*) is a vehement twenty-one page open letter to the president of the Republic that appeared in the journal *L'aurore*. The letter defended Alfred Dreyfus, a Jewish captain in the French army accused of treason and sentenced to life on Devil's Island, and charged that army officials had perjured themselves during the Dreyfus trial. As a result of his role in the scandal, Zola was twice charged for libel, suspended from the Legion d'Honneur, and, on the advice of legal counsel, fled to England. In 1899 the affair was reopened and Zola returned to Paris under a general amnesty. His actions in the case were considered instrumental in the eventual pardon of Dreyfus. In the next few years Zola published several more novels, including three volumes of the unfinished tetralogy "Les quatre évangiles." In 1902 he died during the night of asphyxiation caused by a faulty fireplace chimney.

In the "Rougon-Macquart" cycle Zola applied the methods of science to the novelist's art. F. W. J. Hemmings has remarked that "Zola reduced the craft of fiction to a mechanical technique," and this technique is visible in the author's *ébauches:* plot outlines, character sketches, and a general thesis to be worked out in each individual novel. An exhaustive researcher, Zola investigated the life of various social subgroups for the background of his works: he compiled a dictionary of slang to lend verisimilitude to the dialogue of the lower classes in *L'assommoir;* he learned about the theater and horse racing during the preparatory stages of *Nana;* and he studied a coal mining district during a workers' strike for *Germinal.* By his immersion in a particular milieu, Zola attempted to attain in his fiction the greatest possible fidelity to social fact. However, recent critics have questioned the extent to which Zola's novels actually reflect the guidelines of Naturalism. Brian Nicholas, for instance, has asserted that "the inclinations of the impressionist, the poet of humanity in the mass, presided at the conception of Zola's novels rather than any doctrinaire scientism." Three of the most notable "Rougon-Macquart" novels—*L'assommoir, Nana,* and *Germinal*—have provided critics with evidence that Zola's work displays the concerns of both the scientist and the artist, as well as the conscience of the social reformer. *L'assommoir* traces the life of Gervaise, an industrious laundress with modest dreams whose kindness leads her to financial, moral, and physical ruin; *Nana* narrates the rise and fall of the precociously licentious daughter of Gervaise, who becomes the leading Parisian courtesan and symbolizes the ruin of Parisian society; *Germinal* features the son of Gervaise, Etienne, who becomes the socialist leader of an impoverished mining community. Despite scientific justifications for human behavior in these works, modern critics have emphasized their artistry and point out that Zola's novels evolved from a desire for social change as much as a scientific urge to compile a social record. Such critics find that Zola's genius as both artist and polemist are especially evident in his rendering of crowd scenes, most notably the comical wedding party in *L'assommoir* and the horrifying spectacle of rioting strikers in *Germinal.* Other aspects of Zola's novels that have been closely examined are his complex narrative techniques, his allusions to classical mythology, and the implied religious or philosophical basis of his works. Many critics now agree that Zola's works, once considered simple documentations of the surface of human life, can be rewardingly studied from various and far more sophisticated perspectives.

With Naturalism Zola articulated a theory that affected the course of literature throughout the world. His literary precepts can be seen as an influence on the naturalistic dramas of Henrik Ibsen and Gerhart Hauptmann, on the Italian *verismo* movement, and on such American authors as Stephen Crane, Theodore Dreiser, and Ernest Hemingway. Although the strict scientific conception of literature is no longer popular, or even plausible, the best of the "Rougon-Macquart" novels are regarded as masterpieces that transcend the tenets of Naturalism.

(See also *Contemporary Authors,* Vol. 104.)

## PRINCIPAL WORKS

*Contes à Ninon*  (short stories)  1864
  [*Stories for Ninon,* 1895]
*La confession de Claude*  (novel)  1865
  [*Claude's Confession,* 1882]
*Thérèse Raquin*  (novel)  1867
  [*The Devil's Compact,* 1892]
*Madeleine Férat*  (novel)  1868
  [*Magdalen Férat,* 1880]
*La fortune des Rougon*  (novel)  1871
  [*The Rougon-Macquart Family,* 1879]
*La curée*  (novel)  1872
  [*In the Whirlpool,* 1882]
*Le ventre de Paris*  (novel)  1873
  [*The Markets of Paris,* 1879]
*La conquête de Plassans*  (novel)  1874
  [*The Conquest of Plassans,* 1879; also published as *A Mad Love; or, The Abbé and His Court,* 1882]
*La faute de l'abbé Mouret*  (novel)  1875
  [*Albine; or, The Abbe's Temptation,* 1882]
*Son excellence Eugène Rougon*  (novel)  1876
  [*Eugene Rougon,* 1876]
*L'assommoir*  (novel)  1877
  [*Gervaise,* 1879; also published as *The "Assommoir,"* 1884]
*Une page d'amour*  (novel)  1878
  [*Hélène,* 1878]
*Nana*  (novel)  1880
  [*Nana,* 1880]
*Le roman experimental*  (criticism)  1880
  [*The Experimental Novel,* 1880]
*Les romanciers naturalistes*  (criticism)  1881
*Pot-bouille*  (novel)  1882
  [*Piping Hot,* 1889]
*Au bonheur des dames*  (novel)  1883
  [*The Bonheur des Dames; or, The Shop Girls of Paris,* 1883; published in England as *The Ladies' Paradise,* 1883]
*La joie de vivre*  (novel)  1884
  [*Life's Joys,* 1884]
*Germinal*  (novel)  1885
  [*Germinal,* 1885]
*L'oeuvre*  (novel)  1886

[*His Masterpiece,* 1886]
*La terre* (novel) 1887
[*The Soil,* 1888; also published as *Earth,* 1954]
*La rêve* (novel) 1888
[*The Dream,* 1888]
*La bête humaine* (novel) 1890
[*The Human Brutes,* 1890; also published as *The Human Animals,* 1890]
*L'argent* (novel) 1891
[*Money,* 1891]
*La débâcle* (novel) 1892
[*The Downfall,* 1892]
*Le docteur Pascal* (novel) 1893
[*Doctor Pascal,* 1893]
†*Lourdes* (novel) 1894
[*Lourdes,* 1896]
†*Rome* (novel) 1896
[*Rome,* 1896]
"*J'accuse*" (letter) 1898
["*The Dreyfus Case,*" 1898]
†*Paris* (novel) 1898
[*Paris,* 1898]
‡*Fécondité* (novel) 1899
[*Fruitfulness,* 1900]
‡*Travail* (novel) 1901
[*Labor,* 1901]
‡*Vérité* (novel) 1903
[*Truth,* 1903]

*These volumes comprise the series "Les Rougon-Macquart."

†These volumes comprise the trilogy "Les trois villes."

‡These volumes comprise the unfinished tetralogy "Les quatre evangiles."

---

## Louis Ulbach   (essay date 1868)

[*In the following excerpt from an essay originally published in* Le figaro *in 1868, Ulbach denounces* Thérèse Raquin *and other contemporary novels for their graphic depiction of sordid subject matter. Translated passages from* Thérèse Raquin *are by Leonard Tancock.*]

A monstrous school of novelists, established several years ago, claims to substitute the eloquence of the charnel-house for the eloquence of the flesh, calls upon our most surgical of curiosities, groups together victims of the plague to have us admire their sores, finds its direct inspiration in cholera, its master, and fills our minds with pus.

The cold slabs of the morgue have replaced the sofas of Crébillon; Manon Lescaut has become a sordid kitchen-maid, forsaking the grease for the mud of the streets. Faublas needs to kill, to watch his victims rot in order to conjure up visions of love; or else, by whipping high-class ladies, he acts out the writings of the marquis de Sade (without ever having read them!).

*Germinie Lacerteux,* **Thérèse Raquin,** *La comtesse de Chalis,* and many other novels not worth mentioning (for

I am not trying to hide the fact that I am providing them with publicity), will prove what I am stating.

I am not questioning the intentions, which are good, but I am hoping to show that, in an era which is so blasé, perverted, lethargic and sick, the best of intentions get off track and try to correct matters by means which only serve to corrupt. They look for success in order to have an audience, and they hang out dirty laundry like flags to attract the passers-by.

I respect the writers whose works I am about to trample underfoot: they believe in social regeneration, but in making their little pile of mud, they only mirror themselves in it, before they sweep it away. They want other people to sniff it and everyone see himself reflected in it; they have an affected taste for their own task and they forget about the sewer, all the while keeping the filth outside. (p. 25)

Balzac, the sublime dung-heap on which all these mushrooms are growing, concentrated all the corruptions and all the disgraces in one character, Mme Marneffe; and yet, since he never put Mme Marneffe in a position so visibly grotesque or trivial that her portrait could provoke laughter or disgust, Mme Marneffe was represented on the stage. I defy you to put Fanny on the stage: the principal scene would make her appear ridiculous. And I defy you to put the countess of Chalis there! I defy you to do the same with Germinie Lacerteux or Thérèse Raquin, those impossible phantoms which simply ooze death, having never breathed life, who are but nightmarish visions of reality.

The second reproach I shall address to this literature of violence is that it believes itself to be very malicious, whereas it is in reality very naïve: it is only an illusion.

It is easier to write a brutal novel, full of pus, crime, and prostitution than it is to write a restrained, moderate, watered-down novel, pointing out the sources of shame without uncovering them, moving the reader without nauseating him.

What a handy procedure it is to expose bruised flesh. Anyone can deal with decadent subjects and never miss making an effect. Even the most naïve of the Realists, while describing in a very unimaginative way old Montfaucon, would nauseate an entire generation.

To attract through disgust, to please by what is horrible is a strategy which unfortunately appeals to a very human instinct, but one which is at the same time the lowest and most disreputable instinct, the most universal and yet the most bestial instinct. The crowds which rush to the guillotine or hurry to the morgue, are they really the public that one should captivate, encourage and maintain in the cult of terror and purulence?

Chastity, candor, love in its heroic aspects, hate in all its hypocrisy, the truth of life, after all, cannot be represented without polish; they demand more work, more observation and are of more benefit to the reader. I am not claiming to restrict the domain of the writer. Everything, down to the flesh, is his territory, but tearing off skin is no longer simple observation, it is surgery, and if once, by chance, an écorché can be indispensable to a psychological demonstration, the écorché made into a system is no more than insanity and depravity.

I was saying that all these unhealthy imaginations were poor or lazy imaginations. I would only need to refer to their methods to prove it. They thrive on imitation. *Madame Bovary, Fanny* and *L'affaire Clémenceau* bear the mark of an original and personal talent: so it is that these three superior works have remained models to be imitated, parodied and extended as if to make them grimace. To combine the judicial element with the pornographic element is the entire foundation of the art. Mystery with hysterica! that is the formula.

There is, however, a pitfall in these two words: the courts are a commonplace source of varied and facile episodes, and, in an age of nervous excesses, since one no longer has the keys to passion, passion gives way to nervous spasms. All this is just as effective and more convenient.

Having explained all this, I must own up to the special reason for my anger. My curiosity recently slipped into a pool of mud and blood called *Thérèse Raquin,* whose author, Mr. Zola, is reputed to be a young man of talent. At least, I know that he is ardently aspiring to fame. An enthusiast of crudeness, he published *La confession de Claude,* the idyll of a student and a prostitute. He sees women as Mr. Manet paints them: the colour of mud with pink make-up. Intolerant of any criticism, he practises criticism himself with intolerance, and, at an age when most people are normally only capable of following their desires, Zola entitles his so-called literary studies: *Mes haines* [*My Hates*]!

I do not know if Mr. Zola has the power to write a subtle, delicate, substantial and decent book. To renounce violence, one must have will, wit, ideas and style. But I can already point out one such conversion to the author of *Thérèse Raquin.*

Jules Claretie has also written a book full of erotic and fatal frenzy, but he quickly grew sick of the genre after his own success, and he went searching through history for more realistic tragedies, and for passions which were no less terrible but more heroic. A lot of people die in his *Derniers Montagnards,* but with a cry of hope and a love of freedom! No anger is spared, but with the effect that one is left in a kinder, more tolerant mood.

As for *Thérèse Raquin,* it is the residue of all the horrors which were published previous to it. All the blood and infamies of those works have been drained into it; it is Mother Bancal's bucket.

The subject matter, however, is quite simple: the physical remorse of two lovers who kill the husband in order to be freer to deceive him, but who find that, once the husband is dead (his name was Camille), they no longer dare embrace, for here, according to the author, is the subtle torture which awaits them: "They cried aloud and strained still closer so as not to leave any space between their bodies for the dead man. Yet they could still feel bits of Camille's flesh squashed disgustingly between them, freezing their bodies in places whilst the rest was on fire."

In the end, not managing to *crush* out the drowned man with their kisses, they bite each other, end up loathing each other and kill themselves in a double suicide brought about by their despair at not being able to murder each other.

If I told the author that his idea is immoral, he could be indignant, for the description of remorse is generally taken to be a moralizing spectacle; but if remorse was always limited to physical impressions and to carnal loathings, it would then be no more than a reaction of the temperament, and it would not be remorse. What constitutes the strength and the triumph of goodness is that, even with the flesh appeased and passions spent, goodness awakes and burns brightly in the mind. A *storm in the mind* is a sublime spectacle, whereas a storm in the loins is a very base sight.

The first time that Thérèse sees the man she will love, here is how the liking is presented: "The man's sanguine temperament, his loud voice, his fat laugh, the keen, powerful aroma given off by his whole person, threw the young woman off her balance and plunged her into a sort of nervous anguish."

O Romeo! O Juliette! what prompt and subtle intuition did you have to fall in love so quickly? Thérèse is a woman in need of a lover. On the other hand, Laurent, her accomplice, decides to drown the husband after a walk during which he undergoes the following temptation: "He whistled and kicked the stones, but now and again there was a fierce glint in his eyes as he watched his mistress's swinging hips."

After such stimulation, how could one resist assassinating poor old Camille, that sickly, tacky creature, whose name rhymes with camomil(l)e?

So they throw the husband into the water. From that moment on, Laurent frequents the morgue until such time as his drowned victim might be put on display. The author takes advantage of this occasion to describe for us the sensual pleasures of the morgue and its habitués.

Laurent takes particular delight in looking at the murdered women. One day he falls in love with the corpse of a girl who hanged herself; it is true that her "fresh, plump body took on most delicate hues with the pallor of death." Laurent "lingered over her for a long time, running his eyes up and down her body, lost in a sort of fearful desire."

It appears that society women also go to the morgue; one of them lapses into a state of contemplation while looking at the robust body of a stonemason. "The lady"—writes the author—"went on studying him and, as it were, turning him over with her eyes, weighing him up. She raised the corner of her veil, took one last look, and went away."

As for the street kids, "young louts have their first women in the Morgue."

Since this article may be read just after lunch, I shall skip over the description of Camille's lovely rotting corpse. You can almost feel the worms crawling about.

Once the drowned man is properly buried, the lovers get married, and then their torment begins.

I am not being unfair in recognizing that certain parts of

this analysis of the sensations of two murderers are well observed. Their horrible wedding-night is a very striking tableau. I am not systematically blaming the strident tones, the violent and violet brush-strokes; I am only complaining that they are isolated and unadulterated; what detracts most from this book could have been its strongest point.

But the monotony of the ignoble is the worst possible form of monotony. It is as if, to use a comparison appropriate to this book, the reader were lying under the tap of one of the tables in the morgue, and as if, right down to the last page, he could feel the slow, steady drip of the water used to wash down the dead bodies.

Man and wife, going from one fit of rage to another, from depravity to depravity, end up fighting, each one wanting to denounce the other. Thérèse turns to prostitution, and Laurent, "whose flesh is dead," regrets that he cannot do the same.

Finally, one day, these two slaves of the morgue fall exhausted, poisoned, on top of one another, in front of the chair of Camille Raquin's paralyzed old mother, who silently enjoys this punishment which avenges her son.

This book sums up too faithfully all the putridness of contemporary literature not to provoke a certain amount of anger. I would have said nothing about the work if it had been no more than an individual fantasy, but, the manner is contagious and whatever one reads one keeps coming across it. Let us force our novelists to prove their talent in other ways than by borrowing their subjects from the courts of law and the garbage dump.

At the sale of the pasha who has recently liquidated his gallery just like a European, Mr. Courbet depicted the last word in voluptuous pleasure in the arts by a painting that was put on display, and by another, hung in a toilet, that was shown only to indiscreet ladies and to connoisseurs. The entire shame of this school is in these two canvasses, as it is elsewhere in the novels: weary debauchery and crude anatomy. It is well painted, it is incontestably real, but it is horribly stupid.

When the literature of which I have been talking wants an emblem, it will have Courbet make a copy of these two canvasses. The possible painting will draw the customers to the door, and the other painting will be in the sanctuary, like the muse, the genie, the oracle. (pp. 26-9)

> Louis Ulbach, "Putrid Literature," translated by Barbara Gough, in Critical Essays on Emile Zola, edited by David Baguley, G. K. Hall & Co., 1986, pp. 25-30.

### Robert Harborough Sherard   (essay date 1893)

[*Sherard was an English journalist and biographer who wrote the first English-language study of Zola's life and works. In the following excerpt from that study, Sherard offers an anecdotal account of the origin and composition of* L'assommoir.]

It was at Saint-Aubin-on-the-Sea that Zola evolved the plan and story of the book *L'assommoir,* which was to make his fame and his fortune. Already, on leaving Paris in the early part of that summer, he had made up his mind that his next book should be a study of the people of the Paris faubourgs, an idea which he had long entertained and had ardently desired to put into execution. He knew the people of Paris well. When quite a child, during a visit to Paris, he had spent several weeks with a relation who was a workman himself, and who inhabited one of those immense tenement houses in a poor quarter which he desired to describe. Later on, when starving in Paris, many months had been spent in the poor quarters of the rue de la Pépinière, at Montrouge, in the rue Saint-Jacques, and in the boulevard Montparnasse. He remembered being present at domestic events of 'wonderful colour'—a death and a funeral in a workman's family, a workman's *fête,* workmen's festivities. He had experienced poverty himself; the horror of hunger and cold he could describe with a full knowledge of what he was writing about—the struggle for the day's bread. (pp. 130-31)

His mind was made up to make use of all these souvenirs of his: his book should be a complete monograph of the life of the people. It was decided that it should describe, amongst other things, a typical workman's wedding and a workman's funeral. It should put on the stage all the varieties of workmen—the industrious workman, the lazy drunkard, the honest man, and the low scoundrel who lives on women's shame.

He had brought with him to Saint-Aubin a large collection of notes, having visited, before his departure from Paris, a smithy, the workshop of a gold-chain maker—romanticism probably prompting him in this last choice—and a laundry. He had carefully studied up Delvau's Slang Dictionary, his original intention being to write the book almost entirely in the *argot* used by the faubourg people. It was, indeed, in Delvau's *Dictionnaire de la langue verte* that he found the title of his book *L'assommoir,* that wonderfully expressive term for the crushing, killing effect of the cheap drinking-shop. Nothing, however, was further from his intentions than to write a book against intemperance. Zola has never written books with a purpose. If the title of the book was *L'assommoir,* it was because the drinking-shop is the place where, as a matter of necessity, workmen meet together, and it thus constituted the natural stage for a story in which various types of workmen were to be described. But what was still wanting during the first days of his stay at Saint-Aubin, and from the lack of which he was unable to set to work, was the plot of the story.

'What I want,' he said one afternoon, as he was sitting with a friend on the beach at Saint-Aubin, 'is something very simple.'

Facing him was the sea, sparkling under the sun. The sky above was a deep blue, and as no clouds thickened the atmosphere, the line of horizon was as sharply and clearly defined as though drawn with a compass.

Pointing to this line suddenly, he said: 'What I want to find is something like that—something, I am certain, quite simple—a well-drawn line, quite straight. The effect would be grandiose, no doubt.'

Then he added, that he should probably content himself with the simple story of the life of a woman of the people, who, after having had two children by a lover, marries, later on, another man, and at first behaves well towards her husband, working bravely, and succeeding in setting up in business as a washerwoman. Then the husband would become a drunkard, and she, in consequence, would gradually go down hill to disorder and wretchedness. But there was still something wanting, and it was only when he had hit upon the idea of bringing the lover—Lantier—back into the family, that he could cry out, as he did one afternoon on the beach at Saint-Aubin, 'Eureka!' and that he could say that the 'Assommoir' was already done.

The plot having been decided upon, Zola drew up the plan of the book with the same care and precision that had always characterised his preliminary labour on his novels. And here may be the place to quote what he himself said to Signor Edmondo de Amicis, who visited him in Paris some time after the publication of *L'assommoir,* as to his way of writing a novel.

> 'This is how I do it,' he said. 'Indeed, as a matter of fact, I can hardly be said to "do it"—rather, it does itself. I can't invent facts, lacking absolutely that faculty of imagination. If I sit down to my table to think out the plot of a story, I remain sitting for three days together with my head in my hand, racking my brains, and finding nothing. As a consequence, I have had to give up troubling myself about the subject of my stories. I begin to work on my novel without knowing what events will be described in the course of it, nor what characters will take part in the action, nor what the end and the beginning will be. I know only my principal character—my Rougon or my Macquart, male or female, always an old acquaintance. I occupy myself with him alone, I reflect on his character, I think of the family in which he was born, on his first impressions, and on the class in which I have decided to place his life. That is my most important occupation—to study the people with whom my principal character will have to do, the places which he will have to inhabit, the air which he will have to breathe, his profession, his habits, down to the most trivial occupations with which he will fill up his spare moments.

> 'After spending two or three months in this study, I am master of this particular kind of life, I see it, I feel it, I live in it in imagination, and I am certain of being able to give my novel the special colour and perfume of that class of people. Besides, by living some time as I have done amongst this class of people, I have made the acquaintance of individuals belonging to it, I have heard real facts related, I know what occurs there as a general rule, I have learned the language which they usually talk, I have in my head a quantity of types, of scenes, of fragments of dialogue, of episodes, of occurrences, which form a confused story made up of a thousand unconnected fragments. Then there remains to be done what for me is the most difficult task of all, to attach to a single thread, as best I am able, all these reminiscences and scattered impressions. It is almost always a lengthy task. But I set to work upon it phlegmatically, and instead of using my imagination I use my reasoning faculties. I argue to myself, I write my monologues word for word, just as they occur to me, so that, read by another, they would appear strange. So-and-so does this or that. What would be the natural result of such-and-such an act? Would such an act affect my personage? Certainly. It is therefore logical that this other person should react in such-and-such a manner. Then some other character may intervene there, such a one, for instance, whose acquaintance I made at such a place on such an evening. I research the immediate consequences of even the smallest event, that which would logically be its natural result, the character and the position of my personages being taken into consideration; I work as does a commissary of police who desires to discover the authors of some mysterious crime from some very slight clue. Often, however, very great difficulties stand in my way. Sometimes there are only two more threads to be knotted together, the most simple of consequences to be deduced, and I cannot manage to do it. I tire myself out and worry myself uselessly. Then I give up thinking about it, because I know that I am wasting my time. Two, three, or four days go by. One fine morning, in the end, whilst I am at breakfast and am thinking of something quite different, suddenly my two threads knot themselves together, the deduction is found, and all my difficulties are overcome. Then a flood of light is poured over the whole of my novel. I see it all, and all is finished. I become once more sure of myself. I know that I shall succeed, and there remains for me nothing more but what I consider the most agreeable part of my work. And I set to work upon it quietly, methodically, with my watch in my hand. I write a little every day, three pages of print, not a line more, and I only work in the morning. I write almost without having to make any corrections, because for months I have been thinking it all over, and as soon as I have written them I put the pages aside and do not see them again until they are in print. I can calculate infallibly the date when my book will be finished.'

(pp. 132-37)

*Robert Harborough Sherard, in his* Emile Zola: A Biographical & Critical Study, *Chatto & Windus, 1893, 288 p.*

### Ernest Alfred Vizetelly　(essay date 1904)

*[In the following excerpt, Vizetelly surveys the novels in the "Rougon-Macquart" series as a unified whole.]*

To understand [Zola] aright, let us remember that he made his *débuts* at a time when science was enlarging her domain daily. For him she exercised a fascination equal to that of art. In his youth he had turned eagerly to certain scientific studies even while he was steeping himself in poetry, and later he devoured Flourens, Zimmermann, translations of the great scientists of England and Germany. He saw that there was often a deep poetry in science; he dreamt of making it manifest,—of going further,—of associating science and art, of establishing their co-relation, welding them together even in instances when to some folk they seemed to be antagonistic. His nature . . . was a compound, a hybrid one, by no means unique, but such as is not often observed. "Lewis Carroll" supplies a somewhat approximate instance: in him one found the mathematician elbowing the romancer, only he did not dream of importing *Euclid* into *Alice*. Zola, in doing so, or rather in doing something similar, was not entirely influenced by his own special nature, but was carried along by the spirit of his age, in which everything tended towards science. Those who remember Darwin and Faraday and Huxley and the others, and the thirst that came on so many young men in those days, will not gainsay it.

The literary critics declared, of course, and many of them declare still, that Zola was altogether wrong. Regarding Art as being so distinct, so different from Science that no amalgam could be effected, they laid down and still lay down certain rules as being necessary to salvation. That attitude was and is preposterous to the open mind which holds that no dogmas are of any account, and that of those who frame them one may say in Dante's words:

> Non ragionam di lor, ma guarda e passa.

It is true that some critics have asserted that if there be no finality in science there is a finality in art. But in fiction, with which alone one is concerned here, the form has changed repeatedly, and on each such occasion the loud protests raised by the representatives of old and recognised schools have proved ineffectual. One rule, one dogma after another, has been set aside, and still and ever the evolution has continued. To say that the artist in fiction must do this and must not do that is to expose oneself to the ridicule, at times, even of one's contemporaries, and certainly of posterity. Take a comparatively recent epoch and think of the dogmas and the protests brought forward by the Classiques in their great contest with the Romantiques in France, and remember who, in the end, were vanquished. Thus men of conservative views may protest, but if there be a good cause for any evolution, which one or another writer may essay, it will end by triumphing in spite of all the opposition offered to it.

The art of the novelist has been often likened to that of the painter, but it does not follow that this is the only possible comparison. A novelist may liken himself to a sculptor, in fact to anybody he chooses. Nothing, moreover, is final. The world, as modern scientists have just rediscovered, and as Heraclitus asserted three and twenty centuries ago, is not a being but a becoming. Change is the universal law, even in matter; and if some minds, imprisoned within narrow ideas and formulas, find it impossible to contemplate the possibility of certain changes, they must yield to the broader minds for which everything is possible. The world's changes are reflected in its literature. Science within our own time has profoundly modified the study and the writing of history. As for the novel, the Romanticists spoke no last word, for it was not in their power to do so. Whether Zola had arisen or not, it was fatal that the novel should at last embrace many things which earlier writers of fiction had never dreamt of including in it, that it should, in a word, follow the trend of the modern mind.

Among writers, moreover, there are always many whose aim is not mere amusement. Some openly declare instruction, enlightenment, to be their purpose. Some are only half conscious of their mission, some not at all, and it happens not unfrequently that a lesson is conveyed in books where it has been never intended. At one time the drama was the form of literature which appealed most successfully to the greater number. The novel at last acquired a similar position, and it followed that the writer who wished to reach the greater number had to approach them as a novelist. That had been done long before the time of Zola, who was both a writer with a purpose and one who wished to reach the majority. Now, if an author desire to bring about some reformation of the community, it is natural that he should begin by portraying it. If he wish to elucidate certain social, scientific, and psychological problems for the common good, it is essential that he should in the first case state them. In that event, say some pedants, he must confine himself to treatises of the accepted form. But the author answers no, for such treatises would not reach the greater number, and his purpose would then remain unfulfilled. To reach them he must approach them in the only literary form for which they care: he must embody his views in novels. "I have, in my estimation," said Zola, "certain contributions to make to the thought of the world on certain subjects, and I have chosen the novel as the best means of communication. To tell me that I must not do so is nonsense. I claim it as my right, and who are you to gainsay it?"

But let us pass to another point. The oft-repeated assertion that Zola confined himself to portraying the ulcers and sores of life is contrary to fact. He undoubtedly found more evil than good in the community, and he insisted on the evil because it was that which needed remedying. But he blamed nobody for extolling the higher side of life. He denounced the writers who cast a deceptive and often poisonous glamour over the imperfections of the world, he railed at many of the people who pretended to be very good, for he was not deceived by hypocrisy and cant; but, at the same time, he never held that mankind was naturally evil. He attributed its blemishes to its social systems, its superstitions, the thousand fallacies amid which it was reared, and his whole life was a battle with those fallacies, those superstitions, and those systems.

As he contended against so many generally accepted opinions it was inevitable that his work and even his purpose should be greatly misjudged. Critics took in turn one and another volume of his Rougon-Macquart series, and pronounced condemnation on it. It was only when, after long years, the series was at last finished that some little justice was shown to the author. It should be remembered that no volume of the series is in itself a really complete work. The series indeed is the book, the volumes are but chapters of it. Besides, they ought not to be taken nowadays in the order in which they were originally published. It occasionally happens that writers are unable to produce their works in proper sequence. There have been instances when the second and fourth volumes of some literary undertaking have been published before the first and the third. So it was with the Rougon-Macquart novels. Zola was no walking encyclopædia. Every now and again it happened that he was not ready for the volume which by rights should have followed the one he had just finished. He lacked, at the moment, sufficient knowledge of the subject which that next volume was to embrace. Or else, as also happened at times, his fancy or his feelings or some combination of circumstances carried him onward, inducing him to skip a volume for a time. But he always reverted to it afterwards, like an author who, writing not twenty volumes, but one, has passed over some troublesome chapter, yet harks back and writes it at last, well knowing that his work will lack completeness and intelligibility if the gap be not filled up. (pp. 344-49)

[The] example of the critics who, even since the completion of the series, have followed that same order in judging Zola's work is not one to imitate. By adopting that system one may certainly trace the variations in Zola's general style over a term of years; but if the series is to be judged as a whole one must take its sections in the order in which the author himself desired they should be read. This he indicated in *Le docteur Pascal,* and confirmed by word of mouth to the present writer; and it is unfortunate, perhaps, that the French publishers should still "list" the volumes chronologically, thereby leading many readers astray. Some volumes of course—notably the first and the last—occupy their proper places in the lists, but others have to be taken in a very different order. (pp. 349-50)

In *La fortune des Rougon* (I) the author describes the origin of the Rougons and the Macquarts. One Adélaïde Fouque, a woman of hysterical nature who eventually goes mad,—a variety of disorders being transmitted to most of her descendants,—marries a man named Rougon, and on his death lives with another named Macquart. By the former she has a son, Pierre Rougon; by the latter a son, Antoine, and a daughter, Ursule Macquart. This daughter marries a hatter named Mouret, and thus at the outset of the series the second generation of the family is shown divided into three branches. In the third generation it increases to eleven members; in the fourth to thirteen. In the fifth it dwindles, its vitiated energies now being largely spent; and though there are indications of its continuance in sundry children who do not appear on the scene, the hope of regeneration rests virtually in only one child, a boy three months old when the curtain finally descends. In *La fortune des Rougon,* then, we are shown old Adélaïde Fouque, her children and some of theirs, all more or less poverty-stricken and striving for wealth, which comes with the foundation of the Second Empire. The scene is laid at Plassans . . . and one sees the Imperial *régime* established there by craft and bloodshed.

Next comes *Son excellence Eugène Rougon* (II) which carries one to Paris, where the fortunes of the eldest of the Rougon brothers, first an advocate and at last an all-powerful minister of state, are followed in official and political circles. The court of Napoleon III appears at the Tuileries and at Compiègne, where one meets, among others, a beautiful Italian adventuress, Clorinde Balbi—suggestive of the notorious Countess de Castiglione—with a mother reminiscent of Madame de Montijo. And in

*Zola at work in his study.*

other chapters of the volume the scheming and plotting of the reign, the official jobbery and corruption, are traced for several years.

*La curée* (III) follows, and one turns to Eugène Rougon's younger brother, Aristide, who has assumed the pseudonym of Saccard. With him the reader joins in the great rush for the spoils of the new *régime*. A passion for money and enjoyment seizes on one and all, debauchery reigns in society, and a fever of reckless speculation is kindled by the transformation of Paris under Baron Haussmann and his acolytes. Men and women sell themselves. Renée, Saccard's second wife, passes from mere adultery to incest, becoming a modern Phædra, while Saccard himself leads the life of an eager, gluttonous bird of prey, which he continues in the ensuing volume, *L'argent* (IV), where the Bourse—the money-market—is shown with all its gambling, its thousand tricks and frauds.

So far the series might seem a mere record of roguery, vice, and corruption, but those who know the books are aware that such is not the case. Silvère and Miette stand for love and all the better qualities of humanity in the first volume; there are at least the Martinots and the Berauds in the second and third; and the devoted Madame Caroline, the honest Hamelin, the pious Princess d'Orviedo, the dreamy, generous-hearted Sigismond, the loving Jordans, and the unfortunate Mazaud, all figure in the fourth, amid the scramble for gold in which the other characters participate.

In sharp contrast with that greed for gain is the picture offered by the next volume, *Le rêve* (V), where an immaculate lily arises from the hot-bed of vice, whence later, and as a further contrast, a type of foul shamelessness, Nana, the harlot, is also to spring. But it is best not to anticipate. In the first four volumes the Rougons, under the influence of heredity and surroundings, have shown themselves scoundrels, whereas in Angélique, the heroine of *Le rêve,* a girl of their blood appears who is all purity and candour. She comes upon the scene, precisely at this moment, to emphasise the author's conviction that, whatever he may have had to depict in his solicitude for truth, all is not vice, degradation, and materialism, that there are other aspirations in life besides the thirst for wealth, enjoyment and power. And here, too, the priesthood is shown in its better aspect: the good Abbé Cornille, the proud, heartbroken Bishop d'Hautecœur, in contrast with whom the scheming, unscrupulous Abbé Faujas appears in the next section of the series.

This is *La conquête de Plassans* (VI) which retains one in the provinces (whither one is carried from Paris in *Le rêve*), and one is confronted by a carefully painted picture of middle-class society in a small town, this in its turn contrasting with the previous pictures of life in Paris. And now the baleful results which may attend marriages between cousins are exemplified. Marthe Rougon has married François Mouret, and both have inherited lesions from their common ancestress, Adélaïde Fouque. One of their children, Désirée, physically strong and healthy, is mentally an "innocent"; and they themselves are unhinged, the workings of their heredity being accentuated and hastened by the wiles of Faujas, the priest, who gains

access to their home. He is a secret agent of the imperial government, and thus one again sees the Empire at work in the provinces, utilising the clergy to enforce its authority, and as often as not betrayed by it. In the end all collapses. The maddened Mouret sets fire to his home and perishes in the flames with Abbé Faujas, while Marthe dies of a disorder springing from her inherited hysteria.

Then, the middle class of the provinces having been sketched, that of the metropolis is depicted with an unsparing hand. The career of the Mourets' eldest son, Octave, is followed, first through the pages of *Pot-bouille* (VII), in which he appears as a kind of modern Don Juan, a Don Juan stripped of all poetry, all glamour, a sensualist of our great cities, the man who prowls, not among the unhappy creatures of the streets, but among the women of outward respectability who may help him to acquire position and fortune. The scene is laid in a house of the Rue de Choiseul, in the centre of Paris; and all around Octave gravitate depraved, venal, egotistical, and sickly beings, adulterous households, unscrupulous match-making mothers, *demi-vierges* who will only marry for money, dowry hunters, slatternly servant girls, and that type of the middle-class debauchee who makes those girls his prey. And the pleasing figures in the work are few—poor old Josserand, for instance, and the charming Madame Hédouin, with the prosperous author on the first floor, who drives in his carriage and has two handsome children. At the same time the book pours a stream of light first on all the ignoble shifts to which middle-class folk of small means are put in their insane endeavours to ape their wealthier neighbours, and secondly on the evils that arise from that dowry system which superficial people regard as proving the foresight and wisdom of the French when they embark on the sea of matrimony. As a matter of fact, it frequently happens that this dowry system entirely blights married life. As often as not the dowry itself is a mere snare and delusion—the bride's parents retaining the principal, and merely serving the interest until their death, when, as in the case of Zola's old Vabre, the parental fortune may have entirely disappeared!

In *Au bonheur des dames* (VIII) Octave Mouret appears again, a sensualist still but also a man of enterprise, at the head of a "Grand Magasin de Nouveautés," a Temple of Temptation, which revolutionises trade and panders to the feminine love of finery. Here the *bourgeoisie* is shown elbowing the class immediately below it, a world of *employés,* clerks, shopmen and shop-girls, whose lives, likewise, are full of evil. But again a girl of admirable rectitude, Denise Baudu, comes forward to illumine the novelist's pages, and redeem and ennoble the man who has hitherto regarded her sex as an instrument or a toy.

When Zola has cast Octave Mouret at the feet of Denise, thereby exemplifying a pure woman's influence over man, he again transfers his scene from bustling Paris to a lonely region of the southern provinces, there to follow the career of Octave's brother, Serge. In *La faute de l'abbé Mouret* (IX) the battle is again one between woman, love, and man; but a new factor appears—religion—for Serge is a priest, bound by the unnatural vow of his calling, one of hysterical, mystical temperament also, enslaved by the superstitions of his creed. In his tumble-down parsonage and his little, decaying, forsaken church, amid a semi-savage, brutish peasantry, he long strives to resist the cry of nature. But she at last asserts her might, and the novelist carries the reader into the enchanted garden of the Paradou, where love reigns supreme. Yet the golden hours are brief: the priest is recalled to his religion of death, and he cannot resist the call, for all the training of years which has confirmed and increased his mystical tendency comes back, and he is helpless. Thus the natural life is forsaken for the illusions and dogmas of a creed; and Albine, whom Serge has loved, is left forlorn with her unborn babe, to lie down and die amid the perfume of the flowers with which she has strewn her bed. Serge it is who casts the symbolical pinch of earth upon her coffin, for he has resumed his ministry among the brutish peasants, dedicating all his efforts to slay the sex given him by his God, for instead of living as a man he must obey the command of his Church and live as an eunuch.

After that battle with nature and love, there comes a companion picture: the fall of Hélène Mouret in *Une page d'amour* (X). She has hitherto led an absolutely blameless life, but a sudden passion sweeps her off her feet. A tragic sombreness attends the episode. No glamour is cast over woman's frailty in Zola's pages. If Hélène tastes an hour of intoxication she is punished for it as frightfully as any moralist could desire. Jeanne, her fondly loved daughter, who is devoured by jealous hysteria, dies as the result of her lapse; and it is only afterwards, in pity as it were, that Hélène is granted the chance of beginning her life afresh.

Then the series continues. All the Rougons—excepting one, Pascal, whom the novelist keeps back till the end—have now been dealt with, the Mourets also, and the chronicle of the bastard Macquart branch begins. Antoine Macquart has three children, Lisa, Gervaise, and Jean, and it is Lisa who supplies the next volume of the series, *Le ventre de Paris* (XI), which carries one through and around the great markets of the French metropolis, as well as into the fine pork-butcher's shop, which Lisa keeps with her husband, Quenu. This is a volume redolent of victuals certainly, marked also by the egotism of the shopkeeping and petty trading classes, with yet a glimpse of one of those conspiracies which were frequent in the time of Napoleon III, and a backward glance at the *coup d'état* by which that sovereign had risen to power. The chief figure in the story is Quenu's brother, the unhappy Florent, who has escaped from Cayenne, and whom Lisa, that comfortable egotist, ends by betraying to the authorities. For that ultra-righteous deed,—counselled by Lisa's confessor,—and for the savagery of all the fat fishwives, one is consoled by the presence of honest Madame François and of Cadine, the little flower-girl, and Marjolin, her youthful lover, whose smile brightens many a page.

Then, in *La joie de vivre* (XII), comes Pauline, whose nature is so different from that of her mother, Lisa. She has no egotism in her composition; she would never betray anybody; she is all human devotion and self-sacrifice. With her we are carried to the seashore, to a little fisher hamlet, where her guardian Chanteau dwells; and he, his wife, and his son prey upon her, wrecking her life, though she remains brave and smiling till the end. And how little joy there may be in life is shown not only by her case, but by that of the crippled Chanteau, his embittered, covetous, suspicious wife, his jealous servant, and his weak-minded son, who tries to be this and that, but succeeds in nothing and is consumed by a foolish, unreasoning dread of death. It is to these that Pauline has to minister, for these that she has to sacrifice herself, even as it often happens that the good have to lay down their lives for the unworthy.

Pauline, one has said, is very different from her mother, Lisa. Equally different is Lisa's sister, Gervaise, the pathetic heroine of *L'assommoir* (XIII), with which the family chronicle is continued. Lisa rises, Gervaise falls; so does it happen in many of the world's families. Zola has now descended through several strata of society, and has come to the working classes. A deep pathos lies beneath the picture he traces of them under the bane of drink. At first Gervaise appears so courageous amid her misfortunes that one can readily grant her the compassionate sympathy accorded to every trusting woman whom a coward abandons. There seems hope for her at the outset of her marriage with Coupeau; a possibility, too, that she may prove successful when, industrious and energetic, she starts her little laundry business. But her husband's lazy, drunken ways recoil on her, the return of the rascally Lantier completes her misfortune, and then she rolls down hill, to die at last of starvation. The stage of *L'assommoir* is crowded with typical figures, some of them perchance imperishable, for their names have passed into the French language to serve as designations for one and another degraded character that one encounters in every-day life. Yet all the personages of Zola's work are not depraved. Even in this dark book there are a few who point to the brighter side of human nature, honest Goujet, for instance, and Lalie, the poor, pitiful "little mother." Gervaise and Coupeau themselves are not wholly vile. In the midst of their degradation, when she prowls the boulevard in the snow, when he is dancing madly in his padded cell, one instinctively retraces their careers back to the early days when both had looked so hopefully on life; and one recognises that a fatal environment, more than natural worthlessness, has been the great cause of their downfall.

Nana already appears—in her childhood and her youth—in the pages of *L'assommoir,* but Zola does not pass direct from that work to the later career of Gervaise's daughter. He first takes Gervaise's elder children, her sons by Lantier; and *L'œuvre* (XIV) unfolds the painful story of Claude, the painter, a glimpse of whom has been given previously in *Le ventre de Paris.* Again in *L'œuvre,* one finds a record of downfall, but, whereas in *L'assommoir* it has largely resulted from environment and circumstances, it now proceeds more directly from an evil heredity. Claude stands virtually on the border line that parts insanity from genius, and thus in his career, the old hypotheses of Moreau of Tours, and those subsequently enunciated in England by Nesbit, might find play. In the end, after a life of conflict and misery, insanity triumphs and Claude destroys himself. His tale . . . is linked with a picture of the French art-world. Fortunately a current of human interest flows through the book, for beside Claude the unhappy Christine, his wife, appears: she, like Gervaise, at first being a good, true, and courageous woman, one who commits the irremediable mistake of linking her life with that of a man fated to failure and insanity.

In these last sections of Zola's series the march of degenerescence is hastened; downfall follows downfall; before long that of individuals is to be succeeded by a supreme collapse, that of the *régime* under which they live. Thus, after *L'œuvre,* comes *La bête humaine* (XV), Claude's brother Jacques, an engine-driver, in whom a murderer appears among the Rougon-Macquarts. The hereditary virus, transmitted from Adélaïde Fouque, has turned in him to an insensate craving for woman's blood, and, frankly, his story is horrible. At the same time, while one follows the growth of his abominable disease, many a vivid page arrests attention: awful, yet a masterpiece of colloquial narrative and full of a penetrating psychology, is Severine's account of the murder of President Grandmorin; very human is Jacques' love for his engine, La Lison; and striking are the pictures of the snowstorm, the railway accident, and the death of Jacques and the stoker Pecqueux, at the end of the volume, when their train, crowded with soldiers, is seen rushing driverless, like some great, maddened, blind beast, towards catastrophe and annihilation.

Next the story of Gervaise's third son, Étienne, is unfolded in *Germinal* (XVI), this again a tale of the workers, the hardships, the misery, the degradation of the sweated toilers of the coal-pits, who are maddened by want to revolt. And then, of course, they are shot down by the soldiers at the disposal of the capitalists who batten on the sufferings of labour. A tribute of compassion, a call for justice, a cry of warning to the rich and powerful—such, as Zola himself said, is *Germinal.* Those who wonder at the hatred of the workers for those above them, at the spread of socialism throughout France, need merely read his pages to understand why and how such things have come to pass.

But *Nana* (XVII) now confronts the reader. He has just passed through the world of labour: drunkenness, degradation, insanity, crime, revolution have been indicated successively as resultants of the condition of the masses; and here comes another product of an evil social system, the low-born harlot who, like an unconscious instrument of retribution, ascends from her native dung-heap to poison the *bourgeoisie* and aristocracy—the rulers, the law-givers, to whom the existence of that dung-heap and its evil ferments is due. In *Nana* depravity coruscates. Here is the so-called "life of pleasure" of the world's great cities, the life of indulgence which recruits its votaries among all the aristocracies, all the plutocracies, all the *bourgeoisies,* all the bohemias. To some, Nana may seem to be "a scourge of God"—assuredly the world's Nanas have wrought more evil than its Attilas—"a punishment on men for their lewd and lawless sensuality." In Zola's pages one does not witness merely the ruin and disgrace of the professedly profligate; one sees also how natural, youthful desire when exposed to temptation may ripen into depravity and end in misery. One sees, again, the reflex action of libertinism on married life—how wives end at times by following the example of their husbands, and even "bettering the instruction." From first to last this much-maligned

book is a stupendous warning for both sexes, as great a denunciation of the social evil as ever was penned.

But the scene changes, and in *La terre* (XVIII) appears Jean Macquart, soldier and artisan, who becomes a peasant. He, though a brother of Gervaise, has escaped the hereditary taint, is strong, sensible, hardworking, a man destined, one might think, to a life of useful and happy obscurity. But fate casts him among the Fouans, a family of untutored peasants, barely raised above animality; and a drama of savage greed and egotism is unfolded around him. Old Fouan, being no longer able to till his fields himself, divides his property among his children, who agree to make him an allowance. But he is cheated, ill-treated, robbed of his savings by them, and finally murdered by one of his sons. That same son, Buteau, is consumed by a ravenous earth-hunger, but animal desire is also strong within him. He is both enamoured and jealous of his wife's sister, Françoise, who is Jean Macquart's wife, his passion for her being blended with a craving to appropriate her land. At last she, by violence, becomes his victim, and in a struggle with her sister, who is present, is thrown upon a scythe and mortally injured. That crime is witnessed by old Fouan, and it is for fear lest he should reveal it that he is stifled—then burnt.

From *La terre* Jean Macquart passes to *La débâcle* (XIX), for the time has now come for the great smash-up of that Empire all tinsel without and all rottenness within. War and invasion descend upon France. You follow the retreating soldiers from the Rhine to the Meuse, on that terrible, woeful march to Sedan, where all becomes disaster. You see the wretched Emperor borne along in the baggage train of his army, carried, it was thought, to certain death in the hope that France might then forgive, and allow his son to reign. And you see him under fire, vainly courting death, which will not take him. Then the horrors of Bazeilles, the struggle for the Calvary, the great charge, the hoisting of the white flag, the truce, and the abject surrender follow in swift succession. Next comes the battlefield after the slaughter, with the dreadful Camp of Misery, and later, the efforts of the National Defence, the peace imposed on the vanquished, and then the Commune's horrors crowning all. But from first to last human interest is never absent: one finds it in the friendship of Jean for the unlucky and degenerate Maurice, in the story of Silvine and Prosper, in the bravery of Weiss, the heroism of Henriette, Jean's love for her, and the hope that both, hereafter, may be able to begin life afresh and together, a hope which is blasted by the fatality of civil war, when brother rushes on brother and blindly slays him.

At last comes *Le docteur Pascal* (XX), the zealous scientist who sits in judgment on his family. You see him among his documents, sifting evidence, explaining the heredity of one and another relative, expounding the whole theory of atavism which underlies Zola's series. The old ancestress, Adélaïde Fouque, is still alive, a centenarian, mad, confined for many years in a lunatic asylum. Her son, Antoine Macquart, also survives, still an unscrupulous knave and a confirmed drunkard, until spontaneous combustion destroys him, while hemmorrhage carries off little Charles, the last delicate, degenerate scion of the exhausted stock. Pascal himself would seem to have escaped the hereditary taint; but after a long life of celibacy, spent in the study and practice of medicine, his passions awaken, and he falls in love with Clotilde, his niece. He strives to overcome that passion, he wishes to marry the girl to his friend Ramond, but she will not have it so, and in her turn becomes a temptress. Then the impetuous blood of the Rougons masters them both, and they fall into each other's arms. Previously, old Madame Félicité, Pascal's mother, has tried to use Clotilde as an instrument to effect the destruction of the documents which the doctor has collected, for the family would be dishonoured should they ever see the light. The girl has also tried to convert Pascal to her own religious views; but all in vain. A period of delirious folly ensues, Pascal turns prodigal in his old age, and is at last brought to ruin by a dishonest notary. Then Clotilde and he have to part, and he dies, struck down by heart disease. The young woman survives with a child, his son and hers, who, perhaps, may yet rejuvenate the dwindling race. And we see her nursing her babe and indulging in a thousand hopes, as the curtain at last descends on the history of the Rougon-Macquarts.

Such, then, is Zola's great series: one work in twenty volumes, in whose pages appear twelve hundred human characters. . . . (pp. 350-65)

*Germinal, L'assommoir, La débâcle,* and *La terre* are ranked as the four pillars of the Rougon-Macquart series. From a purely literary standpoint the first is superior to the second, because it contains less slang. The use of slang in dialogue is often advisable, even necessary; but in narrative and descriptive passages it is difficult to defend it unless the story be told in the first person by one who habitually speaks slang. Zola had some such idea in writing *L'assommoir* (which he pictured as a book about the people by one of them), but shrank from carrying it to its logical conclusion, and the result, in a literary sense, was not quite pleasing. However, both *Germinal* and *L'assommoir* are living books, the greatest their author ever penned.

Passing to *La débâcle,* this is certainly a wonderfully truthful panorama of war and its horrors, though the psychology of several of its characters is open to criticism. Too many of them lack robustness; they seem too full of nerves to be regarded as typical. In the case of Maurice, a mere degenerate, the picture is accurate enough; but assuredly many feelings which Zola and others have attributed to soldiers are little known in actual war. The majority of military men are far less sensitive than some have said, and incident often follows incident so rapidly in real battle that there is no time for thought or emotion at all. *La terre* also has faults, the outcome of Zola's reforming purpose, which led him to assemble too many black characters within a small circle; had they been more dispersed among people of an average kind the effect would have been more lifelike. In *Nana* the general blackness of the characters does not seem out of place, for only men and women of a sorry sort gravitate around a harlot. A few more average characters in *La terre,* or, rather, more prominence given to some who scarcely appear in its pages would have greatly improved the book. Here, however, as in *Pot-bouille,* Zola, carried away by his feelings, over-

looked that doctrine of average truth, of which Ste.-Beuve had reminded him apropos of *Thérèse Raquin.* He then admitted that he had piled on the agony unduly, and he made the same mistake in two or three volumes of "Les Rougon-Macquart." But when all is said *La terre* remains one of his strongest and most truthful books.

The savage brutishness of the chief characters in the work may well seem impossible to the ignorant; but although in reading *La terre* one should always bear in mind that Zola never pretended that all peasants were like those in his grim picture, it is certain that his personages, individually, are accurately drawn. Awful is the record of parricides, matricides, fratricides, common murders, murderous assaults, rapes, and offences of inferior degree perpetrated in rural France. And earth hunger, disputes about property, boundaries, inheritances, and so forth, will be found at the bottom of the great majority of cases. But *La terre* does not deal exclusively with the criminal side of peasant life. It pictures many other features: it describes the drawbacks of the small-holdings system, shows agriculture hampered by the extreme subdivision of the soil, traces the march of revolutionary and socialist principles among those who till it; sketching, too, on the way, the treatment which the imperial *régime* accorded to the peasantry.

There is not space here to pass all the Rougon-Macquart volumes in review from a critical point of view. One may say, however, that generally, though not invariably, those dealing with a multiplicity of characters are superior to those in which Zola analyses the feelings and actions of a few. It is acknowledged he excelled in portraying the "crowd." (pp. 379-82)

Without insisting further on the merits or demerits of particular volumes, if we glance at the series as a whole we shall find it to be an unexampled achievement. It is more self-contained than *La comédie humaine,* in writing which Balzac really had no definite plan. As M. Chaumié, French Minister of Public Instruction, has said [at Zola's funeral]:

> In Zola's work one finds all society . . . with the *milieux* in which it displays its activity, the men composing it, the passions which stir and sway them, their vices, sorrows, and miseries, the sufferings too of the disinherited,—the whole forming so striking and so true a picture that after contemplating it those with the poorest like those with the keenest sight must realise the necessity of remedying those sufferings, contending against those vices, and assuaging those sorrows. . . . Thus, what might have been only an admirable literary achievement, an inestimable document on a period, an ever-living picture of a given time . . . acquires greater grandeur, is insured of yet loftier glory, by the generous spirit which inspired it.

Further, though it has been suggested here that some exaggeration and some flaws may appear in the psychology of certain individual characters, the series as a whole responds to Taine's definition of literature as "a living psychology." As M. Paul Bourget has said:

> Zola regarded the novel as a kind of hypothetical

experiment, attempted on positive bases, the first condition for success being that the bases should be accurate and the hypothesis logical. When the hour of justice strikes for that unwearying toiler people will recognise what immense preliminary toil and study lay beneath each of his books. They will also discern his unwavering purpose to inquire fully into the condition of contemporary France, to carry his inquiry as far as possible in order to set the social problem completely and accurately before one. His right to depict all reality (*la réalité totale*), which is that of every sociologist, even of every historian, will not be disputed then.

(pp. 384-85)

*Ernest Alfred Vizetelly, in his* Émile Zola, Novelist and Reformer: An Account of His Life and Work, *1904. Reprint by Books for Libraries Press, 1971, 560 p.*

## George Lukács   (essay date 1940)

[*A Hungarian literary critic and philosopher, Lukács's works reflect his adherence to Marxist ideology. The subjects of his literary criticism are primarily the nineteenth-century Realists—Honoré de Balzac and Leo Tolstoy—and their twentieth-century counterparts—Maxim Gorky and Thomas Mann. In major works such as* Studies in European Realism *(1950) and* The Historical Novel *(1955), Lukács explicated his belief that "unless art can be made creatively consonant with history and human needs, it will always offer a counterworld of escape and marvelous waste." In the following essay first written in 1940, he finds that Zola did not relate the characters in his novels to their social environment and therefore failed in his ambition to provide a realistic depiction of both individuals and society. For a rebuttal of Lukács's criticism of Zola, see the excerpt by Patrick Brady (1981).*]

Emile Zola the novelist is the 'historian of private life' under the Second Empire in France in the same way as Balzac was the historian of private life under the restoration and the July monarchy. Zola himself never disclaimed this heritage. He always protested against the assumption that he had invented a new art form and always regarded himself as the heir and follower of Balzac and Stendhal, the two great realists of the beginning of the nineteenth century. Of the two, he regarded Stendhal as the connecting link with the literature of the eighteenth century. Of course so remarkable and original a writer as Zola could not regard his literary predecessors as mere models to copy; he admired Balzac and Stendhal but vigorously criticized them none the less; he tried to eliminate what he considered dead and antiquated in them and to work out the principles of a creative method which could have a fertilizing influence on the further evolution of realism. (It should be said here that Zola never speaks of realism, but always of naturalism.)

But the further development of realism in Zola's hands took a far more intricate course than Zola himself imagined. Between Balzac and Zola lies the year 1848 and the bloody days of June, the first independent action of the working class, which left so indelible an impression on the ideology of the French *bourgeoisie*, that after it *bourgeois* ideology ceased to play a progressive part in France for a long time. Ideology grew adaptable and developed into mere apologetics on behalf of the *bourgeoisie*.

Zola himself, however, never stooped to be an apologist of the *bourgeois* social order. On the contrary, he fought a courageous battle against the reactionary evolution of French capitalism, first in the literary sphere and later openly in the political. In the course of his life he gradually came ever closer to socialism, although he never got beyond a paler version of Fourier's Utopianism, a version lacking, however, Fourier's brilliantly dialectical social criticism. But the ideology of his own class was too deeply ingrained in his thinking, his principles and his creative method, although the conscious sharpness of his criticism of society was never dulled; on the contrary, it was much more vigorous and progressive than that of the Catholic Royalist Balzac.

Balzac and Stendhal, who had described the ghastly transformation of bourgeois France from the heroic period of the revolution and Napoleon to the romantically hypocritical corruption of the restoration and the no longer even hypocritical philistine filth of the July monarchy, had lived in a society in which the antagonism of bourgeoisie and working-class was not as yet the plainly visible hub around which social evolution moved forward. Hence Balzac and Stendhal could dig down to the very roots of the sharpest contradictions inherent in bourgeois society while the writers who lived after 1848 could not do so: such merciless candour, such sharp criticism would have necessarily driven them to break the link with their own class.

Even the sincerely progressive Zola was incapable of such a rupture.

It is this attitude which is reflected in his methodological conception, in his rejection, as romantic and 'unscientific,' of Balzac's bred-in-the-bone dialectic and prophetic fervour in the exposure of the contradictions of capitalism, for which he, Zola, substitutes a 'scientific' method in which society is conceived as a harmonious entity and the criticism applied to society formulated as a struggle against the diseases attacking its organic unity, a struggle against the 'undesirable features' of capitalism.

Zola says: "The social cycle is identical with the life-cycle: in society as in the human body, there is a solidarity linking the various organs with each other in such a way that if one organ putrefies, the rot spreads to the other organs and results in a very complicated disease."

This 'scientific' conception led Zola to identify mechanically the human body and human society, and he is quite consistent when he criticizes Balzac's great preface to *The Human Comedy* from this angle. In this preface Balzac, as a true dialectician, raises the same question: he asks to what extent the dialectic of race evolution as developed by Geoffroy de Saint Hilaire applies to human society; but at the same time he sharply stresses the new categories created by the specific dialectic of society. Zola thinks that such a conception destroys the 'scientific unity' of the method and that the conception itself is due to the 'romantic confusion' of Balzac's mind. What he then puts in the place of Balzac's ideas, as a 'scientific' result, is the undialectic conception of the organic unity of nature and society; the elimination of antagonisms is regarded as the motive power of social movement and the principle of 'harmony' as the essence of social being. Thus Zola's subjectively most sincere and courageous criticism of society is locked into the magic circle of progressive *bourgeois* narrowmindedness. On this basis of principle, Zola carries on the tradition established by the creative methods of Balzac and Stendhal with great consistence. It is not by accident nor a result of some personal bias in favour of his older friend and comrade-in-arms Flaubert that Zola found in the latter the true realization of all that in Balzac was merely a beginning or an intent.

Zola wrote about *Madame Bovary:* 'It seems that the formula of the modern novel, scattered all over Balzac's colossal *oeuvre,* is here clearly worked out in a book of 400 pages. And with it the code of the modern novel has now been written.'

Zola stresses as the elements of Flaubert's greatness: above all the elimination of romantic traits. 'The composition of the novel lies only in the way in which incidents are chosen and made to follow each other in a certain harmonic order of evolution. The incidents themselves are absolutely average. . . . All out-of-the-ordinary inventions have been excluded. . . . The story is unfolded by relating all that happens from day to day without ever springing any surprises.' According to Zola, Balzac, too, had in his greatest works sometimes achieved this realistic presentation of everyday life. 'But before he could reach the point of concerning himself only with accurate description, he revelled for a long time in inventions and lost himself in the search for false thrills and false magnificence.'

He continues: 'The novelist, if he accepts the basic principle of showing the ordinary course of average lives, must kill the "hero." By "hero" I mean inordinately magnified characters, puppets inflated into giants. Inflated "heroes" of this sort drag down Balzac's novels, because he always believes that he has not made them gigantic enough.' In the naturalist method 'this exaggeration by the artist and this whimsicality of composition are done away with' and 'all heads are brought down to the same level, for the opportunities permitting us to depict a truly superior human being are very rare.'

Here we already see quite clearly the principles on the basis of which Zola criticizes the heritage left by the great realists. Zola repeatedly discusses the great realists, particularly Balzac and Stendhal and constantly reiterates the same basic idea that Balzac and Stendhal were great because, in many details and episodes of their works, they described human passions faithfully and contributed very interesting documents to our knowledge of human passions. But according to Zola both of them, and particularly Stendhal, suffered from a mistaken romanticism. He writes, about the end of *Le rouge et le noir* and Julien Sorel: 'This goes absolutely beyond everyday truth, the truth we strive for; the psychologist Stendhal, no less than the story-teller Alexander Dumas, plunges us up to our necks in the unusual and extraordinary. Seen from the viewpoint of exact truth, Julien Sorel provides me with as many surprises as d'Artagnan.' Zola applies the same criticism to Mathilde de la Mole, all the characters in *The Monastery of Parma,* Balzac's Vautrin and many other Balzac characters.

Zola regards the whole relationship between Julien and Mathilde as mere brain-gymnastics and hair-splitting and both characters as unusual and artificial. He entirely fails to realize that Stendhal could not raise to the highest level of typicality the great conflict which he wanted to depict unless he invented these two absolutely above-average and quite extraordinary characters; only thus could he bring in his criticism of the hypocrisy, duplicity and baseness of the restoration period, and show up the infamously greedy and mean capitalist essence of its feudal-romantic ideology. Only by creating the figure of Mathilde, in whom the romantic ideology of reaction grows into a genuine passion, even though in heroically exaggerated form, could Stendhal raise the plot and the concrete situations to a level on which the contrast between these ideologies and their social basis on the one hand, and the plebeian Jacobinism of the Napoeleon-admirer Julien Sorel on the other, could be fully developed. Similarly, Zola failed to realize that Balzac could not possibly dispense with Vautrin's larger-than-life figure if he wanted the otherwise merely personal and individual catastrophe of Lucien de Rubempré's ambitions to become the tragedy of the whole ruling class of the restoration period; it was only by this device that Balzac was enabled to weave into this tragicomedy the entire tissue of the moribund society of the restoration, from the king meditating a *coup d'état* to the bureaucrat carving a career for himself.

But Zola could not see this. He says of Balzac: "His imagination, that unruly imagination which drove him to exaggeration and with which he wanted to re-create the world in his own image, irritates me more than it attracts me. If the great novelist had had nothing but this his imagination, he would now be merely a pathological case, a curiosity of our literature."

According to Zola, Balzac's greatness and his claim to immortality lay in the fact that he was one of the first who 'possessed a sense of reality.' But Zola arrived at this 'sense of reality' by first cutting out of Balzac's life-work the great contradictions of capitalist society and accepting only the presentation of everyday life which was for Balzac merely a means of throwing the contradictions into bolder relief and giving a total picture of society in motion, complete with all its determinants and antagonisms.

It is most characteristic that Zola (and with him Hippolyte Taine) should speak with the greatest admiration of General Hulot, a character in the novel *La cousine Bette.* But both of them see in him only a masterly portrait of an oversexed man. Neither Zola nor Taine say a word about the artistry with which Balzac traces Hulot's passions to the conditions of life in the Napoleonic era; and yet it would not have been difficult to notice this, for Balzac uses Crével—a character also painted with no less consummate mastery—as a counterfoil to show up the difference between the eroticism of the Napoleonic era and that of the reign of Louis Philippe. Neither Zola, nor Taine mention the doubtful operations with which Hulot tries to make money, although in describing them, Balzac gives an admirable picture of the infamies and horrors of incipient French colonial policy.

In other words both Zola and Taine insulate Hulot's erotic passion from its social basis and thus turn a socially pathological figure into a psychopathological one. It is natural that looking at it from this angle he could see only 'exaggeration' (i.e. romanticism) in the great, socially typical characters created by Balzac and Stendhal.

"Life is simpler than that" Zola says at the end of one of his criticisms of Stendhal. He thus completes the transition from the old realism to the new, from realism proper to naturalism. The decisive social basis of this change is to be found in the fact that the social evolution of the *bourgeoisie* has changed the way of life of writers. The writer no longer participates in the great struggles of his time, but is reduced to a mere spectator and chronicler of public life. Zola understood clearly enough that Balzac himself had to go bankrupt in order to be able to depict Cesar Birotteau; that he had to know from his own experience the whole underworld of Paris in order to create such characters as Rastignac and old Goriot.

In contrast, Zola—and to an even greater extent Flaubert, the true founder of the new realism,—were solitary observers and critical commentators of the social life of their own day. (The courageous public fight put up by Zola in connection with the Dreyfus affair came too late and was too much a mere episode in Zola's life to effect any radical change in his creative method.) Zola's naturalist 'experimental' novels were therefore merely attempts to find a method by which the writer, now reduced to a mere spectator, could again realistically master reality. Naturally Zola never became conscious of this social degradation of the writer; his theory and practice grew out of this social existence without his ever becoming aware of it. On the contrary, inasmuch as he had some inkling of the change in the writer's position in capitalist society, he, as the liberal positivist that he was, regarded it as an advantage, as a step forward, and therefore praised Flaubert's impartiality (which in reality did not exist) as a new trait in the writer's make-up. Lafargue who, in accordance with the traditions of Marx and Engels, severely criticized Zola's creative method and contrasted it with that of Balzac, saw very clearly that Zola was isolated from the social life of his time. Lafargue described Zola's attitude to reality as similar to that of a newspaper reporter and this is perfectly in accordance with Zola's own programmatic statements about the correct creative method in literature.

Of these statements we quote only one, in which he gives his opinion on the proper conception of a good novel:

> A naturalist writer wants to write a novel about the stage. Starting from this point without characters or data, his first concern will be to collect material, to find out what he can about this world he wishes to describe. He may have known a few actors and seen a few performances. . . . Then he will talk to the people best informed on the subject, will collect statements, anecdotes, portraits. But this is not all. He will also read the written documents available. *Finally* he will visit the locations, *spend a few days* in a theatre in order to acquaint himself with the smallest details, pass an evening in an actress' dressing-room and absorb the atmosphere as much as possible. When all this material has been gathered, the novel will take shape of its own accord. All the novelist has to do is to group the facts in a logical sequence. . . . *Interest will no longer be focussed on the* peculiarities of the story—on the contrary, the more general and commonplace the story is, the more typical it will be.

Here we have the new realism, *recte* naturalism, in concentrated essence and in sharp opposition to the traditions of the old realism; a mechanical average takes the place of the dialectic unity of type and individual; description and analysis is substituted for epic situations and epic plots. The tension of the old-type story, the co-operation and clashing of human beings who are both individuals and at the same time representatives of important class tendencies—all these are eliminated and their place is taken by 'average' characters whose individual traits are accidents from the artistic point of view (or in other words have no decisive influence on what happens in the story) and these 'average' characters act without a pattern, either merely side by side or else in completely chaotic fashion.

It was only because he could not always consistently adhere to his own programme that Zola could ever come to be a great writer.

But we must not assume that Zola represents the same 'triumph of realism' of which Engels speaks in connection with Balzac. The analogy is merely formal and the assumption would therefore be wrong. Balzac boldly exposed the contradictions of nascent capitalist society and hence his observation of reality constantly clashed with his political prejudices. But as an honest artist he always depicted only what he himself saw, learned and underwent, concerning himself not at all whether his true-to-life description of the things he saw contradicted his pet ideas. It was out of this conflict that the 'triumph of reality', was born, but then Balzac's *artistic* objectives did not preclude the extensive and penetrating presentation of social reality.

Zola's position was totally different. There is no such wide gap between Zola's social and political views and the social-critical tendencies of his work as there is in Balzac's. True, his observation of facts and of historical evolution did slowly radicalize Zola and bring him closer to Utopian socialism, but this did not amount to a clash between the writer's prejudices and reality.

The contrast in the sphere of art is all the sharper. Zola's method, which hampered not only Zola himself but his whole generation, because it was the result of the writer's position as solitary observer, prevents any profoundly realistic representation of life. Zola's 'scientific' method always seeks the average, and this grey statistical mean, the point at which all internal contradictions are blunted, where the great and the petty, the noble and the base, the beautiful and the ugly are all mediocre 'products' together, spells the doom of great literature.

Zola was a far too naive liberal all his life, far too ardent a believer in *bourgeois* progress, ever to harbour any doubts regarding his own very questionable, positivist 'scientific' method.

Nevertheless the artistic implementation of his method was not achieved without a struggle. Zola the writer was far too conscious of the greatness of modern life (even though the greatness was inhuman) for him to resign himself without a struggle to the grey tedium which would have been the result of a method such as his, if consistently carried through. Zola hated and despised far too much the evil, base, reactionary forces which permeate capitalist society, for him to remain a cold, unsympathetic 'experimenter' such as the positivist-naturalist doctrine required him to be.

As we have seen, the struggle resulting from this was fought out within the framework of Zola's own creative method. In Balzac it was reality and political bias that were at war with each other, in Zola it was the creative method and the 'material' presented. Hence in Zola there is no such universal break-through as the 'triumph of realism' in Balzac, there are only isolated moments, details, in which the author breaks the chains of his own positivist, 'scientific', naturalist dogmas in order to give free scope to his temperament in truly realist fashion.

We can find such a break-through in almost every one of Zola's novels and hence there are admirably life-like *single episodes* in every one of his major books. But they can not permeate the entire work, for the doctrine still triumphs in the general lay-out of each of them. Thus the strange situation is created that Zola, although his life-work is very extensive, has never created a single character who grew to be a type, a by-word, almost a living being, such as for instance the Bovary couple or Homais the apothecary in Flaubert, not to mention the immortal figures given us by such creators of men as Balzac or Dickens.

But there was an urge in Zola, to go beyond the grey average of naturalism in his composition. Thus it is that he created many extraordinarily effective pictures. No reader can fail to be deeply impressed by his admirable descriptions of pits and markets, the stock exchange, a racecourse, a battlefield or a theatre. Perhaps no one has painted more colourfully and suggestively the outer trappings of modern life.

But only the *outer* trappings.

They form a gigantic backdrop in front of which tiny, haphazard people move to and fro and live their haphazard lives. Zola could never achieve what the truly great realists Balzac, Tolstoy or Dickens accomplished: to present social institutions as human relationships and social objects as the vehicles of such relationships. Man and his surroundings are always sharply divided in all Zola's works.

Hence, as soon as he departs from the monotony of naturalism, he is immediately transmuted into a decorative picturesque romanticist, who treads in the footsteps of Victor Hugo with his bombastic monumentalism.

There is a strange element of tragedy here.

Zola, who as we have seen, criticized Balzac and Stendhal so vehemently for their alleged romanticism, was compelled to have recourse to a romanticism of the Victor Hugo stamp in order to escape, in part at least, from the counter-artistic consequences of his own naturalism.

Sometimes Zola himself seemed to realise this discrepancy. The romantic, rhetoric and picturesque artificiality of style produced by the triumph of French naturalism, was at variance with Zola's sincere love of truth. As a decent man and honest writer he felt that he himself was much to blame for this. "I am too much a son of my time, I am too deeply immersed in romanticism for me to dream of emancipating myself from certain rhetorical prejudices. . . . Less artificiality and more solidity—I should like us to be less brilliant and to have more real content. . . . "

But he could find no way out of this dilemma in the sphere of art. On the contrary, the more vigorously he participated in the struggle of opinions, the more rhetorical his style became.

For there are only two roads leading out of the monotonous commonplace of naturalism, which results from the direct, mechanical mirroring of the humdrum reality of capitalism. Either the writer succeeds in revealing the human and social significance of the struggle for life and lifting it to a higher plane by artistic means (as Balzac did)—or else he has to overstress the mere outward scenery of life, rhetorically and picturesquely, and quite independently of the human import of the events depicted (like Victor Hugo).

Such was the romantic dilemma which faced French naturalism. Zola (as before him Flaubert) took the second road because he was in sincere opposition to the ideology of the post-revolutionary *bourgeoisie;* because he hated and despised that glorification of false ideals and false 'great men' which was the fashion of his time and because he was quite determined to expose all this without mercy. But the most honest and sincere determination to fight for such things could not make up for the artistic falsity of the method and the inorganic nature of the presentation resulting from it.

Goethe in his old age had already seen this parting of the ways, the 'romantic' dilemma of the nascent new literature. In the last years of his life he read almost simultaneously Balzac's *The Asses' Skin* and Victor Hugo's *Notre Dame Of Paris.* About Balzac's novel he wrote in his diary:

> I have continued reading *The Asses' Skin* . . . it is an excellent work of the latest literary method and excels among other things by moving to and fro between the impossible and the intolerable with vigour and good taste and succeeds in most consistently making use as a medium of the miraculous and of the strangest states of mind and events, to the details of which one could give much more praise.

In other words, Goethe saw quite clearly that Balzac used the romantic element, the grotesque, the fantastic, the bizarre, the ugly, the ironically or sententiously exaggerated only in order to show up essential human and social relationships. All this was for Balzac merely a means, if a roundabout one, to the creation of a realism which, while absorbing the new aspects of life, would yet preserve the qualities of the older great literature.

Goethe's opinion of Victor Hugo was the exact opposite of his attitude to Balzac. He wrote to Zelter:

> Victor Hugo's *Notre Dame* captivates the reader by its diligent study of the old scenes, customs and events, but the characters show no trace of natural animation. They are lifeless lay figures pulled about by wires; they are cleverly put together, but the wood and steel skeletons support mere stuffed puppets with whom the author deals most cruelly, jerking them into the strangest poses, contorting them, tormenting and whipping them, cutting up their bodies and souls,—but because they have no flesh and blood, all he can do is tear up the rags out of which they are made; all this is done with considerable historical and rhetorical talent and a vivid imagination; without these qualities he could not have produced these abominations. . . .

Of course Zola cannot simply be identified with Victor Hugo, although Hugo, too, had gone a little way in the direction of realism. *Les miserables* and *1793* doubtless show a higher level of characterization than *Notre Dame Of Paris* although of *Les miserables* Flaubert angrily remarked that such a characterization of social conditions and human beings was impermissible in an age in which Balzac had already written his works.

But Hugo was never able to get away from his basic mistake, which was that he portrayed human beings independently of their social environment—and from the resulting puppet-like nature of his characters. The aged Goethe's judgment of Hugo is valid, with some mitigation, in respect of all Hugo's novels. Zola, who followed this tradition, is equally incapable of penetrating and convincing characterization.

Zola depicts with naturalist fidelity the biological and 'psychological' entity of the average human being and this preserves him from treating his characters as arbitrarily as Victor Hugo. But on the one hand this method sets his characterization very narrow limits and on the other hand the combination of two contradictory principles, i.e. of naturalism and romantically rhetorical monumentality again produce a Hugoan discrepancy between characters and environment which he cannot overcome.

Hence Zola's fate is one of the literary tragedies of the nineteenth century. Zola is one of those outstanding personalities whose talents and human qualities destined them for the greatest things, but who have been prevented by capitalism from accomplishing their destiny and finding themselves in a truly realistic art.

This tragic conflict is obvious in Zola's life-work, all the more as capitalism was unable to conquer Zola the man. He trod his path to the end, honourably, indomitably, uncompromisingly. In his youth he fought with courage for the new literature and art (he was a supporter of Manet and the impressionists) and in his riper years he again played the man in the battle against the conspiracy of the French clericals and the French general staff in the Dreyfus affair.

Zola's resolute struggle for the cause of progress will survive many of his one-time fashionable novels, and will place his name in history side by side with that of Voltaire who defended Calas as Zola defended Dreyfus. Surrounded by the fake democracy and corruption of the Third Republic, by the false so-called democrats who let no day pass without betraying the traditions of the great French revolution, Zola stands head and shoulders above them as the model of the courageous and high-principled *bourgeois* who—even if he failed to understand the essence of socialism—did not abandon democracy even when behind it the Socialist demands of the working class were already being voiced.

We should remember this to-day when the Republic has become a mere cover for a conquest-hungry colonial imperialism and a brutal oppression of the metropolitan working class.

The mere memory of Zola's courageous and upright figure is an indictment of the so-called "democracy" represented by the men who rule France to-day. (pp. 85-96)

> *George Lukács, "The Zola Centenary," in his* Studies in European Realism: A Sociological Survey of the Writings of Balzac, Stendhal, Zola, Tolstoy, Gorki and Others, *translated by Edith Bone, Hillway Publishing Co., 1950, pp. 85-96.*

## Victor Brombert (essay date 1961)

[*Brombert is an American critic who has written extensively on modern French literature, including a major study of the works of Gustave Flaubert. In the following excerpt, he analyzes the character of Marc Froment in* Vérité *as a representation of Zola's shift in artistic and moral views late in his life.*]

*Vérité* (1902) is an unsophisticated panegyric to the glory of a schoolteacher who, urged onward by his republican mystique, fights obscurantism and lays the foundations of the new City of Truth and Justice. Characteristic simplifications and amplifications leave little doubt as to the author's own fervor. Zola's intellectual hero, Marc Froment, has a quasi-primitive heroic stature.

> There was a measure of heroism in his deed and he accomplished it with simplicity, out of enthusiasm for the good work he was undertaking. The highest role, the noblest, in a young democracy is that of the primary schoolteacher, so poor, so despised, who is entrusted with the education of the humble and who is to make of them the future happy citizens, the builders of the City of Justice and Peace. His mission suddenly became clear to him: his apostolate of truth, his passion to penetrate the positive truth, to proclaim it loudly, to teach it to everyone.

The tone of the passage, words such as "mission" and

*Portrait of Zola by Edouard Manet.*

"apostolate," the idea of a "truth" to be discovered and disseminated, clearly point to an ideological passion as absolute as a religious faith. The millenaristic social dream is repeatedly suggested by direct references to the *cité future*. Not only are the schoolteachers of the Third Republic called "modern apostles," "apostles of reason," "missionaries of the new humanity," but the novel is part of a tetralogy entitled "Les quatre evangiles" ("The Four Gospels"), the individual titles of which are *Fécondité, Travail, Vérité* and *Justice* [*Vérité* appeared posthumously. The final volume, *Justice,* was never written]. Mathieu, Luc and Marc are the respective heroes of the completed "Evangiles." As for the name Froment (from the Latin *frumentum,* the richest type of wheat), it serves to remind us of Zola's obsession with the theme of fertility. In *Vérité* the fertilizing is exclusively intellectual: the hero sows the seed of enlightenment, the "good word" which will free peoples' minds from error and lies.

The specific error, the specific lie around which the novel crystallizes and against which Marc Froment sets out like a true crusader is the scandal of the Dreyfus case—which Zola transposes by making of a Jewish schoolmaster, a colleague of Marc Froment, the innocent victim of local superstitions, mental indolence and chauvinistic bias. A schoolteacher and a Jew: a predestined target of all the forces of darkness! It is no doubt with a certain measure of contentment that Zola made his "apostle" the defender of a Jew. But although the fictional version of the Dreyfus case is at the heart of the novel (in 1902 all the incidents

were still fresh in readers' minds), Zola seems much more concerned with his own humanitarian dreams than with the legal issues raised by the famous *Affaire.* The attitude of Zola is not unique. Péguy and his friends also experienced this national crisis above all as a spiritual adventure. *"L'affaire Dreyfus, c'est la mystique républicaine,"* Albert Thibaudet explained many years later. Indeed, once the battle had been won and the true culprits denounced, there remained the abstract quest for justice and for the myth of Republican Purity. The priest-ridden town of *Vérité* gives way at the end of the novel to the harmonious city, a new version of Eldorado made secure for future generations by the schoolteacher (now the most honored citizen), by science and by the "irresistible power of ideas."

An unmitigated seriousness inspires the book. One finds here none of the ambiguities that characterize Vallès', Bourget's or Barrès' treatment of the intellectual. Yet there is incongruity in Zola's enthusiasm for Marc Froment and for the "irresistible power of ideas." No one, in a sense, was less prepared than Zola to exalt the heroic virtues of the intellect, or less suited temperamentally to be a leader of the *parti intellectuel.* But literary history is full of such ironies. Just as Bourget, the son of a professor and himself endowed with a potential for scholarship, became sharply critical of much that intellectualism and science stood for; just as Barrès, the dilettantish aesthete, posed as an enemy of culture and was consequently acclaimed by those whom he himself had termed "barbarians"—so Emile Zola, by a twist of fate, found himself at the head of a group with which he had little in common. For Zola felt scant tenderness for professors and for the academic life. He left school after having twice failed the *baccalauréat.* His writings display a consistent suspicion of the academic scholar and are often outspokenly hostile. Particularly unpalatable to him was the spirit that prevailed at the Sorbonne and at the Ecole Normale Supérieure. Professors and professional critics do not fare well in his novels. In *Le docteur Pascal,* the retired teacher living in symbolic isolation in the house next door embodies egoism, cowardice and sterility.

Zola became even more bitter after the unfavorable reception of his novel *Rome.* Pierre, the hero of *Paris,* launches into a lengthy disquisition against the *normaliens:* they are not satisfied with teaching, but want to rule over the world of art, of journalism and of society; they pose as dilettantes, are haunted by the desire to charm, become masters of paradox, and strive mightily to appear skeptical, frivolous and very "Parisian." Even in *Vérité* there are echoes of this same prejudice. Marcilly, the ever-smiling young Député, a former *normalien,* is nothing but a pleasure-seeking *arriviste.* As for Le Barazer, the Inspecteur d'Académie, he is an ardent republican and consequently defends Marc Froment. But his very adroitness is a moral blemish: the prudent "diplomat" is also an "opportunist."

More strictly literary reasons—his concept, for instance, of the modern epic novel—also explain why Zola denied the thinker and the drama of thought any important role in the Rougon-Macquart cycle. When the critic Jules Lemaître, after the publication of *Germinal,* spoke of Zola's "pessimistic epic of human animality" [see Further Reading], Zola replied [in a letter]: "You place man in his mind, I put him in all of his organs. You isolate man from nature, I can't conceive of him away from the earth, whence he comes and where he will return. . . . I firmly believe that I have taken into account all of the organs, the brain as well as the rest. My characters think as much as they should think, as much as one does think in ordinary life." This dialogue with Lemaître he carried into *L'œuvre,* where Sandoz, who is in part an idealized self-portrait, explains why he does not want to write metaphysical novels or novels of ideas: "What a joke, this continuous and exclusive study of the activity of the brain, on the pretext that the brain is the noble organ! . . . Thought, thought, damn it all! thought is the product of the entire body. Let's see a brain think all by itself, let's see what happens to the nobility of the brain when the belly is sick! . . . " Observations such as these are significant. The "thinker" simply did not fit Zola's requirements for heroic stature. Commenting on Théodore de Banville's play, *Deïdamie* (1876), he very seriously asserted that contemporary writers wishing to emulate works of antiquity should use as characters peasants and workers. "Only our workers and our peasants h... the simple and sturdy build of Homer's heroes."

The trilogy "Les trois villes" (*Rome, Lourdes, Paris*) thus marks a turning point in Zola's career as a novelist, a bridge between the completed Rougon-Macquart cycle and "Les Quatre Evangiles." The "intellectual" Froment family, in sharp contrast with the Rougon-Macquarts, imports into Zola's fictional world a new series of themes: crises of conscience, social indignation, intelligence as a dynamic force, moral dedication, spiritual conversions and reconversions. This renewal and, to some extent, broadening of Zola's themes can be diversely interpreted. Malevolent voices immediately suggested that Zola's powers had declined, that he had lost his creative vision and in its stead was purveying artificially contrived "problems." It is still customary today to point to the waning of Zola's imagination and artistic powers after 1892 or 1893. Certainly nothing he wrote after that date can even be compared with the movement and color of *L'assommoir, Germinal* or *La débâcle.*

To equate intellectual themes with artistic decrepitude constitutes, however, a dubious critical judgment. In reality, there are other reasons why Zola turned his energies to the novel of ideas. First among them perhaps was the intellectual mood prevalent in French letters at the turn of the century. Convinced that in spite of her prosperity France was really undergoing a grave moral crisis, many of the serious writers (Barrès, Claudel, Maurras, Anatole France, the young Romain Rolland) set out to diagnose her ills and prescribe appropriate remedies. Bourget's *Le disciple* had set the tone. More specifically, Zola's ire had been aroused by Brunetière's polemics with Berthelot and by his crusade against science. *Paris* is studded with direct and indirect allusions to Brunetière's article on the "bankruptcy of science." Zola felt compelled to counter-attack, and his fiction became ideologically militant. But it is also true that as early as 1890 Zola starts to toy with the idea of a totally different type of novel. "I begin to be tired of my series"—he confides to Jules Lemaître in a letter

thanking him for his review of *La bête humaine.* And, after explaining that he must finish it, he adds this curious remark: "Then I will see, if I am not too old, and if I am not too much afraid of being called a turncoat." This "turncoat" aspect of his work is manifested in "Les trois villes" and "Les quatre evangiles"; Zola himself has best defined it in a letter to Octave Mirbeau: "All this is very utopian, but what do you want? I've been dissecting for forty years; I must be allowed in my old days to dream a little." To embody his dreams in fiction, Zola needed a new type of character: the thinking (or dreaming) protagonist capable of free choice, or critical distance, and driven onward by an urge for syntheses and global visions.

Perhaps Zola himself exaggerates the newness of what he wrote after 1893. His renunciation of the aims and methods of pure naturalism is less far-reaching than he thinks. "Dream" and "dissection" are, in his case, not really irreconcilable. The utopian characteristics of "Les trois villes" and "Les quatre evangiles" only bring to the surface a natural and, at one time, predominant tendency of Zola's character. For Zola's early admirations went to idealistic and visionary artists: Dante, Ronsard, Chénier. He even enjoyed the delicate dreams of a Musset. The Romantics, against whom he openly rebelled, had not only been his spiritual masters, but could claim him as their direct and secretly most faithful heir. He had been brutally unfair to Hugo—but owed him far more than he would ever dare acknowledge: a taste for grandiose visions, sympathy for the "people," a tendency to self-dramatization and self-glorification, and, above all, that inner conviction that the poet is prophet, *vates,* seer, a fierce magus, a voice that announces the truth. Like Hugo, he might have proclaimed:

> *Peuples! écoutez le poète!*
> *Ecoutez le rêveur sacré!*

His earliest projects, for instance the long poem in three cantos to be entitled *La chaîne des êtres,* betray epic ambitions and call for a significant mixture of the scientific and the poetical. In a letter to his friend Baille (June, 1860), Zola explains that the scientific account of creation and the historical account of the progress of civilization are to lead up to a *"magnifique divagation"* in the final canto. The very choice of terms is revealing: "Thus, in the first canto, the scientist; in the second, the philosopher; in the third, the lyric bard; in all three, the poet.—A magnificent idea . . . "

The distance separating the "scientist" from the "lyric bard," the cold observer from the utopian dreamer, never gaped very wide. The naturalistic novels of Zola are saturated with moral and moralizing undertones which point forward to the revolutionary lyricism of his later period. This explains perhaps his determination to equate science with revolution. Docteur Pascal's credo is still a typical eighteenth-century belief in progress, toughened somewhat by Darwinism. In *Paris,* however, the scientist Bertheroy goes much further, proclaiming the religion of science: "Science alone is revolutionary." Hostile to the anarchist intellectual who reasons out murder cold-bloodedly in order to alleviate his boredom (one recognizes Zola's own anti-"intellectual" bias), Bertheroy explains: "Isn't science enough? . . . she alone sweeps away dogmas, carries away the gods, brings light and happiness. . . . It is I, a pensioned and decorated member of the Institute who am the only true revolutionary." These poetics of science, this sentimental, vague, optimistic fatalism were not exactly to the liking of Zola's new socialist friends. It has been suggested that it is in part their admonitions which oriented him toward the "fideistic" characters of "Les quatre evangiles."

The hero of *Vérité*—an intellectual with a non-intellectual temperament—is thus the fictional product of many contradictory strains in Zola's make-up: a long-standing suspicion of the scholar and yet a faith in the revelations of science; a need for epic simplifications and yet the ambition to be a subtle moral diagnostician of France's ills; utopian leanings and militant tendencies colored by an obsession with the physical aspects of human life; a propensity for obvious symbols aggravated by scant gifts for analysis; the temperament of a visionary allured by sweeping syntheses in which science, poetry and revolution all merge— these are some of the reasons that account for Zola's apostolic free-thinker Marc Froment. They also cast light on the idyllic simplicity of his character.

Even the manner in which Zola magnifies and glorifies his character reveals a curious lack of focus. On the one hand, there is a systematic attempt to cluster around the figure of this defender of Truth and Justice some of the conventional tragic themes and attitudes. Marc Froment, an "alien" in the town he adopts, is the solver of a riddle (the novel, at times, takes the form of a detective story) and the healer of a moral disease. His drama is personal (a moral crisis that involves a seeming choice between honor and happiness); but it is also communal: the drama of social responsibility in which the individual assumes and ultimately purifies a common guilt. His is moreover a tragedy of progressive loss and loneliness, as his wife temporarily abandons him and he is deprived of his daughter and of his friends.

Marc Froment's courageous acceptance of personal loss in the pursuit of a higher aim, his ability to dominate his grief for the sake of a passionate commitment to an ideal, soon cease, however, to be presented in the light of an individual experience. The hero, struggling against ignorance, founder of the new City that embodies Zola's dream of a revitalized France, dedicated to the happiness of the community, loses his identity and dissolves into an epic abstraction. Even Zola's style—his mania for recapitulations and repetition of epithets—contributes to the epic climate.

This tendency to proceed from the individual to the group is of course a permanent feature of Zola's novels. In *Vérité*, there is however a more precise reason for this shift in emphasis. Zola's fictionalized account of the Dreyfus case was to be above all a dithyramb in honor of the primary schoolteacher, the *instituteur*. And not only in honor of the *instituteur* Marc Froment (whose humility and sense of vocation are merely representative), but in honor of the entire *"bataillon sacré"* who, in the remotest villages of France, struggle valiantly to conquer ignorance.

Zola's paean of praise to the *instituteur* is of course not an isolated phenomenon. Ever since Condorcet coined the word in 1792 the name has been synonymous with republican virtues. Hugo and Michelet repeatedly proclaimed that this shaper of minds and torch-bearer lighting the road to a better future embodied the highest values of France. During the Third Republic (1870-1940), the *instituteur* truly came to symbolize the myth of Revolution, love of democracy, the religion of progress and the cult of civic virtues. Ferdinand Buisson, himself one of France's idealistic educators, called the *instituteur* the "pioneer of the new regime," and asserted that in a Republic the schoolteacher should be *"chose sacrée."* Clemenceau, in *Le grand Pan,* spoke of the prophets of the New Logos! Caught between the grandeur of his mission and the misery of his condition, the *instituteur* was eventually surrounded by a special mythological aura. Albert Thibaudet recalls a version of *Prometheus Bound* (performed at a Université Populaire in 1903) in which the heroic Prometheus was a persecuted socialist *instituteur*. The *instituteur* also found his way into the novel: Eugène Sue's "lay Parsifal" in *Martin, l'enfant trouvé* (1846); the poor young teacher in Erckmann-Chatrian's *Histoire d'un sous-maître* (1871); the hungry, disheveled hero, driven to madness, in Antonin Lavergne's *Jean Coste* (1901); the idealistic Clauricard, in Jules Romains' *Les hommes de bonne volonté;* the austere, demanding schoolmasters in *La mort de Jean Madec* (1945), whose purity of heart and unshakable faith in the eminent dignity of the common people Brice Parain so powerfully evokes—all moving portraits, no doubt; but none as ambitious as Zola's.

For Zola's treatment is not limited to the lonely struggle and ultimate victory of a representative type. *Vérité,* like *Jean Coste* (and perhaps more convincingly), also insists on the pathos of the *instituteur,* which is brought out by means of a minor character, the embittered Férou who, persecuted by the local priest as well as by the brutal peasants, lives in heroic misery. Son of a shepherd, he is a typical *déclassé,* permanently humiliated and literally spat upon. Through this somewhat excessive image of misery Zola attempts to give his social victim a tragic dignity. Expressions such as "heroic courage," "tragic gravity" are only a prelude to the sordid dénouement. Exasperated to the point of rebellion, Férou is dismissed from his teaching post, then deserts from the army, and is finally shot down like a mad dog by a sergeant in a disciplinary battalion, leaving his wife and two daughters in utter destitution. But if Zola presents this destiny with somewhat clumsy insistence, it is not at all to back the view that rebellion is the only answer to this moneyless and honorless career, but to bring out the martyrdom of his "apostles." For martyrdom is the proof as well as the price of their ideal. If things turn out well in the long run for Marc Froment it is not because his hero must suffer less, but because the truth of the new Gospel has to be victorious. "Glory be to the *instituteur* stricken down in the exercise of his function, a victim of his effort toward more light! . . . " The very tone of such sentences—and they are not rare— suggests once again the evangelic style, and serves to remind the reader that the worn-out Gospel is to be replaced by a newer and better one: the Gospel of Intelligence, which supposedly proclaims the inanity and danger of the Christian "Blessed are the poor in spirit. . . . " No wonder certain contemporary critics, like Lucien-Victor Meunier, considered *Vérité* a "superb book of republican and lay education." Gustave Téry, in *La raison* (May 10, 1903), called the novel "our gospel, our lay breviary"! To more sober readers, however, the end of the novel may well seem a little exuberant, even faintly comical in its very note of triumph. Not only does Marc's own daughter become an *institutrice,* but the fecundity of the new gospel is such that nearly everybody, one gathers, becomes a schoolmaster, marries a schoolmistress and gives birth to a swarm of future sowers of the Truth.

But Zola was not content with this abstract triumph of the *instituteur.* Beyond the tragic dilemma of Marc the individual, beyond the glorification of the "sacred battalion" which ultimately dissolves into mere propaganda, Zola was also quite evidently out to glorify himself. His outline for the novel contains this revealing note: "And at the end he [Marc] is right. *It is my triumph*" [italics Brombert's]. The reference is clearly to Zola's role in the Dreyfus case. Curiously enough, Dreyfus himself, in all the literature inspired by his plight, never appears as a hero or even as an important character. Partly this may be due to his pale, unheroic figure which so much disappointed his most ardent defenders. Nearly all the writers who dealt with the case squarely or episodically (Zola, Anatole France, Romain Rolland, Proust, Martin du Gard) were in fact primarily concerned with the broader political or social issues, or with their own ideological commitment. Zola is one of the few who has at least attempted to present Dreyfus as a suffering creature and not merely as a symbol. But he it is, too, who pushed the furthest his efforts at self-glorification.

Malicious pens and tongues have suggested that all Zola really saw in the famous *Affaire* was the providential occasion to remain in the public eye at a time his muse was deserting him—and that he exploited this occasion to the hilt. Nothing, however, could be further from the truth. What in reality first seduced Zola was neither the abstract problem of Truth and Justice, nor even the role he might play, but the human drama. It is with a novelist's eye that he first surveyed the scene: "What a poignant drama, and what superb characters! In front of these tragically beautiful documents which life brings us, my novelist's heart pounds with passionate admiration." Only later—and gradually—did Zola conceive of the heroic role he might be called upon to play as a writer, as an "intellectual."

There was great *literary* potential in this personal and intellectual involvement. The dramatization of the artist, of the intellectual *self,* was, moreover, not alien to Zola. *Le docteur Pascal* describes the struggle of a scientific mind against the prejudices of family and society, and on another level, the autumnal love affair of a sexagenarian which is not without some echo of Zola's own *arrièresaison* adultery. Docteur Pascal is perhaps the only character Zola extols as an alienated individual (*"je suis à part"*) whose solidarity with the human family is colored by the pride of being "different," "without any communion." Pascal's death is a Socratic death (he continues discussing and dissecting), and this death scene was probably the one Zola had dreamt for himself: sustained by the "heroic idea of work," Pascal dies at his desk. Sandoz, the generous, fer-

tile writer in *L'œuvre,* is another, though less dramatic, self-portrait, whose primary function is to provide Zola's "healthy" views on art as contrasted with Claude Lantier's fatal obsession with beauty unattainable. Centering on the artist's demonic struggle with the angel, filled with theoretical digressions on art, *L'œuvre* takes its place in the tradition of the artist's novel that runs from Balzac to Romain Rolland and Proust. It is to a large extent an echo to Balzac's *Chef-d'œuvre inconnu* and an answer to the Goncourts' *Manette Salomon.* But although Zola succeeds in contrasting Lantier's diseased passion for art with Sandoz' redeeming passion for life, the treatment of the intellectual themes is here also strangely blurred. Sandoz and Lantier represent two different *physiologies,* never the two conflicting poles of a single consciousness. Even Lantier's own grandeur and decadence remain strangely out of focus, for it is never clear whether his anguish and defeat are the result of a Promethean quest for absolutes which drives him to madness and suicide in the best Romantic tradition, or merely—as Zola repeatedly suggests—the price he must pay for his heredity. Thus Zola (perhaps because his theories were at odds with his deeper nature) never truly exploited the drama of the mind. For it is one thing to glorify, and another to dramatize. In spite of the latent themes in *L'œuvre* and in *Le docteur Pascal,* Zola has not succeeded, it would seem, in paying more than lip service to the tragedy of thinking, doubting, or creating.

The case of Marc Froment, in *Vérité,* is conclusive. Surely, Zola has not been sparing in his use of epithets and in his attempts to magnify the figure of his hero. He has in fact rarely been so prodigal with the terms *hero, heroism, heroic* and other laudatory expressions. Though Marc's family life is in danger, he silences this personal anguish with a "heroic effort." He accepts the struggle with a "brave gesture." At the height of the crisis, he shows an "admirable and valiant serenity" and continues teaching with "marvelous" spirit and integrity. He is an "unknown hero" who feels a deep "need for heroism." When victory is at long last achieved, he becomes a "patriarchal" grandfather and indulges in nostalgic reminiscences of the "heroic days." And yet, in spite of these ponderous efforts, in spite of a dramatic situation rich in possibilities and of his own personal involvement—Zola did not succeed in creating, as Bourget had done, a convincing drama of ideas. The moral crisis is merely stated. One finds here no inner conflict.

The sources of this failure must be traced ultimately to Zola's artistic temperament and to the peculiar limitations of his talent. But part of this failure is also self-willed. Zola was so afraid to describe a human being merely as an ambulatory thinking machine, he was so easily antagonized by what he considered the inhuman, arrogant depravity of the thinker, the very concept of the intellectual was in short so alien to him, that he devoted far more effort to "humanizing" Marc Froment than to bringing into sharp relief his supposed anguish. A modest pedagogue in a small provincial town, Marc had originally planned to become a printer. He is a husband, father, grandfather, and finally a venerable patriarch. Zola tirelessly underlines his simplicity, his modesty, his generosity of heart. But, paradoxically, this effort at humanization only waters down the portrait to the point where no psychological tension is possible. The very humanity of the character is obliterated by his exemplary qualities.

Yet Zola's flair for great subjects, which even a Barrès admired, brought him very close to a new theme: *the suffering of others.* It is easy enough to catalogue some of the glaring defects of the novel: clumsy transposition from fact to fancy, unnecessary repetitions, a coarse, unenlightened anti-clericalism, the naïveté of the beliefs. All this is obvious. The real pity, however, is that Zola did not exploit the drama of human solidarity he repeatedly broaches throughout the work. For Marc Froment is a characteristically "modern" hero in his refusal to pursue an exclusively private happiness, his conviction that he is responsible for all the pain and injustice that exist in the world, and his "religion of human solidarity" which is a more apostolic version of that *"fraternité douloureuse"* already experienced by Docteur Pascal. (pp. 68-79)

> Victor Brombert, "Emile Zola and Anatole France: The Lay Apostle and the Lay Saint," *in his* The Intellectual Hero: Studies in the French Novel, 1880-1955, *1961. Reprint by The University of Chicago Press, 1964, pp. 68-93.*

## Brian Nicholas    (essay date 1962)

[*In the following excerpt, Nicholas studies* L'assommoir *as a creative work in which Zola employed scientific documentation as material for his art, citing* L'assommoir *as an example of Zola's artistic achievement in which he delineates the character of Gervaise as the embodiment of her social milieu.*]

Public reaction to the French novel, especially in England, did not distinguish very clearly between the Flaubert of *Madame Bovary* and Zola. Though Zola was more often accused of open materialism both were seen as technically accomplished realists, whose moral attitudes ranged from the indifferent to the subversive. But, though Zola counted himself as Flaubert's artistic disciple, their relationship was tenuous, and the master more than once disclaimed him. The aims of the new 'naturalist' movement, which was being fathered upon him, seemed to him 'puerile' and 'monstrous'. Whereas Flaubert had used 'realism', documentation, only as a means to aesthetic ends, Zola's purpose was that of the dramatic reporter and investigator; while Flaubert was pursuing beauty, Zola, so it seemed, was pursuing scientific truth.

It is not difficult to see what Flaubert objected to in the naturalist programme, or how remote it seemed from his own. The great "Rougon-Macquart" series, to which *L'assommoir* belongs, has as its sub-title 'Histoire naturelle et sociale d'une famille sous le Second Empire'. Its declared purpose was nothing less than a scientific anatomy of a corrupt society, in which social criticism would be combined with the illustration, through several generations, of the complex, topical, but still very dubious 'laws' of heredity and environment. It would be difficult to exaggerate the pretentiousness of theoretical naturalism. Literature was to become a branch of science, a principal agent

of positivism. Taine's dictum that virtue and vice were mere products, like sugar and vitriol, was to be taken up for examination and illustration; the Goncourts, though on the aesthetic wing of the movement, described their novel *Germinie Lacerteux* as a pathological experiment—'la clinique de l'amour'. The claim was everywhere implicit that the novelist was going to become an actual assistant of the doctor and the chemist, not a mere publicist or beneficiary of their findings. The obvious objection—that the novelist can only 'discover' in the behaviour of his characters what he has put there himself—was blandly ignored. The results of the method, applied in its purest form, are almost always artistic failure. Germinie and Zola's early heroines, Thérèse Raquin and Madeleine Férat, are all, in varying degrees, physiological monsters, their actions shored up or explained away at every point with scientific and medical commentary. They lack even the semblance of freedom which the fictional character requires in order to come to life.

But there is another side to Zola's choice of programme for his life's work; whatever his public pronouncements on the subject, all the evidence points to a more reassuring fact—that it was made with a strong sense of artistic expediency. The hereditarily depraved family represented neither an intellectual certainty nor the impulsions of a personal moral vision; rather it acted as a starting point (and something of a cover) for the radical commentator's portrayal of a decadent society. Zola remarks very calmly in his preliminary notes for the series that he must choose a 'tendency' in order to hold his work together, and that 'materialism would probably be the best' for his particular aims and talents. In short an avowed weakness in psychological invention and discrimination led Zola to the choice of violent and rough-hewn characters; and the inclinations of the impressionist, the poet of humanity in the mass, presided at the conception of his novels rather than any doctrinaire scientism. Zola's most successful novels are those where the individual is less important than the society, and can be seen primarily as a product of it. It is in the panoramas of working-class life that the liberal observer can feel at his most secure. Here materialism can be implicit, without being dogmatic or restrictive; in depicting a homogeneous, highly-conditioned society of victims he can stop well short of examining the individual conscience, without implying that it does not, or at least could not, exist. Thus ***Germinal*** has no character who is studied in his own right; it is concerned with individuals only in so far as they contribute to a portrait of the society. The structure of the novel declares this preoccupation. It starts with a long evocation of the mining country, seen through the eyes of a newcomer; and the action which follows is largely amplification, we are taken closer to the picture and shown the details. There is *variety* in the characters, but no concern for moral appraisal; in that what there is to condone appears to be condoned, and what virtue and humanity survive under such appalling conditions are held up for our wonder rather than for our admiration.

Essentially the world of ***L'assommoir*** is the same sort of homogeneous, impressionistically conceived world as that of ***Germinal.*** Though it follows out the fate of a single character, Gervaise is not the tragic heroine chosen and

*Photograph of Jeanne Rozerot, Zola's mistress and mother of his two children, taken by Zola in the countryside near Verneuil.*

set in action because she embodies some particular vision of human destiny or human nature. She is followed because she is illustrative not so much of a human or cosmic as of a social truth. She is not a tragic victim, but a casualty, in a particular milieu where the casualty rate is high. Given the world as it appears in *L'assommoir,* we can imagine other accounts of the same field of events, taking other characters as their centre, which would be equally valid for making Zola's point, if less interesting and efficient. Gervaise's is only one of the disasters that take place in *L'assommoir,* all of them of the same 'status'; she is an example of what is happening, less tellingly, all over the novel. The point being made is a general sociological one, Gervaise is chosen to give it undogmatic illustration. And the manner in which this is done represents perhaps the only successful conversion of the naturalist idea of 'scientific' study of the individual fate to effective creative purpose. The Goncourts' story of Germinie Lacerteux, which profoundly influenced Zola, had attempted a complete and systematic exculpation, and had inevitably foundered in medical terminology and other forms of pleading inimical to the novel. Zola is not concerned with excusing the individual or examining the question of freedom, only with dramatizing and making irrefutable a relationship—the interdependence of the individual with the forces which play on him in a particular situation. By compari-

son with *Germinal, L'assommoir* is a fragmentary and unsystematic plea for moral relativism. Gervaise is not documented from birth to death but is introduced to us already deeply implicated in life, the victim of a violent and unhappy home and mother of two children by the age of eighteen; she is a reclaimed drinker, capable of hard work, but easy-going and a lover of pleasure. Zola sets her down to enact her fate in a society—the working world of Paris—which has precisely her own tendencies. The novel can thus succeed because it has no case to establish, no exact apportioning of responsibilities to perform. This undogmatic quality allows it to produce not a scientific account but a vast and detailed working out of a sociological proposition which is also, in this case, an uncontroversial moral tautology. (pp. 63-6)

The first presentation of Gervaise offers a dual and inconclusive image. Though her personal fortunes are at their lowest ebb she is by no means abandoned to despair. Her routine acceptance of misfortune, her unreflecting pursuit of her daily tasks, her physical strength and courage—all these give an impression of resilience. But at the same time we see, in suggestive impressionistic terms, that dwarfing of the individual which is to be the theme of the novel. As Gervaise waits for Lantier to come home she looks down on a sight still relatively new to her—the vast flow of workers trooping from the faubourgs into Paris; and already, in the tableau of her isolated silhouette against the unknown crowd, we get the sense of the individual only just succeeding in remaining distinct in the larger flux of life. That impression is strengthened by the ensuing scene of the fight in the wash-house, which, while it emphasizes Gervaise's courage, also prefigures much of what is to follow—with its overripe atmosphere, its vulgarity and raucousness, its incidental personal struggle overshadowed by the more permanent reality of the machine, suggesting here the grinding routine of everyday life, the basic communal struggle against dirt. As Gervaise trudges back to her room, 'derrière elle le lavoir reprenait son bruit énorme d'écluse' ('behind her the wash-house returned to its huge monotonous noise, as of a rushing weir'), and as she looks out again on the street she feels a dull fear at the sight of the two landmarks which seem to bound her life— the abattoir and the hospital. The first day recounted establishes an image of Gervaise's fate—it is a buoyant, unreflecting sortie against life, whose symbols, however, are threateningly and incontrovertibly evoked.

The dual image of the contender for mastery and the potential victim is reinforced, and remains unresolved, in the following episodes, which, while they advance the action, repeat the structural pattern. Thus in the second chapter a 'new start' seems to have been made. The lyrical enlargement on which the previous episode closed seems to have been discounted, and with no reference to intervening hardships we have the almost idyllic scene of Gervaise and Coupeau sitting in the *assommoir* together; she now has a job, and Coupeau wants to marry her. But again the scene widens out so that the precarious security of the individual is threatened. As Gervaise prepares to involve herself with Coupeau so the implications of that involvement are impressionistically suggested by a further evocation of the constituents of 'life'. The couple sit, significantly, only just inside the sinister dram-shop, enjoying its most harmless commodity, a plum steeped in brandy; the room is almost empty. But as the lunch hour approaches the crowds flood back—'c'était un envahissement du trottoir, des ruisseaux, de la chaussée'—and the neatly contained idyll is disturbed by the arrival of Coupeau's boisterous workmates, who have come for the stronger products of the silent distilling machine at the back of the bar. As the atmosphere thickens Gervaise has to go outside to breathe. The picture of the milieu, its pressures and oppressiveness, fills out further, after the marriage has been decided, with the visit to Coupeau's relatives in the vast, pullulating tenement-house, which we see through Gervaise's eyes, and which she feels as something bearing down on her physically, ' écrasante, glaciale à ses épaules'. This time, however, she herself discounts her fears as childishness—'c'était toujours sa bête de peur, un enfantillage dont elle souriait ensuite'. We concur in the rejection of fatalism, while retaining the indication of sociological probabilities.

That rejection is apparently confirmed with the beginning of the next episode—the marriage day. We are back in the world of autonomy, the forward-looking world of routine planning: 'Gervaise ne voulait pas de noce. A quoi bon dépenser de l'argent?' While the scene is essentially pictorial, the description of a characteristic working-class celebra-

tion, it is also functional, its structure again moving from the contained, purposeful opening to a wider prospect weighted with threats of invasion and disaster. The dinner is the sort of scrappy festivity, with bad service, mediocre food, squabbles about the bill, which would probably be looked back on as a notable family event. But in spite of Gervaise and Coupeau some of the men start drinking and quarrelling; the party disintegrates in bad humour; and when the couple go out into the streets they are caught up in the drunken uproar of Saturday night. The episode closes on the encounter with the drunken undertaker's assistant, Bazouge, whose lugubrious imprecations frighten Gervaise and spoil for her a whole day of quiet pleasure. Again in terms at once realistic and discreetly symbolic individual enterprise is confronted with the larger and less manageable flux of life.

The opening episodes establish the pattern of action of the whole novel. Gervaise's career is not a regular curve of success and failure, but a series of discontinuous and uncoordinated sallies against life; and her buoyancy depends in a large measure on her inability to make a synthesis, an assessment of probabilities. Thus the threatening image of the slum-house is subsequently discounted, and Gervaise brought over to Coupeau's own cheerful optimism—their greatest wish, we are told without any corrective explanation, was to get a room there. Though the fortunes of the family rise substantially the imagery remains of involvement rather than ascendancy. Indeed the normal line of the success and failure story is deliberately broken: Coupeau's accident precedes the leasing of the shop, and he is already a drinker and waster by the time the laundry establishes a moderate success. When she enters on the lease Gervaise feels she is throwing herself 'au beau milieu d'une machine en branle'; and the image is apposite. Life had threatened from outside; Gervaise, by her very enterprise, draws it closer around her. The alternation of hard work and indulgence, the constant gossip, the stench of clothes and the fumes of the stove, all these work a destructive effect on her will. The laundry, in fact, is only a variant of the *assommoir,* both toxic and anaesthetizing in its effect; Coupeau and Gervaise succumb to the composite fumes of the *quartier,* 'l'air de Paris, où il y a une vraie fumée d'eau de vie et de vin'.

There is much more to **L'assommoir** than the impressionistic outline, and we shall have to return to its detailed portrayal of relations, to the way in which it gives 'life' a more precise definition. But the recurrent, uncommented pattern of enterprise and engulfment, autonomy and invasion, is what gives meaning to, and makes acceptable, the positive steps in Gervaise's downfall. If we examine the presentation of her yielding to Lantier and her return to drinking spirits, we find that each occurs at the end of an episode (and at the end of a day), under conditions of fatigue and pressure amounting almost to physical vertigo. And each is superseded, and as it were ignored, by a return to the world of the practical—in the first case Maman Coupeau's illness and death, in the second the question of Nana's future. The inexorable recurrence of the pattern seems to level out the significance of the individual features, to make them mere variants, outward and not in themselves very momentous signs, of another less personal process. That process could be called organic decay. Gervaise is not seen as an individual with an unbroken moral consciousness, but rather as a willing machine, constantly restarting and redirecting itself, but gradually running down, getting worn out. 'Worn out', indeed, is the definition she finds for herself—'oui, Coupeau et Lantier l'*usaient*, c'était le mot'. For Gervaise the demands of living are so urgent that events are easily assimilated, positions hastily improvised; as action squeezes out awareness, degradation consolidates its hold, almost unfelt. The adequacy of such an account from the moral point of view remains to be discussed; from the point of view of artistic strategy we may note that it is precisely the vitality and sense of freedom which Zola gives his characters that allows him to enforce a materialistic pattern in which moral questions cease to be asked.

Since the later part of the novel relates an obviously irreversible decline it is not without its *longueurs*. But by following up the long chapter devoted to Nana we can see how the structure continues to be exploited both to animate and to neutralize the scene, to give it life and to establish a framework in which the consciences of the characters have diminished significance. At the end of the previous chapter Gervaise's return to drink had reduced her finally to Coupeau's own state of moral insignificance. We now turn to another part of the scene, where life is proceeding normally:

> Nana grandissait, devenait garce. . . . Oui, c'était ça, quinze ans, toutes ses dents et pas de corset. . . .

Nana's activities are not recounted merely in the interests of the novel series, in order to form a transition to the work that bears her name; their significance lies in the reactions they provoke in her parents. For Gervaise and Coupeau exercise the severest moral authority on her at a time when they themselves have forfeited all right to respect. But the account of their accompanying Nana to the workshop and making elaborate arrangements for her surveillance is related without irony. We do not feel the moralist's comparative intention; there is no attempt to use Nana's conduct in order finally to appraise Gervaise's, and Gervaise herself cannot be recalled to an appraisal of her own position. When she openly accuses Nana of selling herself she is stunned by her daughter's retaliation—'tu as fait ce que tu as voulu, je fais ce que je veux'—and her reaction is purely physical: 'Gervaise restait toute pâle, les mains tremblantes, sans savoir ce qu'elle faisait'. And later, when the household have become resigned to Nana's delinquencies Gervaise still makes a moral restriction—Nana can do what she likes, but she musn't come home dressed in fine clothes, 'qu'elle s'habillât au moins comme une ouvrière doit s'habiller' ('she must dress at least in a way fitting for a worker'). Their attitude towards Nana is not so much a revival or survival of the Coupeaus' old *honnêteté*, as a sign of the fact that they have not fully registered their own decline. Certainly it is not conscious self-defence. In a sense they approach this episode with the same self-confidence as they have previous phases of their life. But we feel that this moral activity is growing more and more ritual and meaningless. Indeed Zola, in these last episodes, engages the reader in the same way that

Flaubert engages us in Emma's death: his narrative, having finally categorized the characters, treats them without irony; and we give a sort of numb attention to the detail of what we know to be moral nullities. The Nana episode finally shows the interplay of character, moral conflict, the survival of virtue and conscience, as miniature and automatic features within a wider and more impersonal process. Reminders of the workings of that process may evoke sentiment, but not invite moral reflection. Thus, the precise feelings of Gervaise for Coupeau in the last stages are not investigated; but we are told that when she goes to see him in the asylum she buys a couple of oranges at the door, so as not to go in empty-handed. There is a touch of pathos in the survival of an ingrained working-class habit. But the pathos arises from a spectacle of unresolved status; it is not determined by a consideration of the state of mind of the character. Our reaction is not moral or evaluative; for this is less goodness combating life, than habit ignoring it. Gervaise's very decency is a sort of independent mechanism, a token of how little she has made a synthesis of events, of how much more powerful life is than she to control or keep up with or analyse it.

The structure of the novel, then, suggests a Gervaise acting with only apparent purposefulness inside a larger pattern of pressures and probabilities visible to the sociological observer; and eventually within a process of decay visible to all, but only sporadically to herself. But our analysis so far may have suggested a rather vague and selective impressionism, concerned to distract moral judgment in order to impose a more poetic, humanitarian interpretation of the facts. This, however, would be a completely misleading description of the texture of *L'assommoir*. If Zola places his heroine in a wider perspective, the other characters of the novel subject her to myopic scrutiny. In few other novels do we have such a continuous impression of a life lived in the public gaze, wholly composed of fluid social relations, the subject of unrelenting moral comment and speculation. And, to see how this 'close-up' view of Gervaise both fills out and confirms the broader outline, we must turn to what is perhaps the most distinctive feature of *L'assommoir*—its narrative technique.

The narrative technique, like the structure, has been widely noticed; and it brought Zola criticism from two opposing quarters. While a conservative public objected to the idiom on grounds of brutality and obscenity, Flaubert regarded the style as an artistic aberration. Zola, he said, thought that there were 'strong' words in the same way that the salon blue-stockings of the seventeenth century thought there were 'noble' ones. Zola's general apology, contained in his preface to the novel, was that he had been engaged on a scientific enterprise, 'un travail purement philologique'; in a novel about the people he had to use the language of the people. The argument, however, never went beyond a superficial level of moral and artistic propriety. As in all questions of style much larger issues are involved—and in this case the whole sense of the novel. The nature of the vocabulary is less important than the way in which it is used. For it is not only in the reporting of direct speech that the popular idiom is reproduced; it spreads to, and substantially takes over, the whole narration.

Two pairs of brief quotations, from the beginning and the later part of the novel, will serve to introduce a discussion of the style. The first pair involve Gervaise and her family. At the very beginning of the story Gervaise and her children are waiting for Lantier. . . .

> The two children were fast asleep, with their heads on the same pillow. Claude, who was eight years old, drew in long breaths, his little hands outside the quilt, while Etienne, who was only four, smiled in his sleep, one arm round the neck of his brother. As the mother's tear-filled glance rested on the children she burst out sobbing afresh, then pressed a handkerchief to her mouth to stifle the little sobs that she could not keep down. And barefooted as she was, without thinking of putting on her slippers again, she went back to her post at the window. . . .

In the period of their decline the Coupeaus' relations with their daughter Nana are described as follows. . . .

> Her parents had had to get used to it. The hidings she got made no difference to her. They gave her a good drubbing, but that did not prevent her from making use of their lodgings as a sort of inn, where one could put up by the week. She knew that she would have to pay for her bed by a thrashing, and she came and took her thrashing, when there was anything to be gained by it. And then, you get tired of dealing blows. . . . She came in or she didn't come in; as long as she didn't leave the door open it was all right. Good heavens, decency, like anything else, wears out in time.

The second pair are descriptions of slum lodgings, respectively the room in which Gervaise had lived with Lantier and the attic to which the Coupeaus move after the ruin of the laundry. . . .

> And slowly, her eyes clouded with tears, she looked all round the wretched little lodging-house room, with its walnut chest of drawers in which one of the drawers was wanting, its three cane-bottom chairs, and its greasy little table on which stood a delapidated water jug. They had put in an iron bedstead for the children, which filled up two thirds of the room and blocked up the chest of drawers as well. Gervaise and Lantier's trunk, wide open in the corner, stretched out its empty sides. . . .

> Then, over against Bazouge, was the Coupeaus', a room and a little room looking on the court. . . . One room and a little room, that was all. The Coupeaus had to perch there now. And the larger of the two rooms was a mere handbreadth. Everything had to be done in it. You had to sleep, eat, and all the rest. In the little room there was just space enough for Nana's bed . . . and they left the door open at night so that she shouldn't suffocate. . . . The bed, the table, four chairs; the place was quite full.

What is striking in each case is not so much the change in what is described as the change in narrative standpoint, one might almost say in the very identity of the narrator. The earlier passages are serious and objective, perhaps even with a tendency to sentiment, the later are familiar, confidential, even amused, with no sense of tragedy and a certain moral nonchalance. The transition is significant. Clearly the events of ***L'assommoir*** are not, for the most part, directly related and interpreted by the author as omniscient observer. Nor, on the other hand, do we have a purely 'dramatic' presentation, narrated by identifiable observers distinct from the author. A novel could, of course, be put together in this latter way, as a traveller might piece together recordings from a distant tribe, not in order to distinguish its individual members but to chart its beliefs and moral standards. Such a novel would in fact imitate the anthropological documentary in being willingly removed from concerns of evaluative morality. But our impression of ***L'assommoir*** is of something more serious and more authoritative. Just as the structure shows the individual in a wider perspective of social and physical pressures, so the narrative form actually illustrates the proposition that the relative judgment is the only meaningful one. We are not just set down in the *assommoir* world to listen to the local gossip. Rather the start is in the manner of objective narration: Gervaise is the unknown heroine of a new environment, held up for our inspection and whom, it seems, we are to follow and appraise. When she has her fight in the wash-house it is remarked that she is at a disadvantage in the battle of insults, 'n'ayant pas encore le coup de gosier de Paris' ('she had not got into the Paris way of slanging'). But the burden of what follows is that she becomes so much a conditioned part of her milieu that she can only properly be described in its own colloquial terms. We get not appraisal, but the impression of a forced withdrawal from the attempt at appraisal; we witness a gradual retreat by the novelist, a handing over of his role to a succession of appropriate narrators. The novel is a dramatized admission, and demonstration, of the impossibility of an absolute moral judgment.

The stages of this process, and its precise effect on the reader, are difficult to illustrate in detail; only the broad outline can be indicated. Though the narrative begins in conventional descriptive manner, characterization is from the first built on and limited to the observable; there is no 'inside' information on Gervaise, no authoritative comment. Our picture of her is built up solely through the reactions and opinions she provokes. She is, we gradually learn from her own revelations, already deeply compromised with life; but she is primarily the newcomer to a society, about to make a new start. And it is a society for whom character is equated with performance, whose moral judgments are avowedly discontinuous, continually remodelled in the pattern of experience, expediency and oblivion. As Coupeau says when he strikes up the friendship with Lantier—if one kept grudges for nine or ten years one would end up by not talking to anybody. And as her world does not seek final moral realities, so Gervaise herself willingly disclaims any permanent moral growth—'l'expérience l'avait corrigée un peu, voilà tout'. The novel thus establishes itself as working legitimately in the realm of the provisional. For Coupeau Gervaise is 'joliment courageuse' in her struggle; after their marriage the couple become popular 'à cause de leur gentillesse'; and admiration for Gervaise increases when she insists on nursing Coupeau after his fall—'elle boitait, mais elle avait du chien' ('she limped, it was true, but she had guts'). Her faults too, as her prosperity increases, are noted, but generally excused. . . .

> She was getting fond of good things to eat; on that everyone agreed, but it was not a bad fault, quite the contrary. When you have the income to pay for delicacies it would be silly indeed to eat potato peel.

This last judgment already points to the relative quality of Gervaise's virtue, the way in which her popularity tells us as much about her society as about herself. But a more definitive judgment does not seem to be precluded. In general the early characterization, though fragmentary and speculative, seems at any rate to admit the possibility of a synthesis, of a final portrait. The various views of her are in general clearly attributed, and—even when incorporated in it as indirect speech—remain distinct from the objective narrative. We are invited to assess their validity, to continue our *own* work of appraisal.

But quite early the distinction between narrative and reported opinion begins to be blurred. Thus maxims of common currency begin to appear in the text, without any obvious attribution. When the numbers for the wedding feast are fixed at fifteen the decision is approved by the observation that 'quand on est trop de monde, ça se termine toujours par des disputes'. Goujet's temperance is approved, but so is his refusal to condemn wine, 'car le vin est l'ami de l'ouvrier'. It is in the framework of this proverbial wisdom, the expression of a philosophy by turns realistic and fatalistic, sceptical and superstitious, moralizing and indulgent, that Gervaise's conduct is recounted and that her moral status comes to be gauged. The narrative viewpoint itself is getting imperceptibly closer, becoming inextricably identified with a sort of composite local opinion. In consequence, from being someone whom we are to judge *in the light of* her society's judgments, Gervaise becomes more and more a manifestation of that society, a factor in *its* characterization, a sounding-board for *its* scale of values and reactions. Not, however, exclusively: Zola's achievement is so to have evoked the homogeneity of the milieu, the necessary conditioning of all its inhabitants, that we also recognize these judgments as the only possibly valid ones; they are the nearest we can get to a true perspective. Thus we have the impression of a sharp authoritative focusing of Gervaise, the feeling that Zola has delegated the narration to the only competent observers; yet every judgment points back to the society making it, we watch the judges watching and are made conscious that judge and defendant are part of a larger organism, which is being 'studied' disinterestedly from above.

By the time the Coupeaus take their most controversial moral step—the setting up of the *ménage à trois* with Lantier—the status of the narrative has shifted to that of an anonymous, almost uniformly colloquial commentary. And the comments themselves are inconclusive, precisely because Gervaise's fate is so familiar, so typical of her world, that, though its mechanics can be endlessly annotated, judgment invariably trails off into the relative and the comparative. . . .

> All that, however you took it, hardly seemed the

thing; but there are so many unpleasant things in life, and much worse than that, that the neighbours came to look on the *ménage a trois* as quite natural, quite decent even. For there were no quarrels, and propriety was never outraged. Certainly, if you were to pry into other houses in the neighbourhood, you would get some much nastier shocks.

As the Coupeaus' decline continues judgment may get more severe, but its expression remains reluctant, the nature of its comparisons tendentious. . . .

> No doubt the Coupeaus had only themselves to blame. However hard life may be you can always make your way, with order and economy, like the Lorilleux for instance, who sent in their quarter's rent punctually, folded in bits of dirty paper; but then, the Lorilleux lived like starved spiders—enough to disgust you with work.

A last recapitulation seems to place the blame finally on the Coupeaus and to reject their fatalistic excuses. . . .

> Yes, it was their own fault, no doubt, if they went on from bad to worse. But people don't say those things, especially when they are on their beam-ends. They declared it was their bad luck, that God had it in for them. They kicked up a regular shindy now, indoors.

But the tone of this only serves to mark a final shift in the narrative viewpoint—from inconclusive criticism to acceptance. The Coupeaus' fall loses even its blurred moral contours, and ceases to engage the sustained interest of the *quartier;* not only for us but for them the Coupeaus become intractable to moral comment. They become, rather, local phenomena, an accepted part of the landscape, like the recumbent drunks whom the inhabitants step unthinkingly across on the pavements. They are regrettable, picturesque, sometimes pathetic, but their case is well-known and requires no explanation. The moral 'fall' moves into perspective as a striking case of the familiar social 'downfall' (*dégringolade*)—'enfin un plongeon complet'. The narrative gives up even its sporadic attempts at analysis; as the course of the action becomes more disastrous the account of it becomes, on the whole, coarser, more superficial, more familiar, more garrulous; the tone is by turns resigned, head-shaking, amused, deprecating. Now that they have been categorized the Coupeaus' behaviour is readily explicable, it is allusively referred to popular 'laws'. 'Natural' and 'naturellement' become the recurrent explanatory terms: 'Naturellement on ne peut pas nocer et travailler'; 'naturellement, à measure que la misère et la paresse entraient, la malpropreté entrait aussi'; 'naturellement, lorsqu'on se décatit à ce point, tout l'orgueil de la femme s'en va'. In the same way Lantier's progress is followed with amusement and without surprise—'enfin il n'y a que les hommes de cette espéce qui aient de la chance'—his sort have all the luck. Nana's flight causes as little impression—'dans la maison où chaque mois des filles s'envolaient comme des serins . . . l'accident des Coupeau n'étonna personne' ('in the house, from which girls flew off every month like canaries, the Coupeaus' misfortune surprised no one'). Eventually the Coupeaus become, in another characteristic phrase, something 'qu'il fallait voir'—which you ought to have seen; Gervaise's imitation of Coupeau's delirium becomes, in her last days 'une des curiosités de la maison'. So, when Bazouge finally comes to collect her, we remember that when he was summoned at the time of Maman Coupeau's death he thought, for no particular reason, that it was for Gervaise. Reasonably; for Gervaise's fate is only a foreground feature in a picture littered with death and misery—she follows Maman Coupeau, Mme Bijard, Mme Goujet, Lalie, Coupeau and Père Bru.

The insistence on naturalness alternates with other responses equally remote from moral adjudication. Thus turns in the Coupeaus' fortunes are frequently introduced by the words 'heureusement' and 'malheureusement', which suggest not appraisal but a sort of unreasoned, *ad hoc* sympathy, the subdued encouragement accorded to the losing side. Or else statements are introduced with phrases such as 'il faut dire que', 'le pis était que', 'le plus triste était', 'la vérité était', 'à la vérité'. These do not, of course, introduce the author's interpretations or corrections; indeed their recurrence suggests almost a parody of the definitive narration. Rather they are the glosses of a somewhat knowing raconteur, prompted in his reminiscences to attempt to organize and estimate what he is describing: 'Gervaise appelait ça la paillasse; mais à la vérité ça n'était qu'un tas de paille dans le coin' ('Gervaise called it the mattress, but really it was only a pile of straw in the corner'). The very casualness and lack of vindictiveness of the comment makes it not an arresting pointer to the state of Gervaise's consciousness, but another token of the pathetic ordinariness of the situation. To have sold the bed is 'natural', to refuse to admit it equally so—'ce sont des choses qu'on ne dit pas, surtout quand on est dans la crotte'.

But the growing 'frivolity' of the account can only be appropriate provided that there is no suggestion that it conceals or distorts reality, that there is a 'real' Gervaise behind the seen one whose moral life would require a more serious account. Otherwise the narrative technique would be openly seen as an evasive trick to avoid facing the moral issue. In fact, however, the sardonic narrative corresponds exactly to an increasing coarseness, a decaying awareness, on the part of the characters themselves. And the expression of that correspondence finally secures Gervaise from the focus of an outside moral judgment. Not only does narrative progressively merge with local opinion; ultimately, in certain key passages, it becomes difficult to distinguish the character's reactions from the comments of the observer. When Gervaise goes to see Coupeau in the padded cell the account seems partly to reproduce her own bewildered but unsentimental impressions. But we also feel the presence of the local narrator, looking for words to describe a situation which is by no means a rarity but which one does not often see close up—'Oh! les dames enceintes faisaient bien de rester dehors! . . . un drôle de démolition quand même, s'en aller en se tordant, comme une fille à qui les chatouilles font de l'effet' ('Oh! it was well that women with child were not there to see! . . . a funny way to break down, wriggling about like that, like a girl who is ticklish'). The overlapping, and substantial identity, of the reactions of actor and narrator is such that

Gervaise's feelings are not and cannot be examined for their dignity or adequacy; they are merged with those of her world, they acquire the atoning seal of typicality. Or rather we could say that the view of Gervaise has become so close-up that the possibility of a critical focusing is denied. Having moved nearer out of a scruple for justice, a respect for the relative context, the narrative standpoint is reduced to a mere acquiescence in the facts; the distance necessary for judgment has been whittled away to nothing.

By the same token Gervaise forfeits the claim to personal tragic stature. While tragedy must concern itself to a point with the consciousness of its characters, must assess their own view of their predicament, *L'assommoir* is the story of a decaying, rather than an errant or a suffering conscience. Gervaise is only fitfully aware of her own degradation, for long periods her reactions are blunted and trivial. The final literary advantage of the narrative technique is that, relieved of the necessity of offering events for possible tragic interpretation, it can remain piquant and exhilarating in disaster. Coupeau's drinking bouts with 'ce farceur de Mes-Bottes', 'cet animal Lantier' grown fat off the two shops he has ruined, Nana's drift into prostitution, all these are the objects of racy comic observation. But the possibility of pathos is not thereby excluded. Gervaise's pathos, however, belongs strictly to her lucid intervals of reflection and reminiscence—notably in the finely sustained scene where she is reduced to soliciting; and here, quite appropriately, the narrator is, as it were, sobered into respect. But, with equal propriety, there is no attempt to make the whole cohere into a tragic portrait, because there is no continuous moral consciousness in the subject. The change of tone is no more than a change of expression on the face of the familiar spectator, to whom all is within the field of the natural, who is ready to respond to the phenomena in all their variations.

By his manner of presentation Zola avoids either judging the Coupeaus or fitting them into a dogmatic scheme of necessity. The former would infringe his theoretical, the latter destroy his artistic pretensions. It is significant that 'natural', the keyword of the movement which Zola founded, is here exploited in its colloquial, not its scientific acceptation. The Coupeaus' fate is seen as natural not in a deterministic sense, but in the light of experience, almost even of statistics. They are neither judged nor excused; they are imperceptibly demoted from the status of individual moral beings to that of sociological specimens. And if the stages of the process are elusive and discontinuous this only reinforces the realism of the account. It is remarked at one point that it is no longer any use treating Coupeau as a 'père sans moralité' since drink has taken away from him 'toute conscience du bien et du mal'. And this only states a fact of which we have been becoming increasingly aware as we read. There is in 'real life' a point at which the alcoholic, the criminal or the social wreck ceases to interest the moralist and engages the doctor or the sociologist; and the impossibility of fixing that point does not make the transition from one state to the other any less real; nor need it raise the problem of freedom. Zola has not explicitly denied the existence of the moral world; he has merely dramatized the transition.

A dramatized transition—perhaps the force of the drama has failed to come over in the rather technical discussion to which Zola's own very calculated methods have led us. It may act as some sort of corrective to introduce the final part of our discussion with a fairly detailed account of one of the most famous 'set-pieces' of the novel—Gervaise's birthday feast, which occupies the whole of the central chapter. In addition to being one of Zola's most vigorous pieces of description it illustrates better than any other scene the rigorous subordination of the pictorial to the functional, and provides material for a final and more precise definition of Gervaise's fate at the hands of 'life'.

Though the birthday feast represents Gervaise's moment of triumph in the *quartier* it is in no sense the high point of a continuous curve of happiness and prosperity. The previous chapter had faded on a note of despair and disintegration, with Gervaise's discovery that Coupeau is drinking brandy—'alors elle resta toute froide; elle pensait à son mari, à Goujet, à Lantier, désespérant d'être jamais heureuse'.

The birthday episode starts, as usual, in the unreflecting world of the practical: 'La fête de Gervaise tombait le 19 juin.' And the fame of the Coupeaus' parties, from which one came away 'ronds comme des balles' is condoned by the amused colloquial narrative. There is also explicit moral approval from Virginie. . . .

> When a man drinks all you have it's fool's labour to let everything run away in drink, and not fill your own stomach first.

The prospect of the feast provides an effective basis for a social *entente*. The Lorilleux agree to a reconciliation, the Boches make their peace, Maman Coupeau is good-natured and co-operative—'l'idée de la fête attendrissait tous les coeurs'. Gervaise's generosity answers a 'sacrée envie de nocer' in the whole society; her popularity is a function of its own philosophy of life. And on Gervaise's side good-nature is complemented by a desire for revenge—the Lorilleux are to be readmitted, but they are also to be 'écrasés', put to shame by the splendour of the feast. In this Maman Coupeau is Gervaise's willing accomplice, and an undercurrent of malice sustains their solidarity during the preparations.

But as soon as these start they are overshadowed by threats of disruption: Virginie reports that Lantier has reappeared in the district. Gervaise's reaction is of fatalistic self-pity. . . .

> What did the wretched man want of her? And just now, when she was in the midst of the preparations for the party; she had never had any luck; she couldn't even have a little pleasure in peace.

Another incident loaded with significance, but to which Gervaise makes the stock reaction of indignation and self-pity, is the arrival of an irate customer demanding her washing. Gervaise pretends they are closed to clean the shop. . . .

> As soon as she had gone, Gervaise burst out into abusive language. If you listened to your customers, sure enough you would never have time

to eat a mouthful; you would slave out your very life for their precious sakes! One wasn't a dog on a leash, was one?

She plunges back with renewed enthusiasm into the preparations. When they run out of money Gervaise cannot think what to do; the pawnshop has not been mentioned since the first scene of the novel, and Maman Coupeau is the first to suggest it. Gervaise laughs at herself for not thinking of it, and even calls Maman Coupeau back to give her her wedding ring. . . .

> And when Maman Coupeau had brought back the twenty-five francs she danced for joy. She would buy six bottles of vintage wine . . . the Lorilleux would be squashed flat.

Encouraged by this prospect they complete the preparations; and the party begins with an almost ritual procession of tribute to Gervaise as the guests arrive with their potted plants. The reconciliation with the Lorilleux is ceremoniously carried out, but they have not brought any flowers, and the party spirit does not prevent Gervaise and Maman Coupeau from eagerly watching their reactions to the magnificently laid table, and making pained reflections on the existence of such people. But it is the Lorilleux who are finally condemned in an anonymous comment, which sees their resentment, characteristically, as 'natural', but blames their lack of self-restraint. . . .

> No one, certainly, likes being taken down a peg; and in a family especially, when one succeeds, the others are furious, it's natural enough. Only one keeps it in, one doesn't display it for everyone to see.

The dinner is now ready, but again disaster threatens. Coupeau is missing, and when Gervaise, Virginie and Goujet go to look for him, they see Lantier in a restaurant. When they find Coupeau in the *assommoir* he makes a scene, refusing to be fetched home by women; and when they finally get him out he too sees Lantier and accuses Gervaise of going out specially to attract him. And, though he calms down, the party returns less gaily than it had set out.

Gervaise's fatalistic premonitions receive further support when she finds that there are thirteen people at the table. Seeing a convenient remedy to an urgent situation she calls in from the street Père Bru, the destitute old housepainter who often comes to warm himself by her stove. Not only are their numbers made up, but they can now overeat with a good conscience. The gesture receives sentimental approbation. . . .

> Goujet's eyes filled with tears, he was so touched. The others too were moved, thought she had done very well. . . .

For us, Gervaise's spontaneous good nature, without being appraised, is firmly linked with the superstition and self-indulgence of her world.

The company's humour is restored, though Mme Lorilleux is not too pleased at being placed next to the grubby old worker. And another momentary annoyance, Coupeau's renewed disappearance, is swept away when he returns with a pot of flowers under each arm and embraces his wife: a touching moment which, however, is again placed firmly into naturalistic perspective by Clémence's comment. . . .

> 'Monsieur Coupeau's in good form tonight,' whispered Clémence in Boche's ear. 'He's had just enough to put him in good temper.'

The dinner can now begin; the past is for the moment forgotten, the future can be put out of mind. The door of the shop is closed to keep the neighbours from prying; and the establishment of harmony and domestic security is signalized by the eruption of a more healthy, everyday quarrel among the children; the courses succeed one another, the initial awkwardness of the guests wears off, the wine circulates freely. For a precarious moment they are at peace and safe from the world. They will remain safe only as long as the door is shut, life as it were excluded, the escapist moment judiciously prolonged. But before the giant goose is eaten the ladies complain of the heat, and Coupeau, who no longer cares what the neighbours think, throws open the door on to the street. Gervaise stuffs herself, but Goujet is still touched by her solicitude for old Bru—'dans sa gourmandise elle restait si gentille et si bonne'. The narration reflects the growing mood of harmony, vivacity and self-justification. . . .

> When you're at it, you're at it eh? . . . Why, you could see the corporations getting larger every minute. . . . With their mouths open and their chins bedabbled with grease, they had faces for all the world like backsides, and so red too that you would say they were rich people's belongings, rich people bursting with prosperity. . . . And the wine too, my friends, the wine flowed around the table as water flows in the Seine. . . . Devil take it all! the Jesuits might say what they like, the fruit of the vine was a famous fund all the same. . . . As if the workman, downtrodden, penniless, despised by the bourgeois as he was, had so much fun in his life that anyone had a right to complain if he got a bit boozed from time to time, for the sake of seeing things look rosy.

Even Goujet, normally so sober, is letting himself go; Poisson proposes a toast to Gervaise, and she is loudly acclaimed. In the meantime the feast has attracted the attention of the street; a good-natured crowd assembles, and the Coupeaus' triumph is only increased as they call out to their friends and toast the passers-by.

But the unreal security is already undermined. Eating has given way to singing, but as the company join in the choruses Virginie, who has been out reconnoitring, comes in to warn Gervaise, not without a certain relish, that Lantier is in the area; and shortly after they see him in the crowd which has collected on the opposite pavement. The company are completely immersed in their maudlin emotion at Mme Lerat's ballad; but Coupeau, noticing Gervaise's anxiety, sees what she is looking at, and goes out to deal with Lantier. As the factitious emotion inside the shop increases Gervaise watches with real terror what is going on outside. Coupeau, struck by the fresh air, is not steady enough to fight Lantier, and after several minutes, to Ger-

vaise's surprise, their verbal dispute begins to change tone; the insults give way to friendly banter. At length Coupeau pushes Lantier inside to join the party. The company, hardly recovered from their effusion of tears, look on curiously, but not very comprehendingly. Gervaise herself can hardly believe what has happened; and then, quite suddenly, 'elle avait trouvé ces choses *naturelles*'—just another of life's tricks. Why should she bother herself or make a scene? She welcomes the physical torpor which deadens her moral response, and her pretexts, as she words them to herself, are in harmony with the whole fatalistic and indulgent philosophy of the evening. . . .

> The goose had not quite agreed with her; she had certainly eaten too much; and it hindered her from thinking. A pleasant idleness weighed upon her. . . . Good Lord! what was the use of getting worked up when other folk didn't, and things seemed to settle down of themselves to the general satisfaction. . . . It would really have been out of place to break up the harmony of the dinner, right at the end.

Lantier pays very little attention to her, and he is soon forgotten as Coupeau effects a return to the former atmosphere by striking up *Qué cochon d'enfant;* he adopts a rusty old woman's voice, the ladies poise their knives ready to beat time, the song continues 'au milieu d'une gaieté formidable'. And now the whole neighbourhood joins in. . . .

> The whole street now joined in *Qué cochon d'enfant.* Across the road the little watchmaker, the grocer's boys, the tripe-seller, the fruiterer, all took up the refrain, slapping themselves in chorus. The whole street seemed to be drunk— the very smell of the feast had set them reeling. And it must be said that the party itself was by this time awfully boozed. It had come on little by little, from the first glass of wine after the soup to now, the finishing touch, when they all bawled together, all crammed with food, in the reddish haze of the two smoking lamps. The immense jollity deadened the very sound of the last vehicles passing in the street. . . . Coupeau was at this verse:
>
> L'dimanche à la P'tit'-Villette
> Après la chaleur . . .
>
> At that they fairly raised the roof, and so loud a burst of voices went up into the warm air of the night that these roisterers fell to applauding themselves, feeling that it was an effort impossible to beat.

On this climax the scene fades out. The last paragraph is a postscript: nobody ever managed to remember exactly how the feast ended, but the next day there are some embarrassed attempts at self-justification, and all are able to concur in condemning Clémence, 'une fille à ne pas inviter, décidément', who had finished by showing 'tout ce qu'elle possédait' and being sick over the muslin curtains. The men, at least, had gone out in the street, while Virginie had lain down just for a moment, to guard against any consequences. We hear nothing of Gervaise's excuses, and her memories are very vague; she seems to remember

Goujet sobbing as he left, and Lantier must have stayed to the end; at one moment she had felt a warm breath in her hair—'mais elle ne savait pas si ce souffle venait de Lantier ou de la nuit chaude'.

The next chapter opens in the usual meticulously circumstantial way, but for the first time it does not focus Gervaise's enterprise:

> Le samedi suivant, Coupeau, qui n'était pas rentré dîner, amena Lantier vers dix heures. . . .

It ends with Gervaise, now a resigned physical victim, being pushed towards Lantier's bed, while Coupeau, disgusting and insensible on the floor, 'roulé dans son vomissement', blocks the way to her own.

Clearly the episode is in no sense gratuitous description, since it prepares and enacts a critical incident in Gervaise's fortunes. The structural pattern of previous episodes is repeated, and for the first time with decisive effect. The disastrous infiltration of Lantier takes place at a moment when individual consciousness and power of decision are in abeyance, anaesthetized by the pressure of the milieu; whereas the sober wedding feast ended with Gervaise brought up against the symbols of disaster she is now, literally, invaded by them. The particular quality of this scene is to define more precisely and realistically the nature of this individual helplessness, without sacrificing impressionistic and representative power. Certainly it has that power—in a sense it could be said to be a final image of Gervaise's life, to sum up the fruitless struggle for happiness and success in which she is engaged, to define the terms and narrow limits in which they are possible. The very 'detachability' of the episode is significant. It is a 'set piece', but only in the sense that every episode in Gervaise's life is a set piece, an attempt to carve out an improvised happiness in the face of all the evidence. It supersedes a moment of despair. It is conceived in a mood of resigned self-indulgence. From its very beginnings it is threatened with disaster. It establishes a moment of precarious success, but a success founded on rough-and-ready or impermanent bases—the Lorilleux' greed, Coupeau's propitious dose of alcohol, the general desire to shut out realities; the moment is achieved only by calling on all the resources of the society, exploiting all its most dangerous virtues. And as soon as it is achieved it begins to be undermined: the opening of the doors marks the reassertion of life, the situation passes out of Gervaise's control, personal responsibility and identity dissolve in a haze of fatigue, intoxication and confusion.

The recurrent structure is consummately exploited here: viewed in one light the feast seems a splendid gesture of resilience, a come-back against despair, which ends in unforeseeable disaster; another example of the relentless processes of life which cheat and by-pass the individual will. But the detailed working out of the scene defines the nature of 'life', as well as evoking its movement. The action is rigorously realistic; the dramatic enlargement itself is generated from within—it is alcoholic, rather than lyrical or tragic. And 'life' is not some mysteriously compulsive pressure outside Gervaise, which can only be understood in symbolic terms. Rather here it is little more than the sum of interacting personal weaknesses, which may or may not have a remoter social cause. The very harmony which the idea of the dinner provokes, the conspiratorial escapism, make it a characteristic and conscious gesture of an organically decayed society. And Gervaise in freely proposing it is seen to be a typical constituent part of the organism that destroys her. Her enterprise is a product, not a transcendence of her social condition, her very ability to conceive and manage the dinner is a token of potential disaster.

Gervaise's inherent weaknesses exactly dovetail with the debilitating influences of her society; and both her popularity and her decline are seen as almost automatic functions of that correspondence. Thus even in this scene of triumph and disaster it is clearly enforced that Gervaise has no *moral* ascendancy over her world; indeed the feast presents a uniformly low moral tone, in which Gervaise is scrupulously included. No one is swayed or 'reformed' by Gervaise, and she herself is seen to be made of exactly the same sort of stuff as her fellows. Not only in the case of Coupeau's *bonhomie* is the idealistic and sentimental interpretation discounted; Goujet's view of Gervaise is also implicitly corrected. Gervaise is successively grouped with various characters to point what she shares with them of malice, extravagance, complacency and superstition. In this scene, more strongly than anywhere else in the novel, we have the impression of urban humanity not as a collection of individuals, but as a pool of highly-conditioned materials merely made up in different permutations; the particular blend which constitutes Gervaise happens to be the 'recipe' both for popularity and defeat. An intimate, almost mechanical connection between the two is strongly suggested in visual terms—the same door which serves to publicize Gervaise's triumph to the *quartier* also serves to admit Lantier. So that if the absolute of goodness is demoted into the relative of popularity, the absolute of responsibility is also attenuated. Since Gervaise is called on to act as an individual at a moment when the society are as one man, responsibility radiates out on to them. The postscript is perhaps intended as a last reminder of the moral homogeneity of the society. All the members of the party feel the need to justify themselves, to claim that they remained responsible, retained their individual identity throughout. And the fact that these claims are so obviously invalid stresses the primacy of the group as the irresponsible unit. Their life, in a less spectacular way than the dinner, is a moral orgy from which each saves what face and stature he can; Gervaise's being posed a specific moral problem is an incidental—and representative—piece of bad luck.

'A totally represented world . . . a world practically workable with every part as functional as every other, and with the parts all chosen for direct mutual aid.' Henry James's description of Zola's achievement stresses the density of the realism, the feeling we have of having covered all the ground, of having had the whole subject revealed to us in all its scenic and personal detail. But 'direct mutual aid' also provides an unexpectedly appropriate definition of the moral interdependence, the spreading of the moral burden, which we have seen as characterizing the presentation of Gervaise and her society. And it points to an intimate connection between the aesthetic aim of making the whole take shape from the parts, and the moral implication that the parts can be finally explained in terms of the whole. James goes on to describe the profuseness of the social evocation as 'perpetually delaying access to the private world, the world of the individual'. That limitation, though of little importance in novels whose chief purpose is panoramic, assumes greater significance in *L'assommoir,* where an individual fate is the centre of interest. And the 'delay' is made more striking by the fact that there is some appearance of expedition. Zola seems to want to get at the 'truth' by every available means, the whole air of the novel is serious, comprehensive, authentic. But every approach to Gervaise, as we have seen, dissolves as if inevitably into the relative and inconclusive. The moral objector might assert that Zola, having promised us the scientific truth in all its complexity, restricts himself to means which effectually stop him providing it; that he has merely simplified his world in such a way that he can remain on the surface without appearing superficial.

To such a critic the technical accomplishment of the book would seem a distortion of reality, a concealing of what he most wants to know. The aesthetic impact of the novel's structure is to convey the all-absorbing demands of living, to present Gervaise in her resilience, to temper her irresponsibility by denying her leisure for self-

*Playbill for the stage adaptation of Zola's novel* L'assommoir.

inspection. And, though this may be a legitimate image of working life, it does remain a telescoping of the real, where the margin for reflection, however diminished, is never completely negligible. Moreover, when it *is* studied, the personal consciousness still appears in such a way as to make a moral discrimination impossible; and it would be possible to see this presentation as something of a technical sleight of hand. There is every appearance, in the close scrutiny applied to Gervaise, that her state of mind, her moral stature, are being made the object of critical study. At every moment, for instance, we are reminded of the difference between statement and truth. Thus Gervaise's fatalism and rationalizations about her conduct are not meant to be accepted at their face value; we are not called on (to return to the birthday scene) to believe that what she had to eat *really* prevented her from thinking, or that God was *really* against her. But the possible lines of inquiry which such a self-deception offers are not followed up; in fact all we are allowed to feel about it is its 'typicality'. What Zola does is to give a scrupulous appearance of discounting individual illusions, but only to make way for a broader sociological interpretation which, by implication, substantially repeats the characters' self-deceiving claims. 'Qui dit psychologue', declares Sandoz, Zola's mouthpiece in *L'oeuvre,* 'dit traître à la vérité.' But here the rejection of analysis is conveniently extended to the presumption that the individual conscience has nothing individual to reveal, its expressions are only significant as elements in the characterization of a larger unit. Looking back on *L'assommoir* we are certainly aware of a spiritual homogeneity in excess of what strict realism would allow. It is a world, for instance, where no one is misunderstood and no one shocked, a world full of scandal but devoid of mystery. And the reason for the uniformity of this world, and the apparent completeness of our knowledge of it, is that every one in it has the same sort of mental life; each is placed equally distant, in conformity with a sociological axiom, from self-knowledge and truth. In a different cause from Flaubert, but with some of the same results, Zola too forbids his characters to stray beyond the bounds of the cliché. In such a world attention is easily diverted from questions of personal responsibility to considerations of typicality, without the issue of freedom being specifically faced.

Zola might retort that such criticism was largely irrelevant, since his aim was not a study of freedom and responsibility but an urgent social portrait, which justified and acknowledged the 'delay in access to the private'. He is not proposing the philosophical: 'This had to be'; but the sociological: 'This was, and the measure in which it was typical is its most important aspect.' Zola was much concerned to reject the generalizing speculation which *L'assommoir* provoked, and in his preface he answers, rather inconsequentially, the many critics who had complained that he was betraying the working-class movement by his uniformly unflattering portrayal:

> It is a work of truth, the first novel with a real tang of the people. And it must not be concluded that the people as a whole are bad, for my characters are not bad, they are only ignorant and

corrupted by the atmosphere of hard work and misery in which they live.

But the charge of materialism arises precisely out of the invitation which a work makes to generalization. And in this sense the predicament of the naturalist is that the more accomplished his artistic achievement, the more immoral its implications can be held to be. Thus it is the very congruity of Gervaise with the world she lives in which permits the symmetry, the undogmatic assurance and dramatic power of the birthday scene; but the choice of the easily movable object to meet the barely resistible force is hardly a very searching way of 'studying' the complex question of the interaction of personal and social forces. In this respect the realist (like the popular newspapers today) could be held accountable not only for his presentation of events, but also for his choice of materials. 'On what authority', asked James of *Nana,* 'does M. Zola present nature to us as a combination of the cesspool and the house of prostitution? On the authority of his predilections alone.' After the play he had made of the scientific basis of his works Zola could hardly be surprised if their content was seen as the description of 'nature' and not as historical symbolism or political satire.

But the fact that the artist in Zola appealed against the implications of his own scientific theory is itself significant; and our final impression of him is not of the militant materialist. His best novels are completely undogmatic, their morality is the preliminary humanitarian morality of the liberal reporter; and his rejection of 'psychology' is so clearly seen to be a function of an artistic weakness that it has little power to harm. When carried to excess the 'physiological' approach always defeated itself: thus *La bête humaine* strikes us not as a complacent demonstration of the necessary depravity of railway workers, but as an improbable horror story against a superbly evoked background for which it is largely a pretext. When *L'assommoir* appeared Edmond Goncourt welcomed it as carrying on the 'clinical' work that he and his brother had started in *Germinie Lacerteux*. But he said that the battle for scientific modernity in the novel was only just starting: only when the method had been applied to every human species and every stratum of society would victory be achieved. That would, indeed, involve a definition not only of 'the people as a whole', but of human nature. Zola may have started with that ambition—and certainly *L'assommoir* is still a by-product of comprehensive scientific intentions; but perhaps he is better described by his own words in the preface to the work, where he protests that he is not 'the brutal novelist, the gorger of blood', but 'a worthy bourgeois, a studious artist keeping quietly to himself, and whose one ambition is to leave behind him as broad and living a work as he can'. 'Large et vivant' describes *L'assommoir* more nearly than the abstract labels of materialist or determinist; like *Madame Bovary* it is the supreme product of an aesthetic which proved to have strictly limited potentialities. (pp. 68-97)

> Brian Nicholas, "The Novel as Social Document: 'L'Assommoir' (1877)," in The Moral and the Story, by Ian Gregor and Brian Nicholas, Faber & Faber, 1962, pp. 63-97.

## F. W. J. Hemmings   (essay date 1966)

[*Hemmings is an English biographer and critic who has written extensively on French literature and culture, including two well-received biographies of Zola (see Further Reading). In the following essay, he commends Zola's innovations as a novelist in both his choice of subject matter and his imaginative treatment of sociological issues.*]

Shortly after the conclusion of the Franco-Prussian war a young English reporter on the staff of the *Illustrated London News* found himself at Versailles, with an assignment to cover the deliberations of the National Assembly. One day a French colleague pointed out to him a pale, shabby, worried-looking individual, and said with a snigger: 'Look, there's Zola. You know—the man who believes in Manet!'

At that time Zola had published six novels, besides a volume of short stories and a collection of critical essays. But he was still remembered mainly for the frightful scandal he had caused before the war by his campaign in favour of Manet. He was still thought of by the public at large as the man who insisted there was talent in 'Le déjeuner sur l'herbe' and the rest of the extraordinary daubs perpetrated by this crude barbarian, this practical joker whom no respectable art critic could take seriously.

Zola's defence of Manet had been published as a pamphlet under the title *Une nouvelle manière en peinture,* which could be reasonably translated 'innovations in painting'. This was in 1867, and later the same year Zola had brought out his novel *Thérèse Raquin* which might have been (though it was not) reviewed under the heading 'innovations in fiction'. *Thérèse Raquin* may not be a great work of literature, but nothing quite like it had been written before.

At first it did not sell too well; then someone on the staff of *Le figaro* focused attention on it by publishing a violently hostile article entitled 'Putrid Literature' [see excerpt dated 1868]. Reviewers were a good deal more uninhibited in those days. Zola's novel was referred to as 'a puddle of mud and blood', and he was accused of 'seeing woman as M. Manet paints her, mudcoloured and daubed with pink lipstick'—a side-swipe, no doubt, at Manet's notorious 'Olympia'. Thanks to this calculated rudeness, people started to buy *Thérèse Raquin* and it went rapidly into a second edition. Zola added a preface in which he alluded to the diatribe in *Le figaro* and professed himself amazed that his book should be judged sordid. He was not aware, he said, that he was being any more improper than painters who set out to render a nude model on canvas. In deliberately drawing the analogy—a dubious one, I would say—between the novelist's work and the painter's, and in implicitly accepting his reviewer's comparison between *Thérèse Raquin* and 'Olympia', Zola shows at least what his ambition was: to innovate in the same kind of way as Manet had innovated. And the proof that he was doing this would be that public reaction to *Thérèse Raquin* would be as violently hostile as it had been to 'Olympia' when that picture was exhibited in 1865, three years before.

If we read *Thérèse Raquin* today, almost a century after its publication, few of us are going to be shocked. This is natural enough, since any literary innovation, if it is at all fruitful, is bound in time to lose its power to shock, though if it is at all significant it should retain its power to impress. Zola thought that his principal innovation had been to invent characters without souls, as he put it. What he meant was that his characters are governed entirely by their animal appetites and are therefore incapable of making moral choices. But it is obvious that his characters do make moral choices—bad ones—and suffer the consequences, just as they would if they had been created by a novelist convinced of the spiritual nature of man. Zola prefers to talk about nervous breakdowns and avoids talking about pangs of conscience, and this has its significance, no doubt, but makes little difference to the situation. Thérèse and her lover Laurent conspire to murder Thérèse's husband Camille. The crime escapes detection, but the two murderers end by punishing themselves and each other; both finally commit suicide. The moral law, then, exists, and though it may be temporarily upset, it will in the end re-assert itself. This is not a particularly disturbing thesis, nor a particularly materialistic one.

Yet *Thérèse Raquin* remains a disturbing work; not by reason of its emphatic materialism, which hardly matters, but because of the quality of imagination that Zola manifests here for the first time. *Thérèse Raquin* is a masterpiece of the macabre, sufficiently related to day-to-day reality to avoid the absurdities of the run-of-the-mill horror story. If one is looking for parallels one will turn, perhaps, to Poe or Hawthorne or think of certain scenes in Dickens. With Zola, as with these others, the potency of the effect on the reader derives most probably from the coincidence between some deep-seated private obsession or neurosis in the writer and certain rudimentary psychic fears present, if buried, in most people's minds. In the case of *Thérèse Raquin* the personal origin of some of Zola's more dreadful inventions is demonstrable, as far as such things are demonstrable.

Towards the end of the novel there is a particularly revolting scene where Thérèse and Laurent, having got married after Camille has met his end in what passes as a boating accident, find themselves simultaneously suffering from the hallucination that Camille's drowned corpse is lying between them in bed, preventing them from embracing. They imagine they can feel the clammy wetness and the sponginess of the rotting flesh. They suppose that, even after death, Camille continues to show himself jealous; they have gone to the trouble of killing him, and all to no purpose. In *Germinal,* a novel written many years later, there is a scene in which the hero and heroine, Etienne and Catherine, are trapped below ground when the coal-mine they are working in is flooded. Catherine's man Chaval, a brutal bully, has been killed by Etienne, and his body is floating in the flood-water. Being in the dark, Catherine and Etienne cannot see the corpse, but as they sit on a ledge of rock just above the level of the water, a current keeps washing it against their feet. Zola's comment here was this: 'Chaval would not go away, he wanted to be with them, against them. . . . There was no point in having smashed his head in, if they were to have him come back

between them, obstinately jealous. To the very end he would be there, even dead, to prevent them coming together'.

It is difficult to believe that this is a deliberate echo in *Germinal* of the episode in *Thérèse Raquin.* Both passages are, or bear every sign of being, compulsive representations of the same private neurosis. This is where we touch on what is so individual in Zola's art, so difficult to tease out, and at the same time so fascinating and necessary to study: the irresistible intrusion of personal fantasies in works which Zola did his deliberate utmost to construct as impartial, objective studies.

But even on the level of explicit intention Zola was a portentous innovator: not in *Thérèse Raquin,* and not in fact until ten years later when he started writing the series of masterpieces of which the first was *L'assommoir.* When *Thérèse Raquin* was published Zola, who knew all the tricks of the trade, having been publicity manager in the firm of Hachette for some years, wrote to Hippolyte Taine suggesting he should review the book in the *Journal des Débats;* no doubt he would have liked Taine to champion him as he had championed Manet. Taine was too cautious to rise to the bait, though he did send Zola a long letter of encouragement and advice. Zola had been reading Taine with admiration for some time; what had struck him most was Taine's bold positing of analogies between the physical sciences and what were then called the moral sciences. Everything can be accounted for, according to Taine; a man does not run a temperature for no reason, similarly he does not turn to crime for no reason. The scientist's job—the moral scientist's job—is to analyse the circumstances and to arrive at the causes by deduction.

Taine was, in a sense, tracing the programme of the still embryonic sciences of psychology and sociology. As a strictly academic discipline, sociology came into being within Zola's lifetime, but as far as I know he never read the seminal works of Durkheim and Gabriel Tarde, though Durkheim's *Règles de la méthode sociologique* came out in 1895 and Tarde's *Études de psychologie sociale* in 1898. Nevertheless, in his most important and influential books, which were published in the eighteen-seventies and eighties, Zola proceeded much as a sociologist might; it could be said that he raised sociology to the dignity of art before sociology had acquired the status of a science.

All through the century novelists had been observing and commenting on the social scene, depicting the conflict between old rank and new wealth, the cleavage between the provinces and the capital, the impact of the industrial revolution, the occult power of the Church. But earlier writers had never considered giving these particular aspects of the social scene precedence over the drama of the individual, which remained their central preoccupation. When we read the second part of *Illusions perdues* we are given a lively and horrifying picture of the underworld of journalism in the early days of newspapers; but it is clear that Balzac's real interest, in composing this work, lay in charting the swift rise to fame and sudden fall into ignominy of Lucien de Rubempré, who exists as a highly specific individual, charming, gifted, ambitious, but a snob, weak-willed, sensual, and lacking in moral fibre; we feel that, if a journalistic career had not happened to offer the right framework, Balzac would have cheerfully substituted some other field of activity in which to display Lucien with the good and evil in him. The social problem of an irresponsible and corrupt press manipulated by unscrupulous financiers and shady politicians was comparatively marginal. The difference is one of approach rather than emphasis, as can be realized when one compares this novel of Balzac's with, say, Evelyn Waugh's *Scoop.*

Similarly, Julien Sorel may have been to some extent typical of the young plebeian of the post-Napoleonic period, educated beyond his station and discontented with his lot; but Stendhal's hero is so much more than this—he is both typical and exceptional, as will be, in her turn, Emma Bovary. Flaubert said of her: 'My poor Emma suffers and weeps in twenty villages in France at this very time'. He did not say 'in twenty hundred villages'. In other words, though you could find unhappy wives like Emma, you could not generalize from Emma's predicament and reach valid conclusions about the working of marriage among the bourgeoisie in rural France in the middle of the nineteenth century.

Zola, on the other hand, means us to generalize. He never created a Lucien de Rubempré, a Julien Sorel, or an Emma Bovary. Since he shared the interests of the social scientist, it was to the social problem that he addressed himself first; the characters were to function within the terms of the problem. He kept, of the old-fashioned novel, at any rate the formula of the central character who however was not meant to be regarded as significant in himself; he was intended to be no more than a witness, or perhaps a victim, of the particular social phenomenon that the novel was really about.

We can regard *L'assommoir,* if we like, as conforming to the type of the time-honoured 'fictional biography', like *Le rouge et le noir* or *Madame Bovary,* or like George Moore's *Esther Waters,* written later and to some extent in imitation of *L'assommoir.* Indeed, Zola's first idea for a title was *The Simple Life of Gervaise Macquart.* The book describes Gervaise's career, tells us what she hoped to get out of life, and how grievously disappointed she was in the end.

But is that the subject of the book? Gervaise emerges as a figure for whom one can feel some compassion, some admiration; but her freedom of action is too circumscribed, the choices open to her are too limited, for her to bear by herself the weight of the structure of the book. The point has been made with some force in one of the chapters of Ian Gregor and Brian Nicholas's study, *The Moral and the Story* [see excerpt dated 1962]. Gervaise, it is said here, 'is illustrative not so much of a human or cosmic as of a social truth. She is not a tragic victim, but a casualty, in a particular milieu where the casualty rate is high'. The writers go on to observe, plausibly enough, that the misfortunes that overtake Gervaise could have befallen any other person in that particular milieu: 'The point being made is a general sociological one: Gervaise is chosen to give it undogmatic illustration'. If one agrees that a novel has value chiefly as it provides opportunity for the discussion and elucidation of personal issues of behaviour—as

do all novels that fit into what has been called the 'great tradition'—then one will conclude, with Gregor and Nicholas, that *L'assommoir* belongs to an aesthetic of 'strictly limited potentialities'.

The mistake these critics have made is to suppose that the novel is about Gervaise and that discussion of the novel should centre on her. But Zola rejected the title *La simple vie de Gervaise Macquart.* He substituted the name of the gin-shop that plays a certain part in bringing about Gervaise's downfall, but even this can be misleading: *L'assommoir* is not really about the ravages of drink in the lower classes, though the Victorians supposed it was and for that reason accorded it qualified approval. Drink is a social problem, but not a sociological one. *L'assommoir* really deals with the immovability of class barriers. Gervaise has ambitions to rise out of the proletariat into the class immediately above and, for a while, she succeeds; she opens a laundry business and becomes a small-scale employer of labour. Then the business folds up and she is back where she started.

All Zola's important novels after *L'assommoir* similarly treat of big social issues, like the difficulty of moving from one class to the next one up. I say 'big' because there is a difference between the problems Zola interested himself in and the relatively circumscribed ones that Dickens, for instance, occasionally dealt with. The social scandals exposed by Dickens—unsupervised private schools, bureaucratic red tape, the cumbrous slowness of the law—were susceptible to treatment by reform; Zola was not a reformer—not, at least, when he was writing novels. His themes were, more than anything, historical: the transformation of retail trade with the emergence of the big emporiums; the fatal conservatism of the small farmer at a time of revolutionary changes in food production; the prevalence of belief in faith-healing at the end of a century which had seen more rapid strides in medicine than had any previous century. These gave him the subjects of *Au bonheur des dames, La terre, Lourdes,* three novels unlike anything anyone had written before. (Balzac, who was not a sociologist, ran into endless trouble trying to write his novel on the rural classes in France, and finally abandoned *Les paysans* without finishing it.) And what was the subject of *Germinal?* Zola spelled it out for himself at the beginning of his plan: the novel was to deal with 'the struggle between capital and labour'; this would turn out to be 'the most important question of the twentieth century'.

The innovation was a striking one, not well understood at the time, though Henry James did at least see that the question to be asked about Zola was why he wrote novels at all, instead of devoting himself, as he put it with a touch of irony, 'to an equal task in physics, mathematics, politics, or economics'. It has proved a fruitful innovation. We have only to think of the number of novels currently being written about, for instance, the problem of racial intolerance, whether set in South Africa, the United States, or parts of England. Their authors may never have read a line of Zola but they are nevertheless exploring the country he opened up. Truly, an aesthetic 'of strictly *un*limited potentialities'.

All the same, it is doubtful whether Zola would be as significant a writer as he is if all he had done was to annex sociology to the novel. Many writers, since 1885, have attempted to dramatize 'the struggle between capital and labour', but not even out of Russia has come a second *Germinal.* The impact of *Germinal* depends in the last resort not on the subject but on the way Zola treated his subject. The relative weakness of some of his other novels, like *L'argent* or *La débâcle,* is traceable to the fact that their interest depends on little else but the subject.

Take one I have not so far mentioned: *Nana.* In *Nana* the sociological fact that Zola started from was the well-known one that the large armies of prostitutes which used to patrol the streets of big cities in his day were recruited from the lower classes. And so Nana, the daughter of Gervaise Macquart, born and bred in the slums, exists as a social reality, the 'brutal *fille*', as Henry James unfeelingly described her, 'without a conscience or a soul, with nothing but devouring appetites and impudences' [see *TCLC,* Vol. 21, pp. 415-17]. But if she were totally describable in such terms, would *Nana* still be read? There were any number of novels written in France in the eighteen-seventies and eighties about the lives of prostitutes, before and after *Nana;* well-written books, some of them, but all of them works of pornography in the original meaning of the word, that is, as the dictionary defines it: 'descriptions of the lives and manners of prostitutes and their patrons'. Though their authors—Edmond de Goncourt, Huysmans, Charles-Louis Philippe—were men of talent, these books are seldom opened today.

*Nana,* on the other hand, still has its readers by the thousand, the reason being that it is something more than the fictional biography of a prostitute, because its heroine is something more than a prostitute. At the end of the last-but-one chapter, immediately after Zola has described her breaking out in a fit of tearful repentance when it is borne in on her how many domestic tragedies she has unwittingly caused, he shows her, having recovered her spirits, standing in the hall of her luxurious mansion, buttoning on her gloves. Nana, he wrote, 'was standing alone in the midst of the heaped-up treasures of her house, with a nation of men at her feet. Like those monsters of ancient fable whose fearful lair was strewn with bones, she set her feet on skulls'.

If Manet had chosen to paint this scene, instead of the 'realistic' Nana that he actually did paint, he would have produced something more like a Gustave Moreau than a Manet. Nana, here, transcends the sociological facts. She is a mythical figure belonging to epic poetry, a symbol of the destructiveness of sexual passion, just as the very different figure of Penelope is the mythical embodiment of wifely fidelity in the proto-novel *The Odyssey.* One is at liberty, of course, to postulate some latent dread of sex in Zola, manifesting itself in *Nana;* the creation is personal, but its origins all the same are as diffuse as the origins of the religions of man. Hesiod speaks of Eros as 'him who loosens the limbs and damages the mind', and early Greek vase-paintings show the god of love as no playful putto, but as a formidable figure wielding an axe or a whip. As Thomas Mann asked in his essay on Wagner: 'Is not that Astarte of the Second Empire, called Nana, a symbol and

a myth? How does she come by her name? It is a primitive sound, one of the early, sensual lispings of mankind; Nana was a cognomen of the Babylonian Ishtar. Did Zola know this? All the more remarkable and significant if he did not know it'.

Not only in *Nana,* but in all Zola's major works, beginning with *L'assommoir,* we are aware of this extra dimension, of the fact that beneath the sociological superstructure flow fierce, primitive undercurrents, like an age-old torrent thundering below a solidly constructed, utilitarian modern bridge. Why did he choose to dramatize the 'struggle between capital and labour', in *Germinal,* by showing us a community of miners instead of, for instance, factory workers, who were just as subject to wage-cuts, just as apt to go on strike? He chose the mine because it was important to him that the action of *Germinal* should take place in the bowels of the earth, representing the deep underground tunnels of the subconscious, that 'cellarage' where Hamlet's father's ghost moves around, the hell of Christian and pagan mythologies.

Why, in *La bête humaine,* is there so much furtiveness, deception, spying, and fear of exposure, so that there is scarcely a character who has not some secret to hide from the others? What has all this to do with railways, or even with the growing gap between technological advance and moral progress, Zola's ostensible themes in *La bête humaine?* We know today that at the time he was writing the book, Zola had just embarked on a love affair—his first infidelity in eighteen years of married life. This fact, taken in conjunction with the qualities of *La bête humaine* just mentioned, helps us to realize the extent to which Zola, this allegedly objective reporter on the social scene, used his novels for disguised confession of his own anxieties, which are also our anxieties, unless our private lives have always been so blameless that we have never had anything to hide.

Did he know what he was doing? One comes back to Thomas Mann's words: 'All the more remarkable and significant if he did not know it'. If he had understood himself better, he might have understood better what he was doing, though that would not have helped him and might have inhibited him. He supposed that what he was doing was to show that psychology is only a special branch of physiology; he imagined that he was indicating to legislators and administrators the pressing tasks awaiting their attention; he flattered himself that scientists and economists would look more closely at the unsolved problems to which he drew attention in his books. And all the time what he was chiefly doing was to add his quota to the gods and monsters of that legendary era, the nineteenth century. (pp. 574-75, 577, 580)

*F. W. J. Hemmings, "Emile Zola," in* The Listener, *Vol. LXXV, No. 1934, April 21, 1966, pp. 574-75, 577, 580.*

## Patrick Brady   (essay date 1981)

[*In the following excerpt, Brady defends Zola against detractors associated with Marxist literary criticism, pri-*

*Zola having tea with his children.*

marily the criticism of George Lukács (see essay dated 1940).]

I admire much about the work of George Lukács, but not those passages of his I propose to deal with in the present essay. I have expressed in print my admiration for the *Theory of the Novel* and my reservations about *The Historical Novel* [in *Structuralist Perspectives in Criticism of Fiction* (1978)], but my topic here is something closer to my heart. I wish to take up the defense of a great socialist writer I believe to have been grievously maligned by Lukács, namely the author of *Germinal:* Emile Zola. The distinguished Hungarian critic attacked Zola repeatedly, unmercifully, and unjustly, and I propose to accompany my arguments as to the inaccuracy and incompetence of Lukács' criticism of Zola by a hypothesis as to the reasons why the critic let himself down so badly here. This hypothesis is based on the mode of application of the principle of contradiction: the oversimplification successfully avoided by complementing the principle of reflection with the principle of contradiction returns in the form of an oversimplified and indiscriminate application of the latter. I shall attempt to demonstrate this by a *mise en question* of Lukács' criticism of Zola.

*1. Lukács, Zola, and Mediation: From Reflection to Contradiction.*—We know little of Marx's views on Zola: Prawer's recent and thorough study of Marx's writings on literature [*Karl Marx and World Literature* (1976)], records not a single reference to the great Naturalist. Engels, on the other hand, made a reference to Zola that has become famous, remarking of Balzac "I consider [him] a far greater master of realism than all the Zolas *passés, présents et à venir* [letter to Margaret Harkness, April 1888; quoted in Baxandall and Morawski, eds., *Marx and Engels on Literature and Art* (1973)]. However, there appears to be little or no evidence that Engels had ever read Zola, although he did attend the Free Stage (*Freie Volksbühne*) of Berlin in 1893 and could therefore have seen stage adaptations of some Zola novels. That of course would hardly constitute a valid basis for any informed comment on Zola's novels. Why, then, does Marx ignore Zola? Why does Engels reject him?

The key appears to be provided by the letter I have just quoted, where the passage cited is immediately preceded by the following lines: "I am far from finding fault with your not having written a point-blank socialist novel, a *Tendenzroman* as we Germans call it, to glorify the social and political views of the author. That is not at all what

I mean. *The more the opinions of the author remain hidden, the better for the work of art.*" The principle stated in this last sentence (and it appears to be extremely debatable in the bald and categorical form given to it here by Engels) represents one formulation of what we may term "the principle of contradiction." The development of such a principle represented an attempt to avoid the simplistic (because static and mechanical) perspectives associated with the principle of reflection, which tends to give the impression that the impact of economic conditions on cultural institutions is simple and direct. Marx and Engels apparently sought to prevent any such oversimplification by the development of the notion of mediation into a veritable principle of contradiction, which posits a dynamic, dialectical conception of infrastructural influences and manifestations.

This principle asserts that, "without knowing it himself, an author may speak of one thing to the conscious mind while whispering another to the subconscious." Thus Marx will declare on one occasion: "Eugène Sue has raised himself above the horizon of his own narrow *Weltanschauung.* He has delivered a slap in the face of bourgeois prejudices." The key illustration, however, of the principle of contradiction is provided by Balzac, for whom both Marx and Engels have the greatest admiration. That admiration at first glance appears paradoxical, since Balzac is politically a *légitimiste;* but they admire his profound understanding of social realities, and by explaining the relationship between his political conservatism and his social understanding in terms of the principle of contradiction, they are able to justify this admiration.

Lukács, following Marx and Engels, praises Balzac and denigrates Zola. He extrapolates from their analyses, and his judgments on Zola will constitute an attempt to prove the validity of the principle of contradiction when applied to a non-contradictory author. As in Engels, we find in Lukács not merely the notion that the relationship between consciously-held position and literary creation *may* be contradictory but the affirmation that it *must* be so. The result is a condemnation of Zola which, while influential even beyond Marxist circles, has nevertheless been questioned even by some *Marxist* critics. Thus Bertolt Brecht criticized Lukács' narrow conception of Realism, formulating as follows the dilemma proposed to the modern author by Lukács: "Writers must simply stop at the old masters, produce rich spiritual life, diminish the rapidity of events by narrating slowly, push the individual once more into the middle of events by means of their art, and so on and so on." Such a formula—individualist, idealist, static, and nostalgic—would, if universally accepted, have a petrifying effect on literary evolution, as Brecht pointed out in 1938:

> There is no turning back. We must deal not with what is old and good but with what is new and bad. Our task is not to dismantle technique but to develop it. Man becomes human again not by emerging from the crowd but by plunging himself into it. The crowd rids him of his lack of humanity, so that man becomes human again (not a solitary individual, as before).

According to Brecht, if the individual is crushed in and by modern bourgeois, capitalist, industrialized society, the writer must depict this phenomenon honestly and clearly as an aspect of the alienation characteristic of the modern period. This is precisely what Zola does. (pp. 60-2)

I shall consider three novels by Zola. One has been examined by certain critics in the light of Lukács' principles, the second has been commented on broadly by Lukács himself, while the third provides a passage by Zola which Lukács has criticized in detail.

*2. Lukács, Zola, and Myth: The Case of "Germinal".*—Let us begin to move closer to Lukácsian mediation in relation to the actual text of Zola's novels. The most famous, of course, as well as the most "socialist," is *Germinal.* Henri Mitterand adopts the point of view not of the reader but of the miners, whom he assimilates moreover rather hastily to primitive man:

> Bonnemort portant la main sur Cécile instaure une connexion entre les deux mondes. Cécile morte, il faudra que les dieux remplissent le vide en y instaurant la justice sociale, bienfait obscurément escompté par l'inconscient des mineurs. (Lévi-Strauss: *La Pensée sauvage.*) Mais tout ceci n'est que rêve, magie, simulacre. . . . La révolution se dissout en fantasmes. Le trajet métonymique a échoué.

Mitterand repeats this idea a year later: "La grève a échoué, le monde a repris son immobilité, recouvré son harmonie, résorbé ses contradictions." We must reject such an interpretation, for it is clearly contradicted by the promise of revolution inscribed in the last pages of *Germinal.* Moreover, Etienne himself, far from abandoning the struggle, goes off to look for a better place to continue the struggle (Paris) and a more effective weapon (the law). As for the ideological role of myth, it is far from certain that it is marked by reactionary bourgeois thinking, as Mitterand declares. Bakunin, for example, refused to indulge in a detailed analysis of the conditions of oppression or in the evocation of a better world: he believed in the creative spontaneity of the masses exalted by myth. Pierre Aubéry declares that if Zola was not a Marxist it is because he was a Bakunist—a position which was closer to the state of mind of the working classes of his day. In *Germinal,* the strike fails (that is certain), the revolution dissolves perhaps (that appears debatable), but *Germinal* is not a failure, and it is largely because of its mythic dimension, with its striking, awe-inspiring scenes, that it is a masterpiece.

According to Mitterand, Zola assimilates class conflict to the natural antithesis which opposes light to darkness, the terrestrial to the subterranean—which, he says, has the effect of making class distinctions a natural and eternal phenomenon (not a cultural and transitory one): it amounts to adopting a conservative ideological position. At first glance, this interpretation is persuasive and profound; on closer inspection, however, it appears to be unfair to Zola, and above all illogical. Logically, in order for us to say that Zola does not categorize class distinctions as cultural phenomena, we should be in possession of a complete series of binary oppositions, whereas in fact the series which underlies the interpretation proposed by Mitterand is incomplete and therefore lame and unconvincing:

| Nature | social distinctions |
|---|---|
| Culture | ? |

What is "natural" in **Germinal** is not the distinction between bourgeois and workers (on the contrary, that is continually denounced, for example at the formal dinner at the Hennebeau's place interrupted by the deputation of miners, as a monstrosity of a *cultural* nature), but rather the working class itself. We do in fact have at our disposal a complete series which is otherwise oriented, suggesting that the bourgeoisie as a class is a social and transitory phenomenon:

| Nature | working class |
|---|---|
| Culture | bourgeoisie |

This, in my opinion, is the "ideological message" (if there is one) of **Germinal.**

Ira Shor, strangely insensitive to the role and function of certain aspects of **Germinal** (notably, "descriptions of the Le Voreux mine as a symbolic voracious beast"), finds them "tedious" and "burdensome" [see Further Reading]. However, he defends the novel against Lukács when the latter accuses it of being static and lifeless, lacking in dialectical movement, obsessively bestial, an insult to the miners (Lukács actually espouses this criticism made against Zola by his bourgeois detractors), and pessimistic. Shor concludes that "**Germinal** exceeds Lukács' criteria for great realism."

In a note on Shor's essay, William Berg adds:

> In **Germinal,** imagery becomes no less than an ideological tool, arranged in a dialectical pattern and pointing, finally, to a progressive and optimistic vision of the working class and, indeed, of history. Nearly all these qualities—ideology, dialectical thinking, progressive and optimistic thought—are denied to Zola by Lukács and other Marxist critics [see Further Reading, *TCLC*, Vol. 21].

### 3. Lukács, Zola, and Dialectics: The Case of "L'œuvre."—

*L'œuvre* has been commented on directly by Lukács, who makes the following judgments on this novel: (a) that the theme of the tragedy of the artist is suitable only to the short story, not to the novel, and that *L'œuvre* is consequently a failure; (b) that if this theme could be so adapted as to make it appropriate to the novel form, Zola failed to carry out such necessary adaptation; (c) that Zola found the basic structure of *L'œuvre* in Balzac's short story entitled "Le chef-d'oeuvre inconnu," to which he merely added a few supplementary motivations, which moreover he failed to integrate effectively [*Writer and Critic, and Other Essays*].

As for the first of these assertions, it is far from certain that *L'œuvre* is a failure (it is unquestionably superior in many ways to "Le chef-d'oeuvre inconnu") and, even if it were one, that would not prove that the theme treated is unsuitable to the novel genre, which is a hazardous and arbitrary hypothesis that can probably not even be tested or evaluated, let alone proved. The second assertion is quite false,

as is evident from the manuscripts of Zola's novels (of which Lukács was apparently ignorant): the writing of *L'œuvre* in no way consisted of taking a brief treatment of a theme and developing a longer version of it, since on the contrary he devoted himself in this novel to the writing of a sort of fictionalized autobiography evoking his own sufferings caused by the task of artistic creation (a very different theme from that of Balzac's short story).

The third of Lukács' assertions is quite simply erroneous, as I have shown in detail: Zola's chief sources are not literary but biographical and autobiographical, and even his chief literary source is not "Le chef-d'oeuvre inconnu." [P. Brady, *"L'œuvre" d'Emile Zola, roman sur les arts* (1967)]. If we want to compare *L'œuvre* with a work by Balzac, we find a much more illuminating example in *La cousine Bette,* for it is in *L'œuvre* and *La cousine Bette* that Zola and Balzac respectively describe in the greatest detail the relationships that exist between the Artist, Society, and Woman. An examination of the texts of these two novels reveals that the relationships between the Artist and Society (represented by Woman) are presented in dialectical form by Zola as well as by Balzac, in fact that this dialectical character (or effect) is much more striking in Zola's treatment of it. It is in Balzac's work rather than Zola's that the Artist is *récupéré*, absorbed by society and corrupted by its values, so that social conflict is eliminated. In the Zola novel, on the contrary, the conflict remains in its entirety, irreducible—a situation which is emphasized by Claude Lantier's suicide and Sandoz's endless struggle. Moreover, Zola emphasizes much more clearly the role of Woman, the very type of the human individual subjugated and exploited by Society, which makes her its instrument in the psychological and aesthetic castration, the *embourgeoisement,* and the corruption of the Artist. In Zola, much more than in Balzac, Art is diametrically opposed to the conceptions, values, and goals of bourgeois society.

### 4. Lukács, Zola, and Description: The Case of "Nana."—

Here is Lukács' commentary on the horse-racing scene at Longchamp in **Nana:**

> The racing incident is very loosely joined up with the development of the plot, and could easily be removed. The only connecting link is that one of Nana's many passing admirers is ruined through the exposure of the swindle. The other link connecting this episode with the main theme is even less substantial, and has nothing to do with the plot—and is for this very reason the more characteristic of Zola's style. The winning horse also bears the name "Nana." And Zola makes the most of his opportunity to emphasize this coincidence. The victory of the courtesan Nana's namesake symbolizes her own triumphs in the Parisian *beau monde* and *demi-monde.* [see *TCLC*, Vol. 21, pp. 421-23].

Sandy Petrey's comment on the same passage stresses various signs of social decadence such as the mingling of people belonging to various classes and committed to various moral codes; the transfer of action and initiative from human beings to things; the predominance of mere powerfully valorized signifiers (such as the cry "Nana!") over empty, obscure, or at least ambiguous signifieds; the proliferation of clichés and grammatical confusion: and the decadent mania for Anglicisms [Petrey, "Socio-criticism and 'Les Rougon-Macquart'," *L'esprit créateur* (1974)].

More importantly, perhaps, this passage of *Nana* is also extremely rich in psychoanalytical and archetypal meanings, which Petrey and the sociocritics, like Lukács before them, have done little to bring out.

The day of the Grand Prix de Paris at the Bois de Boulogne is a special occasion, marked by international rivalry of a symbolic order represented by the French and English horses in the race and emphasized by the repeated antipatriotic remarks of La Faloise. The festive, ceremonial character of the occasion, like that of the Comices Agricoles in *Madame Bovary,* indicates that we have left behind the daily routine and monotony of profane time but without really acceding to the high sphere of sacred time. Eliade terms this intermediate sphere "festal" time.

The notion of giving Nana's name to the mare who wins the Grand Prix (but only through a fraud whose discovery leads to the suicide of Vandeuvres) is brilliantly conceived and brilliantly exploited. The two Nanas share more than the same name. Both human and horse are superb creatures, both are female, both have hair of a magnificent tawny colour: the courtesan wears hers in a huge flowing "pony-tail," while the colour of the animal's coat reminds one of a beautiful blonde (it has "une blondeur de fille rousse"). When she sees her, Nana exclaims: "Look! she has my hair!" This completes the depiction of Nana as animal begun at her very first appearance in the novel, where we are told that at the nape of her neck "des cheveux roux mettaient comme une toison de bête."

Both the woman and the animal symbolize sexuality, and the climax of the race sees the courtesan indulging unconsciously in a gesture of sympathetic magic aimed at helping the golden mare. However, she translates this effort of the race into sexual terms ("un balancement des cuisses et des reins," "des coups de ventre") murmuring words of encouragement, and the little English jockey appears to respond phallically ("la cravache haute"). The name "Spirit" given to the English horse which Nana defeats, and the name "Prince" given to Nana's jockey, makes of the event a battle between money, the flesh, and the spirit—a battle won by the flesh and money together, in the form of the golden mare and her jockey, just as the bought and kept woman Nana conquers Paris. This sexual symbolism is reinforced stylistically: the climax of the race is described in a rhythm which suggests sexual climax.

All of these elements and aspects of the scene illustrate and reinforce the central theme of the novel as a whole, namely rampant and triumphant sexuality, its market-related prestige, and its corrupting effects.

*Conclusion.*—Lukács' commentaries on the texts of Zola's *novels* are few in number, poor in quality, arbitrary in their demands, and clouded by an ill-conceived obsession with Zola's purely theoretical pronouncements. It is true that Lukács knows Zola better than Engels did (let alone Marx), and that Mitterand and Duchet are less negative than Lukács, and Petrey less negative still. I believe this

retreat from the denigration of Zola is an inevitable result of greater familiarity with his work and greater objectivity. What needs further development is the study of the psychoanalytical and archetypal aspects of Zola's work, which provide necessary complements to the sociocritical dimension.

It is my belief that if Lukács had known and understood Zola's *novels* better he would have adopted a very different tone when commenting on them, to the advantage both of Zola's reputation and of the reputation of Lukács himself. If such better knowledge seemed superfluous to Lukács, it may be because of his inheriting from Marx and Engels the misapplication to Zola of the principle of contradiction. (62-8)

*Patrick Brady, "Lukács, Zola, and the Principle of Contradiction," in* L'esprit créateur, *Vol. XXI, No. 3, Fall, 1981, pp. 60-8.*

### Suzanne Nalbantian   (essay date 1983)

[*In the following excerpt from her study* Seeds of Decadence in the Late Nineteenth-Century Novel, *Nalbantian examines how Zola used images of excessive consumption and indulgence to depict social and psychological decadence in* Germinal, Nana, *and* L'assommoir.]

In his panoramic view of French society in the wake of the Franco-Prussian war, Emile Zola created a clear definition of decadence by associating it with indulgence and the loss of control. However, his depiction of material excess was to be stylistic not thematic, the tone moral not moralistic, as he evinced the mechanism of that decadence. In 1880 Zola had firmly proclaimed a manifesto of Naturalism in his treatise on the 'experimental novel', adapting the findings of Claude Bernard and the Positivists to his conception of the novel. There he had stated in principle that the rigours of scientific truth were to be brought to the novel form. But at the time of the publication of *Germinal* in 1885, he had to admit that his art had in fact surpassed Naturalist observation, for his method had actually necessitated an 'agrandissement de la verité' (an exaggeration of the truth). In a letter to Henry Céard, he states: 'I have the hypertrophy of the true detail, the leap into the stars from the springboard of exact observation. Truth rises on wings up to the symbol.' In tune with his times, Zola used a physiological metaphor here to illustrate the enlargement process of his artistic expression to which social reality was subject in his fiction. Described in terms of the abnormality of 'hypertrophy' this symbolization became his telling testimony of the decadence within.

Through the hyperbole, Zola actually isolated and catalyzed the elements of his conception of Western decadence which highlighted the contagious quality of an excess whose overall pervasiveness cut through class structures and social distinctions, a germ so to speak which assaulted and affected all the levels of society. The consumption-ailment which debilitates the whole can be identified as the major symptom of Decadence: 'In society as in the human body, there exists a solidarity which unites the different parts, tying together the different organs, such that if one organ decays, all the others are affected and a very complex sickness is announced' [Emile Zola, *Le roman experimental*]. In concentrating on physical analogies such as the capitalist mine in *Germinal,* the body in *Nana* or the alembic of alcohol in *L'assommoir,* to name a few, Zola featured agents of hyperbolic consumption.

The French word 'appétit' serves Zola in a number of ways, both in actual physical connotation and in a figurative one. Ever characteristic is the 'débordement des appétits' (overflow of appetites) in the Zola canon. 'Manger' is the all-purpose word used to render consumption concrete. Zola uses its nineteenth-century Darwinian connotation of struggle for survival to highlight the deterministic quality such consumption assumes. The notion of the 'gros' or flabbiness is frequently used to connote the underlying weakness of will and moral lassitude. What results is a deterioration of character (both stylistically and psychologically) as a general spread of fatigue moves across class distinctions. This aspect of excess is particularly striking in *Germinal,* where the moral inadequacies and debility of a ruling capital class are duplicated in the labour sector in a simultaneous process. This procedure creates a mutual impression of mechanistic void through the omnipresent visual quality of the central image and the structural determinism of the seasonal sequences.

The portrayal of the mine, 'Le Voreux', voracious as the name itself, is from the beginning of the novel conceived as a dark mouth consuming the energy and stamina of the workers it engulfs. The mine is impersonated as a crouching beast with apocalyptic powers and consumptive activity: 'And Le Voreux, at the bottom of its pit, crouched as an evil beast, churned more, exhaled with a longer and heavier breath, the air disturbed by the painful digestion of human flesh.' Throughout the novel it is depicted as 'repu' (stuffed) yet eating with a gluttonous appetite that is never satiated. As characters are destroyed within its midst, the mine itself represents inordinate consumption and in bestial fashion it externalizes the eating away or attrition within the social fabric. A dark womb-like receptacle of human specimens, it churns and gorges the human element and harbours agents of its own destruction as it is ultimately envisaged bursting into an apocalyptic deluge. The mine is the pivot around which destruction occurs; in the process of consumption it is itself consumed.

Zola identifies the destructive forces of the mine as a weakness from within. For if the mine abuses the human services and reduces the workers to beastlike insects, it is also unable to sustain itself. This is evidenced in the initial fact that the mining company has to contract some of its work: 'The worker might be dying of hunger, but the company also was eating into its millions.' For the old mine gives signs of structural weakness. It is as if the seams of Le Voreux, which fall apart, transcribe possible points of vulnerability and waning within the capital class. In terms of imagery, Zola incorporates the decadent stereotype of the Barbarian assault on Byzantium in his description of the mining disaster to suggest the paradoxical situation of capital at its apparent height. This expression of decadence, focused as it is on the condition of the mine, identifies the 'germinal' imagery with the blatantly destructive scene in the vision of the dreamy Etienne Lantier:

And in this awaiting of a new invasion of barbarians regenerating the decayed nations of the old world, reborn was his faith in a coming revolution, the true one, that of the workers, the flames of which would burn up the *fin-de-siècle* with the red glow of the rising sun now drenching the sky in blood.

The rhetoric of *fin-de-siècle* with its purple tones describes a state of transition. The notion of the old order waning into the advent of the new, although still anticipated, is communicated as a dominant mood. This atmospheric effect of a waning age is particularly shared by Zola's contemporary, Thomas Hardy, whose emphasis is less political than moral. In setting a moralistic past against a 'moraline-free' future (to use Nietzsche's terminology) Hardy proceeds . . . to explore the impact of such conflict, not upon society, but upon the individual. In the case of both Zola and Hardy, an analogy is established between an old world and an old edifice. And whether it be the decrepit mine or the crumbling walls of the Oxford edifice, the structures are dramatically conveyed as decaying.

Eschatological paradigms colour Zola's works, as the collapse of the dark mine, Le Voreux, exceeds the proportions of an individual mining catastrophe, representing symbolically a challenge to the system. It is significant and disturbing that action is in the hands of the anarchist Souvarine, whose act of total destruction actually effects the mining collapse and moves the novel to its cataclysmic ending. The attempted and belaboured designs of the characters Etienne Lantier and Rasseneur, the socialist revolutionaries in the variant modes of evolutionist and progressive, are instantaneously surpassed by the nihilistic attitude of Souvarine which surfaces at the end, and gains ascendancy as the name suggests. He is envisaged physically attacking the mine in its entrails and actually creating the deluge. In some ways his response resembles the devastating one of the ominous Father Time in Hardy's *Jude the Obscure.* . . . Like Souvarine, Father Time's dispassionate 'mechanical creep' ('he followed his directions literally without an inquiring gaze at anything') effectuates action in an otherwise stalemate situation of ratiocinative stalling, and thereby precipitates the narrative to the catastrophic forecast of impending doom. In the case of Zola, the image of the mine, collapsing and expiring as a giant monster gorged with human flesh, is hyperbolized in the proportions of an apocalypse, with paradigms of beast and deluge prevailing.

Throughout the novel and leading to the ultimate catastrophe, Zola's technical patterns of duplication and mirroring highlight the decadent process harboured in the mine. If the bourgeois is signified by the brioche cooking in the oven, the working-class household is seen craving and consuming a lower form of bread. The kitchen is another piece of reality which Zola seizes upon in symbolic fashion as a locus of consumption. To use George Poulet's approach to morphological metaphors, the process of consumption here receives another spatial objectification. This milieu and ambience create an exaggerated effect.

The 'immensity' of the Grégoire kitchen and its gourmand table, identifying the bourgeois stereotype, is cast hyperbolically as the centre of activity:

The kitchen was vast [*immense*] and by its scrupulous cleanliness and the arsenal of saucepans, pots and utensils which filled it, you could tell that it was the most important room in the house. It had a goodly smell of food. Racks and cupboards were overflowing [*débordaient*] with provisions.

The plump and spoiled child Cécile is its symbolic product. In contrast, the Maheus are cramped in their household, engaged in eating their crumbs of bread and begging for more to fill their 'ventre vide': 'Catherine was pondering in front of the open cupboard. All there was left was a bit of bread, plenty of cream cheese, but only the merest shave of butter.' Jeanlin's avid hunger is representative of their offspring. It is typical of Zola to express class struggle in the politically charged terms of the 'gras' (fat) versus the 'mince' (thin), as indicated in the notes to the appropriately entitled novel *Le ventre de Paris.* But what is stressed in the later novel, *Germinal,* is the compounding of the consumption process in the society as a whole beyond the issue of class conflict, as a deterministic factor of general decay. The ironic counterparts of the eating process converge most strikingly in the well constructed chapter of the Hennebeau luncheon party for the Grégoires at the time of the strike. The intent is to bring together Cécile Grégoire and Hennebeau's nephew, Paul Négrel, joining the 'corpulent' sector. There the series of courses of an enormous meal is given utmost attention, proceeding with the precision of clockwork. When news of the threatened strike is flashed, the idle and stout Madame Hennebeau responds in irresponsible fashion: 'Oh, so they are on strike. Oh, well, what difference does that make to us? We aren't going to stop eating, right?' Indeed, a whole sardonic chapter passes in the uninterrupted consumption of a menu of truffles to coffee while workers continue their obsessive struggle for bread.

In myriad forms, consumption appears as a focus for excess. The violent and bestial death and emasculation of the company's grocer, Maigrat, symbolic of his function as the source of food, is yet another instance. As the workers take vengeance on one who had cruelly refused to offer them sustenance in times of dire need, they draw attention to the central factor. From their consumptive drive, uncontrollable behaviour erupts. The consumption and the destructive element are joined, and the results are as devastating in this individual instance as the collapse of the mine. In the case of the Maigrat affair, the theme of promiscuity and consumption are linked in the fact that La Mouquette, the symbol of inordinate sexuality, is the agent of the grocer's horrific emasculation.

Such violent forces surge throughout the novel, most readily conveying the destructive and consumptive element at work. Promiscuity is seen to be equally present and contagious in the cornfield as in the bourgeois household. For example, Etienne is disturbed by the frenzy of the love-making in adjacent quarters: 'It wasn't that it prevented him from sleeping, but they pushed so hard that in the end they were damaging the wall.'

The rampant sexuality throughout *Germinal* is likened to a form of consumption, exhaling a heated atmosphere like that of ovens and mines. La Mouquette, the sexual symbol, who has countless affairs and even manages to win Etienne over at one point, is a form of monstrous power. The overt sensualism is an obsessive factor invading the bourgeois sector as well, exemplified in the case of the Hennebeau household. The little interlude describing Madame Hennebeau's adultery and Monsieur Hennebeau's sense of personal failure remains a haunting scene. It is through Hennebeau that Zola expresses the analogy of consumption: in discovering clues to his wife's affair with his nephew Paul Négrel, Hennebeau ponders in disdain that her illicit sexuality has become a form of incessant consumption:

> By now it had become simply a depraved amusement, men had become a habit for her, a recreation, like dessert after a meal. He blamed everything on her, almost exculpating the boy whom she ate into, in this arousal of appetite, as one might bite the first green fruit picked up on the road. Whom would she devour [*mangerait*] next—just how low would she sink, when there were no more obliging nephews?

Ironically, however, the upright and incompetent Hennebeau is envious of the carefree sexual activity of the masses before him.

The deterministic aspect of these various forms of excessive consumption is metonymized in the phrase 'la nécessité du ventre', as the belly becomes the one constant amidst the variables. Its expression as the struggle for survival is highlighted by the symbol of the rabbit, Pologne, which is discovered *eaten* in the fields, and its analogy with the human Jeanlin whose struggle for existence leads him to an unscrupulous killing of a sentry. It is also the inner necessity which returns the workers to work without any progress as they forego the tactics of the strike. And when Etienne contemplates future worker rebellion, he expresses it in the Darwinian terms of future consumption as an unending process of survival and competition:

> Wasn't Darwin then right; wouldn't the world be a battle, the strong ones eating the weak ones, for the beauty and perpetuation of the species? . . . If one class had to be devoured, wouldn't it be the people who would devour [*mangerait*] the bourgeoisie, weary of pleasure?

The activity inherent in the multiple connotations of the word 'manger' converges into the continuous consumption hyperbolized and causing the 'dégringolade' (decadence, downfall) and the 'avachissement' (flabbiness, lack of energy)—powerful words which translate the crumbling and the waning.

This rampant hyperbole has the effect of paling the stylistic delineation of character. This phenomenon has perhaps been overlooked by the classic Marxist objection to Zola's work. Lukács, for example, sees no historical determinism in the individual characters whom he regards as psychologically *private* types with private histories unintegrated in any social process. Interestingly, he objects to the fact that they are not individual or concrete enough as authentic social types. He does not find social institutions dissolved into personal relationships and functioning as bearers of class interests as he does in Balzac. In his

*Studies in European Realism,* Lukács contrasts Zola with his preferred Balzac: 'The basic rule which Balzac follows is to focus attention on the principal factors of the social process in their historical development and to show them in the specific form in which they manifest themselves in different individuals.' He asserts that in Balzac, social forces never appear as superhuman symbols or fantastic monsters as they do in Zola. Nor do social institutions appear 'romanticized' in what he calls the subjective abstraction of Zola's mechanical (rather than dialectical) analogy between the human body and human society.

Lukács eventually attributes Zola's alleged failure as a social realist to the fact that 'the ideology of his own class was too deeply ingrained in his thinking, his principles and his creative method, although the conscious sharpness of his criticism of society was never dulled' [see excerpt dated 1940]. This he contrasts with the case of Balzac who, presumably a Royalist, was subject to the determination of his own historical epoch which made him, in his exposure of the inherent contradictions of nascent capitalism, uninhibited by the artificial effects of class rubric. More recent critics such as Jean Borie [in *Zola et les mythes,* 1971] have also noted Zola's attraction to Utopian socialism—which is not in concordance with their belief that Zola's work reflected the actual process of socialist development.

Critics like Lukács do interpret Zola's work along with that of other Naturalists as evidence of a 'decadent' stage in capitalist literature, but they single out the pejorative connotation of the word 'decadent', as it departs from what they regard as the authentic vision and technique of socialist realism. They do not perceive that it is the captured ambience of decadence in the case of *Germinal,* for example, which determines the plot and diminishes the integrity of the individual character types above and beyond their identification with a class structure. In fact, an Etienne Lantier can be identified with an Idiot or a Jude in common symptoms of weakness, regardless of social milieu.

Specifically, the process of duplication and mirroring in *Germinal* has demonstrated a collective texture of human ineffectuality emerging. The characters remain pallid, sharing common traits of listlessness, self-destructiveness; they are on the verge of waning into oblivion. Their individual identities surface in initial form, soon to fall back into the common pool, as in the case of Etienne who remains always bland and faceless, a pale paradigm of failure.

If the mining environment turns the oldest member of the Maheu family, Bonnemort, into an automaton consumed and conditioned by its operation, it reduces the youngest member, Jeanlin, to the dehumanized condition of an animal, surviving on instinct and impulse in a ruthless race for food and sex. Bonnemort, as suggested by his name, is a living figure of death, whose ancient appearance belies his 58 years. Jeanlin is likened throughout to a roving rabbit force with primitive drives, which eats and multiplies. He assumes, too, the features of a fawn-like creature, reminiscent of a Dionysian archetype which is a familiar motif in Decadent narrative; Etienne contemplates him:

> The young man was silent, his mouth full, troubled. He looked at the child who, with his pointed muzzle, green eyes, long ears, resembles some degenerate with the instinctive intelligence and craftiness of a savage, gradually reverting to man's animal origins. The mine, which had made him what he was, had finished the job by breaking his legs.

Both Bonnemort and Jeanlin are eventually killed by the consuming mine.

Before the mine, humans become insignificant as they lose their individual identities and form a file of shadows trailing into darkness. The fact that Etienne, as the leader of the strike, is not given a central position stresses the failure of individuality amidst greater collective forces. He remains positioned at spatial and psychological distances from his objectives; his long purviews of the mining scenes emblematically remove him from effective involvement in the workers' cause. His character never burgeons; nor has it impact on his surroundings. A similar 'obscurity' of individual character is crystallized in Hardy's Jude. . . . There, a physical distancing also conveys a gap between aspiration and its fulfilment. Etienne's failure is exemplified in the paradigmatic way in which he recovers his initial position as a peregrinative wandering labourer seeking work at the end of the novel, in futile, unprogressive motion.

Etienne's contradictory position contributes to his metaphysical and literary marginality, and as a character he remains very much the observer, like many of the Decadent personae. The hypocrisy with which he espouses the workers' cause while at the same time aspiring to the position of a leader with eventual bourgeois ambitions is an inconsistency which causes his failure. The conflicting tendencies within him, created by the conflicting social climate without, make him inviable and ineffective.

Like the Idiot archetype before him and the Jude figure after him, his character becomes diluted through a prevailing inadequacy caused by passivity and lack of initiative. In fact, in a position analogous to that of the Idiot, Etienne fails both in a 'mission' (here a political one rather than a religious one) and in a relationship with a woman: Catherine. His inability to communicate verbally is stressed repeatedly as a factor contributing to his social ineffectiveness. His reticent and timid nature makes him lose his beloved Catherine to the more aggressive and possessive Chaval, who steals her from under his eyes. His inherited tendency toward alcoholism which surfaces periodically at crucial moments that require full attention is comparable in its effect to the epileptic bouts of the Idiot. It renders him unable to deal with crisis situations.

Etienne's mental activity is also marked by a theoretical and abstract approach which distances him from the reality before him. He is given to musing and dreams, socialist theories and Utopian hopes, instead of action and implementation. Zola's indirect discourse highlights this. Symbolically, also, Etienne is often pictured pondering books and treatises, in static postures.

Yet to overscrutinize the personal deficiencies of an Etienne Lantier is to attribute psychological depth to a character in a novel which is in the very process of transforming individual character into paradigm, released from previous moral codes. The lean and timid Etienne remains a shadowy figure on the verge of assuming a collective identity. What distinguishes Etienne is that he becomes a failure in the development of a new social archetype rather than the weakening of a previous, recognizable model such as the religious one of the Idiot. The character of Etienne is in draft form even as the social structure into which he has been situated.

In the case of *Nana* (1880), often regarded as an ornamental period piece of the Second Empire's blatant 'corruption', it can be seen how the heroine's white body specifically becomes the target of the hyperbole. Nana enacts the 'nervous exaggeration of the sexual instinct'. Her personality is indeed subservient to her physicality as she becomes the personification of sensual excess. The individual character surpasses its individual significance, as it assumes a mythical dimension, conceptualizing whoredom. Character has lost its concreteness here not because it has become a pale paradigm of failure but because it has become a powerful conglomerate of sensual forces and has attained a mythic role. Zola obtains an overt and uncontrolled sensuality debilitating an entire social corpus. The literal and spectacular way in which Nana is shown infecting and destroying an entire society is the effect of stylistic exaggeration. She becomes a living emblem of appetite and waste as she 'feeds' irresponsibly upon the men in her midst and is never satiated. The consumption analogy with sexuality here receives prime treatment:

> What remained, in the hours when she was not indignant, was an ever open *appetite* of expenditure along with a natural contempt for the man who was paying, and a constant caprice of *consumption* and waste which took pride in the ruin of her lovers.

The word 'manger' is used with reference to her voracious sexual appetite as she becomes a 'devourer of men' (*mangeuse d'hommes*) eating up acres of property, heritages and professions by the mouthful—'à chaque bouchée, Nana dévorait un arpent. . . . Le triomphe de Nana fut de l'avoir et de lui manger un journal'. Zola brings a series of victims to Nana's caprices from various segments of society (journalists, bankers, counts) and hyperbolizes her magnetic power of attraction. Her most symbolic conquest is that of Count Muffat; she becomes therewith a catalyst for the decay of the aristocracy. In the metaphor of the golden fly, she is reported to be the agent of corruption as she spreads the squalor from the people to the aristocracy: 'corrupting and disorganizing Paris between her white thighs'. It is as if Zola is demonstrating as literally as possible his dictum: 'if one organ decays, all the others are affected and a very complex sickness is announced.' From the sordid grounds of Naturalism a leap to symbolization has occurred in the presentation of this alluring and 'supernatural' character that vividly engulfs a whole society. Her destructive force reflects the failings of that society.

It is interesting to note that in some respects, Zola is here not far from his Aesthete contender Huysmans in the creation of monstrous metaphors to express sensuality. The 'Grande Vérole' or Pox is the hyperbole of disease in *A rebours*. But where Huysmans resorted to mechanical women and lacquered erotic looking flowers suggesting the pox, Zola created a living, natural creature of sexual excess in the person of Nana. Whereas in Huysmans, the association between the pox and the artificial flower expresses the analogy between sensuality and art as possible avenues of escape from reality, in Zola it is this very reality of the social decay that is the target of his stylistic expression of sensuality.

If Nana is mythic rather than individualized, her character is stylized by exaggerated poses. Though written earlier, *Nana* seems to amalgamate the sensual forces and drives which surface sporadically in *Germinal.* The repeated metonymic images of her haunches, neck and the bed are the realistic parts which undergo hyperbolic treatment and create a cult of sexuality. The Byzantine bed outrageously replaces the altar. The self-infatuation of the narcissistic prototype, a kind of Salomé or *femme fatale,* is captured in physical terms:

> Nana was absorbed in her self-enrapture. She was bending her neck and looking attentively in the mirror at the little brown mark which she had on top of her right haunch. . . . Slowly she opened out her arms, suggesting the torso of a corpulent Venus. She stretched out her figure, examined herself before and behind, stopping to look at the contour of her bosom and at the fullness of her thighs.

Fittingly, she terminates this anatomical self-examination of neck, hips, torso and thighs with motions comparable to a belly dance (*danse du ventre*): the consumption reference returns. The presentation of Nana in her boudoir receives an arabesque and ornamental treatment, comparable to the elaborate sequences and detailed descriptions that were designated as true decadent style by the Aesthetic stylists of the term. But the Dionysian ecstasy which the character Nana achieves in her self-contemplation is devoid of creative energy because of her compulsive self-consciousness. Instead it leads to destruction, evidenced by the facts of the narrative. One of her liaisons results in miscarriage. And the final image of Nana is that of a rotting corpse which . . . portends the decadence of the social structure.

The apocalyptic paradigm also becomes associated with this work, as Nana is likened hyperbolically to the biblical beast of the Revelations in the mind of the infatuated Count Muffat:

> He thought of his old horror of Womankind, of the monster of the Scriptures, of the lubricious and the bestial. Nana was all covered with fine hair, the soft russet made her body velvety; whilst the Beast was apparent in her equine flanks and buttocks, in the fleshy bulges and depressions which endowed her sexuality with the provocative mystery of their shadows. She was indeed the Golden Beast, an unconscious force, whose odour alone corrupted the world.

The language used to describe Nana's bestial allure is provocative in its sensuality and visual effect. The outrageous scene in which the Count prances on all fours before Nana is reminiscent of the image of the Harlot of Babylon and her beast in the Apocalypse, identifying in the waning of Second Empire France a paradigm of moral corruption. . . . [The] biblical reference is invoked directly and elaborated upon in the novel's expression of social decadence.

In the case of two other social and political novels of the 'Rougon-Macquart,' *L'assommoir* (1877) and *L'argent* (1891), the consumption metaphor permeates the language and remains the unifying expression of the decadence which Zola observes. If in *Nana,* the signifier is the body, in *L'assommoir,* it is the drinking dive. The alembic of alcohol in *L'assommoir* receives hyperbolic description and the proliferation of the substance it contains literally translates the Decadent effects. As Nana's sexuality pervades the streets of Paris and destroys the aristocracy, so the liquid of the alembic floods the streets and debilitates the working-class population, contributing to the specific deterioration of a certain worker family:

> The alembic, noiselessly, without a flame, without a disturbance in the reflections of its dull copper, was sweating out alcohol, like a slow and persistent spring which would eventually pour out into the room, spread to the outer boulevards, and inundate the immense cavity of Paris.

Here, Zola is literally enacting the 'hypertrophie du détail vrai', as he focuses on the alembic and its alchemy into symbol. A mysterious quality is ascribed to this container in its transformation from a real observed object into a signifier by the exaggerated spread of its potent fluid. The excessive consumption of alcohol suggested by the obsessive intrusion of this signifier implies the universal weakening of will-power and the aggravation of an already inherent lassitude in the total population not exempting the working class. This is illustrated in particular in two members of the working class, Coupeau and, finally, his wife, Gervaise, the laundress. The Naturalist observation has been transformed into symbolic representation as the alcohol passes through the catalytic container to harbour Decadent effects: 'And the shadow cast by the machine on to the back wall created abominations, figures with tales, monsters opening up their jaws to devour the world.' The symbolic 'leap' has been enacted, and the consumptive power of the drinking dive is expressed through its association with monsters opening their enormous jaws to devour (*avaler*) and with a cauldron 'round as a belly' (*ventre*).

As the reality of the drinking bar L'Assommoir (which harbours the alembic) acquires a symbolic dimension, the word 'assommer' expands semantically into its various connotations. In particular, the signification of weariness is attached to it. The word in its meaning as 'bludgeon' denotes a weapon used to beat and overwhelm. In the context of the novel, it alludes particularly to conjugal quarrels often caused by excessive drinking—when men beat their women. The meanings 'drinking bar—bludgeon—overwhelm' carried by the highly allusive word 'assommoir' describe the situation. Gervaise's attempts to arrest her husband's degeneration are defeated by an over-

whelming sense of fatigue within her, which develops from her many ordeals. The young woman, mistreated and abandoned by her former lover and father of her children, Lantier, is coerced into marriage with a 'vaut rien' of a zinc worker who drains her of her energies, with anguish, while consuming himself in alcoholism. The forces are greater than the pathetic figure can endure, and she appears tired and beleaguered, burdened well beyond her 22 years. As in the case of *Germinal,* an immense fatigue weakens and consumes the human specimen. Zola here generalizes this condition to describe the corrupt society's effect through the analogy of a bludgeon actually used: 'Her dream was to live in an honest society because being in a bad society was like being bashed on the head; it cracked your skull open and reduced a woman to less than nothing.'

Another symbolic aggrandizement is that of the 'machine à vapeur', the steam engine located in the giant laundry shed. In an arresting paragraph describing the laundry scene, Zola conveys the oppressive environment through the cumulative power of detail. The prose follows the same expansive procedure used to describe the mine in *Germinal,* the body in *Nana* and the alembic in *L'assommoir* and markedly echoes these other engrossing descriptions, starting with the static, copulative 'c'était . . . ':

> It was an immense laundry shed, with a flat roof. . . . A heavy moisture rained down, charged with the smell of soap, a stale, dank, persistent aroma; at times the stronger odour of bleach prevailed . . . the steam engine, on the right hand side, white with a fine dew of condensation, puffed and snorted incessantly.

Here not only are the visual qualities magnified, but those of odour and sound are intensified. The combination of odours of bleach and soap with a milky fog of hot steam creates a suffocating atmosphere. In a further spectacular hyperbole, the whiteness of Gervaise's laundry extends like a sheet of blankness across the urban scene mirroring the way the blackness of the mine pervades *Germinal's* rural scene with darkness. Like the mine in *Germinal,* the mechanistic objects in *L'assommoir,* the 'machine à souler' (the alcohol machine) and the 'machine à vapeur' (the steam machine), are envisaged as agents generating excess and consuming the human element in the process.

*L'assommoir* demonstrates the breakdown of resistance, as it were, with respect to a disease. Zola scrutinizes the slow but steady process of decline through the figure of Gervaise. Placed in an environment of already deteriorated specimens, in the company of Lantier and Coupeau, she slowly loses her control as she imbibes the spirit of lassitude around her. Her ambitions of constructing a laundry boutique to support her dependent household are soon defeated; as the debts of her miserable store mount, the more heedless and lax she becomes. In a striking section of the novel, Zola gives physical signs of her moral deterioration. As her lassitude and irresponsibility increase, she becomes more corpulent and sordid: 'she too was getting too fat' (*elle aussi devenait trop grasse*). As in the case of Madame Hennebeau of *Germinal,* though in a different social context, her external flabbiness expresses an inner looseness: 'she let herself go' (*elle s'y abandonnait*), 'she lost her integrity' (*elle perdait de sa probité*), 'they were consuming her' (*ils l'usaient*). The manner by which she becomes oblivious to the increasing sordidness and putridness of smell (*puanteur*) around her is another sign of her deterioration. Zola turns her into a grotesque specimen, drastically expressing her state as one resembling unconsciousness: 'a torpor of lassitude' (*engourdissement de fainéantise*). An accumulation of his favourite 'decadent' synonyms exaggerates this particular case of decline with the alliterative *d* sound prevailing: 'dégringolade' (fall), 'débandade' (slackening), 'débâcle' (collapse), 'démolissement' (demolishing)—all of which seem to be summarized in the powerful word 'assommer'. At the end of the novel, Zola depicts Gervaise in a scene at L'Assommoir where, after fervently seeking the irresponsible Coupeau, she loses her own will-power. Forgetting her myriad responsibilities, she succumbs to the vitriol of the drinking dive, the ultimate catalyst of her decline.

The hyperbole in this novel highlights the process of demoralization through the contagious factors of lassitude and loss of control. This consumption-ailment aggravated by the effect of the alcohol is viewed as spreading from Coupeau to Gervaise and eventually to Nana, who was bred in this environment and used to spy on the drunken scenes. As already seen, it is then transmitted by Nana to the Count Muffat in the subsequent novel. One weakness breeds another, as Zola conveyed in an organic analogy in his theoretical treatise, *Le roman expérimental.* Here it is not a case of duplication as it is in *Germinal,* but of multiplication of effects, and the fluid alcohol is the metaphor for such intemperate proliferation.

Finally, in the novel *L'argent,* the hyperbole is applied to money: wasteful expenditure is viewed in terms of promiscuous speculation and that excessive spending is part of the hyperbole of destructive consumption. If in *L'assommoir* Zola isolates the working-class scene in his scrutiny of consumption, when he comes to the writing of his lesser-known novel, *L'argent,* fourteen years later, he takes on the financial sector. Furthermore, *L'argent* recasts the dialectics of *Germinal* along an ideological plane. Here the focus is no longer on the contending position of labour versus capital, but rather on the process of capital consumption and the resulting deterioration of the productive capacity of society. In presenting the dialects of capitalist behaviour, Zola places money in the pivotal position of love: 'Why make money bear the burden of the corruptions and crimes of which it is the cause? Is love less tainted, that love which creates life?' But the multipile analogies of love and money in this novel express inordinate speculation in the terms of prostitution. Zola is concerned with the distinction between the accumulation of capital and its wasteful expenditure—accumulation being a constructive process whereas excessive spending is part of the hyperbole of destructive consumption.

At the heights of his commercial success, Saccard and his wife Caroline lyrically muse upon their money, envisaging it as a 'pluie d'or', showering all of Paris with dazzle and golden lustre. The hyperboles are applied to gold, depicted as reigning as a king or god over society. Its abuse in overt speculation precipitates financial failures that are likened to an apocalyptic destruction. Zola evokes the spirit of the end of the world. Eschatological imagery is associated with this excess: 'But this time, behind the reddish vapour of the horizon, in the distant crises of the city, there was a great hollow cracking, the rumbling, approaching end of the world.' Zola traces the destruction of a whole financial empire, and the association of empire with the 'banque universelle' (fittingly named) and the portrait of Saccard as its emperor exaggerate the dimensions of its sudden collapse. The vivid description of Paris as a colossal place harbouring a night of debauchery creates a Roman aura of overt decadence: 'like a colossal palace in which debauchery was active until dawn.' As for Saccard, the archetypal speculator, he represents once again a mechanism, a chemistry characteristic of a society propelled by appetite, in which speculation is viewed as a necessary 'fattening' (*l'engrais nécessaire*). Rather than simply determine him as a product of his society, Zola conveys him as its extension. This principal character, as in the case of *Germinal's* Etienne Lantier, is a type rather than a personality. Much less is known of him than of Stendhal's Julien Sorel, for example, whose psychology is explicitly conveyed by his author. As has been seen, Zola subordinates psychology and character to plot and issues in his determination to observe and indicate an eschatological, gruelling spirit of an age, the diagnosis of which seems to be hyperbolic consumption.

Nana's wasteful expenditure is mirrored in that of Saccard's, her male counterpart. Both register factors created by the chronic instability of the time; both serve as personifications of the social body mechanism. Their mythlike identities serve as measurements of the typical condition. What becomes disturbing is that the singularity of their individual cases is anulled as it becomes applicable to the general condition; and the exaggeration which their specific cases imply becomes descriptive of the rule rather than the exception.

Flesh and money blatantly invade Zola's landscapes; and eating along with copulating become the principal activities, as they climactically burst into hyperbolic dimensions consistently throughout the novels. In *Nana,* the body becomes the imperial throne, praised and revered as it proceeds in its increasing conquest and debilitates several sectors of the ruling class, most notably the nobility. In *Germinal,* the mine, physically lodging the private capital, grows to outrageous dimensions of mouth, belly (*ventre*) and beast, consuming in this instance labour and contributing to its 'avachissement' or fatigue. In *L'assommoir,* the destructive meaning of the word 'assommer' receives attention as the wine and alcohol are agents debilitating that working class, already weakened in lethargy. This is paralleled in *L'argent,* where the wine analogy is replaced by the gold one: showers of gold (*pluie d'or*) and liquid money (*l'argent qui coule*) flood the city of Paris, having in their intensity the semblance of a superhuman force.

What ties these various facets of social decadence together is the element of excess, expressed in the stylistic method of magnification. Zola's narrative is infected with the germ of hyperbole just as James's narrative is contaminated by the figure of postponement. In each case, the germ assaults the materiality of the text and becomes ingrained in its structure. It affects the contours of narrative and becomes the telling indicator of the Decadence—whether it be the failure of participation, as in James, or the height of indulgence, as in Zola. In his magnification of selected individual objects—the wine, the body, the alembic, the money—Zola creates explosions of gargantuan proportions, encoding the abnormality of Decadence.

Myriad examples of this process of hyperbole can be located in the gamut of Zola's novels, as an identifying trait of continuous consumption and collective drain. It becomes clear that this observation is not limited to the particular problems of Second Empire France, because the symptom of moral flabbiness detected across the various social sectors is a common concern of modern industrial societies, and is evident as well in the other novelists here considered. Zola's spectacular and grandiose visions of decay, with the histrionics of the crumbling and the ruin, seem to pave the way for the colossal catastrophes envisaged by a Conrad. The French author and his contemporaries used a set of metaphoric devices to convey their sense of decadence. In the particular case of Zola, the loss of moral containment was relentlessly expressed in the hyperbole of consumption. (pp. 55-72)

> Suzanne Nalbantian, "Emile Zola and the Hyperbole of Consumption," in her Seeds of Decadence in the Late Nineteenth-Century Novel: A Crisis in Values, *St. Martin's Press, 1983, pp. 55-72.*

## Philip Walker   (essay date 1984)

[*In the following excerpt, Walker discusses conflicting religious and philosophical doctrines among intellectuals of the mid-nineteenth century, asserting that* Germinal *exemplifies Zola's own contradictory and ambiguous beliefs.*]

No other great novelist that I can think of is more radically incoherent on the philosophical or religious level than Zola. Although the frequent recurrence of a large number of ideas provides his writings with a certain consistency, not even the semblance of a logical system binds them together. The enormous efforts that he made—especially, it would seem in his last years—to arrive at some overall logical order did not get him very far. Obsessed by a multitude of disparate dreams, intuitions, hypotheses, doctrines, torn, as he had himself foreseen [in a letter to Paul Cézanne] at the age of twenty that he would be, between doubt and faith, hope and despair, he never attained to a comprehensive philosophy or religion that he could permanently embrace.

Undoubtedly there were moments when he was persuaded that he had found such a philosophy or religion or at least the basis for it or the key to it. There is no reason to suspect that when, for example, he recorded in "Religion" the divine revelation that Eros is the supreme principle of creation he was not convinced that he had penetrated to the core of things. But such moments never, it would appear, lasted very long. . . . [He] is constantly coming up with new philosophies and new religious faiths. He repeat-

edly formulates his thoughts in forms reminiscent of the Catholic Credos, but never recites the same creed twice. Moreover, it is precisely with respect to the most central questions that he provides us with the most divergent answers. It is impossible to pin him down to any firm definition of God. He entertains wildly conflicting ideas concerning the nature of man, man's relationship with God, the problem of evil, death, history, and progress.

Even toward the end of his career, Zola's philosophical and religious thought was just as unsettled and pervaded by tensions and contradictions as ever before. In December 1893, only five months after the publication of *Le docteur Pascal,* with its ringing manifesto of his religion of life, he composed *Lazare,* with its bitter rejection of life, its intense longing for utter extinction. In August 1898, the same month that he began *Fécondité,* with its deification of life and love—"divine desire"—he disconsolately wrote his friend Fernand Desmoulin, "I have never believed in anything but work . . . " As for "Les quatre evangiles," it is, despite Zola's efforts to make it logically coherent, full of glaring contradictions. The final flowering of his old ambition to be the new prophet whom the world was waiting for, it submits to us not just one new religion, but, rather, a series of largely disparate new faiths, each with a different supreme value, each with a different New Messiah, each with a different vision of the shape of things to come.

Obviously, all Zola's life, that unified, harmonious vision,

*Mine workers, whose travails Zola fictionalized in his novel* Germinal, *pay their last respects at the author's funeral.*

that "one entire Truth which alone can cure my sick soul," eluded his grasp. At the heart of his philosophical and religious thought, we find only a vast cacophony.

This cacophony invades all his major fictional series, including "Les Rougon-Macquart." When we consider this imposing assemblage of twenty novels as a single work (which is the way Zola wanted us to regard it), we can find no more philosophical or religious harmony than we can in the whole corpus of Zola's writings. For example, the optimistic vision of the world conveyed to us by *Au bonheur des dames* and the pessimistic vision of the world conveyed to us by *La bête humaine* are impossible to reconcile logically. Or one might cite among many other possible examples of the contradictory elements inherent in "Les Rougon-Macquart" the clashing soteriological doctrines implicit in it. *La faute de l'abbé Mouret* suggests that happiness is to be achieved through the mystical union with the supreme forces of creation that results from the act of love. *Le rêve,* on the other hand, advances the theory that man can be saved by entertaining the right illusions, that is to say, by the power of the imagination to alter the world, which is nothing but an illusion of the senses, "in such a way that the environment, the so-called grace come from God, will come from man to improve man." Yet in *Le docteur Pascal,* the philosophical conclusion of "Les Rougon-Macquart," Zola places all his trust in the saving powers of reason, science, work, and life.

Any attempt to perceive a logically consistent philosophical or religious core in "Les Rougon-Macquart" will, moreover, find no support in Zola's working notes or numerous letters and articles dealing with the series or with his fiction in general. The Taine-like philosophy that dominates the **"Notes générales sur la marche de l'œuvre"** and **"Notes générales sur la nature de l'œuvre"** that he jotted down while first planning the series in 1868 and 1869 is not at all identical with the Claude Bernard- or Littré-like positivism professed in *Le roman expérimental* (1880). Neither of these different positivistic philosophies goes together with the unanimism with which Zola identifies himself in his letter of July 22, 1885, to Jules Lemaitre—not to mention Zola's effort in his working notes for *Le docteur Pascal* to base the series retroactively on Renan's *Credo* as summarized by Melchior de Vogüé.

As for Zola's individual novels, some, obviously, reflect the contradictions, fissures, and confusions in Zola's philosophical and religious thought more completely and faithfully than others, and *Germinal* would appear to be an excellent, perhaps even the best, example. It certainly does so much more completely and faithfully than, for instance, *La terre,* which is dominated by only one of Zola's competing visions of nature, the vision summarized in the great hymn to the Great Mother in the final pages, or *La bête humaine,* with its unadulterated pessimism. Even *L'assommoir,* with its mingled pessimism and optimism, its incoherent mixture of Zola's more or less competing cults of life, nature, love, science, progress, force, and work, or *La joie de vivre,* with its sharp, unresolved conflict between the quasi-Schopenhauerian elements in Zola's thought and his cult of life, cannot, I suspect, altogether compete with *Germinal* in this regard.

Unlike nearly all of Zola's other creative works, including those novels I have just mentioned, *Germinal* would seem not only to reflect all the major competing philosophical and religious tendencies in Zola's thought but to ascribe to each of them much the same weight it has in Zola's thought in general, that is to say, a weight approximately equal to that of each of the others. The metaphysically skeptical factualist and positivist, the curiously incoherent pessimist, and the even more incoherent optimist would all appear to be equally represented in *Germinal,* just as, in my opinion, they are in Zola's thought considered as a whole.

For this very reason, moreover, *Germinal* would seem to me to testify more strongly than many if not all of Zola's other novels (I will not even mention his short stories, plays, and librettos) to the absoluteness of his failure to work out for himself some faith that he could permanently and consistently embrace, to create a solid, coherent fictional world, or even to impose just any logical order on his thought simply for the sake of order.

I have no idea what others may think of *Germinal's* ability to tolerate, even, in some cases, invite, so many clashing philosophical or religious interpretations. Insofar as I know, this has never received the critical attention that it deserves. Even its full magnitude has never, to the best of my knowledge, been noted by any other commentator. Critics have generally contented themselves with one reading. None that I know of has attempted more than three. Even Zola's philosophical and religious thought in general has not aroused the same widespread attention as some of his other aspects. Although excellent studies, some in considerable depth, have been published on certain important elements of it, we have as yet no satisfactory attempt to present it in its entirety. There are, I suppose, good reasons for this. Since the present revival of critical interest in Zola began, in the fifties, critics have, as a group, been more concerned with his mythopoeic dimensions and structural qualities. The school of thought—represented in France by, among others, Lanson—which tended to regard literature as a vulgarization of philosophy has throughout this same period been out of fashion. Furthermore, many critics have tended not to take Zola very seriously as an intellectual, rather unjustly, I suspect. Moreover, even those about whom this is not necessarily true may be all too easily tempted to dismiss the philosophical and religious contradictions that can be read into *Germinal,* despite their number and violence, as simply further confirmation of the truism that most creative artists are not systematic philosophers or theologians.

In my own personal opinion, however, the philosophical and religious contradictions that we can observe or at least legitimately suspect in *Germinal* must very definitely be included among those factors that make it the exceedingly powerful novel that it is. I am glad that these contradictions are there or at least may very possibly be there, that Zola did not decide while planning *Germinal* to include in it only ideas that would not logically clash, to make it the vehicle of a single consistent vision. Each reader is free to perceive in it a world view congenial to his own. Furthermore, what it lost in systematicness, in unity, it gained in fidelity to Zola's own personality. Indeed, I can think of no other individual novel of Zola's that comes so close to attaining one of his major artistic ideals—to give himself to us, as he once said, "whole, in all my violence and in all my gentleness, such as God made me."

There is also—at least for me—something unutterably poignant in these contradictions. I cannot contemplate them without thinking of the immense, but futile, spiritual and intellectual struggle that produced them, and I find this struggle, which they evoke, every bit as moving as the epic battle for social justice that the novel relates.

Moreover, insofar as Zola was able, in writing *Germinal,* to express the whole range of his mature philosophical and religious thought, with its violent discordancies and lack of any fixed center, he came closer to attaining another, almost equally important artistic aim: that of embodying in his own works the mind of his age, of "being of his own time."

The main outlines of the history of French philosophical and religious thought during Zola's lifetime are well known: the breakdown of the eclectic philosophy of Cousin; the predominance of positivism from around 1850 on; the critical reaction provoked during those same years by that very predominance; the skepticism and pessimism that culminated in the philosophical dilettantism and vogue for Schopenhauer and von Hartmann in the 1880s; the Catholic renaissance and idealistic revival from around 1880 or earlier. What, however, has been less widely remarked is the strong elements of discord and division discernible throughout this entire period both in its philosophical and religious speculations as a whole and in the outlook of many of the individual thinkers behind them.

As D. G. Charlton has emphasized [in *Positivist Thought in France During the Second Empire, 1852-1870*], "The progress of philosophy in the nineteenth century is not so much a succession of pitched battles in which one side or another is triumphant and banishes its opponents from the field, as a debate prolonged throughout the century." As much as ever before, Paris during Zola's lifetime was a seething melting pot of ideas. Everything conspired to make the philosophical and religious setting in which Zola wrote one of rich complexity, controversy, confusion, ambiguity: the widespread rejection of Christianity; the accelerating pace of the scientific revolution; the collapse of eclecticism; the decline of faith in the vast, soaring metaphysical systems and religious-substitutes of the first half of the century; the impact of a host of foreign philosophers, scholars, and writers—Kant, Hegel, Schelling, Fichte, Herder, Creuzer, Strauss, Schopenhauer, von Hartmann, Marx, Nietzsche, J. S. Mill, Spencer, Coleridge, Shelley, Carlyle, Tennyson, Browning, Ruskin, and numerous others; not to mention the influence of a multitude of native thinkers, critics, poets, and novelists propounding a great variety of doctrines, many of which were incompatible—Saint-Simon, Fourier, Cabet, Enfantin, Leroux, Proudhon, Lamennais, Michelet, Quinet, Comte, Hugo, Sainte-Beuve, Lamartine, Vigny, Littré, Bernard, Renan, Taine, Leconte de Lisle, Baudelaire, Flaubert,

Cournot, Lequier, Renouvier, Vacherot, Ravaisson, Simon, Paul Janet, Lachelier, Fouillée, Boutroux, Bergson, Bourget, Barrès, Brunetière, Anatole France. . . .

During the period when positivism was dominant, opposition to positivism was neither dormant nor ineffective; the readers of the Second Empire were solicited by opponents of positivism quite as forceful and alert as the positivist writers whom they attacked. Indeed, Ravaisson, one of the most perspicacious contemporary observers of French philosophy in the 1850s and 1860s, concluded in 1867 that the general tendency of thought at this time was toward idealism. Paul Janet, writing the following year, was equally hopeful, even going so far as to claim that "the spiritualist school is still the most active, the most fecund, I might even say the most progressive of contemporary schools." Meanwhile, initiated by Cournot, Lequier, and Renouvier, neo-criticism had already become a formidable force. In short, the "age of positivism" is also the age of neo-criticism and a revitalized spiritualist philosophy.

Furthermore, during the next fifty years or so, the years of the critical reaction and so-called idealistic revival, positivism not only survived, but was in many ways even more militant than under the Second Empire. Ribot, Dumas, Pierre Janet, and others carried the positivistic outlook into psychology; Richet into physiology; Le Dantec into biology; Espinas, Izoulet, Durkheim, and followers like Levy-Bruhl into sociology; Charles Lalo into aesthetics; Henri Berr and Lacombe into the philosophy of history. Among professional philosophers, it persisted in the generation after Taine, Renan, and Littré in such men as Abel Rey, Goblot, Cresson, Jules de Gaultier.

Although pessimism was particularly widespread in the 1880s, strong pessimistic currents—it need hardly be pointed out—ran through the literature and thought of the whole period.

Throughout Zola's lifetime, moreover, the tradition that had produced in such rich profusion the great optimistic metaphysical systems and secular faiths of the first fifty years or so of the century—the cults of science, social religions, metaphysical religions, occult and neo-pagan religions, cults of history and progress—was far from exhausted. Hugo's prophetic voice kept ringing out at the center of French society until 1885, the year *Germinal* was published. Michelet's visionary *L'oiseau, L'insecte, La mer,* and *La montagne* came out between 1856 and 1867. *L'amour* was published in 1858. The spirit of the great social prophets of the first half of the century lived on in the republican and socialist thought of the second half. Littré, Berthelot, Le Dantec, and many others helped perpetuate the worship of science and progress. As late as 1888, Theophilanthropy, a secular religious cult founded in 1798, still had, as Julien Vinson notes, more than 85,000 adherents. Led by Laromiguiére and Laffitte, Comte's Religion of Humanity was still practiced by a faithful following in the 1890s. Humanitarianism in general remained throughout the whole period (to quote Guérard) "the spiritual backbone of the French nation." Stirred by the passions of the Dreyfus affair, it demonstrated once again its strong secular appeal as the century approached its close. As Paul-Hyacinthe Loyson was to confess in 1910, "It was through the Affair that the men of our generation communicated for the first time in Humanity. For us, Humanity was and remains a religion."

Moreover, the extreme intellectual divisions of Zola's period were by no means confined to explicit oppositions between positivists and anti-positivists, optimists and pessimists, spiritualists and materialists, believers and doubters. Not only the young dilettants described by Bourget in the 1880s, but also most other individual intellectuals, including Taine, Renan, and the other intellectual leaders of Zola's generation, were violently torn between conflicting attitudes and ideas. It was the great age of the "divided mind." When Renan, comparing himself to the legendary hircocervus, half goat, half stag, of the medieval scholastics, wrote, "Each of my halves was forever trying to demolish the other," he could have been speaking not only of himself, but also of a multitude of his most thoughtful contemporaries. (87-92)

In *Essais de psychologie contemporaine,* published in 1883, the year before Zola began *Germinal,* Paul Bourget wrote of the vast confusion that characterized his more thoughtful contemporaries in general. He noted how difficult, if not impossible, it was to inhale the Parisian atmosphere of the day—that atmosphere "supercharged with contrary electricities, where many different, detailed bits of information dart about like a population of invisible atoms"—and maintain any systematic unity in one's own ideas. "We are living in a time of religious and metaphysical collapse," he stated, "when all the old doctrines lie scattered about on the ground. . . . An unprecedented anarchy is now the rule among all those who think." He went on to note how he and his contemporaries, in contrast to eighteenth-century skeptics, had even reached the point of calling into question their own doubts. In 1886, only a year after the publication of *Germinal,* Charles Fuster, struck by much the same phenomena as Bourget, summed them all up very well when he wrote:

> Contemporary life is a long torrent of lava. You will not find anything precise in our ideas, because we entertain all ideas. Current thought—I mean the thought of those people who think (there are precious few)—fed by doctrines which are too opposed to survive together, has been invaded by an inexpressible chaos. In this singular malaise of a thought that has become too refined, too open to all the most contradictory impressions, there is no faith exempt from doubt, no doubt . . . that does not have its moments of faith.

Not only most of the individual ideas, but also most of the philosophical and religious tensions, fissures, and contradictions that can be read into individual Zola novels like *Germinal* as well as into Zola's combined works viewed as a whole are, of course, not only Zola's but those of this whole age—this age when the intellectual and spiritual upheaval provoked by the rise of modern civilization was surely at its peak.

Finally, I must point out that much of what seems to me most admirable in the artistic form of *Germinal* lies precisely in how Zola appears to have consciously or unconsciously coped in it with the artistic problems resulting from his philosophical and religious contradictions.

I have in mind, first of all, the truly masterful way in which he would seem to have managed in *Germinal,* as in *L'assommoir, La joie de vivre,* and several of his other novels, to translate his violent philosophical and religious ambiguity into the very form and substance of his fiction, thus producing, as we know, a veritable feast of ambiguity—an even richer feast indeed, as I have tried to show . . . , than some of us may have at first suspected.

Does *Germinal* belittle or exalt, undermine or reinforce the humanitarian dream of "the great final kiss"? Is *Germinal* a deterministic novel, and, if so, what kind of determinism does it express—scientific determinism, Tainian determinism, pantheistic determinism? Does *Germinal* hold out to us the hope of significant social improvement, or does it not suggest, rather, the tragic futility of the nineteenth-century faith in progress? Is Nature as Zola portrays it in the novel good or bad? Does the novel deify Earth or not? Is the novel pantheistic or not? If it is pantheistic, which of the different kinds of pantheism discernible elsewhere in Zola does it reflect? Must we interpret the novel's emphasis on the sordid, painful side of existence as an expression of Zola's pessimism? Or could it not be motivated by, among other things, his desire, as he put it in his notes for *Le docteur Pascal,* "to show courageously what things are really like, so that I could say that despite everything life is great and good because we live it with so much eagerness"? Is not the novel's repeated insistence on the smallness and frailty of man just another possible expression of Zola's pessimism? Or could it not originate in the rejection of anthropocentrism which marks his essentially optimistic "new faith" based on geology? Is the time of the novel geological time? Or is it some other kind of time—the circular time of the myth of eternal renewal or a time more in accordance with romantic humanitarianism? What is the symbolic meaning, if any, of Etienne and Négrel's fraternal embrace? Does the title *Germinal* reflect the positivistic historian or sociologist in Zola or the optimistic, visionary prophet? To what extent are the optimistic visionary elements of the novel serious prophetic visions, not just mere reveries? Does the novel's structure mirror Zola's philosophical positivism or his scientism—that is to say, his tendency, so typical of his age, to try to "derive" a metaphysics or religion from science? . . . [One] cannot try to answer these questions—or any of the dozens of similar questions which must inevitably occur to anyone contemplating *Germinal* in the light of Zola's philosophical and religious thought—without realizing how wonderfully ambiguous this novel is on the philosophical and religious level.

But I also have in mind the way Zola has managed consciously or unconsciously in *Germinal,* despite its lack of any solid, coherent vision of reality, to achieve an overwhelming realism—partly through the use of illusionistic tricks involving every sort of violence (violent actions, violent contrasts, Expressionistic color, etc.), partly through an intense emphasis on, and fidelity to, that side of reality which our predominantly sensate culture tends to mistake for the whole of reality, and partly through his preoccupation with themes that have to do with those aspects of our modern collective experience that most vitally concern us and therefore seem most real.

I also have in mind how effectively the firm, harmonious artistic structure of **Germinal** offsets—and in a way compensates for—its philosophical and religious ambiguity. As elsewhere in Zola's fiction, his love of stability and order, frustrated on the higher intellectual plane, asserts itself with a vengeance on the aesthetic level—in the rigorous, almost mathematical logic with which nearly everything in this massive, complex work is organized around its central theme; in its tight, geometrical compartmentation; in its powerfully stylized, architectonic use of color; in its strong symmetries, achieved primarily through correspondences of form, emphasis, or arrangement set up between contrasting elements. Even some of the most contradictory elements of the ambiguous and, I might add, largely protean, miragelike world view that, as we have seen, the novel appears to reflect when contemplated in the context of Zola's overall philosophical and religious thought themselves become parts of the harmonious artistic design. The positivistic and visionary elements set off each other in aesthetically pleasing contrapuntal relationships. The optimist counterbalances the pessimist; the doubter, the man of faith; the scientific iconoclast, the advocate of scientist new religions; the serious reformer, the spinner of escapist reveries; the geologist-prophet, the romantic humanitarian; the perpetuator of ancient myths and rites, the radically modern intellectual.

Lastly, I am thinking of the thematic value of **Germinal**'s philosophical and religious ambiguity insofar as it may indeed be interpreted as symptomatic of Zola's confused, unstable (and no doubt always partly unconscious) vision of reality. For some of us, it heightens the impression of being plunged into a world racked by cosmic catastrophe, a world wholly caught up in the process of destruction and renewal. It suggests the immensity, the all-pervasive nature of a process which transforms man's fundamental principles and symbols as well as his external environment. Looking outward through, as it were, Zola's eye, we see this process going on on the socioeconomic level—the Montsou strike, the rise of the proletariat, the war between labor and capital. Reversing our gaze, peering into Zola's eye itself, we glimpse signs of the spiritual and intellectual chaos engendered by the same process. (pp. 93-6)

> *Philip Walker, in his* 'Germinal' and Zola's Philosophical and Religious Thought, *John Benjamins Publishing Company, 1984, 157 p.*

---

## FURTHER READING

Baguley, David, ed. *Critical Essays on Emile Zola.* Boston: G. K. Hall & Co., 1986, 198 p.
    Collection of reviews and essays dating from Zola's lifetime to more recent criticism that features diverse interpretations of Zola's novels.

Becker, George J. "Emile Zola." In his *Master European Realists of the Nineteenth Century,* pp. 93-131. New York: Frederick Ungar Publishing Co., 1982.
    Overview of novels in the "Rougon-Macquart" series.

Beizer, Janet L. "Uncovering *Nana:* The Courtesan's New Clothes." *L'esprit créateur* 25, No. 2 (Summer 1985): 45-56.
    Views Nana—a character often depicted unclothed, though her true identity is continually veiled—as representative of a contradiction of Zola's literary theories. Beizer states: "To Zola's 'one must tell everything,' Nana impertinently replies 'one cannot show all'."

Brown, Frederick. "Zola and Manet: 1866." *The Hudson Review* 61, No. 1 (Spring 1988): 71-92.
    Account of Zola's journalistic works, discussing his association with Hippolyte de Villemessant, editor of the weekly *L'evénement,* as well as relationships with Impressionist painters—notably Edouard Manet—whose works Zola defended.

Buckler, William E. "Emile Zola: *L'assommoir.*" In his *Novels in the Making,* pp. 119-40. Boston: Houghton Mifflin Company, 1961.
    Annotated excerpts of Zola's notes for *L'assommoir.*

Chaitin, Gilbert. "The Voices of the Dead: Love, Death and Politics in Zola's *Fortune de Rougon:* Parts I and II." *Literature and Psychology* 26, Nos. 3, 4 (1976): 131-44, 148-58.
    Psychoanalytical interpretation of *La fortune des Rougon.* Part I analyzes such themes as death, love, and politics "to show in detail how virtually all of the major themes of the ["Rougon-Macquart"] series, natural, psychological and social, have their origin in this first novel"; Part II focuses on sexual imagery, voyeurism, and repression.

Cogman, P. W. M. "The Comic in Zola's *La terre.*" *Forum for Modern Language Studies* 23, No. 2 (April 1987): 161-68.
    Links comic characters in *La terre* to its central thematic concerns: "fertility/fertilisation, sexuality/excretion, authority and respectability and their subversion."

Duncan, Phillip A. "The 'Art' of Landscape in Zola's *L'oeuvre.*" *Symposium* 39, No. 3 (Fall 1985): 167-76.
    Compares cityscapes by the artist-protagonist Claude in *L'oeuvre* to Zola's narrative technique within the novel, concluding that both Claude's paintings and Zola's narration exhibit characteristics of Romanticism, Impressionism, and Symbolism.

*L'esprit créateur,* Special Issue: Zola and Naturalism 25, No. 4 (Winter 1985).
    Features essays by leading Zola critics, including Patrick Brady, David Baguley, and Philip Walker, as well as reviews of new book-length studies of Zola and a retrospective of criticism of Zola's works from 1976-1985 by Brady that updates surveys of Zola studies by Robert Lethbridge and F. W. J. Hemmings (see Further Reading entries below).

Goldberg, M. A. "Zola and Social Revolution: A Study of *Germinal.*" *The Antioch Review* 27, No. 4 (Winter 1967-68): 491-507.
    Interprets *Germinal* as an artistic portrayal of Zola's vision of social revolution.

Goodin, George. "The Flawed Victim." In his *The Poetics of Protest: Literary Form and Political Implication in the Victim-*

*of-Society Novel,* pp. 87-132. Carbondale: Southern Illinois University Press, 1985.

> Discusses Gervaise in *L'assommoir* as a "flawed victim"—a character who possesses a weakness that contributes to his or her own downfall. Goodin asserts that Gervaise's flaw is her divided personality that pits a tendency toward complying with the reckless lifestyle of those around her against her desire to remain independent and committed to hard work.

Hemmings, F. W. J. "The Origin of the Terms *Naturalisme, Naturaliste.*" *French Studies* 8, No. 2 (April 1954): 109-21.

> Traces various meanings of the terms *naturaliste* and *naturalisme.* Hemmings discusses critics and writers who employed these terms prior to Zola and their influence on Zola.

——. "The Present Position of Zola Studies." *French Studies* 10, No. 2 (April 1956): 97-122.

> Overview of studies of Zola's novels, critical essays, and journalistic works, as well as biographical studies of Zola, collections of his correspondences and diaries, and interviews with Zola. For subsequent overviews of Zola criticism and biography, see Further Reading entries under *L'esprit créateur* and Robert Lethbridge.

——. *Emile Zola.* Rev. ed. Oxford: Clarendon Press, 1966, 329 p.

> Standard biography in English.

——. *The Life and Times of Emile Zola.* New York: Charles Scribner's Sons, 1977, 192 p.

> Illustrated biography.

Knapp, Bettina L. *Emile Zola.* New York: Frederick Ungar Publishing Co., 1980, 174 p.

> Biography that focuses on the continued influence of Zola. Knapp asserts in the introduction that Zola's "work remains powerful because he realistically and symbolically searched the heart of humankind and endowed it with the dimensions of eternity."

Lemaître, Jules. "Emile Zola." In his *Literary Impressions,* translated by A. W. Evans, pp. 108-53. London: Daniel O'Connor, 1921.

> Appraises Zola's methods of narration in the "Rougon-Macquart" series. Designating Zola "an epic poet and a pessimistic poet," Lemaître ascribes what he perceives as characteristics of epic poetry to Zola's works such as universalized characters types, exaggeration, repetition, and depiction of the "collective soul of the crowd."

Lethbridge, Robert. "Twenty Years of Zola Studies (1956-1975)." *French Studies* 31, No. 3 (July 1977): 281-93.

> Summation of Zola studies from 1956-1975, continuing Hemmings's survey and preceding Patrick Brady's (see Further Reading entries above).

——, and Keefe, Terry, eds. *Zola and the Craft of Fiction: (Essays in Honour of F. W. J. Hemmings).* Leicester: Leicester University Press, 1990, 166 p.

> Essays in French and English.

Nelson, Brian. *Zola and the Bourgeoisie: A Study of Themes and Techniques in 'Les Rougon-Macquart'.* Totowa, N. J.: Barnes & Noble Books, 1983, 230 p.

> Analysis of Zola's social vision as reflected in his delineation of bourgeois values in the "Rougon-Macquart" series.

Page, Dwight H. "Generation and Degeneration in Emile Zola's *L'assommoir.*" *Philological Papers* 34 (1988): 38-50.

> Interpretation of *L'assommoir,* illustrating "the unity between the textual structure of *L'assommoir* and its ethical and sociological messages."

Parmée, Douglas. Introduction to *The Attack on the Mill, and Other Stories,* by Emile Zola, pp. vii-xxiv. Oxford: Oxford University Press, 1984.

> Stresses unique characteristics of Zola's short fiction not prevalent in his novels, noting especially an ironic tone in the short stories.

Ponterio, Robert. "Souvarine and His Rabbit: Using Images to Define Character in *Germinal.*" *Philological Papers* 35 (1989): 37-45.

> Analyzes the character of Souvarine and the function of the rabbit in *Germinal* as a means to discern "the way associations drawn from various images of the rabbit are integrated into the reader's model of the anarchist."

Root, Winthrop H. *German Criticism of Zola: 1875-1893.* New York: Columbia University Press, 1931, 112 p.

> Analysis of Zola's reception by German critics who were early proponents of Zola's theories of literary Naturalism. This study examines the relation of Zola's theories to German Naturalism.

Schor, Naomi. "Smiles of the Sphinx: Zola and the Riddle of Femininity." In her *Breaking the Chain: Women, Theory, and French Realist Fiction,* pp. 29-47. New York: Columbia University Press, 1985.

> Assessment of Zola's portrayal of women in *Nana* and *Une page d'amour* based on the premise that "in order to bring to light the problematics of femininity which haunts Zola's works, we will have to read Zola *with* Freud, his contemporary: not the Freud of the Oedipus, but of the preoedipus, the author of the essays on the 'riddle of femininity'."

Shor, Ira Neil. "The Novel in History: Lukács and Zola." *CLIO* 2, No. 1 (October 1972): 19-41.

> Summarizes concepts of Georg Lukács's Marxist theory of literary analysis and examines *Germinal, The Debacle,* and *Truth* in view of Lukács's negative appraisals of these works, finding that "of the three novels to be discussed, *Germinal* rises far above Lukács's low estimate, while *The Debacle* and most of *Truth* are more static than *Germinal,* and do show an authorial consciousness frozen in history."

Tilby, Michael. "Emile Zola and His First English Biographer." *Laurels* 59, No. 1 (Spring-Summer 1988): 33-56.

> Questions the reliability of Robert Sherard's biography of Zola (see excerpt dated 1893).

Walker, Philip. *Zola.* London: Routledge & Kegan Paul, 1985, 257 p.

> Critical biography.

Warren, Jill. "Zola's View of Prostitution in *Nana.*" In *The Image of the Prostitute in Modern Literature,* edited by Pierre L. Horn and Mary Beth Pringle, pp. 29-41. New York: Frederick Ungar Publishing Co., 1984.

> Considers the depiction of prostitution in *Nana* indicative of Zola's bourgeois attitudes toward sexuality as well as illustrative of the social decadence that led to the

fall of the Second Empire (1852-1871), concluding that Zola conveys a misogynist viewpoint in the novel.

*Yale French Studies, Special Issue: Zola,* No. 42 (1969). Critical essays by noted Zola scholars, including Naomi Schor, F. W. J. Hemmings, Philip Walker, and Henri Mitterand.

# Twentieth-Century Literary Criticism

Cumulative Indexes
Volumes 1-41

# This Index Includes References to Entries in These Gale Series

***Children's Literature Review*** includes excerpts from reviews, criticism, and commentary on works of authors and illustrators who create books for children.

***Classical and Medieval Literature Criticism*** offers excerpts of criticism on the works of world authors from classical antiquity through the fourteenth century.

***Contemporary Authors*** series encompasses five related series. ***Contemporary Authors*** provides biographical and bibliographical information on more than 97,000 writers of fiction, nonfiction, poetry, journalism, drama, and film. ***Contemporary Authors New Revision Series*** provides completely updated information on active authors covered in previously published volumes of *CA*. ***Contemporary Authors Permanent Series*** consists of updated listings for deceased and inactive authors removed from the original volumes 9-36 when those volumes were revised. ***Contemporary Authors Autobiography Series*** presents specially commissioned autobiographies by leading contemporary writers. ***Contemporary Authors Bibliographical Series*** contains primary and secondary bibliographies as well as analytical bibliographical essays by authorities on major modern authors.

***Contemporary Literary Criticism*** presents excerpts of criticism on the works of novelists, poets, dramatists, short story writers, scriptwriters, and other creative writers who are now living or who have died since 1960.

***Dictionary of Literary Biography*** comprises three related series. ***Dictionary of Literary Biography*** furnishes illustrated overviews of authors' lives and works and places them in the larger perspective of literary history. ***Dictionary of Literary Biography Documentary Series*** illuminates the careers of major figures through a selection of literary documents, including letters, interviews, and photographs. ***Dictionary of Literary Biography Yearbook*** summarizes the past year's literary activity and includes updated and new entries on individual authors. A cumulative index to authors and articles is included in each new volume. ***Concise Dictionary of Literary Biography,*** a six-volume series, collects revised and updated sketches on major American authors that were originally presented in *Dictionary of Literary Biography.*

***Drama Criticism*** provides excerpts of criticism on the works of playwrights of all nationalities and periods of literary history.

***Literature Criticism from 1400 to 1800*** compiles significant passages from the most noteworthy criticism on authors of the fifteenth through the eighteenth centuries.

***Nineteenth-Century Literature Criticism*** offers significant passages from criticism on authors who died between 1800 and 1899.

***Poetry Criticism*** presents excerpts of criticism on the works of poets from all eras, movements, and nationalities.

***Short Story Criticism*** combines excerpts of criticism on short fiction by writers of all eras and nationalities.

***Something about the Author*** series encompasses three related series. ***Something about the Author*** contains well-illustrated biographical sketches on authors and illustrators of juvenile and young adult literature from all eras. ***Something about the Author Autobiography Series*** presents specially commissioned autobiographies by prominent authors and illustrators of books for children and young adults. ***Authors & Artists for Young Adults*** provides high school and junior high school students with profiles of their favorite creative artists.

***Twentieth-Century Literary Criticism*** contains critical excerpts by the most significant commentators on poets, novelists, short story writers, dramatists, and philosophers who died between 1900 and 1960.

***Yesterday's Authors of Books for Children*** contains heavily illustrated entries on children's writers who died before 1961. Complete in two volumes.

# Literary Criticism Series
# Cumulative Author Index

This index lists all author entries in the Gale Literary Criticism Series and includes cross-references to other Gale sources. References in the index are identified as follows:

**AAYA:** *Authors & Artists for Young Adults,* Volumes 1-6
**CAAS:** *Contemporary Authors Autobiography Series,* Volumes 1-13
**CA:** *Contemporary Authors* (original series), Volumes 1-132
**CABS:** *Contemporary Authors Bibliographical Series,* Volumes 1-3
**CANR:** *Contemporary Authors New Revision Series,* Volumes 1-33
**CAP:** *Contemporary Authors Permanent Series,* Volumes 1-2
**CA-R:** *Contemporary Authors* (revised editions), Volumes 1-44
**CDALB:** *Concise Dictionary of American Literary Biography,* Volumes 1-6
**CLC:** *Contemporary Literary Criticism,* Volumes 1-65
**CLR:** *Children's Literature Review,* Volumes 1-24
**CMLC:** *Classical and Medieval Literature Criticism,* Volumes 1-7
**DC:** *Drama Criticism,* Volume 1
**DLB:** *Dictionary of Literary Biography,* Volumes 1-104
**DLB-DS:** *Dictionary of Literary Biography Documentary Series,* Volumes 1-8
**DLB-Y:** *Dictionary of Literary Biography Yearbook,* Volumes 1980-1988
**LC:** *Literature Criticism from 1400 to 1800,* Volumes 1-16
**NCLC:** *Nineteenth-Century Literature Criticism,* Volumes 1-31
**PC:** *Poetry Criticism,* Volumes 1-2
**SAAS:** *Something about the Author Autobiography Series,* Volumes 1-12
**SATA:** *Something about the Author,* Volumes 1-64
**SSC:** *Short Story Criticism,* Volumes 1-7
**TCLC:** *Twentieth-Century Literary Criticism,* Volumes 1-41
**YABC:** *Yesterday's Authors of Books for Children,* Volumes 1-2

A. E. 1867-1935 . . . . . . . . . . . . . TCLC 3, 10
See also Russell, George William
See also DLB 19

Abbey, Edward 1927-1989 . . . . . . CLC 36, 59
See also CANR 2; CA 45-48;
obituary CA 128

Abbott, Lee K., Jr. 19??- . . . . . . . . . . CLC 48

Abe, Kobo 1924- . . . . . . . . . . . CLC 8, 22, 53
See also CANR 24; CA 65-68

Abell, Kjeld 1901-1961 . . . . . . . . . . . CLC 15
See also obituary CA 111

Abish, Walter 1931- . . . . . . . . . . . . . . CLC 22
See also CA 101

Abrahams, Peter (Henry) 1919- . . . . . CLC 4
See also CA 57-60

Abrams, M(eyer) H(oward) 1912- . . . CLC 24
See also CANR 13; CA 57-60; DLB 67

Abse, Dannie 1923- . . . . . . . . . . . CLC 7, 29
See also CAAS 1; CANR 4; CA 53-56;
DLB 27

Achebe, (Albert) Chinua(lumogu)
1930- . . . . . . . . CLC 1, 3, 5, 7, 11, 26, 51
See also CLR 20; CANR 6, 26; CA 1-4R;
SATA 38, 40

Acker, Kathy 1948- . . . . . . . . . . . . . CLC 45
See also CA 117, 122

Ackroyd, Peter 1949- . . . . . . . . . CLC 34, 52
See also CA 123, 127

Acorn, Milton 1923- . . . . . . . . . . . . . CLC 15
See also CA 103; DLB 53

Adamov, Arthur 1908-1970 . . . . . . CLC 4, 25
See also CAP 2; CA 17-18;
obituary CA 25-28R

Adams, Alice (Boyd) 1926- . . . CLC 6, 13, 46
See also CANR 26; CA 81-84; DLB-Y 86

Adams, Douglas (Noel) 1952- . . . CLC 27, 60
See also CA 106; DLB-Y 83

Adams, Henry (Brooks)
1838-1918 . . . . . . . . . . . . . . . . . . TCLC 4
See also CA 104; DLB 12, 47

Adams, Richard (George)
1920- . . . . . . . . . . . . . . . . . CLC 4, 5, 18
See also CLR 20; CANR 3; CA 49-52;
SATA 7

Adamson, Joy(-Friederike Victoria)
1910-1980 . . . . . . . . . . . . . . . . . . CLC 17
See also CANR 22; CA 69-72;
obituary CA 93-96; SATA 11;
obituary SATA 22

Adcock, (Kareen) Fleur 1934- . . . . . . CLC 41
See also CANR 11; CA 25-28R; DLB 40

Addams, Charles (Samuel)
1912-1988 . . . . . . . . . . . . . . . . . CLC 30
See also CANR 12; CA 61-64;
obituary CA 126

Adler, C(arole) S(chwerdtfeger)
1932- . . . . . . . . . . . . . . . . . . . . . . CLC 35
See also CANR 19; CA 89-92; SATA 26

Adler, Renata 1938- . . . . . . . . . . . . CLC 8, 31
See also CANR 5, 22; CA 49-52

Ady, Endre 1877-1919 . . . . . . . . . . . TCLC 11
See also CA 107

Agee, James 1909-1955 . . . . . . . . TCLC 1, 19
See also CA 108; DLB 2, 26;
CDALB 1941-1968

Agnon, S(hmuel) Y(osef Halevi)
1888-1970 . . . . . . . . . . . . . . CLC 4, 8, 14
See also CAP 2; CA 17-18;
obituary CA 25-28R

Ai 1947- . . . . . . . . . . . . . . . . . . . . . CLC 4, 14
See also CA 85-88

Aickman, Robert (Fordyce)
1914-1981 . . . . . . . . . . . . . . . . . . CLC 57
See also CANR 3; CA 7-8R

**Aiken, Conrad (Potter)**
1889-1973 ........ **CLC 1, 3, 5, 10, 52**
See also CANR 4; CA 5-8R;
obituary CA 45-48; SATA 3, 30; DLB 9,
45

**Aiken, Joan (Delano)** 1924-........ **CLC 35**
See also CLR 1, 19; CANR 4; CA 9-12R;
SAAS 1; SATA 2, 30

**Ainsworth, William Harrison**
1805-1882 ............... **NCLC 13**
See also SATA 24; DLB 21

**Ajar, Emile** 1914-1980
See Gary, Romain

**Akhmadulina, Bella (Akhatovna)**
1937- ...................... **CLC 53**
See also CA 65-68

**Akhmatova, Anna**
1888-1966 ....... **CLC 11, 25, 64; PC 2**
See also CAP 1; CA 19-20;
obituary CA 25-28R

**Aksakov, Sergei Timofeyvich**
1791-1859 ................. **NCLC 2**

**Aksenov, Vassily (Pavlovich)** 1932-
See Aksyonov, Vasily (Pavlovich)

**Aksyonov, Vasily (Pavlovich)**
1932- ................... **CLC 22, 37**
See also CANR 12; CA 53-56

**Akutagawa Ryunosuke**
1892-1927 ................ **TCLC 16**
See also CA 117

**Alain** 1868-1951 ................ **TCLC 41**
See also Chartier, Emile-Auguste

**Alain-Fournier** 1886-1914 ......... **TCLC 6**
See also Fournier, Henri Alban
See also DLB 65

**Alarcon, Pedro Antonio de**
1833-1891 ................. **NCLC 1**

**Alas (y Urena), Leopoldo (Enrique Garcia)**
1852-1901 ................. **TCLC 29**
See also CA 113

**Albee, Edward (Franklin III)**
1928- ... **CLC 1, 2, 3, 5, 9, 11, 13, 25, 53**
See also CANR 8; CA 5-8R; DLB 7;
CDALB 1941-1968

**Alberti, Rafael** 1902- .............. **CLC 7**
See also CA 85-88

**Alcott, Amos Bronson** 1799-1888 .. **NCLC 1**
See also DLB 1

**Alcott, Louisa May** 1832-1888 .... **NCLC 6**
See also CLR 1; YABC 1; DLB 1, 42, 79;
CDALB 1865-1917

**Aldanov, Mark** 1887-1957 ....... **TCLC 23**
See also CA 118

**Aldington, Richard** 1892-1962...... **CLC 49**
See also CA 85-88; DLB 20, 36

**Aldiss, Brian W(ilson)**
1925- ................ **CLC 5, 14, 40**
See also CAAS 2; CANR 5; CA 5-8R;
SATA 34; DLB 14

**Alegria, Fernando** 1918-........... **CLC 57**
See also CANR 5; CA 11-12R

**Aleixandre, Vicente** 1898-1984 ... **CLC 9, 36**
See also CANR 26; CA 85-88;
obituary CA 114

**Alepoudelis, Odysseus** 1911-
See Elytis, Odysseus

**Aleshkovsky, Yuz** 1929-........... **CLC 44**
See also CA 121, 128

**Alexander, Lloyd (Chudley)** 1924- .. **CLC 35**
See also CLR 1, 5; CANR 1; CA 1-4R;
SATA 3, 49; DLB 52

**Alger, Horatio, Jr.** 1832-1899..... **NCLC 8**
See also SATA 16; DLB 42

**Algren, Nelson** 1909-1981 .... **CLC 4, 10, 33**
See also CANR 20; CA 13-16R;
obituary CA 103; DLB 9; DLB-Y 81, 82;
CDALB 1941-1968

**Alighieri, Dante** 1265-1321 ....... **CMLC 3**

**Allard, Janet** 1975-.............. **CLC 59**

**Allen, Edward** 1948-.............. **CLC 59**

**Allen, Roland** 1939-
See Ayckbourn, Alan

**Allen, Woody** 1935- .......... **CLC 16, 52**
See also CANR 27; CA 33-36R; DLB 44

**Allende, Isabel** 1942- .......... **CLC 39, 57**
See also CA 125

**Alleyne, Carla D.** 1975?- .......... **CLC 65**

**Allingham, Margery (Louise)**
1904-1966 ................... **CLC 19**
See also CANR 4; CA 5-8R;
obituary CA 25-28R; DLB 77

**Allingham, William** 1824-1889 ... **NCLC 25**
See also DLB 35

**Allston, Washington** 1779-1843.... **NCLC 2**
See also DLB 1

**Almedingen, E. M.** 1898-1971...... **CLC 12**
See also Almedingen, Martha Edith von
See also SATA 3

**Almedingen, Martha Edith von** 1898-1971
See Almedingen, E. M.
See also CANR 1; CA 1-4R

**Alonso, Damaso** 1898- ............ **CLC 14**
See also CA 110; obituary CA 130

**Alta** 1942-...................... **CLC 19**
See also CA 57-60

**Alter, Robert B(ernard)** 1935-...... **CLC 34**
See also CANR 1; CA 49-52

**Alther, Lisa** 1944-.............. **CLC 7, 41**
See also CANR 12; CA 65-68

**Altman, Robert** 1925-............. **CLC 16**
See also CA 73-76

**Alvarez, A(lfred)** 1929-.......... **CLC 5, 13**
See also CANR 3; CA 1-4R; DLB 14, 40

**Alvarez, Alejandro Rodriguez** 1903-1965
See Casona, Alejandro
See also obituary CA 93-96

**Amado, Jorge** 1912-........... **CLC 13, 40**
See also CA 77-80

**Ambler, Eric** 1909-............. **CLC 4, 6, 9**
See also CANR 7; CA 9-12R; DLB 77

**Amichai, Yehuda** 1924- ...... **CLC 9, 22, 57**
See also CA 85-88

**Amiel, Henri Frederic** 1821-1881 .. **NCLC 4**

**Amis, Kingsley (William)**
1922- ...... **CLC 1, 2, 3, 5, 8, 13, 40, 44**
See also CANR 8; CA 9-12R; DLB 15, 27

**Amis, Martin** 1949- ....... **CLC 4, 9, 38, 62**
See also CANR 8, 27; CA 65-68; DLB 14

**Ammons, A(rchie) R(andolph)**
1926- ......... **CLC 2, 3, 5, 8, 9, 25, 57**
See also CANR 6; CA 9-12R; DLB 5

**Anand, Mulk Raj** 1905-........... **CLC 23**
See also CA 65-68

**Anaya, Rudolfo A(lfonso)** 1937- .... **CLC 23**
See also CAAS 4; CANR 1; CA 45-48;
DLB 82

**Andersen, Hans Christian**
1805-1875 ............ **NCLC 7; SSC 6**
See also CLR 6; YABC 1, 1

**Anderson, Jessica (Margaret Queale)**
19??-........................ **CLC 37**
See also CANR 4; CA 9-12R

**Anderson, Jon (Victor)** 1940- ....... **CLC 9**
See also CANR 20; CA 25-28R

**Anderson, Lindsay** 1923- .......... **CLC 20**
See also CA 125

**Anderson, Maxwell** 1888-1959 ..... **TCLC 2**
See also CA 105; DLB 7

**Anderson, Poul (William)** 1926- .... **CLC 15**
See also CAAS 2; CANR 2, 15; CA 1-4R;
SATA 39; DLB 8

**Anderson, Robert (Woodruff)**
1917- ...................... **CLC 23**
See also CA 21-24R; DLB 7

**Anderson, Roberta Joan** 1943-
See Mitchell, Joni

**Anderson, Sherwood**
1876-1941 ...... **TCLC 1, 10, 24; SSC 1**
See also CAAS 3; CA 104, 121; DLB 4, 9;
DLB-DS 1

**Andrade, Carlos Drummond de**
1902-1987 ................... **CLC 18**
See also CA 123

**Andrewes, Lancelot** 1555-1626 ....... **LC 5**

**Andrews, Cicily Fairfield** 1892-1983
See West, Rebecca

**Andreyev, Leonid (Nikolaevich)**
1871-1919 ................. **TCLC 3**
See also CA 104

**Andrezel, Pierre** 1885-1962
See Dinesen, Isak; Blixen, Karen
(Christentze Dinesen)

**Andric, Ivo** 1892-1975 ............. **CLC 8**
See also CA 81-84; obituary CA 57-60

**Angelique, Pierre** 1897-1962
See Bataille, Georges

**Angell, Roger** 1920- .............. **CLC 26**
See also CANR 13; CA 57-60

**Angelou, Maya** 1928-....... **CLC 12, 35, 64**
See also CANR 19; CA 65-68; SATA 49;
DLB 38

**Annensky, Innokenty** 1856-1909... **TCLC 14**
See also CA 110

**Anouilh, Jean (Marie Lucien Pierre)**
1910-1987 ...... **CLC 1, 3, 8, 13, 40, 50**
See also CA 17-20R; obituary CA 123

**Anthony, Florence** 1947-
See Ai

**Anthony (Jacob), Piers** 1934- ...... CLC 35
See also Jacob, Piers A(nthony)
D(illingham)
See also DLB 8

**Antoninus, Brother** 1912-
See Everson, William (Oliver)

**Antonioni, Michelangelo** 1912- ..... CLC 20
See also CA 73-76

**Antschel, Paul** 1920-1970...... CLC 10, 19
See also Celan, Paul
See also CA 85-88

**Anwar, Chairil** 1922-1949 ........ TCLC 22
See also CA 121

**Apollinaire, Guillaume**
1880-1918 ................. TCLC 3, 8
See also Kostrowitzki, Wilhelm Apollinaris
de

**Appelfeld, Aharon** 1932- ....... CLC 23, 47
See also CA 112

**Apple, Max (Isaac)** 1941-........ CLC 9, 33
See also CANR 19; CA 81-84

**Appleman, Philip (Dean)** 1926-..... CLC 51
See also CANR 6; CA 13-16R

**Apuleius, (Lucius) (Madaurensis)**
125?-175?.................. CMLC 1

**Aquin, Hubert** 1929-1977........ CLC 15
See also CA 105; DLB 53

**Aragon, Louis** 1897-1982........ CLC 3, 22
See also CA 69-72; obituary CA 108;
DLB 72

**Arbuthnot, John** 1667-1735.......... LC 1

**Archer, Jeffrey (Howard)** 1940- .... CLC 28
See also CANR 22; CA 77-80

**Archer, Jules** 1915- ............ CLC 12
See also CANR 6; CA 9-12R; SAAS 5;
SATA 4

**Arden, John** 1930- ......... CLC 6, 13, 15
See also CAAS 4; CA 13-16R; DLB 13

**Arenas, Reinaldo** 1943- ........... CLC 41
See also CA 124, 128

**Aretino, Pietro** 1492-1556 ......... LC 12

**Arguedas, Jose Maria**
1911-1969 ............... CLC 10, 18
See also CA 89-92

**Argueta, Manlio** 1936-........... CLC 31

**Ariosto, Ludovico** 1474-1533........ LC 6

**Aristophanes**
c. 450 B.C.-c. 385 B.C. ...... CMLC 4

**Arlt, Roberto** 1900-1942 ........ TCLC 29
See also CA 123

**Armah, Ayi Kwei** 1939-........ CLC 5, 33
See also CANR 21; CA 61-64

**Armatrading, Joan** 1950-.......... CLC 17
See also CA 114

**Arnim, Achim von (Ludwig Joachim von**
**Arnim)** 1781-1831 .......... NCLC 5
See also DLB 90

**Arnold, Matthew** 1822-1888 ... NCLC 6, 29
See also DLB 32, 57

**Arnold, Thomas** 1795-1842 ...... NCLC 18
See also DLB 55

**Arnow, Harriette (Louisa Simpson)**
1908-1986 ............... CLC 2, 7, 18
See also CANR 14; CA 9-12R;
obituary CA 118; SATA 42, 47; DLB 6

**Arp, Jean** 1887-1966.............. CLC 5
See also CA 81-84; obituary CA 25-28R

**Arquette, Lois S(teinmetz)** 1934-
See Duncan (Steinmetz Arquette), Lois
See also SATA 1

**Arrabal, Fernando** 1932- ... CLC 2, 9, 18, 58
See also CANR 15; CA 9-12R

**Arrick, Fran** 19??- ............... CLC 30

**Artaud, Antonin** 1896-1948 ..... TCLC 3, 36
See also CA 104

**Arthur, Ruth M(abel)** 1905-1979.... CLC 12
See also CANR 4; CA 9-12R;
obituary CA 85-88; SATA 7;
obituary SATA 26

**Artsybashev, Mikhail Petrarch**
1878-1927 ................. TCLC 31

**Arundel, Honor (Morfydd)**
1919-1973 .................. CLC 17
See also CAP 2; CA 21-22;
obituary CA 41-44R; SATA 4;
obituary SATA 24

**Asch, Sholem** 1880-1957 ......... TCLC 3
See also CA 105

**Ashbery, John (Lawrence)**
1927- ... CLC 2, 3, 4, 6, 9, 13, 15, 25, 41
See also CANR 9; CA 5-8R; DLB 5;
DLB-Y 81

**Ashton-Warner, Sylvia (Constance)**
1908-1984 .................. CLC 19
See also CA 69-72; obituary CA 112

**Asimov, Isaac** 1920-.... CLC 1, 3, 9, 19, 26
See also CLR 12; CANR 2, 19; CA 1-4R;
SATA 1, 26; DLB 8

**Astley, Thea (Beatrice May)**
1925- ...................... CLC 41
See also CANR 11; CA 65-68

**Aston, James** 1906-1964
See White, T(erence) H(anbury)

**Asturias, Miguel Angel**
1899-1974 ............... CLC 3, 8, 13
See also CAP 2; CA 25-28;
obituary CA 49-52

**Atheling, William, Jr.** 1921-1975
See Blish, James (Benjamin)

**Atherton, Gertrude (Franklin Horn)**
1857-1948 ................... TCLC 2
See also CA 104; DLB 9, 78

**Atwood, Margaret (Eleanor)**
1939- .... CLC 2, 3, 4, 8, 13, 15, 25, 44;
SSC 2
See also CANR 3, 24; CA 49-52; SATA 50;
DLB 53

**Aubin, Penelope** 1685-1731? ......... LC 9
See also DLB 39

**Auchincloss, Louis (Stanton)**
1917- ............. CLC 4, 6, 9, 18, 45
See also CANR 6; CA 1-4R; DLB 2;
DLB-Y 80

**Auden, W(ystan) H(ugh)**
1907-1973 ..... CLC 1, 2, 3, 4, 6, 9, 11,
14, 43; PC 1
See also CANR 5; CA 9-12R;
obituary CA 45-48; DLB 10, 20

**Audiberti, Jacques** 1899-1965 ...... CLC 38
See also obituary CA 25-28R

**Auel, Jean M(arie)** 1936-.......... CLC 31
See also CANR 21; CA 103

**Augier, Emile** 1820-1889 ........ NCLC 31

**Augustine, St.** 354-430........... CMLC 6

**Austen, Jane** 1775-1817.... NCLC 1, 13, 19

**Auster, Paul** 1947-............... CLC 47
See also CANR 23; CA 69-72

**Austin, Mary (Hunter)**
1868-1934 .................. TCLC 25
See also CA 109; DLB 9

**Averroes** 1126-1198 ............. CMLC 7

**Avison, Margaret** 1918-.......... CLC 2, 4
See also CA 17-20R; DLB 53

**Ayckbourn, Alan** 1939- .... CLC 5, 8, 18, 33
See also CA 21-24R; DLB 13

**Aydy, Catherine** 1937-
See Tennant, Emma

**Ayme, Marcel (Andre)** 1902-1967... CLC 11
See also CA 89-92; DLB 72

**Ayrton, Michael** 1921-1975......... CLC 7
See also CANR 9, 21; CA 5-8R;
obituary CA 61-64

**Azorin** 1874-1967................ CLC 11
See also Martinez Ruiz, Jose

**Azuela, Mariano** 1873-1952........ TCLC 3
See also CA 104

**"Bab"** 1836-1911
See Gilbert, (Sir) W(illiam) S(chwenck)

**Babel, Isaak (Emmanuilovich)**
1894-1941 ................. TCLC 2, 13
See also CA 104

**Babits, Mihaly** 1883-1941 ........ TCLC 14
See also CA 114

**Bacchelli, Riccardo** 1891-1985 ..... CLC 19
See also CA 29-32R; obituary CA 117

**Bach, Richard (David)** 1936-....... CLC 14
See also CANR 18; CA 9-12R; SATA 13

**Bachman, Richard** 1947-
See King, Stephen (Edwin)

**Bacovia, George** 1881-1957 ....... TCLC 24

**Bagehot, Walter** 1826-1877 ...... NCLC 10
See also DLB 55

**Bagnold, Enid** 1889-1981......... CLC 25
See also CANR 5; CA 5-8R;
obituary CA 103; SATA 1, 25; DLB 13

**Bagryana, Elisaveta** 1893-......... CLC 10

**Bailey, Paul** 1937- .............. CLC 45
See also CANR 16; CA 21-24R; DLB 14

**Baillie, Joanna** 1762-1851 ........ NCLC 2

**Bainbridge, Beryl**
1933- .... CLC 4, 5, 8, 10, 14, 18, 22, 62
See also CANR 24; CA 21-24R; DLB 14

**Baker, Elliott** 1922-............ CLC 8, 61
See also CANR 2; CA 45-48

**Baker, Nicholson** 1957-.......... CLC 61

**Baker, Russell (Wayne)** 1925-...... **CLC 31**
See also CANR 11; CA 57-60

**Bakshi, Ralph** 1938-............. **CLC 26**
See also CA 112

**Bakunin, Mikhail (Alexandrovich)**
1814-1876 ................ **NCLC 25**

**Baldwin, James (Arthur)**
1924-1987 ..... **CLC 1, 2, 3, 4, 5, 8, 13,**
**15, 17, 42, 50; DC 1**
See also CANR 3,24; CA 1-4R;
obituary CA 124; CABS 1; SATA 9, 54;
DLB 2, 7, 33; DLB-Y 87;
CDALB 1941-1968; AAYA 4

**Ballard, J(ames) G(raham)**
1930-......... **CLC 3, 6, 14, 36; SSC 1**
See also CANR 15; CA 5-8R; DLB 14

**Balmont, Konstantin Dmitriyevich**
1867-1943 ................. **TCLC 11**
See also CA 109

**Balzac, Honore de**
1799-1850 ............ **NCLC 5; SSC 5**

**Bambara, Toni Cade** 1939- ........ **CLC 19**
See also CA 29-32R; DLB 38

**Bandanes, Jerome** 1937- ......... **CLC 59**

**Banim, John** 1798-1842 ......... **NCLC 13**

**Banim, Michael** 1796-1874 ...... **NCLC 13**

**Banks, Iain** 1954-............... **CLC 34**
See also CA 123

**Banks, Lynne Reid** 1929-......... **CLC 23**
See also Reid Banks, Lynne

**Banks, Russell** 1940- ............ **CLC 37**
See also CANR 19; CA 65-68

**Banville, John** 1945-.............. **CLC 46**
See also CA 117, 128; DLB 14

**Banville, Theodore (Faullain) de**
1832-1891 ................. **NCLC 9**

**Baraka, Imamu Amiri**
1934-........ **CLC 1, 2, 3, 5, 10, 14, 33**
See also Jones, (Everett) LeRoi
See also DLB 5, 7, 16, 38;
CDALB 1941-1968

**Barbellion, W. N. P.** 1889-1919 ... **TCLC 24**

**Barbera, Jack** 1945-.............. **CLC 44**
See also CA 110

**Barbey d'Aurevilly, Jules Amedee**
1808-1889 ................. **NCLC 1**

**Barbusse, Henri** 1873-1935 ........ **TCLC 5**
See also CA 105; DLB 65

**Barea, Arturo** 1897-1957 ........ **TCLC 14**
See also CA 111

**Barfoot, Joan** 1946- .............. **CLC 18**
See also CA 105

**Baring, Maurice** 1874-1945 ....... **TCLC 8**
See also CA 105; DLB 34

**Barker, Clive** 1952- .............. **CLC 52**
See also CA 121

**Barker, George (Granville)**
1913-..................... **CLC 8, 48**
See also CANR 7; CA 9-12R; DLB 20

**Barker, Howard** 1946-............. **CLC 37**
See also CA 102; DLB 13

**Barker, Pat** 1943-................ **CLC 32**
See also CA 117, 122

**Barlow, Joel** 1754-1812 ........ **NCLC 23**
See also DLB 37

**Barnard, Mary (Ethel)** 1909-....... **CLC 48**
See also CAP 2; CA 21-22

**Barnes, Djuna (Chappell)**
1892-1982 ... **CLC 3, 4, 8, 11, 29; SSC 3**
See also CANR 16; CA 9-12R;
obituary CA 107; DLB 4, 9, 45

**Barnes, Julian** 1946-.............. **CLC 42**
See also CANR 19; CA 102

**Barnes, Peter** 1931- ............ **CLC 5, 56**
See also CA 65-68; DLB 13

**Baroja (y Nessi), Pio** 1872-1956 .... **TCLC 8**
See also CA 104

**Barondess, Sue K(aufman)** 1926-1977
See Kaufman, Sue
See also CANR 1; CA 1-4R;
obituary CA 69-72

**Barrett, (Roger) Syd** 1946-
See Pink Floyd

**Barrett, William (Christopher)**
1913-...................... **CLC 27**
See also CANR 11; CA 13-16R

**Barrie, (Sir) J(ames) M(atthew)**
1860-1937 .................. **TCLC 2**
See also CLR 16; YABC 1; CA 104;
DLB 10

**Barrol, Grady** 1953-
See Bograd, Larry

**Barry, Philip (James Quinn)**
1896-1949 ................. **TCLC 11**
See also CA 109; DLB 7

**Barth, John (Simmons)**
1930-...... **CLC 1, 2, 3, 5, 7, 9, 10, 14,**
**27, 51**
See also CANR 5, 23; CA 1-4R; CABS 1;
DLB 2

**Barthelme, Donald**
1931-1989 ..... **CLC 1, 2, 3, 5, 6, 8, 13,**
**23, 46, 59; SSC 2**
See also CANR 20; CA 21-24R, 129;
SATA 7; DLB 2; DLB-Y 80

**Barthelme, Frederick** 1943-....... **CLC 36**
See also CA 114, 122; DLB-Y 85

**Barthes, Roland** 1915-1980 ....... **CLC 24**
See also obituary CA 97-100

**Barzun, Jacques (Martin)** 1907- .... **CLC 51**
See also CANR 22; CA 61-64

**Bashkirtseff, Marie** 1859-1884 ... **NCLC 27**

**Bassani, Giorgio** 1916-............ **CLC 9**
See also CA 65-68

**Bataille, Georges** 1897-1962 ....... **CLC 29**
See also CA 101; obituary CA 89-92

**Bates, H(erbert) E(rnest)**
1905-1974 ................. **CLC 46**
See also CA 93-96; obituary CA 45-48

**Baudelaire, Charles**
1821-1867 ......... **NCLC 6, 29; PC 1**

**Baudrillard, Jean** 1929-........... **CLC 60**

**Baum, L(yman) Frank** 1856-1919 ... **TCLC 7**
See also CLR 15; CA 108; SATA 18;
DLB 22

**Baumbach, Jonathan** 1933-...... **CLC 6, 23**
See also CAAS 5; CANR 12; CA 13-16R;
DLB-Y 80

**Bausch, Richard (Carl)** 1945- ...... **CLC 51**
See also CA 101

**Baxter, Charles** 1947-............. **CLC 45**
See also CA 57-60

**Baxter, James K(eir)** 1926-1972 .... **CLC 14**
See also CA 77-80

**Bayer, Sylvia** 1909-1981
See Glassco, John

**Beagle, Peter S(oyer)** 1939-........ **CLC 7**
See also CANR 4; CA 9-12R; DLB-Y 80

**Beard, Charles A(ustin)**
1874-1948 ................. **TCLC 15**
See also CA 115; SATA 18; DLB 17

**Beardsley, Aubrey** 1872-1898 ..... **NCLC 6**

**Beattie, Ann** 1947- ... **CLC 8, 13, 18, 40, 63**
See also CA 81-84; DLB-Y 82

**Beattie, James** 1735-1803 ....... **NCLC 25**

**Beauvoir, Simone (Lucie Ernestine Marie**
**Bertrand) de**
1908-1986 ... **CLC 1, 2, 4, 8, 14, 31, 44,**
**50**
See also CANR 28; CA 9-12R;
obituary CA 118; DLB 72; DLB-Y 86

**Becker, Jurek** 1937-............. **CLC 7, 19**
See also CA 85-88; DLB 75

**Becker, Walter** 1950-............. **CLC 26**

**Beckett, Samuel (Barclay)**
1906-1989 ..... **CLC 1, 2, 3, 4, 6, 9, 10,**
**11, 14, 18, 29, 57, 59**
See also CA 5-8R; DLB 13, 15

**Beckford, William** 1760-1844 .... **NCLC 16**
See also DLB 39

**Beckman, Gunnel** 1910-........... **CLC 26**
See also CANR 15; CA 33-36R; SATA 6

**Becque, Henri** 1837-1899........ **NCLC 3**

**Beddoes, Thomas Lovell**
1803-1849 ................. **NCLC 3**

**Beecher, Catharine Esther**
1800-1878 ................. **NCLC 30**
See also DLB 1

**Beecher, John** 1904-1980.......... **CLC 6**
See also CANR 8; CA 5-8R;
obituary CA 105

**Beer, Johann** 1655-1700............. **LC 5**

**Beer, Patricia** 1919?-.............. **CLC 58**
See also CANR 13; CA 61-64; DLB 40

**Beerbohm, (Sir Henry) Max(imilian)**
1872-1956 ................ **TCLC 1, 24**
See also CA 104; DLB 34

**Behan, Brendan**
1923-1964 ............ **CLC 1, 8, 11, 15**
See also CA 73-76; DLB 13

**Behn, Aphra** 1640?-1689 ............ **LC 1**
See also DLB 39, 80

**Behrman, S(amuel) N(athaniel)**
1893-1973 ................. **CLC 40**
See also CAP 1; CA 15-16;
obituary CA 45-48; DLB 7, 44

**Beiswanger, George Edwin** 1931-
See Starbuck, George (Edwin)

Belasco, David   1853-1931 ........ TCLC 3
See also CA 104; DLB 7

Belcheva, Elisaveta   1893-
See Bagryana, Elisaveta

Belinski, Vissarion Grigoryevich
1811-1848 ................. NCLC 5

Belitt, Ben   1911-................. CLC 22
See also CAAS 4; CANR 7; CA 13-16R;
DLB 5

Bell, Acton   1820-1849
See Bronte, Anne

Bell, Currer   1816-1855
See Bronte, Charlotte

Bell, Madison Smartt   1957-........ CLC 41
See also CA 111

Bell, Marvin (Hartley)   1937-..... CLC 8, 31
See also CA 21-24R; DLB 5

Bellamy, Edward   1850-1898 ...... NCLC 4
See also DLB 12

Belloc, (Joseph) Hilaire (Pierre Sebastien
Rene Swanton)
1870-1953 ............... TCLC 7, 18
See also YABC 1; CA 106; DLB 19

Bellow, Saul
1915- ..... CLC 1, 2, 3, 6, 8, 10, 13, 15,
25, 33, 34, 63
See also CA 5-8R; CABS 1; DLB 2, 28;
DLB-Y 82; DLB-DS 3;
CDALB 1941-1968

Belser, Reimond Karel Maria de   1929-
See Ruyslinck, Ward

Bely, Andrey   1880-1934.......... TCLC 7
See also CA 104

Benary-Isbert, Margot   1889-1979... CLC 12
See also CLR 12; CANR 4; CA 5-8R;
obituary CA 89-92; SATA 2;
obituary SATA 21

Benavente (y Martinez), Jacinto
1866-1954 .................. TCLC 3
See also CA 106

Benchley, Peter (Bradford)
1940- ..................... CLC 4, 8
See also CANR 12; CA 17-20R; SATA 3

Benchley, Robert   1889-1945 ....... TCLC 1
See also CA 105; DLB 11

Benedikt, Michael   1935- ........ CLC 4, 14
See also CANR 7; CA 13-16R; DLB 5

Benet, Juan   1927-................. CLC 28

Benet, Stephen Vincent
1898-1943 ................... TCLC 7
See also YABC 1; CA 104; DLB 4, 48

Benet, William Rose   1886-1950 ... TCLC 28
See also CA 118; DLB 45

Benford, Gregory (Albert)   1941-.... CLC 52
See also CANR 12, 24; CA 69-72;
DLB-Y 82

Benjamin, Walter   1892-1940 ..... TCLC 39

Benn, Gottfried   1886-1956........ TCLC 3
See also CA 106; DLB 56

Bennett, Alan   1934-.............. CLC 45
See also CA 103

Bennett, (Enoch) Arnold
1867-1931 ............... TCLC 5, 20
See also CA 106; DLB 10, 34

Bennett, George Harold   1930-
See Bennett, Hal
See also CA 97-100

Bennett, Hal   1930-................ CLC 5
See also Bennett, George Harold
See also DLB 33

Bennett, Jay   1912-................ CLC 35
See also CANR 11; CA 69-72; SAAS 4;
SATA 27, 41

Bennett, Louise (Simone)   1919-..... CLC 28
See also Bennett-Coverly, Louise Simone

Bennett-Coverly, Louise Simone   1919-
See Bennett, Louise (Simone)
See also CA 97-100

Benson, E(dward) F(rederic)
1867-1940 .................. TCLC 27
See also CA 114

Benson, Jackson J.   1930-......... CLC 34
See also CA 25-28R

Benson, Sally   1900-1972 .......... CLC 17
See also CAP 1; CA 19-20;
obituary CA 37-40R; SATA 1, 35;
obituary SATA 27

Benson, Stella   1892-1933........ TCLC 17
See also CA 117; DLB 36

Bentley, E(dmund) C(lerihew)
1875-1956 ................. TCLC 12
See also CA 108; DLB 70

Bentley, Eric (Russell)   1916-...... CLC 24
See also CANR 6; CA 5-8R

Berger, John (Peter)   1926- ...... CLC 2, 19
See also CA 81-84; DLB 14

Berger, Melvin (H.)   1927-........ CLC 12
See also CANR 4; CA 5-8R; SAAS 2;
SATA 5

Berger, Thomas (Louis)
1924- .......... CLC 3, 5, 8, 11, 18, 38
See also CANR 5; CA 1-4R; DLB 2;
DLB-Y 80

Bergman, (Ernst) Ingmar   1918-..... CLC 16
See also CA 81-84

Bergson, Henri   1859-1941....... TCLC 32

Bergstein, Eleanor   1938-........... CLC 4
See also CANR 5; CA 53-56

Berkoff, Steven   1937-............. CLC 56
See also CA 104

Bermant, Chaim   1929-........... CLC 40
See also CANR 6; CA 57-60

Bernanos, (Paul Louis) Georges
1888-1948 .................. TCLC 3
See also CA 104; DLB 72

Bernard, April   19??-.............. CLC 59

Bernhard, Thomas
1931-1989 ............ CLC 3, 32, 61
See also CA 85-88,; obituary CA 127,
DLB 85

Berriault, Gina   1926-............. CLC 54
See also CA 116

Berrigan, Daniel J.   1921-.......... CLC 4
See also CAAS 1; CANR 11; CA 33-36R;
DLB 5

Berrigan, Edmund Joseph Michael, Jr.
1934-1983
See Berrigan, Ted
See also CANR 14; CA 61-64;
obituary CA 110

Berrigan, Ted   1934-1983 ......... CLC 37
See also Berrigan, Edmund Joseph Michael,
Jr.
See also DLB 5

Berry, Chuck   1926- .............. CLC 17

Berry, Wendell (Erdman)
1934- ............. CLC 4, 6, 8, 27, 46
See also CA 73-76; DLB 5, 6

Berryman, John
1914-1972 ..... CLC 1, 2, 3, 4, 6, 8, 10,
13, 25, 62
See also CAP 1; CA 15-16;
obituary CA 33-36R; CABS 2; DLB 48;
CDALB 1941-1968

Bertolucci, Bernardo   1940-........ CLC 16
See also CA 106

Bertrand, Aloysius   1807-1841 .... NCLC 31

Bertran de Born   c. 1140-1215..... CMLC 5

Besant, Annie (Wood)   1847-1933 ... TCLC 9
See also CA 105

Bessie, Alvah   1904-1985........... CLC 23
See also CANR 2; CA 5-8R;
obituary CA 116; DLB 26

Beti, Mongo   1932-................ CLC 27
See also Beyidi, Alexandre

Betjeman, (Sir) John
1906-1984 ........ CLC 2, 6, 10, 34, 43
See also CA 9-12R; obituary CA 112;
DLB 20; DLB-Y 84

Betti, Ugo   1892-1953 ............. TCLC 5
See also CA 104

Betts, Doris (Waugh)   1932-.... CLC 3, 6, 28
See also CANR 9; CA 13-16R; DLB-Y 82

Bialik, Chaim Nachman
1873-1934 .................. TCLC 25

Bidart, Frank   19??-............... CLC 33

Bienek, Horst   1930-............. CLC 7, 11
See also CA 73-76; DLB 75

Bierce, Ambrose (Gwinett)
1842-1914?................. TCLC 1, 7
See also CA 104; DLB 11, 12, 23, 71, 74;
CDALB 1865-1917

Billington, Rachel   1942-........... CLC 43
See also CA 33-36R

Binyon, T(imothy) J(ohn)   1936- .... CLC 34
See also CA 111

Bioy Casares, Adolfo   1914-..... CLC 4, 8, 13
See also CANR 19; CA 29-32R

Birch, Allison   1974?- ............. CLC 65

Bird, Robert Montgomery
1806-1854 ................. NCLC 1

Birdwell, Cleo   1936-
See DeLillo, Don

Birney (Alfred) Earle
1904- ................. CLC 1, 4, 6, 11
See also CANR 5, 20; CA 1-4R

**Bishop, Elizabeth**
    1911-1979 ...... **CLC 1, 4, 9, 13, 15, 32**
    See also CANR 26; CA 5-8R;
    obituary CA 89-92; CABS 2;
    obituary SATA 24; DLB 5

**Bishop, John**  1935- ............... **CLC 10**
    See also CA 105

**Bissett, Bill**  1939- ................ **CLC 18**
    See also CANR 15; CA 69-72; DLB 53

**Bitov, Andrei (Georgievich)**  1937- ... **CLC 57**

**Biyidi, Alexandre**  1932-
    See Beti, Mongo
    See also CA 114, 124

**Bjornson, Bjornstjerne (Martinius)**
    1832-1910 ............... **TCLC 7, 37**
    See also CA 104

**Blackburn, Paul**  1926-1971 ...... **CLC 9, 43**
    See also CA 81-84; obituary CA 33-36R;
    DLB 16; DLB-Y 81

**Black Elk**  1863-1950 ............ **TCLC 33**

**Blackmore, R(ichard) D(oddridge)**
    1825-1900 ................. **TCLC 27**
    See also CA 120; DLB 18

**Blackmur, R(ichard) P(almer)**
    1904-1965 ................. **CLC 2, 24**
    See also CAP 1; CA 11-12;
    obituary CA 25-28R; DLB 63

**Blackwood, Algernon (Henry)**
    1869-1951 ................... **TCLC 5**
    See also CA 105

**Blackwood, Caroline**  1931- ....... **CLC 6, 9**
    See also CA 85-88; DLB 14

**Blair, Eric Arthur**  1903-1950
    See Orwell, George
    See also CA 104; SATA 29

**Blais, Marie-Claire**
    1939- ............. **CLC 2, 4, 6, 13, 22**
    See also CAAS 4; CA 21-24R; DLB 53

**Blaise, Clark**  1940- ............... **CLC 29**
    See also CAAS 3; CANR 5; CA 53-56R;
    DLB 53

**Blake, Nicholas**  1904-1972
    See Day Lewis, C(ecil)

**Blake, William**  1757-1827 ....... **NCLC 13**
    See also SATA 30

**Blasco Ibanez, Vicente**
    1867-1928 ................. **TCLC 12**
    See also CA 110

**Blatty, William Peter**  1928- ......... **CLC 2**
    See also CANR 9; CA 5-8R

**Blessing, Lee**  1949- ............... **CLC 54**

**Blish, James (Benjamin)**
    1921-1975 ................. **CLC 14**
    See also CANR 3; CA 1-4R;
    obituary CA 57-60; DLB 8

**Blixen, Karen (Christentze Dinesen)**
    1885-1962
    See Dinesen, Isak
    See also CAP 2; CA 25-28; SATA 44

**Bloch, Robert (Albert)**  1917- ....... **CLC 33**
    See also CANR 5; CA 5-8R; SATA 12;
    DLB 44

**Blok, Aleksandr (Aleksandrovich)**
    1880-1921 .................. **TCLC 5**
    See also CA 104

**Bloom, Harold**  1930- .......... **CLC 24, 65**
    See also CA 13-16R; DLB 67

**Blount, Roy (Alton), Jr.**  1941- ..... **CLC 38**
    See also CANR 10; CA 53-56

**Bloy, Leon**  1846-1917............ **TCLC 22**
    See also CA 121

**Blume, Judy (Sussman Kitchens)**
    1938- .................... **CLC 12, 30**
    See also CLR 2, 15; CANR 13; CA 29-32R;
    SATA 2, 31; DLB 52

**Blunden, Edmund (Charles)**
    1896-1974 ................. **CLC 2, 56**
    See also CAP 2; CA 17-18;
    obituary CA 45-48; DLB 20

**Bly, Robert (Elwood)**
    1926- ......... **CLC 1, 2, 5, 10, 15, 38**
    See also CA 5-8R; DLB 5

**Bochco, Steven**  1944?- ............ **CLC 35**

**Bodker, Cecil**  1927- .............. **CLC 21**
    See also CLR 23; CANR 13; CA 73-76;
    SATA 14

**Boell, Heinrich (Theodor)**  1917-1985
    See Boll, Heinrich
    See also CANR 24; CA 21-24R;
    obituary CA 116

**Bogan, Louise**  1897-1970..... **CLC 4, 39, 46**
    See also CA 73-76; obituary CA 25-28R;
    DLB 45

**Bogarde, Dirk**  1921- .............. **CLC 19**
    See also Van Den Bogarde, Derek (Jules
    Gaspard Ulric) Niven
    See also DLB 14

**Bogosian, Eric**  1953- ............. **CLC 45**

**Bograd, Larry**  1953- .............. **CLC 35**
    See also CA 93-96; SATA 33

**Bohl de Faber, Cecilia**  1796-1877
    See Caballero, Fernan

**Boiardo, Matteo Maria**  1441-1494 .... **LC 6**

**Boileau-Despreaux, Nicolas**
    1636-1711 .................... **LC 3**

**Boland, Eavan (Aisling)**  1944-...... **CLC 40**
    See also DLB 40

**Boll, Heinrich (Theodor)**
    1917-1985 ... **CLC 2, 3, 6, 9, 11, 15, 27,**
    **39**
    See also Boell, Heinrich (Theodor)
    See also DLB 69; DLB-Y 85

**Bolt, Robert (Oxton)**  1924- ........ **CLC 14**
    See also CA 17-20R; DLB 13

**Bond, Edward**  1934-....... **CLC 4, 6, 13, 23**
    See also CA 25-28R; DLB 13

**Bonham, Frank**  1914-............. **CLC 12**
    See also CANR 4; CA 9-12R; SAAS 3;
    SATA 1, 49

**Bonnefoy, Yves**  1923-........ **CLC 9, 15, 58**
    See also CA 85-88

**Bontemps, Arna (Wendell)**
    1902-1973 ................. **CLC 1, 18**
    See also CLR 6; CANR 4; CA 1-4R;
    obituary CA 41-44R; SATA 2, 44;
    obituary SATA 24; DLB 48, 51

**Booth, Martin**  1944-............. **CLC 13**
    See also CAAS 2; CA 93-96

**Booth, Philip**  1925-............... **CLC 23**
    See also CANR 5; CA 5-8R; DLB-Y 82

**Booth, Wayne C(layson)**  1921- ..... **CLC 24**
    See also CAAS 5; CANR 3; CA 1-4R;
    DLB 67

**Borchert, Wolfgang**  1921-1947 ..... **TCLC 5**
    See also CA 104; DLB 69

**Borges, Jorge Luis**
    1899-1986 ... **CLC 1, 2, 3, 4, 6, 8, 9, 10,**
    **13, 19, 44, 48; SSC 4**
    See also CANR 19; CA 21-24R; DLB-Y 86

**Borowski, Tadeusz**  1922-1951 ...... **TCLC 9**
    See also CA 106

**Borrow, George (Henry)**
    1803-1881 .................. **NCLC 9**
    See also DLB 21, 55

**Bosschere, Jean de**  1878-1953..... **TCLC 19**
    See also CA 115

**Boswell, James**  1740-1795........... **LC 4**

**Bottoms, David**  1949-............. **CLC 53**
    See also CANR 22; CA 105; DLB-Y 83

**Boucolon, Maryse**  1937-
    See Conde, Maryse
    See also CA 110

**Bourget, Paul (Charles Joseph)**
    1852-1935 ................. **TCLC 12**
    See also CA 107

**Bourjaily, Vance (Nye)**  1922- .... **CLC 8, 62**
    See also CAAS 1; CANR 2; CA 1-4R;
    DLB 2

**Bourne, Randolph S(illiman)**
    1886-1918 ................. **TCLC 16**
    See also CA 117; DLB 63

**Bova, Ben(jamin William)**  1932-.... **CLC 45**
    See also CLR 3; CANR 11; CA 5-8R;
    SATA 6; DLB-Y 81

**Bowen, Elizabeth (Dorothea Cole)**
    1899-1973 ..... **CLC 1, 3, 6, 11, 15, 22;**
    **SSC 3**
    See also CAP 2; CA 17-18;
    obituary CA 41-44R; DLB 15

**Bowering, George**  1935-........ **CLC 15, 47**
    See also CANR 10; CA 21-24R; DLB 53

**Bowering, Marilyn R(uthe)**  1949-... **CLC 32**
    See also CA 101

**Bowers, Edgar**  1924- .............. **CLC 9**
    See also CANR 24; CA 5-8R; DLB 5

**Bowie, David**  1947- ............... **CLC 17**
    See also Jones, David Robert

**Bowles, Jane (Sydney)**  1917-1973.... **CLC 3**
    See also CAP 2; CA 19-20;
    obituary CA 41-44R

**Bowles, Paul (Frederick)**
    1910- ........ **CLC 1, 2, 19, 53; SSC 3**
    See also CAAS 1; CANR 1, 19; CA 1-4R;
    DLB 5, 6

**Box, Edgar**  1925-
    See Vidal, Gore

**Boyd, William**  1952-.......... **CLC 28, 53**
    See also CA 114, 120

**Boyle, Kay**  1903- .. **CLC 1, 5, 19, 58; SSC 5**
    See also CAAS 1; CA 13-16R; DLB 4, 9, 48

**Boyle, Patrick**  19??-.............. **CLC 19**

Boyle, Thomas Coraghessan
    1948- .................... CLC 36, 55
    See also CA 120; DLB-Y 86

Brackenridge, Hugh Henry
    1748-1816 ................. NCLC 7
    See also DLB 11, 37

Bradbury, Edward P.   1939-
    See Moorcock, Michael

Bradbury, Malcolm (Stanley)
    1932- .................... CLC 32, 61
    See also CANR 1; CA 1-4R; DLB 14

Bradbury, Ray(mond Douglas)
    1920- ........... CLC 1, 3, 10, 15, 42
    See also CANR 2; CA 1-4R; SATA 11;
    DLB 2, 8

Bradford, Gamaliel   1863-1932..... TCLC 36
    See also DLB 17

Bradley, David (Henry), Jr.   1950- .. CLC 23
    See also CANR 26; CA 104; DLB 33

Bradley, John Ed   1959-........... CLC 55

Bradley, Marion Zimmer   1930-..... CLC 30
    See also CANR 7; CA 57-60; DLB 8

Bradstreet, Anne   1612-1672......... LC 4
    See also DLB 24; CDALB 1640-1865

Bragg, Melvyn   1939- ............. CLC 10
    See also CANR 10; CA 57-60; DLB 14

Braine, John (Gerard)
    1922-1986 .............. CLC 1, 3, 41
    See also CANR 1; CA 1-4R;
    obituary CA 120; DLB 15; DLB-Y 86

Brammer, Billy Lee   1930?-1978
    See Brammer, William

Brammer, William   1930?-1978 ..... CLC 31
    See also obituary CA 77-80

Brancati, Vitaliano   1907-1954..... TCLC 12
    See also CA 109

Brancato, Robin F(idler)   1936-..... CLC 35
    See also CANR 11; CA 69-72; SATA 23

Brand, Millen   1906-1980.......... CLC 7
    See also CA 21-24R; obituary CA 97-100

Branden, Barbara   19??- ........... CLC 44

Brandes, Georg (Morris Cohen)
    1842-1927 ................. TCLC 10
    See also CA 105

Brandys, Kazimierz   1916-......... CLC 62

Branley, Franklyn M(ansfield)
    1915- ...................... CLC 21
    See also CLR 13; CANR 14; CA 33-36R;
    SATA 4

Brathwaite, Edward   1930-......... CLC 11
    See also CANR 11; CA 25-28R; DLB 53

Brautigan, Richard (Gary)
    1935-1984 .... CLC 1, 3, 5, 9, 12, 34, 42
    See also CA 53-56; obituary CA 113;
    SATA 56; DLB 2, 5; DLB-Y 80, 84

Brecht, (Eugen) Bertolt (Friedrich)
    1898-1956 ........ TCLC 1, 6, 13, 35
    See also CA 104; DLB 56

Bremer, Fredrika   1801-1865 ..... NCLC 11

Brennan, Christopher John
    1870-1932 ................. TCLC 17
    See also CA 117

Brennan, Maeve   1917-............ CLC 5
    See also CA 81-84

Brentano, Clemens (Maria)
    1778-1842 ................. NCLC 1
    See also DLB 90

Brenton, Howard   1942-........... CLC 31
    See also CA 69-72; DLB 13

Breslin, James   1930-
    See Breslin, Jimmy
    See also CA 73-76

Breslin, Jimmy   1930-........... CLC 4, 43
    See also Breslin, James

Bresson, Robert   1907-........... CLC 16
    See also CA 110

Breton, Andre   1896-1966... CLC 2, 9, 15, 54
    See also CAP 2; CA 19-20;
    obituary CA 25-28R; DLB 65

Breytenbach, Breyten   1939-..... CLC 23, 37
    See also CA 113, 129

Bridgers, Sue Ellen   1942- ......... CLC 26
    See also CANR 11; CA 65-68; SAAS 1;
    SATA 22; DLB 52

Bridges, Robert   1844-1930........ TCLC 1
    See also CA 104; DLB 19

Bridie, James   1888-1951 .......... TCLC 3
    See also Mavor, Osborne Henry
    See also DLB 10

Brin, David   1950-............... CLC 34
    See also CANR 24; CA 102

Brink, Andre (Philippus)
    1935- ................... CLC 18, 36
    See also CA 104

Brinsmead, H(esba) F(ay)   1922- .... CLC 21
    See also CANR 10; CA 21-24R; SAAS 5;
    SATA 18

Brittain, Vera (Mary)   1893?-1970... CLC 23
    See also CAP 1; CA 15-16;
    obituary CA 25-28R

Broch, Hermann   1886-1951....... TCLC 20
    See also CA 117; DLB 85

Brock, Rose   1923-
    See Hansen, Joseph

Brodkey, Harold   1930-............ CLC 56
    See also CA 111

Brodsky, Iosif Alexandrovich   1940-
    See Brodsky, Joseph (Alexandrovich)
    See also CA 41-44R

Brodsky, Joseph (Alexandrovich)
    1940- ........ CLC 4, 6, 13, 36, 50
    See also Brodsky, Iosif Alexandrovich

Brodsky, Michael (Mark)   1948- .... CLC 19
    See also CANR 18; CA 102

Bromell, Henry   1947-............ CLC 5
    See also CANR 9; CA 53-56

Bromfield, Louis (Brucker)
    1896-1956 ................. TCLC 11
    See also CA 107; DLB 4, 9

Broner, E(sther) M(asserman)
    1930- ...................... CLC 19
    See also CANR 8, 25; CA 17-20R; DLB 28

Bronk, William   1918-............ CLC 10
    See also CANR 23; CA 89-92

Bronte, Anne   1820-1849......... NCLC 4
    See also DLB 21

Bronte, Charlotte   1816-1855 .... NCLC 3, 8
    See also DLB 21

Bronte, (Jane) Emily   1818-1848 .. NCLC 16
    See also DLB 21, 32

Brooke, Frances   1724-1789 ......... LC 6
    See also DLB 39

Brooke, Henry   1703?-1783 ......... LC 1
    See also DLB 39

Brooke, Rupert (Chawner)
    1887-1915 ............TCLC 2, 7
    See also CA 104; DLB 19

Brooke-Rose, Christine   1926-...... CLC 40
    See also CA 13-16R; DLB 14

Brookner, Anita   1928-...... CLC 32, 34, 51
    See also CA 114, 120; DLB-Y 87

Brooks, Cleanth   1906-............ CLC 24
    See also CA 17-20R; DLB 63

Brooks, Gwendolyn
    1917- ........... CLC 1, 2, 4, 5, 15, 49
    See also CANR 1; CA 1-4R; SATA 6;
    DLB 5, 76; CDALB 1941-1968

Brooks, Mel   1926-............... CLC 12
    See also Kaminsky, Melvin
    See also CA 65-68; DLB 26

Brooks, Peter   1938-.............. CLC 34
    See also CANR 1; CA 45-48

Brooks, Van Wyck   1886-1963...... CLC 29
    See also CANR 6; CA 1-4R; DLB 45, 63

Brophy, Brigid (Antonia)
    1929- .................. CLC 6, 11, 29
    See also CAAS 4; CANR 25; CA 5-8R;
    DLB 14

Brosman, Catharine Savage   1934-.... CLC 9
    See also CANR 21; CA 61-64

Broughton, T(homas) Alan   1936- ... CLC 19
    See also CANR 2, 23; CA 45-48

Broumas, Olga   1949-............ CLC 10
    See also CANR 20; CA 85-88

Brown, Charles Brockden
    1771-1810 ................. NCLC 22
    See also DLB 37, 59, 73;
    CDALB 1640-1865

Brown, Christy   1932-1981........ CLC 63
    See also CA 105; obituary CA 104

Brown, Claude   1937- ............ CLC 30
    See also CA 73-76

Brown, Dee (Alexander)   1908- .. CLC 18, 47
    See also CAAS 6; CANR 11; CA 13-16R;
    SATA 5; DLB-Y 80

Brown, George Douglas   1869-1902
    See Douglas, George

Brown, George Mackay   1921-.... CLC 5, 28
    See also CAAS 6; CANR 12; CA 21-24R;
    SATA 35; DLB 14, 27

Brown, Rita Mae   1944-........ CLC 18, 43
    See also CANR 2, 11; CA 45-48

Brown, Rosellen   1939-............ CLC 32
    See also CANR 14; CA 77-80

Brown, Sterling A(llen)
    1901-1989 ........... CLC 1, 23, 59
    See also CANR 26; CA 85-88;
    obituary CA 27; DLB 48, 51, 63

Brown, William Wells
    1816?-1884............. NCLC 2; DC 1
    See also DLB 3, 50

**Browne, Jackson** 1950- .......... CLC 21
See also CA 120

**Browning, Elizabeth Barrett**
1806-1861 ............... NCLC 1, 16
See also DLB 32

**Browning, Robert**
1812-1889 ............ NCLC 19; PC 2
See also YABC 1; DLB 32

**Browning, Tod** 1882-1962 ......... CLC 16
See also obituary CA 117

**Bruccoli, Matthew J(oseph)** 1931- .. CLC 34
See also CANR 7; CA 9-12R

**Bruce, Lenny** 1925-1966 .......... CLC 21
See also Schneider, Leonard Alfred

**Brunner, John (Kilian Houston)**
1934- ..................... CLC 8, 10
See also CAAS 8; CANR 2; CA 1-4R

**Brutus, Dennis** 1924- ............. CLC 43
See also CANR 2; CA 49-52

**Bryan, C(ourtlandt) D(ixon) B(arnes)**
1936- ...................... CLC 29
See also CANR 13; CA 73-76

**Bryant, William Cullen**
1794-1878 .................. NCLC 6
See also DLB 3, 43, 59; CDALB 1640-1865

**Bryusov, Valery (Yakovlevich)**
1873-1924 ................. TCLC 10
See also CA 107

**Buchan, Sir John** 1875-1940 ...... TCLC 41
See also YABC 2; brief entry CA 108;
DLB 34, 70

**Buchanan, George** 1506-1582 ........ LC 4

**Buchheim, Lothar-Gunther** 1918- .... CLC 6
See also CA 85-88

**Buchner, (Karl) Georg**
1813-1837 ................. NCLC 26

**Buchwald, Art(hur)** 1925-.......... CLC 33
See also CANR 21; CA 5-8R; SATA 10

**Buck, Pearl S(ydenstricker)**
1892-1973 ............... CLC 7, 11, 18
See also CANR 1; CA 1-4R;
obituary CA 41-44R; SATA 1, 25; DLB 9

**Buckler, Ernest** 1908-1984........ CLC 13
See also CAP 1; CA 11-12;
obituary CA 114; SATA 47

**Buckley, Vincent (Thomas)**
1925-1988 ................. CLC 57
See also CA 101

**Buckley, William F(rank), Jr.**
1925- .................. CLC 7, 18, 37
See also CANR 1, 24; CA 1-4R; DLB-Y 80

**Buechner, (Carl) Frederick**
1926- ................. CLC 2, 4, 6, 9
See also CANR 11; CA 13-16R; DLB-Y 80

**Buell, John (Edward)** 1927-........ CLC 10
See also CA 1-4R; DLB 53

**Buero Vallejo, Antonio** 1916- ... CLC 15, 46
See also CANR 24; CA 106

**Bukowski, Charles** 1920- .... CLC 2, 5, 9, 41
See also CA 17-20R; DLB 5

**Bulgakov, Mikhail (Afanas'evich)**
1891-1940 ............... TCLC 2, 16
See also CA 105

**Bullins, Ed** 1935- ............. CLC 1, 5, 7
See also CANR 24; CA 49-52; DLB 7, 38

**Bulwer-Lytton, (Lord) Edward (George Earle**
**Lytton)** 1803-1873 .......... NCLC 1
See also Lytton, Edward Bulwer
See also DLB 21

**Bunin, Ivan (Alexeyevich)**
1870-1953 ............ TCLC 6; SSC 5
See also CA 104

**Bunting, Basil** 1900-1985.... CLC 10, 39, 47
See also CANR 7; CA 53-56;
obituary CA 115; DLB 20

**Bunuel, Luis** 1900-1983 ........... CLC 16
See also CA 101; obituary CA 110

**Bunyan, John** 1628-1688 ............ LC 4
See also DLB 39

**Burgess (Wilson, John) Anthony**
1917- ..... CLC 1, 2, 4, 5, 8, 10, 13, 15,
22, 40, 62
See also Wilson, John (Anthony) Burgess
See also DLB 14

**Burke, Edmund** 1729-1797.......... LC 7

**Burke, Kenneth (Duva)** 1897- .... CLC 2, 24
See also CA 5-8R; DLB 45, 63

**Burney, Fanny** 1752-1840 ....... NCLC 12
See also DLB 39

**Burns, Robert** 1759-1796............ LC 3

**Burns, Tex** 1908?-
See L'Amour, Louis (Dearborn)

**Burnshaw, Stanley** 1906- ..... CLC 3, 13, 44
See also CA 9-12R; DLB 48

**Burr, Anne** 1937- ................ CLC 6
See also CA 25-28R

**Burroughs, Edgar Rice**
1875-1950 ................ TCLC 2, 32
See also CA 104; SATA 41; DLB 8

**Burroughs, William S(eward)**
1914- ..... CLC 1, 2, 5, 15, 22, 42
See also CANR 20; CA 9-12R; DLB 2, 8,
16; DLB-Y 81

**Busch, Frederick** 1941- ... CLC 7, 10, 18, 47
See also CAAS 1; CA 33-36R; DLB 6

**Bush, Ronald** 19??-............... CLC 34

**Butler, Octavia E(stelle)** 1947- ..... CLC 38
See also CANR 12, 24; CA 73-76; DLB 33

**Butler, Samuel** 1612-1680 .......... LC 16
See also DLB 101

**Butler, Samuel** 1835-1902 ...... TCLC 1, 33
See also CA 104; DLB 18, 57

**Butor, Michel (Marie Francois)**
1926- ............... CLC 1, 3, 8, 11, 15
See also CA 9-12R

**Buzo, Alexander** 1944-........... CLC 61
See also CANR 17; CA 97-100

**Buzzati, Dino** 1906-1972 .......... CLC 36
See also obituary CA 33-36R

**Byars, Betsy** 1928-............... CLC 35
See also CLR 1, 16; CANR 18; CA 33-36R;
SAAS 1; SATA 4, 46; DLB 52

**Byatt, A(ntonia) S(usan Drabble)**
1936- ................... CLC 19, 65
See also CANR 13, 33; CA 13-16R;
DLB 14

**Byrne, David** 1953?-.............. CLC 26

**Byrne, John Keyes** 1926-
See Leonard, Hugh
See also CA 102

**Byron, George Gordon (Noel), Lord Byron**
1788-1824 ............... NCLC 2, 12

**Caballero, Fernan** 1796-1877..... NCLC 10

**Cabell, James Branch** 1879-1958 ... TCLC 6
See also CA 105; DLB 9, 78

**Cable, George Washington**
1844-1925 ............ TCLC 4; SSC 4
See also CA 104; DLB 12, 74

**Cabrera Infante, G(uillermo)**
1929- ................... CLC 5, 25, 45
See also CANR 29; CA 85-88

**CAEdmon** fl. 658-680............ CMLC 7

**Cage, John (Milton, Jr.)** 1912- ..... CLC 41
See also CANR 9; CA 13-16R

**Cain, G.** 1929-
See Cabrera Infante, G(uillermo)

**Cain, James M(allahan)**
1892-1977 ............... CLC 3, 11, 28
See also CANR 8; CA 17-20R;
obituary CA 73-76

**Caldwell, Erskine (Preston)**
1903-1987 ........ CLC 1, 8, 14, 50, 60
See also CAAS 1; CANR 2; CA 1-4R;
obituary CA 121; DLB 9, 86

**Caldwell, (Janet Miriam) Taylor (Holland)**
1900-1985 ............... CLC 2, 28, 39
See also CANR 5; CA 5-8R;
obituary CA 116

**Calhoun, John Caldwell**
1782-1850 ................. NCLC 15
See also DLB 3

**Calisher, Hortense** 1911-.... CLC 2, 4, 8, 38
See also CANR 1, 22; CA 1-4R; DLB 2

**Callaghan, Morley (Edward)**
1903-1990 .......... CLC 3, 14, 41, 65
See also CANR 33; CA 9-12R;
obituary CA 132; DLB 68

**Calvino, Italo**
1923-1985 .... CLC 5, 8, 11, 22, 33, 39;
SSC 3
See also CANR 23; CA 85-88;
obituary CA 116

**Cameron, Carey** 1952-............ CLC 59

**Cameron, Peter** 1959-.............. CLC 44
See also CA 125

**Campana, Dino** 1885-1932........ TCLC 20
See also CA 117

**Campbell, John W(ood), Jr.**
1910-1971 ................. CLC 32
See also CAP 2; CA 21-22;
obituary CA 29-32R; DLB 8

**Campbell, (John) Ramsey** 1946- .... CLC 42
See also CANR 7; CA 57-60

**Campbell, (Ignatius) Roy (Dunnachie)**
1901-1957 .................. TCLC 5
See also CA 104; DLB 20

**Campbell, Thomas** 1777-1844 .... NCLC 19

**Campbell, (William) Wilfred**
1861-1918 .................. TCLC 9
See also CA 106

**Camus, Albert**
    1913-1960 ... **CLC 1, 2, 4, 9, 11, 14, 32,**
                                                        **63**
    See also CA 89-92; DLB 72

**Canby, Vincent** 1924-............. **CLC 13**
    See also CA 81-84

**Canetti, Elias** 1905- ......... **CLC 3, 14, 25**
    See also CANR 23; CA 21-24R; DLB 85

**Canin, Ethan** 1960-.............. **CLC 55**

**Cape, Judith** 1916-
    See Page, P(atricia) K(athleen)

**Capek, Karel**
    1890-1938 .......... **TCLC 6, 37; DC 1**
    See also CA 104

**Capote, Truman**
    1924-1984 ..... **CLC 1, 3, 8, 13, 19, 34,**
                                        **38, 58; SSC 2**
    See also CANR 18; CA 5-8R;
        obituary CA 113; DLB 2; DLB-Y 80, 84;
        CDALB 1941-1968

**Capra, Frank** 1897-.............. **CLC 16**
    See also CA 61-64

**Caputo, Philip** 1941-.............. **CLC 32**
    See also CA 73-76

**Card, Orson Scott** 1951- .... **CLC 44, 47, 50**
    See also CA 102

**Cardenal, Ernesto** 1925-........... **CLC 31**
    See also CANR 2; CA 49-52

**Carducci, Giosue** 1835-1907...... **TCLC 32**

**Carew, Thomas** 1595?-1640........ **LC 13**

**Carey, Ernestine Gilbreth** 1908-.... **CLC 17**
    See also CA 5-8R; SATA 2

**Carey, Peter** 1943-................ **CLC 40, 55**
    See also CA 123, 127

**Carleton, William** 1794-1869...... **NCLC 3**

**Carlisle, Henry (Coffin)** 1926-...... **CLC 33**
    See also CANR 15; CA 13-16R

**Carlson, Ron(ald F.)** 1947-........ **CLC 54**
    See also CA 105

**Carlyle, Thomas** 1795-1881...... **NCLC 22**
    See also DLB 55

**Carman, (William) Bliss**
    1861-1929 ................... **TCLC 7**
    See also CA 104

**Carpenter, Don(ald Richard)**
    1931-...................... **CLC 41**
    See also CANR 1; CA 45-48

**Carpentier (y Valmont), Alejo**
    1904-1980......... **CLC 8, 11, 38**
    See also CANR 11; CA 65-68;
        obituary CA 97-100

**Carr, Emily** 1871-1945........... **TCLC 32**
    See also DLB 68

**Carr, John Dickson** 1906-1977...... **CLC 3**
    See also CANR 3; CA 49-52;
        obituary CA 69-72

**Carr, Virginia Spencer** 1929-....... **CLC 34**
    See also CA 61-64

**Carrier, Roch** 1937-.............. **CLC 13**
    See also DLB 53

**Carroll, James (P.)** 1943-.......... **CLC 38**
    See also CA 81-84

**Carroll, Jim** 1951- .............. **CLC 35**
    See also CA 45-48

**Carroll, Lewis** 1832-1898........ **NCLC 2**
    See also Dodgson, Charles Lutwidge
    See also CLR 2; DLB 18

**Carroll, Paul Vincent** 1900-1968.... **CLC 10**
    See also CA 9-12R; obituary CA 25-28R;
        DLB 10

**Carruth, Hayden** 1921- ... **CLC 4, 7, 10, 18**
    See also CANR 4; CA 9-12R; SATA 47;
        DLB 5

**Carter, Angela (Olive)** 1940-..... **CLC 5, 41**
    See also CANR 12; CA 53-56; DLB 14

**Carver, Raymond**
    1938-1988 .......... **CLC 22, 36, 53, 55**
    See also CANR 17; CA 33-36R;
        obituary CA 126; DLB-Y 84, 88

**Cary, (Arthur) Joyce (Lunel)**
    1888-1957 ................ **TCLC 1, 29**
    See also CA 104; DLB 15

**Casanova de Seingalt, Giovanni Jacopo**
    1725-1798 ................... **LC 13**

**Casares, Adolfo Bioy** 1914-
    See Bioy Casares, Adolfo

**Casely-Hayford, J(oseph) E(phraim)**
    1866-1930 ................. **TCLC 24**
    See also CA 123

**Casey, John** 1880-1964
    See O'Casey, Sean

**Casey, John** 1939- .............. **CLC 59**
    See also CANR 23; CA 69-72

**Casey, Michael** 1947-.............. **CLC 2**
    See also CA 65-68; DLB 5

**Casey, Warren** 1935- ............. **CLC 12**
    See also Jacobs, Jim and Casey, Warren
    See also CA 101

**Casona, Alejandro** 1903-1965 ...... **CLC 49**
    See also Alvarez, Alejandro Rodriguez

**Cassavetes, John** 1929-........... **CLC 20**
    See also CA 85-88, 127

**Cassill, R(onald) V(erlin)** 1919-... **CLC 4, 23**
    See also CAAS 1; CANR 7; CA 9-12R;
        DLB 6

**Cassity, (Allen) Turner** 1929- .... **CLC 6, 42**
    See also CANR 11; CA 17-20R

**Castaneda, Carlos** 1935?-.......... **CLC 12**
    See also CA 25-28R

**Castedo, Elena** 1937- ............. **CLC 65**
    See also CA 132

**Castelvetro, Lodovico** 1505-1571..... **LC 12**

**Castiglione, Baldassare** 1478-1529 ... **LC 12**

**Castro, Rosalia de** 1837-1885 ..... **NCLC 3**

**Cather, Willa (Sibert)**
    1873-1947 ...... **TCLC 1, 11, 31; SSC 2**
    See also CA 104; SATA 30; DLB 9, 54;
        DLB-DS 1; CDALB 1865-1917

**Catton, (Charles) Bruce**
    1899-1978 ................... **CLC 35**
    See also CANR 7; CA 5-8R;
        obituary CA 81-84; SATA 2;
        obituary SATA 24; DLB 17

**Cauldwell, Frank** 1923-
    See King, Francis (Henry)

**Caunitz, William** 1935- .......... **CLC 34**

**Causley, Charles (Stanley)** 1917-..... **CLC 7**
    See also CANR 5; CA 9-12R; SATA 3;
        DLB 27

**Caute, (John) David** 1936-........ **CLC 29**
    See also CAAS 4; CANR 1; CA 1-4R;
        DLB 14

**Cavafy, C(onstantine) P(eter)**
    1863-1933 ................ **TCLC 2, 7**
    See also CA 104

**Cavanna, Betty** 1909-.............. **CLC 12**
    See also CANR 6; CA 9-12R; SATA 1, 30

**Cayrol, Jean** 1911-................ **CLC 11**
    See also CA 89-92; DLB 83

**Cela, Camilo Jose** 1916-...... **CLC 4, 13, 59**
    See also CAAS 10; CANR 21; CA 21-24R

**Celan, Paul** 1920-1970...... **CLC 10, 19, 53**
    See also Antschel, Paul
    See also DLB 69

**Celine, Louis-Ferdinand**
    1894-1961 ..... **CLC 1, 3, 4, 7, 9, 15, 47**
    See also Destouches,
        Louis-Ferdinand-Auguste
    See also DLB 72

**Cellini, Benvenuto** 1500-1571 ........ **LC 7**

**Cendrars, Blaise** 1887-1961........ **CLC 18**
    See also Sauser-Hall, Frederic

**Cernuda, Luis (y Bidon)**
    1902-1963 ................... **CLC 54**
    See also CA 89-92

**Cervantes (Saavedra), Miguel de**
    1547-1616 ................... **LC 6**

**Cesaire, Aime (Fernand)** 1913-.. **CLC 19, 32**
    See also CANR 24; CA 65-68

**Chabon, Michael** 1965?-........... **CLC 55**

**Chabrol, Claude** 1930-............. **CLC 16**
    See also CA 110

**Challans, Mary** 1905-1983
    See Renault, Mary
    See also CA 81-84; obituary CA 111;
        SATA 23; obituary SATA 36

**Chambers, Aidan** 1934-........... **CLC 35**
    See also CANR 12; CA 25-28R; SATA 1

**Chambers, James** 1948-
    See Cliff, Jimmy

**Chambers, Robert W.** 1865-1933... **TCLC 41**

**Chandler, Raymond** 1888-1959 ... **TCLC 1, 7**
    See also CA 104

**Channing, William Ellery**
    1780-1842 ................. **NCLC 17**
    See also DLB 1, 59

**Chaplin, Charles (Spencer)**
    1889-1977 ................... **CLC 16**
    See also CA 81-84; obituary CA 73-76;
        DLB 44

**Chapman, Graham** 1941?- ......... **CLC 21**
    See also Monty Python
    See also CA 116; obituary CA 169

**Chapman, John Jay** 1862-1933..... **TCLC 7**
    See also CA 104

**Chappell, Fred** 1936-............. **CLC 40**
    See also CAAS 4; CANR 8; CA 5-8R;
        DLB 6

**Char, Rene (Emile)**
1907-1988 .......... **CLC 9, 11, 14, 55**
See also CA 13-16R; obituary CA 124

**Charles I** 1600-1649 .............. **LC 13**

**Chartier, Emile-Auguste** 1868-1951
See Alain

**Charyn, Jerome** 1937- ........ **CLC 5, 8, 18**
See also CAAS 1; CANR 7; CA 5-8R;
DLB-Y 83

**Chase, Mary (Coyle)** 1907-1981 ...... **DC 1**
See also CA 77-80, 105; SATA 17, 29

**Chase, Mary Ellen** 1887-1973 ....... **CLC 2**
See also CAP 1; CA 15-16;
obituary CA 41-44R; SATA 10

**Chateaubriand, Francois Rene de**
1768-1848 .................. **NCLC 3**

**Chatier, Emile-Auguste** 1868-1951
See Alain

**Chatterji, Bankim Chandra**
1838-1894 ................. **NCLC 19**

**Chatterji, Saratchandra**
1876-1938 ................. **TCLC 13**
See also CA 109

**Chatterton, Thomas** 1752-1770 ....... **LC 3**

**Chatwin, (Charles) Bruce**
1940-1989 ............. **CLC 28, 57, 59**
See also CA 85-88,; obituary CA 127

**Chayefsky, Paddy** 1923-1981 ....... **CLC 23**
See also CA 9-12R; obituary CA 104;
DLB 7, 44; DLB-Y 81

**Chayefsky, Sidney** 1923-1981
See Chayefsky, Paddy
See also CANR 18

**Chedid, Andree** 1920- ............. **CLC 47**

**Cheever, John**
1912-1982 ..... **CLC 3, 7, 8, 11, 15, 25,
64; SSC 1**
See also CANR 5, 27; CA 5-8R;
obituary CA 106; CABS 1; DLB 2;
DLB-Y 80, 82; CDALB 1941-1968

**Cheever, Susan** 1943- .......... **CLC 18, 48**
See also CA 103; DLB-Y 82

**Chekhov, Anton (Pavlovich)**
1860-1904 ...... **TCLC 3, 10, 31; SSC 2**
See also CA 104, 124

**Chernyshevsky, Nikolay Gavrilovich**
1828-1889 ................... **NCLC 1**

**Cherry, Caroline Janice** 1942-
See Cherryh, C. J.

**Cherryh, C. J.** 1942- ............. **CLC 35**
See also CANR 10; CA 65-68; DLB-Y 80

**Chesnutt, Charles Waddell**
1858-1932 ...... **TCLC 5, 39; SSC 7**
See also CA 106, 125; DLB 12, 50, 78

**Chester, Alfred** 1929?-1971 ........ **CLC 49**
See also obituary CA 33-36R

**Chesterton, G(ilbert) K(eith)**
1874-1936 .......... **TCLC 1, 6; SSC 1**
See also CA 104; SATA 27; DLB 10, 19,
34, 70

**Ch'ien Chung-shu** 1910- .......... **CLC 22**

**Child, Lydia Maria** 1802-1880 .... **NCLC 6**
See also DLB 1, 74

**Child, Philip** 1898-1978 .......... **CLC 19**
See also CAP 1; CA 13-14; SATA 47

**Childress, Alice** 1920-.......... **CLC 12, 15**
See also CLR 14; CANR 3; CA 45-48;
SATA 7, 48; DLB 7, 38

**Chislett, (Margaret) Anne** 1943?- ... **CLC 34**

**Chitty, (Sir) Thomas Willes** 1926- .. **CLC 11**
See also Hinde, Thomas
See also CA 5-8R

**Chomette, Rene** 1898-1981
See Clair, Rene
See also obituary CA 103

**Chopin, Kate (O'Flaherty)**
1851-1904 ................ **TCLC 5, 14**
See also CA 104, 122; DLB 12;
CDALB 1865-1917

**Christie, (Dame) Agatha (Mary Clarissa)**
1890-1976 ...... **CLC 1, 6, 8, 12, 39, 48**
See also CANR 10; CA 17-20R;
obituary CA 61-64; SATA 36; DLB 13

**Christie, (Ann) Philippa** 1920-
See Pearce, (Ann) Philippa
See also CANR 4; CA 7-8

**Christine de Pizan** 1365?-1431?....... **LC 9**

**Chulkov, Mikhail Dmitrievich**
1743-1792 ................... **LC 2**

**Churchill, Caryl** 1938- ......... **CLC 31, 55**
See also CANR 22; CA 102; DLB 13

**Churchill, Charles** 1731?-1764........ **LC 3**

**Chute, Carolyn** 1947-............. **CLC 39**
See also CA 123

**Ciardi, John (Anthony)**
1916-1986 ............ **CLC 10, 40, 44**
See also CAAS 2; CANR 5; CA 5-8R;
obituary CA 118; SATA 1, 46; DLB 5;
DLB-Y 86

**Cicero, Marcus Tullius**
106 B.C.-43 B.C............. **CMLC 3**

**Cimino, Michael** 1943?-........... **CLC 16**
See also CA 105

**Cioran, E. M.** 1911-............... **CLC 64**
See also CA 25-28R

**Clair, Rene** 1898-1981 ............ **CLC 20**
See also Chomette, Rene

**Clampitt, Amy** 19??-............... **CLC 32**
See also CA 110

**Clancy, Tom** 1947-............... **CLC 45**
See also CA 125

**Clare, John** 1793-1864 ........... **NCLC 9**
See also DLB 55

**Clark, (Robert) Brian** 1932-........ **CLC 29**
See also CA 41-44R

**Clark, Eleanor** 1913- ........... **CLC 5, 19**
See also CA 9-12R; DLB 6

**Clark, John Pepper** 1935- ......... **CLC 38**
See also CANR 16; CA 65-68

**Clark, Mavis Thorpe** 1912?- ....... **CLC 12**
See also CANR 8; CA 57-60; SAAS 5;
SATA 8

**Clark, Walter Van Tilburg**
1909-1971 .................. **CLC 28**
See also CA 9-12R; obituary CA 33-36R;
SATA 8; DLB 9

**Clarke, Arthur C(harles)**
1917- ...... **CLC 1, 4, 13, 18, 35; SSC 3**
See also CANR 2; CA 1-4R; SATA 13

**Clarke, Austin** 1896-1974......... **CLC 6, 9**
See also CANR 14; CAP 2; CA 29-32;
obituary CA 49-52; DLB 10, 20, 53

**Clarke, Austin (Ardinel) C(hesterfield)**
1934-..................... **CLC 8, 53**
See also CANR 14; CA 25-28R; DLB 53

**Clarke, Gillian** 1937-............. **CLC 61**
See also CA 106; DLB 40

**Clarke, Marcus (Andrew Hislop)**
1846-1881 ................. **NCLC 19**

**Clarke, Shirley** 1925-............. **CLC 16**

**Clash, The** ....................... **CLC 30**

**Claudel, Paul (Louis Charles Marie)**
1868-1955 ............... **TCLC 2, 10**
See also CA 104

**Clavell, James (duMaresq)**
1924-..................... **CLC 6, 25**
See also CANR 26; CA 25-28R

**Clayman. Gregory** 1974?-.......... **CLC 65**

**Cleaver, (Leroy) Eldridge** 1935- .... **CLC 30**
See also CANR 16; CA 21-24R

**Cleese, John** 1939-............... **CLC 21**
See also Monty Python
See also CA 112, 116

**Cleland, John** 1709-1789 ............ **LC 2**
See also DLB 39

**Clemens, Samuel Langhorne**
1835-1910 ...... **TCLC 6, 12, 19; SSC 6**
See also Twain, Mark
See also YABC 2; CA 104; DLB 11, 12, 23,
64, 74; CDALB 1865-1917

**Cliff, Jimmy** 1948-............... **CLC 21**

**Clifton, Lucille** 1936-............. **CLC 19**
See also CLR 5; CANR 2, 24; CA 49-52;
SATA 20; DLB 5, 41

**Clough, Arthur Hugh** 1819-1861.. **NCLC 27**
See also DLB 32

**Clutha, Janet Paterson Frame** 1924-
See Frame (Clutha), Janet (Paterson)
See also CANR 2; CA 1-4R

**Coburn, D(onald) L(ee)** 1938- ...... **CLC 10**
See also CA 89-92

**Cocteau, Jean (Maurice Eugene Clement)**
1889-1963 ........ **CLC 1, 8, 15, 16, 43**
See also CAP 2; CA 25-28; DLB 65

**Codrescu, Andrei** 1946-........... **CLC 46**
See also CANR 13; CA 33-36R

**Coetzee, J(ohn) M.** 1940-....... **CLC 23, 33**
See also CA 77-80

**Cohen, Arthur A(llen)**
1928-1986 ............... **CLC 7, 31**
See also CANR 1, 17; CA 1-4R;
obituary CA 120; DLB 28

**Cohen, Leonard (Norman)**
1934-..................... **CLC 3, 38**
See also CANR 14; CA 21-24R; DLB 53

**Cohen, Matt** 1942-............... **CLC 19**
See also CA 61-64; DLB 53

**Cohen-Solal, Annie** 19??-.......... **CLC 50**

**Colegate, Isabel** 1931- ............ **CLC 36**
See also CANR 8, 22; CA 17-20R; DLB 14**

Coleridge, Samuel Taylor
    1772-1834 . . . . . . . . . . . . . . . . . NCLC 9

Coleridge, Sara  1802-1852 . . . . . . NCLC 31

Coles, Don  1928- . . . . . . . . . . . . . CLC 46
    See also CA 115

Colette (Sidonie-Gabrielle)
    1873-1954 . . . . . . . . . . . . . TCLC 1, 5, 16
    See also CA 104; DLB 65

Collett, (Jacobine) Camilla (Wergeland)
    1813-1895 . . . . . . . . . . . . . . . . NCLC 22

Collier, Christopher  1930- . . . . . . . . CLC 30
    See also CANR 13; CA 33-36R; SATA 16

Collier, James L(incoln)  1928- . . . . . CLC 30
    See also CLR 3; CANR 4; CA 9-12R;
    SATA 8

Collier, Jeremy  1650-1726 . . . . . . . . . . LC 6

Collins, Hunt  1926-
    See Hunter, Evan

Collins, Linda  19??- . . . . . . . . . . . . . CLC 44
    See also CA 125

Collins, Tom  1843-1912
    See Furphy, Joseph

Collins, (William) Wilkie
    1824-1889 . . . . . . . . . . . . . . NCLC 1, 18
    See also DLB 18, 70

Collins, William  1721-1759 . . . . . . . . . LC 4

Colman, George  1909-1981
    See Glassco, John

Colter, Cyrus  1910- . . . . . . . . . . . . . CLC 58
    See also CANR 10; CA 65-68; DLB 33

Colton, James  1923-
    See Hansen, Joseph

Colum, Padraic  1881-1972 . . . . . . . . CLC 28
    See also CA 73-76; obituary CA 33-36R;
    SATA 15; DLB 19

Colvin, James  1939-
    See Moorcock, Michael

Colwin, Laurie  1945- . . . . . . . CLC 5, 13, 23
    See also CANR 20; CA 89-92; DLB-Y 80

Comfort, Alex(ander)  1920- . . . . . . . . CLC 7
    See also CANR 1; CA 1-4R

Compton-Burnett, Ivy
    1892-1969 . . . . . . . CLC 1, 3, 10, 15, 34
    See also CANR 4; CA 1-4R;
    obituary CA 25-28R; DLB 36

Comstock, Anthony  1844-1915 . . . . TCLC 13
    See also CA 110

Conde, Maryse  1937- . . . . . . . . . . . . CLC 52
    See also Boucolon, Maryse

Condon, Richard (Thomas)
    1915- . . . . . . . . . . . . CLC 4, 6, 8, 10, 45
    See also CAAS 1; CANR 2, 23; CA 1-4R

Congreve, William  1670-1729 . . . . . . . . LC 5
    See also DLB 39

Connell, Evan S(helby), Jr.
    1924- . . . . . . . . . . . . . . . . CLC 4, 6, 45
    See also CAAS 2; CANR 2; CA 1-4R;
    DLB 2; DLB-Y 81

Connelly, Marc(us Cook)
    1890-1980 . . . . . . . . . . . . . . . . . CLC 7
    See also CA 85-88; obituary CA 102;
    obituary SATA 25; DLB 7; DLB-Y 80

Conner, Ralph  1860-1937 . . . . . . . . TCLC 31

Conrad, Joseph
    1857-1924 . . . . . . . . . TCLC 1, 6, 13, 25
    See also CA 104; SATA 27; DLB 10, 34

Conroy, Pat  1945-. . . . . . . . . . . . . . CLC 30
    See also CANR 24; CA 85-88; DLB 6

Constant (de Rebecque), (Henri) Benjamin
    1767-1830 . . . . . . . . . . . . . . . . . NCLC 6

Cook, Michael  1933- . . . . . . . . . . . . CLC 58
    See also CA 93-96; DLB 53

Cook, Robin  1940- . . . . . . . . . . . . . . CLC 14
    See also CA 108, 111

Cooke, Elizabeth  1948- . . . . . . . . . . . CLC 55

Cooke, John Esten  1830-1886 . . . . . NCLC 5
    See also DLB 3

Cooney, Ray  19??- . . . . . . . . . . . . . . CLC 62

Cooper, J. California  19??- . . . . . . . . CLC 56
    See also CA 125

Cooper, James Fenimore
    1789-1851 . . . . . . . . . . . . . NCLC 1, 27
    See also SATA 19; DLB 3;
    CDALB 1640-1865

Coover, Robert (Lowell)
    1932- . . . . . . . . . . . CLC 3, 7, 15, 32, 46
    See also CANR 3; CA 45-48; DLB 2;
    DLB-Y 81

Copeland, Stewart (Armstrong)
    1952- . . . . . . . . . . . . . . . . . . . CLC 26
    See also The Police

Coppard, A(lfred) E(dgar)
    1878-1957 . . . . . . . . . . . . . . . . . TCLC 5
    See also YABC 1; CA 114

Coppee, Francois  1842-1908 . . . . . . TCLC 25

Coppola, Francis Ford  1939- . . . . . . . CLC 16
    See also CA 77-80; DLB 44

Corcoran, Barbara  1911- . . . . . . . . . CLC 17
    See also CAAS 2; CANR 11; CA 21-24R;
    SATA 3; DLB 52

Corman, Cid  1924- . . . . . . . . . . . . . . CLC 9
    See also Corman, Sidney
    See also CAAS 2; DLB 5

Corman, Sidney  1924-
    See Corman, Cid
    See also CA 85-88

Cormier, Robert (Edmund)
    1925- . . . . . . . . . . . . . . . . . CLC 12, 30
    See also CLR 12; CANR 5, 23; CA 1-4R;
    SATA 10, 45; DLB 52

Corn, Alfred (Dewitt III)  1943-. . . . . CLC 33
    See also CA 104; DLB-Y 80

Cornwell, David (John Moore)
    1931- . . . . . . . . . . . . . . . . . . CLC 9, 15
    See also le Carre, John
    See also CANR 13; CA 5-8R

Corso, (Nunzio) Gregory  1930-. . . CLC 1, 11
    See also CA 5-8R; DLB 5, 16

Cortazar, Julio
    1914-1984 . . . . . CLC 2, 3, 5, 10, 13, 15,
                   33, 34; SSC 7
    See also CANR 12; CA 21-24R

Corvo, Baron  1860-1913
    See Rolfe, Frederick (William Serafino
    Austin Lewis Mary)

Cosic, Dobrica  1921- . . . . . . . . . . . . CLC 14
    See also CA 122

Costain, Thomas B(ertram)
    1885-1965 . . . . . . . . . . . . . . . . . CLC 30
    See also CA 5-8R; obituary CA 25-28R;
    DLB 9

Costantini, Humberto  1924?-1987. . . CLC 49
    See also obituary CA 122

Costello, Elvis  1955-. . . . . . . . . . . . . CLC 21

Cotter, Joseph Seamon, Sr.
    1861-1949 . . . . . . . . . . . . . . . . TCLC 28
    See also CA 124; DLB 50

Couperus, Louis (Marie Anne)
    1863-1923 . . . . . . . . . . . . . . . . TCLC 15
    See also CA 115

Courtenay, Bryce  1933-. . . . . . . . . . . CLC 59

Cousteau, Jacques-Yves  1910-. . . . . . CLC 30
    See also CANR 15; CA 65-68; SATA 38

Coward, (Sir) Noel (Pierce)
    1899-1973 . . . . . . . . . . . CLC 1, 9, 29, 51
    See also CAP 2; CA 17-18;
    obituary CA 41-44R; DLB 10

Cowley, Malcolm  1898-1989 . . . . . . . CLC 39
    See also CANR 3; CA 5-6R;
    obituary CA 128; DLB 4, 48; DLB-Y 81

Cowper, William  1731-1800. . . . . . . NCLC 8

Cox, William Trevor  1928- . . . . . . CLC 9, 14
    See also Trevor, William
    See also CANR 4; CA 9-12R

Cozzens, James Gould
    1903-1978 . . . . . . . . . . . . . CLC 1, 4, 11
    See also CANR 19; CA 9-12R;
    obituary CA 81-84; DLB 9; DLB-Y 84;
    DLB-DS 2; CDALB 1941-1968

Crabbe, George  1754-1832. . . . . . . NCLC 26

Crace, Douglas  1944- . . . . . . . . . . . . CLC 58

Crane, (Harold) Hart
    1899-1932 . . . . . . . . . . . . . . . TCLC 2, 5
    See also CA 104; DLB 4, 48

Crane, R(onald) S(almon)
    1886-1967 . . . . . . . . . . . . . . . . . CLC 27
    See also CA 85-88; DLB 63

Crane, Stephen
    1871-1900 . . . . . TCLC 11, 17, 32; SSC 7
    See also YABC 2; CA 109; DLB 12, 54, 78;
    CDALB 1865-1917

Craven, Margaret  1901-1980. . . . . . . CLC 17
    See also CA 103

Crawford, F(rancis) Marion
    1854-1909 . . . . . . . . . . . . . . . . TCLC 10
    See also CA 107; DLB 71

Crawford, Isabella Valancy
    1850-1887 . . . . . . . . . . . . . . . . NCLC 12
    See also DLB 92

Crayencour, Marguerite de  1903-1987
    See Yourcenar, Marguerite

Creasey, John  1908-1973. . . . . . . . . CLC 11
    See also CANR 8; CA 5-8R;
    obituary CA 41-44R; DLB 77

Crebillon, Claude Prosper Jolyot de (fils)
    1707-1777 . . . . . . . . . . . . . . . . . . LC 1

Creeley, Robert (White)
    1926- . . . . . . . . CLC 1, 2, 4, 8, 11, 15, 36
    See also CANR 23; CA 1-4R; DLB 5, 16

**Crews, Harry (Eugene)**
1935- .................. CLC **6, 23, 49**
See also CANR 20; CA 25-28R; DLB 6

**Crichton, (John) Michael**
1942- ................... CLC **2, 6, 54**
See also CANR 13; CA 25-28R; SATA 9;
DLB-Y 81

**Crispin, Edmund** 1921-1978........ CLC **22**
See also Montgomery, Robert Bruce
See also DLB 87

**Cristofer, Michael** 1946- ......... CLC **28**
See also CA 110; DLB 7

**Croce, Benedetto** 1866-1952 ...... TCLC **37**
See also CA 120

**Crockett, David (Davy)**
1786-1836 ................. NCLC **8**
See also DLB 3, 11

**Croker, John Wilson** 1780-1857 .. NCLC **10**

**Cronin, A(rchibald) J(oseph)**
1896-1981 ................... CLC **32**
See also CANR 5; CA 1-4R;
obituary CA 102; obituary SATA 25, 47

**Cross, Amanda** 1926-
See Heilbrun, Carolyn G(old)

**Crothers, Rachel** 1878-1953....... TCLC **19**
See also CA 113; DLB 7

**Crowley, Aleister** 1875-1947 ....... TCLC **7**
See also CA 104

**Crowley, John** 1942-
See also CA 61-64; DLB-Y 82

**Crumb, Robert** 1943- ............. CLC **17**
See also CA 106

**Cryer, Gretchen** 1936?- ........... CLC **21**
See also CA 114, 123

**Csath, Geza** 1887-1919.......... TCLC **13**
See also CA 111

**Cudlip, David** 1933- ............. CLC **34**

**Cullen, Countee** 1903-1946 ..... TCLC **4, 37**
See also CA 108, 124; SATA 18; DLB 4,
48, 51; CDALB 1917-1929

**Cummings, E(dward) E(stlin)**
1894-1962 ......... CLC **1, 3, 8, 12, 15**
See also CA 73-76; DLB 4, 48

**Cunha, Euclides (Rodrigues) da**
1866-1909 .................. TCLC **24**
See also CA 123

**Cunningham, J(ames) V(incent)**
1911-1985 ................. CLC **3, 31**
See also CANR 1; CA 1-4R;
obituary CA 115; DLB 5

**Cunningham, Julia (Woolfolk)**
1916- ..................... CLC **12**
See also CANR 4, 19; CA 9-12R; SAAS 2;
SATA 1, 26

**Cunningham, Michael** 1952- ....... CLC **34**

**Currie, Ellen** 19??- ............... CLC **44**

**Dabrowska, Maria (Szumska)**
1889-1965 ................. CLC **15**
See also CA 106

**Dabydeen, David** 1956?-........... CLC **34**
See also CA 106

**Dacey, Philip** 1939- .............. CLC **51**
See also CANR 14; CA 37-40R

**Dagerman, Stig (Halvard)**
1923-1954 ................. TCLC **17**
See also CA 117

**Dahl, Roald** 1916-............ CLC **1, 6, 18**
See also CLR 1, 7; CANR 6; CA 1-4R;
SATA 1, 26

**Dahlberg, Edward** 1900-1977... CLC **1, 7, 14**
See also CA 9-12R; obituary CA 69-72;
DLB 48

**Daly, Elizabeth** 1878-1967......... CLC **52**
See also CAP 2; CA 23-24;
obituary CA 25-28R

**Daly, Maureen** 1921-............. CLC **17**
See also McGivern, Maureen Daly
See also SAAS 1; SATA 2

**Daniken, Erich von** 1935-
See Von Daniken, Erich

**Dannay, Frederic** 1905-1982
See Queen, Ellery
See also CANR 1; CA 1-4R;
obituary CA 107

**D'Annunzio, Gabriele**
1863-1938 ................ TCLC **6, 40**
See also CA 104

**Dante (Alighieri)**
See Alighieri, Dante

**Danziger, Paula** 1944- ............ CLC **21**
See also CLR 20; CA 112, 115; SATA 30,
36

**Dario, Ruben** 1867-1916 .......... TCLC **4**
See also Sarmiento, Felix Ruben Garcia
See also CA 104

**Darley, George** 1795-1846........ NCLC **2**

**Daryush, Elizabeth** 1887-1977.... CLC **6, 19**
See also CANR 3; CA 49-52; DLB 20

**Daudet, (Louis Marie) Alphonse**
1840-1897 ................. NCLC **1**

**Daumal, Rene** 1908-1944........ TCLC **14**
See also CA 114

**Davenport, Guy (Mattison, Jr.)**
1927- ................... CLC **6, 14, 38**
See also CANR 23; CA 33-36R

**Davidson, Donald (Grady)**
1893-1968 ............... CLC **2, 13, 19**
See also CANR 4; CA 5-8R;
obituary CA 25-28R; DLB 45

**Davidson, John** 1857-1909....... TCLC **24**
See also CA 118; DLB 19

**Davidson, Sara** 1943-............. CLC **9**
See also CA 81-84

**Davie, Donald (Alfred)**
1922- ................CLC **5, 8, 10, 31**
See also CAAS 3; CANR 1; CA 1-4R;
DLB 27

**Davies, Ray(mond Douglas)** 1944- .. CLC **21**
See also CA 116

**Davies, Rhys** 1903-1978........... CLC **23**
See also CANR 4; CA 9-12R;
obituary CA 81-84

**Davies, (William) Robertson**
1913- ........... CLC **2, 7, 13, 25, 42**
See also CANR 17; CA 33-36R; DLB 68

**Davies, W(illiam) H(enry)**
1871-1940 ................. TCLC **5**
See also CA 104; DLB 19

**Davis, H(arold) L(enoir)**
1896-1960 ................... CLC **49**
See also obituary CA 89-92; DLB 9

**Davis, Rebecca (Blaine) Harding**
1831-1910 .................. TCLC **6**
See also CA 104; DLB 74

**Davis, Richard Harding**
1864-1916 ................. TCLC **24**
See also CA 114; DLB 12, 23, 78, 79

**Davison, Frank Dalby** 1893-1970 ... CLC **15**
See also obituary CA 116

**Davison, Peter** 1928- ............. CLC **28**
See also CAAS 4; CANR 3; CA 9-12R;
DLB 5

**Davys, Mary** 1674-1732............. LC **1**
See also DLB 39

**Dawson, Fielding** 1930- ............ CLC **6**
See also CA 85-88

**Day, Clarence (Shepard, Jr.)**
1874-1935 ................. TCLC **25**
See also CA 108; DLB 11

**Day, Thomas** 1748-1789............. LC **1**
See also YABC 1; DLB 39

**Day Lewis, C(ecil)**
1904-1972 ............... CLC **1, 6, 10**
See also CAP 1; CA 15-16;
obituary CA 33-36R; DLB 15, 20

**Dazai Osamu** 1909-1948 ........ TCLC **11**
See also Tsushima Shuji

**De Crayencour, Marguerite** 1903-1987
See Yourcenar, Marguerite

**Deer, Sandra** 1940-............... CLC **45**

**De Ferrari, Gabriella** 19??- ........ CLC **65**

**Defoe, Daniel** 1660?-1731 ........... LC **1**
See also SATA 22; DLB 39

**De Hartog, Jan** 1914-............. CLC **19**
See also CANR 1; CA 1-4R

**Deighton, Len** 1929-....... CLC **4, 7, 22, 46**
See also Deighton, Leonard Cyril
See also DLB 87

**Deighton, Leonard Cyril** 1929-
See Deighton, Len
See also CANR 19; CA 9-12R

**De la Mare, Walter (John)**
1873-1956 ................... TCLC **4**
See also CLR 23; CA 110; SATA 16;
DLB 19

**Delaney, Shelagh** 1939- ........... CLC **29**
See also CA 17-20R; DLB 13

**Delany, Mary (Granville Pendarves)**
1700-1788 ................... LC **12**

**Delany, Samuel R(ay, Jr.)**
1942- ................... CLC **8, 14, 38**
See also CA 81-84; DLB 8, 33

**De la Roche, Mazo** 1885-1961 ..... CLC **14**
See also CA 85-88; DLB 68

**Delbanco, Nicholas (Franklin)**
1942- .................... CLC **6, 13**
See also CAAS 2; CA 17-20R; DLB 6

**del Castillo, Michel** 1933- ......... CLC **38**
See also CA 109

**Deledda, Grazia** 1871-1936 ....... TCLC **23**
See also CA 123

**Delibes (Setien), Miguel** 1920- ... **CLC 8, 18**
See also CANR 1; CA 45-48

**DeLillo, Don**
1936- ........ **CLC 8, 10, 13, 27, 39, 54**
See also CANR 21; CA 81-84; DLB 6

**De Lisser, H(erbert) G(eorge)**
1878-1944 .................. **TCLC 12**
See also CA 109

**Deloria, Vine (Victor), Jr.** 1933-.... **CLC 21**
See also CANR 5, 20; CA 53-56; SATA 21

**Del Vecchio, John M(ichael)**
1947- ...................... **CLC 29**
See also CA 110

**de Man, Paul** 1919-1983 ......... **CLC 55**
See also obituary CA 111; DLB 67

**De Marinis, Rick** 1934-........... **CLC 54**
See also CANR 9, 25; CA 57-60

**Demby, William** 1922-........... **CLC 53**
See also CA 81-84; DLB 33

**Denby, Edwin (Orr)** 1903-1983 ..... **CLC 48**
See also obituary CA 110

**Dennis, John** 1657-1734........... **LC 11**

**Dennis, Nigel (Forbes)** 1912-........ **CLC 8**
See also CA 25-28R; obituary CA 129;
DLB 13, 15

**De Palma, Brian** 1940-........... **CLC 20**
See also CA 109

**De Quincey, Thomas** 1785-1859 ... **NCLC 4**

**Deren, Eleanora** 1908-1961
See Deren, Maya
See also obituary CA 111

**Deren, Maya** 1908-1961........... **CLC 16**
See also Deren, Eleanora

**Derleth, August (William)**
1909-1971 ................... **CLC 31**
See also CANR 4; CA 1-4R;
obituary CA 29-32R; SATA 5; DLB 9

**Derrida, Jacques** 1930-........... **CLC 24**
See also CA 124, 127

**Desai, Anita** 1937- ........... **CLC 19, 37**
See also CA 81-84

**De Saint-Luc, Jean** 1909-1981
See Glassco, John

**De Sica, Vittorio** 1902-1974 ....... **CLC 20**
See also obituary CA 117

**Desnos, Robert** 1900-1945........ **TCLC 22**
See also CA 121

**Destouches, Louis-Ferdinand-Auguste**
1894-1961
See Celine, Louis-Ferdinand
See also CA 85-88

**Deutsch, Babette** 1895-1982 ....... **CLC 18**
See also CANR 4; CA 1-4R;
obituary CA 108; SATA 1;
obituary SATA 33; DLB 45

**Devenant, William** 1606-1649 ....... **LC 13**

**Devkota, Laxmiprasad**
1909-1959 .................. **TCLC 23**
See also CA 123

**DeVoto, Bernard (Augustine)**
1897-1955 .................. **TCLC 29**
See also CA 113; DLB 9

**De Vries, Peter**
1910- ........ **CLC 1, 2, 3, 7, 10, 28, 46**
See also CA 17-20R; DLB 6; DLB-Y 82

**Dexter, Pete** 1943-............ **CLC 34, 55**
See also CA 127

**Diamond, Neil (Leslie)** 1941-....... **CLC 30**
See also CA 108

**Dick, Philip K(indred)**
1928-1982 ................ **CLC 10, 30**
See also CANR 2, 16; CA 49-52;
obituary CA 106; DLB 8

**Dickens, Charles**
1812-1870 .......... **NCLC 3, 8, 18, 26**
See also SATA 15; DLB 21, 55, 70

**Dickey, James (Lafayette)**
1923- ........ **CLC 1, 2, 4, 7, 10, 15, 47**
See also CANR 10; CA 9-12R; CABS 2;
DLB 5; DLB-Y 82; DLB-DS 7

**Dickey, William** 1928-......... **CLC 3, 28**
See also CANR 24; CA 9-12R; DLB 5

**Dickinson, Charles** 1952-......... **CLC 49**

**Dickinson, Emily (Elizabeth)**
1830-1886 .......... **NCLC 21; PC 1**
See also SATA 29; DLB 1;
CDALB 1865-1917

**Dickinson, Peter (Malcolm de Brissac)**
1927- .................... **CLC 12, 35**
See also CA 41-44R; SATA 5; DLB 87

**Didion, Joan** 1934-..... **CLC 1, 3, 8, 14, 32**
See also CANR 14; CA 5-8R; DLB 2;
DLB-Y 81, 86; CDALB 1968-1987

**Dillard, Annie** 1945-............ **CLC 9, 60**
See also CANR 3; CA 49-52; SATA 10;
DLB-Y 80

**Dillard, R(ichard) H(enry) W(ilde)**
1937- ...................... **CLC 5**
See also CAAS 7; CANR 10; CA 21-24R;
DLB 5

**Dillon, Eilis** 1920-................ **CLC 17**
See also CAAS 3; CANR 4; CA 9-12R;
SATA 2

**Dinesen, Isak**
1885-1962 ......... **CLC 10, 29; SSC 7**
See also Blixen, Karen (Christentze
Dinesen)
See also CANR 22

**Disch, Thomas M(ichael)** 1940-... **CLC 7, 36**
See also CAAS 4; CANR 17; CA 21-24R;
SATA 54; DLB 8

**Disraeli, Benjamin** 1804-1881 ..... **NCLC 2**
See also DLB 21, 55

**Dixon, Paige** 1911-
See Corcoran, Barbara

**Dixon, Stephen** 1936-............ **CLC 52**
See also CANR 17; CA 89-92

**Doblin, Alfred** 1878-1957........ **TCLC 13**
See also Doeblin, Alfred

**Dobrolyubov, Nikolai Alexandrovich**
1836-1861 .................. **NCLC 5**

**Dobyns, Stephen** 1941-........... **CLC 37**
See also CANR 2, 18; CA 45-48

**Doctorow, E(dgar) L(aurence)**
1931- ..... **CLC 6, 11, 15, 18, 37, 44, 65**
See also CANR 2, 33; CA 45-48; DLB 2,
28; DLB-Y 80; CDALB 1968-1987

**Dodgson, Charles Lutwidge** 1832-1898
See Carroll, Lewis
See also YABC 2

**Doeblin, Alfred** 1878-1957........ **TCLC 13**
See also CA 110; DLB 66

**Doerr, Harriet** 1910- ............. **CLC 34**
See also CA 117, 122

**Donaldson, Stephen R.** 1947-....... **CLC 46**
See also CANR 13; CA 89-92

**Donleavy, J(ames) P(atrick)**
1926- ............. **CLC 1, 4, 6, 10, 45**
See also CANR 24; CA 9-12R; DLB 6

**Donnadieu, Marguerite** 1914-
See Duras, Marguerite

**Donne, John** 1572?-1631 ...... **LC 10; PC 1**

**Donnell, David** 1939?- ............ **CLC 34**

**Donoso, Jose** 1924-....... **CLC 4, 8, 11, 32**
See also CA 81-84

**Donovan, John** 1928-............. **CLC 35**
See also CLR 3; CA 97-100; SATA 29

**Doolittle, Hilda** 1886-1961
See H(ilda) D(oolittle)
See also CA 97-100; DLB 4, 45

**Dorfman, Ariel** 1942-............. **CLC 48**
See also CA 124

**Dorn, Ed(ward Merton)** 1929-... **CLC 10, 18**
See also CA 93-96; DLB 5

**Dos Passos, John (Roderigo)**
1896-1970 ... **CLC 1, 4, 8, 11, 15, 25, 34**
See also CANR 3; CA 1-4R;
obituary CA 29-32R; DLB 4, 9;
DLB-DS 1

**Dostoevski, Fedor Mikhailovich**
1821-1881 ....... **NCLC 2, 7, 21; SSC 2**

**Doughty, Charles (Montagu)**
1843-1926 .................. **TCLC 27**
See also CA 115; DLB 19, 57

**Douglas, George** 1869-1902....... **TCLC 28**

**Douglas, Keith** 1920-1944 ........ **TCLC 40**
See also DLB 27

**Douglass, Frederick** 1817-1895.... **NCLC 7**
See also SATA 29; DLB 1, 43, 50;
CDALB 1640-1865

**Dourado, (Waldomiro Freitas) Autran**
1926- .................... **CLC 23, 60**
See also CA 25-28R

**Dove, Rita** 1952-.................. **CLC 50**
See also CA 109

**Dowson, Ernest (Christopher)**
1867-1900 .................. **TCLC 4**
See also CA 105; DLB 19

**Doyle, (Sir) Arthur Conan**
1859-1930 ................ **TCLC 7, 26**
See also CA 104, 122; SATA 24; DLB 18,
70

**Dr. A** 1933-
See Silverstein, Alvin and Virginia B(arbara
Opshelor) Silverstein

**Drabble, Margaret**
1939- ........ **CLC 2, 3, 5, 8, 10, 22, 53**
See also CANR 18; CA 13-16R; SATA 48;
DLB 14

**Drayton, Michael** 1563-1631........ **LC 8**

**Dreiser, Theodore (Herman Albert)**
    1871-1945 . . . . . . . . . . **TCLC 10, 18, 35**
    See also CA 106; SATA 48; DLB 9, 12;
    DLB-DS 1; CDALB 1865-1917

**Drexler, Rosalyn** 1926- . . . . . . . . . . **CLC 2, 6**
    See also CA 81-84

**Dreyer, Carl Theodor** 1889-1968. . . . **CLC 16**
    See also obituary CA 116

**Drieu La Rochelle, Pierre**
    1893-1945 . . . . . . . . . . . . . . . . . . **TCLC 21**
    See also CA 117; DLB 72

**Droste-Hulshoff, Annette Freiin von**
    1797-1848 . . . . . . . . . . . . . . . . . **NCLC 3**

**Drummond, William Henry**
    1854-1907 . . . . . . . . . . . . . . . . . **TCLC 25**
    See also DLB 92

**Drummond de Andrade, Carlos** 1902-1987
    See Andrade, Carlos Drummond de

**Drury, Allen (Stuart)** 1918- . . . . . . . . **CLC 37**
    See also CANR 18; CA 57-60

**Dryden, John** 1631-1700 . . . . . . . . . . . **LC 3**

**Duberman, Martin** 1930- . . . . . . . . . . . **CLC 8**
    See also CANR 2; CA 1-4R

**Dubie, Norman (Evans, Jr.)** 1945- . . **CLC 36**
    See also CANR 12; CA 69-72

**Du Bois, W(illiam) E(dward) B(urghardt)**
    1868-1963 . . . . . . . . . . **CLC 1, 2, 13, 64**
    See also CA 85-88; SATA 42; DLB 47, 50,
    91; CDALB 1865-1917

**Dubus, Andre** 1936- . . . . . . . . . . . **CLC 13, 36**
    See also CANR 17; CA 21-24R

**Ducasse, Isidore Lucien** 1846-1870
    See Lautreamont, Comte de

**Duclos, Charles Pinot** 1704-1772 . . . . . **LC 1**

**Dudek, Louis** 1918- . . . . . . . . . . . **CLC 11, 19**
    See also CANR 1; CA 45-48; DLB 88

**Dudevant, Amandine Aurore Lucile Dupin**
    1804-1876
    See Sand, George

**Duerrenmatt, Friedrich**
    1921- . . . . . . . . . **CLC 1, 4, 8, 11, 15, 43**
    See also CA 17-20R; DLB 69

**Duffy, Bruce** 19??- . . . . . . . . . . . . . . . **CLC 50**

**Duffy, Maureen** 1933- . . . . . . . . . . . . **CLC 37**
    See also CA 25-28R; DLB 14

**Dugan, Alan** 1923- . . . . . . . . . . . . . . **CLC 2, 6**
    See also CA 81-84; DLB 5

**Duhamel, Georges** 1884-1966 . . . . . . . **CLC 8**
    See also CA 81-84; obituary CA 25-28R;
    DLB 65

**Dujardin, Edouard (Emile Louis)**
    1861-1949 . . . . . . . . . . . . . . . . . **TCLC 13**
    See also CA 109

**Duke, Raoul** 1939-
    See Thompson, Hunter S(tockton)

**Dumas, Alexandre (Davy de la Pailleterie)**
    **(pere)** 1802-1870. . . . . . . . . . **NCLC 11**
    See also SATA 18

**Dumas, Alexandre (fils)**
    1824-1895 . . . . . . . . . . . . . **NCLC 9; DC 1**

**Dumas, Henry** 1918-1968 . . . . . . . . . **CLC 62**

**Dumas, Henry (L.)** 1934-1968. . . . . . . **CLC 6**
    See also CA 85-88; DLB 41

**Du Maurier, Daphne** 1907- . . . **CLC 6, 11, 59**
    See also CANR 6; CA 5-8R;
    obituary CA 128; SATA 27

**Dunbar, Paul Laurence**
    1872-1906 . . . . . . . . . . . . . . . **TCLC 2, 12**
    See also CA 104, 124; SATA 34; DLB 50,
    54, 78; CDALB 1865-1917

**Duncan (Steinmetz Arquette), Lois**
    1934- . . . . . . . . . . . . . . . . . . . . . **CLC 26**
    See also Arquette, Lois S(teinmetz)
    See also CANR 2; CA 1-4R; SAAS 2;
    SATA 1, 36

**Duncan, Robert (Edward)**
    1919-1988 . . . **CLC 1, 2, 4, 7, 15, 41, 55;**
                                                              **PC 2**
    See also CANR 28; CA 9-12R;
    obituary CA 124; DLB 5, 16

**Dunlap, William** 1766-1839 . . . . . . **NCLC 2**
    See also DLB 30, 37, 59

**Dunn, Douglas (Eaglesham)**
    1942- . . . . . . . . . . . . . . . . . . . . **CLC 6, 40**
    See also CANR 2; CA 45-48; DLB 40

**Dunn, Elsie** 1893-1963
    See Scott, Evelyn

**Dunn, Stephen** 1939- . . . . . . . . . . . . . **CLC 36**
    See also CANR 12; CA 33-36R

**Dunne, Finley Peter** 1867-1936. . . . **TCLC 28**
    See also CA 108; DLB 11, 23

**Dunne, John Gregory** 1932-. . . . . . . . **CLC 28**
    See also CANR 14; CA 25-28R; DLB-Y 80

**Dunsany, Lord (Edward John Moreton Drax
    Plunkett)** 1878-1957. . . . . . . . . **TCLC 2**
    See also CA 104; DLB 10

**Durang, Christopher (Ferdinand)**
    1949- . . . . . . . . . . . . . . . . . . . **CLC 27, 38**
    See also CA 105

**Duras, Marguerite**
    1914- . . . . . . . . . **CLC 3, 6, 11, 20, 34, 40**
    See also CA 25-28R; DLB 83

**Durban, Pam** 1947-. . . . . . . . . . . . . . . **CLC 39**
    See also CA 123

**Durcan, Paul** 1944-. . . . . . . . . . . . . . . **CLC 43**

**Durrell, Lawrence (George)**
    1912-1990 . . . . **CLC 1, 4, 6, 8, 13, 27, 41**
    See also CA 9-12R; DLB 15, 27

**Durrenmatt, Friedrich**
    1921- . . . . . . . . . . **CLC 1, 4, 8, 11, 15, 43**
    See also Duerrenmatt, Friedrich
    See also DLB 69

**Dutt, Toru** 1856-1877. . . . . . . . . . . **NCLC 29**

**Dwight, Timothy** 1752-1817. . . . . . **NCLC 13**
    See also DLB 37

**Dworkin, Andrea** 1946- . . . . . . . . . . . **CLC 43**
    See also CANR 16; CA 77-80

**Dylan, Bob** 1941- . . . . . . . . . . **CLC 3, 4, 6, 12**
    See also CA 41-44R; DLB 16

**Eagleton, Terry** 1943-. . . . . . . . . . . . . **CLC 63**

**East, Michael** 1916-
    See West, Morris L.

**Eastlake, William (Derry)** 1917-. . . . . **CLC 8**
    See also CAAS 1; CANR 5; CA 5-8R;
    DLB 6

**Eberhart, Richard** 1904-. . . **CLC 3, 11, 19, 56**
    See also CANR 2; CA 1-4R; DLB 48;
    CDALB 1941-1968

**Eberstadt, Fernanda** 1960-. . . . . . . . **CLC 39**

**Echegaray (y Eizaguirre), Jose (Maria Waldo)**
    1832-1916 . . . . . . . . . . . . . . . . . . **TCLC 4**
    See also CA 104

**Echeverria, (Jose) Esteban (Antonino)**
    1805-1851 . . . . . . . . . . . . . . . . **NCLC 18**

**Eckert, Allan W.** 1931- . . . . . . . . . . . **CLC 17**
    See also CANR 14; CA 13-16R; SATA 27,
    29

**Eco, Umberto** 1932-. . . . . . . . . . **CLC 28, 60**
    See also CANR 12; CA 77-80

**Eddison, E(ric) R(ucker)**
    1882-1945 . . . . . . . . . . . . . . . . . **TCLC 15**
    See also CA 109

**Edel, Leon (Joseph)** 1907-. . . . . . **CLC 29, 34**
    See also CANR 1, 22; CA 1-4R

**Eden, Emily** 1797-1869 . . . . . . . . . **NCLC 10**

**Edgar, David** 1948-. . . . . . . . . . . . . . . **CLC 42**
    See also CANR 12; CA 57-60; DLB 13

**Edgerton, Clyde** 1944- . . . . . . . . . . . . **CLC 39**
    See also CA 118

**Edgeworth, Maria** 1767-1849. . . . . . **NCLC 1**
    See also SATA 21

**Edmonds, Helen (Woods)** 1904-1968
    See Kavan, Anna
    See also CA 5-8R; obituary CA 25-28R

**Edmonds, Walter D(umaux)** 1903- . . **CLC 35**
    See also CANR 2; CA 5-8R; SAAS 4;
    SATA 1, 27; DLB 9

**Edson, Russell** 1905- . . . . . . . . . . . . . **CLC 13**
    See also CA 33-36R

**Edwards, G(erald) B(asil)**
    1899-1976 . . . . . . . . . . . . . . . . . . **CLC 25**
    See also obituary CA 110

**Edwards, Gus** 1939-. . . . . . . . . . . . . . **CLC 43**
    See also CA 108

**Edwards, Jonathan** 1703-1758. . . . . . . **LC 7**
    See also DLB 24

**Ehle, John (Marsden, Jr.)** 1925-. . . . **CLC 27**
    See also CA 9-12R

**Ehrenburg, Ilya (Grigoryevich)**
    1891-1967 . . . . . . . . . . . . **CLC 18, 34, 62**
    See also CA 102; obituary CA 25-28R

**Eich, Guenter** 1907-1971
    See also CA 111; obituary CA 93-96

**Eich, Gunter** 1907-1971. . . . . . . . . . . **CLC 15**
    See also Eich, Guenter
    See also DLB 69

**Eichendorff, Joseph Freiherr von**
    1788-1857 . . . . . . . . . . . . . . . . . **NCLC 8**
    See also DLB 90

**Eigner, Larry** 1927- . . . . . . . . . . . . . . . **CLC 9**
    See also Eigner, Laurence (Joel)
    See also DLB 5

**Eigner, Laurence (Joel)** 1927-
    See Eigner, Larry
    See also CANR 6; CA 9-12R

**Eiseley, Loren (Corey)** 1907-1977. . . . **CLC 7**
    See also CANR 6; CA 1-4R;
    obituary CA 73-76

**Eisenstadt, Jill** 1963- . . . . . . . . . . . . . **CLC 50**

**Ekeloef, Gunnar (Bengt)** 1907-1968
See Ekelof, Gunnar (Bengt)
See also obituary CA 25-28R

**Ekelof, Gunnar (Bengt)** 1907-1968 .. **CLC 27**
See also Ekeloef, Gunnar (Bengt)

**Ekwensi, Cyprian (Odiatu Duaka)**
1921- ........................ **CLC 4**
See also CANR 18; CA 29-32R

**Eliade, Mircea** 1907-1986 ......... **CLC 19**
See also CA 65-68; obituary CA 119

**Eliot, George** 1819-1880.... **NCLC 4, 13, 23**
See also DLB 21, 35, 55

**Eliot, John** 1604-1690 ............. **LC 5**
See also DLB 24

**Eliot, T(homas) S(tearns)**
1888-1965 .... **CLC 1, 2, 3, 6, 9, 10, 13,
15, 24, 34, 41, 55, 57**
See also CA 5-8R; obituary CA 25-28R;
DLB 7, 10, 45, 63; DLB-Y 88

**Elizabeth** 1866-1941 ............. **TCLC 41**
See also Russell, Mary Annette Beauchamp

**Elkin, Stanley (Lawrence)**
1930- .......... **CLC 4, 6, 9, 14, 27, 51**
See also CANR 8; CA 9-12R; DLB 2, 28;
DLB-Y 80

**Elledge, Scott** 19??- .............. **CLC 34**

**Elliott, George P(aul)** 1918-1980..... **CLC 2**
See also CANR 2; CA 1-4R;
obituary CA 97-100

**Elliott, Janice** 1931- .............. **CLC 47**
See also CANR 8; CA 13-16R; DLB 14

**Elliott, Sumner Locke** 1917- ....... **CLC 38**
See also CANR 2, 21; CA 5-8R

**Ellis, A. E.** 19??- .................. **CLC 7**

**Ellis, Alice Thomas** 19??- .......... **CLC 40**

**Ellis, Bret Easton** 1964- .......... **CLC 39**
See also CA 118, 123

**Ellis, (Henry) Havelock**
1859-1939 ................. **TCLC 14**
See also CA 109

**Ellis, Trey** 1964- ................. **CLC 55**

**Ellison, Harlan (Jay)** 1934- ... **CLC 1, 13, 42**
See also CANR 5; CA 5-8R; DLB 8

**Ellison, Ralph (Waldo)**
1914- ................ **CLC 1, 3, 11, 54**
See also CANR 24; CA 9-12R; DLB 2, 76;
CDALB 1941-1968

**Ellmann, Lucy** 1956- ............. **CLC 61**
See also CA 128

**Ellmann, Richard (David)**
1918-1987 ................. **CLC 50**
See also CANR 2; CA 1-4R;
obituary CA 122; DLB-Y 87

**Elman, Richard** 1934- ............. **CLC 19**
See also CAAS 3; CA 17-20R

**Eluard, Paul** 1895-1952 ....... **TCLC 7, 41**
See also Grindel, Eugene

**Elyot, (Sir) Thomas** 1490?-1546 ..... **LC 11**

**Elytis, Odysseus** 1911- ........ **CLC 15, 49**
See also CA 102

**Emecheta, (Florence Onye) Buchi**
1944- .................... **CLC 14, 48**
See also CA 81-84

**Emerson, Ralph Waldo**
1803-1882 .................. **NCLC 1**
See also DLB 1, 59, 73; CDALB 1640-1865

**Empson, William**
1906-1984 ....... **CLC 3, 8, 19, 33, 34**
See also CA 17-20R; obituary CA 112;
DLB 20

**Enchi, Fumiko (Veda)** 1905-1986 ... **CLC 31**
See also obituary CA 121

**Ende, Michael** 1930- .............. **CLC 31**
See also CLR 14; CA 118, 124; SATA 42;
DLB 75

**Endo, Shusaku** 1923- ..... **CLC 7, 14, 19, 54**
See also CANR 21; CA 29-32R

**Engel, Marian** 1933-1985.......... **CLC 36**
See also CANR 12; CA 25-28R; DLB 53

**Engelhardt, Frederick** 1911-1986
See Hubbard, L(afayette) Ron(ald)

**Enright, D(ennis) J(oseph)**
1920- ................... **CLC 4, 8, 31**
See also CANR 1; CA 1-4R; SATA 25;
DLB 27

**Enzensberger, Hans Magnus**
1929- ..................... **CLC 43**
See also CA 116, 119

**Ephron, Nora** 1941- ......... **CLC 17, 31**
See also CANR 12; CA 65-68

**Epstein, Daniel Mark** 1948- ........ **CLC 7**
See also CANR 2; CA 49-52

**Epstein, Jacob** 1956- ............. **CLC 19**
See also CA 114

**Epstein, Joseph** 1937- ............. **CLC 39**
See also CA 112, 119

**Epstein, Leslie** 1938- ............. **CLC 27**
See also CANR 23; CA 73-76

**Equiano, Olaudah** 1745?-1797 ...... **LC 16**
See also DLB 37, 50

**Erasmus, Desiderius** 1469?-1536..... **LC 16**

**Erdman, Paul E(mil)** 1932- ........ **CLC 25**
See also CANR 13; CA 61-64

**Erdrich, Louise** 1954- .......... **CLC 39, 54**
See also CA 114

**Erenburg, Ilya (Grigoryevich)** 1891-1967
See Ehrenburg, Ilya (Grigoryevich)

**Erickson, Steve** 1950- ............. **CLC 64**
See also CA 129

**Eseki, Bruno** 1919-
See Mphahlele, Ezekiel

**Esenin, Sergei (Aleksandrovich)**
1895-1925 ................... **TCLC 4**
See also CA 104

**Eshleman, Clayton** 1935- ........... **CLC 7**
See also CAAS 6; CA 33-36R; DLB 5

**Espriu, Salvador** 1913-1985......... **CLC 9**
See also obituary CA 115

**Estleman, Loren D.** 1952- ......... **CLC 48**
See also CA 85-88

**Evans, Marian** 1819-1880
See Eliot, George

**Evans, Mary Ann** 1819-1880
See Eliot, George

**Evarts, Esther** 1900-1972
See Benson, Sally

**Everett, Percival L.** 1957?- ........ **CLC 57**
See also CA 129

**Everson, Ronald G(ilmour)** 1903- ... **CLC 27**
See also CA 17-20R; DLB 88

**Everson, William (Oliver)**
1912- ................... **CLC 1, 5, 14**
See also CANR 20; CA 9-12R; DLB 5, 16

**Evtushenko, Evgenii (Aleksandrovich)** 1933-
See Yevtushenko, Yevgeny

**Ewart, Gavin (Buchanan)**
1916- ................... **CLC 13, 46**
See also CANR 17; CA 89-92; DLB 40

**Ewers, Hanns Heinz** 1871-1943 ... **TCLC 12**
See also CA 109

**Ewing, Frederick R.** 1918-
See Sturgeon, Theodore (Hamilton)

**Exley, Frederick (Earl)** 1929- .... **CLC 6, 11**
See also CA 81-84; DLB-Y 81

**Ezekiel, Nissim** 1924- ............. **CLC 61**
See also CA 61-64

**Ezekiel, Tish O'Dowd** 1943- ....... **CLC 34**

**Fagen, Donald** 1948- .............. **CLC 26**

**Fair, Ronald L.** 1932- ............. **CLC 18**
See also CANR 25; CA 69-72; DLB 33

**Fairbairns, Zoe (Ann)** 1948- ....... **CLC 32**
See also CANR 21; CA 103

**Fairfield, Cicily Isabel** 1892-1983
See West, Rebecca

**Fallaci, Oriana** 1930- ............. **CLC 11**
See also CANR 15; CA 77-80

**Faludy, George** 1913- ............. **CLC 42**
See also CA 21-24R

**Fante, John** 1909-1983............. **CLC 60**
See also CANR 23; CA 69-72;
obituary CA 109; DLB-Y 83

**Farah, Nuruddin** 1945- ............ **CLC 53**
See also CA 106

**Fargue, Leon-Paul** 1876-1947 ..... **TCLC 11**
See also CA 109

**Farigoule, Louis** 1885-1972
See Romains, Jules

**Farina, Richard** 1937?-1966......... **CLC 9**
See also CA 81-84; obituary CA 25-28R

**Farley, Walter** 1920- ............. **CLC 17**
See also CANR 8; CA 17-20R; SATA 2, 43;
DLB 22

**Farmer, Philip Jose** 1918- ....... **CLC 1, 19**
See also CANR 4; CA 1-4R; DLB 8

**Farrell, J(ames) G(ordon)**
1935-1979 ................... **CLC 6**
See also CA 73-76; obituary CA 89-92;
DLB 14

**Farrell, James T(homas)**
1904-1979 ............ **CLC 1, 4, 8, 11**
See also CANR 9; CA 5-8R,
obituary CA 89-92; DLB 4, 9, 86;
DLB-DS 2

**Farrell, M. J.** 1904-
See Keane, Molly

**Fassbinder, Rainer Werner**
1946-1982 ................. **CLC 20**
See also CA 93-96; obituary CA 106

**Fast, Howard (Melvin)** 1914- ...... **CLC 23**
See also CANR 1; CA 1-4R; SATA 7;
DLB 9

**Faulkner, William (Cuthbert)**
1897-1962 .... **CLC 1, 3, 6, 8, 9, 11, 14,**
**18, 28, 52; SSC 1**
See also CA 81-84; DLB 9, 11, 44;
DLB-Y 86; DLB-DS 2

**Fauset, Jessie Redmon**
1884?-1961................ **CLC 19, 54**
See also CA 109; DLB 51

**Faust, Irvin** 1924-................. **CLC 8**
See also CA 33-36R; DLB 2, 28; DLB-Y 80

**Fearing, Kenneth (Flexner)**
1902-1961 ................... **CLC 51**
See also CA 93-96; DLB 9

**Federman, Raymond** 1928- ...... **CLC 6, 47**
See also CANR 10; CA 17-20R; DLB-Y 80

**Federspiel, J(urg) F.** 1931-......... **CLC 42**

**Feiffer, Jules** 1929-........... **CLC 2, 8, 64**
See also CANR 30; CA 17-20R; SATA 8,
61; DLB 7, 44; AAYA 3

**Feinberg, David B.** 1956-.......... **CLC 59**

**Feinstein, Elaine** 1930-............ **CLC 36**
See also CAAS 1; CA 69-72; DLB 14, 40

**Feke, Gilbert David** 1976?- ........ **CLC 65**

**Feldman, Irving (Mordecai)** 1928-.... **CLC 7**
See also CANR 1; CA 1-4R

**Fellini, Federico** 1920-............ **CLC 16**
See also CA 65-68

**Felsen, Gregor** 1916-
See Felsen, Henry Gregor

**Felsen, Henry Gregor** 1916- ....... **CLC 17**
See also CANR 1; CA 1-4R; SAAS 2;
SATA 1

**Fenton, James (Martin)** 1949-...... **CLC 32**
See also CA 102; DLB 40

**Ferber, Edna** 1887-1968........... **CLC 18**
See also CA 5-8R; obituary CA 25-28R;
SATA 7; DLB 9, 28, 86

**Ferlinghetti, Lawrence (Monsanto)**
1919?- ......... **CLC 2, 6, 10, 27; PC 1**
See also CANR 3; CA 5-8R; DLB 5, 16;
CDALB 1941-1968

**Ferrier, Susan (Edmonstone)**
1782-1854 .................. **NCLC 8**

**Ferrigno, Robert** 19??-............ **CLC 65**

**Feuchtwanger, Lion** 1884-1958 ..... **TCLC 3**
See also CA 104; DLB 66

**Feydeau, Georges** 1862-1921...... **TCLC 22**
See also CA 113

**Ficino, Marsilio** 1433-1499 ........ **LC 12**

**Fiedler, Leslie A(aron)**
1917- .................. **CLC 4, 13, 24**
See also CANR 7; CA 9-12R; DLB 28, 67

**Field, Andrew** 1938-............. **CLC 44**
See also CANR 25; CA 97-100

**Field, Eugene** 1850-1895 ......... **NCLC 3**
See also SATA 16; DLB 21, 23, 42

**Fielding, Henry** 1707-1754 .......... **LC 1**
See also DLB 39, 84

**Fielding, Sarah** 1710-1768.......... **LC 1**
See also DLB 39

**Fierstein, Harvey** 1954-........... **CLC 33**
See also CA 123, 129

**Figes, Eva** 1932-................. **CLC 31**
See also CANR 4; CA 53-56; DLB 14

**Finch, Robert (Duer Claydon)**
1900-...................... **CLC 18**
See also CANR 9, 24; CA 57-60; DLB 88

**Findley, Timothy** 1930- ........... **CLC 27**
See also CANR 12; CA 25-28R; DLB 53

**Fink, Janis** 1951-
See Ian, Janis

**Firbank, Louis** 1944-
See Reed, Lou
See also CA 117

**Firbank, (Arthur Annesley) Ronald**
1886-1926 .................. **TCLC 1**
See also CA 104; DLB 36

**Fisher, Roy** 1930-................. **CLC 25**
See also CANR 16; CA 81-84; DLB 40

**Fisher, Rudolph** 1897-1934 ....... **TCLC 11**
See also CA 107; DLB 51

**Fisher, Vardis (Alvero)** 1895-1968.... **CLC 7**
See also CA 5-8R; obituary CA 25-28R;
DLB 9

**FitzGerald, Edward** 1809-1883 .... **NCLC 9**
See also DLB 32

**Fitzgerald, F(rancis) Scott (Key)**
1896-1940 .... **TCLC 1, 6, 14, 28; SSC 6**
See also CA 110, 123; DLB 4, 9, 86;
DLB-Y 81; DLB-DS 1;
CDALB 1917-1929

**Fitzgerald, Penelope** 1916-... **CLC 19, 51, 61**
See also CAAS 10; CA 85-88,; DLB 14

**Fitzgerald, Robert (Stuart)**
1910-1985 ................... **CLC 39**
See also CANR 1; CA 2R;
obituary CA 114; DLB-Y 80

**FitzGerald, Robert D(avid)** 1902-... **CLC 19**
See also CA 17-20R

**Flanagan, Thomas (James Bonner)**
1923-.................... **CLC 25, 52**
See also CA 108; DLB-Y 80

**Flaubert, Gustave**
1821-1880 ............ **NCLC 2, 10, 19**

**Fleming, Ian (Lancaster)**
1908-1964 ................. **CLC 3, 30**
See also CA 5-8R; SATA 9; DLB 87

**Fleming, Thomas J(ames)** 1927- .... **CLC 37**
See also CANR 10; CA 5-8R; SATA 8

**Fletcher, John Gould** 1886-1950... **TCLC 35**
See also CA 107; DLB 4, 45

**Flieg, Hellmuth**
See Heym, Stefan

**Flying Officer X** 1905-1974
See Bates, H(erbert) E(rnest)

**Fo, Dario** 1929-.................. **CLC 32**
See also CA 116

**Follett, Ken(neth Martin)** 1949- .... **CLC 18**
See also CANR 13; CA 81-84; DLB-Y 81

**Fontane, Theodor** 1819-1898 ..... **NCLC 26**

**Foote, Horton** 1916-.............. **CLC 51**
See also CA 73-76; DLB 26

**Forbes, Esther** 1891-1967.......... **CLC 12**
See also CAP 1; CA 13-14;
obituary CA 25-28R; SATA 2; DLB 22

**Forche, Carolyn** 1950- ............ **CLC 25**
See also CA 109, 117; DLB 5

**Ford, Ford Madox**
1873-1939 ............ **TCLC 1, 15, 39**
See also CA 104; DLB 34

**Ford, John** 1895-1973............. **CLC 16**
See also obituary CA 45 48

**Ford, Richard** 1944-.............. **CLC 46**
See also CANR 11; CA 69-72

**Foreman, Richard** 1937-........... **CLC 50**
See also CA 65-68

**Forester, C(ecil) S(cott)**
1899-1966 ................... **CLC 35**
See also CA 73-76; obituary CA 25-28R;
SATA 13

**Forman, James D(ouglas)** 1932- .... **CLC 21**
See also CANR 4, 19; CA 9-12R; SATA 8,
21

**Fornes, Maria Irene** 1930-...... **CLC 39, 61**
See also CANR 28; CA 25-28R; DLB 7

**Forrest, Leon** 1937- ............... **CLC 4**
See also CAAS 7; CA 89-92; DLB 33

**Forster, E(dward) M(organ)**
1879-1970 .... **CLC 1, 2, 3, 4, 9, 10, 13,**
**15, 22, 45**
See also CAP 1; CA 13-14;
obituary CA 25-28R; SATA 57; DLB 34

**Forster, John** 1812-1876 ........ **NCLC 11**

**Forsyth, Frederick** 1938-...... **CLC 2, 5, 36**
See also CA 85-88; DLB 87

**Forten (Grimke), Charlotte L(ottie)**
1837-1914 .................. **TCLC 16**
See also Grimke, Charlotte L(ottie) Forten
See also DLB 50

**Foscolo, Ugo** 1778-1827.......... **NCLC 8**

**Fosse, Bob** 1925-1987............. **CLC 20**
See also Fosse, Robert Louis

**Fosse, Robert Louis** 1925-1987
See Bob Fosse
See also CA 110, 123

**Foster, Stephen Collins**
1826-1864 ................. **NCLC 26**

**Foucault, Michel** 1926-1984 .... **CLC 31, 34**
See also CANR 23; CA 105;
obituary CA 113

**Fouque, Friedrich (Heinrich Karl) de La**
Motte 1777-1843 ........... **NCLC 2**

**Fournier, Henri Alban** 1886-1914
See Alain-Fournier
See also CA 104

**Fournier, Pierre** 1916-............ **CLC 11**
See also Gascar, Pierre
See also CANR 16; CA 89-92

**Fowles, John (Robert)**
1926- .... **CLC 1, 2, 3, 4, 6, 9, 10, 15, 33**
See also CANR 25; CA 5-8R; SATA 22;
DLB 14

**Fox, Paula** 1923-................ **CLC 2, 8**
See also CLR 1; CANR 20; CA 73-76;
SATA 17; DLB 52

Fox, William Price (Jr.) 1926- ..... CLC 22
See also CANR 11; CA 17-20R; DLB 2;
DLB-Y 81

Foxe, John 1516?-1587............. LC 14

Frame (Clutha), Janet (Paterson)
1924- ................CLC 2, 3, 6, 22
See also Clutha, Janet Paterson Frame

France, Anatole 1844-1924 ....... TCLC 9
See also Thibault, Jacques Anatole Francois

Francis, Claude 19??-............. CLC 50

Francis, Dick 1920- ........ CLC 2, 22, 42
See also CANR 9; CA 5-8R; DLB 87

Francis, Robert (Churchill)
1901-1987 ................... CLC 15
See also CANR 1; CA 1-4R;
obituary CA 123

Frank, Anne 1929-1945 ......... TCLC 17
See also CA 113; SATA 42

Frank, Elizabeth 1945-........... CLC 39
See also CA 121, 126

Franklin, (Stella Maria Sarah) Miles
1879-1954 ................... TCLC 7
See also CA 104

Fraser, Antonia (Pakenham)
1932- ...................... CLC 32
See also CA 85-88; SATA 32

Fraser, George MacDonald 1925-.... CLC 7
See also CANR 2; CA 45-48

Fraser, Sylvia 1935-.............. CLC 64
See also CANR 1, 16; CA 45-48

Frayn, Michael 1933-...... CLC 3, 7, 31, 47
See also CA 5-8R; DLB 13, 14

Fraze, Candida 19??- ............. CLC 50
See also CA 125

Frazer, Sir James George
1854-1941 .................. TCLC 32
See also CA 118

Frazier, Ian 1951-............... CLC 46
See also CA 130

Frederic, Harold 1856-1898...... NCLC 10
See also DLB 12, 23

Frederick the Great 1712-1786 ...... LC 14

Fredman, Russell (Bruce) 1929-
See also CLR 20

Fredro, Aleksander 1793-1876..... NCLC 8

Freeling, Nicolas 1927- ........... CLC 38
See also CANR 1, 17; CA 49-52; DLB 87

Freeman, Douglas Southall
1886-1953 .................. TCLC 11
See also CA 109; DLB 17

Freeman, Judith 1946-........... CLC 55

Freeman, Mary (Eleanor) Wilkins
1852-1930 ............ TCLC 9; SSC 1
See also CA 106; DLB 12, 78

Freeman, R(ichard) Austin
1862-1943 .................. TCLC 21
See also CA 113; DLB 70

French, Marilyn 1929-...... CLC 10, 18, 60
See also CANR 3; CA 69-72

Freneau, Philip Morin 1752-1832.. NCLC 1
See also DLB 37, 43

Friedman, B(ernard) H(arper)
1926- ...................... CLC 7
See also CANR 3; CA 1-4R

Friedman, Bruce Jay 1930-.... CLC 3, 5, 56
See also CANR 25; CA 9-12R; DLB 2, 28

Friel, Brian 1929-........... CLC 5, 42, 59
See also CA 21-24R; DLB 13

Friis-Baastad, Babbis (Ellinor)
1921-1970 .................. CLC 12
See also CA 17-20R; SATA 7

Frisch, Max (Rudolf)
1911- ........ CLC 3, 9, 14, 18, 32, 44
See also CA 85-88; DLB 69

Fromentin, Eugene (Samuel Auguste)
1820-1876 ................. NCLC 10

Frost, Robert (Lee)
1874-1963 ... CLC 1, 3, 4, 9, 10, 13, 15,
26, 34, 44; PC 1
See also CA 89-92; SATA 14; DLB 54;
DLB-DS 7; CDALB 1917-1929

Fry, Christopher 1907-....... CLC 2, 10, 14
See also CANR 9; CA 17-20R; DLB 13

Frye, (Herman) Northrop 1912-.... CLC 24
See also CANR 8; CA 5-8R; DLB 67, 68

Fuchs, Daniel 1909-............ CLC 8, 22
See also CAAS 5; CA 81-84; DLB 9, 26, 28

Fuchs, Daniel 1934-.............. CLC 34
See also CANR 14; CA 37-40R

Fuentes, Carlos
1928-....... CLC 3, 8, 10, 13, 22, 41, 60
See also CANR 10; CA 69-72

Fugard, Athol 1932-... CLC 5, 9, 14, 25, 40
See also CA 85-88

Fugard, Sheila 1932- ............. CLC 48
See also CA 125

Fuller, Charles (H., Jr.)
1939-................ CLC 25; DC 1
See also CA 108, 112; DLB 38

Fuller, John (Leopold) 1937-...... CLC 62
See also CANR 9; CA 21-22R; DLB 40

Fuller, (Sarah) Margaret
1810-1850 ................. NCLC 5
See also Ossoli, Sarah Margaret (Fuller
marchesa d')
See also DLB 1, 59, 73; CDALB 1640-1865

Fuller, Roy (Broadbent) 1912-.... CLC 4, 28
See also CA 5-8R; DLB 15, 20

Fulton, Alice 1952-.............. CLC 52
See also CA 116

Furphy, Joseph 1843-1912........ TCLC 25

Futrelle, Jacques 1875-1912 ...... TCLC 19
See also CA 113

Gaboriau, Emile 1835-1873...... NCLC 14

Gadda, Carlo Emilio 1893-1973 .... CLC 11
See also CA 89-92

Gaddis, William
1922-........ CLC 1, 3, 6, 8, 10, 19, 43
See also CAAS 4; CANR 21; CA 17-20R;
DLB 2

Gaines, Ernest J. 1933-...... CLC 3, 11, 18
See also CANR 6, 24; CA 9-12R; DLB 2,
33; DLB-Y 80

Gale, Zona 1874-1938 ........... TCLC 7
See also CA 105; DLB 9, 78

Gallagher, Tess 1943-......... CLC 18, 63
See also CA 106

Gallant, Mavis
1922-.......... CLC 7, 18, 38; SSC 5
See also CA 69-72; DLB 53

Gallant, Roy A(rthur) 1924-....... CLC 17
See also CANR 4; CA 5-8R; SATA 4

Gallico, Paul (William) 1897-1976 ... CLC 2
See also CA 5-8R; obituary CA 69-72;
SATA 13; DLB 9

Galsworthy, John 1867-1933...... TCLC 1
See also CA 104; DLB 10, 34

Galt, John 1779-1839............ NCLC 1

Galvin, James 1951-.............. CLC 38
See also CANR 26; CA 108

Gamboa, Frederico 1864-1939..... TCLC 36

Gann, Ernest K(ellogg) 1910-...... CLC 23
See also CANR 1; CA 1-4R

Garcia Lorca, Federico
1899-1936.................TCLC 1, 7
See also CA 104

Garcia Marquez, Gabriel (Jose)
1928-.... CLC 2, 3, 8, 10, 15, 27, 47, 55
See also CANR 10; CA 33-36R

Gardam, Jane 1928-.............. CLC 43
See also CLR 12; CANR 2, 18; CA 49-52;
SATA 28, 39; DLB 14

Gardner, Herb 1934- ............. CLC 44

Gardner, John (Champlin, Jr.)
1933-1982 .... CLC 2, 3, 5, 7, 8, 10, 18,
28, 34; SSC 7
See also CA 65-68; obituary CA 107;
obituary SATA 31, 40; DLB 2; DLB-Y 82

Gardner, John (Edmund) 1926-..... CLC 30
See also CANR 15; CA 103

Garfield, Leon 1921-.............. CLC 12
See also CA 17-20R; SATA 1, 32

Garland, (Hannibal) Hamlin
1860-1940 .................. TCLC 3
See also CA 104; DLB 12, 71, 78

Garneau, Hector (de) Saint Denys
1912-1943 ................. TCLC 13
See also CA 111; DLB 88

Garner, Alan 1935-............... CLC 17
See also CLR 20; CANR 15; CA 73-76;
SATA 18

Garner, Hugh 1913-1979 ......... CLC 13
See also CA 69-72; DLB 68

Garnett, David 1892-1981 ......... CLC 3
See also CANR 17; CA 5-8R;
obituary CA 103; DLB 34

Garrett, George (Palmer, Jr.)
1929-.................CLC 3, 11, 51
See also CAAS 5; CANR 1; CA 1-4R;
DLB 2, 5; DLB-Y 83

Garrick, David 1717-1779 .......... LC 15
See also DLB 84

Garrigue, Jean 1914-1972 ........ CLC 2, 8
See also CANR 20; CA 5-8R;
obituary CA 37-40R

Garvey, Marcus 1887-1940 ....... TCLC 41
See also CA 124; brief entry CA 120

Gary, Romain 1914-1980......... CLC 25
See also Kacew, Romain

Gascar, Pierre 1916-............. CLC 11
See also Fournier, Pierre

Gascoyne, David (Emery) 1916- .... CLC 45
See also CANR 10; CA 65-68; DLB 20

Gaskell, Elizabeth Cleghorn
1810-1865 ................. NCLC 5
See also DLB 21

Gass, William H(oward)
1924 .......... CLC 1, 2, 8, 11, 15, 39
See also CA 17-20R; DLB 2

Gates, Henry Louis, Jr. 1950-...... CLC 65
See also CANR 25; CA 109; DLB 67

Gautier, Theophile 1811-1872 ..... NCLC 1

Gaye, Marvin (Pentz) 1939-1984 ... CLC 26
See also obituary CA 112

Gebler, Carlo (Ernest) 1954-....... CLC 39
See also CA 119

Gee, Maggie 19??- ............... CLC 57

Gee, Maurice (Gough) 1931-....... CLC 29
See also CA 97-100; SATA 46

Gelbart, Larry 1923?-.......... CLC 21, 61
See also CA 73-76

Gelber, Jack 1932-........ CLC 1, 6, 14, 60
See also CANR 2; CA 1-4R; DLB 7

Gellhorn, Martha (Ellis) 1908- .. CLC 14, 60
See also CA 77-80; DLB-Y 82

Genet, Jean
1910-1986 ... CLC 1, 2, 5, 10, 14, 44, 46
See also CANR 18; CA 13-16R; DLB 72;
DLB-Y 86

Gent, Peter 1942-................ CLC 29
See also CA 89-92; DLB 72; DLB-Y 82

George, Jean Craighead 1919-...... CLC 35
See also CLR 1; CA 5-8R; SATA 2;
DLB 52

George, Stefan (Anton)
1868-1933 ............... TCLC 2, 14
See also CA 104

Gerhardi, William (Alexander) 1895-1977
See Gerhardie, William (Alexander)

Gerhardie, William (Alexander)
1895-1977 ................... CLC 5
See also CANR 18; CA 25-28R;
obituary CA 73-76; DLB 36

Gertler, T(rudy) 1946?- ........... CLC 34
See also CA 116

Gessner, Friedrike Victoria 1910-1980
See Adamson, Joy(-Friederike Victoria)

Ghelderode, Michel de
1898-1962 ................ CLC 6, 11
See also CA 85-88

Ghiselin, Brewster 1903-.......... CLC 23
See also CANR 13; CA 13-16R

Ghose, Zulfikar 1935-............. CLC 42
See also CA 65-68

Ghosh, Amitav 1943- ............. CLC 44

Giacosa, Giuseppe 1847-1906 ...... TCLC 7
See also CA 104

Gibbon, Lewis Grassic 1901-1935... TCLC 4
See also Mitchell, James Leslie

Gibbons, Kaye 1960- ............. CLC 50

Gibran, (Gibran) Kahlil
1883-1931 ................TCLC 1, 9
See also CA 104

Gibson, William 1914-............ CLC 23
See also CANR 9; CA 9-12R; DLB 7

Gibson, William 1948-......... CLC 39, 63
See also CA 126

Gide, Andre (Paul Guillaume)
1869-1951 ............ TCLC 5, 12, 36
See also CA 104, 124; DLB 65

Gifford, Barry (Colby) 1946-....... CLC 34
See also CANR 9; CA 65-68

Gilbert, (Sir) W(illiam) S(chwenck)
1836-1911 .................. TCLC 3
See also CA 104; SATA 36

Gilbreth, Ernestine 1908-
See Carey, Ernestine Gilbreth

Gilbreth, Frank B(unker), Jr.
1911- ..................... CLC 17
See also CA 9-12R; SATA 2

Gilchrist, Ellen 1935-.......... CLC 34, 48
See also CA 113, 116

Giles, Molly 1942- ............... CLC 39
See also CA 126

Gilliam, Terry (Vance) 1940-
See Monty Python
See also CA 108, 113

Gilliatt, Penelope (Ann Douglass)
1932- .............. CLC 2, 10, 13, 53
See also CA 13-16R; DLB 14

Gilman, Charlotte (Anna) Perkins (Stetson)
1860-1935 ............... TCLC 9, 37
See also CA 106

Gilmour, David 1944-
See Pink Floyd

Gilpin, William 1724-1804 ...... NCLC 30

Gilroy, Frank D(aniel) 1925-........ CLC 2
See also CA 81-84; DLB 7

Ginsberg, Allen
1926- ........ CLC 1, 2, 3, 4, 6, 13, 36
See also CANR 2; CA 1-4R; DLB 5, 16;
CDALB 1941-1968

Ginzburg, Natalia 1916-...... CLC 5, 11, 54
See also CA 85-88

Giono, Jean 1895-1970.......... CLC 4, 11
See also CANR 2; CA 45-48;
obituary CA 29-32R; DLB 72

Giovanni, Nikki 1943- ..... CLC 2, 4, 19, 64
See also CLR 6; CAAS 6; CANR 18;
CA 29-32R; SATA 24; DLB 5, 41

Giovene, Andrea 1904-............. CLC 7
See also CA 85-88

Gippius, Zinaida (Nikolayevna) 1869-1945
See Hippius, Zinaida
See also CA 106

Giraudoux, (Hippolyte) Jean
1882-1944 ................. TCLC 2, 7
See also CA 104; DLB 65

Gironella, Jose Maria 1917- ....... CLC 11
See also CA 101

Gissing, George (Robert)
1857-1903 ............... TCLC 3, 24
See also CA 105; DLB 18

Gladkov, Fyodor (Vasilyevich)
1883-1958 ................. TCLC 27

Glanville, Brian (Lester) 1931- ...... CLC 6
See also CANR 3; CA 5-8R; SATA 42;
DLB 15

Glasgow, Ellen (Anderson Gholson)
1873?-1945................ TCLC 2, 7
See also CA 104; DLB 9, 12

Glassco, John 1909-1981 .......... CLC 9
See also CANR 15; CA 13-16R;
obituary CA 102; DLB 68

Glasser, Ronald J. 1940?- ......... CLC 37

Glendinning, Victoria 1937-........ CLC 50
See also CA 120

Glissant, Edouard 1928-........... CLC 10

Gloag, Julian 1930- ............. CLC 40
See also CANR 10; CA 65-68

Gluck, Louise (Elisabeth)
1943-................. CLC 7, 22, 44
See also CA 33-36R; DLB 5

Gobineau, Joseph Arthur (Comte) de
1816-1882 ................ NCLC 17

Godard, Jean-Luc 1930-........... CLC 20
See also CA 93-96

Godden, (Margaret) Rumer 1907-... CLC 53
See also CLR 20; CANR 4, 27; CA 7-8R;
SATA 3, 36

Godwin, Gail 1937-........ CLC 5, 8, 22, 31
See also CANR 15; CA 29-32R; DLB 6

Godwin, William 1756-1836...... NCLC 14
See also DLB 39

Goethe, Johann Wolfgang von
1749-1832 ............... NCLC 4, 22

Gogarty, Oliver St. John
1878-1957 ................ TCLC 15
See also CA 109; DLB 15, 19

Gogol, Nikolai (Vasilyevich)
1809-1852 ..... NCLC 5, 15, 31; DC 1;
SSC 4
See also CAAS 1, 4

Gokceli, Yasar Kemal 1923-
See Kemal, Yashar

Gold, Herbert 1924-....... CLC 4, 7, 14, 42
See also CANR 17; CA 9-12R; DLB 2;
DLB-Y 81

Goldbarth, Albert 1948-......... CLC 5, 38
See also CANR 6; CA 53-56

Goldberg, Anatol 1910-1982 ....... CLC 34
See also obituary CA 117

Goldemberg, Isaac 1945- ......... CLC 52
See also CANR 11; CA 69-72

Golding, William (Gerald)
1911- ..... CLC 1, 2, 3, 8, 10, 17, 27, 58
See also CANR 13; CA 5-8R; DLB 15

Goldman, Emma 1869-1940...... TCLC 13
See also CA 110

Goldman, William (W.) 1931- .... CLC 1, 48
See also CA 9-12R; DLB 44

Goldmann, Lucien 1913-1970 ...... CLC 24
See also CAP 2; CA 25-28

Goldoni, Carlo 1707-1793 .......... LC 4

Goldsberry, Steven 1949-......... CLC 34

Goldsmith, Oliver   1728?-1774 . . . . . . . . LC 2
   See also SATA 26; DLB 39

Gombrowicz, Witold
   1904-1969 . . . . . . . . . . . CLC 4, 7, 11, 49
   See also CAP 2; CA 19-20;
   obituary CA 25-28R

Gomez de la Serna, Ramon
   1888-1963 . . . . . . . . . . . . . . . . . CLC 9
   See also obituary CA 116

Goncharov, Ivan Alexandrovich
   1812-1891 . . . . . . . . . . . . . . . . . NCLC 1

Goncourt, Edmond (Louis Antoine Huot) de
   1822-1896 . . . . . . . . . . . . . . . . NCLC 7

Goncourt, Jules (Alfred Huot) de
   1830-1870 . . . . . . . . . . . . . . . . NCLC 7

Gontier, Fernande   19??- . . . . . . . . . . CLC 50

Goodman, Paul   1911-1972 . . . . CLC 1, 2, 4, 7
   See also CAP 2; CA 19-20;
   obituary CA 37-40R

Gordimer, Nadine
   1923- . . . . . . . CLC 3, 5, 7, 10, 18, 33, 51
   See also CANR 3; CA 5-8R

Gordon, Adam Lindsay
   1833-1870 . . . . . . . . . . . . . . . NCLC 21

Gordon, Caroline
   1895-1981 . . . . . . . . . . . . CLC 6, 13, 29
   See also CAP 1; CA 11-12;
   obituary CA 103; DLB 4, 9; DLB-Y 81

Gordon, Charles William   1860-1937
   See Conner, Ralph
   See also CA 109

Gordon, Mary (Catherine)
   1949- . . . . . . . . . . . . . . . . . CLC 13, 22
   See also CA 102; DLB 6; DLB-Y 81

Gordon, Sol   1923- . . . . . . . . . . . . . . . CLC 26
   See also CANR 4; CA 53-56; SATA 11

Gordone, Charles   1925- . . . . . . . . . . CLC 1, 4
   See also CA 93-96; DLB 7

Gorenko, Anna Andreyevna   1889?-1966
   See Akhmatova, Anna

Gorky, Maxim   1868-1936 . . . . . . . . TCLC 8
   See also Peshkov, Alexei Maximovich

Goryan, Sirak   1908-1981
   See Saroyan, William

Gosse, Edmund (William)
   1849-1928 . . . . . . . . . . . . . . . . TCLC 28
   See also CA 117; DLB 57

Gotlieb, Phyllis (Fay Bloom)
   1926- . . . . . . . . . . . . . . . . . . . . CLC 18
   See also CANR 7; CA 13-16R; DLB 88

Gould, Lois   1938?- . . . . . . . . . . . . CLC 4, 10
   See also CA 77-80

Gourmont, Remy de   1858-1915 . . . . TCLC 17
   See also CA 109

Govier, Katherine   1948- . . . . . . . . . . CLC 51
   See also CANR 18; CA 101

Goyen, (Charles) William
   1915-1983 . . . . . . . . . . . CLC 5, 8, 14, 40
   See also CANR 6; CA 5-8R;
   obituary CA 110; DLB 2; DLB-Y 83

Goytisolo, Juan   1931- . . . . . . . CLC 5, 10, 23
   See also CA 85-88

Gozzi, (Conte) Carlo   1720-1806 . . NCLC 23

Grabbe, Christian Dietrich
   1801-1836 . . . . . . . . . . . . . . . . NCLC 2

Grace, Patricia   1937- . . . . . . . . . . . CLC 56

Gracian y Morales, Baltasar
   1601-1658 . . . . . . . . . . . . . . . . LC 15

Gracq, Julien   1910- . . . . . . . . . . CLC 11, 48
   See also Poirier, Louis
   See also DLB 83

Grade, Chaim   1910-1982 . . . . . . . . . CLC 10
   See also CA 93-96; obituary CA 107

Graham, Jorie   1951- . . . . . . . . . . . . . CLC 48
   See also CA 111

Graham, R(obert) B(ontine) Cunninghame
   1852-1936 . . . . . . . . . . . . . . . . TCLC 19

Graham, W(illiam) S(ydney)
   1918-1986 . . . . . . . . . . . . . . . . CLC 29
   See also CA 73-76; obituary CA 118;
   DLB 20

Graham, Winston (Mawdsley)
   1910- . . . . . . . . . . . . . . . . . . . CLC 23
   See also CANR 2, 22; CA 49-52;
   obituary CA 118

Granville-Barker, Harley
   1877-1946 . . . . . . . . . . . . . . . . TCLC 2
   See also CA 104

Grass, Gunter (Wilhelm)
   1927- . . CLC 1, 2, 4, 6, 11, 15, 22, 32, 49
   See also CANR 20; CA 13-16R; DLB 75

Grau, Shirley Ann   1929- . . . . . . . . . CLC 4, 9
   See also CANR 22; CA 89-92; DLB 2

Graves, Richard Perceval   1945- . . . . CLC 44
   See also CANR 9, 26; CA 65-68

Graves, Robert (von Ranke)
   1895-1985 . . . CLC 1, 2, 6, 11, 39, 44, 45
   See also CANR 5; CA 5-8R;
   obituary CA 117; SATA 45; DLB 20;
   DLB-Y 85

Gray, Alasdair   1934- . . . . . . . . . . . . . CLC 41
   See also CA 123

Gray, Amlin   1946- . . . . . . . . . . . . . . . CLC 29

Gray, Francine du Plessix   1930- . . . . CLC 22
   See also CAAS 2; CANR 11; CA 61-64

Gray, John (Henry)   1866-1934 . . . . TCLC 19
   See also CA 119

Gray, Simon (James Holliday)
   1936- . . . . . . . . . . . . . . . CLC 9, 14, 36
   See also CAAS 3; CA 21-24R; DLB 13

Gray, Spalding   1941- . . . . . . . . . . . . . CLC 49

Gray, Thomas   1716-1771 . . . . . . . LC 4; PC 2

Grayson, Richard (A.)   1951- . . . . . . . CLC 38
   See also CANR 14; CA 85-88

Greeley, Andrew M(oran)   1928- . . . . CLC 28
   See also CAAS 7; CANR 7; CA 5-8R

Green, Hannah   1932- . . . . . . . . CLC 3, 7, 30
   See also Greenberg, Joanne
   See also CA 73-76

Green, Henry   1905-1974 . . . . . . . CLC 2, 13
   See also Yorke, Henry Vincent
   See also DLB 15

Green, Julien (Hartridge)   1900- . . CLC 3, 11
   See also CA 21-24R; DLB 4, 72

Green, Paul (Eliot)   1894-1981 . . . . . . CLC 25
   See also CANR 3; CA 5-8R;
   obituary CA 103; DLB 7, 9; DLB-Y 81

Greenberg, Ivan   1908-1973
   See Rahv, Philip
   See also CA 85-88

Greenberg, Joanne (Goldenberg)
   1932- . . . . . . . . . . . . . . . . CLC 3, 7, 30
   See also Green, Hannah
   See also CANR 14; CA 5-8R; SATA 25

Greenberg, Richard   1959?- . . . . . . . . CLC 57

Greene, Bette   1934- . . . . . . . . . . . . . CLC 30
   See also CLR 2; CANR 4; CA 53-56;
   SATA 8

Greene, Gael   19??- . . . . . . . . . . . . . . . CLC 8
   See also CANR 10; CA 13-16R

Greene, Graham (Henry)
   1904- . . . . . CLC 1, 3, 6, 9, 14, 18, 27, 37
   See also CA 13-16R; SATA 20; DLB 13, 15;
   DLB-Y 85

Gregor, Arthur   1923- . . . . . . . . . . . . . CLC 9
   See also CANR 11; CA 25-28R; SATA 36

Gregory, Lady (Isabella Augusta Persse)
   1852-1932 . . . . . . . . . . . . . . . . TCLC 1
   See also CA 104; DLB 10

Grendon, Stephen   1909-1971
   See Derleth, August (William)

Grenville, Kate   1950- . . . . . . . . . . . . . CLC 61
   See also CA 118

Greve, Felix Paul Berthold Friedrich
   1879-1948
   See Grove, Frederick Philip
   See also CA 104

Grey, (Pearl) Zane   1872?-1939 . . . . . TCLC 6
   See also CA 104; DLB 9

Grieg, (Johan) Nordahl (Brun)
   1902-1943 . . . . . . . . . . . . . . . . TCLC 10
   See also CA 107

Grieve, C(hristopher) M(urray)   1892-1978
   See MacDiarmid, Hugh
   See also CA 5-8R; obituary CA 85-88

Griffin, Gerald   1803-1840 . . . . . . . . NCLC 7

Griffin, Peter   1942- . . . . . . . . . . . . . . CLC 39

Griffiths, Trevor   1935- . . . . . . . . . CLC 13, 52
   See also CA 97-100; DLB 13

Grigson, Geoffrey (Edward Harvey)
   1905-1985 . . . . . . . . . . . . . . . . CLC 7, 39
   See also CANR 20; CA 25-28R;
   obituary CA 118; DLB 27

Grillparzer, Franz   1791-1872 . . . . . . NCLC 1

Grimke, Charlotte L(ottie) Forten   1837-1914
   See Forten (Grimke), Charlotte L(ottie)
   See also CA 117, 124

Grimm, Jakob (Ludwig) Karl
   1785-1863 . . . . . . . . . . . . . . . . . NCLC 3
   See also SATA 22; DLB 90

Grimm, Wilhelm Karl   1786-1859 . . NCLC 3
   See also SATA 22; DLB 90

Grimmelshausen, Johann Jakob Christoffel
   von   1621-1676 . . . . . . . . . . . . . . LC 6

Grindel, Eugene   1895-1952
   See also brief entry CA 104

Grossman, Vasily (Semenovich)
   1905-1964 . . . . . . . . . . . . . . . . . CLC 41
   See also CA 124, 130

**Grove, Frederick Philip**
  1879-1948 .................. TCLC 4
  See also Greve, Felix Paul Berthold
    Friedrich

**Grumbach, Doris (Isaac)**
  1918- ................. CLC 13, 22, 64
  See also CAAS 2; CANR 9; CA 5-8R

**Grundtvig, Nicolai Frederik Severin**
  1783-1872 ................. NCLC 1

**Grunwald, Lisa** 1959- ............. CLC 44
  See also CA 120

**Guare, John** 1938- .......... CLC 8, 14, 29
  See also CANR 21; CA 73-76; DLB 7

**Gudjonsson, Halldor Kiljan** 1902-
  See Laxness, Halldor (Kiljan)
  See also CA 103

**Guest, Barbara** 1920- .............. CLC 34
  See also CANR 11; CA 25-28R; DLB 5

**Guest, Judith (Ann)** 1936- ....... CLC 8, 30
  See also CANR 15; CA 77-80

**Guild, Nicholas M.** 1944- .......... CLC 33
  See also CA 93-96

**Guillen, Jorge** 1893-1984 .......... CLC 11
  See also CA 89-92; obituary CA 112

**Guillen, Nicolas** 1902-1989 ........ CLC 48
  See also CA 116, 125; obituary CA 129

**Guillevic, (Eugene)** 1907- .......... CLC 33
  See also CA 93-96

**Guiney, Louise Imogen**
  1861-1920 ................. TCLC 41
  See also DLB 54

**Guiraldes, Ricardo** 1886-1927 ..... TCLC 39

**Gunn, Bill** 1934-1989 .............. CLC 5
  See also Gunn, William Harrison
  See also DLB 38

**Gunn, Thom(son William)**
  1929- ................ CLC 3, 6, 18, 32
  See also CANR 9; CA 17-20R; DLB 27

**Gunn, William Harrison** 1934-1989
  See Gunn, Bill
  See also CANR 12, 25; CA 13-16R;
    obituary CA 128

**Gurney, A(lbert) R(amsdell), Jr.**
  1930- ................ CLC 32, 50, 54
  See also CA 77-80

**Gurney, Ivor (Bertie)** 1890-1937 ... TCLC 33

**Gustafson, Ralph (Barker)** 1909- .... CLC 36
  See also CANR 8; CA 21-24R; DLB 88

**Guthrie, A(lfred) B(ertram), Jr.**
  1901- ....................... CLC 23
  See also CA 57-60; DLB 6

**Guthrie, Woodrow Wilson** 1912-1967
  See Guthrie, Woody
  See also CA 113; obituary CA 93-96

**Guthrie, Woody** 1912-1967 ........ CLC 35
  See also Guthrie, Woodrow Wilson

**Guy, Rosa (Cuthbert)** 1928- ........ CLC 26
  See also CLR 13; CANR 14; CA 17-20R;
    SATA 14; DLB 33

**Haavikko, Paavo (Juhani)**
  1931- .................... CLC 18, 34
  See also CA 106

**Hacker, Marilyn** 1942- ....... CLC 5, 9, 23
  See also CA 77-80

**Haggard, (Sir) H(enry) Rider**
  1856-1925 ................. TCLC 11
  See also CA 108; SATA 16; DLB 70

**Haig-Brown, Roderick L(angmere)**
  1908-1976 .................. CLC 21
  See also CANR 4; CA 5-8R;
    obituary CA 69-72; SATA 12; DLB 88

**Hailey, Arthur** 1920- .............. CLC 5
  See also CANR 2; CA 1-4R; DLB-Y 82

**Hailey, Elizabeth Forsythe** 1938- ... CLC 40
  See also CAAS 1; CANR 15; CA 93-96

**Haines, John** 1924- ............... CLC 58
  See also CANR 13; CA 19-20R; DLB 5

**Haldeman, Joe** 1943- .............. CLC 61
  See also CA 53-56; DLB 8

**Haley, Alex (Palmer)** 1921- ...... CLC 8, 12
  See also CA 77-80; DLB 38

**Haliburton, Thomas Chandler**
  1796-1865 ................. NCLC 15
  See also DLB 11

**Hall, Donald (Andrew, Jr.)**
  1928- ............ CLC 1, 13, 37, 59
  See also CAAS 7; CANR 2; CA 5-8R;
    SATA 23; DLB 5

**Hall, James Norman** 1887-1951 ... TCLC 23
  See also CA 123; SATA 21

**Hall, (Marguerite) Radclyffe**
  1886-1943 ................. TCLC 12
  See also CA 110

**Hall, Rodney** 1935- .............. CLC 51
  See also CA 109

**Halpern, Daniel** 1945- ............ CLC 14
  See also CA 33-36R

**Hamburger, Michael (Peter Leopold)**
  1924- .................... CLC 5, 14
  See also CAAS 4; CANR 2; CA 5-8R;
    DLB 27

**Hamill, Pete** 1935- ............... CLC 10
  See also CANR 18; CA 25-28R

**Hamilton, Edmond** 1904-1977 ...... CLC 1
  See also CANR 3; CA 1-4R; DLB 8

**Hamilton, Gail** 1911-
  See Corcoran, Barbara

**Hamilton, Ian** 1938- .............. CLC 55
  See also CA 106; DLB 40

**Hamilton, Mollie** 1909?-
  See Kaye, M(ary) M(argaret)

**Hamilton, (Anthony Walter) Patrick**
  1904-1962 .................. CLC 51
  See also obituary CA 113; DLB 10

**Hamilton, Virginia (Esther)** 1936-... CLC 26
  See also CLR 1, 11; CANR 20; CA 25-28R;
    SATA 4; DLB 33, 52

**Hammett, (Samuel) Dashiell**
  1894-1961 ........ CLC 3, 5, 10, 19, 47
  See also CA 81-84; DLB-DS 6

**Hammon, Jupiter** 1711?-1800? .... NCLC 5
  See also DLB 31, 50

**Hamner, Earl (Henry), Jr.** 1923- ... CLC 12
  See also CA 73-76; DLB 6

**Hampton, Christopher (James)**
  1946- ...................... CLC 4
  See also CA 25-28R; DLB 13

**Hamsun, Knut** 1859-1952....... TCLC 2, 14
  See also Pedersen, Knut

**Handke, Peter** 1942- .. CLC 5, 8, 10, 15, 38
  See also CA 77-80; DLB 85

**Hanley, James** 1901-1985 ... CLC 3, 5, 8, 13
  See also CA 73-76; obituary CA 117

**Hannah, Barry** 1942- .......... CLC 23, 38
  See also CA 108, 110; DLB 6

**Hansberry, Lorraine (Vivian)**
  1930-1965 ................. CLC 17, 62
  See also CA 109; obituary CA 25-28R;
    CABS 3; DLB 7, 38; CDALB 1941-1968

**Hansen, Joseph** 1923- ............. CLC 38
  See also CANR 16; CA 29-32R

**Hansen, Martin** 1909-1955 ....... TCLC 32

**Hanson, Kenneth O(stlin)** 1922- .... CLC 13
  See also CANR 7; CA 53-56

**Hardenberg, Friedrich (Leopold Freiherr) von**
  1772-1801
  See Novalis

**Hardwick, Elizabeth** 1916- ........ CLC 13
  See also CANR 3; CA 5-8R; DLB 6

**Hardy, Thomas**
  1840-1928 ... TCLC 4, 10, 18, 32; SSC 2
  See also CA 104, 123; SATA 25; DLB 18,
    19

**Hare, David** 1947- ............. CLC 29, 58
  See also CA 97-100; DLB 13

**Harlan, Louis R(udolph)** 1922- ..... CLC 34
  See also CANR 25; CA 21-24R

**Harling, Robert** 1951?- ............ CLC 53

**Harmon, William (Ruth)** 1938- ..... CLC 38
  See also CANR 14; CA 33-36R

**Harper, Frances Ellen Watkins**
  1825-1911 ................. TCLC 14
  See also CA 111, 125; DLB 50

**Harper, Michael S(teven)** 1938- .. CLC 7, 22
  See also CANR 24; CA 33-36R; DLB 41

**Harris, Christie (Lucy Irwin)**
  1907- ...................... CLC 12
  See also CANR 6; CA 5-8R; SATA 6;
    DLB 88

**Harris, Frank** 1856-1931 ........ TCLC 24
  See also CAAS 1; CA 109

**Harris, George Washington**
  1814-1869 ................. NCLC 23
  See also DLB 3, 11

**Harris, Joel Chandler** 1848-1908 ... TCLC 2
  See also YABC 1; CA 104; DLB 11, 23, 42,
    78, 91

**Harris, John (Wyndham Parkes Lucas)**
  Beynon 1903-1969 .......... CLC 19
  See also Wyndham, John
  See also CA 102; obituary CA 89-92

**Harris, MacDonald** 1921- .......... CLC 9
  See also Heiney, Donald (William)

**Harris, Mark** 1922- .............. CLC 19
  See also CAAS 3; CANR 2; CA 5-8R;
    DLB 2; DLB-Y 80

**Harris, (Theodore) Wilson** 1921-.... CLC 25
  See also CANR 11, 27; CA 65-68

**Harrison, Harry (Max)** 1925- ...... CLC 42
  See also CANR 5, 21; CA 1-4R; SATA 4;
    DLB 8

**Harrison, James (Thomas)** 1937-
See Harrison, Jim
See also CANR 8; CA 13-16R

**Harrison, Jim** 1937-........ **CLC 6, 14, 33**
See also Harrison, James (Thomas)
See also DLB-Y 82

**Harrison, Tony** 1937-............. **CLC 43**
See also CA 65-68; DLB 40

**Harriss, Will(ard Irvin)** 1922-...... **CLC 34**
See also CA 111

**Harte, (Francis) Bret(t)**
1836?-1902................ **TCLC 1, 25**
See also CA 104; SATA 26; DLB 12, 64,
74, 79; CDALB 1865-1917

**Hartley, L(eslie) P(oles)**
1895-1972 ................. **CLC 2, 22**
See also CA 45-48; obituary CA 37-40R;
DLB 15

**Hartman, Geoffrey H.** 1929-....... **CLC 27**
See also CA 117, 125; DLB 67

**Haruf, Kent** 19??-................ **CLC 34**

**Harwood, Ronald** 1934-.......... **CLC 32**
See also CANR 4; CA 1-4R; DLB 13

**Hasek, Jaroslav (Matej Frantisek)**
1883-1923 ................... **TCLC 4**
See also CA 104, 129

**Hass, Robert** 1941-............ **CLC 18, 39**
See also CANR 30; CA 111

**Hastings, Selina** 19??- ............ **CLC 44**

**Hauptmann, Gerhart (Johann Robert)**
1862-1946 ................... **TCLC 4**
See also CA 104; DLB 66

**Havel, Vaclav** 1936-........ **CLC 25, 58, 65**
See also CA 104

**Haviaras, Stratis** 1935- ........... **CLC 33**
See also CA 105

**Hawkes, John (Clendennin Burne, Jr.)**
1925- ...... **CLC 1, 2, 3, 4, 7, 9, 14, 15,
27, 49**
See also CANR 2; CA 1-4R; DLB 2, 7;
DLB-Y 80

**Hawking, Stephen (William)**
1948-....................... **CLC 63**
See also CA 126, 129

**Hawthorne, Julian** 1846-1934 ..... **TCLC 25**

**Hawthorne, Nathaniel**
1804-1864 ... **NCLC 2, 10, 17, 23; SSC 3**
See also YABC 2; DLB 1, 74;
CDALB 1640-1865

**Hayashi Fumiko** 1904-1951...... **TCLC 27**

**Haycraft, Anna** 19??-
See Ellis, Alice Thomas
See also CA 122

**Hayden, Robert (Earl)**
1913-1980 ............ **CLC 5, 9, 14, 37**
See also CANR 24; CA 69-72;
obituary CA 97-100; CABS 2; SATA 19;
obituary SATA 26; DLB 5, 76;
CDALB 1941-1968

**Hayman, Ronald** 1932-............ **CLC 44**
See also CANR 18; CA 25-28R

**Haywood, Eliza (Fowler)** 1693?-1756.. **LC 1**
See also DLB 39

**Hazlitt, William** 1778-1830 ...... **NCLC 29**

**Hazzard, Shirley** 1931- ........... **CLC 18**
See also CANR 4; CA 9-12R; DLB-Y 82

**H(ilda) D(oolittle)**
1886-1961 ........ **CLC 3, 8, 14, 31, 34**
See also Doolittle, Hilda

**Head, Bessie** 1937-1986........... **CLC 25**
See also CANR 25; CA 29-32R;
obituary CA 119

**Headon, (Nicky) Topper** 1956?- .... **CLC 30**
See also The Clash

**Heaney, Seamus (Justin)**
1939- ............ **CLC 5, 7, 14, 25, 37**
See also CANR 25; CA 85-88; DLB 40

**Hearn, (Patricio) Lafcadio (Tessima Carlos)**
1850-1904 .................... **TCLC 9**
See also CA 105; DLB 12, 78

**Hearne, Vicki** 1946-............. **CLC 56**

**Hearon, Shelby** 1931-............. **CLC 63**
See also CANR 18; CA 25-28

**Heat Moon, William Least** 1939-... **CLC 29**

**Hebert, Anne** 1916- ......... **CLC 4, 13, 29**
See also CA 85-88; DLB 68

**Hecht, Anthony (Evan)**
1923- .................. **CLC 8, 13, 19**
See also CANR 6; CA 9-12R; DLB 5

**Hecht, Ben** 1894-1964 ............. **CLC 8**
See also CA 85-88; DLB 7, 9, 25, 26, 28, 86

**Hedayat, Sadeq** 1903-1951........ **TCLC 21**
See also CA 120

**Heidegger, Martin** 1889-1976 ...... **CLC 24**
See also CA 81-84; obituary CA 65-68

**Heidenstam, (Karl Gustaf) Verner von**
1859-1940 .................... **TCLC 5**
See also CA 104

**Heifner, Jack** 1946-.............. **CLC 11**
See also CA 105

**Heijermans, Herman** 1864-1924 ... **TCLC 24**
See also CA 123

**Heilbrun, Carolyn G(old)** 1926-..... **CLC 25**
See also CANR 1, 28; CA 45-48

**Heine, Harry** 1797-1856
See Heine, Heinrich

**Heine, Heinrich** 1797-1856 ....... **NCLC 4**
See also DLB 90

**Heinemann, Larry C(urtiss)** 1944- .. **CLC 50**
See also CA 110

**Heiney, Donald (William)** 1921-..... **CLC 9**
See also Harris, MacDonald
See also CANR 3; CA 1-4R

**Heinlein, Robert A(nson)**
1907-1988 ...... **CLC 1, 3, 8, 14, 26, 55**
See also CANR 1, 20; CA 1-4R;
obituary CA 125; SATA 9, 56; DLB 8

**Heller, Joseph**
1923- ........ **CLC 1, 3, 5, 8, 11, 36, 63**
See also CANR 8; CA 5-8R; CABS 1;
DLB 2, 28; DLB-Y 80

**Hellman, Lillian (Florence)**
1905?-1984..... **CLC 2, 4, 8, 14, 18, 34,
44, 52; DC 1**
See also CA 13-16R; obituary CA 112;
DLB 7; DLB-Y 84

**Helprin, Mark** 1947- ..... **CLC 7, 10, 22, 32**
See also CA 81-84; DLB-Y 85

**Hemans, Felicia** 1793-1835 ...... **NCLC 29**

**Hemingway, Ernest (Miller)**
1899-1961 ... **CLC 1, 3, 6, 8, 10, 13, 19,
30, 34, 39, 41, 44, 50, 61; SSC 1**
See also CA 77-80; DLB 4, 9; DLB-Y 81,
87; DLB-DS 1; CDALB 1917-1929

**Hempel, Amy** 1951-............... **CLC 39**
See also CA 118

**Henley, Beth** 1952-................ **CLC 23**
See also Henley, Elizabeth Becker
See also CABS 3; DLB-Y 86

**Henley, Elizabeth Becker** 1952-
See Henley, Beth
See also CA 107

**Henley, William Ernest**
1849-1903 ................... **TCLC 8**
See also CA 105; DLB 19

**Hennissart, Martha**
See Lathen, Emma
See also CA 85-88

**Henry, O.** 1862-1910 ... **TCLC 1, 19; SSC 5**
See Porter, William Sydney
See also YABC 2; CA 104; DLB 12, 78, 79;
CDALB 1865-1917

**Henry VIII** 1491-1547............. **LC 10**

**Hentoff, Nat(han Irving)** 1925-..... **CLC 26**
See also CLR 1; CAAS 6; CANR 5, 25;
CA 1-4R; SATA 27, 42; AAYA 4

**Heppenstall, (John) Rayner**
1911-1981 ................... **CLC 10**
See also CANR 29; CA 1-4R;
obituary CA 103

**Herbert, Frank (Patrick)**
1920-1986 .......... **CLC 12, 23, 35, 44**
See also CANR 5; CA 53-56;
obituary CA 118; SATA 9, 37, 47; DLB 8

**Herbert, Zbigniew** 1924- ........ **CLC 9, 43**
See also CA 89-92

**Herbst, Josephine** 1897-1969....... **CLC 34**
See also CA 5-8R; obituary CA 25-28R;
DLB 9

**Herder, Johann Gottfried von**
1744-1803 ................. **NCLC 8**

**Hergesheimer, Joseph**
1880-1954 ................. **TCLC 11**
See also CA 109; DLB 9

**Herlagnez, Pablo de** 1844-1896
See Verlaine, Paul (Marie)

**Herlihy, James Leo** 1927-.......... **CLC 6**
See also CANR 2; CA 1-4R

**Hermogenes** fl.c. 175-............. **CMLC 6**

**Hernandez, Jose** 1834-1886...... **NCLC 17**

**Herrick, Robert** 1591-1674 ........ **LC 13**

**Herriot, James** 1916-............. **CLC 12**
See also Wight, James Alfred
See also AAYA 1

**Herrmann, Dorothy** 1941-......... **CLC 44**
See also CA 107

**Hersey, John (Richard)**
1914- .............. **CLC 1, 2, 7, 9, 40**
See also CA 17-20R; SATA 25; DLB 6

**Herzen, Aleksandr Ivanovich**
1812-1870 ................. **NCLC 10**

**Herzl, Theodor** 1860-1904........ **TCLC 36**

Author Index

Herzog, Werner 1942-............ CLC 16
See also CA 89-92

Hesiod  c. 8th Century B.C.- ...... CMLC 5

Hesse, Hermann
    1877-1962 .... CLC 1, 2, 3, 6, 11, 17, 25
    See also CAP 2; CA 17-18; SATA 50;
    DLB 66

Heyen, William 1940- ......... CLC 13, 18
See also CAAS 9; CA 33-36R; DLB 5

Heyerdahl, Thor 1914-............ CLC 26
See also CANR 5, 22; CA 5-8R; SATA 2,
52

Heym, Georg (Theodor Franz Arthur)
    1887-1912 .................. TCLC 9
    See also CA 106

Heym, Stefan 1913-.............. CLC 41
See also CANR 4; CA 9-12R; DLB 69

Heyse, Paul (Johann Ludwig von)
    1830-1914 .................. TCLC 8
    See also CA 104

Hibbert, Eleanor (Burford) 1906-.... CLC 7
See also CANR 9, 28; CA 17-20R; SATA 2

Higgins, George V(incent)
    1939- ................CLC 4, 7, 10, 18
    See also CAAS 5; CANR 17; CA 77-80;
    DLB 2; DLB-Y 81

Higginson, Thomas Wentworth
    1823-1911 .................. TCLC 36
    See also DLB 1, 64

Highsmith, (Mary) Patricia
    1921- ................CLC 2, 4, 14, 42
    See also CANR 1, 20; CA 1-4R

Highwater, Jamake 1942- ......... CLC 12
See also CLR 17; CAAS 7; CANR 10;
    CA 65-68; SATA 30, 32; DLB 52;
    DLB-Y 85

Hijuelos, Oscar 1951- ............ CLC 65
See also CA 123

Hikmet (Ran), Nazim 1902-1963.... CLC 40
See also obituary CA 93-96

Hildesheimer, Wolfgang 1916- ..... CLC 49
See also CA 101; DLB 69

Hill, Geoffrey (William)
    1932-................CLC 5, 8, 18, 45
    See also CANR 21; CA 81-84; DLB 40

Hill, George Roy 1922-............ CLC 26
See also CA 110, 122

Hill, Susan B. 1942-.............. CLC 4
See also CANR 29; CA 33-36R; DLB 14

Hillerman, Tony 1925-............ CLC 62
See also CANR 21; CA 29-32R; SATA 6

Hilliard, Noel (Harvey) 1929-...... CLC 15
See also CANR 7; CA 9-12R

Hilton, James 1900-1954........ TCLC 21
See also CA 108; SATA 34; DLB 34, 77

Himes, Chester (Bomar)
    1909-1984 ........ CLC 2, 4, 7, 18, 58
    See also CANR 22; CA 25-28R;
    obituary CA 114; DLB 2, 76

Hinde, Thomas 1926-........... CLC 6, 11
See also Chitty, (Sir) Thomas Willes

Hine, (William) Daryl 1936-....... CLC 15
See also CANR 1, 20; CA 1-4R; DLB 60

Hinton, S(usan) E(loise) 1950- ..... CLC 30
See also CLR 3, 23; CA 81-84; SATA 19,
58; AAYA 2

Hippius (Merezhkovsky), Zinaida
    (Nikolayevna) 1869-1945...... TCLC 9
    See also Gippius, Zinaida (Nikolayevna)

Hiraoka, Kimitake 1925-1970
See Mishima, Yukio
See also CA 97-100; obituary CA 29-32R

Hirsch, Edward (Mark) 1950-... CLC 31, 50
See also CANR 20; CA 104

Hitchcock, (Sir) Alfred (Joseph)
    1899-1980 .................. CLC 16
    See also obituary CA 97-100; SATA 27;
    obituary SATA 24

Hoagland, Edward 1932-.......... CLC 28
See also CANR 2; CA 1-4R; SATA 51;
DLB 6

Hoban, Russell C(onwell) 1925- .. CLC 7, 25
See also CLR 3; CANR 23; CA 5-8R;
SATA 1, 40; DLB 52

Hobson, Laura Z(ametkin)
    1900-1986 ................ CLC 7, 25
    See also CA 17-20R; obituary CA 118;
    SATA 52; DLB 28

Hochhuth, Rolf 1931-........ CLC 4, 11, 18
See also CA 5-8R

Hochman, Sandra 1936-.......... CLC 3, 8
See also CA 5-8R; DLB 5

Hochwalder, Fritz 1911-1986 ...... CLC 36
See also CA 29-32R; obituary CA 120

Hocking, Mary (Eunice) 1921-..... CLC 13
See also CANR 18; CA 101

Hodgins, Jack 1938-.............. CLC 23
See also CA 93-96; DLB 60

Hodgson, William Hope
    1877-1918 .................. TCLC 13
    See also CA 111; DLB 70

Hoffman, Alice 1952-.............. CLC 51
See also CA 77-80

Hoffman, Daniel (Gerard)
    1923- .................. CLC 6, 13, 23
    See also CANR 4; CA 1-4R; DLB 5

Hoffman, Stanley 1944-............ CLC 5
See also CA 77-80

Hoffman, William M(oses) 1939- ... CLC 40
See also CANR 11; CA 57-60

Hoffmann, Ernst Theodor Amadeus
    1776-1822 .................. NCLC 2
    See also SATA 27; DLB 90

Hoffmann, Gert 1932- ............ CLC 54

Hofmannsthal, Hugo (Laurenz August
    Hofmann Edler) von
    1874-1929 .................. TCLC 11
    See also CA 106; DLB 81

Hogg, James 1770-1835.......... NCLC 4

Holbach, Paul Henri Thiry, Baron d'
    1723-1789 .................. LC 14

Holberg, Ludvig 1684-1754 ......... LC 6

Holden, Ursula 1921-.............. CLC 18
See also CAAS 8; CANR 22; CA 101

Holderlin, (Johann Christian) Friedrich
    1770-1843 ................. NCLC 16

Holdstock, Robert (P.) 1948-....... CLC 39

Holland, Isabelle 1920- ........... CLC 21
See also CANR 10, 25; CA 21-24R;
SATA 8

Holland, Marcus 1900-1985
See Caldwell, (Janet Miriam) Taylor
(Holland)

Hollander, John 1929-...... CLC 2, 5, 8, 14
See also CANR 1; CA 1-4R; SATA 13;
DLB 5

Holleran, Andrew 1943?-.......... CLC 38

Hollinghurst, Alan 1954-.......... CLC 55
See also CA 114

Hollis, Jim 1916-
See Summers, Hollis (Spurgeon, Jr.)

Holmes, John Clellon 1926-1988.... CLC 56
See also CANR 4; CA 9-10R;
obituary CA 125; DLB 16

Holmes, Oliver Wendell
    1809-1894 .................. NCLC 14
    See also SATA 34; DLB 1;
    CDALB 1640-1865

Holt, Victoria 1906-
See Hibbert, Eleanor (Burford)

Holub, Miroslav 1923-............. CLC 4
See also CANR 10; CA 21-24R

Homer  c. 8th century B.C.-....... CMLC 1

Honig, Edwin 1919-.............. CLC 33
See also CAAS 8; CANR 4; CA 5-8R;
DLB 5

Hood, Hugh (John Blagdon)
    1928-.................... CLC 15, 28
    See also CANR 1; CA 49-52; DLB 53

Hood, Thomas 1799-1845........ NCLC 16

Hooker, (Peter) Jeremy 1941-...... CLC 43
See also CANR 22; CA 77-80; DLB 40

Hope, A(lec) D(erwent) 1907-.... CLC 3, 51
See also CA 21-24R

Hope, Christopher (David Tully)
    1944- ...................... CLC 52
    See also CA 106

Hopkins, Gerard Manley
    1844-1889 .................. NCLC 17
    See also DLB 35, 57

Hopkins, John (Richard) 1931-...... CLC 4
See also CA 85-88

Hopkins, Pauline Elizabeth
    1859-1930 .................. TCLC 28
    See also DLB 50

Horgan, Paul 1903- ............. CLC 9, 53
See also CANR 9; CA 13-16R; SATA 13;
DLB-Y 85

Horovitz, Israel 1939-............ CLC 56
See also CA 33-36R; DLB 7

Horwitz, Julius 1920-1986......... CLC 14
See also CANR 12; CA 9-12R;
obituary CA 119

Hospital, Janette Turner 1942-..... CLC 42
See also CA 108

Hostos (y Bonilla), Eugenio Maria de
    1893-1903 ................. TCLC 24
    See also CA 123

Hougan, Carolyn 19??-............ CLC 34

Household, Geoffrey (Edward West)
1900-1988 .................. CLC 11
See also CA 77-80; obituary CA 126;
SATA 14, 59; DLB 87

Housman, A(lfred) E(dward)
1859-1936 .......... TCLC 1, 10; PC 2
See also CA 104, 125; DLB 19

Housman, Laurence  1865-1959 ..... TCLC 7
See also CA 106; SATA 25; DLB 10

Howard, Elizabeth Jane  1923- ... CLC 7, 29
See also CANR 8; CA 5-8R

Howard, Maureen  1930- ..... CLC 5, 14, 46
See also CA 53-56; DLB-Y 83

Howard, Richard  1929- ...... CLC 7, 10, 47
See also CANR 25; CA 85-88; DLB 5

Howard, Robert E(rvin)
1906-1936 ................... TCLC 8
See also CA 105

Howe, Fanny  1940- ............... CLC 47
See also CA 117; SATA 52

Howe, Julia Ward  1819-1910 ..... TCLC 21
See also CA 117; DLB 1

Howe, Tina  1937- ................. CLC 48
See also CA 109

Howell, James  1594?-1666......... LC 13

Howells, William Dean
1837-1920 ........... TCLC 7, 17, 41
See also brief entry CA 104; DLB 12, 64,
74, 79; CDALB 1865-1917

Howes, Barbara  1914- ............ CLC 15
See also CAAS 3; CA 9-12R; SATA 5

Hrabal, Bohumil  1914-............ CLC 13
See also CA 106

Hubbard, L(afayette) Ron(ald)
1911-1986 ................... CLC 43
See also CANR 22; CA 77-80;
obituary CA 118

Huch, Ricarda (Octavia)
1864-1947 .................. TCLC 13
See also CA 111; DLB 66

Huddle, David  1942- ............. CLC 49
See also CA 57-60

Hudson, W(illiam) H(enry)
1841-1922 .................. TCLC 29
See also CA 115; SATA 35

Hueffer, Ford Madox  1873-1939
See Ford, Ford Madox

Hughart, Barry  1934-............. CLC 39

Hughes, David (John)  1930- ....... CLC 48
See also CA 116, 129; DLB 14

Hughes, Edward James  1930-
See Hughes, Ted

Hughes, (James) Langston
1902-1967 .... CLC 1, 5, 10, 15, 35, 44;
PC 1; SSC 6
See also CLR 17; CANR 1; CA 1-4R;
obituary CA 25-28R; SATA 4, 33;
DLB 4, 7, 48, 51, 86; CDALB 1929-1941

Hughes, Richard (Arthur Warren)
1900-1976 .................. CLC 1, 11
See also CANR 4; CA 5-8R;
obituary CA 65-68; SATA 8;
obituary SATA 25; DLB 15

Hughes, Ted  1930- ..... CLC 2, 4, 9, 14, 37
See also CLR 3; CANR 1; CA 1-4R;
SATA 27, 49; DLB 40

Hugo, Richard F(ranklin)
1923-1982 .............. CLC 6, 18, 32
See also CANR 3; CA 49-52;
obituary CA 108; DLB 5

Hugo, Victor Marie
1802-1885 ............ NCLC 3, 10, 21
See also SATA 47

Huidobro, Vicente  1893-1948 ..... TCLC 31

Hulme, Keri  1947- ............... CLC 39
See also CA 125

Hulme, T(homas) E(rnest)
1883-1917 .................. TCLC 21
See also CA 117; DLB 19

Hume, David  1711-1776............ LC 7

Humphrey, William  1924-........ CLC 45
See also CA 77-80; DLB 6

Humphreys, Emyr (Owen)  1919-.... CLC 47
See also CANR 3, 24; CA 5-8R; DLB 15

Humphreys, Josephine  1945-.... CLC 34, 57
See also CA 121, 127

Hunt, E(verette) Howard (Jr.)
1918- ....................... CLC 3
See also CANR 2; CA 45-48

Hunt, (James Henry) Leigh
1784-1859 .................. NCLC 1

Hunter, Evan  1926- ........... CLC 11, 31
See also CANR 5; CA 5-8R; SATA 25;
DLB-Y 82

Hunter, Kristin (Eggleston)  1931-... CLC 35
See also CLR 3; CANR 13; CA 13-16R;
SATA 12; DLB 33

Hunter, Mollie (Maureen McIlwraith)
1922- ....................... CLC 21
See also McIlwraith, Maureen Mollie
Hunter

Hunter, Robert  ?-1734............. LC 7

Hurston, Zora Neale
1891-1960 ....... CLC 7, 30, 61; SSC 4
See also CA 85-88; DLB 51, 86

Huston, John (Marcellus)
1906-1987 ................... CLC 20
See also CA 73-76; obituary CA 123;
DLB 26

Hutten, Ulrich von  1488-1523....... LC 16

Huxley, Aldous (Leonard)
1894-1963 .. CLC 1, 3, 4, 5, 8, 11, 18, 35
See also CA 85-88; DLB 36

Huysmans, Charles Marie Georges
1848-1907
See Huysmans, Joris-Karl
See also CA 104

Huysmans, Joris-Karl  1848-1907 ... TCLC 7
See also Huysmans, Charles Marie Georges

Hwang, David Henry  1957-........ CLC 55
See also CA 127

Hyde, Anthony  1946?-............ CLC 42

Hyde, Margaret O(ldroyd)  1917- ... CLC 21
See also CLR 23; CANR 1; CA 1-4R;
SAAS 8; SATA 1, 42

Hynes, James  1956?-............. CLC 65

Ian, Janis  1951- ................. CLC 21
See also CA 105

Ibarguengoitia, Jorge  1928-1983.... CLC 37
See also obituary CA 113, 124

Ibsen, Henrik (Johan)
1828-1906 ......... TCLC 2, 8, 16, 37
See also CA 104

Ibuse, Masuji  1898-.............. CLC 22
See also CA 127

Ichikawa, Kon  1915-.............. CLC 20
See also CA 121

Idle, Eric  1943-.................. CLC 21
See also Monty Python
See also CA 116

Ignatow, David  1914-..... CLC 4, 7, 14, 40
See also CAAS 3; CA 9-12R; DLB 5

Ihimaera, Witi (Tame)  1944-....... CLC 46
See also CA 77-80

Ilf, Ilya  1897-1937 .............. TCLC 21

Immermann, Karl (Lebrecht)
1796-1840 .................. NCLC 4

Ingalls, Rachel  19??-.............. CLC 42
See also CA 123, 127

Ingamells, Rex  1913-1955 ........ TCLC 35

Inge, William (Motter)
1913-1973 .............. CLC 1, 8, 19
See also CA 9-12R; DLB 7;
CDALB 1941-1968

Innaurato, Albert  1948-........ CLC 21, 60
See also CA 115, 122

Innes, Michael  1906-
See Stewart, J(ohn) I(nnes) M(ackintosh)

Ionesco, Eugene
1912- ........ CLC 1, 4, 6, 9, 11, 15, 41
See also CA 9-12R; SATA 7

Iqbal, Muhammad  1877-1938 ..... TCLC 28

Irving, John (Winslow)
1942- ................ CLC 13, 23, 38
See also CANR 28; CA 25-28R; DLB 6;
DLB-Y 82

Irving, Washington
1783-1859 ......... NCLC 2, 19; SSC 2
See also YABC 2; DLB 3, 11, 30, 59, 73,
74; CDALB 1640-1865

Isaacs, Susan  1943- .............. CLC 32
See also CANR 20; CA 89-92

Isherwood, Christopher (William Bradshaw)
1904-1986 ........ CLC 1, 9, 11, 14, 44
See also CA 13-16R; obituary CA 117;
DLB 15; DLB-Y 86

Ishiguro, Kazuo  1954- ...... CLC 27, 56, 59
See also CA 120

Ishikawa Takuboku  1885-1912 .... TCLC 15
See also CA 113

Iskander, Fazil (Abdulovich)
1929-...................... CLC 47
See also CA 102

Ivanov, Vyacheslav (Ivanovich)
1866-1949 .................. TCLC 33
See also CA 122

Ivask, Ivar (Vidrik)  1927-......... CLC 14
See also CANR 24; CA 37-40R

Jackson, Jesse 1908-1983 ......... CLC 12
See also CANR 27; CA 25-28R;
obituary CA 109; SATA 2, 29, 48

Jackson, Laura (Riding) 1901- ...... CLC 7
See also Riding, Laura
See also CANR 28; CA 65-68; DLB 48

Jackson, Shirley 1919-1965..... CLC 11, 60
See also CANR 4; CA 1-4R;
obituary CA 25-28R; SATA 2; DLB 6;
CDALB 1941-1968

Jacob, (Cyprien) Max 1876-1944 ... TCLC 6
See also CA 104

Jacob, Piers A(nthony) D(illingham) 1934-
See Anthony (Jacob), Piers
See also CA 21-24R

Jacobs, Jim 1942- and Casey, Warren
1942- ............................. CLC 12
See also CA 97-100

Jacobs, Jim 1942-
See Jacobs, Jim and Casey, Warren
See also CA 97-100

Jacobs, W(illiam) W(ymark)
1863-1943 ................... TCLC 22
See also CA 121

Jacobsen, Josephine 1908-......... CLC 48
See also CANR 23; CA 33-36R

Jacobson, Dan 1929- ........... CLC 4, 14
See also CANR 2, 25; CA 1-4R; DLB 14

Jagger, Mick 1944-................ CLC 17

Jakes, John (William) 1932- ....... CLC 29
See also CANR 10; CA 57-60; DLB-Y 83

James, C(yril) L(ionel) R(obert)
1901-1989 .................... CLC 33
See also CA 117, 125; obituary CA 128

James, Daniel 1911-1988
See Santiago, Danny
See also obituary CA 125

James, Henry (Jr.)
1843-1916 ......... TCLC 2, 11, 24, 40
See also CA 104, 132; DLB 12, 71, 74;
CDALB 1865-1917

James, M(ontague) R(hodes)
1862-1936 ................... TCLC 6
See also CA 104

James, P(hyllis) D(orothy)
1920- ..................... CLC 18, 46
See also CANR 17; CA 21-24R

James, William 1842-1910..... TCLC 15, 32
See also CA 109

Jami, Nur al-Din 'Abd al-Rahman
1414-1492 ..................... LC 9

Jandl, Ernst 1925- ............... CLC 34

Janowitz, Tama 1957- ............ CLC 43
See also CA 106

Jarrell, Randall
1914-1965 ....... CLC 1, 2, 6, 9, 13, 49
See also CLR 6; CANR 6; CA 5-8R;
obituary CA 25-28R; CABS 2; SATA 7;
DLB 48, 52; CDALB 1941-1968

Jarry, Alfred 1873-1907........ TCLC 2, 14
See also CA 104

Jeake, Samuel, Jr. 1889-1973
See Aiken, Conrad

Jean Paul 1763-1825 ........... NCLC 7

Jeffers, (John) Robinson
1887-1962 ........ CLC 2, 3, 11, 15, 54
See also CA 85-88; DLB 45;
CDALB 1917-1929

Jefferson, Thomas 1743-1826 .... NCLC 11
See also DLB 31; CDALB 1640-1865

Jellicoe, (Patricia) Ann 1927- ...... CLC 27
See also CA 85-88; DLB 13

Jenkins, (John) Robin 1912- ....... CLC 52
See also CANR 1; CA 4R; DLB 14

Jennings, Elizabeth (Joan)
1926-..................... CLC 5, 14
See also CAAS 5; CANR 8; CA 61-64;
DLB 27

Jennings, Waylon 1937-........... CLC 21

Jensen, Johannes 1873-1950 ..... TCLC 41

Jensen, Laura (Linnea) 1948- ...... CLC 37
See also CA 103

Jerome, Jerome K. 1859-1927..... TCLC 23
See also CA 119; DLB 10, 34

Jerrold, Douglas William
1803-1857 ................... NCLC 2

Jewett, (Theodora) Sarah Orne
1849-1909 ........ TCLC 1, 22; SSC 6
See also CA 108, 127; SATA 15; DLB 12,
74

Jewsbury, Geraldine (Endsor)
1812-1880 ................. NCLC 22
See also DLB 21

Jhabvala, Ruth Prawer
1927-................... CLC 4, 8, 29
See also CANR 2, 29; CA 1-4R

Jiles, Paulette 1943-........... CLC 13, 58
See also CA 101

Jimenez (Mantecon), Juan Ramon
1881-1958 ................... TCLC 4
See also CA 104

Joel, Billy 1949-................. CLC 26
See also Joel, William Martin

Joel, William Martin 1949-
See Joel, Billy
See also CA 108

Johnson, B(ryan) S(tanley William)
1933-1973 ................. CLC 6, 9
See also CANR 9; CA 9-12R;
obituary CA 53-56; DLB 14, 40

Johnson, Charles (Richard)
1948-............... CLC 7, 51, 65
See also CA 116; DLB 33

Johnson, Denis 1949-............. CLC 52
See also CA 117, 121

Johnson, Diane 1934-....... CLC 5, 13, 48
See also CANR 17; CA 41-44R; DLB-Y 80

Johnson, Eyvind (Olof Verner)
1900-1976 ................... CLC 14
See also CA 73-76; obituary CA 69-72

Johnson, James Weldon
1871-1938 ............... TCLC 3, 19
See also Johnson, James William
See also CA 104, 125; SATA 31; DLB 51;
CDALB 1917-1929

Johnson, James William 1871-1938
See Johnson, James Weldon
See also SATA 31

Johnson, Joyce 1935-............. CLC 58
See also CA 125, 129

Johnson, Lionel (Pigot)
1867-1902 .................. TCLC 19
See also CA 117; DLB 19

Johnson, Marguerita 1928-
See Angelou, Maya

Johnson, Pamela Hansford
1912-1981 .............. CLC 1, 7, 27
See also CANR 2, 28; CA 1-4R,
obituary CA 104; DLB 15

Johnson, Samuel 1709-1784........ LC 15
See also DLB 39, 95

Johnson, Uwe
1934-1984 ........... CLC 5, 10, 15, 40
See also CANR 1; CA 1-4R;
obituary CA 112; DLB 75

Johnston, George (Benson) 1913- ... CLC 51
See also CANR 5, 20; CA 1-4R; DLB 88

Johnston, Jennifer 1930- ........... CLC 7
See also CA 85-88; DLB 14

Jolley, Elizabeth 1923-............. CLC 46
See also CA 127

Jones, D(ouglas) G(ordon) 1929-.... CLC 10
See also CANR 13; CA 29-32R, 113;
DLB 53

Jones, David
1895-1974 ........ CLC 2, 4, 7, 13, 42
See also CANR 28; CA 9-12R;
obituary CA 53-56; DLB 20

Jones, David Robert 1947-
See Bowie, David
See also CA 103

Jones, Diana Wynne 1934- ........ CLC 26
See also CLR 23; CANR 4, 26; CA 49-52;
SAAS 7; SATA 9

Jones, Gayl 1949-............... CLC 6, 9
See also CANR 27; CA 77-80; DLB 33

Jones, James 1921-1977.... CLC 1, 3, 10, 39
See also CANR 6; CA 1-4R;
obituary CA 69-72; DLB 2

Jones, (Everett) LeRoi
1934- ........ CLC 1, 2, 3, 5, 10, 14, 33
See also Baraka, Amiri; Baraka, Imamu
Amiri
See also CA 21-24R

Jones, Louis B. 19??- ............. CLC 65

Jones, Madison (Percy, Jr.) 1925- ... CLC 4
See also CAAS 11; CANR 7; CA 13-16R

Jones, Mervyn 1922- .......... CLC 10, 52
See also CAAS 5; CANR 1; CA 45-48

Jones, Mick 1956?-............... CLC 30
See also The Clash

Jones, Nettie 19??-................ CLC 34

Jones, Preston 1936-1979 ......... CLC 10
See also CA 73-76; obituary CA 89-92;
DLB 7

Jones, Robert F(rancis) 1934-....... CLC 7
See also CANR 2; CA 49-52

Jones, Rod 1953- ................ CLC 50
See also CA 128

Jones, Terry 1942?- .............. CLC 21
See also Monty Python
See also CA 112, 116; SATA 51

**Jong, Erica** 1942- ......... **CLC 4, 6, 8, 18**
See also CANR 26; CA 73-76; DLB 2, 5, 28

**Jonson, Ben(jamin)** 1572-1637 ....... **LC 6**
See also DLB 62

**Jordan, June** 1936- ......... **CLC 5, 11, 23**
See also CLR 10; CANR 25; CA 33-36R;
SATA 4; DLB 38; AAYA 2

**Jordan, Pat(rick M.)** 1941- ....... **CLC 37**
See also CANR 25; CA 33-36R

**Josipovici, Gabriel (David)**
1940- ..................... **CLC 6, 43**
See also CAAS 8; CA 37-40R; DLB 14

**Joubert, Joseph** 1754-1824 ....... **NCLC 9**

**Jouve, Pierre Jean** 1887-1976 ...... **CLC 47**
See also obituary CA 65-68

**Joyce, James (Augustine Aloysius)**
1882-1941 ...... **TCLC 3, 8, 16, 26, 35;**
**SSC 3**
See also CA 104, 126; DLB 10, 19, 36

**Jozsef, Attila** 1905-1937 ......... **TCLC 22**
See also CA 116

**Juana Ines de la Cruz** 1651?-1695 .... **LC 5**

**Julian of Norwich** 1342?-1416? ....... **LC 6**

**Just, Ward S(wift)** 1935- ........ **CLC 4, 27**
See also CA 25-28R

**Justice, Donald (Rodney)** 1925- .. **CLC 6, 19**
See also CANR 26; CA 5-8R; DLB-Y 83

**Kacew, Romain** 1914-1980
See Gary, Romain
See also CA 108; obituary CA 102

**Kacewgary, Romain** 1914-1980
See Gary, Romain

**Kadare, Ismail** 1936- ............. **CLC 52**

**Kadohata, Cynthia** 19??- .......... **CLC 59**

**Kafka, Franz**
1883-1924 .... **TCLC 2, 6, 13, 29; SSC 5**
See also CA 105, 126; DLB 81

**Kahn, Roger** 1927- ............... **CLC 30**
See also CA 25-28R; SATA 37

**Kaiser, (Friedrich Karl) Georg**
1878-1945 .................. **TCLC 9**
See also CA 106

**Kaletski, Alexander** 1946- ......... **CLC 39**
See also CA 118

**Kallman, Chester (Simon)**
1921-1975 ................... **CLC 2**
See also CANR 3; CA 45-48;
obituary CA 53-56

**Kaminsky, Melvin** 1926-
See Brooks, Mel
See also CANR 16; CA 65-68

**Kaminsky, Stuart** 1934- .......... **CLC 59**
See also CANR 29; CA 73-76

**Kane, Paul** 1941-
See Simon, Paul

**Kanin, Garson** 1912- .............. **CLC 22**
See also CANR 7; CA 5-8R; DLB 7

**Kaniuk, Yoram** 1930- ............. **CLC 19**

**Kant, Immanuel** 1724-1804 ...... **NCLC 27**

**Kantor, MacKinlay** 1904-1977 ...... **CLC 7**
See also CA 61-64; obituary CA 73-76;
DLB 9

**Kaplan, David Michael** 1946- ...... **CLC 50**

**Kaplan, James** 19??- .............. **CLC 59**

**Karamzin, Nikolai Mikhailovich**
1766-1826 .................. **NCLC 3**

**Karapanou, Margarita** 1946- ....... **CLC 13**
See also CA 101

**Karl, Frederick R(obert)** 1927- ..... **CLC 34**
See also CANR 3; CA 5-8R

**Kassef, Romain** 1914-1980
See Gary, Romain

**Katz, Steve** 1935- ................ **CLC 47**
See also CANR 12; CA 25-28R; DLB-Y 83

**Kauffman, Janet** 1945- ............ **CLC 42**
See also CA 117; DLB-Y 86

**Kaufman, Bob (Garnell)**
1925-1986 ................... **CLC 49**
See also CANR 22; CA 41-44R;
obituary CA 118; DLB 16, 41

**Kaufman, George S(imon)**
1889-1961 .................. **CLC 38**
See also CA 108; obituary CA 93-96; DLB 7

**Kaufman, Sue** 1926-1977 ........ **CLC 3, 8**
See also Barondess, Sue K(aufman)

**Kavan, Anna** 1904-1968 ........ **CLC 5, 13**
See also Edmonds, Helen (Woods)
See also CANR 6; CA 5-8R

**Kavanagh, Patrick (Joseph Gregory)**
1905-1967 ................... **CLC 22**
See also CA 123; obituary CA 25-28R;
DLB 15, 20

**Kawabata, Yasunari**
1899-1972 ........... **CLC 2, 5, 9, 18**
See also CA 93-96; obituary CA 33-36R

**Kaye, M(ary) M(argaret)** 1909?- .... **CLC 28**
See also CANR 24; CA 89-92

**Kaye, Mollie** 1909?-
See Kaye, M(ary) M(argaret)

**Kaye-Smith, Sheila** 1887-1956 ..... **TCLC 20**
See also CA 118; DLB 36

**Kazan, Elia** 1909- ........... **CLC 6, 16, 63**
See also CA 21-24R

**Kazantzakis, Nikos**
1885?-1957 ............. **TCLC 2, 5, 33**
See also CA 105

**Kazin, Alfred** 1915- ........... **CLC 34, 38**
See also CAAS 7; CANR 1; CA 1-4R;
DLB 67

**Keane, Mary Nesta (Skrine)** 1904-
See Keane, Molly
See also CA 108, 114

**Keane, Molly** 1904- .............. **CLC 31**
See also Keane, Mary Nesta (Skrine)

**Keates, Jonathan** 19??- ............ **CLC 34**

**Keaton, Buster** 1895-1966 ........ **CLC 20**

**Keaton, Joseph Francis** 1895-1966
See Keaton, Buster

**Keats, John** 1795-1821 ...... **NCLC 8; PC 1**

**Keene, Donald** 1922- ............. **CLC 34**
See also CANR 5; CA 1-4R

**Keillor, Garrison** 1942- ........... **CLC 40**
See also Keillor, Gary (Edward)
See also CA 111; SATA 58; DLB-Y 87;
AAYA 2

**Keillor, Gary (Edward)**
See Keillor, Garrison
See also CA 111, 117

**Kell, Joseph** 1917-
See Burgess (Wilson, John) Anthony

**Keller, Gottfried** 1819-1890 ...... **NCLC 2**

**Kellerman, Jonathan (S.)** 1949- ..... **CLC 44**
See also CANR 29; CA 106

**Kelley, William Melvin** 1937- ...... **CLC 22**
See also CANR 27; CA 77-80; DLB 33

**Kellogg, Marjorie** 1922- ............ **CLC 2**
See also CA 81-84

**Kelly, M. T.** 1947- ................ **CLC 55**
See also CANR 19; CA 97-100

**Kelman, James** 1946- ............. **CLC 58**

**Kemal, Yashar** 1922- .......... **CLC 14, 29**
See also CA 89-92

**Kemble, Fanny** 1809-1893 ....... **NCLC 18**
See also DLB 32

**Kemelman, Harry** 1908- ............ **CLC 2**
See also CANR 6; CA 9-12R; DLB 28

**Kempe, Margery** 1373?-1440? ........ **LC 6**

**Kempis, Thomas á** 1380-1471 ....... **LC 11**

**Kendall, Henry** 1839-1882 ....... **NCLC 12**

**Keneally, Thomas (Michael)**
1935- ...... **CLC 5, 8, 10, 14, 19, 27, 43**
See also CANR 10; CA 85-88

**Kennedy, John Pendleton**
1795-1870 ................. **NCLC 2**
See also DLB 3

**Kennedy, Joseph Charles** 1929- ...... **CLC 8**
See also Kennedy, X. J.
See also CANR 4, 30; CA 1-4R; SATA 14

**Kennedy, William (Joseph)**
1928- .............. **CLC 6, 28, 34, 53**
See also CANR 14; CA 85-88; SATA 57;
DLB-Y 85; AAYA 1

**Kennedy, X. J.** 1929- ........... **CLC 8, 42**
See also Kennedy, Joseph Charles
See also CAAS 9; DLB 5

**Kerouac, Jack**
1922-1969 .... **CLC 1, 2, 3, 5, 14, 29, 61**
See also Kerouac, Jean-Louis Lebris de
See also DLB 2, 16; DLB-DS 3;
CDALB 1941-1968

**Kerouac, Jean-Louis Lebris de** 1922-1969
See Kerouac, Jack
See also CANR 26; CA 5-8R;
obituary CA 25-28R; CDALB 1941-1968

**Kerr, Jean** 1923- ................. **CLC 22**
See also CANR 7; CA 5-8R

**Kerr, M. E.** 1927- .............. **CLC 12, 35**
See also Meaker, Marijane
See also SAAS 1; AAYA 2

**Kerr, Robert** 1970?- ........... **CLC 55, 59**

**Kerrigan, (Thomas) Anthony**
1918- ..................... **CLC 4, 6**
See also CAAS 11; CANR 4; CA 49-52

**Kesey, Ken (Elton)**
1935- ......... **CLC 1, 3, 6, 11, 46, 64**
See also CANR 22; CA 1-4R; DLB 2, 16;
CDALB 1968-1987

**Kesselring, Joseph (Otto)**
1902-1967 .................. **CLC 45**

Kessler, Jascha (Frederick) 1929-.... CLC 4
See also CANR 8; CA 17-20R

Kettelkamp, Larry 1933-.......... CLC 12
See also CANR 16; CA 29-32R; SAAS 3;
SATA 2

Kherdian, David 1931-........... CLC 6, 9
See also CLR 24; CAAS 2; CA 21-24R;
SATA 16

Khlebnikov, Vclimir (Vladimirovich)
1885-1922 .................. TCLC 20
See also CA 117

Khodasevich, Vladislav (Felitsianovich)
1886-1939 .................. TCLC 15
See also CA 115

Kielland, Alexander (Lange)
1849-1906 ................... TCLC 5
See also CA 104

Kiely, Benedict 1919-.......... CLC 23, 43
See also CANR 2; CA 1-4R; DLB 15

Kienzle, William X(avier) 1928- .... CLC 25
See also CAAS 1; CANR 9; CA 93-96

Killens, John Oliver 1916-........ CLC 10
See also CAAS 2; CANR 26; CA 77-80,
123; DLB 33

Killigrew, Anne 1660-1685........... LC 4

Kincaid, Jamaica 1949?- .......... CLC 43
See also CA 125

King, Francis (Henry) 1923-..... CLC 8, 53
See also CANR 1; CA 1-4R; DLB 15

King, Stephen (Edwin)
1947-.............. CLC 12, 26, 37, 61
See also CANR 1, 30; CA 61-64; SATA 9,
55; DLB-Y 80; AAYA 1

Kingman, (Mary) Lee 1919-........ CLC 17
See also Natti, (Mary) Lee
See also CA 5-8R; SAAS 3; SATA 1

Kingsley, Sidney 1906-............ CLC 44
See also CA 85-88; DLB 7

Kingsolver, Barbara 1955-......... CLC 55
See also CA 129

Kingston, Maxine Hong
1940-.................. CLC 12, 19, 58
See also CANR 13; CA 69-72; SATA 53;
DLB-Y 80

Kinnell, Galway
1927-........ CLC 1, 2, 3, 5, 13, 29
See also CANR 10; CA 9-12R; DLB 5;
DLB-Y 87

Kinsella, Thomas 1928- ...... CLC 4, 19, 43
See also CANR 15; CA 17-20R; DLB 27

Kinsella, W(illiam) P(atrick)
1935-.................. CLC 27, 43
See also CAAS 7; CANR 21; CA 97-100

Kipling, (Joseph) Rudyard
1865-1936 ......... TCLC 8, 17; SSC 5
See also YABC 2; CA 105, 120; DLB 19, 34

Kirkup, James 1918- .............. CLC 1
See also CAAS 4; CANR 2; CA 1-4R;
SATA 12; DLB 27

Kirkwood, James 1930-1989 ........ CLC 9
See also CANR 6; CA 1-4R;
obituary CA 128

Kis, Danilo 1935-1989 ............ CLC 57
See also CA 118, 129; brief entry CA 109

Kivi, Aleksis 1834-1872 ........ NCLC 30

Kizer, Carolyn (Ashley) 1925-... CLC 15, 39
See also CAAS 5; CANR 24; CA 65-68;
DLB 5

Klappert, Peter 1942-............ CLC 57
See also CA 33-36R; DLB 5

Klausner, Amos 1939-
See Oz, Amos

Klein, A(braham) M(oses)
1909-1972 .................. CLC 19
See also CA 101; obituary CA 37-40R;
DLB 68

Klein, Norma 1938-1989 ......... CLC 30
See also CLR 2, 19; CANR 15; CA 41-44R;
obituary CA 128; SAAS 1; SATA 7, 57;
AAYA 2

Klein, T.E.D. 19??-............... CLC 34
See also CA 119

Kleist, Heinrich von 1777-1811.... NCLC 2
See also DLB 90

Klima, Ivan 1931-................ CLC 56
See also CANR 17; CA 25-28R

Klimentev, Andrei Platonovich 1899-1951
See Platonov, Andrei (Platonovich)
See also CA 108

Klinger, Friedrich Maximilian von
1752-1831 .................. NCLC 1

Klopstock, Friedrich Gottlieb
1724-1803 ................. NCLC 11

Knebel, Fletcher 1911-............ CLC 14
See also CAAS 3; CANR 1; CA 1-4R;
SATA 36

Knight, Etheridge 1931-........... CLC 40
See also CANR 23; CA 21-24R; DLB 41

Knight, Sarah Kemble 1666-1727 ..... LC 7
See also DLB 24

Knowles, John 1926- ...... CLC 1, 4, 10, 26
See also CA 17-20R; SATA 8; DLB 6;
CDALB 1968-1987

Koch, C(hristopher) J(ohn) 1932- ... CLC 42
See also CA 127

Koch, Kenneth 1925- ......... CLC 5, 8, 44
See also CANR 6; CA 1-4R; DLB 5

Kochanowski, Jan 1530-1584........ LC 10

Kock, Charles Paul de
1794-1871 ................. NCLC 16

Koestler, Arthur
1905-1983 ....... CLC 1, 3, 6, 8, 15, 33
See also CANR 1; CA 1-4R;
obituary CA 109; DLB-Y 83

Kohout, Pavel 1928-.............. CLC 13
See also CANR 3; CA 45-48

Kolmar, Gertrud 1894-1943 ...... TCLC 40

Konigsberg, Allen Stewart 1935-
See Allen, Woody

Konrad, Gyorgy 1933-.......... CLC 4, 10
See also CA 85-88

Konwicki, Tadeusz 1926-..... CLC 8, 28, 54
See also CAAS 9; CA 101

Kopit, Arthur (Lee) 1937- .... CLC 1, 18, 33
See also CA 81-84; CABS 3; DLB 7

Kops, Bernard 1926-.............. CLC 4
See also CA 5-8R; DLB 13

Kornbluth, C(yril) M. 1923-1958.... TCLC 8
See also CA 105; DLB 8

Korolenko, Vladimir (Galaktionovich)
1853-1921 ................. TCLC 22
See also CA 121

Kosinski, Jerzy (Nikodem)
1933-........ CLC 1, 2, 3, 6, 10, 15, 53
See also CANR 9; CA 17-20R; DLB 2;
DLB-Y 82

Kostelanetz, Richard (Cory) 1940-... CLC 28
See also CAAS 8; CA 13-16R

Kostrowitzki, Wilhelm Apollinaris de
1880-1918
See Apollinaire, Guillaume
See also CA 104

Kotlowitz, Robert 1924-............ CLC 4
See also CA 33-36R

Kotzebue, August (Friedrich Ferdinand) von
1761-1819 ................. NCLC 25

Kotzwinkle, William 1938- ... CLC 5, 14, 35
See also CLR 6; CANR 3; CA 45-48;
SATA 24

Kozol, Jonathan 1936-............ CLC 17
See also CANR 16; CA 61-64

Kozoll, Michael 1940?-............ CLC 35

Kramer, Kathryn 19??-............ CLC 34

Kramer, Larry 1935- .............. CLC 42
See also CA 124, 126

Krasicki, Ignacy 1735-1801....... NCLC 8

Krasinski, Zygmunt 1812-1859 .... NCLC 4

Kraus, Karl 1874-1936............. TCLC 5
See also CA 104

Kreve, Vincas 1882-1954 ......... TCLC 27

Kristofferson, Kris 1936-.......... CLC 26
See also CA 104

Krizanc, John 1956-.............. CLC 57

Krleza, Miroslav 1893-1981........ CLC 8
See also CA 97-100; obituary CA 105

Kroetsch, Robert (Paul)
1927-.................. CLC 5, 23, 57
See also CANR 8; CA 17-20R; DLB 53

Kroetz, Franz Xaver 1946- ........ CLC 41
See also CA 130

Kropotkin, Peter 1842-1921....... TCLC 36
See also CA 119

Krotkov, Yuri 1917-.............. CLC 19
See also CA 102

Krumgold, Joseph (Quincy)
1908-1980 ................. CLC 12
See also CANR 7; CA 9-12R;
obituary CA 101; SATA 1, 48;
obituary SATA 23

Krutch, Joseph Wood 1893-1970.... CLC 24
See also CANR 4; CA 1-4R;
obituary CA 25-28R; DLB 63

Krylov, Ivan Andreevich
1768?-1844.................. NCLC 1

Kubin, Alfred 1877-1959 ......... TCLC 23
See also CA 112; DLB 81

Kubrick, Stanley 1928-............ CLC 16
See also CA 81-84; DLB 26

**Kumin, Maxine (Winokur)**
1925- ................. **CLC 5, 13, 28**
See also CAAS 8; CANR 1, 21; CA 1-4R;
SATA 12; DLB 5

**Kundera, Milan** 1929- ..... **CLC 4, 9, 19, 32**
See also CANR 19; CA 85-88; AAYA 2

**Kunitz, Stanley J(asspon)**
1905- ................... **CLC 6, 11, 14**
See also CANR 26; CA 41-44R; DLB 48

**Kunze, Reiner** 1933-.............. **CLC 10**
See also CA 93-96; DLB 75

**Kuprin, Aleksandr (Ivanovich)**
1870-1938 .................. **TCLC 5**
See also CA 104

**Kureishi, Hanif** 1954-............ **CLC 64**

**Kurosawa, Akira** 1910-............ **CLC 16**
See also CA 101

**Kuttner, Henry** 1915-1958........ **TCLC 10**
See also CA 107; DLB 8

**Kuzma, Greg** 1944-................ **CLC 7**
See also CA 33-36R

**Kuzmin, Mikhail** 1872?-1936...... **TCLC 40**

**Labrunie, Gerard** 1808-1855
See Nerval, Gerard de

**Laclos, Pierre Ambroise Francois Choderlos**
de 1741-1803 .............. **NCLC 4**

**La Fayette, Marie (Madelaine Pioche de la
Vergne, Comtesse) de**
1634-1693 .................... **LC 2**

**Lafayette, Rene**
See Hubbard, L(afayette) Ron(ald)

**Laforgue, Jules** 1860-1887........ **NCLC 5**

**Lagerkvist, Par (Fabian)**
1891-1974 .......... **CLC 7, 10, 13, 54**
See also CA 85-88; obituary CA 49-52

**Lagerlof, Selma (Ottiliana Lovisa)**
1858-1940 ................. **TCLC 4, 36**
See also CLR 7; CA 108; SATA 15

**La Guma, (Justin) Alex(ander)**
1925-1985 ................... **CLC 19**
See also CANR 25; CA 49-52;
obituary CA 118

**Lamartine, Alphonse (Marie Louis Prat) de**
1790-1869 ................. **NCLC 11**

**Lamb, Charles** 1775-1834........ **NCLC 10**
See also SATA 17

**Lamming, George (William)**
1927- ..................... **CLC 2, 4**
See also CANR 26; CA 85-88

**LaMoore, Louis Dearborn** 1908?-
See L'Amour, Louis (Dearborn)

**L'Amour, Louis (Dearborn)**
1908 1988 ............... **CLC 25, 55**
See also CANR 3, 25; CA 1-4R;
obituary CA 125; DLB-Y 80

**Lampedusa, (Prince) Giuseppe (Maria
Fabrizio) Tomasi di**
1896-1957 ................. **TCLC 13**
See also CA 111

**Lampman, Archibald** 1861-1899 .. **NCLC 25**
See also DLB 92

**Lancaster, Bruce** 1896-1963........ **CLC 36**
See also CAP 1; CA 9-12; SATA 9

**Landis, John (David)** 1950-........ **CLC 26**
See also CA 112, 122

**Landolfi, Tommaso** 1908-1979... **CLC 11, 49**
See also CA 127; obituary CA 117

**Landon, Letitia Elizabeth**
1802-1838 ................. **NCLC 15**

**Landor, Walter Savage**
1775-1864 ................. **NCLC 14**

**Landwirth, Heinz** 1927-
See Lind, Jakov
See also CANR 7; CA 11-12R

**Lane, Patrick** 1939-.............. **CLC 25**
See also CA 97-100; DLB 53

**Lang, Andrew** 1844-1912........ **TCLC 16**
See also CA 114; SATA 16

**Lang, Fritz** 1890-1976 .......... **CLC 20**
See also CANR 30; CA 77-80;
obituary CA 69-72

**Langer, Elinor** 1939- ............ **CLC 34**
See also CA 121

**Lanier, Sidney** 1842-1881 ........ **NCLC 6**
See also SATA 18; DLB 64

**Lanyer, Aemilia** 1569-1645 ........ **LC 10**

**Lao Tzu** c. 6th-3rd century B.C.... **CMLC 7**

**Lapine, James** 1949-.............. **CLC 39**
See also CA 123, 130

**Larbaud, Valery** 1881-1957........ **TCLC 9**
See also CA 106

**Lardner, Ring(gold Wilmer)**
1885-1933 ................. **TCLC 2, 14**
See also CA 104; DLB 11, 25, 86;
CDALB 1917-1929

**Larkin, Philip (Arthur)**
1922-1985 ... **CLC 3, 5, 8, 9, 13, 18, 33,
39, 64**
See also CANR 24; CA 5-8R;
obituary CA 117; DLB 27

**Larra (y Sanchez de Castro), Mariano Jose de**
1809-1837 ................. **NCLC 17**

**Larsen, Eric** 1941- .............. **CLC 55**

**Larsen, Nella** 1891-1964 .......... **CLC 37**
See also CA 125; DLB 51

**Larson, Charles R(aymond)** 1938-... **CLC 31**
See also CANR 4; CA 53-56

**Latham, Jean Lee** 1902-........... **CLC 12**
See also CANR 7; CA 5-8R; SATA 2

**Lathen, Emma** ..................... **CLC 2**
See also Hennissart, Martha; Latsis, Mary
J(ane)

**Latsis, Mary J(ane)**............... **CLC 2**
See also Lathen, Emma
See also CA 85-88

**Lattimore, Richmond (Alexander)**
1906-1984 ................... **CLC 3**
See also CANR 1; CA 1-4R;
obituary CA 112

**Laughlin, James** 1914-............ **CLC 49**
See also CANR 9; CA 21-24R; DLB 48

**Laurence, (Jean) Margaret (Wemyss)**
1926-1987 .. **CLC 3, 6, 13, 50, 62; SSC 7**
See also CA 5-8R; obituary CA 121;
SATA 50; DLB 53

**Laurent, Antoine** 1952- .......... **CLC 50**

**Lautreamont, Comte de**
1846-1870 ................. **NCLC 12**

**Lavin, Mary** 1912-...... **CLC 4, 18; SSC 4**
See also CA 9-12R; DLB 15

**Lawler, Raymond (Evenor)** 1922-... **CLC 58**
See also CA 103

**Lawrence, D(avid) H(erbert)**
1885-1930 .... **TCLC 2, 9, 16, 33; SSC 4**
See also CA 104, 121; DLB 10, 19, 36

**Lawrence, T(homas) E(dward)**
1888-1935 ................. **TCLC 18**
See also CA 115

**Lawson, Henry (Archibald Hertzberg)**
1867-1922 ................. **TCLC 27**
See also CA 120

**Laxness, Halldor (Kiljan)** 1902-.... **CLC 25**
See also Gudjonsson, Halldor Kiljan

**Laye, Camara** 1928-1980........ **CLC 4, 38**
See also CANR 25; CA 85-88;
obituary CA 97-100

**Layton, Irving (Peter)** 1912-..... **CLC 2, 15**
See also CANR 2; CA 1-4R; DLB 88

**Lazarus, Emma** 1849-1887........ **NCLC 8**

**Leacock, Stephen (Butler)**
1869-1944 ................. **TCLC 2**
See also CA 104; DLB 92

**Lear, Edward** 1812-1888 ........ **NCLC 3**
See also CLR 1; SATA 18; DLB 32

**Lear, Norman (Milton)** 1922-...... **CLC 12**
See also CA 73-76

**Leavis, F(rank) R(aymond)**
1895-1978 ................... **CLC 24**
See also CA 21-24R; obituary CA 77-80

**Leavitt, David** 1961?-............ **CLC 34**
See also CA 116, 122

**Lebowitz, Fran(ces Ann)**
1951?- ................... **CLC 11, 36**
See also CANR 14; CA 81-84

**Le Carre, John** 1931-... **CLC 3, 5, 9, 15, 28**
See also Cornwell, David (John Moore)
See also DLB 87

**Le Clezio, J(ean) M(arie) G(ustave)**
1940- ..................... **CLC 31**
See also CA 116, 128; DLB 83

**Leconte de Lisle, Charles-Marie-Rene**
1818-1894 ................. **NCLC 29**

**Leduc, Violette** 1907-1972........ **CLC 22**
See also CAP 1; CA 13-14;
obituary CA 33-36R

**Ledwidge, Francis** 1887-1917...... **TCLC 23**
See also CA 123; DLB 20

**Lee, Andrea** 1953- .............. **CLC 36**
See also CA 125

**Lee, Andrew** 1917-
See Auchincloss, Louis (Stanton)

**Lee, Don L.** 1942-................ **CLC 2**
See also Madhubuti, Haki R.
See also CA 73-76

**Lee, George Washington**
1894-1976 ................... **CLC 52**
See also CA 125; DLB 51

**Lee, (Nelle) Harper** 1926-...... **CLC 12, 60**
See also CA 13-16R; SATA 11; DLB 6;
CDALB 1941-1968

**Lee, Lawrence** 1903- ............. **CLC 34**
See also CA 25-28R

**Lee, Manfred B(ennington)**
1905-1971 ................... **CLC 11**
See also Queen, Ellery
See also CANR 2; CA 1-4R;
obituary CA 29-32R

**Lee, Stan** 1922-.................. **CLC 17**
See also CA 108, 111

**Lee, Tanith** 1947-................ **CLC 46**
See also CA 37-40R; SATA 8

**Lee, Vernon** 1856-1935 .......... **TCLC 5**
See also Paget, Violet
See also DLB 57

**Lee-Hamilton, Eugene (Jacob)**
1845-1907 ................. **TCLC 22**
See also CA 117

**Leet, Judith** 1935- ............... **CLC 11**

**Le Fanu, Joseph Sheridan**
1814-1873 ................. **NCLC 9**
See also DLB 21, 70

**Leffland, Ella** 1931- ............. **CLC 19**
See also CA 29-32R; DLB-Y 84

**Leger, (Marie-Rene) Alexis Saint-Leger**
1887-1975 .................. **CLC 11**
See also Perse, St.-John
See also CA 13-16R; obituary CA 61-64

**Le Guin, Ursula K(roeber)**
1929- .............. **CLC 8, 13, 22, 45**
See also CLR 3; CANR 9; CA 21-24R;
SATA 4, 52; DLB 8, 52;
CDALB 1968-1987

**Lehmann, Rosamond (Nina)** 1901- ... **CLC 5**
See also CANR 8; CA 77-80; DLB 15

**Leiber, Fritz (Reuter, Jr.)** 1910-.... **CLC 25**
See also CANR 2; CA 45-48; SATA 45;
DLB 8

**Leimbach, Marti** 1963-............. **CLC 65**

**Leino, Eino** 1878-1926 .......... **TCLC 24**

**Leiris, Michel** 1901-.............. **CLC 61**
See also CA 119, 128

**Leithauser, Brad** 1953-............. **CLC 27**
See also CANR 27; CA 107

**Lelchuk, Alan** 1938-................ **CLC 5**
See also CANR 1; CA 45-48

**Lem, Stanislaw** 1921-........ **CLC 8, 15, 40**
See also CAAS 1; CA 105

**Lemann, Nancy** 1956-............. **CLC 39**
See also CA 118

**Lemonnier, (Antoine Louis) Camille**
1844-1913 ................. **TCLC 22**
See also CA 121

**Lenau, Nikolaus** 1802-1850 ...... **NCLC 16**

**L'Engle, Madeleine** 1918- ......... **CLC 12**
See also CLR 1, 14; CANR 3, 21; CA 1-4R;
SATA 1, 27; DLB 52; AAYA 1

**Lengyel, Jozsef** 1896-1975.......... **CLC 7**
See also CA 85-88; obituary CA 57-60

**Lennon, John (Ono)**
1940-1980 ............... **CLC 12, 35**
See also CA 102

**Lennon, John Winston** 1940-1980
See Lennon, John (Ono)

**Lennox, Charlotte Ramsay**
1729?-1804................. **NCLC 23**
See also DLB 39

**Lentricchia, Frank (Jr.)** 1940-...... **CLC 34**
See also CANR 19; CA 25-28R

**Lenz, Siegfried** 1926-............. **CLC 27**
See also CA 89-92; DLB 75

**Leonard, Elmore** 1925-......... **CLC 28, 34**
See also CANR 12, 28; CA 81-84

**Leonard, Hugh** 1926-............. **CLC 19**
See also Byrne, John Keyes
See also DLB 13

**Leopardi, (Conte) Giacomo (Talegardo**
**Francesco di Sales Saverio Pietro)**
1798-1837 ................. **NCLC 22**

**Lerman, Eleanor** 1952-............. **CLC 9**
See also CA 85-88

**Lerman, Rhoda** 1936-............. **CLC 56**
See also CA 49-52

**Lermontov, Mikhail Yuryevich**
1814-1841 ................. **NCLC 5**

**Leroux, Gaston** 1868-1927........ **TCLC 25**
See also CA 108

**Lesage, Alain-Rene** 1668-1747........ **LC 2**

**Leskov, Nikolai (Semyonovich)**
1831-1895 ................. **NCLC 25**

**Lessing, Doris (May)**
1919- .... **CLC 1, 2, 3, 6, 10, 15, 22, 40;**
**SSC 6**
See also CA 9-12R; DLB 15; DLB-Y 85

**Lessing, Gotthold Ephraim**
1729-1781 ................... **LC 8**

**Lester, Richard** 1932-............. **CLC 20**

**Lever, Charles (James)**
1806-1872 ................. **NCLC 23**
See also DLB 21

**Leverson, Ada** 1865-1936........ **TCLC 18**
See also CA 117

**Levertov, Denise**
1923- ......... **CLC 1, 2, 3, 5, 8, 15, 28**
See also CANR 3, 29; CA 1-4R; DLB 5

**Levi, Peter (Chad Tiger)** 1931-..... **CLC 41**
See also CA 5-8R; DLB 40

**Levi, Primo** 1919-1987......... **CLC 37, 50**
See also CANR 12; CA 13-16R;
obituary CA 122

**Levin, Ira** 1929- ................ **CLC 3, 6**
See also CANR 17; CA 21-24R

**Levin, Meyer** 1905-1981 .......... **CLC 7**
See also CANR 15; CA 9-12R;
obituary CA 104; SATA 21;
obituary SATA 27; DLB 9, 28; DLB-Y 81

**Levine, Norman** 1924- ............ **CLC 54**
See also CANR 14; CA 73-76; DLB 88

**Levine, Philip** 1928-... **CLC 2, 4, 5, 9, 14, 33**
See also CANR 9; CA 9-12R; DLB 5

**Levinson, Deirdre** 1931-........... **CLC 49**
See also CA 73-76

**Levi-Strauss, Claude** 1908- ........ **CLC 38**
See also CANR 6; CA 1-4R

**Levitin, Sonia** 1934-.............. **CLC 17**
See also CANR 14; CA 29-32R; SAAS 2;
SATA 4

**Lewes, George Henry**
1817-1878 ................. **NCLC 25**
See also DLB 55

**Lewis, Alun** 1915-1944............ **TCLC 3**
See also CA 104; DLB 20

**Lewis, C(ecil) Day** 1904-1972
See Day Lewis, C(ecil)

**Lewis, C(live) S(taples)**
1898-1963 ......... **CLC 1, 3, 6, 14, 27**
See also CLR 3; CA 81-84; SATA 13;
DLB 15

**Lewis (Winters), Janet** 1899-....... **CLC 41**
See also Winters, Janet Lewis
See also CANR 29; CAP 1; CA 9-10R;
DLB-Y 87

**Lewis, Matthew Gregory**
1775-1818 ................. **NCLC 11**
See also DLB 39

**Lewis, (Harry) Sinclair**
1885-1951 ........ **TCLC 4, 13, 23, 39**
See also CA 104; DLB 9; DLB-DS 1;
CDALB 1917-1929

**Lewis, (Percy) Wyndham**
1882?-1957..............**TCLC 2, 9**
See also CA 104; DLB 15

**Lewisohn, Ludwig** 1883-1955...... **TCLC 19**
See also CA 73-76, 107;
obituary CA 29-32R; DLB 4, 9, 28

**L'Heureux, John (Clarke)** 1934-.... **CLC 52**
See also CANR 23; CA 15-16R

**Lieber, Stanley Martin** 1922-
See Lee, Stan

**Lieberman, Laurence (James)**
1935-..................... **CLC 4, 36**
See also CANR 8; CA 17-20R

**Li Fei-kan** 1904-................. **CLC 18**
See also Pa Chin
See also CA 105

**Lightfoot, Gordon (Meredith)**
1938-...................... **CLC 26**
See also CA 109

**Ligotti, Thomas** 1953- ............ **CLC 44**
See also CA 123

**Liliencron, Detlev von**
1844-1909 ................. **TCLC 18**
See also CA 117

**Lima, Jose Lezama** 1910-1976
See Lezama Lima, Jose

**Lima Barreto, (Alfonso Henriques de)**
1881-1922 ................. **TCLC 23**
See also CA 117

**Lincoln, Abraham** 1809-1865..... **NCLC 18**

**Lind, Jakov** 1927-.......... **CLC 1, 2, 4, 27**
See also Landwirth, Heinz
See also CAAS 4; CA 9-12R

**Lindsay, David** 1876-1945........ **TCLC 15**
See also CA 113

**Lindsay, (Nicholas) Vachel**
1879-1931 ................. **TCLC 17**
See also CA 114; SATA 40; DLB 54;
CDALB 1865-1917

**Linney, Romulus** 1930- ........... **CLC 51**
See also CA 1-4R

**Li Po** 701-763.................. **CMLC 2**

**Lipsius, Justus**　1547-1606 . . . . . . . . . **LC 16**

**Lipsyte, Robert (Michael)**　1938- . . . . **CLC 21**
See also CLR 23; CANR 8; CA 17-20R;
SATA 5

**Lish, Gordon (Jay)**　1934- . . . . . . . . . **CLC 45**
See also CA 113, 117

**Lispector, Clarice**　1925-1977 . . . . . . **CLC 43**
See also obituary CA 116

**Littell, Robert**　1935?- . . . . . . . . . . . . **CLC 42**
See also CA 109, 112

**Liu E**　1857-1909 . . . . . . . . . . . . . . . **TCLC 15**
See also CA 115

**Lively, Penelope**　1933- . . . . . . . . **CLC 32, 50**
See also CLR 7; CANR 29; CA 41-44R;
SATA 7; DLB 14

**Livesay, Dorothy**　1909- . . . . . . . . **CLC 4, 15**
See also CAAS 8; CA 25-28R; DLB 68

**Lizardi, Jose Joaquin Fernandez de**
1776-1827 . . . . . . . . . . . . . . . . **NCLC 30**

**Llewellyn, Richard**　1906-1983 . . . . . . **CLC 7**
See also Llewellyn Lloyd, Richard (Dafydd
Vyvyan)
See also DLB 15

**Llewellyn Lloyd, Richard (Dafydd Vyvyan)**
1906-1983
See Llewellyn, Richard
See also CANR 7; CA 53-56;
obituary CA 111; SATA 11, 37

**Llosa, Mario Vargas**　1936-
See Vargas Llosa, Mario

**Lloyd, Richard Llewellyn**　1906-
See Llewellyn, Richard

**Locke, John**　1632-1704 . . . . . . . . . . . . **LC 7**
See also DLB 31

**Lockhart, John Gibson**
1794-1854 . . . . . . . . . . . . . . . . . **NCLC 6**

**Lodge, David (John)**　1935- . . . . . . . . **CLC 36**
See also CANR 19; CA 17-20R; DLB 14

**Loewinsohn, Ron(ald William)**
1937- . . . . . . . . . . . . . . . . . . . . . **CLC 52**
See also CA 25-28R

**Logan, John**　1923- . . . . . . . . . . . . . . . **CLC 5**
See also CA 77-80; obituary CA 124; DLB 5

**Lo Kuan-chung**　1330?-1400? . . . . . . . . **LC 12**

**Lombino, S. A.**　1926-
See Hunter, Evan

**London, Jack**
1876-1916 . . . . . . **TCLC 9, 15, 39; SSC 4**
See also London, John Griffith
See also SATA 18; DLB 8, 12, 78;
CDALB 1865-1917

**London, John Griffith**　1876-1916
See London, Jack
See also CA 110, 119

**Long, Emmett**　1925-
See Leonard, Elmore

**Longbaugh, Harry**　1931-
See Goldman, William (W.)

**Longfellow, Henry Wadsworth**
1807-1882 . . . . . . . . . . . . . . . . . **NCLC 2**
See also SATA 19; DLB 1, 59;
CDALB 1640-1865

**Longley, Michael**　1939- . . . . . . . . . . **CLC 29**
See also CA 102; DLB 40

**Longus**　fl. c. 2nd century- . . . . . . . . **CMLC 7**

**Lopate, Phillip**　1943- . . . . . . . . . . . . **CLC 29**
See also CA 97-100; DLB-Y 80

**Lopez Portillo (y Pacheco), Jose**
1920- . . . . . . . . . . . . . . . . . . . . . **CLC 46**
See also CA 129

**Lopez y Fuentes, Gregorio**
1897-1966 . . . . . . . . . . . . . . . . . **CLC 32**

**Lord, Bette Bao**　1938- . . . . . . . . . . . . **CLC 23**
See also CA 107; SATA 58

**Lorde, Audre (Geraldine)**　1934- . . . . . **CLC 18**
See also CANR 16, 26; CA 25-28R;
DLB 41

**Loti, Pierre**　1850-1923 . . . . . . . . . . . **TCLC 11**
See also Viaud, (Louis Marie) Julien

**Lovecraft, H(oward) P(hillips)**
1890-1937 . . . . . . . . **TCLC 4, 22; SSC 3**
See also CA 104

**Lovelace, Earl**　1935- . . . . . . . . . . . . . **CLC 51**
See also CA 77-80

**Lowell, Amy**　1874-1925 . . . . . . . . **TCLC 1, 8**
See also CA 104; DLB 54

**Lowell, James Russell**　1819-1891 . . **NCLC 2**
See also DLB 1, 11, 64, 79;
CDALB 1640-1865

**Lowell, Robert (Traill Spence, Jr.)**
1917-1977 . . . **CLC 1, 2, 3, 4, 5, 8, 9, 11,
15, 37**
See also CANR 26; CA 9-12R;
obituary CA 73-76; CABS 2; DLB 5

**Lowndes, Marie (Adelaide) Belloc**
1868-1947 . . . . . . . . . . . . . . . . **TCLC 12**
See also CA 107; DLB 70

**Lowry, (Clarence) Malcolm**
1909-1957 . . . . . . . . . . . . . . **TCLC 6, 40**
See also CA 105, 131; DLB 15

**Loy, Mina**　1882-1966 . . . . . . . . . . . . **CLC 28**
See also CA 113; DLB 4, 54

**Lucas, Craig** . . . . . . . . . . . . . . . . . . . . **CLC 64**

**Lucas, George**　1944- . . . . . . . . . . . . . **CLC 16**
See also CANR 30; CA 77-80; SATA 56;
AAYA 1

**Lucas, Victoria**　1932-1963
See Plath, Sylvia

**Ludlam, Charles**　1943-1987 . . . . . **CLC 46, 50**
See also CA 85-88; obituary CA 122

**Ludlum, Robert**　1927- . . . . . . . . . **CLC 22, 43**
See also CANR 25; CA 33-36R; DLB-Y 82

**Ludwig, Ken**　19??- . . . . . . . . . . . . . . **CLC 60**

**Ludwig, Otto**　1813-1865 . . . . . . . . . **NCLC 4**

**Lugones, Leopoldo**　1874-1938 . . . . . **TCLC 15**
See also CA 116

**Lu Hsun**　1881-1936 . . . . . . . . . . . . . **TCLC 3**

**Lukacs, Georg**　1885-1971 . . . . . . . . . **CLC 24**
See also Lukacs, Gyorgy

**Lukacs, Gyorgy**　1885-1971
See Lukacs, Georg
See also CA 101; obituary CA 29-32R

**Luke, Peter (Ambrose Cyprian)**
1919- . . . . . . . . . . . . . . . . . . . . . **CLC 38**
See also CA 81-84; DLB 13

**Lurie (Bishop), Alison**
1926- . . . . . . . . . . . . . . **CLC 4, 5, 18, 39**
See also CANR 2, 17; CA 1-4R; SATA 46;
DLB 2

**Lustig, Arnost**　1926- . . . . . . . . . . . . . **CLC 56**
See also CA 69-72; SATA 56; AAYA 3

**Luther, Martin**　1483-1546 . . . . . . . . . . **LC 9**

**Luzi, Mario**　1914- . . . . . . . . . . . . . . . **CLC 13**
See also CANR 9; CA 61-64

**Lynn, Kenneth S(chuyler)**　1923- . . . . **CLC 50**
See also CANR 3, 27; CA 1-4R

**Lytle, Andrew (Nelson)**　1902- . . . . . . **CLC 22**
See also CA 9-12R; DLB 6

**Lyttelton, George**　1709-1773 . . . . . . . **LC 10**

**Lytton, Edward Bulwer**　1803-1873
See Bulwer-Lytton, (Lord) Edward (George
Earle Lytton)
See also SATA 23

**Maas, Peter**　1929- . . . . . . . . . . . . . . . **CLC 29**
See also CA 93-96

**Macaulay, (Dame Emile) Rose**
1881-1958 . . . . . . . . . . . . . . . . . **TCLC 7**
See also CA 104; DLB 36

**MacBeth, George (Mann)**
1932- . . . . . . . . . . . . . . . . . . **CLC 2, 5, 9**
See also CA 25-28R; SATA 4; DLB 40

**MacCaig, Norman (Alexander)**
1910- . . . . . . . . . . . . . . . . . . . . . **CLC 36**
See also CANR 3; CA 9-12R; DLB 27

**MacCarthy, Desmond**　1877-1952 . . **TCLC 36**

**MacDermot, Thomas H.**　1870-1933
See Redcam, Tom

**MacDiarmid, Hugh**
1892-1978 . . . . . . . . **CLC 2, 4, 11, 19, 63**
See also Grieve, C(hristopher) M(urray)
See also DLB 20

**Macdonald, Cynthia**　1928- . . . . . . **CLC 13, 19**
See also CANR 4; CA 49-52

**MacDonald, George**　1824-1905 . . . . . **TCLC 9**
See also CA 106; SATA 33; DLB 18

**MacDonald, John D(ann)**
1916-1986 . . . . . . . . . . . **CLC 3, 27, 44**
See also CANR 1, 19; CA 1-4R;
obituary CA 121; DLB 8; DLB-Y 86

**Macdonald, (John) Ross**
1915-1983 . . . . . . **CLC 1, 2, 3, 14, 34, 41**
See also Millar, Kenneth
See also DLB-DS 6

**MacEwen, Gwendolyn (Margaret)**
1941-1987 . . . . . . . . . . . . . . **CLC 13, 55**
See also CANR 7, 22; CA 9-12R;
obituary CA 124; SATA 50, 55; DLB 53

**Machado (y Ruiz), Antonio**
1875-1939 . . . . . . . . . . . . . . . . . **TCLC 3**
See also CA 104

**Machado de Assis, (Joaquim Maria)**
1839-1908 . . . . . . . . . . . . . . . . **TCLC 10**
See also CA 107

**Machen, Arthur (Llewellyn Jones)**
1863-1947 . . . . . . . . . . . . . . . . . **TCLC 4**
See also CA 104; DLB 36

**Machiavelli, Niccolo**　1469-1527 . . . . . . **LC 8**

MacInnes, Colin 1914-1976...... CLC 4, 23
See also CANR 21; CA 69-72;
obituary CA 65-68; DLB 14

MacInnes, Helen (Clark)
1907-1985 ............... CLC 27, 39
See also CANR 1, 28; CA 1-4R;
obituary CA 65-68, 117; SATA 22, 44;
DLB 87

Macintosh, Elizabeth 1897-1952
See Tey, Josephine
See also CA 110

Mackenzie, (Edward Montague) Compton
1883-1972 ................... CLC 18
See also CAP 2; CA 21-22;
obituary CA 37-40R; DLB 34

Mac Laverty, Bernard 1942-....... CLC 31
See also CA 116, 118

MacLean, Alistair (Stuart)
1922-1987 .......... CLC 3, 13, 50, 63
See also CANR 28; CA 57-60;
obituary CA 121; SATA 23, 50

MacLeish, Archibald
1892-1982 ............... CLC 3, 8, 14
See also CA 9-12R; obituary CA 106;
DLB 4, 7, 45; DLB-Y 82

MacLennan, (John) Hugh
1907- ..................... CLC 2, 14
See also CA 5-8R; DLB 68

MacLeod, Alistair 1936- .......... CLC 56
See also CA 123; DLB 60

Macleod, Fiona 1855-1905
See Sharp, William

MacNeice, (Frederick) Louis
1907-1963 .......... CLC 1, 4, 10, 53
See also CA 85-88; DLB 10, 20

Macpherson, (Jean) Jay 1931-...... CLC 14
See also CA 5-8R; DLB 53

MacShane, Frank 1927-.......... CLC 39
See also CANR 3; CA 11-12R

Macumber, Mari 1896-1966
See Sandoz, Mari (Susette)

Madach, Imre 1823-1864........ NCLC 19

Madden, (Jerry) David 1933- .... CLC 5, 15
See also CAAS 3; CANR 4; CA 1-4R;
DLB 6

Madhubuti, Haki R. 1942-.......... CLC 6
See also Lee, Don L.
See also CANR 24; CA 73-76; DLB 5, 41

Maeterlinck, Maurice 1862-1949 ... TCLC 3
See also CA 104

Mafouz, Naguib 1912-
See Mahfuz, Najib

Maginn, William 1794-1842....... NCLC 8

Mahapatra, Jayanta 1928-......... CLC 33
See also CAAS 9; CANR 15; CA 73-76

Mahfuz Najib 1912-........... CLC 52, 55
See also DLB-Y 88

Mahon, Derek 1941-.............. CLC 27
See also CA 113, 128; DLB 40

Mailer, Norman
1923- ...... CLC 1, 2, 3, 4, 5, 8, 11, 14,
28, 39
See also CANR 28; CA 9-12R; CABS 1;
DLB 2, 16, 28; DLB-Y 80, 83;
DLB-DS 3; CDALB 1968-1987

Maillet, Antonine 1929-........... CLC 54
See also CA 115, 120; DLB 60

Mais, Roger 1905-1955 .......... TCLC 8
See also CA 105, 124

Maitland, Sara (Louise) 1950-...... CLC 49
See also CANR 13; CA 69-72

Major, Clarence 1936-....... CLC 3, 19, 48
See also CAAS 6; CANR 13, 25;
CA 21-24R; DLB 33

Major, Kevin 1949- .............. CLC 26
See also CLR 11; CANR 21; CA 97-100;
SATA 32; DLB 60

Malamud, Bernard
1914-1986 ..... CLC 1, 2, 3, 5, 8, 9, 11,
18, 27, 44
See also CANR 28; CA 5-8R;
obituary CA 118; CABS 1; DLB 2, 28;
DLB-Y 80, 86; CDALB 1941-1968

Malherbe, Francois de 1555-1628..... LC 5

Mallarme, Stephane 1842-1898.... NCLC 4

Mallet-Joris, Francoise 1930-...... CLC 11
See also CANR 17; CA 65-68; DLB 83

Maloff, Saul 1922-................ CLC 5
See also CA 33-36R

Malone, Louis 1907-1963
See MacNeice, (Frederick) Louis

Malone, Michael (Christopher)
1942-..................... CLC 43
See also CANR 14; CA 77-80

Malory, (Sir) Thomas ?-1471....... LC 11
See also SATA 33, 59

Malouf, David 1934- ............. CLC 28

Malraux, (Georges-) Andre
1901-1976 ...... CLC 1, 4, 9, 13, 15, 57
See also CAP 2; CA 21-24;
obituary CA 69-72; DLB 72

Malzberg, Barry N. 1939-.......... CLC 7
See also CAAS 4; CANR 16; CA 61-64;
DLB 8

Mamet, David (Alan)
1947-1987 .......... CLC 9, 15, 34, 46
See also CANR 15; CA 81-84, 124;
CABS 3; DLB 7; AAYA 3

Mamoulian, Rouben 1898-........ CLC 16
See also CA 25-28R; obituary CA 124

Mandelstam, Osip (Emilievich)
1891?-1938?............... TCLC 2, 6
See also CA 104

Mander, Jane 1877-1949 ........ TCLC 31

Mandiargues, Andre Pieyre de
1909- ..................... CLC 41
See also CA 103; DLB 83

Mangan, James Clarence
1803-1849 ............... NCLC 27

Manley, (Mary) Delariviere
1672?-1724................... LC 1
See also DLB 39, 80

Mann, (Luiz) Heinrich 1871-1950... TCLC 9
See also CA 106; DLB 66

Mann, Thomas
1875-1955 ...... TCLC 2, 8, 14, 21, 35;
SSC 5
See also CA 104, 128; DLB 66

Manning, Frederic 1882-1935 ..... TCLC 25
See also CA 124

Manning, Olivia 1915-1980...... CLC 5, 19
See also CANR 29; CA 5-8R;
obituary CA 101

Mano, D. Keith 1942- .......... CLC 2, 10
See also CAAS 6; CANR 26; CA 25-28R;
DLB 6

Mansfield, Katherine
1888-1923 ............. TCLC 2, 8, 39
See also CA 104

Manso, Peter 1940-.............. CLC 39
See also CA 29-32R

Manzoni, Alessandro 1785-1873.. NCLC 29

Mapu, Abraham (ben Jekutiel)
1808-1867 ................ NCLC 18

Marat, Jean Paul 1743-1793....... LC 10

Marcel, Gabriel (Honore)
1889-1973 .................. CLC 15
See also CA 102; obituary CA 45-48

Marchbanks, Samuel 1913-
See Davies, (William) Robertson

Marie de l'Incarnation 1599-1672.... LC 10

Marinetti, F(ilippo) T(ommaso)
1876-1944 .................. TCLC 10
See also CA 107

Marivaux, Pierre Carlet de Chamblain de
(1688-1763).................... LC 4

Markandaya, Kamala 1924-...... CLC 8, 38
See also Taylor, Kamala (Purnaiya)

Markfield, Wallace (Arthur) 1926-... CLC 8
See also CAAS 3; CA 69-72; DLB 2, 28

Markham, Robert 1922-
See Amis, Kingsley (William)

Marks, J. 1942-
See Highwater, Jamake

Marley, Bob 1945-1981 ........... CLC 17
See also Marley, Robert Nesta

Marley, Robert Nesta 1945-1981
See Marley, Bob
See also CA 107; obituary CA 103

Marlowe, Christopher 1564-1593 ..... DC 1
See also DLB 62

Marmontel, Jean-Francois
1723-1799 .................... LC 2

Marquand, John P(hillips)
1893-1960 ............... CLC 2, 10
See also CA 85-88; DLB 9

Marquez, Gabriel Garcia 1928-
See Garcia Marquez, Gabriel

Marquis, Don(ald Robert Perry)
1878-1937 ................... TCLC 7
See also CA 104; DLB 11, 25

Marryat, Frederick 1792-1848 .... NCLC 3
See also DLB 21

Marsh, (Dame Edith) Ngaio
1899-1982 ................. CLC 7, 53
See also CANR 6; CA 9-12R; DLB 77

Marshall, Garry 1935?-........... CLC 17
See also CA 111; AAYA 3

Marshall, Paule 1929- ..... CLC 27; SSC 3
See also CANR 25; CA 77-80; DLB 33

Marsten, Richard    1926-
See Hunter, Evan

Martin, Steve    1945?- . . . . . . . . . . . . CLC 30
See also CANR 30; CA 97-100

Martin du Gard, Roger
1881-1958 . . . . . . . . . . . . . . . . . TCLC 24
See also CA 118; DLB 65

Martineau, Harriet    1802-1876. . . . NCLC 26
See also YABC 2; DLB 21, 55

Martinez Ruiz, Jose    1874-1967
See Azorin
See also CA 93-96

Martinez Sierra, Gregorio
1881-1947 . . . . . . . . . . . . . . . . . . TCLC 6
See also CA 104, 115

Martinez Sierra, Maria (de la O'LeJarraga)
1880?-1974. . . . . . . . . . . . . . . . . . TCLC 6
See also obituary CA 115

Martinson, Harry (Edmund)
1904-1978 . . . . . . . . . . . . . . . . . . CLC 14
See also CA 77-80

Marvell, Andrew    1621-1678. . . . . . . . . LC 4

Marx, Karl (Heinrich)
1818-1883 . . . . . . . . . . . . . . . . . NCLC 17

Masaoka Shiki    1867-1902 . . . . . . . . TCLC 18

Masefield, John (Edward)
1878-1967 . . . . . . . . . . . . . . . CLC 11, 47
See also CAP 2; CA 19-20;
obituary CA 25-28R; SATA 19; DLB 10,
19

Maso, Carole    19??- . . . . . . . . . . . . . . CLC 44

Mason, Bobbie Ann
1940- . . . . . . . . . . . . . CLC 28, 43; SSC 4
See also CANR 11; CA 53-56; SAAS 1;
DLB-Y 87

Mason, Nick    1945-. . . . . . . . . . . . . . . CLC 35
See also Pink Floyd

Mason, Tally    1909-1971
See Derleth, August (William)

Masters, Edgar Lee
1868?-1950. . . . . . . . . TCLC 2, 25; PC 1
See also CA 104; DLB 54;
CDALB 1865-1917

Masters, Hilary    1928- . . . . . . . . . . . . CLC 48
See also CANR 13; CA 25-28R

Mastrosimone, William    19??- . . . . . . CLC 36

Matheson, Richard (Burton)
1926- . . . . . . . . . . . . . . . . . . . . . CLC 37
See also CA 97-100; DLB 8, 44

Mathews, Harry    1930-. . . . . . . . . . CLC 6, 52
See also CAAS 6; CANR 18; CA 21-24R

Mathias, Roland (Glyn)    1915-. . . . . . CLC 45
See also CANR 19; CA 97-100; DLB 27

Matthews, Greg    1949- . . . . . . . . . . . . CLC 45

Matthews, William    1942-. . . . . . . . . CLC 40
See also CANR 12; CA 29-32R; DLB 5

Matthias, John (Edward)    1941 . . . . . . CLC 9
See also CA 33-36R

Matthiessen, Peter
1927- . . . . . . . . . . . CLC 5, 7, 11, 32, 64
See also CANR 21; CA 9-12R; SATA 27;
DLB 6

Maturin, Charles Robert
1780?-1824. . . . . . . . . . . . . . . . . NCLC 6

Matute, Ana Maria    1925- . . . . . . . . CLC 11
See also CA 89-92

Maugham, W(illiam) Somerset
1874-1965 . . . . . . . . . . . . . CLC 1, 11, 15
See also CA 5-8R; obituary CA 25-28R;
DLB 10, 36

Maupassant, (Henri Rene Albert) Guy de
1850-1893 . . . . . . . . . . . NCLC 1; SSC 1

Mauriac, Claude    1914-. . . . . . . . . . . . CLC 9
See also CA 89-92; DLB 83

Mauriac, Francois (Charles)
1885-1970 . . . . . . . . . . . . . CLC 4, 9, 56
See also CAP 2; CA 25-28; DLB 65

Mavor, Osborne Henry    1888-1951
See Bridie, James
See also CA 104

Maxwell, William (Keepers, Jr.)
1908- . . . . . . . . . . . . . . . . . . . . . CLC 19
See also CA 93-96; DLB-Y 80

May, Elaine    1932- . . . . . . . . . . . . . . CLC 16
See also CA 124; DLB 44

Mayakovsky, Vladimir (Vladimirovich)
1893-1930 . . . . . . . . . . . . . . TCLC 4, 18
See also CA 104

Mayhew, Henry    1812-1887 . . . . . . NCLC 31
See also DLB 18, 55

Maynard, Joyce    1953-. . . . . . . . . . . . CLC 23
See also CA 111, 129

Mayne, William (James Carter)
1928- . . . . . . . . . . . . . . . . . . . . . CLC 12
See also CA 9-12R; SATA 6

Mayo, Jim    1908?-
See L'Amour, Louis (Dearborn)

Maysles, Albert    1926- and Maysles, David
1926- . . . . . . . . . . . . . . . . . . . . . CLC 16
See also CA 29-32R

Maysles, Albert    1926- . . . . . . . . . . . CLC 16
See also Maysles, Albert and Maysles,
David
See also CA 29-32R

Maysles, David    1932-. . . . . . . . . . . . CLC 16
See also Maysles, Albert and Maysles,
David

Mazer, Norma Fox    1931- . . . . . . . . CLC 26
See also CLR 23; CANR 12; CA 69-72;
SAAS 1; SATA 24

McAuley, James (Phillip)
1917-1976 . . . . . . . . . . . . . . . . . . CLC 45
See also CA 97-100

McBain, Ed    1926-
See Hunter, Evan

McBrien, William    1930- . . . . . . . . . CLC 44
See also CA 107

McCaffrey, Anne    1926 . . . . . . . . . . CLC 17
See also CANR 15; CA 25-28R; SATA 8;
DLB 8

McCarthy, Cormac    1933-. . . . . . . . CLC 4, 57
See also CANR 10; CA 13-16R; DLB 6

McCarthy, Mary (Therese)
1912-1989-. . . CLC 1, 3, 5, 14, 24, 39, 59
See also CANR 16; CA 5-8R;
obituary CA 129; DLB 2; DLB-Y 81

McCartney, (James) Paul
1942- . . . . . . . . . . . . . . . . . . CLC 12, 35

McCauley, Stephen    19??-. . . . . . . . . CLC 50

McClure, Michael    1932- . . . . . . . . CLC 6, 10
See also CANR 17; CA 21-24R; DLB 16

McCorkle, Jill (Collins)    1958-. . . . . . CLC 51
See also CA 121; DLB-Y 87

McCourt, James    1941-. . . . . . . . . . . . CLC 5
See also CA 57-60

McCoy, Horace    1897-1955 . . . . . . . TCLC 28
See also CA 108; DLB 9

McCrae, John    1872-1918. . . . . . . . . TCLC 12
See also CA 109; DLB 92

McCullers, (Lula) Carson (Smith)
1917-1967 . . . . . . . CLC 1, 4, 10, 12, 48
See also CANR 18; CA 5-8R;
obituary CA 25-28R; CABS 1; SATA 27;
DLB 2, 7; CDALB 1941-1968

McCullough, Colleen    1938?- . . . . . . . CLC 27
See also CANR 17; CA 81-84

McElroy, Joseph (Prince)
1930- . . . . . . . . . . . . . . . . . . . CLC 5, 47
See also CA 17-20R

McEwan, Ian (Russell)    1948- . . . . . . CLC 13
See also CANR 14; CA 61-64; DLB 14

McFadden, David    1940-. . . . . . . . . . . CLC 48
See also CA 104; DLB 60

McFarland, Dennis    1956- . . . . . . . . . CLC 65

McGahern, John    1934-. . . . . . . . CLC 5, 9, 48
See also CANR 29; CA 17-20R; DLB 14

McGinley, Patrick    1937-. . . . . . . . . . CLC 41
See also CA 120, 127

McGinley, Phyllis    1905-1978 . . . . . . CLC 14
See also CANR 19; CA 9-12R;
obituary CA 77-80; SATA 2, 44;
obituary SATA 24; DLB 11, 48

McGinniss, Joe    1942-. . . . . . . . . . . . CLC 32
See also CANR 26; CA 25-28R

McGivern, Maureen Daly    1921-
See Daly, Maureen
See also CA 9-12R

McGrath, Patrick    1950-. . . . . . . . . . . CLC 55

McGrath, Thomas    1916- . . . . . . . CLC 28, 59
See also CANR 6; CA 9-12R, 130;
SATA 41

McGuane, Thomas (Francis III)
1939- . . . . . . . . . . . . . . . CLC 3, 7, 18, 45
See also CANR 5, 24; CA 49-52; DLB 2;
DLB-Y 80

McGuckian, Medbh    1950-. . . . . . . . . CLC 48
See also DLB 40

McHale, Tom    1941-1982. . . . . . . . . CLC 3, 5
See also CA 77-80; obituary CA 106

McIlvanney, William    1936-. . . . . . . . CLC 42
See also CA 25-28R; DLB 14

McIlwraith, Maureen Mollie Hunter    1922-
See Hunter, Mollie
See also CA 29-32R; SATA 2

McInerney, Jay    1955- . . . . . . . . . . . . CLC 34
See also CA 116, 123

McIntyre, Vonda N(eel)    1948- . . . . . CLC 18
See also CANR 17; CA 81-84

McKay, Claude
1889-1948 . . . . . . . . . . TCLC 7, 41; PC 2
See also CA 104, 124; DLB 4, 45, 51

**McKuen, Rod** 1933-............. CLC 1, 3
See also CA 41-44R

**McLuhan, (Herbert) Marshall**
1911-1980 ................... CLC 37
See also CANR 12; CA 9-12R;
obituary CA 102; DLB 88

**McManus, Declan Patrick** 1955-
See Costello, Elvis

**McMillan, Terry** 1951- ....... CLC 50, 61

**McMurtry, Larry (Jeff)**
1936- .......... CLC 2, 3, 7, 11, 27, 44
See also CANR 19; CA 5-8R; DLB 2;
DLB-Y 80, 87; CDALB 1968-1987

**McNally, Terrence** 1939-...... CLC 4, 7, 41
See also CANR 2; CA 45-48; DLB 7

**McPhee, John** 1931-............. CLC 36
See also CANR 20; CA 65-68

**McPherson, James Alan** 1943- ..... CLC 19
See also CANR 24; CA 25-28R; DLB 38

**McPherson, William** 1939- ........ CLC 34
See also CA 57-60

**McSweeney, Kerry** 19??-.......... CLC 34

**Mead, Margaret** 1901-1978........ CLC 37
See also CANR 4; CA 1-4R;
obituary CA 81-84; SATA 20

**Meaker, M. J.** 1927-
See Kerr, M. E.; Meaker, Marijane

**Meaker, Marijane** 1927-
See Kerr, M. E.
See also CA 107; SATA 20

**Medoff, Mark (Howard)** 1940- ... CLC 6, 23
See also CANR 5; CA 53-56; DLB 7

**Megged, Aharon** 1920-............. CLC 9
See also CANR 1; CA 49-52

**Mehta, Ved (Parkash)** 1934- ....... CLC 37
See also CANR 2, 23; CA 1-4R

**Mellor, John** 1953?-
See The Clash

**Meltzer, Milton** 1915- ............ CLC 26
See also CLR 13; CA 13-16R; SAAS 1;
SATA 1, 50; DLB 61

**Melville, Herman**
1819-1891 ...... NCLC 3, 12, 29; SSC 1
See also SATA 59; DLB 3, 74;
CDALB 1640-1865

**Membreno, Alejandro** 1972- ....... CLC 59

**Mencken, H(enry) L(ouis)**
1880-1956 ................... TCLC 13
See also CA 105, 125; DLB 11, 29, 63;
CDALB 1917-1929

**Mercer, David** 1928-1980........... CLC 5
See also CANR 23; CA 9-12R;
obituary CA 102; DLB 13

**Meredith, George** 1828-1909...... TCLC 17
See also CA 117; DLB 18, 35, 57

**Meredith, William (Morris)**
1919- .............. CLC 4, 13, 22, 55
See also CANR 6; CA 9-12R; DLB 5

**Merezhkovsky, Dmitri**
1865-1941 ................. TCLC 29

**Merimee, Prosper**
1803-1870 ........... NCLC 6; SSC 7

**Merkin, Daphne** 1954-............ CLC 44
See also CANR 123

**Merrill, James (Ingram)**
1926- ........ CLC 2, 3, 6, 8, 13, 18, 34
See also CANR 10; CA 13-16R; DLB 5;
DLB-Y 85

**Merton, Thomas (James)**
1915-1968 ............ CLC 1, 3, 11, 34
See also CANR 22; CA 5-8R;
obituary CA 25-28R; DLB 48; DLB-Y 81

**Merwin, W(illiam) S(tanley)**
1927- ...... CLC 1, 2, 3, 5, 8, 13, 18, 45
See also CANR 15; CA 13-16R; DLB 5

**Metcalf, John** 1938-.............. CLC 37
See also CA 113; DLB 60

**Mew, Charlotte (Mary)**
1870-1928 .................. TCLC 8
See also CA 105; DLB 19

**Mewshaw, Michael** 1943-.......... CLC 9
See also CANR 7; CA 53-56; DLB-Y 80

**Meyer-Meyrink, Gustav** 1868-1932
See Meyrink, Gustav
See also CA 117

**Meyers, Jeffrey** 1939- ............. CLC 39
See also CA 73-76

**Meynell, Alice (Christiana Gertrude**
**Thompson)** 1847-1922 ........ TCLC 6
See also CA 104; DLB 19

**Meyrink, Gustav** 1868-1932...... TCLC 21
See also Meyer-Meyrink, Gustav

**Michaels, Leonard** 1933-......... CLC 6, 25
See also CANR 21; CA 61-64

**Michaux, Henri** 1899-1984 ...... CLC 8, 19
See also CA 85-88; obituary CA 114

**Michelangelo** 1475-1564........... LC 12

**Michelet, Jules** 1798-1874....... NCLC 31

**Michener, James A(lbert)**
1907- ............ CLC 1, 5, 11, 29, 60
See also CANR 21; CA 5-8R; DLB 6

**Mickiewicz, Adam** 1798-1855 ..... NCLC 3

**Middleton, Christopher** 1926- ...... CLC 13
See also CANR 29; CA 13-16R; DLB 40

**Middleton, Stanley** 1919-........ CLC 7, 38
See also CANR 21; CA 25-28R; DLB 14

**Migueis, Jose Rodrigues** 1901-..... CLC 10

**Mikszath, Kalman** 1847-1910 ..... TCLC 31

**Miles, Josephine (Louise)**
1911-1985 ........ CLC 1, 2, 14, 34, 39
See also CANR 2; CA 1-4R;
obituary CA 116; DLB 48

**Mill, John Stuart** 1806-1873..... NCLC 11
See also DLB 55

**Millar, Kenneth** 1915-1983 ........ CLC 14
See also Macdonald, Ross
See also CANR 16; CA 9-12R;
obituary CA 110; DLB 2; DLB-Y 83;
DLB-DS 6

**Millay, Edna St. Vincent**
1892-1950 ................... TCLC 4
See also CA 103; DLB 45;
CDALB 1917-1929

**Miller, Arthur**
1915- ...... CLC 1, 2, 6, 10, 15, 26, 47;
DC 1
See also CANR 2, 30; CA 1-4R; CABS 3;
DLB 7; CDALB 1941-1968

**Miller, Henry (Valentine)**
1891-1980 ...... CLC 1, 2, 4, 9, 14, 43
See also CA 9-12R; obituary CA 97-100;
DLB 4, 9; DLB-Y 80; CDALB 1929-1941

**Miller, Jason** 1939?-.............. CLC 2
See also CA 73-76; DLB 7

**Miller, Sue** 19??-................. CLC 44

**Miller, Walter M(ichael), Jr.**
1923- ...................... CLC 4, 30
See also CA 85-88; DLB 8

**Millhauser, Steven** 1943-....... CLC 21, 54
See also CA 108, 110, 111; DLB 2

**Millin, Sarah Gertrude** 1889-1968 .. CLC 49
See also CA 102; obituary CA 93-96

**Milne, A(lan) A(lexander)**
1882-1956 ................... TCLC 6
See also CLR 1; YABC 1; CA 104;
DLB 10, 77

**Milner, Ron(ald)** 1938-............ CLC 56
See also CANR 24; CA 73-76; DLB 38

**Milosz Czeslaw**
1911- ........... CLC 5, 11, 22, 31, 56
See also CANR 23; CA 81-84

**Milton, John** 1608-1674............. LC 9

**Miner, Valerie (Jane)** 1947-........ CLC 40
See also CA 97-100

**Minot, Susan** 1956- ............... CLC 44

**Minus, Ed** 1938-................. CLC 39

**Miro (Ferrer), Gabriel (Francisco Victor)**
1879-1930 ................... TCLC 5
See also CA 104

**Mishima, Yukio**
1925-1970 .... CLC 2, 4, 6, 9, 27; DC 1;
SSC 4
See also Hiraoka, Kimitake

**Mistral, Gabriela** 1889-1957 ....... TCLC 2
See also CA 104

**Mitchell, James Leslie** 1901-1935
See Gibbon, Lewis Grassic
See also CA 104; DLB 15

**Mitchell, Joni** 1943-.............. CLC 12
See also CA 112

**Mitchell (Marsh), Margaret (Munnerlyn)**
1900-1949 ................... TCLC 11
See also CA 109, 125; DLB 9

**Mitchell, S. Weir** 1829-1914...... TCLC 36

**Mitchell, W(illiam) O(rmond)**
1914- ...................... CLC 25
See also CANR 15; CA 77-80; DLB 88

**Mitford, Mary Russell** 1787-1855.. NCLC 4

**Mitford, Nancy** 1904-1973........ CLC 44
See also CA 9-12R

**Miyamoto Yuriko** 1899-1951...... TCLC 37

**Mo, Timothy** 1950-............... CLC 46
See also CA 117

**Modarressi, Taghi** 1931- .......... CLC 44
See also CA 121

**Modiano, Patrick (Jean)** 1945-..... CLC 18
See also CANR 17; CA 85-88; DLB 83

**Mofolo, Thomas (Mokopu)**
1876-1948 ................... TCLC 22
See also CA 121

**Mohr, Nicholasa** 1935-............ **CLC 12**
See also CLR 22; CANR 1; CA 49-52;
SAAS 8; SATA 8

**Mojtabai, A(nn) G(race)**
1938-................**CLC 5, 9, 15, 29**
See also CA 85-88

**Moliere** 1622-1673 ............... **LC 10**

**Molnar, Ferenc** 1878-1952....... **TCLC 20**
See also CA 109

**Momaday, N(avarre) Scott**
1934-....................**CLC 2, 19**
See also CANR 14; CA 25-28R; SATA 30,
48

**Monroe, Harriet** 1860-1936...... **TCLC 12**
See also CA 109; DLB 54, 91

**Montagu, Elizabeth** 1720-1800 .... **NCLC 7**

**Montagu, Lady Mary (Pierrepont) Wortley**
1689-1762 ..................... **LC 9**

**Montague, John (Patrick)**
1929-....................**CLC 13, 46**
See also CANR 9; CA 9-12R; DLB 40

**Montaigne, Michel (Eyquem) de**
1533-1592 .................... **LC 8**

**Montale, Eugenio** 1896-1981... **CLC 7, 9, 18**
See also CANR 30; CA 17-20R;
obituary CA 104

**Montgomery, Marion (H., Jr.)**
1925-.................... **CLC 7**
See also CANR 3; CA 1-4R; DLB 6

**Montgomery, Robert Bruce** 1921-1978
See Crispin, Edmund
See also CA 104

**Montherlant, Henri (Milon) de**
1896-1972 ................. **CLC 8, 19**
See also CA 85-88; obituary CA 37-40R;
DLB 72

**Montisquieu, Charles-Louis de Secondat**
1689-1755 ..................... **LC 7**

**Monty Python**.................. **CLC 21**

**Moodie, Susanna (Strickland)**
1803-1885 ................. **NCLC 14**

**Mooney, Ted** 1951-.............. **CLC 25**

**Moorcock, Michael (John)**
1939-.............. **CLC 5, 27, 58**
See also CAAS 5; CANR 2, 17; CA 45-48;
DLB 14

**Moore, Brian**
1921-......... **CLC 1, 3, 5, 7, 8, 19, 32**
See also CANR 1, 25; CA 1-4R

**Moore, George (Augustus)**
1852-1933 .................. **TCLC 7**
See also CA 104; DLB 10, 18, 57

**Moore, Lorrie** 1957-.......... **CLC 39, 45**
See also Moore, Marie Lorena

**Moore, Marianne (Craig)**
1887-1972 ... **CLC 1, 2, 4, 8, 10, 13, 19,
47**
See also CANR 3; CA 1-4R;
obituary CA 33-36R; SATA 20; DLB 45;
CDALB 1929-1941

**Moore, Marie Lorena** 1957-
See Moore, Lorrie
See also CA 116

**Moore, Thomas** 1779-1852....... **NCLC 6**

**Morand, Paul** 1888-1976 ......... **CLC 41**
See also obituary CA 69-72; DLB 65

**Morante, Elsa** 1918-1985....... **CLC 8, 47**
See also CA 85-88; obituary CA 117

**Moravia, Alberto**
1907-........ **CLC 2, 7, 11, 18, 27, 46**
See also Pincherle, Alberto

**More, Hannah** 1745-1833 ....... **NCLC 27**

**More, Henry** 1614-1687............ **LC 9**

**More, (Sir) Thomas** 1478-1535 ..... **LC 10**

**Moreas, Jean** 1856-1910 ......... **TCLC 18**

**Morgan, Berry** 1919-............. **CLC 6**
See also CA 49-52; DLB 6

**Morgan, Edwin (George)** 1920-..... **CLC 31**
See also CANR 3; CA 7-8R; DLB 27

**Morgan, (George) Frederick**
1922-..................... **CLC 23**
See also CANR 21; CA 17-20R

**Morgan, Janet** 1945-............. **CLC 39**
See also CA 65-68

**Morgan, Lady** 1776?-1859....... **NCLC 29**

**Morgan, Robin** 1941-............. **CLC 2**
See also CA 69-72

**Morgan, Seth** 1949-1990 ......... **CLC 65**
See also CA 132

**Morgenstern, Christian (Otto Josef Wolfgang)**
1871-1914 .................. **TCLC 8**
See also CA 105

**Moricz, Zsigmond** 1879-1942 ..... **TCLC 33**

**Morike, Eduard (Friedrich)**
1804-1875 ................. **NCLC 10**

**Mori Ogai** 1862-1922............ **TCLC 14**
See also Mori Rintaro

**Mori Rintaro** 1862-1922
See Mori Ogai
See also CA 110

**Moritz, Karl Philipp** 1756-1793 ...... **LC 2**

**Morris, Julian** 1916-
See West, Morris L.

**Morris, Steveland Judkins** 1950-
See Wonder, Stevie
See also CA 111

**Morris, William** 1834-1896 ....... **NCLC 4**
See also DLB 18, 35, 57

**Morris, Wright (Marion)**
1910-............. **CLC 1, 3, 7, 18, 37**
See also CANR 21; CA 9-12R; DLB 2;
DLB-Y 81

**Morrison, James Douglas** 1943-1971
See Morrison, Jim
See also CA 73-76

**Morrison, Jim** 1943-1971......... **CLC 17**
See also Morrison, James Douglas

**Morrison, Toni** 1931-..... **CLC 4, 10, 22, 55**
See also CANR 27; CA 29-32R; DLB 6, 33;
DLB-Y 81; CDALB 1968-1987; AAYA 1

**Morrison, Van** 1945-............. **CLC 21**
See also CA 116

**Mortimer, John (Clifford)**
1923-.................... **CLC 28, 43**
See also CANR 21; CA 13-16R; DLB 13

**Mortimer, Penelope (Ruth)** 1918-.... **CLC 5**
See also CA 57-60

**Mosher, Howard Frank** 19??-...... **CLC 62**

**Mosley, Nicholas** 1923-........... **CLC 43**
See also CA 69-72; DLB 14

**Moss, Howard**
1922-1987 .......... **CLC 7, 14, 45, 50**
See also CANR 1; CA 1-4R;
obituary CA 123; DLB 5

**Motion, Andrew (Peter)** 1952-...... **CLC 47**
See also DLB 40

**Motley, Willard (Francis)**
1912-1965 ................. **CLC 18**
See also CA 117; obituary CA 106; DLB 76

**Mott, Michael (Charles Alston)**
1930-.................... **CLC 15, 34**
See also CAAS 7; CANR 7, 29; CA 5-8R

**Mowat, Farley (McGill)** 1921- ..... **CLC 26**
See also CLR 20; CANR 4, 24; CA 1-4R;
SATA 3, 55; DLB 68; AAYA 1

**Mphahlele, Es'kia** 1919-
See Mphahlele, Ezekiel

**Mphahlele, Ezekiel** 1919-......... **CLC 25**
See also CA 81-84

**Mqhayi, S(amuel) E(dward) K(rune Loliwe)**
1875-1945 ................. **TCLC 25**

**Mrozek, Slawomir** 1930- ....... **CLC 3, 13**
See also CAAS 10; CANR 29; CA 13-16R

**Mtwa, Percy** 19??-.............. **CLC 47**

**Mueller, Lisel** 1924-........... **CLC 13, 51**
See also CA 93-96

**Muir, Edwin** 1887-1959........... **TCLC 2**
See also CA 104; DLB 20

**Muir, John** 1838-1914 .......... **TCLC 28**

**Mujica Lainez, Manuel**
1910-1984 .................. **CLC 31**
See also CA 81-84; obituary CA 112

**Mukherjee, Bharati** 1940-......... **CLC 53**
See also CA 107; DLB 60

**Muldoon, Paul** 1951-............. **CLC 32**
See also CA 113, 129; DLB 40

**Mulisch, Harry (Kurt Victor)**
1927-..................... **CLC 42**
See also CANR 6, 26; CA 9-12R

**Mull, Martin** 1943-.............. **CLC 17**
See also CA 105

**Munford, Robert** 1737?-1783......... **LC 5**
See also DLB 31

**Munro, Alice (Laidlaw)**
1931-........ **CLC 6, 10, 19, 50; SSC 3**
See also CA 33-36R; SATA 29; DLB 53

**Munro, H(ector) H(ugh)** 1870-1916
See Saki
See also CA 104; DLB 34

**Murasaki, Lady** c. 11th century-... **CMLC 1**

**Murdoch, (Jean) Iris**
1919-...... **CLC 1, 2, 3, 4, 6, 8, 11, 15,
22, 31, 51**
See also CANR 8; CA 13-16R; DLB 14

**Murphy, Richard** 1927-........... **CLC 41**
See also CA 29-32R; DLB 40

**Murphy, Sylvia** 19??-............. **CLC 34**

**Murphy, Thomas (Bernard)** 1935-... **CLC 51**
See also CA 101

**Murray, Les(lie) A(llan)**   1938-  .....  **CLC 40**
See also CANR 11, 27; CA 21-24R

**Murry, John Middleton**
1889-1957 ..................  **TCLC 16**
See also CA 118

**Musgrave, Susan**   1951-  ........  **CLC 13, 54**
See also CA 69-72

**Musil, Robert (Edler von)**
1880-1942 ..................  **TCLC 12**
See also CA 109; DLB 81

**Musset, (Louis Charles) Alfred de**
1810-1857 ..................  **NCLC 7**

**Myers, Walter Dean**   1937-  ........  **CLC 35**
See also CLR 4, 16; CANR 20; CA 33-36R;
SAAS 2; SATA 27, 41; DLB 33; AAYA 4

**Nabokov, Vladimir (Vladimirovich)**
1899-1977  ....  **CLC 1, 2, 3, 6, 8, 11, 15,**
**23, 44, 46, 64**
See also CANR 20; CA 5-8R;
obituary CA 69-72; DLB 2; DLB-Y 80;
DLB-DS 3; CDALB 1941-1968

**Nagy, Laszlo**   1925-1978 ...........  **CLC 7**
See also CA 129; obituary CA 112

**Naipaul, Shiva(dhar Srinivasa)**
1945-1985 ...............  **CLC 32, 39**
See also CA 110, 112; obituary CA 116;
DLB-Y 85

**Naipaul, V(idiadhar) S(urajprasad)**
1932-  .........  **CLC 4, 7, 9, 13, 18, 37**
See also CANR 1; CA 1-4R; DLB-Y 85

**Nakos, Ioulia**   1899?-
See Nakos, Lilika

**Nakos, Lilika**   1899?-  .............  **CLC 29**

**Nakou, Lilika**   1899?-
See Nakos, Lilika

**Narayan, R(asipuram) K(rishnaswami)**
1906-  ........  **CLC 7, 28, 47**
See also CA 81-84

**Nash, (Fredric) Ogden**   1902-1971  ..  **CLC 23**
See also CAP 1; CA 13-14;
obituary CA 29-32R; SATA 2, 46;
DLB 11

**Nathan, George Jean**   1882-1958 ...  **TCLC 18**
See also CA 114

**Natsume, Kinnosuke**   1867-1916
See Natsume, Soseki
See also CA 104

**Natsume, Soseki**   1867-1916 .....  **TCLC 2, 10**
See also Natsume, Kinnosuke

**Natti, (Mary) Lee**   1919-
See Kingman, (Mary) Lee
See also CANR 2; CA 7-8R

**Naylor, Gloria**   1950-  .........  **CLC 28, 52**
See also CANR 27; CA 107

**Neff, Debra**   1972-................  **CLC 59**

**Neihardt, John G(neisenau)**
1881-1973 ..................  **CLC 32**
See also CAP 1; CA 13-14; DLB 9, 54

**Nekrasov, Nikolai Alekseevich**
1821-1878 ..................  **NCLC 11**

**Nelligan, Emile**   1879-1941 .......  **TCLC 14**
See also CA 114; DLB 92

**Nelson, Willie**   1933-..............  **CLC 17**
See also CA 107

**Nemerov, Howard**   1920-  ....  **CLC 2, 6, 9, 36**
See also CANR 1, 27; CA 1-4R; CABS 2;
DLB 5, 6; DLB-Y 83

**Neruda, Pablo**
1904-1973 .....  **CLC 1, 2, 5, 7, 9, 28, 62**
See also CAP 2; CA 19-20;
obituary CA 45-48

**Nerval, Gerard de**   1808-1855 ......  **NCLC 1**

**Nervo, (Jose) Amado (Rulz de)**
1870-1919 ..................  **TCLC 11**
See also CA 109

**Neufeld, John (Arthur)**   1938-  ......  **CLC 17**
See also CANR 11; CA 25-28R; SAAS 3;
SATA 6

**Neville, Emily Cheney**   1919-.......  **CLC 12**
See also CANR 3; CA 5-8R; SAAS 2;
SATA 1

**Newbound, Bernard Slade**   1930-
See Slade, Bernard
See also CA 81-84

**Newby, P(ercy) H(oward)**
1918-  ....................  **CLC 2, 13**
See also CA 5-8R; DLB 15

**Newlove, Donald**   1928-  ...........  **CLC 6**
See also CANR 25; CA 29-32R

**Newlove, John (Herbert)**   1938-.....  **CLC 14**
See also CANR 9, 25; CA 21-24R

**Newman, Charles**   1938-..........  **CLC 2, 8**
See also CA 21-24R

**Newman, Edwin (Harold)**   1919-  ....  **CLC 14**
See also CANR 5; CA 69-72

**Newton, Suzanne**   1936-...........  **CLC 35**
See also CANR 14; CA 41-44R; SATA 5

**Ngema, Mbongeni**   1955-  .........  **CLC 57**

**Ngugi, James (Thiong'o)**
1938-  ................  **CLC 3, 7, 13, 36**
See also Ngugi wa Thiong'o; Wa Thiong'o,
Ngugi
See also CANR 27; CA 81-84

**Ngugi wa Thiong'o**   1938-...  **CLC 3, 7, 13, 36**
See also Ngugi, James (Thiong'o); Wa
Thiong'o, Ngugi

**Nichol, B(arrie) P(hillip)**   1944-.....  **CLC 18**
See also CA 53-56; DLB 53

**Nichols, John (Treadwell)**   1940-  ....  **CLC 38**
See also CAAS 2; CANR 6; CA 9-12R;
DLB-Y 82

**Nichols, Peter (Richard)**
1927-  ..................  **CLC 5, 36, 65**
See also CANR 33; CA 104; DLB 13

**Nicolas, F.R.E.**   1927-
See Freeling, Nicolas

**Niedecker, Lorine**   1903-1970 ....  **CLC 10, 42**
See also CAP 2; CA 25-28; DLB 48

**Nietzsche, Friedrich (Wilhelm)**
1844-1900 ..............  **TCLC 10, 18**
See also CA 107, 121

**Nievo, Ippolito**   1831-1861 .......  **NCLC 22**

**Nightingale, Anne Redmon**   1943-
See Redmon (Nightingale), Anne
See also CA 103

**Nin, Anais**
1903-1977 ......  **CLC 1, 4, 8, 11, 14, 60**
See also CANR 22; CA 13-16R;
obituary CA 69-72; DLB 2, 4

**Nissenson, Hugh**   1933-...........  **CLC 4, 9**
See also CANR 27; CA 17-20R; DLB 28

**Niven, Larry**   1938-................  **CLC 8**
See also Niven, Laurence Van Cott
See also DLB 8

**Niven, Laurence Van Cott**   1938-
See Niven, Larry
See also CANR 14; CA 21-24R

**Nixon, Agnes Eckhardt**   1927-......  **CLC 21**
See also CA 110

**Nizan, Paul**   1905-1940...........  **TCLC 40**
See also DLB 72

**Nkosi, Lewis**   1936-...............  **CLC 45**
See also CANR 27; CA 65-68

**Nodier, (Jean) Charles (Emmanuel)**
1780-1844 ..................  **NCLC 19**

**Nolan, Christopher**   1965-..........  **CLC 58**
See also CA 111

**Nordhoff, Charles**   1887-1947 ......  **TCLC 23**
See also CA 108; SATA 23; DLB 9

**Norman, Marsha**   1947-  ...........  **CLC 28**
See also CA 105; CABS 3; DLB-Y 84

**Norris, (Benjamin) Frank(lin)**
1870-1902 ..................  **TCLC 24**
See also CA 110; DLB 12, 71;
CDALB 1865-1917

**Norris, Leslie**   1921-  .............  **CLC 14**
See also CANR 14; CAP 1; CA 11-12;
DLB 27

**North, Andrew**   1912-
See Norton, Andre

**North, Christopher**   1785-1854
See Wilson, John

**Norton, Alice Mary**   1912-
See Norton, Andre
See also CANR 2; CA 1-4R; SATA 1, 43

**Norton, Andre**   1912-  .............  **CLC 12**
See also Norton, Mary Alice
See also DLB 8, 52

**Norway, Nevil Shute**   1899-1960
See Shute (Norway), Nevil
See also CA 102; obituary CA 93-96

**Norwid, Cyprian Kamil**
1821-1883 ..................  **NCLC 17**

**Nossack, Hans Erich**   1901-1978 .....  **CLC 6**
See also CA 93-96; obituary CA 85-88;
DLB 69

**Nova, Craig**   1945-................  **CLC 7, 31**
See also CANR 2; CA 45-48

**Novak, Joseph**   1933-
See Kosinski, Jerzy (Nikodem)

**Novalis**   1772-1801 .............  **NCLC 13**

**Nowlan, Alden (Albert)**   1933-......  **CLC 15**
See also CANR 5; CA 9-12R; DLB 53

**Noyes, Alfred**   1880-1958 .........  **TCLC 7**
See also CA 104; DLB 20

**Nunn, Kem**   19??-................  **CLC 34**

**Nye, Robert**   1939-  .............  **CLC 13, 42**
See also CANR 29; CA 33-36R; SATA 6;
DLB 14**

**Nyro, Laura**   1947- . . . . . . . . . . . . . . **CLC 17**

**Oates, Joyce Carol**
1938- . . . . .  **CLC 1, 2, 3, 6, 9, 11, 15, 19,
33, 52; SSC 6**
See also CANR 25; CA 5-8R; DLB 2, 5;
DLB-Y 81; CDALB 1968-1987

**O'Brien, Darcy**   1939- . . . . . . . . . . . . **CLC 11**
See also CANR 8; CA 21-24R

**O'Brien, Edna**
1936- . . . . . . . . .  **CLC 3, 5, 8, 13, 36, 65**
See also CANR 6; CA 1-4R; DLB 14

**O'Brien, Fitz-James**   1828?-1862 . . **NCLC 21**
See also DLB 74

**O'Brien, Flann**
1911-1966 . . . . . . .  **CLC 1, 4, 5, 7, 10, 47**
See also O Nuallain, Brian

**O'Brien, Richard**   19??- . . . . . . . . . . . **CLC 17**
See also CA 124

**O'Brien, (William) Tim(othy)**
1946- . . . . . . . . . . . . . . . . . **CLC 7, 19, 40**
See also CA 85-88; DLB-Y 80

**Obstfelder, Sigbjorn**   1866-1900 . . . . **TCLC 23**
See also CA 123

**O'Casey, Sean**
1880-1964 . . . . . . . .  **CLC 1, 5, 9, 11, 15**
See also CA 89-92; DLB 10

**Ochs, Phil**   1940-1976 . . . . . . . . . . . . **CLC 17**
See also obituary CA 65-68

**O'Connor, Edwin (Greene)**
1918-1968 . . . . . . . . . . . . . . . . . . **CLC 14**
See also CA 93-96; obituary CA 25-28R

**O'Connor, (Mary) Flannery**
1925-1964 . . .  **CLC 1, 2, 3, 6, 10, 13, 15,
21; SSC 1**
See also CANR 3; CA 1-4R; DLB 2;
DLB-Y 80; CDALB 1941-1968

**O'Connor, Frank**
1903-1966 . . . . . . . .  **CLC 14, 23; SSC 5**
See also O'Donovan, Michael (John)
See also CA 93-96

**O'Dell, Scott**   1903- . . . . . . . . . . . . . . **CLC 30**
See also CLR 1, 16; CANR 12; CA 61-64;
SATA 12; DLB 52

**Odets, Clifford**   1906-1963 . . . . . . . **CLC 2, 28**
See also CA 85-88; DLB 7, 26

**O'Donovan, Michael (John)**
1903-1966 . . . . . . . . . . . . . . . . . . **CLC 14**
See also O'Connor, Frank
See also CA 93-96

**Oe, Kenzaburo**   1935- . . . . . . . . . . **CLC 10, 36**
See also CA 97-100

**O'Faolain, Julia**   1932- . . . . . . . **CLC 6, 19, 47**
See also CAAS 2; CANR 12; CA 81-84;
DLB 14

**O'Faolain, Sean**   1900- . . . . .  **CLC 1, 7, 14, 32**
See also CANR 12; CA 61-64; DLB 15

**O'Flaherty, Liam**
1896-1984 . . . . . . . . .  **CLC 5, 34; SSC 6**
See also CA 101; obituary CA 113; DLB 36;
DLB-Y 84

**O'Grady, Standish (James)**
1846-1928 . . . . . . . . . . . . . . . . . **TCLC 5**
See also CA 104

**O'Grady, Timothy**   1951- . . . . . . . . . **CLC 59**

**O'Hara, Frank**   1926-1966 . . . . . **CLC 2, 5, 13**
See also CA 9-12R; obituary CA 25-28R;
DLB 5, 16; CDALB 1929-1941

**O'Hara, John (Henry)**
1905-1970 . . . . . . .  **CLC 1, 2, 3, 6, 11, 42**
See also CA 5-8R; obituary CA 25-28R;
DLB 9; DLB-DS 2; CDALB 1929-1941

**O'Hara Family**
See Banim, John and Banim, Michael

**O'Hehir, Diana**   1922- . . . . . . . . . . . . **CLC 41**
See also CA 93-96

**Okigbo, Christopher (Ifenayichukwu)**
1932-1967 . . . . . . . . . . . . . . . . . . **CLC 25**
See also CA 77-80

**Olds, Sharon**   1942- . . . . . . . . . . . **CLC 32, 39**
See also CANR 18; CA 101

**Olesha, Yuri (Karlovich)**
1899-1960 . . . . . . . . . . . . . . . . . . **CLC 8**
See also CA 85-88

**Oliphant, Margaret (Oliphant Wilson)**
1828-1897 . . . . . . . . . . . . . . . . **NCLC 11**
See also DLB 18

**Oliver, Mary**   1935- . . . . . . . . . . . . **CLC 19, 34**
See also CANR 9; CA 21-24R; DLB 5

**Olivier, (Baron) Laurence (Kerr)**
1907- . . . . . . . . . . . . . . . . . . . . . . **CLC 20**
See also CA 111, 129

**Olsen, Tillie**   1913- . . . . . . . . . . . . . **CLC 4, 13**
See also CANR 1; CA 1-4R; DLB 28;
DLB-Y 80

**Olson, Charles (John)**
1910-1970 . . . . .  **CLC 1, 2, 5, 6, 9, 11, 29**
See also CAP 1; CA 15-16;
obituary CA 25-28R; CABS 2; DLB 5, 16

**Olson, Theodore**   1937-
See Olson, Toby

**Olson, Toby**   1937- . . . . . . . . . . . . . . **CLC 28**
See also CANR 9; CA 65-68

**Ondaatje, (Philip) Michael**
1943- . . . . . . . . . . . . . . . **CLC 14, 29, 51**
See also CA 77-80; DLB 60

**Oneal, Elizabeth**   1934- . . . . . . . . . . . **CLC 30**
See also Oneal, Zibby
See also CLR 13; CA 106; SATA 30

**Oneal, Zibby**   1934- . . . . . . . . . . . . . . **CLC 30**
See also Oneal, Elizabeth

**O'Neill, Eugene (Gladstone)**
1888-1953 . . . . . . . . . . . . . **TCLC 1, 6, 27**
See also CA 110; DLB 7;
CDALB 1929-1941

**Onetti, Juan Carlos**   1909- . . . . . . . **CLC 7, 10**
See also CA 85-88

**O'Nolan, Brian**   1911-1966
See O'Brien, Flann

**O Nuallain, Brian**   1911-1966
See O'Brien, Flann
See also CAP 2; CA 21-22;
obituary CA 25-28R

**Oppen, George**   1908-1984 . . . . **CLC 7, 13, 34**
See also CANR 8; CA 13-16R;
obituary CA 113; DLB 5

**Orlovitz, Gil**   1918-1973 . . . . . . . . . . **CLC 22**
See also CA 77-80; obituary CA 45-48;
DLB 2, 5

**Ortega y Gasset, Jose**   1883-1955 . . . **TCLC 9**
See also CA 106, 130

**Ortiz, Simon J.**   1941- . . . . . . . . . . . . **CLC 45**

**Orton, Joe**   1933?-1967 . . . . . . . **CLC 4, 13, 43**
See also Orton, John Kingsley
See also DLB 13

**Orton, John Kingsley**   1933?-1967
See Orton, Joe
See also CA 85-88

**Orwell, George**
1903-1950 . . . . . . . . .  **TCLC 2, 6, 15, 31**
See also Blair, Eric Arthur
See also DLB 15

**Osborne, John (James)**
1929- . . . . . . . . . . . . . **CLC 1, 2, 5, 11, 45**
See also CANR 21; CA 13-16R; DLB 13

**Osborne, Lawrence**   1958- . . . . . . . . . **CLC 50**

**Osceola**   1885-1962
See Dinesen, Isak; Blixen, Karen
(Christentze Dinesen)

**Oshima, Nagisa**   1932- . . . . . . . . . . . . **CLC 20**
See also CA 116

**Oskison, John M.**   1874-1947 . . . . . . **TCLC 35**

**Ossoli, Sarah Margaret (Fuller marchesa d')**
1810-1850
See Fuller, (Sarah) Margaret
See also SATA 25

**Ostrovsky, Alexander**
1823-1886 . . . . . . . . . . . . . . . . **NCLC 30**

**Otero, Blas de**   1916- . . . . . . . . . . . . . **CLC 11**
See also CA 89-92

**Ovid**   43 B.C.-c. 18 A.D. . . . . **CMLC 7; PC 2**

**Owen, Wilfred (Edward Salter)**
1893-1918 . . . . . . . . . . . . . . . . **TCLC 5, 27**
See also CA 104; DLB 20

**Owens, Rochelle**   1936- . . . . . . . . . . . . **CLC 8**
See also CAAS 2; CA 17-20R

**Owl, Sebastian**   1939-
See Thompson, Hunter S(tockton)

**Oz, Amos**   1939- . . .  **CLC 5, 8, 11, 27, 33, 54**
See also CANR 27; CA 53-56

**Ozick, Cynthia**   1928- . . . . . .  **CLC 3, 7, 28, 62**
See also CANR 23; CA 17-20R; DLB 28;
DLB-Y 82

**Ozu, Yasujiro**   1903-1963 . . . . . . . . . . **CLC 16**
See also CA 112

**Pa Chin**   1904- . . . . . . . . . . . . . . . . . . **CLC 18**
See also Li Fei-kan

**Pack, Robert**   1929- . . . . . . . . . . . . . . **CLC 13**
See also CANR 3; CA 1-4R; DLB 5

**Padgett, Lewis**   1915-1958
See Kuttner, Henry

**Padilla, Heberto**   1932- . . . . . . . . . . . **CLC 38**
See also CA 123

**Page, Jimmy**   1944- . . . . . . . . . . . . . . **CLC 12**

**Page, Louise**   1955- . . . . . . . . . . . . . . **CLC 40**

**Page, P(atricia) K(athleen)**
1916- . . . . . . . . . . . . . . . . . . . **CLC 7, 18**
See also CANR 4, 22; CA 53-56; DLB 68

**Paget, Violet**   1856-1935
See Lee, Vernon
See also CA 104

Palamas, Kostes  1859-1943 . . . . . . . . TCLC 5
See also CA 105

Palazzeschi, Aldo  1885-1974 . . . . . . . CLC 11
See also CA 89-92; obituary CA 53-56

Paley, Grace  1922- . . . . . . . . . . CLC 4, 6, 37
See also CANR 13; CA 25-28R; DLB 28

Palin, Michael  1943- . . . . . . . . . . . . . CLC 21
See also Monty Python
Scc also CA 107

Palliser, Charles  1948?- . . . . . . . . . . CLC 65

Palma, Ricardo  1833-1919 . . . . . . . TCLC 29
See also CANR 123

Pancake, Breece Dexter  1952-1979
See Pancake, Breece D'J

Pancake, Breece D'J  1952-1979 . . . . CLC 29
See also obituary CA 109

Papadiamantis, Alexandros
1851-1911 . . . . . . . . . . . . . . . . . TCLC 29

Papini, Giovanni  1881-1956 . . . . . . . TCLC 22
See also CA 121

Paracelsus  1493-1541 . . . . . . . . . . . . . . LC 14

Parini, Jay (Lee)  1948- . . . . . . . . . . . CLC 54
See also CA 97-100

Parker, Dorothy (Rothschild)
1893-1967 . . . . . . . . . . . CLC 15; SSC 2
See also CAP 2; CA 19-20;
obituary CA 25-28R; DLB 11, 45. 86

Parker, Robert B(rown)  1932- . . . . . . CLC 27
See also CANR 1, 26; CA 49-52

Parkin, Frank  1940- . . . . . . . . . . . . . CLC 43

Parkman, Francis  1823-1893 . . . . . NCLC 12
See also DLB 1, 30

Parks, Gordon (Alexander Buchanan)
1912- . . . . . . . . . . . . . . . . . . . . CLC 1, 16
See also CANR 26; CA 41-44R; SATA 8;
DLB 33

Parnell, Thomas  1679-1718 . . . . . . . . . LC 3

Parra, Nicanor  1914- . . . . . . . . . . . . . CLC 2
See also CA 85-88

Pasolini, Pier Paolo
1922-1975 . . . . . . . . . . . . . . CLC 20, 37
See also CA 93-96; obituary CA 61-64

Pastan, Linda (Olenik)  1932- . . . . . . CLC 27
See also CANR 18; CA 61-64; DLB 5

Pasternak, Boris
1890-1960 . . . . . . . . . . CLC 7, 10, 18, 63
See also CA 127; obituary CA 116

Patchen, Kenneth  1911-1972 . . . CLC 1, 2, 18
See also CANR 3; CA 1-4R;
obituary CA 33-36R; DLB 16, 48

Pater, Walter (Horatio)
1839-1894 . . . . . . . . . . . . . . . . . NCLC 7
See also DLB 57

Paterson, Andrew Barton
1864-1941 . . . . . . . . . . . . . . . . . TCLC 32

Paterson, Katherine (Womeldorf)
1932- . . . . . . . . . . . . . . . . . CLC 12, 30
See also CLR 7; CANR 28; CA 21-24R;
SATA 13, 53; DLB 52; AAYA 1

Patmore, Coventry Kersey Dighton
1823-1896 . . . . . . . . . . . . . . . . . NCLC 9
See also DLB 35

Paton, Alan (Stewart)
1903-1988 . . . . . . . . . . CLC 4, 10, 25, 55
See also CANR 22; CAP 1; CA 15-16;
obituary CA 125; SATA 11

Paulding, James Kirke  1778-1860. . NCLC 2
See also DLB 3, 59, 74

Paulin, Tom  1949- . . . . . . . . . . . . . . CLC 37
See also CA 123; DLB 40

Paustovsky, Konstantin (Georgievich)
1892-1968 . . . . . . . . . . . . . . . . . CLC 40
See also CA 93-96; obituary CA 25-28R

Paustowsky, Konstantin (Georgievich)
1892-1968
See Paustovsky, Konstantin (Georgievich)

Pavese, Cesare  1908-1950 . . . . . . . . TCLC 3
See also CA 104

Pavic, Milorad  1929- . . . . . . . . . . . . CLC 60

Payne, Alan  1932-
See Jakes, John (William)

Paz, Octavio
1914- . . . . . . CLC 3, 4, 6, 10, 19, 51, 65;
PC 1
See also CANR 32; CA 73-76

Peacock, Molly  1947-. . . . . . . . . . . . CLC 60
See also CA 103

Peacock, Thomas Love
1785-1886 . . . . . . . . . . . . . . . . . NCLC 22

Peake, Mervyn  1911-1968 . . . . . . . CLC 7, 54
See also CANR 3; CA 5-8R;
obituary CA 25-28R; SATA 23; DLB 15

Pearce, (Ann) Philippa  1920-. . . . . . . CLC 21
See also Christie, (Ann) Philippa
See also CLR 9; CA 5-8R; SATA 1

Pearl, Eric  1934-
See Elman, Richard

Pearson, T(homas) R(eid)  1956- . . . . CLC 39
See also CA 120, 130

Peck, John  1941- . . . . . . . . . . . . . . . CLC 3
See also CANR 3; CA 49-52

Peck, Richard  1934-. . . . . . . . . . . . . CLC 21
See also CLR 15; CANR 19; CA 85-88;
SAAS 2; SATA 18; AAYA 1

Peck, Robert Newton  1928-. . . . . . . . CLC 17
See also CA 81-84; SAAS 1; SATA 21;
AAYA 3

Peckinpah, (David) Sam(uel)
1925-1984 . . . . . . . . . . . . . . . . . CLC 20
See also CA 109; obituary CA 114

Pedersen, Knut  1859-1952
See Hamsun, Knut
See also CA 104, 109, 119

Peguy, Charles (Pierre)
1873-1914 . . . . . . . . . . . . . . . . . TCLC 10
See also CA 107

Pepys, Samuel  1633-1703. . . . . . . . . . LC 11

Percy, Walker
1916-1990 . . . CLC 2, 3, 6, 8, 14, 18, 47,
65
See also CANR 1, 23; CA 1-4R;
obituary CA 131; DLB 2; DLB-Y 80

Perec, Georges  1936-1982 . . . . . . . . CLC 56
See also DLB 83

Pereda, Jose Maria de
1833-1906 . . . . . . . . . . . . . . . . . TCLC 16

Perelman, S(idney) J(oseph)
1904-1979 . . . CLC 3, 5, 9, 15, 23, 44, 49
See also CANR 18; CA 73-76;
obituary CA 89-92; DLB 11, 44

Peret, Benjamin  1899-1959 . . . . . . . TCLC 20
See also CA 117

Peretz, Isaac Leib  1852?-1915. . . . . TCLC 16
See also CA 109

Perez, Galdos Benito  1853-1920 . . . TCLC 27
See also CA 125

Perrault, Charles  1628-1703 . . . . . . . . LC 2
See also SATA 25

Perse, St.-John  1887-1975 . . . . CLC 4, 11, 46
See also Leger, (Marie-Rene) Alexis
Saint-Leger

Pesetsky, Bette  1932-. . . . . . . . . . . . CLC 28

Peshkov, Alexei Maximovich  1868-1936
See Gorky, Maxim
See also CA 105

Pessoa, Fernando (Antonio Nogueira)
1888-1935 . . . . . . . . . . . . . . . . . TCLC 27
See also CA 125

Peterkin, Julia (Mood)  1880-1961. . . CLC 31
See also CA 102; DLB 9

Peters, Joan K.  1945-. . . . . . . . . . . . CLC 39

Peters, Robert L(ouis)  1924-. . . . . . . . CLC 7
See also CAAS 8; CA 13-16R

Petofi, Sandor  1823-1849. . . . . . . . NCLC 21

Petrakis, Harry Mark  1923-. . . . . . . . CLC 3
See also CANR 4, 30; CA 9-12R

Petrov, Evgeny  1902-1942 . . . . . . . TCLC 21

Petry, Ann (Lane)  1908- . . . . . . CLC 1, 7, 18
See also CLR 12; CAAS 6; CANR 4;
CA 5-8R; SATA 5; DLB 76

Petursson, Halligrimur  1614-1674 . . . . LC 8

Philipson, Morris (H.)  1926-. . . . . . . CLC 53
See also CANR 4; CA 1-4R

Phillips, Jayne Anne  1952- . . . . . CLC 15, 33
See also CANR 24; CA 101; DLB-Y 80

Phillips, Robert (Schaeffer)  1938-. . . CLC 28
See also CANR 8; CA 17-20R

Pica, Peter  1925-
See Aldiss, Brian W(ilson)

Piccolo, Lucio  1901-1969. . . . . . . . . CLC 13
See also CA 97-100

Pickthall, Marjorie (Lowry Christie)
1883-1922 . . . . . . . . . . . . . . . . . TCLC 21
See also CA 107; DLB 92

Pico della Mirandola, Giovanni
1463-1494 . . . . . . . . . . . . . . . . . LC 15

Piercy, Marge
1936- . . . . . . . . CLC 3, 6, 14, 18, 27, 62
See also CAAS 1; CANR 13; CA 21-24R

Pilnyak, Boris  1894-1937?. . . . . . . TCLC 23

Pincherle, Alberto  1907- . . . . . . . CLC 11, 18
See also Moravia, Alberto
See also CA 25-28R

Pineda, Cecile  1942-. . . . . . . . . . . . . CLC 39
See also CA 118

Pinero, Miguel (Gomez)
1946-1988 . . . . . . . . . . . . . . . CLC 4, 55
See also CANR 29; CA 61-64;
obituary CA 125

Pinero, Sir Arthur Wing
　1855-1934 . . . . . . . . . . . . . . . . . TCLC 32
　See also CA 110; DLB 10

Pinget, Robert　1919- . . . . . . . CLC 7, 13, 37
　See also CA 85-88; DLB 83

Pink Floyd . . . . . . . . . . . . . . . . . . . . . CLC 35

Pinkney, Edward　1802-1828 . . . . . NCLC 31

Pinkwater, D(aniel) M(anus)
　1941- . . . . . . . . . . . . . . . . . . . . . . CLC 35
　See also Pinkwater, Manus
　See also CLR 4; CANR 12; CA 29-32R;
　　SAAS 3; SATA 46; AAYA 1

Pinkwater, Manus　1941-
　See Pinkwater, D(aniel) M(anus)
　See also SATA 8

Pinsky, Robert　1940- . . . . . . . . CLC 9, 19, 38
　See also CAAS 4; CA 29-32R; DLB-Y 82

Pinter, Harold
　1930- . . . . . CLC 1, 3, 6, 9, 11, 15, 27, 58
　See also CA 5-8R; DLB 13

Pirandello, Luigi　1867-1936 . . . . . TCLC 4, 29
　See also CA 104

Pirsig, Robert M(aynard)　1928- . . . CLC 4, 6
　See also CA 53-56; SATA 39

Pisarev, Dmitry Ivanovich
　1840-1868 . . . . . . . . . . . . . . . . . NCLC 25

Pix, Mary (Griffith)　1666-1709 . . . . . . . LC 8
　See also DLB 80

Plaidy, Jean　1906-
　See Hibbert, Eleanor (Burford)

Plant, Robert　1948- . . . . . . . . . . . . . CLC 12

Plante, David (Robert)
　1940- . . . . . . . . . . . . . . . . . CLC 7, 23, 38
　See also CANR 12; CA 37-40R; DLB-Y 83

Plath, Sylvia
　1932-1963 . . . . CLC 1, 2, 3, 5, 9, 11, 14,
　　　　　　　　　　17, 50, 51, 62; PC 1
　See also CAP 2; CA 19-20; DLB 5, 6;
　　CDALB 1941-1968

Platonov, Andrei (Platonovich)
　1899-1951 . . . . . . . . . . . . . . . . . TCLC 14
　See also Klimentov, Andrei Platonovich
　See also CA 108

Platt, Kin　1911- . . . . . . . . . . . . . . . CLC 26
　See also CANR 11; CA 17-20R; SATA 21

Plimpton, George (Ames)　1927- . . . . . CLC 36
　See also CA 21-24R; SATA 10

Plomer, William (Charles Franklin)
　1903-1973 . . . . . . . . . . . . . . . . . CLC 4, 8
　See also CAP 2; CA 21-22; SATA 24;
　　DLB 20

Plumly, Stanley (Ross)　1939- . . . . . . CLC 33
　See also CA 108, 110; DLB 5

Poe, Edgar Allan
　1809-1849 . . . NCLC 1, 16; PC 1; SSC 1
　See also SATA 23; DLB 3, 59, 73, 74;
　　CDALB 1640-1865

Pohl, Frederik　1919- . . . . . . . . . . . . CLC 18
　See also CAAS 1; CANR 11; CA 61-64;
　　SATA 24; DLB 8

Poirier, Louis　1910-
　See Gracq, Julien
　See also CA 122, 126

Poitier, Sidney　1924?- . . . . . . . . . . . CLC 26
　See also CA 117

Polanski, Roman　1933- . . . . . . . . . . CLC 16
　See also CA 77-80

Poliakoff, Stephen　1952- . . . . . . . . . CLC 38
　See also CA 106; DLB 13

Police, The . . . . . . . . . . . . . . . . . . . . . CLC 26

Pollitt, Katha　1949- . . . . . . . . . . . . . CLC 28
　See also CA 120, 122

Pollock, Sharon　19??- . . . . . . . . . . . . CLC 50
　See also DLB 60

Pomerance, Bernard　1940- . . . . . . . . CLC 13
　See also CA 101

Ponge, Francis (Jean Gaston Alfred)
　1899- . . . . . . . . . . . . . . . . . . . . CLC 6, 18
　See also CA 85-88; obituary CA 126

Pontoppidan, Henrik　1857-1943 . . . TCLC 29
　See also obituary CA 126

Poole, Josephine　1933- . . . . . . . . . . . CLC 17
　See also CANR 10; CA 21-24R; SAAS 2;
　　SATA 5

Popa, Vasko　1922- . . . . . . . . . . . . . . CLC 19
　See also CA 112

Pope, Alexander　1688-1744 . . . . . . . . . LC 3

Porter, Gene Stratton　1863-1924 . . TCLC 21
　See also CA 112

Porter, Katherine Anne
　1890-1980 . . . . . CLC 1, 3, 7, 10, 13, 15,
　　　　　　　　　　　　　　27; SSC 4
　See also CANR 1; CA 1-4R;
　　obituary CA 101; obituary SATA 23, 39;
　　DLB 4, 9; DLB-Y 80

Porter, Peter (Neville Frederick)
　1929- . . . . . . . . . . . . . . . . . . CLC 5, 13, 33
　See also CA 85-88; DLB 40

Porter, William Sydney　1862-1910
　See Henry, O.
　See also YABC 2; CA 104; DLB 12, 78, 79;
　　CDALB 1865-1917

Post, Melville D.　1871-1930 . . . . . . TCLC 39
　See also brief entry CA 110

Potok, Chaim　1929- . . . . . . . CLC 2, 7, 14, 26
　See also CANR 19; CA 17-20R; SATA 33;
　　DLB 28

Potter, Dennis (Christopher George)
　1935- . . . . . . . . . . . . . . . . . . . . . . CLC 58
　See also CA 107

Pound, Ezra (Loomis)
　1885-1972 . . . . . CLC 1, 2, 3, 4, 5, 7, 10,
　　　　　　　　　　　　13, 18, 34, 48, 50
　See also CA 5-8R; obituary CA 37-40R;
　　DLB 4, 45, 63; CDALB 1917-1929

Povod, Reinaldo　1959- . . . . . . . . . . . CLC 44

Powell, Anthony (Dymoke)
　1905- . . . . . . . . . . . CLC 1, 3, 7, 9, 10, 31
　See also CANR 1; CA 1-4R; DLB 15

Powell, Padgett　1952- . . . . . . . . . . . . CLC 34
　See also CA 126

Powers, J(ames) F(arl)
　1917- . . . . . . . . . . CLC 1, 4, 8, 57; SSC 4
　See also CANR 2; CA 1-4R

Pownall, David　1938- . . . . . . . . . . . . CLC 10
　See also CA 89-92; DLB 14

Powys, John Cowper
　1872-1963 . . . . . . . . . . . CLC 7, 9, 15, 46
　See also CA 85-88; DLB 15

Powys, T(heodore) F(rancis)
　1875-1953 . . . . . . . . . . . . . . . . . . TCLC 9
　See also CA 106; DLB 36

Prager, Emily　1952- . . . . . . . . . . . . . CLC 56

Pratt, E(dwin) J(ohn)　1883-1964 . . . . CLC 19
　See also obituary CA 93-96; DLB 92

Premchand　1880-1936 . . . . . . . . . . TCLC 21

Preussler, Otfried　1923- . . . . . . . . . . CLC 17
　See also CA 77-80; SATA 24

Prevert, Jacques (Henri Marie)
　1900-1977 . . . . . . . . . . . . . . . . . . CLC 15
　See also CANR 29; CA 77-80;
　　obituary CA 69-72; obituary SATA 30

Prevost, Abbe (Antoine Francois)
　1697-1763 . . . . . . . . . . . . . . . . . . . . LC 1

Price, (Edward) Reynolds
　1933- . . . . . . . . . CLC 3, 6, 13, 43, 50, 63
　See also CANR 1; CA 1-4R; DLB 2

Price, Richard　1949- . . . . . . . . . . . CLC 6, 12
　See also CANR 3; CA 49-52; DLB-Y 81

Prichard, Katharine Susannah
　1883-1969 . . . . . . . . . . . . . . . . . . CLC 46
　See also CAP 1; CA 11-12

Priestley, J(ohn) B(oynton)
　1894-1984 . . . . . . . . . . . CLC 2, 5, 9, 34
　See also CA 9-12R; obituary CA 113;
　　DLB 10, 34, 77; DLB-Y 84

Prince (Rogers Nelson)　1958?- . . . . . CLC 35

Prince, F(rank) T(empleton)　1912- . . CLC 22
　See also CA 101; DLB 20

Prior, Matthew　1664-1721 . . . . . . . . . . LC 4

Pritchard, William H(arrison)
　1932- . . . . . . . . . . . . . . . . . . . . . . CLC 34
　See also CANR 23; CA 65-68

Pritchett, V(ictor) S(awdon)
　1900- . . . . . . . . . . . . . . CLC 5, 13, 15, 41
　See also CA 61-64; DLB 15

Probst, Mark　1925- . . . . . . . . . . . . . CLC 59
　See also CA 130

Procaccino, Michael　1946-
　See Cristofer, Michael

Prokosch, Frederic　1908-1989 . . . . CLC 4, 48
　See also CA 73-76; obituary CA 128;
　　DLB 48

Prose, Francine　1947- . . . . . . . . . . . . CLC 45
　See also CA 109, 112

Proust, Marcel　1871-1922 . . TCLC 7, 13, 33
　See also CA 104, 120; DLB 65

Pryor, Richard　1940- . . . . . . . . . . . . CLC 26
　See also CA 122

Przybyszewski, Stanislaw
　1868-1927 . . . . . . . . . . . . . . . . . TCLC 36
　See also DLB 66

Puig, Manuel
　1932-1990 . . . . . . . . CLC 3, 5, 10, 28, 65
　See also CANR 2, 32; CA 45-48

Purdy, A(lfred) W(ellington)
　1918- . . . . . . . . . . . . . . . CLC 3, 6, 14, 50
　See also CA 81-84

**Purdy, James (Amos)**
1923- ............ **CLC 2, 4, 10, 28, 52**
See also CAAS 1; CANR 19; CA 33-36R;
DLB 2

**Pushkin, Alexander (Sergeyevich)**
1799-1837 .............. **NCLC 3, 27**

**P'u Sung-ling** 1640-1715 ............ **LC 3**

**Puzo, Mario** 1920- ........ **CLC 1, 2, 6, 36**
See also CANR 4; CA 65-68; DLB 6

**Pym, Barbara (Mary Crampton)**
1913-1980 ............ **CLC 13, 19, 37**
See also CANR 13; CAP 1; CA 13-14;
obituary CA 97-100; DLB 14; DLB-Y 87

**Pynchon, Thomas (Ruggles, Jr.)**
1937- ..... **CLC 2, 3, 6, 9, 11, 18, 33, 62**
See also CANR 22; CA 17-20R; DLB 2

**Quarrington, Paul** 1954?- .......... **CLC 65**
See also CA 129

**Quasimodo, Salvatore** 1901-1968 ... **CLC 10**
See also CAP 1; CA 15-16;
obituary CA 25-28R

**Queen, Ellery** 1905-1982 ........ **CLC 3, 11**
See also Dannay, Frederic; Lee, Manfred
B(ennington)

**Queneau, Raymond**
1903-1976 ............ **CLC 2, 5, 10, 42**
See also CA 77-80; obituary CA 69-72;
DLB 72

**Quin, Ann (Marie)** 1936-1973 ....... **CLC 6**
See also CA 9-12R; obituary CA 45-48;
DLB 14

**Quinn, Simon** 1942-
See Smith, Martin Cruz
See also CANR 6, 23; CA 85-88

**Quiroga, Horacio (Sylvestre)**
1878-1937 ................. **TCLC 20**
See also CA 117

**Quoirez, Francoise** 1935-
See Sagan, Francoise
See also CANR 6; CA 49-52

**Rabe, David (William)** 1940-... **CLC 4, 8, 33**
See also CA 85-88; CABS 3; DLB 7

**Rabelais, Francois** 1494?-1553....... **LC 5**

**Rabinovitch, Sholem** 1859-1916
See Aleichem, Sholom
See also CA 104

**Rachen, Kurt von** 1911-1986
See Hubbard, L(afayette) Ron(ald)

**Radcliffe, Ann (Ward)** 1764-1823 .. **NCLC 6**
See also DLB 39

**Radiguet, Raymond** 1903-1923 .... **TCLC 29**
See also DLB 65

**Radnoti, Miklos** 1909-1944 ....... **TCLC 16**
See also CA 118

**Rado, James** 1939- .............. **CLC 17**
See also CA 105

**Radomski, James** 1932-
See Rado, James

**Radvanyi, Netty Reiling** 1900-1983
See Seghers, Anna
See also CA 85-88; obituary CA 110

**Rae, Ben** 1935-
See Griffiths, Trevor

**Raeburn, John** 1941- ............ **CLC 34**
See also CA 57-60

**Ragni, Gerome** 1942- ............ **CLC 17**
See also CA 105

**Rahv, Philip** 1908-1973 ........... **CLC 24**
See also Greenberg, Ivan

**Raine, Craig** 1944- ............... **CLC 32**
See also CANR 29; CA 108; DLB 40

**Raine, Kathleen (Jessie)** 1908- ... **CLC 7, 45**
See also CA 85-88; DLB 20

**Rainis, Janis** 1865-1929 ......... **TCLC 29**

**Rakosi, Carl** 1903- .............. **CLC 47**
See also Rawley, Callman
See also CAAS 5

**Ramos, Graciliano** 1892-1953 ..... **TCLC 32**

**Rampersad, Arnold** 19??- .......... **CLC 44**

**Ramuz, Charles-Ferdinand**
1878-1947 ................. **TCLC 33**

**Rand, Ayn** 1905-1982 ....... **CLC 3, 30, 44**
See also CANR 27; CA 13-16R;
obituary CA 105

**Randall, Dudley (Felker)** 1914- ...... **CLC 1**
See also CANR 23; CA 25-28R; DLB 41

**Ransom, John Crowe**
1888-1974 ........ **CLC 2, 4, 5, 11, 24**
See also CANR 6; CA 5-8R;
obituary CA 49-52; DLB 45, 63

**Rao, Raja** 1909- .............. **CLC 25, 56**
See also CA 73-76

**Raphael, Frederic (Michael)**
1931- ..................... **CLC 2, 14**
See also CANR 1; CA 1-4R; DLB 14

**Rathbone, Julian** 1935- .......... **CLC 41**
See also CA 101

**Rattigan, Terence (Mervyn)**
1911-1977 ................... **CLC 7**
See also CA 85-88; obituary CA 73-76;
DLB 13

**Ratushinskaya, Irina** 1954- ....... **CLC 54**
See also CA 129

**Raven, Simon (Arthur Noel)**
1927- ..................... **CLC 14**
See also CA 81-84

**Rawley, Callman** 1903-
See Rakosi, Carl
See also CANR 12; CA 21-24R

**Rawlings, Marjorie Kinnan**
1896-1953 .................. **TCLC 4**
See also YABC 1; CA 104; DLB 9, 22

**Ray, Satyajit** 1921- .............. **CLC 16**
See also CA 114

**Read, Herbert (Edward)** 1893-1968 .. **CLC 4**
See also CA 85-88; obituary CA 25-28R;
DLB 20

**Read, Piers Paul** 1941- ...... **CLC 4, 10, 25**
See also CA 21-24R; SATA 21; DLB 14

**Reade, Charles** 1814-1884 ........ **NCLC 2**
See also DLB 21

**Reade, Hamish** 1936-
See Gray, Simon (James Holliday)

**Reading, Peter** 1946- ............. **CLC 47**
See also CA 103; DLB 40

**Reaney, James** 1926- ............. **CLC 13**
See also CA 41-44R; SATA 43; DLB 68

**Rebreanu, Liviu** 1885-1944 ...... **TCLC 28**

**Rechy, John (Francisco)**
1934- ................. **CLC 1, 7, 14, 18**
See also CAAS 4; CANR 6; CA 5-8R;
DLB-Y 82

**Redcam, Tom** 1870-1933 ........ **TCLC 25**

**Redgrove, Peter (William)**
1932- ..................... **CLC 6, 41**
See also CANR 3; CA 1-4R; DLB 40

**Redmon (Nightingale), Anne**
1943- ..................... **CLC 22**
See also Nightingale, Anne Redmon
See also DLB-Y 86

**Reed, Ishmael**
1938- ........ **CLC 2, 3, 5, 6, 13, 32, 60**
See also CANR 25; CA 21-24R; DLB 2, 5,
33

**Reed, John (Silas)** 1887-1920 ...... **TCLC 9**
See also CA 106

**Reed, Lou** 1944- ................. **CLC 21**

**Reeve, Clara** 1729-1807 ......... **NCLC 19**
See also DLB 39

**Reid, Christopher** 1949- ........... **CLC 33**
See also DLB 40

**Reid Banks, Lynne** 1929-
See Banks, Lynne Reid
See also CANR 6, 22; CA 1-4R; SATA 22

**Reiner, Max** 1900-
See Caldwell, (Janet Miriam) Taylor
(Holland)

**Reizenstein, Elmer Leopold** 1892-1967
See Rice, Elmer

**Remark, Erich Paul** 1898-1970
See Remarque, Erich Maria

**Remarque, Erich Maria**
1898-1970 ................... **CLC 21**
See also CA 77-80; obituary CA 29-32R;
DLB 56

**Remizov, Alexey (Mikhailovich)**
1877-1957 ................. **TCLC 27**
See also CA 125

**Renan, Joseph Ernest**
1823-1892 ................. **NCLC 26**

**Renard, Jules** 1864-1910 ........ **TCLC 17**
See also CA 117

**Renault, Mary** 1905-1983 .... **CLC 3, 11, 17**
See also Challans, Mary
See also DLB-Y 83

**Rendell, Ruth** 1930- ........... **CLC 28, 48**
See also Vine, Barbara
See also CA 109; DLB 87

**Renoir, Jean** 1894-1979 ........... **CLC 20**
See also CA 129; obituary CA 85-88

**Resnais, Alain** 1922- .............. **CLC 16**

**Reverdy, Pierre** 1899-1960 ........ **CLC 53**
See also CA 97-100; obituary CA 89-92

**Rexroth, Kenneth**
1905-1982 ...... **CLC 1, 2, 6, 11, 22, 49**
See also CANR 14; CA 5-8R;
obituary CA 107; DLB 16, 48; DLB-Y 82;
CDALB 1941-1968

**Reyes, Alfonso** 1889-1959 ....... **TCLC 33**

...atharine Maria
...67 ................... NCLC 19
...LB 1, 74

...1931- ............... CLC 7
...A 97-100

...iorgos Stylianou 1900-1971
..., George
...ANR 5; CA 5-8R;
... CA 33-36R

...ge 1900-1971 ....... CLC 5, 11
...eferiades, Giorgos Stylianou

...(Wolf) 1937- ....... CLC 3, 10
...ANR 20; CA 25-28R; DLB-Y 86

...1945- ................. CLC 35

...t Clark 1945-
... SATA 8
...Bob

...a 1900-1983 ....... CLC 7, 110
...advanyi, Netty Reiling
...LB 69

...rick (Lewis) 1936- ..... CLC 18
...ANR 8; CA 13-16R; DLB-Y 84

...lav 1901-1986 ..... CLC 34, 44
...A 127

... c. 966-1017? ....... CMLC 6

..., Jr. 1928- ..... CLC 1, 2, 4, 8
...A 13-16R; DLB 2

...enne Pivert de
...6 ................... NCLC 16

...n (Jose) 1902-1982 .... CLC 8
...ANR 8; CA 5-8R;
...CA 105

...s Annaeus
...5 A.D. ............... CMLC 6

...old Sédar 1906- ...... CLC 54
...A 116

...rd) Rod(man)
...5 ................... CLC 30
... 65-68; obituary CA 57-60;

...07-
...c, (Eugene)

...t W(illiam)
...8 ................... TCLC 15
... 115; SATA 20

...1952- ................. CLC 43
... 121, 127

... Propper
...r .................... CLC 27
...NR 7; CA 5-8R;
...A 108

...Evan) Thompson
...5 ................... TCLC 31
... 109; SATA 18; DLB 92

...ee 1918- ......... CLC 19, 61
...AS 1; CA 89-92; DLB 6

...ise de Marie de
...hantal 1626-1696 ..... LC 11

...Harvey)
... CLC 2, 4, 6, 8, 10, 15, 53;
... PC 2
...NR 3; CA 1-4R;
...A 53-56; CABS 2; SATA 10;
...DALB 1941-1968

Shaara, Michael (Joseph) 1929- .... CLC 15
See also CA 102; obituary CA 125;
DLB-Y 83

Shackleton, C. C. 1925-
See Aldiss, Brian W(ilson)

Shacochis, Bob 1951- ............. CLC 39
See also CA 119, 124

Shaffer, Anthony 1926- ........... CLC 19
See also CA 110, 116; DLB 13

Shaffer, Peter (Levin)
1926- .......... CLC 5, 14, 18, 37, 60
See also CANR 25; CA 25-28R; DLB 13

Shalamov, Varlam (Tikhonovich)
1907?-1982 ..................... CLC 18
See also obituary CA 105

Shamlu, Ahmad 1925- ............. CLC 10

Shammas, Anton 1951- ............ CLC 55

Shange, Ntozake 1948- ....... CLC 8, 25, 38
See also CA 85-88; DLB 38

Shapcott, Thomas W(illiam) 1935- .. CLC 38
See also CA 69-72

Shapiro, Karl (Jay) 1913- .. CLC 4, 8, 15, 53
See also CAAS 6; CANR 1; CA 1-4R;
DLB 48

Sharp, William 1855-1905 ....... TCLC 39

Sharpe, Tom 1928- ............... CLC 36
See also CA 114; DLB 14

Shaw, (George) Bernard
1856-1950 ........... TCLC 3, 9, 21
See also CA 104, 109, 119; DLB 10, 57

Shaw, Henry Wheeler
1818-1885 .................. NCLC 15
See also DLB 11

Shaw, Irwin 1913-1984 ...... CLC 7, 23, 34
See also CANR 21; CA 13-16R;
obituary CA 112; DLB 6; DLB-Y 84;
CDALB 1941-1968

Shaw, Robert 1927-1978 ........... CLC 5
See also CANR 4; CA 1-4R;
obituary CA 81-84; DLB 13, 14

Shawn, Wallace 1943- ............. CLC 41
See also CA 112

Sheed, Wilfrid (John Joseph)
1930- ............ CLC 2, 4, 10, 53
See also CA 65-68; DLB 6

Sheffey, Asa 1913-1980
See Hayden, Robert (Earl)

Sheldon, Alice (Hastings) B(radley)
1915-1987
See Tiptree, James, Jr.
See also CA 108; obituary CA 122

Shelley, Mary Wollstonecraft Godwin
1797-1851 ..................... NCLC 14
See also SATA 29

Shelley, Percy Bysshe
1792-1822 ..................... NCLC 18

Shepard, Jim 19??- ................ CLC 36

Shepard, Lucius 19??- ............. CLC 34
See also CA 128

Shepard, Sam
1943- ......... CLC 4, 6, 17, 34, 41, 44
See also CANR 22; CA 69-72; DLB 7

Shepherd, Michael 1927-
See Ludlum, Robert

Sherburne, Zoa (Morin) 1912- ...... CLC 30
See also CANR 3; CA 1-4R; SATA 3

Sheridan, Frances 1724-1766 ........ LC 7
See also DLB 39, 84

Sheridan, Richard Brinsley
1751-1816 ............. NCLC 5; DC 1
See also DLB 89

Sherman, Jonathan Marc 1970?- .... CLC 55

Sherman, Martin 19??- ............. CLC 19
See also CA 116

Sherwin, Judith Johnson 1936- ... CLC 7, 15
See also CA 25-28R

Sherwood, Robert E(mmet)
1896-1955 .................... TCLC 3
See also CA 104; DLB 7, 26

Shiel, M(atthew) P(hipps)
1865-1947 ..................... TCLC 8
See also CA 106

Shiga, Naoya 1883-1971 ........... CLC 33
See also CA 101; obituary CA 33-36R

Shimazaki, Haruki 1872-1943
See Shimazaki, Toson
See also CA 105

Shimazaki, Toson 1872-1943 ....... TCLC 5
See also Shimazaki, Haruki

Sholokhov, Mikhail (Aleksandrovich)
1905-1984 ................. CLC 7, 15
See also CA 101; obituary CA 112;
SATA 36

Sholom Aleichem 1859-1916 .... TCLC 1, 35
See also Rabinovitch, Sholem

Shreve, Susan Richards 1939- ...... CLC 23
See also CAAS 5; CANR 5; CA 49-52;
SATA 41, 46

Shue, Larry 1946-1985 ............ CLC 52
See also obituary CA 117

Shulman, Alix Kates 1932- ...... CLC 2, 10
See also CA 29-32R; SATA 7

Shuster, Joe 1914- ............... CLC 21

Shute (Norway), Nevil 1899-1960 ... CLC 30
See also Norway, Nevil Shute
See also CA 102; obituary CA 93-96

Shuttle, Penelope (Diane) 1947- ..... CLC 7
See also CA 93-96; DLB 14, 40

Siegel, Jerome 1914- ............. CLC 21
See also CA 116

Sienkiewicz, Henryk (Adam Aleksander Pius)
1846-1916 ..................... TCLC 3
See also CA 104

Sigal, Clancy 1926- ............... CLC 7
See also CA 1-4R

Sigourney, Lydia (Howard Huntley)
1791-1865 ..................... NCLC 21
See also DLB 1, 42, 73

Siguenza y Gongora, Carlos de
1645-1700 ..................... LC 8

Sigurjonsson, Johann 1880-1919 ... TCLC 27

Sikelianos, Angeles 1884-1951 ..... TCLC 39

Silkin, Jon 1930- ............. CLC 2, 6, 43
See also CAAS 5; CA 5-8R; DLB 27

Silko, Leslie Marmon 1948- ....... CLC 23
See also CA 115, 122

Reyes y Basoalto, Ricardo Eliecer Neftali
1904-1973
See Neruda, Pablo

Reymont, Wladyslaw Stanislaw
1867-1925 ..................... TCLC 5
See also CA 104

Reynolds, Jonathan 1942?- ...... CLC 6, 38
See also CANR 28; CA 65-68

Reynolds, (Sir) Joshua 1723-1792 .... LC 15

Reynolds, Michael (Shane) 1937- ... CLC 44
See also CANR 9; CA 65-68

Reznikoff, Charles 1894-1976 ....... CLC 9
See also CAP 2; CA 33-36;
obituary CA 61-64; DLB 28, 45

Rezzori, Gregor von 1914- ........ CLC 25
See also CA 122

Rhys, Jean
1890-1979 ...... CLC 2, 4, 6, 14, 19, 51
See also CA 25-28R; obituary CA 85-88;
DLB 36

Ribeiro, Darcy 1922- ............. CLC 34
See also CA 33-36R

Ribeiro, Joao Ubaldo (Osorio Pimentel)
1941- ......................... CLC 10
See also CA 81-84

Ribman, Ronald (Burt) 1932- ....... CLC 7
See also CA 21-24R

Rice, Anne 1941- ................. CLC 41
See also CANR 12; CA 65-68

Rice, Elmer 1892-1967 .......... CLC 7, 49
See also CAP 2; CA 21-22;
obituary CA 25-28R; DLB 4, 7

Rice, Tim 1944- .................. CLC 21
See also CA 103

Rich, Adrienne (Cecile)
1929- ....... CLC 3, 6, 7, 11, 18, 36
See also CANR 20; CA 9-12R; DLB 5, 67

Richard, Keith 1943- ............. CLC 17
See also CA 107

Richards, David Adam 1950- ...... CLC 59
See also CA 93-96; DLB 53

Richards, I(vor) A(rmstrong)
1893-1979 ............... CLC 14, 24
See also CA 41-44R; obituary CA 89-92;
DLB 27

Richards, Keith 1943-
See Richard, Keith
See also CA 107

Richardson, Dorothy (Miller)
1873-1957 ..................... TCLC 3
See also CA 104; DLB 36

Richardson, Ethel 1870-1946
See Richardson, Henry Handel
See also CA 105

Richardson, Henry Handel
1870-1946 ..................... TCLC 4
See also Richardson, Ethel

Richardson, Samuel 1689-1761 ....... LC 1
See also DLB 39

Richler, Mordecai
1931- ....... CLC 3, 5, 9, 13, 18, 46
See also CLR 17; CA 65-68; SATA 27, 44;
DLB 53

Richter, Conrad (Michael)
1890-1968 ............. CLC 30
See also CANR 23; CA 5-8R;
obituary CA 25-28R; SATA 3; DLB 9

Richter, Johann Paul Friedrich 1763-1825
See Jean Paul

Riddell, Mrs. J. H. 1832-1906 ..... TCLC 40

Riding, Laura 1901- ............ CLC 3, 7
See also Jackson, Laura (Riding)

Riefenstahl, Berta Helene Amalia
1902- ......................... CLC 16
See also Riefenstahl, Leni
See also CA 108

Riefenstahl, Leni 1902- ........... CLC 16
See also Riefenstahl, Berta Helene Amalia
See also CA 108

Rilke, Rainer Maria
1875-1926 ........ TCLC 1, 6, 19; PC 2
See also CA 104, 132; DLB 81

Rimbaud, (Jean Nicolas) Arthur
1854-1891 ................. NCLC 4

Ringwood, Gwen(dolyn Margaret) Pharis
1910-1984 ..................... CLC 48
See also obituary CA 112

Rio, Michel 19??- ................ CLC 43

Ritsos, Yannis 1909- ...... CLC 6, 13, 31
See also CA 77-80

Ritter, Erika 1948?- ............. CLC 52

Rivera, Jose Eustasio 1889-1928 ... TCLC 35

Rivers, Conrad Kent 1933-1968 ..... CLC 1
See also CA 85-88; DLB 41

Rizal, Jose 1861-1896 ........... NCLC 27

Roa Bastos, Augusto 1917- ........ CLC 45

Robbe-Grillet, Alain
1922- ...... CLC 1, 2, 4, 6, 8, 10, 14, 43
See also CA 9-12R; DLB 83

Robbins, Harold 1916- ............. CLC 5
See also CANR 26; CA 73-76

Robbins, Thomas Eugene 1936-
See Robbins, Tom
See also CA 81-84

Robbins, Tom 1936- ......... CLC 9, 32, 64
See also Robbins, Thomas Eugene
See also CANR 29; CA 81-84; DLB-Y 80

Robbins, Trina 1938- ............. CLC 21

Roberts, (Sir) Charles G(eorge) D(ouglas)
1860-1943 ..................... TCLC 8
See also CA 105; SATA 29; DLB 92

Roberts, Kate 1891-1985 .......... CLC 15
See also CA 107; obituary CA 116

Roberts, Keith (John Kingston)
1935- ......................... CLC 14
See also CA 25-28R

Roberts, Kenneth 1885-1957 ...... TCLC 23
See also CA 109; DLB 9

Roberts, Michele (B.) 1949- ....... CLC 48
See also CA 115

Robinson, Edwin Arlington
1869-1935 ............. TCLC 5; PC 1
See also CA 104; DLB 54;
CDALB 1865-1917

Robinson, Henry Crabb
1775-1867 ................. NCLC 15

Robinson, Jill 1936- ............. CLC 10
See also CA 102

Robinson, Kim Stanley 19??- ...... CLC 34
See also CA 126

Robinson, Marilynne 1944- ........ CLC 25
See also CA 116

Robinson, Smokey 1940- .......... CLC 21

Robinson, William 1940-
See Robinson, Smokey
See also CA 116

Robison, Mary 1949- ............. CLC 42
See also CA 113, 116

Roddenberry, Gene 1921- ......... CLC 17
See also CANR 110; SATA 45

Rodgers, Mary 1931- ............. CLC 12
See also CLR 20; CANR 8; CA 49-52;
SATA 8

Rodgers, W(illiam) R(obert)
1909-1969 ..................... CLC 7
See also CA 85-88; DLB 20

Rodman, Howard 19??- ............ CLC 65

Rodriguez, Claudio 1934- ......... CLC 10

Roethke, Theodore (Huebner)
1908-1963 ...... CLC 1, 3, 8, 11, 19, 46
See also CA 81-84; CABS 2; SAAS 1;
DLB 5; CDALB 1941-1968

Rogers, Sam 1943-
See Shepard, Sam

Rogers, Thomas (Hunton) 1931- .... CLC 57
See also CA 89-92

Rogers, Will(iam Penn Adair)
1879-1935 ..................... TCLC 8
See also CA 105; DLB 11

Rogin, Gilbert 1929- ............. CLC 18
See also CANR 15; CA 65-68

Rohan, Koda 1867-1947 .......... TCLC 22
See also CA 121

Rohmer, Eric 1920- .............. CLC 16
See also Scherer, Jean-Marie Maurice

Rohmer, Sax 1883-1959 .......... TCLC 28
See also Ward, Arthur Henry Sarsfield
See also CA 108; DLB 70

Roiphe, Anne (Richardson)
1935- ....................... CLC 3, 9
See also CA 89-92; DLB-Y 80

Rolfe, Frederick (William Serafino Austin
Lewis Mary) 1860-1913 ...... TCLC 12
See also CA 107; DLB 34

Rolland, Romain 1866-1944 ....... TCLC 23
See also CA 118; DLB 65

Rolvaag, O(le) E(dvart)
1876-1931 ..................... TCLC 17
See also CA 117; DLB 9

Romains, Jules 1885-1972 .......... CLC 7
See also CA 85-88

Romero, Jose Ruben 1890-1952 ... TCLC 14
See also CA 114

Ronsard, Pierre de 1524-1585 ....... LC 6

Rooke, Leon 1934- ............ CLC 25, 34
See also CANR 23; CA 25-28R

Roper, William 1498-1578 ........ LC 10

Rosa, Joao Guimaraes 1908-1967 ... CLC 23
See also obituary CA 89-92

Rosen, Richard (Dean) 1949-....... CLC 39
See also CA 77-80

Rosenberg, Isaac 1890-1918....... TCLC 12
See also CA 107; DLB 20

Rosenblatt, Joe 1933-.............. CLC 15
See also Rosenblatt, Joseph

Rosenblatt, Joseph 1933-
See Rosenblatt, Joe
See also CA 89-92

Rosenfeld, Samuel 1896-1963
See Tzara, Tristan
See also obituary CA 89-92

Rosenthal, M(acha) L(ouis) 1917-... CLC 28
See also CAAS 6; CANR 4; CA 1-4R;
SATA 59; DLB 5

Ross, (James) Sinclair 1908-...... CLC 13
See also CA 73-76; DLB 88

Rossetti, Christina Georgina
1830-1894 .................. NCLC 2
See also SATA 20; DLB 35

Rossetti, Dante Gabriel
1828-1882 .................. NCLC 4
See also DLB 35

Rossetti, Gabriel Charles Dante 1828-1882
See Rossetti, Dante Gabriel

Rossner, Judith (Perelman)
1935- .................CLC 6, 9, 29
See also CA 17-20R; DLB 6

Rostand, Edmond (Eugene Alexis)
1868-1918 .............TCLC 6, 37
See also CA 104, 126

Roth, Henry 1906-........CLC 2, 6, 11
See also CAP 1; CA 11-12; DLB 28

Roth, Joseph 1894-1939.......... TCLC 33
See also DLB 85

Roth, Philip (Milton)
1933- ...... CLC 1, 2, 3, 4, 6, 9, 15, 22,
                                   31, 47
See also CANR 1, 22; CA 1-4R; DLB 2, 28;
DLB-Y 82

Rothenberg, James 1931-....... CLC 57

Rothenberg, Jerome 1931-....... CLC 6, 57
See also CANR 1; CA 45-48; DLB 5

Roumain, Jacques 1907-1944...... TCLC 19
See also CA 117

Rourke, Constance (Mayfield)
1885-1941 .................. TCLC 12
See also YABC 1; CA 107

Rousseau, Jean-Baptiste 1671-1741 ... LC 9

Rousseau, Jean-Jacques 1712-1778... LC 14

Roussel, Raymond 1877-1933 ..... TCLC 20
See also CA 117

Rovit, Earl (Herbert) 1927-........ CLC 7
See also CANR 12; CA 5-8R

Rowe, Nicholas 1674-1718........... LC 8

Rowson, Susanna Haswell
1762-1824 .................. NCLC 5
See also DLB 37

Roy, Gabrielle 1909-1983...... CLC 10, 14
See also CANR 5; CA 53-56;
obituary CA 110; DLB 68

Rozewicz, Tadeusz 1921-........CLC 9, 23
See also CA 108

Ruark, Gibbons 1941-.............. CLC 3
See also CANR 14; CA 33-36R

Rubens, Bernice 192?-......... CLC 19, 31
See also CA 25-28R; DLB 14

Rudkin, (James) David 1936-...... CLC 14
See also CA 89-92; DLB 13

Rudnik, Raphael 1933-............. CLC 7
See also CA 29-32R

Ruiz, Jose Martinez 1874-1967
See Azorin

Rukeyser, Muriel
1913-1980........CLC 6, 10, 15, 27
See also CANR 26; CA 5-8R;
obituary CA 93-96; obituary SATA 22;
DLB 48

Rule, Jane (Vance) 1931-......... CLC 27
See also CANR 12; CA 25-28R; DLB 60

Rulfo, Juan 1918-1986............. CLC 8
See also CANR 26; CA 85-88;
obituary CA 118

Runyon, (Alfred) Damon
1880-1946 .................. TCLC 10
See also CA 107; DLB 11

Rush, Norman 1933-.............. CLC 44
See also CA 121, 126

Rushdie, (Ahmed) Salman
1947- ...... CLC 23, 31, 55, 59
See also CA 108, 111

Rushforth, Peter (Scott) 1945-..... CLC 19
See also CA 101

Ruskin, John 1819-1900......... TCLC 20
See also CA 114; SATA 24; DLB 55

Russ, Joanna 1937-.............. CLC 15
See also CANR 11; CA 25-28R; DLB 8

Russell, George William 1867-1935
See A. E.
See also CA 104

Russell, (Henry) Ken(neth Alfred)
1927- .................. CLC 16
See also CA 105

Russell, Mary Annette Beauchamp 1866-1941
See Elizabeth

Russell, Willy 1947-.............. CLC 60

Rutherford, Mark 1831-1913...... TCLC 25
See also CA 121; DLB 18

Ruyslinck, Ward 1929-............ CLC 14
See also CA 25-28R

Ryan, Cornelius (John) 1920-1974 ... CLC 7
See also CA 69-72; obituary CA 53-56

Ryan, Michael 1946-............. CLC 65
See also CA 49-52; DLB-Y 82

Rybakov, Anatoli 1911?-....... CLC 23, 53
See also CA 126

Ryder, Jonathan 1927-
See Ludlum, Robert

Ryga, George 1932-.............. CLC 14
See also CA 101; obituary CA 124; DLB 60

Sévine, Marquise de Marie de
Rabutin-Chantal 1626-1696..... LC 11

Saba, Umberto 1883-1957 ........ TCLC 33

Sabato, Ernesto 1911-........ CLC 10, 23
See also CA 97-100

Sacher-Masoch, Leopold von
1836?-1895................. NCLC 31

Sachs, Marilyn (Stickle) 1927-..... CLC 35
See also CLR 2; CANR 13; CA 17-20R;
SAAS 2; SATA 3, 52

Sachs, Nelly 1891-1970 .......... CLC 14
See also CAP 2; CA 17-18;
obituary CA 25-28R

Sackler, Howard (Oliver)
1929-1982 ................ CLC 14
See also CA 61-64; obituary CA 108; DLB 7

Sade, Donatien Alphonse Francois, Comte de
1740-1814 ................. NCLC 3

Sadoff, Ira 1945-................. CLC 9
See also CANR 5, 21; CA 53-56

Safire, William 1929-............. CLC 10
See also CA 17-20R

Sagan, Carl (Edward) 1934-...... CLC 30
See also CANR 11; CA 25-28R; SATA 58

Sagan, Francoise
1935- ............. CLC 3, 6, 9, 17, 36
See also Quoirez, Francoise
See also CANR 6; DLB 83

Sahgal, Nayantara (Pandit) 1927-... CLC 41
See also CANR 11; CA 9-12R

Saint, H(arry) F. 1941- .......... CLC 50

Sainte-Beuve, Charles Augustin
1804-1869 ................. NCLC 5

Sainte-Marie, Beverly 1941-1972?
See Sainte-Marie, Buffy
See also CA 107

Sainte-Marie, Buffy 1941-....... CLC 17
See also Sainte-Marie, Beverly

Saint-Exupery, Antoine (Jean Baptiste Marie
Roger) de 1900-1944 ........ TCLC 2
See also CLR 10; CA 108; SATA 20;
DLB 72

Saintsbury, George 1845-1933..... TCLC 31
See also DLB 57

Sait Faik (Abasiyanik)
1906-1954 ................. TCLC 23

Saki 1870-1916 ................ TCLC 3
See also Munro, H(ector) H(ugh)
See also CA 104

Salama, Hannu 1936-............ CLC 18

Salamanca, J(ack) R(ichard)
1922- ................CLC 4, 15
See also CA 25-28R

Salinas, Pedro 1891-1951......... TCLC 17
See also CA 117

Salinger, J(erome) D(avid)
1919- ....... CLC 1, 3, 8, 12, 56; SSC 2
See also CA 5-8R; DLB 2;
CDALB 1941-1968

Salter, James 1925-........ CLC 7, 52, 59
See also CA 73-76

Saltus, Edgar (Evertson)
1855-1921 ................. TCLC 8
See also CA 105

Saltykov, Mikhail Evgrafovich
1826-1889 ................. NCLC 16

Samarakis, Antonis 1919- ......... CLC 5
See also CA 25-28R

Sanchez, Florencio 1875-1910..... TCLC 37

Sanchez, Luis Rafael 1936-........ CLC 23

Sanchez, Sonia 1934-.............. CLC 5
See also CANR 24; CA 33-36R; SATA 22;
DLB 41

Sand, George 1804-1876......... NCLC 2

Sandburg, Carl (August)
1878-1967 ... CLC 1, 4, 10, 15, 35; PC 2
See also CA 5-8R; obituary CA 25-28R;
SATA 8; DLB 17, 54; CDALB 1865-1917

Sandburg, Charles August 1878-1967
See Sandburg, Carl (August)

Sanders, (James) Ed(ward) 1939-... CLC 53
See also CANR 13; CA 15-16R, 103;
DLB 16

Sanders, Lawrence 1920-......... CLC 41
See also CA 81-84

Sandoz, Mari (Susette) 1896-1966 .. CLC 28
See also CANR 17; CA 1-4R;
obituary CA 25-28R; SATA 5; DLB 9

Saner, Reg(inald Anthony) 1931-.... CLC 9
See also CA 65-68

Sannazaro, Jacopo 1456?-1530 ....... LC 8

Sansom, William 1912-1976....... CLC 2, 6
See also CA 5-8R; obituary CA 65-68

Santayana, George 1863-1952..... TCLC 40
See also CA 115; DLB 54, 71

Santiago, Danny 1911-............ CLC 33
See also CA 125

Santmyer, Helen Hooven
1895-1986 ................. CLC 33
See also CANR 15; CA 1-4R;
obituary CA 118; DLB-Y 84

Santos, Bienvenido N(uqui) 1911-.. CLC 22
See also CANR 19; CA 101

Sappho c. 6th-century B.C.-...... CMLC 3

Sarduy, Severo 1937-.............. CLC 6
See also CA 89-92

Sargeson, Frank 1903-1982 ....... CLC 31
See also CA 106, 25-28R; obituary CA 106

Sarmiento, Felix Ruben Garcia 1867-1916
See Dario, Ruben
See also CA 104

Saroyan, William
1908-1981 ..... CLC 1, 8, 10, 29, 34, 56
See also CA 5-8R; obituary CA 103;
SATA 23; obituary SATA 24; DLB 7, 9;
DLB-Y 81

Sarraute, Nathalie
1902- .........CLC 1, 2, 4, 8, 10, 31
See also CANR 23; CA 9-12R; DLB 83

Sarton, Eleanore Marie 1912-
See Sarton, (Eleanor) May

Sarton, (Eleanor) May
1912- ............CLC 4, 14, 49
See also CANR 1; CA 1-4R; SATA 36;
DLB 48; DLB-Y 81

Sartre, Jean-Paul (Charles Aymard)
1905-1980 ... CLC 1, 4, 7, 9, 13, 18, 24,
                                   44, 50, 52
See also CANR 21; CA 9-12R;
obituary CA 97-100; DLB 72

Sassoon, Siegfried (Lorraine)
1886-1967 ................. CLC 36
See also CA 104; obituary CA 25-28R;
DLB 20

Saul, John (W. III) 1942-......... CLC 46
See also CANR 16; CA 81-84

Saura, Carlos 1932-.............. CLC 20
See also CA 114

Sauser-Hall, Frederic-Louis
1887-1961 .................. CLC 18
See also Cendrars, Blaise
See also CA 102; obituary CA 93-96

Savage, Thomas 1915-............ CLC 40
See also CA 126

Savan, Glenn 19??-.............. CLC 50

Sayers, Dorothy L(eigh)
1893-1957 ...............TCLC 2, 15
See also CA 104, 119; DLB 10, 36, 77

Sayers, Valerie 19??-............. CLC 50

Sayles, John (Thomas)
1950- .............CLC 7, 10, 14
See also CA 57-60; DLB 44

Scammell, Michael 19??-......... CLC 34

Scannell, Vernon 1922-........... CLC 49
See also CANR 8; CA 5-8R; DLB 27

Schaeffer, Susan Fromberg
1941- .............CLC 6, 11, 22
See also CANR 18; CA 49-52; SATA 22;
DLB 28

Schell, Jonathan 1943-........... CLC 35
See also CANR 12; CA 73-76

Schelling, Friedrich Wilhelm Joseph von
1775-1854 ................ NCLC 30
See also DLB 90

Scherer, Jean-Marie Maurice 1920-
See Rohmer, Eric
See also CA 110

Schevill, James (Erwin) 1920-...... CLC 7
See also CA 5-8R

Schisgal, Murray (Joseph) 1926-.... CLC 6
See also CA 21-24R

Schlee, Ann 1934-.............. CLC 35
See also CA 101; SATA 36, 44

Schlegel, August Wilhelm von
1767-1845 ................ NCLC 15

Schlegel, Johann Elias (von)
1719?-1749.................. LC 5

Schmidt, Arno 1914-1979......... CLC 56
See also obituary CA 109; DLB 69

Schmitz, Ettore 1861-1928
See Svevo, Italo
See also CA 104, 122

Schnackenberg, Gjertrud 1953-..... CLC 40
See also CA 116

Schneider, Leonard Alfred 1925-1966
See Bruce, Lenny
See also CA 89-92

Schnitzler, Arthur 1862-1931 ...... TCLC 4
See also CA 104; DLB 81

Schor, Sandra 1932?-1990 ........ CLC 65
See also CA 132

Schorer, Mark 1908-1977 ......... CLC 9
See also CANR 7; CA 5-8R;
obituary CA 73-76

Schrader, Paul (Joseph) 1946-..... CLC 26
See also CA 37-40R; DLB 44

Schreiner (
Albert
See also

Schulberg,
1914-
See also
28; DI

Schulz, Bru
See also
obituary

Schulz, Ch
See also

Schuyler,
See also

Schwartz,
1913-
See also

Schwartz,
See also

Schwartz-I
See also

Schwarz-I
See also

Schwob, (
1867
See also

Sciascia,
192
See als

Scoppett
See als

Scorsese,
See al

Scotland

Scott, D
186
See al

Scott, E
See al
48

Scott, F
18
See a

Scott, J
See a

Scott, F
See
DI

Scott, S
See a

Scribe,
17
See a

Scuder

Sealy,

Seare,
See

Sebest

Sebest
See

Sedgwick, C
1789-1
See also

Seelye, John
See also

Seferiades,
See Seferi
See also

Seferis, Geo
See also

Segal, Erich
1923-
See also

Seger, Bob

Seger, Rober
See Seger,

Seghers, Ann
See also R
See also D

Seidel, Frede
See also

Seifert, Jaros
See also

Sei Shonago

Selby, Huber

Senancour, Eti
1770-184

Sender, Ramo
See also CA
obituary

Seneca, Luciu
4 B.C.-6

Senghor, Léo
See also CA

Serling, (Edw
1924-197
See also CA
DLB 26

Serpieres 19
See Guillev

Service, Robe
1874-195
See also CA

Seth, Vikram
See also CA

Seton, Cynthia
1926-198
See also CA

Seton, Ernest
1860-194
See also CA

Settle, Mary I
See also CA

Sevigne, Marq
Rabutin-C

Sexton, Anne (
1928-197

See also CA
obituary C
DLB 5; C

**Sillanpaa, Franz Eemil** 1888-1964... **CLC 19**
See also CA 129; obituary CA 93-96

**Sillitoe, Alan**
1928- ......... **CLC 1, 3, 6, 10, 19, 57**
See also CAAS 2; CANR 8, 26; CA 9-12R;
DLB 14

**Silone, Ignazio** 1900-1978 ......... **CLC 4**
See also CAAS 2; CANR 26; CAP 2;
CA 25-28, 11-12R,; obituary CA 81-84

**Silver, Joan Micklin** 1935- ........ **CLC 20**
See also CA 114, 121

**Silverberg, Robert** 1935- .......... **CLC 7**
See also CAAS 3; CANR 1, 20; CA 1-4R;
SATA 13; DLB 8

**Silverstein, Alvin** 1933- ........... **CLC 17**
See also CANR 2; CA 49-52; SATA 8

**Silverstein, Virginia B(arbara Opshelor)**
1937- ........................ **CLC 17**
See also CANR 2; CA 49-52; SATA 8

**Simak, Clifford D(onald)**
1904-1988 ............... **CLC 1, 55**
See also CANR 1; CA 1-4R;
obituary CA 125; DLB 8

**Simenon, Georges (Jacques Christian)**
1903-1989 ...... **CLC 1, 2, 3, 8, 18, 47**
See also CA 85-88; obituary CA 129;
DLB 72

**Simenon, Paul** 1956?-
See The Clash

**Simic, Charles** 1938-...... **CLC 6, 9, 22, 49**
See also CAAS 4; CANR 12; CA 29-32R

**Simmons, Charles (Paul)** 1924-..... **CLC 57**
See also CA 89-92

**Simmons, Dan** 1948-.............. **CLC 44**

**Simmons, James (Stewart Alexander)**
1933-...................... **CLC 43**
See also CA 105; DLB 40

**Simms, William Gilmore**
1806-1870 ................. **NCLC 3**
See also DLB 3, 30, 59, 73

**Simon, Carly** 1945-.............. **CLC 26**
See also CA 105

**Simon, Claude (Henri Eugene)**
1913- ................ **CLC 4, 9, 15, 39**
See also CA 89-92; DLB 83

**Simon, (Marvin) Neil**
1927- ............... **CLC 6, 11, 31, 39**
See also CA 21-24R; DLB 7

**Simon, Paul** 1941- ............... **CLC 17**
See also CA 116

**Simonon, Paul** 1956?-
See The Clash

**Simpson, Louis (Aston Marantz)**
1923- ................ **CLC 4, 7, 9, 32**
See also CAAS 4; CANR 1; CA 1-4R;
DLB 5

**Simpson, Mona (Elizabeth)** 1957-... **CLC 44**
See also CA 122

**Simpson, N(orman) F(rederick)**
1919- ...................... **CLC 29**
See also CA 11-14R; DLB 13

**Sinclair, Andrew (Annandale)**
1935- .................... **CLC 2, 14**
See also CAAS 5; CANR 14; CA 9-12R;
DLB 14

**Sinclair, Mary Amelia St. Clair** 1865?-1946
See Sinclair, May
See also CA 104

**Sinclair, May** 1865?-1946 ...... **TCLC 3, 11**
See also Sinclair, Mary Amelia St. Clair
See also DLB 36

**Sinclair, Upton (Beall)**
1878-1968 ........... **CLC 1, 11, 15, 63**
See also CANR 7; CA 5-8R;
obituary CA 25-28R; SATA 9; DLB 9

**Singer, Isaac Bashevis**
1904-.... **CLC 1, 3, 6, 9, 11, 15, 23, 38;**
**SSC 3**
See also CLR 1; CANR 1; CA 1-4R;
SATA 3, 27; DLB 6, 28, 52;
CDALB 1941-1968

**Singer, Israel Joshua** 1893-1944 ... **TCLC 33**

**Singh, Khushwant** 1915-.......... **CLC 11**
See also CANR 6; CA 9-12R

**Sinyavsky, Andrei (Donatevich)**
1925- ...................... **CLC 8**
See also CA 85-88

**Sirin, V.**
See Nabokov, Vladimir (Vladimirovich)

**Sissman, L(ouis) E(dward)**
1928-1976 ................. **CLC 9, 18**
See also CANR 13; CA 21-24R;
obituary CA 65-68; DLB 5

**Sisson, C(harles) H(ubert)** 1914-..... **CLC 8**
See also CAAS 3; CANR 3; CA 1-4R;
DLB 27

**Sitwell, (Dame) Edith** 1887-1964... **CLC 2, 9**
See also CA 9-12R; DLB 20

**Sjoewall, Maj** 1935-
See Wahloo, Per
See also CA 61-64, 65-68

**Sjowall, Maj** 1935-
See Wahloo, Per

**Skelton, Robin** 1925- ............. **CLC 13**
See also CAAS 5; CA 5-8R; DLB 27, 53

**Skolimowski, Jerzy** 1938- ......... **CLC 20**

**Skolimowski, Yurek** 1938-
See Skolimowski, Jerzy

**Skram, Amalie (Bertha)**
1847-1905 ................. **TCLC 25**

**Skrine, Mary Nesta** 1904-
See Keane, Molly

**Skvorecky, Josef (Vaclav)**
1924- .................... **CLC 15, 39**
See also CAAS 1; CANR 10; CA 61-64

**Slade, Bernard** 1930- .......... **CLC 11, 46**
See also Newbound, Bernard Slade
See also DLB 53

**Slaughter, Carolyn** 1946-.......... **CLC 56**
See also CA 85-88

**Slaughter, Frank G(ill)** 1908- ...... **CLC 29**
See also CANR 5; CA 5-8R

**Slavitt, David (R.)** 1935- ........ **CLC 5, 14**
See also CAAS 3; CA 21-24R; DLB 5, 6

**Slesinger, Tess** 1905-1945 ....... **TCLC 10**
See also CA 107

**Slessor, Kenneth** 1901-1971........ **CLC 14**
See also CA 102; obituary CA 89-92

**Slowacki, Juliusz** 1809-1849 ..... **NCLC 15**

**Smart, Christopher** 1722-1771........ **LC 3**

**Smart, Elizabeth** 1913-1986........ **CLC 54**
See also CA 81-84; obituary CA 118;
DLB 88

**Smiley, Jane (Graves)** 1949-....... **CLC 53**
See also CA 104

**Smith, A(rthur) J(ames) M(arshall)**
1902-1980 .................. **CLC 15**
See also CANR 4; CA 1-4R;
obituary CA 102; DLB 88

**Smith, Betty (Wehner)** 1896-1972... **CLC 19**
See also CA 5-8R; obituary CA 33-36R;
SATA 6; DLB-Y 82

**Smith, Cecil Lewis Troughton** 1899-1966
See Forester, C(ecil) S(cott)

**Smith, Charlotte (Turner)**
1749-1806 ................. **NCLC 23**
See also DLB 39

**Smith, Clark Ashton** 1893-1961 .... **CLC 43**

**Smith, Dave** 1942- ............. **CLC 22, 42**
See also Smith, David (Jeddie)
See also CAAS 7; CANR 1; DLB 5

**Smith, David (Jeddie)** 1942-
See Smith, Dave
See also CANR 1; CA 49-52

**Smith, Florence Margaret** 1902-1971
See Smith, Stevie
See also CAP 2; CA 17-18;
obituary CA 29-32R

**Smith, Iain Crichton** 1928- ........ **CLC 64**
See also DLB 40

**Smith, John** 1580?-1631............. **LC 9**
See also DLB 24, 30

**Smith, Lee** 1944-................. **CLC 25**
See also CA 114, 119; DLB-Y 83

**Smith, Martin Cruz** 1942-.......... **CLC 25**
See also CANR 6; CA 85-88

**Smith, Martin William** 1942-
See Smith, Martin Cruz

**Smith, Mary-Ann Tirone** 1944-..... **CLC 39**
See also CA 118

**Smith, Patti** 1946- ............... **CLC 12**
See also CA 93-96

**Smith, Pauline (Urmson)**
1882-1959 ................. **TCLC 25**
See also CA 29-32R; SATA 27

**Smith, Rosamond** 1938-
See Oates, Joyce Carol

**Smith, Sara Mahala Redway** 1900-1972
See Benson, Sally

**Smith, Stevie** 1902-1971.... **CLC 3, 8, 25, 44**
See also Smith, Florence Margaret
See also DLB 20

**Smith, Wilbur (Addison)** 1933-..... **CLC 33**
See also CANR 7; CA 13-16R

**Smith, William Jay** 1918- .......... **CLC 6**
See also CA 5-8R; SATA 2; DLB 5

**Smolenskin, Peretz** 1842-1885.... **NCLC 30**

**Smollett, Tobias (George)** 1721-1771 .. **LC 2**
See also DLB 39

**Snodgrass, W(illiam) D(e Witt)**
1926- ................. **CLC 2, 6, 10, 18**
See also CANR 6; CA 1-4R; DLB 5

Snow, C(harles) P(ercy)
1905-1980 ...... **CLC 1, 4, 6, 9, 13, 19**
See also CA 5-8R; obituary CA 101;
DLB 15, 77

Snyder, Gary (Sherman)
1930- ...... **CLC 1, 2, 5, 9, 32**
See also CANR 30; CA 17-20R; DLB 5, 16

Snyder, Zilpha Keatley 1927- ...... **CLC 17**
See also CA 9-12R; SAAS 2; SATA 1, 28

Sobol, Joshua 19??- ...... **CLC 60**

Soderberg. Hjalmar 1869-1941 .... **TCLC 39**

Sodergran, Edith 1892-1923...... **TCLC 31**

Sokolov, Raymond 1941- ...... **CLC 7**
See also CA 85-88

Sologub, Fyodor 1863-1927........ **TCLC 9**
See also Teternikov, Fyodor Kuzmich
See also CA 104

Solomos, Dionysios 1798-1857 ... **NCLC 15**

Solwoska, Mara 1929-
See French, Marilyn
See also CANR 3; CA 69-72

Solzhenitsyn, Aleksandr I(sayevich)
1918- ... **CLC 1, 2, 4, 7, 9, 10, 18, 26, 34**
See also CA 69-72

Somers, Jane 1919-
See Lessing, Doris (May)

Sommer, Scott 1951- ...... **CLC 25**
See also CA 106

Sondheim, Stephen (Joshua)
1930- ...... **CLC 30, 39**
See also CA 103

Sontag, Susan 1933-... **CLC 1, 2, 10, 13, 31**
See also CA 17-20R; DLB 2, 67

Sophocles
c. 496? B.C.-c. 406? B.C...... **CMLC 2;
DC 1**

Sorrentino, Gilbert
1929- ...... **CLC 3, 7, 14, 22, 40**
See also CANR 14; CA 77-80; DLB 5;
DLB-Y 80

Soto, Gary 1952-...... **CLC 32**
See also CA 119, 125; DLB 82

Souster, (Holmes) Raymond
1921- ...... **CLC 5, 14**
See also CANR 13; CA 13-16R; DLB 88

Southern, Terry 1926- ...... **CLC 7**
See also CANR 1; CA 1-4R; DLB 2

Southey, Robert 1774-1843 ...... **NCLC 8**
See also SATA 54

Southworth, Emma Dorothy Eliza Nevitte
1819-1899 ...... **NCLC 26**

Soyinka, Akinwande Oluwole 1934-
See Soyinka, Wole

Soyinka, Wole 1934- .. **CLC 3, 5, 14, 36, 44**
See also CA 13-16R; DLB-Y 86

Spackman, W(illiam) M(ode)
1905- ...... **CLC 46**
See also CA 81-84

Spacks, Barry 1931-...... **CLC 14**
See also CA 29-32R

Spanidou, Irini 1946- ...... **CLC 44**

Spark, Muriel (Sarah)
1918- ...... **CLC 2, 3, 5, 8, 13, 18, 40**
See also CANR 12; CA 5-8R; DLB 15

Spencer, Elizabeth 1921-...... **CLC 22**
See also CA 13-16R; SATA 14; DLB 6

Spencer, Scott 1945-...... **CLC 30**
See also CA 113; DLB-Y 86

Spender, Stephen (Harold)
1909- ...... **CLC 1, 2, 5, 10, 41**
See also CA 9-12R; DLB 20

Spengler, Oswald 1880-1936 ...... **TCLC 25**
See also CA 118

Spenser, Edmund 1552?-1599 ...... **LC 5**

Spicer, Jack 1925-1965 ...... **CLC 8, 18**
See also CA 85-88; DLB 5, 16

Spielberg, Peter 1929- ...... **CLC 6**
See also CANR 4; CA 5-8R; DLB-Y 81

Spielberg, Steven 1947- ...... **CLC 20**
See also CA 77-80; SATA 32

Spillane, Frank Morrison 1918-
See Spillane, Mickey
See also CA 25-28R

Spillane, Mickey 1918- ...... **CLC 3, 13**
See also Spillane, Frank Morrison

Spinoza, Benedictus de 1632-1677 .... **LC 9**

Spinrad, Norman (Richard) 1940-... **CLC 46**
See also CANR 20; CA 37-40R; DLB 8

Spitteler, Carl (Friedrich Georg)
1845-1924 ...... **TCLC 12**
See also CA 109

Spivack, Kathleen (Romola Drucker)
1938- ...... **CLC 6**
See also CA 49-52

Spoto, Donald 1941-...... **CLC 39**
See also CANR 11; CA 65-68

Springsteen, Bruce 1949-...... **CLC 17**
See also CA 111

Spurling, Hilary 1940-...... **CLC 34**
See also CANR 25; CA 104

Squires, (James) Radcliffe 1917-... **CLC 51**
See also CANR 6, 21; CA 1-4R

Stael-Holstein, Anne Louise Germaine Necker,
Baronne de 1766-1817...... **NCLC 3**

Stafford, Jean 1915-1979 ...... **CLC 4, 7, 19**
See also CANR 3; CA 1-4R;
obituary CA 85-88; obituary SATA 22;
DLB 2

Stafford, William (Edgar)
1914- ...... **CLC 4, 7, 29**
See also CAAS 3; CANR 5, 22; CA 5-8R;
DLB 5

Stannard, Martin 1947-...... **CLC 44**

Stanton, Maura 1946- ...... **CLC 9**
See also CANR 15; CA 89-92

Stapledon, (William) Olaf
1886-1950 ...... **TCLC 22**
See also CA 111; DLB 15

Starbuck, George (Edwin) 1931-... **CLC 53**
See also CANR 23; CA 21-22R

Stark, Richard 1933-
See Westlake, Donald E(dwin)

Stead, Christina (Ellen)
1902-1983 ...... **CLC 2, 5, 8, 32**
See also CA 13-16R; obituary CA 109

Steele, Timothy (Reid) 1948-...... **CLC 45**
See also CANR 16; CA 93-96

Steffens, (Joseph) Lincoln
1866-1936 ...... **TCLC 20**
See also CA 117; SAAS 1

Stegner, Wallace (Earle) 1909- ... **CLC 9, 49**
See also CANR 1, 21; CA 1-4R; DLB 9

Stein, Gertrude 1874-1946... **TCLC 1, 6, 28**
See also CA 104; DLB 4, 54, 86;
CDALB 1917-1929

Steinbeck, John (Ernst)
1902-1968 ...... **CLC 1, 5, 9, 13, 21, 34,
45, 59**
See also CANR 1; CA 1-4R;
obituary CA 25-28R; SATA 9; DLB 7, 9;
DLB-DS 2; CDALB 1929-1941

Steinem, Gloria 1934-...... **CLC 63**
See also CANR 28; CA 53-56

Steiner, George 1929-...... **CLC 24**
See also CA 73-76; DLB 67

Steiner, Rudolf(us Josephus Laurentius)
1861-1925 ...... **TCLC 13**
See also CA 107

Stendhal 1783-1842...... **NCLC 23**

Stephen, Leslie 1832-1904...... **TCLC 23**
See also CANR 9; CA 21-24R, 123;
DLB 57

Stephens, James 1882?-1950 ...... **TCLC 4**
See also CA 104; DLB 19

Stephens, Reed
See Donaldson, Stephen R.

Steptoe, Lydia 1892-1982
See Barnes, Djuna

Sterchi, Beat 1949-...... **CLC 65**

Sterling, George 1869-1926 ...... **TCLC 20**
See also CA 117; DLB 54

Stern, Gerald 1925- ...... **CLC 40**
See also CA 81-84

Stern, Richard G(ustave) 1928-... **CLC 4, 39**
See also CANR 1, 25; CA 1-4R; DLB 87

Sternberg, Jonas 1894-1969
See Sternberg, Josef von

Sternberg, Josef von 1894-1969..... **CLC 20**
See also CA 81-84

Sterne, Laurence 1713-1768...... **LC 2**
See also DLB 39

Sternheim, (William Adolf) Carl
1878-1942 ...... **TCLC 8**
See also CA 105

Stevens, Mark 19??-...... **CLC 34**

Stevens, Wallace 1879-1955..... **TCLC 3, 12**
See also CA 104, 124; DLB 54

Stevenson, Anne (Katharine)
1933- ...... **CLC 7, 33**
See also Elvin, Anne Katharine Stevenson
See also CANR 9; CA 17-18R; DLB 40

Stevenson, Robert Louis
1850-1894 ...... **NCLC 5, 14**
See also CLR 10, 11; YABC 2; DLB 18, 57

Reyes y Basoalto, Ricardo Eliecer Neftali
 1904-1973
 See Neruda, Pablo

Reymont, Wladyslaw Stanislaw
 1867-1925 .................. TCLC 5
 See also CA 104

Reynolds, Jonathan 1942?- ...... CLC 6, 38
 See also CANR 28; CA 65-68

Reynolds, (Sir) Joshua 1723-1792.... LC 15

Reynolds, Michael (Shane) 1937- ... CLC 44
 See also CANR 9; CA 65-68

Reznikoff, Charles 1894-1976 ....... CLC 9
 See also CAP 2; CA 33-36;
  obituary CA 61-64; DLB 28, 45

Rezzori, Gregor von 1914-......... CLC 25
 See also CA 122

Rhys, Jean
 1890-1979 ...... CLC 2, 4, 6, 14, 19, 51
 See also CA 25-28R; obituary CA 85-88;
  DLB 36

Ribeiro, Darcy 1922-............. CLC 34
 See also CA 33-36R

Ribeiro, Joao Ubaldo (Osorio Pimentel)
 1941-....................... CLC 10
 See also CA 81-84

Ribman, Ronald (Burt) 1932- ....... CLC 7
 See also CA 21-24R

Rice, Anne 1941- ................ CLC 41
 See also CANR 12; CA 65-68

Rice, Elmer 1892-1967......... CLC 7, 49
 See also CAP 2; CA 21-22;
  obituary CA 25-28R; DLB 4, 7

Rice, Tim 1944- ................. CLC 21
 See also CA 103

Rich, Adrienne (Cecile)
 1929-......... CLC 3, 6, 7, 11, 18, 36
 See also CANR 20; CA 9-12R; DLB 5, 67

Richard, Keith 1943- ............. CLC 17
 See also CA 107

Richards, David Adam 1950-....... CLC 59
 See also CA 93-96; DLB 53

Richards, I(vor) A(rmstrong)
 1893-1979 .............. CLC 14, 24
 See also CA 41-44R; obituary CA 89-92;
  DLB 27

Richards, Keith 1943-
 See Richard, Keith
 See also CA 107

Richardson, Dorothy (Miller)
 1873-1957 ................. TCLC 3
 See also CA 104; DLB 36

Richardson, Ethel 1870-1946
 See Richardson, Henry Handel
 See also CA 105

Richardson, Henry Handel
 1870-1946 ................. TCLC 4
 See also Richardson, Ethel

Richardson, Samuel 1689-1761 ....... LC 1
 See also DLB 39

Richler, Mordecai
 1931-......... CLC 3, 5, 9, 13, 18, 46
 See also CLR 17; CA 65-68; SATA 27, 44;
  DLB 53

Richter, Conrad (Michael)
 1890-1968 ................. CLC 30
 See also CANR 23; CA 5-8R;
  obituary CA 25-28R; SATA 3; DLB 9

Richter, Johann Paul Friedrich 1763-1825
 See Jean Paul

Riddell, Mrs. J. H. 1832-1906..... TCLC 40

Riding, Laura 1901-............. CLC 3, 7
 See also Jackson, Laura (Riding)

Riefenstahl, Berta Helene Amalia
 1902-....................... CLC 16
 See also Riefenstahl, Leni
 See also CA 108

Riefenstahl, Leni 1902- ........... CLC 16
 See also Riefenstahl, Berta Helene Amalia
 See also CA 108

Rilke, Rainer Maria
 1875-1926 ....... TCLC 1, 6, 19; PC 2
 See also CA 104, 132; DLB 81

Rimbaud, (Jean Nicolas) Arthur
 1854-1891 .................. NCLC 4

Ringwood, Gwen(dolyn Margaret) Pharis
 1910-1984 .................. CLC 48
 See also obituary CA 112

Rio, Michel 19??-................. CLC 43

Ritsos, Yannis 1909-........ CLC 6, 13, 31
 See also CA 77-80

Ritter, Erika 1948?-.............. CLC 52

Rivera, Jose Eustasio 1889-1928... TCLC 35

Rivers, Conrad Kent 1933-1968...... CLC 1
 See also CA 85-88; DLB 41

Rizal, Jose 1861-1896........... NCLC 27

Roa Bastos, Augusto 1917- ....... CLC 45

Robbe-Grillet, Alain
 1922-...... CLC 1, 2, 4, 6, 8, 10, 14, 43
 See also CA 9-12R; DLB 83

Robbins, Harold 1916-............. CLC 5
 See also CANR 26; CA 73-76

Robbins, Thomas Eugene 1936-
 See Robbins, Tom
 See also CA 81-84

Robbins, Tom 1936-......... CLC 9, 32, 64
 See also Robbins, Thomas Eugene
 See also CANR 29; CA 81-84; DLB-Y 80

Robbins, Trina 1938-............. CLC 21

Roberts, (Sir) Charles G(eorge) D(ouglas)
 1860-1943 .................. TCLC 8
 See also CA 105; SATA 29; DLB 92

Roberts, Kate 1891-1985 .......... CLC 15
 See also CA 107; obituary CA 116

Roberts, Keith (John Kingston)
 1935-...................... CLC 14
 See also CA 25-28R

Roberts, Kenneth 1885-1957 ..... TCLC 23
 See also CA 109; DLB 9

Roberts, Michele (B.) 1949-........ CLC 48
 See also CA 115

Robinson, Edwin Arlington
 1869-1935 ............. TCLC 5; PC 1
 See also CA 104; DLB 54;
  CDALB 1865-1917

Robinson, Henry Crabb
 1775-1867 ................ NCLC 15

Robinson, Jill 1936-............. CLC 10
 See also CA 102

Robinson, Kim Stanley 19??-....... CLC 34
 See also CA 126

Robinson, Marilynne 1944-........ CLC 25
 See also CA 116

Robinson, Smokey 1940-.......... CLC 21

Robinson, William 1940-
 See Robinson, Smokey
 See also CA 116

Robison, Mary 1949-............. CLC 42
 See also CA 113, 116

Roddenberry, Gene 1921-......... CLC 17
 See also CANR 110; SATA 45

Rodgers, Mary 1931-............. CLC 12
 See also CLR 20; CANR 8; CA 49-52;
  SATA 8

Rodgers, W(illiam) R(obert)
 1909-1969 .................. CLC 7
 See also CA 85-88; DLB 20

Rodman, Howard 19??- ........... CLC 65

Rodriguez, Claudio 1934-......... CLC 10

Roethke, Theodore (Huebner)
 1908-1963 ...... CLC 1, 3, 8, 11, 19, 46
 See also CA 81-84; CABS 2; SAAS 1;
  DLB 5; CDALB 1941-1968

Rogers, Sam 1943-
 See Shepard, Sam

Rogers, Thomas (Hunton) 1931-.... CLC 57
 See also CA 89-92

Rogers, Will(iam Penn Adair)
 1879-1935 .................. TCLC 8
 See also CA 105; DLB 11

Rogin, Gilbert 1929-............. CLC 18
 See also CANR 15; CA 65-68

Rohan, Koda 1867-1947.......... TCLC 22
 See also CA 121

Rohmer, Eric 1920- ............. CLC 16
 See also Scherer, Jean-Marie Maurice

Rohmer, Sax 1883-1959......... TCLC 28
 See also Ward, Arthur Henry Sarsfield
 See also CA 108; DLB 70

Roiphe, Anne (Richardson)
 1935-...................... CLC 3, 9
 See also CA 89-92; DLB-Y 80

Rolfe, Frederick (William Serafino Austin
  Lewis Mary) 1860-1913...... TCLC 12
 See also CA 107; DLB 34

Rolland, Romain 1866-1944....... TCLC 23
 See also CA 118; DLB 65

Rolvaag, O(le) E(dvart)
 1876-1931 ................. TCLC 17
 See also CA 117; DLB 9

Romains, Jules 1885-1972.......... CLC 7
 See also CA 85-88

Romero, Jose Ruben 1890-1952 ... TCLC 14
 See also CA 114

Ronsard, Pierre de 1524-1585........ LC 6

Rooke, Leon 1934-............ CLC 25, 34
 See also CANR 23; CA 25-28R

Roper, William 1498-1578.......... LC 10

Rosa, Joao Guimaraes 1908-1967 ... CLC 23
 See also obituary CA 89-92

**Rosen, Richard (Dean)** 1949-...... CLC 39
See also CA 77-80

**Rosenberg, Isaac** 1890-1918....... TCLC 12
See also CA 107; DLB 20

**Rosenblatt, Joe** 1933-............ CLC 15
See also Rosenblatt, Joseph

**Rosenblatt, Joseph** 1933-
See Rosenblatt, Joe
See also CA 89-92

**Rosenfeld, Samuel** 1896-1963
See Tzara, Tristan
See also obituary CA 89-92

**Rosenthal, M(acha) L(ouis)** 1917-... CLC 28
See also CAAS 6; CANR 4; CA 1-4R;
SATA 59; DLB 5

**Ross, (James) Sinclair** 1908-....... CLC 13
See also CA 73-76; DLB 88

**Rossetti, Christina Georgina**
1830-1894 .................. NCLC 2
See also SATA 20; DLB 35

**Rossetti, Dante Gabriel**
1828-1882 .................. NCLC 4
See also DLB 35

**Rossetti, Gabriel Charles Dante** 1828-1882
See Rossetti, Dante Gabriel

**Rossner, Judith (Perelman)**
1935-.................. CLC 6, 9, 29
See also CANR 18; CA 17-20R; DLB 6

**Rostand, Edmond (Eugene Alexis)**
1868-1918 ................ TCLC 6, 37
See also CA 104, 126

**Roth, Henry** 1906-........... CLC 2, 6, 11
See also CAP 1; CA 11-12; DLB 28

**Roth, Joseph** 1894-1939......... TCLC 33
See also DLB 85

**Roth, Philip (Milton)**
1933-...... CLC 1, 2, 3, 4, 6, 9, 15, 22,
31, 47
See also CANR 1, 22; CA 1-4R; DLB 2, 28;
DLB-Y 82

**Rothenberg, James** 1931-.......... CLC 57

**Rothenberg, Jerome** 1931-....... CLC 6, 57
See also CANR 1; CA 45-48; DLB 5

**Roumain, Jacques** 1907-1944...... TCLC 19
See also CA 117

**Rourke, Constance (Mayfield)**
1885-1941 .................. TCLC 12
See also YABC 1; CA 107

**Rousseau, Jean-Baptiste** 1671-1741 ... LC 9

**Rousseau, Jean-Jacques** 1712-1778... LC 14

**Roussel, Raymond** 1877-1933 ..... TCLC 20
See also CA 117

**Rovit, Earl (Herbert)** 1927-......... CLC 7
See also CANR 12; CA 5-8R

**Rowe, Nicholas** 1674-1718........... LC 8

**Rowson, Susanna Haswell**
1762-1824 .................. NCLC 5
See also DLB 37

**Roy, Gabrielle** 1909-1983....... CLC 10, 14
See also CANR 5; CA 53-56;
obituary CA 110; DLB 68

**Rozewicz, Tadeusz** 1921-........ CLC 9, 23
See also CA 108

**Ruark, Gibbons** 1941- ............. CLC 3
See also CANR 14; CA 33-36R

**Rubens, Bernice** 192?- ......... CLC 19, 31
See also CA 25-28R; DLB 14

**Rudkin, (James) David** 1936- ...... CLC 14
See also CA 89-92; DLB 13

**Rudnik, Raphael** 1933-............. CLC 7
See also CA 29-32R

**Ruiz, Jose Martinez** 1874-1967
See Azorin

**Rukeyser, Muriel**
1913-1980 .......... CLC 6, 10, 15, 27
See also CANR 26; CA 5-8R;
obituary CA 93-96; obituary SATA 22;
DLB 48

**Rule, Jane (Vance)** 1931-.......... CLC 27
See also CANR 12; CA 25-28R; DLB 60

**Rulfo, Juan** 1918-1986............. CLC 8
See also CANR 26; CA 85-88;
obituary CA 118

**Runyon, (Alfred) Damon**
1880-1946 ................. TCLC 10
See also CA 107; DLB 11

**Rush, Norman** 1933-.............. CLC 44
See also CA 121, 126

**Rushdie, (Ahmed) Salman**
1947- .............. CLC 23, 31, 55, 59
See also CA 108, 111

**Rushforth, Peter (Scott)** 1945- ..... CLC 19
See also CA 101

**Ruskin, John** 1819-1900......... TCLC 20
See also CA 114; SATA 24; DLB 55

**Russ, Joanna** 1937-.............. CLC 15
See also CANR 11; CA 25-28R; DLB 8

**Russell, George William** 1867-1935
See A. E.
See also CA 104

**Russell, (Henry) Ken(neth Alfred)**
1927- ..................... CLC 16
See also CA 105

**Russell, Mary Annette Beauchamp** 1866-1941
See Elizabeth

**Russell, Willy** 1947-.............. CLC 60

**Rutherford, Mark** 1831-1913..... TCLC 25
See also CA 121; DLB 18

**Ruyslinck, Ward** 1929-............ CLC 14

**Ryan, Cornelius (John)** 1920-1974 ... CLC 7
See also CA 69-72; obituary CA 53-56

**Ryan, Michael** 1946- ............. CLC 65
See also CA 49-52; DLB-Y 82

**Rybakov, Anatoli** 1911?- ....... CLC 23, 53
See also CA 126

**Ryder, Jonathan** 1927-
See Ludlum, Robert

**Ryga, George** 1932- .............. CLC 14
See also CA 101; obituary CA 124; DLB 60

**Séviné, Marquise de Marie de
Rabutin-Chantal** 1626-1696..... LC 11

**Saba, Umberto** 1883-1957 ........ TCLC 33

**Sabato, Ernesto** 1911- ......... CLC 10, 23
See also CA 97-100

**Sacher-Masoch, Leopold von**
1836?-1895................ NCLC 31

**Sachs, Marilyn (Stickle)** 1927-..... CLC 35
See also CLR 2; CANR 13; CA 17-20R;
SAAS 2; SATA 3, 52

**Sachs, Nelly** 1891-1970 ........... CLC 14
See also CAP 2; CA 17-18;
obituary CA 25-28R

**Sackler, Howard (Oliver)**
1929-1982 ................. CLC 14
See also CA 61-64; obituary CA 108; DLB 7

**Sade, Donatien Alphonse Francois, Comte de**
1740-1814 ................. NCLC 3

**Sadoff, Ira** 1945-................. CLC 9
See also CANR 5, 21; CA 53-56

**Safire, William** 1929-............ CLC 10
See also CA 17-20R

**Sagan, Carl (Edward)** 1934-....... CLC 30
See also CANR 11; CA 25-28R; SATA 58

**Sagan, Francoise**
1935- ............. CLC 3, 6, 9, 17, 36
See also Quoirez, Francoise
See also CANR 6; DLB 83

**Sahgal, Nayantara (Pandit)** 1927-... CLC 41
See also CANR 11; CA 9-12R

**Saint, H(arry) F.** 1941- ........... CLC 50

**Sainte-Beuve, Charles Augustin**
1804-1869 ................. NCLC 5

**Sainte-Marie, Beverly** 1941-1972?
See Sainte-Marie, Buffy
See also CA 107

**Sainte-Marie, Buffy** 1941-......... CLC 17
See also Sainte-Marie, Beverly

**Saint-Exupery, Antoine (Jean Baptiste Marie
Roger) de** 1900-1944 ......... TCLC 2
See also CLR 10; CA 108; SATA 20;
DLB 72

**Saintsbury, George** 1845-1933..... TCLC 31
See also DLB 57

**Sait Faik (Abasiyanik)**
1906-1954 ................. TCLC 23

**Saki** 1870-1916.................. TCLC 3
See also Munro, H(ector) H(ugh)
See also CA 104

**Salama, Hannu** 1936-............. CLC 18

**Salamanca, J(ack) R(ichard)**
1922-.................... CLC 4, 15
See also CA 25-28R

**Salinas, Pedro** 1891-1951......... TCLC 17
See also CA 117

**Salinger, J(erome) D(avid)**
1919-....... CLC 1, 3, 8, 12, 56; SSC 2
See also CA 5-8R; DLB 2;
CDALB 1941-1968

**Salter, James** 1925-.......... CLC 7, 52, 59
See also CA 73-76

**Saltus, Edgar (Evertson)**
1855-1921 .................. TCLC 8
See also CA 105

**Saltykov, Mikhail Evgrafovich**
1826-1889 ................. NCLC 16

**Samarakis, Antonis** 1919- .......... CLC 5
See also CA 25-28R

**Sanchez, Florencio** 1875-1910..... TCLC 37

**Sanchez, Luis Rafael** 1936-....... CLC 23

Sanchez, Sonia 1934- . . . . . . . . . . . . **CLC 5**
 See also CANR 24; CA 33-36R; SATA 22;
 DLB 41

Sand, George 1804-1876. . . . . . . . . **NCLC 2**

Sandburg, Carl (August)
 1878-1967 . . . **CLC 1, 4, 10, 15, 35; PC 2**
 See also CA 5-8R; obituary CA 25-28R;
 SATA 8; DLB 17, 54; CDALB 1865-1917

Sandburg, Charles August 1878-1967
 See Sandburg, Carl (August)

Sanders, (James) Ed(ward) 1939- . . . **CLC 53**
 See also CANR 13; CA 15-16R, 103;
 DLB 16

Sanders, Lawrence 1920- . . . . . . . . . **CLC 41**
 See also CA 81-84

Sandoz, Mari (Susette) 1896-1966 . . **CLC 28**
 See also CANR 17; CA 1-4R;
 obituary CA 25-28R; SATA 5; DLB 9

Saner, Reg(inald Anthony) 1931- . . . . **CLC 9**
 See also CA 65-68

Sannazaro, Jacopo 1456?-1530 . . . . . . . **LC 8**

Sansom, William 1912-1976. . . . . . . **CLC 2, 6**
 See also CA 5-8R; obituary CA 65-68

Santayana, George 1863-1952 . . . . . **TCLC 40**
 See also CA 115; DLB 54, 71

Santiago, Danny 1911- . . . . . . . . . . . . **CLC 33**
 See also CA 125

Santmyer, Helen Hooven
 1895-1986 . . . . . . . . . . . . . . . . . **CLC 33**
 See also CANR 15; CA 1-4R;
 obituary CA 118; DLB-Y 84

Santos, Bienvenido N(uqui) 1911- . . . **CLC 22**
 See also CANR 19; CA 101

Sappho c. 6th-century B.C.- . . . . . . . **CMLC 3**

Sarduy, Severo 1937- . . . . . . . . . . . . . **CLC 6**
 See also CA 89-92

Sargeson, Frank 1903-1982 . . . . . . . **CLC 31**
 See also CA 106, 25-28R; obituary CA 106

Sarmiento, Felix Ruben Garcia 1867-1916
 See Dario, Ruben
 See also CA 104

Saroyan, William
 1908-1981 . . . . . **CLC 1, 8, 10, 29, 34, 56**
 See also CA 5-8R; obituary CA 103;
 SATA 23; obituary SATA 24; DLB 7, 9;
 DLB-Y 81

Sarraute, Nathalie
 1902- . . . . . . . . . . **CLC 1, 2, 4, 8, 10, 31**
 See also CANR 23; CA 9-12R; DLB 83

Sarton, Eleanore Marie 1912-
 See Sarton, (Eleanor) May

Sarton, (Eleanor) May
 1912- . . . . . . . . . . . . . . . . . **CLC 4, 14, 49**
 See also CANR 1; CA 1-4R; SATA 36;
 DLB 48; DLB-Y 81

Sartre, Jean-Paul (Charles Aymard)
 1905-1980 . . . **CLC 1, 4, 7, 9, 13, 18, 24,**
           **44, 50, 52**
 See also CANR 21; CA 9-12R;
 obituary CA 97-100; DLB 72

Sassoon, Siegfried (Lorraine)
 1886-1967 . . . . . . . . . . . . . . . . . **CLC 36**
 See also CA 104; obituary CA 25-28R;
 DLB 20

Saul, John (W. III) 1942- . . . . . . . . . **CLC 46**
 See also CANR 16; CA 81-84

Saura, Carlos 1932- . . . . . . . . . . . . . . **CLC 20**
 See also CA 114

Sauser-Hall, Frederic-Louis
 1887-1961 . . . . . . . . . . . . . . . . . **CLC 18**
 See also Cendrars, Blaise
 See also CA 102; obituary CA 93-96

Savage, Thomas 1915- . . . . . . . . . . . . **CLC 40**
 See also CA 126

Savan, Glenn 19??- . . . . . . . . . . . . . . **CLC 50**

Sayers, Dorothy L(eigh)
 1893-1957 . . . . . . . . . . . . . . **TCLC 2, 15**
 See also CA 104, 119; DLB 10, 36, 77

Sayers, Valerie 19??- . . . . . . . . . . . . . **CLC 50**

Sayles, John (Thomas)
 1950- . . . . . . . . . . . . . . . . . **CLC 7, 10, 14**
 See also CA 57-60; DLB 44

Scammell, Michael 19??- . . . . . . . . . . **CLC 34**

Scannell, Vernon 1922- . . . . . . . . . . . **CLC 49**
 See also CANR 8; CA 5-8R; DLB 27

Schaeffer, Susan Fromberg
 1941- . . . . . . . . . . . . . . . **CLC 6, 11, 22**
 See also CANR 18; CA 49-52; SATA 22;
 DLB 28

Schell, Jonathan 1943- . . . . . . . . . . . **CLC 35**
 See also CANR 12; CA 73-76

Schelling, Friedrich Wilhelm Joseph von
 1775-1854 . . . . . . . . . . . . . . . . **NCLC 30**
 See also DLB 90

Scherer, Jean-Marie Maurice 1920-
 See Rohmer, Eric
 See also CA 110

Schevill, James (Erwin) 1920- . . . . . . **CLC 7**
 See also CA 5-8R

Schisgal, Murray (Joseph) 1926- . . . . . **CLC 6**
 See also CA 21-24R

Schlee, Ann 1934- . . . . . . . . . . . . . . . **CLC 35**
 See also CA 101; SATA 36, 44

Schlegel, August Wilhelm von
 1767-1845 . . . . . . . . . . . . . . . . **NCLC 15**

Schlegel, Johann Elias (von)
 1719?-1749. . . . . . . . . . . . . . . . . . . **LC 5**

Schmidt, Arno 1914-1979. . . . . . . . . **CLC 56**
 See also obituary CA 109; DLB 69

Schmitz, Ettore 1861-1928
 See Svevo, Italo
 See also CA 104, 122

Schnackenberg, Gjertrud 1953- . . . . . **CLC 40**
 See also CA 116

Schneider, Leonard Alfred 1925-1966
 See Bruce, Lenny
 See also CA 89-92

Schnitzler, Arthur 1862-1931 . . . . . . **TCLC 4**
 See also CA 104; DLB 81

Schor, Sandra 1932?-1990 . . . . . . . . . **CLC 65**
 See also CA 132

Schorer, Mark 1908-1977 . . . . . . . . . **CLC 9**
 See also CANR 7; CA 5-8R;
 obituary CA 73-76

Schrader, Paul (Joseph) 1946- . . . . . . **CLC 26**
 See also CA 37-40R; DLB 44

Schreiner (Cronwright), Olive (Emilie
 Albertina) 1855-1920. . . . . . . . . . **TCLC 9**
 See also CA 105; DLB 18

Schulberg, Budd (Wilson)
 1914- . . . . . . . . . . . . . . . . . . **CLC 7, 48**
 See also CANR 19; CA 25-28R; DLB 6, 26,
 28; DLB-Y 81

Schulz, Bruno 1892-1942. . . . . . . . . **TCLC 5**
 See also CA 115, 123

Schulz, Charles M(onroe) 1922- . . . . **CLC 12**
 See also CANR 6; CA 9-12R; SATA 10

Schuyler, James (Marcus)
 1923- . . . . . . . . . . . . . . . . . . **CLC 5, 23**
 See also CA 101; DLB 5

Schwartz, Delmore
 1913-1966 . . . . . . . . . . . **CLC 2, 4, 10, 45**
 See also CAP 2; CA 17-18;
 obituary CA 25-28R; DLB 28, 48

Schwartz, John Burnham 1925- . . . . **CLC 59**

Schwartz, Lynne Sharon 1939- . . . . . **CLC 31**
 See also CA 103

Schwarz-Bart, Andre 1928- . . . . . . . **CLC 2, 4**
 See also CA 89-92

Schwarz-Bart, Simone 1938- . . . . . . . . **CLC 7**
 See also CA 97-100

Schwob, (Mayer Andre) Marcel
 1867-1905 . . . . . . . . . . . . . . . . **TCLC 20**
 See also CA 117

Sciascia, Leonardo
 1921-1989 . . . . . . . . . . . . . . **CLC 8, 9, 41**
 See also CA 85-88

Scoppettone, Sandra 1936- . . . . . . . . **CLC 26**
 See also CA 5-8R; SATA 9

Scorsese, Martin 1942- . . . . . . . . . . . **CLC 20**
 See also CA 110, 114

Scotland, Jay 1932-
 See Jakes, John (William)

Scott, Duncan Campbell
 1862-1947 . . . . . . . . . . . . . . . . . **TCLC 6**
 See also CA 104; DLB 92

Scott, Evelyn 1893-1963. . . . . . . . . . . **CLC 43**
 See also CA 104; obituary CA 112; DLB 9,
 48

Scott, F(rancis) R(eginald)
 1899-1985 . . . . . . . . . . . . . . . . . **CLC 22**
 See also CA 101; obituary CA 114; DLB 88

Scott, Joanna 19??- . . . . . . . . . . . . . . **CLC 50**
 See also CA 126

Scott, Paul (Mark) 1920-1978 . . . . **CLC 9, 60**
 See also CA 81-84; obituary CA 77-80;
 DLB 14

Scott, Sir Walter 1771-1832 . . . . . **NCLC 15**
 See also YABC 2

Scribe, (Augustin) Eugene
 1791-1861 . . . . . . . . . . . . . . . . **NCLC 16**

Scudery, Madeleine de 1607-1701 . . . . . **LC 2**

Sealy, I. Allan 1951- . . . . . . . . . . . . . **CLC 55**

Seare, Nicholas 1925-
 See Trevanian; Whitaker, Rodney

Sebestyen, Igen 1924-
 See Sebestyen, Ouida

Sebestyen, Ouida 1924- . . . . . . . . . . . **CLC 30**
 See also CLR 17; CA 107; SATA 39

Sedgwick, Catharine Maria
  1789-1867 ................. NCLC **19**
  See also DLB 1, 74

Seelye, John 1931- ................ CLC **7**
  See also CA 97-100

Seferiades, Giorgos Stylianou 1900-1971
  See Seferis, George
  See also CANR 5; CA 5-8R;
    obituary CA 33-36R

Seferis, George 1900-1971 ...... CLC **5, 11**
  See also Seferiades, Giorgos Stylianou

Segal, Erich (Wolf) 1937- ....... CLC **3, 10**
  See also CANR 20; CA 25-28R; DLB-Y 86

Seger, Bob 1945- ................ CLC **35**

Seger, Robert Clark 1945-
  See Seger, Bob

Seghers, Anna 1900-1983 ...... CLC **7, 110**
  See also Radvanyi, Netty Reiling
  See also DLB 69

Seidel, Frederick (Lewis) 1936- ..... CLC **18**
  See also CANR 8; CA 13-16R; DLB-Y 84

Seifert, Jaroslav 1901-1986 ..... CLC **34, 44**
  See also CA 127

Sei Shonagon c. 966-1017? ........ CMLC **6**

Selby, Hubert, Jr. 1928- ..... CLC **1, 2, 4, 8**
  See also CA 13-16R; DLB 2

Senacour, Etienne Pivert de
  1770-1846 ................. NCLC **16**

Sender, Ramon (Jose) 1902-1982 .... CLC **8**
  See also CANR 8; CA 5-8R;
    obituary CA 105

Seneca, Lucius Annaeus
  4 B.C.-65 A.D. .............. CMLC **6**

Senghor, Léopold Sédar 1906- ...... CLC **54**
  See also CA 116

Serling, (Edward) Rod(man)
  1924-1975 .................. CLC **30**
  See also CA 65-68; obituary CA 57-60;
    DLB 26

Serpieres 1907-
  See Guillevic, (Eugene)

Service, Robert W(illiam)
  1874-1958 .................. TCLC **15**
  See also CA 115; SATA 20

Seth, Vikram 1952- ............... CLC **43**
  See also CA 121, 127

Seton, Cynthia Propper
  1926-1982 .................. CLC **27**
  See also CANR 7; CA 5-8R;
    obituary CA 108

Seton, Ernest (Evan) Thompson
  1860-1946 .................. TCLC **31**
  See also CA 109; SATA 18; DLB 92

Settle, Mary Lee 1918- ........ CLC **19, 61**
  See also CAAS 1; CA 89-92; DLB 6

Sevigne, Marquise de Marie de
  Rabutin-Chantal 1626-1696 ..... LC **11**

Sexton, Anne (Harvey)
  1928-1974 ... CLC **2, 4, 6, 8, 10, 15, 53;**
                               PC **2**
  See also CANR 3; CA 1-4R;
    obituary CA 53-56; CABS 2; SATA 10;
    DLB 5; CDALB 1941-1968

Shaara, Michael (Joseph) 1929- .... CLC **15**
  See also CA 102; obituary CA 125;
    DLB-Y 83

Shackleton, C. C. 1925-
  See Aldiss, Brian W(ilson)

Shacochis, Bob 1951- ............. CLC **39**
  See also CA 119, 124

Shaffer, Anthony 1926- ........... CLC **19**
  See also CA 110, 116; DLB 13

Shaffer, Peter (Levin)
  1926- .......... CLC **5, 14, 18, 37, 60**
  See also CANR 25; CA 25-28R; DLB 13

Shalamov, Varlam (Tikhonovich)
  1907?-1982 ................. CLC **18**
  See also obituary CA 105

Shamlu, Ahmad 1925- ............ CLC **10**

Shammas, Anton 1951- ............ CLC **55**

Shange, Ntozake 1948- ...... CLC **8, 25, 38**
  See also CA 85-88; DLB 38

Shapcott, Thomas W(illiam) 1935- .. CLC **38**
  See also CA 69-72

Shapiro, Karl (Jay) 1913- .. CLC **4, 8, 15, 53**
  See also CAAS 6; CANR 1; CA 1-4R;
    DLB 48

Sharp, William 1855-1905 ........ TCLC **39**

Sharpe, Tom 1928- ................ CLC **36**
  See also CA 114; DLB 14

Shaw, (George) Bernard
  1856-1950 ............. TCLC **3, 9, 21**
  See also CA 104, 109, 119; DLB 10, 57

Shaw, Henry Wheeler
  1818-1885 ................. NCLC **15**
  See also DLB 11

Shaw, Irwin 1913-1984 ....... CLC **7, 23, 34**
  See also CANR 21; CA 13-16R;
    obituary CA 112; DLB 6; DLB-Y 84;
    CDALB 1941-1968

Shaw, Robert 1927-1978 ........... CLC **5**
  See also CANR 4; CA 1-4R;
    obituary CA 81-84; DLB 13, 14

Shawn, Wallace 1943- ............ CLC **41**
  See also CA 112

Sheed, Wilfrid (John Joseph)
  1930- ................ CLC **2, 4, 10, 53**
  See also CA 65-68; DLB 6

Sheffey, Asa 1913-1980
  See Hayden, Robert (Earl)

Sheldon, Alice (Hastings) B(radley)
  1915-1987
  See Tiptree, James, Jr.
  See also CA 108; obituary CA 122

Shelley, Mary Wollstonecraft Godwin
  1797-1851 ................. NCLC **14**
  See also SATA 29

Shelley, Percy Bysshe
  1792-1822 ................. NCLC **18**

Shepard, Jim 19??- ............... CLC **36**

Shepard, Lucius 19??- ............ CLC **34**
  See also CA 128

Shepard, Sam
  1943- ......... CLC **4, 6, 17, 34, 41, 44**
  See also CANR 22; CA 69-72; DLB 7

Shepherd, Michael 1927-
  See Ludlum, Robert

Sherburne, Zoa (Morin) 1912- ...... CLC **30**
  See also CANR 3; CA 1-4R; SATA 3

Sheridan, Frances 1724-1766 ........ LC **7**
  See also DLB 39, 84

Sheridan, Richard Brinsley
  1751-1816 ............. NCLC **5; DC 1**
  See also DLB 89

Sherman, Jonathan Marc 1970?- .... CLC **55**

Sherman, Martin 19??- ............ CLC **19**
  See also CA 116

Sherwin, Judith Johnson 1936- ... CLC **7, 15**
  See also CA 25-28R

Sherwood, Robert E(mmet)
  1896-1955 .................. TCLC **3**
  See also CA 104; DLB 7, 26

Shiel, M(atthew) P(hipps)
  1865-1947 .................. TCLC **8**
  See also CA 106

Shiga, Naoya 1883-1971 .......... CLC **33**
  See also CA 101; obituary CA 33-36R

Shimazaki, Haruki 1872-1943
  See Shimazaki, Toson
  See also CA 105

Shimazaki, Toson 1872-1943 ...... TCLC **5**
  See also Shimazaki, Haruki

Sholokhov, Mikhail (Aleksandrovich)
  1905-1984 ................. CLC **7, 15**
  See also CA 101; obituary CA 112;
    SATA 36

Sholom Aleichem 1859-1916 .... TCLC **1, 35**
  See also Rabinovitch, Sholem

Shreve, Susan Richards 1939- ...... CLC **23**
  See also CAAS 5; CANR 5; CA 49-52;
    SATA 41, 46

Shue, Larry 1946-1985 ............ CLC **52**
  See also obituary CA 117

Shulman, Alix Kates 1932- ...... CLC **2, 10**
  See also CA 29-32R; SATA 7

Shuster, Joe 1914- ............... CLC **21**

Shute (Norway), Nevil 1899-1960 ... CLC **30**
  See also Norway, Nevil Shute
  See also CA 102; obituary CA 93-96

Shuttle, Penelope (Diane) 1947- ..... CLC **7**
  See also CA 93-96; DLB 14, 40

Siegel, Jerome 1914- ............. CLC **21**
  See also CA 116

Sienkiewicz, Henryk (Adam Aleksander Pius)
  1846-1916 .................. TCLC **3**
  See also CA 104

Sigal, Clancy 1926- ............... CLC **7**
  See also CA 1-4R

Sigourney, Lydia (Howard Huntley)
  1791-1865 ................. NCLC **21**
  See also DLB 1, 42, 73

Siguenza y Gongora, Carlos de
  1645-1700 .................... LC **8**

Sigurjonsson, Johann 1880-1919 ... TCLC **27**

Sikelianos, Angeles 1884-1951 ..... TCLC **39**

Silkin, Jon 1930- ............... CLC **2, 6, 43**
  See also CAAS 5; CA 5-8R; DLB 27

Silko, Leslie Marmon 1948- ....... CLC **23**
  See also CA 115, 122

Sillanpaa, Franz Eemil 1888-1964... **CLC 19**
See also CA 129; obituary CA 93-96

Sillitoe, Alan
1928- ......... **CLC 1, 3, 6, 10, 19, 57**
See also CAAS 2; CANR 8, 26; CA 9-12R;
DLB 14

Silone, Ignazio 1900-1978 ......... **CLC 4**
See also CAAS 2; CANR 26; CAP 2;
CA 25-28, 11-12R,; obituary CA 81-84

Silver, Joan Micklin 1935- ....... **CLC 20**
See also CA 114, 121

Silverberg, Robert 1935- ......... **CLC 7**
See also CAAS 3; CANR 1, 20; CA 1-4R;
SATA 13; DLB 8

Silverstein, Alvin 1933- ............ **CLC 17**
See also CANR 2; CA 49-52; SATA 8

Silverstein, Virginia B(arbara Opshelor)
1937- ......................... **CLC 17**
See also CANR 2; CA 49-52; SATA 8

Simak, Clifford D(onald)
1904-1988 ............ **CLC 1, 55**
See also CANR 1; CA 1-4R;
obituary CA 125; DLB 8

Simenon, Georges (Jacques Christian)
1903-1989 ....... **CLC 1, 2, 3, 8, 18, 47**
See also CA 85-88; obituary CA 129;
DLB 72

Simenon, Paul 1956?-
See The Clash

Simic, Charles 1938-...... **CLC 6, 9, 22, 49**
See also CAAS 4; CANR 12; CA 29-32R

Simmons, Charles (Paul) 1924- ..... **CLC 57**
See also CA 89-92

Simmons, Dan 1948-............. **CLC 44**

Simmons, James (Stewart Alexander)
1933- ...................... **CLC 43**
See also CA 105; DLB 40

Simms, William Gilmore
1806-1870 ................. **NCLC 3**
See also DLB 3, 30, 59, 73

Simon, Carly 1945-.............. **CLC 26**
See also CA 105

Simon, Claude (Henri Eugene)
1913- ............... **CLC 4, 9, 15, 39**
See also CA 89-92; DLB 83

Simon, (Marvin) Neil
1927- ............... **CLC 6, 11, 31, 39**
See also CA 21-24R; DLB 7

Simon, Paul 1941- .............. **CLC 17**
See also CA 116

Simonon, Paul 1956?-
See The Clash

Simpson, Louis (Aston Marantz)
1923- ................ **CLC 4, 7, 9, 32**
See also CAAS 4; CANR 1; CA 1-4R;
DLB 5

Simpson, Mona (Elizabeth) 1957-... **CLC 44**
See also CA 122

Simpson, N(orman) F(rederick)
1919- ....................... **CLC 29**
See also CA 11-14R; DLB 13

Sinclair, Andrew (Annandale)
1935- ................... **CLC 2, 14**
See also CAAS 5; CANR 14; CA 9-12R;
DLB 14

Sinclair, Mary Amelia St. Clair 1865?-1946
See Sinclair, May
See also CA 104

Sinclair, May 1865?-1946 ...... **TCLC 3, 11**
See also Sinclair, Mary Amelia St. Clair
See also DLB 36

Sinclair, Upton (Beall)
1878-1968 ........... **CLC 1, 11, 15, 63**
See also CANR 7; CA 5-8R;
obituary CA 25-28R; SATA 9; DLB 9

Singer, Isaac Bashevis
1904- .... **CLC 1, 3, 6, 9, 11, 15, 23, 38;**
                                      **SSC 3**
See also CLR 1; CANR 1; CA 1-4R;
SATA 3, 27; DLB 6, 28, 52;
CDALB 1941-1968

Singer, Israel Joshua 1893-1944 ... **TCLC 33**

Singh, Khushwant 1915-.......... **CLC 11**
See also CANR 6; CA 9-12R

Sinyavsky, Andrei (Donatevich)
1925- ....................... **CLC 8**
See also CA 85-88

Sirin, V.
See Nabokov, Vladimir (Vladimirovich)

Sissman, L(ouis) E(dward)
1928-1976 ................. **CLC 9, 18**
See also CANR 13; CA 21-24R;
obituary CA 65-68; DLB 5

Sisson, C(harles) H(ubert) 1914-..... **CLC 8**
See also CAAS 3; CANR 3; CA 1-4R;
DLB 27

Sitwell, (Dame) Edith 1887-1964... **CLC 2, 9**
See also CA 9-12R; DLB 20

Sjoewall, Maj 1935-
See Wahloo, Per
See also CA 61-64, 65-68

Sjowall, Maj 1935-
See Wahloo, Per

Skelton, Robin 1925- ............. **CLC 13**
See also CAAS 5; CA 5-8R; DLB 27, 53

Skolimowski, Jerzy 1938- ......... **CLC 20**

Skolimowski, Yurek 1938-
See Skolimowski, Jerzy

Skram, Amalie (Bertha)
1847-1905 ................. **TCLC 25**

Skrine, Mary Nesta 1904-
See Keane, Molly

Skvorecky, Josef (Vaclav)
1924- ................... **CLC 15, 39**
See also CAAS 1; CANR 10; CA 61-64

Slade, Bernard 1930- .......... **CLC 11, 46**
See also Newbound, Bernard Slade
See also DLB 53

Slaughter, Carolyn 1946-.......... **CLC 56**
See also CA 85-88

Slaughter, Frank G(ill) 1908- ...... **CLC 29**
See also CANR 5; CA 5-8R

Slavitt, David (R.) 1935- ........ **CLC 5, 14**
See also CAAS 3; CA 21-24R; DLB 5, 6

Slesinger, Tess 1905-1945 ........ **TCLC 10**
See also CA 107

Slessor, Kenneth 1901-1971 ....... **CLC 14**
See also CA 102; obituary CA 89-92

Slowacki, Juliusz 1809-1849 ..... **NCLC 15**

Smart, Christopher 1722-1771........ **LC 3**

Smart, Elizabeth 1913-1986........ **CLC 54**
See also CA 81-84; obituary CA 118;
DLB 88

Smiley, Jane (Graves) 1949- ....... **CLC 53**
See also CA 104

Smith, A(rthur) J(ames) M(arshall)
1902-1980 ................... **CLC 15**
See also CANR 4; CA 1-4R;
obituary CA 102; DLB 88

Smith, Betty (Wehner) 1896-1972... **CLC 19**
See also CA 5-8R; obituary CA 33-36R;
SATA 6; DLB-Y 82

Smith, Cecil Lewis Troughton 1899-1966
See Forester, C(ecil) S(cott)

Smith, Charlotte (Turner)
1749-1806 ................. **NCLC 23**
See also DLB 39

Smith, Clark Ashton 1893-1961 .... **CLC 43**

Smith, Dave 1942- ............. **CLC 22, 42**
See also Smith, David (Jeddie)
See also CAAS 7; CANR 1; DLB 5

Smith, David (Jeddie) 1942-
See Smith, Dave
See also CANR 1; CA 49-52

Smith, Florence Margaret 1902-1971
See Smith, Stevie
See also CAP 2; CA 17-18;
obituary CA 29-32R

Smith, Iain Crichton 1928- ........ **CLC 64**
See also DLB 40

Smith, John 1580?-1631............. **LC 9**
See also DLB 24, 30

Smith, Lee 1944-.................. **CLC 25**
See also CA 114, 119; DLB-Y 83

Smith, Martin Cruz 1942-......... **CLC 25**
See also CANR 6; CA 85-88

Smith, Martin William 1942-
See Smith, Martin Cruz

Smith, Mary-Ann Tirone 1944-..... **CLC 39**
See also CA 118

Smith, Patti 1946- .............. **CLC 12**
See also CA 93-96

Smith, Pauline (Urmson)
1882-1959 ................. **TCLC 25**
See also CA 29-32R; SATA 27

Smith, Rosamond 1938-
See Oates, Joyce Carol

Smith, Sara Mahala Redway 1900-1972
See Benson, Sally

Smith, Stevie 1902-1971.... **CLC 3, 8, 25, 44**
See also Smith, Florence Margaret
See also DLB 20

Smith, Wilbur (Addison) 1933-..... **CLC 33**
See also CANR 7; CA 13-16R

Smith, William Jay 1918- .......... **CLC 6**
See also CA 5-8R; SATA 2; DLB 5

Smolenskin, Peretz 1842-1885.... **NCLC 30**

Smollett, Tobias (George) 1721-1771 .. **LC 2**
See also DLB 39

Snodgrass, W(illiam) D(e Witt)
1926- ............... **CLC 2, 6, 10, 18**
See also CANR 6; CA 1-4R; DLB 5

Snow, C(harles) P(ercy)
1905-1980 ....... CLC 1, 4, 6, 9, 13, 19
See also CA 5-8R; obituary CA 101;
DLB 15, 77

Snyder, Gary (Sherman)
1930- .............. CLC 1, 2, 5, 9, 32
See also CANR 30; CA 17-20R; DLB 5, 16

Snyder, Zilpha Keatley 1927- ...... CLC 17
See also CA 9-12R; SAAS 2; SATA 1, 28

Sobol, Joshua 19??- .............. CLC 60

Soderberg. Hjalmar 1869-1941 .... TCLC 39

Sodergran, Edith 1892-1923...... TCLC 31

Sokolov, Raymond 1941-........... CLC 7
See also CA 85-88

Sologub, Fyodor 1863-1927........ TCLC 9
See also Teternikov, Fyodor Kuzmich
See also CA 104

Solomos, Dionysios 1798-1857 ... NCLC 15

Solwoska, Mara 1929-
See French, Marilyn
See also CANR 3; CA 69-72

Solzhenitsyn, Aleksandr I(sayevich)
1918- ... CLC 1, 2, 4, 7, 9, 10, 18, 26, 34
See also CA 69-72

Somers, Jane 1919-
See Lessing, Doris (May)

Sommer, Scott 1951- .............. CLC 25
See also CA 106

Sondheim, Stephen (Joshua)
1930- .................... CLC 30, 39
See also CA 103

Sontag, Susan 1933-... CLC 1, 2, 10, 13, 31
See also CA 17-20R; DLB 2, 67

Sophocles
c. 496? B.C.-c. 406? B.C...... CMLC 2;
DC 1

Sorrentino, Gilbert
1929- ............ CLC 3, 7, 14, 22, 40
See also CANR 14; CA 77-80; DLB 5;
DLB-Y 80

Soto, Gary 1952-................. CLC 32
See also CA 119, 125; DLB 82

Souster, (Holmes) Raymond
1921- .................... CLC 5, 14
See also CANR 13; CA 13-16R; DLB 88

Southern, Terry 1926- ............. CLC 7
See also CANR 1; CA 1-4R; DLB 2

Southey, Robert 1774-1843 ....... NCLC 8
See also SATA 54

Southworth, Emma Dorothy Eliza Nevitte
1819-1899 ................ NCLC 26

Soyinka, Akinwande Oluwole 1934-
See Soyinka, Wole

Soyinka, Wole 1934- .. CLC 3, 5, 14, 36, 44
See also CA 13-16R; DLB-Y 86

Spackman, W(illiam) M(ode)
1905-....................... CLC 46
See also CA 81-84

Spacks, Barry 1931-.............. CLC 14
See also CA 29-32R

Spanidou, Irini 1946-............ CLC 44

Spark, Muriel (Sarah)
1918- ........ CLC 2, 3, 5, 8, 13, 18, 40
See also CANR 12; CA 5-8R; DLB 15

Spencer, Elizabeth 1921-.......... CLC 22
See also CA 13-16R; SATA 14; DLB 6

Spencer, Scott 1945-.............. CLC 30
See also CA 113; DLB-Y 86

Spender, Stephen (Harold)
1909- ............. CLC 1, 2, 5, 10, 41
See also CA 9-12R; DLB 20

Spengler, Oswald 1880-1936 ..... TCLC 25
See also CA 118

Spenser, Edmund 1552?-1599 ........ LC 5

Spicer, Jack 1925-1965 ......... CLC 8, 18
See also CA 85-88; DLB 5, 16

Spielberg, Peter 1929- ............ CLC 6
See also CANR 4; CA 5-8R; DLB-Y 81

Spielberg, Steven 1947- .......... CLC 20
See also CA 77-80; SATA 32

Spillane, Frank Morrison 1918-
See Spillane, Mickey
See also CA 25-28R

Spillane, Mickey 1918- ......... CLC 3, 13
See also Spillane, Frank Morrison

Spinoza, Benedictus de 1632-1677 .... LC 9

Spinrad, Norman (Richard) 1940-... CLC 46
See also CANR 20; CA 37-40R; DLB 8

Spitteler, Carl (Friedrich Georg)
1845-1924 .................. TCLC 12
See also CA 109

Spivack, Kathleen (Romola Drucker)
1938- ....................... CLC 6
See also CA 49-52

Spoto, Donald 1941-.............. CLC 39
See also CANR 11; CA 65-68

Springsteen, Bruce 1949-.......... CLC 17
See also CA 111

Spurling, Hilary 1940-............ CLC 34
See also CANR 25; CA 104

Squires, (James) Radcliffe 1917-.... CLC 51
See also CANR 6, 21; CA 1-4R

Stael-Holstein, Anne Louise Germaine Necker,
Baronne de 1766-1817....... NCLC 3

Stafford, Jean 1915-1979 ..... CLC 4, 7, 19
See also CANR 3; CA 1-4R;
obituary CA 85-88; obituary SATA 22;
DLB 2

Stafford, William (Edgar)
1914- ................... CLC 4, 7, 29
See also CAAS 3; CANR 5, 22; CA 5-8R;
DLB 5

Stannard, Martin 1947-........... CLC 44

Stanton, Maura 1946- ............. CLC 9
See also CANR 15; CA 89-92

Stapledon, (William) Olaf
1886-1950 .................. TCLC 22
See also CA 111; DLB 15

Starbuck, George (Edwin) 1931-.... CLC 53
See also CANR 23; CA 21-22R

Stark, Richard 1933-
See Westlake, Donald E(dwin)

Stead, Christina (Ellen)
1902-1983 ............. CLC 2, 5, 8, 32
See also CA 13-16R; obituary CA 109

Steele, Timothy (Reid) 1948-....... CLC 45
See also CANR 16; CA 93-96

Steffens, (Joseph) Lincoln
1866-1936 ................. TCLC 20
See also CA 117; SAAS 1

Stegner, Wallace (Earle) 1909- ... CLC 9, 49
See also CANR 1, 21; CA 1-4R; DLB 9

Stein, Gertrude 1874-1946... TCLC 1, 6, 28
See also CA 104; DLB 4, 54, 86;
CDALB 1917-1929

Steinbeck, John (Ernst)
1902-1968 ..... CLC 1, 5, 9, 13, 21, 34,
45, 59
See also CANR 1; CA 1-4R;
obituary CA 25-28R; SATA 9; DLB 7, 9;
DLB-DS 2; CDALB 1929-1941

Steinem, Gloria 1934-............. CLC 63
See also CANR 28; CA 53-56

Steiner, George 1929-............. CLC 24
See also CA 73-76; DLB 67

Steiner, Rudolf(us Josephus Laurentius)
1861-1925 .................. TCLC 13
See also CA 107

Stendhal 1783-1842............. NCLC 23

Stephen, Leslie 1832-1904........ TCLC 23
See also CANR 9; CA 21-24R, 123;
DLB 57

Stephens, James 1882?-1950 ....... TCLC 4
See also CA 104; DLB 19

Stephens, Reed
See Donaldson, Stephen R.

Steptoe, Lydia 1892-1982
See Barnes, Djuna

Sterchi, Beat 1949-............... CLC 65

Sterling, George 1869-1926 ....... TCLC 20
See also CA 117; DLB 54

Stern, Gerald 1925- .............. CLC 40
See also CA 81-84

Stern, Richard G(ustave) 1928-... CLC 4, 39
See also CANR 1, 25; CA 1-4R; DLB 87

Sternberg, Jonas 1894-1969
See Sternberg, Josef von

Sternberg, Josef von 1894-1969..... CLC 20
See also CA 81-84

Sterne, Laurence 1713-1768.......... LC 2
See also DLB 39

Sternheim, (William Adolf) Carl
1878-1942 .................. TCLC 8
See also CA 105

Stevens, Mark 19??-.............. CLC 34

Stevens, Wallace 1879-1955..... TCLC 3, 12
See also CA 104, 124; DLB 54

Stevenson, Anne (Katharine)
1933- .................... CLC 7, 33
See also Elvin, Anne Katharine Stevenson
See also CANR 9; CA 17-18R; DLB 40

Stevenson, Robert Louis
1850-1894 ............... NCLC 5, 14
See also CLR 10, 11; YABC 2; DLB 18, 57

**Stewart, J(ohn) I(nnes) M(ackintosh)**
1906- .................. **CLC 7, 14, 32**
See also CAAS 3; CA 85-88

**Stewart, Mary (Florence Elinor)**
1916- ..................... **CLC 7, 35**
See also CANR 1; CA 1-4R; SATA 12

**Stewart, Will** 1908-
See Williamson, Jack
See also CANR 23; CA 17-18R

**Still, James** 1906-............... **CLC 49**
See also CANR 10, 26; CA 65-68;
SATA 29; DLB 9

**Sting** 1951-
See The Police

**Stitt, Milan** 1941-............... **CLC 29**
See also CA 69-72

**Stoker, Abraham**
See Stoker, Bram
See also CA 105; SATA 29

**Stoker, Bram** 1847-1912 ......... **TCLC 8**
See also Stoker, Abraham
See also SATA 29; DLB 36, 70

**Stolz, Mary (Slattery)** 1920-....... **CLC 12**
See also CANR 13; CA 5-8R; SAAS 3;
SATA 10

**Stone, Irving** 1903-1989........... **CLC 7**
See also CAAS 3; CANR 1; CA 1-4R, 129;
SATA 3

**Stone, Robert (Anthony)**
1937?- ................. **CLC 5, 23, 42**
See also CANR 23; CA 85-88

**Stoppard, Tom**
1937- ... **CLC 1, 3, 4, 5, 8, 15, 29, 34, 63**
See also CA 81-84; DLB 13; DLB-Y 85

**Storey, David (Malcolm)**
1933- .................. **CLC 2, 4, 5, 8**
See also CA 81-84; DLB 13, 14

**Storm, Hyemeyohsts** 1935-......... **CLC 3**
See also CA 81-84

**Storm, (Hans) Theodor (Woldsen)**
1817-1888 ................. **NCLC 1**

**Storni, Alfonsina** 1892-1938 ....... **TCLC 5**
See also CA 104

**Stout, Rex (Todhunter)** 1886-1975 ... **CLC 3**
See also CA 61-64

**Stow, (Julian) Randolph** 1935- .. **CLC 23, 48**
See also CA 13-16R

**Stowe, Harriet (Elizabeth) Beecher**
1811-1896 ................. **NCLC 3**
See also YABC 1; DLB 1, 12, 42, 74;
CDALB 1865-1917

**Strachey, (Giles) Lytton**
1880-1932 ................. **TCLC 12**
See also CA 110

**Strand, Mark** 1934- ......... **CLC 6, 18, 41**
See also CA 21-24R; SATA 41; DLB 5

**Straub, Peter (Francis)** 1943- ...... **CLC 28**
See also CA 85-88; DLB-Y 84

**Strauss, Botho** 1944- ............. **CLC 22**

**Straussler, Tomas** 1937-
See Stoppard, Tom

**Streatfeild, (Mary) Noel** 1897- ..... **CLC 21**
See also CA 81-84; obituary CA 120;
SATA 20, 48

**Stribling, T(homas) S(igismund)**
1881-1965 .................. **CLC 23**
See also obituary CA 107; DLB 9

**Strindberg, (Johan) August**
1849-1912 ............. **TCLC 1, 8, 21**
See also CA 104

**Stringer, Arthur** 1874-1950 ...... **TCLC 37**
See also DLB 92

**Strugatskii, Arkadii (Natanovich)**
1925- ..................... **CLC 27**
See also CA 106

**Strugatskii, Boris (Natanovich)**
1933- ..................... **CLC 27**
See also CA 106

**Strummer, Joe** 1953?-
See The Clash

**Stuart, (Hilton) Jesse**
1906-1984 ........ **CLC 1, 8, 11, 14, 34**
See also CA 5-8R; obituary CA 112;
SATA 2; obituary SATA 36; DLB 9, 48;
DLB-Y 84

**Sturgeon, Theodore (Hamilton)**
1918-1985 ................ **CLC 22, 39**
See also CA 81-84; obituary CA 116;
DLB 8; DLB-Y 85

**Styron, William**
1925- .......... **CLC 1, 3, 5, 11, 15, 60**
See also CANR 6; CA 5-8R; DLB 2;
DLB-Y 80; CDALB 1968-1987

**Sudermann, Hermann** 1857-1928 .. **TCLC 15**
See also CA 107

**Sue, Eugene** 1804-1857 .......... **NCLC 1**

**Sukenick, Ronald** 1932-..... **CLC 3, 4, 6, 48**
See also CAAS 8; CA 25-28R; DLB-Y 81

**Suknaski, Andrew** 1942- .......... **CLC 19**
See also CA 101; DLB 53

**Sully Prudhomme, Rene**
1839-1907 ................. **TCLC 31**

**Su Man-shu** 1884-1918........... **TCLC 24**
See also CA 123

**Summers, Andrew James** 1942-
See The Police

**Summers, Andy** 1942-
See The Police

**Summers, Hollis (Spurgeon, Jr.)**
1916- ....................... **CLC 10**
See also CANR 3; CA 5-8R; DLB 6

**Summers, (Alphonsus Joseph-Mary Augustus)**
Montague 1880-1948 ....... **TCLC 16**
See also CA 118

**Sumner, Gordon Matthew** 1951-
See The Police

**Surtees, Robert Smith**
1805-1864 ................ **NCLC 14**
See also DLB 21

**Susann, Jacqueline** 1921-1974...... **CLC 3**
See also CA 65-68; obituary CA 53-56

**Suskind, Patrick** 1949-............ **CLC 44**

**Sutcliff, Rosemary** 1920-.......... **CLC 26**
See also CLR 1; CA 5-8R; SATA 6, 44

**Sutro, Alfred** 1863-1933........... **TCLC 6**
See also CA 105; DLB 10

**Sutton, Henry** 1935-
See Slavitt, David (R.)

**Svevo, Italo** 1861-1928........ **TCLC 2, 35**
See also Schmitz, Ettore

**Swados, Elizabeth** 1951- .......... **CLC 12**
See also CA 97-100

**Swados, Harvey** 1920-1972 ........ **CLC 5**
See also CANR 6; CA 5-8R;
obituary CA 37-40R; DLB 2

**Swarthout, Glendon (Fred)** 1918- ... **CLC 35**
See also CANR 1; CA 1-4R; SATA 26

**Swenson, May** 1919-1989..... **CLC 4, 14, 61**
See also CA 5-8R; obituary CA 130;
SATA 15; DLB 5

**Swift, Graham** 1949- ............. **CLC 41**
See also CA 117, 122

**Swift, Jonathan** 1667-1745.......... **LC 1**
See also SATA 19; DLB 39

**Swinburne, Algernon Charles**
1837-1909 .............. **TCLC 8, 36**
See also CA 105; DLB 35, 57

**Swinfen, Ann** 19??-............... **CLC 34**

**Swinnerton, Frank (Arthur)**
1884-1982 .................. **CLC 31**
See also obituary CA 108; DLB 34

**Symons, Arthur (William)**
1865-1945 ................. **TCLC 11**
See also CA 107; DLB 19, 57

**Symons, Julian (Gustave)**
1912- ................. **CLC 2, 14, 32**
See also CAAS 3; CANR 3; CA 49-52;
DLB 87

**Synge, (Edmund) John Millington**
1871-1909 ................**TCLC 6, 37**
See also CA 104; DLB 10, 19

**Syruc, J.** 1911-
See Milosz, Czeslaw

**Szirtes, George** 1948-............. **CLC 46**
See also CANR 27; CA 109

**Tabori, George** 1914-............. **CLC 19**
See also CANR 4; CA 49-52

**Tagore, (Sir) Rabindranath**
1861-1941 ................. **TCLC 3**
See also Thakura, Ravindranatha
See also CA 120

**Taine, Hippolyte Adolphe**
1828-1893 ................ **NCLC 15**

**Talese, Gaetano** 1932-
See Talese, Gay

**Talese, Gay** 1932-................ **CLC 37**
See also CANR 9; CA 1-4R

**Tallent, Elizabeth (Ann)** 1954- ..... **CLC 45**
See also CA 117

**Tally, Ted** 1952-................. **CLC 42**
See also CA 120, 124

**Tamayo y Baus, Manuel**
1829-1898 ................. **NCLC 1**

**Tammsaare, A(nton) H(ansen)**
1878-1940 ................. **TCLC 27**

**Tan, Amy** 1952- ................. **CLC 59**

**Tanizaki, Jun'ichiro**
1886-1965.......... **CLC 8, 14, 28**
See also CA 93-96; obituary CA 25-28R

**Tarbell, Ida** 1857-1944.......... **TCLC 40**
See also CA 122; DLB 47

**Tarkington, (Newton) Booth**
1869-1946 . . . . . . . . . . . . . . . . . . **TCLC 9**
See also CA 110; SATA 17; DLB 9

**Tasso, Torquato** 1544-1595 . . . . . . . . . **LC 5**

**Tate, (John Orley) Allen**
1899-1979 . . . . **CLC 2, 4, 6, 9, 11, 14, 24**
See also CA 5-8R; obituary CA 85-88;
DLB 4, 45, 63

**Tate, James** 1943- . . . . . . . . . . . **CLC 2, 6, 25**
See also CA 21-24R; DLB 5

**Tavel, Ronald** 1940- . . . . . . . . . . . . . . **CLC 6**
See also CA 21-24R

**Taylor, C(ecil) P(hillip)** 1929-1981 . . **CLC 27**
See also CA 25-28R; obituary CA 105

**Taylor, Edward** 1644?-1729 . . . . . . . . **LC 11**
See also DLB 24

**Taylor, Eleanor Ross** 1920- . . . . . . . . **CLC 5**
See also CA 81-84

**Taylor, Elizabeth** 1912-1975 . . . **CLC 2, 4, 29**
See also CANR 9; CA 13-16R; SATA 13

**Taylor, Henry (Splawn)** 1917- . . . . . . **CLC 44**
See also CAAS 7; CA 33-36R; DLB 5

**Taylor, Kamala (Purnaiya)** 1924-
See Markandaya, Kamala
See also CA 77-80

**Taylor, Mildred D(elois)** 1943- . . . . . **CLC 21**
See also CLR 9; CANR 25; CA 85-88;
SAAS 5; SATA 15; DLB 52

**Taylor, Peter (Hillsman)**
1917- . . . . . . . . . . . **CLC 1, 4, 18, 37, 44, 50**
See also CANR 9; CA 13-16R; DLB-Y 81

**Taylor, Robert Lewis** 1912- . . . . . . . . **CLC 14**
See also CANR 3; CA 1-4R; SATA 10

**Teasdale, Sara** 1884-1933 . . . . . . . . . **TCLC 4**
See also CA 104; SATA 32; DLB 45

**Tegner, Esaias** 1782-1846 . . . . . . . . **NCLC 2**

**Teilhard de Chardin, (Marie Joseph) Pierre**
1881-1955 . . . . . . . . . . . . . . . . . . **TCLC 9**
See also CA 105

**Tennant, Emma** 1937- . . . . . . . . **CLC 13, 52**
See also CAAS 9; CANR 10; CA 65-68;
DLB 14

**Tennyson, Alfred** 1809-1892 . . . . . **NCLC 30**
See also DLB 32

**Teran, Lisa St. Aubin de** 19??- . . . . . **CLC 36**

**Terkel, Louis** 1912-
See Terkel, Studs
See also CANR 18; CA 57-60

**Terkel, Studs** 1912- . . . . . . . . . . . . . . **CLC 38**
See also Terkel, Louis

**Terry, Megan** 1932- . . . . . . . . . . . . . . **CLC 19**
See also CA 77-80; CABS 3; DLB 7

**Tertz, Abram** 1925-
See Sinyavsky, Andrei (Donatevich)

**Tesich, Steve** 1943?- . . . . . . . . . . . . . . **CLC 40**
See also CA 105; DLB-Y 83

**Tesich, Stoyan** 1943?-
See Tesich, Steve

**Teternikov, Fyodor Kuzmich** 1863-1927
See Sologub, Fyodor
See also CA 104

**Tevis, Walter** 1928-1984 . . . . . . . . . . **CLC 42**
See also CA 113

**Tey, Josephine** 1897-1952 . . . . . . . **TCLC 14**
See also Mackintosh, Elizabeth

**Thackeray, William Makepeace**
1811-1863 . . . . . . . . . . . . **NCLC 5, 14, 22**
See also SATA 23; DLB 21, 55

**Thakura, Ravindranatha** 1861-1941
See Tagore, (Sir) Rabindranath
See also CA 104

**Thelwell, Michael (Miles)** 1939- . . . . **CLC 22**
See also CA 101

**Theroux, Alexander (Louis)**
1939- . . . . . . . . . . . . . . . . . . . . **CLC 2, 25**
See also CANR 20; CA 85-88

**Theroux, Paul**
1941- . . . . . . . . . **CLC 5, 8, 11, 15, 28, 46**
See also CANR 20; CA 33-36R; SATA 44;
DLB 2

**Thesen, Sharon** 1946- . . . . . . . . . . . . **CLC 56**

**Thibault, Jacques Anatole Francois**
1844-1924
See France, Anatole
See also CA 106

**Thiele, Colin (Milton)** 1920- . . . . . . . **CLC 17**
See also CANR 12; CA 29-32R; SAAS 2;
SATA 14

**Thomas, Audrey (Grace)**
1935- . . . . . . . . . . . . . . . . . **CLC 7, 13, 37**
See also CA 21-24R; DLB 60

**Thomas, D(onald) M(ichael)**
1935- . . . . . . . . . . . . . . . . **CLC 13, 22, 31**
See also CANR 17; CA 61-64; DLB 40

**Thomas, Dylan (Marlais)**
1914-1953 . . . . . **TCLC 1, 8; PC 2; SSC 3**
See also CA 104, 120; SATA 60; DLB 13,
20

**Thomas, Edward (Philip)**
1878-1917 . . . . . . . . . . . . . . . . . **TCLC 10**
See also CA 106; DLB 19

**Thomas, John Peter** 1928-
See Thomas, Piri

**Thomas, Joyce Carol** 1938- . . . . . . . . **CLC 35**
See also CLR 19; CA 113, 116; SAAS 7;
SATA 40; DLB 33

**Thomas, Lewis** 1913- . . . . . . . . . . . . . **CLC 35**
See also CA 85-88

**Thomas, Piri** 1928- . . . . . . . . . . . . . . . **CLC 17**
See also CA 73-76

**Thomas, R(onald) S(tuart)**
1913- . . . . . . . . . . . . . . . . **CLC 6, 13, 48**
See also CAAS 4; CA 89-92; DLB 27

**Thomas, Ross (Elmore)** 1926- . . . . . . **CLC 39**
See also CANR 22; CA 33-36R

**Thompson, Ernest** 1860-1946
See Seton, Ernest (Evan) Thompson

**Thompson, Francis (Joseph)**
1859-1907 . . . . . . . . . . . . . . . . . . **TCLC 4**
See also CA 104; DLB 19

**Thompson, Hunter S(tockton)**
1939- . . . . . . . . . . . . . . . . **CLC 9, 17, 40**
See also CANR 23; CA 17-20R

**Thompson, Judith** 1954- . . . . . . . . . . . **CLC 39**

**Thomson, James** 1700-1748 . . . . . . . . **LC 16**
See also DLB 95

**Thomson, James** 1834-1882 . . . . . . **NCLC 18**
See also DLB 35

**Thoreau, Henry David**
1817-1862 . . . . . . . . . . . . . . **NCLC 7, 21**
See also DLB 1; CDALB 1640-1865

**Thurber, James (Grover)**
1894-1961 . . . . . . . **CLC 5, 11, 25; SSC 1**
See also CANR 17; CA 73-76; SATA 13;
DLB 4, 11, 22

**Thurman, Wallace** 1902-1934 . . . . . . **TCLC 6**
See also CA 104, 124; DLB 51

**Tieck, (Johann) Ludwig**
1773-1853 . . . . . . . . . . . . . . . . . . **NCLC 5**
See also DLB 90

**Tilghman, Christopher** 1948?- . . . . . . **CLC 65**

**Tillinghast, Richard** 1940- . . . . . . . . . **CLC 29**
See also CANR 26; CA 29-32R

**Timrod, Henry** 1828-1867 . . . . . . . **NCLC 25**

**Tindall, Gillian** 1938- . . . . . . . . . . . . . . **CLC 7**
See also CANR 11; CA 21-24R

**Tiptree, James, Jr.** 1915-1987 . . . **CLC 48, 50**
See also Sheldon, Alice (Hastings) B(radley)
See also DLB 8

**Tocqueville, Alexis (Charles Henri Maurice**
**Clerel, Comte) de** 1805-1859 . . **NCLC 7**

**Tolkien, J(ohn) R(onald) R(euel)**
1892-1973 . . . . . . . **CLC 1, 2, 3, 8, 12, 38**
See also CAP 2; CA 17-18;
obituary CA 45-48; SATA 2, 24, 32;
obituary SATA 24; DLB 15

**Toller, Ernst** 1893-1939 . . . . . . . . . . **TCLC 10**
See also CA 107

**Tolson, Melvin B(eaunorus)**
1900?-1966 . . . . . . . . . . . . . . . . . . **CLC 36**
See also CA 124; obituary CA 89-92;
DLB 48, 124

**Tolstoy, (Count) Alexey Nikolayevich**
1883-1945 . . . . . . . . . . . . . . . . . **TCLC 18**
See also CA 107

**Tolstoy, (Count) Leo (Lev Nikolaevich)**
1828-1910 . . . . . . . . . **TCLC 4, 11, 17, 28**
See also CA 104, 123; SATA 26

**Tomlin, Lily** 1939- . . . . . . . . . . . . . . . **CLC 17**

**Tomlin, Mary Jean** 1939-
See Tomlin, Lily
See also CA 117

**Tomlinson, (Alfred) Charles**
1927- . . . . . . . . . . . . . **CLC 2, 4, 6, 13, 45**
See also CA 5-8R; DLB 40

**Toole, John Kennedy**
1937-1969 . . . . . . . . . . . . . . . . **CLC 19, 64**
See also CA 104; DLB-Y 81

**Toomer, Jean**
1894-1967 . . . . . **CLC 1, 4, 13, 22; SSC 1**
See also CA 85-88; DLB 45, 51

**Torrey, E. Fuller** 19??- . . . . . . . . . . . . **CLC 34**
See also CA 119

**Tournier, Michel** 1924- . . . . . . **CLC 6, 23, 36**
See also CANR 3; CA 49-52; SATA 23;
DLB 83

**Townsend, Sue** 1946- . . . . . . . . . . . . . **CLC 61**
See also CA 119, 127; SATA 48, 55

Townshend, Peter (Dennis Blandford)
        1945-..................... CLC 17, 42
        See also CA 107

Tozzi, Federigo  1883-1920........ TCLC 31

Traill, Catharine Parr
        1802-1899 ................. NCLC 31
        See also DLB 99

Trakl, Georg  1887-1914........... TCLC 5
        See also CA 104

Transtromer, Tomas (Gosta)
        1931-.................. CLC 52, 65
        See also CA 129; brief entry CA 117

Traven, B.  1890-1969........... CLC 8, 11
        See also CAP 2; CA 19-20;
        obituary CA 25-28R; DLB 9, 56

Tremain, Rose  1943-............. CLC 42
        See also CA 97-100; DLB 14

Tremblay, Michel  1942-.......... CLC 29
        See also CA 116; DLB 60

Trevanian  1925-................. CLC 29
        See also CA 108

Trevor, William  1928-..... CLC 7, 9, 14, 25
        See also Cox, William Trevor
        See also DLB 14

Trifonov, Yuri (Valentinovich)
        1925-1981 ................... CLC 45
        See also obituary CA 103, 126

Trilling, Lionel  1905-1975.... CLC 9, 11, 24
        See also CANR 10; CA 9-12R;
        obituary CA 61-64; DLB 28, 63

Trogdon, William  1939-
        See Heat Moon, William Least
        See also CA 115, 119

Trollope, Anthony  1815-1882 ..... NCLC 6
        See also SATA 22; DLB 21, 57

Trollope, Frances  1780-1863 ..... NCLC 30
        See also DLB 21

Trotsky, Leon (Davidovich)
        1879-1940................. TCLC 22
        See also CA 118

Trotter (Cockburn), Catharine
        1679-1749 ................... LC 8
        See also DLB 84

Trow, George W. S.  1943-........ CLC 52
        See also CA 126

Troyat, Henri  1911-............. CLC 23
        See also CANR 2; CA 45-48

Trudeau, G(arretson) B(eekman)  1948-
        See Trudeau, Garry
        See also CA 81-84; SATA 35

Trudeau, Garry  1948-............ CLC 12
        See also Trudeau, G(arretson) B(eekman)

Truffaut, Francois  1932-1984....... CLC 20
        See also CA 81-84; obituary CA 113

Trumbo, Dalton  1905-1976 ........ CLC 19
        See also CANR 10; CA 21-24R;
        obituary CA 69-72; DLB 26

Trumbull, John  1750-1831....... NCLC 30
        See also DLB 31

Tryon, Thomas  1926-........... CLC 3, 11
        See also CA 29-32R

Ts'ao Hsueh-ch'in  1715?-1763........ LC 1

Tsushima Shuji  1909-1948
        See Dazai Osamu
        See also CA 107

Tsvetaeva (Efron), Marina (Ivanovna)
        1892-1941 ................ TCLC 7, 35
        See also CA 104, 128

Tunis, John R(oberts)  1889-1975 ... CLC 12
        See also CA 61-64; SATA 30, 37; DLB 22

Tuohy, Frank  1925-............. CLC 37
        See also DLB 14

Tuohy, John Francis  1925-
        See Tuohy, Frank
        See also CANR 3; CA 5-8R

Turco, Lewis (Putnam)  1934- ... CLC 11, 63
        See also CANR 24; CA 13-16R; DLB-Y 84

Turgenev, Ivan
        1818-1883 .......... NCLC 21; SSC 7

Turner, Frederick  1943-......... CLC 48
        See also CANR 12; CA 73-76; DLB 40

Tutuola, Amos  1920- ........ CLC 5, 14, 29
        See also CA 9-12R

Twain, Mark
        1835-1910 ... TCLC 6, 12, 19, 36; SSC 6
        See also Clemens, Samuel Langhorne
        See also YABC 2; DLB 11, 12, 23, 64, 74

Tyler, Anne
        1941-........ CLC 7, 11, 18, 28, 44, 59
        See also CANR 11; CA 9-12R; SATA 7;
        DLB 6; DLB-Y 82

Tyler, Royall  1757-1826......... NCLC 3
        See also DLB 37

Tynan (Hinkson), Katharine
        1861-1931 ................. TCLC 3
        See also CA 104

Tytell, John  1939- ............. CLC 50
        See also CA 29-32R

Tzara, Tristan  1896-1963......... CLC 47
        See also Rosenfeld, Samuel

Uhry, Alfred  1947?-............. CLC 55
        See also CA 127

Unamuno (y Jugo), Miguel de
        1864-1936 ................ TCLC 2, 9
        See also CA 104

Underwood, Miles  1909-1981
        See Glassco, John

Undset, Sigrid  1882-1949......... TCLC 3
        See also CA 104

Ungaretti, Giuseppe
        1888-1970 .............. CLC 7, 11, 15
        See also CAP 2; CA 19-20;
        obituary CA 25-28R

Unger, Douglas  1952-............. CLC 34
        See also CA 130

Unger, Eva  1932-
        See Figes, Eva

Updike, John (Hoyer)
        1932- ...... CLC 1, 2, 3, 5, 7, 9, 13, 15,
                                23, 34, 43
        See also CANR 4; CA 1-4R; CABS 2;
        DLB 2, 5; DLB-Y 80, 82; DLB-DS 3

Urdang, Constance (Henriette)
        1922-........................ CLC 47
        See also CANR 9, 24; CA 21-24R

Uris, Leon (Marcus)  1924-....... CLC 7, 32
        See also CANR 1; CA 1-4R; SATA 49

Ustinov, Peter (Alexander)  1921-.... CLC 1
        See also CANR 25; CA 13-16R; DLB 13

Vaculik, Ludvik  1926-............. CLC 7
        See also CA 53-56

Valenzuela, Luisa  1938-.......... CLC 31
        See also CA 101

Valera (y Acala-Galiano), Juan
        1824-1905 ................. TCLC 10
        See also CA 106

Valery, Paul (Ambroise Toussaint Jules)
        1871-1945 ................ TCLC 4, 15
        See also CA 104, 122

Valle-Inclan (y Montenegro), Ramon (Maria)
        del  1866-1936................ TCLC 5
        See also CA 106

Vallejo, Cesar (Abraham)
        1892-1938 ................... TCLC 3
        See also CA 105

Van Ash, Cay  1918-............. CLC 34

Vance, Jack  1916?-............. CLC 35
        See also DLB 8

Vance, John Holbrook  1916?-
        See Vance, Jack
        See also CANR 17; CA 29-32R

Van Den Bogarde, Derek (Jules Gaspard
        Ulric) Niven  1921-
        See Bogarde, Dirk
        See also CA 77-80

Vandenburgh, Jane  19??-.......... CLC 59

Vanderhaeghe, Guy  1951- ......... CLC 41
        See also CA 113

Van der Post, Laurens (Jan)  1906-... CLC 5
        See also CA 5-8R

Van de Wetering, Janwillem
        1931-..................... CLC 47
        See also CANR 4; CA 49-52

Van Dine, S. S.  1888-1939....... TCLC 23

Van Doren, Carl (Clinton)
        1885-1950 ................. TCLC 18
        See also CA 111

Van Doren, Mark  1894-1972..... CLC 6, 10
        See also CANR 3; CA 1-4R;
        obituary CA 37-40R; DLB 45

Van Druten, John (William)
        1901-1957 ................... TCLC 2
        See also CA 104; DLB 10

Van Duyn, Mona  1921-....... CLC 3, 7, 63
        See also CANR 7; CA 9-12R; DLB 5

Van Itallie, Jean-Claude  1936- ...... CLC 3
        See also CAAS 2; CANR 1; CA 45-48;
        DLB 7

Van Ostaijen, Paul  1896-1928..... TCLC 33

Van Peebles, Melvin  1932- ...... CLC 2, 20
        See also CA 85-88

Vansittart, Peter  1920-........... CLC 42
        See also CANR 3; CA 1-4R

Van Vechten, Carl  1880-1964 ...... CLC 33
        See also obituary CA 89-92; DLB 4, 9, 51

Van Vogt, A(lfred) E(lton)  1912-..... CLC 1
        See also CANR 28; CA 21-24R; SATA 14;
        DLB 8

**Varda, Agnes** 1928- .............. CLC **16**
See also CA 116, 122

**Vargas Llosa, (Jorge) Mario (Pedro)**
1936- ....... CLC **3, 6, 9, 10, 15, 31, 42**
See also CANR 18; CA 73-76

**Vassilikos, Vassilis** 1933-......... CLC **4, 8**
See also CA 81-84

**Vaughn, Stephanie** 19??- .......... CLC **62**

**Vazov, Ivan** 1850-1921........... TCLC **25**
See also CA 121

**Veblen, Thorstein Bunde**
1857-1929 .................. TCLC **31**
See also CA 115

**Verga, Giovanni** 1840-1922 ....... TCLC **3**
See also CA 104, 123

**Verhaeren, Emile (Adolphe Gustave)**
1855-1916 .................. TCLC **12**
See also CA 109

**Verlaine, Paul (Marie)**
1844-1896 ............. NCLC **2; PC 2**

**Verne, Jules (Gabriel)** 1828-1905 ... TCLC **6**
See also CA 110; SATA 21

**Very, Jones** 1813-1880.......... NCLC **9**
See also DLB 1

**Vesaas, Tarjei** 1897-1970......... CLC **48**
See also obituary CA 29-32R

**Vian, Boris** 1920-1959 ........... TCLC **9**
See also CA 106; DLB 72

**Viaud, (Louis Marie) Julien** 1850-1923
See Loti, Pierre
See also CA 107

**Vicker, Angus** 1916-
See Felsen, Henry Gregor

**Vidal, Eugene Luther, Jr.** 1925-
See Vidal, Gore

**Vidal, Gore**
1925- ........ CLC **2, 4, 6, 8, 10, 22, 33**
See also CANR 13; CA 5-8R; DLB 6

**Viereck, Peter (Robert Edwin)**
1916- ........................ CLC **4**
See also CANR 1; CA 1-4R; DLB 5

**Vigny, Alfred (Victor) de**
1797-1863 ................. NCLC **7**

**Vilakazi, Benedict Wallet**
1905-1947 ................. TCLC **37**

**Villiers de l'Isle Adam, Jean Marie Mathias**
**Philippe Auguste, Comte de**
1838-1889 ................. NCLC **3**

**Vinci, Leonardo da** 1452-1519...... LC **12**

**Vine, Barbara** 1930-............. CLC **50**
See also Rendell, Ruth

**Vinge, Joan (Carol) D(ennison)**
1948- ..................... CLC **30**
See also CA 93-96; SATA 36

**Visconti, Luchino** 1906-1976....... CLC **16**
See also CA 81-84; obituary CA 65-68

**Vittorini, Elio** 1908-1966...... CLC **6, 9, 14**
See also obituary CA 25-28R

**Vizinczey, Stephen** 1933-.......... CLC **40**

**Vliet, R(ussell) G(ordon)**
1929-1984 .................. CLC **22**
See also CANR 18; CA 37-40R;
obituary CA 112

**Voight, Ellen Bryant** 1943-........ CLC **54**
See also CANR 11; CA 69-72

**Voigt, Cynthia** 1942- ............. CLC **30**
See also CANR 18; CA 106; SATA 33, 48;
AAYA 3

**Voinovich, Vladimir (Nikolaevich)**
1932- .................... CLC **10, 49**
See also CA 81-84

**Voltaire** 1694-1778 ............... LC **14**

**Von Daeniken, Erich** 1935-
See Von Daniken, Erich
See also CANR 17; CA 37-40R

**Von Daniken, Erich** 1935-......... CLC **30**
See also Von Daeniken, Erich

**Vonnegut, Kurt, Jr.**
1922- ...... CLC **1, 2, 3, 4, 5, 8, 12, 22,**
**40, 60**
See also CANR 1; CA 1-4R; DLB 2, 8;
DLB-Y 80; DLB-DS 3;
CDALB 1968-1987

**Vorster, Gordon** 1924- ............ CLC **34**

**Voznesensky, Andrei** 1933- ... CLC **1, 15, 57**
See also CA 89-92

**Waddington, Miriam** 1917- ........ CLC **28**
See also CANR 12, 30; CA 21-24R;
DLB 68

**Wagman, Fredrica** 1937- .......... CLC **7**
See also CA 97-100

**Wagner, Richard** 1813-1883....... NCLC **9**

**Wagner-Martin, Linda** 1936-....... CLC **50**

**Wagoner, David (Russell)**
1926- ................... CLC **3, 5, 15**
See also CAAS 3; CANR 2; CA 1-4R;
SATA 14; DLB 5

**Wah, Fred(erick James)** 1939-...... CLC **44**
See also CA 107; DLB 60

**Wahloo, Per** 1926-1975 ............ CLC **7**
See also CA 61-64

**Wahloo, Peter** 1926-1975
See Wahloo, Per

**Wain, John (Barrington)**
1925- ............... CLC **2, 11, 15, 46**
See also CAAS 4; CANR 23; CA 5-8R;
DLB 15, 27

**Wajda, Andrzej** 1926-............. CLC **16**
See also CA 102

**Wakefield, Dan** 1932-............. CLC **7**
See also CAAS 7; CA 21-24R

**Wakoski, Diane**
1937- .......... CLC **2, 4, 7, 9, 11, 40**
See also CAAS 1; CANR 9; CA 13-16R;
DLB 5

**Walcott, Derek (Alton)**
1930- ......... CLC **2, 4, 9, 14, 25, 42**
See also CANR 26; CA 89-92; DLB-Y 81

**Waldman, Anne** 1945- ............. CLC **7**
See also CA 37-40R; DLB 16

**Waldo, Edward Hamilton** 1918-
See Sturgeon, Theodore (Hamilton)

**Walker, Alice**
1944- ...... CLC **5, 6, 9, 19, 27, 46, 58;**
**SSC 5**
See also CANR 9, 27; CA 37-40R;
SATA 31; DLB 6, 33; CDALB 1968-1988

**Walker, David Harry** 1911-....... CLC **14**
See also CANR 1; CA 1-4R; SATA 8

**Walker, Edward Joseph** 1934-
See Walker, Ted
See also CANR 12; CA 21-24R

**Walker, George F.** 1947-....... CLC **44, 61**
See also CANR 21; CA 103; DLB 60

**Walker, Joseph A.** 1935- ........ CLC **19**
See also CANR 26; CA 89-92; DLB 38

**Walker, Margaret (Abigail)**
1915- .................... CLC **1, 6**
See also CANR 26; CA 73-76; DLB 76

**Walker, Ted** 1934- ............... CLC **13**
See also Walker, Edward Joseph
See also DLB 40

**Wallace, David Foster** 1962-....... CLC **50**

**Wallace, Irving** 1916-........... CLC **7, 13**
See also CAAS 1; CANR 1; CA 1-4R

**Wallant, Edward Lewis**
1926-1962 .................. CLC **5, 10**
See also CANR 22; CA 1-4R; DLB 2, 28

**Walpole, Horace** 1717-1797......... LC **2**
See also DLB 39

**Walpole, (Sir) Hugh (Seymour)**
1884-1941 .................. TCLC **5**
See also CA 104; DLB 34

**Walser, Martin** 1927-............. CLC **27**
See also CANR 8; CA 57-60; DLB 75

**Walser, Robert** 1878-1956........ TCLC **18**
See also CA 118; DLB 66

**Walsh, Gillian Paton** 1939-
See Walsh, Jill Paton
See also CA 37-40R; SATA 4

**Walsh, Jill Paton** 1939-........... CLC **35**
See also CLR 2; SAAS 3

**Wambaugh, Joseph (Aloysius, Jr.)**
1937- .................... CLC **3, 18**
See also CA 33-36R; DLB 6; DLB-Y 83

**Ward, Arthur Henry Sarsfield** 1883-1959
See Rohmer, Sax
See also CA 108

**Ward, Douglas Turner** 1930-....... CLC **19**
See also CA 81-84; DLB 7, 38

**Warhol, Andy** 1928-1987.......... CLC **20**
See also CA 89-92; obituary CA 121

**Warner, Francis (Robert le Plastrier)**
1937- ..................... CLC **14**
See also CANR 11; CA 53-56

**Warner, Marina** 1946-............ CLC **59**
See also CANR 21; CA 65-68

**Warner, Rex (Ernest)** 1905-1986.... CLC **45**
See also CA 89-92; obituary CA 119;
DLB 15

**Warner, Susan** 1819-1885 ....... NCLC **31**
See also DLB 3, 42

**Warner, Sylvia Townsend**
1893-1978 ................. CLC **7, 19**
See also CANR 16; CA 61-64;
obituary CA 77-80; DLB 34

**Warren, Mercy Otis** 1728-1814... NCLC **13**
See also DLB 31

**Warren, Robert Penn**
      1905-1989 ... CLC **1, 4, 6, 8, 10, 13, 18,**
                                    **39, 53, 59; SSC 4**
      See also CANR 10; CA 13-16R. 129. 130;
      SATA 46; DLB 2, 48; DLB-Y 80;
      CDALB 1968-1987

**Warton, Thomas**   1728-1790........ LC **15**

**Washington, Booker T(aliaferro)**
      1856-1915 ................. TCLC **10**
      See also CA 114, 125; SATA 28

**Wassermann, Jakob**   1873-1934..... TCLC **6**
      See also CA 104; DLB 66

**Wasserstein, Wendy**   1950-...... CLC **32, 59**
      See also CA 121; CABS 3

**Waterhouse, Keith (Spencer)**
      1929-................. CLC **47**
      See also CA 5-8R; DLB 13, 15

**Waters, Roger**   1944-
      See Pink Floyd

**Wa Thiong'o, Ngugi**
      1938-............... CLC **3, 7, 13, 36**
      See also Ngugi, James (Thiong'o); Ngugi wa
      Thiong'o

**Watkins, Paul**   1964-............. CLC **55**

**Watkins, Vernon (Phillips)**
      1906-1967 ................. CLC **43**
      See also CAP 1; CA 9-10;
      obituary CA 25-28R; DLB 20

**Waugh, Auberon (Alexander)**   1939-.. CLC **7**
      See also CANR 6, 22; CA 45-48; DLB 14

**Waugh, Evelyn (Arthur St. John)**
      1903-1966 .. CLC **1, 3, 8, 13, 19, 27, 44**
      See also CANR 22; CA 85-88;
      obituary CA 25-28R; DLB 15

**Waugh, Harriet**   1944-............ CLC **6**
      See also CANR 22; CA 85-88

**Webb, Beatrice (Potter)**
      1858-1943 ................. TCLC **22**
      See also CA 117

**Webb, Charles (Richard)**   1939-...... CLC **7**
      See also CA 25-28R

**Webb, James H(enry), Jr.**   1946-.... CLC **22**
      See also CA 81-84

**Webb, Mary (Gladys Meredith)**
      1881-1927 ................. TCLC **24**
      See also CA 123; DLB 34

**Webb, Phyllis**   1927-.............. CLC **18**
      See also CANR 23; CA 104; DLB 53

**Webb, Sidney (James)**
      1859-1947 ................. TCLC **22**
      See also CA 117

**Webber, Andrew Lloyd**   1948-...... CLC **21**

**Weber, Lenora Mattingly**
      1895-1971 ................. CLC **12**
      See also CAP 1; CA 19-20;
      obituary CA 29-32R; SATA 2;
      obituary SATA 26

**Webster, Noah**   1758-1843 ....... NCLC **30**
      See also DLB 1, 37, 42, 43, 73

**Wedekind, (Benjamin) Frank(lin)**
      1864-1918 ................. TCLC **7**
      See also CA 104

**Weidman, Jerome**   1913-............ CLC **7**
      See also CANR 1; CA 1-4R; DLB 28

**Weil, Simone**   1909-1943......... TCLC **23**
      See also CA 117

**Weinstein, Nathan Wallenstein**   1903?-1940
      See West, Nathanael
      See also CA 104

**Weir, Peter**   1944-................ CLC **20**
      See also CA 113, 123

**Weiss, Peter (Ulrich)**
      1916-1982 .............. CLC **3, 15, 51**
      See also CANR 3; CA 45-48;
      obituary CA 106; DLB 69

**Weiss, Theodore (Russell)**
      1916-.................... CLC **3, 8, 14**
      See also CAAS 2; CA 9-12R; DLB 5

**Welch, (Maurice) Denton**
      1915-1948 ................. TCLC **22**
      See also CA 121

**Welch, James**   1940-......... CLC **6, 14, 52**
      See also CA 85-88

**Weldon, Fay**
      1933-......... CLC **6, 9, 11, 19, 36, 59**
      See also CANR 16; CA 21-24R; DLB 14

**Wellek, Rene**   1903-.............. CLC **28**
      See also CAAS 7; CANR 8; CA 5-8R;
      DLB 63

**Weller, Michael**   1942-......... CLC **10, 53**
      See also CA 85-88

**Weller, Paul**   1958-............... CLC **26**

**Wellershoff, Dieter**   1925-......... CLC **46**
      See also CANR 16; CA 89-92

**Welles, (George) Orson**
      1915-1985 ................. CLC **20**
      See also CA 93-96; obituary CA 117

**Wellman, Mac**   1945-............. CLC **65**

**Wellman, Manly Wade**   1903-1986 .. CLC **49**
      See also CANR 6, 16; CA 1-4R;
      obituary CA 118; SATA 6, 47

**Wells, Carolyn**   1862-1942 ....... TCLC **35**
      See also CA 113; DLB 11

**Wells, H(erbert) G(eorge)**
      1866-1946 ...... TCLC **6, 12, 19; SSC 6**
      See also CA 110, 121; SATA 20; DLB 34,
      70

**Wells, Rosemary**   1943-........... CLC **12**
      See also CLR 16; CA 85-88; SAAS 1;
      SATA 18

**Welty, Eudora (Alice)**
      1909-.... CLC **1, 2, 5, 14, 22, 33; SSC 1**
      See also CA 9-12R; CABS 1; DLB 2;
      DLB-Y 87; CDALB 1941-1968

**Wen I-to**   1899-1946 ............. TCLC **28**

**Werfel, Franz (V.)**   1890-1945 ...... TCLC **8**
      See also CA 104; DLB 81

**Wergeland, Henrik Arnold**
      1808-1845 ................. NCLC **5**

**Wersba, Barbara**   1932-............ CLC **30**
      See also CLR 3; CANR 16; CA 29-32R;
      SAAS 2; SATA 1, 58; DLB 52

**Wertmuller, Lina**   1928-............ CLC **16**
      See also CA 97-100

**Wescott, Glenway**   1901-1987....... CLC **13**
      See also CANR 23; CA 13-16R;
      obituary CA 121; DLB 4, 9

**Wesker, Arnold**   1932- ........ CLC **3, 5, 42**
      See also CAAS 7; CANR 1; CA 1-4R;
      DLB 13

**Wesley, Richard (Errol)**   1945-....... CLC **7**
      See also CA 57-60; DLB 38

**Wessel, Johan Herman**   1742-1785 .... LC **7**

**West, Anthony (Panther)**
      1914-1987 ................... CLC **50**
      See also CANR 3, 19; CA 45-48; DLB 15

**West, Jessamyn**   1907-1984 ...... CLC **7, 17**
      See also CA 9-12R; obituary CA 112;
      obituary SATA 37; DLB 6; DLB-Y 84

**West, Morris L(anglo)**   1916-..... CLC **6, 33**
      See also CA 5-8R; obituary CA 124

**West, Nathanael**   1903?-1940.... TCLC **1, 14**
      See also Weinstein, Nathan Wallenstein
      See also CA 125, 140; DLB 4, 9, 28

**West, Paul**   1930- ............. CLC **7, 14**
      See also CAAS 7; CANR 22; CA 13-16R;
      DLB 14

**West, Rebecca**   1892-1983 .. CLC **7, 9, 31, 50**
      See also CANR 19; CA 5-8R;
      obituary CA 109; DLB 36; DLB-Y 83

**Westall, Robert (Atkinson)**   1929-... CLC **17**
      See also CLR 13; CANR 18; CA 69-72;
      SAAS 2; SATA 23

**Westlake, Donald E(dwin)**
      1933-.................... CLC **7, 33**
      See also CANR 16; CA 17-20R

**Westmacott, Mary**   1890-1976
      See Christie, (Dame) Agatha (Mary
      Clarissa)

**Whalen, Philip**   1923-........... CLC **6, 29**
      See also CANR 5; CA 9-12R; DLB 16

**Wharton, Edith (Newbold Jones)**
      1862-1937 ....... TCLC **3, 9, 27; SSC 6**
      See also CA 104; DLB 4, 9, 12, 78;
      CDALB 1865-1917

**Wharton, William**   1925-........ CLC **18, 37**
      See also CA 93-96; DLB-Y 80

**Wheatley (Peters), Phillis**
      1753?-1784..................... LC **3**
      See also DLB 31, 50; CDALB 1640-1865

**Wheelock, John Hall**   1886-1978.... CLC **14**
      See also CANR 14; CA 13-16R;
      obituary CA 77-80; DLB 45

**Whelan, John**   1900-
      See O'Faolain, Sean

**Whitaker, Rodney**   1925-
      See Trevanian

**White, E(lwyn) B(rooks)**
      1899-1985............. CLC **10, 34, 39**
      See also CLR 1; CANR 16; CA 13-16R;
      obituary CA 116; SATA 2, 29, 44;
      obituary SATA 44; DLB 11, 22

**White, Edmund III**   1940-.......... CLC **27**
      See also CANR 3, 19; CA 45-48

**White, Patrick (Victor Martindale)**
      1912-1990 ..... CLC **3, 4, 5, 7, 9, 18, 65**
      See also CA 81-84; obituary CA 132

**White, T(erence) H(anbury)**
      1906-1964 ................... CLC **30**
      See also CA 73-76; SATA 12

**White, Terence de Vere**   1912-....... CLC **49**
      See also CANR 3; CA 49-52**

**White, Walter (Francis)**
1893-1955 ................. TCLC 15
See also CA 115, 124; DLB 51

**White, William Hale** 1831-1913
See Rutherford, Mark
See also CA 121

**Whitehead, E(dward) A(nthony)**
1933- ........................ CLC 5
See also CA 65-68

**Whitemore, Hugh** 1936-........... CLC 37

**Whitman, Sarah Helen**
1803-1878 ................. NCLC 19
See also DLB 1

**Whitman, Walt** 1819-1892..... NCLC 4, 31
See also SATA 20; DLB 3, 64;
CDALB 1640-1865

**Whitney, Phyllis A(yame)** 1903-.... CLC 42
See also CANR 3, 25; CA 1-4R; SATA 1,
30

**Whittemore, (Edward) Reed (Jr.)**
1919- ........................ CLC 4
See also CAAS 8; CANR 4; CA 9-12R;
DLB 5

**Whittier, John Greenleaf**
1807-1892 ................. NCLC 8
See also DLB 1; CDALB 1640-1865

**Wicker, Thomas Grey** 1926-
See Wicker, Tom
See also CANR 21; CA 65-68

**Wicker, Tom** 1926-................ CLC 7
See also Wicker, Thomas Grey

**Wideman, John Edgar**
1941- ................. CLC 5, 34, 36
See also CANR 14; CA 85-88; DLB 33

**Wiebe, Rudy (H.)** 1934-...... CLC 6, 11, 14
See also CA 37-40R; DLB 60

**Wieland, Christoph Martin**
1733-1813 ................. NCLC 17

**Wieners, John** 1934-.............. CLC 7
See also CA 13-16R; DLB 16

**Wiesel, Elie(zer)** 1928-..... CLC 3, 5, 11, 37
See also CAAS 4; CANR 8; CA 5-8R;
SATA 56; DLB 83; DLB-Y 87

**Wiggins, Marianne** 1948-.......... CLC 57

**Wight, James Alfred** 1916-
See Herriot, James
See also CA 77-80; SATA 44

**Wilbur, Richard (Purdy)**
1921- ............. CLC 3, 6, 9, 14, 53
See also CANR 2; CA 1-4R; CABS 2;
SATA 9; DLB 5

**Wild, Peter** 1940-................ CLC 14
See also CA 37-40R; DLB 5

**Wilde, Oscar (Fingal O'Flahertie Wills)**
1854-1900 ......... TCLC 1, 8, 23, 41
See also CA 119; brief entry CA 104;
SATA 24; DLB 10, 19, 34, 57

**Wilder, Billy** 1906-.............. CLC 20
See also Wilder, Samuel
See also DLB 26

**Wilder, Samuel** 1906-
See Wilder, Billy
See also CA 89-92

**Wilder, Thornton (Niven)**
1897-1975 ..... CLC 1, 5, 6, 10, 15, 35;
DC 1
See also CA 13-16R; obituary CA 61-64;
DLB 4, 7, 9

**Wiley, Richard** 1944-............. CLC 44
See also CA 121, 129

**Wilhelm, Kate** 1928-.............. CLC 7
See also CAAS 5; CANR 17; CA 37-40R;
DLB 8

**Willard, Nancy** 1936-........... CLC 7, 37
See also CLR 5; CANR 10; CA 89-92;
SATA 30, 37; DLB 5, 52

**Williams, C(harles) K(enneth)**
1936-....................... CLC 33, 56
See also CA 37-40R; DLB 5

**Williams, Charles (Walter Stansby)**
1886-1945 ................. TCLC 1, 11
See also CA 104

**Williams, Ella Gwendolen Rees** 1890-1979
See Rhys, Jean

**Williams, (George) Emlyn**
1905-1987 ................. CLC 15
See also CA 104, 123; DLB 10, 77

**Williams, Hugo** 1942-............. CLC 42
See also CA 17-20R; DLB 40

**Williams, John A(lfred)** 1925-.... CLC 5, 13
See also CAAS 3; CANR 6, 26; CA 53-56;
DLB 2, 33

**Williams, Jonathan (Chamberlain)**
1929- ....................... CLC 13
See also CANR 8; CA 9-12R; DLB 5

**Williams, Joy** 1944-.............. CLC 31
See also CANR 22; CA 41-44R

**Williams, Norman** 1952- .......... CLC 39
See also CA 118

**Williams, Paulette** 1948-
See Shange, Ntozake

**Williams, Tennessee**
1911-1983 .... CLC 1, 2, 5, 7, 8, 11, 15,
19, 30, 39, 45
See also CA 5-8R; obituary CA 108; DLB 7;
DLB-Y 83; DLB-DS 4;
CDALB 1941-1968

**Williams, Thomas (Alonzo)** 1926-... CLC 14
See also CANR 2; CA 1-4R

**Williams, Thomas Lanier** 1911-1983
See Williams, Tennessee

**Williams, William Carlos**
1883-1963 .... CLC 1, 2, 5, 9, 13, 22, 42
See also CA 89-92; DLB 4, 16, 54, 86

**Williamson, David** 1932- ......... CLC 56

**Williamson, Jack** 1908- .......... CLC 29
See also Williamson, John Stewart
See also DLB 8

**Williamson, John Stewart** 1908-
See Williamson, Jack
See also CANR 123; CA 17-20R

**Willingham, Calder (Baynard, Jr.)**
1922- .................... CLC 5, 51
See also CANR 3; CA 5-8R; DLB 2, 44

**Wilson, A(ndrew) N(orman)** 1950- .. CLC 33
See also CA 112, 122; DLB 14

**Wilson, Andrew** 1948-
See Wilson, Snoo

**Wilson, Angus (Frank Johnstone)**
1913- ............. CLC 2, 3, 5, 25, 34
See also CANR 21; CA 5-8R; DLB 15

**Wilson, August** 1945-....... CLC 39, 50, 63
See also CA 115, 122

**Wilson, Brian** 1942-.............. CLC 12

**Wilson, Colin** 1931-............. CLC 3, 14
See also CAAS 5; CANR 1, 122; CA 1-4R;
DLB 14

**Wilson, Edmund**
1895-1972 .......... CLC 1, 2, 3, 8, 24
See also CANR 1; CA 1-4R;
obituary CA 37-40R; DLB 63

**Wilson, Ethel Davis (Bryant)**
1888-1980 ................. CLC 13
See also CA 102; DLB 68

**Wilson, John** 1785-1854......... NCLC 5

**Wilson, John (Anthony) Burgess** 1917-
See Burgess, Anthony
See also CANR 2; CA 1-4R

**Wilson, Lanford** 1937-....... CLC 7, 14, 36
See also CA 17-20R; DLB 7

**Wilson, Robert (M.)** 1944-........ CLC 7, 9
See also CANR 2; CA 49-52

**Wilson, Sloan** 1920-.............. CLC 32
See also CANR 1; CA 1-4R

**Wilson, Snoo** 1948-................ CLC 33
See also CA 69-72

**Wilson, William S(mith)** 1932- ..... CLC 49
See also CA 81-84

**Winchilsea, Anne (Kingsmill) Finch, Countess**
of 1661-1720.................. LC 3

**Winters, Janet Lewis** 1899-
See Lewis (Winters), Janet
See also CAP 1; CA 9-10

**Winters, (Arthur) Yvor**
1900-1968 ............... CLC 4, 8, 32
See also CAP 1; CA 11-12;
obituary CA 25-28R; DLB 48

**Winterson, Jeannette** 1959-........ CLC 64

**Wiseman, Frederick** 1930-........ CLC 20

**Wister, Owen** 1860-1938 ........ TCLC 21
See also CA 108; DLB 9, 78

**Witkiewicz, Stanislaw Ignacy**
1885-1939 .................. TCLC 8
See also CA 105; DLB 83

**Wittig, Monique** 1935?-............ CLC 22
See also CA 116; DLB 83

**Wittlin, Joseph** 1896-1976........ CLC 25
See also Wittlin, Jozef

**Wittlin, Jozef** 1896-1976
See Wittlin, Joseph
See also CANR 3; CA 49-52;
obituary CA 65-68

**Wodehouse, (Sir) P(elham) G(renville)**
1881-1975 ... CLC 1, 2, 5, 10, 22; SSC 2
See also CANR 3; CA 45-48;
obituary CA 57-60; SATA 22; DLB 34

**Woiwode, Larry (Alfred)** 1941-... CLC 6, 10
See also CANR 16; CA 73-76; DLB 6

**Wojciechowska, Maia (Teresa)**
1927- ....................... CLC 26
See also CLR 1; CANR 4; CA 9-12R;
SAAS 1; SATA 1, 28

Wolf, Christa   1929-  . . . . . . . **CLC 14, 29, 58**
See also CA 85-88; DLB 75

Wolfe, Gene (Rodman)   1931-. . . . . . . **CLC 25**
See also CAAS 9; CANR 6; CA 57-60;
DLB 8

Wolfe, George C.   1954-  . . . . . . . . . . **CLC 49**

Wolfe, Thomas (Clayton)
1900-1938  . . . . . . . . . . . . **TCLC 4, 13, 29**
See also CA 104; DLB 9; DLB-Y 85;
DLB-DS 2

Wolfe, Thomas Kennerly, Jr.   1931-
See Wolfe, Tom
See also CANR 9; CA 13-16R

Wolfe, Tom   1931-. . .   **CLC 1, 2, 9, 15, 35, 51**
See also Wolfe, Thomas Kennerly, Jr.

Wolff, Geoffrey (Ansell)   1937-  . . . . . **CLC 41**
See also CA 29-32R

Wolff, Tobias (Jonathan Ansell)
1945-  . . . . . . . . . . . . . . . . . . . **CLC 39, 64**
See also CA 114, 117

Wolfram von Eschenbach
c. 1170-c. 1220  . . . . . . . . . . . . . . **CMLC 5**

Wolitzer, Hilma   1930-. . . . . . . . . . . . **CLC 17**
See also CANR 18; CA 65-68; SATA 31

Wollstonecraft (Godwin), Mary
1759-1797  . . . . . . . . . . . . . . . . . . . **LC 5**
See also DLB 39

Wonder, Stevie   1950-. . . . . . . . . . . . . **CLC 12**
See also Morris, Steveland Judkins

Wong, Jade Snow   1922-. . . . . . . . . . . **CLC 17**
See also CA 109

Woodcott, Keith   1934-
See Brunner, John (Kilian Houston)

Woolf, (Adeline) Virginia
1882-1941  . . . . . . . **TCLC 1, 5, 20; SSC 7**
See also CA 130; brief entry CA 104;
DLB 36

Woollcott, Alexander (Humphreys)
1887-1943  . . . . . . . . . . . . . . . . . . **TCLC 5**
See also CA 105; DLB 29

Wordsworth, Dorothy
1771-1855  . . . . . . . . . . . . . . . . **NCLC 25**

Wordsworth, William   1770-1850. . **NCLC 12**

Wouk, Herman   1915-. . . . . . . . . **CLC 1, 9, 38**
See also CANR 6; CA 5-8R; DLB-Y 82

Wright, Charles   1935-  . . . . . . . **CLC 6, 13, 28**
See also CAAS 7; CA 29-32R; DLB-Y 82

Wright, Charles (Stevenson)   1932- . . **CLC 49**
See also CA 9-12R; DLB 33

Wright, James (Arlington)
1927-1980  . . . . . . . . . . . **CLC 3, 5, 10, 28**
See also CANR 4; CA 49-52;
obituary CA 97-100; DLB 5

Wright, Judith   1915-  . . . . . . . . . **CLC 11, 53**
See also CA 13-16R; SATA 14

Wright, L(aurali) R.   1939-. . . . . . . . . **CLC 44**

Wright, Richard (Nathaniel)
1908-1960 . . .   **CLC 1, 3, 4, 9, 14, 21, 48;**
**SSC 2**
See also CA 108; DLB 76; DLB-DS 2

Wright, Richard B(ruce)   1937-  . . . . . . **CLC 6**
See also CA 85-88; DLB 53

Wright, Rick   1945-
See Pink Floyd

Wright, Stephen   1946-. . . . . . . . . . . **CLC 33**

Wright, Willard Huntington   1888-1939
See Van Dine, S. S.
See also CA 115

Wright, William   1930-. . . . . . . . . . . **CLC 44**
See also CANR 7, 23; CA 53-56

Wu Ch'eng-en   1500?-1582?  . . . . . . . . . **LC 7**

Wu Ching-tzu   1701-1754 . . . . . . . . . . . **LC 2**

Wurlitzer, Rudolph   1938?-. . . . . **CLC 2, 4, 15**
See also CA 85-88

Wycherley, William   1640?-1716 . . . . . . **LC 8**
See also DLB 80

Wylie (Benet), Elinor (Morton Hoyt)
1885-1928  . . . . . . . . . . . . . . . . . . **TCLC 8**
See also CA 105; DLB 9, 45

Wylie, Philip (Gordon)   1902-1971. . . **CLC 43**
See also CAP 2; CA 21-22;
obituary CA 33-36R; DLB 9

Wyndham, John   1903-1969 . . . . . . . . **CLC 19**
See also Harris, John (Wyndham Parkes
Lucas) Beynon

Wyss, Johann David   1743-1818 . . **NCLC 10**
See also SATA 27, 29

Yanovsky, Vassily S(emenovich)
1906-1989 . . . . . . . . . . . . . . . . **CLC 2, 18**
See also CA 97-100; obituary CA 129

Yates, Richard   1926- . . . . . . . . **CLC 7, 8, 23**
See also CANR 10; CA 5-8R; DLB 2;
DLB-Y 81

Yeats, William Butler
1865-1939 . . . . . . . . **TCLC 1, 11, 18, 31**
See also CANR 10; CA 104; DLB 10, 19

Yehoshua, A(braham) B.
1936-  . . . . . . . . . . . . . . . . . . . **CLC 13, 31**
See also CA 33-36R

Yep, Laurence (Michael)   1948-. . . . . **CLC 35**
See also CLR 3, 17; CANR 1; CA 49-52;
SATA 7; DLB 52

Yerby, Frank G(arvin)   1916-. . . **CLC 1, 7, 22**
See also CANR 16; CA 9-12R; DLB 76

Yevtushenko, Yevgeny (Alexandrovich)
1933-  . . . . . . . . . . . . **CLC 1, 3, 13, 26, 51**
See also CA 81-84

Yezierska, Anzia   1885?-1970. . . . . . **CLC 46**
See also CA 126; obituary CA 89-92;
DLB 28

Yglesias, Helen   1915-. . . . . . . . . . **CLC 7, 22**
See also CANR 15; CA 37-40R

Yorke, Henry Vincent   1905-1974
See Green, Henry
See also CA 85-88; obituary CA 49-52

Young, Al   1939-. . . . . . . . . . . . . . . . **CLC 19**
See also CANR 26; CA 29-32R; DLB 33

Young, Andrew   1885-1971. . . . . . . . . **CLC 5**
See also CANR 7; CA 5-8R

Young, Edward   1683-1765. . . . . . . . . . . **LC 3**

Young, Neil   1945-. . . . . . . . . . . . . . . **CLC 17**
See also CA 110

Yourcenar, Marguerite
1903-1987 . . . . . . . . . . . . . **CLC 19, 38, 50**
See also CANR 23; CA 69-72; DLB 72;
DLB-Y 88

Yurick, Sol   1925-. . . . . . . . . . . . . . . . **CLC 6**
See also CANR 25; CA 13-16R

Zamyatin, Yevgeny Ivanovich
1884-1937 . . . . . . . . . . . . . . . **TCLC 8, 37**
See also CA 105

Zangwill, Israel   1864-1926. . . . . . . **TCLC 16**
See also CA 109; DLB 10

Zappa, Francis Vincent, Jr.   1940-
See Zappa, Frank
See also CA 108

Zappa, Frank   1940- . . . . . . . . . . . . . **CLC 17**
See also Zappa, Francis Vincent, Jr.

Zaturenska, Marya   1902-1982. . . . **CLC 6, 11**
See also CANR 22; CA 13-16R;
obituary CA 105

Zelazny, Roger   1937-. . . . . . . . . . . . . **CLC 21**
See also CANR 26; CA 21-24R; SATA 39,
59; DLB 8

Zhdanov, Andrei A(lexandrovich)
1896-1948 . . . . . . . . . . . . . . . . . **TCLC 18**
See also CA 117

Ziegenhagen, Eric   1970-. . . . . . . . . . **CLC 55**

Zimmerman, Robert   1941-
See Dylan, Bob

Zindel, Paul   1936- . . . . . . . . . . . . . **CLC 6, 26**
See also CLR 3; CA 73-76; SATA 16, 58;
DLB 7, 52

Zinoviev, Alexander   1922-. . . . . . . . . **CLC 19**
See also CAAS 10; CA 116

Zola, Emile   1840-1902 . . . **TCLC 1, 6, 21, 41**
See also brief entry CA 104

Zoline, Pamela   1941-. . . . . . . . . . . . . **CLC 62**

Zorrilla y Moral, Jose   1817-1893. . **NCLC 6**

Zoshchenko, Mikhail (Mikhailovich)
1895-1958 . . . . . . . . . . . . . . . . . **TCLC 15**
See also CA 115

Zuckmayer, Carl   1896-1977. . . . . . . **CLC 18**
See also CA 69-72; DLB 56

Zukofsky, Louis
1904-1978 . . . . . . . **CLC 1, 2, 4, 7, 11, 18**
See also CA 9-12R; obituary CA 77-80;
DLB 5

Zweig, Paul   1935-1984. . . . . . . . **CLC 34, 42**
See also CA 85-88; obituary CA 113

Zweig, Stefan   1881-1942 . . . . . . . . . **TCLC 17**
See also CA 112; DLB 81

# *TCLC* Cumulative Nationality Index

## AMERICAN

Adams, Henry **4**
Agee, James **1, 19**
Anderson, Maxwell **2**
Anderson, Sherwood **1, 10, 24**
Atherton, Gertrude **2**
Austin, Mary **25**
Barry, Philip **11**
Baum, L. Frank **7**
Beard, Charles A. **15**
Belasco, David **3**
Benchley, Robert **1**
Benét, Stephen Vincent **7**
Benét, William Rose **28**
Bierce, Ambrose **1, 7**
Black Elk **33**
Bourne, Randolph S. **16**
Bradford, Gamaliel **36**
Bromfield, Louis **11**
Burroughs, Edgar Rice **2, 32**
Cabell, James Branch **6**
Cable, George Washington **4**
Cather, Willa **1, 11, 31**
Chambers, Robert W. **41**
Chandler, Raymond **1, 7**
Chapman, John Jay **7**
Chesnutt, Charles Waddell **5, 39**
Chopin, Kate **5, 14**
Comstock, Anthony **13**
Cotter, Joseph Seamon, Sr. **28**
Crane, Hart **2, 5**
Crane, Stephen **11, 17, 32**
Crawford, F. Marion **10**
Crothers, Rachel **19**
Cullen, Countee **4, 37**
Davis, Rebecca Harding **6**
Davis, Richard Harding **24**
Day, Clarence **25**
DeVoto, Bernard **29**

Dreiser, Theodore **10, 18, 35**
Dunbar, Paul Laurence **2, 12**
Dunne, Finley Peter **28**
Fisher, Rudolph **11**
Fitzgerald, F. Scott **1, 6, 14, 28**
Fletcher, John Gould **35**
Forten, Charlotte L. **16**
Freeman, Douglas Southall **11**
Freeman, Mary Wilkins **9**
Futrelle, Jacques **19**
Gale, Zona **7**
Garland, Hamlin **3**
Gilman, Charlotte Perkins **9, 37**
Glasgow, Ellen **2, 7**
Goldman, Emma **13**
Grey, Zane **6**
Guiney, Louise Imogen **41**
Hall, James Norman **23**
Harper, Frances Ellen Watkins **14**
Harris, Joel Chandler **2**
Harte, Bret **1, 25**
Hawthorne, Julian **25**
Hearn, Lafcadio **9**
Henry, O. **1, 19**
Hergesheimer, Joseph **11**
Higginson, Thomas Wentworth **36**
Hopkins, Pauline Elizabeth **28**
Howard, Robert E. **8**
Howe, Julia Ward **21**
Howells, William Dean **7, 17, 41**
James, Henry **2, 11, 24, 40**
James, William **15, 32**
Jewett, Sarah Orne **1, 22**
Johnson, James Weldon **3, 19**
Kornbluth, C. M. **8**
Kuttner, Henry **10**
Lardner, Ring **2, 14**
Lewis, Sinclair **4, 13, 23, 39**
Lewisohn, Ludwig **19**

Lindsay, Vachel **17**
London, Jack **9, 15, 39**
Lovecraft, H. P. **4, 22**
Lowell, Amy **1, 8**
Marquis, Don **7**
Masters, Edgar Lee **2, 25**
McCoy, Horace **28**
McKay, Claude **7, 41**
Mencken, H. L. **13**
Millay, Edna St. Vincent **4**
Mitchell, Margaret **11**
Mitchell, S. Weir **36**
Monroe, Harriet **12**
Muir, John **28**
Nathan, George Jean **18**
Nordhoff, Charles **23**
Norris, Frank **24**
O'Neill, Eugene **1, 6, 27**
Oskison, John M. **35**
Porter, Gene Stratton **21**
Post, Melville **39**
Rawlings, Marjorie Kinnan **4**
Reed, John **9**
Roberts, Kenneth **23**
Robinson, Edwin Arlington **5**
Rogers, Will **8**
Rölvaag, O. E. **17**
Rourke, Constance **12**
Runyon, Damon **10**
Saltus, Edgar **8**
Santayana, George **40**
Sherwood, Robert E. **3**
Slesinger, Tess **10**
Steffens, Lincoln **20**
Stein, Gertrude **1, 6, 28**
Sterling, George **20**
Stevens, Wallace **3, 12**
Tarbell, Ida **40**
Tarkington, Booth **9**

515

Teasdale, Sara  4
Thurman, Wallace  6
Twain, Mark  6, 12, 19, 36
Van Dine, S. S.  23
Van Doren, Carl  18
Veblen, Thorstein  31
Washington, Booker T.  10
Wells, Carolyn  35
West, Nathanael  1, 14
Wharton, Edith  3, 9, 27
White, Walter  15
Wister, Owen  21
Wolfe, Thomas  4, 13, 29
Woollcott, Alexander  5
Wylie, Elinor  8

**ARGENTINE**
Arlt, Roberto  29
Güiraldes, Ricardo  39
Lugones, Leopoldo  15
Storni, Alfonsina  5

**AUSTRALIAN**
Brennan, Christopher John  17
Franklin, Miles  7
Furphy, Joseph  25
Ingamells, Rex  35
Lawson, Henry  27
Paterson, A. B.  32
Richardson, Henry Handel  4

**AUSTRIAN**
Broch, Hermann  20
Hofmannsthal, Hugo von  11
Kafka, Franz  2, 6, 13, 29
Kraus, Karl  5
Kubin, Alfred  23
Meyrink, Gustav  21
Musil, Robert  12
Roth, Joseph  33
Schnitzler, Arthur  4
Steiner, Rudolf  13
Trakl, Georg  5
Werfel, Franz  8
Zweig, Stefan  17

**BELGIAN**
Bosschère, Jean de  19
Lemonnier, Camille  22
Maeterlinck, Maurice  3
Van Ostaijen, Paul  33
Verhaeren, Émile  12

**BRAZILIAN**
Cunha, Euclides da  24
Lima Barreto  23
Machado de Assis, Joaquim Maria  10
Ramos, Graciliano  32

**BULGARIAN**
Vazov, Ivan  25

**CANADIAN**
Campbell, Wilfred  9
Carman, Bliss  7
Carr, Emily  32
Connor, Ralph  31
Drummond, William Henry  25
Garneau, Hector Saint- Denys  13
Grove, Frederick Philip  4
Leacock, Stephen  2
McCrae, John  12

Nelligan, Emile  14
Pickthall, Marjorie  21
Roberts, Charles G. D.  8
Scott, Duncan Campbell  6
Service, Robert W.  15
Seton, Ernest Thompson  31
Stringer, Arthur  37

**CHILEAN**
Huidobro, Vicente  31
Mistral, Gabriela  2

**CHINESE**
Liu E  15
Lu Hsün  3
Su Man-shu  24
Wen I-to  28

**COLOMBIAN**
Rivera, Jose Eustasio  35

**CZECHOSLOVAKIAN**
Čapek, Karel  6, 37
Hašek, Jaroslav  4

**DANISH**
Brandes, Georg  10
Hansen, Martin A.  32
Jensen, Johannes  41
Pontopiddan, Henrik  29

**DUTCH**
Couperus, Louis  15
Frank, Anne  17
Heijermans, Herman  24

**ENGLISH**
Barbellion, W. N. P.  24
Baring, Maurice  8
Beerbohm, Max  1, 24
Belloc, Hilaire  7, 18
Bennett, Arnold  5, 20
Benson, E. F.  27
Benson, Stella  17
Bentley, E. C.  12
Besant, Annie  9
Blackmore, R. D.  27
Blackwood, Algernon  5
Bridges, Robert  1
Brooke, Rupert  2, 7
Butler, Samuel  1, 33
Chesterton, G. K.  1, 6
Conrad, Joseph  1, 6, 13, 25
Coppard, A. E.  5
Crowley, Aleister  7
De la Mare, Walter  4
Doughty, Charles  27
Douglas, Keith  40
Dowson, Ernest  4
Doyle, Arthur Conan  7, 26
Eddison, E. R.  15
Elizabeth  41
Ellis, Havelock  14
Firbank, Ronald  1
Ford, Ford Madox  1, 15, 39
Freeman, R. Austin  21
Galsworthy, John  1
Gilbert, W. S.  3
Gissing, George  3
Gosse, Edmund  28
Granville-Barker, Harley  2
Gray, John  19

Gurney, Ivor  33
Haggard, H. Rider  11
Hall, Radclyffe  12
Hardy, Thomas  4, 10, 18, 32
Henley, William Ernest  8
Hilton, James  21
Hodgson, William Hope  13
Housman, A. E.  1, 10
Housman, Laurence  7
Hudson, W. H.  29
Hulme, T. E.  21
Jacobs, W. W.  22
James, M. R.  6
Jerome, Jerome K.  23
Johnson, Lionel  19
Kaye-Smith, Sheila  20
Kipling, Rudyard  8, 17
Lawrence, D. H.  2, 9, 16, 33
Lawrence, T. E.  18
Lee, Vernon  5
Lee-Hamilton, Eugene  22
Leverson, Ada  18
Lewis, Wyndham  2, 9
Lindsay, David  15
Lowndes, Marie Belloc  12
Lowry, Malcolm  6, 40
Macaulay, Rose  7
MacCarthy, Desmond  36
Manning, Frederic  25
Meredith, George  17
Mew, Charlotte  8
Meynell, Alice  6
Milne, A. A.  6
Murry, John Middleton  16
Noyes, Alfred  7
Orwell, George  2, 6, 15, 31
Owen, Wilfred  5, 27
Pinero, Arthur Wing  32
Powys, T. F.  9
Richardson, Dorothy  3
Rohmer, Sax  28
Rolfe, Frederick  12
Rosenberg, Isaac  12
Ruskin, John  20
Rutherford, Mark  25
Saintsbury, George  31
Saki  3
Sayers, Dorothy L.  2, 15
Shiel, M. P.  8
Sinclair, May  3, 11
Stapledon, Olaf  22
Stephen, Leslie  23
Strachey, Lytton  12
Summers, Montague  16
Sutro, Alfred  6
Swinburne, Algernon Charles  8, 36
Symons, Arthur  11
Thomas, Edward  10
Thompson, Francis  4
Van Druten, John  2
Walpole, Hugh  5
Webb, Beatrice  22
Webb, Mary  24
Webb, Sidney  22
Welch, Denton  22
Wells, H. G.  6, 12, 19
Williams, Charles  1, 11
Woolf, Virginia  1, 5, 20
Zangwill, Israel  16

**ESTONIAN**
Tammsaare, A. H.  27

**FINNISH**
Leino, Eino  24
Södergran, Edith  31

**FRENCH**
Alain  41
Alain-Fournier  6
Apollinaire, Guillaume  3, 8
Artaud, Antonin  3, 36
Barbusse, Henri  5
Bergson, Henri  32
Bernanos, Georges  3
Bloy, Léon  22
Bourget, Paul  12
Claudel, Paul  2, 10
Colette  1, 5, 16
Coppée, François  25
Daumal, René  14
Desnos, Robert  22
Drieu La Rochelle, Pierre  21
Dujardin, Edouard  13
Eluard, Paul  7, 41
Fargue, Léon-Paul  11
Feydeau, Georges  22
France, Anatole  9
Gide, André  5, 12, 36
Giraudoux, Jean  2, 7
Gourmont, Remy de  17
Huysmans, Joris-Karl  7
Jacob, Max  6
Jarry, Alfred  2, 14
Larbaud, Valéry  9
Leroux, Gaston  25
Loti, Pierre  11
Martin du Gard, Roger  24
Moréas, Jean  18
Nizan, Paul  40
Péguy, Charles  10
Péret, Benjamin  20
Proust, Marcel  7, 13, 33
Radiguet, Raymond  29
Renard, Jules  17
Rolland, Romain  23
Rostand, Edmond  6, 37
Roussel, Raymond  20
Saint-Exupéry, Antoine de  2
Schwob, Marcel  20
Sully Prudhomme  31
Teilhard de Chardin, Pierre  9
Valéry, Paul  4, 15
Verne, Jules  6
Vian, Boris  9
Weil, Simone  23
Zola, Emile  1, 6, 21, 41

**GERMAN**
Benjamin, Walter  39
Benn, Gottfried  3
Borchert, Wolfgang  5
Brecht, Bertolt  1, 6, 13, 35
Döblin, Alfred  13
Ewers, Hanns Heinz  12
Feuchtwanger, Lion  3
George, Stefan  2, 14
Hauptmann, Gerhart  4
Heym, Georg  9
Heyse, Paul  8
Huch, Ricarda  13
Kaiser, Georg  9
Kolmar, Gertrud  40
Liliencron, Detlev von  18
Mann, Heinrich  9

Mann, Thomas  2, 8, 14, 21, 35
Morgenstern, Christian  8
Nietzsche, Friedrich  10, 18
Rilke, Rainer Maria  1, 6, 19
Spengler, Oswald  25
Sternheim, Carl  8
Sudermann, Hermann  15
Toller, Ernst  10
Wassermann, Jakob  6
Wedekind, Frank  7

**GHANIAN**
Casely-Hayford, J. E.  24

**GREEK**
Cavafy, C. P.  2, 7
Kazantzakis, Nikos  2, 5, 33
Palamas, Kostes  5
Papadiamantis, Alexandros  29
Sikelianos, Angeles  39

**HAITIAN**
Roumain, Jacques  19

**HUNGARIAN**
Ady, Endre  11
Babits, Mihály  14
Csáth, Géza  13
Herzl, Theodor  36
Hungarian Literature of the Twentieth
  Century  26
József, Attila  22
Mikszáth, Kálmán  31
Molnár, Ferenc  20
Móricz, Zsigmond  33
Radnóti, Miklós  16

**ICELANDIC**
Sigurjónsson, Jóhann  27

**INDIAN**
Chatterji, Saratchandra  13
Iqbal, Muhammad  28
Premchand  21
Tagore, Rabindranath  3

**INDONESIAN**
Anwar, Chairil  22

**IRANIAN**
Hedayat, Sadeq  21

**IRISH**
A. E.  3, 10
Cary, Joyce  1, 29
Dunsany, Lord  2
Gogarty, Oliver St. John  15
Gregory, Lady  1
Harris, Frank  24
Joyce, James  3, 8, 16, 26, 35
Ledwidge, Francis  23
Moore, George  7
O'Grady, Standish  5
Riddell, Mrs. J. H.  40
Shaw, Bernard  3, 9, 21
Stephens, James  4
Stoker, Bram  8
Synge, J. M.  6, 37
Tynan, Katharine  3
Wilde, Oscar  1, 8, 23, 41
Yeats, William Butler  1, 11, 18, 31

**ITALIAN**
Betti, Ugo  5
Brancati, Vitaliano  12
Campana, Dino  20
Carducci, Giosuè  32
Croce, Benedetto  37
D'Annunzio, Gabriele  6, 40
Deledda, Grazia  23
Giacosa, Giuseppe  7
Lampedusa, Giuseppe Tomasi di  13
Marinetti, F. T.  10
Papini, Giovanni  22
Pavese, Cesare  3
Pirandello, Luigi  4, 29
Saba, Umberto  33
Svevo, Italo  2, 35
Tozzi, Federigo  31
Verga, Giovanni  3

**JAMAICAN**
De Lisser, H. G.  12
Garvey, Marcus  41
Mais, Roger  8
Redcam, Tom  25

**JAPANESE**
Akutagawa Ryūnosuke  16
Dazai Osamu  11
Hayashi Fumiko  27
Ishikawa Takuboku  15
Masaoka Shiki  18
Miyamoto Yuriko  37
Mori Ōgai  14
Natsume, Sōseki  2, 10
Rohan, Kōda  22
Shimazaki, Tōson  5

**LATVIAN**
Rainis, Janis  29

**LEBANESE**
Gibran, Kahlil  1, 9

**LESOTHAN**
Mofolo, Thomas  22

**LITHUANIAN**
Krévé, Vincas  27

**MEXICAN**
Azuela, Mariano  3
Gamboa, Frederico  36
Nervo, Amado  11
Reyes, Alfonso  33
Romero, José Rubén  14

**NATIVE AMERICAN**
See American

**NEPALI**
Devkota, Laxmiprasad  23

**NEW ZEALAND**
Mander, Jane  31
Mansfield, Katherine  2, 8, 39

**NICARAGUAN**
Darío, Rubén  4

**NIGERIAN**
Nigerian Literature of the Twentieth
  Century  30

Nationality Index

## NORWEGIAN
Bjørnson, Bjørnstjerne   7, 37
Grieg, Nordhal   10
Hamsun, Knut   2, 14
Ibsen, Henrik   2, 8, 16, 37
Kielland, Alexander   5
Lie, Jonas   5
Obstfelder, Sigbjørn   23
Skram, Amalie   25
Undset, Sigrid   3

## PAKISTANI
Iqbal, Muhammad   28

## PERUVIAN
Palma, Ricardo   29
Vallejo, César   3

## POLISH
Asch, Sholem   3
Borowski, Tadeusz   9
Peretz, Isaac Leib   16
Przybyszewski, Stanisław   36
Reymont, Władysław Stanisław   5
Schulz, Bruno   5
Sienkiewitz, Henryk   3
Singer, Israel Joshua   33
Witkiewicz, Stanisław Ignacy   8

## PORTUGUESE
Pessoa, Fernando   27

## PUERTO RICAN
Hostos, Eugenio María de   24

## RUMANIAN
Bacovia, George   24
Rebreanu, Liviu   28

## RUSSIAN
Aldanov, Mark   23
Andreyev, Leonid   3
Annensky, Innokenty   14
Artsybashev, Mikhail   31
Babel, Isaak   2, 13
Balmont, Konstantin Dmitriyevich   11
Bely, Andrey   7
Blok, Aleksandr   5
Bryusov, Valery   10
Bulgakov, Mikhail   2, 16
Bunin, Ivan   6
Chekhov, Anton   3, 10, 31
Esenin, Sergei   4
Gladkov, Fyodor   27
Gorky, Maxim   8
Hippius, Zinaida   9
Ilf, Ilya   21
Ivanov, Vyacheslav   33
Khlebnikov, Velimir   20
Khodasevich, Vladislav   15
Korolenko, Vladimir   22
Kropotkin, Peter   36
Kuprin, Aleksandr   5
Kuzmin, Mikhail   40
Mandelstam, Osip   2, 6
Mayakovsky, Vladimir   4, 18
Merezhkovsky, Dmitri   29
Petrov, Evgeny   21
Pilnyak, Boris   23
Platonov, Andrei   14
Remizov, Alexey   27
Sologub, Fyodor   9

Tolstoy, Alexey Nikolayevich   18
Tolstoy, Leo   4, 11, 17, 28
Trotsky, Leon   22
Tsvetaeva, Marina   7, 35
Zamyatin, Yevgeny Ivanovich   8, 37
Zhdanov, Andrei   18
Zoshchenko, Mikhail   15

## SCOTTISH
Barrie, J. M.   2
Bridie, James   3
Brown, George Douglas   28
Buchan, Sir John   41
Davidson, John   24
Frazer, James   32
Gibbon, Lewis Grassic   4
Graham, R. B. Cunninghame   19
Lang, Andrew   16
MacDonald, George   9
Muir, Edwin   2
Sharp. William   39
Tey, Josephine   14

## SOUTH AFRICAN
Campbell, Roy   5
Mqhayi, S. E. K.   25
Schreiner, Olive   9
Smith, Pauline   25
Vilakazi, Benedict Wallet   37

## SPANISH
Alas, Leopoldo   29
Barea, Arturo   14
Baroja, Pío   8
Benavente, Jacinto   3
Blasco Ibáñez, Vicente   12
Echegaray, José   4
García Lorca, Federico   1, 7
Jiménez, Juan Ramón   4
Machado, Antonio   3
Martínez Sierra, Gregorio   6
Miró, Gabriel   5
Ortega y Gasset, José   9
Pereda, José María de   16
Pérez, Galdós, Benito   27
Salinas, Pedro   17
Unamuno, Miguel de   2, 9
Valera, Juan   10
Valle-Inclán, Ramón del   5

## SWEDISH
Dagerman, Stig   17
Heidenstam, Verner von   5
Lagerlöf, Selma   4, 36
Soderberg, Hjalmar   39
Strindberg, August   1, 8, 21

## SWISS
Ramuz, Charles-Ferdinand   33
Spitteler, Carl   12
Walser, Robert   18

## TURKISH
Sait Faik   23

## UKRAINIAN
Bialik, Chaim Nachman   25
Sholom Aleichem   1, 35

## URUGUAYAN
Quiroga, Horacio   20
Sánchez, Florencio   37

## WELSH
Davies, W. H.   5
Lewis, Alun   3
Machen, Arthur   4
Thomas, Dylan   1, 8

# *TCLC* Title Index to Volume 41

*Aandens Stadier* (*The Stages of the Mind*) (Jensen)  **41**:294

*Aarstiderne* (*The Book of the Seasons*) (Jensen)  **41**:294

*The Adventures of a Modest Man* (Chambers)  **41**:95

*Adventures of Elizabeth in Rügen* (Elizabeth)  **41**:122-23, 130, 132

*Æsteik og Udvikling* (*Esthetics and Evolution*) (Jensen)  **41**:295

"After the Defeat at Manilla" (Jensen)  **41**:292

"After the Winter" (McKay)  **41**:344

"The Agricultural Show" (McKay)  **41**:329-30

"Ailleurs ici partout" (Eluard)  **41**:153

*Ailsa Paige* (Chambers)  **41**:95-7

*Alain on Happiness* (Alain)  See *Propos sur le bonheur*

*All the Dogs of My Life* (Elizabeth)  **41**:131

"The American James" (Howells)  **41**:266

*L'amour la poésie* (Eluard)  **41**:150

"L'amoureuse" (Eluard)  **41**:154

"Andreas Olufsen" (Jensen)  **41**:308

*Animals and Their Masters, Masters and Their Animals* (Eluard)  See *Les animaux et leurs hommes, les hommes et leurs animaux*

*Les animaux et leurs hommes, les hommes et leurs animaux* (*Animals and Their Masters, Masters and Their Animals*) (Eluard)  **41**:152-53

*Annie Kilburn* (Howells)  **41**:269

*Anthology of Writings on Art* (Eluard)  See *Ecrits sur l'art*

"An Appeal to the Intelligentsia" (Garvey)  **41**:198

*An Appeal to the Soul of White America* (Garvey)  **41**:179

*The April Baby's Book of Tunes* (Elizabeth)  **41**:122

*April Hopes* (Howells)  **41**:286

"Arbejderen" (Jensen)  **41**:303

*L'argent* (Zola)  **41**:412, 439, 448-49

"Les armes de la douleur" (Eluard)  **41**:168

*Ashes of Empire* (Chambers)  **41**:91

*L'assommoir* (Zola)  **41**:408-09, 413, 415, 422, 425-29, 431, 435-39, 444, 448-49, 451, 453

"Astræa" (Guiney)  **41**:215, 222, 229

"Athassel Abbey" (Guiney)  **41**:205

*Au bonheur des dames* (Zola)  **41**:412, 438, 451

*Augustus* (Buchan)  **41**:59-60, 63-4

"Bakmandens Hund" ("The Dog of the Man from the Bak Farm") (Jensen)  **41**:308

"The Ballad of Kenelm" (Guiney)  **41**:205, 207, 214

"A Ballad of Metz" (Guiney)  **41**:206

*The Ballad of Reading Gaol, and Other Poems* (Wilde)  **41**:358, 397

*Banana Bottom* (McKay)  **41**:322-25, 328, 330, 335, 340-43

*Banjo* (McKay)  **41**:317-18, 320-23, 325, 328-29, 335, 338-40, 342

"Beati Mortui" (Guiney)  **41**:215

"En Beboer af Jorden" ("An Inhabitant of the Soil") (Jensen)  **41**:307

*The Benefactress* (Elizabeth)  **41**:122, 130

"Beside Hazlitt's Grave" (Guiney)  **41**:216

*La bête humaine* (Zola)  **41**:414, 422, 436, 439, 451

"The Birthday of the Infanta" (Wilde)  **41**:375, 378

"Bitte-Selgen" (Jensen)  **41**:308

*The Blanket of the Dark* (Buchan)  **41**:39

"Blasons des fleurs et des fruits" (Eluard)  **41**:156

*Blasons des fleurs et des fruits* (Eluard)  **41**:151

*Blessed Edmund Campion* (Guiney)  **41**:219

"Bo'l" (Jensen)  **41**:308

"Bondefangeren" (Jensen)  **41**:303

*The Book of the Seasons* (Jensen)  See *Aarstiderne*

"Borderlands" (Guiney)  **41**:214, 221-22, 227

*A Boy's Town* (Howells)  **41**:275

*Bræen* (*The Glacier, Ice*) (Jensen)  **41**:290-91, 293-95

"Brownskin Blues" (McKay)  **41**:329

"The Bull Fight" (Jensen)  **41**:292

"The Burden of Itys" (Wilde)  **41**:378

*Cahiers de Lorient* (Alain)  **41**:29

*A Cambric Mask* (Chambers)  **41**:95

"The Canterville Ghost" (Wilde)  **41**:359

*Capitale de la douleur* (Eluard)  **41**:150, 154

*The Caravaners* (Elizabeth)  **41**:122-23, 128, 130-31

*Cardigan* (Chambers)  **41**:94, 101

*Castle Gay* (Buchan)  **41**:38, 41, 45, 74

"Catholicism in England: A Non-Scientific Survey" (Guiney)  **41**:219

"Cecil" (Jensen)  **41**:307

"Celle de toujours, toute" ("She Who Is of Always, All"; "She of All Time, All") (Eluard)  **41**:147

"Chaluz Castle" (Guiney)  **41**:207

*A Chance Acquaintance* (Howells)  **41**:234

*Chanson complète* (*Total Song*) (Eluard)  **41**:158

"Charondas" (Guiney)  **41**:206

*Le château des pauvres* (Eluard)  **41**:151

"A Chouan" (Guiney)  **41**:207

*Christine* (Elizabeth)  **41**:131

"Christofer Columbus" (Jensen)  **41**:300

*Christopher and Columbus* (Elizabeth)  **41**:124

*Christopher Columbus* (Jensen)  **41**:295, 298

*Cimbrernes Tog* (*The Cimbrians; The Raids of the Cimbri*) (Jensen)  **41**:295, 298

*The Cimbrians* (Jensen)
See *Cimbrernes Tog*

"Les cinq rondels du tout jeune homme" (Eluard)  **41**:150

"Le cinquième poème visible" (Eluard)  **41**:157

"Le coeur sur l'arbre" (Eluard)  **41**:153

*Comme deux gouttes d'eau* (Eluard)  **41**:150

"Comments on the Art of Knowing Others and Oneself" (Alain)  **41**:21

*The Common Law* (Chambers)  **41**:97, 111

*La confession de Claude* (Zola)  **41**:407

*La conquête de Plassans* (Zola)  **41**:412

*Constab Ballads* (McKay)  **41**:319, 328, 343

*Corps mémorable* (Eluard)  **41**:151

*A Counterfeit Presentment* (Howells)  **41**:263

"Courage" (Eluard)  **41**:168

*Cours naturel* (Eluard)  **41**:156, 167

"The Court of the Dragon" (Chambers)  **41**:88, 101, 103-08

*The Courts of the Morning* (Buchan)  **41**:38, 41, 44, 53-6, 67

"Couvre-feu" (Eluard)  **41**:152, 161

"Crazy Mary" (McKay)  **41**:329

"The Critic as Artist" (Wilde)  **41**:376-77, 379, 381-82

*Criticism and Fiction* (Howells)  **41**:255-56, 284

"Critique de la poésie" (Eluard)  **41**:151

*La curée* (Zola)  **41**:412

*The Dancing Floor* (Buchan)  **41**:38, 41, 44-5, 54

*The Danger Mark* (Chambers)  **41**:92, 95-6, 101

*Danskere* (Jensen)  **41**:296

"Daybreak" (Guiney)  **41**:213

*La débâcle* (Zola)  **41**:414-15, 422, 439

*Defiance* (Jensen)
See *Trods*

"The Delights of an Incognito" (Guiney)  **41**:209

"The Demoiselle d'Ys" (Chambers)  **41**:87-8, 94, 101, 103, 106, 110

"A Description of Himmerland" (Jensen)
See "Himmerlands Beskrivelse"

"Despotisms" (Guiney)  **41**:221

*Les dessous d'une vie ou la pyramide humaine* (Eluard)  **41**:150

*Le devoir et l'inquiétude* (*Duty and Anguish*) (Eluard)  **41**:153

"The Devoted Friend" (Wilde)  **41**:383

*Dictionnaire abrégé du Surréalisme* (Eluard)  **41**:153

*Les dieux* (*The Gods*) (Alain)  **41**:23-5, 30

*Digte* (Jensen)  **41**:301

"Dissertation on Man" (Garvey)  **41**:183

*Le docteur Pascal* (Zola)  **41**:411, 414, 421, 424, 450-51, 453

*Dr. Breen's Practice* (Howells)  **41**:234

"The Dog of the Man from the Bak Farm" (Jensen)
See "Bakmandens Hund"

*Donner à voir* (Eluard)  **41**:163

*Le dur désir de durer* (Eluard)  **41**:151

*The Dutchess of Padua* (Wilde)  **41**:354, 376

*Duty and Anguish* (Eluard)
See *Le devoir et l'inquiétude*

*Dyrenes Forvandling* (*The Transformation of the Animals*) (Jensen)  **41**:294

*Ecrits sur l'art* (*Anthology of Writings on Art*) (Eluard)  **41**:149, 152

"L'égalité des sexes" ("The Equality of the Sexes") (Eluard)  **41**:160

"The Eggs of the Silver Moon" (Chambers)  **41**:114

*Einar Elkær* (Jensen)  **41**:296, 303

*Eksotiske Noveller* (*Exotic Tales*) (Jensen)  **41**:294

*Eléments d'une doctrine radicale* (Alain)  **41**:13

*Elizabeth and Her German Garden* (*German Garden*) (Elizabeth)  **41**:117-18, 121-22, 124, 127, 129-31, 138-39

"Elses Bryllup" (*Else's Wedding*) (Jensen)  **41**:306

*Else's Wedding* (Jensen)
See "Elses Bryllup"

"The Emigrant" (Jensen)  **41**:308

*The Enchanted April* (Elizabeth)  **41**:124-25, 129, 132, 137

"An Encounter with a Pickpocket" (Guiney)  **41**:209

*England and Yesterday* (Guiney)  **41**:208-09

*Entretiens au bord de la mer* (Alain)  **41**:30

*Entretiens chez le sculpteur* (Alain)  **41**:30

"L'envoi" (Wilde)  **41**:367

"The Equality of the Sexes" (Eluard)
See "L'égalité des sexes"

*Esthetics and Evolution* (Jensen)
See *Æsteik og Udvikling*

"Et Møde" (Jensen)  **41**:303

*Exotic Tales* (Jensen)
See *Eksotiske Noveller*

"The Face of Peace" (Eluard)  **41**:149

*Facile* (Eluard)  **41**:150

"Fact and the Mystic" (Guiney)  **41**:207

*The Fall of the King* (Jensen)
See *Kongens Fald*

"The Far Island" (Buchan)  **41**:73

*Father* (Elizabeth)  **41**:130, 132

*La faute de l'abbé Mouret* (Zola)  **41**:412, 451

*Fécondité* (Zola)  **41**:421, 450

*The Fighting Chance* (Chambers)  **41**:92, 95-6, 101

*Fire* (Jensen)
See *Det tabte Land*

*Fire and Ice* (Jensen)  **41**:291, 297-98

*The Firing Line* (Chambers)  **41**:92, 95, 101

"First in the World" (Eluard)  **41**:147

"The Fisherman and His Soul" (Wilde)  **41**:381-82

"Five Cards for Christmastide" (Guiney)  **41**:217

"Flame-Heart" (McKay)  **41**:344

"Flavian: A Clerical Portrait" (Guiney)  **41**:220

"Fool-Proof" (Eluard)  **41**:149

"A Foot-Note to a Famous Lyric" (Guiney)  **41**:207

*La fortune des Rougon* (Zola)  **41**:411

"Four Colloquies" (Guiney)  **41**:207

*Fräulein Schmidt and Mr. Anstruther* (Elizabeth)  **41**:122-23, 132, 136

*The Free Fishers* (Buchan)  **41**:39

"A Friend's Song for Limdisius" (Guiney)  **41**:205

"A Friend's Song for Simoisius" (Guiney)  **41**:218

"Gabriel Péri" (Eluard)  **41**:161, 168

*The Gap in the Curtain* (Buchan)  **41**:38, 41, 44

"Garden Chidings" (Guiney)  **41**:207

*German Garden* (Elizabeth)
See *Elizabeth and Her German Garden*

*Germinal* (Zola)  **41**:414-15, 421-22, 425-26, 437-49, 451-54

*Gingertown* (McKay)  **41**:318, 328-30, 336, 342

*The Glacier* (Jensen)
See *Bræen*

"Gloucester Harbor" (Guiney)  **41**:203, 206

*The Gods* (Alain)
See *Les dieux*

"The Golddigger" (Jensen)
See "Guldgraveren"

*Goose-Quill Papers* (Guiney)  **41**:209-10

*The Gothic Renaissance* (Jensen)
See *Den gotiske Renaissance*

*Den gotiske Renaissance* (*The Gothic Renaissance*) (Jensen)  **41**:300-01, 308-09

"Graabølle" (Jensen)  **41**:308

*The Green Mouse* (Chambers)  **41**:95

*Greenmantle* (Buchan)  **41**:36-8, 41-2, 53-5, 64, 66-7, 81-3

*Grey Weather: Moorland Tales of My Own People* (Buchan)  **41**:34, 72

"The Grove of Ashtaroth" (Buchan)  **41**:34

"Guernica" (Eluard)  **41**:164, 166-67

"Guldgraveren" ("The Golddigger") (Jensen)  **41**:307

*The Half-Hearted* (Buchan)  **41**:41-4, 46

"La halte des heures" (Eluard)  **41**:157

*Happy Ending: The Collected Lyrics of Louise Imogen Guiney* (Guiney)  **41**:212, 214-15, 219, 229

"The Happy Prince" (Wilde)  **41**:389

*The Happy Prince, and Other Tales* (Wilde)  **41**:376

"The Harbor-Master" (Chambers)  **41**:102

*Harlem: Negro Metropolis* (McKay)  **41**:328, 330, 335

*Harlem Shadows* (McKay)  **41**:316, 328, 336, 343

"The Harlot's House" (Wilde)  **41**:397

*A Hazard of New Fortunes* (Howells)  **41**:269

"Hedebonden" ("The Moorland Peasant") (Jensen)  **41**:308

*Heroines of Fiction* (Howells)  **41**:277

"Hr. Jesper" ("Sir Jesper") (Jensen)  **41**:308

"Hiball" (McKay)  **41**:342

*Himmerland People* (Jensen)  **41**:306, 309

*Himmerland Stories: Third Collection* (Jensen)  **41**:306

"Himmerlands Beskrivelse" ("A Description of Himmerland") (Jensen)  **41**:308

*Himmerlandshistorier* (*Tales from Himmerland*) (Jensen)  **41**:294, 296

*Histoire de mes pensées* (Alain)  **41**:7, 10, 26, 28, 30

*Hjulet* (*The Wheel*) (Jensen)  **41**:291, 294, 296, 301-03

*Holding Fast* (Eluard)
See *A toute épreuve*

"Home-Thoughts" (McKay)  **41**:344

*Home to Harlem* (McKay)  **41**:317-18, 320-22, 325, 328-29, 334-40

"The Horse Dealer" (Jensen)
See "Prangeren"

*A House of Pomegranates* (Wilde)  **41**:376

*The House of the Four Winds* (Buchan)  **41**:38, 41, 44-6, 74

*Huntingtower* (Buchan)  **41**:38, 41, 46, 49, 74-5

"Hverrestens-Ajes" (Jensen)  **41**:308
*Ice* (Jensen)
  See *Bræen*
*An Ideal Husband* (Wilde)  **41**:397
*Les idées et les âges* (Alain)  **41**:3, 28, 30
"Identités" (Eluard)  **41**:156
"If We Must Die" (McKay)  **41**:318-19, 345
*L'immaculée conception* (Eluard)  **41**:152
*The Importance of Being Earnest* (Wilde)
  **41**:388
"In Leinster" (Guiney)  **41**:207
*In Order to Live on This Earth* (Eluard)
  See *Pour vivre ici*
"In Quest of the Dingue" (Chambers)  **41**:102
*In Search of the Unknown* (Chambers)  **41**:95,
  100, 102, 113-14
"In the Darkness" (Jensen)  **41**:306-07
*In the Mountains* (Elizabeth)  **41**:131, 136
*In the Quarter* (Chambers)  **41**:87-90, 94, 114
"In Ulster" (Guiney)  **41**:207
*Indian Summer* (Howells)  **41**:256, 263, 269,
  286
"An Inhabitant of the Soil" (Jensen)
  See "En Beboer af Jorden"
"Inquirendo" (Guiney)  **41**:208
*Introduction to Our Epoch* (Jensen)
  See *Introduktion till vor Tidsalder*
*Introduction to Sally* (*Sally*) (Elizabeth)
  **41**:125
*Introduktion till vor Tidsalder* (*Introduction to
  Our Epoch*) (Jensen)  **41**:294
*Iole* (Chambers)  **41**:95
"Is the Ux Extinct?" (Chambers)  **41**:102
*The Island of Sheep* (*The Man from the
  Norlands*) (Buchan)  **41**:38, 41, 53-8, 67
*The Jasmine Farm* (Elizabeth)  **41**:129, 132
"Jens" (Jensen)  **41**:307
"Joan Miró" (Eluard)  **41**:149
*John Burnet of Barns* (Buchan)  **41**:34
*John Macnab* (Buchan)  **41**:38, 41, 44-5, 47,
  49, 51
*Le joie de vivre* (Zola)  **41**:413, 451, 453
*Jørgine* (Jensen)  **41**:306, 308
"The Key to Grief" (Chambers)  **41**:102
*A King and a Few Dukes* (Chambers)  **41**:88
*The King in Yellow* (Chambers)  **41**:87-90, 94,
  101-02, 104, 107-08, 113-14
"The Kings" (Guiney)  **41**:204, 207-08, 221-22
"Kirsten's Last Journey" (Jensen)
  See "Kirstens sidste Rejse"
"Kirstens sidste Rejse" ("Kirsten's Last
  Journey") (Jensen)  **41**:307
"The Knight Errant" (Guiney)  **41**:205, 221,
  227
*Kongens Fald* (*The Fall of the King*) (Jensen)
  **41**:293-94, 296, 306, 309-13
"The Ladies of the Lake" (Chambers)  **41**:114
*The Lady of the :Aroostook:* (Howells)  **41**:234,
  266
*The Landlord at Lion's Head* (Howells)
  **41**:286
*Den lange Rejse* (*The Long Journey*) (Jensen)
  **41**:291-99, 302
"The Last Faun" (Guiney)  **41**:207
*Lazare* (Zola)  **41**:450
*Une leçon de morale* (Eluard)  **41**:151
"The Lemnian" (Buchan)  **41**:34
*Letters Home* (Howells)  **41**:256
*The Letters of Oscar Wilde* (Wilde)  **41**:372
*Lettres à Sergio Solmi sur la philosophie de
  Kant* (Alain)  **41**:11

"Liberté" ("Liberty") (Eluard)  **41**:151, 161,
  168
"Liberty" (Eluard)
  See "Liberté"
*Life of Scott* (Buchan)
  See *Sir Walter Scott*
"Lille Ahasverus" (Jensen)  **41**:303
"The Lindby Marksman" (Jensen)
  See "Lindby-Skytten"
"Lindby-Skytten" ("The Lindby Marksman")
  (Jensen)  **41**:307
"Lines on Various Fly-Leaves" (Guiney)
  **41**:209
*Lingéres légères* (Eluard)  **41**:151
*A l'intérieur de la vie* (*Within Life's Limits*)
  (Eluard)  **41**:157
*A Little English Gallery* (Guiney)  **41**:208-09
"Little Sheik" (McKay)  **41**:329
*Le livre ouvert, 1938-1940* (*The Open Book*)
  (Eluard)  **41**:156-57, 159-60
*The Long Journey* (Jensen)
  See *Den lange Rejse*
*A Long Way from Home* (McKay)  **41**:325,
  328, 335, 343, 345
*Une longue réflexion amoureuse* (Eluard)
  **41**:151
"Lord Arthur Savile's Crime" (Wilde)
  **41**:359-60, 362, 397
*Lorraine* (Chambers)  **41**:88, 91
*A Lost Lady of Old Years* (Buchan)  **41**:34
*The Lost Land* (Jensen)
  See *Det tabte Land*
*Lourdes* (Zola)  **41**:422, 438
*Love* (Elizabeth)  **41**:125, 127, 137
"Lover Loquitur" (Guiney)  **41**:206
*Lovers' Saint Ruth's, and Three Other Tales*
  (Guiney)  **41**:209
"Love's Morning Star" (Garvey)  **41**:198
*Madame d'Ora* (Jensen)  **41**:291, 294, 296,
  300, 303
*The Maid at Arms* (Chambers)  **41**:94
*The Maids of Paradise* (Chambers)  **41**:91
"The Maker of Moons" (Chambers)  **41**:102,
  107
*The Maker of Moons* (Chambers)  **41**:88, 90,
  94, 100, 104, 106-08, 114
"The Man at the Next Table" (Chambers)
  **41**:104
*The Man from the Norlands* (Buchan)
  See *The Island of Sheep*
*The Marquis of Montrose* (Buchan)  **41**:60
*Mars; or, The Truth about War* (Alain)
  See *Mars ou la guerre jugée*
*Mars ou la guerre jugée* (*Mars; or, The Truth
  about War*) (Alain)  **41**:2-3, 5, 10, 16, 25
*The Martyr's Idyl, and Shorter Poems* (Guiney)
  **41**:207-08, 214
"The Mask" (Chambers)  **41**:101, 103-06, 108,
  110, 114
"A Matter of Interest" (Chambers)  **41**:113-14
"Mattie and Her Sweetman" (McKay)  **41**:329
"Médieuses" (Eluard)  **41**:159
*Médieuses* (Eluard)  **41**:150, 159
*Le meilleur choix de poèmes est celui que l'on
  fait pour soi* (Eluard)  **41**:152
*Memoir of Prosper Mérimée* (Guiney)  **41**:209
*Memory Hold-the-Door* (*Pilgrim's Way*)
  (Buchan)  **41**:59, 63, 66, 77-8, 81, 84
*Mes haines* (*My Hates*) (Zola)  **41**:407
"The Messenger" (Chambers)  **41**:88, 102
*Midwinter* (Buchan)  **41**:39

*The Minister's Charge; or, The Apprenticeship
  of Lemuel Barker* (Howells)  **41**:256, 268-
  69, 286
"Le miroir d'un moment" (Eluard)  **41**:154
*Miscellanies* (Wilde)  **41**:367
*Mr. Skeffington* (Elizabeth)  **41**:131-32
*Mr. Standfast* (Buchan)  **41**:38, 41-2, 48, 50,
  54, 57-8, 64, 66-7, 73, 77, 80
"The Model Millionaire" (Wilde)  **41**:359
*A Modern Instance* (Howells)  **41**:233-34, 247,
  252, 262-63, 265-66, 270, 275, 277
*:Monsieur Henri:: A Foot-Note to French
  History* (Guiney)  **41**:207-08
"Monsunen" (Jensen)  **41**:303
*Montrose* (Buchan)  **41**:59-63
*The Moon Endureth* (Buchan)  **41**:34-5, 37,
  41, 73
"The Moorland Peasant" (Jensen)
  See "Hedebonden"
"The Motor" (Guiney)  **41**:221
*Mountain Meadow* (Buchan)
  See *Sick Heart River*
*Mourir de ne pas mourir* (Eluard)  **41**:150,
  154, 160
*My Hates* (Zola)
  See *Mes haines*
*My Year in a Log Cabin* (Howells)  **41**:253
*The Mystery of Choice* (Chambers)  **41**:88, 90,
  94, 102, 106, 113-14
"Myten som Kunstform" (Jensen)  **41**:309
*Nana* (Zola)  **41**:414-15, 436, 439, 442-44,
  447-49
"Near-White" (McKay)  **41**:329
*Les nécessités de la vie et les conséquences des
  rêves* (Eluard)  **41**:153
"A Negro Writer to His Critics" (McKay)
  **41**:336
*The Negroes in America* (McKay)  **41**:331-32,
  335
"The Negro's Tragedy" (McKay)  **41**:318
*New Himmerland Stories* (Jensen)  **41**:306, 308
*The New World* (Jensen)
  See *Den ny Verden*
"Newman's Littlemore: A Few Addenda"
  (Guiney)  **41**:220
"Nigger Lover" (McKay)  **41**:329
"Nine Brasenose Worthies" (Buchan)  **41**:59
"No-Man's-Land" (Buchan)  **41**:37, 73
*Norne-Gæst* (Jensen)  **41**:295
"North and South" (McKay)  **41**:318-19
"A Notable Collection of Relics for Oxford"
  (Guiney)  **41**:220
"Notes générales sur la marche de l'œuvre"
  (Zola)  **41**:451
"Notre vie" (Eluard)  **41**:161
"Nous sommes" ("We Are") (Eluard)  **41**:147,
  158
*Une nouvelle manière en peinture* (Zola)
  **41**:436
"Nuits partagées" ("Shared Nights") (Eluard)
  **41**:149, 155, 158
*Den ny Verden* (*The New World*) (Jensen)
  **41**:290, 300-01, 303
"October Night" (Jensen)
  See "Oktobernat"
*L'oeuvre* (Zola)  **41**:413-14, 422, 424, 435, 442
"Of the Golden Age" (Guiney)  **41**:207
"Oktobernat" ("October Night") (Jensen)
  **41**:306
*Oliver Cromwell* (Buchan)  **41**:39, 51, 59, 62-3
"On Dying Considered as a Dramatic
  Situation" (Guiney)  **41**:209

"On Leaving Winchester" (Guiney) **41**:208, 216

"On Teaching One's Grandmother How to Suck Eggs" (Guiney) **41**:209-10

"On the Loneliness of Priests" (Guiney) **41**:220

*152 proverbes mis au goût du jour* (Eluard) **41**:153

*Onze chapîtres sur Platon* (Alain) **41**:3

*The Open Book* (Eluard)
See *Le livre ouvert, 1938-1940*

"An Open Letter to the Moon" (Guiney) **41**:210

"Open Time" (Guiney) **41**:205

"An Outdoor Litany" (Guiney) **41**:214

"The Outgoing of the Tide" (Buchan) **41**:73

*Outsiders* (Chambers) **41**:91, 95

"Paa Memphis Station" (Jensen) **41**:304, 306

*Une page d'amour* (Zola) **41**:413

*Paris* (Zola) **41**:421-22

"Passeur" (Chambers) **41**:88

*The Pastor's Wife* (Elizabeth) **41**:119, 122-24, 132, 134, 136-37

*The Path of the King* (Buchan) **41**:37-8

*The Paths and the Roads of Poetry* (Eluard)
See *Les sentiers et les routes de la poésie*

*Patrins, to Which Is Added an Inquirendo into the Wit & Other Good Parts of His Late Majesty King Charles the Second* (Guiney) **41**:209-11, 219

"Pen, Pencil, and Poison" (Wilde) **41**:359

"Peter Rugg the Bostonian" (Guiney) **41**:207

"Un Peu d'Amour" (Chambers) **41**:113-14

*Le phénix* (*The Phoenix*) (Eluard) **41**:151-52, 158

*The Philosophy and Opinions of Marcus Garvey; or, Africa for the Africans* (Garvey) **41**:187, 190-91, 194, 199

*The Phoenix* (Eluard)
See *Le phénix*

"Physics of Poetry" (Eluard)
See "Physique de la poésie"

*Physics of Poetry* (Eluard)
See *Physique de la poésie*

"Physique de la poésie" ("Physics of Poetry") (Eluard) **41**:149

*Physique de la poésie* (*Physics of Poetry*) (Eluard) **41**:164

*The Picture of Dorian Gray* (Wilde) **41**:347-403

*Pilgrim's Way* (Buchan)
See *Memory Hold-the-Door*

"Planting the Poplar" (Guiney) **41**:218, 229

"A Pleasant Evening" (Chambers) **41**:88, 102

*Poèmes* (Eluard) **41**:153

*Poèmes politiques* (Eluard) **41**:151, 162

*Poèmes pour la paix* (Eluard) **41**:150, 153-54

*Poems, Scots and English* (Buchan) **41**:72

"La poésie doit avoir pour but la vérité pratique" (Eluard) **41**:162

*Poésie et vérité* (Eluard) **41**:162

"Poésie ininterrompue" (Eluard) **41**:151, 153

*Poésie involontaire et poésie intentionelle* (Eluard) **41**:151-52

"Poetic Evidence" (Eluard) **41**:144

*Poetic Meditations* (Garvey) **41**:198

"The Poet's Chart" (Guiney) **41**:207-08

*Police!!!* (Chambers) **41**:102, 113-14

"Pompe Funebre" (Chambers) **41**:88

*The Portrait of Mr. W. H.* (Wilde) **41**:359, 371, 375-77, 381, 389, 398

*Portraits de famille* (Alain) **41**:30

*Pot-bouille* (Zola) **41**:412, 415

"Potowatomis Datter" (Jensen) **41**:303-04

"Pour vivre ici" (Eluard) **41**:152, 169

*Pour vivre ici* (*In Order to Live on This Earth*) (Eluard) **41**:154

*Pouvoir tout dire* (Eluard) **41**:152

*The Power-House* (Buchan) **41**:38, 40-1, 53, 65, 67-8, 70-1

"Prangeren" ("The Horse Dealer") (Jensen) **41**:308

*Première anthologie vivante de la poésie du passé* (Eluard) **41**:152

*Premières vues anciennes* (Eluard) **41**:152

*Prester John* (Buchan) **41**:34-6, 38, 41, 44, 49

*A Prince of the Captivity* (Buchan) **41**:41-2, 44-5, 54, 58, 67, 80

*The Princess Priscilla's Fortnight* (Elizabeth) **41**:122-23

"Printemps" (Eluard) **41**:158

*De profundis* (Wilde) **41**:358, 361, 374, 376, 396-97

*Les propos d'Alain* (Alain) **41**:3

*Propos de littérature* (Alain) **41**:27

*Propos sur le bonheur* (*Alain on Happiness*) (Alain) **41**:3, 21-2, 29

*Propos sur le christianisme* (Alain) **41**:3

*Propos sur l'éducation* (Alain) **41**:9, 29

"The Provider" (Guiney) **41**:209

"The Purple Emperor" (Chambers) **41**:102, 113-14

*Quatre-vingt-un chapîtres sur l'esprit et les passions* (Alain) **41**:3

"Quiet Mogens" (Jensen)
See "Den stille Mogens"

*The Raids of the Cimbri* (Jensen)
See *Cimbrernes Tog*

*Ralentir travaux* (Eluard) **41**:152

*The Reckoning* (Chambers) **41**:94

*Recusant Poets* (Guiney) **41**:217, 221, 223-24

*The Red Republic* (Chambers) **41**:88, 91, 101

"Règnes" (Eluard) **41**:160

"The Repairer of Reputations" (Chambers) **41**:101, 103-09, 114

*Répétitions* (Eluard) **41**:150

"The Resurrection of the Negro" (Garvey) **41**:184

*Le rêve* (Zola) **41**:412, 451

"The Riding of Ninemileburn" (Buchan) **41**:73

*The Rise of Silas Lapham* (Howells) **41**:231-87

"The Rise of Silas Needham" (Howells) **41**:267

"The Rise of the Tide" (Guiney) **41**:207

"The Rival Singers" (Guiney) **41**:206

*A Roadside Harp* (Guiney) **41**:204-05, 207-08, 210, 213-14

*Robert Emmet: A Survey of His Rebellion and of His Romance* (Guiney) **41**:218, 220

*Le roman expérimental* (Zola) **41**:444, 449, 451

*Rome* (Zola) **41**:421-22

*La rose publique* (Eluard) **41**:150

"Rue Barrée" (Chambers) **41**:88, 94

*The Runagates Club* (Buchan) **41**:41, 44

"St. Frideswide's Day in Oxford" (Guiney) **41**:220

*Sally* (Elizabeth)
See *Introduction to Sally*

*Salomé* (Wilde) **41**:377

*Salute to Adventurers* (Buchan) **41**:38

"Sanctuary" (Guiney) **41**:218, 221-22, 225

*Scholar Gipsies* (Buchan) **41**:34

"The Scot's Tongue" (Buchan) **41**:72

"The Search" (Guiney) **41**:207

"Seeing" (Eluard) **41**:149

*Selected Poems* (McKay) **41**:318-19, 344

*Les sentiers et les routes de la poésie* (*The Paths and the Roads of Poetry*) (Eluard) **41**:152, 161

"The Serpent's Crown" (Guiney) **41**:207

"Shared Nights" (Eluard)
See "Nuits partagées"

"She of All Time, All" (Eluard)
See "Celle de toujours, toute"

"She Who Is of Always, All" (Eluard)
See "Celle de toujours, toute"

*The Ship* (Jensen)
See *Skibet*

"The Shrine of St. Edward the Confessor" (Guiney) **41**:220

*Sick Heart River* (*Mountain Meadow*) (Buchan) **41**:40-1, 43, 45, 47, 50, 53, 57-8, 73

"The Silent Land" (Chambers) **41**:88, 107

"Sir Jesper" (Jensen)
See "Hr. Jesper"

*Sir Quixote of the Moors* (Buchan) **41**:33

*Sir Walter Raleigh* (Buchan) **41**:59

*Sir Walter Scott* (*Life of Scott*) (Buchan) **41**:45, 59-63

*Skibet* (*The Ship*) (Jensen) **41**:290-91, 295

*The Slayer of Souls* (Chambers) **41**:102, 114

"The Sluggards" (Jensen)
See "Syvsoverne"

"The Snow Fairy" (McKay) **41**:344

*The Solitary Summer* (Elizabeth) **41**:117-18, 122, 128, 130

*Some Ladies in Haste* (Chambers) **41**:90, 95

*Son excellence Eugène Rougon* (Zola) **41**:411

*Songs at the Start* (Guiney) **41**:203, 206, 210, 212, 216

*Songs of Jamaica* (McKay) **41**:319, 328, 335, 343

*Souvenirs* (Alain) **41**:26

"The Spanish Needle" (McKay) **41**:344

*The Special Messenger* (Chambers) **41**:95

"The Sphinx without a Secret" (Wilde) **41**:359

*Spinoza* (Alain) **41**:3

"Spring" (Guiney) **41**:203

"Spring in New Hampshire" (McKay) **41**:344

*Spring in New Hampshire, and Other Poems* (McKay) **41**:344

*The Stages of the Mind* (Jensen)
See *Aandens Stadier*

"The Still of the Year" (Guiney) **41**:214

"Den stille Mogens" ("Quiet Mogens") (Jensen) **41**:307

"The Strange Burial of Sue" (McKay) **41**:329-30

"Streams of Water in the South" (Buchan) **41**:72-3

"The Street of Our Lady of the Fields" (Chambers) **41**:94

"The Street of the First Shell" (Chambers) **41**:88, 94

"The Street of the Four Winds" (Chambers) **41**:88, 94, 104

"Summum Bonum" (Guiney) **41**:207, 221

*Système des beaux-arts* (Alain) **41**:3, 6, 24, 28, 30

"Syvsoverne" ("The Sluggards") (Jensen) **41**:307-08

*Det tabte Land* (*Fire; The Lost Land*) (Jensen)
  **41:**294-95
*Tales from Himmerland* (Jensen)
  See *Himmerlandshistorier*
"A Talisman" (Guiney)   **41:**216
*The Talkers* (Chambers)   **41:**102
"Tarpeia" (Guiney)   **41:**204, 207, 227, 229
*Le temps déborde* (Eluard)   **41:**151, 153, 161
*La terre* (Zola)   **41:**414-15, 438, 451
"La terre est bleue comme une orange..."
  (Eluard)   **41:**169
*Their Wedding Journey* (Howells)   **41:**234, 263
*Thérèse Raquin* (Zola)   **41:**406-07, 415, 436-37
"The Third Eye" (Chambers)   **41:**113
*The Thirty-Nine Steps* (Buchan)   **41:**35-8, 41,
  53-4, 56, 64-5, 68-71, 73, 78-80
"Thomas i Spanggaarden" ("Thomas of the
  Spang Farm") (Jensen)   **41:**307
"Thomas of the Spang Farm" (Jensen)
  See "Thomas i Spanggaarden"
"Three and Thirty Years" (Jensen)
  See "Tre og tredive Aar"
*The Three Hostages* (Buchan)   **41:**38, 41-2, 44,
  46, 52, 55-8, 67-8, 71, 79-82
"To a Dog's Memory" (Guiney)   **41:**205, 221
"To an Ideal" (Guiney)   **41:**221-23
"To an Unknown Priest" (Guiney)   **41:**220
"To One Who Would Not Spare Himself"
  (Guiney)   **41:**220
*To Tell Everything* (Eluard)
  See *Tout dire*
"To the White Fiends" (McKay)   **41:**324, 345
"Tordenkalven" (Jensen)   **41:**307
*Total Song* (Eluard)
  See *Chanson complète*
"Tout dire" (Eluard)   **41:**157
*Tout dire* (*To Tell Everything*) (Eluard)
  **41:**157
*A toute épreuve* (*Holding Fast*) (Eluard)
  **41:**150, 156
*A Tracer of Lost Persons* (Chambers)   **41:**95,
  102, 114
*The Tragedy of White Injustice* (Garvey)
  **41:**185, 198
*The Transformation of the Animals* (Jensen)
  See *Dyrenes Forvandling*
*Travail* (Zola)   **41:**421
*A Traveler from Altruria* (Howells)   **41:**261,
  269
"Tre og tredive Aar" ("Three and Thirty
  Years") (Jensen)   **41:**307
*The Tree of Heaven* (Chambers)   **41:**90, 95,
  102, 114
*Trial by Lynching* (McKay)   **41:**331
*Trods* (*Defiance*) (Jensen)   **41:**292
"The Tropics in New York" (McKay)   **41:**344
"Truant" (McKay)   **41:**329, 342
"Tryste Noël" (Guiney)   **41:**207
*Tuscan Cities* (Howells)   **41:**263
"Two Irish Peasant Songs" (Guiney)   **41:**214
*The Undiscovered Country* (Howells)   **41:**233-
  34
"L'univers solitude" (Eluard)   **41:**156
"Vandmøllen" ("The Water Mill") (Jensen)
  **41:**308
*Le ventre de Paris* (Zola)   **41:**413, 445
*Vera* (Elizabeth)   **41:**124, 130-31, 137
*Vera; or, The Nihilists* (Wilde)   **41:**354, 376
"Vergniaud in the Tumbril" (Guiney)   **41:**207
*Vérité* (Zola)   **41:**420-21, 423-24
"La victoire de Guernica" (Eluard)   **41:**151,
  163-64, 167

*La vie immédiate* (Eluard)   **41:**150-51, 154,
  158, 162
"The Vigil-at-Arms" (Guiney)   **41:**221
*Vigiles de l'esprit* (Alain)   **41:**7
*Vingt leçons sur les beaux-arts* (Alain)   **41:**30
"Vivre" (Eluard)   **41:**159
"The Watcher by the Threshold" (Buchan)
  **41:**73
*The Watcher by the Threshold, and Other Tales*
  (Buchan)   **41:**35, 37, 73
"The Water Mill" (Jensen)
  See "Vandmøllen"
"We Are" (Eluard)
  See "Nous sommes"
"What American Catholics Lack" (Guiney)
  **41:**220
*The Wheel* (Jensen)
  See *Hjulet*
"When I Pounded the Pavement" (McKay)
  **41:**329
"When on the Marge of Evening" (Guiney)
  **41:**221
"The White City" (McKay)   **41:**336
"The White House" (McKay)   **41:**336, 345
"White Man's Solution for the Negro Problem
  in America" (Garvey)   **41:**188
*The White Sail, and Other Poems* (Guiney)
  **41:**203-04, 206-07, 213
"The White Shadow" (Chambers)   **41:**113
"Whitmans Apoteosis" (Jensen)   **41:**301
"The Wild Ride" (Guiney)   **41:**204, 213, 217
*The Witch of Ellangowan* (Chambers)   **41:**89
*Witch Wood* (Buchan)   **41:**39, 72-3, 75-6
*With the Band* (Chambers)   **41:**88
*Within Life's Limits* (Eluard)
  See *A l'intérieur de la vie*
*A Woman of No Importance* (Wilde)   **41:**397
*A Woman's Reason* (Howells)   **41:**263
"Wombwell" (Jensen)   **41:**307
"The Wooing Pine" (Guiney)   **41:**206-07
"Writ in My Lord Clarendon," *His History of
  the Rebellion* (Guiney)   **41:**217
"The Yellow Sign" (Chambers)   **41:**87, 100-
  01, 103, 105-06, 110
*Les yeux fertiles* (Eluard)   **41:**163
*A Young Man in a Hurry* (Chambers)   **41:**95
*The Younger Set* (Chambers)   **41:**92, 95, 101